CRIME IN THE UNITED STATES

CRIME IN THE UNITED STATES

2015
NINTH EDITION
EDITED BY SHANA HERTZ HATTIS

 **Bernan** Press

Lanham • Boulder • New York • London

Published by Bernan Press
An imprint of The Rowman & Littlefield Publishing Group, Inc.
4501 Forbes Boulevard, Suite 200, Lanham, Maryland 20706
www.rowman.com
800-865-3457; info@bernan.com

Unit A, Whitacre Mews, 26-34 Stannary Street, London SE11 4AB

ISBN: 978-1-59888-765-5
eISBN: 978-1-59888-766-2

∞™ The paper used in this publication meets the minimum requirements of American National Standard for Information Sciences Permanence of Paper for Printed Library Materials, ANSI/NISO Z39.48-1992.

Printed in the United States of America

CONTENTS

SECTION V: LAW ENFORCEMENT PERSONNEL 395

SECTION VI: HATE CRIMES 581

SECTION I

SUMMARY OF THE UNIFORM CRIME REPORTING (UCR) PROGRAM

SUMMARY OF THE UNIFORM CRIME REPORTING (UCR) PROGRAM

Bernan Press is proud to present its ninth edition of *Crime in the United States*. This title was formerly published by the Federal Bureau of Investigation (FBI), but is no longer available in printed form from the government. This edition contains final data from 2013, the most current year for which data is available.

This section describes the history of the UCR program, which collects the data used in *Crime in the United States*. It also examines the best way to use the data in this publication.

About the UCR Program

The UCR program's primary objective is to generate reliable information for use in law enforcement administration, operation, and management; however, over the course of the program, its data has stood out as one of the country's leading social indicators.

The UCR program is a nationwide, cooperative statistical effort of more than 18,000 city, university and college, county, state, tribal, and federal law enforcement agencies voluntarily reporting data on crimes brought to their attention. Since 1930, the FBI has administered the UCR program and continued to assess and monitor the nature and type of crime in the nation. Criminologists, sociologists, legislators, municipal planners, the media, and other students of criminal justice use the data for varied research and planning purposes. In 2013, law enforcement agencies active in the UCR program represented more than 309 million United States inhabitants, or 98.0 percent of the total population. The coverage amounted to 98.8 percent of the population in metropolitan statistical areas, 92.9 percent of the population in cities outside metropolitan areas, and 93.5 percent of the population in nonmetropolitan counties. These percentages represent slight decreases from the coverage from 2012.

Note for Users

It is important for UCR data users to remember that the FBI's primary objective is to generate a reliable set of crime statistics for use in law enforcement administration, operation, and management. The FBI does not provide a ranking of agencies; instead, it provides alphabetical tabulations of states, metropolitan statistical areas, cities with over 10,000 inhabitants, suburban and rural counties, and selected colleges and universities. Law enforcement officials use these data for their designed purposes. Additionally, the public relies on these data for information about the fluctuations in levels of crime from year to year, while criminologists, sociologists, legislators, city planners, media outlets, and other students of criminal justice use them for a variety of research and planning purposes. Since crime is a sociological phenomenon influenced by a variety of factors, the FBI discourages data users from ranking agencies and using the data as a measurement of the effectiveness of law enforcement.

To ensure that data are uniformly reported, the FBI provides contributing law enforcement agencies with a handbook that explains how to classify and score offenses and provides uniform crime offense definitions. Acknowledging that offense definitions may vary from state to state, the FBI cautions agencies to report offenses according to the guidelines provided in the handbook, rather than by local or state statutes. Most agencies make a good faith effort to comply with established guidelines.

The UCR program publishes the statistics most commonly requested by data users. More information regarding the availability of UCR program data is available by telephone at (304) 625-4995, by fax at (304) 625-3566, or by e-mail at cjis_comm@leo.gov. Data requests via e-mail cannot be processed without the requester's full name, mailing address, and contact telephone number.

Variables Affecting Crime: Caution Against Ranking

Until data users examine all the variables that affect crime in a town, city, county, state, region, or college or university, they can make no meaningful comparisons. In each edition of *Crime in the United States*, many entities—including news media, tourism agencies, and other organizations with an interest in crime in the nation—use reported figures to compile rankings of cities and counties. However, these rankings are merely a quick choice made by that data user; they provide no insight into the many variables that mold the crime in a particular town, city, county, state, or region. Consequently, these rankings may lead to simplistic and/or incomplete analyses, which can create misleading perceptions and thus adversely affect cities, counties, and their residents.

Considering Other Characteristics of a Jurisdiction

To assess criminality and law enforcement's response from jurisdiction to jurisdiction, data users must consider many variables, some of which (despite having significant impact on crime) are not readily measurable or applicable among all locales. Geographic and demographic factors specific to each jurisdiction must be considered and applied in order to make an accurate and complete assessment of crime in that jurisdiction. Several sources of information are available to help the researcher explore the variables that affect crime in a particular locale. The U.S. Census Bureau data, for example, can help the user better understand the makeup of a locale's population. The transience of the population, its racial and ethnic makeup, and its composition by age and gender, educational levels, and prevalent family structures are all key factors in assessing and understanding crime.

Local chambers of commerce, planning offices, and similar entities provide information regarding the economic and cultural makeup of cities and counties. Understanding a jurisdiction's industrial/economic base, its dependence upon neighboring jurisdictions, its transportation system, its economic dependence on nonresidents (such as tourists and convention attendees), and its proximity to military installations, correctional institutions, and other types of facilities all contribute to accurately gauging and interpreting the crime known to and reported by law enforcement.

The strength (including personnel and other resources) and aggressiveness of a jurisdiction's law enforcement agency are also key factors in understanding the nature and extent of crime occurring in that area. Although information pertaining to the number of sworn and civilian employees can be found in this publication, it cannot be used alone as an assessment of the emphasis that a community places on enforcing the law. For example, one city may report more crime than another comparable city because its law enforcement agency identifies more offenses. Attitudes of citizens toward crime and their crime reporting practices—especially for minor offenses—also have an impact on the volume of crimes known to police.

Making Valid Crime Assessments

It is essential for all data users to become as well educated as possible about understanding and quantifying the nature and extent of crime in the United States and in the jurisdictions represented by law enforcement contributors to the UCR program. Valid assessments are possible only with careful study and analysis of the various unique conditions that affect each local law enforcement jurisdiction.

Some factors that are known to affect the volume and type of crime occurring from place to place are:

- Population density and degree of urbanization

- Variations in composition of population, particularly in the concentration of youth

- Stability of the population with respect to residents' mobility, commuting patterns, and transient factors

- Modes of transportation and highway systems

- Economic conditions, including median income, poverty level, and job availability

- Cultural factors and educational, recreational, and religious characteristics

- Family conditions, with respect to divorce and family cohesiveness

- Climate

- Effective strength of law enforcement agencies

- Administrative and investigative emphases of law enforcement

- Policies of other components of the criminal justice system (that is, prosecutorial, judicial, correctional, and probational policies)

- Residents' attitudes toward crime

- Crime reporting practices of residents

Although many of the listed factors equally affect the crime of a particular area, the UCR program makes no attempt to relate them to the data presented. **The data user is therefore cautioned against comparing statistical data of individual reporting units from cities, counties, metropolitan areas, states, or colleges or universities solely on the basis on their population coverage or student enrollment.** Until data users examine all the variables that affect crime in a town, city, county, state, region, or college or university, they can make no meaningful comparisons.

Historical Background

Since 1930, the FBI has administered the UCR program; the agency continues to assess and monitor the nature and type of crime in the nation. Data users look to the UCR program for various research and planning purposes.

Recognizing a need for national crime statistics, the International Association of Chiefs of Police (IACP) formed the Committee on Uniform Crime Records in the 1920s to develop a system of uniform crime statistics. After studying state criminal codes and making an evaluation of the recordkeeping practices in use, the committee completed a plan for crime reporting that became the foundation of the UCR program in 1929. The plan included standardized offense definitions for seven main offense classifications known as Part I crimes to gauge fluctuations in the overall volume and rate of crime. Developers also instituted the Hierarchy Rule as the main reporting procedure for what is now known as the Summary Reporting System of the UCR program.

Seven main offense classifications, known as Part I crimes, were chosen to gauge the state of crime in the nation. These seven offense classifications included the violent crimes of murder and nonnegligent manslaughter, rape, robbery, and aggravated assault; also included were the property crimes of burglary, larceny-theft, and motor vehicle theft. By congressional mandate, arson was added as the eighth Part I offense category. Data collection for arson began in 1979.

During the early planning of the program, it was recognized that the differences among criminal codes precluded a mere aggregation of state statistics to arrive at a national total. Also, because of the variances in punishment for the same offenses in different states, no distinction between felony and misdemeanor crimes was possible. To avoid these problems and provide nationwide uniformity in crime reporting, standardized offense definitions were developed. Law enforcement agencies use these to submit data without regard for local statutes. UCR program offense definitions can be found in Appendix I.

In January 1930, 400 cities (representing 20 million inhabitants in 43 states) began participating in the UCR program. Congress enacted Title 28, Section 534, of the *United States Code* that same year, which authorized the attorney general to gather crime information. The attorney general, in turn, designated the FBI to serve as the national clearinghouse for the collected crime data. Since then, data based on uniform classifications and procedures for reporting have been obtained annually from the nation's law enforcement agencies.

Advisory Groups

Providing vital links between local law enforcement and the FBI for the UCR program are the Criminal Justice Information Systems Committees of the IACP and the National Sheriffs' Association (NSA). The IACP represents the thousands of police departments nationwide, as it has since the program began. The NSA encourages sheriffs throughout the country to participate fully in the program. Both committees serve the program in advisory capacities.

In 1988, a Data Providers' Advisory Policy Board was established. This board operated until 1993, when it combined with the National Crime Information Center Advisory Policy Board to form a single Advisory Policy Board (APB) to address all FBI criminal justice information services. The current APB works to ensure continuing emphasis on UCR-related issues. The Association of State Uniform Crime Reporting Programs (ASUCRP) focuses on UCR issues within individual state law enforcement associations and also promotes interest in the UCR program. These organizations foster widespread and responsible use of uniform crime statistics and lend assistance to data contributors.

Redesign of UCR

Although UCR data collection was originally conceived as a tool for law enforcement administration, the data were widely used by other entities involved in various forms of social planning by the 1980s. Recognizing the need for more detailed crime statistics, law enforcement called for a thorough evaluative study to modernize the UCR program. The FBI formulated a comprehensive three-phase redesign effort. The Bureau of Justice Statistics (BJS) agency in the Department of Justice responsible for funding criminal justice information projects, agreed to underwrite the first two phases. These phases were conducted by an independent contractor and structured to determine what, if any, changes should be made to the current program. The third phase would involve implementation of the changes identified.

The final report, the Blueprint for the Future of the Uniform Crime Reporting Program, was released in the summer of 1985. It specifically outlined recommendations for an expanded, improved UCR program to meet future informational needs. There were three recommended areas of enhancement to the UCR program:

- Offenses and arrests would be reported using an incident-based system

- Data would be collected on two levels. Agencies in level one would report important details about those offenses comprising the Part I crimes, their victims, and arrestees. Level two would consist of law enforcement agencies covering populations of more than 100,000 and a sampling of smaller agencies that would collect expanded detail on all significant offenses

- A quality assurance program would be introduced

In January 1986, Phase III of the redesign effort began, guided by the general recommendations set forth in the Blueprint. The FBI selected an experimental site to implement the redesigned program, while contractors developed new data guidelines and system specifications. Upon selecting the South Carolina Law Enforcement Division (SLED), which enlisted the cooperation of nine local law enforcement agencies, the FBI developed automated data capture specifications to adapt the SLED's state system to the national UCR program's standards, and the BJS funded the revisions. The pilot demonstration ran from March 1 through September 30, 1987, and resulted in further refinement of the guidelines and specifications.

From March 1 through March 3, 1988, the FBI held a national UCR conference to present the new system to law enforcement and to obtain feedback on its acceptability. Attendees of the conference passed three overall recommendations without dissent: first, that there be established a new, incident-based national crime reporting system; second, that the FBI manage this program, and third, that an Advisory Policy Board composed of law enforcement executives be formed to assist in directing and implementing the new program. Furthermore, attendees recommended that the implementation of national incident-based reporting proceed at a pace commensurate with the resources and limitations of contributing law enforcement agencies.

Establishing the NIBRS

From March 1988 through January 1989, the FBI developed and assumed management of the UCR program's National Incident-Based Reporting System (NIBRS), and by April 1989, the first test of NIBRS data was submitted to the national UCR program. Over the next few years, the national lUCR program published information about the redesigned program in five documents:

- *Uniform Crime Reporting Handbook*, NIBRS Edition (1992) provides a nontechnical program overview focusing on definitions, policies, and procedures of the IBRS

- *Data Submission Specifications* (May 1992) is used by local and state systems personnel, who are responsible for preparing magnetic media for submission to the FBI

- *Approaches to Implementing an Incident-Based System* (July 1992) is a guide for system designers

- *Error Message Manual* (revised December 1999) contains designations of mandatory and optional data elements, data element edits, and error messages

- *Data Collection Guidelines* (revised August 2000) contains a system overview and descriptions of the offense codes, reports, data elements, and data values used in the system

As more agencies inquired about the NIBRS, the FBI, in May 2002, made the *Handbook for Acquiring a Records Management System (RMS) That Is Compatible with the NIBRS* available to agencies considering or developing automated incident-based records management systems. The handbook, developed under the sponsorship of the FBI and the BJS, provides instructions for planning and conducting a system acquisition and offers guidelines on preparing an agency for conversion to the new system and to the NIBRS.

The National UCR Program staff has also presented additional documents, including the *National Incident-Based Reporting System (NIBRS) Technical Specification* (Version 1.1, dated September 17, 2014) and the *National Incident-Based Reporting System (NIBRS) User Manual* (Version 1.0, dated January 17, 2013.)

Originally designed with 52 data elements, the redesigned NIBRS captures up to 57 data elements via 6 types of data segments: administrative, offense, victim property, offender, and arrestee. Although, in the late 1980s, the FBI committed to hold all changes to the NIBRS in abeyance until a substantial amount of contributors implemented the system, modifications have been necessary. The system's flexibility has allowed the collection of four additional pieces of information to be captured within an incident: bias-motivated offenses (1990), the presence of gang activity (1997), data for law enforcement officers killed and assaulted (2003), and data on cargo theft (2005). The system has also allowed the addition of new codes to further specify location types and property types (2010).

The FBI began accepting NIBRS data from a handful of agencies in January 1989. As more contributing law enforcement agencies become educated about the rich data available through incident-based reporting and as resources permit, more agencies are implementing the NIBRS. Based on the 2012 data submissions, 15 states submit all their data via the NIBRS and 32 state UCR Programs are certified for NIBRS participation.

Suspension of the *Crime Index* and the *Modified Crime Index*

In June 2004, the CJIS APB approved discontinuing the use of the *Crime Index* in the UCR program and its publications and directed the FBI to publish a violent crime total and a property crime total. The *Crime Index*, first published in *Crime in the United States* in 1960, was the title used for a simple aggregation of the seven main offense classifications (Part I offenses) in the Summary Reporting System. The Modified Crime Index was the number of Crime Index offenses plus arson.

For several years, the CJIS Division studied the appropriateness and usefulness of these indices and brought the matter before many advisory groups including the UCR Subcommittee of the CJIS APB, the ASUCRP, and a meeting of leading criminologists and sociologists hosted by the BJS. In short, the *Crime Index* and the *Modified Crime Index* were not true indicators of the degrees of criminality because they were always driven upward by the offense with the highest number, typically larceny-theft. The sheer volume of those offenses overshadowed more serious but less frequently committed offenses, creating a bias against a jurisdiction with a high number of larceny-thefts but a low number of other serious crimes such as murder and rape.

Recent Developments in UCR Program

In the fall of 2011, the APB recommended, and FBI Director Robert Mueller III approved, changing the definition of rape. Since 1929, in the SRS, rape had been defined as "the carnal knowledge of a female forcibly and against her will," (*UCR Handbook*, 2004, p.19). Beginning with the 2013 data collection, the SRS definition for the violent crime of rape will be: "Penetration, no matter how slight, of the vagina or anus with any body part or object, or oral penetration by a sex organ of another person, without the consent of the victim." This definition can be found in the *Summary Reporting System [SRS] User Manual*, Version 1.0, dated June 20, 2013. The FBI is developing reporting options for law enforcement agencies to meet this requirement, which will be built into the redeveloped data collection system.

In addition to approving the new definition of rape for the SRS, the APB and Director Mueller approved removing the word "forcible" from the name of the offense and also replacing the phrase "against the person's will" with "without the consent of the victim" in other sex-related offenses in the SRS, the NIBRS, the Hate Crime Statistics Program, and Cargo Theft.

In response to a directive by the U.S. Government's Office of Management and Budget, the national UCR Program has expanded its data collection categories for race from four (White, Black, American Indian or Alaska Native, and Asian or Other Pacific Islander) to five (White, Black or African American, American Indian or Alaska Native, Asian, and Native Hawaiian or Other Pacific Islander). Also, the ethnicity categories have changed from "Hispanic" to "Hispanic or Latino" and from "Non-Hispanic" to "Not Hispanic or Latino." These changes are reflected in data presented for 2012.

The national UCR Program staff continues to develop data collection methods to comply with both the William Wilberforce Trafficking Victims Protection Reauthorization Act of 2008 and the Matthew Shepard and James Byrd, Jr. Hate Crime Prevention Act of 2009. As a result, the FBI will begin accepting data on human trafficking as well as data on crimes motivated by "gender and gender identity" bias and "crimes committed by, and crimes directed against, juveniles" from contributors in January 2013.

UCR Redevelopment Project Update

To streamline the program's database management and quality control activities, the FBI created the UCR Redevelopment Project (UCRRP). The UCRRP's goal is to improve the efficiency, usability, and maintainability of the UCR Program's submission processes, databases, and quality control activities. Through the UCRRP, the UCR Program will improve customer service by decreasing the time it takes to analyze data and by decreasing the time needed to release and publish crime data. The program will also enhance its external data query tool so that the public can view and analyze more published UCR data from the Internet.

Another major goal of the UCRRP is to reduce, to the point of elimination, the exchange of printed materials between submitting agencies and the FBI. Beginning with the 2013 data collections, all data was to be submitted electronically, and after July 2013, the UCR Program no longer accepted paper submissions or the electronic submission of documents (for example, Portable Document Format files). The UCRRP has begun working with agencies to help them adopt electronic submissions via the NIBRS, electronic SRS, or Extensible Markup Language.

UNIFORM CRIME REPORTING PROGRAM CHANGES DEFINITION OF RAPE

For the first time in the more than 80-year history of the Uniform Crime Reporting (UCR) Program, the FBI has changed the definition of a Part 1 offense. In December 2011, then FBI Director Robert S. Mueller, III, approved revisions to the UCR Program's definition of rape as recommended by the FBI's Criminal Justice Information Services (CJIS) Division Advisory Policy Board (APB), which is made up of representatives from all facets of law enforcement.

Beginning in 2013, rape is defined for Summary UCR purposes as, "Penetration, no matter how slight, of the vagina or anus with any body part or object, or oral penetration by a sex organ of another person, without the consent of the victim." The new definition updated the 80-year-old historical definition of rape which was "carnal knowledge of a female forcibly and against her will." Effectively, the revised definition expands rape to include both male and female victims and offenders, and reflects the various forms of sexual penetration understood to be rape, especially nonconsenting acts of sodomy, and sexual assaults with objects.

"This new, more inclusive definition will provide us with a more accurate understanding of the scope and volume of these crimes," said Attorney General Eric Holder. Proponents of the new definition and of the omission of the term "forcible" say that the changes broaden the scope of the previously narrow definitions by capturing (1) data without regard to gender, (2) the penetration of any bodily orifice, penetration by any object or body part, and (3) offenses in which physical force is not involved. Now, for example, instances in which offenders use drugs or alcohol or incidents in which offenders sodomize victims of the same gender will be counted as rape for statistical purposes.

It has long been the UCR Program's mission to collect and publish data regarding the scope and nature of crime in the nation, including those for rape. Since the FBI began collecting data using the revised definition of rape in January 2013, program officials expected that the number of reported rapes would rise. According to David Cuthbertson, former FBI Assistant Director of the CJIS Division, "As we implement this change, the FBI is confident that the number of victims of this heinous crime will be more accurately reflected in national crime statistics."

HOW THE CHANGES AFFECT RAPE DATA IN *CRIME IN THE UNITED STATES*

Because of the changes to the definition, readers will see some differences in this year's *Crime in the United States* publication. First, although the revised definition for rape was approved in 2011 and implemented in 2013, not all state and local agencies have been able to effect the change in their records management systems. The UCR Program is encouraging law enforcement agencies to use the revised definition; however, some agencies currently can report the offense based only on the legacy definition. Therefore, rape data collected under both definitions are used in this publication. Footnotes for tables in *Crime in the United States* indicate which (or both) definition(s) of rape is being used in each of the tables.

Second, as this is the first year for publishing rape data collected by the UCR Program under the revised definition, showing 2-, 5-, and 10-year trends with these data is not possible.

Third, because the revised definition, unlike the legacy definition, includes offenses of rape, sodomy, sexual assaults with objects, and offenses in which males were the victims, the number of rape offenses may appear to increase for various agencies or in certain aggregations. Except where comparisons are made based on the same definitions of rape, readers are cautioned against assuming increases in rape numbers are due to an increase of violence or number of sexual assaults, but rather, the increase may simply be a reflection of the more inclusive definition.

Expanded Offense Tables

Expanded offense data are the details of the various offenses that the Uniform Crime Reporting Program collects beyond the count of how many crimes law enforcement agencies report. These details may include the type of weapon used in a crime, the type or value of items stolen, and so forth. Expanded homicide data provide supplemental details about murders such as the age, sex, and race of both the victim and the offender, the weapon used in the homicide, the circumstances surrounding the offense, and the relationship of the victim to the offender. In addition, expanded data includes trends (for example, 2-year comparisons) and rates per 100,000 inhabitants.

Expanded offense data, including expanded homicide data, are information collected in addition to the reports of the number of crimes known. As a result, law enforcement agencies can report an offense without providing the supplemental data about that offense. These additional tables can be found at http://www.fbi.gov/about-us/cjis/ucr/crime-in-the-u.s/2013/crime-in-the-u.s.-2013/offenses-known-to-law-enforcement/expanded-offense/expandedoffensemain_final.

About the Editor

Shana Hertz Hattis is a consulting writer-editor for Bernan Press. She holds a master of science in education degree in from Northwestern University and a bachelor's degree in journalism from the same university. She has previously edited *Vital Statistics of the United States: Births, Life Expectancy, Deaths, and Selected Health Data* and several volumes of *Crime in the United States* for Bernan.

SECTION II

OFFENSES KNOWN TO POLICE

VIOLENT CRIME

- MURDER
- FORCIBLE RAPE
- ROBBERY
- AGGRAVATED ASSAULT

PROPERTY CRIME

- BURGLARY
- LARCENY-THEFT
- MOTOR VEHICLE THEFT
- ARSON

VIOLENT CRIME

Figure 2.1 Violent Crime Rates by Offense and Region, 2013

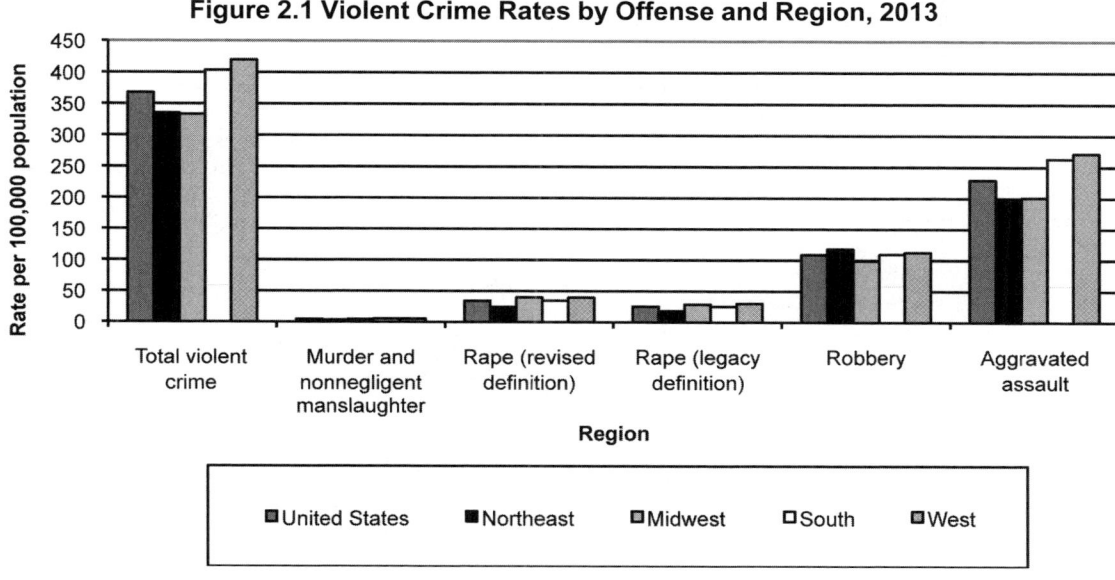

Definition

Violent crime consists of four offenses: murder and nonnegligent manslaughter, rape, robbery, and aggravated assault. According to the Uniform Crime Reporting (UCR) program, run by the Federal Bureau of Investigation (FBI), violent crimes involve either the use of force or the threat of force.

Data Collection

The data presented in *Crime in the United States* reflect the Hierarchy Rule, which counts only the most serious offense in a multiple-offense criminal incident. In descending order of severity, the violent crimes are murder and nonnegligent manslaughter, rape, robbery, and aggravated assault; these are followed by the property crimes of burglary, larceny-theft, and motor vehicle theft. Arson is also considered a property crime, but the Hierarchy Rule does not apply to the arson offense. In cases in which arson occurs in conjunction with another violent or property crime, the arson and the additional crime are reported. More information on the expanded violent crime tables (which are available online but not included in this publication) can be found in Section I.

IMPORTANT NOTE: RAPE DATA

In 2013, the FBI UCR Program initiated the collection of rape data within the Summary Reporting System under a revised definition. The definition changed to the revised UCR definition below.

- Legacy UCR definition of rape: The carnal knowledge of a female forcibly and against her will.

- Revised UCR definition of rape: Penetration, no matter how slight, of the vagina or anus with any body part or object, or oral penetration by a sex organ of another person, without the consent of the victim.

For more information, please see http://www.fbi.gov/about-us/cjis/ucr/crime-in-the-u.s/2013/crime-in-the-u.s.-2013/rape-addendum/rape_addendum_final.

National Volume, Trends, and Rate

In 2013, an estimated 1,163,146 violent crimes occurred in the United States, a decrease of 4.2 percent from the 2012 estimate. An estimated 367.9 violent crimes were committed per 100,000 inhabitants in 2013, a decline of 5.1 percent since 2012. Aggravated assaults accounted for 62.3 percent of violent crimes, the highest percentage of violent crimes reported to law enforcement. Robbery accounted for 29.7 percent of violent crimes, rape (legacy definition) accounted for 6.9 percent of violent crimes (representing no change from 2012), and murder accounted for 1.2 percent of violent crimes (a proportion that has not changed since 2009). (Table 1)

Occurrences in all four violent crime categories decreased from 2012 to 2013, a change in the trend from the previous year. Murder decreased 4.4 percent, rape (legacy definition) decreased 6.3 percent, aggravated assault decreased 5.0 percent, and robbery decreased 2.8 percent. (Tables 1 and 1A)

In longer-term trends, the 2013 estimated violent crime total was 12.3 percent below the 2009 level and 14.5 percent below the 2004 level. The 5-year and 10-year trend data also showed that the violent crime rate decreased 14.8 percent between 2009 and 2013 and decreased 20.6 percent between 2004 and 2013. (Tables 1 and 1A)

In 2013, offenders used firearms in 69.0 percent of the nation's murders, 40.0 percent of robberies, and 21.6 percent of aggravated assaults. Although the largest percentage of murders and robberies were committed with firearms, weapons such as clubs and blunt objects accounted for the majority (32.2 percent) of aggravated assaults. (Weapons data are not collected for rape offenses.) (Expanded Homicide Table 7, Expanded Offense Robbery Table 3, and Expanded Aggravated Assault Table; see http://www.fbi.gov/about-us/cjis/ucr/crime-in-the-u.s/2013/crime-in-the-u.s.-2013/offenses-known-to-law-enforcement/expanded-offense/expandedoffensemain for more information)

Many violent crimes are committed by people in known relationships. Figure 2 shows the number of murder victims who knew their offender. In the figure, the relationship categories of husband and wife include common-law spouses and ex-spouses. The categories of mother, father, sister, brother, son, and daughter include stepparents, stepchildren, and stepsiblings. The category of "acquaintance" includes homosexual relationships and the composite category of other known-to-victim offenders.

Regional Offense Trends and Rate

The UCR program divides the United States into four regions: the Northeast, the South, the Midwest, and the West. (More details concerning geographic regions are provided in Appendix III.) The population distribution of the regions can be found in Table 3, and the estimated volume and rate of violent crime by region are provided in Table 4.

THE NORTHEAST

The Northeast accounted for an estimated 17.7 percent of the nation's population in 2013 and an estimated 16.1 percent of its violent crimes. The estimated number of violent crimes decreased 4.3 percent from 2012 to 2013. Murder decreased 7.0 percent in the Northeast. Rape (legacy definition) decreased 9.5 percent. Robberies declined 2.5 percent. Aggravated assaults decreased 4.8 percent from 2012. In 2013, there were an estimated 335.1 violent crimes per 100,000 inhabitants. (Tables 3 and 4)

THE MIDWEST

With an estimated 21.4 percent of the total population of the United States, the Midwest accounted for 19.4 percent of the nation's estimated number of violent crimes in 2013. The region had a 3.9 percent decrease in violent crime from 2012 to 2013. The estimated number of aggravated assaults decreased 6.3 percent and the estimated number of robberies fell 4.0 percent, while the number of murders dropped 3.4 percent and the estimated number of rapes (legacy definition) declined 10.3 percent. The rate of violent crime per 100,000 inhabitants in the Midwest was 403.5, a decrease of 4.8 percent from 2012 to 2013. (Tables 3 and 4)

THE SOUTH

The South, the nation's most populous region, accounted for 37.4 percent of the nation's population in 2013. Approximately 41.1 percent of violent crimes in 2013 occurred in the South. Violent crime decreased 3.9 percent, while the estimated number of murders fell 4.3 percent and the estimated number of rapes (legacy definition) fell 5.7 percent. Robberies dropped 1.6 percent, while aggravated assault and decreased by 4.7 percent. The estimated rate of violent crime in the South was 403.5 incidents per 100,000 inhabitants in 2013. (Tables 3 and 4)

THE WEST

With 23.5 percent of the nation's population in 2013, the West also accounted for an estimated 23.5 percent of the nation's violent crime. Violent crime in the West decreased 4.1 percent from 2012 to 2013. All four violent offense categories decreased in number from 2012 to 2013. Murders fell 4.5 percent, rapes (legacy definition) decreased 1.3 percent, robberies declined 4.0 percent, and aggravated assault fell 4.5 percent. The region's violent crime rate in 2013 was 367.4 per 100,000 inhabitants. (Tables 3 and 4)

Community Types

The UCR program aggregates crime data into three community types: metropolitan statistical areas (MSAs), cities outside MSAs, and nonmetropolitan counties outside MSAs. Appendix III provides additional information regarding community types. In 2013, approximately 85.1 percent of the nation's population lived in MSAs. Residents of cities outside MSAs accounted for 6.0 percent of the country's population, and residents living in nonmetropolitan counties accounted for 8.8 percent of the population. (Table 2)

In the areas reporting violent crimes to the UCR Program, approximately 85.6 percent of these crimes occurred in MSAs, while 5.3 percent occurred in cities outside MSAs and 3.8 percent occurred in nonmetropolitan counties. By community type, the violent crime rates were estimated at 397.4 incidents per 100,000 inhabitants in MSAs, 376.7 incidents per 100,000 inhabitants in cities outside MSAs, and 180.8 incidents per 100,000 inhabitants in nonmetropolitan counties. The last figure represents an increase from the 2012 figure. (Table 2)

Population Groups: Trends and Rates

In the UCR program, data are also aggregated into population groups; these groups are described in more detail in Appendix III. The nation's cities had an overall decrease of 4.5 percent in the estimated number of violent crimes from 2012 to 2013. By city population group, cities with 25,000 to 49,999 (Group IV) and those with 100,000 to 249,999 (Group II) inhabitants had the largest percentage declines in the estimated number of violent crimes (6.4 percent and 5.7 percent, respectively). (Table 12)

The law enforcement agencies in the nation's cities collectively reported a rate of 449.7 violent crimes per 100,000 inhabitants in 2013. Law enforcement agencies in the subset of cities with 500,000 to 999,999 inhabitants reported the highest violent crime rate, 831.1 violent crimes per 100,000 inhabitants; the violent crime rate for all cities with 250,000 or more inhabitants was 734.7 per 100,000 inhabitants. Agencies in cities with 10,000 to 24,999 inhabitants reported the lowest violent crime rate (268.7 incidents per 100,000 inhabitants). Law enforcement agencies in the nation's metropolitan counties reported a collective violent crime rate of 256.1 per 100,000 inhabitants, while agencies in nonmetropolitan counties reported a collective rate of 178.5 violent crimes per 100,000 inhabitants. (Table 16)

MURDER

Figure 2.2 Murder Victims, Known Relationship to Offender, 2013

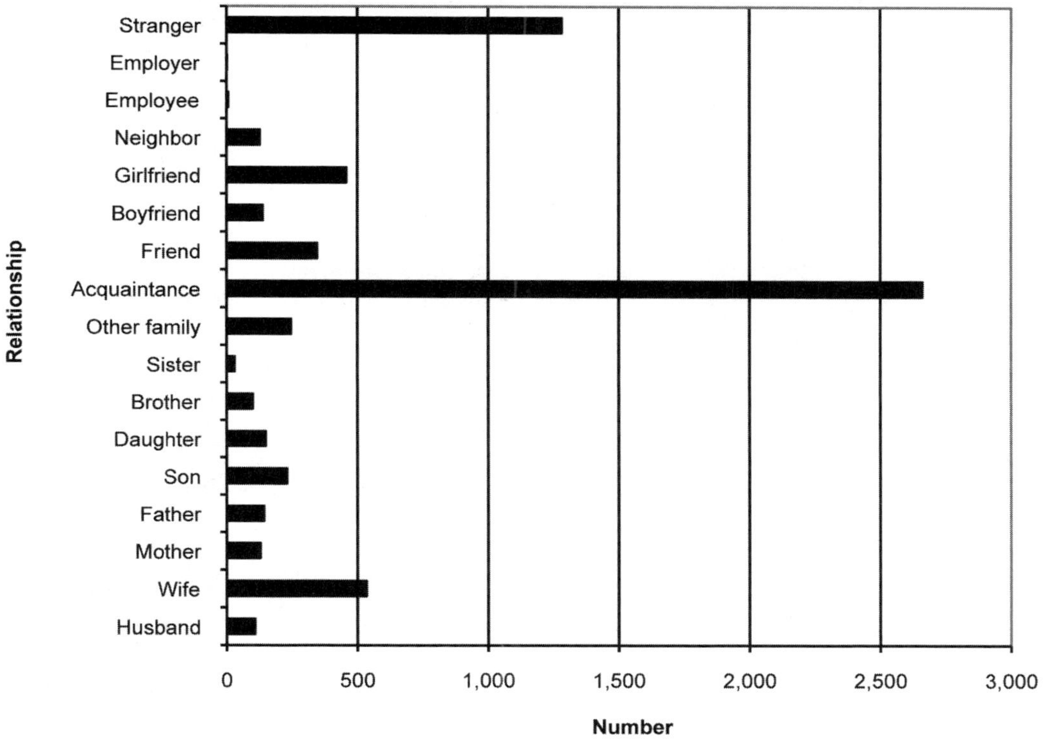

Note. The relationship categories of husband and wife include both common-law and ex-spouses. The categories of mother, father, sister, brother, son, and daughter include stepparents, stepchildren, and stepsiblings. The category of acquaintance includes homosexual relationships and the composite category of other known to victim.

Definition

The UCR program defines murder and non-negligent manslaughter as the willful (non-negligent) killing of one human being by another. The classification of this offense is based solely on police investigation, rather than on the determination of a court, medical examiner, coroner, jury, or other judicial body. The UCR program does not include the following situations under this offense classification: deaths caused by negligence, suicide, or accident; justifiable homicides; and attempts to murder or assaults to murder, which are considered aggravated assaults.

Data Collection/Supplementary Homicide Reports (SHR)

The UCR program's *Supplementary Homicide Report* (SHR) provides information about murder victims and offenders by age, sex, and race; the types of weapons used in the murders; the relationships of the victims to the offenders; and the circumstances surrounding the incident. Law enforcement agencies are asked to complete an SHR for each murder reported to the UCR program. Data from SHRs can be viewed in the Expanded Homicide Data section, found on the FBI Web site: http://www.fbi.gov/about-us/cjis/ucr/crime-in-the-u.s/2013/crime-in-the-u.s.-2013/offenses-known-to-law-enforcement/expanded-homicide. More information on these reports and the expanded homicide tables can be found in Section I. Highlights from these tables have been included below.

National Volume, Trends, and Rates

An estimated 14.196 persons were murdered nationwide in 2013. This number was a 4.4 percent decrease from the 2012 estimate, a 7.8 percent decrease from the 2009 figure, and a 12.1 percent decrease from the 2004 estimate. The 2013 murder rate, 4.5 offenses per 100,000 inhabitants, was a 5.1 percent decrease from the 2012 rate. Murder accounted for 1.2 percent of the overall estimated number of violent crimes in 2013, a percentage it has maintained for 5 years. (Tables 1 and 1A)

Regional Offense Trends and Rates

The UCR program divides the United States into four regions: the Northeast, the South, the Midwest, and the West. (More details concerning geographic regions are provided in Appendix III.) In 2013, nearly 44 percent (43.8 percent) of murders were reported in the South, the country's most populous region. The West reported 21.0 percent of murders, 21.4 percent of murders were reported in the Midwest, and 13.8 percent of murders were reported in the Northeast.

THE NORTHEAST

In 2013, the Northeast accounted for an estimated 17.7 percent of the nation's population and 13.8 percent of its estimated number of murders. With an estimated 1,953 murders, the Northeast saw a 7.0 percent decrease from its 2012 figure. The offense rate for the Northeast was 3.5 murders per 100,000 inhabitants, a decline from 3.9 murders per 100,000 inhabitants in 2012. (Tables 3 and 4)

THE MIDWEST

The Midwest accounted for an estimated 21.4 percent of the nation's total population and 21.4 percent of the country's estimated number of murders in 2013. The Midwest reported an estimated 3,042 murders in 2013. The region experienced a rate of 4.5 murders per 100,000 inhabitants in 2013, slightly below its 2012 rate. (Tables 3 and 4)

THE SOUTH

The South accounted for an estimated 37.4 percent of the nation's population in 2013 and 43.8 percent of the nation's murders, the highest proportion among the four regions. The estimated 6,222 murders, however, represented a 4.3 percent decrease from the 2012 figure. The region's estimated rate of 5.3 murders per 100,000 inhabitants represented a decrease of 5.2 percent from the estimated rate for 2012. (Tables 3 and 4)

THE WEST

The West accounted for an estimated 23.5 percent of the nation's population and 21.0 percent of the estimated number of murders in 2013. The West experienced an estimated 2,979 murders, a 4.5 percent decrease from the 2012 estimate. The region's murder rate was 4.0 per 100,000 inhabitants. (Tables 3 and 4)

Community Types

The UCR program aggregates data for three community types: metropolitan statistical areas (MSAs), cities outside MSAs, and nonmetropolitan counties outside MSAs. (See Appendix III for definitions.) In 2013, MSAs accounted for 85.2 percent of the nation's population and 88.4 percent of the estimated total number of murders. MSAs experienced a rate of 4.7 murders per 100,000 inhabitants in 2013, down from a rate of 4.5 per 100,000 inhabitants in 2012. Cities outside MSAs accounted for 6.0 percent of the U.S. population and (with an estimated 714 murders) accounted for 5.0 percent of the estimated murders in the nation. The murder rate for cities outside MSAs was 3.7 per 100,000 inhabitants. In 2013, approximately 6.6 percent of the nation's population lived in nonmetropolitan counties outside MSAs. An estimated 934 murders took place in these counties, accounting for 6.6 percent of the nation's estimated total. (Table 2)

Population Groups: Trends and Rates

The UCR program uses the following population group designations in its data presentations: cities (grouped according to population size) and counties (classified as either metropolitan or nonmetropolitan). A breakdown of these classifications is provided in Appendix III.

From 2012 to 2013, the nation's cities experienced a 6.1 percent decrease in homicides. One city groups experienced an increase (1.0 percent in cities with 100,000 to 249,999 inhabitants). The city groups with the greatest decreases in homicides were cities with 1,000,000 or more inhabitants (14.4 percent) and cities with 10,000 to 24,999 inhabitants (13.7 percent). Metropolitan counties experienced an increase in homicides of 2.1 percent from 2012 to 2013, while nonmetropolitan counties experienced an increase of 0.6 percent. (Table 12)

In 2013, cities collectively had a rate of 5.2 murders per 100,000 inhabitants. Cities with 250,000 to 499,999 inhabitants had the highest murder rate (11.0 murders per 100,000 inhabitants). Cities with 10,000 to 24,999 inhabitants had the lowest murder rate, with 2.5 murders per 100,000 inhabitants. The homicide rate for metropolitan counties and nonmetropolitan counties was the same, 3.4 murders per 100,000 inhabitants. Suburban areas had a homicide rate of 2.9 per 100,000 inhabitants. (Table 16)

Supplementary Homicide Reports Data

VICTIMS/OFFENDERS

Based on 2013 supplemental homicide data (where the ages, sexes, or races of the murder victims were identified), 90.6 percent of victims were over 18 years of age, 21.2 percent were under 22 years of age, 8.4 percent were under 18 years of age, and the age of 1.0 percent of the victims was unknown. Of the 12,253 murder victims represented in the 2013 expanded tables whose gender was identified, 77.7 percent were male. Concerning race, 45.2 percent of victims were White, 51.1 percent were Black, and 3.7 percent were of other races. Race was unknown for 147 victims. For murders in which the gender of the offender was identified, 64.3 percent were males; the sex of offenders for 28.0 percent of homicides was unknown. For the offenders for whom race was identified, 38.0 percent were Black, 31.1 percent were White, and 1.8 percent were other races; 4,112 offenders were of unknown race. (Expanded Homicide Data Tables 1, 2, and 3)

VICTIM-OFFENDER RELATIONSHIPS

For incidents in which the victim-offender relationship was specified (including the designation of "unknown"), 13.6 percent of victims were slain by family members, 10.5 percent were murdered by strangers, and 30.5 percent were killed by acquaintances (neighbor, friend, boyfriend, employer, etc.). (Expanded Homicide Data Table 10)

CIRCUMSTANCES/WEAPONS

Concerning the known circumstances surrounding murders, and including murders with unknown circumstances, 26.5 percent of victims were murdered during arguments (including romantic triangles) and brawls in 2013. Felony circumstances (rape, robbery, burglary, etc.) accounted for 15.6 percent of murders. Circumstances were unknown for 36.2 percent of reported homicides. Of the homicides for which the type of weapon was specified, 69.0 percent involved the use of firearms. Of the identified firearms used, handguns comprised 68.4 percent of the total. (Expanded Homicide Data Tables 8 and 12)

Justifiable Homicide

Certain willful killings must be reported as justifiable, or excusable, homicide. In the UCR program, justifiable homicide is defined as, and is limited to, the following:

- The killing of a felon by a peace officer in the line of duty

- The killing of a felon, during the commission of a felony, by a private citizen

Because these killings are determined by law enforcement investigation to be justifiable, they are tabulated separately from murder and nonnegligent manslaughter. Law enforcement reported 742 justifiable homicides in 2013. Of those, law enforcement officers justifiably killed 461 individuals, and private citizens justifiably killed 281 individuals. (Expanded Homicide Data Tables 14 and 15)

RAPE

Figure 2.3 State with the Highest and Lowest Rates of Rape per 100,000 Inhabitants (Revised Definition), 2013

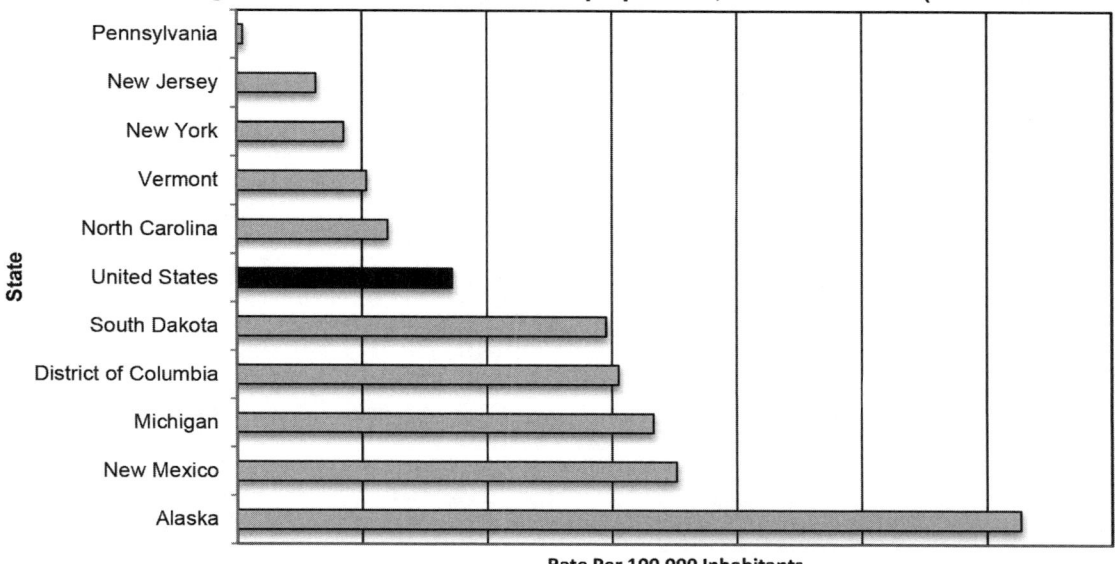

Rate Per 100,000 Inhabitants

Definition

In 2013, the FBI UCR Program initiated collection of rape data under a revised definition within the Summary Reporting System. Previously, offense data for forcible rape was collected under the legacy UCR definition: the carnal knowledge of a female forcibly and against her will. Beginning with the 2013 data year, the term "forcible" was removed from the offense title, and the definition was changed. The revised UCR definition of rape is: Penetration, no matter how slight, of the vagina or anus with any body part or object, or oral penetration by a sex organ of another person, without the consent of the victim. Attempts or assaults to commit rape are also included; however, statutory rape and incest are excluded. See Rape Addendum for details.

All rape data submitted in 2013—whether collected under the revised definition or the legacy definition—are presented in this publication. However, because only one year of rape data has been collected under the revised definition, the overview presented here discusses only legacy definition rape data.

DATA COLLECTION

- The UCR Program counts one offense for each victim of a rape, attempted rape, or assault with intent to rape, regardless of the victim's age. Sexual relations without the victim's consent which involves a familial offender is counted as a rape and not an act of incest. All other crimes of a sexual nature are considered to be Part II offenses; as such, the UCR Program collects only arrest data for those crimes. The offense of statutory rape, in which no force is used but the female victim is under the age of consent, is included in the arrest total for the sex offenses category.

- For this overview only, the FBI deviated from standard procedure and manually calculated the 2012 and 2013 rates of females raped based on the national female population provided by the U.S. Census Bureau.

National Volume, Trends, and Rates

In 2013, the estimated number of rapes (legacy definition, 79,770) decreased 6.3 percent from the 2012 estimate. The estimated volume of rapes in 2013 was 10.6 percent lower than in 2009 and 16.1 percent lower than in 2004. (Tables 1 and 1A)

Regional Offense Trends and Rates

The UCR program divides the United States into four regions: the Northeast, the South, the Midwest, and the West. (More details concerning geographic regions are provided in Appendix III) Regional analysis offers estimates of the volume of female rapes, the percent change from the previous year's estimate, and the rate of rape per 100,000 female inhabitants in each region.

NORTHEAST

The Northeast made up 17.7 percent of the U.S. population in 2013. An estimated 10,054 rapes of females (legacy definition)—12.6 percent of the national total—occurred in the Northeast. This was a decrease of 9.4 percent from the 2012 estimated figure. (Tables 3 and 4)

MIDWEST

The Midwest accounted for 21.4 percent of the U.S. population in 2013. Of all the rapes (legacy definition) in the nation, 24.4 percent occurred in the Midwest in 2013. The 2013 estimate (19,437 rapes) represented a decrease of 8.9 percent from the 2012 estimate. (Tables 3 and 4)

SOUTH

The South, the nation's most populous region, accounted for an estimated 37.4 percent of the nation's population in 2013; the region also accounted for an estimated 37.8 percent of the nation's estimated number of rapes (legacy definition). An estimated 30,128 female victims reported rape in the South in 2013, down 5.1 percent from the 31,760 rapes reported in 2012. (Tables 3 and 4)

WEST

The West accounted for 23.5 percent of the nation's population in 2013. The region also accounted for 25.3 percent of the nation's total number of estimated rapes (legacy definition) with an estimated 20,151 offenses. The West saw a 0.6 percent decline in rapes from 2012 to 2013. (Tables 3 and 4)

Community Types

Using the U.S. Office of Management and Budget's designations, the UCR program aggregates crime data by type of community in which the offenses occur: metropolitan statistical areas (MSAs), cities outside MSAs, and nonmetropolitan counties outside MSAs. (Appendix IIIIV provides more detailed information about community types.)

MSAS

In 2013, MSAs accounted for 85.2 percent of the nation's population and 83.5 percent of the nation's estimated number of rapes (legacy definition). An estimated 66,640 females were forcibly raped in metropolitan areas. (Table 2)

CITIES OUTSIDE MSAS

Cities outside MSAs are mostly incorporated areas that are served by city law enforcement agencies. Although accounting for only 6.0 percent of the U.S. population in 2013, cities outside MSAs accounted for 9.0 percent of the nation's estimated rapes (legacy definition, 7,161 estimated offenses). (Table 2)

NONMETROPOLITAN COUNTIES

In 2013, approximately 8.8 percent of the nation's population lived in nonmetropolitan counties outside MSAs (counties made up of mostly non-incorporated areas that are served by noncity law enforcement agencies). Collectively, these areas had an estimated 5,969 rapes (legacy definition), representing 4.4 percent of the nation's estimated total. (Table 2)

Population Groups: Trends and Rates

The UCR program uses the following population group designations in its data presentations: cities (grouped according to population size) and counties (classified as either metropolitan or nonmetropolitan). A breakdown of these classifications is provided in Appendix III.

From 2012 to 2013, the nation's cities experienced a 4.8 percent decrease in rapes (see table notes for classification details). Cities with 100,000 to 249,999 inhabitants experienced the greatest decline (9.8 percent). Metropolitan counties experienced a decrease in rapes of 8.2 percent from 2012 to 2013, while nonmetropolitan counties experienced decrease of 8.5 percent. (Table 12)

In 2013, cities collectively had a rate of 25.4 rapes (legacy definition) per 100,000 inhabitants. Cities with 500,000 to 999,999 inhabitants had the highest rate of rape (35.6 rapes per 100,000 inhabitants). Cities with 25,000 to 49,999 inhabitants had the lowest rate, with 21.2 rapes per 100,000 inhabitants. The rape rate for metropolitan counties was 16.5 per 100,000 inhabitants, and for nonmetropolitan counties, it was 18.5 per 100,000 inhabitants. Suburban areas had a rape rate of 17.6 per 100,000 inhabitants. (Table 16)

ROBBERY

Figure 2.4 Robberies, by Location and Percent Distribution, 2013

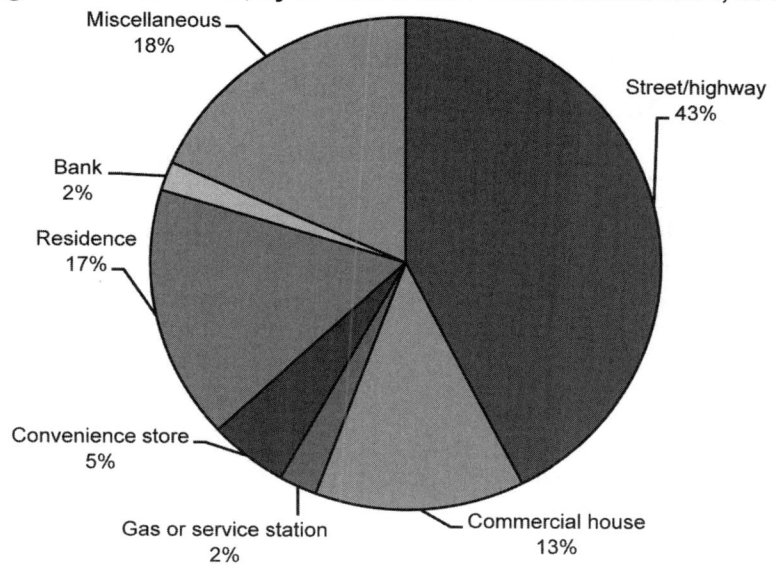

Definition

The UCR program defines robbery as the taking or attempt to take anything of value from the care, custody, or control of a person or persons by force or threat of force or violence and/or by putting the victim in fear.

National Volume, Trends, and Rates

In 2013, the estimated robbery total (345,034) decreased 2.8 percent from the 2012 estimate. The 5-year robbery trend (2009 data compared with 2013 data) showed a decrease of 15.6 percent. The 2013 estimated robbery rate (109.1 per 100,000 inhabitants) showed a decrease of 3.5 percent when compared with the 2012 rate. (Tables 1 and 1A)

Regional Offense Trends and Rates

The UCR program divides the United States into four regions: the Northeast, the South, the Midwest, and the West. (More details concerning geographic regions are provided in Appendix III.)

NORTHEAST

The Northeast, with an estimated 17.7 percent of the nation's population in 2013, accounted for 19.1 percent of the nation's estimated number of robberies. The estimated number of robberies decreased 2.5 percent from 2012. The rate for this region was 118.1 robberies per 100,000 inhabitants, down from 121.4 robberies per 100,000 inhabitants in 2012. (Tables 3 and 4)

MIDWEST

The Midwest accounted for 21.4 percent of the total population of the United States and 19.4 percent of its estimated number of robberies in 2013. An estimated 66,945 robberies occurred in the Midwest in 2013, a 4.0 percent decrease from the estimated figure from 2012. The region's robbery rate was 99.1 robberies per 100,000 inhabitants in 2013. (Tables 3 and 4)

SOUTH

The South, the nation's most highly populated region, accounted for an estimated 37.4 percent of the nation's population and 37.6 percent of the nation's estimated number of robberies in 2013. Robberies accounted for an estimated 129,825 violent crimes in this region in 2013, representing a 1.6 percent decrease from the 2012 figure. The 2013 robbery rate in the South was 109.7 per 100,000 inhabitants, down 2.5 percent from 2012. (Tables 3 and 4)

WEST

The West was home to an estimated 23.5 percent of the nation's population and accounted for 23.8 percent of the nation's estimated number of robberies in 2013. The estimated number of robberies (82,199) in the region in 2013 represented a 4.0 percent decrease from the 2012 figure. The rate of robberies per 100,000 inhabitants in the West was 110.7, a 5.0 percent decrease from the 2012 rate. (Tables 3 and 4)

Community Types

The UCR program aggregates data for three community types: metropolitan statistical areas (MSAs), cities outside MSAs, and nonmetropolitan counties outside MSAs. MSAs include a central city or urbanized area with at least 50,000 inhabitants, as well as the county that contains the principal city and other adjacent counties that have, as defined by the U.S. Office of Management and Budget, a high degree of social and economic integration as measured through commuting. Cities outside MSAs are mostly incorporated areas, and nonmetropolitan counties are made up of mostly unincorporated areas served by non-city law enforcement.

In 2013, MSAs were home to an estimated 85.2 percent of the nation's population, and 95.8 percent of the nation's estimated number of robberies took place in these areas. Robberies in MSAs occurred at a rate of 123.4 per 100,000 inhabitants. Cities outside MSAs accounted for 6.0 percent of the U.S. population and accounted for 2.5 percent of the estimated number of robberies in the nation. The robbery rate for cities outside MSAs was 50.3 per 100,000 inhabitants. Nonmetropolitan counties made up 8.8 percent of the nation's estimated population and 0.9 percent of the nation's estimated robberies, at a rate of 11.8 robberies per 100,000 inhabitants. (Table 2)

Population Groups: Trends and Rates

The national UCR program aggregates data by various population groups, which include cities, metropolitan counties, and nonmetropolitan counties. A definition of these groups can be found in Appendix III. The number of robberies in cities as a whole decreased by 3.0 percent between 2012 and 2013. Among the population groups labeled *city*, those cities with fewer than 10,000 inhabitants had the greatest decrease in the number of robberies (5.8 percent). Nonmetropolitan counties had a 10.4 percent decrease in the estimated number of robberies, and metropolitan counties showed a 2.1 percent decrease. The number of robberies in suburban areas fell 2.7 percent. (Table 12)

Among the population groups, the nation's cities collectively had a rate of 145.7 robberies per 100,000 inhabitants. Of the population groups and subsets designated *city*, those 250,000 to 499,999 inhabitants had the highest rate (288.8 per 100,000 inhabitants), while those with fewer than 10,000 inhabitants had the lowest rate (44.7 per 100,000 inhabitants) of robberies. Of the two county groups, metropolitan counties had a rate of 53.0 robberies per 100,000 inhabitants, a slight decrease from 2012; while nonmetropolitan counties had a rate of 10.8 robberies per 100,000 inhabitants, a decrease from the rate of 12.7 in 2012. Suburban areas had a robbery rate of 55.9 per 100,000 inhabitants, down from the 2012 rate of 57.8. (Table 16)

Offense Analysis

The UCR program collects supplemental data about robberies to document the use of weapons, the dollar loss associated with the offense, and the location types.

ROBBERY BY WEAPON

Firearms were used in 40.0 percent of robberies in 2013. Strong-arm robberies accounted for 43.6 percent of the total. Offenders used knives or cutting instruments in 7.6 percent of these crimes. In the remaining 8.8 percent of the robberies, the offenders used other types of weapons. (Table 19)

LOSS BY DOLLAR VALUE

Based on the supplemental reports from law enforcement agencies, robberies cost victims, collectively, an estimated $404 million in 2013. The average loss per robbery was $1,167. Average dollar losses were the highest for banks, which suffered an average loss of $3,542 per offense. Gas and service stations lost an average of $830 per offense. Commercial houses, which include supermarkets, department stores, and restaurants, had average losses of $1,808 per offense. An average of $1,480 was taken from residences. An average of $1,171 was lost in each offense against convenience stores, up from an average of $706 in 2012. (Tables 1 and 23)

ROBBERY TRENDS BY LOCATION

Among the location types, residence robberies had the greatest percentage decrease from 2012 to 2013, declining 3.5 percent. Robberies that occurred at convenience stores decreased 3.0 percent; those that occurred at banks decreased 0.9 percent; and those that occurred on streets and highways decreased 3.1 percent. The number of robberies that occurred at commercial decreased 0.9 percent, while those that occurred at gas or service stations decreased 1.1 percent. (Table 23)

By location type, the greatest proportion of robberies in 2013 occurred on streets and highways (42.5 percent). Robbers targeted commercial houses in 13.3 percent of offenses and struck residences in 16.6 percent of offenses. Convenience stores accounted for 5.0 percent of robberies, followed by gas and service stations (2.4 percent) and banks (1.9 percent). (Table 23)

AGGRAVATED ASSAULT

Figure 2.5 Number and Rate of Aggravated Assaults, 1992–2013

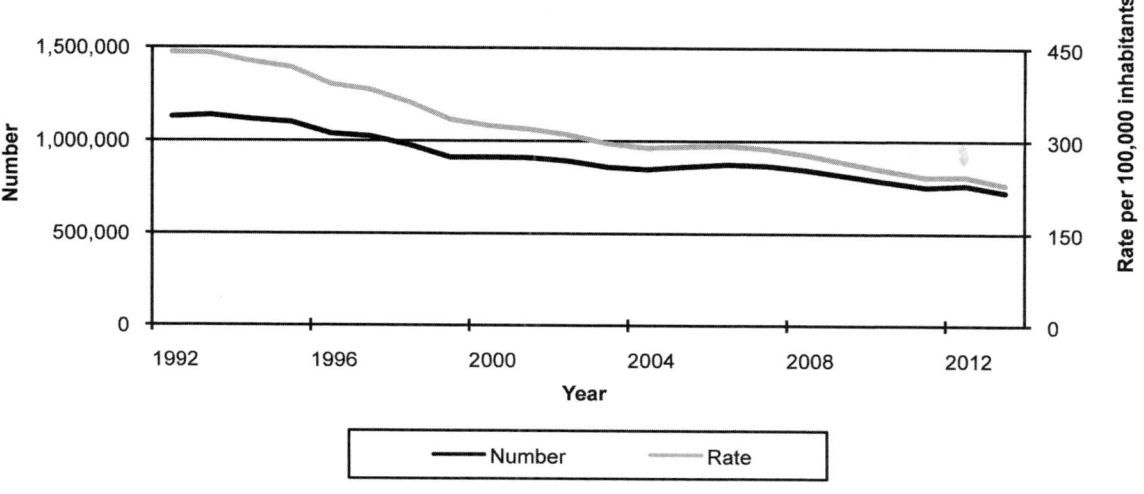

Definition

The UCR program defines aggravated assault as an unlawful attack by one person upon another for the purpose of inflicting severe or aggravated bodily injury. This type of assault is usually accompanied by the use of a weapon or by other means likely to produce death or great bodily harm. Attempted aggravated assaults that involve the display or threat of a gun, knife, or other weapon are included in this crime category because serious personal injury would likely result if these assaults were completed. When aggravated assault and larceny-theft occur together, the offense falls under the category of robbery.

National Volume, Trends, and Rates

In 2013, estimated occurrences of aggravated assaults totaled 724,149, a 5.0 percent decrease from the 2012 figure and a 14.5 percent decline when compared with the estimate for 2004. The estimated rate of aggravated assault in 2013 was 229.1 per 100,000 inhabitants, a 20.6 percent drop from 2004. (Tables 1 and 1A)

Among the four types of violent crime offenses (murder, rape, robbery, and aggravated assault), aggravated assault typically has the highest rate of occurrence. This trend continued in 2013 with aggravated assault accounting for 62.2 percent of all violent crimes. (Table 1)

Regional Offense Trends and Rates

The UCR program divides the United States into four regions: the Northeast, the South, the Midwest, and the West. (More details concerning geographic regions are provided in Appendix III.)

NORTHEAST

The region with the smallest proportion of the nation's population (an estimated 17.7 percent in 2013) also accounted for the smallest proportion of the nation's estimated number of aggravated assaults (15.1 percent). Occurrences of aggravated assault decreased 4.8 percent from 2012 to 2013, dropping to an estimated 109,395 incidents. The region continued to have the lowest aggravated assault rate in the nation, at 195.5 incidents per 100,000 inhabitants. (Tables 3 and 4)

MIDWEST

With 21.4 percent of the nation's total population in 2013, the Midwest accounted for approximately 18.8 percent of the nation's estimated number of aggravated assaults. Occurrences of this offense decreased 6.3 percent from the estimated total for 2012, dropping to an estimated 135,803 incidents. The region's aggravated assault rate, at 201.0 incidents per 100,000 inhabitants, represented a 6.6 percent decrease from the 2012 rate. (Tables 3 and 4)

SOUTH

The South, the nation's most highly populated region, accounted for an estimated 43.0 percent of the nation's population in 2013 and the largest amount of the nation's estimated number of aggravated assaults (43.0 percent). From 2012 to 2013, the estimated number of aggravated assaults decreased 4.7 percent, to a total of 311,465 incidents. The rate of aggravated assaults decreased to 263.1 per 100,000 inhabitants. (Tables 3 and 4)

WEST

In 2013, the West was home to an estimated 23.5 percent of the nation's population. The region accounted for 23.1 percent of the nation's estimated number of aggravated assaults. From 2012 to 2013, the estimated number of offenses decreased 4.5 percent to 167,486 incidents. The rate, estimated at 225.6 offenses per 100,000 inhabitants, represented a drop of 5.5 percent from the rate of 2012. (Tables 3 and 4)

Community Types

The UCR program aggregates data for three community types: metropolitan statistical areas (MSAs), cities outside MSAs, and nonmetropolitan counties outside MSAs. MSAs include a central city or urbanized area with at least 50,000 inhabitants, as well as the county that contains the principal city and other adjacent counties that have a high degree of social and economic integration as measured through commuting. Cities outside MSAs are mostly incorporated areas, and nonmetropolitan counties are made up of mostly unincorporated areas. (For additional information about community types, see Appendix III.)

In 2013, 85.2 percent of the nation's population lived in MSAs, where the rate of aggravated assault was an estimated 235.6 per 100,000 inhabitants. Cities outside MSAs (with 6.0 percent of the U.S. population) had the highest rate of aggravated assault at 271.6 offenses per 100,000 inhabitants. Nonmetropolitan counties accounted for 8.8 percent of the U.S. population and had an offense rate of 136.4 aggravated assaults per 100,000 inhabitants. (Table 2)

Population Groups: Trends and Rates

From 2012 to 2013, the number of aggravated assaults decreased for all cities. Cities with 25,000 to 49,999 inhabitants experienced the greatest decrease (8.0 percent), followed by cities with 100,000 to 249,999 and 250,000 to 499,999, both of which decreased 6.5 percent. In metropolitan counties, the number of aggravated assaults dropped by 3.5 percent; in nonmetropolitan counties, this number decreased by 4.3 percent. Aggravated assaults in suburban areas decreased 4.7 percent from 2012 to 2013. (Table 12)

Aggravated assault occurred at an estimated rate of 229.1 offenses per 100,000 inhabitants nationwide. The collective rate for cities was 265.3 aggravated assaults per 100,000 inhabitants. Among city population groups, rates ranged from a high of 483.1 offenses per 100,000 inhabitants (in cities with 500,000 to 999,999 inhabitants) to a low of 177.3 offenses per 100,000 inhabitants (in cities with 10,000 to 24,999 inhabitants). The aggravated assault rate was 175.7 in metropolitan counties and 135.8 in nonmetropolitan counties. It was 163.9 in suburban areas. (Table 16)

Offense Analysis

AGGRAVATED ASSAULT BY WEAPON

Of the aggravated assault offenses for which law enforcement agencies provided expanded data in 2013, 27.0 percent involved personal weapons such as hands, fists, and/or feet; 21.6 percent were committed with firearms; 19.1 percent involved knives or other cutting instruments; and 32.2 percent involved other weapons. (Table 19)

PROPERTY CRIME

Figure 2.6 Percent Change of Property Crimes, 1992–2013

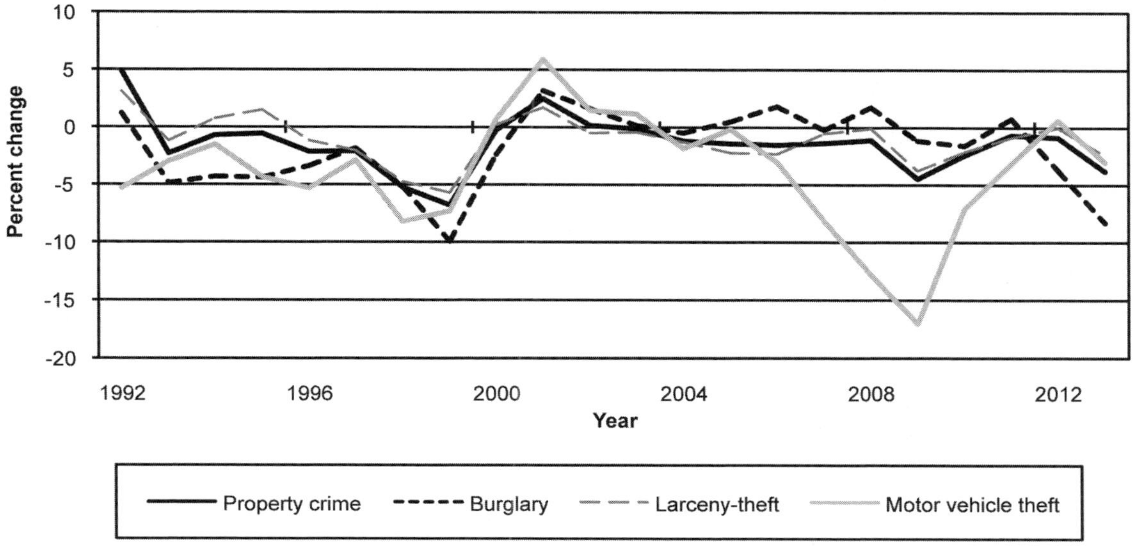

Definition

The UCR program's definition of property crime includes the offenses of burglary, larceny-theft, motor vehicle theft, and arson. The object of theft-type offenses is the taking of money or property without the use of force or threat of force against the victims. Property crime includes arson because the offense involves the destruction of property; however, arson victims may be subjected to force. Because of limited participation and the varying collection procedures conducted by local law enforcement agencies, only limited data are available for arson. Arson statistics are included in the trend, clearance, and arrest tables in *Crime in the United States*, but they are not included in any estimated volume data. More information on the expanded arson tables (which are available online but not included in this publication) can be found in Section I.

Data Collection

The data presented in *Crime in the United States* reflect the Hierarchy Rule, which counts only the most serious offense in a multiple-offense criminal incident. In descending order of severity, the violent crimes are murder and nonnegligent manslaughter, rape, robbery, and aggravated assault; these are followed by the property crimes of burglary, larceny-theft, and motor vehicle theft. The Hierarchy Rule does not apply to the offense of arson.

National Volume, Trends, and Rates

An estimated 8,632,512 property crimes were committed in the United States in 2013, representing a 3.8 percent decrease from the 2012 (2-year trend) estimate, a 7.5 percent decrease from the 2009 (5-year trend) estimate, and a 16.3 percent decrease from the 2004 (10-year trend) estimate. (Tables 1 and 1A)

From 2012 to 2013, motor vehicle theft decreased 3.3 percent. Larceny-theft decreased 13.4 percent from 2004 to 2013, 5.3 percent from 2009 to 2013, and 2.7 percent from 2012 to 2013. Burglary declined 10.1 percent from 2004, 12.5 percent from 2009, and 8.6 percent from 2012. (Tables 1 and 1A)

The estimated property crime rate per 100,000 inhabitants in 2013 was 2,730.7 a 4.8 percent decrease from the 2012 rate, an 10.2 percent decrease from the 2009 rate, and a 22.3 percent decrease from the 2004 rate. The rate of burglaries per 100,000 residents fell 16.5 percent from 2004 to 2013.The motor vehicle theft rates per 100,000 residents fell 43.5 percent from 2004 to 2013. (Tables 1 and 1A)

Regional Offense Trends and Rates

The UCR program separates the United States into four regions: the Northeast, the Midwest, the South, and the West. (Geographic breakdowns can be found in Appendix III.) Property crime data collected by the UCR program and aggregated by region reflected the following results.

NORTHEAST

The Northeast region accounted for 17.7 percent of the nation's population in 2013. The region also accounted for 12.7 percent of the nation's estimated number of property crimes in 2013. Law enforcement in the Northeast saw a 5.6 percent decrease in the estimated number of property crimes from 2012 to 2013. The property crime rate for the Northeast, estimated at 1,960.4 incidents per 100,000 inhabitants, was 5.9 percent less than the 2012 rate. (Tables 3 and 4)

MIDWEST

The Midwest, with 21.4 percent of the U.S. population in 2013, accounted for 20.0 percent of the nation's estimated number of property crimes. Law enforcement in the Midwest saw the number of property crimes decrease 7.7 percent from 2012 to 2013. The rate of property crime in the Midwest in 2013, estimated at 2,560.4 incidents per 100,000 inhabitants, represented an 8.0 percent decrease from the 2012 rate. (Tables 3 and 4)

SOUTH

The South, the nation's most populous region, accounted for 37.4 percent of the U.S. population in 2013. The region also accounted for an estimated 42.4 percent of the nation's property crimes. The South experienced a 3.4 percent decrease in its estimated number of property crimes from 2012 to 2013. The 2013 property crime rate, an estimated 3,094.8 incidents per 100,000 inhabitants, dropped 4.3 percent from the 2012 rate. (Tables 3 and 4)

WEST

In 2013, the West accounted for 23.5 percent of the nation's population. The West also accounted for 24.8 percent of the nation's estimated number of property crimes. From 2012 to 2013, the estimated number of property crimes in this region decreased 1.5 percent. The estimated property crime rate in the West in 2013, 2,885.4 incidents per 100,000 inhabitants, was a 2.5 percent decrease from the 2012 rate. (Tables 3 and 4)

Community Types

The UCR program aggregates data by three community types: metropolitan statistical areas (MSAs), cities outside metropolitan areas, and nonmetropolitan counties. (Additional in-depth information regarding community types can be found in Appendix III.) In 2013, 85.2 percent of the U.S. population lived in MSAs. The property crime rate for MSAs was 2,815.7 per 100,000 inhabitants. Cities outside metropolitan areas, which accounted for 6.0 percent of the total population in 2013, had a property crime rate of 3,417.2 per 100,000 inhabitants. Nonmetropolitan counties, with 8.8 percent of the nation's population in 2013, had a property crime rate of 1,440.4 per 100,000 inhabitants. (Table 2)

Population Groups: Trends and Rates

The UCR program organizes the agencies that contribute data into population groups, which include cities, metropolitan counties, and nonmetropolitan counties. (Appendix III provides further details about these groups.) From 2012 to 2013, law enforcement in the nation's cities collectively reported a 3.6 percent decrease in the number of property crimes. Most city groups experienced decreases in the number of property crimes; cities with fewer than 10,000 residents had the greatest decline, 5.5 percent. Metropolitan counties also experienced a decrease of 5.5 percent from 2012 to 2013, while property crime in nonmetropolitan counties dropped 8.0 percent. (Table 12)

The nation's cities collectively had a property crime rate of 3,196.7 incidents per 100,000 inhabitants in 2013. Nonmetropolitan counties had a rate of 1,424.4 incidents per 100,000 inhabitants, and metropolitan counties had a rate of 1,929.3 incidents per 100,000 inhabitants. The rate was 2,204.6 in suburban areas. (Table 16)

Offense Analysis

The estimated dollar loss attributing to property crimes, not including arson, in 2013 was $16.6 billion. Among the individual property crime categories, the dollar losses were an estimated $4.5 billion for burglary, $7.6 billion for larceny-theft, and more than $4.1 billion for motor vehicle theft. In 2013, the average dollar value per motor vehicle stolen in the United States was $6,1019. The average dollar value of property taken during burglaries was $2,322, and during larceny-thefts, $1,259. (Tables 1 and 23) Arson had an average dollar loss of $14.390. Arsons of industrial/manufacturing structures had the highest average dollar loss ($126.606), followed by "other commercial" structures. (Expanded Arson Table 2)

BURGLARY

Figure 2.7 Burglary, by Location and Time, 2013

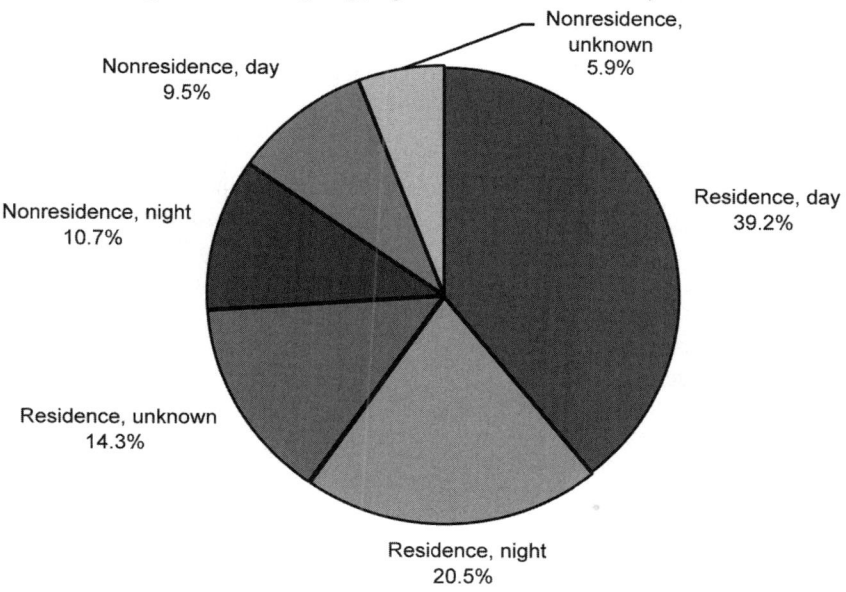

- Nonresidence, unknown 5.9%
- Nonresidence, day 9.5%
- Nonresidence, night 10.7%
- Residence, unknown 14.3%
- Residence, night 20.5%
- Residence, day 39.2%

Definition

The UCR program defines burglary as the unlawful entry of a structure to commit a felony or theft. To classify an offense as a burglary, the use of force to gain entry need not have occurred. The program has three subclassifications for burglary: forcible entry, unlawful entry where no force is used, and attempted forcible entry. The UCR definition of "structure" includes, but is not limited to, apartments, barns, house trailers or houseboats (when used as permanent dwellings), offices, railroad cars (but not automobiles), stables, and vessels (such as ships).

National Volume, Trends, and Rate

In 2013, there were an estimated 1,928,465 burglaries—a decrease of 8.6 percent when compared with 2012 data. There was a decrease of 12.5 percent in the number of burglaries in 2013 when compared with the 2009 estimate, and a decrease of 10.1 percent when compared with the 2004 estimate. Burglary accounted for 22.3 percent of the estimated number of property crimes committed in 2013. The burglary rate for the United States in 2013 was 610.0 incidents per 100,000 inhabitants, a 9.3 percent decrease from the 2012 rate. (Tables 1 and 1A)

Regional Offense Trends and Rates

The UCR program divides the United States into four regions: the Northeast, the Midwest, the South, and the West. (Details regarding these regions can be found in Appendix III.) An analysis of burglary data by region showed the following details.

NORTHEAST

In 2013, 17.7 percent of the nation's population lived in the Northeast. This region accounted for 10.8 percent of the estimated total number of burglary offenses in the nation in 2013. The region's burglary rate, an estimated 372.4 offenses per 100,000 inhabitants, represented a decrease of 12.3 percent from the 2012 rate. (Tables 3 and 4)

MIDWEST

The Midwest accounted for 21.4 percent of the nation's population in 2013. This region accounted for 19.9 percent of the nation's estimated number of burglaries. In this region, the estimated number of burglaries dropped 12.1 percent from 2012 to 2013. The Midwest had a burglary rate of 567.4 offenses per 100,000 inhabitants, a 12.4 percent decrease from the 2012 rate. (Tables 3 and 4)

SOUTH

The South, the nation's most highly populated region (37.4 percent of all inhabitants), had the most burglaries in 2013 (an estimated 871,095); however, this represented an 8.2 percent drop from its estimate in 2012. With 37.4 percent of the nation's population, this region accounted for 45.2 percent of all burglaries in the United States. The estimated rate of burglary in the South was 735.8 incidents per 100,000 inhabitants, an 9.0 percent decrease from the 2012 rate. (Tables 3 and 4)

WEST

The West accounted for 23.5 percent of the nation's population in 2013. This region accounted for an estimated 24.2 percent of the nation's burglaries. The region's burglary rate was 627.2, a 5.6 percent increase from the 2012 rate. The total number of burglaries (465,758) represented a 4.7 percent decrease from the 2012 estimate. (Tables 3 and 4)

Community Types

The UCR program aggregates data by three community types: metropolitan statistical areas (MSAs), cities outside MSAs, and nonmetropolitan counties. (See Appendix III for more information regarding community types.) In 2013, 85.2 percent of the U.S. population lived in MSAs, and an estimated 84.8 percent of all burglaries occurred in this type of community. Inhabitants of cities outside MSAs accounted for 6.0 percent of the total population in 2013 and 6.7 percent of the estimated number of burglaries; nonmetropolitan counties, with 8.8 percent of the U.S. population, accounted for 6.6 percent of all burglaries. The burglary rates per 100,000 inhabitants were 613.3 in MSAs, 737.9 in cities outside MSAs, and 491.0 in nonmetropolitan counties. (Table 2)

Population Groups: Trends and Rates

In addition to analyzing data by region and community type, the UCR program aggregates crime statistics by population groups. Cities are categorized into six groups based on the number of inhabitants; counties are categorized into two groups, metropolitan and nonmetropolitan. (Appendix III offers further details regarding these population groups.)

An examination of data from law enforcement agencies showed that the nation's cities experienced a collective 8.5 percent decrease in burglaries from 2012 to 2013. Burglaries decreased in all city groups, with cities of 10,000 to 24,999 inhabitants posting the greatest decrease (9.5 percent). The volume of burglaries decreased 8.9 percent in metropolitan counties, 9.2 percent in nonmetropolitan counties, and 9.4 percent in suburban areas. (Table 12)

The UCR program calculates burglary rates for population groups from the information provided by participating agencies that submitted all 12 months of offense data for the year. In 2013, the nation's cities had 658.1 offenses per 100,000 inhabitants. Cities with 500,000 to 999,999 inhabitants had the highest burglary rate at 958.5 incidents per 100,000 inhabitants. Cities with 10,000 to 24,999 inhabitants had the lowest burglary rate—537.5 incidents per 100,000 inhabitants. Metropolitan counties had a rate of 564.7 per 100,000 inhabitants, and nonmetropolitan counties had a rate of 478.9 per 100,000 inhabitants. The rate in suburban areas was 494.5 per 100,000 inhabitants. (Table 16)

Offense Analysis

The UCR program requests that participating law enforcement agencies provide details regarding the nature of burglaries in their jurisdictions, such as type of entry, type of structure, time of day, and dollar loss associated with each offense.

Of all burglaries in 2013, 59.2 percent involved forcible entry, 34.3 percent were unlawful entries (without force), and the remainder (6.4 percent) comprised forcible entry attempts. (Table 19)

Victims of burglary offenses suffered an estimated $4.5 billion in lost property in 2013; overall, the average dollar loss per burglary offense was $2,322. (Tables 1 and 23)

As in the past, burglars targeted residences more often than nonresidential structures. In 2013, burglaries of residential properties accounted for 74.0 percent of all burglary offenses. Law enforcement agencies were unable to determine the time of day for 20.2 percent of all reported burglaries. However, of the burglaries for which time of day could be established, most burglaries of residences (39.2 percent of all reported burglaries) occurred during the day, while most burglaries of nonresidential structures (10.7 percent of all reported burglaries) occurred at night. (Table 23)

LARCENY-THEFT

Figure 2.8 Larceny-Theft, Percent Distribution, 2013

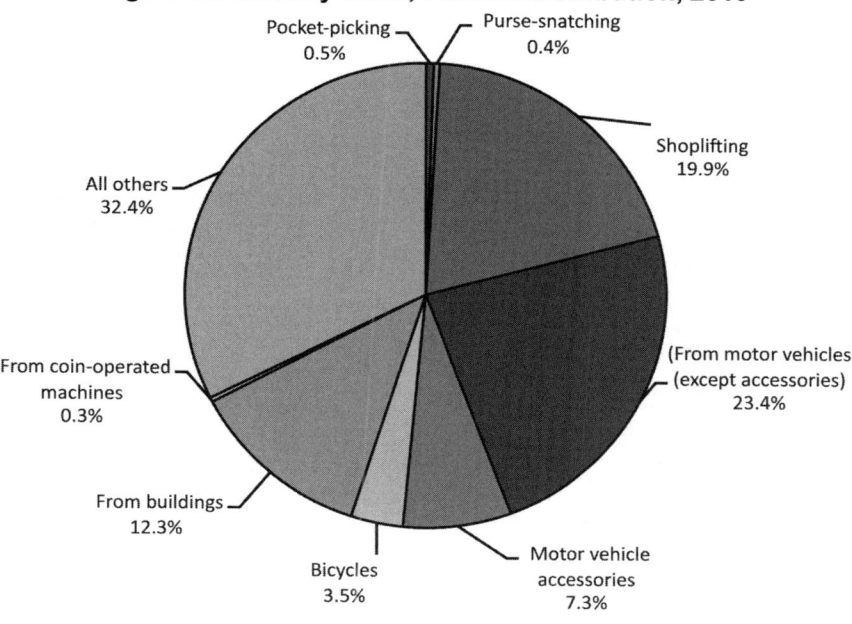

Pocket-picking 0.5%
Purse-snatching 0.4%
Shoplifting 19.9%
All others 32.4%
(From motor vehicles (except accessories) 23.4%
From coin-operated machines 0.3%
From buildings 12.3%
Bicycles 3.5%
Motor vehicle accessories 7.3%

Definition

The UCR program defines larceny-theft as the unlawful taking, carrying, leading, or riding away of property from the possession or constructive possession of another. Examples are thefts of bicycles, motor vehicle parts and accessories, shoplifting, pocket picking, or the stealing of any property or article not taken by force and violence or by fraud. Attempted larcenies are included. Embezzlement, confidence games, forgery, check fraud, and so on, are excluded from this category.

National Volume, Trends, and Rates

Larceny-thefts accounted for an estimated 69.6 percent of property crimes in 2013—an estimated 6,004,453 larceny-thefts nationwide. The estimated number of larceny-thefts declined 2.7 from 2012 to 2013. The 2013 estimate showed a 13.4 percent decline compared with the 2004 estimate. The trend data also showed decreases in the larceny-theft rates per 100,000 inhabitants during these periods. The rate of larceny-thefts declined 3.4 percent from 2012 to 2013 and 19.6 percent from 2004 to 2013. (Tables 1 and 1A)

Regional Offense Trends and Rates

The UCR program defines four regions within the United States: the Northeast, the Midwest, the South, and the West. (See Appendix III for a geographical description of each region.)

NORTHEAST

The Northeast was the region with the smallest proportion (17.7 percent) of the U.S. population in 2013. The region also experienced the fewest larceny-thefts in the country, accounting for only 13.8 percent of all larceny-thefts. The estimated number of offenses in 2013 (825,630) represented a 3.5 percent decline from 2012, and the estimated rate—1,475.8 incidents per 100,000 inhabitants—represented a 3.8 percent decline. (Tables 3 and 4)

MIDWEST

With 21.4 percent of the U.S. population in 2013, the Midwest accounted for an estimated 20.3 percent of the nation's larceny-thefts. The estimated number of offenses (1,217,580) declined 6.5 percent compared with the 2012 data, and the estimated rate of occurrences (1,802.5 incidents per 100,000 inhabitants) declined 6.8 percent. (Tables 3 and 4)

SOUTH

With more than one-third of the U.S. population in 2013 (37.4 percent), the South had the nation's highest proportion of larceny-theft offenses: an estimated 42.5 percent. (Estimated offenses in this region totaled 2,550,709, a 1.6 percent decrease from the 2012 estimate. The South's larceny-theft rate—estimated at 2,154.6 offenses per 100,000 inhabitants—decreased 2.5 percent from the 2012 estimate. (Tables 3 and 4)

WEST

In 2013, an estimated 23.5 percent of the U.S. population lived in the West. This region was also where 23.5 percent of the nation's estimated number of larceny-thefts took place. Occurrences of larceny-theft decreased 0.6 percent from 2012 to 2013 to an estimated total of 1,410,534 offenses. The region's larceny-theft rate, estimated at 1,899.6 offenses per 100,000 inhabitants, was a decrease of 1.6 percent from the 2012 rate. (Tables 3 and 4)

Community Types

The UCR program aggregates data for three community types: metropolitan statistical areas (MSAs), cities outside MSAs, and nonmetropolitan counties outside MSAs. MSAs include a central city or urbanized area with at least 50,000 inhabitants, as well as the county that contains the principal city and other adjacent counties that share a high degree of social and economic integration as measured through commuting. Cities outside MSAs are mostly incorporated areas, and nonmetropolitan counties are composed of unincorporated areas. (See Appendix III for more information regarding community types.)

In 2013, MSAs were home to an estimated 85.2 percent of the nation's population and again experienced 87.1 percent of the nation's larceny-theft incidents. Cities outside MSAs accounted for 6.0 percent of the U.S. population and 7.5 percent of larceny-theft offenses. Nonmetropolitan counties, which were home to 8.8 percent of the nation's population, accounted for 3.7 percent of the estimated number of larceny-theft offenses. The larceny-theft rates per 100,000 inhabitants were 1,961.7 in MSAs, 2,541.8 in cities outside MSAs, and 857.8 in nonmetropolitan counties. (Table 2)

Population Groups: Trends and Rates

In cities, collectively, occurrences of larceny-theft decreased 2.1 percent between 2012 and 2013. Cities with fewer than 10,000 inhabitants experienced the greatest decrease (4.9 percent). Cities with 500,000 to 999,999 inhabitants showed an increase in larceny-theft (0.3 percent). Larceny-theft continued to show decline in counties and suburban areas—nonmetropolitan counties experienced the greatest drop in larceny thefts, decreasing 7.6 percent, followed by metropolitan counties and suburban areas, with larceny-theft decreasing 3.9 percent in both classifications. (Table 12)

Based on reports of larceny-theft offenses from U.S. law enforcement agencies that submitted 12 months of complete data for 2013, this offense occurred at a rate of 1,915.5 offenses per 100,000 inhabitants. The collective rate for cities was 2,270.0 offenses per 100,000 inhabitants. Among city population groups, cities with 500,000 to 999,000 inhabitants had the highest larceny-theft rate, 3,041.9 incidents per 100,000 inhabitants. Cities with 10,000 to 24,999 inhabitants had the lowest rate, at 2,055.2. In metropolitan counties, the rate was 1,253.4 incidents per 100,000 inhabitants; in nonmetropolitan counties, the rate was 853.3 incidents per 100,000 inhabitants. The rate in suburban areas was 1,561.1 incidents per 100,000 inhabitants. (Table 16)

Offense Analysis

DISTRIBUTION

Table 23 provides a further breakdown of larceny-theft offenses, including shoplifting, thefts from buildings, thefts of motor vehicle accessories, thefts of bicycles, thefts from coin-operated machines, purse snatching, and pocket picking. The "all other" category, which includes the less-defined types of larceny-theft, accounted for 32.4 percent of all offenses in 2013.

LOSS BY DOLLAR VALUE

Larceny-theft offenses cost victims an estimated $7.6 billion dollars in 2013. The average value of property stolen was $1,259 per offense, $272 more than in 2012. Larceny-theft from buildings had the highest average dollar loss per offense at $1,384. Thefts from motor vehicles (except accessories) had an average dollar loss of $937 per offense; thefts of motor vehicle accessories, $556; purse snatching, $467; pocket picking, $514; thefts from coin-operated machines, $448; thefts of bicycles, $420; and shoplifting, $207. (Tables 1 and 23)

Offenses in which the stolen property was valued at more than $200 accounted for 46.8 percent of all larceny-thefts in 2013, up 0.2 percent from 2012. Table 23 provides further analysis, including the average dollar value per offense of all offenses in the overall category of property crime. (Table 23)

MOTOR VEHICLE THEFT

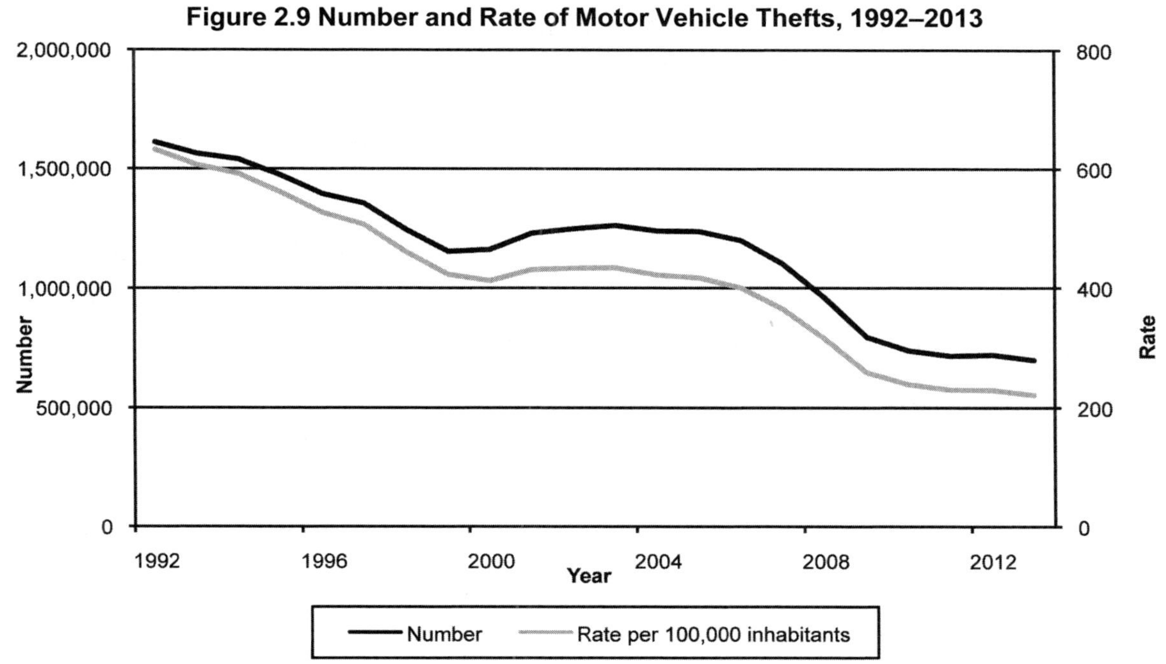

Figure 2.9 Number and Rate of Motor Vehicle Thefts, 1992–2013

Definition

The UCR program defines motor vehicle theft as the theft or attempted theft of a motor vehicle. The offense includes the stealing of automobiles, trucks, buses, motorcycles, snowmobiles, etc. The taking of a motor vehicle for temporary use by a person or persons with lawful access is excluded.

National Volume, Trends, and Rates

In 2013, an estimated 699,594 motor vehicle thefts took place in the United States. The estimated number of motor vehicle thefts decreased 3.3 percent when compared with data from 2012, decreased 12.1 percent when compared with 2009 figures, and decreased 43.5 percent when compared with 2004 figures. (Tables 1 and 1A)

The estimated rate of motor vehicle theft in 2013 was 221.3 incidents per 100,000 inhabitants. In the 2-year, 5-year, and 10-year trend data, this rate showed decline: the 2013 rate was 4.0 percent lower than the 2012 rate, 14.6 percent lower than the 2009 rate, and 47.5 percent lower than the 2004 rate. (Tables 1 and 1A)

Regional Offense Trends and Rates

In order to analyze crime by geographic area, the UCR program divides the United States into four regions: the Northeast, the Midwest, the South, and the West. (Appendix III provides a map delineating the regions.) This section provides a regional overview of motor vehicle theft.

NORTHEAST

The Northeast accounted for an estimated 17.7 percent of the nation's population in 2013. The region also accounted for an estimated 9.0 percent of its motor vehicle thefts. An estimated 62,764 motor vehicle thefts occurred in the Northeast in 2013, a 10.0 percent drop in occurrences from 2012. The estimated rate of 112.2 motor vehicle thefts per 100,000 inhabitants in the Northeast in 2013 represented a 10.3 percent decline from the 2012 rate. (Tables 3 and 4)

MIDWEST

An estimated 21.4 percent of the country's population resided in the Midwest in 2013. The region accounted for 18.4 percent of the nation's motor vehicle thefts. The Midwest had an estimated 128,619 motor vehicle thefts in 2013, a decrease of 4.7 percent from the previous year's total. The motor vehicle theft rate was estimated at 190.4 motor vehicles stolen per 100,000 inhabitants, a decrease of 5.1 percent from the 2012 rate. (Tables 3 and 4)

SOUTH

The South, the nation's most populous region, was home to an estimated 37.4 percent of the U.S. population in 2013 and accounted for 34.6 percent of the nation's motor vehicle thefts. The estimated 241,976 motor vehicle thefts in the South was down 3.7 percent from the 2012 estimate. Motor vehicles in the South were stolen at an estimated rate of 204.4 offenses per 100,000 inhabitants in 2013, a rate that was 4.6 percent lower than the 2012 rate. (Tables 3 and 4)

WEST

With approximately 23.5 percent of the U.S. population in 2013, the West accounted for the highest percentage (38.1 percent) of all motor vehicle thefts in the nation in 2013. An estimated 266,235 motor vehicle thefts occurred in this region. This number represented a 0.3 percent decrease from the previous year's estimate. The region's 2013 rate of 358.5 motor vehicles stolen per 100,000 inhabitants was 1.3 percent lower than the 2012 rate. (Tables 3 and 4)

Community Types

The UCR program aggregates data by three community types: metropolitan statistical areas (MSAs), cities outside MSAs, and nonmetropolitan counties. MSAs are areas that include a principal city or urbanized area with at least 50,000 inhabitants and the county that contains the principal city and other adjacent counties that have, as defined by the U.S. Office of Management and Budget, a high degree of economic and social integration.

In 2013, the vast majority (85.2 percent) of the U.S. population resided in MSAs, where approximately 92.1 percent of motor vehicle thefts occurred. For 2013, the UCR program estimated an overall rate of 240.7 motor vehicles stolen per 100,000 MSA inhabitants. Cities outside MSAs accounted for 3.5 percent of motor vehicle thefts, and nonmetropolitan counties also accounted for 3.5 percent of motor vehicle thefts. The UCR program estimated a 2013 rate of 137.6 motor vehicles stolen for every 100,000 inhabitants in cities outside MSAs, and a rate of 91.6 motor vehicles stolen per 100,000 inhabitants in nonmetropolitan counties. (Table 2)

Population Groups: Trends and Rates

The UCR program aggregates data by various population groups, which include cities, metropolitan counties, and nonmetropolitan counties. (A definition of these groups can be found in Appendix III.)

In cities, collectively, the number of motor vehicle thefts decreased 2.7 percent from 2012 to 2013. The number of motor vehicle thefts decreased in all city groups, with the exception of cities with 100,000 to 249,999 residents, where the rate increased 0.7 percent. Cities with 1 million or more inhabitants again experienced the greatest decline at 7.2 percent. Nonmetropolitan counties experienced a decrease of 4.7 percent, metropolitan counties experienced a decrease of 6.6 percent, and suburban areas experienced a decrease of 4.9 percent. (Table 12)

In 2013, cities had a collective motor vehicle theft rate of 268.6 per 100,000 inhabitants. Among the population groups, cities with 500,000 to 999,999 inhabitants experienced the highest rate of motor vehicle thefts with 522.4 motor vehicle thefts per 100,000 inhabitants. Conversely, the nation's smallest cities, those with populations under 10,000, had the lowest rate of motor vehicle theft with 130.2 incidents per 100,000 in population. Within the county groups, metropolitan counties had a rate of 157.3 motor vehicles stolen per 100,000 inhabitants, while nonmetropolitan counties had a rate of 92.3 incidents per 100,000 inhabitants. Suburban areas had a rate of 148.9 per 100,000 inhabitants. (Table 16)

Offense Analysis

Based on the reports of law enforcement agencies, the UCR program estimated the combined value of motor vehicles stolen nationwide in 2013 at approximately $4.1 billion. In 2013, the average dollar value per motor vehicle stolen in the United States was $5,972. (Tables 1 and 23) Automobiles were, by far, the most frequently stolen vehicles, accounting for 73.9 percent of all vehicles stolen. Trucks and buses accounted for 15.2 percent of stolen vehicles, and other vehicles accounted for 11.0 percent of stolen vehicles. (Expanded Motor Vehicle Theft Table)

By type of vehicle, automobiles were stolen at a rate of 170.3 cars per 100,000 inhabitants in 2013. Trucks and buses were stolen at a rate of 35.0 vehicles per 100,000 inhabitants, and other types of vehicles were stolen at a rate of 25.3 vehicles per 100,000 inhabitants. (Table 19)

ARSON

Figure 2.10 Average Dollar Amount of Arson Damage, by Property Type, 2013

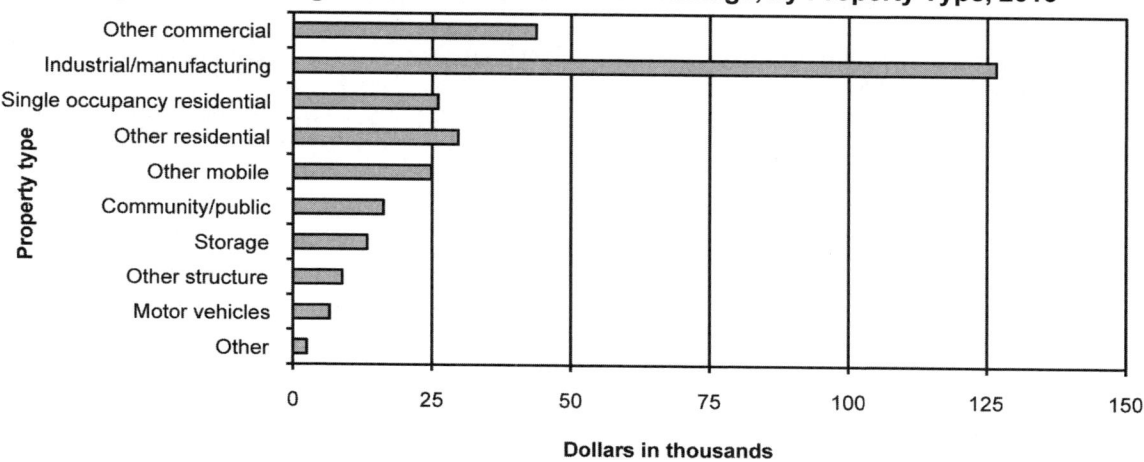

Dollars in thousands

Definition

The UCR program defines arson as any willful or malicious burning or attempt to burn (with or without intent to defraud) a dwelling house, public building, motor vehicle, aircraft, or personal property of another, etc.

Data Collection

Only fires that investigators determined were willfully set (not fires labeled as "suspicious" or "of unknown origin") are included in this arson data collection. Points to consider regarding arson statistics include:

National offense rates per 100,000 inhabitants (found in Tables 1, 2, and 4) do not include arson data; the FBI presents rates for arson separately. Arson rates are calculated based upon data received from all law enforcement agencies that provide the UCR program with data for 12 complete months.

Arson data collection does not include estimates for arson, because the degree of reporting arson offenses varies from agency to agency. Because of this unevenness of reporting, arson offenses are excluded from Tables 1 through 7, all of which contain offense estimations.

The number of arsons reported by individual law enforcement agencies is available in Tables 8 through 11. Arson trend data (which indicate year-to-year changes) can be found in Tables 12 through 15.

Population Groups: Trends and Rates

The number of arsons reported in cities 2013 was 14.2 percent lower than the number reported in 2012. Among the population groups labeled city, the subset with 1 million or more inhabitants had the only increase (1.8 percent). Cities with 25,000 to 49,999 inhabitants reported the largest year-to-year decrease, 23.1 percent. Agencies in the nation's metropolitan counties reported a 10.9 percent decrease in the number of arsons, while those in nonmetropolitan counties reported an 11.4 percent decrease. Those in suburban areas reported a 15.4 percent decline. (Table 12)

Arson rates in this paragraph were based on information received from 13,010 agencies that provided 12 months of complete arson data to the UCR program. An examination of data indicated that in 2013, the highest rate among non-subset city groups—27.9 arsons per 100,000 inhabitants—was reported in cities with 500,000 to 999,999 inhabitants. Cities with 10,000 to 24,999 inhabitants had the lowest rate of arson at 11.2 per 100,000 inhabitants. Metropolitan counties had 11.8 arsons per 100,000 inhabitants, and nonmetropolitan counties had 11.2 arsons per 100,000 inhabitants, the lowest of all the population groups. The rate in suburban areas was 11.5 per 100,000 inhabitants. (Expanded Arson Table 1)

Offense Analysis

The UCR program breaks down arson offenses into three property categories: structural, mobile, and other. In addition, the structural property type is broken down into seven types of structures, and the mobile property type consists of two subgroupings. The program also collects information on the estimated dollar value of the damaged property.

Property Type

The total number of arsons decreased in 2013. Arsons for the structural property type decreased 14.3 percent, other arsons dropped 13.9 percent, while arsons for the mobile property type dropped 10.4 percent from 2012 to 2013. (Table 15)

DISTRIBUTION BY PROPERTY TYPE

Arsons involving structures (residential, storage, public, etc.) accounted for 45.9 percent of the total number of arson offenses in 2013; arsons involving mobile property accounted for 23.8 percent of offenses; and other types of property (such

33

as crops, timber, fences, etc.) accounted for 30.3 percent of reported arsons. Of the arsons involving structures, 65.1 percent involved residential properties. Of the residential arsons, 74.2 percent were single-occupancy residences. Approximately 16.6 percent of structures were not in use when the arson occurred. Mobile arsons accounted for 23.8 percent of all arsons. Within this category, 94.5 percent of offenses involved the burning of motor vehicles. (Expanded Arson Table 2)

DOLLAR LOSS

In monetary terms, the average dollar loss in 2013 for arson was $14,390. The average dollar loss for a structural arson was $25,761. Within the structural arson category, the industrial/manufacturing subcategory had the highest average dollar loss at $126,606. Within that same category, single-occupancy dwellings had an average dollar loss of $26,080. Mobile property had an average dollar loss of $7,686. Other property types had an average dollar loss of $2,463. (Expanded Arson Table 2)

Table 1.   Violent Crime in the United States, by Volume and Rate Per 100,000 Inhabitants, 1994–2013

(Number, rate per 100,000 population.)

Year	Population[1]	Violent crime		Murder and nonnegligent manslaughter		Rape (legacy definition)[2]		Robbery		Aggravated assault	
		Number	Rate	Number	Rate	Number	Rate	Number	Rate	Number	Rate
1994	260,327,021	1,857,670	713.6	23,326	9.0	102,216	39.3	618,949	237.8	1,113,179	427.6
1995	262,803,276	1,798,792	684.5	21,606	8.2	97,470	37.1	580,509	220.9	1,099,207	418.3
1996	265,228,572	1,688,540	636.6	19,645	7.4	96,252	36.3	535,594	201.9	1,037,049	391.0
1997	267,783,607	1,636,096	611.0	18,208	6.8	96,153	35.9	498,534	186.2	1,023,201	382.1
1998	270,248,003	1,533,887	567.6	16,974	6.3	93,144	34.5	447,186	165.5	976,583	361.4
1999	272,690,813	1,426,044	523.0	15,522	5.7	89,411	32.8	409,371	150.1	911,740	334.3
2000	281,421,906	1,425,486	506.5	15,586	5.5	90,178	32.0	408,016	145.0	911,706	324.0
2001 [3]	285,317,559	1,439,480	504.5	16,037	5.6	90,863	31.8	423,557	148.5	909,023	318.6
2002	287,973,924	1,423,677	494.4	16,229	5.6	95,235	33.1	420,806	146.1	891,407	309.5
2003	290,788,976	1,383,676	475.8	16,528	5.7	93,883	32.3	414,235	142.5	859,030	295.4
2004	293,656,842	1,360,088	463.2	16,148	5.5	95,089	32.4	401,470	136.7	847,381	288.6
2005	296,507,061	1,390,745	469.0	16,740	5.6	94,347	31.8	417,438	140.8	862,220	290.8
2006	299,398,484	1,435,123	479.3	17,309	5.8	94,472	31.6	449,246	150.0	874,096	292.0
2007	301,621,157	1,422,970	471.8	17,128	5.7	92,160	30.6	447,324	148.3	866,358	287.2
2008	304,059,724	1,394,461	458.6	16,465	5.4	90,750	29.8	443,563	145.9	843,683	277.5
2009	307,006,550	1,325,896	431.9	15,399	5.0	89,241	29.1	408,742	133.1	812,514	264.7
2010 [4]	309,330,219	1,251,248	404.5	14,722	4.8	85,593	27.7	369,089	119.3	781,844	252.8
2011	311,587,816	1,206,005	387.1	14,661	4.7	84,175	27.0	354,746	113.9	752,423	241.5
2012	313,914,040	1,214,462	386.9	14,827	4.7	84,376	26.9	354,520	112.9	760,739	242.3
2013	316,128,839	1,163,146	367.9	14,196	4.5	79,770	25.2	345,031	109.1	724,149	229.1

1 Populations are U.S. Census Bureau provisional estimates as of July 1 for each year except 2000 and 2010, which are decennial census counts.   2 The figures shown in this column for the offense of rape were estimated using the legacy Uniform Crime Reporting definition of rape. See chapter notes for more detail.   3 The murder and nonnegligent homicides that occurred as a result of the events of September 11, 2001, are not included in this table.   4 The crime figures have been adjusted.

Table 1A.   Property Crime in the United States, by Volume and Rate Per 100,000 Inhabitants, 1994–2013

(Number, rate per 100,000 population.)

Year	Property crime		Burglary		Larceny-theft		Motor vehicle theft	
	Number	Rate	Number	Rate	Number	Rate	Number	Rate
1994	12,131,873	4,660.2	2,712,774	1,042.1	7,879,812	3,026.9	1,539,287	591.3
1995	12,063,935	4,590.5	2,593,784	987.0	7,997,710	3,043.2	1,472,441	560.3
1996	11,805,323	4,451.0	2,506,400	945.0	7,904,685	2,980.3	1,394,238	525.7
1997	11,558,475	4,316.3	2,460,526	918.8	7,743,760	2,891.8	1,354,189	505.7
1998	10,951,827	4,052.5	2,332,735	863.2	7,376,311	2,729.5	1,242,781	459.9
1999	10,208,334	3,743.6	2,100,739	770.4	6,955,520	2,550.7	1,152,075	422.5
2000	10,182,584	3,618.3	2,050,992	728.8	6,971,590	2,477.3	1,160,002	412.2
2001	10,437,189	3,658.1	2,116,531	741.8	7,092,267	2,485.7	1,228,391	430.5
2002	10,455,277	3,630.6	2,151,252	747.0	7,057,379	2,450.7	1,246,646	432.9
2003	10,442,862	3,591.2	2,154,834	741.0	7,026,802	2,416.5	1,261,226	433.7
2004	10,319,386	3,514.1	2,144,446	730.3	6,937,089	2,362.3	1,237,851	421.5
2005	10,174,754	3,431.5	2,155,448	726.9	6,783,447	2,287.8	1,235,859	416.8
2006	10,019,601	3,346.6	2,194,993	733.1	6,626,363	2,213.2	1,198,245	400.2
2007	9,882,212	3,276.4	2,190,198	726.1	6,591,542	2,185.4	1,100,472	364.9
2008	9,774,152	3,214.6	2,228,887	733.0	6,586,206	2,166.1	959,059	315.4
2009	9,337,060	3,041.3	2,203,313	717.7	6,338,095	2,064.5	795,652	259.2
2010	9,112,625	2,945.9	2,168,459	701.0	6,204,601	2,005.8	739,565	239.1
2011	9,052,743	2,905.4	2,185,140	701.3	6,151,095	1,974.10	716,508	230.0
2012	8,975,438	2,859.2	2,103,787	670.2	6,150,598	1,959.30	721,053	229.7
2013	8,632,512	2,730.7	1,928,465	610.0	6,004,453	1,899.40	699,594	221.3

Table 1B.   Violent Crime in the United States, Percent Change in Volume and Rate Per 100,000 Inhabitants for 2 Years, 5 Years, and 10 Years, 2004–2013

(Percent change.)

Year	Violent crime		Murder and nonnegligent manslaughter		Rape (legacy definition)[1]		Robbery	
	Number	Rate	Number	Rate	Number	Rate	Number	Rate
2004–2013	-14.5	-20.6	-12.1	-18.3	-16.1	-22.1	-14.1	-20.2
2009–2013	-12.3	-14.8	-7.8	-10.5	-10.6	-13.2	-15.6	-18.0
2012–2013	-4.2	-5.1	-4.2	-5.1	-6.3	-7.0	-2.8	-3.5

1 The figures shown in this column for the offense of rape were estimated using the legacy Uniform Crime Reporting definition of rape. See chapter notes for more detail.

Table 1C.   Property Crime in the United States, Percent Change in Volume and Rate Per 100,000 Inhabitants for 2 Years, 5 Years, and 10 Years, 2004–2013

(Percent change.)

Year	Property crime		Burglary		Larceny-theft		Motor vehicle theft	
	Number	Rate	Number	Rate	Number	Rate	Number	Rate
2004–2013	-16.3	-22.3	-10.1	-16.5	-13.4	-19.6	-43.5	-47.5
2009–2013	-7.5	-10.2	-12.5	-15.0	-5.3	-8.0	-12.1	-14.6
2012–2013	-3.8	-4.8	-8.6	-9.3	-2.7	-3.4	-3.3	-4.0

Table 2.   Crime in the United States, by Community Type, 2013

(Number, percent, rate per 100,000 population)

Area	Murder and nonnegligent manslaughter	Rape (revised definition)[1]	Robbery	Aggravated assault	Burglary	Larceny-theft	Motor vehicle theft
United States	14,196	108,612	345,031	724,149	1,928,465	6,004,453	699,594
Rate per 100,000 inhabitants	4.5	34.4	109.1	229.1	610.0	1,899.4	221.3
Metropolitan Statistical Areas	X	X	X	X	X	X	X
Area actually reporting (percent)[2]	12,495	46,965	330,671	629,873	1,635,957	5,228,622	644,175
Estimated total (percent)	12,548	90,739	332,161	634,340	1,650,943	5,280,799	647,827
Rate per 100,000 inhabitants	4.7	33.7	123.4	235.6	613.3	1,961.7	240.7
Cities Outside Metropolitan Areas	X	X	X	X	X	X	X
Area actually reporting (percent)[2]	654	5,256	8,763	48,512	129,969	449,937	24,519
Estimated total (percent)	714	9,724	9,581	51,781	140,654	484,530	26,225
Rate per 100,000 inhabitants	3.7	51.0	50.3	271.6	737.9	2,541.8	137.6
Nonmetropolitan Counties	X	X	X	X	X	X	X
Area actually reporting (percent)[2]	870	5,830	3,068	35,688	127,915	225,019	24,160
Estimated total (percent)	934	8,149	3,289	38,028	136,868	239,124	25,542
Rate per 100,000 inhabitants	3.4	29.2	11.8	136.4	491.0	857.8	91.6

Note: Although arson data are included in the trend and clearance tables, sufficient data are not available to estimate totals for this offense. Therefore, no arson data are published in this table.   X = Not applicable.   1 Population figures are U.S. Census Bureau provisional estimates as of July 1, 2013.   2 The percentage reported under "Area actually reporting" is based upon the population covered by agencies providing 3 months or more of crime reports to the FBI.

Table 3.   Crime in the United States, Population and Offense Distribution, by Region, 2013

(Percent distribution.)

Region	Population	Violent crime	Murder and nonnegligent manslaughter	Rape (revised definition)[1]	Rape (legacy definition)[2]	Robbery	Aggravated assault	Property crime	Burglary	Larceny-theft	Motor vehicle theft
United States[3]	100.0	100.0	100.0	100.0	100.0	100.0	100.0	100.0	100.0	100.0	100.0
Northeast	17.7	16.1	13.8	12.5	12.6	19.1	15.1	12.7	10.8	13.8	9.0
Midwest	21.4	19.4	21.4	24.8	24.4	19.4	18.8	20.0	19.9	20.3	18.4
South	37.4	41.1	43.8	37.8	37.8	37.6	43.0	42.4	45.2	42.5	34.6
West	23.5	23.5	21.0	24.9	25.3	23.8	23.1	24.8	24.2	23.5	38.1

Note: Although arson data are included in the trend and clearance tables, sufficient data are not available to estimate totals for this offense. Therefore, no arson data are published in this table.   1 The figures shown in this column for the offense of rape were estimated using the revised Uniform Crime Reporting (UCR) definition of rape. See chapter notes for more detail.   2 The figures shown in this column for the offense of rape were estimated using the legacy Uniform Crime Reporting (UCR) definition of rape. See chapter notes for more detail.   3 Because of rounding, the percentages may not add to 100.0.

Table 4. Crime, by Region, Geographic Division, and State, 2012–2013

(Number, rate per 100,000 population, percent.)

Area	Population[1]	Violent crime[2]		Murder and nonnegligent manslaughter		Rape (revised definition)[3]		Rape (legacy definition)[4]	
		Number	Rate	Number	Rate	Number	Rate	Number	Rate
United States [5,6,7,8,9]									
2012	313,873,685	1,217,067	387.8	14,866	4.7	NA	NA	85,141	27.1
2013	316,128,839	1,163,146	367.9	14,196	4.5	108,612	34.4	79,770	25.2
Percent change	X	-4.4	-5.1	-4.5	-5.2	NA	NA	-6.3	-7.0
Northeast [5,6,7,8]									
2012	55,771,792	195,891	351.2	2,101	3.8	NA	NA	11,107	19.9
2013	55,943,073	187,464	335.1	1,953	3.5	13,623	24.4	10,054	18.0
Percent change	X	-4.3	-4.6	-7.0	-7.3	NA	NA	-9.5	-9.8
New England[5,6,7,8]									
2012	14,563,443	45,245	310.7	323	2.2	NA	NA	3,864	26.5
2013	14,618,806	43,740	299.2	310	2.1	5,376	36.8	3,978	27.2
Percent change	X	-3.3	-3.7	-4.0	-4.4	NA	NA	+3.0	+2.6
Connecticut[6]									
2012	3,591,765	10,183	283.5	117	3.3	NA	NA	933	26.0
2013	3,596,080	9,153	254.5	86	2.4	955	26.6	668	18.6
Percent change	X	-10.1	-10.2	-26.5	-26.6	NA	NA	-28.4	-28.5
Maine[6,8]									
2012	1,328,501	1,626	122.4	26	2.0	NA	NA	372	28.0
2013	1,328,302	1,615	121.6	24	1.8	447	33.7	344	25.9
Percent change	X	-0.7	-0.7	-7.7	-7.7	NA	NA	-7.5	-7.5
Massachusetts[6]									
2012	6,645,303	27,047	407.0	121	1.8	NA	NA	1,650	24.8
2013	6,692,824	27,038	404.0	137	2.0	2,718	40.6	2,089	31.2
Percent change	X	*	-0.7	+13.2	+12.4	NA	NA	+26.6	+25.7
New Hampshire[7]									
2012	1,321,617	2,841	215.0	15	1.1	NA	NA	486	36.8
2013	1,323,459	2,642	199.6	22	1.7	686	51.8	479	36.2
Percent change	X	-7.0	-7.1	+46.7	+46.5	NA	NA	-1.4	-1.6
Rhode Island[7]									
2012	1,050,304	2,657	253.0	36	3.4	NA	NA	292	27.8
2013	1,051,511	2,572	244.6	31	2.9	440	41.8	307	29.2
Percent change	X	-3.2	-3.3	-13.9	-14.0	NA	NA	+5.1	+5.0
Vermont[7]									
2012	625,953	891	142.3	8	1.3	NA	NA	131	20.9
2013	626,630	720	114.9	10	1.6	130	20.7	91	14.5
Percent change	X	-19.2	-19.3	+25.0	+24.9	NA	NA	-30.5	-30.6
Middle Atlantic[5,7,8]									
2012	41,208,349	150,646	365.6	1,778	4.3	NA	NA	7,243	17.6
2013	41,324,267	143,724	347.8	1,643	4.0	8,247	20.0	6,076	14.7
Percent change	X	-4.6	-4.9	-7.6	-7.9	NA	NA	-16.1	-16.3
New Jersey									
2012	8,867,749	25,727	290.1	388	4.4	NA	NA	1,035	11.7
2013	8,899,339	25,415	285.6	401	4.5	1,120	12.6	861	9.7
Percent change	X	-1.2	-1.6	+3.4	+3.0	NA	NA	-16.8	-17.1
New York[3]									
2012	19,576,125	79,535	406.3	683	3.5	NA	NA	2,837	14.5
2013	19,651,127	76,596	389.8	648	3.3	3,353	17.1	2,577	13.1
Percent change	X	-3.7	-4.1	-5.1	-5.5	NA	NA	-9.2	-9.5
Pennsylvania[7,8]									
2012	12,764,475	45,384	355.5	707	5.5	NA	NA	3,371	26.4
2013	12,773,801	41,713	326.6	594	4.7	3,774	29.5	2,638	20.7
Percent change	X	-8.1	-8.2	-16.0	-16.0	NA	NA	-21.7	-21.8
Midwest [5,6,7,8]									
2012	67,321,425	239,436	355.7	3,148	4.7	NA	NA	21,678	32.2
2013	67,547,890	225,227	333.4	3,042	4.5	26,929	39.9	19,437	28.8
Percent change	X	-5.9	-6.2	-3.4	-3.7	NA	NA	-10.3	-10.6
East North Central[5,6,7,8]									
2012	46,566,078	172,143	369.7	2,425	5.2	NA	NA	14,918	32.0
2013	46,662,180	160,988	345.0	2,309	4.9	18,726	40.1	13,648	29.2
Percent change	X	-6.5	-6.7	-4.8	-5.0	NA	NA	-8.5	-8.7
Illinois[6]									
2012	12,868,192	53,556	416.2	770	6.0	NA	NA	3,581	27.8
2013	12,882,135	47,987	372.5	706	5.5	4,263	33.1	3,276	25.4
Percent change	X	-10.4	-10.5	-8.3	-8.4	NA	NA	-8.5	-8.6
Indiana[6]									
2012	6,537,782	22,544	344.8	307	4.7	NA	NA	1,661	25.4
2013	6,570,902	22,991	349.9	355	5.4	2,142	32.6	1,646	25.0
Percent change	X	+2.0	+1.5	+15.6	+15.1	NA	NA	-0.9	-1.4
Michigan[7]									
2012	9,882,519	44,962	455.0	701	7.1	NA	NA	4,635	46.9
2013	9,895,622	42,536	429.8	631	6.4	6,593	66.6	4,606	46.5

Table 4.   Crime, by Region, Geographic Division, and State, 2012–2013— continued

(Number, rate per 100,000 population, percent.)

Area	Population[1]	Violent crime[2]		Murder and nonnegligent manslaughter[*]		Rape (revised definition)[3]		Rape (legacy definition)[4]	
		Number	Rate	Number	Rate	Number	Rate	Number	Rate
Percent change	X	-5.4	-5.5	-10.0	-10.1	NA	NA	-0.6	-0.8
Ohio[6]									
2012	11,553,031	34,827	301.5	478	4.1	NA	NA	3,813	33.0
2013	11,570,808	31,904	275.7	455	3.9	4,041	34.9	2,824	24.4
Percent change	X	-8.4	-8.5	-4.8	-5.0	NA	NA	-25.9	-26.1
Wisconsin[6,8]									
2012	5,724,554	16,254	283.9	169	3.0	NA	NA	1,228	21.5
2013	5,742,713	15,570	271.1	162	2.8	1,687	29.4	1,296	22.6
Percent change	X	-4.2	-4.5	-4.1	-4.4	NA	NA	+5.5	+5.2
West North Central [5,6,7]									
2012	20,755,347	67,293	324.2	723	3.5	NA	NA	6,760	32.6
2013	20,885,710	64,239	307.6	733	3.5	8,203	39.3	5,789	27.7
Percent change	X	-4.5	-5.1	+1.4	+0.8	NA	NA	-14.4	-14.9
Iowa[7]									
2012	3,075,039	8,167	265.6	49	1.6	NA	NA	901	29.3
2013	3,090,416	8,062	260.9	43	1.4	1,083	35.0	757	24.5
Percent change	X	-1.3	-1.8	-12.2	-12.7	NA	NA	-16.0	-16.4
Kansas[6]									
2012	2,885,398	10,292	356.7	85	2.9	NA	NA	1,105	38.3
2013	2,893,957	9,478	327.5	112	3.9	1,195	41.3	835	28.9
Percent change	X	-7.9	-8.2	+31.8	+31.4	NA	NA	-24.4	-24.7
Minnesota[7]									
2012	5,379,646	12,419	230.9	99	1.8	NA	NA	1,638	30.4
2013	5,420,380	12,100	223.2	114	2.1	2,008	37.0	1,403	25.9
Percent change	X	-2.6	-3.3	+15.2	+14.3	NA	NA	-14.3	-15.0
Missouri[7]									
2012	6,024,522	27,189	451.3	390	6.5	NA	NA	1,527	25.3
2013	6,044,171	25,509	422.0	371	6.1	2,287	37.8	1,599	26.5
Percent change	X	-6.2	-6.5	-4.9	-5.2	NA	NA	+4.7	+4.4
Nebraska[6]									
2012	1,855,350	4,802	258.8	52	2.8	NA	NA	710	38.3
2013	1,868,516	4,712	252.2	57	3.1	801	42.9	616	33.0
Percent change	X	-1.9	-2.6	+9.6	+8.8	NA	NA	-13.2	-13.9
North Dakota[7]									
2012	701,345	1,723	245.7	25	3.6	NA	NA	279	39.8
2013	723,393	1,854	256.3	16	2.2	330	45.6	230	31.8
Percent change	X	+7.6	+4.3	-36.0	-38.0	NA	NA	-17.6	-20.1
South Dakota[7]									
2012	834,047	2,701	323.8	23	2.8	NA	NA	600	71.9
2013	844,877	2,524	298.7	20	2.4	499	59.1	349	41.3
Percent change	X	-6.6	-7.8	-13.0	-14.2	NA	NA	-41.8	-42.6
South [5,6,7,9]									
2012	117,253,992	497,113	424.0	6,499	5.5	NA	NA	31,940	27.2
2013	118,383,453	477,640	403.5	6,222	5.3	41,028	34.7	30,128	25.4
Percent change	X	-3.9	-4.8	-4.3	-5.2	NA	NA	-5.7	-6.6
South Atlantic [5,7,9]									
2012	61,186,832	255,319	417.3	3,312	5.4	NA	NA	14,741	24.1
2013	61,783,647	244,019	395.0	3,194	5.2	19,104	30.9	13,801	22.3
Percent change	X	-4.4	-5.3	-3.6	-4.5	NA	NA	-6.4	-7.3
Delaware[7]									
2012	917,053	5,048	550.5	56	6.1	NA	NA	249	27.2
2013	925,749	4,435	479.1	39	4.2	380	41.0	266	28.7
Percent change	X	-12.1	-13.0	-30.4	-31.0	NA	NA	+6.8	+5.8
District of Columbia[7,9]									
2012	633,427	7,866	1,241.8	88	13.9	NA	NA	236	37.3
2013	646,449	8,287	1,281.9	103	15.9	395	61.1	276	42.7
Percent change	X	+5.4	+3.2	+17.0	+14.7	NA	NA	+16.9	+14.6
Florida[7]									
2012	19,320,749	94,087	487.0	1,009	5.2	NA	NA	5,260	27.2
2013	19,552,860	89,948	460.0	972	5.0	6,760	34.6	4,722	24.1
Percent change	X	-4.4	-5.5	-3.7	-4.8	NA	NA	-10.2	-11.3
Georgia									
2012	9,915,646	37,675	380.0	583	5.9	NA	NA	2,143	21.6
2013	9,992,167	35,943	359.7	556	5.6	2,582	25.8	1,984	19.9
Percent change	X	-4.6	-5.3	-4.6	-5.4	NA	NA	-7.4	-8.1
Maryland									
2012	5,884,868	28,086	477.3	373	6.3	NA	NA	1,237	21.0
2013	5,928,814	27,734	467.8	381	6.4	1,532	25.8	1,177	19.9
Percent change	X	-1.3	-2.0	+2.1	+1.4	NA	NA	-4.9	-5.6
North Carolina									
2012	9,748,364	34,464	353.5	479	4.9	NA	NA	1,984	20.4
2013	9,848,060	33,152	336.6	469	4.8	2,369	24.1	1,821	18.5
Percent change	X	-3.8	-4.8	-2.1	-3.1	NA	NA	-8.2	-9.1
South Carolina[7]									

Table 4.   Crime, by Region, Geographic Division, and State, 2012–2013— continued

(Number, rate per 100,000 population, percent.)

Area	Population[1]	Violent crime[2]		Murder and nonnegligent manslaughter		Rape (revised definition)[3]		Rape (legacy definition)[4]	
		Number	Rate	Number	Rate	Number	Rate	Number	Rate
2012	4,723,417	26,474	560.5	332	7.0	NA	NA	1,712	36.2
2013	4,774,839	23,625	494.8	297	6.2	2,171	45.5	1,518	31.8
Percent change	X	-10.8	-11.7	-10.5	-11.5	NA	NA	-11.3	-12.3
Virginia[7]									
2012	8,186,628	15,676	191.5	322	3.9	NA	NA	1,505	18.4
2013	8,260,405	15,524	187.9	316	3.8	2,262	27.4	1,581	19.1
Percent change	X	-1.0	-1.9	-1.9	-2.7	NA	NA	+5.0	+4.1
West Virginia[7]									
2012	1,856,680	5,943	320.1	70	3.8	NA	NA	415	22.4
2013	1,854,304	5,371	289.7	61	3.3	653	35.2	456	24.6
Percent change	X	-9.6	-9.5	-12.9	-12.7	NA	NA	+9.9	+10.0
East South Central [5,6,7]									
2012	18,638,622	80,527	432.0	1,156	6.2	NA	NA	5,474	29.4
2013	18,716,202	74,601	398.6	1,037	5.5	6,936	37.1	4,911	26.2
Percent change	X	-7.4	-7.7	-10.3	-10.7	NA	NA	-10.3	-10.7
Alabama[7]									
2012	4,817,528	21,693	450.3	342	7.1	NA	NA	1,296	26.9
2013	4,833,722	20,210	418.1	347	7.2	2,044	42.3	1,428	29.5
Percent change	X	-6.8	-7.1	+1.5	+1.1	NA	NA	+10.2	+9.8
Kentucky[6]									
2012	4,379,730	9,852	224.9	201	4.6	NA	NA	1,312	30.0
2013	4,395,295	8,737	198.8	167	3.8	1,611	36.7	1,126	25.6
Percent change	X	-11.3	-11.6	-16.9	-17.2	NA	NA	-14.2	-14.5
Mississippi[6]									
2012	2,986,450	7,769	260.1	213	7.1	NA	NA	819	27.4
2013	2,991,207	7,999	267.4	195	6.5	930	31.1	715	23.9
Percent change	X	+3.0	+2.8	-8.5	-8.6	NA	NA	-12.7	-12.8
Tennessee[7]									
2012	6,454,914	41,213	638.5	400	6.2	NA	NA	2,047	31.7
2013	6,495,978	37,655	579.7	328	5.0	2,351	36.2	1,642	25.3
Percent change	X	-8.6	-9.2	-18.0	-18.5	NA	NA	-19.8	-20.3
West South Central [5,6,7]									
2012	37,428,538	161,267	430.9	2,031	5.4	NA	NA	11,725	31.3
2013	37,883,604	159,020	419.8	1,991	5.3	14,988	39.6	11,416	30.1
Percent change	X	-1.4	-2.6	-2.0	-3.1	NA	NA	-2.6	-3.8
Arkansas[7]									
2012	2,949,828	13,851	469.6	174	5.9	NA	NA	1,233	41.8
2013	2,959,373	13,191	445.7	159	5.4	1,423	48.1	993	33.6
Percent change	X	-4.8	-5.1	-8.6	-8.9	NA	NA	-19.5	-19.7
Louisiana[6]									
2012	4,602,134	22,839	496.3	489	10.6	NA	NA	1,155	25.1
2013	4,625,470	23,609	510.4	498	10.8	1,619	35.0	1,244	26.9
Percent change	X	+3.4	+2.8	+1.8	+1.3	NA	NA	+7.7	+7.2
Oklahoma[6]									
2012	3,815,780	18,102	474.4	220	5.8	NA	NA	1,622	42.5
2013	3,850,568	16,484	428.1	195	5.1	2,180	56.6	1,675	43.5
Percent change	X	-8.9	-9.8	-11.4	-12.2	NA	NA	+3.3	+2.3
Texas[6]									
2012	26,060,796	106,475	408.6	1,148	4.4	NA	NA	7,715	29.6
2013	26,448,193	105,736	399.8	1,139	4.3	9,766	36.9	7,504	28.4
Percent change	X	-0.7	-2.1	-0.8	-2.2	NA	NA	-2.7	-4.2
West [5,6,7,8]									
2012	73,526,476	284,627	387.1	3,118	4.2	NA	NA	20,416	27.8
2013	74,254,423	272,815	367.4	2,979	4.0	27,032	36.4	20,151	27.1
Percent change	X	-4.1	-5.1	-4.5	-5.4	NA	NA	-1.3	-2.3
Mountain [5,6,7,8]									
2012	22,611,082	85,702	379.0	875	3.9	NA	NA	8,308	36.7
2013	22,881,245	84,139	367.7	938	4.1	11,541	50.4	8,491	37.1
Percent change	X	-1.8	-3.0	+7.2	+5.9	NA	NA	+2.2	+1.0
Arizona[6,8]									
2012	6,551,149	28,077	428.6	358	5.5	NA	NA	2,282	34.8
2013	6,626,624	26,892	405.8	357	5.4	3,050	46.0	2,343	35.4
Percent change	X	-4.2	-5.3	-0.3	-1.4	NA	NA	+2.7	+1.5
Colorado[7]									
2012	5,189,458	15,951	307.4	152	2.9	NA	NA	2,122	40.9
2013	5,268,367	15,342	291.2	178	3.4	2,934	55.7	2,050	38.9
Percent change	X	-3.8	-5.3	+17.1	+15.4	NA	NA	-3.4	-4.8
Idaho[7]									
2012	1,595,590	3,348	209.8	30	1.9	NA	NA	495	31.0
2013	1,612,136	3,300	204.7	27	1.7	655	40.6	457	28.3
Percent change	X	-1.4	-2.4	-10.0	-10.9	NA	NA	-7.7	-8.6
Montana[7]									
2012	1,005,494	2,803	278.8	29	2.9	NA	NA	392	39.0

Table 4.   Crime, by Region, Geographic Division, and State, 2012–2013— continued

(Number, rate per 100,000 population, percent.)

Area	Population[1]	Violent crime[2]		Murder and nonnegligent manslaughter		Rape (revised definition)[3]		Rape (legacy definition)[4]	
		Number	Rate	Number	Rate	Number	Rate	Number	Rate
2013	1,015,165	2,444	240.7	22	2.2	410	40.4	287	28.3
Percent change	X	-12.8	-13.6	-24.1	-24.9	NA	NA	-26.8	-27.5
Nevada									
2012	2,754,354	16,763	608.6	124	4.5	NA	NA	931	33.8
2013	2,790,136	16,496	591.2	163	5.8	1,418	50.8	1,090	39.1
Percent change	X	-1.6	-2.9	+31.5	+29.8	NA	NA	+17.1	+15.6
New Mexico									
2012	2,083,540	11,660	559.6	116	5.6	NA	NA	957	45.9
2013	2,085,287	12,443	596.7	125	6.0	1,465	70.3	1,126	54.0
Percent change	X	+6.7	+6.6	+7.8	+7.7	NA	NA	+17.7	+17.6
Utah[6]									
2012	2,854,871	5,939	208.0	52	1.8	NA	NA	975	34.2
2013	2,900,872	6,070	209.2	49	1.7	1,422	49.0	994	34.3
Percent change	X	+2.2	+0.6	-5.8	-7.3	NA	NA	+1.9	+0.3
Wyoming									
2012	576,626	1,161	201.3	14	2.4	-100.0	NA	154	26.7
2013	582,658	1,152	197.7	17	2.9	187	32.1	144	24.7
Percent change	X	-0.8	-1.8	+21.4	+20.2	NA	NA	-6.5	-7.5
Pacific [5,6,7,8]									
2012	50,915,394	198,925	390.7	2,243	4.4	NA	NA	12,108	23.8
2013	51,373,178	188,676	367.3	2,041	4.0	15,491	30.2	11,660	22.7
Percent change	X	-5.2	-6.0	-9.0	-9.8	NA	NA	-3.7	-4.6
Alaska[7]									
2012	730,307	4,412	604.1	30	4.1	NA		583	79.8
2013	735,132	4,430	602.6	34	4.6	922	125.4	644	87.6
Percent change	X	+0.4	-0.3	+13.3	+12.6	NA	NA	+10.5	+9.7
California									
2012	37,999,878	160,944	423.5	1,884	5.0	NA	NA	7,837	20.6
2013	38,332,521	151,879	396.2	1,746	4.6	9,714	25.3	7,464	19.5
Percent change	X	-5.6	-6.5	-7.3	-8.1	NA	NA	-4.8	-5.6
Hawaii									
2012	1,390,090	3,378	243.0	21	1.5	NA	NA	279	20.1
2013	1,404,054	3,444	245.3	21	1.5	385	27.4	296	21.1
Percent change	X	+2.0	+0.9	*	-1.0	NA	NA	+6.1	+5.0
Oregon[6]									
2012	3,899,801	9,638	247.1	91	2.3	NA	NA	1,159	29.7
2013	3,930,065	9,546	242.9	80	2.0	1,897	48.3	1,459	37.1
Percent change	X	-1.0	-1.7	-12.1	-12.8	NA	NA	+25.9	+24.9
Washington[6,8]									
2012	6,895,318	20,553	298.1	217	3.1	NA	NA	2,250	32.6
2013	6,971,406	19,377	277.9	160	2.3	2,573	36.9	1,797	25.8
Percent change	X	-5.7	-6.8	-26.3	-27.1	NA	NA	-20.1	-21.0
Puerto Rico									
2012	3,651,545	10,041	275.0	978	26.8	NA	NA	32	0.9
2013	3,615,086	9,320	257.8	883	24.4	34	0.9	26	0.7
Percent change	X	-7.2	-6.2	-9.7	-8.8	NA	NA	-18.8	-17.9

Table 4.   Crime, by Region, Geographic Division, and State, 2012–2013

(Number, rate per 100,000 population, percent.)

Area	Robbery		Aggravated assault		Property crime		Burglary		Larceny-theft		Motor vehicle theft	
	Number	Rate	Number	Rate	Number	Rate	Number	Rate	Number	Rate	Number	Rate
United States [5,6,7,8,9]												
2012	355,051	113.1	762,009	242.8	9,001,992	2,868.0	2,109,932	672.2	6,168,874	1,965.4	723,186	230.4
2013	345,031	109.1	724,149	229.1	8,632,512	2,730.7	1,928,465	610.0	6,004,453	1,899.4	699,594	221.3
Percent change	-2.8	-3.5	-5.0	-5.6	-4.1	-4.8	-8.6	-9.3	-2.7	-3.4	-3.3	-4.0
Northeast [5,6,7,8]												
2012	67,737	121.5	114,946	206.1	1,161,969	2,083.4	236,761	424.5	855,437	1,533.8	69,771	125.1
2013	66,062	118.1	109,395	195.5	1,096,709	1,960.4	208,315	372.4	825,630	1,475.8	62,764	112.2
Percent change	-2.5	-2.8	-4.8	-5.1	-5.6	-5.9	-12.0	-12.3	-3.5	-3.8	-10.0	-10.3
New England [5,6,7,8]												
2012	11,984	82.3	29,074	199.6	328,658	2,256.7	72,994	501.2	234,804	1,612.3	20,860	143.2
2013	11,977	81.9	27,475	187.9	307,315	2,102.2	63,966	437.6	223,584	1,529.4	19,765	135.2
Percent change	-0.1	-0.4	-5.5	-5.9	-6.5	-6.8	-12.4	-12.7	-4.8	-5.1	-5.2	-5.6
Connecticut [6]												
2012	3,709	103.3	5,424	151.0	77,169	2,148.5	14,787	411.7	55,904	1,556.4	6,478	180.4
2013	3,530	98.2	4,869	135.4	70,990	1,974.1	12,892	358.5	51,876	1,442.6	6,222	173.0
Percent change	-4.8	-4.9	-10.2	-10.3	-8.0	-8.1	-12.8	-12.9	-7.2	-7.3	-4.0	-4.1
Maine [6,8]												
2012	420	31.6	808	60.8	33,398	2,514.0	7,476	562.7	24,931	1,876.6	991	74.6
2013	335	25.2	912	68.7	30,447	2,292.2	6,483	488.1	23,050	1,735.3	914	68.8
Percent change	-20.2	-20.2	+12.9	+12.9	-8.8	-8.8	-13.3	-13.3	-7.5	-7.5	-7.8	-7.8
Massachusetts [6]												
2012	6,555	98.6	18,721	281.7	143,325	2,156.8	34,635	521.2	99,453	1,496.6	9,237	139.0
2013	6,706	100.2	18,106	270.5	137,285	2,051.2	30,735	459.2	97,428	1,455.7	9,122	136.3
Percent change	+2.3	+1.6	-3.3	-4.0	-4.2	-4.9	-11.3	-11.9	-2.0	-2.7	-1.2	-1.9
New Hampshire [7]												
2012	471	35.6	1,869	141.4	32,074	2,426.9	5,988	453.1	25,024	1,893.4	1,062	80.4
2013	649	49.0	1,492	112.7	29,040	2,194.3	4,936	373.0	23,164	1,750.3	940	71.0
Percent change	+37.8	+37.6	-20.2	-20.3	-9.5	-9.6	-17.6	-17.7	-7.4	-7.6	-11.5	-11.6
Rhode Island [7]												
2012	715	68.1	1,614	153.7	27,039	2,574.4	5,929	564.5	18,478	1,759.3	2,632	250.6
2013	684	65.0	1,550	147.4	25,678	2,442.0	5,607	533.2	17,838	1,696.4	2,233	212.4
Percent change	-4.3	-4.4	-4.0	-4.1	-5.0	-5.1	-5.4	-5.5	-3.5	-3.6	-15.2	-15.3
Vermont [7]												
2012	114	18.2	638	101.9	15,653	2,500.7	4,179	667.6	11,014	1,759.6	460	73.5
2013	73	11.6	546	87.1	13,875	2,214.2	3,313	528.7	10,228	1,632.2	334	53.3
Percent change	-36.0	-36.0	-14.4	-14.5	-11.4	-11.5	-20.7	-20.8	-7.1	-7.2	-27.4	-27.5
Middle Atlantic [5,7,8]												
2012	55,753	135.3	85,872	208.4	833,311	2,022.2	163,767	397.4	620,633	1,506.1	48,911	118.7
2013	54,085	130.9	81,920	198.2	789,394	1,910.2	144,349	349.3	602,046	1,456.9	42,999	104.1
Percent change	-3.0	-3.3	-4.6	-4.9	-5.3	-5.5	-11.9	-12.1	-3.0	-3.3	-12.1	-12.3
New Jersey												
2012	11,385	128.4	12,919	145.7	181,481	2,046.5	42,338	477.4	122,662	1,383.2	16,481	185.9
2013	12,082	135.8	12,071	135.6	167,556	1,882.8	35,873	403.1	117,936	1,325.2	13,747	154.5
Percent change	+6.1	+5.7	-6.6	-6.9	-7.7	-8.0	-15.3	-15.6	-3.9	-4.2	-16.6	-16.9
New York [3]												
2012	28,633	146.3	47,382	242.0	375,268	1,917.0	64,389	328.9	293,562	1,499.6	17,317	88.5
2013	27,241	138.6	46,130	234.7	358,598	1,824.8	56,442	287.2	286,674	1,458.8	15,482	78.8
Percent change	-4.9	-5.2	-2.6	-3.0	-4.4	-4.8	-12.3	-12.7	-2.3	-2.7	-10.6	-10.9
Pennsylvania [7,8]												
2012	15,735	123.3	25,571	200.3	276,562	2,166.7	57,040	446.9	204,409	1,601.4	15,113	118.4
2013	14,762	115.6	23,719	185.7	263,240	2,060.8	52,034	407.3	197,436	1,545.6	13,770	107.8
Percent change	-6.2	-6.3	-7.2	-7.3	-4.8	-4.9	-8.8	-8.8	-3.4	-3.5	-8.9	-9.0
Midwest [5,6,7,8]												
2012	69,716	103.6	144,894	215.2	1,873,378	2,782.7	436,009	647.7	1,302,359	1,934.5	135,010	200.5
2013	66,945	99.1	135,803	201.0	1,729,496	2,560.4	383,297	567.4	1,217,580	1,802.5	128,619	190.4
Percent change	-4.0	-4.3	-6.3	-6.6	-7.7	-8.0	-12.1	-12.4	-6.5	-6.8	-4.7	-5.1
East North Central [5,6,7,8]												
2012	56,592	121.5	98,208	210.9	1,291,164	2,772.8	317,592	682.0	880,582	1,891.0	92,990	199.7
2013	54,137	116.0	90,894	194.8	1,175,272	2,518.7	273,270	585.6	815,378	1,747.4	86,624	185.6
Percent change	-4.3	-4.5	-7.4	-7.6	-9.0	-9.2	-14.0	-14.1	-7.4	-7.6	-6.8	-7.0
Illinois [6]												
2012	19,480	151.4	29,725	231.0	332,706	2,585.5	71,100	552.5	235,314	1,828.6	26,292	204.3
2013	17,722	137.6	26,283	204.0	292,983	2,274.3	58,237	452.1	213,813	1,659.8	20,933	162.5
Percent change	-9.0	-9.1	-11.6	-11.7	-11.9	-12.0	-18.1	-18.2	-9.1	-9.2	-20.4	-20.5
Indiana [6]												
2012	6,601	101.0	13,975	213.8	197,994	3,028.5	47,689	729.4	136,668	2,090.4	13,637	208.6
2013	7,108	108.2	13,882	211.3	187,536	2,854.0	42,909	653.0	130,423	1,984.9	14,204	216.2
Percent change	+7.7	+7.1	-0.7	-1.2	-5.3	-5.8	-10.0	-10.5	-4.6	-5.1	+4.2	+3.6
Michigan [7]												
2012	10,423	105.5	29,203	295.5	249,249	2,522.1	65,560	663.4	158,609	1,604.9	25,080	253.8
2013	10,105	102.1	27,194	274.8	230,334	2,327.6	56,344	569.4	149,423	1,510.0	24,567	248.3
Percent change	-3.1	-3.2	-6.9	-7.0	-7.6	-7.7	-14.1	-14.2	-5.8	-5.9	-2.0	-2.2

Table 4.   Crime, by Region, Geographic Division, and State, 2012–2013— continued

(Number, rate per 100,000 population, percent.)

Area	Robbery		Aggravated assault		Property crime		Burglary		Larceny-theft		Motor vehicle theft	
	Number	Rate	Number	Rate	Number	Rate	Number	Rate	Number	Rate	Number	Rate
Ohio[6]												
2012	15,396	133.3	15,140	131.0	370,435	3,206.4	105,312	911.6	245,372	2,123.9	19,751	171.0
2013	14,368	124.2	14,257	123.2	338,731	2,927.5	91,433	790.2	227,766	1,968.5	19,532	168.8
Percent change	-6.7	-6.8	-5.8	-6.0	-8.6	-8.7	-13.2	-13.3	-7.2	-7.3	-1.1	-1.3
Wisconsin[6,8]												
2012	4,692	82.0	10,165	177.6	140,780	2,459.2	27,931	487.9	104,619	1,827.5	8,230	143.8
2013	4,834	84.2	9,278	161.6	125,688	2,188.7	24,347	424.0	93,953	1,636.0	7,388	128.6
Percent change	+3.0	+2.7	-8.7	-9.0	-10.7	-11.0	-12.8	-13.1	-10.2	-10.5	-10.2	-10.5
West North Central [5,6,7]												
2012	13,124	63.2	46,686	224.9	582,214	2,805.1	118,417	570.5	421,777	2,032.1	42,020	202.5
2013	12,808	61.3	44,909	215.0	554,224	2,653.6	110,027	526.8	402,202	1,925.7	41,995	201.1
Percent change	-2.4	-3.0	-3.8	-4.4	-4.8	-5.4	-7.1	-7.7	-4.6	-5.2	-0.1	-0.7
Iowa[7]												
2012	962	31.3	6,255	203.4	70,357	2,288.0	17,201	559.4	49,116	1,597.2	4,040	131.4
2013	939	30.4	6,323	204.6	67,800	2,193.9	15,868	513.5	47,686	1,543.0	4,246	137.4
Percent change	-2.4	-2.9	+1.1	+0.6	-3.6	-4.1	-7.7	-8.2	-2.9	-3.4	+5.1	+4.6
Kansas[6]												
2012	1,493	51.7	7,609	263.7	91,066	3,156.1	18,874	654.1	65,413	2,267.0	6,779	234.9
2013	1,350	46.6	7,181	248.1	85,280	2,946.8	17,375	600.4	61,264	2,117.0	6,641	229.5
Percent change	-9.6	-9.8	-5.6	-5.9	-6.4	-6.6	-7.9	-8.2	-6.3	-6.6	-2.0	-2.3
Minnesota[7]												
2012	3,475	64.6	7,207	134.0	138,152	2,568.1	25,378	471.7	104,316	1,939.1	8,458	157.2
2013	3,674	67.8	6,909	127.5	131,195	2,420.4	22,713	419.0	100,516	1,854.4	7,966	147.0
Percent change	+5.7	+4.9	-4.1	-4.9	-5.0	-5.7	-10.5	-11.2	-3.6	-4.4	-5.8	-6.5
Missouri[7]												
2012	5,782	96.0	19,490	323.5	199,813	3,316.7	42,510	705.6	140,971	2,340.0	16,332	271.1
2013	5,484	90.7	18,055	298.7	189,606	3,137.0	38,865	643.0	134,416	2,223.9	16,325	270.1
Percent change	-5.2	-5.5	-7.4	-7.7	-5.1	-5.4	-8.6	-8.9	-4.6	-5.0	*	-0.4
Nebraska[6]												
2012	1,128	60.8	2,912	157.0	51,203	2,759.7	8,745	471.3	38,301	2,064.4	4,157	224.1
2013	1,040	55.7	2,999	160.5	49,018	2,623.4	8,900	476.3	35,655	1,908.2	4,463	238.9
Percent change	-7.8	-8.5	+3.0	+2.3	-4.3	-4.9	+1.8	+1.1	-6.9	-7.6	+7.4	+6.6
North Dakota[7]												
2012	127	18.1	1,292	184.2	14,297	2,038.5	2,429	346.3	10,687	1,523.8	1,181	168.4
2013	162	22.4	1,446	199.9	15,148	2,094.0	2,934	405.6	10,798	1,492.7	1,416	195.7
Percent change	+27.6	+23.7	+11.9	+8.5	+6.0	+2.7	+20.8	+17.1	+1.0	-2.0	+19.9	+16.2
South Dakota[7]												
2012	157	18.8	1,921	230.3	17,326	2,077.3	3,280	393.3	12,973	1,555.4	1,073	128.6
2013	159	18.8	1,996	236.2	16,177	1,914.7	3,372	399.1	11,867	1,404.6	938	111.0
Percent change	+1.3	*	+3.9	+2.6	-6.6	-7.8	+2.8	+1.5	-8.5	-9.7	-12.6	-13.7
South [5,6,7,9]												
2012	131,951	112.5	326,723	278.6	3,791,837	3,233.9	948,407	808.8	2,592,195	2,210.8	251,235	214.3
2013	129,825	109.7	311,465	263.1	3,663,780	3,094.8	871,095	735.8	2,550,709	2,154.6	241,976	204.4
Percent change	-1.6	-2.5	-4.7	-5.6	-3.4	-4.3	-8.2	-9.0	-1.6	-2.5	-3.7	-4.6
South Atlantic [5,7,9]												
2012	71,555	116.9	165,711	270.8	1,928,811	3,152.3	470,928	769.7	1,330,920	2,175.2	126,963	207.5
2013	69,577	112.6	157,447	254.8	1,849,711	2,993.9	430,544	696.9	1,301,807	2,107.0	117,360	190.0
Percent change	-2.8	-3.7	-5.0	-5.9	-4.1	-5.0	-8.6	-9.5	-2.2	-3.1	-7.6	-8.5
Delaware[7]												
2012	1,498	163.3	3,245	353.9	30,707	3,348.4	7,389	805.7	21,880	2,385.9	1,438	156.8
2013	1,226	132.4	2,904	313.7	28,379	3,065.5	6,131	662.3	20,916	2,259.4	1,332	143.9
Percent change	-18.2	-18.9	-10.5	-11.3	-7.6	-8.4	-17.0	-17.8	-4.4	-5.3	-7.4	-8.2
District of Columbia[7,9]												
2012	4,037	637.3	3,505	553.3	30,757	4,855.7	3,519	555.5	23,575	3,721.8	3,663	578.3
2013	4,078	630.8	3,830	592.5	31,083	4,808.3	3,316	513.0	24,533	3,795.0	3,234	500.3
Percent change	+1.0	-1.0	+9.3	+7.1	+1.1	-1.0	-5.8	-7.7	+4.1	+2.0	-11.7	-13.5
Florida[7]												
2012	23,889	123.6	63,929	330.9	632,988	3,276.2	153,563	794.8	442,095	2,288.2	37,330	193.2
2013	23,200	118.7	61,054	312.3	607,172	3,105.3	138,916	710.5	433,344	2,216.3	34,912	178.6
Percent change	-2.9	-4.0	-4.5	-5.6	-4.1	-5.2	-9.5	-10.6	-2.0	-3.1	-6.5	-7.6
Georgia												
2012	12,502	126.1	22,447	226.4	339,473	3,423.6	86,992	877.3	223,875	2,257.8	28,606	288.5
2013	12,488	125.0	20,915	209.3	334,399	3,346.6	82,258	823.2	225,315	2,254.9	26,826	268.5
Percent change	-0.1	-0.9	-6.8	-7.5	-1.5	-2.2	-5.4	-6.2	+0.6	-0.1	-6.2	-6.9
Maryland												
2012	10,173	172.9	16,303	277.0	162,309	2,758.1	33,803	574.4	113,550	1,929.5	14,956	254.1
2013	10,048	169.5	16,128	272.0	157,913	2,663.5	31,949	538.9	112,546	1,898.3	13,418	226.3
Percent change	-1.2	-2.0	-1.1	-1.8	-2.7	-3.4	-5.5	-6.2	-0.9	-1.6	-10.3	-10.9
North Carolina												
2012	9,392	96.3	22,609	231.9	328,594	3,370.8	99,323	1,018.9	213,151	2,186.5	16,120	165.4
2013	9,349	94.9	21,513	218.4	308,049	3,128.0	90,702	921.0	202,741	2,058.7	14,606	148.3
Percent change	-0.5	-1.5	-4.8	-5.8	-6.3	-7.2	-8.7	-9.6	-4.9	-5.8	-9.4	-10.3
South Carolina[7]												
2012	4,511	95.5	19,919	421.7	181,049	3,833.0	45,222	957.4	122,340	2,590.1	13,487	285.5
2013	3,972	83.2	17,838	373.6	173,049	3,624.2	40,958	857.8	119,511	2,502.9	12,580	263.5

Table 4.   Crime, by Region, Geographic Division, and State, 2012–2013— continued

(Number, rate per 100,000 population, percent.)

Area	Robbery		Aggravated assault		Property crime		Burglary		Larceny-theft		Motor vehicle theft	
	Number	Rate	Number	Rate	Number	Rate	Number	Rate	Number	Rate	Number	Rate
Percent change	-11.9	-12.9	-10.4	-11.4	-4.4	-5.4	-9.4	-10.4	-2.3	-3.4	-6.7	-7.7
Virginia[7]												
2012	4,718	57.6	9,131	111.5	178,434	2,179.6	29,651	362.2	139,654	1,705.9	9,129	111.5
2013	4,565	55.3	9,062	109.7	170,654	2,065.9	26,640	322.5	135,478	1,640.1	8,536	103.3
Percent change	-3.2	-4.1	-0.8	-1.6	-4.4	-5.2	-10.2	-11.0	-3.0	-3.9	-6.5	-7.3
West Virginia[7]												
2012	835	45.0	4,623	249.0	44,500	2,396.8	11,466	617.6	30,800	1,658.9	2,234	120.3
2013	651	35.1	4,203	226.7	39,013	2,103.9	9,674	521.7	27,423	1,478.9	1,916	103.3
Percent change	-22.0	-21.9	-9.1	-9.0	-12.3	-12.2	-15.6	-15.5	-11.0	-10.9	-14.2	-14.1
East South Central [5,6,7]												
2012	18,995	101.9	54,902	294.6	583,536	3,130.8	161,673	867.4	387,973	2,081.6	33,890	181.8
2013	17,610	94.1	51,043	272.7	553,979	2,959.9	144,636	772.8	376,524	2,011.8	32,819	175.4
Percent change	-7.3	-7.7	-7.0	-7.4	-5.1	-5.5	-10.5	-10.9	-3.0	-3.4	-3.2	-3.6
Alabama[7]												
2012	5,020	104.2	15,035	312.1	168,878	3,505.5	47,481	985.6	111,523	2,314.9	9,874	205.0
2013	4,648	96.2	13,787	285.2	161,993	3,351.3	42,429	877.8	108,993	2,254.8	10,571	218.7
Percent change	-7.4	-7.7	-8.3	-8.6	-4.1	-4.4	-10.6	-10.9	-2.3	-2.6	+7.1	+6.7
Kentucky[6]												
2012	3,547	81.0	4,792	109.4	112,800	2,575.5	29,877	682.2	76,199	1,739.8	6,724	153.5
2013	3,246	73.9	4,198	95.5	103,857	2,362.9	26,213	596.4	71,612	1,629.3	6,032	137.2
Percent change	-8.5	-8.8	-12.4	-12.7	-7.9	-8.3	-12.3	-12.6	-6.0	-6.4	-10.3	-10.6
Mississippi[6]												
2012	2,277	76.2	4,460	149.3	83,933	2,810.5	28,084	940.4	51,520	1,725.1	4,329	145.0
2013	2,409	80.5	4,680	156.5	81,500	2,724.7	24,995	835.6	52,117	1,742.3	4,388	146.7
Percent change	+5.8	+5.6	+4.9	+4.8	-2.9	-3.1	-11.0	-11.1	+1.2	+1.0	+1.4	+1.2
Tennessee[7]												
2012	8,151	126.3	30,615	474.3	217,925	3,376.1	56,231	871.1	148,731	2,304.2	12,963	200.8
2013	7,307	112.5	28,378	436.9	206,629	3,180.9	50,999	785.1	143,802	2,213.7	11,828	182.1
Percent change	-10.4	-10.9	-7.3	-7.9	-5.2	-5.8	-9.3	-9.9	-3.3	-3.9	-8.8	-9.3
West South Central [5,6,7]												
2012	41,401	110.6	106,110	283.5	1,279,490	3,418.5	315,806	843.8	873,302	2,333.3	90,382	241.5
2013	42,638	112.6	102,975	271.8	1,260,090	3,326.2	295,915	781.1	872,378	2,302.8	91,797	242.3
Percent change	+3.0	+1.8	-3.0	-4.1	-1.5	-2.7	-6.3	-7.4	-0.1	-1.3	+1.6	+0.3
Arkansas[7]												
2012	2,310	78.3	10,134	343.5	109,389	3,708.3	32,673	1,107.6	70,982	2,406.3	5,734	194.4
2013	2,258	76.3	9,781	330.5	106,613	3,602.6	30,485	1,030.1	70,450	2,380.6	5,678	191.9
Percent change	-2.3	-2.6	-3.5	-3.8	-2.5	-2.9	-6.7	-7.0	-0.7	-1.1	-1.0	-1.3
Louisiana[6]												
2012	5,458	118.6	15,737	342.0	162,673	3,534.7	42,037	913.4	112,764	2,450.3	7,872	171.1
2013	5,548	119.9	16,319	352.8	165,686	3,582.0	41,184	890.4	115,342	2,493.6	9,160	198.0
Percent change	+1.6	+1.1	+3.7	+3.2	+1.9	+1.3	-2.0	-2.5	+2.3	+1.8	+16.4	+15.8
Oklahoma[6]												
2012	3,248	85.1	13,012	341.0	130,969	3,432.3	36,094	945.9	83,131	2,178.6	11,744	307.8
2013	3,031	78.7	11,583	300.8	126,057	3,273.7	33,348	866.1	81,495	2,116.4	11,214	291.2
Percent change	-6.7	-7.5	-11.0	-11.8	-3.8	-4.6	-7.6	-8.4	-2.0	-2.9	-4.5	-5.4
Texas[6]												
2012	30,385	116.6	67,227	258.0	876,459	3,363.1	205,002	786.6	606,425	2,327.0	65,032	249.5
2013	31,801	120.2	65,292	246.9	861,734	3,258.2	190,898	721.8	605,091	2,287.8	65,745	248.6
Percent change	+4.7	+3.1	-2.9	-4.3	-1.7	-3.1	-6.9	-8.2	-0.2	-1.7	+1.1	-0.4
West [5,6,7,8]												
2012	85,647	116.5	175,446	238.6	2,174,808	2,957.9	488,755	664.7	1,418,883	1,929.8	267,170	363.4
2013	82,199	110.7	167,486	225.6	2,142,527	2,885.4	465,758	627.2	1,410,534	1,899.6	266,235	358.5
Percent change	-4.0	-5.0	-4.5	-5.5	-1.5	-2.5	-4.7	-5.6	-0.6	-1.6	-0.3	-1.3
Mountain [5,6,7,8]												
2012	19,151	84.7	57,368	253.7	681,093	3,012.2	148,958	658.8	475,875	2,104.6	56,260	248.8
2013	18,588	81.2	56,122	245.3	676,136	2,955.0	144,129	629.9	474,704	2,074.6	57,303	250.4
Percent change	-2.9	-4.1	-2.2	-3.3	-0.7	-1.9	-3.2	-4.4	-0.2	-1.4	+1.9	+0.7
Arizona[6,8]												
2012	7,383	112.7	18,054	275.6	231,701	3,536.8	52,911	807.7	159,808	2,439.4	18,982	289.8
2013	6,702	101.1	17,490	263.9	225,243	3,399.1	48,533	732.4	159,272	2,403.5	17,438	263.2
Percent change	-9.2	-10.3	-3.1	-4.2	-2.8	-3.9	-8.3	-9.3	-0.3	-1.5	-8.1	-9.2
Colorado[7]												
2012	3,392	65.4	10,285	198.2	139,355	2,685.3	26,163	504.2	101,091	1,948.0	12,101	233.2
2013	3,151	59.8	9,963	189.1	140,057	2,658.5	25,081	476.1	102,443	1,944.5	12,533	237.9
Percent change	-7.1	-8.5	-3.1	-4.6	+0.5	-1.0	-4.1	-5.6	+1.3	-0.2	+3.6	+2.0
Idaho[7]												
2012	243	15.2	2,580	161.7	31,825	1,994.6	7,240	453.8	23,203	1,454.2	1,382	86.6
2013	220	13.6	2,596	161.0	30,055	1,864.3	6,640	411.9	21,879	1,357.1	1,536	95.3
Percent change	-9.5	-10.4	+0.6	-0.4	-5.6	-6.5	-8.3	-9.2	-5.7	-6.7	+11.1	+10.0
Montana[7]												
2012	202	20.1	2,180	216.8	26,102	2,595.9	3,920	389.9	20,484	2,037.2	1,698	168.9
2013	204	20.1	1,931	190.2	25,953	2,556.5	4,064	400.3	20,039	1,974.0	1,850	182.2
Percent change	+1.0	*	-11.4	-12.3	-0.6	-1.5	+3.7	+2.7	-2.2	-3.1	+9.0	+7.9
Nevada												

Table 4. Crime, by Region, Geographic Division, and State, 2012–2013— continued

(Number, rate per 100,000 population, percent.)

Area	Robbery Number	Robbery Rate	Aggravated assault Number	Aggravated assault Rate	Property crime Number	Property crime Rate	Burglary Number	Burglary Rate	Larceny-theft Number	Larceny-theft Rate	Motor vehicle theft Number	Motor vehicle theft Rate
2012	4,918	178.6	10,790	391.7	77,510	2,814.1	22,120	803.1	45,372	1,647.3	10,018	363.7
2013	5,183	185.8	10,060	360.6	79,177	2,837.7	23,047	826.0	46,132	1,653.4	9,998	358.3
Percent change	+5.4	+4.0	-6.8	-8.0	+2.2	+0.8	+4.2	+2.9	+1.7	+0.4	-0.2	-1.5
New Mexico												
2012	1,847	88.6	8,740	419.5	75,094	3,604.2	21,384	1,026.3	48,247	2,315.6	5,463	262.2
2013	1,810	86.8	9,382	449.9	77,256	3,704.8	21,476	1,029.9	49,875	2,391.8	5,905	283.2
Percent change	-2.0	-2.1	+7.3	+7.3	+2.9	+2.8	+0.4	+0.3	+3.4	+3.3	+8.1	+8.0
Utah[6]												
2012	1,105	38.7	3,807	133.4	86,284	3,022.3	13,095	458.7	67,157	2,352.4	6,032	211.3
2013	1,243	42.8	3,784	130.4	85,586	2,950.4	13,333	459.6	64,788	2,233.4	7,465	257.3
Percent change	+12.5	+10.7	-0.6	-2.2	-0.8	-2.4	+1.8	+0.2	-3.5	-5.1	+23.8	+21.8
Wyoming												
2012	61	10.6	932	161.6	13,222	2,293.0	2,125	368.5	10,513	1,823.2	584	101.3
2013	75	12.9	916	157.2	12,809	2,198.4	1,955	335.5	10,276	1,763.6	578	99.2
Percent change	+23.0	+21.7	-1.7	-2.7	-3.1	-4.1	-8.0	-9.0	-2.3	-3.3	-1.0	-2.1
Pacific [5,6,7,8]												
2012	66,496	130.6	118,078	231.9	1,493,715	2,933.7	339,797	667.4	943,008	1,852.1	210,910	414.2
2013	63,611	123.8	111,364	216.8	1,466,391	2,854.4	321,629	626.1	935,830	1,821.6	208,932	406.7
Percent change	-4.3	-5.2	-5.7	-6.5	-1.8	-2.7	-5.3	-6.2	-0.8	-1.6	-0.9	-1.8
Alaska[7]												
2012	630	86.3	3,169	433.9	20,037	2,743.6	2,950	403.9	15,565	2,131.3	1,522	208.4
2013	624	84.9	3,128	425.5	21,210	2,885.2	2,916	396.7	16,599	2,258.0	1,695	230.6
Percent change	-1.0	-1.6	-1.3	-1.9	+5.9	+5.2	-1.2	-1.8	+6.6	+5.9	+11.4	+10.6
California												
2012	56,521	148.7	94,702	249.2	1,049,465	2,761.8	245,767	646.8	635,090	1,671.3	168,608	443.7
2013	53,640	139.9	89,029	232.3	1,018,907	2,658.1	232,058	605.4	621,557	1,621.5	165,292	431.2
Percent change	-5.1	-5.9	-6.0	-6.8	-2.9	-3.8	-5.6	-6.4	-2.1	-3.0	-2.0	-2.8
Hawaii												
2012	1,125	80.9	1,953	140.5	43,419	3,123.5	7,653	550.5	31,901	2,294.9	3,865	278.0
2013	1,131	80.6	1,996	142.2	42,875	3,053.7	7,533	536.5	31,658	2,254.8	3,684	262.4
Percent change	+0.5	-0.5	+2.2	+1.2	-1.3	-2.2	-1.6	-2.5	-0.8	-1.7	-4.7	-5.6
Oregon[6]												
2012	2,419	62.0	5,969	153.1	126,417	3,241.6	22,051	565.4	94,114	2,413.3	10,252	262.9
2013	2,397	61.0	5,610	142.7	124,737	3,173.9	20,769	528.5	94,106	2,394.5	9,862	250.9
Percent change	-0.9	-1.7	-6.0	-6.7	-1.3	-2.1	-5.8	-6.5	*	-0.8	-3.8	-4.5
Washington[6,8]												
2012	5,801	84.1	12,285	178.2	254,377	3,689.1	61,376	890.1	166,338	2,412.3	26,663	386.7
2013	5,819	83.5	11,601	166.4	258,662	3,710.3	58,353	837.0	171,910	2,465.9	28,399	407.4
Percent change	+0.3	-0.8	-5.6	-6.6	+1.7	+0.6	-4.9	-6.0	+3.3	+2.2	+6.5	+5.3
Puerto Rico												
2012	6,298	172.5	2,733	74.8	51,679	1,415.3	15,287	418.6	30,545	836.5	5,847	160.1
2013	6,016	166.4	2,395	66.3	48,851	1,351.3	13,961	386.2	29,360	812.2	5,530	153.0
Percent change	-4.5	-3.5	-12.4	-11.5	-5.5	-4.5	-8.7	-7.8	-3.9	-2.9	-5.4	-4.5

Note: Although arson data are included in the trend and clearance tables, sufficient data are not available to estimate totals for this offense. Therefore, no arson data are published in this table.   NA = Not available.   X = Not applicable.   * = Less than one-tenth of 1 percent.   1 Population figures are U.S. Census Bureau provisional estimates as of July 1, 2013.   2 The violent crime figures include the offenses of murder, rape (legacy definition), robbery, and aggravated assault.   3 The figures shown in this column for the offense of rape were estimated using the revised Uniform Crime Reporting (UCR) definition of rape. See chapter notes for more detail.   4 The figures shown in this column for the offense of rape were estimated using the legacy Uniform Crime Reporting (UCR) definition of rape. See chapter notes for more detail.   5 The crime figures have been adjusted.   6 Agencies within this state submitted rape data according to both the revised UCR definition of rape and the legacy UCR definition of rape. 7 This state's agencies submitted rape data according to the revised UCR definition of rape.   8 Because of changes in the state/local agency's reporting practices, figures are not comparable to previous years' data.   9 Includes offenses reported by the Zoological Police and the Metro Transit Police.

Table 5.   Crime,[1] by State and Area, 2013

(Number, percent, rate per 100,000 population.)

Area	Murder and nonnegligent manslaughter	Rape (revised definition)[e]	Robbery	Aggravated assault	Burglary	Larceny-theft	Motor vehicle theft
Alabama [3]							
Metropolitan statistical area							
Area actually reporting	280	1,454	4,130	10,373	32,452	86,012	8,468
Estimated total	283	1,507	4,208	10,666	33,451	88,269	8,696
Cities outside metropolitan areas							
Area actually reporting	33	282	348	2,022	5,317	14,897	1,182
Estimated total	35	299	367	2,139	5,605	15,637	1,245
Nonmetropolitan counties							
Area actually reporting	29	236	72	974	3,347	5,048	625
Estimated total	29	238	73	982	3,373	5,087	630
State total	347	2,044	4,648	13,787	42,429	108,993	10,571
Rate per 100,000 inhabitants	7.2	42.3	96.2	285.2	877.8	2,254.8	218.7
Alaska [3]							
Metropolitan statistical area							
Area actually reporting	15	454	569	1,696	1,523	11,912	1,041
Cities outside metropolitan areas							
Area actually reporting	1	98	33	636	407	2,950	249
Estimated total	1	101	34	659	421	3,054	258
Nonmetropolitan counties							
Area actually reporting	18	367	21	773	972	1,633	396
State total	34	922	624	3,128	2,916	16,599	1,695
Rate per 100,000 inhabitants	4.6	125.4	84.9	425.5	396.7	2,258.0	230.6
Arizona [4,5]							
Metropolitan statistical area							
Area actually reporting	315		6,567	15,516	44,933	152,271	16,035
Estimated total	315	2,406	6,575	15,536	45,003	152,558	16,056
Cities outside metropolitan areas							
Area actually reporting	36		102	1,406	2,465	4,901	1,054
Estimated total	41	631	115	1,591	2,789	5,546	1,193
Nonmetropolitan counties							
Area actually reporting	1	13	12	363	741	1,168	189
State total	357	3,050	6,702	17,490	48,533	159,272	17,438
Rate per 100,000 inhabitants	5.4	46.0	101.1	263.9	732.4	2,403.5	263.2
Arkansas [3]							
Metropolitan statistical area							
Area actually reporting	100	898	1,852	6,781	18,297	47,716	3,875
Estimated total	101	928	1,865	6,978	18,856	48,636	3,991
Cities outside metropolitan areas							
Area actually reporting	25	272	316	1,590	6,846	13,112	775
Estimated total	27	294	342	1,719	7,402	14,176	838
Nonmetropolitan counties							
Area actually reporting	29	186	47	1,001	3,903	7,052	784
Estimated total	31	201	51	1,084	4,227	7,638	849
State total	159	1,423	2,258	9,781	30,485	70,450	5,678
Rate per 100,000 inhabitants	5.4	48.1	76.3	330.5	1,030.1	2,380.6	191.9
California							
Metropolitan statistical area							
Area actually reporting	1,711		53,239	86,136	225,528	609,730	163,051
Estimated total	1,711	9,349	53,247	86,152	225,576	609,857	163,081
Cities outside metropolitan areas							
Area actually reporting	15	141	244	1,261	2,848	7,146	852
Nonmetropolitan counties							
Area actually reporting	20	224	149	1,616	3,634	4,554	1,359
State total	1,746	9,714	53,640	89,029	232,058	621,557	165,292
Rate per 100,000 inhabitants	4.6	25.3	139.9	232.3	605.4	1,621.5	431.2
Colorado [3]							
Metropolitan statistical area							
Area actually reporting	154	2,620	3,073	8,995	22,739	92,275	11,894
Estimated total	156	2,651	3,085	9,087	22,972	93,108	11,998
Cities outside metropolitan areas							
Area actually reporting	14	176	53	516	1,275	6,897	314
Estimated total	15	187	57	550	1,359	7,353	335
Nonmetropolitan counties							
Area actually reporting	7	94	9	318	732	1,933	195
Estimated total	7	96	9	326	750	1,982	200
State total	178	2,934	3,151	9,963	25,081	102,443	12,533
Rate per 100,000 inhabitants	3.4	55.7	59.8	189.1	476.1	1,944.5	237.9
Connecticut [4]							
Metropolitan statistical area							
Area actually reporting	80	842	3,456	4,501	11,328	47,504	5,695

Table 5.   Crime,[1] by State and Area, 2013— continued

(Number, percent, rate per 100,000 population.)

Area	Murder and nonnegli-gent manslaughter	Rape (revised definition)[2]	Robbery	Aggravated assault	Burglary	Larceny-theft	Motor vehicle theft
Cities outside metropolitan areas							
Area actually reporting	0	31	21	96	297	1,659	115
Nonmetropolitan counties							
Area actually reporting	6	82	53	272	1,267	2,713	412
State total	86	955	3,530	4,869	12,892	51,876	6,222
Rate per 100,000 inhabitants	2.4	26.6	98.2	135.4	358.5	1,442.6	173.0
Delaware [3]							
Metropolitan statistical area							
Area actually reporting	39	379	1,226	2,903	6,131	20,915	1,332
Cities outside metropolitan areas							
Area actually reporting							
State total	0	1	0	1	0	1	0
Rate per 100,000 inhabitants	39	380	1,226	2,904	6,131	20,916	1,332
	4.2	41.0	132.4	313.7	662.3	2,259.4	143.9
District of Columbia [3,6]							
Metropolitan statistical area							
Area actually reporting	103	395	4,078	3,830	3,316	24,533	3,234
Cities outside metropolitan areas							
Nonmetropolitan counties							
District total	103	395	4,078	3,830	3,316	24,533	3,234
Rate per 100,000 inhabitants	15.9	61.1	630.8	592.5	513.0	3,795.0	500.3
Florida [3]							
Metropolitan statistical area							
Area actually reporting	936	6,543	22,839	58,183	133,415	421,479	34,175
Estimated total							
Cities outside metropolitan areas	9	53	185	870	1,529	4,710	266
Area actually reporting	9	55	192	902	1,585	4,881	276
Estimated total							
Nonmetropolitan counties	25	152	159	1,853	3,685	6,571	434
Area actually reporting	27	162	169	1,969	3,916	6,984	461
State total	972	6,760	23,200	61,054	138,916	433,344	34,912
Rate per 100,000 inhabitants	5.0	34.6	118.7	312.3	710.5	2,216.3	178.6
Georgia							
Metropolitan statistical area							
Area actually reporting	479		11,456	16,585	68,360	186,099	24,765
Estimated total	480	2,154	11,511	16,673	68,678	187,372	24,884
Cities outside metropolitan areas							
Area actually reporting	36		700	2,179	6,501	22,199	735
Estimated total	39	256	762	2,371	7,073	24,152	800
Nonmetropolitan counties							
Area actually reporting	34		197	1,717	5,972	12,658	1,048
Estimated total	37	172	215	1,871	6,507	13,791	1,142
State total	556	2,582	12,488	20,915	82,258	225,315	26,826
Rate per 100,000 inhabitants	5.6	25.8	125.0	209.3	823.2	2,254.9	268.5
Hawaii							
Metropolitan statistical area							
Area actually reporting	12	273	1,011	1,553	5,661	26,292	3,196
Cities outside metropolitan areas							
Nonmetropolitan counties							
Area actually reporting	9	112	120	443	1,872	5,366	488
State total	21	385	1,131	1,996	7,533	31,658	3,684
Rate per 100,000 inhabitants	1.5	27.4	80.6	142.2	536.5	2,254.8	262.4
Idaho [3]							
Metropolitan statistical area							
Area actually reporting	13	474	178	1,774	4,409	15,890	1,083
Estimated total	13	474	178	1,775	4,411	15,897	1,083
Cities outside metropolitan areas							
Area actually reporting	6	98	30	447	1,113	4,078	222
Nonmetropolitan counties							
Area actually reporting	8	83	12	374	1,116	1,904	231
State total	27	655	220	2,596	6,640	21,879	1,536
Rate per 100,000 inhabitants	1.7	40.6	13.6	161.0	411.9	1,357.1	95.3
Illinois [4]							
Metropolitan statistical area							
Area actually reporting	672		17,272	23,387	50,706	189,093	19,946
Estimated total	680	3,737	17,502	23,844	51,966	194,673	20,249
Cities outside metropolitan areas							
Area actually reporting	19		166	1,582	3,712	13,021	396
Estimated total	22	412	192	1,832	4,298	15,077	459
Nonmetropolitan counties							
Area actually reporting	4		26	569	1,849	3,808	211
Estimated total	4	114	28	607	1,973	4,063	225

Table 5.   Crime,[1] by State and Area, 2013— continued

(Number, percent, rate per 100,000 population.)

Area	Murder and nonnegligent manslaughter	Rape (revised definition)[2]	Robbery	Aggravated assault	Burglary	Larceny-theft	Motor vehicle theft
State total	706	4,263	17,722	26,283	58,237	213,813	20,933
Rate per 100,000 inhabitants	5.5	33.1	137.6	204.0	452.1	1,659.8	162.5
Indiana [4]							
Metropolitan statistical area							
Area actually reporting	306		6,762	11,535	34,748	102,557	12,156
Estimated total	319	1,852	6,924	12,099	36,980	110,263	12,872
Cities outside metropolitan areas							
Area actually reporting	10		95	646	2,236	10,679	616
Estimated total	13	159	124	841	2,911	13,902	802
Nonmetropolitan counties							
Area actually reporting	17		44	695	2,227	4,618	391
Estimated total	23	131	60	942	3,018	6,258	530
State total	355	2,142	7,108	13,882	42,909	130,423	14,204
Rate per 100,000 inhabitants	5.4	32.6	108.2	211.3	653.0	1,984.9	216.2
Iowa [3]							
Metropolitan statistical area							
Area actually reporting	28	714	820	4,025	10,301	33,836	3,129
Estimated total	28	723	822	4,080	10,428	34,161	3,161
Cities outside metropolitan areas							
Area actually reporting	6	247	97	1,585	3,258	10,088	662
Estimated total	7	270	106	1,736	3,568	11,048	725
Nonmetropolitan counties							
Area actually reporting	7	79	10	443	1,635	2,163	314
Estimated total	8	90	11	507	1,872	2,477	360
State total	43	1,083	939	6,323	15,868	47,686	4,246
Rate per 100,000 inhabitants	1.4	35.0	30.4	204.6	513.5	1,543.0	137.4
Kansas [4]							
Metropolitan statistical area							
Area actually reporting	79	781	1,163	4,998	11,467	44,275	5,426
Estimated total	79	784	1,164	5,012	11,502	44,438	5,440
Cities outside metropolitan areas							
Area actually reporting	15	296	162	1,519	3,799	13,191	813
Estimated total	16	312	171	1,604	4,010	13,925	858
Nonmetropolitan counties							
Area actually reporting	16	95	14	542	1,789	2,785	329
Estimated total	17	99	15	565	1,863	2,901	343
State total	112	1,195	1,350	7,181	17,375	61,264	6,641
Rate per 100,000 inhabitants	3.9	41.3	46.6	248.1	600.4	2,117.0	229.5
Kentucky [4]							
Metropolitan statistical area							
Area actually reporting	95	848	2,737	3,130	17,632	54,088	4,496
Estimated total	95	851	2,744	3,135	17,680	54,258	4,508
Cities outside metropolitan areas							
Area actually reporting	11	169	315	422	3,046	11,202	544
Estimated total	11	176	328	440	3,175	11,675	567
Nonmetropolitan counties							
Area actually reporting	59	569	169	607	5,218	5,531	932
Estimated total	61	584	174	623	5,358	5,679	957
State total	167	1,611	3,246	4,198	26,213	71,612	6,032
Rate per 100,000 inhabitants	3.8	36.7	73.9	95.5	596.4	1,629.3	137.2
Louisiana [4]							
Metropolitan statistical area							
Area actually reporting	453		5,050	13,112	35,041	97,724	8,106
Estimated total	456	1,284	5,087	13,261	35,385	99,191	8,168
Cities outside metropolitan areas							
Area actually reporting	19		285	1,254	2,686	7,761	295
Estimated total	24	134	364	1,604	3,435	9,926	377
Nonmetropolitan counties							
Area actually reporting	17		91	1,371	2,228	5,868	580
Estimated total	18	201	97	1,454	2,364	6,225	615
State total	498	1,619	5,548	16,319	41,184	115,342	9,160
Rate per 100,000 inhabitants	10.8	35.0	119.9	352.8	890.4	2,493.6	198.0
Maine [4,5]							
Metropolitan statistical area							
Area actually reporting	13	250	270	548	3,785	14,734	525
Cities outside metropolitan areas							
Area actually reporting	3	117	50	237	1,408	5,980	202
Nonmetropolitan counties							
Area actually reporting	8	80	15	127	1,290	2,336	187
State total	24	447	335	912	6,483	23,050	914
Rate per 100,000 inhabitants	1.8	33.7	25.2	68.7	488.1	1,735.3	68.8

Table 5.   Crime,[1] by State and Area, 2013— continued

(Number, percent, rate per 100,000 population.)

Area	Murder and nonnegligent manslaughter	Rape (revised definition)[2]	Robbery	Aggravated assault	Burglary	Larceny-theft	Motor vehicle theft
Maryland							
Metropolitan statistical area							
Area actually reporting	380	1,499	9,960	15,740	31,049	110,069	13,333
Cities outside metropolitan areas							
Area actually reporting	0	13	71	194	313	1,382	21
Nonmetropolitan counties							
Area actually reporting	1	20	17	194	587	1,095	64
State total	381	1,532	10,048	16,128	31,949	112,546	13,418
Rate per 100,000 inhabitants	6.4	25.8	169.5	272.0	538.9	1,898.3	226.3
Massachusetts [4]							
Metropolitan statistical area							
Area actually reporting	136		6,609	17,645	29,863	94,792	8,941
Estimated total	137	2,659	6,663	17,838	30,207	95,912	9,038
Cities outside metropolitan areas							
Area actually reporting	0		35	214	425	1,224	68
Estimated total	0	59	43	265	526	1,516	84
Nonmetropolitan counties							
Area actually reporting	0	0	0	3	2	0	0
State total	137	2,718	6,706	18,106	30,735	97,428	9,122
Rate per 100,000 inhabitants	2.0	40.6	100.2	270.5	459.2	1,455.7	136.3
Michigan [3]							
Metropolitan statistical area							
Area actually reporting	596	4,962	9,930	24,679	48,923	126,298	23,405
Estimated total	597	4,995	9,973	24,802	49,238	127,412	23,530
Cities outside metropolitan areas							
Area actually reporting	8	492	69	764	1,884	10,616	290
Estimated total	9	546	77	849	2,094	11,799	322
Nonmetropolitan counties							
Area actually reporting	24	1,010	53	1,482	4,813	9,807	687
Estimated total	25	1,052	55	1,543	5,012	10,212	715
State total	631	6,593	10,105	27,194	56,344	149,423	24,567
Rate per 100,000 inhabitants	6.4	66.6	102.1	274.8	569.4	1,510.0	248.3
Minnesota [3]							
Metropolitan statistical area							
Area actually reporting	94	1,514	3,576	5,628	18,230	82,949	6,834
Estimated total	94	1,514	3,576	5,629	18,232	82,964	6,835
Cities outside metropolitan areas							
Area actually reporting	9	245	81	783	1,962	11,404	585
Nonmetropolitan counties							
Area actually reporting	11	249	17	497	2,519	6,148	546
State total	114	2,008	3,674	6,909	22,713	100,516	7,966
Rate per 100,000 inhabitants	2.1	37.0	67.8	127.5	419.0	1,854.4	147.0
Mississippi [4]							
Metropolitan statistical area							
Area actually reporting	74		1,363	1,895	10,137	24,041	2,347
Estimated total	77	460	1,441	2,161	11,410	26,910	2,601
Cities outside metropolitan areas							
Area actually reporting	45		538	813	5,031	11,991	703
Estimated total	67	265	798	1,206	7,465	17,793	1,043
Nonmetropolitan counties							
Area actually reporting	25		83	642	2,992	3,625	364
Estimated total	51	205	170	1,313	6,120	7,414	744
State total	195	930	2,409	4,680	24,995	52,117	4,388
Rate per 100,000 inhabitants	6.5	31.1	80.5	156.5	835.6	1,742.3	146.7
Missouri [3]							
Metropolitan statistical area							
Area actually reporting	310	1,955	5,176	14,317	30,232	106,390	14,277
Cities outside metropolitan areas	310	1,956	5,177	14,320	30,242	106,435	14,280
Area actually reporting							
Estimated total	17	173	256	2,073	4,319	20,400	1,018
Nonmetropolitan counties	17	174	257	2,079	4,332	20,463	1,021
Area actually reporting							
Estimated total	44	157	50	1,656	4,291	7,518	1,024
State total	371	2,287	5,484	18,055	38,865	134,416	16,325
Rate per 100,000 inhabitants	6.1	37.8	90.7	298.7	643.0	2,223.9	270.1
Montana [3]							
Metropolitan statistical area							
Area actually reporting	5	131	143	645	2,164	9,837	944
Cities outside metropolitan areas							
Area actually reporting	12	166	42	612	923	5,628	415
Estimated total	12	170	43	627	946	5,770	425
Nonmetropolitan counties							

Table 5.   Crime,[1] by State and Area, 2013— continued

(Number, percent, rate per 100,000 population.)

Area	Murder and nonnegligent manslaughter	Rape (revised definition)[2]	Robbery	Aggravated assault	Burglary	Larceny-theft	Motor vehicle theft
Area actually reporting	5	103	17	625	904	4,202	456
Estimated total	5	109	18	659	954	4,432	481
State total	22	410	204	1,931	4,064	20,039	1,850
Rate per 100,000 inhabitants	2.2	40.4	20.1	190.2	400.3	1,974.0	182.2
Nebraska [4]							
Metropolitan statistical area							
Area actually reporting	53		992	2,436	6,499	26,152	3,917
Estimated total	53	503	993	2,439	6,518	26,238	3,925
Cities outside metropolitan areas							
Area actually reporting	1		35	388	1,414	6,567	323
Estimated total	1	233	39	433	1,580	7,336	361
Nonmetropolitan counties							
Area actually reporting	2		6	100	631	1,638	139
Estimated total	3	65	8	127	802	2,081	177
State total	57	801	1,040	2,999	8,900	35,655	4,463
Rate per 100,000 inhabitants	3.1	42.9	55.7	160.5	476.3	1,908.2	238.9
Nevada							
Metropolitan statistical area							
Area actually reporting	143	1,290	5,124	9,267	21,274	42,622	9,529
Cities outside metropolitan areas							
Area actually reporting	10	49	24	199	577	1,243	176
Nonmetropolitan counties							
Area actually reporting	10		34	582	1,171	2,220	287
Estimated total	10	79	35	594	1,196	2,267	293
State total	163	1,418	5,183	10,060	23,047	46,132	9,998
Rate per 100,000 inhabitants	5.8	50.8	185.8	360.6	826.0	1,653.4	358.3
New Hampshire [3]							
Metropolitan statistical area							
Area actually reporting	13	367	508	921	2,813	13,915	571
Estimated total	13	378	515	944	2,888	14,333	587
Cities outside metropolitan areas							
Area actually reporting	8	247	117	407	1,549	7,259	268
Estimated total	9	284	134	467	1,778	8,333	308
Nonmetropolitan counties							
Area actually reporting)	0	6	0	13	27	66	2
Estimated total	0	24	0	81	270	498	45
State total	22	686	649	1,492	4,936	23,164	940
Rate per 100,000 inhabitants	1.7	51.8	49.0	112.7	373.0	1,750.3	71.0
New Jersey							
Metropolitan statistical area							
Area actually reporting	400		12,059	12,045	35,779	117,601	13,717
Estimated total	401	1,120	12,082	12,071	35,873	117,936	13,747
Cities outside metropolitan areas							
Nonmetropolitan counties							
State total	401	1,120	12,082	12,071	35,873	117,936	13,747
Rate per 100,000 inhabitants	4.5	12.6	135.8	135.6	403.1	1,325.2	154.5
New Mexico							
Metropolitan statistical area							
Area actually reporting	69	999	1,507	6,111	14,610	35,010	4,529
Estimated total							
Cities outside metropolitan areas	31		251	2,501	4,508	12,401	921
Area actually reporting	31	355	254	2,527	4,554	12,528	930
Estimated total							
Nonmetropolitan counties	19		37	560	1,741	1,760	336
Area actually reporting	25	111	49	744	2,312	2,337	446
Estimated total	125	1,465	1,810	9,382	21,476	49,875	5,905
State total	6.0	70.3	86.8	449.9	1,029.9	2,391.8	283.2
New York							
Metropolitan statistical area							
Area actually reporting	626		26,913	44,671	50,561	265,122	14,872
Estimated total	627	2,998	26,959	44,754	50,808	266,372	14,927
Cities outside metropolitan areas							
Area actually reporting	3		209	731	2,431	11,385	225
Estimated total	3	157	218	763	2,539	11,891	235
Nonmetropolitan counties							
Area actually reporting	18	198	64	613	3,095	8,411	320
State total	648	3,353	27,241	46,130	56,442	286,674	15,482
Rate per 100,000 inhabitants	3.3	17.1	138.6	234.7	287.2	1,458.8	78.8
North Carolina							
Metropolitan statistical area							
Area actually reporting	352		7,776	16,254	65,304	158,115	11,656

Table 5.   Crime,[1] by State and Area, 2013— continued

(Number, percent, rate per 100,000 population.)

Area	Murder and nonnegligent manslaughter	Rape (revised definition)[2]	Robbery	Aggravated assault	Burglary	Larceny-theft	Motor vehicle theft
Estimated total	353	1,841	7,830	16,403	65,970	160,141	11,762
Cities outside metropolitan areas							
Area actually reporting	51		937	2,529	8,423	23,035	1,088
Estimated total	55	243	1,012	2,732	9,100	24,888	1,175
Nonmetropolitan counties							
Area actually reporting	58		480	2,250	14,788	16,756	1,579
Estimated total	61	285	507	2,378	15,632	17,712	1,669
State total	469	2,369	9,349	21,513	90,702	202,741	14,606
Rate per 100,000 inhabitants	4.8	24.1	94.9	218.4	921.0	2,058.7	148.3
North Dakota [3]							
Metropolitan statistical area							
Area actually reporting	7	198	110	862	1,699	6,182	521
Cities outside metropolitan areas							
Area actually reporting	6	108	46	434	777	3,445	612
Estimated total	6	109	47	440	788	3,495	621
Nonmetropolitan counties							
Area actually reporting	3	23	5	143	444	1,113	272
Estimated total	3	23	5	144	447	1,121	274
State total	16	330	162	1,446	2,934	10,798	1,416
Rate per 100,000 inhabitants	2.2	45.6	22.4	199.9	405.6	1,492.7	195.7
Ohio [4]							
Metropolitan statistical area							
Area actually reporting	409	2,727	13,349	12,184	74,511	175,070	17,482
Estimated total	418	3,411	13,695	12,570	77,792	187,702	18,049
Cities outside metropolitan areas							
Area actually reporting	9	246	446	712	6,226	23,211	586
Estimated total	11	339	531	848	7,417	27,651	698
Nonmetropolitan counties							
Area actually reporting	24	250	130	770	5,714	11,396	721
Estimated total	26	291	142	839	6,224	12,413	785
State total	455	4,041	14,368	14,257	91,433	227,766	19,532
Rate per 100,000 inhabitants	3.9	34.9	124.2	123.2	790.2	1,968.5	168.8
Oklahoma [4]							
Metropolitan statistical area							
Area actually reporting	156	1,653	2,700	8,497	23,527	58,338	9,078
Cities outside metropolitan areas							
Area actually reporting	21	407	292	2,446	7,002	19,046	1,454
Nonmetropolitan counties							
Area actually reporting	18	120	39	640	2,819	4,111	682
State total	195	2,180	3,031	11,583	33,348	81,495	11,214
Rate per 100,000 inhabitants	5.1	56.6	78.7	300.8	866.1	2,116.4	291.2
Oregon [4]							
Metropolitan statistical area							
Area actually reporting	58		2,234	4,674	16,988	80,581	8,688
Estimated total	58	1,548	2,242	4,689	17,050	80,905	8,716
Cities outside metropolitan areas							
Area actually reporting	7		122	564	2,127	9,543	661
Estimated total	7	217	125	580	2,187	9,811	680
Nonmetropolitan counties							
Area actually reporting	15		29	331	1,486	3,289	452
Estimated total	15	132	30	341	1,532	3,390	466
State total	80	1,897	2,397	5,610	20,769	94,106	9,862
Rate per 100,000 inhabitants	2.0	48.3	61.0	142.7	528.5	2,394.5	250.9
Pennsylvania [3,5]							
Metropolitan statistical area							
Area actually reporting	553	3,308	14,464	21,664	46,396	180,021	13,010
Estimated total	553	3,317	14,496	21,740	46,574	180,941	13,047
Cities outside metropolitan areas							
Area actually reporting	6	121	168	1,339	2,091	9,383	277
Estimated total	6	124	173	1,376	2,149	9,641	285
Nonmetropolitan counties							
Area actually reporting	35	333	93	603	3,311	6,854	438
State total	594	3,774	14,762	23,719	52,034	197,436	13,770
Rate per 100,000 inhabitants	4.7	29.5	115.6	185.7	407.3	1,545.6	107.8
Puerto Rico							
Metropolitan statistical area							
Area actually reporting	845	33	5,889	2,219	13,267	28,257	5,433
Cities outside metropolitan areas							
Area actually reporting	38	1	127	176	694	1,103	97
Total	883	34	6,016	2,395	13,961	29,360	5,530
Rate per 100,000 inhabitants	24.4	0.9	166.4	66.3	386.2	812.2	153.0

Table 5.   Crime,[1] by State and Area, 2013— continued

(Number, percent, rate per 100,000 population.)

Area	Murder and nonnegligent manslaughter	Rape (revised definition)[2]	Robbery	Aggravated assault	Burglary	Larceny-theft	Motor vehicle theft
Rhode Island [3]							
Metropolitan statistical area							
Area actually reporting	31	425	684	1,538	5,606	17,809	2,207
Cities outside metropolitan areas							
Nonmetropolitan counties							
Area actually reporting	0	15	0	12	1	29	26
State total	31	440	684	1,550	5,607	17,838	2,233
Rate per 100,000 inhabitants	2.9	41.8	65.0	147.4	533.2	1,696.4	212.4
South Carolina [3]							
Metropolitan statistical area							
Area actually reporting	209	1,795	3,440	14,455	32,985	100,739	10,817
Estimated total	209	1,797	3,447	14,488	33,057	101,059	10,836
Cities outside metropolitan areas							
Area actually reporting	37	151	323	1,400	2,796	8,710	447
Estimated total	38	154	330	1,432	2,859	8,907	457
Nonmetropolitan counties							
Area actually reporting	50	220	195	1,918	5,042	9,545	1,287
State total	297	2,171	3,972	17,838	40,958	119,511	12,580
Rate per 100,000 inhabitants	6.2	45.5	83.2	373.6	857.8	2,502.9	263.5
South Dakota [3]							
Metropolitan statistical area							
Area actually reporting	5	267	119	838	1,971	6,789	509
Estimated total	5	268	119	840	1,979	6,814	511
Cities outside metropolitan areas							
Area actually reporting	7	195	29	977	1,005	4,060	330
Estimated total	7	203	30	1,020	1,049	4,239	345
Nonmetropolitan counties							
Area actually reporting	6	22	8	106	268	635	64
Estimated total	8	28	10	136	344	814	82
State total	20	499	159	1,996	3,372	11,867	938
Rate per 100,000 inhabitants	2.4	59.1	18.8	236.2	399.1	1,404.6	111.0
Tennessee [3]							
Metropolitan statistical area							
Area actually reporting	274	1,989	6,854	23,330	39,978	117,086	9,564
Estimated total	275	1,997	6,867	23,412	40,121	117,744	9,598
Cities outside metropolitan areas							
Area actually reporting	17	189	331	2,617	4,697	16,671	880
Nonmetropolitan counties							
Area actually reporting	36	165	109	2,349	6,181	9,387	1,350
State total	328	2,351	7,307	28,378	50,999	143,802	11,828
Rate per 100,000 inhabitants	5.0	36.2	112.5	436.9	785.1	2,213.7	182.1
Texas [4]							
Metropolitan statistical area							
Area actually reporting	1,037		31,004	58,295	169,961	556,848	62,315
Estimated total	1,037	8,669	31,020	58,339	170,112	557,452	62,364
Cities outside metropolitan areas							
Area actually reporting	50		625	4,394	11,056	33,426	1,689
Estimated total	51	663	637	4,501	11,325	34,222	1,727
Nonmetropolitan counties							
Area actually reporting	50		141	2,406	9,284	13,166	1,623
Estimated total	51	434	144	2,452	9,461	13,417	1,654
State total	1,139	9,766	31,801	65,292	190,898	605,091	65,745
Rate per 100,000 inhabitants	4.3	36.9	120.2	246.9	721.8	2,287.8	248.6
Utah [4]							
Metropolitan statistical area							
Area actually reporting	37	1,242	1,213	3,270	12,209	59,737	7,109
Estimated total	37	1,244	1,215	3,276	12,237	59,879	7,124
Cities outside metropolitan areas							
Area actually reporting	4	128	9	229	544	2,837	156
Estimated total	4	133	9	239	568	2,962	163
Nonmetropolitan counties							
Area actually reporting	8	44	18	261	513	1,890	173
Estimated total	8	45	19	269	528	1,947	178
State total	49	1,422	1,243	3,784	13,333	64,788	7,465
Rate per 100,000 inhabitants	1.7	49.0	42.8	130.4	459.6	2,233.4	257.3
Vermont [3]							
Metropolitan statistical area							
Area actually reporting	3	40	31	183	961	4,351	77
Cities outside metropolitan areas							
Area actually reporting	1	49	29	255	1,099	4,154	152
Nonmetropolitan counties	1	49	29	255	1,100	4,159	152
Area actually reporting							

Table 5.   Crime,[1] by State and Area, 2013— continued

(Number, percent, rate per 100,000 population.)

Area	Murder and nonnegligent manslaughter	Rape (revised definition)[2]	Robbery	Aggravated assault	Burglary	Larceny-theft	Motor vehicle theft
Estimated total	6	41	13	108	1,252	1,718	105
State total	10	130	73	546	3,313	10,228	334
Rate per 100,000 inhabitants	1.6	20.7	11.6	87.1	528.7	1,632.2	53.3
Virginia [3]							
Metropolitan statistical area							
Area actually reporting	271	1,887	4,311	7,979	22,448	121,447	7,684
Estimated total	271	1,888	4,312	7,982	22,456	121,497	7,687
Cities outside metropolitan areas							
Area actually reporting	9	107	153	384	1,354	6,645	261
Nonmetropolitan counties							
Area actually reporting	36	267	100	696	2,830	7,336	588
State total	316	2,262	4,565	9,062	26,640	135,478	8,536
Rate per 100,000 inhabitants	3.8	27.4	55.3	109.7	322.5	1,640.1	103.3
Washington [4,5]							
Metropolitan statistical area							
Area actually reporting	139	2,322	5,615	10,578	52,137	158,431	26,852
Cities outside metropolitan areas							
Area actually reporting	10	146	164	606	3,166	9,051	936
Estimated total	10	148	166	615	3,212	9,183	950
Nonmetropolitan counties							
Area actually reporting	11	103	38	408	3,004	4,296	597
State total	160	2,573	5,819	11,601	58,353	171,910	28,399
Rate per 100,000 inhabitants	2.3	36.9	83.5	166.4	837.0	2,465.9	407.4
West Virginia [3]							
Metropolitan statistical area							
Area actually reporting	28	438	513	2,350	6,620	18,624	1,297
Estimated total	29	465	549	2,535	7,042	20,327	1,389
Cities outside metropolitan areas							
Area actually reporting	5	44	39	384	661	2,515	96
Estimated total	7	62	55	541	931	3,543	135
Nonmetropolitan counties							
Area actually reporting	22	111	41	994	1,500	3,133	346
Estimated total	25	126	47	1,127	1,701	3,553	392
State total	61	653	651	4,203	9,674	27,423	1,916
Rate per 100,000 inhabitants	3.3	35.2	35.1	226.7	521.7	1,478.9	103.3
Wisconsin [4,5]							
Metropolitan statistical area							
Area actually reporting	143		4,706	7,825	19,037	74,026	6,550
Estimated total	143	1,278	4,725	7,873	19,245	75,179	6,592
Cities outside metropolitan areas							
Area actually reporting	8		78	843	2,043	13,132	335
Estimated total	8	247	80	869	2,106	13,540	345
Nonmetropolitan counties							
Area actually reporting	11		29	529	2,959	5,170	445
Estimated total	11	162	29	536	2,996	5,234	451
State total	162	1,687	4,834	9,278	24,347	93,953	7,388
Rate per 100,000 inhabitants	2.8	29.4	84.2	161.6	424.0	1,636.0	128.6
Wyoming							
Metropolitan statistical area							
Area actually reporting	4	40	30	302	818	3,948	227
Cities outside metropolitan areas							
Area actually reporting	4		42	452	823	5,102	254
Estimated total	4	107	43	465	847	5,254	262
Nonmetropolitan counties							
Area actually reporting	8		2	138	269	995	82
Estimated total	9	40	2	149	290	1,074	89
State total	17	187	75	916	1,955	10,276	578
Rate per 100,000 inhabitants	2.9	32.1	12.9	157.2	335.5	1,763.6	99.2

Note: Although arson data are included in the trend and clearance tables, sufficient data are not available to estimate totals for this offense. Therefore, no arson data are published in this table.   1 The violent crime figures include the offenses of murder, rape (revised definition), robbery, and aggravated assault.   2 The figures shown in this column for the offense of rape were estimated using the revised Uniform Crime Reporting (UCR) definition of rape. See chapter notes for more detail.   3 This state's agencies submitted rape data according to the revised UCR definition of rape.   4 Agencies within this state submitted rape data according to both the revised UCR definition of rape and the legacy UCR definition of rape.   5 Because of changes in the state/local agency's reporting practices, figures are not comparable to previous years' data. 6 Includes offenses reported by the Zoological Police and the Metro Transit Police.

Table 6.   Crime, by Selected Metropolitan Statistical Area, 2013

(Number, percent, rate per 100,000 population.)

Area	Murder and nonnegligent manslaughter	Rape[1]	Robbery	Aggravated assault	Burglary	Larceny-theft	Motor vehicle theft
Abilene, TX, MSA							
City of Abilene	1	37	125	314	1,055	3,460	254
Total area actually reporting	1	43	128	388	1,323	3,907	292
Rate per 100,000 inhabitants	0.6	25.6	76.1	230.8	787.0	2,324.0	173.7
Akron, OH, MSA							
City of Akron	23	160	528	859	3,096	5,922	631
Total area actually reporting	35	256	660	1,052	4,798	13,252	865
Estimated total	36	270	695	1,090	5,122	14,520	921
Rate per 100,000 inhabitants	5.1	38.4	98.8	154.9	728.1	2,064.1	130.9
Albany, GA, MSA							
City of Albany	8	21	183	537	1,319	3,169	173
Total area actually reporting	9	36	215	750	1,963	4,658	275
Estimated total	9	37	223	762	2,010	4,813	292
Rate per 100,000 inhabitants	5.7	23.5	141.7	484.2	1,277.3	3,058.5	185.6
Albany, OR, MSA							
City of Albany	0	8	27	5	252	1,625	142
Total area actually reporting	1	18	45	33	750	2,976	292
Rate per 100,000 inhabitants	0.8	15.1	37.8	27.7	629.4	2,497.6	245.1
Albany-Schenectady-Troy, NY, MSA							
City of Albany	8	30	227	526	705	3,243	142
City of Schenectady	8	31	203	365	769	1,878	153
City of Troy	1	14	145	211	593	1,305	87
Total area actually reporting	24	131	716	1,467	3,738	15,787	650
Rate per 100,000 inhabitants	2.7	14.9	81.7	167.3	426.3	1,800.4	74.1
Albuquerque, NM, MSA							
City of Albuquerque	37	439	1,046	2,803	7,297	20,229	3,005
Total area actually reporting	50	527	1,183	4,167	9,466	23,767	3,597
Estimated total	53	573	1,239	4,835	10,350	26,272	3,849
Rate per 100,000 inhabitants	5.9	63.5	137.3	535.7	1,146.7	2,910.6	426.4
Alexandria, LA, MSA							
City of Alexandria	6	11	156	630	1,130	2,561	189
Total area actually reporting	11	46	181	951	1,967	4,642	420
Estimated total	12	48	188	980	2,033	4,922	432
Rate per 100,000 inhabitants	7.8	31.0	121.5	633.6	1,314.3	3,182.1	279.3
Allentown-Bethlehem-Easton, PA-NJ, MSA							
City of Allentown, PA	12	64	329	223	1,263	2,724	337
City of Bethlehem, PA	4	27	74	78	365	1,601	44
Total area actually reporting	24	170	540	802	3,723	13,649	801
Estimated total	24	170	540	802	3,724	13,655	801
Rate per 100,000 inhabitants	2.9	20.5	65.2	96.8	449.4	1,647.9	96.7
Altoona, PA, MSA							
City of Altoona	2	25	29	75	259	733	43
Total area actually reporting	2	36	33	197	393	1,680	73
Estimated total	2	36	34	199	396	1,698	74
Rate per 100,000 inhabitants	1.6	28.3	26.8	156.6	311.6	1,336.2	58.2
Amarillo, TX, MSA							
City of Amarillo	9	214	242	821	1,816	5,643	695
Total area actually reporting	9	221	250	885	1,998	6,178	743
Rate per 100,000 inhabitants	3.5	84.9	96.0	340.0	767.6	2,373.4	285.4
Ames, IA, MSA							
City of Ames	0	34	11	43	224	1,181	34
Total area actually reporting	0	46	14	67	310	1,470	52
Estimated total	0	48	15	77	331	1,561	57
Rate per 100,000 inhabitants	0.0	52.2	16.3	83.8	360.2	1,698.6	62.0
Anchorage, AK, MSA							
City of Anchorage	14	408	522	1,491	1,318	9,845	869
Total area actually reporting	15	419	528	1,535	1,398	10,722	927
Rate per 100,000 inhabitants	4.8	133.2	167.9	488.0	444.4	3,408.6	294.7
Ann Arbor, MI, MSA							
City of Ann Arbor	3	48	49	147	410	2,021	94
Total area actually reporting	11	187	161	720	1,508	5,525	376
Rate per 100,000 inhabitants	3.1	52.9	45.6	203.9	427.0	1,564.3	106.5
Anniston-Oxford-Jacksonville, AL, MSA							
City of Anniston	5	39	78	339	770	1,120	98

Table 6.   Crime, by Selected Metropolitan Statistical Area, 2013— continued

(Number, percent, rate per 100,000 population.)

Area	Murder and nonnegligent manslaughter	Rape[1]	Robbery	Aggravated assault	Burglary	Larceny-theft	Motor vehicle theft
City of Oxford	2	6	6	36	166	704	40
City of Jacksonville	0	3	10	22	137	439	13
Total area actually reporting	8	64	103	447	1,366	2,814	189
Rate per 100,000 inhabitants	6.8	54.8	88.1	382.4	1,168.6	2,407.3	161.7
Appleton, WI, MSA							
City of Appleton	1	28	14	133	186	1,088	30
Total area actually reporting	1	38	19	227	459	2,651	68
Rate per 100,000 inhabitants	0.4	16.6	8.3	98.9	200.0	1,155.3	29.6
Athens-Clarke County, GA, MSA							
City of Athens-Clarke County	2	37	125	240	967	2,912	195
Total area actually reporting	2	52	133	347	1,376	4,388	271
Estimated total	2	52	134	349	1,384	4,422	274
Rate per 100,000 inhabitants	1.0	26.3	67.9	176.8	701.0	2,239.7	138.8
Atlanta-Sandy Springs-Roswell, GA, MSA							
City of Atlanta	84	105	2,363	2,965	5,938	17,158	4,432
City of Sandy Springs	6	14	105	61	526	2,063	150
City of Roswell	1	17	72	54	476	1,556	75
City of Alpharetta	2	2	23	20	128	1,074	26
Cit of Marietta	5	12	127	306	457	1,861	181
Total area actually reporting	323	1,074	8,697	11,302	44,496	119,994	18,557
Estimated total	324	1,077	8,714	11,329	44,591	120,386	18,593
Rate per 100,000 inhabitants	5.9	19.5	158.1	205.6	809.1	2,184.4	337.4
Atlantic City-Hammonton, NJ, MSA							
City of Atlantic City	3	9	367	306	393	2,011	71
City of Hammonton	0	0	1	7	47	95	9
Total area actually reporting	8	38	520	659	1,741	6,226	232
Rate per 100,000 inhabitants	2.9	13.8	188.3	238.7	630.6	2,255.0	84.0
Augusta-Richmond County, GA-SC, MSA							
Total area actually reporting	32	169	597	834	5,097	14,032	1,676
Estimated total	32	171	612	857	5,179	14,369	1,707
Rate per 100,000 inhabitants	5.5	29.5	105.5	147.8	893.0	2,477.7	294.3
Austin-Round Rock, TX, MSA							
City of Austin	26	217	763	2,117	6,550	32,948	2,169
City of Round Rock	2	24	37	86	297	2,086	45
Total area actually reporting	52	436	999	3,604	10,017	46,639	2,977
Estimated total	52	437	1,001	3,609	10,035	46,713	2,983
Rate per 100,000 inhabitants	2.8	23.3	53.3	192.0	534.0	2,485.7	158.7
Bakersfield, CA, MSA							
City of Bakersfield	24	43	708	1,082	4,605	9,272	2,937
Total area actually reporting	61	171	1,285	3,452	10,728	16,851	5,802
Rate per 100,000 inhabitants	7.1	19.8	149.0	400.4	1,244.3	1,954.4	672.9
Baltimore-Columbia-Towson, MD, MSA							
City of Baltimore	233	298	3,734	4,460	7,391	18,946	4,452
Total area actually reporting	278	647	6,303	10,324	16,662	59,726	7,086
Rate per 100,000 inhabitants	10.0	23.3	227.4	372.5	601.2	2,155.2	255.7
Bangor, ME, MSA							
City of Bangor	3	10	35	22	243	1,564	37
Total area actually reporting	6	23	56	55	812	3,439	88
Rate per 100,000 inhabitants	3.9	15.0	36.5	35.8	528.9	2,240.0	57.3
Barnstable Town, MA, MSA							
City of Barnstable	0	18	30	254	289	835	67
Total area actually reporting	2	89	78	772	1,785	3,219	199
Rate per 100,000 inhabitants	0.9	41.2	36.1	357.7	827.0	1,491.3	92.2
Baton Rouge, LA, MSA[2]							
City of Baton Rouge	49	74	974	1,030	3,264	7,648	506
Total area actually reporting	83	177	1,378	2,482	7,831	21,810	1,019
Estimated total	84	180	1,388	2,521	7,921	22,194	1,035
Rate per 100,000 inhabitants	10.2	22.0	169.3	307.6	966.4	2,707.6	126.3
Bay City, MI, MSA							
City of Bay City	0	62	21	134	210	674	54
Total area actually reporting	2	119	29	166	502	1,636	114
Rate per 100,000 inhabitants	1.9	111.4	27.2	155.5	470.1	1,532.1	106.8
Beaumont-Port Arthur, TX, MSA							
City of Beaumont	16	59	419	731	1,922	3,987	283
City of Port Arthur	5	18	121	215	726	1,537	127

Table 6.   Crime, by Selected Metropolitan Statistical Area, 2013— continued

(Number, percent, rate per 100,000 population.)

Area	Murder and nonnegligent manslaughter	Rape[1]	Robbery	Aggravated assault	Burglary	Larceny-theft	Motor vehicle theft
Total area actually reporting	35	116	628	1,398	4,075	8,811	755
Rate per 100,000 inhabitants	8.6	28.6	154.7	344.3	1,003.6	2,169.9	185.9
Bend-Redmond, OR, MSA							
City of Bend	1	21	22	138	267	1,913	87
City of Redmond	0	11	15	61	157	867	43
Total area actually reporting	3	46	41	274	632	3,443	177
Rate per 100,000 inhabitants	1.8	28.0	25.0	166.9	384.9	2,097.1	107.8
Billings, MT, MSA							
City of Billings	4	39	81	236	989	4,074	541
Total area actually reporting	4	49	84	302	1,206	4,733	652
Rate per 100,000 inhabitants	2.4	29.7	51.0	183.2	731.6	2,871.2	395.5
Binghamton, NY, MSA							
City of Binghamton	3	19	101	161	525	1,767	57
Total area actually reporting	8	55	158	315	1,323	5,313	155
Rate per 100,000 inhabitants	3.2	22.2	63.7	127.1	533.7	2,143.5	62.5
Birmingham-Hoover, AL, MSA							
City of Birmingham	63	178	969	1,642	4,018	8,661	1,478
City of Hoover	2	9	34	29	344	2,144	108
Total area actually reporting	91	481	1,671	3,579	10,890	26,788	2,946
Estimated total	93	506	1,712	3,723	11,366	27,971	3,060
Rate per 100,000 inhabitants	8.2	44.4	150.3	326.9	997.9	2,455.9	268.7
Bismarck, ND, MSA							
City of Bismarck	1	26	15	152	334	1,289	107
Total area actually reporting	3	72	22	397	560	2,081	221
Rate per 100,000 inhabitants	2.4	58.0	17.7	319.5	450.7	1,675.0	177.9
Blacksburg-Christiansburg-Radford, VA, MSA							
City of Blacksburg	0	7	4	20	91	417	15
City of Christiansburg	1	13	3	13	53	478	14
City of Radford	0	11	7	73	75	321	11
Total area actually reporting	2	79	20	213	558	2,795	103
Rate per 100,000 inhabitants	1.1	44.0	11.1	118.6	310.8	1,556.9	57.4
Bloomington, IL, MSA							
City of Bloomington	2	57	59	281	402	1,446	53
Total area actually reporting	4	88	94	397	809	2,801	89
Estimated total	4	91	102	413	852	2,995	99
Rate per 100,000 inhabitants	2.1	48.0	53.9	218.0	449.8	1,581.2	52.3
Bloomington, IN, MSA							
City of Bloomington	2	34	78	161	516	1,942	148
Total area actually reporting	3	56	87	261	860	3,062	213
Estimated total	3	59	90	274	935	3,239	232
Rate per 100,000 inhabitants	1.8	36.1	55.0	167.5	571.5	1,979.9	141.8
Bloomsburg-Berwick, PA, MSA							
City of Bloomsburg Town	0	9	3	29	56	173	2
City of Berwick	0	1	3	29	106	284	11
Total area actually reporting	1	18	11	184	331	1,129	32
Rate per 100,000 inhabitants	1.2	21.2	12.9	216.3	389.1	1,327.1	37.6
Boise City, ID, MSA							
City of Boise	3	123	45	429	825	3,703	213
Total area actually reporting	6	313	84	1,049	2,301	8,179	529
Estimated total	6	313	84	1,050	2,303	8,186	529
Rate per 100,000 inhabitants	0.9	48.3	13.0	162.1	355.5	1,263.5	81.7
Boston-Cambridge-Newton, MA-NH, MSA							
City of Boston, MA	39	279	1,868	2,851	3,096	13,147	1,610
City of Cambridge, MA	2	24	114	221	401	2,402	104
City of Newton, MA	0	11	18	45	205	584	18
City of Framingham, MA	0	4	23	145	217	735	73
City of Waltham, MA	1	22	28	90	212	694	46
Total area actually reporting	85	1,286	4,427	10,596	16,118	65,135	5,966
Estimated total	86	1,308	4,464	10,728	16,370	66,047	6,034
Rate per 100,000 inhabitants	1.8	28.0	95.4	229.3	349.9	1,411.5	129.0
Boston, MA, MD							
Total area actually reporting	61	640	2,900	5,999	7,689	29,226	2,765
Estimated total	62	656	2,933	6,119	7,902	29,920	2,825
Rate per 100,000 inhabitants	3.2	33.8	151.0	315.0	406.8	1,540.4	145.4
Cambridge-Newton-Framingham, MA, MD							

Table 6.　Crime, by Selected Metropolitan Statistical Area, 2013— continued

(Number, percent, rate per 100,000 population.)

Area	Murder and nonnegligent manslaughter	Rape[1]	Robbery	Aggravated assault	Burglary	Larceny-theft	Motor vehicle theft
Total area actually reporting	21	456	1,400	4,226	7,234	29,160	2,932
Rate per 100,000 inhabitants	0.9	19.7	60.5	182.7	312.7	1,260.6	126.8
Rockingham County-Strafford County, NH, MD							
Total area actually reporting	3	190	127	371	1,195	6,749	269
Estimated total	3	196	131	383	1,234	6,967	277
Rate per 100,000 inhabitants	0.7	46.3	30.9	90.4	291.4	1,645.0	65.4
Boulder, CO, MSA							
City of Boulder	0	38	40	140	612	2,236	100
Total area actually reporting	0	136	65	343	1,038	4,922	251
Estimated total	2	162	74	420	1,232	5,514	333
Rate per 100,000 inhabitants	0.6	52.2	23.8	135.3	397.0	1,776.8	107.3
Bowling Green, KY, MSA							
City of Bowling Green	2	59	69	71	455	2,272	125
Total area actually reporting	2	72	76	86	775	2,837	177
Rate per 100,000 inhabitants	1.2	44.1	46.5	52.6	474.2	1,735.8	108.3
Bremerton-Silverdale, WA, MSA							
City of Bremerton	1	35	55	136	452	1,354	140
Total area actually reporting	2	119	105	481	1,931	5,126	512
Rate per 100,000 inhabitants	0.8	46.3	40.9	187.2	751.7	1,995.4	199.3
Bridgeport-Stamford-Norwalk, CT, MSA							
City of Bridgeport	11	82	584	720	1,191	2,610	663
City of Stamford	1	28	160	145	354	1,435	149
City of Norwalk	0	14	61	164	245	1,377	106
City of Danbury	2	25	53	28	221	972	64
City of Stratford	0	8	41	25	251	1,042	136
Total area actually reporting	14	175	943	1,120	2,955	10,644	1,319
Rate per 100,000 inhabitants	1.5	19.0	102.4	121.6	320.8	1,155.6	143.2
Brownsville-Harlingen, TX, MSA							
City of Brownsville	1	61	136	275	1,140	6,441	257
City of Harlingen	2	21	59	182	496	2,012	76
Total area actually reporting	6	126	244	633	2,761	11,587	496
Rate per 100,000 inhabitants	1.4	30.0	58.1	150.7	657.5	2,759.2	118.1
Brunswick, GA, MSA [2]							
City of Brunswick	3	4	38	117	331	732	47
Total area actually reporting	7	19	111		1,195	2,989	162
Estimated total	7	19	113		1,209	3,045	167
Rate per 100,000 inhabitants	6.2	16.7	99.3		1,062.9	2,677.1	146.8
Buffalo-Cheektowaga-Niagara Falls, NY, MSA							
City of Buffalo	47	145	1,322	1,735	3,458	8,076	957
City of Cheektowaga Town	0	11	48	99	345	2,271	73
City of Niagara Falls	3	12	166	403	746	1,949	112
Total area actually reporting	59	241	1,744	2,839	6,525	23,046	1,473
Rate per 100,000 inhabitants	5.2	21.2	153.6	250.1	574.9	2,030.4	129.8
Burlington, NC, MSA							
City of Burlington	0	16	100	246	546	1,977	112
Total area actually reporting	3	33	147	410	1,311	3,433	225
Rate per 100,000 inhabitants	1.9	21.3	94.7	264.2	844.6	2,211.8	145.0
California-Lexington Park, MD, MSA							
Total area actually reporting	3	6	62	171	640	1,730	119
Rate per 100,000 inhabitants	2.7	5.4	56.2	155.0	580.3	1,568.5	107.9
Canton-Massillon, OH, MSA							
City of Canton	11	72	357	233	1,218	2,597	438
City of Massillon	0	14	31	24	249	695	31
Total area actually reporting	12	137	479	445	2,651	7,321	698
Estimated total	12	138	482	448	2,680	7,434	703
Rate per 100,000 inhabitants	3.0	34.2	119.3	110.9	663.3	1,839.9	174.0
Cape Coral-Fort Myers, FL, MSA							
City of Cape Coral	3	7	40	147	803	2,427	145
City of Fort Myers	10	45	185	512	392	1,726	161
Total area actually reporting	25	150	577	1,432	3,779	9,808	813
Rate per 100,000 inhabitants	3.8	22.9	87.9	218.2	575.9	1,494.6	123.9
Cape Girardeau, MO-IL, MSA							
City of Cape Girardeau, MO	5	12	85	156	446	1,487	57
Total area actually reporting	7	23	100	348	738	2,136	107
Rate per 100,000 inhabitants	7.2	23.6	102.6	356.9	756.8	2,190.5	109.7

Table 6. Crime, by Selected Metropolitan Statistical Area, 2013— continued

(Number, percent, rate per 100,000 population.)

Area	Murder and nonnegligent manslaughter	Rape[1]	Robbery	Aggravated assault	Burglary	Larceny-theft	Motor vehicle theft
Carson City, NV, MSA							
Total area actually reporting	4	0	17	112	202	654	68
Rate per 100,000 inhabitants	7.3	0.0	30.9	203.9	367.7	1,190.5	123.8
Casper, WY, MSA							
City of Casper	2	7	15	64	294	1,657	85
Total area actually reporting	3	11	17	138	377	1,879	111
Rate per 100,000 inhabitants	3.8	13.8	21.3	172.5	471.3	2,349.0	138.8
Cedar Rapids, IA, MSA[3]							
City of Cedar Rapids	4	46	90	252	977	3,433	297
Total area actually reporting	4	68	98	323	1,302	4,256	356
Estimated total	4	74	99	362	1,395	4,435	380
Rate per 100,000 inhabitants	1.5	28.1	37.6	137.3	529.2	1,682.6	144.2
Chambersburg-Waynesboro, PA, MSA[3]							
City of Chambersburg	0	3	46	37	127	660	23
City of Waynesboro[3]	1	3	11	9	40	199	3
Total area actually reporting	4	35	80	111	528	2,314	89
Rate per 100,000 inhabitants	2.6	23.1	52.8	73.2	348.2	1,525.9	58.7
Champaign-Urbana, IL, MSA							
City of Champaign	4	39	119	492	506	1,698	71
City of Urbana	2	27	66	46	354	1,211	40
Total area actually reporting	9	116	217	767	1,385	4,260	166
Estimated total	9	117	220	772	1,400	4,326	170
Rate per 100,000 inhabitants	3.8	50.0	93.9	329.6	597.7	1,847.0	72.6
Charleston, North Charleston, SC, MSA							
City of Charleston	7	29	72	123	305	2,725	162
City of North Charleston	13	56	196	428	892	4,409	503
Total area actually reporting	51	201	502	1,785	4,396	16,155	1,697
Estimated total	51	202	505	1,797	4,422	16,271	1,704
Rate per 100,000 inhabitants	7.2	28.4	71.0	252.8	622.1	2,289.0	239.7
Charlotte-Concord-Gastonia, NC-SC, MSA							
City of Charlotte-Mecklenburg, NC	59	230	1,805	2,999	6,439	22,274	1,856
City of Concord, NC	7	9	50	56	414	2,033	102
City of Gastonia, NC	6	22	150	332	752	2,873	241
City of Rock Hill, SC	4	49	78	241	396	2,066	121
Total area actually reporting	121	531	2,646	6,049	15,766	49,171	3,567
Estimated total	122	535	2,665	6,097	15,963	49,867	3,600
Rate per 100,000 inhabitants	5.2	23.0	114.4	261.8	685.4	2,141.0	154.6
Charlottesville, VA, MSA							
City of Charlottesville	1	20	63	127	200	1,218	53
Total area actually reporting	4	89	97	240	675	3,439	173
Rate per 100,000 inhabitants	1.8	39.6	43.2	106.8	300.5	1,530.7	77.0
Chattanooga, TN-GA, MSA							
City of Chattanooga, TN	18	64	385	1,225	2,317	8,165	986
Total area actually reporting	22	124	491	2,122	4,469	14,833	1,644
Rate per 100,000 inhabitants	4.1	22.9	90.7	392.1	825.8	2,740.8	303.8
Cheyenne, WY, MSA							
City of Cheyenne	1	12	12	108	279	1,698	88
Total area actually reporting	1	20	13	164	441	2,069	116
Rate per 100,000 inhabitants	1.0	20.9	13.6	171.5	461.1	2,163.4	121.3
Chicago-Naperville, Elgin, IL-IN-WI, MSA[4,5]							
City of Chicago, IL[4,5]	414		11,815		17,775	65,497	12,636
City of Naperville, IL	0	7	21	77	225	1,610	34
City of Elgin, IL	3	56	63	114	351	1,462	89
City of Gary, IN	54	47	327	455	1,454	2,533	732
City of Arlington Heights, IL	0	7	7	28	125	659	16
City of Evanston, IL	1	10	63	115	361	1,474	67
City of Schaumburg, IL	0	15	30	26	175	1,928	73
City of Skokie, IL	0	9	58	90	285	1,221	69
City of Des Plaines, IL	2	7	12	35	153	595	43
City of Hoffman Estates, IL	0	16	21	18	102	426	20
Total area actually reporting	604		15,897		39,565	161,090	19,034
Estimated total	608		15,998		40,196	163,715	19,191
Rate per 100,000 inhabitants	6.4		167.7		421.4	1,716.4	201.2
Chicago-Naperville-Arlington Heights, IL, MD[4,5]							
Total area actually reporting	493		14,486		31,123	127,700	16,344
Estimated total	496		14,569		31,574	129,707	16,452

Table 6.   Crime, by Selected Metropolitan Statistical Area, 2013— continued

(Number, percent, rate per 100,000 population.)

Area	Murder and nonnegligent manslaughter	Rape[1]	Robbery	Aggravated assault	Burglary	Larceny-theft	Motor vehicle theft
Rate per 100,000 inhabitants	6.8		198.7		430.7	1,769.2	224.4
Elgin, IL, MD							
Total area actually reporting	9	147	207	712	1,441	7,549	251
Estimated total	9	150	217	732	1,496	7,792	264
Rate per 100,000 inhabitants	1.4	23.8	34.5	116.4	237.8	1,238.8	42.0
Gary, IN, MD							
Total area actually reporting	81	141	795	1,332	4,126	14,337	2,059
Estimated total	82	146	801	1,356	4,240	14,663	2,092
Rate per 100,000 inhabitants	11.6	20.6	113.1	191.5	598.8	2,070.7	295.4
Lake County-Kenosha County, IL-WI, MD							
Total area actually reporting	21	187	409	737	2,875	11,504	380
Estimated total	21	188	411	741	2,886	11,553	383
Rate per 100,000 inhabitants	2.4	21.6	47.3	85.2	331.9	1,328.5	44.0
Chico, CA, MSA							
City of Chico	2	41	95	161	622	1,568	382
Total area actually reporting	13	79	148	394	1,685	3,642	896
Rate per 100,000 inhabitants	5.8	35.5	66.6	177.2	757.8	1,637.8	402.9
Cincinnati, OH-KY-IN, MSA							
City of Cincinnati, OH	70	199	1,610	947	5,467	10,488	1,276
Total area actually reporting	101	666	2,667	2,507	15,444	46,181	2,983
Estimated total	103	691	2,716	2,584	16,013	48,133	3,098
Rate per 100,000 inhabitants	4.8	32.3	127.1	120.9	749.5	2,252.9	145.0
Clarksville, TN-KY, MSA							
City of Clarksville, TN	6	84	115	543	1,020	2,965	156
Total area actually reporting	14	133	163	718	1,818	4,894	277
Estimated total	14	133	164	719	1,823	4,912	278
Rate per 100,000 inhabitants	5.0	47.7	58.8	257.8	653.6	1,761.0	99.7
Cleveland, TN, MSA							
City of Cleveland	1	27	32	279	414	1,912	114
Total area actually reporting	1	37	37	444	833	2,669	233
Rate per 100,000 inhabitants	0.8	31.2	31.2	374.5	702.7	2,251.4	196.5
Coeur d'Alene, ID, MSA							
City of Coeur d'Alene	0	53	20	184	359	1,259	117
Total area actually reporting	3	80	31	345	916	2,845	228
Rate per 100,000 inhabitants	2.1	55.5	21.5	239.2	635.1	1,972.6	158.1
College Station-Bryan, TX, MSA							
City of College Station	0	34	37	308	432	1,750	48
City of Bryan	2	31	75	250	539	1,683	89
Total area actually reporting	5	78	122	676	1,317	4,383	200
Rate per 100,000 inhabitants	2.1	32.9	51.4	285.0	555.3	1,848.0	84.3
Colorado Springs, CO, MSA							
City of Colorado Springs	26	370	418	1,079	3,726	12,521	1,928
Total area actually reporting	42	496	463	1,495	4,755	15,149	2,224
Estimated total	42	498	464	1,500	4,768	15,228	2,231
Rate per 100,000 inhabitants	6.2	73.4	68.4	221.0	702.4	2,243.3	328.7
Columbia, MO, MSA							
City of Columbia	5	67	112	232	703	3,490	166
Total area actually reporting	5	78	128	357	889	4,497	227
Rate per 100,000 inhabitants	2.9	45.7	75.0	209.1	520.7	2,634.1	133.0
Columbia, SC, MSA							
City of Columbia	8	58	331	555	1,398	5,800	791
Total area actually reporting	37	324	836	3,375	5,905	20,147	2,672
Estimated total	37	325	838	3,385	5,927	20,246	2,678
Rate per 100,000 inhabitants	4.7	41.0	105.6	426.7	747.1	2,552.2	337.6
Columbus, GA-AL, MSA							
City of Columbus, GA	22	36	481	483	3,355	8,012	1,108
Total area actually reporting	30	70	530	668	4,233	9,866	1,403
Estimated total	30	70	532	672	4,245	9,914	1,407
Rate per 100,000 inhabitants	9.5	22.2	168.5	212.8	1,344.4	3,139.9	445.6
Columbus, IN, MSA							
City of Columbus	1	17	19	45	241	1,754	129
Total area actually reporting	5	23	21	99	350	2,142	182
Rate per 100,000 inhabitants	6.2	28.7	26.2	123.6	436.9	2,674.1	227.2

Table 6.   Crime, by Selected Metropolitan Statistical Area, 2013— continued

(Number, percent, rate per 100,000 population.)

Area	Murder and nonnegligent manslaughter	Rape[1]	Robbery	Aggravated assault	Burglary	Larceny-theft	Motor vehicle theft
Corpus Christi, TX, MSA[3]							
City of Corpus Christi	18	147	390	1,384	2,595	11,519	487
Total area actually reporting	24	198	432	1,660	3,750	14,382	700
Rate per 100,000 inhabitants	5.4	44.8	97.7	375.6	848.4	3,254.0	158.4
Corvallis, OR, MSA							
City of Corvallis	0	10	16	38	195	1,354	38
Total area actually reporting	0	13	25	66	290	1,849	80
Rate per 100,000 inhabitants	0.0	15.0	28.8	75.9	333.5	2,126.5	92.0
Crestview-Fort Walton Beach-Destin, FL, MSA							
City of Crestview	0	39	44	97	149	612	41
City of Fort Walton Beach	2	3	14	37	93	535	33
Total area actually reporting	7	120	125	792	1,197	4,469	263
Rate per 100,000 inhabitants	2.8	47.5	49.5	313.5	473.8	1,768.9	104.1
Cumberland, MD-WV, MSA							
City of Cumberland, MD	1	20	44	95	323	991	27
Total area actually reporting	4	34	66	188	624	1,996	69
Estimated total	4	34	67	191	631	2,031	71
Rate per 100,000 inhabitants	3.9	33.4	65.9	187.9	620.7	1,997.8	69.8
Dallas-Fort Worth-Arlington, TX, MSA							
City of Dallas	143	543	4,202	3,442	14,516	30,374	7,384
City of Fort Worth	48	523	1,256	2,593	8,316	23,557	2,399
City of Arlington	18	105	562	1,152	3,181	10,879	940
City of Plano	3	84	106	196	944	4,730	256
City of Irving	2	24	186	318	1,137	4,444	594
City of Denton	1	93	52	192	472	2,203	102
City of Richardson	2	15	60	51	539	2,068	151
Total area actually reporting	303	2,167	8,225	11,970	47,750	141,018	17,930
Estimated total	303	2,169	8,229	11,981	47,789	141,174	17,943
Rate per 100,000 inhabitants	4.4	31.8	120.8	175.8	701.3	2,071.8	263.3
Dallas-Plano-Irving, TX, MD							
Total area actually reporting	213	1,321	5,981	6,800	30,888	86,243	12,988
Estimated total	213	1,323	5,984	6,808	30,918	86,363	12,998
Rate per 100,000 inhabitants	4.7	29.4	132.8	151.1	686.1	1,916.5	288.4
Fort Worth-Arlington, TX, MD							
Total area actually reporting	90	846	2,244	5,170	16,862	54,775	4,942
Estimated total	90	846	2,245	5,173	16,871	54,811	4,945
Rate per 100,000 inhabitants	3.9	36.7	97.3	224.1	731.0	2,375.0	214.3
Dalton, GA, MSA							
City of Dalton	0	7	12	47	201	1,063	55
Total area actually reporting	2	32	30	271	860	2,805	225
Estimated total	2	33	33	276	878	2,879	232
Rate per 100,000 inhabitants	1.4	23.1	23.1	193.1	614.4	2,014.7	162.4
Daphne-Fairhope-Foley, AL, MSA							
City of Daphne	1	3	5	22	89	421	16
City of Fairhope	0	6	6	28	144	515	19
City of Foley	0	4	10	41	111	656	22
Total area actually reporting	1	48	67	311	939	3,749	204
Rate per 100,000 inhabitants	0.5	24.8	34.7	160.9	485.7	1,939.3	105.5
Davenport-Moline-Rock Island, IA-IL, MSA							
City of Davenport, IA	2	88	167	397	961	3,048	239
City of Moline, IL	0	8	13	100	235	1,127	27
City of Rock Island, IL	5	2	32	161	227	741	38
Total area actually reporting	7	143	241	975	1,949	7,087	375
Estimated total	7	145	247	988	1,984	7,240	383
Rate per 100,000 inhabitants	1.8	37.8	64.4	257.4	516.9	1,886.4	99.8
Dayton, OH, MSA							
City of Dayton	28	107	518	577	2,613	4,427	615
Total area actually reporting	44	326	876	914	6,840	18,013	1,398
Estimated total	44	330	885	923	6,921	18,329	1,412
Rate per 100,000 inhabitants	5.5	41.1	110.2	114.9	861.9	2,282.6	175.8
Decatur, AL, MSA							
City of Decatur	5	12	26	106	569	1,831	153
Total area actually reporting	7	37	38	215	1,040	2,665	239
Estimated total	7	37	39	218	1,050	2,698	242
Rate per 100,000 inhabitants	4.5	24.0	25.3	141.3	680.4	1,748.4	156.8
Decatur, IL, MSA							

Table 6.   Crime, by Selected Metropolitan Statistical Area, 2013— continued

(Number, percent, rate per 100,000 population.)

Area	Murder and nonnegligent manslaughter	Rape[1]	Robbery	Aggravated assault	Burglary	Larceny-theft	Motor vehicle theft
City of Decatur	5	9	84	253	793	1,512	64
Total area actually reporting	5	19	87	311	892	1,832	82
Rate per 100,000 inhabitants	4.6	17.3	79.2	283.0	811.8	1,667.3	74.6
Deltona-Daytona Beach-Ormond Beach, FL, MSA							
City of Daytona Beach	4	57	195	543	745	2,912	367
City of Ormond Beach	0	10	17	105	259	1,055	72
Total area actually reporting	26	179	455	1,685	4,129	13,326	1,105
Estimated total	26	180	457	1,690	4,142	13,372	1,109
Rate per 100,000 inhabitants	4.3	30.0	76.3	282.1	691.3	2,231.9	185.1
Denver-Aurora-Broomfield, CO, MSA							
City of Denver	40	514	1,132	2,401	4,918	15,306	3,487
City of Aurora	23	224	468	721	1,981	7,805	1,000
City of Lakewood	6	107	113	398	872	5,397	623
City of Broomfield	1	12	6	14	106	1,054	44
Total area actually reporting	99	1,427	2,125	5,196	12,468	53,444	8,041
Estimated total	99	1,427	2,125	5,197	12,472	53,466	8,043
Rate per 100,000 inhabitants	3.7	53.0	78.9	193.0	463.1	1,985.1	298.6
Des Moines-West Des Moines, IA, MSA							
City of Des Moines	11	90	211	714	2,311	6,854	850
City of West Des Moines	1	16	12	61	205	1,377	76
Total area actually reporting	14	159	247	1,177	3,536	11,762	1,190
Rate per 100,000 inhabitants	2.3	26.7	41.4	197.4	592.9	1,972.2	199.5
Detroit-Warren-Livonia, MI, MSA							
City of Detroit	316	618	4,774	8,796	11,754	17,188	11,893
City of Warren	3	127	166	383	887	2,037	584
City of Dearborn	2	33	126	186	399	2,328	377
City of Livonia	0	18	34	96	285	1,498	178
City of Troy	0	17	7	38	222	1,250	78
City of Farmington Hills	1	14	21	36	245	773	96
City of Southfield	2	39	121	100	443	1,393	284
City of Taylor	3	49	76	219	470	1,404	209
City of Novi	2	7	11	28	96	833	37
Total area actually reporting	411	2,156	7,052	14,828	26,182	65,268	19,151
Estimated total	411	2,161	7,058	14,845	26,226	65,422	19,168
Rate per 100,000 inhabitants	9.6	50.3	164.3	345.5	610.4	1,522.6	446.1
Detroit-Livonia-Dearborn, MI, MD							
Total area actually reporting	364	1,117	5,867	11,343	17,357	35,330	15,497
Estimated total	364	1,122	5,873	11,360	17,401	35,484	15,514
Rate per 100,000 inhabitants	20.4	62.8	328.7	635.9	974.0	1,986.2	868.4
Warren-Troy-Farmington Hills, MI, MD							
Total area actually reporting	47	1,039	1,185	3,485	8,825	29,938	3,654
Rate per 100,000 inhabitants	1.9	41.4	47.2	138.8	351.6	1,192.7	145.6
Dothan, AL, MSA							
City of Dothan	4	16	77	232	580	1,770	107
Total area actually reporting	9	61	101	404	1,103	2,818	224
Estimated total	9	62	104	412	1,127	2,896	231
Rate per 100,000 inhabitants	6.1	41.8	70.2	278.1	760.6	1,954.6	155.9
Dover, DE, MSA							
City of Dover	1	16	58	191	88	1,919	86
Total area actually reporting	4	92	146	532	769	4,104	184
Rate per 100,000 inhabitants	2.4	54.2	86.0	313.4	453.1	2,418.0	108.4
Dubuque, IA, MSA							
City of Dubuque	0	14	36	82	409	1,172	60
Total area actually reporting	0	16	37	100	481	1,332	81
Rate per 100,000 inhabitants	0.0	16.7	38.6	104.4	502.3	1,391.1	84.6
Duluth, MN-WI, MSA							
City of Duluth, MN	2	52	72	216	643	3,484	156
Total area actually reporting	4	121	115	414	1,742	7,365	430
Rate per 100,000 inhabitants	1.4	43.2	41.0	147.8	621.8	2,628.8	153.5
East Stroudsburg, PA, MSA							
Total area actually reporting	8	49	57	504	1,138	2,886	102
Rate per 100,000 inhabitants	4.8	29.1	33.9	299.4	676.1	1,714.7	60.6
Eau Claire, WI, MSA							
City of Eau Claire	1	22	14	86	235	1,287	48
Total area actually reporting	2	34	23	146	475	2,212	88
Rate per 100,000 inhabitants	1.2	20.7	14.0	88.8	288.8	1,345.0	53.5

Table 6.   Crime, by Selected Metropolitan Statistical Area, 2013— continued

(Number, percent, rate per 100,000 population.)

Area	Murder and nonnegligent manslaughter	Rape[1]	Robbery	Aggravated assault	Burglary	Larceny-theft	Motor vehicle theft
El Centro, CA, MSA							
City of El Centro	1	7	54	82	416	1,499	124
Total area actually reporting	2	29	102	384	1,387	3,759	552
Estimated total	2	30	110	400	1,435	3,886	582
Rate per 100,000 inhabitants	1.1	16.9	61.8	224.8	806.4	2,183.7	327.0
Elizabethtown-Fort Knox, KY, MSA							
City of Elizabethtown	0	9	10	16	182	881	25
Total area actually reporting	2	35	23	58	519	1,640	76
Rate per 100,000 inhabitants	1.3	23.2	15.3	38.5	344.4	1,088.3	50.4
Elmira, NY, MSA							
City of Elmira	0	2	29	50	224	790	13
Total area actually reporting	0	7	37	107	351	1,670	27
Rate per 100,000 inhabitants	0.0	7.9	41.6	120.2	394.2	1,875.6	30.3
El Paso, TX, MSA							
City of El Paso	10	176	457	1,879	1,771	12,993	794
Total area actually reporting	12	236	496	2,181	2,364	15,006	961
Rate per 100,000 inhabitants	1.4	28.0	58.9	258.9	280.7	1,781.6	114.1
Erie, PA, MSA							
City of Erie	3	60	175	219	1,017	2,093	98
Total area actually reporting	4	89	227	364	1,707	4,782	173
Estimated total	4	89	228	366	1,711	4,804	174
Rate per 100,000 inhabitants	1.4	31.7	81.3	130.5	610.1	1,713.0	62.0
Eugene, OR, MSA							
City of Eugene	0	68	195	139	1,539	5,773	608
Total area actually reporting	4	104	240	336	2,537	9,564	999
Estimated total	4	105	242	340	2,552	9,643	1,006
Rate per 100,000 inhabitants	1.1	29.5	67.9	95.4	716.2	2,706.3	282.3
Fairbanks, AK, MSA							
City of Fairbanks	0	34	37	142	116	1,050	103
Total area actually reporting	0	35	41	161	125	1,190	114
Rate per 100,000 inhabitants	0.0	100.7	118.0	463.4	359.8	3,425.3	328.1
Fargo, ND-MN, MSA							
City of Fargo, ND	3	71	58	314	701	2,342	166
Total area actually reporting	4	93	69	402	1,098	3,694	276
Rate per 100,000 inhabitants	1.8	41.9	31.1	180.9	494.2	1,662.7	124.2
Farmington, NM, MSA							
City of Farmington	3	49	43	196	297	1,285	92
Total area actually reporting	6	94	60	465	618	1,969	168
Rate per 100,000 inhabitants	4.7	73.7	47.0	364.6	484.5	1,543.7	131.7
Fayetteville, NC, MSA							
City of Fayetteville	25	65	586	494	3,279	8,351	631
Total area actually reporting	30	86	767	970	5,514	12,166	884
Rate per 100,000 inhabitants	7.9	22.7	202.9	256.6	1,458.5	3,217.9	233.8
Fayetteville-Springdale-Rogers, AR-MO, MSA							
City of Fayetteville, AR	3	33	33	270	538	2,473	160
City of Springdale, AR	3	77	29	245	473	2,056	122
City of Rogers, AR	0	31	11	166	225	1,453	31
City of Bentonville, AR	0	12	2	47	117	557	12
Total area actually reporting	12	262	88	1,245	2,429	8,491	490
Estimated total	12	265	91	1,265	2,490	8,631	498
Rate per 100,000 inhabitants	2.5	54.3	18.6	259.2	510.2	1,768.5	102.0
Flagstaff, AZ, MSA							
City of Flagstaff	1	25	43	177	220	2,594	55
Total area actually reporting	3	57	54	337	473	3,594	102
Rate per 100,000 inhabitants	2.2	41.6	39.4	246.0	345.3	2,623.4	74.5
Flint, MI, MSA							
City of Flint	48	145	447	1,267	1,941	2,000	320
Total area actually reporting	57	341	699	1,906	4,574	7,053	784
Estimated total	57	341	699	1,907	4,576	7,059	785
Rate per 100,000 inhabitants	13.7	81.9	167.8	457.7	1,098.4	1,694.4	188.4
Florence, SC, MSA							
City of Florence	2	29	69	193	456	2,376	104
Total area actually reporting	11	87	163	718	2,137	6,690	533
Estimated total	11	87	164	722	2,146	6,729	535

Table 6.   Crime, by Selected Metropolitan Statistical Area, 2013— continued

(Number, percent, rate per 100,000 population.)

Area	Murder and nonnegligent manslaughter	Rape[1]	Robbery	Aggravated assault	Burglary	Larceny-theft	Motor vehicle theft
Rate per 100,000 inhabitants	5.3	42.0	79.2	348.5	1,036.0	3,248.5	258.3
Florence-Muscle Shoals, AL, MSA							
City of Florence	3	28	56	120	324	1,380	103
City of Muscle Shoals	0	5	18	35	109	539	45
Total area actually reporting	5	72	93	350	937	3,103	287
Rate per 100,000 inhabitants	3.4	49.0	63.3	238.3	637.9	2,112.6	195.4
Fond du Lac, WI, MSA							
City of Fond du Lac	1	31	11	111	126	1,021	31
Total area actually reporting	1	40	17	142	250	1,355	46
Rate per 100,000 inhabitants	1.0	39.2	16.7	139.3	245.2	1,329.0	45.1
Fort Collins-Loveland, CO, MSA							
City of Fort Collins	0	57	37	263	531	3,137	140
Total area actually reporting	2	138	66	440	934	5,631	247
Rate per 100,000 inhabitants	0.6	43.7	20.9	139.3	295.7	1,782.5	78.2
Fort Smith, AR-OK, MSA							
City of Fort Smith, AR	4	79	94	429	975	3,447	199
Total area actually reporting	6	129	116	871	2,154	6,162	423
Rate per 100,000 inhabitants	2.1	45.9	41.3	310.0	766.7	2,193.4	150.6
Fort Wayne, IN, MSA							
City of Fort Wayne	31	95	447	376	2,396	7,025	386
Total area actually reporting	34	121	496	458	2,859	8,777	495
Estimated total	34	124	499	472	2,939	8,967	516
Rate per 100,000 inhabitants	8.0	29.2	117.7	111.3	693.0	2,114.5	121.7
Fresno, CA, MSA							
City of Fresno	40	53	903	1,556	5,223	13,304	4,057
Total area actually reporting	57	163	1,221	3,427	9,102	21,257	6,339
Rate per 100,000 inhabitants	6.0	17.1	127.9	359.1	953.8	2,227.5	664.3
Gadsden, AL, MSA							
City of Gadsden	6	47	104	267	830	1,904	200
Total area actually reporting	8	80	112	376	1,274	2,601	282
Estimated total	8	83	119	397	1,337	2,805	300
Rate per 100,000 inhabitants	7.7	79.5	114.0	380.5	1,281.3	2,688.2	287.5
Gainesville, FL, MSA							
City of Gainesville	6	62	155	583	742	4,000	244
Total area actually reporting	10	115	238	1,103	1,548	6,095	366
Rate per 100,000 inhabitants	3.7	42.5	88.0	407.7	572.2	2,253.0	135.3
Gainesville, GA, MSA							
City of Gainesville	1	21	39	54	209	1,230	66
Total area actually reporting	7	45	69	172	901	3,005	292
Rate per 100,000 inhabitants	3.7	24.0	36.8	91.8	481.1	1,604.5	155.9
Gettysburg, PA, MSA [3]							
City of Gettysburg	0	8	8	11	28	110	3
Total area actually reporting	0	25	17	57	289	943	40
Estimated total	0	25	17	58	291	952	40
Rate per 100,000 inhabitants	0.0	24.6	16.8	57.2	286.9	938.5	39.4
Glens Falls, NY, MSA							
City of Glens Falls	0	2	3	17	50	288	5
Total area actually reporting	1	16	13	96	344	1,676	31
Rate per 100,000 inhabitants	0.8	12.5	10.1	74.7	267.8	1,304.7	24.1
Goldsboro, NC, MSA							
City of Goldsboro	5	3	67	208	571	1,670	103
Total area actually reporting	8	5	102	367	1,392	2,831	222
Estimated total	8	5	104	372	1,413	2,906	226
Rate per 100,000 inhabitants	6.4	4.0	83.1	297.4	1,129.7	2,323.3	180.7
Grand Forks, ND-MN, MSA							
City of Grand Forks, ND	0	30	25	89	191	1,084	68
Total area actually reporting	1	54	27	128	351	1,681	108
Rate per 100,000 inhabitants	1.0	53.7	26.9	127.4	349.3	1,672.6	107.5
Grand Island, NE, MSA							
City of Grand Island	1	36	8	91	526	1,759	104
Total area actually reporting	1	39	9	101	665	2,030	122
Estimated total	1	41	10	104	680	2,092	128
Rate per 100,000 inhabitants	1.2	48.7	11.9	123.6	808.0	2,485.8	152.1

Table 6.   Crime, by Selected Metropolitan Statistical Area, 2013— continued

(Number, percent, rate per 100,000 population.)

Area	Murder and nonnegligent manslaughter	Rape[1]	Robbery	Aggravated assault	Burglary	Larceny-theft	Motor vehicle theft
Grand Junction, CO, MSA							
City of Grand Junction	2	63	48	149	298	2,141	113
Total area actually reporting	4	136	54	270	558	3,087	185
Estimated total	4	136	54	271	560	3,101	186
Rate per 100,000 inhabitants	2.7	91.1	36.2	181.6	375.2	2,077.8	124.6
Grand Rapids-Wyoming, MI, MSA							
City of Grand Rapids	17	82	471	756	1,621	4,315	252
City of Wyoming	0	59	68	182	392	1,140	115
Total area actually reporting	24	669	651	1,695	4,454	14,464	723
Estimated total	24	672	655	1,706	4,482	14,563	734
Rate per 100,000 inhabitants	2.4	66.4	64.7	168.6	442.8	1,438.8	72.5
Grants Pass, OR, MSA							
City of Grants Pass	1	11	35	63	477	1,844	236
Total area actually reporting	3	11	37	85	772	2,229	363
Rate per 100,000 inhabitants	3.6	13.2	44.5	102.2	928.3	2,680.3	436.5
Great Falls, MT, MSA							
City of Great Falls	0	30	18	101	393	2,186	104
Total area actually reporting	0	35	19	130	451	2,374	122
Rate per 100,000 inhabitants	0.0	42.6	23.1	158.2	548.7	2,888.2	148.4
Greeley, CO, MSA							
City of Greeley	2	74	68	347	475	2,558	186
Total area actually reporting	2	116	81	583	869	3,930	340
Estimated total	2	119	83	591	889	4,056	352
Rate per 100,000 inhabitants	0.7	44.3	30.9	220.0	330.9	1,509.7	131.0
Green Bay, WI, MSA							
City of Green Bay	2	52	79	367	575	2,001	98
Total area actually reporting	2	72	102	446	947	4,221	157
Estimated total	2	76	105	461	1,024	4,474	171
Rate per 100,000 inhabitants	0.6	24.3	33.6	147.4	327.4	1,430.4	54.7
Greensboro-High Point, NC, MSA							
City of Greensboro	27	70	496	856	2,972	8,063	502
City of High Point	2	30	178	346	1,206	2,970	313
Total area actually reporting	35	136	795	1,588	7,241	17,130	1,171
Estimated total	35	136	796	1,590	7,251	17,164	1,173
Rate per 100,000 inhabitants	4.7	18.3	107.3	214.3	977.2	2,313.2	158.1
Greenville, NC, MSA							
City of Greenville	7	20	175	353	1,157	2,573	132
Total area actually reporting	11	33	223	525	1,742	3,891	201
Estimated total	11	33	225	530	1,761	3,958	204
Rate per 100,000 inhabitants	6.3	18.9	129.0	304.0	1,010.0	2,270.1	117.0
Greenville-Anderson-Mauldin, SC, MSA							
City of Greenville	3	35	118	299	666	2,384	211
City of Anderson	2	21	43	212	510	1,767	140
City of Mauldin	0	10	8	22	75	302	33
City of Easley	1	4	10	60	165	1,066	60
Total area actually reporting	46	478	738	3,526	8,622	23,050	2,597
Estimated total	46	478	739	3,530	8,631	23,089	2,599
Rate per 100,000 inhabitants	5.4	56.1	86.7	414.1	1,012.5	2,708.7	304.9
Gulfport-Biloxi-Pascagoula, MS, MSA							
City of Greenville	3	35	118	299	666	2,384	211
City of Anderson	2	21	43	212	510	1,767	140
City of Mauldin	0	10	8	22	75	302	33
City of Easley	1	4	10	60	165	1,066	60
Total area actually reporting	46	478	738	3,526	8,622	23,050	2,597
Estimated total	46	478	739	3,530	8,631	23,089	2,599
Rate per 100,000 inhabitants	5.4	56.1	86.7	414.1	1,012.5	2,708.7	304.9
Hagerstown-Martinsburg, MD-WV, MSA							
City of Hagerstown, MD	5	10	101	128	375	1,051	72
City of Martinsburg, WV	1	8	27	34	97	702	28
Total area actually reporting	8	48	181	363	1,332	4,125	270
Rate per 100,000 inhabitants	3.1	18.6	70.2	140.8	516.8	1,600.4	104.8
Hammond, LA, MSA							
City of Hammond	3	14	77	157	902	1,322	81
Total area actually reporting	12	57	156	862	2,421	4,210	326
Rate per 100,000 inhabitants	9.7	45.9	125.6	694.0	1,949.1	3,389.5	262.5

Table 6.   Crime, by Selected Metropolitan Statistical Area, 2013— continued

(Number, percent, rate per 100,000 population.)

Area	Murder and nonnegligent manslaughter	Rape[1]	Robbery	Aggravated assault	Burglary	Larceny-theft	Motor vehicle theft
Hanford-Corcoran, CA MSA							
City of Hanford	2	10	63	224	345	1,401	193
City of Corcoran	0	2	10	59	103	215	46
Total area actually reporting	6	35	123	561	858	2,413	452
Rate per 100,000 inhabitants	4.0	23.1	81.3	370.9	567.3	1,595.3	298.8
Harrisburg-Carlisle, PA, MSA							
City of Harrisburg	11	56	388	272	613	1,655	158
City of Carlisle	0	15	19	14	60	547	3
Total area actually reporting	18	176	607	855	2,327	9,079	393
Estimated total	18	176	608	857	2,333	9,108	394
Rate per 100,000 inhabitants	3.3	31.8	109.8	154.7	421.3	1,644.6	71.1
Harrisonburg, VA, MSA							
City of Harrisonburg	1	18	16	71	206	1,126	35
Total area actually reporting	1	34	17	114	361	1,603	58
Rate per 100,000 inhabitants	0.8	26.2	13.1	87.9	278.4	1,236.0	44.7
Hartford-West Hartford-East Hartford, CT, MSA							
City of Hartford	23	53	557	840	981	3,416	639
City of West Hartford	0	2	35	8	176	1,120	83
City of East Hartford	1	31	63	87	327	998	120
City of Middletown	0	12	22	26	87	666	74
Total area actually reporting	35	259	1,046	1,366	3,998	16,853	1,679
Rate per 100,000 inhabitants	3.4	25.3	102.2	133.4	390.5	1,646.1	164.0
Hilton Head Island-Bluffton-Beaufort, SC, MSA							
City of Bluffton	0	2	13	34	61	300	18
City of Beaufort	0	6	28	119	126	659	19
Total area actually reporting	6	84	134	731	1,321	4,077	277
Rate per 100,000 inhabitants	3.0	42.7	68.1	371.5	671.3	2,071.9	140.8
Hinesville, GA, MSA							
City of Hinesville	3	8	42	67	351	1,035	58
Total area actually reporting	5	16	51	158	651	1,499	109
Rate per 100,000 inhabitants	6.0	19.3	61.5	190.4	784.7	1,806.9	131.4
Homosassa Spring, FL, MSA							
Total area actually reporting	5	45	65	413	631	1,911	107
Estimated total	5	46	69	422	653	1,989	113
Rate per 100,000 inhabitants	3.6	33.0	49.6	303.1	469.0	1,428.4	81.2
Hot Springs, AR, MSA							
City of Hot Springs	7	25	57	51	721	2,294	166
Total area actually reporting	9	70	74	306	1,547	3,370	261
Rate per 100,000 inhabitants	9.3	72.0	76.2	314.9	1,592.2	3,468.4	268.6
Houma-Thibodaux, LA, MSA							
City of Houma	5	16	67	116	243	1,272	59
City of Thibodaux	1	4	7	56	93	577	13
Total area actually reporting	23	41	130	432	1,414	5,087	239
Rate per 100,000 inhabitants	11.0	19.6	62.1	206.4	675.5	2,430.2	114.2
Houston-The Woodlands-Sugar Land, TX, MSA[3]							
City of Houston	214	618	9,891	10,270	23,733	73,591	13,595
City of Sugar Land	1	6	35	66	256	1,311	46
City of Baytown	4	19	126	136	916	2,373	364
City of Conroe	1	29	60	126	416	1,550	105
Total area actually reporting	373	1,441	14,656	18,641	49,637	146,193	23,297
Estimated total	373	1,441	14,656	18,642	49,639	146,202	23,298
Rate per 100,000 inhabitants	5.9	22.9	233.3	296.8	790.3	2,327.6	370.9
Huntsville, AL, MSA							
City of Huntsville	24	87	391	1,005	1,884	6,629	703
Total area actually reporting	27	187	466	1,421	3,190	10,393	998
Rate per 100,000 inhabitants	6.2	43.0	107.2	327.0	734.2	2,391.9	229.7
Idaho Falls, ID, MSA							
City of Idaho Falls	0	31	19	74	304	1,210	109
Total area actually reporting	3	48	24	143	535	1,828	164
Rate per 100,000 inhabitants	2.2	34.9	17.4	104.0	388.9	1,328.9	119.2
Indianapolis-Carmel-Anderson, IN, MSA							
City of Indianapolis	129	656	3,800	5,894	13,445	26,156	5,005
City of Carmel	0	4	11	5	128	573	43
City of Anderson	5	36	103	56	605	1,829	230
Total area actually reporting	141	767	4,056		16,199	39,292	6,110
Estimated total	148	807	4,162		17,235	43,790	6,496

Table 6.   Crime, by Selected Metropolitan Statistical Area, 2013— continued

(Number, percent, rate per 100,000 population.)

Area	Murder and nonnegligent manslaughter	Rape[1]	Robbery	Aggravated assault	Burglary	Larceny-theft	Motor vehicle theft
Rate per 100,000 inhabitants	7.6	41.5	213.8		885.4	2,249.6	333.7
Iowa City, IA, MSA							
City of Iowa City	0	28	56	144	357	1,411	82
Total area actually reporting	0	88	71	314	576	2,465	137
Estimated total	0	88	71	314	576	2,466	137
Rate per 100,000 inhabitants	0.0	54.8	44.3	195.7	359.0	1,537.0	85.4
Jackson, MI, MSA							
City of Jackson	4	59	61	246	433	1,220	79
Total area actually reporting	5	134	80	418	869	2,827	147
Estimated total	5	136	83	427	892	2,910	156
Rate per 100,000 inhabitants	3.1	84.7	51.7	266.0	555.8	1,813.1	97.2
Jackson, MS, MSA							
City of Jackson	50	110	845	626	3,366	5,864	1,054
Total area actually reporting	57	140	954	860	4,668	9,167	1,331
Estimated total	58	154	995	984	5,277	10,615	1,439
Rate per 100,000 inhabitants	10.0	26.6	171.6	169.7	910.0	1,830.6	248.2
Jackson, TN, MSA							
City of Jackson	11	40	151	723	815	2,484	156
Total area actually reporting	11	58	168	972	1,263	3,276	236
Rate per 100,000 inhabitants	8.4	44.4	128.5	743.7	966.3	2,506.5	180.6
Jacksonville, FL, MSA							
City of Jacksonville	93	452	1,424	3,277	7,069	24,361	1,577
Total area actually reporting	99	583	1,646	4,576	9,453	33,478	2,043
Rate per 100,000 inhabitants	7.1	41.9	118.2	328.5	678.6	2,403.5	146.7
Janesville-Beloit, WI, MSA							
City of Janesville	0	41	25	100	330	1,576	37
City of Beloit	1	16	36	76	320	830	45
Total area actually reporting	2	69	70	227	899	2,969	118
Rate per 100,000 inhabitants	1.2	43.0	43.6	141.4	559.8	1,848.9	73.5
Jefferson City, MO, MSA							
City of Jefferson City	0	7	36	157	235	1,162	49
Total area actually reporting	2	19	54	351	709	2,418	116
Rate per 100,000 inhabitants	1.3	12.6	35.9	233.2	471.0	1,606.2	77.1
Johnson City, TN, MSA							
City of Johnson City	2	23	50	222	399	2,097	76
Total area actually reporting	7	46	70	537	1,146	3,828	183
Rate per 100,000 inhabitants	3.5	22.8	34.7	266.6	568.9	1,900.3	90.8
Johnstown, PA, MSA							
City of Johnstown	7	2	44	76	277	497	28
Total area actually reporting	12	15	67	159	600	1,853	87
Rate per 100,000 inhabitants	8.5	10.6	47.6	112.9	425.9	1,315.3	61.8
Jonesboro, AR, MSA							
City of Jonesboro	2	36	58	217	979	1,930	86
Total area actually reporting	2	63	65	310	1,390	2,815	116
Estimated total	2	64	67	321	1,423	2,892	121
Rate per 100,000 inhabitants	1.6	51.2	53.6	256.7	1,138.0	2,312.8	96.8
Joplin, MO, MSA							
City of Joplin	1	35	55	149	617	3,055	253
Total area actually reporting	4	66	73	378	1,451	5,639	495
Rate per 100,000 inhabitants	2.3	37.9	41.9	217.0	832.9	3,237.0	284.1
Kahului-Wailuku-Lahaina, HI, MSA							
Total area actually reporting	1	45	97	307	948	4,314	442
Rate per 100,000 inhabitants	0.6	28.2	60.8	192.3	593.8	2,702.1	276.9
Kankakee, IL, MSA							
City of Kankakee	4	23	70	99	285	743	35
Total area actually reporting	6	52	84	200	586	2,009	72
Estimated total	6	54	90	212	620	2,160	80
Rate per 100,000 inhabitants	5.3	47.9	79.8	187.9	549.4	1,914.1	70.9
Kansas City, MO-KS, MSA[1]							
City of Kansas City, MO	99	377	1,662	3,726	6,412	13,949	4,287
City of Overland Park, KS	2	33	45	204	404	2,846	280
City of Kansas City, KS	28	83	238	382	1,617	4,566	1,045
Total area actually reporting	152	861	2,380	6,202	13,830	44,395	8,393
Estimated total	152	862	2,381	6,206	13,843	44,456	8,397

Table 6.   Crime, by Selected Metropolitan Statistical Area, 2013— continued

(Number, percent, rate per 100,000 population.)

Area	Murder and nonnegligent manslaughter	Rape[1]	Robbery	Aggravated assault	Burglary	Larceny-theft	Motor vehicle theft
Rate per 100,000 inhabitants	7.4	42.1	116.2	302.8	675.5	2,169.2	409.7
Kennewick-Richland, WA, MSA							
City of Kennewick	2	34	43	161	444	1,876	158
City of Richland	3	17	11	64	205	927	35
Total area actually reporting	9	88	88	418	1,293	4,533	410
Rate per 100,000 inhabitants	3.3	32.2	32.2	152.8	472.7	1,657.4	149.9
Kingsport-Bristol-Bristol, TN-VA, MSA							
City of Kingsport, TN	0	16	31	220	381	2,151	125
City of Bristol, TN	1	10	8	77	186	888	50
City of Bristol, VA	0	6	7	46	61	462	20
Total area actually reporting	5	112	73	782	1,552	6,350	369
Estimated total	5	113	74	784	1,558	6,385	371
Rate per 100,000 inhabitants	1.6	36.5	23.9	253.5	503.8	2,064.7	120.0
Kingston, NY, MSA							
City of Kingston	1	4	25	44	112	565	10
Total area actually reporting	3	31	52	208	590	2,636	55
Rate per 100,000 inhabitants	1.7	17.1	28.6	114.4	324.5	1,449.9	30.3
Knoxville, TN, MSA							
City of Knoxville	18	139	415	969	2,275	8,424	739
Total area actually reporting	30	251	613	2,105	6,159	18,232	1,504
Estimated total	31	259	626	2,187	6,302	18,890	1,538
Rate per 100,000 inhabitants	3.6	30.4	73.4	256.6	739.4	2,216.2	180.4
Kokomo, IN, MSA							
City of Kokomo	2	18	66	99	496	1,600	114
Total area actually reporting	2	18	68	130	581	1,753	128
Rate per 100,000 inhabitants	2.4	21.7	81.8	156.4	699.1	2,109.3	154.0
La Crosse-Onalaska, WI-MN, MSA[4]							
City of La Crosse, WI	1	20	29	57	305	1,200	43
City of Onalaska, WI	0	0	0	8	26	401	2
Total area actually reporting	2	26	29	110	443	1,994	70
Rate per 100,000 inhabitants	1.5	19.1	21.3	80.9	325.9	1,467.1	51.5
Lafayette, LA, MSA							
City of Lafayette	8	17	272	571	1,276	5,995	297
Total area actually reporting	23	83	504	1,543	3,731	11,720	1,012
Estimated total	24	85	513	1,579	3,814	12,074	1,027
Rate per 100,000 inhabitants	5.0	17.8	107.5	330.9	799.3	2,530.4	215.2
Lafayette, West Lafayette, IN, MSA							
City of Lafayette	2	35	67	285	718	2,466	232
City of West Lafayette	0	6	6	25	90	430	16
Total area actually reporting	3	56	81	349	1,055	3,895	282
Estimated total	3	60	87	372	1,158	4,202	312
Rate per 100,000 inhabitants	1.4	28.8	41.7	178.4	555.5	2,015.6	149.7
Lake Havasu City-Kingman, AZ, MSA							
City of Lake Havasu City	1	17	11	58	285	899	68
City of Kingman	1	11	19	97	398	1,159	64
Total area actually reporting	9	34	68	314	1,833	4,500	396
Estimated total	9	35	71	322	1,861	4,616	405
Rate per 100,000 inhabitants	4.4	17.1	34.6	157.0	907.4	2,250.6	197.5
Lakeland-Winter Haven, FL, MSA							
City of Lakeland	7	52	143	258	1,130	4,082	198
City of Winter Haven	2	24	46	143	353	1,180	44
Total area actually reporting	20	177	396	1,694	4,929	12,280	906
Rate per 100,000 inhabitants	3.2	28.4	63.6	272.0	791.4	1,971.6	145.5
Lancaster, PA, MSA [3]							
City of Lancaster	5	53	249	190	441	2,165	86
Total area actually reporting	9	132	340	424	1,741	7,814	290
Rate per 100,000 inhabitants	1.7	25.0	64.3	80.2	329.3	1,478.0	54.9
Lansing-East Lansing, MI, MSA							
City of Lansing	8	127	256	813	1,268	2,329	363
City of East Lansing	0	31	24	54	150	552	97
Total area actually reporting	14	301	366	1,134	2,368	6,689	673
Estimated total	15	314	383	1,181	2,488	7,114	721
Rate per 100,000 inhabitants	3.2	67.3	82.1	253.0	533.1	1,524.2	154.5
Laredo, TX, MSA							
City of Laredo	3	75	207	742	1,425	8,685	372

Table 6.   Crime, by Selected Metropolitan Statistical Area, 2013— continued

(Number, percent, rate per 100,000 population.)

Area	Murder and nonnegligent manslaughter	Rape[1]	Robbery	Aggravated assault	Burglary	Larceny-theft	Motor vehicle theft
Total area actually reporting	4	80	211	838	1,536	8,952	391
Rate per 100,000 inhabitants	1.5	30.4	80.2	318.7	584.2	3,404.6	148.7
Las Cruces, NM, MSA							
City of Las Cruces	6	27	74	225	724	3,454	171
Total area actually reporting	8	74	89	515	1,387	4,541	314
Estimated total	8	76	91	541	1,421	4,637	324
Rate per 100,000 inhabitants	3.7	35.3	42.3	251.5	660.7	2,155.9	150.6
Las Vegas-Henderson-Paradise, NV, MSA							
City of Las Vegas Metropolitan Police Department	97	705	4,072	6,500	14,785	26,548	6,635
City of Henderson	8	45	160	154	1,405	3,416	537
Total area actually reporting	116	855	4,716	8,048	18,568	34,302	8,246
Rate per 100,000 inhabitants	5.7	42.2	232.8	397.3	916.5	1,693.2	407.0
Lawrence, KS, MSA							
City of Lawrence	1	50	74	213	493	2,959	173
Total area actually reporting	1	57	75	238	622	3,334	196
Rate per 100,000 inhabitants	0.9	50.3	66.2	209.9	548.6	2,940.8	172.9
Lawton, OK, MSA							
City of Lawton	13	80	168	658	1,485	3,313	229
Total area actually reporting	13	91	169	677	1,663	3,541	250
Rate per 100,000 inhabitants	9.7	68.2	126.6	507.3	1,246.2	2,653.4	187.3
Lebanon, PA, MSA							
City of Lebanon	2	2	62	37	139	623	23
Total area actually reporting	2	14	96	131	378	2,049	66
Rate per 100,000 inhabitants	1.5	10.3	70.8	96.5	278.6	1,510.1	48.6
Lewiston, ID-WA, MSA							
City of Lewiston, ID	0	8	8	33	264	853	52
Total area actually reporting	0	11	21	81	426	1,531	93
Rate per 100,000 inhabitants	0.0	17.8	34.0	131.0	689.1	2,476.5	150.4
Lewiston-Auburn, ME, MSA							
City of Lewiston	0	25	20	44	313	848	56
City of Auburn	0	10	10	12	197	858	17
Total area actually reporting	1	46	36	72	703	2,122	99
Rate per 100,000 inhabitants	0.9	42.8	33.5	67.0	654.1	1,974.5	92.1
Lexington-Fayette, KY, MSA							
City of Lexington[1]	18	134	467	327	2,574	9,042	831
Total area actually reporting	24	185	584	463	3,814	13,376	1,017
Estimated total	24	185	584	463	3,816	13,384	1,018
Rate per 100,000 inhabitants	4.9	37.8	119.3	94.6	779.8	2,735.2	208.0
Lima, OH, MSA							
City of Lima	3	42	78	243	582	1,255	95
Total area actually reporting	3	49	86	259	907	2,443	145
Estimated total	3	50	88	261	921	2,499	147
Rate per 100,000 inhabitants	2.9	47.6	83.8	248.6	877.1	2,380.0	140.0
Lincoln, NE, MSA							
City of Lincoln	5	142	212	631	1,423	7,625	306
Total area actually reporting	5	152	214	660	1,547	8,153	326
Rate per 100,000 inhabitants	1.6	48.5	68.3	210.5	493.4	2,600.3	104.0
Little Rock-North Little Rock-Conway, AR, MSA							
City of Little Rock	35	119	944	1,679	3,794	10,655	1,080
City of North Little Rock	13	11	138	299	864	2,762	275
City of Conway	1	22	49	167	367	2,299	108
Total area actually reporting	55	268	1,262	3,100	8,566	23,279	2,257
Estimated total	56	294	1,270	3,266	9,031	23,982	2,360
Rate per 100,000 inhabitants	7.7	40.7	175.6	451.6	1,248.9	3,316.4	326.4
Logan, UT-ID, MSA							
City of Logan, UT	0	20	0	15	138	700	22
Total area actually reporting	1	33	0	38	256	1,227	48
Rate per 100,000 inhabitants	0.8	25.4	0.0	29.3	197.1	944.9	37.0
Longview, TX, MSA							
City of Longview	5	38	148	249	615	2,481	195
Total area actually reporting	12	86	189	614	1,740	5,054	385
Estimated total	12	86	190	616	1,747	5,080	387
Rate per 100,000 inhabitants	5.5	39.4	87.0	282.2	800.4	2,327.4	177.3
Longview, WA, MSA							

Table 6.   Crime, by Selected Metropolitan Statistical Area, 2013— continued

(Number, percent, rate per 100,000 population.)

Area	Murder and nonnegligent manslaughter	Rape[1]	Robbery	Aggravated assault	Burglary	Larceny-theft	Motor vehicle theft
City of Longview	0	38	48	84	512	1,734	175
Total area actually reporting	1	101	61	199	910	2,859	288
Rate per 100,000 inhabitants	1.0	98.9	59.7	194.8	890.7	2,798.3	281.9
Los Angeles-Long Beach-Anaheim, CA, MSA							
City of Los Angeles	251	764	7,885	7,624	15,728	55,734	14,382
City of Long Beach	34	103	1,118	1,091	3,776	6,868	2,355
City of Anaheim	11	82	437	600	1,412	6,518	1,681
City of Santa Ana	13	51	463	594	803	4,163	1,459
City of Irvine	2	12	38	61	583	2,553	149
City of Glendale	1	8	75	97	563	2,384	251
City of Torrance	1	16	76	94	591	1,833	362
City of Pasadena	3	25	162	244	939	2,553	287
City of Orange	4	8	64	71	473	1,673	272
City of Costa Mesa	1	46	94	111	512	2,748	296
City of Burbank	0	13	51	107	285	1,926	219
City of Carson	3	15	148	234	514	1,248	489
City of Santa Monica	7	27	120	170	573	2,806	165
City of Newport Beach	2	7	13	51	454	1,600	104
City of Tustin	1	6	36	57	213	1,147	113
City of Monterey Park	0	8	60	36	316	637	209
City of Gardena	0	16	144	85	298	726	307
City of Arcadia	0	1	37	39	376	1,080	62
City of Fountain Valley	0	9	20	63	262	835	73
Total area actually reporting	594	2,176	18,776	24,880	58,588	185,313	46,168
Rate per 100,000 inhabitants	4.5	16.6	142.9	189.3	445.8	1,410.2	351.3
Anaheim-Santa Ana-Irvine, CA, MD							
Total area actually reporting	51	424	1,993	3,574	10,416	44,001	7,233
Rate per 100,000 inhabitants	1.6	13.6	63.9	114.6	334.0	1,410.9	231.9
Los Angeles-Long Beach-Glendale, CA, MD							
Total area actually reporting	543	1,752	16,783	21,306	48,172	141,312	38,935
Rate per 100,000 inhabitants	5.4	17.5	167.5	212.6	480.6	1,410.0	388.5
Louisville/Jefferson County, KY-IN, MSA							
City of Louisville Metro, KY	48	160	1,427	2,009	6,920	19,835	2,025
Total area actually reporting	61	262	1,727		9,801	29,576	2,782
Estimated total	62	271	1,741		10,034	30,252	2,848
Rate per 100,000 inhabitants	4.9	21.6	138.5		798.0	2,405.9	226.5
Lubbock, TX, MSA							
City of Lubbock	5	88	388	1,348	2,608	8,103	846
Total area actually reporting	9	116	390	1,464	2,934	8,908	933
Rate per 100,000 inhabitants	3.0	38.6	129.7	486.8	975.5	2,961.7	310.2
Lynchburg, VA, MSA							
City of Lynchburg	1	36	73	220	349	1,538	87
Total area actually reporting	5	83	89	314	738	3,174	206
Rate per 100,000 inhabitants	1.9	32.3	34.7	122.3	287.3	1,235.8	80.2
Macon, GA, MSA							
City of Macon	18	46	231	288	1,993	4,318	489
Total area actually reporting	23	72	308	497	2,876	7,438	812
Estimated total	23	72	308	497	2,878	7,445	813
Rate per 100,000 inhabitants	9.9	30.9	132.3	213.4	1,235.8	3,196.8	349.1
Madera, CA, MSA							
City of Madera	7	28	107	426	589	1,010	256
Total area actually reporting	13	59	132	813	1,454	1,930	550
Rate per 100,000 inhabitants	8.5	38.6	86.4	532.2	951.7	1,263.3	360.0
Madison, WI, MSA [3]							
City of Madison	5	76	296	507	1,382	6,094	253
Total area actually reporting	11	166	369	812	2,341	11,360	433
Estimated total	11	166	369	813	2,345	11,386	434
Rate per 100,000 inhabitants	1.8	26.5	58.9	129.9	374.6	1,818.7	69.3
Manchester-Nashua, NH, MSA							
City of Manchester	4	91	295	357	894	3,141	159
City of Nashua	6	32	61	83	323	1,857	68
Total area actually reporting	10	177	381	550	1,618	7,166	302
Estimated total	10	182	384	561	1,654	7,366	310
Rate per 100,000 inhabitants	2.5	45.1	95.1	138.9	409.4	1,823.3	76.7
Manhattan, KS, MSA							
Total area actually reporting	6	28	20	137	332	1,324	73
Estimated total	6	28	20	138	335	1,336	74

Table 6.   Crime, by Selected Metropolitan Statistical Area, 2013— continued

(Number, percent, rate per 100,000 population.)

Area	Murder and nonnegligent manslaughter	Rape[1]	Robbery	Aggravated assault	Burglary	Larceny-theft	Motor vehicle theft
Rate per 100,000 inhabitants	6.0	28.2	20.1	138.9	337.2	1,344.8	74.5
Mankato-North Mankato, MN, MSA[4]							
City of Mankato[4]	1	18	31	57	312	1,395	46
City of North Mankato[4]	0	4	2	16	65	188	17
Total area actually reporting	2	37	39	101	530	1,995	103
Rate per 100,000 inhabitants	2.0	37.5	39.5	102.3	536.7	2,020.2	104.3
Mansfield, OH, MSA							
City of Mansfield	0	33	82	54	982	2,111	74
Total area actually reporting	1	48	108	69	1,649	3,861	120
Estimated total	1	49	111	72	1,678	3,974	125
Rate per 100,000 inhabitants	0.8	40.0	90.7	58.8	1,370.6	3,246.0	102.1
McAllen-Edinburg-Mission, TX, MSA							
City of McAllen	2	6	83	80	536	4,652	236
City of Edinburg	1	30	50	196	738	3,299	255
City of Mission	0	4	32	36	447	2,321	177
Total area actually reporting	22	197	469	1,661	6,417	22,286	1,564
Rate per 100,000 inhabitants	2.7	24.0	57.2	202.7	783.3	2,720.3	190.9
Medford, OR, MSA							
City of Medford	1	37	99	346	575	4,075	163
Total area actually reporting	4	72	131	525	1,145	6,739	296
Rate per 100,000 inhabitants	1.9	34.6	63.0	252.5	550.7	3,241.0	142.4
Memphis, TN-MS-AR, MSA							
City of Memphis	124	437	3,133	7,200	11,825	25,295	2,684
Total area actually reporting	138	605	3,444	9,073	15,683	35,897	3,424
Estimated total	139	617	3,468	9,165	16,117	36,837	3,517
Rate per 100,000 inhabitants	10.3	45.8	257.3	680.0	1,195.8	2,733.1	260.9
Merced, CA, MSA							
City of Merced	5	19	133	399	644	1,608	395
Total area actually reporting	27	78	231	1,219	2,097	4,657	1,342
Rate per 100,000 inhabitants	10.2	29.5	87.3	460.9	792.8	1,760.7	507.4
Miami-Fort Lauderdale-West Pompano Beach, FL, MSA							
City of Miami	71	96	2,216	2,562	3,993	15,021	1,914
City of Fort Lauderdale	13	73	701	669	2,654	6,429	567
City of Pompano Beach	15	29	281	376	1,024	3,453	386
City of West Palm Beach	7	64	273	475	1,220	3,580	329
City of Miami Beach	4	53	377	485	950	8,425	376
City of Boca Raton	4	8	54	99	464	1,744	94
City of Deerfield Beach	2	28	105	170	624	1,606	156
City of Delray Beach	0	29	147	311	588	2,308	211
City of Jupiter	0	7	36	84	163	864	67
Total area actually reporting	383	1,824	11,062	18,238	44,416	156,375	14,980
Rate per 100,000 inhabitants	6.6	31.2	189.2	311.9	759.7	2,674.6	256.2
Fort Lauderdale-Pompano Beach-Deerfield Beach, FL, MD							
Total area actually reporting	80	568	2,981	4,449	15,934	43,855	3,931
Rate per 100,000 inhabitants	4.3	30.8	161.7	241.4	864.4	2,379.1	213.3
Miami-Miami Beach-Kendall, FL, MD							
Total area actually reporting	229	813	6,370	9,835	18,943	82,490	8,331
Rate per 100,000 inhabitants	8.7	30.9	242.2	373.9	720.1	3,135.8	316.7
West Palm Beach-Boca Raton-Delray Beach, FL, MD							
Total area actually reporting	74	443	1,711	3,954	9,539	30,030	2,718
Rate per 100,000 inhabitants	5.4	32.3	124.6	288.0	694.9	2,187.6	198.0
Midland, TX, MSA							
City of Midland	5	22	63	260	568	2,459	164
Total area actually reporting	6	25	70	336	788	3,056	266
Rate per 100,000 inhabitants	3.9	16.0	44.9	215.7	505.8	1,961.8	170.8
Milwaukee-Waukesha-West Allis, WI, MSA							
City of Milwaukee	104	401	3,284	4,405	6,491	16,138	4,384
City of Waukesha	1	23	25	41	210	1,079	38
City of West Allis	1	14	104	77	631	2,128	92
Total area actually reporting	110	526	3,678	4,862	9,144	33,120	4,962
Estimated total	110	533	3,692	4,891	9,259	33,908	4,986
Rate per 100,000 inhabitants	7.0	33.9	234.9	311.2	589.2	2,157.7	317.3
Minneapolis-St. Paul-Bloomington, MN-WI, MSA							
City of Minneapolis, MN	36	385	1,856	1,761	4,601	13,182	1,575
City of St. Paul, MN	14	218	716	1,252	2,769	6,443	1,761

Table 6.   Crime, by Selected Metropolitan Statistical Area, 2013— continued

(Number, percent, rate per 100,000 population.)

Area	Murder and nonnegligent manslaughter	Rape[1]	Robbery	Aggravated assault	Burglary	Larceny-theft	Motor vehicle theft
City of Bloomington, MN	1	17	49	61	193	2,990	100
City of Plymouth, MN	0	21	5	23	186	903	52
City of Eagan, MN	0	2	14	21	163	1,087	37
City of Eden Prairie, MN	1	10	7	21	83	788	23
Total area actually reporting	87	1,226	3,340	4,809	15,041	68,577	5,986
Estimated total	87	1,226	3,341	4,812	15,050	68,642	5,989
Rate per 100,000 inhabitants	2.5	35.5	96.7	139.2	435.5	1,986.2	173.3
Missoula, MT, MSA							
City of Missoula	1	32	39	146	418	2,341	131
Total area actually reporting	1	47	40	213	507	2,730	170
Rate per 100,000 inhabitants	0.9	41.9	35.7	190.1	452.5	2,436.4	151.7
Mobile, AL, MSA [6]							
City of Mobile[6]	29	88	459	965	3,207	9,123	681
Total area actually reporting	40	169	658	1,559	4,953	12,504	1,228
Rate per 100,000 inhabitants	9.7	40.8	158.9	376.5	1,196.2	3,019.8	296.6
Modesto, CA, MSA							
City of Modesto	14	72	450	1,168	2,251	6,349	1,389
Total area actually reporting	33	126	741	1,816	5,133	11,936	3,469
Rate per 100,000 inhabitants	6.3	24.0	141.3	346.2	978.5	2,275.3	661.3
Monroe, LA, MSA							
City of Monroe	6	29	147	334	1,467	2,822	82
Total area actually reporting	17	46	195	746	2,659	5,679	229
Estimated total	17	47	199	763	2,698	5,846	236
Rate per 100,000 inhabitants	9.5	26.4	111.6	427.9	1,513.2	3,278.9	132.4
Monroe, MI, MSA							
City of Monroe	1	25	23	61	151	521	42
Total area actually reporting	5	104	57	224	830	2,303	217
Estimated total	5	108	62	239	869	2,442	233
Rate per 100,000 inhabitants	3.3	71.6	41.1	158.4	575.9	1,618.3	154.4
Morgantown, WV, MSA							
City of Morgantown	0	18	31	45	176	485	20
Total area actually reporting	1	61	44	225	463	1,403	94
Estimated total	1	65	50	252	518	1,681	106
Rate per 100,000 inhabitants	0.7	48.0	36.9	186.2	382.7	1,241.9	78.3
Morristown, TN, MSA							
City of Morristown	2	11	25	124	134	1,375	74
Total area actually reporting	2	36	39	291	658	2,652	170
Rate per 100,000 inhabitants	1.7	31.2	33.8	252.3	570.5	2,299.3	147.4
Mount Vernon-Anacortes, WA, MSA							
City of Mount Vernon	1	15	31	42	258	1,276	128
City of Anacortes	0	6	3	12	127	402	30
Total area actually reporting	4	40	64	146	1,195	3,659	338
Rate per 100,000 inhabitants	3.4	33.6	53.8	122.7	1,004.2	3,074.7	284.0
Muncie, IN, MSA							
City of Muncie	0	29	96	163	532	2,321	154
Total area actually reporting	0	34	100	189	700	2,821	179
Rate per 100,000 inhabitants	0.0	28.9	85.0	160.7	595.3	2,399.2	152.2
Muskegon, MI, MSA							
City of Muskegon	3	47	70	205	649	1,262	59
Total area actually reporting	10	159	146	485	1,337	4,553	227
Rate per 100,000 inhabitants	5.9	93.7	86.0	285.7	787.6	2,682.0	133.7
Myrtle Beach-Conway-North Myrtle Beach, SC-NC, MSA							
City of Myrtle Beach, SC	2	49	186	238	608	3,497	470
City of Conway, SC	3	11	19	80	111	727	42
City of North Myrtle Beach, SC	0	14	20	86	279	1,153	136
Total area actually reporting	14	229	411	1,283	4,113	11,943	1,400
Estimated total	14	230	416	1,296	4,163	12,124	1,409
Rate per 100,000 inhabitants	3.5	57.3	103.6	322.7	1,036.5	3,018.7	350.8
Napa, CA, MSA							
City of Napa	2	26	47	180	304	975	130
Total area actually reporting	2	37	83	295	605	1,732	237
Rate per 100,000 inhabitants	1.4	26.4	59.3	210.7	432.2	1,237.3	169.3
Naples-Immokalee-Marco Island, FL, MSA							
City of Naples	0	9	7	23	101	438	12
City of Marco Island	0	0	0	4	31	145	1

Table 6.   Crime, by Selected Metropolitan Statistical Area, 2013— continued

(Number, percent, rate per 100,000 population.)

Area	Murder and nonnegligent manslaughter	Rape[1]	Robbery	Aggravated assault	Burglary	Larceny-theft	Motor vehicle theft
Total area actually reporting	12	82	114	577	1,121	3,884	231
Rate per 100,000 inhabitants	3.6	24.3	33.8	171.2	332.6	1,152.4	68.5
Nashville-Davidson--Murfreesboro--Franklin, TN, MSA							
City of Nashville	35	437	1,611	4,529	5,613	17,650	1,197
City of Murfreesboro	4	54	130	517	742	3,131	178
City of Franklin	0	19	20	78	90	873	25
Total area actually reporting	59	747	2,013	7,586	10,270	34,923	2,255
Rate per 100,000 inhabitants	3.4	42.8	115.3	434.6	588.3	2,000.6	129.2
New Bern, NC, MSA							
City of New Bern	0	7	43	70	525	992	50
Total area actually reporting	1	31	68	240	1,422	2,207	134
Estimated total	1	32	70	251	1,488	2,298	143
Rate per 100,000 inhabitants	0.8	24.8	54.3	194.8	1,154.8	1,783.4	111.0
New Haven-Milford, CT, MSA							
City of New Haven	19	76	770	778	1,082	4,233	753
City of Milford	0	1	23	18	148	1,302	105
Total area actually reporting	27	156	1,350	1,579	3,485	16,783	2,467
Rate per 100,000 inhabitants	3.3	19.3	166.9	195.2	430.9	2,075.0	305.0
New Orleans-Metairie, LA, MSA							
City of New Orleans	156	176	1,138	1,495	3,203	9,179	2,143
Total area actually reporting	235	321	1,805	3,511	7,853	27,676	3,530
Rate per 100,000 inhabitants	19.0	25.9	145.7	283.3	633.8	2,233.5	284.9
New York-Newark-Jersey City, NY-NJ-PA, MSA							
City of New York, NY	335	1,112	19,170	31,767	16,606	117,931	7,434
City of Newark, NJ	112	45	2,433	926	2,074	3,997	2,894
City of Jersey City, NJ	20	35	717	883	1,052	3,046	738
City of White Plains, NY	1	3	28	46	77	1,134	21
City of New Brunswick, NJ	3	19	165	116	546	1,032	87
City of Lakewood Township, NJ	2	5	34	52	186	768	44
Total area actually reporting	687	1,915	31,055	44,046	49,197	249,355	21,475
Estimated total	688	1,920	31,094	44,100	49,360	250,083	21,519
Rate per 100,000 inhabitants	3.5	9.6	156.0	221.2	247.6	1,254.4	107.9
Dutchess County-Putnam County, NY, MD							
Total area actually reporting	12	40	156	422	910	4,184	107
Estimated total	12	41	160	429	927	4,281	110
Rate per 100,000 inhabitants	3.0	10.3	40.3	108.0	233.4	1,077.8	27.7
Nassau County-Suffolk County, NY, MD							
Total area actually reporting	51	93	1,714	2,133	5,944	32,781	2,064
Estimated total	51	93	1,715	2,135	5,948	32,803	2,065
Rate per 100,000 inhabitants	1.8	3.3	60.0	74.8	208.3	1,148.6	72.3
Newark, NJ-PA, MD							
Total area actually reporting	177	229	5,022	3,070	9,249	26,580	6,673
Rate per 100,000 inhabitants	7.1	9.2	201.1	122.9	370.3	1,064.2	267.2
New York-Jersey City-White Plains, NY-NJ, MD							
Total area actually reporting	447	1,553	24,163	38,421	33,094	185,810	12,631
Estimated total	448	1,557	24,197	38,466	33,236	186,419	12,671
Rate per 100,000 inhabitants	3.2	11.0	170.6	271.2	234.3	1,314.1	89.3
Niles-Benton Harbor, MI, MSA							
City of Niles	0	14	6	34	45	241	18
City of Benton Harbor	3	22	60	140	304	377	25
Total area actually reporting	3	143	112	436	1,108	2,948	162
Estimated total	3	144	113	440	1,118	2,983	166
Rate per 100,000 inhabitants	1.9	92.3	72.4	282.1	716.8	1,912.4	106.4
North Port-Sarasota-Bradenton, FL, MSA							
City of North Port	0	26	15	67	264	687	13
City of Sarasota	4	31	151	227	564	2,023	155
City of Bradenton	9	17	115	210	438	1,480	86
City of Venice	0	3	4	30	95	338	13
Total area actually reporting	20	295	646	2,114	4,932	14,885	798
Rate per 100,000 inhabitants	2.7	40.5	88.7	290.2	677.1	2,043.5	109.6
Norwich-New London, CT, MSA							
City of Norwich	1	14	29	86	306	644	52
City of New London	3	23	50	223	236	494	61
Total area actually reporting	4	60	98	393	787	2,650	153
Rate per 100,000 inhabitants	2.7	41.1	67.1	268.9	538.5	1,813.2	104.7

Table 6.   Crime, by Selected Metropolitan Statistical Area, 2013— continued

(Number, percent, rate per 100,000 population.)

Area	Murder and nonnegligent manslaughter	Rape[1]	Robbery	Aggravated assault	Burglary	Larceny-theft	Motor vehicle theft
Ocala, FL, MSA [5]							
City of Ocala	6	25	92	209	530	2,306	53
Total area actually reporting	17	148	170	1,118	1,866		273
Rate per 100,000 inhabitants	5.0	43.8	50.3	331.1	552.6		80.9
Ocean City, NJ, MSA							
City of Ocean City	0	3	3	6	88	346	6
Total area actually reporting	0	22	64	165	844	3,044	67
Rate per 100,000 inhabitants	0.0	22.9	66.6	171.6	878.0	3,166.4	69.7
Odessa, TX, MSA							
City of Odessa	2	56	143	879	764	3,147	463
Total area actually reporting	3	58	177	951	1,165	4,498	644
Rate per 100,000 inhabitants	2.0	39.3	120.0	645.0	790.1	3,050.6	436.8
Ogden-Clearfield, UT, MSA [2]							
City of Ogden	2	78	111	225	578	3,153	274
City of Clearfield	0	12	4	23	99	495	36
Total area actually reporting	8	328	184	493		11,547	879
Estimated total	8	329	185	496		11,614	836
Rate per 100,000 inhabitants	1.3	53.0	29.8	79.9		1,871.3	142.8
Oklahoma City, OK, MSA							
City of Oklahoma City	62	450	1,191	3,295	8,016	20,387	4,076
Total area actually reporting	78	695	1,430	4,414	12,856	33,747	5,434
Rate per 100,000 inhabitants	5.9	52.8	108.7	335.5	977.3	2,565.3	413.1
Olympia-Tumwater, WA, MSA							
City of Olympia	0	18	38	75	382	1,284	123
City of Tumwater	0	10	5	26	161	421	30
Total area actually reporting	3	76	101	338	1,998	4,548	462
Rate per 100,000 inhabitants	1.1	29.1	38.7	129.5	765.7	1,742.9	177.0
Omaha-Council Bluffs, NE-IA, MSA							
City of Omaha, NE	42	184	718	1,505	3,509	12,519	3,080
City of Council Bluffs, IA	0	75	80	429	947	3,126	541
Total area actually reporting	47	341	851	2,218	5,481	19,372	4,083
Estimated total	47	342	851	2,222	5,492	19,422	4,086
Rate per 100,000 inhabitants	5.3	38.3	95.2	248.6	614.6	2,173.4	457.2
Orlando-Kissimmee-Sanford, FL, MSA							
City of Orlando	17	126	573	1,600	3,485	11,984	1,020
City of Kissimmee	3	36	132	371	802	2,042	119
City of Sanford	5	36	132	274	994	2,202	236
Total area actually reporting	89	936	2,776	8,370	19,883	52,568	4,557
Estimated total	89	939	2,788	8,396	19,952	52,808	4,575
Rate per 100,000 inhabitants	3.9	41.5	123.3	371.3	882.4	2,335.4	202.3
Oshkosh-Neenah, WI, MSA							
City of Oshkosh	0	9	23	123	219	1,163	39
City of Neenah	0	4	3	34	55	441	9
Total area actually reporting	0	20	29	221	429	2,416	72
Rate per 100,000 inhabitants	0.0	11.8	17.1	130.4	253.1	1,425.5	42.5
Owensboro, KY, MSA							
City of Owensboro	0	47	49	44	373	1,553	106
Total area actually reporting	0	56	52	53	529	1,932	127
Rate per 100,000 inhabitants	0.0	48.1	44.6	45.5	454.0	1,657.9	109.0
Oxnard-Thousand Oaks-Ventura, CA, MSA							
City of Oxnard	15	10	328	298	974	3,436	664
City of Thousand Oaks	0	7	42	90	291	1,222	91
City of Ventura	6	21	99	136	745	3,025	257
City of Camarillo	0	6	25	42	205	849	76
Total area actually reporting	34	85	607	903	3,210	11,690	1,500
Rate per 100,000 inhabitants	4.0	10.1	72.2	107.4	381.8	1,390.5	178.4
Palm Bay-Melbourne-Titusville, FL, MSA							
City of Palm Bay	3	21	43	384	517	1,326	115
City of Melbourne	6	61	136	454	741	2,526	110
City of Titusville	3	32	72	221	545	903	156
Total area actually reporting	20	277	470	2,122	3,751	10,952	690
Rate per 100,000 inhabitants	3.6	50.3	85.4	385.5	681.4	1,989.5	125.3
Panama City, FL, MSA							
City of Panama City	3	10	65	244	377	1,803	119
City of Lynn Haven	8	90	164	715	1,433	5,551	322
City of Panama City Beach	4.2	47.6	86.7	378.0	757.5	2,934.3	170.2

Table 6.   Crime, by Selected Metropolitan Statistical Area, 2013— continued

(Number, percent, rate per 100,000 population.)

Area	Murder and nonnegligent manslaughter	Rape[1]	Robbery	Aggravated assault	Burglary	Larceny-theft	Motor vehicle theft
Parkersburg-Vienna, WV, MSA							
City of Parkersburg	0	21	12	94	343	982	57
City of Vienna	0	0	0	10	18	273	8
Total area actually reporting	0	36	13	211	572	1,518	93
Estimated total	0	37	14	218	585	1,586	96
Rate per 100,000 inhabitants	0.0	40.0	15.2	235.9	633.1	1,716.5	103.9
Pensacola-Ferry Pass-Brent, FL, MSA							
City of Pensacola	3	27	69	290	466	2,035	112
Total area actually reporting	29	197	458	1,695	3,882	11,099	855
Rate per 100,000 inhabitants	6.2	42.2	98.2	363.4	832.3	2,379.6	183.3
Peoria, IL, MSA							
City of Peoria	16	24	275	469	1,123	3,098	194
Total area actually reporting	21	80	317	834	2,102	6,007	278
Estimated total	22	85	332	864	2,185	6,377	298
Rate per 100,000 inhabitants	5.8	22.3	87.2	226.9	573.8	1,674.6	78.3
Philadelphia-Camden-Wilmington, PA-NJ-DE-MD, MSA							
City of Philadelphia, PA	247	1,279	7,562	7,986	10,408	37,253	5,791
City of Wilmington, DE	19	24	453	665	960	2,387	371
Total area actually reporting	426	2,157	11,916	15,512	28,590	110,507	10,267
Estimated total	426	2,158	11,921	15,525	28,621	110,663	10,273
Rate per 100,000 inhabitants	7.1	35.8	197.5	257.2	474.2	1,833.3	170.2
Camden, NJ, MD							
Total area actually reporting	84	201	1,516	2,233	6,597	21,144	1,489
Rate per 100,000 inhabitants	6.7	16.0	120.6	177.6	524.7	1,681.6	118.4
Montgomery County-Bucks County-Chester County, PA, MD							
Total area actually reporting	26	289	875	1,610	5,620	26,478	1,170
Estimated total							
Rate per 100,000 inhabitants	1.4	15.3	46.2	85.1	297.0	1,399.1	61.8
Philadelphia, PA, MD							
Total area actually reporting	278	1,461	8,366	9,718	12,404	47,178	6,460
Estimated total	278	1,461	8,367	9,721	12,411	47,212	6,461
Rate per 100,000 inhabitants	13.1	69.1	395.7	459.7	586.9	2,232.8	305.6
Wilmington, DE-MD-NJ, MD							
Total area actually reporting	40	213	1,074	2,129	4,579	15,441	1,094
Rate per 100,000 inhabitants	5.6	29.7	149.6	296.5	637.7	2,150.5	152.4
Phoenix-Mesa-Scottsdale, AZ, MSA							
City of Phoenix	118	635	3,233	5,506	16,747	36,983	6,355
City of Mesa	22	203	478	1,104	2,357	9,607	952
City of Scottsdale	4	37	101	195	1,093	4,465	208
City of Tempe	3	62	224	542	1,276	6,113	487
Total area actually reporting	212	1,291	5,055	10,646	32,054	97,294	
Estimated total	212	1,292	5,057	10,651	32,071	97,363	
Rate per 100,000 inhabitants	4.8	29.5	115.3	242.8	731.0	2,219.4	
Pittsburgh, PA, MSA [3]							
City of Pittsburgh	45	78	956	1,180	2,173	7,258	616
Total area actually reporting	97	363	1,964	4,445	8,603	33,004	1,801
Estimated total	97	367	1,976	4,473	8,669	33,343	1,815
Rate per 100,000 inhabitants	4.1	15.5	83.7	189.5	367.2	1,412.4	76.9
Pittsfield, MA, MSA							
City of Pittsfield	0	31	29	51	481	827	44
Total area actually reporting	1	72	46	230	974	1,956	89
Estimated total	1	75	53	254	1,017	2,095	101
Rate per 100,000 inhabitants	0.8	57.7	40.8	195.4	782.4	1,611.8	77.7
Pocatello, ID, MSA							
City of Pocatello	0	21	27	147	278	1,415	83
Total area actually reporting	1	24	30	187	346	2,044	100
Rate per 100,000 inhabitants	1.2	28.4	35.5	221.3	409.6	2,419.5	118.4
Portland-South Portland, ME, MSA							
City of Portland	1	21	85	70	383	2,160	69
City of South Portland	0	10	13	37	113	722	26
Total area actually reporting	6	152	178	421	2,270	9,173	338
Rate per 100,000 inhabitants	1.2	29.3	34.3	81.1	437.4	1,767.5	65.1
Portland-Vancouver-Hillsboro, OR-WA, MSA							
City of Portland, OR	14	234	917	1,776	4,128	22,216	3,289

Table 6.   Crime, by Selected Metropolitan Statistical Area, 2013— continued

(Number, percent, rate per 100,000 population.)

Area	Murder and nonnegligent manslaughter	Rape[1]	Robbery	Aggravated assault	Burglary	Larceny-theft	Motor vehicle theft
City of Vancouver, WA	2	74	146	371	1,007	3,950	976
City of Hillsboro, OR	0	29	55	57	311	1,723	126
City of Beaverton, OR	1	20	22	81	175	1,213	83
Total area actually reporting	32	712	1,696	3,350	10,955	51,143	6,850
Estimated total	32	715	1,702	3,361	11,002	51,388	6,871
Rate per 100,000 inhabitants	1.4	30.9	73.5	145.2	475.2	2,219.4	296.8
Port St. Lucie, FL, MSA							
City of Port St. Lucie	1	21	40	241	722	1,666	73
Total area actually reporting	15	87	234	1,134	2,590	6,740	405
Rate per 100,000 inhabitants	3.4	19.9	53.6	259.6	592.9	1,542.9	92.7
Prescott, AZ, MSA							
City of Prescott	0	7	11	106	182	855	48
Total area actually reporting	3	52	31	439	894	3,158	235
Rate per 100,000 inhabitants	1.4	24.3	14.5	204.9	417.3	1,474.0	109.7
Providence-Warwick, RI-MA, MSA							
City of Providence, RI	12	97	365	641	1,828	5,184	962
City of Warwick RI	4	35	15	39	282	1,648	85
Total area actually reporting	40	683	1,293	3,412	8,780	26,013	3,072
Rate per 100,000 inhabitants	2.5	42.6	80.6	212.6	547.1	1,621.0	191.4
Provo-Orem, UT, MSA							
City of Provo	1	82	21	56	329	2,373	108
City of Orem	2	13	7	11	192	1,789	98
Total area actually reporting	6	154	49	185	1,296	8,784	455
Rate per 100,000 inhabitants	1.1	27.4	8.7	32.9	230.8	1,564.4	81.0
Pueblo, CO, MSA							
City of Pueblo	2	165	211	633	1,900	5,168	528
Total area actually reporting	5	171	219	668	2,117	6,112	606
Rate per 100,000 inhabitants	3.1	105.4	134.9	411.6	1,304.4	3,765.9	373.4
Punta Gorda, FL, MSA							
City of Punta Gorda	0	2	2	17	36	256	4
Total area actually reporting	1	39	35	315	784	2,511	114
Rate per 100,000 inhabitants	0.6	23.8	21.4	192.2	478.2	1,531.7	69.5
Racine, WI, MSA							
City of Racine	1	21	179	96	1,211	1,704	95
Total area actually reporting	2	29	197	126	1,476	3,180	146
Rate per 100,000 inhabitants	1.0	14.9	101.2	64.7	758.0	1,633.2	75.0
Raleigh, NC, MSA							
City of Raleigh	12	79	605	987	3,157	9,278	705
Total area actually reporting	33	152	814	1,630	6,909	19,134	1,269
Estimated total	33	154	820	1,646	6,976	19,369	1,280
Rate per 100,000 inhabitants	2.7	12.7	67.8	136.0	576.6	1,600.9	105.8
Rapid City, SD, MSA							
City of Rapid City	2	63	48	285	578	1,902	149
Total area actually reporting	2	104	50	361	811	2,442	186
Rate per 100,000 inhabitants	1.4	73.8	35.5	256.2	575.5	1,732.8	132.0
Reading, PA, MSA							
City of Reading	11	50	328	354	1,040	1,465	294
Total area actually reporting	11	95	421	695	1,880	5,368	476
Estimated total	11	96	423	699	1,890	5,421	478
Rate per 100,000 inhabitants	2.7	23.2	102.2	168.9	456.7	1,310.0	115.5
Redding, CA, MSA							
City of Redding	3	66	131	505	1,088	2,790	502
Total area actually reporting	7	97	165	1,029	1,754	3,623	903
Rate per 100,000 inhabitants	3.9	54.1	92.0	573.5	977.6	2,019.3	503.3
Reno, NV, MSA							
City of Reno	7	33	327	825	1,633	4,909	881
Total area actually reporting	12	85	416	1,208	2,684	7,542	1,244
Rate per 100,000 inhabitants	2.8	19.5	95.6	277.6	616.7	1,732.9	285.8
Richmond, VA, MSA							
City of Richmond	37	43	624	623	1,817	5,949	938
Total area actually reporting	77	249	1,128	1,575	5,533	22,329	1,899
Rate per 100,000 inhabitants	6.2	20.0	90.8	126.8	445.4	1,797.4	152.9
Riverside-San Bernardino-Ontario, CA, MSA							
City of Riverside	10	78	495	747	1,978	6,912	1,718

Table 6.   Crime, by Selected Metropolitan Statistical Area, 2013— continued

(Number, percent, rate per 100,000 population.)

Area	Murder and nonnegligent manslaughter	Rape[1]	Robbery	Aggravated assault	Burglary	Larceny-theft	Motor vehicle theft
City of San Bernardino	45	74	794	1,036	2,673	4,025	2,691
City of Ontario	9	31	167	246	830	2,586	1,091
City of Corona	9	14	65	74	644	2,305	490
City of Victorville	9	36	202	404	1,461	2,067	637
City of Temecula	3	11	39	38	711	1,897	240
City of Chino	4	7	47	200	518	1,249	277
City of Redlands	2	15	84	114	605	2,047	368
Total area actually reporting	219	758	4,736	8,924	33,572	67,684	21,476
Rate per 100,000 inhabitants	5.0	17.3	107.8	203.2	764.4	1,541.1	489.0
Roanoke, VA, MSA							
City of Roanoke	9	44	142	262	628	3,636	180
Total area actually reporting	16	98	173	455	1,104	6,180	325
Rate per 100,000 inhabitants	5.1	31.5	55.6	146.1	354.6	1,985.1	104.4
Rochester, MN, MSA							
City of Rochester	0	50	54	110	429	2,026	103
Total area actually reporting	0	65	56	180	714	2,625	144
Rate per 100,000 inhabitants	0.0	30.8	26.5	85.3	338.2	1,243.2	68.2
Rochester, NY, MSA							
City of Rochester	42	92	918	1,055	2,587	6,855	609
Total area actually reporting	52	202	1,209	1,606	5,609	19,458	1,013
Estimated total	52	202	1,211	1,610	5,619	19,517	1,015
Rate per 100,000 inhabitants	4.8	18.6	111.7	148.5	518.2	1,799.9	93.6
Rockford, IL, MSA							
City of Rockford	19	145	394	1,507	2,001	4,666	372
Total area actually reporting	25	193	440	1,736	2,630	6,673	478
Estimated total	26	199	457	1,770	2,723	7,088	500
Rate per 100,000 inhabitants	7.5	57.7	132.5	513.3	789.7	2,055.6	145.0
Rocky Mount, NC, MSA							
City of Rocky Mount	4	16	154	425	992	2,179	111
Total area actually reporting	16	23	184	574	1,781	3,142	202
Estimated total	16	24	190	589	1,843	3,361	212
Rate per 100,000 inhabitants	10.5	15.8	125.1	387.9	1,213.7	2,213.3	139.6
Rome, GA, MSA							
City of Rome	2	19	69	157	413	1,681	84
Total area actually reporting	4	27	79	258	875	2,923	190
Rate per 100,000 inhabitants	4.2	28.1	82.2	268.4	910.3	3,040.9	197.7
Sacramento—Roseville—Arden-Arcade, CA, MSA							
City of Sacramento	34	95	1,158	1,850	3,886	11,233	2,861
City of Roseville	1	13	64	183	482	2,623	238
City of Folsom	0	7	35	56	240	1,024	72
Total area actually reporting	91	469	2,848	5,799	14,681	38,144	8,416
Rate per 100,000 inhabitants	4.1	21.2	128.7	262.0	663.2	1,723.2	380.2
Saginaw, MI, MSA							
City of Saginaw	29	64	129	763	746	644	102
Total area actually reporting	38	149	190	1,113	1,373	2,708	225
Rate per 100,000 inhabitants	19.2	75.2	95.9	562.0	693.3	1,367.5	113.6
Salem, OR, MSA							
City of Salem	7	47	138	328	983	5,143	656
Total area actually reporting	14	100	214	604	2,042	9,640	1,144
Rate per 100,000 inhabitants	3.5	25.1	53.6	151.4	511.9	2,416.5	286.8
Salinas, CA, MSA							
City of Salinas	24	36	451	490	1,148	2,720	1,488
Total area actually reporting	47	82	655	1,010	2,706	6,036	2,198
Rate per 100,000 inhabitants	10.9	19.0	152.0	234.4	628.0	1,400.8	510.1
Salisbury, MD, MSA							
City of Salisbury, MD	0	17	99	210	336	1,420	50
Total area actually reporting	11	176	315	1,204	3,355	8,793	395
Rate per 100,000 inhabitants	2.9	45.7	81.8	312.5	870.8	2,282.4	102.5
Salt Lake City, UT, MSA							
City of Salt Lake City	7	204	422	842	2,068	9,517	1,876
Total area actually reporting	20	654	964	2,433	7,778	36,235	5,619
Estimated total	20	654	964	2,433	7,780	36,244	5,620
Rate per 100,000 inhabitants	1.8	57.3	84.4	213.1	681.4	3,174.4	492.2
San Antonio-New Braunfels, TX, MSA							
City of San Antonio	72	663	2,192	5,901	14,850	58,567	6,577

Table 6. Crime, by Selected Metropolitan Statistical Area, 2013— continued

(Number, percent, rate per 100,000 population.)

Area	Murder and nonnegligent manslaughter	Rape[1]	Robbery	Aggravated assault	Burglary	Larceny-theft	Motor vehicle theft
City of New Braunfels	3	16	24	104	351	1,673	129
Total area actually reporting	105	889	2,429	7,013	19,289	73,244	7,703
Estimated total	105	889	2,430	7,015	19,295	73,269	7,705
Rate per 100,000 inhabitants	4.6	39.1	107.0	308.9	849.6	3,226.3	339.3
San Diego-Carlsbad, CA, MSA							
City of San Diego	39	316	1,456	3,492	6,355	19,230	6,143
City of Carlsbad	1	23	44	153	525	1,436	124
Total area actually reporting	71	668	3,054	7,384	13,970	45,034	11,272
Rate per 100,000 inhabitants	2.2	20.8	95.3	230.3	435.7	1,404.6	351.6
San Francisco-Oakland-Hayward, CA, MSA							
City of San Francisco	48	161	4,202	2,653	5,931	36,527	5,366
City of Oakland	90	180	4,922	2,792	5,058	13,285	6,833
City of Hayward	5	33	333	218	1,051	2,122	1,671
City of Berkeley	4	26	410	122	1,055	3,658	664
City of San Leandro	3	26	251	114	761	2,287	912
City of Redwood City	1	26	66	97	507	1,138	226
City of San Ramon	0	0	14	13	171	485	104
City of Pleasanton	0	3	29	28	185	979	117
City of Walnut Creek	0	4	31	43	364	1,634	163
City of South San Francisco	0	5	39	74	268	739	181
City of San Rafael	0	26	77	103	366	1,114	332
Total area actually reporting	216	853	13,255	10,807	30,011	102,174	28,500
Rate per 100,000 inhabitants	4.8	19.0	294.6	240.2	667.0	2,271.0	633.5
Oakland-Hayward-Berkeley, CA, MD							
Total area actually reporting	155	510	8,339	6,696	19,520	51,645	20,319
Rate per 100,000 inhabitants	5.8	19.2	313.4	251.6	733.6	1,940.8	763.6
San Francisco-Redwood City-South San Francisco, CA, MD							
Total area actually reporting	59	295	4,780	3,806	9,137	47,520	7,532
Rate per 100,000 inhabitants	3.7	18.7	302.4	240.8	578.0	3,006.2	476.5
San Rafael, CA, MD							
Total area actually reporting	2	48	136	305	1,354	3,009	649
Rate per 100,000 inhabitants	0.8	18.6	52.8	118.5	525.9	1,168.7	252.1
San Jose-Sunnyvale-Santa Clara, CA, MSA							
City of San Jose	38	270	1,095	1,812	5,173	12,411	7,926
City of Sunnyvale	4	16	51	73	574	1,456	404
City of Santa Clara	0	13	55	104	461	2,169	393
City of Mountain View	0	13	32	112	294	1,277	135
City of Milpitas	1	8	56	28	291	1,491	285
City of Palo Alto	0	4	29	21	242	1,174	67
City of Cupertino	0	3	23	15	179	584	49
Total area actually reporting	57	414	1,533	2,779	8,960	26,038	10,269
Rate per 100,000 inhabitants	3.0	21.6	80.1	145.1	467.9	1,359.9	536.3
San Luis Obispo-Paso Robles-Arroyo Grande, CA, MSA							
City of San Luis Obispo	0	34	26	101	328	1,384	63
City of Paso Robles	2	8	6	87	211	595	42
City of Arroyo Grande	0	5	4	22	137	288	30
Total area actually reporting	5	106	81	877	1,642	4,167	399
Rate per 100,000 inhabitants	1.8	38.3	29.3	316.8	593.2	1,505.3	144.1
Santa Cruz-Watsonville, CA, MSA							
City of Santa Cruz	4	33	85	285	552	2,383	228
City of Watsonville	3	20	71	143	218	824	266
Total area actually reporting	11	78	199	714	1,640	5,477	1,023
Rate per 100,000 inhabitants	4.1	29.1	74.2	266.2	611.3	2,041.7	381.3
Santa Maria-Santa Barbara, CA, MSA							
City of Santa Maria	3	34	122	331	647	1,557	730
City of Santa Barbara	2	32	82	246	459	2,091	120
Total area actually reporting	6	153	285	972	2,249	6,429	1,146
Rate per 100,000 inhabitants	1.4	35.2	65.6	223.9	518.0	1,480.8	264.0
Santa Rosa, CA, MSA							
City of Santa Rosa	3	42	105	391	638	2,559	309
Total area actually reporting	9	126	242	1,405	1,804	5,693	721
Rate per 100,000 inhabitants	1.8	25.5	48.9	283.9	364.5	1,150.4	145.7
Savannah, GA, MSA							
City of Savannah-Chatham Metropolitan	30	49	414	358	2,125	5,608	725
Total area actually reporting	36	68	500	554	2,854	7,512	870
Rate per 100,000 inhabitants	9.8	18.6	136.4	151.2	778.7	2,049.7	237.4

Table 6.   Crime, by Selected Metropolitan Statistical Area, 2013— continued

(Number, percent, rate per 100,000 population.)

Area	Murder and nonnegligent manslaughter	Rape[1]	Robbery	Aggravated assault	Burglary	Larceny-theft	Motor vehicle theft
Scranton—Wilkes-Barre—Hazleton, PA, MSA							
City of Scranton	2	18	71	75	549	1,614	114
City of Wilkes-Barre	12	30	110	56	317	969	103
City of Hazleton	1	2	26	54	242	358	31
Total area actually reporting	24	114	324	813	2,590	9,105	517
Estimated total	24	117	333	834	2,639	9,359	528
Rate per 100,000 inhabitants	4.3	20.8	59.1	148.1	468.5	1,661.4	93.7
Seattle-Tacoma-Bellevue, WA, MSA							
City of Seattle	19	153	1,601	1,985	7,384	24,189	4,310
City of Tacoma	10	144	524	1,088	3,086	8,200	2,024
City of Bellevue	1	20	48	56	688	3,013	248
City of Everett	1	42	192	208	1,129	4,702	1,034
City of Kent	2	58	160	99	1,061	3,669	870
City of Renton	3	27	101	123	859	3,396	683
City of Auburn	5	34	110	144	798	2,474	672
City of Lakewood	2	41	90	277	674	1,770	207
City of Redmond	0	24	3	12	193	1,402	70
Total area actually reporting	78	1,136	4,032	6,397	31,505	94,993	18,291
Rate per 100,000 inhabitants	2.2	31.6	112.0	177.8	875.4	2,639.6	508.3
Seattle-Bellevue-Everett, WA, MD							
Total area actually reporting	53	794	3,082	4,039	22,959	73,547	14,024
Rate per 100,000 inhabitants	1.9	28.6	110.9	145.3	826.2	2,646.5	504.6
Tacoma-Lakewood, WA, MD							
Total area actually reporting	25	342	950	2,358	8,546	21,446	4,267
Rate per 100,000 inhabitants	3.0	41.7	115.9	287.7	1,042.5	2,616.2	520.5
Sebastian-Vero Beach, FL, MSA							
City of Sebastian	1	7	5	42	77	373	10
City of Vero Beach	1	9	6	32	103	388	8
Total area actually reporting	4	40	41	334	680	2,215	88
Rate per 100,000 inhabitants	2.8	28.2	28.9	235.4	479.2	1,561.1	62.0
Sebring, FL, MSA							
City of Sebring	2	2	9	44	123	378	12
Total area actually reporting	4	23	52	270	861	1,960	139
Estimated total	4	26	63	295	926	2,186	156
Rate per 100,000 inhabitants	4.1	26.4	64.1	300.1	942.0	2,223.8	158.7
Sheboygan, WI, MSA							
City of Sheboygan	1	20	14	97	187	1,023	31
Total area actually reporting	1	27	19	116	261	1,740	61
Rate per 100,000 inhabitants	0.9	23.5	16.5	100.9	227.1	1,513.7	53.1
Sherman-Denison, TX, MSA							
City of Sherman	2	4	21	93	312	958	46
City of Denison	4	11	15	64	145	646	53
Total area actually reporting	7	26	42	249	724	2,166	170
Estimated total	7	26	43	251	730	2,189	172
Rate per 100,000 inhabitants	5.7	21.2	35.0	204.5	594.8	1,783.6	140.1
Shreveport-Bossier City, LA, MSA							
City of Shreveport	26	84	376	911	2,360	6,720	504
City of Bossier City	6	20	65	303	473	2,554	155
Total area actually reporting	35	130	462	1,750	3,541	11,431	826
Estimated total	35	131	465	1,763	3,572	11,562	832
Rate per 100,000 inhabitants	7.8	29.1	103.4	392.1	794.5	2,571.6	185.1
Sioux City, IA-NE-SD M.S.A							
City of Sioux City, IA	3	46	40	235	604	2,814	240
Total area actually reporting	4	62	45	305	816	3,513	292
Estimated total	4	63	45	307	826	3,549	295
Rate per 100,000 inhabitants	2.4	37.2	26.6	181.2	487.5	2,094.5	174.1
Sioux Falls, SD, MSA							
City of Sioux Falls	3	138	67	428	870	3,796	264
Total area actually reporting	3	159	68	475	1,141	4,262	317
Rate per 100,000 inhabitants	1.2	65.8	28.1	196.6	472.2	1,763.8	131.2
South Bend-Mishawaka, IN-MI, MSA							
City of South Bend, IN	9	93	363	199	1,468	3,096	326
City of Mishawaka, IN	0	20	61	55	305	2,259	140
Total area actually reporting	11	155	444	356	2,453	6,595	547
Estimated total	11	158	448	368	2,483	6,707	559
Rate per 100,000 inhabitants	3.4	49.5	140.3	115.3	777.9	2,101.2	175.1

Table 6.   Crime, by Selected Metropolitan Statistical Area, 2013— continued

(Number, percent, rate per 100,000 population.)

Area	Murder and nonnegligent manslaughter	Rape[1]	Robbery	Aggravated assault	Burglary	Larceny-theft	Motor vehicle theft
Spartanburg, SC, MSA							
City of Spartanburg	3	24	130	370	490	2,060	118
Total area actually reporting	9	147	292	1,031	2,559	6,882	597
Estimated total	9	147	292	1,033	2,563	6,898	598
Rate per 100,000 inhabitants	2.8	46.0	91.4	323.3	802.0	2,158.6	187.1
Spokane-Spokane Valley, WA, MSA							
City of Spokane	11	166	518	745	3,889	13,352	2,290
City of Spokane Valley	1	35	81	114	961	3,862	490
Total area actually reporting	20	253	659	1,031	6,426	20,999	3,330
Rate per 100,000 inhabitants	3.7	47.3	123.1	192.7	1,200.7	3,923.8	622.2
Springfield, IL, MSA							
City of Springfield	4	71	287	829	1,300	4,439	166
Total area actually reporting	34	153	336	1,057	1,676	5,334	788
Estimated total	35	158	351	1,087	1,759	5,703	808
Rate per 100,000 inhabitants	16.5	74.4	165.3	511.8	828.2	2,685.2	380.4
Springfield, MA, MSA							
City of Springfield	22	89	598	964	2,360	4,018	735
Total area actually reporting	28	326	907	1,990	4,779	12,006	1,291
Estimated total	28	329	913	2,011	4,817	12,130	1,302
Rate per 100,000 inhabitants	4.5	52.4	145.3	320.1	766.7	1,930.6	207.2
Springfield, MO, MSA							
City of Springfield	12	281	395	1,206	2,313	11,232	1,146
Total area actually reporting	14	340	427	1,607	3,655	15,113	1,483
Rate per 100,000 inhabitants	3.1	75.9	95.3	358.7	815.8	3,373.4	331.0
Springfield, OH, MSA							
City of Springfield	6	46	208	167	1,304	2,923	236
Total area actually reporting	6	54	220	198	1,691	3,997	282
Estimated total	6	54	220	198	1,694	4,010	283
Rate per 100,000 inhabitants	4.4	39.4	160.4	144.4	1,235.1	2,923.7	206.3
State College, PA, MSA							
City of State College	0	5	13	23	101	596	10
Total area actually reporting	0	37	23	84	316	1,824	27
Rate per 100,000 inhabitants	0.0	23.8	14.8	54.1	203.3	1,173.7	17.4
Staunton-Waynesboro, VA, MSA							
City of Staunton	1	15	5	29	71	510	17
City of Waynesboro	0	15	8	23	101	553	34
Total area actually reporting	2	52	25	120	341	1,623	77
Rate per 100,000 inhabitants	1.7	43.7	21.0	100.8	286.4	1,363.1	64.7
St. Cloud, MN, MSA							
City of St. Cloud	1	56	46	147	371	2,308	163
Total area actually reporting	2	89	50	181	605	3,812	250
Rate per 100,000 inhabitants	1.0	46.5	26.1	94.5	315.9	1,990.3	130.5
St. George, UT, MSA [2]							
City of St. George	1	39	11	82	475	1,184	69
Total area actually reporting	2	57	16	128		2,004	111
Estimated total	2	58	17	131		2,070	118
Rate per 100,000 inhabitants	1.4	39.2	11.5	88.6		1,399.4	79.8
St. Joseph, MO-KS, MSA							
City of St. Joseph, MO	1	61	85	227	805	3,237	296
Total area actually reporting	2	73	88	299	1,046	3,722	330
Rate per 100,000 inhabitants	1.6	56.8	68.5	232.8	814.5	2,898.2	257.0
St. Louis, MO-IL, MSA							
City of St. Louis, MO	120	333	1,457	3,167	4,305	13,452	3,330
City of St. Charles, MO	0	17	27	69	201	1,502	67
Total area actually reporting	201	961	2,804	7,945	14,779	52,256	6,059
Estimated total	203	981	2,860	8,059	15,095	53,631	6,136
Rate per 100,000 inhabitants	7.2	35.0	102.0	287.4	538.4	1,912.9	218.9
Stockton-Lodi, CA, MSA							
City of Stockton	32	91	1,088	2,411	4,189	8,748	2,143
City of Lodi	1	11	89	186	634	1,302	365
Total area actually reporting	47	135	1,477	3,321	7,538	17,069	3,996
Rate per 100,000 inhabitants	6.6	19.0	208.4	468.6	1,063.7	2,408.6	563.9
Sumter, SC, MSA							
City of Sumter	2	13	72	300	637	1,249	128
Total area actually reporting	7	51	108	564	1,382	2,277	255

Table 6.   Crime, by Selected Metropolitan Statistical Area, 2013— continued

(Number, percent, rate per 100,000 population.)

Area	Murder and nonnegligent manslaughter	Rape[1]	Robbery	Aggravated assault	Burglary	Larceny-theft	Motor vehicle theft
Rate per 100,000 inhabitants	6.4	46.9	99.4	518.8	1,271.4	2,094.7	234.6
Syracuse, NY, MSA							
City of Syracuse	21	75	400	696	1,781	4,298	394
Total area actually reporting	28	128	503	1,051	3,367	12,385	645
Rate per 100,000 inhabitants	4.2	19.4	76.1	159.0	509.3	1,873.5	97.6
Tallahassee, FL, MSA							
City of Tallahassee	11	160	387	840	2,082	5,594	440
Total area actually reporting	17	223	454	1,509	3,252	8,979	606
Estimated total	17	223	455	1,511	3,257	8,995	607
Rate per 100,000 inhabitants	4.5	58.9	120.1	398.8	859.7	2,374.2	160.2
Tampa-St. Petersburg-Clearwater, FL, MSA							
City of Tampa	28	78	580	1,411	1,950	6,320	553
City of St. Petersburg	15	155	634	1,575	2,742	9,315	1,124
City of Clearwater	4	50	177	387	851	3,284	181
City of Largo	3	47	94	208	650	2,134	140
Total area actually reporting	123	890	2,607	7,768	17,794	56,266	4,411
Rate per 100,000 inhabitants	4.3	31.0	90.8	270.5	619.5	1,959.0	153.6
Terre Haute, IN, MSA							
City of Terre Haute	4	22	54	97	850	2,130	281
Total area actually reporting	5	36	61	156	1,249	3,453	390
Estimated total	6	41	69	186	1,383	3,861	430
Rate per 100,000 inhabitants	3.5	23.7	39.9	107.5	799.4	2,231.8	248.6
Texarkana, TX-AR, MSA							
City of Texarkana, TX	2	21	71	235	470	1,725	105
Total area actually reporting	6	78	120	635	1,465	4,132	290
Rate per 100,000 inhabitants	4.0	51.9	79.9	422.7	975.2	2,750.6	193.0
The Villages, FL, MSA							
Total area actually reporting	2	14	22	137	317	612	53
Estimated total	2	15	24	142	330	658	57
Rate per 100,000 inhabitants	1.9	14.3	22.9	135.7	315.5	629.0	54.5
Toledo, OH, MSA [7]							
City of Toledo[7]	28	129	962	1,783	5,357		1,064
Total area actually reporting	29	198	1,030	1,908	6,479		1,256
Estimated total	30	209	1,057	1,937	6,728		1,299
Rate per 100,000 inhabitants	4.9	34.3	173.4	317.7	1,103.5		213.1
Topeka, KS, MSA							
City of Topeka	11	33	172	396	1,238	4,679	569
Total area actually reporting	13	47	175	572	1,668	5,832	677
Estimated total	13	49	176	581	1,689	5,932	686
Rate per 100,000 inhabitants	5.5	20.9	75.0	247.7	720.1	2,528.9	292.5
Trenton, NJ, MSA							
City of Trenton	37	13	525	547	996	909	416
Total area actually reporting	40	31	685	762	1,936	4,867	688
Rate per 100,000 inhabitants	10.8	8.4	185.5	206.3	524.2	1,317.9	186.3
Tucson, AZ, MSA							
City of Tucson	47	216	1,002	2,103	4,957	27,440	2,190
Total area actually reporting	71	333	1,225	2,705	7,550	37,897	3,030
Rate per 100,000 inhabitants	7.1	33.3	122.5	270.6	755.3	3,791.0	303.1
Tulsa, OK, MSA							
City of Tulsa	60	373	994	2,400	5,935	12,654	2,389
Total area actually reporting	64	565	1,093	3,240	8,439	19,762	3,264
Rate per 100,000 inhabitants	6.7	58.8	113.8	337.5	879.0	2,058.3	340.0
Tuscaloosa, AL, MSA							
City of Tuscaloosa	8	44	161	221	1,165	3,196	151
Total area actually reporting	16	78	230	555	1,991	5,335	354
Estimated total	16	79	233	564	2,018	5,422	361
Rate per 100,000 inhabitants	6.8	33.7	99.4	240.7	861.1	2,313.6	154.0
Tyler, TX, MSA							
City of Tyler	5	43	53	275	825	3,111	180
Total area actually reporting	8	56	78	458	1,568	4,498	343
Estimated total	8	57	79	461	1,578	4,539	346
Rate per 100,000 inhabitants	3.7	26.2	36.4	212.2	726.5	2,089.8	159.3
Utica-Rome, NY, MSA							
City of Utica	7	27	102	225	449	1,997	82

Table 6.   Crime, by Selected Metropolitan Statistical Area, 2013— continued

(Number, percent, rate per 100,000 population.)

Area	Murder and nonnegligent manslaughter	Rape[1]	Robbery	Aggravated assault	Burglary	Larceny-theft	Motor vehicle theft
City of Rome	4	0	23	20	157	470	35
Total area actually reporting	17	58	146	440	1,289	5,033	185
Estimated total	17	58	149	445	1,301	5,101	187
Rate per 100,000 inhabitants	5.7	19.5	50.0	149.3	436.6	1,711.8	62.8
Vallejo-Fairfield, CA, MSA							
City of Vallejo	25	30	424	540	2,972	1,553	1,209
City of Fairfield	3	13	165	317	735	2,170	629
Total area actually reporting	31	79	718	1,173	4,666	6,473	2,394
Rate per 100,000 inhabitants	7.3	18.7	169.5	276.9	1,101.6	1,528.2	565.2
Victoria, TX, MSA							
City of Victoria	1	53	58	284	507	1,908	64
Total area actually reporting	3	70	61	351	717	2,312	108
Rate per 100,000 inhabitants	3.1	71.5	62.3	358.5	732.4	2,361.6	110.3
Vineland-Bridgeton, NJ, MSA							
City of Vineland	1	14	84	109	594	1,681	61
City of Bridgeton	2	12	165	161	376	763	47
Total area actually reporting	4	41	382	427	1,785	4,939	190
Rate per 100,000 inhabitants	2.5	25.9	241.3	269.8	1,127.7	3,120.4	120.0
Virginia Beach-Norfolk-Newport News, VA-NC, MSA							
City of Virginia Beach, VA	17	140	304	269	1,407	9,374	445
City of Norfolk, VA	28	134	414	842	2,039	8,006	767
City of Newport News, VA	15	56	246	478	991	4,247	344
City of Hampton, VA	22	21	120	129	722	3,525	226
City of Portsmouth, VA	12	47	177	354	1,535	3,615	205
Total area actually reporting	118	562	1,534	2,960	9,025	39,821	2,541
Estimated total	118	563	1,537	2,974	9,109	39,937	2,552
Rate per 100,000 inhabitants	6.9	32.9	89.9	173.9	532.5	2,334.8	149.2
Visalia-Porterville, CA, MSA							
City of Visalia	8	31	156	305	1,218	3,016	619
City of Porterville	8	8	44	134	472	801	233
Total area actually reporting	42	86	438	1,585	4,458	7,870	
Rate per 100,000 inhabitants	9.2	18.9	96.1	347.9	978.6	1,727.6	
Waco, TX, MSA							
City of Waco	4	58	142	311	1,508	3,751	163
Total area actually reporting	7	112	179	575	2,129	6,045	321
Estimated total	7	114	182	584	2,160	6,168	331
Rate per 100,000 inhabitants	2.7	44.1	70.5	226.2	836.5	2,388.5	128.2
Warner Robins, GA, MSA							
City of Warner Robins	4	17	138	205	854	3,191	168
Total area actually reporting	8	32	185	475	1,600	5,205	272
Estimated total	8	33	192	487	1,641	5,376	287
Rate per 100,000 inhabitants	4.3	17.6	102.5	260.1	876.4	2,871.3	153.3
Washington-Arlington-Alexandria, DC-VA-MD-WV, MSA							
City of Washington, D.C.	103	393	3,660	3,724	3,314	23,108	3,147
City of Alexandria, VA	5	21	118	114	249	2,427	291
City of Frederick, MD	1	7	98	222	227	1,504	61
Total area actually reporting	222	1,320	8,397	9,721	17,317	100,443	11,002
Estimated total	222	1,321	8,399	9,733	17,341	100,567	11,008
Rate per 100,000 inhabitants	3.7	22.2	141.3	163.8	291.8	1,692.1	185.2
Silver Spring-Frederick-Rockville, MD, MD							
Total area actually reporting	14	153	953	1,263	3,470	15,861	1,063
Rate per 100,000 inhabitants	1.1	12.2	75.7	100.4	275.8	1,260.5	84.5
Washington-Arlington-Alexandria, DC-VA-MD-WV, MD							
Total area actually reporting	208	1,167	7,444	8,458	13,847	84,582	9,939
Estimated total	208	1,168	7,446	8,470	13,871	84,706	9,945
Rate per 100,000 inhabitants	4.4	24.9	158.9	180.8	296.1	1,808.1	212.3
Watertown-Fort Drum, NY, MSA							
City of Watertown	0	12	16	81	169	953	43
Total area actually reporting	0	14	16	107	338	1,825	80
Estimated total	0	14	18	111	348	1,880	82
Rate per 100,000 inhabitants	0.0	11.5	14.8	91.2	286.0	1,545.3	67.4
Wausau, WI, MSA							
City of Wausau	2	11	13	59	217	725	28
Total area actually reporting	2	17	17	88	462	1,529	53
Estimated total	2	17	18	89	467	1,565	54

Table 6.   Crime, by Selected Metropolitan Statistical Area, 2013— continued

(Number, percent, rate per 100,000 population.)

Area	Murder and nonnegligent manslaughter	Rape[1]	Robbery	Aggravated assault	Burglary	Larceny-theft	Motor vehicle theft
Rate per 100,000 inhabitants	1.5	12.6	13.3	65.9	345.8	1,158.9	40.0
Wichita, KS, MSA							
City of Wichita	15	244	468	2,338	3,933	14,885	1,984
Total area actually reporting	22	331	499	2,765	5,157	18,875	2,278
Estimated total	22	332	499	2,768	5,165	18,910	2,281
Rate per 100,000 inhabitants	3.5	52.1	78.3	434.4	810.6	2,967.6	358.0
Wichita Falls, TX, MSA							
City of Wichita Falls	7	29	124	241	995	3,277	286
Total area actually reporting	7	41	132	329	1,248	3,767	333
Estimated total	7	42	134	334	1,267	3,844	339
Rate per 100,000 inhabitants	4.6	27.8	88.6	220.8	837.7	2,541.4	224.1
Williamsport, PA, MSA							
City of Williamsport	5	10	47	48	228	902	28
Total area actually reporting	6	30	59	106	541	1,949	57
Rate per 100,000 inhabitants	5.1	25.5	50.2	90.3	460.7	1,659.6	48.5
Wilmington, NC, MSA							
City of Wilmington	7	39	253	388	1,645	3,569	335
Total area actually reporting	9	65	296	590	2,650	6,319	481
Estimated total	9	65	298	594	2,669	6,385	484
Rate per 100,000 inhabitants	3.4	24.4	111.7	222.6	1,000.1	2,392.5	181.4
Winchester, VA-WV, MSA							
City of Winchester, VA	1	25	29	34	106	867	33
Total area actually reporting	3	61	41	139	404	2,064	125
Estimated total	3	61	41	140	406	2,072	125
Rate per 100,000 inhabitants	2.3	46.3	31.1	106.2	307.9	1,571.1	94.8
Winston-Salem, NC, MSA							
City of Winston-Salem	15	80	439	892	3,883	8,359	611
Total area actually reporting	23	141	619	1,628	7,201	14,651	1,064
Estimated total	23	142	622	1,636	7,235	14,769	1,070
Rate per 100,000 inhabitants	3.5	21.8	95.4	251.0	1,110.0	2,265.8	164.2
Worcester, MA-CT, MSA							
City of Worcester, MA	9	22	483	1,236	1,916	3,924	399
Total area actually reporting	14	263	688	2,597	4,331	11,595	877
Estimated total	14	267	696	2,625	4,381	11,758	891
Rate per 100,000 inhabitants	1.6	31.3	81.6	307.8	513.7	1,378.6	104.5
Yakima, WA, MSA							
City of Yakima	9	37	144	281	1,194	2,896	594
Total area actually reporting	16	73	191	439	2,267	4,958	1,140
Rate per 100,000 inhabitants	6.4	29.4	76.8	176.5	911.6	1,993.7	458.4
York-Hanover, PA, MSA							
City of York	12	33	174	129	486	905	90
City of Hanover	1	1	8	14	36	465	4
Total area actually reporting	19	101	270	592	1,377	6,299	261
Estimated total	19	101	271	595	1,384	6,334	262
Rate per 100,000 inhabitants	4.3	23.0	61.8	135.7	315.7	1,445.0	59.8
Yuba City, CA, MSA							
City of Yuba City	2	15	39	118	438	1,210	332
Total area actually reporting	7	54	85	370	1,389	2,866	826
Rate per 100,000 inhabitants	4.2	32.1	50.5	219.7	824.8	1,701.8	490.5
Yuma, AZ, MSA							
City of Yuma	5	46	64	472	805	2,348	222
Total area actually reporting	12	67	72	657	1,560	3,379	382
Estimated total	12	68	74	662	1,577	3,449	387
Rate per 100,000 inhabitants	5.9	33.7	36.7	327.9	781.2	1,708.5	191.7

1 The rape figures in this table are an aggregate total of the data submitted using both the revised and legacy Uniform Crime Reporting (UCR) definitions. See chapter notes for further information.   2 The FBI determined that the agency's data were overreported. Consequently, those data are not included in this table.   3 Because of changes in the state/local agency's reporting practices, figures are not comparable to previous years' data.   4 The data collection methodology for the offense of rape used by Chicago, Illinois does not comply with national UCR Program guidelines. Consequently, its figures for rape and violent crime (of which rape is a part) are not published in this table.   5 The FBI determined that the agency's data were underreported. Consequently, those data are not included in this table.   6 The population for the city of Mobile, Alabama, includes 55,819 inhabitants from the jurisdiction of the Mobile County Sheriff's Department.   7 The FBI determined that the agency did not follow national Uniform Crime Reporting Program guidelines for reporting an offense. Consequently, this figure is not included in this table.

Table 7. Offense Analysis, United States, 2009–2013

(Number.)

Classification	2009	2010	2011	2012[1]	2013
Murder	15,399	14,722	14,661	14,856	14,196
Rape (revised definition) [2]	89,241	85,593	84,175	84,376	X
Rape (legacy definition) [3]	X	X	X	X	108,612
Robbery [4]	408,742	369,089	354,746	355,051	345,031
By location					
Street/highway	174,886	159,307	155,218	154,289	146,472
Commercial house	55,980	48,804	46,156	47,151	45,751
Gas or service station	9,881	8,549	8,539	8,660	8,352
Convenience store	21,983	19,282	18,108	18,180	17,099
Residence	69,280	63,779	60,138	59,979	57,362
Bank	8,829	8,034	7,038	6,666	6.510
Miscellaneous	67,903	61,333	59,549	60,126	63,483
Burglary [4]	2,203,313	2,168,459	2,185,140	2,109,932	1,928,465
By location					
Residence (dwelling)	1,599,047	1,602,056	1,628,656	1,571,635	1,425,732
Residence, night	445,983	445,480	442,390	429,662	394,352
Residence, day	819,725	825,163	859,299	832,944	755,178
Residence, unknown	333,339	331,414	326,967	309,028	275,702
Nonresidence (store, office, etc.)	604,266	566,403	556,484	538,297	502,733
Nonresidence, night	255,147	233,765	227,446	220,784	205,639
Nonresidence, day	200,924	192,985	196,461	192,963	183,031
Nonresidence, unknown	148,195	139,652	132,577	124,550	114,063
Larceny-theft (except motor vehicle theft) [4]	6,338,095	6,204,601	6,151,095	6,168,874	6,004,453
By type					
Pocket-picking	26,631	24,231	26,518	29,550	32,345
Purse-snatching	30,493	28,137	27,082	26,407	25,802
Shoplifting	1,149,406	1,064,608	1,077,791	1,147,679	1,196,166
From motor vehicles (except accessories)	1,727,583	1,638,670	1,523,950	1,480,790	1,402,352
Motor vehicle accessories	573,270	549,905	497,980	467,369	438,055
Bicycles	212,362	206,677	216,987	223,786	212,358
From buildings	704,184	699,599	728,050	745,238	738,246
From coin-operated machines	26,085	20,309	19,536	17,240	15,866
All others	1,888,080	1,972,464	2,033,200	2,030,815	1,943,262
By value					
Under $50	2,833,851	2,811,555	2,850,302	2,872,445	2,812,486
$50 to $200	1,443,919	1,421,342	1,399,484	1,398,870	1,339,125
Over $200	2,060,325	1,971,705	1,901,309	1,897,560	1,852,841
Motor vehicle theft	795,652	739,565	716,508	721,053	699,594

1 The crime figures have been adjusted.   2 The figures shown in this column for the offense of rape were estimated using the revised Uniform Crime Reporting (UCR) definition of rape. See chapter notes for more detail.   3 The figures shown in this column for the offense of rape were estimated using the legacy Uniform Crime Reporting (UCR) definition of rape. See chapter notes for more detail.   4 Because of rounding, the number of offenses may not add to the total.

Table 8.   Offenses Known to Law Enforcement, by Selected State and City, 2013

(Number.)

State/city	Violent crime	Murder and nonnegligent manslaughter	Rape (revised definition)[1]	Robbery	Aggravated assault	Burglary	Larceny-theft	Motor vehicle theft	Arson[2]
Alabama									
Abbeville	11	1	1	2	7	21	39	3	
Adamsville	19	1	0	7	11	58	252	11	
Addison	1	0	1	0	0	6	17	2	
Alabaster	44	0	2	11	31	70	544	26	
Alexander City	119	2	16	12	89	121	510	30	
Aliceville	7	0	0	2	5	16	26	6	
Andalusia	34	1	4	6	23	95	379	17	
Anniston	461	5	39	78	339	770	1,120	98	
Arab	32	0	5	4	23	166	414	60	
Ardmore	2	0	0	0	2	7	23	1	
Arley	3	0	0	0	3	12	11	4	
Ashford	2	0	0	0	2	8	46	0	
Ashland	9	0	0	1	8	24	35	4	
Ashville	10	0	1	0	9	35	48	5	
Athens	16	0	1	11	4	116	627	12	
Atmore	52	2	4	9	37	41	150	10	
Auburn	115	2	6	35	72	346	1,514	70	
Bay Minette	47	0	3	5	39	33	221	18	
Bear Creek	4	0	0	0	4	2	8	2	
Bessemer	527	3	15	161	348	725	2,265	209	
Birmingham	2,852	63	178	969	1,642	4,018	8,661	1,478	
Blountsville	6	0	3	0	3	14	49	8	
Brent	16	0	1	3	12	12	72	6	
Brewton	47	0	7	2	38	43	202	13	
Bridgeport	13	0	1	0	12	0	6	0	
Brilliant	4	0	0	2	2	8	13	2	
Butler	6	0	0	1	5	15	22	3	
Camp Hill	22	1	2	1	18	13	14	2	
Carbon Hill	14	0	1	5	8	30	78	13	
Cedar Bluff	20	0	1	1	18	63	122	6	
Centre	21	0	4	2	15	41	194	19	
Centreville	0	0	0	0	0	9	25	2	
Chickasaw	53	0	5	13	35	152	230	19	
Childersburg	1	0	0	1	0	42	59	3	
Citronelle	22	2	0	2	18	45	106	18	0
Clanton	52	0	2	10	40	66	512	19	
Clayton	8	0	0	1	7	22	18	1	
Coaling	10	0	0	1	9	22	63	7	
Collinsville	6	0	1	1	4	24	38	3	
Cordova	15	0	4	0	11	10	34	4	
Creola	10	0	1	1	8	9	46	1	
Crossville	0	0	0	0	0	5	17	3	
Cullman	31	2	6	7	16	110	493	30	
Dadeville	17	0	3	1	13	34	107	10	
Daleville	17	0	5	1	11	25	64	14	
Daphne	31	1	3	5	22	89	421	16	
Dauphin Island	4	0	2	0	2	13	50	2	
Decatur	149	5	12	26	106	569	1,831	153	
Demopolis	47	1	3	4	39	43	246	4	1
Dora	21	0	6	1	14	32	80	15	
Dothan	334	4	16	78	236	591	1,802	109	
Double Springs	5	0	0	0	5	6	19	2	
Douglas	1	0	0	0	1	21	37	3	
East Brewton	22	0	1	0	21	18	36	6	
Eclectic	11	0	2	0	9	14	46	0	
Elba	29	0	4	6	19	46	108	3	
Enterprise	112	2	11	25	74	154	573	47	3
Eufaula	78	0	4	11	63	143	328	25	
Eutaw	46	0	2	4	40	19	54	4	
Evergreen	37	0	5	2	30	59	150	14	
Fairfield	181	4	12	67	98	284	650	73	
Fairhope	40	0	6	6	28	144	515	19	
Fayette	11	0	1	2	8	7	51	8	
Flomaton	9	0	4	1	4	14	32	3	
Florala	10	0	4	1	5	5	25	3	
Florence	207	3	28	56	120	324	1,380	103	
Foley	55	0	4	10	41	111	656	22	
Fyffe	3	0	0	0	3	2	16	1	
Gadsden	424	6	47	104	267	830	1,904	200	14
Gardendale	53	1	2	7	43	103	546	15	
Geneva	13	0	2	2	9	47	93	10	
Georgiana	12	0	0	0	12	17	36	4	
Glencoe	13	0	2	1	10	42	60	5	
Grant	4	0	0	0	4	17	30	4	
Greenville	0	0	0	0	0	0	0	0	
Guin	16	0	0	1	15	13	43	2	

Table 8.   Offenses Known to Law Enforcement, by Selected State and City, 2013— continued

(Number.)

State/city	Violent crime	Murder and nonnegligent manslaughter	Rape (revised definition)	Robbery	Aggravated assault	Burglary	Larceny-theft	Motor vehicle theft	Arson[2]
Gulf Shores	51	0	4	5	42	97	531	21	
Guntersville	48	0	5	10	33	99	477	27	
Gurley	4	0	2	0	2	8	16	2	
Hackleburg	3	0	0	0	3	10	15	4	
Hamilton	12	0	1	1	10	29	86	9	
Hanceville	16	0	1	1	14	28	60	13	
Hartford	13	0	0	1	12	17	64	3	
Hartselle	19	0	0	4	15	63	277	20	
Headland	7	0	1	2	4	29	60	2	
Helena	18	0	6	1	11	20	140	9	
Henagar	3	0	0	0	3	14	25	7	
Hokes Bluff	3	0	0	0	3	11	17	7	
Hoover	74	2	9	34	29	344	2,144	108	1
Hueytown	26	1	3	2	20	116	502	28	
Huntsville	1,507	24	87	391	1,005	1,884	6,629	703	
Ider	5	0	2	0	3	12	22	4	
Irondale	46	0	5	12	29	116	312	35	
Jackson	34	0	5	4	25	45	158	5	
Jacksonville	35	0	3	10	22	137	439	13	
Jasper	113	1	7	26	79	199	743	39	
Jemison	13	2	1	1	9	31	98	2	
Kinsey	2	0	0	1	1	10	14	1	
Lafayette	19	0	4	1	14	15	48	7	
Lake View	6	0	0	0	6	3	12	1	
Lanett	75	1	4	13	57	138	300	35	
Leeds	57	2	4	17	34	72	440	28	
Leesburg	10	0	1	0	9	16	41	4	
Leighton	8	0	4	1	3	15	12	0	
Level Plains	11	0	3	1	7	7	31	2	
Lincoln	31	2	5	5	19	97	244	33	
Linden	16	0	2	1	13	28	17	2	
Livingston	18	0	1	2	15	35	57	6	
Loxley	17	0	2	2	13	40	108	22	
Luverne	11	0	1	0	10	13	47	8	
Madison	133	2	17	27	87	214	947	39	
Maplesville	4	0	1	0	3	12	22	2	
Margaret	4	0	1	0	3	14	12	2	
McIntosh	10	0	0	0	10	7	15	0	
Midfield	47	0	2	20	25	103	150	28	
Midland City	16	0	2	1	13	27	51	3	
Millbrook	54	1	11	17	25	171	517	38	
Mobile	1,541	29	88	459	965	3,207	9,123	681	
Monroeville	78	3	6	6	63	85	357	26	
Montevallo	15	0	4	3	8	54	156	9	
Moody	21	0	0	2	19	53	165	18	
Morris	5	0	2	1	2	10	20	2	
Moulton	5	0	3	1	1	33	46	3	
Moundville	3	0	0	0	3	23	38	6	
Mountain Brook	12	1	1	9	1	71	213	10	
Mount Vernon	28	0	3	2	23	35	53	10	
Muscle Shoals	58	0	5	18	35	109	539	45	
Napier Field	4	0	1	0	3	6	17	3	
New Brockton	5	0	0	0	5	18	20	1	
New Hope	17	0	1	0	16	15	30	7	
Newton	3	0	0	0	3	9	26	1	
Northport	114	0	20	32	62	162	525	41	
Notasulga	7	0	0	0	7	19	13	4	
Odenville	21	0	3	0	18	19	37	7	
Oneonta	21	0	4	0	17	21	172	16	
Opelika	165	3	13	37	112	309	1,146	54	
Owens Crossroads	1	0	0	0	1	3	16	2	
Oxford	62	2	7	8	45	206	874	50	
Ozark	86	0	14	17	55	160	686	32	
Pelham	26	0	6	10	10	45	362	24	
Pell City	66	1	4	10	51	80	443	31	
Phenix City	211	5	23	46	137	702	1,432	270	
Piedmont	20	0	3	3	14	48	153	16	
Pine Hill	6	0	1	1	4	6	9	0	
Pleasant Grove	19	1	1	3	14	39	89	12	
Powell	8	0	0	1	7	10	14	4	
Prattville	86	2	24	30	30	248	957	79	
Priceville	6	0	4	0	2	10	16	1	
Prichard	469	4	12	134	319	607	687	213	0
Ragland	5	0	0	1	4	13	17	0	
Rainbow City	14	0	1	4	9	67	178	21	
Rainsville	15	0	1	0	14	19	101	10	
Red Bay	10	0	2	0	8	14	31	1	
Reform	6	0	1	0	5	13	37	1	

Table 8. Offenses Known to Law Enforcement, by Selected State and City, 2013— continued

(Number.)

State/city	Violent crime	Murder and nonnegligent manslaughter	Rape (revised definition)[1]	Robbery	Aggravated assault	Burglary	Larceny-theft	Motor vehicle theft	Arson[2]
Riverside	8	0	1	0	7	20	65	5	
Robertsdale	28	0	4	2	22	59	174	11	
Russellville	42	2	9	5	26	81	244	20	
Samson	19	1	1	2	15	22	81	4	
Saraland	37	0	7	6	24	67	487	32	
Sardis City	0	0	0	0	0	12	25	4	0
Satsuma	15	0	2	0	13	21	83	14	
Scottsboro	64	0	5	4	55	117	464	24	
Selma	245	3	16	42	184	469	1,058	103	
Sheffield	80	2	7	10	61	119	315	30	
Silverhill	0	0	0	0	0	7	32	2	
Slocomb	4	0	0	0	4	15	25	1	
Snead	3	0	1	0	2	16	33	6	
Southside	10	0	5	0	5	46	101	9	
Springville	5	0	1	1	3	23	82	5	
Sulligent	4	0	0	0	4	7	43	0	
Sumiton	14	0	2	1	11	16	124	12	
Summerdale	9	0	2	1	6	18	47	11	
Sylacauga	55	2	13	10	30	153	444	24	5
Sylvania	1	0	0	0	1	2	19	2	
Talladega	129	0	6	20	103	526	731	47	
Tallassee		0		1	66	86	203	7	
Tarrant	18	1	3	7	7	169	234	13	
Taylor	1	0	0	0	1	1	12	1	
Thorsby	3	0	0	1	2	4	7	0	
Town Creek	7	0	0	0	7	12	16	1	
Trinity	5	0	1	0	4	10	28	6	
Troy	132	3	15	18	96	225	630	52	
Tuscaloosa	434	8	44	161	221	1,165	3,196	151	
Tuscumbia	47	0	7	4	36	73	265	35	
Tuskegee	82	2	7	10	63	190	317	45	
Valley	79	2	10	9	58	164	408	50	
Valley Head	1	0	0	0	1	5	10	2	
Vance	4	0	0	1	3	15	22	4	
Vestavia Hills	17	0	0	6	11	116	404	24	
Warrior	9	0	1	1	7	11	50	10	
Weaver	24	1	6	1	16	42	66	7	
Wedowee	9	0	2	0	7	9	18	3	
Wetumpka	40	0	2	8	30	57	344	8	
Winfield	23	0	1	1	21	26	91	8	
Woodstock	2	0	0	1	1	7	23	2	
York	21	0	2	1	18	21	36	4	
Alaska									
Anchorage	2,435	14	408	522	1,491	1,318	9,845	869	74
Bethel	56	0	10	2	44	26	78	45	17
Bristol Bay Borough	1	1	0	0	0	0	3	6	0
Cordova	9	0	0	0	9	0	33	2	0
Craig	27	0	0	0	27	4	21	1	1
Dillingham	47	0	16	1	30	2	28	12	0
Fairbanks	213	0	34	37	142	116	1,050	103	4
Haines	7	0	0	0	7	12	48	2	0
Homer	63	0	0	1	62	15	213	10	0
Juneau	134	0	18	15	101	101	926	36	10
Kenai	30	0	6	1	23	47	236	18	0
Ketchikan	32	0	4	1	27	16	256	6	0
Kodiak	87	0	1	4	82	36	235	19	2
Kotzebue	85	0	24	3	58	25	110	33	3
Nome	34	0	4	1	29	10	40	6	0
North Pole	19	0	1	1	17	6	67	6	2
North Slope Borough	79	0	9	1	69	34	72	15	2
Palmer	20	0	7	0	13	13	145	5	2
Petersburg	6	0	0	0	6	16	69	3	0
Seward	6	0	0	1	5	13	97	5	0
Sitka	7	0	0	0	7	21	174	12	1
Skagway	3	0	0	0	3	1	9	0	0
Soldotna	19	0	5	2	12	8	138	8	1
Unalaska	15	0	2	0	13	3	66	5	1
Valdez	16	0	0	0	16	11	82	4	0
Wasilla	42	1	4	6	31	64	520	43	1
Wrangell	6	0	0	0	6	6	16	1	0
Arizona									
Bisbee	74	1		0	72	8	202	7	
Buckeye	49	1		17	30	334	925	69	
Bullhead City	76	0		25	51	363	1,252	101	
Camp Verde	33	0		0	31	57	185	17	
Casa Grande	229	5		57	155	474	1,415	86	

Table 8. Offenses Known to Law Enforcement, by Selected State and City, 2013— continued

(Number.)

State/city	Violent crime	Murder and nonnegligent manslaughter	Rape (revised definition)	Robbery	Aggravated assault	Burglary	Larceny-theft	Motor vehicle theft	Arson[2]
Chandler	575	2		162	359	993	4,628	279	
Chino Valley	50	1		2	46	34	163	10	
Clarkdale	5	0		0	4	19	32	0	
Clifton	11	0		0	11	8	31	3	
Coolidge	66	0		13	48	144	488	30	
Cottonwood	44	0		3	40	40	346	15	
Eagar	15	0		1	14	25	75	6	
El Mirage	86	1		18	63	297	802	74	
Eloy	72	1		7	56	156	311	39	
Flagstaff	246	1		43	177	220	2,594	55	
Florence	24	1		2	21	29	168	1	
Fredonia	3	0		0	3	4	8	0	
Gilbert	193	1	14	47	131	647	2,672	153	
Glendale	905	13		335	508	2,410	10,166	1,050	
Globe	77	0		7	70	122	365	1	
Goodyear	94	4		20	54	433	1,201	82	
Holbrook	49	0		6	43	109	237	16	
Huachuca City	0	0	0	0	0	4	8	1	
Jerome	3	0		0	3	5	16	0	
Kearny	8	0		0	8	16	14	0	
Kingman	128	1		19	97	398	1,159	64	
Lake Havasu City	87	1		11	58	285	899	68	
Mammoth	5	0		0	5	5	20	1	
Marana	37	1		10	22	134	882	40	
Maricopa	62	0		6	46	155	633	31	
Mesa	1,807	22		478	1,104	2,357	9,607	952	
Miami	19	0		1	18	52	27	3	
Nogales	39	0		5	34	94	372	57	
Page	59	1		4	52	48	391	28	
Paradise Valley	13	0		0	12	63	146	6	
Payson	56	1		3	48	94	368	21	
Peoria	254	4		59	175	717	2,906	207	
Phoenix	9,492	118		3,233	5,506	16,747	36,983	6,355	
Pima	4	0		0	4	11	42	3	
Pinetop-Lakeside	34	0		1	31	21	170	2	
Prescott	124	0		11	106	182	855	48	
Prescott Valley	82	0		6	70	109	612	30	
Quartzsite	16	0		0	16	19	70	4	
Sahuarita	17	0		1	14	37	304	8	
San Luis	37	1		3	29	139	345	55	
Scottsdale	337	4		101	195	1,093	4,465	208	
Sedona	20	0		1	13	41	171	5	
Show Low	125	0		6	113	73	494	10	
Snowflake-Taylor	21	0		2	19	37	68	4	
Somerton	15	0		1	14	48	119	20	
South Tucson	150	5		40	89	104	714	31	
Springerville	9	0		0	7	13	44	3	
St. Johns	19	0		0	16	44	76	7	
Surprise	149	0		49	86	402	1,572	146	
Tempe	831	3		224	542	1,276	6,113	487	
Thatcher	1	0		0	1	31	113	0	
Tolleson	37	1		10	25	194	441	41	
Tucson	3,368	47		1,002	2,103	4,957	27,440	2,190	
Wickenburg	15	0		1	11	81	108	8	
Willcox	11	0		3	5	37	210	16	
Williams	12	0		2	8	25	70	2	
Winslow	95	1		10	83	57	318	10	
Yuma	587	5	46	64	472	805	2,348	222	
Arkansas									
Arkadelphia	40	1	6	4	29	93	255	10	2
Ashdown	11	0	3	1	7	21	150	2	1
Ash Flat	1	1	0	0	0	4	14	1	0
Atkins	2	0	0	0	2	29	63	7	0
Bald Knob	3	0	1	0	2	28	115	9	1
Barling	19	0	1	0	18	17	76	7	1
Bay	1	0	1	0	0	15	18	0	0
Bearden	4	0	0	0	4	16	13	3	0
Beebe	19	0	3	3	13	110	183	21	0
Bella Vista	26	0	8	1	17	55	73	5	1
Benton	107	0	12	18	77	313	976	81	4
Bentonville	61	0	12	2	47	117	557	12	2
Berryville	7	0	2	0	5	71	206	8	0
Blytheville	235	3	12	53	167	535	695	51	6
Booneville	4	0	2	0	2	38	122	5	0
Bradford	3	0	0	0	3	9	18	0	1
Brinkley	13	0	0	6	7	28	43	3	1
Brookland	2	0	0	0	2	14	14	5	1

Table 8.   Offenses Known to Law Enforcement, by Selected State and City, 2013— continued

(Number.)

State/city	Violent crime	Murder and nonnegligent manslaughter	Rape (revised definition)[1]	Robbery	Aggravated assault	Burglary	Larceny-theft	Motor vehicle theft	Arson[2]
Bryant	12	0	5	7	0	204	668	33	0
Bull Shoals	8	0	1	0	7	9	18	1	0
Cabot	55	0	11	13	31	393	486	44	0
Caddo Valley	1	0	1	0	0	8	29	1	0
Camden	63	0	7	14	42	129	345	10	1
Cammack Village	0	0	0	0	0	7	11	0	0
Caraway	6	0	0	1	5	9	0	0	1
Carlisle	12	0	3	2	7	34	25	2	0
Cave City	4	0	2	0	2	16	25	5	1
Cave Springs	5	0	0	0	5	15	11	0	0
Centerton	19	0	2	1	16	18	44	1	1
Charleston	11	0	2	0	9	11	20	0	0
Cherokee Village	8	0	6	0	2	39	55	2	0
Clarendon	2	0	0	0	2	8	10	1	0
Clarksville	15	0	8	0	7	86	283	5	2
Clinton	3	0	1	0	2	9	41	8	0
Conway	239	1	22	49	167	367	2,299	108	6
Corning	13	0	1	0	12	24	14	2	3
Cotter	2	0	0	0	2	0	14	0	0
Crossett	27	0	3	2	22	160	171	7	3
Danville	3	0	1	0	2	6	8	1	0
Dardanelle	21	0	5	5	11	94	130	10	0
Decatur	9	0	1	0	8	12	12	0	0
De Queen	11	0	4	1	6	58	133	13	1
Dermott	3	0	0	0	3	21	7	0	1
Des Arc	0	0	0	0	0	4	7	1	0
De Witt	20	0	1	2	17	51	78	4	0
Diaz	6	0	0	0	6	18	15	2	0
Dover	2	0	2	0	0	14	31	1	1
Dumas	11	0	0	5	6	33	43	5	0
Earle	4	0	0	1	3	39	46	2	1
El Dorado	164	1	13	17	133	364	565	53	4
England	22	0	2	5	15	30	63	4	0
Eudora	8	0	0	0	8	36	53	5	2
Fairfield Bay	5	0	1	0	4	18	28	2	0
Farmington	22	1	7	1	13	16	66	2	1
Fayetteville	339	3	33	33	270	538	2,473	160	7
Flippin	3	1	0	0	2	9	69	0	0
Fordyce	16	0	3	1	12	71	136	5	3
Forrest City	135	3	4	29	99	338	715	27	4
Fort Smith	606	4	79	94	429	975	3,447	199	9
Gassville	1	0	0	0	1	9	31	2	0
Gentry	6	0	1	0	5	12	16	0	0
Glenwood	7	0	0	0	7	21	39	1	0
Gosnell	25	0	1	0	24	45	30	2	0
Gravette	4	0	1	0	3	23	24	3	0
Greenbrier	0	0	0	0	0	2	5	1	0
Green Forest	14	0	3	1	10	16	61	3	0
Greenland	6	2	0	0	4	8	12	1	0
Greenwood	19	0	0	0	19	28	27	1	0
Greers Ferry	3	0	0	0	3	6	14	3	1
Gurdon	12	1	0	0	11	26	19	0	0
Hamburg	22	0	0	0	22	26	24	0	1
Hampton	5	0	0	1	4	12	21	0	0
Hardy	2	0	0	0	2	13	30	3	0
Harrisburg	10	0	2	0	8	24	56	0	1
Harrison	71	0	13	2	56	168	502	22	2
Heber Springs	18	0	2	2	14	125	184	14	1
Helena-West Helena	148	3	16	42	87	347	486	13	15
Highfill	0	0	0	0	0	2	5	0	1
Highland	1	0	0	0	1	2	4	0	0
Hope	82	2	13	10	57	189	340	18	5
Hot Springs	140	7	25	57	51	721	2,294	166	3
Hoxie	6	0	2	1	3	6	11	3	0
Jacksonville	217	3	9	23	182	339	1,035	69	6
Jonesboro	313	2	36	58	217	979	1,930	86	12
Kensett	3	0	0	1	2	16	31	4	0
Lake City	3	0	0	1	2	4	2	2	0
Lakeview	1	0	0	0	1	3	9	0	0
Lake Village	31	1	0	1	29	33	77	3	1
Lamar	3	0	3	0	0	13	23	1	0
Leachville	5	0	1	0	4	7	9	2	0
Lepanto	10	0	1	0	9	12	46	2	0
Lincoln	3	0	0	1	2	13	9	1	0
Little Rock	2,777	35	119	944	1,679	3,794	10,655	1,080	93
Lonoke	32	0	2	5	25	56	158	2	0
Lowell	6	0	3	0	3	35	108	9	0
Magnolia	48	0	2	7	39	280	222	8	4

Table 8.   Offenses Known to Law Enforcement, by Selected State and City, 2013— continued

(Number.)

State/city	Violent crime	Murder and nonnegligent manslaughter	Rape (revised definition)[1]	Robbery	Aggravated assault	Burglary	Larceny-theft	Motor vehicle theft	Arson[2]
Malvern	8	1	1	2	4	22	25	2	0
Marianna	8	0	2	6	0	99	95	4	3
Marion	91	0	13	8	70	144	244	17	5
Marmaduke	4	0	1	0	3	8	27	2	1
Marvell	2	0	0	0	2	7	10	1	0
Maumelle	20	0	3	6	11	74	281	13	0
Mayflower	6	0	1	0	5	6	43	8	0
McCrory	0	0	0	0	0	5	27	0	0
McGehee	57	0	2	2	53	111	68	2	0
McRae	1	0	0	0	1	11	15	0	0
Mena	21	0	4	0	17	94	219	6	0
Mineral Springs	1	0	0	0	1	16	11	0	0
Monette	3	0	1	0	2	4	10	0	0
Monticello	47	0	4	2	41	120	354	21	1
Morrilton	18	1	2	0	15	40	310	6	3
Mountain Home	24	0	21	0	3	46	507	14	0
Mountain View	10	0	0	0	10	23	88	2	0
Mulberry	10	0	2	2	6	33	54	0	1
Murfreesboro	0	0	0	0	0	0	8	0	0
Nashville	5	0	0	0	5	112	176	2	1
Newport	28	0	7	16	5	190	406	13	2
North Little Rock	461	13	11	138	299	864	2,762	275	10
Ola	3	0	0	1	2	6	21	0	0
Osceola	99	0	12	7	80	188	258	13	2
Ozark	18	0	8	1	9	51	97	5	0
Pangburn	0	0	0	0	0	11	21	1	0
Paragould	127	0	23	18	86	483	1,073	136	11
Paris	35	0	2	2	31	112	114	12	0
Pea Ridge	6	0	2	1	3	18	44	1	1
Perryville	1	0	0	0	1	3	22	0	0
Piggott	9	0	2	0	7	87	65	1	0
Plummerville	7	0	1	1	5	5	11	0	0
Pottsville	6	0	1	0	5	18	27	3	1
Prairie Grove	14	0	2	0	12	16	64	1	0
Quitman	0	0	0	0	0	7	19	0	1
Redfield	1	0	1	0	0	6	15	0	0
Rison	2	0	0	0	2	32	8	2	0
Rogers	208	0	31	11	166	225	1,453	31	1
Russellville	94	0	14	16	64	227	832	91	3
Salem	8	0	0	0	8	19	23	0	0
Sheridan	13	0	2	0	11	60	132	4	2
Sherwood	130	1	10	17	102	356	868	66	1
Siloam Springs	46	0	8	1	37	155	346	13	2
Springdale	354	3	77	29	245	473	2,056	122	13
Stamps	4	0	0	2	2	12	20	2	1
Star City	12	0	3	0	9	15	16	0	1
Stuttgart	44	1	1	10	32	210	222	19	8
Swifton	0	0	0	0	0	4	8	1	0
Texarkana	305	2	17	44	242	409	1,237	58	2
Trumann	60	0	8	4	48	173	404	12	5
Van Buren	107	0	10	6	91	256	609	27	2
Vilonia	6	0	2	0	4	45	56	3	0
Waldron	16	0	2	1	13	75	119	4	2
Walnut Ridge	6	0	0	0	6	27	54	1	0
Ward	28	0	2	1	25	49	71	5	0
Warren	22	0	3	5	14	79	42	2	0
White Hall	5	1	1	0	3	37	59	6	1
Wynne	33	5	5	4	19	166	286	6	1
California									
Adelanto	198	2		52	129	381	372	133	17
Agoura Hills	19	0		10	7	109	185	12	7
Alameda	158	0		85	63	287	1,285	330	17
Albany	29	0		24	4	94	388	75	7
Alhambra	163	1		81	72	344	1,196	234	7
Aliso Viejo	25	0		4	19	71	224	20	3
Alturas	28	1		2	21	23	46	2	0
American Canyon	54	0		31	19	91	387	32	2
Anaheim	1,130	11		437	600	1,412	6,518	1,681	35
Anderson	63	0		9	46	147	454	120	5
Antioch	946	12		352	557	1,351	1,872	1,217	57
Apple Valley	185	3		58	112	596	775	223	22
Arcadia	77	0		37	39	376	1,080	62	3
Arcata	67	3		15	42	147	634	60	14
Arroyo Grande	31	0		4	22	137	288	30	0
Artesia	63	2		28	33	91	177	55	1
Arvin	153	2		16	134	323	308	113	15
Atascadero	97	1		24	60	119	400	25	7

Table 8.   Offenses Known to Law Enforcement, by Selected State and City, 2013— continued

(Number.)

State/city	Violent crime	Murder and nonnegligent manslaughter	Rape (revised definition)[1]	Robbery	Aggravated assault	Burglary	Larceny-theft	Motor vehicle theft	Arson[2]
Atherton	10	0		1	8	34	78	3	1
Atwater	182	1		22	152	361	804	158	5
Auburn	49	0		13	34	86	190	26	7
Avalon	4	0		2	2	13	57	18	1
Avenal	62	0		6	52	63	67	17	2
Azusa	246	2		36	204	256	671	171	6
Bakersfield	1,857	24		708	1,082	4,605	9,272	2,937	193
Baldwin Park	220	5		74	135	280	727	363	8
Banning	129	2		26	92	355	323	130	0
Barstow	229	3		45	168	329	354	102	11
Bear Valley	12	0		0	11	10	101	0	0
Beaumont	85	1		20	56	180	1,015	103	6
Bell	208	0		81	117	124	334	77	0
Bellflower	279	1		105	164	427	968	487	13
Bell Gardens	120	1		56	60	141	351	271	2
Belmont	27	1		4	17	129	269	39	1
Belvedere	0	0		0	0	5	20	1	0
Benicia	30	0		8	18	134	199	50	8
Berkeley	562	4		410	122	1,055	3,658	664	16
Beverly Hills	77	0		29	43	239	899	41	4
Big Bear Lake	56	0		5	46	77	126	12	1
Biggs	16	0		0	16	11	18	5	0
Bishop	28	0		4	24	24	80	4	0
Blythe	65	1		20	40	223	435	35	25
Bradbury	1	0		0	1	5	9	2	0
Brawley	61	0		7	49	301	854	56	36
Brea	64	2		22	36	205	939	66	3
Brentwood	89	0		20	58	253	848	113	5
Brisbane	5	0		1	4	19	73	6	1
Broadmoor	14	0		2	9	20	29	6	0
Buellton	7	0		1	3	15	46	1	0
Buena Park	221	2		80	126	361	1,435	369	2
Burbank	171	0		51	107	285	1,926	219	6
Burlingame	37	0		12	23	148	472	45	5
Calabasas	20	0		6	11	84	222	7	7
Calexico	92	0		27	65	362	837	275	3
California City	87	0		9	74	425	239	19	0
Calimesa	14	0		5	9	44	106	15	0
Calistoga	9	0		1	7	27	45	3	0
Camarillo	73	0		25	42	205	849	76	9
Campbell	106	2		24	68	341	1,016	206	11
Canyon Lake	3	0		0	3	34	109	14	0
Capitola	38	1		4	30	41	532	27	2
Carlsbad	221	1		44	153	525	1,436	124	10
Carmel	9	0		2	5	32	70	3	0
Carpinteria	21	0		4	14	50	191	20	0
Carson	400	3		148	234	514	1,248	489	9
Cathedral City	149	4		44	92	399	417	302	1
Central Marin	41	0		12	24	276	358	61	1
Ceres	133	1		41	82	355	1,026	339	14
Cerritos	82	0		42	36	374	1,210	218	6
Chico	299	2		95	161	622	1,568	382	37
Chino	258	4		47	200	518	1,249	277	4
Chino Hills	63	0		11	47	315	615	87	4
Chowchilla	81	0		7	71	196	213	43	7
Chula Vista	595	2		248	316	971	3,532	781	35
Citrus Heights	320	7		76	218	483	1,825	345	14
City of Angels	9	0		1	7	28	26	3	0
Claremont	37	0		23	12	280	546	68	5
Clayton	2	0		2	0	37	54	10	0
Clearlake	125	2		21	89	309	292	89	13
Cloverdale	5	0		0	5	44	102	12	1
Clovis	181	0		47	111	879	2,220	305	12
Coachella	118	2		56	58	358	634	380	5
Coalinga	131	0		6	118	169	282	34	12
Colma	5	0		1	3	13	238	22	1
Colton	161	2		69	84	532	1,018	386	1
Colusa	10	0		2	4	47	71	20	0
Commerce	83	1		39	41	101	515	277	6
Compton	1,242	36		360	820	579	1,160	799	39
Concord	407	1		159	235	825	2,764	768	9
Corcoran	71	0		10	59	103	215	46	2
Corning	47	0		4	43	89	173	38	2
Corona	162	9		65	74	644	2,305	490	9
Coronado	11	0		4	5	57	470	28	4
Costa Mesa	252	1		94	111	512	2,748	296	13
Cotati	35	0		6	29	31	41	7	0
Covina	138	0		52	77	369	818	157	9

Table 8.   Offenses Known to Law Enforcement, by Selected State and City, 2013— continued

(Number.)

State/city	Violent crime	Murder and nonnegligent manslaughter	Rape (revised definition)[1]	Robbery	Aggravated assault	Burglary	Larceny-theft	Motor vehicle theft	Arson[2]
Crescent City	94	0		13	74	61	125	16	0
Cudahy	111	0		38	69	64	174	82	1
Culver City	161	0		88	66	174	1,327	115	1
Cupertino	41	0		23	15	179	584	49	15
Cypress	50	0		17	29	148	689	97	6
Daly City	223	0		90	118	352	1,190	291	26
Dana Point	70	0		10	51	133	429	24	0
Danville	17	0		2	12	94	291	28	2
Davis	103	3		20	49	723	967	87	10
Delano	309	6		81	218	713	793	443	51
Del Mar	16	0		3	12	34	134	11	0
Del Rey Oaks	5	0		3	2	10	29	0	0
Desert Hot Springs	277	2		63	209	487	475	141	3
Diamond Bar	62	0		25	34	344	476	66	1
Dinuba	214	0		20	188	333	446	92	5
Dixon	35	0		1	30	103	263	45	1
Dorris	1	0		0	1	3	11	3	0
Dos Palos	89	1		2	55	56	100	54	0
Downey	326	7		171	136	573	1,873	846	9
Duarte	41	1		19	20	97	214	55	0
Dublin	70	0		15	54	168	494	77	5
Dunsmuir	4	0		1	3	9	24	1	0
East Palo Alto	347	8		80	248	236	231	130	0
Eastvale	63	1		18	35	203	667	135	1
El Cajon	386	2		143	212	493	1,775	462	17
El Centro	144	1		54	82	416	1,499	124	3
El Cerrito	92	0		63	29	280	717	123	1
Elk Grove	469	0		99	364	544	2,229	190	11
El Monte	340	3		155	168	568	1,038	576	11
El Segundo	37	0		19	18	143	343	52	6
Emeryville	132	0		70	60	135	1,362	154	2
Encinitas	127	1		21	96	258	752	71	1
Escalon	10	0		0	9	58	114	19	2
Escondido	596	6		201	350	717	2,476	772	12
Etna	1	0		0	1	0	3	0	1
Eureka	192	2		73	100	399	1,506	182	25
Exeter	20	1		4	12	72	158	19	2
Fairfax	13	0		1	9	30	68	6	1
Fairfield	498	3		165	317	735	2,170	629	20
Farmersville	47	0		15	31	104	119	35	2
Ferndale	4	0		0	4	10	15	1	0
Fillmore	26	0		4	21	26	106	20	7
Firebaugh	70	0		3	61	18	28	3	3
Folsom	98	0		35	56	240	1,024	72	10
Fontana	725	10		202	480	872	2,217	999	9
Fort Bragg	53	0		2	50	94	282	15	4
Fort Jones	1	0		0	1	5	4	0	0
Fortuna	41	0		4	35	85	321	23	2
Foster City	15	0		3	10	69	216	20	4
Fountain Valley	92	0		20	63	262	835	73	5
Fowler	37	0		2	32	29	96	41	2
Fremont	273	1		136	111	944	2,484	669	21
Fresno	2,552	40		903	1,556	5,223	13,304	4,057	184
Fullerton	372	0		107	236	627	2,873	359	27
Galt	63	2		15	39	190	263	64	4
Gardena	245	0		144	85	298	726	307	7
Garden Grove	455	5		137	297	637	2,221	539	29
Gilroy	180	3		51	111	222	1,283	235	10
Glendale	181	1		75	97	563	2,384	251	5
Glendora	65	2		30	26	173	1,096	71	6
Goleta	43	0		9	27	137	301	13	1
Gonzales	24	0		7	15	35	55	19	2
Grand Terrace	38	0		16	21	77	143	59	2
Grass Valley	115	0		10	103	131	551	69	5
Greenfield	89	1		31	56	62	141	56	3
Gridley	72	1		1	66	53	115	23	6
Grover Beach	39	0		7	25	94	174	35	1
Guadalupe	10	0		1	8	12	29	11	0
Gustine	39	0		5	32	50	55	20	8
Hanford	299	2		63	224	345	1,401	193	11
Hawaiian Gardens	56	1		21	32	47	106	52	1
Hawthorne	580	6		299	243	523	1,333	386	6
Hayward	589	5		333	218	1,051	2,122	1,671	21
Healdsburg	25	0		2	20	47	181	8	0
Hemet	447	4		173	246	1,110	2,294	559	1
Hercules	22	0		6	14	83	143	48	0
Hermosa Beach	27	0		6	17	119	395	35	0
Hesperia	371	1		83	270	869	1,052	409	15

Table 8.   Offenses Known to Law Enforcement, by Selected State and City, 2013— continued

(Number.)

State/city	Violent crime	Murder and nonnegligent manslaughter	Rape (revised definition)[1]	Robbery	Aggravated assault	Burglary	Larceny-theft	Motor vehicle theft	Arson[2]
Hidden Hills	2	0		2	0	6	1	0	0
Highland	191	3		56	124	480	527	355	9
Hillsborough	0	0		0	0	32	23	2	0
Hollister	195	4		26	151	185	312	73	7
Holtville	12	0		1	9	26	67	9	0
Hughson	7	0		1	6	50	77	20	1
Huntington Beach	362	2		100	229	793	3,796	345	25
Huntington Park	359	1		197	155	220	1,003	589	5
Huron	71	1		16	52	96	134	41	2
Imperial	7	0		1	6	18	53	15	0
Imperial Beach	133	1		25	101	125	228	101	3
Indian Wells	7	0		2	5	48	116	8	0
Indio	468	1		120	313	792	1,335	572	9
Industry	51	0		18	29	110	705	226	1
Inglewood	739	14		326	370	637	1,441	640	23
Ione	6	0		1	5	28	65	8	1
Irvine	113	2		38	61	583	2,553	149	10
Irwindale	20	0		4	15	40	145	44	3
Isleton	9	0		3	6	23	23	0	0
Jackson	23	0		2	19	60	112	7	5
Jurupa Valley	267	3		75	177	570	1,732	763	2
Kensington	5	0		0	5	36	35	14	2
Kerman	45	0		9	34	120	233	83	1
King City	68	5		20	43	84	93	24	2
Kingsburg	23	0		2	18	111	162	54	2
La Canada Flintridge	12	0		3	9	96	196	11	1
Lafayette	21	0		6	15	110	275	28	0
Laguna Beach	41	0		5	33	87	356	26	5
Laguna Hills	53	0		12	38	75	390	43	1
Laguna Niguel	57	0		13	40	95	500	29	1
Laguna Woods	5	0		1	2	22	100	10	2
La Habra	88	0		33	47	185	856	114	0
La Habra Heights	3	0		0	2	33	20	2	0
Lake Elsinore	103	3		32	66	418	858	218	1
Lake Forest	105	2		23	68	150	620	43	1
Lakeport	14	0		1	11	60	192	20	0
Lake Shastina	2	0		0	2	4	4	2	0
Lakewood	225	2		110	102	419	1,356	287	9
La Mesa	181	1		64	109	354	1,381	233	3
La Mirada	72	1		14	48	207	520	114	3
Lancaster	832	9		261	522	1,062	2,030	403	49
La Palma	10	0		8	2	80	221	25	3
La Puente	143	3		48	80	149	219	125	5
La Quinta	68	0		26	37	402	1,002	90	4
La Verne	37	0		21	15	158	548	47	1
Lawndale	162	1		51	101	151	172	96	4
Lemon Grove	145	1		45	91	120	279	110	2
Lemoore	111	0		28	77	112	408	88	5
Lincoln	25	0		7	12	183	326	44	7
Lindsay	40	0		12	27	99	161	50	2
Livermore	270	0		44	214	387	1,275	168	15
Livingston	33	2		2	28	39	127	30	1
Lodi	287	1		89	186	634	1,302	365	15
Loma Linda	61	0		10	50	166	402	153	3
Lomita	66	0		17	47	114	231	69	1
Lompoc	188	0		31	140	311	660	80	17
Long Beach	2,346	34		1,118	1,091	3,776	6,868	2,355	97
Los Alamitos	24	0		11	11	108	213	39	0
Los Altos	23	0		13	5	79	262	17	4
Los Altos Hills	2	0		0	1	47	35	1	3
Los Angeles	16,524	251		7,885	7,624	15,728	55,734	14,382	1,430
Los Banos	109	1		31	74	257	696	107	4
Los Gatos	25	0		5	17	132	376	43	5
Lynwood	436	2		189	231	325	649	554	12
Madera	568	7		107	426	589	1,010	256	0
Malibu	28	0		11	14	81	246	23	1
Mammoth Lakes	18	0		5	13	33	113	6	1
Manhattan Beach	64	0		34	25	194	623	36	1
Manteca	212	0		79	129	489	1,883	327	22
Marina	50	0		13	33	234	298	28	4
Martinez	53	0		17	33	202	441	181	0
Marysville	87	0		17	60	135	269	135	6
Maywood	112	4		32	72	52	132	136	2
McFarland	65	1		18	44	88	58	128	12
Mendota	38	1		15	21	75	176	43	18
Menifee	99	3		21	69	391	979	310	3
Menlo Park	53	0		18	32	180	436	28	3
Merced	556	5		133	399	644	1,608	395	104

Table 8. **Offenses Known to Law Enforcement, by Selected State and City, 2013— continued**

(Number.)

State/city	Violent crime	Murder and nonnegligent manslaughter	Rape (revised definition)[1]	Robbery	Aggravated assault	Burglary	Larceny-theft	Motor vehicle theft	Arson[2]
Mill Valley	11	0		2	9	78	143	8	0
Milpitas	93	1		56	28	291	1,491	285	8
Mission Viejo	62	0		22	36	156	802	40	4
Modesto	1,704	14		450	1,168	2,251	6,349	1,389	62
Monrovia	57	0		23	33	128	592	86	0
Montague	2	0		0	2	5	11	0	1
Montclair	187	2		79	95	288	962	373	14
Montebello	183	2		81	89	711	549	496	47
Monterey	120	1		38	71	220	835	53	2
Monterey Park	104	0		60	36	316	637	209	0
Monte Sereno	1	0		0	0	14	18	1	0
Moorpark	37	0		7	27	68	315	26	3
Moraga	11	0		0	7	37	92	21	1
Moreno Valley	638	10		312	285	1,822	3,224	826	4
Morgan Hill	63	1		10	41	162	416	98	2
Morro Bay	31	0		1	27	57	105	9	1
Mountain View	157	0		32	112	294	1,277	135	4
Mount Shasta	5	0		2	3	14	48	7	0
Murrieta	70	1		21	38	285	1,149	206	8
Napa	255	2		47	180	304	975	130	16
National City	314	1		137	165	286	1,189	415	7
Needles	15	1		5	8	88	88	32	1
Nevada City	26	0		1	22	36	78	15	0
Newark	123	1		40	73	231	658	173	2
Newman	36	0		4	32	38	124	36	2
Newport Beach	73	2		13	51	454	1,600	104	11
Norco	42	1		7	32	149	367	78	3
Norwalk	407	6		150	235	420	1,262	564	10
Novato	107	0		30	72	215	496	125	20
Oakdale	50	0		14	27	239	503	84	2
Oakland	7,984	90		4,922	2,792	5,058	13,285	6,833	140
Oakley	70	0		19	47	137	266	94	3
Oceanside	634	9		182	402	677	3,417	400	24
Ojai	14	0		3	7	15	80	8	2
Ontario	453	9		167	246	830	2,586	1,091	28
Orange	147	4		64	71	473	1,673	272	15
Orange Cove	212	0		8	189	272	483	125	0
Orinda	10	0		0	10	103	103	8	0
Orland	27	0		5	19	52	107	16	3
Oroville	78	2		26	40	258	593	160	10
Oxnard	651	15		328	298	974	3,436	664	36
Pacifica	66	0		7	51	114	361	71	3
Pacific Grove	22	0		7	13	84	207	17	5
Palmdale	759	10		257	465	1,049	1,928	367	28
Palm Desert	110	2		30	71	572	1,511	132	4
Palm Springs	255	0		99	137	712	1,342	296	9
Palo Alto	54	0		29	21	242	1,174	67	10
Palos Verdes Estates	6	0		0	5	54	89	4	2
Paradise	68	1		7	49	214	242	74	0
Paramount	222	3		122	89	266	863	504	7
Parlier	91	2		18	65	111	156	108	15
Pasadena	434	3		162	244	939	2,553	287	27
Paso Robles	103	2		6	87	211	595	42	4
Patterson	41	1		26	12	206	327	98	3
Perris	241	6		102	132	489	1,067	482	3
Petaluma	179	0		31	131	159	778	76	12
Pico Rivera	207	3		65	132	262	924	335	11
Piedmont	20	0		13	7	116	126	50	2
Pinole	69	2		30	28	128	475	82	2
Pismo Beach	22	0		3	14	146	159	12	0
Pittsburg	185	4		111	68	567	826	629	5
Placentia	66	2		16	42	173	531	80	1
Placerville	63	0		7	53	92	172	30	0
Pleasant Hill	55	0		40	14	206	1,110	153	3
Pleasanton	60	0		29	28	185	979	117	10
Pomona	809	29		295	454	847	2,591	956	17
Porterville	194	8		44	134	472	801	233	5
Port Hueneme	57	1		11	41	112	251	42	1
Poway	90	0		16	66	170	360	45	2
Rancho Cordova	352	5		101	235	478	1,499	225	2
Rancho Cucamonga	331	1		128	188	1,374	1,972	478	17
Rancho Mirage	26	0		8	17	156	443	37	0
Rancho Palos Verdes	30	0		7	22	175	369	36	0
Rancho Santa Margarita	17	0		6	8	77	200	13	1
Red Bluff	146	3		19	115	291	570	77	3
Redding	585	2		146	388	742	2,483	549	5
Redlands	215	2		84	114	605	2,047	368	21
Redondo Beach	160	1		43	112	309	1,146	133	1

Table 8. Offenses Known to Law Enforcement, by Selected State and City, 2013— continued

(Number.)

State/city	Violent crime	Murder and nonnegligent manslaughter	Rape (revised definition)	Robbery	Aggravated assault	Burglary	Larceny-theft	Motor vehicle theft	Arson[2]
Redwood City	190	1		66	97	507	1,138	226	13
Reedley	157	0		25	125	173	244	112	1
Rialto	434	4		192	219	798	1,148	771	20
Richmond	1,112	16		407	654	1,631	1,685	1,510	23
Ridgecrest	154	4		24	117	212	313	45	11
Rio Dell	11	0		0	11	21	22	3	0
Rio Vista	32	0		4	25	113	117	15	2
Ripon	15	0		5	9	66	253	23	1
Riverbank	37	0		13	23	208	400	77	1
Riverside	1,330	10		495	747	1,978	6,912	1,718	75
Rocklin	62	0		17	40	273	678	60	6
Rohnert Park	180	1		24	139	136	487	64	4
Rolling Hills	0	0		0	0	5	6	0	0
Rolling Hills Estates	3	0		1	2	29	82	7	0
Rosemead	149	0		65	78	288	615	164	3
Roseville	261	1		64	183	482	2,623	238	17
Ross	1	0		0	1	21	24	3	0
Sacramento	3,137	34		1,158	1,850	3,886	11,233	2,861	164
Salinas	1,001	24		451	490	1,148	2,720	1,488	36
San Bernardino	1,949	45		794	1,036	2,673	4,025	2,691	87
San Bruno	102	1		35	58	131	780	91	1
San Clemente	56	0		21	32	209	582	53	2
Sand City	3	0		0	3	14	81	4	0
San Diego	5,303	39		1,456	3,492	6,355	19,230	6,143	178
San Dimas	65	0		18	43	176	463	67	1
San Fernando	85	0		28	55	69	258	72	2
San Francisco	7,064	48		4,202	2,653	5,931	36,527	5,866	227
San Gabriel	103	1		31	66	175	493	56	1
Sanger	146	2		25	104	179	433	114	1
San Jacinto	124	5		64	49	469	1,092	244	0
San Jose	3,215	38		1,095	1,812	5,173	12,411	7,926	133
San Juan Capistrano	57	0		13	44	115	302	22	2
San Leandro	394	3		251	114	761	2,287	912	10
San Luis Obispo	161	0		26	101	328	1,384	63	44
San Marcos	214	0		62	133	299	931	170	7
San Marino	20	0		3	15	83	140	1	0
San Mateo	239	0		85	125	309	1,601	155	12
San Pablo	200	0		102	96	305	512	353	4
San Rafael	206	0		77	103	366	1,114	332	19
San Ramon	27	0		14	13	171	485	104	10
Santa Ana	1,121	13		463	594	803	4,163	1,459	33
Santa Barbara	362	2		82	246	459	2,091	120	17
Santa Clara	172	0		55	104	461	2,169	393	18
Santa Clarita	276	2		97	158	704	1,760	249	17
Santa Cruz	407	4		85	285	552	2,383	228	21
Santa Fe Springs	75	0		28	44	135	830	241	2
Santa Maria	490	3		122	331	647	1,557	730	13
Santa Monica	324	7		120	170	573	2,806	165	21
Santa Paula	108	6		33	63	103	358	75	6
Santa Rosa	541	3		105	391	638	2,559	309	25
Santee	156	0		31	120	170	888	107	3
Saratoga	14	0		4	7	89	123	10	2
Sausalito	10	0		2	6	71	226	12	1
Scotts Valley	11	0		2	8	56	220	11	3
Seal Beach	16	0		8	7	93	336	33	1
Seaside	120	4		21	88	150	390	51	0
Sebastopol	23	0		3	18	55	83	8	4
Selma	191	0		35	146	218	589	249	2
Shafter	58	1		13	37	209	251	85	8
Sierra Madre	13	0		1	11	58	65	6	0
Signal Hill	32	0		14	16	95	379	80	2
Simi Valley	132	3		31	89	344	1,233	132	16
Solana Beach	27	0		5	21	93	180	21	0
Soledad	73	0		15	52	105	100	47	0
Solvang	7	0		0	4	21	45	4	0
Sonoma	38	0		11	24	63	139	10	1
Sonora	13	0		6	5	74	213	17	11
South El Monte	88	1		35	48	117	208	119	4
South Gate	496	2		223	256	406	1,379	913	6
South Lake Tahoe	116	3		16	89	171	368	46	2
South Pasadena	29	0		16	10	170	347	51	20
South San Francisco	118	0		39	74	268	739	181	25
Stallion Springs	9	0		0	9	1	15	0	0
Stanton	112	1		45	58	137	409	156	3
St. Helena	6	0		0	6	25	45	2	0
Stockton	3,622	32		1,088	2,411	4,189	8,748	2,143	88
Suisun City	64	1		35	25	132	379	119	2
Sunnyvale	144	4		51	73	574	1,456	404	14

Table 8.   Offenses Known to Law Enforcement, by Selected State and City, 2013— continued

(Number.)

State/city	Violent crime	Murder and nonnegligent manslaughter	Rape (revised definition)[1]	Robbery	Aggravated assault	Burglary	Larceny-theft	Motor vehicle theft	Arson[2]
Susanville	83	2		11	67	148	215	21	6
Sutter Creek	4	0		0	4	15	40	3	1
Taft	60	0		0	58	84	210	37	0
Tehachapi	41	0		7	29	183	174	28	0
Temecula	91	3		39	38	711	1,897	240	9
Temple City	48	1		11	31	179	264	33	0
Thousand Oaks	139	0		42	90	291	1,222	91	12
Tiburon	2	0		0	2	19	68	0	0
Torrance	187	1		76	94	591	1,833	362	6
Tracy	152	0		57	88	353	1,648	235	12
Truckee	18	0		2	16	67	99	7	3
Tulare	430	6		77	332	909	1,333	371	23
Tulelake	1	0		0	1	4	4	0	0
Turlock	310	2		80	216	627	1,578	425	44
Tustin	100	1		36	57	213	1,147	113	5
Twentynine Palms	74	2		5	58	153	159	41	1
Ukiah	116	0		15	93	190	347	27	2
Union City	218	2		92	121	416	886	332	4
Upland	163	0		67	87	589	1,246	399	4
Vacaville	201	1		66	120	267	1,598	231	17
Vallejo	1,019	25		424	540	2,972	1,553	1,209	54
Ventura	262	6		99	136	745	3,025	257	20
Vernon	22	0		13	9	28	187	106	0
Victorville	651	9		202	404	1,461	2,067	637	20
Villa Park	6	0		0	6	30	56	0	3
Visalia	500	8		156	305	1,218	3,016	619	5
Vista	445	1		140	276	390	1,326	329	6
Walnut	37	0		10	26	220	207	36	0
Walnut Creek	78	0		31	43	364	1,634	163	1
Waterford	29	2		4	22	78	104	42	0
Watsonville	237	3		71	143	218	824	266	9
Weed	26	0		3	17	33	74	3	0
West Covina	231	1		106	122	615	2,254	501	2
West Hollywood	216	0		68	134	292	1,044	99	2
Westlake Village	11	0		3	7	40	102	6	1
Westminster	283	0		84	186	420	1,720	336	8
Westmorland	2	0		1	0	2	4	0	0
West Sacramento	205	1		98	90	380	894	209	9
Wheatland	0	0		0	0	16	28	5	0
Whittier	223	3		73	130	455	1,675	253	4
Wildomar	40	0		11	27	166	287	83	1
Williams	5	0		3	2	24	35	8	1
Willits	30	0		1	28	6	35	20	2
Willows	17	0		3	12	54	116	9	0
Windsor	105	0		8	88	52	209	8	4
Winters	8	1		3	4	27	76	12	2
Woodlake	10	1		1	7	39	79	16	0
Woodland	272	1		48	207	510	1,238	194	34
Yorba Linda	30	0		6	19	172	482	46	1
Yountville	1	0		0	0	17	34	6	0
Yreka	49	1		2	44	71	193	14	2
Yuba City	174	2		39	118	438	1,210	332	16
Yucaipa	107	0		31	69	262	534	130	13
Yucca Valley	86	3		15	61	141	234	54	2
Colorado									
Arvada	163	0	33	34	96	331	2,138	197	22
Aspen	14	0	5	0	9	17	286	11	0
Ault	0	0	0	0	0	0	0	2	0
Aurora	1,436	23	224	468	721	1,981	7,805	1,000	80
Avon	9	0	3	0	6	12	124	4	1
Basalt	2	0	0	0	2	11	50	2	0
Berthoud	3	0	1	1	1	13	28	4	0
Black Hawk	6	0	3	2	1	2	195	8	0
Blue River	1	0	0	1	0	0	4	0	0
Boulder	218	0	38	40	140	612	2,236	100	27
Bow Mar	0	0	0	0	0	3	7	0	0
Breckenridge	22	1	4	2	15	19	328	2	1
Broomfield	33	1	12	6	14	106	1,054	44	4
Brush	6	0	1	1	4	10	19	7	0
Buena Vista	0	0	0	0	0	0	4	1	0
Burlington	11	0	3	0	8	23	71	4	1
Campo	0	0	0	0	0	0	0	0	0
Canon City	80	0	3	7	70	94	482	19	7
Carbondale	11	0	6	0	5	5	80	2	1
Castle Rock	45	0	12	6	27	83	448	25	7
Cedaredge	0	0	0	0	0	13	16	0	0
Centennial	141	6	25	20	90	186	936	72	16

Table 8. Offenses Known to Law Enforcement, by Selected State and City, 2013— continued

(Number.)

State/city	Violent crime	Murder and nonnegligent manslaughter	Rape (revised definition)[1]	Robbery	Aggravated assault	Burglary	Larceny-theft	Motor vehicle theft	Arson[2]
Center	10	0	0	2	8	16	33	0	0
Central City	4	0	0	0	4	2	40	3	0
Cherry Hills Village	1	0	0	0	1	13	37	5	0
Colorado Springs	1,893	26	370	418	1,079	3,726	12,521	1,928	62
Columbine Valley	0	0	0	0	0	3	4	0	0
Commerce City	156	1	36	20	99	250	1,113	183	7
Cortez	18	2	4	0	12	16	321	11	1
Craig	18	0	6	0	12	47	182	9	2
Crested Butte	0	0	0	0	0	7	14	0	0
Cripple Creek	9	0	2	1	6	11	60	4	0
Dacono	1	0	0	0	1	0	0	1	0
Del Norte	1	0	0	0	1	4	28	1	0
Delta	25	0	16	1	8	52	303	25	1
Denver	4,087	40	514	1,132	2,401	4,918	15,306	3,487	96
Dillon	2	0	0	0	2	0	18	0	0
Durango	47	0	14	2	31	52	396	16	3
Eagle	8	0	3	0	5	2	73	2	1
Eaton	6	0	0	0	6	2	1	0	0
Edgewater	2	1	0	0	1	6	65	6	0
Elizabeth	1	0	1	0	0	1	18	0	0
Empire	2	0	0	0	2	2	2	0	0
Erie	11	0	1	1	9	15	84	4	0
Estes Park	5	0	0	0	5	4	40	0	0
Evans	69	0	2	5	62	80	237	24	5
Fairplay	3	0	1	0	2	3	8	0	0
Federal Heights	55	0	17	8	30	81	476	71	2
Firestone	2	0	1	0	1	6	83	2	0
Florence	3	0	0	1	2	5	19	3	1
Fort Collins	357	0	57	37	263	531	3,137	140	12
Fort Lupton	3	0	2	0	1	6	14	4	0
Fort Morgan	33	0	21	2	10	51	318	14	3
Fountain	78	0	19	7	52	127	457	35	5
Frederick	6	0	5	1	0	6	74	4	0
Frisco	8	0	0	0	8	3	36	3	0
Fruita	20	0	11	2	7	34	158	9	2
Garden City	19	0	2	2	15	4	25	7	0
Georgetown	2	0	0	0	2	2	3	2	0
Glendale	47	0	8	19	20	45	370	36	0
Glenwood Springs	26	0	4	3	19	50	353	24	0
Golden	33	1	5	6	21	43	334	25	3
Granby	5	0	1	0	4	6	47	1	0
Grand Junction	262	2	63	48	149	298	2,141	113	26
Greeley	491	2	74	68	347	475	2,558	186	26
Greenwood Village	19	0	0	4	15	63	388	15	3
Gunnison	17	1	3	0	13	24	156	9	2
Hayden	0	0	0	0	0	9	10	3	0
Hotchkiss	2	0	1	0	1	3	13	5	0
Hudson	6	0	2	0	4	1	24	5	0
Idaho Springs	16	0	3	0	13	8	48	1	0
Ignacio	0	0	0	0	0	0	0	0	0
Johnstown	4	0	2	1	1	11	69	4	0
Keenesburg	10	0	1	0	9	9	17	1	0
Kersey	6	0	2	0	4	8	17	0	0
Kiowa	1	0	1	0	0	0	0	0	0
Lafayette	50	0	12	5	33	58	374	17	8
La Junta	16	1	2	2	11	105	261	11	3
Lakeside	5	0	0	3	2	0	548	0	0
Lakewood	624	6	107	113	398	872	5,397	623	28
Lamar	15	1	3	2	9	60	203	5	0
La Salle	6	0	0	0	6	6	10	2	0
La Veta	5	2	2	0	1	4	7	0	0
Leadville	13	0	1	0	12	8	13	7	2
Limon	7	0	0	1	6	2	13	0	0
Littleton	44	1	17	6	20	213	959	106	7
Lone Tree	5	0	0	1	4	30	601	6	0
Longmont	226	0	76	19	131	266	1,634	109	64
Louisville	18	0	0	1	17	64	229	16	0
Loveland	150	1	42	19	88	184	1,423	58	17
Mancos	1	0	0	0	1	0	0	1	0
Manitou Springs	14	1	3	1	9	29	100	4	0
Mead	7	0	1	0	6	11	46	6	1
Meeker	1	0	0	0	1	5	17	0	1
Milliken	5	0	3	0	2	4	39	2	0
Minturn	1	0	0	0	1	0	4	1	0
Monte Vista	16	0	2	2	12	69	111	3	1
Montrose	48	0	1	4	43	79	496	14	3
Monument	5	0	3	0	2	32	139	2	1
Morrison	2	0	0	0	2	0	3	1	0

Table 8. Offenses Known to Law Enforcement, by Selected State and City, 2013— continued

(Number.)

State/city	Violent crime	Murder and nonnegligent manslaughter	Rape (revised definition)	Robbery	Aggravated assault	Burglary	Larceny-theft	Motor vehicle theft	Arson[2]
Mount Crested Butte	1	0	0	0	1	0	10	0	0
New Castle	3	0	2	0	1	6	40	3	0
Northglenn	95	0	22	10	63	144	824	135	4
Oak Creek	0	0	0	0	0	3	12	0	0
Pagosa Springs	10	0	3	0	7	15	54	6	1
Paonia	0	0	0	0	0	1	15	0	0
Parachute	6	0	1	1	4	11	10	1	0
Parker	53	0	20	4	29	74	427	21	10
Pueblo	1,011	2	165	211	633	1,900	5,168	528	30
Rangely	4	0	0	0	4	3	10	0	0
Rifle	36	5	13	0	18	36	258	10	0
Rocky Ford	2	0	1	0	1	7	8	0	0
Salida	11	0	0	0	11	30	180	8	1
Sheridan	13	0	1	3	9	36	357	45	1
Silt	5	0	1	1	3	9	51	2	0
Silverthorne	6	0	1	0	5	11	83	4	0
Snowmass Village	0	0	0	0	0	1	37	0	0
South Fork	0	0	0	0	0	0	0	0	0
Springfield	3	0	1	0	2	4	12	0	0
Steamboat Springs	37	0	6	0	31	29	184	14	2
Sterling	27	0	17	1	9	115	354	11	2
Stratton	1	0	0	1	0	8	6	2	0
Telluride	6	0	1	1	4	9	96	2	1
Thornton	331	5	67	53	206	431	2,513	352	15
Timnath	0	0	0	0	0	1	21	1	0
Trinidad	8	0	1	2	5	27	96	3	2
Vail	18	0	1	0	17	16	251	8	0
Walsenburg	18	0	3	6	9	20	72	0	2
Walsh	2	0	0	0	2	0	0	0	0
Westminster	214	2	26	52	134	382	2,283	322	15
Wheat Ridge	103	0	12	19	72	179	806	143	8
Windsor	6	0	0	0	6	38	131	3	2
Woodland Park	10	0	2	0	8	11	179	5	2
Wray	1	0	0	0	1	0	4	0	0
Yuma	2	0	1	0	1	1	14	1	0
Connecticut									
Ansonia	33	0	5	16	12	59	284	50	1
Avon	12	0	8	3	1	20	117	6	1
Berlin	14	0	5	4	5	41	225	11	1
Bethel	3	0	2	0	1	31	143	6	2
Bloomfield	46	1	9	10	26	51	391	22	1
Branford	16	0	0	3	13	55	539	40	1
Bridgeport	1,397	11		584	720	1,191	2,610	663	31
Bristol	82	2	15	45	20	310	963	127	6
Brookfield	9	0	0	0	9	16	141	5	0
Canton	2	0	2	0	0	15	56	1	0
Cheshire	2	0	0	1	1	28	166	10	1
Clinton	21	1	6	2	12	58	208	0	2
Coventry	9	1	1	2	5	39	101	6	0
Cromwell	9	0	0	8	1	16	257	4	0
Danbury	108	2		53	28	221	972	64	2
Darien	2	0	0	0	2	13	65	2	0
Derby	22	0	2	11	9	51	240	25	3
East Hampton	5	0	0	0	5	43	93	3	0
East Hartford	182	1	31	63	87	327	998	120	9
East Haven	29	0	3	12	14	95	558	101	2
Easton	1	0	0	0	1	15	14	1	0
East Windsor	16	1	3	8	4	48	260	9	4
Enfield	50	0		19	30	142	690	25	0
Fairfield	28	0	5	16	7	173	936	39	1
Farmington	20	0	3	11	6	47	591	20	0
Glastonbury	17	0	0	5	12	66	201	7	0
Granby	5	0	2	0	3	21	75	2	0
Greenwich	12	0	2	6	4	77	340	42	3
Groton	7	0	0	0	7	6	124	4	4
Groton Long Point	0	0		0	0	0	3	0	0
Groton Town	47	0	17	8	22	75	492	18	7
Guilford	5	0		0	4	28	218	7	0
Hamden	319	0	12	62	245	234	1,047	77	1
Hartford	1,473	23		557	840	981	3,416	639	45
Madison	2	0	1	0	1	16	96	0	0
Manchester	101	3		50	32	221	1,231	53	3
Meriden	175	0		85	71	385	972	146	5
Middlebury	1	0	0	0	1	10	53	5	0
Middletown	60	0	12	22	26	87	666	74	0
Milford	42	0		23	18	148	1,302	105	0
Monroe	1	0	0	1	0	25	123	9	0

Table 8. Offenses Known to Law Enforcement, by Selected State and City, 2013— continued

(Number.)

State/city	Violent crime	Murder and nonnegligent manslaughter	Rape (revised definition)[1]	Robbery	Aggravated assault	Burglary	Larceny-theft	Motor vehicle theft	Arson[2]
Naugatuck	33	0	10	13	10	200	507	60	0
New Britain	264	1		110	133	610	1,415	236	7
New Canaan	4	0	3	1	0	12	106	5	0
New Haven	1,643	19	76	770	778	1,082	4,233	753	15
Newington	23	0		9	8	78	613	34	0
New London	299	3	23	50	223	236	494	61	6
New Milford	27	0	5	5	17	9	286	13	5
Newtown	2	0	2	0	0	23	96	4	1
North Branford	5	0	2	0	3	14	144	12	1
North Haven	22	0	4	14	4	50	387	33	0
Norwalk	239	0	14	61	164	245	1,377	106	3
Norwich	130	1		29	86	306	644	52	7
Old Saybrook	7	0	2	0	5	11	98	3	1
Orange	10	0	0	9	1	25	290	14	0
Plainfield	15	0	2	3	10	6	87	16	4
Plainville	45	0		12	25	76	396	16	1
Plymouth	9	0	3	0	6	52	140	14	4
Portland	10	0		0	10	9	29	5	0
Putnam	26	0	5	2	19	29	141	7	3
Redding	2	0	0	0	2	13	32	0	0
Ridgefield	0	0	0	0	0	7	69	0	0
Rocky Hill	9	0		7	1	27	256	15	0
Seymour	16	0	4	6	6	69	146	17	0
Shelton	18	0	3	7	8	111	296	40	0
Simsbury	6	0	2	2	2	24	128	6	0
Southington	34	0	12	15	7	139	614	42	8
South Windsor	13	0		6	3	61	316	10	0
Stamford	334	1	28	160	145	354	1,435	149	5
Stonington	10	0	4	2	4	92	300	8	1
Stratford	74	0	8	41	25	251	1,042	136	2
Suffield	6	0	4	0	2	26	66	6	0
Thomaston	6	0	0	2	4	46	57	5	0
Torrington	59	0	15	11	33	94	728	34	1
Trumbull	9	0	0	9	0	84	433	31	0
Vernon	47	0	8	13	26	64	186	16	3
Wallingford	17	1	5	7	4	77	531	27	0
Waterbury	410	5		242	161	566	3,381	689	2
Waterford	41	0	0	6	35	72	421	7	0
Watertown	32	0	4	3	25	60	298	43	0
West Hartford	45	0	2	35	8	176	1,120	83	0
West Haven	290	2		68	220	178	1,095	243	0
Weston	1	0	1	0	0	13	24	0	0
Westport	2	0	0	1	1	47	198	11	0
Wethersfield	17	0	3	6	8	44	313	28	0
Willimantic	33	0	5	14	14	58	251	52	1
Wilton	0	0	0	0	0	26	81	6	0
Winchester	14	0	3	0	11	36	150	6	1
Windsor	25	1	3	14	7	48	353	18	1
Windsor Locks	18	0	7	7	4	42	175	11	0
Wolcott	4	0	2	2	0	43	220	34	1
Woodbridge	5	0	0	2	3	14	65	17	0
Delaware									
Bethany Beach	2	0	0	0	2	9	80	0	0
Blades	7	0	0	1	6	18	22	0	0
Bridgeville	9	0	0	1	8	8	40	1	0
Camden	7	0	1	3	3	9	268	2	0
Cheswold	6	0	1	1	4	2	12	2	0
Clayton	8	0	3	0	5	9	44	0	0
Dagsboro	4	0	0	1	3	4	32	1	0
Delaware City	4	0	1	0	3	18	36	3	0
Delmar	5	0	1	1	3	7	43	3	0
Dewey Beach	17	0	3	2	12	13	74	0	0
Dover	266	1	16	58	191	88	1,919	86	0
Elsmere	25	0	0	6	19	44	103	9	0
Felton	5	0	0	2	3	3	26	0	0
Fenwick Island	0	0	0	0	0	5	9	0	0
Georgetown	48	0	5	19	24	77	296	6	0
Greenwood	8	0	1	1	6	8	20	1	0
Harrington	25	0	3	7	15	32	128	3	0
Laurel	54	0	2	20	32	60	130	5	0
Lewes	6	0	0	0	6	14	58	3	0
Middletown	48	0	5	16	27	45	281	9	0
Milford	83	1	12	19	51	88	483	20	0
Millsboro	14	0	1	1	12	41	133	6	0
Milton	17	0	3	2	12	37	43	2	0
Newark	117	0	7	30	80	103	710	14	2
New Castle	19	0	1	4	14	51	237	5	0

Table 8.   Offenses Known to Law Enforcement, by Selected State and City, 2013— continued

(Number.)

State/city	Violent crime	Murder and nonnegligent manslaughter	Rape (revised definition)	Robbery	Aggravated assault	Burglary	Larceny-theft	Motor vehicle theft	Arson[2]
Newport	10	0	1	4	5	14	47	3	0
Ocean View	2	0	0	0	2	37	25	0	0
Rehoboth Beach	11	0	1	1	9	23	119	7	0
Seaford	75	0	12	14	49	92	439	9	0
Selbyville	11	0	0	1	10	18	50	2	0
Smyrna	69	0	7	18	44	52	267	9	0
Wilmington	1,161	19	24	453	665	960	2,387	371	2
Wyoming	5	0	2	1	2	6	15	1	0
District of Columbia									
Washington	7,880	103	393	3,660	3,724	3,314	23,108	3,147	
Florida									
Alachua	36	0	2	2	32	40	120	6	1
Altamonte Springs	150	0	8	37	105	300	1,180	84	3
Altha	1	0	0	0	1	3	0	0	0
Apalachicola	1	0	0	0	1	8	27	0	0
Apopka	178	1	11	57	109	231	1,202	94	6
Arcadia	82	2	3	9	68	43	123	6	4
Astatula	4	0	1	0	3	15	9	2	0
Atlantic Beach	61	0	6	13	42	89	245	19	0
Atlantis	9	0	0	1	8	7	0	0	0
Auburndale	55	0	13	12	30	137	454	18	1
Aventura	56	0	2	27	27	76	1,910	43	0
Bal Harbour Village	0	0	0	0	0	13	20	2	0
Bartow	93	1	5	16	71	157	812	37	2
Bay Harbor Islands	6	0	0	1	5	4	41	4	0
Belleair	2	0	0	1	1	22	61	4	1
Belleair Beach	4	0	0	0	4	9	11	1	0
Belleair Bluffs	5	0	1	0	4	10	32	0	0
Belle Glade	348	5	19	52	272	285	498	42	4
Belle Isle	18	0	3	4	11	71	124	4	0
Belleview	19	0	1	12	6	75	129	2	1
Biscayne Park	2	0	0	0	2	19	4	2	0
Blountstown	5	0	0	1	4	5	40	1	0
Boca Raton	165	4	8	54	99	464	1,744	94	2
Bonifay	10	0	0	3	7	2	45	4	0
Bowling Green	7	0	0	1	6	17	35	4	0
Boynton Beach	367	8	8	100	251	611	2,278	117	3
Bradenton	351	9	17	115	210	438	1,480	86	9
Bradenton Beach	1	0	1	0	0	5	31	1	0
Brooksville	71	0	2	14	55	67	242	7	1
Bunnell	62	0	0	11	51	43	57	18	0
Cape Coral	197	3	7	40	147	803	2,427	145	4
Carrabelle	6	0	0	0	6	6	8	3	0
Casselberry	151	0	13	35	103	195	901	42	3
Cedar Key	0	0	0	0	0	5	15	1	0
Chattahoochee	23	0	1	2	20	26	30	3	0
Chiefland	4	0	0	2	2	123	148	1	0
Chipley	15	0	1	1	13	29	118	7	0
Clearwater	618	4	50	177	387	851	3,284	181	14
Clermont	84	0	5	11	68	165	667	47	0
Clewiston	51	0	3	7	41	58	230	12	3
Cocoa	321	3	26	65	227	312	802	53	9
Cocoa Beach	83	1	5	13	64	79	613	14	1
Coconut Creek	80	0	10	26	44	278	1,132	68	0
Cooper City	50	0	3	11	36	105	436	17	0
Coral Gables	84	0	3	39	42	391	1,740	83	1
Coral Springs	237	0	24	99	114	389	2,067	109	9
Crescent City	19	0	0	5	14	17	46	2	0
Crestview	180	0	39	44	97	149	612	41	6
Cross City	7	0	1	1	5	16	42	2	0
Cutler Bay	135	1	10	55	69	226	1,382	86	1
Dade City	37	0	5	0	32	61	202	15	1
Dania	189	3	16	75	95	308	951	130	1
Davenport	5	0	0	1	4	34	36	3	1
Davie	306	1	26	93	186	651	2,480	262	7
Daytona Beach	799	4	57	195	543	745	2,912	367	5
Daytona Beach Shores	16	0	0	2	14	35	107	7	0
Deerfield Beach	305	2	28	105	170	624	1,606	156	2
De Funiak Springs	37	0	5	2	30	99	250	4	1
Deland	149	4	3	44	98	247	1,065	39	2
Delray Beach	487	0	29	147	311	588	2,308	211	6
Doral	79	0	5	18	56	196	1,993	118	2
Dunedin	92	0	12	14	66	185	565	21	2
Dunnellon	9	0	0	0	9	13		1	0
Eatonville	30	1	1	2	26	29	46	13	0
Edgewater	21	1	0	3	17	149	395	32	0

Table 8.   Offenses Known to Law Enforcement, by Selected State and City, 2013— continued

(Number.)

State/city	Violent crime	Murder and nonnegligent manslaughter	Rape (revised definition)[1]	Robbery	Aggravated assault	Burglary	Larceny-theft	Motor vehicle theft	Arson[2]
Edgewood	1	0	0	1	0	24	27	2	0
El Portal	15	1	0	7	7	65	23	9	0
Eustis	52	0	2	9	41	133	485	15	1
Fellsmere	8	0	0	1	7	21	62	6	0
Fernandina Beach	36	0	3	7	26	61	227	7	0
Flagler Beach	16	0	2	3	11	18	63	7	0
Florida City	345	1	2	137	205	317	981	58	2
Fort Lauderdale	1,456	13	73	701	669	2,654	6,429	567	30
Fort Myers	752	10	45	185	512	392	1,726	161	16
Fort Pierce	588	7	29	113	439	624	1,560	114	13
Fort Walton Beach	56	2	3	14	37	93	535	33	1
Fruitland Park	13	0	1	3	9	48	132	6	2
Gainesville	806	6	62	155	583	742	4,000	244	13
Golden Beach	1	0	0	0	1	7	6	0	0
Graceville	4	2	0	0	2	5	18	3	0
Greenacres City	184	2	7	65	110	316	967	85	2
Green Cove Springs	49	0	9	6	34	49	162	10	1
Gretna	9	0	0	0	9	11	2	0	0
Gulf Breeze	3	0	0	0	3	16	80	2	1
Gulfport	48	0	4	17	27	116	362	28	10
Gulf Stream	0	0	0	0	0	0	15	0	0
Haines City	64	1	6	12	45	157	494	18	0
Hallandale	279	6	17	91	165	402	1,322	140	2
Havana	3	0	0	0	3	5	23	1	0
Hialeah	774	13	41	231	489	763	5,079	708	12
Hialeah Gardens	42	0	1	13	28	66	679	55	0
Highland Beach	1	0	0	0	1	4	28	0	0
High Springs	21	0	2	3	16	53	106	4	0
Hillsboro Beach	0	0	0	0	0	0	20	1	0
Holly Hill	80	0	7	25	48	162	413	51	2
Hollywood	720	16	63	253	388	1,500	4,478	572	6
Holmes Beach	5	0	2	0	3	13	92	6	0
Homestead	917	2	32	342	541	900	2,223	151	10
Howey-in-the-Hills	3	0	0	0	3	1	1	1	0
Hypoluxo	9	0	3	1	5	9	35	1	0
Indialantic	3	0	0	0	3	20	41	0	0
Indian Creek Village	0	0	0	0	0	0	0	0	0
Indian Harbour Beach	1	0	0	1	0	37	123	4	0
Indian River Shores	0	0	0	0	0	3	14	0	0
Indian Rocks Beach	10	0	1	0	9	14	79	2	0
Indian Shores	4	0	0	0	4	6	48	0	0
Interlachen	4	0	0	1	3	8	53	3	1
Jacksonville	5,246	93	452	1,424	3,277	7,069	24,361	1,577	97
Jacksonville Beach	113	0	21	24	68	115	735	40	6
Jasper	11	0	0	2	9	30	24	6	0
Jennings	3	0	0	3	0	4	4	0	0
Juno Beach	2	0	1	1	0	15	61	1	0
Jupiter	127	0	7	36	84	163	864	67	2
Jupiter Inlet Colony	0	0	0	0	0	0	2	1	0
Jupiter Island	0	0	0	0	0	3	8	2	0
Kenneth City	29	0	4	7	18	19	115	12	1
Key Biscayne	4	0	0	0	4	15	226	19	0
Key Colony Beach	0	0	0	0	0	3	8	0	0
Key West	179	0	20	37	122	263	1,111	101	3
Kissimmee	542	3	36	132	371	802	2,042	119	2
Lady Lake	23	0	0	6	17	37	151	14	0
Lake Alfred	17	0	1	4	12	65	89	11	3
Lake City	188	3	2	29	154	216	801	26	4
Lake Clarke Shores	5	0	0	1	4	28	39	2	0
Lake Hamilton	2	0	0	0	2	17	46	16	0
Lake Helen	5	1	2	0	2	17	48	4	0
Lakeland	460	7	52	143	258	1,130	4,082	198	4
Lake Mary	17	0	2	3	12	66	212	12	0
Lake Park	67	1	9	24	33	96	680	55	1
Lake Placid	9	0	2	2	5	16	99	6	0
Lake Wales	48	1	3	15	29	186	396	21	1
Lake Worth	459	4	45	171	239	584	1,338	140	18
Lantana	75	0	6	26	43	102	399	18	0
Largo	352	3	47	94	208	650	2,134	140	6
Lauderdale-by-the-Sea	11	0	1	3	7	37	83	6	1
Lauderdale Lakes	336	5	31	108	192	539	1,076	95	3
Lauderhill	459	6	21	172	260	946	1,609	169	13
Lawtey	0	0	0	0	0	3	2	0	0
Leesburg	172	0	8	31	133	239	680	33	2
Lighthouse Point	8	0	1	1	6	63	188	11	0
Live Oak	70	0	1	16	53	186	139	12	2
Longboat Key	5	0	0	1	4	18	57	0	0
Longwood	69	0	2	10	57	101	260	19	0

Table 8.   Offenses Known to Law Enforcement, by Selected State and City, 2013— continued

(Number.)

State/city	Violent crime	Murder and nonnegligent manslaughter	Rape (revised definition)	Robbery	Aggravated assault	Burglary	Larceny-theft	Motor vehicle theft	Arson[2]
Lynn Haven	63	0	3	4	56	61	460	14	0
Madeira Beach	30	0	4	2	24	27	176	1	0
Madison	51	0	2	10	39	66	155	2	0
Maitland	23	0	1	5	17	139	296	28	0
Manalapan	2	0	0	0	2	3	20	0	0
Mangonia Park	79	0	7	24	48	39	164	16	0
Marco Island	4	0	0	0	4	31	145	1	1
Margate	123	1	1	35	86	409	694	57	3
Marianna	77	0	2	13	62	64	200	5	0
Mascotte	16	0	1	1	14	49	95	4	0
Medley	6	0	0	1	5	20	177	28	0
Melbourne	657	6	61	136	454	741	2,526	110	18
Melbourne Beach	4	0	0	0	4	23	15	1	0
Melbourne Village	0	0	0	0	0	1	17	0	0
Mexico Beach	8	0	1	1	6	6	33	2	0
Miami	4,945	71	96	2,216	2,562	3,993	15,021	1,914	89
Miami Beach	919	4	53	377	485	950	8,425	376	6
Miami Gardens	921	23	15	322	561	1,128	3,054	478	17
Miami Lakes	30	0	4	10	16	86	504	51	0
Miami Shores	42	0	2	30	10	126	345	20	0
Miami Springs	31	0	6	7	18	79	401	38	0
Milton	25	0	6	6	13	128	182	7	1
Minneola	24	0	1	3	20	75	123	7	1
Miramar	476	4	37	162	273	1,070	1,862	232	14
Monticello	19	0	1	1	17	14	9	0	1
Mount Dora	55	1	6	8	40	89	309	13	1
Naples	39	0	9	7	23	101	438	12	0
Neptune Beach	14	0	2	1	11	39	167	10	0
New Port Richey	115	1	5	32	77	205	478	31	6
New Smyrna Beach	104	0	5	20	79	240	735	36	1
Niceville	19	0	0	2	17	38	128	8	0
North Bay Village	8	0	1	2	5	20	98	14	0
North Lauderdale	209	1	13	67	128	436	677	56	2
North Miami	540	7	30	234	269	590	1,862	286	11
North Miami Beach	322	4	24	152	142	544	1,017	116	13
North Palm Beach	14	0	0	6	8	45	138	8	1
North Port	108	0	26	15	67	264	687	13	1
North Redington Beach	1	0	0	1	0	1	16	1	0
Oakland	19	0	1	0	18	33	58	3	0
Oakland Park	296	2	17	112	165	609	1,408	113	4
Ocala	332	6	25	92	209	530	2,306	53	9
Ocean Ridge	8	0	0	3	5	13	28	2	0
Ocoee	162	2	18	43	99	280	882	58	3
Okeechobee	21	0	0	1	20	31	362	18	0
Oldsmar	30	0	4	5	21	48	368	10	0
Opa Locka	495	11	17	125	342	348	764	193	4
Orange City	15	1	0	2	12	49	382	12	0
Orange Park	46	1	6	8	31	51	197	8	0
Orlando	2,316	17	126	573	1,600	3,485	11,984	1,020	29
Ormond Beach	132	0	10	17	105	259	1,055	72	2
Oviedo	57	0	8	6	43	120	345	14	0
Pahokee	29	1	0	3	25	17	57	4	1
Palatka	87	0	6	26	55	178	483	23	0
Palm Bay	451	3	21	43	384	517	1,326	115	14
Palm Beach	6	0	0	1	5	32	119	6	0
Palm Beach Gardens	70	0	6	27	37	216	1,246	54	2
Palm Beach Shores	1	0	0	0	1	12	36	5	0
Palmetto	125	1	15	22	87	125	398	14	1
Palmetto Bay	38	2	2	15	19	140	571	33	0
Palm Springs	143	0	5	36	102	287	821	66	2
Panama City	322	3	10	65	244	377	1,803	119	6
Panama City Beach	99	0	19	32	48	222	1,015	1	3
Parker	20	0	1	2	17	47	94	8	0
Parkland	22	0	3	3	16	58	178	6	0
Pembroke Park	51	0	5	20	26	151	244	32	2
Pembroke Pines	275	0	11	87	177	775	3,042	206	4
Pensacola	389	3	27	69	290	466	2,035	112	7
Perry	128	1	6	3	118	47	133	4	5
Pinellas Park	252	1	21	53	177	418	2,176	90	5
Plantation	311	2	17	124	168	711	2,256	149	0
Plant City	185	2	7	36	140	344	1,117	113	3
Pompano Beach	819	7	64	273	475	1,220	3,580	329	13
Ponce Inlet	1	0	0	0	1	6	35	2	0
Port Orange	51	1	0	7	43	240	1,232	88	0
Port Richey	26	0	1	5	20	26	355	7	1
Port St. Joe	23	0	1	0	22	34	17	1	0
Port St. Lucie	303	1	21	40	241	722	1,666	73	4
Punta Gorda	21	0	2	2	17	36	256	4	0

Table 8.   Offenses Known to Law Enforcement, by Selected State and City, 2013— continued

(Number.)

State/city	Violent crime	Murder and nonnegligent manslaughter	Rape (revised definition)[1]	Robbery	Aggravated assault	Burglary	Larceny-theft	Motor vehicle theft	Arson[2]
Quincy	46	1	2	7	36	78	235	4	2
Redington Beaches	3	0	0	0	3	5	12	0	0
Riviera Beach	340	6	9	59	266	326	560	88	4
Rockledge	63	0	15	8	40	116	360	14	3
Royal Palm Beach	116	0	12	39	65	119	832	36	2
Safety Harbor	29	0	5	1	23	56	172	5	0
Sanford	447	5	36	132	274	994	2,202	236	0
Sanibel	5	0	0	1	4	53	148	4	0
Sarasota	413	4	31	151	227	564	2,023	155	7
Satellite Beach	34	0	0	2	32	38	116	4	0
Sea Ranch Lakes	1	0	0	0	1	4	9	1	0
Sebastian	55	1	7	5	42	77	373	10	0
Sebring	57	2	2	9	44	123	378	12	5
Seminole	43	0	2	8	33	48	438	11	1
Sewall's Point	0	0	0	0	0	7	13	0	0
Shalimar	0	0	0	0	0	3	4	2	0
South Bay	73	0	2	16	55	78	76	3	3
South Daytona	39	2	0	7	30	112	373	43	1
South Miami	93	1	2	40	50	149	734	19	0
South Palm Beach	0	0	0	0	0	5	5	1	0
South Pasadena	4	0	1	0	3	12	102	3	0
Southwest Ranches	9	0	3	2	4	42	98	14	0
Springfield	43	1	4	8	30	76	209	9	1
Starke	43	1	4	5	33	11	174	7	1
St. Augustine	99	0	6	19	74	91	703	32	1
St. Augustine Beach	7	0	0	2	5	65	94	6	0
St. Cloud	139	2	9	18	110	222	717	21	2
St. Pete Beach	45	0	4	5	36	34	322	20	0
St. Petersburg	2,379	15	155	634	1,575	2,742	9,315	1,124	51
Stuart	54	0	5	11	38	66	568	19	0
Sunny Isles Beach	34	0	5	8	21	48	440	23	0
Sunrise	265	2	22	112	129	773	2,392	124	4
Surfside	7	1	0	1	5	14	93	9	0
Sweetwater	68	0	3	16	49	58	813	59	2
Tallahassee	1,398	11	160	387	840	2,082	5,594	440	7
Tamarac	200	1	14	71	114	444	724	79	2
Tampa	2,097	28	78	580	1,411	1,950	6,320	553	81
Tarpon Springs	100	1	9	24	66	115	549	29	1
Tavares	55	1	0	3	51	102	150	28	1
Temple Terrace	71	0	6	19	46	148	484	23	0
Tequesta	7	1	0	2	4	39	42	2	0
Titusville	328	3	32	72	221	545	903	156	6
Treasure Island	15	0	0	1	14	39	201	9	0
Trenton	5	0	0	0	5	13	18	0	0
Umatilla	14	0	0	1	13	23	39	3	0
Valparaiso	5	0	0	1	4	8	36	4	0
Venice	37	0	3	4	30	95	338	13	1
Vero Beach	48	1	9	6	32	103	388	8	3
Village of Pinecrest	16	0	0	4	12	92	464	24	2
Virginia Gardens	5	0	0	1	4	2	21	6	0
Waldo	17	0	0	1	16	5	17	2	0
Wauchula	20	0	0	3	17	53	97	7	0
Webster	11	0	0	2	9	5	15	1	0
Wellington	126	0	17	27	82	260	900	99	1
West Melbourne	48	1	1	11	35	72	534	16	0
West Miami	8	0	0	1	7	10	62	4	0
Weston	47	2	5	4	36	78	395	16	4
West Palm Beach	701	15	29	281	376	1,024	3,453	386	21
West Park	109	2	9	36	62	276	351	78	5
White Springs	6	0	0	2	4	11	8	3	0
Wildwood	36	1	1	9	25	55	118	8	1
Williston	15	0	0	4	11	18	61	3	1
Wilton Manors	79	0	3	39	37	157	420	31	0
Windermere	0	0	0	0	0	1	37	0	0
Winter Garden	178	2	13	25	138	226	1,135	51	0
Winter Haven	215	2	24	46	143	353	1,180	44	4
Winter Park	100	1	9	17	73	242	782	42	5
Winter Springs	51	0	5	7	39	86	268	15	4
Zephyrhills	47	0	3	9	35	158	815	29	0
Georgia									
Abbeville	3	0		2	1	3	16	3	0
Adairsville	13	0		1	12	15	31	6	0
Adel	18	0		5	8	64	121	4	0
Adrian	0	0		0	0	0	2	0	0
Alapaha	5	0		1	4	0	6	0	0
Albany	749	8		183	537	1,319	3,169	173	19
Alma	24	0		8	14	45	158	5	

Table 8.   Offenses Known to Law Enforcement, by Selected State and City, 2013— continued

(Number.)

State/city	Violent crime	Murder and nonnegligent manslaughter	Rape (revised definition)[1]	Robbery	Aggravated assault	Burglary	Larceny-theft	Motor vehicle theft	Arson[2]
Alpharetta	47	2		23	20	128	1,074	26	2
Alto	0	0		0	0	16	10	2	
Americus	231	0		40	191	605	613	28	1
Aragon	3	0		0	3	8	40	3	0
Arcade	4	1		0	3	4	29	2	
Arlington	61	0		3	58	52	71	1	
Ashburn	40	2		5	31	55	121	8	
Athens-Clarke County	404	2		125	240	967	2,912	195	18
Atlanta	5,517	84		2,363	2,965	5,938	17,158	4,432	71
Attapulgus	0	0		0	0	1	1	0	0
Austell	40	0		4	34	37	139	15	0
Bainbridge	88	1		7	79	128	430	10	
Baldwin	3	0		0	1	14	30	5	0
Ball Ground	1	0		0	1	4	8	0	0
Barnesville	9	0		2	7	41	275	11	
Baxley	15	0		2	13	84	201	4	0
Berlin	0	0		0	0	0	0	0	0
Blackshear	14	0		3	8	27	118	5	0
Blairsville	0	0		0	0	0	21	0	0
Blakely	32	0		4	28	57	143	5	0
Bloomingdale	3	0		0	2	18	39	5	
Blue Ridge	3	0		0	3	5	18	0	
Blythe	0	0		0	0	5	8	1	0
Boston	11	0		1	9	11	36	1	0
Bowdon	16	0		0	16	13	58	2	0
Braselton	13	0		4	4	24	93	10	0
Braswell	0	0		0	0	0	0	0	0
Bremen	11	0		1	8	21	145	7	0
Brooklet	3	0		0	3	5	6	0	0
Brunswick	162	3		38	117	331	732	47	3
Buchanan	5	0		0	5	11	30	2	
Buena Vista	8	0		0	8	18	55	2	0
Butler	5	0		0	5	6	16	2	1
Byron	8	0		0	8	50	89	11	0
Cairo	29	1		7	13	43	172	7	1
Calhoun	44	0		7	30	104	662	18	0
Canton	23	0		11	11	59	326	21	
Carrollton	124	1		31	78	147	895	48	3
Cartersville	51	0		8	40	164	718	45	
Cave Spring	2	0		0	2	3	12	3	0
Cedartown	53	0		21	30	211	689	20	0
Centerville	19	0		11	8	88	323	5	4
Chatsworth	10	0		1	9	27	127	8	
Chattahoochee Hills	0	0		0	0	15	14	10	
Chickamauga	6	0		0	6	12	52	4	
Clarkston	67	0		53	13	139	146	27	
Claxton	8	1		3	3	43	104	1	0
Clayton	14	0		0	14	28	64	5	
Cleveland	14	0		1	10	38	168	0	0
Climax	0	0		0	0	0	0	0	0
Cochran	14	0		3	10	62	181	4	0
College Park	324	4		155	152	402	993	269	5
Colquitt	8	0		2	6	19	49	1	0
Columbus	1,022	22		481	483	3,355	8,012	1,108	37
Commerce	24	0		1	23	27	84	4	0
Conyers	103	4		34	58	163	831	52	6
Coolidge	0	0		0	0	3	1	0	0
Cordele	87	0		31	47	215	618	14	1
Cornelia	6	0		0	5	16	163	7	0
Covington	47	1		11	31	143	592	26	0
Cuthbert	2	0		2	0	19	36	0	0
Dalton	66	0		12	47	201	1,063	55	4
Danielsville	0	0		0	0	1	19	2	0
Dawson	30	0		3	26	85	0	0	0
Decatur	40	1		28	11	127	528	35	0
Demorest	0	0		0	0	5	14	2	0
Dillard	0	0		0	0	1	6	0	
Doerun	6	0		1	4	18	25	0	0
Donalsonville	7	0		2	5	15	90	1	0
Doraville	44	0		20	22	75	301	31	
Douglas	100	2		26	57	95	763	25	0
Douglasville	213	1		46	154	238	1,651	110	11
Dublin	85	2		30	48	235	915	36	0
Duluth	42	1		19	18	91	545	19	
Dunwoody	57	1		30	24	249	1,521	68	
East Ellijay	7	0		1	6	3	84	0	0
Eastman	56	0		9	43	83	358	9	0
East Point	420	12		252	144	938	2,221	746	

Table 8.   Offenses Known to Law Enforcement, by Selected State and City, 2013— continued

(Number.)

State/city	Violent crime	Murder and nonnegligent manslaughter	Rape (revised definition)	Robbery	Aggravated assault	Burglary	Larceny-theft	Motor vehicle theft	Arson[2]
Eatonton	36	0		3	32	43	170	4	
Edison	0	0		0	0	5	12	0	
Elberton	59	0		4	54	46	259	4	
Ellaville	9	0		0	7	4	13	0	0
Ellijay	1	0		0	1	7	14	1	
Emerson	3	0		0	3	9	45	4	0
Ephesus	0	0		0	0	0	0	0	0
Eton	0	0		0	0	2	16	0	0
Euharlee	1	0		0	1	13	106	8	0
Fairburn	52	0		23	24	114	343	52	3
Fairmount	1	0		0	0	2	3	0	0
Fayetteville	30	0		20	10	66	422	25	0
Fitzgerald	52	1		13	32	189	295	16	
Flowery Branch	1	0		0	1	15	75	5	
Folkston	9	0		1	8	18	48	7	0
Forsyth	16	0		4	11	26	195	11	0
Fort Oglethorpe	28	0		2	26	58	618	19	0
Fort Valley	104	1		10	90	123	300	13	0
Franklin	4	0		0	2	7	17	0	0
Franklin Springs	0	0		0	0	3	6	0	0
Gainesville	115	1		39	54	209	1,230	66	4
Garden City	159	0		37	122	156	237	31	
Glennville	15	0		3	12	30	107	1	
Glenwood	3	1		2	0	0	2	2	0
Gordon	0	0		0	0	1	20	1	0
Gray	3	0		0	3	9	55	4	
Greensboro	22	0		1	20	26	132	4	0
Greenville	0	0		0	0	10	15	3	0
Griffin	186	3		59	110	373	1,464	45	1
Grovetown	4	0		3	0	54	142	17	0
Hahira	3	0		0	3	8	28	10	
Hampton	9	0		3	6	29	79	5	0
Hapeville	74	4		40	30	60	384	88	
Harlem	3	0		0	2	7	28	3	
Harrison	0	0		0	0	0	0	0	0
Hazlehurst	7	1		4	2	25	152	3	0
Helen	6	0		0	6	9	51	2	0
Helena	5	0		3	2	7	21	1	
Hinesville	120	3		42	67	351	1,035	58	9
Hiram	9	0		3	6	19	425	8	0
Hoboken	1	0		0	1	3	2	1	0
Holly Springs	4	0		0	3	24	63	11	0
Homeland	0	0		0	0	0	0	0	0
Homerville	20	0		4	16	67	128	7	0
Jackson	20	0		3	16	36	51	8	0
Jefferson	11	2		1	6	20	121	8	0
Jeffersonville	0	0		0	0	4	5	0	0
Jesup	53	0		19	33	117	694	15	0
Johns Creek	37	4		11	18	136	468	15	1
Jonesboro	19	0		9	10	65	146	14	0
Kennesaw	34	0		7	27	72	415	16	0
Kingsland	84	0		5	75	100	353	15	1
Lafayette	16	0		0	15	54	343	14	
Lagrange	99	4		43	47	346	1,308	80	6
Lakeland	10	1		1	6	25	38	10	0
Lake Park	2	0		0	2	3	10	1	0
Lavonia	20	0		2	18	13	127	2	0
Lawrenceville	65	0		38	20	161	645	65	2
Lilburn	39	1		16	22	67	618	28	0
Lincolnton	7	0		2	5	4	37	1	
Locust Grove	10	0		4	6	37	286	10	0
Loganville	16	0		1	15	38	250	16	2
Lookout Mountain	0	0		0	0	5	13	1	
Lumber City	4	0		1	3	7	11	1	0
Lumpkin	0	0		0	0	0	0	0	0
Macon	583	18		231	288	1,993	4,318	489	43
Madison	15	0		4	11	57	161	5	0
Manchester	18	0		2	13	42	119	14	1
Marietta	450	5		127	306	457	1,861	181	2
McCaysville	2	0		0	1	4	22	1	
McDonough	56	2		23	25	104	691	42	2
McIntyre	2	0		0	2	3	19	0	0
McRae	17	0		1	16	25	44	2	0
Meigs	6	0		0	6	8	16	0	
Midville	0	0		0	0	0	0	0	0
Midway	10	0		3	6	22	45	4	0
Milledgeville	61	1		23	33	219	629	28	2
Milton	8	0		1	3	37	382	0	0

Table 8.   Offenses Known to Law Enforcement, by Selected State and City, 2013— continued

(Number.)

State/city	Violent crime	Murder and nonnegligent manslaughter	Rape (revised definition)[1]	Robbery	Aggravated assault	Burglary	Larceny-theft	Motor vehicle theft	Arson[2]
Monroe	97	1		22	73	384	636	37	
Montezuma	19	0		1	18	59	93	7	1
Morrow	33	0		17	14	58	764	33	0
Moultrie	92	2		33	51	238	736	27	
Mount Airy	3	0		0	3	2	13	0	
Nashville	27	0		5	20	81	186	5	1
Nelson	1	0		0	1	3	6	1	
Newnan	117	1		28	82	213	830	39	2
Newton	2	1		0	1	1	9	0	
Nicholls	14	0		3	11	13	22	1	0
Norcross	80	1		40	31	157	481	59	
Oakwood	12	0		3	9	28	256	9	0
Ocilla	23	0		7	13	24	103	10	
Oglethorpe	34	0		11	23	87	104	2	
Oxford	0	0		0	0	14	18	0	
Patterson	0	0		0	0	0	4	0	
Pavo	9	0		0	9	1	2	0	0
Peachtree City	23	0		6	16	25	375	39	3
Pelham	5	0		1	4	19	141	4	0
Pembroke	4	0		0	4	11	40	0	
Perry	35	0		7	26	62	175	14	
Pine Mountain	4	0		0	2	9	43	1	0
Pooler	35	0		16	15	150	388	26	
Porterdale	24	0		0	24	13	45	6	
Port Wentworth	8	0		1	7	28	77	13	1
Poulan	2	0		0	2	5	18	1	
Powder Springs	150	1		8	133	206	501	21	
Quitman	46	1		8	35	60	152	6	
Ray City	0	0		0	0	0	3	0	0
Reynolds	0	0		0	0	0	0	0	0
Richmond Hill	10	1		4	5	39	170	9	0
Ringgold	7	0		2	4	16	166	8	0
Riverdale	81	0		40	41	170	590	66	
Rochelle	1	0		0	0	20	26	0	0
Rockmart	31	1		7	21	91	328	7	1
Rome	247	2		69	157	413	1,681	84	21
Rossville	76	0		12	61	155	487	66	
Roswell	144	1		72	54	476	1,556	75	
Sandersville	29	1		15	11	51	232	6	1
Sandy Springs	186	6		105	61	526	2,063	150	7
Savannah-Chatham Metropolitan	851	30		414	358	2,125	5,608	725	30
Screven	2	0		0	2	3	12	2	0
Senoia	2	0		0	1	11	32	2	0
Shiloh	0	0		0	0	1	0	0	0
Sky Valley	0	0		0	0	3	0	0	0
Smyrna	183	2		72	98	360	1,237	145	
Snellville	34	0		10	23	56	727	37	4
Social Circle	18	0		2	16	62	140	5	
Sparks	10	0		2	8	31	62	3	0
Sparta	13	0		0	13	15	18	4	
Springfield	1	0		1	0	14	46	2	0
Statesboro	88	2		49	26	263	1,061	37	3
Statham	24	0		0	24	103	307	33	
St. Marys	75	0		6	66	103	409	10	2
Summerville	0	0		0	0	0	46	4	
Suwanee	15	0		8	5	134	245	12	0
Sylvania	17	0		8	9	28	91	4	
Talbotton	1	0		1	0	8	16	1	0
Tallulah Falls	0	0		0	0	0	1	0	0
Tennille	11	0		3	8	20	49	1	
Thomasville	88	0		25	54	281	863	22	3
Thunderbolt	10	2		1	6	21	58	9	
Tifton	150	0		56	81	258	975	22	8
Tignall	1	0		0	1	0	3	0	0
Toccoa	57	2		9	45	40	502	6	2
Trenton	1	0		0	1	2	13	4	
Trion	13	0		1	12	10	29	2	
Tunnel Hill	0	0		0	0	1	22	0	
Tybee Island	0	0		0	0	9	62	1	0
Tyrone	5	0		0	5	8	87	4	0
Union City	205	3		116	79	409	1,183	211	5
Union Point	8	0		1	7	24	60	2	0
Vidalia	92	4		19	68	140	550	20	
Villa Rica	43	2		11	26	70	544	25	0
Walthourville	11	0		0	10	59	96	5	
Warm Springs	0	0		0	0	7	16	0	
Warner Robins	364	4		138	205	854	3,191	168	7
Warrenton	12	0		2	10	21	51	0	

Table 8.   Offenses Known to Law Enforcement, by Selected State and City, 2013— continued

(Number.)

State/city	Violent crime	Murder and nonnegligent manslaughter	Rape (revised definition)[1]	Robbery	Aggravated assault	Burglary	Larceny-theft	Motor vehicle theft	Arson[2]
Washington	31	0		0	31	23	92	8	
Watkinsville	1	0		0	1	13	56	0	0
Waverly Hall	0	0		0	0	3	4	1	0
Waycross	64	1		27	35	114	817	15	6
Waynesboro	32	0		7	23	32	90	12	0
West Point	21	0		9	12	35	95	8	0
Willacoochee	4	0		1	3	14	23	0	0
Winder	59	0		11	42	111	489	39	
Winterville	0	0		0	0	4	7	0	
Woodbury	2	0		0	2	4	18	1	
Woodstock	20	0		6	11	47	534	13	0
Wrens	10	0		1	7	8	71	0	0
Idaho									
Aberdeen	2	0	1	0	1	1	12	3	0
American Falls	4	0	1	1	2	10	46	2	0
Bellevue	0	0	0	0	0	11	7	1	0
Blackfoot	23	1	6	1	15	83	346	20	2
Boise	600	3	123	45	429	825	3,703	213	48
Bonners Ferry	13	0	0	1	12	10	42	0	0
Buhl	7	0	1	0	6	16	52	0	2
Caldwell	133	0	19	6	108	190	892	46	5
Cascade	0	0	0	0	0	3	21	1	0
Challis	0	0	0	0	0	0	6	0	0
Chubbuck	34	0	2	3	29	39	553	11	1
Coeur d'Alene	257	0	53	20	184	359	1,259	117	8
Cottonwood	1	0	0	0	1	0	7	0	0
Emmett	8	1	0	0	7	40	48	0	0
Filer	3	0	1	0	2	6	2	2	0
Fruitland	5	0	0	1	4	26	47	7	2
Garden City	65	0	21	5	39	63	347	15	7
Gooding	3	0	1	0	2	15	34	2	0
Grangeville	4	0	0	0	4	17	37	2	0
Hagerman	0	0	0	0	0	0	7	1	0
Hailey	14	1	1	0	12	29	42	1	0
Heyburn	3	0	0	0	3	18	22	2	0
Homedale	9	0	1	0	8	16	35	1	0
Idaho Falls	124	0	31	19	74	304	1,210	109	6
Jerome	30	0	7	3	20	59	128	18	0
Kamiah	3	0	0	1	2	5	11	0	0
Kellogg	8	0	2	0	6	30	34	9	0
Ketchum	3	0	0	0	3	5	44	2	0
Kimberly	1	0	0	0	1	16	10	0	0
Lewiston	49	0	8	8	33	264	853	52	1
McCall	15	0	3	1	11	19	62	1	0
Meridian	115	0	33	5	77	193	812	25	17
Montpelier	5	0	0	0	5	9	50	1	0
Moscow	25	1	8	2	14	116	607	26	3
Mountain Home	39	1	11	0	27	24	175	3	3
Nampa	202	1	42	16	143	434	1,319	123	15
Orofino	7	0	1	0	6	23	43	0	0
Osburn	3	1	0	0	2	8	5	2	0
Parma	0	0	0	0	0	9	9	2	0
Payette	19	0	5	0	14	69	166	5	0
Pinehurst	2	0	1	0	1	14	7	1	0
Pocatello	195	0	21	27	147	278	1,415	83	7
Ponderay	1	0	0	0	1	9	66	3	0
Post Falls	71	1	9	5	56	100	650	53	1
Preston	5	0	1	0	4	11	36	2	0
Priest River	1	0	0	0	1	14	21	4	0
Rathdrum	9	0	1	0	8	56	86	8	0
Rexburg	7	0	0	0	7	29	157	7	0
Rigby	5	0	0	0	5	19	51	3	0
Rupert	11	0	0	1	10	31	102	3	1
Salmon	8	0	1	0	7	11	25	4	0
Sandpoint	19	0	0	0	19	65	265	5	0
Shelley	1	0	0	0	1	11	32	0	0
Shoshone	13	0	1	0	12	2	2	0	0
Soda Springs	14	0	0	1	13	18	19	0	0
Spirit Lake	6	0	2	0	4	6	17	1	0
St. Anthony	4	0	0	0	4	5	21	0	0
St. Maries	9	0	0	1	8	10	18	4	0
Sun Valley	8	0	0	0	8	1	8	1	0
Twin Falls	118	0	18	10	90	196	1,073	51	7
Wendell	6	0	1	0	5	6	19	1	0
Wilder	3	0	0	0	3	6	11	0	0
Illinois									

Table 8.   Offenses Known to Law Enforcement, by Selected State and City, 2013— continued

(Number.)

State/city	Violent crime	Murder and nonnegligent manslaughter	Rape (revised definition)[1]	Robbery	Aggravated assault	Burglary	Larceny-theft	Motor vehicle theft	Arson[2]
Addison	40	1		5	26	97	527	16	5
Albany	0	0		0	0	0	5	0	0
Albers	0	0		0	0	0	0	0	0
Albion	0	0		0	0	8	22	3	1
Algonquin	18	0		2	13	33	475	11	6
Alsip	42	0		16	17	114	423	27	2
Altamont	5	0		1	4	10	51	1	1
Alton	108	0		34	65	309	912	51	3
Amboy	8	0		0	7	8	16	0	0
Anna	21	0		1	19	35	92	4	0
Antioch	16	1		1	10	21	217	0	0
Arlington Heights	42	0		7	28	125	659	16	6
Arthur	2	0		0	1	8	34	0	0
Ashland	1	0		0	1	4	9	0	0
Ashton	0	0		0	0	0	0	0	0
Athens	0	0		0	0	4	9	0	0
Atwood	1	0		0	0	2	5	0	0
Aurora	601	4		119	425	576	2,285	111	20
Aviston	0	0		0	0	0	2	0	0
Bannockburn	0	0		0	0	1	32	0	0
Barrington	2	0		0	0	19	116	3	0
Barrington Hills	0	0		0	0	2	8	2	0
Bartlett	18	1		5	11	22	240	8	2
Bartonville	14	0		1	12	47	174	7	0
Batavia	20	0		1	19	42	304	5	3
Beardstown	8	0		1	7	5	18	4	0
Beecher	1	0		0	1	8	52	0	0
Bellwood	132	3		42	83	110	238	37	0
Belvidere	29	3		3	18	62	300	13	0
Benld	0	0		0	0	1	0	0	0
Bensenville	25	0		5	13	55	193	15	6
Benton	16	0		3	13	53	126	1	0
Berkeley	13	0		4	8	14	75	3	1
Berwyn	117	2		61	48	342	777	79	4
Bethalto	39	1		1	28	28	123	6	0
Blandinsville	0	0		0	0	0	4	0	0
Bloomingdale	10	0		5	4	41	585	5	2
Bloomington	399	2		59	281	402	1,446	53	8
Blue Island	108	0		57	45	163	407	78	0
Blue Mound	5	0		0	5	5	11	0	1
Bluffs	0	0		0	0	7	3	0	0
Bolingbrook	174	1		38	118	118	952	61	7
Bradley	26	0		4	20	63	599	7	1
Braidwood	7	0		1	6	19	48	2	1
Bridgeview	30	0		11	17	53	434	33	3
Broadview	32	0		19	9	41	292	12	0
Brookfield	17	0		5	8	74	278	11	1
Buda	1	0		0	1	0	0	0	0
Buffalo Grove	8	0		1	7	38	285	10	1
Bull Valley	0	0		0	0	1	2	0	0
Burbank	78	2		23	52	52	393	15	1
Burnham	16	0		6	6	37	98	25	0
Burr Ridge	2	1		1	0	15	93	3	0
Byron	0	0		0	0	3	49	0	0
Cahokia	65	1		19	38	218	469	0	2
Cairo	120	2		4	112	57	155	12	22
Cambridge	3	0		0	3	4	5	0	0
Campton Hills	0	0		0	0	5	42	0	0
Canton	27	0		1	19	67	289	11	2
Carbondale	244	2		41	187	272	731	28	8
Carlinville	15	1		1	12	27	134	4	1
Carlyle	15	0		0	14	3	61	0	0
Carol Stream	29	0		7	19	54	385	15	11
Carpentersville	26	0		17	7	108	437	12	2
Carrollton	2	1		0	1	8	21	2	0
Carthage	1	0		0	1	12	6	0	0
Cary	11	0		4	6	16	114	1	1
Caseyville	61	0		5	55	33	71	11	0
Central City	2	0		0	2	9	28	0	0
Centralia	67	0		7	51	237	564	18	0
Champaign	654	4		119	492	506	1,698	71	9
Channahon	0	0		0	0	10	70	3	0
Charleston	22	0		2	17	18	70	0	0
Chebanse	1	0		0	1	1	0	0	0
Chenoa	4	0		1	3	8	18	1	0
Cherry Valley	18	0		4	13	25	309	9	0
Chester	14	0		1	11	7	34	1	3
Chicago		414		11,815		17,775	65,497	12,636	403

Table 8. Offenses Known to Law Enforcement, by Selected State and City, 2013— continued

(Number.)

State/city	Violent crime	Murder and nonnegligent manslaughter	Rape (revised definition)[1]	Robbery	Aggravated assault	Burglary	Larceny-theft	Motor vehicle theft	Arson[2]
Chicago Ridge	22	0		10	8	47	579	32	0
Chillicothe	13	0		1	12	20	118	2	0
Cicero	346	3		162	167	503	1,044	283	16
Clarendon Hills	0	0		0	0	6	55	0	0
Coal City	6	0		1	5	14	103	1	2
Coal Valley	8	0		0	7	4	23	1	0
Cobden	8	0		0	8	5	12	1	0
Colchester	2	0		0	2	0	1	1	0
Colfax	1	0		0	1	3	8	0	0
Collinsville	33	0		6	22	133	614	33	1
Colona	1	0		0	1	14	52	2	0
Columbia	10	1		2	5	33	57	1	0
Cortland	2	0		0	2	0	20	0	1
Country Club Hills	44	1		26	10	88	436	30	2
Countryside	4	0		4	0	13	151	9	1
Crest Hill	26	1		12	8	84	230	13	1
Crete	18	0		3	14	26	130	5	2
Crystal Lake	47	0		7	33	66	701	17	6
Danvers	1	0		0	1	3	7	0	0
Darien	12	0		3	6	52	199	4	0
Davis	0	0		0	0	0	2	0	0
Decatur	351	5		84	253	793	1,512	64	20
Deer Creek	0	0		0	0	2	8	0	0
Deerfield	2	0		1	1	25	159	0	0
De Kalb	204	2		28	142	181	1,006	31	11
Delavan	1	0		0	1	13	16	0	0
De Pue	2	0		0	2	1	8	0	0
De Soto	4	0		0	4	0	5	0	0
Des Plaines	56	2		12	35	153	595	43	8
Diamond	0	0		0	0	0	19	0	0
Divernon	0	0		0	0	6	10	0	0
Dixmoor	20	1		8	10	63	76	25	0
Dixon	13	0		0	4	41	316	6	12
Dolton	166	0		123	40	455	887	160	0
Downers Grove	25	1		7	16	115	588	16	3
Dupo	32	0		1	31	18	47	4	7
Du Quoin	8	0		0	8	15	78	4	2
Dwight	3	0		0	3	8	40	1	2
Earlville	2	0		0	2	7	31	0	0
East Alton	13	0		0	8	51	178	7	0
East Dubuque	15	0		0	15	4	14	4	0
East Dundee	1	0		0	0	10	88	3	0
East Hazel Crest	3	0		3	0	9	23	1	1
East Moline	63	0		6	53	98	376	14	4
Easton	0	0		0	0	0	1	0	0
East Peoria	85	0		6	59	186	476	17	3
Edwardsville	15	0		3	11	40	357	9	0
Effingham	24	1		2	19	48	357	8	0
Elburn	2	0		0	2	14	28	0	1
Eldorado	10	0		0	10	42	101	10	0
Elgin	236	3		63	114	351	1,462	89	14
Elizabeth	2	0		0	2	0	1	0	0
Elk Grove Village	25	0		7	14	89	501	34	3
Elmhurst	12	0		4	6	57	476	22	1
Elmwood	2	0		0	2	15	11	0	0
Elmwood Park	29	0		11	18	68	258	37	1
El Paso	2	0		0	0	16	39	0	0
Elwood	3	0		0	3	2	15	2	0
Erie	3	0		1	2	3	14	0	0
Eureka	7	0		1	4	13	69	0	0
Evanston	189	1		63	115	361	1,474	67	12
Evergreen Park	28	0		20	8	62	545	10	1
Fairbury	3	0		0	3	22	67	0	0
Fairfield	17	0		0	13	42	86	0	1
Fairmont City	3	0		1	2	10	36	3	0
Fairview Heights	34	0		10	20	66	639	24	5
Farmington	8	0		0	7	9	59	3	0
Fayetteville	1	0		0	1	5	5	0	0
Findlay	0	0		0	0	2	3	1	0
Fisher	3	0		0	3	7	17	0	1
Flora	5	0		0	5	19	142	1	0
Flossmoor	15	1		9	4	33	120	4	0
Forest Park	42	0		17	25	91	637	54	7
Forest View	1	0		1	0	14	25	11	0
Fox Lake	14	0		1	10	23	182	0	0
Fox River Grove	5	0		1	2	1	52	1	0
Frankfort	11	0		1	6	25	177	0	1
Franklin Grove	0	0		0	0	3	11	1	0

Table 8.   Offenses Known to Law Enforcement, by Selected State and City, 2013— continued

(Number.)

State/city	Violent crime	Murder and nonnegligent manslaughter	Rape (revised definition)[1]	Robbery	Aggravated assault	Burglary	Larceny-theft	Motor vehicle theft	Arson[2]
Franklin Park	21	0		3	11	46	213	50	4
Freeburg	11	0		1	10	14	34	1	0
Fulton	4	0		0	4	20	36	2	1
Galena	1	0		0	1	2	32	2	0
Galesburg	125	2		11	87	227	891	22	1
Geneseo	7	0		0	5	10	87	1	0
Geneva	5	0		1	3	13	220	2	3
Genoa	6	0		0	3	9	36	0	1
Germantown	0	0		0	0	4	12	0	0
Gibson City	3	1		0	2	14	27	0	0
Gilberts	1	0		0	1	4	42	2	0
Gillespie	11	0		0	10	4	54	2	0
Gilman	2	0		0	2	5	33	1	0
Girard	10	0		0	10	12	22	2	0
Glasford	3	0		0	3	1	0	0	0
Glen Carbon	11	0		0	9	15	61	0	1
Glencoe	0	0		0	0	6	65	1	0
Glendale Heights	40	0		8	16	49	428	11	1
Glen Ellyn	9	1		3	1	55	228	8	1
Glenview	22	0		5	14	77	401	7	3
Glenwood	13	0		11	2	41	151	13	0
Godfrey	12	0		0	11	45	200	3	0
Godley	3	0		1	1	2	4	0	0
Goodfield	0	0		0	0	2	47	2	0
Grafton	0	0		0	0	3	8	1	1
Grandview	0	0		0	0	16	13	1	0
Granite City	174	4		32	123	312	493	49	15
Grantfork	0	0		0	0	1	3	0	0
Granville	0	0		0	0	1	1	0	0
Grayslake	31	0		10	10	67	267	14	2
Grayville	6	0		0	6	2	10	0	3
Greenfield	1	0		0	1	1	3	0	0
Greenup	19	0		0	19	3	30	0	3
Greenville	4	0		1	3	21	99	7	0
Gurnee	38	0		20	9	65	1,368	21	0
Hampshire	5	0		1	4	7	24	0	1
Hampton	2	0		0	1	8	16	0	0
Hanover	0	0		0	0	1	7	0	0
Hanover Park	37	0		4	29	66	243	13	0
Harrisburg	47	0		4	38	115	53	9	1
Hartford	4	0		0	4	3	34	1	0
Harvard	4	0		1	3	20	104	2	1
Harvey	407	10		273	114	493	737	192	10
Harwood Heights	12	0		3	8	24	109	10	0
Havana	20	0		1	17	18	78	3	0
Hawthorn Woods	1	0		0	1	2	17	0	0
Hazel Crest	56	0		40	10	117	327	45	2
Henry	6	1		0	3	4	26	1	0
Herrin	1	0		1	0	217	254	14	1
Herscher	1	0		0	0	2	12	0	2
Heyworth	5	0		0	3	5	21	1	0
Hickory Hills	10	0		0	7	27	151	13	1
Highland Park	23	0		3	16	27	276	4	0
Highwood	10	1		1	6	6	43	1	0
Hillsboro	29	0		0	29	17	44	2	1
Hillsdale	0	0		0	0	0	0	0	0
Hinsdale	2	0		0	1	28	135	2	0
Hodgkins	5	0		1	4	1	259	6	0
Hoffman Estates	55	0		21	18	102	426	20	2
Homer	0	0		0	0	1	6	0	0
Homer Glen	5	0		0	4	43	136	5	0
Hometown	6	0		4	2	8	60	2	0
Homewood	45	1		32	11	48	625	10	0
Hoopeston	32	0		1	23	48	151	3	0
Hopedale	1	0		0	1	4	3	0	0
Hudson	0	0		0	0	6	12	1	0
Huntley	4	0		0	4	25	161	1	1
Indian Head Park	2	0		1	0	3	10	0	0
Inverness	1	0		0	1	7	17	0	0
Irving	2	0		0	2	0	6	0	0
Irvington	1	0		0	1	3	9	0	0
Island Lake	6	0		1	3	16	50	1	0
Itasca	3	0		1	1	7	101	4	0
Jacksonville	39	1		2	27	93	334	2	2
Jerome	11	0		0	11	8	30	1	0
Jerseyville	20	0		0	15	52	232	5	0
Joliet	557	10		158	340	724	2,337	156	51
Justice	10	0		3	7	21	75	15	0

Table 8.   Offenses Known to Law Enforcement, by Selected State and City, 2013— continued

(Number.)

State/city	Violent crime	Murder and nonnegligent manslaughter	Rape (revised definition)[1]	Robbery	Aggravated assault	Burglary	Larceny-theft	Motor vehicle theft	Arson[2]
Kankakee	196	4		70	99	285	743	35	10
Kenilworth	0	0		0	0	3	17	0	0
Kewanee	30	0		0	19	43	362	1	1
Kildeer	2	0		0	1	9	34	0	0
Kincaid	1	0		0	1	3	6	0	0
Kingston	0	0		0	0	3	5	0	0
Knoxville	0	0		0	0	13	38	0	0
Lacon	2	0		0	2	2	7	0	1
La Grange	15	0		8	4	24	88	7	0
La Grange Park	1	0		0	1	11	73	1	0
La Harpe	0	0		0	0	6	13	0	0
Lake in the Hills	15	0		0	11	13	76	4	5
Lakemoor	1	0		0	1	15	26	1	0
Lake Villa	6	0		0	6	7	62	1	3
Lakewood	1	0		0	1	7	5	0	0
Lake Zurich	3	0		1	2	27	279	2	0
Lansing	109	0		57	36	157	939	74	3
La Salle	12	0		0	10	22	146	2	0
Lawrenceville	14	0		1	11	20	60	4	4
Leland	2	0		0	2	2	4	0	0
Leland Grove	0	0		0	0	1	6	1	0
Lemont	13	0		2	10	32	226	2	2
Lexington	1	0		0	1	2	3	0	0
Libertyville	6	1		0	5	25	200	6	0
Lincoln	50	0		6	32	96	320	16	3
Lincolnshire	4	0		0	3	8	48	2	0
Lincolnwood	10	0		4	6	47	475	19	2
Lindenhurst	4	1		0	0	10	38	0	0
Lisle	13	0		4	5	37	185	7	0
Litchfield	9	0		1	8	39	169	8	0
Loami	1	0		0	1	2	6	0	0
Lockport	23	0		5	14	37	218	8	3
Lombard	41	0		17	21	68	837	11	1
Lovington	2	0		0	1	11	7	0	0
Lyons	15	0		6	6	37	155	4	1
Machesney Park	58	0		2	41	101	377	22	2
Macomb	55	0		3	39	117	277	5	0
Mahomet	10	0		0	9	16	40	0	0
Malta	0	0		0	0	1	5	0	0
Manhattan	3	0		0	2	3	34	0	0
Maple Park	2	0		0	2	0	1	0	0
Marengo	3	0		0	2	14	59	3	1
Marine	0	0		0	0	2	3	2	0
Marion	7	0		7	0	150	6	38	12
Maroa	2	0		0	1	5	7	0	1
Marseilles	7	0		0	6	34	65	3	0
Martinsville	0	0		0	0	10	15	0	1
Maryville	6	0		1	5	16	60	0	0
Mascoutah	5	1		1	2	9	48	1	0
Matteson	73	0		44	21	60	768	51	0
Mattoon	41	1		4	28	101	267	4	19
Maywood	207	6		90	93	295	447	102	6
McCook	3	0		0	2	2	23	13	0
McHenry	37	0		6	24	30	395	9	0
McLean	0	0		0	0	3	2	0	0
Melrose Park	43	1		13	21	81	291	79	3
Mendota	11	0		0	8	33	81	0	0
Merrionette Park	0	0		0	0	5	38	0	0
Metropolis	37	0		1	34	31	174	3	1
Midlothian	40	0		20	16	111	178	25	3
Milan	8	0		1	7	27	93	3	1
Minonk	0	0		0	0	4	21	1	0
Minooka	4	0		1	3	12	111	0	0
Mokena	10	0		5	5	28	146	4	7
Moline	121	0		13	100	235	1,127	27	9
Monmouth	56	0		2	45	61	297	15	1
Montgomery	18	0		0	12	63	294	8	2
Monticello	7	0		0	5	3	11	1	1
Morris	19	0		4	11	39	311	8	0
Morrison	11	0		2	6	17	31	0	0
Morton	18	0		1	17	41	113	1	0
Morton Grove	31	0		7	21	63	331	15	2
Mount Carmel	18	0		0	18	37	164	4	1
Mount Carroll	0	0		0	0	6	30	0	1
Mount Morris	1	0		0	1	1	22	0	1
Mount Prospect	21	1		11	8	67	524	19	0
Mount Pulaski	0	0		0	0	1	10	0	0
Mount Vernon	217	0		37	160	240	691	13	3

Table 8.   Offenses Known to Law Enforcement, by Selected State and City, 2013— continued

(Number.)

State/city	Violent crime	Murder and nonnegligent manslaughter	Rape (revised definition)[1]	Robbery	Aggravated assault	Burglary	Larceny-theft	Motor vehicle theft	Arson[2]
Mount Zion	6	0		1	3	4	25	1	0
Moweaqua	2	0		0	2	2	7	0	0
Mundelein	16	0		2	8	34	245	2	1
Naperville	105	0		21	77	225	1,610	34	2
Nashville	8	0		5	2	6	43	1	0
Neoga	2	0		0	2	6	9	2	1
New Athens	1	0		1	0	13	38	0	0
New Lenox	21	0		0	17	37	227	6	2
Newton	3	0		0	3	11	34	3	2
Niles	35	0		8	26	63	637	20	0
Nokomis	20	0		0	20	5	34	2	0
Normal	115	1		29	73	257	1,018	19	2
Norridge	19	0		16	3	53	557	11	0
North Aurora	21	0		4	14	39	179	3	0
Northbrook	8	0		1	2	57	417	5	5
North Chicago	58	2		7	41	45	70	4	4
Northfield	2	0		1	1	2	47	1	0
Northlake	10	0		3	7	42	325	9	1
North Riverside	22	0		6	16	8	436	10	0
Norwood	0	0		0	0	0	0	0	0
Oak Brook	4	0		3	0	27	510	9	0
Oakbrook Terrace	2	0		1	0	22	68	3	0
Oak Forest	37	1		15	16	98	331	8	3
Oak Lawn	81	1		30	44	113	940	29	2
Oak Park	126	0		86	37	457	1,133	59	0
Oakwood Hills	3	0		0	3	2	15	0	0
Oblong	18	0		0	18	10	13	0	0
O'Fallon	34	0		4	24	54	481	11	1
Oglesby	5	1		0	4	12	65	3	0
Okawville	1	0		1	0	2	15	1	0
Olney	30	0		1	18	81	216	9	2
Olympia Fields	3	0		2	0	8	170	6	1
Oquawka	2	0		0	2	4	1	0	1
Oregon	7	1		1	4	6	62	3	0
Orion	1	0		0	1	3	6	0	1
Orland Park	17	0		3	9	64	1,250	18	0
Oswego	18	0		3	5	49	402	8	2
Ottawa	13	0		5	8	36	350	0	2
Palatine	33	0		12	13	27	622	15	6
Palestine	7	0		0	7	7	9	0	0
Palos Heights	6	0		2	4	17	134	6	1
Palos Hills	13	0		3	10	15	137	7	1
Palos Park	0	0		0	0	8	22	1	0
Pana	12	1		1	10	35	59	7	0
Paris	29	0		2	27	45	118	9	2
Park City	11	0		8	3	34	90	8	0
Park Forest	94	1		48	36	138	307	26	2
Park Ridge	15	0		6	8	99	360	10	3
Patoka	0	0		0	0	0	3	0	0
Pawnee	0	0		0	0	1	5	1	0
Paxton	4	1		1	2	14	43	4	1
Pekin	120	4		9	100	167	708	7	5
Peoria	784	16		275	469	1,123	3,098	194	37
Peoria Heights	24	0		2	19	33	106	3	0
Peotone	7	0		0	5	5	32	4	0
Peru	13	0		1	7	26	156	1	1
Phoenix	10	0		3	7	16	26	2	0
Pierron	0	0		0	0	0	0	0	0
Pinckneyville	12	0		0	10	3	19	2	0
Pingree Grove	2	0		0	2	11	21	0	0
Plainfield	20	1		5	13	54	367	5	3
Plano	2	0		1	1	25	90	3	1
Pleasant Plains	0	0		0	0	2	4	0	0
Polo	6	2		0	1	4	15	1	0
Pontiac	51	4		8	34	51	298	8	2
Pontoon Beach	6	0		2	4	11	69	5	0
Posen	17	2		8	7	56	82	12	4
Princeton	12	1		4	4	30	137	4	0
Prospect Heights	27	0		5	16	35	98	8	0
Quincy	188	1		18	142	231	1,027	50	8
Raleigh	0	0		0	0	3	3	0	0
Rantoul	106	0		10	79	140	232	12	2
Red Bud	14	0		0	14	13	21	0	0
Richmond	6	0		0	6	8	20	0	1
Richton Park	42	0		19	19	85	243	17	0
Riverdale	183	1		119	53	209	249	39	1
River Forest	15	0		5	9	91	198	1	0
River Grove	5	1		0	4	41	134	10	0

Table 8.   Offenses Known to Law Enforcement, by Selected State and City, 2013— continued

(Number.)

State/city	Violent crime	Murder and nonnegligent manslaughter	Rape (revised definition)[1]	Robbery	Aggravated assault	Burglary	Larceny-theft	Motor vehicle theft	Arson[2]
Riverside	15	0		1	12	33	118	4	1
Riverton	16	0		0	14	18	47	3	2
Riverwoods	1	0		0	1	4	19	0	0
Robbins	39	0		10	28	45	65	25	3
Robinson	30	0		1	19	29	105	6	0
Rochester	4	1		0	2	5	12	0	0
Rockdale	2	0		1	1	2	8	2	0
Rock Falls	21	0		3	14	53	90	5	4
Rockford	2,065	19	145	394	1,507	2,001	4,666	372	107
Rock Island	200	5		32	161	227	741	38	7
Rockton	3	0		0	3	7	114	0	0
Rolling Meadows	23	0		6	11	21	243	2	0
Romeoville	30	1		10	16	117	610	27	2
Roodhouse	0	0		0	0	3	12	0	0
Roscoe	11	0		0	11	36	97	3	4
Roselle	10	0		2	5	30	203	11	0
Rosemont	15	0		3	9	8	212	3	1
Round Lake	27	0		7	16	40	139	2	2
Round Lake Beach	37	1		5	25	85	532	12	2
Round Lake Heights	8	0		0	6	3	28	1	0
Round Lake Park	16	0		7	9	20	90	0	1
Roxana	6	0		1	1	8	63	7	0
Ruma	0	0		0	0	0	0	0	0
Rushville	2	0		0	2	13	23	2	0
Salem	6	0		1	2	54	298	8	2
Sauget	10	0		1	4	5	87	9	0
Sauk Village	72	2		21	41	247	203	27	5
Savanna	17	0		0	16	21	72	8	1
Schaumburg	71	0		30	26	175	1,928	73	6
Schiller Park	9	0		0	3	40	185	16	0
Seneca	21	0		0	21	14	58	0	0
Sherman	2	0		0	2	3	19	3	0
Shiloh	25	0		7	13	37	163	7	0
Shorewood	18	0		1	13	34	121	3	2
Silvis	25	0		6	17	27	229	5	0
Skokie	157	0		58	90	285	1,221	69	5
Sleepy Hollow	1	0		0	1	5	35	0	0
Smithton	0	0		0	0	0	10	0	0
South Barrington	0	0		0	0	7	67	1	0
South Beloit	16	0		3	12	26	80	4	2
South Chicago Heights	12	0		6	6	12	93	2	0
South Elgin	30	1		6	20	18	269	6	1
South Holland	55	0		39	11	77	300	39	1
South Jacksonville	1	0		0	1	8	29	0	1
South Pekin	8	0		0	8	9	13	0	0
South Roxana	3	0		0	1	19	13	2	0
Sparta	8	0		0	8	34	98	3	0
Springfield	1,191	4		287	829	1,300	4,439	166	44
Spring Grove	1	0		0	0	4	24	2	0
Stanford	0	0		0	0	1	0	0	0
St. Anne	0	0		0	0	3	25	0	0
Staunton	8	0		0	7	3	43	0	1
St. Charles	20	0		2	17	58	473	8	6
Steger	32	0		16	15	51	331	12	1
Sterling	25	0		2	14	84	514	14	1
Stickney	8	0		3	4	6	57	9	1
Stockton	4	0		1	2	9	17	0	1
Stonington	1	0		0	1	2	0	1	1
Streamwood	41	1		11	24	81	572	10	0
Streator	20	0		0	20	54	296	2	1
Stronghurst	0	0		0	0	1	0	0	0
Summit	40	0		19	20	45	171	41	12
Swansea	28	1		16	7	58	209	13	1
Sycamore	11	0		2	8	14	251	5	0
Taylorville	25	0		1	12	38	159	9	0
Teutopolis	0	0		0	0	2	6	1	0
Thomasboro	10	0		0	6	10	17	0	0
Thornton	1	0		1	0	7	23	0	0
Tinley Park	46	1		10	20	113	758	28	1
Tolono	5	0		1	3	12	19	0	0
Tonica	0	0		0	0	1	14	0	0
Tower Lakes	0	0		0	0	0	3	0	0
Troy	14	1		0	12	17	65	2	0
Tuscola	26	0		0	26	14	40	2	1
Urbana	141	2		66	46	354	1,211	40	11
Valmeyer	0	0		0	0	3	12	0	0
Vandalia	27	0		3	18	44	79	4	0
Vernon Hills	14	0		2	10	25	459	2	1

Table 8.   Offenses Known to Law Enforcement, by Selected State and City, 2013— continued

(Number.)

State/city	Violent crime	Murder and nonnegligent manslaughter	Rape (revised definition)	Robbery	Aggravated assault	Burglary	Larceny-theft	Motor vehicle theft	Arson[2]
Vienna	8	0		0	8	4	15	0	0
Villa Park	27	0		13	9	44	371	26	3
Virden	10	0		0	9	11	41	3	0
Virginia	0	0		0	0	0	0	0	0
Wamac	10	0		1	9	43	64	1	0
Warrensburg	5	0		0	5	0	9	1	0
Warrenville	5	0		0	2	31	96	5	0
Washington	24	0		5	19	56	129	0	2
Washington Park	114	2		28	83	47	74	17	0
Watseka	13	0		2	7	32	120	2	1
Wauconda	4	0		0	4	19	102	3	0
Waukegan	405	3		172	199	681	1,766	62	14
Waverly	4	0		0	4	2	2	0	0
Wayne	0	0		0	0	3	6	0	0
Westchester	14	0		7	5	68	160	5	0
West Chicago	33	2		7	16	57	303	28	3
West City	4	0		1	3	2	77	1	0
West Dundee	4	0		1	0	7	226	0	0
Westmont	26	1		8	13	56	234	13	3
Wheaton	32	0		7	21	51	398	6	5
Wheeling	38	1		3	27	70	376	17	4
White Hall	7	0		0	7	15	23	2	2
Willisville	0	0		0	0	0	0	0	0
Willowbrook	6	0		3	3	14	133	7	0
Willow Springs	4	0		1	3	1	27	0	0
Wilmington	5	0		0	4	16	29	4	0
Winfield	2	0		1	1	6	36	0	0
Winnebago	1	0		0	1	6	35	0	0
Winnetka	7	0		1	6	15	113	2	0
Winthrop Harbor	16	0		3	6	21	84	3	0
Witt	0	0		0	0	3	9	0	0
Wood Dale	9	0		4	4	30	163	7	0
Woodhull	0	0		0	0	0	0	0	0
Wood River	31	0		6	19	65	450	9	0
Woodstock	17	1		1	7	20	301	4	2
Worth	8	0		3	4	19	63	14	1
Yorkville	12	0		0	4	33	170	7	0
Zion	146	5		34	88	243	520	37	5
Indiana									
Albion	0	0		0	0	0	0	0	0
Alexandria	6	0		2	2	18	96	7	1
Anderson	200	5		103	56	605	1,829	230	55
Angola	6	1		2	1	25	358	4	0
Auburn	11	0		0	6	34	203	12	0
Aurora	20	0		0	18	16	193	4	0
Batesville	26	0		1	24	25	82	4	0
Bedford	70	0		2	63	60	360	32	1
Beech Grove	33	0		14	15	92	383	64	7
Berne	1	0		0	1	5	23	3	0
Bloomington	275	2		78	161	516	1,942	148	35
Boonville	20	0		0	20	23	165	9	4
Bremen	15	0		0	15	11	44	4	0
Brownsburg	33	0		5	27	55	304	26	1
Carmel	20	0		11	5	128	573	43	0
Cedar Lake	13	0		1	9	57	179	12	1
Chesterfield	1	0		0	1	5	43	3	0
Clarksville	122	5		27	83	172	1,310	47	4
Clinton	16	0		0	15	27	50	5	0
Columbia City	4	0		1	2	13	121	7	0
Columbus	82	1		19	45	241	1,754	129	3
Crawfordsville	23	0	4	4	15	112	400	21	4
Cumberland	20	0		12	8	26	158	8	3
Danville	30	0		3	25	15	67	7	0
Decatur	10	0		2	5	15	161	10	0
Delphi	13	0		3	8	13	47	2	0
Dyer	11	0		5	6	17	167	13	0
East Chicago	196	10		91	81	301	936	225	2
Edinburgh	14	0	1	2	11	19	433	3	0
Ellettsville	25	0		1	24	20	55	1	0
Elwood	7	0		0	7	78	188	19	1
Evansville	564	5		211	294	996	4,371	492	48
Fairmount	4	0		0	4	5	3	1	0
Fishers	16	0		7	7	78	719	29	1
Fort Wayne	949	31	95	447	376	2,396	7,025	386	25
Franklin	69	0		8	59	54	853	9	1
Garrett	2	0		0	1	56	209	16	0
Gary	883	54		327	455	1,454	2,533	732	67

Table 8. Offenses Known to Law Enforcement, by Selected State and City, 2013— continued

(Number.)

State/city	Violent crime	Murder and nonnegligent manslaughter	Rape (revised definition)	Robbery	Aggravated assault	Burglary	Larceny-theft	Motor vehicle theft	Arson[2]
Goshen	30	1		10	11	198	830	70	5
Greenfield	12	0		8	3	40	350	17	
Greensburg	32	0		3	27	13	44	2	0
Greenwood	200	1	1	9	189	175	1,645	88	5
Griffith	30	0		18	10	100	411	54	0
Hagerstown	3	0	0	0	3	11	20	3	0
Hammond	654	9		228	380	608	2,221	406	33
Hartford City	6	0		3	2	55	188	4	0
Highland	9	0		4	5	119	585	54	3
Hobart	61	1		13	45	143	1,309	85	3
Huntington	27	0		3	16	60	304	9	2
Indianapolis	10,479	129	656	3,800	5,894	13,445	26,156	5,005	317
Jasper	48	0	0	0	48	28	101	6	0
Jeffersonville	349	1		43	301	328	1,211	139	0
Knox	6	0		0	5	6	38	0	1
Kokomo	185	2		66	99	496	1,600	114	5
Lafayette	389	2	35	67	285	718	2,466	232	13
Lake Station	50	0		9	35	103	417	61	0
La Porte	44	1	2	16	25	150	690	29	2
Lawrenceburg	8	0		0	7	15	164	0	0
Ligonier	0	0		0	0	1	14	3	0
Linton	0	0	0	0	0	0	181	1	0
Long Beach	0	0	0	0	0	3	5	3	0
Lowell	18	0	0	0	18	11	93	1	0
Marion	80	4		34	35	162	911	75	4
Martinsville	7	0		1	4	82	594	36	1
Merrillville	99	3		33	62	246	979	112	2
Mishawaka	136	0		61	55	305	2,259	140	12
Mooresville	7	0	1	0	6	31	245	30	0
Mount Vernon	12	0		2	10	117	211	19	0
Muncie	288	0		96	163	532	2,321	154	24
Nappanee	3	0		1	1	27	81	5	1
New Albany	87	0		27	47	354	1,514	134	3
New Haven	24	0		13	9	83	422	27	0
New Whiteland	6	0	0	2	4	7	16	3	0
North Judson	6	0		0	5	4	41	1	1
North Liberty	0	0		0	0	3	7	0	0
North Manchester	11	0		0	4	19	89	0	0
North Vernon	22	0		0	20	38	338	16	0
Peru	21	1		2	17	52	76	5	0
Plainfield	50	0	2	7	41	78	755	53	0
Plymouth	7	0	1	2	4	17	290	9	0
Portage	70	0		13	49	124	697	45	0
Porter	1	0		0	1	9	71	6	0
Portland	1	0	0	0	1	12	214	18	0
Rensselaer	26	0		2	21	20	196	2	0
Rushville	10	0		1	4	48	234	8	0
Schererville	20	0		9	10	53	589	32	0
Scottsburg	28	0		5	22	45	248	7	0
Sellersburg		0		3		17	77	15	0
Seymour	100	0		6	87	143	958	100	2
Shelbyville		0		3		55	365	28	0
South Bend	664	9	93	363	199	1,468	3,096	326	25
South Whitley	1	0		0	0	2	29	1	0
Speedway	29	2		20	5	87	495	46	0
Tell City	4	0	1	1	2	22	108	7	0
Terre Haute	177	4	22	54	97	850	2,130	281	52
Tipton	14	0		3	11	31	107	5	0
Valparaiso	33	0		7	24	87	555	23	0
Walkerton	1	0		0	0	12	27	5	0
Warsaw	106	0		1	99	49	382	16	2
Washington	43	1		2	34	143	572	40	1
Waterloo	11	0	1	0	10	12	62	4	6
Westfield	21	2	1	5	13	64	412	12	1
West Lafayette	37	0		6	25	90	430	16	0
Whitestown	19	0		0	19	11	98	5	0
Whiting	4	0		0	4	10	132	20	0
Winchester	1	0		0	1	37	198	6	0
Winona Lake	12	0	0	0	12	8	19	0	0
Zionsville	2	0		1	1	10	50	3	0
Iowa									
Adel	7	0	0	0	7	23	45	2	0
Albia	8	0	0	0	8	8	45	5	1
Algona	15	0	1	0	14	31	28	1	0
Altoona	19	0	1	4	14	47	506	14	1
Ames	88	0	34	11	43	224	1,181	34	10
Anamosa	2	0	0	0	2	15	77	2	0

Table 8.   Offenses Known to Law Enforcement, by Selected State and City, 2013— continued

(Number.)

State/city	Violent crime	Murder and nonnegligent manslaughter	Rape (revised definition)[1]	Robbery	Aggravated assault	Burglary	Larceny-theft	Motor vehicle theft	Arson[2]
Ankeny	43	0	5	4	34	118	543	36	4
Bettendorf	86	0	8	7	71	84	399	12	4
Bloomfield	6	0	1	0	5	0	11	6	0
Blue Grass	0	0	0	0	0	1	7	0	0
Boone	77	0	11	1	65	63	186	15	0
Buffalo	5	0	0	0	5	1	6	2	0
Camanche	5	0	1	0	4	7	28	0	0
Carlisle	5	0	3	0	2	12	7	3	1
Carroll	6	0	2	0	4	23	90	11	2
Carter Lake	19	0	3	0	16	40	96	25	1
Cedar Falls	52	0	19	3	30	80	391	24	3
Cedar Rapids	392	4	46	90	252	977	3,433	297	19
Centerville	28	0	5	2	21	68	107	13	7
Chariton	18	0	2	2	14	47	93	5	3
Charles City	19	0	4	0	15	25	103	3	0
Cherokee	14	1	1	0	12	23	54	2	0
Clarinda	26	0	1	0	25	67	111	11	4
Clear Lake	6	0	1	0	5	45	179	8	0
Clinton	178	0	21	18	139	206	795	45	11
Clive	28	0	0	3	25	43	277	18	0
Coralville	44	0	15	11	18	74	542	11	4
Council Bluffs	584	0	75	80	429	947	3,126	541	28
Cresco	5	0	2	0	3	10	25	0	1
Davenport	654	2	88	167	397	961	3,048	239	30
Decorah	1	0	0	0	1	9	52	3	0
Denison	4	0	0	2	2	16	58	10	1
Des Moines	1,026	11	90	211	714	2,311	6,854	850	33
De Witt	8	0	0	0	8	35	41	3	0
Dubuque	132	0	14	36	82	409	1,172	60	26
Dyersville	10	0	0	1	9	8	46	3	1
Eagle Grove	14	0	1	1	12	16	21	3	1
Eldora	21	0	1	1	19	20	32	2	1
Eldridge	13	0	0	4	9	10	30	4	0
Emmetsburg	1	0	0	0	1	4	2	1	0
Estherville	24	0	4	0	20	20	42	4	0
Evansdale	21	0	6	0	15	37	49	2	0
Fairfield	13	0	1	1	11	165	163	9	2
Forest City	3	0	0	0	3	3	18	4	0
Fort Dodge	157	0	15	13	129	141	881	84	12
Fort Madison	52	0	8	1	43	66	166	12	1
Glenwood	28	1	5	1	21	29	55	13	1
Grinnell	34	0	1	1	32	68	136	6	2
Grundy Center	0	0	0	0	0	0	10	0	0
Hampton	3	0	2	0	1	1	16	0	0
Hawarden	2	0	0	0	2	7	12	1	0
Hiawatha	4	0	1	0	3	36	63	7	1
Humboldt	4	0	0	0	4	7	34	10	0
Indianola	73	0	8	1	64	76	254	19	13
Iowa City	228	0	28	56	144	357	1,411	82	7
Iowa Falls	3	0	1	1	1	6	131	1	1
Jefferson	1	0	1	0	0	11	53	0	2
Johnston	7	0	2	0	5	44	125	9	3
Keokuk	103	0	8	1	94	113	363	27	1
Le Claire	16	0	0	0	16	5	27	1	0
Le Mars	10	0	3	1	6	61	159	10	8
Leon	5	0	1	1	3	0	27	1	0
Lisbon	3	0	0	0	3	2	13	0	0
Manchester	13	0	3	0	10	18	67	4	2
Maquoketa	21	0	5	2	14	32	140	6	1
Marengo	3	0	0	1	2	1	2	0	0
Marion	56	0	15	5	36	117	439	17	5
Marshalltown	172	0	2	5	165	165	533	37	4
Mason City	30	1	8	4	17	216	884	30	7
Monticello	9	0	0	0	9	11	25	2	0
Mount Vernon	5	0	3	1	1	2	36	1	0
Muscatine	146	1	29	2	114	115	401	23	8
New Hampton	2	0	0	0	2	2	20	0	0
Newton	41	0	16	1	24	76	409	18	4
North Liberty	44	0	15	0	29	15	93	11	1
Norwalk	10	0	2	0	8	7	66	1	1
Oelwein	34	0	2	3	29	35	96	6	0
Orange City	3	0	0	0	3	13	37	3	0
Osage	8	0	2	0	6	33	20	1	0
Osceola	10	0	0	0	10	19	91	14	0
Oskaloosa	49	1	6	2	40	65	157	8	0
Ottumwa	74	0	19	5	50	283	835	69	10
Pella	35	0	1	1	33	63	88	2	2
Perry	29	0	4	0	25	27	143	8	1

Table 8.   Offenses Known to Law Enforcement, by Selected State and City, 2013— continued

(Number.)

State/city	Violent crime	Murder and nonnegligent manslaughter	Rape (revised definition)[1]	Robbery	Aggravated assault	Burglary	Larceny-theft	Motor vehicle theft	Arson[2]
Pleasant Hill	6	0	1	0	5	36	67	8	1
Prairie City	3	0	0	0	3	17	16	1	0
Red Oak	19	1	1	0	17	114	138	6	3
Sergeant Bluff	15	0	0	1	14	12	53	1	0
Sheldon	10	0	0	1	9	27	38	4	0
Shenandoah	3	0	1	0	2	7	65	9	0
Sioux City	324	3	46	40	235	604	2,814	240	7
Spencer	19	0	17	1	1	78	164	4	0
Spirit Lake	9	0	1	0	8	94	101	5	1
State Center	0	0	0	0	0	5	7	1	0
Storm Lake	54	0	3	0	51	46	208	11	11
Story City	2	0	0	0	2	13	19	0	0
Toledo	46	0	2	0	44	6	35	2	0
Urbandale	67	0	5	7	55	129	516	25	2
Vinton	4	0	0	0	4	24	48	3	1
Walcott	3	0	1	0	2	3	9	0	1
Washington	54	0	8	3	43	16	58	7	1
Waukee	10	0	1	0	9	36	97	1	1
Waukon	1	0	0	0	1	2	3	0	0
Waverly	54	0	5	1	48	26	83	8	0
Webster City	28	0	1	1	26	40	124	12	0
West Burlington	7	0	0	1	6	31	274	8	0
West Des Moines	90	1	16	12	61	205	1,377	76	3
West Liberty	7	0	0	0	7	14	21	1	1
Williamsburg	1	0	0	1	0	8	12	0	0
Wilton	3	0	1	0	2	8	10	1	0
Windsor Heights	10	0	2	1	7	33	153	6	1
Winterset	6	0	2	0	4	46	67	2	1
Kansas									
Abilene	11	0	1	0	10	36	113	6	2
Andover	8	0	3	0	5	21	328	15	1
Anthony	14	0	0	0	14	15	25	5	0
Arkansas City	87	0	11	4	72	117	366	20	4
Arma	5	0	1	0	4	11	15	1	0
Atchison	33	0	6	1	26	87	257	13	2
Atwood	4	0	1	0	3	7	17	2	0
Auburn	0	0	0	0	0	0	0	0	0
Augusta	33	0	5	1	27	48	315	9	0
Baldwin City	0	0	0	0	0	20	51	7	0
Basehor	0	0	0	0	0	11	36	4	0
Baxter Springs	5	0	0	0	5	27	76	2	3
Bel Aire	9	0	3	2	4	13	80	2	1
Belleville	6	0	0	0	6	15	51	3	0
Beloit	14	0	5	0	9	3	12	1	0
Bentley	0	0	0	0	0	0	1	0	0
Benton	0	0	0	0	0	1	4	0	0
Bonner Springs	24	1	3	2	18	71	254	27	2
Bucklin	0	0	0	0	0	0	0	0	0
Burlington	4	0	1	0	3	2	26	3	0
Burrton	1	0	0	0	1	8	8	0	1
Caney	1	0	0	0	1	8	19	6	0
Chanute	38	1	3	0	34	49	270	12	2
Chase	0	0	0	0	0	0	0	0	0
Clay Center	16	0	0	1	15	29	41	1	0
Clearwater	3	0	0	0	3	9	33	3	1
Coffeyville	100	0	9	6	85	174	432	25	4
Colby	19	1	4	1	13	21	91	8	1
Columbus	1	0	1	0	0	25	61	8	1
Concordia	27	0	6	0	21	42	148	8	2
Council Grove	6	0	0	0	6	14	33	2	0
Derby	36	1	5	2	28	113	416	23	3
Dodge City	68	1	11	11	45	193	618	45	2
Edwardsville	13	0	2	1	10	29	56	7	1
El Dorado	52	1	2	2	47	84	258	16	0
Ellsworth	2	0	0	0	2	17	43	5	0
Elwood	4	0	1	0	3	13	22	2	0
Enterprise	0	0	0	0	0	5	20	0	0
Eudora	8	0	2	0	6	18	58	2	0
Fairway	4	0	1	0	3	5	31	2	0
Fort Scott	57	0	6	4	47	78	217	13	3
Frontenac	4	0	0	1	3	46	47	1	0
Galena	15	0	1	0	14	43	65	11	5
Garden City	124	0	19	11	94	82	588	26	9
Garnett	4	0	3	0	1	24	75	5	0
Girard	4	0	2	0	2	13	37	2	0
Goddard	7	0	0	0	7	34	114	10	0
Grandview Plaza	3	0	1	0	2	10	26	0	0

Table 8.   Offenses Known to Law Enforcement, by Selected State and City, 2013— continued

(Number.)

State/city	Violent crime	Murder and nonnegligent manslaughter	Rape (revised definition)	Robbery	Aggravated assault	Burglary	Larceny-theft	Motor vehicle theft	Arson[2]
Great Bend	74	0	14	4	56	141	468	27	4
Halstead	3	0	0	0	3	40	34	2	0
Hays	71	0	6	3	62	54	446	19	3
Herington	7	0	1	0	6	14	37	5	0
Hesston	2	0	0	0	2	18	49	2	1
Hiawatha	8	1	0	0	7	14	92	7	1
Hill City	3	0	0	0	3	5	14	1	1
Hillsboro	1	0	0	0	1	5	25	1	0
Hoisington	14	0	2	1	11	21	58	3	1
Holcomb	3	0	0	0	3	5	16	0	0
Holton	7	0	2	0	5	12	24	1	0
Horton	5	0	2	0	3	11	22	2	0
Hugoton	4	0	0	0	4	4	15	0	0
Hutchinson	251	3	39	27	182	435	1,695	134	17
Inman	1	0	1	0	0	3	5	0	0
Iola	24	0	5	1	18	64	235	10	3
Junction City	147	1	13	14	119	121	497	20	5
Kansas City	731	28		238	382	1,617	4,566	1,045	56
Kingman	9	0	1	0	8	5	33	2	0
Lansing	21	0	2	1	18	63	61	20	1
Larned	14	0	4	1	9	20	88	7	2
Lawrence	338	1	50	74	213	493	2,959	173	19
Leavenworth	234	0	28	25	181	252	770	67	6
Leawood	13	0	1	2	10	47	320	17	1
Lebo	0	0	0	0	0	0	0	0	0
Lenexa	58	0	9	11	38	106	713	76	1
Le Roy	0	0	0	0	0	1	0	0	0
Liberal	53	0	5	6	42	115	365	19	2
Lindsborg	6	0	0	0	6	18	44	2	0
Louisburg	2	0	0	0	2	34	39	0	1
Maize	6	0	0	2	4	9	32	3	1
Maple Hill	0	0	0	0	0	0	0	0	1
Marion	3	0	1	0	2	9	32	0	0
Marysville	6	0	1	0	5	7	47	3	1
McLouth	3	0	0	0	3	4	15	0	0
McPherson	41	0	7	3	31	211	349	37	2
Medicine Lodge	5	0	0	0	5	17	31	1	0
Mission	21	0		5	14	35	274	55	2
Mission Hills	0	0	0	0	0	9	27	7	1
Mulvane	8	0	0	2	6	14	113	8	0
Neodesha	9	0	2	0	7	12	41	2	0
Newton	123	0	28	8	87	126	518	20	5
North Newton	0	0	0	0	0	0	10	0	0
Norton	6	0	0	0	6	14	34	0	0
Oakley	3	0	0	0	3	3	18	0	0
Oberlin	0	0	0	0	0	3	15	2	0
Olathe	185	2		23	123	217	1,877	179	19
Osage City	3	0	0	0	3	11	26	3	2
Osawatomie	16	0	1	0	15	22	68	6	1
Oswego	2	0	1	0	1	5	13	1	1
Ottawa	30	0	8	2	20	82	223	18	2
Overland Park	284	2		45	204	404	2,846	280	15
Paola	18	0	4	1	13	16	169	4	1
Park City	10	1	2	1	6	49	132	14	0
Peabody	1	0	0	0	1	20	10	2	1
Pittsburg	96	1	19	16	60	208	797	36	3
Plainville	0	0	0	0	0	6	6	0	0
Prairie Village	10	0	1	2	7	51	147	23	0
Pratt	19	1	1	1	16	70	203	9	1
Rose Hill	6	0	1	0	5	5	45	1	2
Russell	24	0	3	0	21	33	38	7	0
Salina	155	1	39	24	91	322	1,513	115	15
Scott City	14	0	2	1	11	8	36	3	1
Scranton	1	0	0	0	1	2	12	1	0
Sedgwick	1	0	0	0	1	3	15	0	0
Seneca	2	0	1	0	1	6	22	3	0
Shawnee	87	2	15	17	53	170	760	157	8
South Hutchinson	7	0	0	1	6	25	48	3	0
Spring Hill	5	0	1	1	3	17	68	6	1
St. John	9	0	2	0	7	5	9	0	0
St. Marys	4	0	0	1	3	11	15	3	2
Stockton	3	0	0	0	3	8	3	0	0
Tonganoxie	13	0	3	0	10	13	61	7	0
Topeka	612	11		172	396	1,238	4,679	569	7
Ulysses	13	0	0	1	12	15	48	4	0
Valley Center	15	0	3	0	12	11	69	2	0
Victoria	0	0	0	0	0	3	4	0	0
Wa Keeney	0	0	0	0	0	2	12	2	0

Table 8. Offenses Known to Law Enforcement, by Selected State and City, 2013— continued

(Number.)

State/city	Violent crime	Murder and nonnegligent manslaughter	Rape (revised definition)	Robbery	Aggravated assault	Burglary	Larceny-theft	Motor vehicle theft	Arson[2]
Wamego	4	0	0	0	4	16	53	4	3
Waterville	0	0	0	0	0	0	1	0	0
Wathena	3	0	1	0	2	4	9	0	0
Waverly	0	0	0	0	0	0	0	0	0
Wellington	34	0	2	3	29	95	324	31	1
Wellsville	4	0	1	1	2	2	20	0	0
Westwood	0	0	0	0	0	11	27	4	0
Wichita	3,065	15	244	468	2,338	3,933	14,885	1,984	113
Winchester	0	0	0	0	0	0	7	0	0
Yates Center	0	0	0	0	0	8	4	2	1
Kentucky									
Adairville	0	0	0	0	0	0	0	0	0
Albany	0	0	0	0	0	0	0	0	0
Alexandria	5	0	1	4	0	16	177	5	0
Anchorage	0	0	0	0	0	11	33	2	0
Ashland	41	0	8	14	19	171	832	36	2
Auburn	3	0	1	0	2	4	10	1	0
Audubon Park	0	0	0	0	0	9	22	5	0
Barbourville	8	0	1	6	1	11	17	2	0
Bardstown	13	0	2	5	6	77	232	6	3
Bardwell	0	0	0	0	0	0	0	0	0
Beattyville	2	0	0	1	1	3	6	3	0
Beaver Dam	2	0	0	0	2	3	39	4	0
Bellevue	10	1	5	1	3	66	108	9	3
Benham	0	0	0	0	0	0	3	0	0
Benton	2	0	0	0	2	22	48	1	0
Berea	11	0	1	5	5	101	262	11	0
Bloomfield	0	0	0	0	0	2	4	1	0
Bowling Green	201	2	59	69	71	455	2,272	125	2
Brandenburg	0	0	0	0	0	4	14	1	0
Brownsville	1	0	1	0	0	1	1	1	0
Burkesville	2	0	0	2	0	7	2	1	0
Burnside	1	0	0	0	1	8	25	1	0
Cadiz	5	0	1	1	3	25	69	1	0
Calvert City	1	0	0	0	1	6	20	1	0
Campbellsville	47	0	13	15	19	83	233	6	0
Carlisle	2	0	0	1	1	0	24	2	0
Carrollton	3	0	2	0	1	14	49	2	1
Catlettsburg	5	0	1	2	2	11	25	2	0
Cave City	5	0	1	2	2	10	36	1	1
Central City	6	0	0	1	5	7	75	0	0
Clarkson	0	0	0	0	0	1	3	1	0
Clay	0	0	0	0	0	1	1	0	0
Clay City	1	0	1	0	0	9	6	1	1
Cloverport	0	0	0	0	0	0	0	0	0
Coal Run Village	0	0	0	0	0	10	60	1	0
Cold Spring	5	0	0	5	0	10	146	2	0
Columbia	5	0	0	1	4	22	40	2	0
Corbin	16	0	5	7	4	66	175	10	3
Covington	241	2	36	131	72	592	1,095	158	22
Cumberland	7	0	1	1	5	3	5	1	0
Cynthiana	14	0	4	4	6	56	229	10	0
Danville	39	3	8	12	16	169	408	17	1
Dawson Springs	1	0	1	0	0	8	28	1	1
Dayton	21	0	6	5	10	67	163	9	2
Earlington	0	0	0	0	0	0	0	0	0
Eddyville	0	0	0	0	0	6	21	0	0
Edgewood	3	0	3	0	0	10	100	4	0
Edmonton	1	0	0	1	0	3	3	0	0
Elizabethtown	35	0	9	10	16	182	881	25	3
Elkton	4	0	0	2	2	5	24	0	0
Elsmere	15	0	4	4	7	72	126	7	0
Eminence	2	0	1	0	1	7	25	1	0
Erlanger	27	1	10	11	5	94	428	33	0
Evarts	0	0	0	0	0	4	8	0	0
Falmouth	2	0	0	1	1	15	37	2	0
Ferguson	0	0	0	0	0	3	6	0	0
Flatwoods	1	0	0	1	0	14	19	6	1
Flemingsburg	0	0	0	0	0	6	37	4	0
Florence	62	0	11	36	15	182	1,278	73	5
Fort Mitchell	4	1	0	3	0	9	73	9	0
Fort Thomas	9	0	4	3	2	55	129	10	1
Fort Wright	19	0	1	18	0	27	315	9	0
Frankfort	81	1	14	35	31	246	857	59	2
Franklin	14	0	2	6	6	47	241	5	0
Fulton	10	0	3	2	5	15	53	3	0
Gamaliel	0	0	0	0	0	0	0	0	0

Table 8.   Offenses Known to Law Enforcement, by Selected State and City, 2013— continued

(Number.)

State/city	Violent crime	Murder and nonnegligent manslaughter	Rape (revised definition)	Robbery	Aggravated assault	Burglary	Larceny-theft	Motor vehicle theft	Arson[2]
Georgetown	78	3	16	36	23	176	874	38	2
Glasgow	30	0	5	3	22	55	269	14	2
Graymoor-Devondale	1	0	0	1	0	8	19	3	0
Grayson	2	0	0	0	2	17	46	2	0
Greensburg	0	0	0	0	0	7	18	1	0
Greenup	0	0	0	0	0	1	3	0	0
Greenville	1	0	0	0	1	6	7	0	0
Guthrie	0	0	0	0	0	3	7	2	0
Hardinsburg	2	0	1	0	1	8	9	0	0
Harlan	14	0	1	7	6	20	67	3	0
Harrodsburg	16	0	5	3	8	71	152	5	0
Hartford	1	0	0	0	1	3	2	2	0
Hawesville	0	0	0	0	0	2	5	0	0
Hazard	30	4	3	6	17	46	205	12	2
Henderson	66	0	8	28	30	147	808	59	1
Heritage Creek	0	0	0	0	0	0	1	0	0
Highland Heights	1	0	0	0	1	18	51	1	0
Hillview	14	0	1	7	6	43	106	6	0
Hodgenville	1	0	0	0	1	6	16	1	0
Hopkinsville	107	5	19	28	55	341	890	38	3
Hurstbourne Acres	0	0	0	0	0	4	3	0	0
Independence	22	1	9	5	7	53	125	8	0
Indian Hills	0	0	0	0	0	18	27	2	0
Irvine	0	0	0	0	0	3	2	0	0
Irvington	0	0	0	0	0	2	7	2	0
Jackson	3	0	0	1	2	13	27	2	0
Jamestown	0	0	0	0	0	5	7	0	0
Jeffersontown	37	0	10	21	6	237	415	46	0
Jenkins	0	0	0	0	0	0	0	0	0
La Grange	4	0	1	0	3	21	89	11	1
Lakeside Park-Crestview Hills	4	0	0	3	1	11	98	6	0
Lancaster	4	0	0	0	4	23	75	2	0
Lawrenceburg	17	0	3	2	12	26	67	6	0
Lebanon	9	0	1	1	7	54	65	4	0
Lebanon Junction	4	0	1	0	3	10	12	2	0
Leitchfield	10	0	1	0	9	78	162	7	1
Lewisburg	1	0	0	0	1	2	1	0	0
Lewisport	3	0	3	0	0	1	2	0	0
Lexington	946	18	134	467	327	2,574	9,042	831	46
Liberty	0	0	0	0	0	3	18	3	1
London	8	0	5	3	0	35	212	13	2
Louisa	1	0	0	0	1	10	25	1	0
Louisville Metro	3,644	48		1,427	2,009	6,920	19,835	2,025	237
Loyall	0	0	0	0	0	4	2	0	0
Ludlow	8	0	4	3	1	58	110	9	1
Lynnview	1	0	0	1	0	2	10	0	0
Madisonville	26	0	7	8	11	80	323	17	2
Manchester	2	0	0	1	1	7	18	4	0
Marion	6	0	2	1	3	14	36	3	0
Martin	0	0	0	0	0	2	1	0	0
Mayfield	32	0	4	9	19	64	183	6	1
Maysville	14	0	4	6	4	87	290	12	1
McKee	0	0	0	0	0	1	1	0	0
Meadow Vale	1	0	0	1	0	1	6	0	0
Middlesboro	28	0	6	15	7	58	539	16	1
Monticello	5	0	0	2	3	60	90	5	1
Morehead	11	1	0	5	5	17	125	6	1
Morganfield	4	0	0	0	4	5	24	1	0
Morgantown	2	0	0	0	2	10	52	4	0
Mortons Gap	0	0	0	0	0	1	0	0	0
Mount Sterling	15	0	1	6	8	59	306	16	1
Mount Vernon	3	0	0	3	0	7	15	3	0
Mount Washington	3	0	1	0	2	40	86	5	0
Muldraugh	3	0	2	0	1	5	14	3	0
Munfordville	1	0	0	1	0	4	5	0	0
Murray	38	0	12	7	19	109	449	12	5
New Haven	1	0	0	0	1	0	3	0	0
Newport	63	0	14	37	12	217	754	56	5
Nicholasville	70	1	11	34	24	254	840	37	1
Northfield	0	0	0	0	0	1	8	0	0
Oak Grove	22	0	4	8	10	85	153	13	2
Olive Hill	1	0	0	0	1	7	16	1	0
Owensboro	140	0	47	49	44	373	1,553	106	7
Owenton	0	0	0	0	0	5	6	2	0
Owingsville	1	0	0	0	1	10	10	1	0
Paducah	72	0	13	25	34	132	1,020	45	4
Paintsville	3	0	0	3	0	11	79	1	0
Paris	16	0	3	6	7	81	206	11	2

Table 8. Offenses Known to Law Enforcement, by Selected State and City, 2013— continued

(Number.)

State/city	Violent crime	Murder and nonnegligent manslaughter	Rape (revised definition)[1]	Robbery	Aggravated assault	Burglary	Larceny-theft	Motor vehicle theft	Arson[2]
Park Hills	3	0	1	2	0	16	32	2	0
Pembroke	0	0	0	0	0	5	7	0	0
Perryville	0	0	0	0	0	1	5	0	0
Pewee Valley	0	0	0	0	0	2	3	0	0
Pikeville	5	0	1	3	1	41	417	14	1
Pineville	2	0	0	2	0	13	44	2	0
Pioneer Village	0	0	0	0	0	5	6	1	0
Powderly	0	0	0	0	0	2	8	2	0
Prestonsburg	10	0	2	1	7	15	41	7	0
Princeton	8	0	1	3	4	34	85	3	1
Prospect	0	0	0	0	0	13	36	0	0
Providence	7	0	0	2	5	14	25	4	0
Raceland	3	0	0	1	2	9	23	0	0
Radcliff	46	1	16	12	17	155	458	22	3
Ravenna	0	0	0	0	0	3	9	1	0
Richmond	95	0	9	49	37	350	1,125	50	4
Russell	4	1	0	2	1	8	48	0	0
Russell Springs	3	0	0	1	2	14	41	1	0
Russellville	13	0	7	2	4	52	174	13	0
Salyersville	1	1	0	0	0	0	1	0	0
Science Hill	0	0	0	0	0	2	1	0	0
Scottsville	4	0	2	1	1	27	58	3	0
Shelbyville	32	0	5	18	9	78	252	12	2
Shepherdsville	25	0	8	5	12	81	232	32	0
Shively	93	2	9	66	16	178	397	77	1
Silver Grove	1	0	0	1	0	9	21	1	0
Simpsonville	1	0	0	1	0	4	13	0	0
Smiths Grove	0	0	0	0	0	0	8	0	0
Somerset	23	0	5	11	7	71	391	18	1
Southgate	6	1	1	4	0	17	43	3	0
South Shore	0	0	0	0	0	0	2	0	0
Springfield	6	0	0	2	4	9	10	4	0
Stanford	6	0	3	2	1	5	14	8	0
Stanton	1	0	0	1	0	15	33	0	0
St. Matthews	31	1	1	23	6	129	559	13	0
Strathmoor Village	0	0	0	0	0	2	0	0	0
Sturgis	1	0	0	1	0	1	6	0	0
Taylor Mill	1	0	1	0	0	15	54	4	1
Taylorsville	0	0	0	0	0	6	14	1	0
Tompkinsville	1	0	0	0	1	0	1	3	0
Trenton	0	0	0	0	0	0	0	0	0
Uniontown	0	0	0	0	0	7	15	1	0
Vanceburg	1	0	0	0	1	0	9	2	0
Versailles	32	0	6	9	17	122	390	22	0
Villa Hills	0	0	0	0	0	4	30	3	0
Vine Grove	9	0	6	0	3	19	58	1	1
Warsaw	1	0	0	0	1	3	10	0	0
Wayland	0	0	0	0	0	1	2	0	0
West Buechel	14	0	0	14	0	16	450	10	0
West Liberty	1	0	0	1	0	6	17	0	0
West Point	4	0	1	0	3	5	22	2	0
Wheelwright	0	0	0	0	0	0	0	0	0
Whitesburg	0	0	0	0	0	0	0	0	0
Wilder	3	0	0	1	2	9	53	4	0
Williamsburg	7	1	1	2	3	29	67	6	0
Williamstown	2	0	1	0	1	23	50	6	0
Wilmore	0	0	0	0	0	22	26	1	1
Winchester	52	0	7	13	32	145	755	35	2
Worthington	0	0	0	0	0	1	3	0	0
Louisiana									
Abbeville	120	2		10	99	191	358	10	
Addis	8	0		0	8	0	1	0	0
Alexandria	803	6		156	630	1,130	2,561	189	
Amite	81	0		8	73	70	352	15	0
Baker	31	1	4	6	20	78	392	16	1
Bastrop	155	2		31	117	370	830	65	
Baton Rouge	2,127	49		974	1,030	3,264	7,648	506	103
Bernice	1	0	0	0	1	3	10	0	0
Berwick	2	1		1	0	12	50	4	
Blanchard	0	0		0	0	5	27	2	0
Bogalusa	106	1		25	74	199	361	32	2
Bossier City	394	6		65	303	473	2,554	155	9
Breaux Bridge	11	0		6	5	43	428	10	0
Broussard	30	0		2	27	128	152	14	
Brusly	3	0		1	2	0	0	0	0
Carencro	31	0		8	23	43	253	12	0
Church Point	11	0		3	8	14	63	2	0

Table 8.   Offenses Known to Law Enforcement, by Selected State and City, 2013— continued

(Number.)

State/city	Violent crime	Murder and nonnegligent manslaughter	Rape (revised definition)	Robbery	Aggravated assault	Burglary	Larceny-theft	Motor vehicle theft	Arson[2]
Clarence	0	0		0	0	0	0	0	0
Clinton	1	0		0	1	0	1	0	0
Cottonport	17	0		1	16	4	5	0	2
Coushatta	9	0		1	8	10	40	0	0
Covington	40	0		10	30	45	277	13	1
Delta	3	0		0	3	0	0	0	0
Denham Springs	60	0		10	48	194	768	14	0
De Quincy	0	0	0	0	0	15	46	1	0
De Ridder	78	0		5	70	69	216	6	1
Epps	0	0		0	0	0	0	0	0
Erath	20	0		0	20	3	11	3	0
Eunice	98	0		16	74	196	402	15	
Farmerville	19	0		1	18	51	196	2	0
Ferriday	18	0		5	13	61	119	1	0
Fisher	2	0		0	2	1	0	0	0
Florien	1	0		0	1	0	0	0	0
Folsom	1	0		1	0	6	11	2	0
Franklin	60	1		7	52	61	302	5	
Franklinton	22	0		9	12	48	127	8	0
French Settlement	2	0		0	2	2	17	1	0
Georgetown	0	0		0	0	0	0	0	0
Golden Meadow	0	0		0	0	3	0	0	0
Gonzales	66	0	5	16	45	63	684	25	0
Grambling	15	0		1	14	112	0	0	1
Gramercy	13	0		0	13	6	56	1	0
Greenwood	10	0		1	9	16	62	6	0
Gretna	67	2		24	38	98	414	41	4
Hammond	251	3		77	157	902	1,322	81	0
Harahan	15	1		4	8	35	102	3	1
Haughton	3	0		0	3	0	3	0	0
Hodge	2	0		2	0	6	5	0	
Houma	204	5		67	116	243	1,272	59	7
Independence	21	0		4	17	29	101	2	0
Iowa	62	0		1	60	10	50	13	
Jeanerette	14	0		1	13	19	83	5	
Jena	3	0		1	2	3	0	0	0
Jennings	30	0	0	6	24	53	254	5	2
Jonesville	20	0		0	19	55	52	2	0
Kaplan	22	0		3	18	18	73	0	0
Kenner	193	7		94	74	342	1,848	132	8
Kentwood	29	0		4	23	136	79	9	0
Killian	1	0		0	1	18	17	0	0
Kinder	13	0		2	11	0	51	2	
Lafayette	868	8		272	571	1,276	5,995	297	19
Lake Arthur	3	1	0	0	2	7	6	3	0
Lake Charles	547	11		178	327	1,974	1,356	205	
Lake Providence	29	0		7	18	10	19	3	0
Leesville	29	0		4	24	13	230	7	
Livonia	1	0		0	1	0	1	0	0
Lutcher	13	0		1	12	4	22	2	0
Mandeville	24	0		10	13	39	229	6	0
Mansfield	47	0		1	45	104	201	3	
Many	33	3		5	25	15	183	1	1
Marion	1	0		1	0	13	19	0	0
Marksville	77	0		6	70	75	267	12	
Minden	31	1		7	21	55	207	12	
Monroe	516	6		147	334	1,467	2,822	82	0
Montgomery	8	0		0	8	20	1	2	0
Montpelier	1	0		0	1	0	4	0	0
Moreauville	1	0		0	1	3	4	0	0
Morgan City	60	3		8	42	54	398	10	
Napoleonville	1	0		0	1	0	0	0	0
Natchitoches	149	1		27	113	513	928	14	3
New Orleans	2,965	156		1,138	1,495	3,203	9,179	2,143	
North Hodge	2	0		0	2	1	8	0	
Norwood	3	0		0	3	0	0	0	0
Oak Grove	5	0		0	5	6	65	1	0
Oil City	2	0		0	2	2	6	0	0
Opelousas	299	2		75	193	275	899	41	2
Patterson	10	1		0	9	6	88	2	
Pearl River	15	0		2	13	14	54	4	0
Pineville	81	0		9	68	158	711	28	2
Plaquemine	46	4	0	3	39	54	266	7	0
Pollock	1	0		0	1	3	6	1	0
Ponchatoula	38	1		4	33	111	221	8	0
Port Vincent	0	0		0	0	5	26	1	0
Rayne	37	1		18	18	66	248	3	0
Roseland	3	0		0	2	4	6	4	0

Table 8.   Offenses Known to Law Enforcement, by Selected State and City, 2013— continued

(Number.)

State/city	Violent crime	Murder and nonnegligent manslaughter	Rape (revised definition)[1]	Robbery	Aggravated assault	Burglary	Larceny-theft	Motor vehicle theft	Arson[2]
Ruston	90	1		20	66	189	596	13	2
Scott	18	1		3	12	46	171	18	0
Shreveport	1,397	26		376	911	2,360	6,720	504	80
Slidell	96	5		16	66	183	1,297	68	1
St. Francisville	4	0		1	3	17	46	1	0
St. Gabriel	24	0		2	20	23	49	4	0
Sulphur	140	0		15	114	258	843	36	1
Thibodaux	68	1		7	56	93	577	13	2
Tickfaw	1	0		0	1	2	17	1	0
Vidalia	21	1		2	18	30	129	2	0
Vinton	8	0	1	2	5	18	33	0	1
Walker	38	0		10	27	42	294	5	0
West Monroe	94	2		7	78	178	873	22	6
Westwego	23	0		1	19	48	180	11	1
Wilson	0	0		0	0	3	0	0	0
Winnfield	81	1		8	70	92	194	13	0
Zachary	39	0		4	34	63	416	18	1
Zwolle	7	0		2	5	17	35	4	0
Maine									
Ashland	0	0		0	0	7	4	1	0
Auburn	32	0	10	10	12	197	858	17	2
Augusta	68	1	25	16	26	206	969	31	5
Baileyville	10	0		0	10	9	22	1	0
Bangor	70	3		35	22	243	1,564	37	4
Bar Harbor	3	0	0	2	1	19	59	1	0
Bath	8	0		1	5	26	262	2	6
Belfast	9	1		0	8	29	124	1	0
Berwick	8	0		0	5	37	84	2	2
Biddeford	119	1		24	75	149	972	18	6
Boothbay Harbor	1	0		0	1	9	50	1	1
Brewer	7	0		2	5	44	251	3	0
Bridgton	7	0		1	5	6	25	2	0
Brownville	1	0		1	0	10	11	2	0
Brunswick	23	0		4	11	90	409	10	0
Bucksport	8	0		0	8	25	48	5	0
Buxton	11	0		0	10	25	68	5	1
Calais	11	0		0	9	18	138	0	0
Camden	2	0		0	1	14	66	1	0
Cape Elizabeth	0	0		0	0	26	70	2	2
Caribou	6	0		1	5	26	80	6	0
Carrabassett Valley	0	0	0	0	0	4	44	0	0
Clinton	4	0		0	2	11	25	2	0
Cumberland	1	0		0	1	11	7	1	0
Damariscotta	2	0		0	1	1	32	0	1
Dexter	5	0		2	3	20	77	4	0
Dixfield	1	0		0	1	15	50	0	1
Dover-Foxcroft	9	0		1	8	22	103	6	2
East Millinocket	0	0		0	0	8	49	0	0
Eastport	3	0		0	3	6	9	1	0
Eliot	4	0		1	1	4	31	0	0
Ellsworth	5	1		1	3	57	209	8	0
Fairfield	6	0		0	4	49	192	5	0
Falmouth	5	1		1	2	19	106	3	2
Farmington	14	0	3	0	11	23	184	3	0
Fort Fairfield	4	0		0	4	8	38	2	0
Fort Kent	2	0		0	2	0	11	1	0
Freeport	3	1		0	2	25	129	4	0
Fryeburg	5	0		1	3	9	32	0	1
Gardiner	10	0		0	7	23	140	1	0
Gorham	14	0		1	11	36	121	7	3
Gouldsboro	1	0		0	1	2	13	0	0
Greenville	4	0		0	4	10	31	0	1
Hallowell	4	0		0	3	10	48	2	0
Hampden	4	0		1	2	18	97	4	0
Holden	1	0		0	1	32	50	0	0
Houlton	6	0		0	4	27	115	1	0
Islesboro	0	0		0	0	3	2	0	0
Jay	3	0		1	1	30	80	3	1
Kennebunk	7	0		1	5	30	102	2	0
Kennebunkport	1	0		0	0	17	47	0	0
Kittery	11	0		3	2	12	153	3	1
Lewiston	89	0	25	20	44	313	848	56	23
Limestone	3	0		0	3	5	9	2	3
Lincoln	2	0		1	1	54	142	5	0
Lisbon	5	0	3	1	1	14	80	4	0
Livermore Falls	2	0		0	2	15	71	2	0
Machias	8	0		2	5	7	37	0	1

Table 8.   Offenses Known to Law Enforcement, by Selected State and City, 2013— continued

(Number.)

State/city	Violent crime	Murder and nonnegligent manslaughter	Rape (revised definition)[1]	Robbery	Aggravated assault	Burglary	Larceny-theft	Motor vehicle theft	Arson[2]
Madawaska	2	0		0	1	3	32	1	0
Madison	4	0	2	0	2	21	73	9	0
Mechanic Falls	6	0		0	5	11	19	1	1
Mexico	3	0		0	1	51	75	3	0
Milbridge	2	0		1	1	1	6	0	0
Millinocket	3	0		1	1	24	52	1	0
Milo	18	0		0	18	21	58	3	0
Monmouth	1	0	0	0	1	16	34	5	0
Mount Desert	0	0		0	0	5	27	0	0
Newport	2	0		2	0	12	85	0	0
North Berwick	3	0		0	3	14	17	1	1
Norway	9	0		0	2	27	109	2	0
Oakland	3	0	3	0	0	24	72	6	0
Ogunquit	1	0		0	1	5	33	0	0
Old Orchard Beach	11	0	7	0	4	67	183	5	1
Old Town	11	1		2	7	22	127	3	0
Orono	3	0		1	1	33	152	1	0
Oxford	4	0		0	3	21	193	4	0
Paris	2	0		0	2	23	95	4	0
Phippsburg	0	0		0	0	3	9	0	0
Pittsfield	0	0		0	0	3	41	3	1
Portland	177	1		85	70	383	2,160	69	6
Presque Isle	13	0		1	8	9	150	2	0
Rangeley	1	0		0	1	10	17	1	0
Richmond	0	0		0	0	5	15	1	0
Rockland	8	0		0	7	31	203	7	0
Rockport	0	0		0	0	4	17	1	0
Rumford	6	0		2	2	48	168	3	1
Sabattus	6	0		0	3	33	44	3	0
Saco	24	0	7	8	9	133	363	12	4
Sanford	70	0		12	39	135	642	26	8
Scarborough	17	0	7	2	8	66	343	11	0
Searsport	0	0		0	0	17	45	3	0
Skowhegan	18	0	9	2	7	86	386	26	3
South Berwick	4	0		0	0	12	57	3	0
South Portland	60	0	10	13	37	113	722	26	0
Southwest Harbor	0	0		0	0	13	37	0	0
Swan's Island	0	0		0	0	5	7	1	0
Thomaston	0	0		0	0	7	55	0	0
Topsham	4	0		1	2	27	117	10	1
Van Buren	0	0		0	0	6	7	2	0
Veazie	1	0		1	0	8	55	0	0
Waldoboro	4	0		1	1	19	51	0	1
Washburn	1	0		0	1	8	27	1	0
Waterville	43	0	15	13	15	105	684	15	1
Wells	5	0	3	0	2	42	77	3	0
Westbrook	38	1		6	20	78	485	20	1
Wilton	5	0		0	5	16	28	1	0
Windham	9	0		2	7	53	248	12	2
Winslow	11	0	6	2	3	33	112	5	0
Winter Harbor	1	0		0	1	1	4	0	0
Winthrop	3	0		1	2	36	94	2	0
Wiscasset	8	0		1	5	15	37	1	0
Yarmouth	6	0		1	3	19	52	1	1
York	8	0	3	1	4	53	161	5	2
Maryland									
Aberdeen	50	0		20	26	77	413	16	4
Annapolis	169	4		63	94	169	821	66	13
Baltimore	8,725	233		3,734	4,460	7,391	18,946	4,452	277
Baltimore City Sheriff	0	0		0	0	0	0	0	0
Bel Air	47	0		11	34	44	316	5	2
Berlin	5	0		1	4	28	69	0	0
Berwyn Heights	7	0		5	2	17	33	2	0
Bladensburg	95	1		43	49	106	230	71	0
Boonsboro	2	0		1	1	4	16	2	0
Bowie	61	0		28	27	155	661	66	4
Brentwood	1	0		0	1	4	10	2	0
Brunswick	8	0		0	8	15	60	0	0
Cambridge	119	0		31	86	95	510	6	12
Capitol Heights	15	0		3	12	26	20	17	0
Centreville	6	0		5	1	21	51	2	1
Chestertown	27	0		13	14	36	104	4	2
Cheverly	29	0		12	16	24	118	25	0
Chevy Chase Village	0	0		0	0	4	35	5	0
Colmar Manor	12	0		2	10	2	37	4	0
Cottage City	4	0		0	4	8	16	5	0
Crisfield	11	0		4	7	3	38	0	1

Table 8.   Offenses Known to Law Enforcement, by Selected State and City, 2013— continued

(Number.)

State/city	Violent crime	Murder and nonnegligent manslaughter	Rape (revised definition)[1]	Robbery	Aggravated assault	Burglary	Larceny-theft	Motor vehicle theft	Arson[2]
Cumberland	160	1		44	95	323	991	27	6
Delmar	10	0		1	9	25	57	1	2
Denton	13	0		4	8	34	241	0	0
District Heights	6	0		3	3	35	86	19	0
Easton	41	0		15	20	74	252	2	0
Edmonston	7	0		1	6	8	40	8	0
Elkton	194	0		40	143	186	828	28	4
Fairmount Heights	0	0		0	0	1	0	2	0
Federalsburg	41	0		2	39	16	64	4	0
Forest Heights	4	0		0	4	38	22	4	0
Frederick	328	1		98	222	227	1,504	61	8
Frostburg	19	0		4	12	43	170	2	0
Fruitland	20	0		5	13	18	231	0	1
Glenarden	9	0		3	6	24	57	15	0
Greenbelt	106	0		66	35	192	545	107	0
Greensboro	9	0		1	7	18	37	0	1
Hagerstown	244	5		101	128	375	1,051	72	27
Hampstead	6	0		1	3	14	60	1	2
Hancock	1	0		0	1	3	30	0	0
Havre de Grace	35	0		11	21	54	321	17	1
Hurlock	4	0		0	4	17	26	2	0
Hyattsville	76	0		56	19	114	938	57	0
Landover Hills	10	0		6	4	9	39	11	0
La Plata	45	0		6	39	47	227	5	3
Laurel	147	0		67	76	145	596	82	1
Lonaconing	0	0		0	0	0	1	0	0
Luke	0	0		0	0	0	0	0	0
Manchester	5	0		1	4	10	16	1	0
Morningside	6	0		3	3	20	26	6	0
Mount Rainier	50	0		35	14	64	170	46	0
New Carrollton	46	2		16	28	40	188	39	1
North East	7	0		2	5	14	107	9	0
Oakland	1	0		1	0	2	35	0	0
Ocean City	83	2		20	50	154	1,036	33	2
Ocean Pines	30	0		0	30	35	112	1	0
Oxford	0	0		0	0	1	5	0	0
Perryville	13	0		4	9	24	96	8	1
Pocomoke City	49	0		3	46	17	164	2	1
Princess Anne	22	0		5	14	37	140	7	3
Ridgely	10	0		2	8	10	36	1	1
Rising Sun	3	0		0	3	7	22	0	0
Riverdale Park	51	0		16	35	30	79	24	0
Rock Hall	4	0		2	2	3	14	1	0
Salisbury	326	0		99	210	336	1,420	50	11
Seat Pleasant	34	1		11	21	31	94	27	0
Smithsburg	1	0		0	1	5	14	0	2
Snow Hill	15	0		1	13	17	48	1	0
St. Michaels	2	0		0	2	5	40	1	0
Sykesville	4	0		1	3	4	16	4	1
Takoma Park	60	1		37	20	125	301	42	1
Taneytown	6	0		0	6	12	61	0	2
Thurmont	11	0		2	9	30	52	1	0
Trappe	4	0		0	4	2	18	0	0
University Park	2	0		1	1	20	49	7	0
Upper Marlboro	1	0		1	0	1	13	3	0
Westminster	88	2		13	73	113	726	10	2
Massachusetts									
Abington	48	0	5	7	36	82	201	14	1
Acton	8	0	1	2	5	31	144	3	0
Acushnet	19	0	2	0	17	27	40	7	2
Adams	21	0	3	3	15	40	109	8	1
Agawam	41	0	12	3	26	105	130	35	1
Amesbury	42	0	3	2	37	40	191	8	2
Amherst	70	0	23	3	44	76	274	17	5
Andover	20	0	3	1	16	39	255	20	0
Arlington	55	3	7	10	35	126	365	25	3
Ashburnham	5	0	2	1	2	20	44	1	0
Ashby	7	0	1	1	5	23	18	2	0
Ashland	18	0	2	0	16	91	109	6	0
Athol	53	0	7	3	43	55	97	2	4
Attleboro	108	0	16	16	76	171	702	69	2
Auburn	47	0	4	7	36	77	437	16	1
Avon	10	0		4	6	29	220	3	
Ayer	12	0	1	1	10	51	84	2	0
Barnstable	302	0	18	30	254	289	835	67	8
Barre	26	0	6	0	20	23	27	3	1
Becket	4	0		0	4	20	7	0	

Table 8.   Offenses Known to Law Enforcement, by Selected State and City, 2013— continued

(Number.)

State/city	Violent crime	Murder and nonnegligent manslaughter	Rape (revised definition)[1]	Robbery	Aggravated assault	Burglary	Larceny-theft	Motor vehicle theft	Arson[2]
Bedford	6	0	1	3	2	11	62	1	0
Belchertown	21	0	4	1	16	41	121	5	0
Bellingham	35	0	3	8	24	55	225	11	3
Belmont	24	0	4	2	18	56	172	13	3
Berkley	9	0	0	1	8	21	23	1	0
Berlin	0	0	0	0	0	0	14	0	0
Bernardston	4	0	0	1	3	2	11	2	0
Beverly	88	0	7	9	72	77	469	28	1
Billerica	48	0	7	8	33	88	352	28	5
Blackstone	17	0	3	2	12	20	60	4	0
Bolton	9	0	0	2	7	18	25	1	0
Boston	5,037	39		1,868	2,851	3,096	13,147	1,610	
Bourne	91	0	14	8	69	215	235	15	4
Boxborough	8	0	0	1	7	4	17	3	0
Boxford	4	0	0	1	3	9	23	2	0
Braintree	83	0	5	18	60	97	648	26	1
Brewster	7	0	0	0	7	50	78	4	1
Brimfield	1	0	0	0	1	9	12	0	0
Brockton	1,162	9	87	228	838	865	2,100	224	20
Brookline	85	0	6	16	63	107	549	20	1
Burlington	33	0	3	6	24	32	453	16	0
Cambridge	361	2	24	114	221	401	2,402	104	10
Canton	59	0	3	7	49	43	140	5	1
Carver	35	0	6	1	28	56	123	6	2
Charlton	22	0	4	2	16	33	77	3	1
Chatham	11	0	0	0	11	20	101	2	1
Chelmsford	22	0	1	4	17	49	422	17	0
Chelsea	458	5	28	175	250	209	874	151	4
Chicopee	272	1	22	81	168	459	995	109	4
Chilmark	1	0	0	0	1	1	7	0	0
Clinton	10	0	0	2	8	9	31	0	0
Cohasset	9	0	0	0	9	20	46	3	0
Concord	17	0	1	1	15	20	162	2	0
Dalton	5	0	2	0	3	20	48	1	2
Danvers	51	1	3	6	41	54	684	23	0
Dartmouth	49	0	5	9	35	157	732	25	1
Dedham	15	0	3	7	5	47	446	25	0
Deerfield	7	0	0	2	5	16	67	3	0
Dennis	80	0	13	8	59	211	276	18	3
Dighton	10	0		2	7	14	16	0	0
Douglas	10	0	1	0	9	33	21	4	0
Dover	2	0	0	0	2	5	31	0	0
Dracut	20	0	4	8	8	75	392	27	0
Dudley	34	0	3	0	31	39	48	3	0
Dunstable	7	0	1	1	5	6	15	1	0
Duxbury	2	0	0	0	2	16	43	0	0
East Bridgewater	31	0	0	2	29	33	158	9	0
East Brookfield	5	0	0	0	5	3	11	2	0
Eastham	11	0	0	0	11	16	82	2	1
Easthampton	19	0	3	2	14	35	118	6	2
East Longmeadow	28	0	3	0	25	58	227	12	1
Easton	33	0	5	6	22	67	160	19	0
Edgartown	8	0	0	0	8	32	89	8	0
Egremont	1	0		0	1	2	21	0	0
Erving	6	0	1	0	5	6	15	1	2
Essex	0	0		0	0	7	19	3	0
Everett	202	1	19	61	121	186	621	91	0
Fairhaven	64	1	7	5	51	66	285	13	0
Fall River	944	0	73	225	646	698	1,443	223	32
Falmouth	102	2	11	18	71	467	392	40	2
Fitchburg	307	2	33	35	237	275	705	80	7
Framingham	172	0	4	23	145	217	735	73	3
Franklin	7	0	0	6	1	31	138	2	0
Freetown	21	0	3	2	16	54	74	9	2
Gardner	93	0	13	10	70	190	366	15	2
Georgetown	3	0	1	0	2	17	46	1	0
Gill	1	0	0	0	1	5	7	0	0
Gloucester	22	0	9	0	13	33	345	5	0
Goshen	0	0	0	0	0	1	1	0	0
Grafton	22	0	2	4	16	40	76	5	0
Granby	9	0	0	0	9	13	58	4	0
Granville	2	0		0	2	4	4	0	
Great Barrington	30	0	8	1	21	27	88	9	1
Groton	8	0	2	0	6	35	51	0	0
Groveland	1	0	0	1	0	6	11	0	0
Halifax	8	0	2	0	6	32	41	4	0
Hamilton	3	0	0	0	3	8	41	1	0
Hampden	3	0	0	1	2	18	33	4	0

Table 8.   Offenses Known to Law Enforcement, by Selected State and City, 2013— continued

(Number.)

State/city	Violent crime	Murder and nonnegligent manslaughter	Rape (revised definition)[3]	Robbery	Aggravated assault	Burglary	Larceny-theft	Motor vehicle theft	Arson[2]
Hanover	2	0	2	0	0	34	171	6	0
Hanson	19	0	3	1	15	23	57	6	0
Hardwick	5	0	1	0	4	8	20	3	0
Harvard	4	0	2	0	2	23	14	0	3
Harwich	24	0	2	1	21	120	124	7	0
Hatfield	5	0	1	2	2	4	6	0	0
Haverhill	414	2	25	57	330	431	1,052	135	5
Hingham	17	0	2	2	13	84	287	11	0
Holbrook	39	0		11	28	74	100	9	
Holden	8	0	1	1	6	21	71	4	0
Holliston	14	0	0	0	14	25	44	6	1
Holyoke	419	4	42	108	265	484	2,067	113	9
Hopedale	18	0	2	0	16	23	32	2	1
Hopkinton	3	0	1	0	2	6	86	1	1
Hubbardston	6	0	0	0	6	20	21	3	0
Hudson	16	0	2	1	13	33	169	7	0
Hull	42	1	5	0	36	42	95	4	2
Ipswich	10	0	0	0	10	20	96	6	1
Kingston	20	0	3	3	14	28	152	11	0
Lakeville	10	1	2	1	6	62	115	6	0
Lancaster	8	0	3	1	4	30	48	2	1
Lawrence	776	1		283	473	433	1,012	828	
Lee	7	0	3	0	4	23	72	3	0
Leicester	13	0	1	0	12	17	223	10	1
Lenox	4	0	1	0	3	35	83	2	1
Leominster	263	1	25	34	203	244	939	52	5
Lexington	17	0	0	3	14	45	185	2	2
Lincoln	6	1	1	1	3	8	29	0	1
Littleton	9	0	4	0	5	15	75	2	1
Longmeadow	14	0	2	3	9	27	121	8	1
Lowell	625	4	40	192	389	759	2,300	320	18
Ludlow	32	0	7	8	17	78	232	10	0
Lunenburg	22	0	5	1	16	62	145	3	0
Lynn	814	2	39	189	584	510	1,635	253	7
Lynnfield	2	0	0	1	1	14	111	8	0
Malden	205	1	3	79	122	240	618	87	3
Manchester-by-the-Sea	9	0	1	0	8	5	23	0	0
Mansfield	47	0	8	3	36	144	196	12	2
Marblehead	17	0	1	0	16	21	134	4	0
Marion	7	0	1	1	5	9	60	0	0
Marlborough	156	0	18	17	121	119	605	32	2
Marshfield	54	0	5	3	46	29	186	14	2
Mashpee	45	0	4	3	38	61	214	9	2
Mattapoisett	6	0	1	1	4	16	45	5	0
Maynard	13	0	0	0	13	14	79	6	0
Medfield	12	0	2	0	10	16	42	0	0
Medford	112	0	10	29	73	160	672	66	2
Medway	1	0	0	0	1	20	89	2	0
Melrose	21	0	3	4	14	69	181	12	0
Mendon	5	0	0	0	5	17	39	1	0
Merrimac	11	0	0	1	10	24	29	3	0
Methuen	106	0	4	30	72	177	830	120	1
Middleboro	70	1	6	7	56	126	300	17	1
Middleton	11	0	0	0	11	4	70	1	0
Milford	58	0	13	7	38	56	449	17	1
Millbury	38	0	7	5	26	58	206	11	4
Millville	2	0	1	1	0	5	27	0	0
Milton	21	1	1	9	10	95	285	11	0
Monson	27	0	3	0	24	35	53	13	1
Montague	45	0	4	3	38	72	147	3	2
Monterey	0	0	0	0	0	1	2	1	0
Nahant	8	0	1	0	7	4	13	1	0
Nantucket	41	0	8	3	30	29	286	15	0
Natick	36	1	2	3	30	62	468	14	2
New Bedford	1,039	6	100	256	677	916	2,186	335	20
Newburyport	31	0	3	3	25	15	154	8	0
Newton	74	0	11	18	45	205	584	18	4
Norfolk	0	0	0	0	0	13	28	0	0
North Adams	133	1	21	8	103	175	395	15	1
Northampton	130	0	29	14	87	126	647	27	4
North Andover	10	0	0	0	10	26	440	13	0
North Attleboro	2	0	0	2	0	31	366	9	0
Northborough	18	0	1	4	13	38	140	4	0
Northbridge	38	0	15	1	22	93	210	5	2
North Brookfield	34	0	3	0	31	12	15	2	0
North Reading	12	0	0	3	9	17	112	5	0
Norton	8	0	0	2	6	36	53	1	0
Norwell	12	0	1	0	11	28	89	5	0

Table 8.   Offenses Known to Law Enforcement, by Selected State and City, 2013— continued

(Number.)

State/city	Violent crime	Murder and nonnegligent manslaughter	Rape (revised definition)[1]	Robbery	Aggravated assault	Burglary	Larceny-theft	Motor vehicle theft	Arson[2]
Norwood	18	0	1	9	8	85	281	20	2
Oak Bluffs	18	0	0	0	18	26	107	4	0
Orange	25	0	5	3	17	52	110	4	4
Orleans	9	0	1	1	7	24	123	1	1
Oxford	27	0	1	4	22	42	160	10	1
Palmer	38	0	8	5	25	88	111	11	0
Paxton	4	0	2	0	2	10	14	1	0
Peabody	115	0	14	24	77	121	877	63	2
Pelham	0	0	0	0	0	4	1	0	0
Pembroke	33	0	2	3	28	38	114	7	0
Pepperell	22	0	1	1	20	32	89	5	1
Pittsfield	111	0	31	29	51	481	827	44	3
Plainville	2	0	0	1	1	31	101	4	0
Plymouth	184	0	9	18	157	236	540	30	1
Plympton	7	0	1	1	5	17	24	1	0
Princeton	7	0	1	0	6	14	17	1	0
Provincetown	17	0	1	0	16	17	85	3	1
Quincy	361	0	35	87	239	461	1,113	73	4
Randolph	176	0	16	31	129	126	374	36	2
Raynham	26	0	2	9	15	68	310	17	1
Reading	10	0	0	3	7	51	122	11	0
Rehoboth	13	0	1	1	11	51	83	9	0
Revere	317	0	19	82	216	182	813	166	8
Rochester	3	0	1	0	2	18	28	4	0
Rockport	6	0	1	1	4	5	3	0	0
Rowley	6	0	1	1	4	7	14	3	0
Rutland	25	1	3	1	20	11	37	4	0
Salem	128	0	3	22	103	135	1,058	45	8
Salisbury	45	1	7	5	32	57	113	8	0
Sandwich	31	0	8	1	22	70	181	8	1
Saugus	80	0	10	15	55	84	527	37	2
Scituate	24	0	3	3	18	26	105	4	0
Seekonk	33	1	0	4	28	50	280	21	0
Sharon	1	0	0	0	1	26	46	4	0
Sherborn	3	0	1	1	1	13	23	3	2
Shirley	11	0	0	0	11	20	23	1	0
Shrewsbury	6	0	0	2	4	54	204	11	0
Somerset	28	0	3	2	23	45	208	10	0
Somerville	191	0	18	51	122	426	998	101	21
Southampton	4	0	2	1	1	9	36	1	0
Southborough	2	0	1	0	1	31	24	3	0
Southbridge	82	0	11	14	57	149	236	22	10
South Hadley	38	0	4	4	30	97	167	12	1
Southwick	8	0	0	1	7	41	70	11	2
Spencer	29	0	4	1	24	34	116	11	0
Springfield	1,673	22	89	598	964	2,360	4,018	735	56
Sterling	12	0	3	1	8	21	48	3	0
Stockbridge	4	0	0	0	4	15	20	0	0
Stoneham	11	0	0	2	9	52	154	11	1
Stoughton	80	1	9	15	55	74	422	36	0
Stow	4	0	0	1	3	7	17	0	0
Sturbridge	30	0	7	5	18	25	146	4	2
Sudbury	0	0	0	0	0	12	80	2	0
Sutton	4	0	1	0	3	46	55	5	0
Swampscott	26	0	1	5	20	58	204	4	0
Swansea	34	1	5	7	21	54	279	17	2
Taunton	209	0	15	52	142	433	485	44	5
Templeton	22	0	2	2	18	21	57	3	0
Tewksbury	141	0	14	9	118	68	398	36	2
Townsend	7	0	2	2	3	60	57	0	0
Truro	5	0	0	0	5	12	23	0	0
Tyngsboro	16	0	0	2	14	26	97	6	1
Upton	7	0	1	1	5	22	35	3	0
Uxbridge	21	0	3	2	16	52	115	9	2
Wakefield	49	0	11	1	37	66	233	14	0
Wales	1	0	0	0	1	4	4	2	0
Walpole	11	0	1	3	7	36	279	6	0
Waltham	141	1	22	28	90	212	694	46	6
Ware	42	0	2	3	37	36	198	4	5
Wareham	163	0	20	21	122	222	554	30	12
Warren	33	0	2	1	30	17	39	4	0
Watertown	53	0	6	5	42	61	388	12	0
Wayland	5	0	0	0	5	16	24	2	0
Webster	122	0	9	21	92	85	319	22	8
Wellesley	15	0	0	1	14	54	142	6	0
Wellfleet	4	0	0	0	4	13	24	1	2
Westborough	14	0	3	3	8	15	131	3	0
West Boylston	5	0	4	0	1	23	83	3	0

Table 8.   Offenses Known to Law Enforcement, by Selected State and City, 2013— continued

(Number.)

State/city	Violent crime	Murder and nonnegligent manslaughter	Rape (revised definition)[1]	Robbery	Aggravated assault	Burglary	Larceny-theft	Motor vehicle theft	Arson[2]
West Bridgewater	23	0	1	4	18	23	111	8	2
Westfield	103	1	20	25	57	174	464	23	3
Westford	14	0	3	1	10	26	93	2	3
Westhampton	0	0		0	0	3	2	0	
Westminster	9	0	0	0	9	17	169	3	0
West Newbury	6	0	1	0	5	6	18	0	0
Weston	3	0	0	0	3	14	49	2	0
Westport	27	0	3	2	22	64	124	10	1
West Springfield	163	0	22	40	101	250	985	86	6
West Tisbury	1	0	0	0	1	8	16	2	0
Westwood	20	0	4	4	12	17	87	7	0
Weymouth	195	1	23	27	144	145	604	35	4
Whately	6	0	0	0	6	3	11	3	0
Whitman	53	0	8	3	42	43	164	10	1
Wilbraham	17	0	4	1	12	52	170	13	1
Williamsburg	4	0	0	0	4	12	22	2	0
Williamstown	14	0	3	1	10	43	173	0	0
Wilmington	29	0	5	6	18	65	180	8	2
Winchendon	50	0	4	2	44	19	189	9	5
Winchester	10	0	0	2	8	25	167	2	0
Winthrop	58	0	2	4	52	82	117	12	2
Woburn	83	0	12	15	56	91	469	21	1
Worcester	1,750	9	22	483	1,236	1,916	3,924	399	7
Wrentham	8	0	1	0	7	48	206	8	0
Yarmouth	202	0	17	8	177	200	446	22	2
Michigan									
Akron	1	0	0	0	1	3	3	0	0
Albion	58	0	10	13	35	86	144	10	3
Allegan	17	0	9	1	7	6	72	5	1
Allen Park	35	0	7	4	24	100	474	88	4
Alma	22	1	8	3	10	27	180	1	1
Almont	8	0	3	1	4	21	27	3	0
Alpena	46	0	17	1	28	39	219	2	2
Ann Arbor	247	3	48	49	147	410	2,021	94	12
Armada	1	0	1	0	0	0	8	0	0
Auburn Hills	61	0	8	17	36	52	680	27	0
Bad Axe	14	0	7	0	7	3	56	1	0
Bangor	13	0	1	0	12	11	55	2	0
Barryton	0	0	0	0	0	0	4	0	0
Barry Township	0	0	0	0	0	5	18	0	0
Bath Township	19	0	5	1	13	38	92	15	2
Bay City	217	0	62	21	134	210	674	54	5
Belding	7	0	2	0	5	27	122	2	1
Bellaire	0	0	0	0	0	0	5	1	0
Belleville	4	0	1	0	3	15	61	8	1
Benton Harbor	225	3	22	60	140	304	377	25	10
Benton Township	157	0	17	33	107	263	894	47	4
Berkley	12	0	5	3	4	28	115	5	0
Berrien Springs-Oronoko Township	13	0	7	2	4	15	48	2	1
Beverly Hills	6	0	1	3	2	17	100	4	0
Big Rapids	29	0	12	1	16	28	169	3	2
Birch Run	6	0	0	1	5	22	56	4	0
Birmingham	14	0	4	6	4	31	195	13	0
Bloomfield Hills	1	0	1	0	0	7	27	2	0
Bloomfield Township	23	0	3	9	11	74	333	28	1
Boyne City	10	0	4	0	6	8	70	0	2
Breckenridge	1	0	1	0	0	2	19	0	0
Bridgeport Township	41	1	3	4	33	73	104	15	1
Brighton	2	0	0	2	0	10	131	6	1
Bronson	4	0	2	0	2	13	50	2	1
Brown City	3	0	1	1	1	9	25	1	0
Brownstown Township	56	0	15	12	29	102	255	62	4
Buena Vista Township	99	1	5	10	83	110	141	14	4
Burr Oak	8	0	5	0	3	2	6	0	1
Burton	119	2	21	34	62	346	847	46	4
Cadillac	46	1	13	2	30	78	338	7	2
Calumet	4	0	3	0	1	2	9	0	0
Cambridge Township	1	0	0	0	1	0	18	0	0
Canton Township	94	0	18	16	60	173	968	109	8
Capac	4	0	2	0	2	10	31	0	0
Carleton	9	0	1	0	8	11	16	2	0
Caro	26	1	3	0	22	25	131	1	0
Carrollton Township	20	0	6	2	12	25	79	1	0
Caseville	0	0	0	0	0	1	23	0	0
Cass City	3	0	2	0	1	4	57	1	0
Cassopolis	2	0	0	1	1	5	19	0	0

Table 8.   Offenses Known to Law Enforcement, by Selected State and City, 2013— continued

(Number.)

State/city	Violent crime	Murder and nonnegligent manslaughter	Rape (revised definition)	Robbery	Aggravated assault	Burglary	Larceny-theft	Motor vehicle theft	Arson[2]
Cedar Springs	13	0	4	2	7	13	76	1	0
Center Line	37	0	4	10	23	46	162	26	2
Central Lake	0	0	0	0	0	2	9	0	0
Charlevoix	4	0	1	1	2	8	120	3	1
Charlotte	28	0	5	3	20	33	212	6	0
Cheboygan	20	0	10	0	10	24	163	5	1
Chelsea	11	0	1	1	9	15	41	3	0
Chesaning	3	0	0	0	3	1	13	1	0
Chesterfield Township	119	0	6	16	97	90	593	43	0
Chikaming Township	3	0	0	0	3	13	52	0	1
Chocolay Township	0	0	0	0	0	6	31	2	0
Clare	18	0	4	1	13	12	83	2	0
Clawson	10	0	3	1	6	8	72	15	0
Clayton Township	12	1	4	0	7	34	41	1	0
Clay Township	11	0	4	0	7	24	117	5	0
Clinton Township	285	5	56	60	164	420	1,480	234	17
Clio	4	0	0	1	3	49	50	3	0
Coleman	2	0	2	0	0	6	43	2	0
Colon	2	0	0	1	1	0	15	0	1
Columbia Township	18	0	5	0	13	10	21	1	1
Concord	1	1	0	0	0	1	8	0	0
Corunna	5	0	1	0	4	9	29	2	1
Covert Township	9	0	2	0	7	32	43	3	0
Croswell	9	0	2	0	7	7	70	1	1
Crystal Falls	1	0	0	0	1	2	15	1	0
Davison Township	27	0	8	2	17	203	181	8	3
Dearborn	347	2	33	126	186	399	2,328	377	14
Dearborn Heights	212	1	20	66	125	341	765	232	6
Denton Township	9	0	2	0	7	11	81	2	0
Detroit	14,504	316	618	4,774	8,796	11,754	17,188	11,893	611
Dewitt	5	0	0	1	4	13	21	1	1
Dryden Township	2	0	2	0	0	9	26	4	1
East Grand Rapids	3	0	1	0	2	25	112	1	0
East Lansing	109	0	31	24	54	150	552	97	98
Eastpointe	295	1	33	69	192	337	534	295	5
Eaton Rapids	8	0	3	0	5	10	69	1	0
Eau Claire	0	0	0	0	0	0	7	0	0
Edmore	0	0	0	0	0	0	0	0	0
Elk Rapids	2	0	0	1	1	1	36	0	0
Elkton	0	0	0	0	0	2	3	0	0
Elsie	0	0	0	0	0	0	8	0	0
Emmett Township	54	0	6	9	39	87	542	15	2
Escanaba	26	0	16	1	9	39	580	9	2
Essexville	2	0	1	0	1	17	62	3	1
Evart	6	0	1	0	5	12	41	1	0
Farmington	13	1	0	1	11	26	85	4	1
Farmington Hills	72	1	14	21	36	245	773	96	8
Fenton	17	0	5	1	11	56	258	16	2
Ferndale	42	0	4	16	22	89	319	55	2
Flat Rock	17	0	3	3	11	24	100	17	1
Flint	1,907	48	145	447	1,267	1,941	2,000	320	110
Flint Township	336	0	29	114	193	560	1,309	95	5
Flushing	5	0	0	2	3	22	77	3	0
Forsyth Township	12	0	4	1	7	11	71	1	0
Fowlerville	10	1	1	2	6	17	82	6	1
Frankenmuth	10	0	2	1	7	10	79	5	0
Frankfort	2	0	2	0	0	6	29	1	0
Franklin	2	1	0	0	1	9	23	2	0
Fraser	29	0	4	5	20	60	308	25	1
Fremont	5	0	2	1	2	10	148	2	0
Frost Township	0	0	0	0	0	14	7	0	0
Fruitport	34	0	10	7	17	31	491	12	0
Garden City	80	2	11	18	49	155	327	59	3
Gaylord	8	0	4	0	4	38	213	8	0
Genesee Township	118	0	16	18	84	124	231	38	11
Gibraltar	8	0	2	0	6	13	47	6	0
Gladstone	5	0	3	0	2	10	68	0	0
Gladwin	15	0	3	0	12	10	94	2	0
Grand Beach	0	0	0	0	0	2	0	0	0
Grand Blanc	12	0	4	2	6	37	74	28	0
Grand Blanc Township	63	0	11	14	38	164	403	42	2
Grand Haven	29	0	13	3	13	37	236	3	5
Grand Ledge	6	0	2	0	4	13	90	1	0
Grand Rapids	1,326	17	82	471	756	1,621	4,315	252	62
Grandville	26	0	4	10	12	66	630	22	0
Grayling	8	0	1	0	7	3	97	0	0
Green Oak Township	22	0	7	4	11	52	164	15	0
Greenville	33	0	18	3	12	39	306	0	1

Table 8. Offenses Known to Law Enforcement, by Selected State and City, 2013— continued

(Number.)

State/city	Violent crime	Murder and nonnegligent manslaughter	Rape (revised definition)[1]	Robbery	Aggravated assault	Burglary	Larceny-theft	Motor vehicle theft	Arson[2]
Grosse Ile Township	4	0	2	0	2	13	30	1	0
Grosse Pointe	5	0	0	1	4	11	76	10	0
Grosse Pointe Farms	7	0	0	4	3	20	57	12	0
Grosse Pointe Park	18	1	0	5	12	22	171	56	2
Grosse Pointe Shores	0	0	0	0	0	6	13	0	0
Grosse Pointe Woods	19	0	2	4	13	36	163	21	1
Hamburg Township	5	0	1	0	4	33	121	8	2
Hampton Township	13	0	7	2	4	92	175	7	0
Hamtramck	366	3	13	159	191	244	334	236	5
Hancock	4	0	3	0	1	6	36	2	0
Harbor Beach	6	0	1	0	5	24	21	0	0
Harbor Springs	1	0	1	0	0	5	23	0	0
Harper Woods	169	2	7	58	102	124	680	175	2
Hart	4	0	1	0	3	13	125	0	0
Hartford	10	0	0	1	9	6	26	2	0
Hastings	14	0	10	0	4	25	112	6	0
Hazel Park	76	0	13	24	39	90	283	63	2
Highland Park	187	6	16	67	98	155	267	155	10
Hillsdale	32	0	13	0	19	32	132	4	0
Holland	137	0	37	7	93	188	858	23	5
Holly	9	0	2	1	6	26	63	3	3
Hopkins	0	0	0	0	0	1	3	0	0
Houghton	8	1	7	0	0	5	106	0	1
Howard City	6	0	4	0	2	16	42	3	0
Howell	28	0	13	2	13	17	158	9	2
Huntington Woods	1	0	0	1	0	12	49	4	0
Huron Township	38	0	10	1	27	52	129	22	0
Imlay City	14	0	2	3	9	11	68	2	1
Inkster	396	15	25	73	283	447	457	130	19
Ionia	21	2	14	0	5	30	175	3	4
Iron River	5	0	3	0	2	30	83	12	0
Ironwood	13	0	1	0	12	16	73	2	0
Ishpeming	8	0	0	1	7	11	83	6	0
Ishpeming Township	0	0	0	0	0	0	10	1	0
Jackson	370	4	59	61	246	433	1,220	79	15
Jonesville	2	0	0	1	1	3	66	2	0
Kalkaska	0	0	0	0	0	0	25	0	0
Keego Harbor	5	0	1	0	4	13	41	3	0
Kentwood	141	2	34	23	82	238	932	43	6
Kinde	0	0	0	0	0	0	0	0	0
Kinross Township	3	0	1	0	2	10	17	0	1
Laingsburg	2	0	1	0	1	4	10	0	0
Lake Linden	1	0	0	0	1	1	12	0	0
Lake Odessa	5	0	2	1	2	2	16	1	0
Lake Orion	2	0	0	1	1	3	36	1	0
Lansing	1,204	8	127	256	813	1,268	2,329	363	31
Lapeer	42	0	17	1	24	33	338	4	2
Lapeer Township	1	0	0	0	1	4	21	1	0
Lathrup Village	3	0	0	2	1	10	55	5	0
Laurium	1	0	1	0	0	3	20	1	0
Lawton	4	0	2	0	2	7	25	0	0
Lennon	0	0	0	0	0	2	8	0	0
Lincoln Park	232	1	19	51	161	299	895	149	5
Lincoln Township	18	0	8	0	10	21	147	5	0
Linden	8	0	2	1	5	5	22	0	0
Litchfield	2	0	0	0	2	4	24	2	1
Livonia	148	0	18	34	96	285	1,498	178	11
Lowell	26	0	7	0	19	13	110	4	1
Ludington	25	0	14	1	10	38	156	3	0
Luna Pier	1	0	1	0	0	6	27	1	0
Mackinac Island	2	0	0	0	2	3	204	1	0
Mackinaw City	3	0	2	0	1	4	33	0	0
Madison Heights	78	0	10	17	51	107	656	99	6
Madison Township	7	0	2	1	4	4	74	0	0
Mancelona	2	0	0	0	2	3	11	1	0
Manistee	11	0	3	0	8	33	122	3	0
Manistique	7	0	2	0	5	12	66	1	1
Marlette	7	0	3	0	4	1	26	0	0
Marquette	19	0	9	2	8	31	284	6	0
Marshall	16	0	4	2	10	17	133	5	0
Marysville	2	0	0	1	1	30	152	3	0
Mason	7	0	2	1	4	34	122	11	0
Mattawan	1	0	0	1	0	3	24	1	0
Mayville	1	0	0	0	1	3	13	0	0
Melvindale	34	0	6	5	23	60	215	32	3
Memphis	4	0	0	0	4	4	7	1	1
Menominee	20	0	10	0	10	38	150	3	0
Meridian Township	116	4	22	31	59	168	739	24	4

Table 8.   Offenses Known to Law Enforcement, by Selected State and City, 2013— continued

(Number.)

State/city	Violent crime	Murder and nonnegligent manslaughter	Rape (revised definition)[1]	Robbery	Aggravated assault	Burglary	Larceny-theft	Motor vehicle theft	Arson[2]
Metamora Township	2	0	0	0	2	14	27	1	0
Michiana	0	0	0	0	0	0	0	0	0
Milan	11	1	6	0	4	19	113	8	0
Milford	12	0	4	1	7	26	62	2	0
Monroe	110	1	25	23	61	151	521	42	1
Montrose Township	11	0	5	0	6	112	79	2	0
Morenci	5	0	2	0	3	4	22	2	0
Morrice	0	0	0	0	0	1	10	0	0
Mount Morris	25	0	2	6	17	10	76	2	3
Mount Morris Township	149	4	31	39	75	352	488	56	6
Mount Pleasant	58	0	10	10	38	76	399	16	6
Mundy Township	23	1	2	3	17	189	153	7	1
Munising	2	0	1	0	1	4	36	2	0
Muskegon	325	3	47	70	205	649	1,262	59	10
Muskegon Heights	206	3	27	45	131	203	449	55	6
Napoleon Township	2	0	0	0	2	20	37	0	0
Nashville	2	0	1	0	1	3	18	5	0
Negaunee	2	0	1	0	1	20	65	2	0
Newaygo	18	0	11	0	7	10	66	2	4
New Baltimore	9	0	2	0	7	7	59	2	2
Niles	54	0	14	6	34	45	241	18	2
Northfield Township	15	0	10	0	5	42	71	6	0
North Muskegon	5	0	1	0	4	3	75	5	0
Northville	4	0	1	1	2	9	41	1	0
Northville Township	18	0	5	0	13	51	299	14	1
Novi	48	2	7	11	28	96	833	37	1
Oakley	3	0	3	0	0	3	0	0	0
Oak Park	180	2	19	61	98	207	480	121	7
Olivet	1	0	0	0	1	2	7	1	0
Orchard Lake	3	0	0	2	1	6	27	2	0
Oscoda Township	20	1	12	0	7	112	121	4	1
Otisville	0	0	0	0	0	1	7	0	0
Otsego	8	0	3	0	5	8	57	1	0
Ovid	1	0	0	0	1	0	5	3	0
Owosso	55	0	16	2	37	86	339	7	3
Oxford	6	0	1	1	4	6	25	2	0
Paw Paw	11	0	2	0	9	19	115	1	0
Pentwater	0	0	0	0	0	0	13	1	0
Perry	2	0	2	0	0	9	15	1	0
Petoskey	1	0	0	0	1	14	59	4	1
Pinckney	0	0	0	0	0	3	34	2	0
Pinconning	0	0	0	0	0	1	15	0	1
Pittsfield Township	69	1	13	16	39	79	602	43	1
Plainwell	10	0	4	3	3	5	34	3	0
Pleasant Ridge	5	0	0	4	1	8	14	1	0
Plymouth	14	0	3	2	9	13	75	1	4
Plymouth Township	18	0	5	3	10	46	231	19	0
Portage	88	1	22	12	53	162	1,408	36	2
Port Huron	179	3	25	31	120	227	632	53	4
Potterville	0	0	0	0	0	6	68	0	0
Raisin Township	0	0	0	0	0	0	9	1	0
Reading	0	0	0	0	0	0	10	0	0
Redford Township	244	1	35	71	137	479	731	328	9
Reed City	7	0	2	1	4	8	45	2	0
Reese	1	0	0	0	1	1	9	11	0
Richfield Township, Genesee County	10	0	7	0	3	34	55	5	0
Richfield Township, Roscommon County	10	0	4	1	5	10	37	4	1
Richland	0	0	0	0	0	0	0	1	0
Richmond	17	0	5	0	12	8	112	1	1
River Rouge	84	0	4	23	57	98	142	41	14
Riverview	19	0	6	4	9	23	117	9	3
Rochester	9	0	1	0	8	18	89	2	0
Rockford	7	0	5	0	2	11	76	1	0
Rockwood	2	0	0	1	1	2	28	2	0
Rogers City	3	0	2	0	1	7	37	0	0
Romeo	5	0	0	0	5	3	31	1	0
Romulus	138	1	26	18	93	175	420	103	11
Roosevelt Park	7	0	3	2	2	15	245	6	1
Roseville	218	0	47	69	102	345	1,433	194	6
Royal Oak	99	0	21	21	57	120	607	64	1
Saginaw	985	29	64	129	763	746	644	102	18
Saginaw Township	96	0	9	26	61	132	705	32	0
Saline	11	0	1	1	9	30	96	3	1
Sand Lake	0	0	0	0	0	3	8	0	0
Sandusky	4	0	1	0	3	4	38	1	0
Saugatuck-Douglas	5	0	1	0	4	13	48	1	0
Sault Ste. Marie	36	0	15	1	20	37	351	9	0

Table 8.   Offenses Known to Law Enforcement, by Selected State and City, 2013— continued

(Number.)

State/city	Violent crime	Murder and nonnegligent manslaughter	Rape (revised definition)[1]	Robbery	Aggravated assault	Burglary	Larceny-theft	Motor vehicle theft	Arson[2]
Sebewaing	2	0	0	0	2	1	19	2	0
Shepherd	4	0	0	0	4	2	19	0	1
Somerset Township	1	0	0	1	0	3	23	2	0
Southfield	262	2	39	121	100	443	1,393	284	6
Southgate	85	0	12	25	48	119	833	100	4
South Haven	3	0	1	1	1	5	9	0	0
South Lyon	17	0	7	1	9	14	80	3	0
Sparta	14	0	7	1	6	5	77	1	1
Spring Arbor Township	1	0	0	0	1	7	47	3	0
Springfield	13	0	4	3	6	36	91	9	1
Spring Lake-Ferrysburg	4	0	2	0	2	18	56	1	0
Stanton	2	0	1	0	1	5	8	0	2
St. Charles	11	0	1	1	9	11	27	1	1
St. Clair	6	0	1	1	4	10	76	1	0
Sterling Heights	244	0	30	25	189	330	1,957	199	10
St. Ignace	5	0	3	0	2	10	73	1	0
St. Johns	8	0	5	1	2	30	77	5	2
St. Joseph Township	19	0	6	1	12	32	108	3	1
St. Louis	8	0	6	0	2	17	43	2	4
Stockbridge	5	0	2	1	2	6	28	1	0
Sumpter Township	14	0	2	1	11	39	60	9	1
Swartz Creek	10	0	1	2	7	26	79	4	0
Sylvan Lake	10	0	0	0	10	10	36	2	0
Tawas	10	0	4	2	4	13	76	2	0
Taylor	347	3	49	76	219	470	1,404	209	25
Thetford Township	3	0	3	0	0	8	9	2	0
Thomas Township	9	0	0	0	9	28	133	5	0
Three Rivers	54	0	14	6	34	64	250	12	3
Tittabawassee Township	15	0	6	0	9	21	69	2	1
Trenton	25	0	4	5	16	39	187	23	2
Troy	62	0	17	7	38	222	1,250	78	2
Tuscarora Township	5	0	0	0	5	2	82	1	1
Unadilla Township	6	1	3	0	2	2	25	2	0
Union City	2	0	2	0	0	16	36	0	0
Utica	25	0	5	2	18	19	149	13	0
Van Buren Township	63	1	10	12	40	109	485	70	3
Vassar	6	0	0	0	6	3	23	1	0
Vicksburg	7	0	3	1	3	9	51	0	1
Walker	40	0	10	6	24	76	583	19	3
Walled Lake	26	0	5	1	20	14	53	6	1
Warren	679	3	127	166	383	887	2,037	584	41
Waterford Township	135	0	36	21	78	275	818	64	1
Wayne	121	2	15	26	78	140	276	63	7
West Bloomfield Township	43	0	9	7	27	144	544	17	5
West Branch	3	0	0	0	3	3	42	1	0
Westland	363	1	66	93	203	564	1,553	282	14
White Cloud	8	0	3	0	5	13	46	0	0
Whitehall	6	0	2	0	4	3	60	1	1
White Lake Township	22	1	3	2	16	80	347	7	3
White Pigeon	6	0	4	0	2	2	38	1	0
Williamston	2	0	1	1	0	8	13	0	0
Wixom	20	1	3	5	11	31	210	24	3
Wolverine Lake	3	0	2	1	0	6	13	0	0
Woodhaven	17	0	3	4	10	17	146	20	0
Wyandotte	56	0	6	12	38	115	402	53	7
Wyoming	309	0	59	68	182	392	1,140	115	8
Yale	5	0	1	1	3	19	30	0	0
Ypsilanti	163	3	22	34	104	222	408	41	1
Zeeland	4	0	1	1	2	57	63	2	2
Zilwaukee	1	0	0	0	1	1	7	1	0
Minnesota									
Albany	4	0	2	0	2	2	25	1	0
Albert Lea	35	0	3	0	32	52	381	14	2
Alexandria	35	1	8	1	25	45	301	17	0
Annandale	0	0	0	0	0	1	23	0	0
Anoka	37	0	15	9	13	55	487	23	2
Appleton	2	0	1	0	1	7	32	0	0
Apple Valley	49	2	11	18	18	106	1,031	26	5
Arden Hills	4	0	0	2	2	19	119	10	2
Austin	61	0	12	7	42	138	570	46	1
Avon	1	0	0	0	1	10	12	1	0
Babbitt	2	0	1	0	1	5	48	0	0
Baxter	8	0	0	0	8	13	388	1	0
Bayport	0	0	0	0	0	1	18	0	0
Becker	5	0	0	0	5	6	32	1	1
Belgrade	0	0	0	0	0	0	0	0	0
Belle Plaine	4	0	2	0	2	4	78	1	1

Table 8.   Offenses Known to Law Enforcement, by Selected State and City, 2013— continued

(Number.)

State/city	Violent crime	Murder and nonnegligent manslaughter	Rape (revised definition)	Robbery	Aggravated assault	Burglary	Larceny-theft	Motor vehicle theft	Arson[2]
Bemidji	44	0	13	3	28	67	1,050	31	1
Benson	5	0	0	0	5	12	80	0	0
Big Lake	17	0	0	2	15	21	83	3	1
Blackduck	1	0	0	0	1	1	14	0	0
Blaine	49	0	10	12	27	148	1,508	61	7
Blooming Prairie	0	0	0	0	0	0	1	1	0
Bloomington	128	1	17	49	61	193	2,990	100	17
Blue Earth	1	0	0	0	1	7	26	3	1
Brainerd	55	0	16	5	34	105	622	23	17
Breckenridge	5	0	1	0	4	11	43	0	0
Brooklyn Center	132	2	14	67	49	207	1,440	73	10
Brooklyn Park	248	3	33	86	126	421	1,875	160	4
Brownton	0	0	0	0	0	2	3	2	0
Buffalo	21	0	9	2	10	31	297	9	0
Burnsville	95	3	4	27	61	216	1,576	80	2
Caledonia	7	0	1	0	6	1	0	1	0
Cambridge	14	0	1	1	12	28	258	16	1
Canby	0	0	0	0	0	4	13	0	
Cannon Falls	5	0	1	2	2	15	96	4	0
Centennial Lakes	10	0	0	3	7	7	87	11	1
Champlin	20	0	6	3	11	40	333	6	0
Chaska	17	0	12	0	5	28	244	7	0
Chisholm	2	0	0	1	1	12	124	2	0
Cloquet	30	0	7	5	18	49	416	18	0
Cold Spring	1	0	0	0	1	3	22	1	0
Columbia Heights	39	0	2	13	24	100	358	27	1
Coon Rapids	94	0	31	15	48	183	1,530	53	9
Corcoran	0	0	0	0	0	0	0	0	0
Cottage Grove	25	0	5	11	9	82	578	23	4
Crookston	13	0	5	0	8	16	56	11	0
Crosby	3	0	1	0	2	6	12	2	0
Crystal	30	0	5	17	8	61	424	35	3
Dawson	1	0	0	0	1	2	12	0	0
Dayton	1	0	1	0	0	16	50	10	0
Deephaven	2	0	0	0	2	3	22	0	0
Detroit Lakes	14	1	4	0	9	43	374	24	0
Dilworth	3	0	1	0	2	13	166	5	0
Duluth	342	2	52	72	216	643	3,484	156	23
Eagan	37	0	2	14	21	163	1,087	37	5
Eagle Lake	4	0	0	2	2	7	20	1	0
East Grand Forks	10	0	2	2	6	40	218	11	2
Echo	0	0	0	0	0	2	0	0	0
Eden Prairie	39	1	10	7	21	83	788	23	3
Edina	16	0	7	5	4	80	835	22	1
Elk River	11	0	6	2	3	56	402	13	2
Elmore	8	0	3	0	5	7	2	0	0
Ely	7	0	3	0	4	3	50	2	0
Eveleth	11	0	2	0	9	28	94	13	1
Fairmont	6	0	1	1	4	53	237	6	0
Falcon Heights	6	0	0	2	4	17	86	5	0
Faribault	90	1	17	10	62	118	631	34	5
Farmington	16	0	0	2	14	33	154	5	3
Fergus Falls	37	0	0	3	34	102	370	12	0
Floodwood	1	0	0	0	1	0	32	0	0
Forest Lake	19	0	9	5	5	67	269	30	0
Fridley	77	0	14	18	45	157	1,018	72	3
Gilbert	0	0	0	0	0	1	1	0	0
Glencoe	1	0	1	0	0	19	76	1	1
Glenwood	3	0	1	0	2	6	47	0	0
Golden Valley	16	0	4	5	7	59	378	14	4
Goodview	7	0	1	1	5	3	35	6	0
Grand Rapids	33	0	15	2	16	38	479	18	3
Granite Falls	5	2	1	0	2	5	28	3	0
Hallock	0	0	0	0	0	0	0	0	0
Hastings	32	0	10	5	17	57	428	22	4
Hermantown	4	0	2	0	2	56	302	14	2
Hibbing	4	0	0	0	4	1	5	0	0
Hokah	0	0	0	0	0	4	12	0	0
Hopkins	34	0	5	11	18	71	342	37	0
Houston	4	0	0	0	4	4	6	1	0
Hoyt Lakes	1	0	1	0	0	0	0	0	0
Hutchinson	35	0	9	0	26	27	348	9	0
International Falls	16	0	5	1	10	43	160	9	3
Inver Grove Heights	83	0	8	9	66	96	614	51	5
Isanti	8	0	2	0	6	10	84	4	0
Janesville	0	0	0	0	0	4	12	1	0
Jordan	6	0	3	0	3	5	54	1	0
Kasson	2	0	2	0	0	9	33	3	0

Table 8.   Offenses Known to Law Enforcement, by Selected State and City, 2013— continued

(Number.)

State/city	Violent crime	Murder and nonnegligent manslaughter	Rape (revised definition)[1]	Robbery	Aggravated assault	Burglary	Larceny-theft	Motor vehicle theft	Arson[2]
Kimball	0	0	0	0	0	0	0	0	0
La Crescent	0	0	0	0	0	0	0	0	0
Lake City	6	0	2	0	4	25	91	7	1
Lake Crystal	2	0	1	0	1	17	21	4	0
Lakefield	3	0	1	0	2	5	13	0	0
Lakes Area	11	0	3	1	7	18	107	11	0
Lakeville	15	0	1	5	9	110	594	20	0
Lauderdale	2	0	0	1	1	9	24	4	0
Lester Prairie	3	0	1	0	2	3	24	0	0
Le Sueur	5	0	0	0	5	14	44	2	0
Lewiston	0	0	0	0	0	1	1	0	0
Lino Lakes	15	0	2	0	13	27	140	5	1
Litchfield	5	0	2	0	3	18	72	5	0
Little Canada	23	0	4	5	14	66	143	37	10
Little Falls	10	0	1	0	9	19	170	6	0
Long Prairie	3	0	0	0	3	2	64	0	0
Madison Lake	1	0	0	0	1	4	16	2	0
Mankato	107	1	18	31	57	312	1,395	46	5
Maple Grove	28	0	6	10	12	113	944	30	4
Mapleton	0	0	0	0	0	4	14	1	0
Maplewood	75	1	17	23	34	283	1,854	158	2
Marshall	22	0	5	0	17	67	306	15	3
Medina	5	0	3	0	2	8	74	5	0
Melrose	2	0	1	1	0	7	15	2	0
Mendota Heights	9	0	1	2	6	33	249	3	1
Milaca	1	0	1	0	0	0	51	1	0
Minneapolis	4,038	36	385	1,856	1,761	4,601	13,182	1,575	124
Minnetonka	13	0	2	4	7	118	718	27	9
Minnetrista	3	0	0	0	3	13	43	0	0
Montevideo	10	1	2	0	7	27	100	5	0
Montgomery	8	0	1	0	7	11	64	2	2
Moorhead	38	1	3	6	28	158	645	44	6
Moose Lake	8	0	2	0	6	4	111	1	0
Morris	9	0	4	1	4	9	85	7	0
Mounds View	23	1	5	2	15	46	283	19	7
Mountain Lake	3	0	0	1	2	3	4	0	0
New Brighton	17	0	2	6	9	76	436	36	2
New Hope	24	1	4	9	10	55	374	25	4
Newport	5	0	0	3	2	20	93	5	0
New Prague	7	0	1	1	5	8	102	4	1
New Richland	1	0	0	0	1	1	0	0	0
New Ulm	15	0	4	0	11	41	131	13	0
North Branch	13	0	1	1	11	47	282	10	4
Northfield	18	0	6	2	10	41	225	3	2
North Mankato	22	0	4	2	16	65	188	17	2
North Oaks	1	0	0	0	1	11	24	4	1
North St. Paul	5	0	1	2	2	39	191	21	0
Oakdale	55	1	18	8	28	136	980	50	8
Oak Park Heights	1	0	0	0	1	6	228	5	0
Olivia	2	0	0	0	2	12	56	1	1
Orono	4	1	0	0	3	44	197	5	0
Ortonville	0	0	0	0	0	0	2	0	0
Osakis	1	0	0	0	1	3	26	1	0
Osseo	0	0	0	0	0	0	0	0	2
Owatonna	36	0	5	6	25	114	538	28	0
Park Rapids	13	0	2	5	6	31	172	14	2
Paynesville	3	0	0	0	3	6	36	4	0
Plainview	4	0	2	0	2	1	5	0	0
Plymouth	49	0	21	5	23	186	903	52	6
Princeton	8	0	1	0	7	8	150	2	0
Prior Lake	20	0	5	3	12	62	365	15	3
Proctor	6	0	2	1	3	17	100	3	0
Ramsey	32	1	20	2	9	49	312	18	0
Red Wing	35	0	14	2	19	68	447	24	5
Redwood Falls	19	1	6	1	11	11	110	4	3
Richfield	88	2	9	49	28	165	763	47	6
Robbinsdale	33	0	1	16	16	71	210	26	0
Rochester	214	0	50	54	110	429	2,026	103	8
Rogers	16	0	4	3	9	19	192	13	0
Roseau	0	0	0	0	0	5	52	5	0
Rosemount	9	2	2	0	5	38	199	6	1
Roseville	52	1	13	18	20	179	1,232	70	0
Sartell	4	0	2	0	2	27	280	7	0
Sauk Centre	2	0	0	0	2	13	95	1	0
Sauk Rapids	12	0	5	1	6	28	168	19	2
Savage	35	0	5	9	21	97	494	9	2
Shakopee	53	2	12	11	28	108	882	34	1
Shoreview	12	2	1	0	9	47	231	16	8

Table 8.   Offenses Known to Law Enforcement, by Selected State and City, 2013— continued

(Number.)

State/city	Violent crime	Murder and nonnegligent manslaughter	Rape (revised definition)	Robbery	Aggravated assault	Burglary	Larceny-theft	Motor vehicle theft	Arson[2]
Silver Bay	3	0	2	0	1	0	1	0	0
Silver Lake	0	0	0	0	0	3	9	0	0
Slayton	1	0	0	0	1	5	12	0	0
Sleepy Eye	3	0	1	0	2	0	2	0	0
South Lake Minnetonka	16	1	9	0	6	20	92	8	0
South St. Paul	88	0	15	9	64	88	378	56	42
Springfield	0	0	0	0	0	0	0	0	0
Spring Grove	0	0	0	0	0	0	0	0	0
Spring Lake Park	29	0	3	11	15	41	216	20	0
St. Anthony	9	0	2	5	2	51	306	16	1
Staples	7	0	2	0	5	19	69	0	0
St. Charles	4	0	1	0	3	3	12	0	0
St. Cloud	250	1	56	46	147	371	2,308	163	25
St. Francis	6	0	1	1	4	22	92	5	0
Stillwater	16	0	6	4	6	45	262	13	2
St. James	10	0	5	0	5	22	54	5	0
St. Joseph	2	0	2	0	0	1	38	1	0
St. Louis Park	68	1	5	25	37	188	1,037	63	7
St. Paul	2,200	14	218	716	1,252	2,769	6,443	1,761	112
St. Paul Park	15	1	0	2	12	27	95	11	1
St. Peter	22	1	5	2	14	36	191	10	0
Thief River Falls	11	0	7	0	4	15	136	8	1
Tracy	0	0	0	0	0	0	0	0	0
Two Harbors	5	0	0	1	4	10	60	2	0
Vadnais Heights	17	0	5	5	7	28	234	32	2
Virginia	37	0	5	4	28	78	429	17	1
Wabasha	5	0	0	0	5	9	27	1	0
Wadena	4	0	2	0	2	0	22	1	0
Waite Park	22	0	6	6	10	44	666	25	1
Warroad	0	0	0	0	0	2	54	1	0
Waseca	5	0	3	0	2	30	165	7	0
Wayzata	4	0	0	3	1	16	82	7	0
Wells	0	0	0	0	0	7	17	0	0
West Hennepin	6	0	1	0	5	7	29	1	0
West St. Paul	84	1	11	16	56	63	856	43	3
Wheaton	0	0	0	0	0	0	0	0	0
White Bear Lake	44	0	8	7	29	128	495	29	1
White Bear Township	3	0	1	2	0	26	118	4	1
Willmar	42	0	8	7	27	54	501	24	4
Windom	5	0	2	0	3	12	52	7	0
Winnebago	2	0	0	0	2	5	11	2	0
Winona	30	0	2	4	24	75	298	23	0
Winsted	2	0	2	0	0	10	14	0	0
Woodbury	21	0	0	7	14	184	1,166	36	0
Worthington	25	0	4	2	19	30	123	6	1
Wyoming	3	0	0	0	3	11	58	5	0
Zumbrota	1	0	0	0	1	9	42	8	0
Mississippi									
Aberdeen	9	0		4	4	40	127	5	0
Amory	5	0		2	2	81	181	3	2
Batesville	18	2		5	10	72	360	15	1
Biloxi	213	3	36	90	84	703	1,482	131	6
Byhalia	10	0		0	10	19	51	1	0
Byram	16	1	1	7	7	62	178	16	0
Cleveland	62	6		18	36	130	607	12	4
Columbia	18	0	3	2	13	37	143	0	0
D'Iberville	9	0		1	4	75	569	19	0
Flowood	38	0		4	29	86	300	6	0
Fulton	0	0		0	0	7	74	1	0
Gautier	48	0		12	35	235	394	34	2
Greenville	99	7		70	5	824	1,616	87	60
Greenwood	83	4		27	45	297	632	16	0
Gulfport	153	1	18	64	70	654	2,670	125	19
Hattiesburg	157	4		46	64	442	2,224	90	3
Horn Lake	35	1		14	16	134	419	25	6
Iuka	4	0		0	3	21	46	1	0
Jackson	1,631	50		845	626	3,366	5,864	1,054	124
Laurel	59	2		33	19	295	611	20	2
Long Beach	14	0		0	12	45	254	17	0
Louisville	10	0		4	6	22	60	0	0
Madison	16	0		2	14	10	151	2	0
McComb	79	1		32	46	179	498	35	0
Meridian	233	3	29	129	72	902	1,327	186	6
Ocean Springs	33	0		7	26	99	455	27	1
Olive Branch	66	0	2	17	47	359	521	36	1
Pascagoula	130	2		26	82	304	1,116	45	7
Pass Christian	8	0		4	2	39	133	7	3

Table 8.   Offenses Known to Law Enforcement, by Selected State and City, 2013— continued

(Number.)

State/city	Violent crime	Murder and nonnegligent manslaughter	Rape (revised definition)[1]	Robbery	Aggravated assault	Burglary	Larceny-theft	Motor vehicle theft	Arson[2]
Petal	0	0		0	0	45	57	7	0
Philadelphia	47	1	0	10	36	74	146	4	0
Picayune	39	1		9	27	77	339	20	2
Poplarville	8	0		1	7	28	41	1	0
Ridgeland	40	0		19	21	46	601	15	0
Southaven	168	0		20	139	210	1,189	56	3
Starkville	42	1		11	29	125	472	11	0
Vicksburg	110	5		14	68	275	915	70	6
West Point	54	1		14	34	162	229	1	0
Wiggins	8	0		2	3	29	84	3	0
Missouri									
Adrian	3	0	0	0	3	11	29	1	0
Advance	1	1	0	0	0	5	16	0	0
Anderson	14	1	3	0	10	31	68	6	1
Annapolis	0	0	0	0	0	0	2	1	0
Appleton City	0	0	0	0	0	3	9	1	0
Arbyrd	0	0	0	0	0	0	0	0	0
Archie	0	0	0	0	0	2	1	0	0
Arnold	36	0	5	10	21	42	602	30	0
Ash Grove	2	0	0	0	2	3	25	2	0
Ashland	19	0	1	0	18	9	67	2	0
Aurora	60	0	3	3	54	142	345	24	2
Auxvasse	2	0	0	0	2	6	32	1	0
Ava	9	0	1	0	8	35	87	4	0
Ballwin	22	1	2	2	17	29	213	8	1
Battlefield	0	0	0	0	0	23	67	2	0
Bella Villa	2	0	0	0	2	0	8	0	0
Belle	12	0	1	0	11	2	21	1	0
Bellefontaine Neighbors	36	2	3	4	27	146	158	45	2
Bellerive	0	0	0	0	0	0	0	0	0
Bel-Nor	2	0	0	1	1	4	40	1	0
Bel-Ridge	39	0	1	3	35	50	64	10	1
Belton	83	0	16	14	53	120	467	39	5
Berkeley	58	2	6	15	35	129	202	27	0
Bernie	0	0	0	0	0	2	18	0	0
Bertrand	1	0	0	1	0	15	8	3	0
Bethany	6	0	1	0	5	8	62	5	0
Beverly Hills	15	0	0	6	9	13	9	3	0
Billings	1	0	0	0	1	5	16	1	0
Birch Tree	0	0	0	0	0	0	2	0	0
Bismarck	1	0	0	0	1	3	0	3	1
Blackburn	0	0	0	0	0	0	0	0	0
Bloomfield	5	0	0	0	5	11	25	2	0
Blue Springs	133	1	31	19	82	197	1,132	128	4
Bolivar	45	0	14	3	28	77	337	15	2
Bonne Terre	7	0	2	0	5	11	20	9	0
Boonville	31	0	2	0	29	33	218	14	2
Bowling Green	5	0	1	0	4	22	96	1	0
Branson	160	2	6	22	130	95	1,105	61	3
Branson West	11	0	0	0	11	1	70	4	0
Braymer	0	0	0	0	0	2	8	0	0
Breckenridge Hills	25	0	2	13	10	80	87	17	0
Brentwood	12	0	4	5	3	24	263	11	0
Bridgeton	100	0	7	24	69	87	886	40	0
Brookfield	4	0	2	0	2	39	96	9	0
Brunswick	4	1	0	0	3	2	4	1	0
Bucklin	2	0	0	0	2	3	1	0	0
Buckner	3	0	2	1	0	15	32	4	0
Buffalo	5	0	0	0	5	15	126	4	0
Butler	11	0	2	0	9	23	161	6	0
Butterfield Village	0	0	0	0	0	0	4	0	0
Byrnes Mill	5	0	2	0	3	8	31	0	0
Cabool	4	0	2	0	2	10	47	1	0
California	7	0	1	4	2	19	70	1	0
Calverton Park	5	0	1	0	4	7	11	0	0
Camdenton	15	0	2	0	13	17	218	8	0
Cameron	36	0	10	3	23	30	133	3	3
Campbell	5	0	1	0	4	22	65	2	0
Canalou	0	0	0	0	0	6	0	0	0
Canton	6	0	2	0	4	16	57	2	2
Cape Girardeau	258	5	12	85	156	446	1,487	57	6
Cardwell	0	0	0	0	0	5	1	0	0
Carl Junction	6	0	0	0	6	46	119	12	1
Carrollton	4	0	1	0	3	7	52	13	0
Carterville	5	0	1	1	3	3	11	3	0
Carthage	29	1	5	4	19	65	391	15	2
Caruthersville	89	1	5	12	71	90	152	14	4

Table 8.   Offenses Known to Law Enforcement, by Selected State and City, 2013— continued

(Number.)

State/city	Violent crime	Murder and nonnegligent manslaughter	Rape (revised definition)[1]	Robbery	Aggravated assault	Burglary	Larceny-theft	Motor vehicle theft	Arson[2]
Cassville	12	0	0	1	11	20	234	5	0
Center	0	0	0	0	0	1	1	0	0
Centralia	9	0	0	1	8	20	67	7	0
Chaffee	6	0	1	0	5	9	35	2	1
Charlack	8	0	1	4	3	12	25	5	0
Charleston	35	0	1	4	30	40	113	6	1
Chesterfield	25	0	2	6	17	61	608	16	0
Chillicothe	23	0	2	1	20	38	211	8	3
Clarkton	9	0	0	0	9	4	15	0	0
Claycomo	7	0	0	0	7	2	35	6	0
Clayton	13	0	3	4	6	43	154	13	0
Cleveland	0	0	0	0	0	2	3	0	0
Clever	16	0	1	0	15	5	9	1	0
Clinton	41	0	3	6	32	79	318	17	0
Cole Camp	2	0	0	0	2	3	20	1	1
Columbia	416	5	67	112	232	703	3,490	166	14
Concordia	3	0	1	0	2	13	31	2	0
Conway	0	0	0	0	0	0	7	2	0
Cool Valley	3	0	1	1	1	3	35	4	0
Corder	0	0	0	0	0	1	1	0	0
Cottleville	1	0	0	0	1	4	42	0	0
Country Club Hills	11	0	0	3	8	12	24	2	0
Crane	1	0	0	0	1	2	9	1	0
Creighton	0	0	0	0	0	0	0	0	0
Crestwood	7	0	0	1	6	24	224	6	0
Creve Coeur	17	0	1	7	9	25	192	13	1
Crocker	16	0	0	0	16	11	27	2	1
Crystal City	6	0	0	1	5	34	264	8	1
Cuba	10	0	1	2	7	19	135	10	1
Delta	0	0	0	0	0	0	0	0	0
Desloge	16	0	1	1	14	31	279	10	1
De Soto	21	0	1	3	17	39	266	8	0
Des Peres	5	0	0	3	2	21	482	5	0
Dexter	20	0	1	3	16	40	255	8	0
Diamond	4	0	0	2	2	3	9	1	0
Dixon	9	0	0	0	9	13	46	7	0
Doniphan	24	0	2	4	18	14	163	10	0
Doolittle	0	0	0	0	0	1	6	0	0
Drexel	3	0	0	0	3	3	7	2	0
Duenweg	6	0	0	0	6	15	19	4	0
Duquesne	2	0	0	0	2	15	40	1	0
East Prairie	2	0	0	1	1	19	70	0	0
Edgar Springs	0	0	0	0	0	0	0	0	0
Edina	0	0	0	0	0	2	3	0	0
Edmundson	2	0	0	0	2	20	50	4	0
Eldon	14	0	1	1	12	43	169	7	0
El Dorado Springs	19	0	0	2	17	26	209	7	0
Ellington	2	0	1	0	1	4	6	0	0
Ellisville	4	0	0	3	1	20	79	4	0
Ellsinore	3	0	0	0	3	0	1	0	0
Elsberry	9	0	0	0	9	5	19	2	0
Eminence	0	0	0	0	0	0	1	0	1
Emma	0	0	0	0	0	1	0	0	0
Essex	1	0	0	0	1	3	12	0	0
Eureka	6	0	0	2	4	7	196	5	0
Excelsior Springs	24	0	4	7	13	80	331	26	0
Exeter	1	0	0	0	1	2	6	0	0
Fair Grove	5	0	0	0	5	5	29	1	0
Fair Play	0	0	0	0	0	1	0	0	0
Fairview	0	0	0	0	0	0	0	0	0
Farmington	51	0	7	3	41	62	701	25	1
Fayette	4	0	0	0	4	1	12	2	0
Ferguson	101	2	3	54	42	300	749	77	0
Ferrelview	1	0	0	0	1	7	22	1	0
Festus	49	0	3	5	41	31	220	11	2
Fleming	0	0	0	0	0	0	0	0	0
Flordell Hills	7	0	1	4	2	16	8	4	0
Florissant	85	2	3	32	48	234	699	60	1
Foley	0	0	0	0	0	0	0	0	0
Fordland	1	0	0	0	1	4	4	0	0
Foristell	0	0	0	0	0	3	16	0	0
Forsyth	2	0	0	2	0	12	54	4	0
Fredericktown	27	1	5	1	20	37	197	12	0
Freeman	0	0	0	0	0	0	0	0	0
Frontenac	5	0	0	1	4	13	45	1	0
Fulton	44	0	0	4	40	76	403	17	2
Galena	0	0	0	0	0	3	1	0	0
Gallatin	2	0	0	0	2	2	5	0	0

Table 8.   Offenses Known to Law Enforcement, by Selected State and City, 2013— continued

(Number.)

State/city	Violent crime	Murder and nonnegligent manslaughter	Rape (revised definition)[1]	Robbery	Aggravated assault	Burglary	Larceny-theft	Motor vehicle theft	Arson[2]
Garden City	2	0	0	0	2	0	13	3	0
Gerald	0	0	0	0	0	5	19	1	0
Gideon	2	0	0	0	2	0	2	0	0
Gladstone	48	1	3	15	29	89	382	42	2
Glasgow	0	0	0	0	0	1	4	0	0
Glendale	3	0	0	0	3	5	48	4	0
Glen Echo Park	1	0	0	0	1	1	0	0	0
Goodman	0	0	0	0	0	7	3	6	1
Gower	3	0	1	2	0	3	17	2	0
Grain Valley	16	0	5	1	10	25	135	15	0
Granby	8	0	0	0	8	20	14	2	0
Grandin	0	0	0	0	0	0	0	0	0
Grandview	106	2	15	31	58	220	500	94	5
Greendale	0	0	0	0	0	8	12	3	0
Greenfield	2	0	0	1	1	4	19	0	0
Greenville	0	0	0	0	0	5	5	1	0
Greenwood	4	0	0	0	4	13	18	4	0
Hallsville	2	0	0	1	1	4	26	1	0
Hamilton	2	0	0	0	2	5	24	1	1
Hannibal	74	1	13	11	49	135	874	32	1
Harrisonville	16	0	5	2	9	57	301	17	1
Hartville	0	0	0	0	0	0	3	1	0
Hawk Point	1	0	0	0	1	1	30	0	0
Hayti	15	0	2	4	9	50	182	6	2
Hayti Heights	0	0	0	0	0	0	3	0	0
Hazelwood	95	1	4	30	60	142	723	42	0
Henrietta	3	0	0	0	3	0	1	0	0
Herculaneum	2	0	0	0	2	8	61	2	1
Hermann	8	0	1	0	7	5	48	2	0
Higginsville	3	0	1	0	2	8	59	6	0
Highlandville	1	0	0	0	1	1	3	1	0
Hillsboro	4	0	1	2	1	12	59	5	0
Hillsdale	20	0	1	1	18	20	12	4	1
Holcomb	0	0	0	0	0	0	0	0	0
Holden	4	0	2	0	2	16	80	2	0
Hollister	13	0	2	0	11	18	75	7	0
Holt	0	0	0	0	0	2	6	1	0
Holts Summit	5	0	1	0	4	25	57	0	0
Hornersville	3	0	0	0	3	7	5	0	2
Houston	0	0	0	0	0	21	116	5	0
Howardville	1	0	0	0	1	0	0	0	0
Humansville	6	0	0	0	6	6	8	0	0
Hurley	0	0	0	0	0	0	0	0	0
Iberia	0	0	0	0	0	0	1	0	0
Independence	543	7	51	122	363	1,167	5,149	792	30
Indian Point	1	0	0	0	1	0	0	1	0
Iron Mountain Lake	5	0	0	0	5	2	6	2	0
Ironton	1	0	0	0	1	7	12	4	0
Jackson	16	0	2	3	11	48	211	8	0
Jasper	8	0	0	2	6	18	18	0	1
Jefferson City	200	0	7	36	157	235	1,162	49	6
Jennings	159	7	6	48	98	258	449	75	5
Jonesburg	3	0	0	0	3	2	8	3	0
Joplin	240	1	35	55	149	617	3,055	253	14
Kahoka	0	0	0	0	0	2	5	1	0
Kansas City	5,864	99	377	1,662	3,726	6,412	13,949	4,287	207
Kearney	12	0	3	1	8	15	109	9	1
Kennett	40	0	1	11	28	154	541	33	1
Kimberling City	7	0	0	0	7	12	25	2	0
Kimmswick	0	0	0	0	0	0	0	0	0
King City	0	0	0	0	0	0	0	0	0
Kinloch	15	2	0	1	12	9	3	3	0
Kirksville	43	1	2	3	37	115	377	12	3
Kirkwood	20	1	5	4	10	48	498	10	0
Knob Noster	7	0	1	0	6	13	37	3	1
Ladue	8	0	0	2	6	21	109	1	0
La Grange	1	0	0	0	1	2	3	2	0
Lake Lotawana	0	0	0	0	0	9	26	2	0
Lake Ozark	4	0	0	0	4	2	60	0	0
Lakeshire	3	0	0	0	3	11	8	0	0
Lake St. Louis	10	0	3	3	4	34	219	7	0
Lake Tapawingo	0	0	0	0	0	5	7	1	0
Lake Waukomis	0	0	0	0	0	1	9	1	0
Lake Winnebago	0	0	0	0	0	0	3	0	0
Lamar	13	0	5	0	8	19	117	3	0
La Monte	0	0	0	0	0	0	3	0	0
La Plata	1	0	0	0	1	5	2	0	0
Lathrop	3	0	0	0	3	9	28	3	0

Table 8.   Offenses Known to Law Enforcement, by Selected State and City, 2013— continued

(Number.)

State/city	Violent crime	Murder and nonnegligent manslaughter	Rape (revised definition)	Robbery	Aggravated assault	Burglary	Larceny-theft	Motor vehicle theft	Arson[2]
Laurie	6	0	0	0	6	6	20	0	0
Lawson	8	0	0	0	8	11	71	7	0
Leadington	1	0	0	0	1	2	3	2	0
Leadwood	15	0	0	0	15	10	11	3	0
Leasburg	0	0	0	0	0	0	0	0	0
Lebanon	70	0	8	2	60	91	574	19	0
Lee's Summit	91	0	18	15	58	267	1,582	109	0
Leeton	0	0	0	0	0	0	3	0	0
Liberal	1	0	1	0	0	3	5	0	0
Liberty	58	1	8	10	39	106	400	31	6
Licking	2	0	0	0	2	3	44	2	0
Lincoln	3	0	1	0	2	5	24	3	0
Linn	1	0	0	0	1	2	10	2	0
Linn Creek	0	0	0	0	0	1	4	1	0
Lone Jack	0	0	0	0	0	5	10	1	0
Louisiana	5	0	0	0	5	2	13	0	0
Lowry City	0	0	0	0	0	0	0	0	0
Macon	9	0	1	0	8	37	125	4	0
Malden	9	0	0	1	8	23	57	4	1
Manchester	9	0	2	2	5	22	289	7	0
Mansfield	2	0	0	0	2	7	55	2	0
Maplewood	22	0	3	6	13	28	544	25	1
Marble Hill	7	0	0	0	7	9	42	0	0
Marceline	33	0	1	1	31	26	32	4	1
Marionville	4	0	0	1	3	18	77	3	0
Marshall	24	0	2	5	17	65	226	14	1
Marshfield	28	0	0	0	28	44	262	5	0
Marston	1	0	0	0	1	7	0	0	0
Marthasville	0	0	0	0	0	0	6	0	0
Martinsburg	0	0	0	0	0	0	0	0	0
Maryland Heights	47	0	3	10	34	71	472	20	3
Maryville	33	0	0	4	29	24	151	7	0
Matthews	3	0	0	0	3	3	18	1	0
Maysville	2	0	0	0	2	1	2	0	0
Memphis	0	0	0	0	0	2	12	3	0
Merriam Woods	0	0	0	0	0	3	0	1	0
Mexico	45	0	4	8	33	86	306	8	1
Milan	5	0	0	0	5	4	11	2	1
Miller	6	0	1	0	5	0	0	0	0
Miner	11	0	1	0	10	11	44	5	0
Miramiguoa	1	0	0	0	1	0	0	0	0
Moberly	29	1	1	8	19	78	488	14	1
Moline Acres	15	0	0	7	8	37	107	11	0
Monett	11	0	0	3	8	90	351	21	0
Monroe City	2	0	0	0	2	13	24	1	0
Montgomery City	4	0	0	0	4	12	45	2	0
Morehouse	1	0	0	0	1	1	2	1	1
Morley	2	0	0	1	1	1	10	1	0
Mosby	3	0	1	0	2	6	29	5	0
Moscow Mills	9	0	0	0	9	7	14	2	0
Mound City	0	0	0	0	0	6	12	1	0
Mountain Grove	17	0	0	0	17	30	158	5	0
Mountain View	15	1	3	1	10	11	95	8	0
Mount Vernon	13	0	1	2	10	18	156	7	1
Napoleon	0	0	0	0	0	0	0	0	0
Neosho	30	0	6	3	21	82	444	22	5
Nevada	46	0	4	4	38	146	570	40	2
New Bloomfield	0	0	0	0	0	3	1	0	0
Newburg	0	0	0	0	0	0	2	0	0
New Florence	0	0	0	0	0	0	17	1	0
New Franklin	8	0	1	0	7	8	6	2	1
New Haven	3	0	1	0	2	4	27	1	0
New London	2	0	0	0	2	2	10	1	0
New Madrid	0	0	0	0	0	6	34	2	0
New Melle	1	0	0	0	1	1	1	0	0
Niangua	0	0	0	0	0	0	0	0	0
Nixa	18	0	3	6	9	48	301	16	1
Noel	8	0	2	0	6	12	17	4	0
Norborne	1	0	0	1	0	0	0	0	0
Normandy	24	1	3	4	16	32	72	8	0
North Kansas City	24	0	4	15	5	29	259	44	0
Northmoor	2	0	0	0	2	4	9	3	0
Northwoods	44	0	1	14	29	48	84	14	0
Norwood	4	0	0	0	4	5	7	0	0
Oak Grove	6	0	1	1	4	19	126	12	0
Oakland	2	0	0	0	2	0	1	1	0
Oakview Village	1	0	0	0	1	0	1	1	0
Odessa	3	0	1	0	2	17	70	4	1

Table 8.   Offenses Known to Law Enforcement, by Selected State and City, 2013— continued

(Number.)

State/city	Violent crime	Murder and nonnegligent manslaughter	Rape (revised definition)[1]	Robbery	Aggravated assault	Burglary	Larceny-theft	Motor vehicle theft	Arson[2]
O'Fallon	63	1	7	6	49	139	1,059	20	0
Old Monroe	0	0	0	0	0	0	0	0	0
Olivette	13	0	0	7	6	35	81	4	1
Oregon	0	0	0	0	0	1	0	0	0
Oronogo	2	0	1	0	1	4	19	2	0
Orrick	1	0	1	0	0	2	3	1	1
Osage Beach	22	0	1	1	20	23	187	1	1
Osceola	7	0	0	1	6	3	19	1	0
Overland	51	2	3	19	27	139	445	19	1
Owensville	1	0	1	0	0	2	14	1	0
Ozark	48	0	4	4	40	76	542	20	1
Pacific	17	0	0	1	16	25	137	3	0
Pagedale	39	0	4	8	27	34	69	6	4
Palmyra	0	0	0	0	0	6	70	2	1
Parkville	11	0	4	1	6	9	86	6	1
Parma	2	0	0	0	2	6	13	0	0
Pasadena Park	1	0	0	0	1	5	2	0	0
Peculiar	9	0	0	0	9	17	68	6	0
Perry	0	0	0	0	0	0	4	2	0
Perryville	15	0	1	1	13	25	124	15	1
Pevely	37	0	0	2	35	19	108	3	0
Piedmont	4	0	0	0	4	6	30	1	1
Pierce City	0	0	0	0	0	8	20	5	0
Pilot Knob	1	0	0	0	1	1	1	0	0
Pine Lawn	41	0	6	6	29	62	49	6	2
Pineville	1	0	0	0	1	0	0	0	0
Platte City	5	0	0	2	3	5	63	6	0
Platte Woods	0	0	0	0	0	1	7	3	0
Plattsburg	3	0	1	0	2	7	26	0	0
Pleasant Hill	2	0	0	0	2	24	88	7	0
Pleasant Hope	1	0	0	0	1	0	2	0	0
Pleasant Valley	5	0	2	0	3	9	38	4	0
Polo	0	0	0	0	0	1	6	0	0
Poplar Bluff	77	0	3	18	56	248	1,063	53	12
Portageville	1	0	0	0	1	1	19	0	0
Potosi	5	0	0	1	4	18	171	8	0
Purdy	3	0	0	0	3	6	14	3	0
Puxico	1	1	0	0	0	0	1	2	0
Qulin	0	0	0	0	0	0	5	0	0
Randolph	0	0	0	0	0	0	2	0	0
Raymore	16	1	2	4	9	29	358	13	0
Raytown	113	1	4	36	72	244	939	119	8
Reeds Spring	1	0	0	1	0	7	10	0	0
Republic	39	0	6	2	31	50	346	13	0
Rich Hill	8	0	1	0	7	9	22	3	0
Richland	9	0	2	2	5	19	40	2	2
Richmond	10	0	2	0	8	51	221	8	2
Richmond Heights	23	0	2	13	8	52	524	10	0
Riverside	6	0	1	2	3	8	108	20	1
Riverview	30	0	2	8	20	59	73	16	3
Rockaway Beach	4	0	0	0	4	3	3	0	0
Rock Hill	6	0	0	0	6	15	67	1	0
Rock Port	0	0	0	0	0	1	7	1	0
Rogersville	1	0	0	0	1	12	87	5	0
Rolla	65	0	6	9	50	76	583	18	5
Rosebud	0	0	0	0	0	0	0	0	0
Salem	8	0	0	1	7	39	206	11	0
Salisbury	2	0	0	0	2	4	11	1	0
Sarcoxie	3	0	0	0	3	13	34	2	0
Savannah	3	0	0	0	3	16	24	3	0
Scott City	14	0	0	0	14	41	106	1	1
Sedalia	122	0	7	14	101	329	1,110	63	2
Seligman	0	0	0	0	0	0	0	0	0
Senath	2	0	0	0	2	1	19	0	0
Seneca	5	0	0	0	5	15	46	3	1
Seymour	15	0	0	1	14	13	37	2	0
Shelbina	0	0	0	0	0	9	16	2	0
Shrewsbury	3	0	1	2	0	6	59	5	0
Sikeston	329	2	1	30	296	219	724	29	12
Silex	0	0	0	0	0	2	3	0	0
Slater	2	0	0	0	2	5	34	2	0
Smithville	9	0	4	0	5	10	85	2	0
Southwest City	5	0	0	0	5	10	16	2	0
Sparta	3	0	0	0	3	6	19	3	0
Springfield	1,894	12	281	395	1,206	2,313	11,232	1,146	63
St. Ann	89	0	3	7	79	71	307	29	1
St. Charles	113	0	17	27	69	201	1,502	67	12
St. Clair	13	0	1	1	11	48	250	17	1

Table 8.   Offenses Known to Law Enforcement, by Selected State and City, 2013— continued

(Number.)

State/city	Violent crime	Murder and nonnegligent manslaughter	Rape (revised definition)[1]	Robbery	Aggravated assault	Burglary	Larceny-theft	Motor vehicle theft	Arson[2]
Steele	35	0	1	7	27	34	64	3	1
Steelville	3	0	0	0	3	13	56	6	0
Ste. Genevieve	16	0	0	1	15	10	78	0	1
Stewartsville	0	0	0	0	0	0	0	0	0
St. James	5	0	1	0	4	12	84	1	0
St. John	27	0	1	11	15	43	140	11	1
St. Joseph	374	1	61	85	227	805	3,237	296	16
St. Louis	5,077	120	333	1,457	3,167	4,305	13,452	3,330	179
St. Marys	2	0	0	0	2	0	4	0	0
Stover	14	0	0	0	14	4	34	1	1
St. Peters	117	0	11	10	96	135	1,118	30	6
Strafford	8	0	1	0	7	10	71	1	1
Strasburg	0	0	0	0	0	0	0	0	0
St. Robert	19	1	1	7	10	57	301	13	1
Sturgeon	0	0	0	0	0	1	0	0	0
Sugar Creek	12	0	2	4	6	58	155	23	2
Sullivan	35	0	3	7	25	54	351	6	0
Summersville	1	0	0	0	1	5	4	2	0
Sunset Hills	10	0	0	3	7	29	127	13	0
Sweet Springs	2	0	0	0	2	3	11	0	0
Tarkio	0	0	0	0	0	5	13	1	0
Terre du Lac	5	0	0	0	5	4	8	3	0
Thayer	0	0	0	0	0	2	13	1	0
Tipton	0	0	0	0	0	6	14	1	0
Town and Country	6	2	2	2	0	15	99	1	0
Trenton	39	1	2	1	35	37	119	5	0
Trimble	5	0	0	2	3	2	3	0	0
Troy	28	0	1	1	26	30	293	8	1
Truesdale	7	0	0	0	7	11	3	1	0
Union	48	0	0	2	46	78	450	21	0
Unionville	0	0	0	0	0	7	20	3	0
University City	190	3	19	69	99	317	980	72	9
Urbana	2	0	0	1	1	1	3	0	0
Van Buren	0	0	0	0	0	2	9	1	0
Vandalia	15	0	5	0	10	6	78	4	0
Velda City	12	0	0	1	11	34	19	4	0
Velda Village Hills	6	0	1	0	5	12	10	3	0
Verona	1	0	0	0	1	7	2	1	0
Versailles	15	0	0	0	15	5	69	2	0
Viburnum	1	0	0	0	1	4	11	0	3
Vienna	0	0	0	0	0	5	16	0	0
Vinita Park	4	0	0	0	4	12	43	6	2
Walnut Grove	1	0	0	0	1	1	3	0	0
Wardell	5	0	1	0	4	2	1	0	0
Warrensburg	36	0	9	6	21	92	454	29	8
Warrenton	53	0	7	6	40	45	350	2	3
Warsaw	18	0	0	0	18	14	81	3	0
Warson Woods	1	0	1	0	0	2	17	0	0
Washburn	0	0	0	0	0	2	1	0	0
Washington	16	0	1	2	13	52	472	10	0
Waynesville	15	0	0	2	13	25	87	1	1
Weatherby Lake	2	0	0	0	2	3	22	0	0
Webb City	16	0	0	0	16	51	508	26	0
Webster Groves	24	1	3	5	15	66	168	6	2
Wellston	76	0	3	20	53	24	72	12	3
Wellsville	2	0	0	0	2	2	2	2	0
Wentzville	40	1	10	9	20	67	504	11	0
Weston	3	0	1	0	2	6	21	1	0
West Plains	33	0	5	4	24	140	590	24	0
Wheaton	0	0	0	0	0	1	3	0	0
Willard	7	0	1	0	6	19	54	6	0
Willow Springs	12	0	2	2	8	19	66	2	0
Winfield	6	0	0	0	6	2	15	1	1
Winona	9	0	1	1	7	7	29	2	0
Wood Heights	0	0	0	0	0	1	5	1	0
Woodson Terrace	12	0	1	5	6	44	73	22	0
Wright City	16	0	1	2	13	23	46	2	0
Montana									
Baker	1	0	1	0	0	0	7	1	0
Belgrade	24	0	4	1	19	21	133	6	2
Billings	360	4	39	81	236	989	4,074	541	7
Boulder	7	0	0	0	7	1	7	0	1
Bozeman	67	0	24	6	37	106	1,042	52	7
Bridger	0	0	0	0	0	0	4	1	0
Columbia Falls	5	0	3	0	2	5	120	9	0
Columbus	1	0	0	0	1	3	39	6	0
Conrad	6	0	1	0	5	0	35	1	0

Table 8.   Offenses Known to Law Enforcement, by Selected State and City, 2013— continued

(Number.)

State/city	Violent crime	Murder and nonnegligent manslaughter	Rape (revised definition)[1]	Robbery	Aggravated assault	Burglary	Larceny-theft	Motor vehicle theft	Arson[2]
Cut Bank	11	0	2	0	9	24	68	5	0
Deer Lodge	5	0	1	1	3	8	78	6	0
Dillon	6	0	2	0	4	0	27	3	0
East Helena	2	0	0	0	2	6	12	1	0
Ennis	0	0	0	0	0	1	1	1	0
Eureka	0	0	0	0	0	1	14	0	0
Fort Benton	3	1	0	0	2	1	7	2	0
Glasgow	6	0	1	0	5	7	50	4	0
Glendive	11	0	2	1	8	22	132	10	1
Great Falls	149	0	30	18	101	393	2,186	104	5
Hamilton	24	0	5	0	19	22	172	4	2
Havre	34	1	9	2	22	33	401	22	6
Helena	112	0	21	9	82	180	1,069	25	14
Hot Springs	1	0	1	0	0	3	5	2	0
Joliet	0	0	0	0	0	1	4	1	0
Kalispell	47	0	14	6	27	99	823	27	2
Laurel	15	0	2	1	12	19	145	18	0
Lewistown	37	0	9	0	28	10	56	8	0
Libby	3	0	0	0	3	9	47	2	0
Livingston	20	0	3	0	17	10	74	5	0
Manhattan	2	0	0	0	2	3	8	0	1
Miles City	15	0	1	1	13	14	128	9	0
Missoula	218	1	32	39	146	418	2,341	131	13
Plains	3	0	0	0	3	2	7	0	0
Polson	24	0	3	1	20	25	260	24	1
Red Lodge	1	0	0	0	1	3	28	3	0
Ronan City	15	0	2	0	13	5	47	0	0
Sidney	14	0	1	0	13	4	52	4	2
Stevensville	5	0	0	0	5	2	26	2	1
Thompson Falls	0	0	0	0	0	3	30	3	0
Troy	0	0	0	0	0	6	6	0	0
West Yellowstone	1	0	1	0	0	1	1	0	0
Whitefish	19	3	2	0	14	26	191	11	1
Wolf Point	16	0	1	3	12	12	75	8	0
Nebraska									
Alliance	20	0	8	1	11	57	76	3	1
Ashland	2	0		0	2	2	15	0	0
Aurora	1	0	1	0	0	17	12	2	0
Beatrice	66	0	21	2	43	76	308	8	2
Bellevue	70	0	13	28	29	138	717	108	5
Bennington	0	0		0	0	12	11	3	0
Blair	8	0	5	2	1	30	84	5	1
Bridgeport	0	0		0	0	5	20	0	0
Broken Bow	6	0	6	0	0	5	28	0	0
Central City	1	0	0	0	1	7	55	1	0
Chadron	9	0	2	0	7	17	162	7	2
Columbus	22	1	6	2	13	70	433	7	2
Cozad	4	0	1	0	3	6	31	2	0
Crete	15	0		2	10	43	162	7	3
Falls City	2	0		0	2	15	41	5	2
Fremont	45	0	27	3	15	99	535	22	8
Gering	0	0		0	0	39	135	10	0
Gordon	7	0	1	0	6	0	22	1	0
Gothenburg	1	0	0	0	1	14	74	2	0
Grand Island	136	1		8	91	526	1,759	104	7
Hastings	54	0	23	4	27	198	689	35	4
Holdrege	6	0	3	0	3	29	90	3	0
Imperial	5	0		0	5	4	11	0	0
Kearney	56	0	16	5	35	134	663	28	5
Kimball	18	0		0	18	2	8	0	0
La Vista	7	0	1	3	3	27	170	18	1
Lexington	27	0	11	3	13	39	226	10	4
Lincoln	990	5		212	631	1,423	7,625	306	40
Madison	3	0	0	0	3	8	8	2	0
McCook	10	0	7	0	3	38	166	11	0
Milford	0	0		0	0	8	18	0	1
Minden	3	0	1	0	2	9	45	3	0
Mitchell	0	0	0	0	0	3	17	1	0
Nebraska City	6	0	3	0	3	38	132	9	0
Norfolk	30	0	19	1	10	135	675	54	1
Ogallala	3	0	2	0	1	9	121	7	0
Omaha	2,449	42		718	1,505	3,509	12,519	3,080	83
O'Neill	0	0		0	0	0	6	1	0
Papillion	10	0	5	4	1	34	322	17	1
Plattsmouth	3	0	2	0	1	7	103	12	0
Ralston	6	1	2	2	1	33	160	20	2
Scottsbluff	41	0	10	6	25	127	578	15	1

Table 8.   Offenses Known to Law Enforcement, by Selected State and City, 2013— continued

(Number.)

State/city	Violent crime	Murder and nonnegligent manslaughter	Rape (revised definition)[1]	Robbery	Aggravated assault	Burglary	Larceny-theft	Motor vehicle theft	Arson[2]
Seward	6	0	1	0	5	8	75	2	0
South Sioux City	13	0		1	12	14	232	4	0
Superior	1	0		0	1	1	10	1	0
Valentine	8	0	1	0	7	5	17	3	0
Valley	4	0		0	1	8	35	2	0
Wahoo	2	0	0	0	2	16	38	1	1
West Point	0	0	0	0	0	0	1	0	0
Wilber	0	0	0	0	0	4	19	2	0
York	1	0		0	1	20	162	14	0
Nevada									
Boulder City	22	2		1	15	52	105	22	2
Carlin	16	1		1	14	8	18	6	0
Elko	89	7		12	50	276	607	95	0
Fallon	23	0		0	21	63	285	17	1
Henderson	367	8		160	154	1,405	3,416	537	22
Las Vegas Metropolitan Police Department	11,374	97		4,072	6,500	14,785	26,548	6,635	257
Lovelock	19	0		1	14	26	20	6	0
Mesquite	11	2		0	9	52	178	20	2
North Las Vegas	1,806	7		463	1,251	2,050	2,936	983	7
Reno	1,154	14		305	767	1,411	4,901	868	18
Sparks	271	2		70	156	559	1,710	253	13
West Wendover	23	0		6	15	38	79	20	0
Winnemucca	17	0		2	15	48	97	11	1
Yerington	4	0		1	0	26	51	3	0
New Hampshire									
Alexandria	0	0	0	0	0	2	8	0	0
Alstead	0	0	0	0	0	1	3	0	0
Alton	9	0	4	1	4	26	66	5	0
Amherst	7	0	2	0	5	25	264	1	1
Antrim	8	0	4	1	3	9	43	1	0
Ashland	5	0	1	1	3	8	48	6	0
Atkinson	1	0	0	0	1	11	9	0	0
Auburn	2	0	0	0	2	32	39	1	1
Barnstead	5	0	1	0	4	20	30	3	0
Barrington	1	0	0	0	1	24	66	2	0
Bartlett	3	0	0	0	3	17	31	1	0
Bedford	12	0	5	4	3	42	290	3	2
Belmont	25	2	5	4	14	53	156	15	1
Bennington	2	0	1	0	1	7	35	8	0
Berlin	22	0	10	4	8	36	94	7	4
Bethlehem	1	0	1	0	0	6	16	2	0
Boscawen	7	0	2	1	4	19	38	3	0
Bow	6	0	2	1	3	30	60	3	0
Brentwood	2	0	0	0	2	10	33	2	0
Bristol	8	0	3	0	5	30	55	5	1
Campton	16	0	6	1	9	16	48	4	0
Candia	6	0	1	0	5	13	33	0	1
Canterbury	1	0	0	0	1	2	17	0	0
Carroll	1	0	0	0	1	11	45	0	0
Center Harbor	1	0	0	0	1	3	18	1	0
Charlestown	4	0	2	0	2	8	15	2	0
Chester	6	0	1	2	3	19	38	3	0
Claremont	41	0	13	8	20	67	350	20	2
Colebrook	8	0	2	1	5	14	45	1	0
Concord	103	0	33	15	55	166	844	14	9
Conway	38	0	13	7	18	57	367	8	1
Dalton	2	0	0	0	2	8	6	0	0
Danville	0	0	0	0	0	9	26	0	0
Deerfield	3	0	1	0	2	7	39	5	0
Deering	3	0	0	0	3	3	14	1	0
Derry	57	0	22	5	30	135	535	27	13
Dover	49	0	22	6	21	77	475	12	2
Dublin	0	0	0	0	0	4	7	0	0
Dunbarton	3	0	1	0	2	9	20	1	0
Durham	27	0	10	0	17	11	103	3	6
Effingham	4	0	0	0	4	2	14	1	0
Enfield	15	0	8	1	6	7	30	1	0
Epping	7	0	5	2	0	18	199	8	2
Epsom	2	0	2	0	0	16	49	2	0
Exeter	22	1	8	3	10	13	112	1	0
Farmington	22	0	7	5	10	47	132	7	3
Franconia	1	0	0	0	1	4	14	2	0
Freedom	1	0	1	0	0	3	3	1	0
Fremont	1	0	0	0	1	8	9	1	0
Gilford	8	0	2	1	5	25	146	9	0

Table 8. Offenses Known to Law Enforcement, by Selected State and City, 2013— continued

(Number.)

State/city	Violent crime	Murder and nonnegligent manslaughter	Rape (revised definition)[1]	Robbery	Aggravated assault	Burglary	Larceny-theft	Motor vehicle theft	Arson[2]
Gilmanton	2	0	0	0	2	28	17	3	1
Goffstown	13	0	1	5	7	58	289	7	0
Gorham	6	0	3	2	1	7	58	0	1
Grantham	2	0	0	0	2	4	16	0	0
Greenland	4	0	1	0	3	7	28	1	0
Hampstead	6	0	1	0	5	31	53	5	0
Hampton	30	1	7	7	15	48	266	15	1
Hampton Falls	5	0	1	2	2	12	19	1	0
Hancock	1	0	0	0	1	0	7	0	0
Hanover	19	0	14	1	4	17	157	1	2
Haverhill	14	0	6	3	5	29	83	3	0
Henniker	6	0	1	0	5	10	34	1	3
Hillsborough	13	0	2	0	11	12	91	2	0
Hinsdale	5	1	1	2	1	16	96	3	0
Hooksett	21	0	7	6	8	72	357	7	2
Hopkinton	10	0	0	0	10	7	48	2	0
Hudson	41	0	10	8	23	66	299	9	4
Jaffrey	13	0	1	2	10	15	46	2	1
Keene	70	1	13	23	33	106	883	17	6
Kingston	2	0	2	0	0	13	36	9	0
Laconia	71	2	10	19	40	112	478	19	8
Lancaster	6	1	4	0	1	10	63	6	1
Lebanon	48	0	19	6	23	46	409	8	7
Lee	8	0	2	1	5	10	16	1	1
Lincoln	1	0	1	0	0	13	60	3	0
Lisbon	1	0	0	0	1	5	7	0	0
Litchfield	6	0	1	0	5	24	29	3	1
Londonderry	32	0	6	11	15	59	228	14	2
Loudon	3	0	3	0	0	22	100	9	2
Madison	0	0	0	0	0	11	30	3	0
Manchester	747	4	91	295	357	894	3,141	159	45
Marlborough	0	0	0	0	0	13	18	1	0
Meredith	3	1	1	1	0	48	122	5	0
Merrimack	6	0	1	3	2	28	193	8	0
Middleton	6	0	0	1	5	8	19	1	1
Milford	24	0	10	2	12	25	241	9	6
Milton	16	0	5	0	11	24	70	8	1
Mont Vernon	2	0	1	0	1	7	8	1	0
Moultonborough	7	0	4	0	3	15	52	3	0
Nashua	182	6	32	61	83	323	1,857	68	9
New Boston	5	0	4	0	1	5	23	1	1
Newbury	0	0	0	0	0	3	10	1	0
New Durham	2	0	2	0	0	6	52	3	0
Newfields	0	0	0	0	0	4	18	0	0
New Hampton	1	0	1	0	0	3	42	1	0
Newington	3	0	0	3	0	3	272	3	0
New Ipswich	2	0	0	0	2	18	47	1	3
New London	0	0	0	0	0	9	18	1	0
Newport	16	0	6	0	10	28	175	7	0
Newton	9	0	1	1	7	9	45	0	1
Northfield	8	0	0	0	8	18	98	3	0
North Hampton	4	0	1	1	2	11	30	1	0
Northumberland	9	0	4	0	5	12	34	1	0
Northwood	9	0	8	1	0	18	44	0	0
Nottingham	4	0	0	0	4	23	26	3	0
Orford	0	0	0	0	0	3	2	0	0
Ossipee	13	0	0	0	13	5	98	3	0
Pelham	20	0	5	1	14	27	117	7	0
Pembroke	15	0	9	0	6	12	58	7	1
Peterborough	6	0	2	1	3	21	84	4	4
Plaistow	5	0	0	2	3	16	151	15	0
Plymouth	15	0	5	1	9	15	172	8	23
Portsmouth	50	0	14	15	21	51	496	20	3
Raymond	17	0	5	3	9	24	111	11	0
Rindge	8	0	4	0	4	7	113	1	0
Rochester	105	0	25	20	60	159	1,104	24	11
Rollinsford	2	0	0	1	1	4	41	1	0
Rye	3	0	3	0	0	4	53	0	0
Salem	48	0	4	14	30	65	765	35	2
Sanbornton	1	0	0	0	1	11	47	0	0
Sandown	1	0	1	0	0	11	17	4	2
Sandwich	0	0	0	0	0	5	23	0	0
Seabrook	31	0	3	7	21	25	233	11	0
Somersworth	47	1	14	11	21	53	410	6	4
South Hampton	0	0	0	0	0	3	5	0	0
Strafford	5	0	0	0	5	6	20	0	1
Stratham	2	0	1	0	1	3	55	0	0
Sugar Hill	1	0	1	0	0	2	1	0	0

Table 8.   Offenses Known to Law Enforcement, by Selected State and City, 2013— continued

(Number.)

State/city	Violent crime	Murder and nonnegligent manslaughter	Rape (revised definition)[1]	Robbery	Aggravated assault	Burglary	Larceny-theft	Motor vehicle theft	Arson[2]
Sunapee	6	0	3	0	3	3	15	0	0
Thornton	0	0	0	0	0	5	17	3	0
Tilton	10	0	4	5	1	29	188	5	0
Troy	1	0	0	0	1	6	18	0	0
Wakefield	5	0	3	0	2	33	58	3	0
Warner	6	0	0	0	6	4	26	1	0
Washington	1	0	0	0	1	6	7	0	0
Waterville Valley	0	0	0	0	0	7	34	2	0
Weare	15	0	4	0	11	14	44	4	1
Webster	0	0	0	0	0	7	25	0	0
Wilton	3	0	1	0	2	10	50	5	0
Winchester	7	0	2	0	5	25	77	3	0
Windham	15	0	2	3	10	33	82	5	2
Wolfeboro	7	0	5	0	2	10	82	2	0
Woodstock	1	0	0	0	1	4	32	3	3
New Jersey									
Aberdeen Township	19	0		13	6	42	185	10	0
Absecon	21	0		4	15	91	169	6	0
Allendale	0	0		0	0	6	29	2	0
Allenhurst	0	0		0	0	20	18	1	0
Allentown	3	0		0	3	12	6	0	0
Alpha	1	0		0	1	15	15	1	1
Alpine	0	0		0	0	6	2	2	0
Andover Township	1	0		0	1	10	23	0	0
Asbury Park	264	6		126	123	196	616	30	3
Atlantic City	685	3		367	306	393	2,011	71	2
Atlantic Highlands	0	0		0	0	18	58	1	0
Audubon	10	0		9	1	34	359	2	0
Audubon Park	0	0		0	0	5	25	1	0
Avalon	2	0		0	2	30	197	0	0
Avon-by-the-Sea	1	0		0	1	37	33	0	0
Barnegat Light	2	0		0	1	3	3	0	0
Barnegat Township	17	0		4	11	61	135	5	1
Barrington	3	0		0	1	26	36	10	0
Bay Head	0	0		0	0	5	28	3	0
Bayonne	138	0		50	88	142	599	87	1
Beach Haven	0	0		0	0	12	103	2	0
Beachwood	7	1		1	5	21	164	3	0
Bedminster Township	1	0		0	1	9	33	4	0
Belleville	112	0		62	49	152	523	164	3
Bellmawr	16	0		9	7	57	174	13	0
Belmar	8	0		1	4	51	195	3	0
Belvidere	2	0		0	2	10	19	1	1
Bergenfield	16	0		6	10	16	87	2	0
Berkeley Heights Township	1	0		0	1	9	77	3	0
Berlin	14	1		1	12	24	123	4	0
Berlin Township	5	0		1	4	37	168	4	9
Bernards Township	2	0		1	0	33	83	4	0
Bernardsville	2	0		0	2	13	29	2	0
Beverly	14	0		7	7	13	42	7	0
Blairstown Township	1	0		0	1	20	20	0	1
Bloomfield	137	1		90	43	199	735	160	0
Bloomingdale	2	0		0	2	6	42	0	0
Bogota	5	0		1	4	12	37	2	0
Boonton	9	0		5	4	19	92	0	0
Boonton Township	2	0		0	2	1	11	0	0
Bordentown	0	0		0	0	13	22	3	0
Bordentown Township	16	0		3	12	33	113	3	0
Bound Brook	16	0		10	6	61	160	3	2
Bradley Beach	4	0		2	1	13	113	3	0
Branchburg Township	4	0		1	3	22	108	3	0
Brick Township	89	1		24	60	252	911	20	2
Bridgeton	340	2		165	161	376	763	47	3
Bridgewater Township	16	1		8	6	70	448	20	0
Brielle	2	0		0	2	5	35	3	0
Brigantine	3	0		0	2	54	118	0	0
Brooklawn	18	0		10	6	23	140	6	0
Buena	16	0		0	15	31	47	0	2
Burlington	60	1		33	20	74	168	13	0
Burlington Township	28	0		12	10	53	307	15	1
Butler	11	0		1	7	11	29	2	1
Byram Township	0	0		0	0	7	25	3	0
Caldwell	8	0		2	5	20	44	2	1
Califon	0	0		0	0	0	6	0	0
Cape May	4	0		0	4	25	121	2	1
Cape May Point	0	0		0	0	2	13	0	0
Carlstadt	8	0		1	6	8	92	25	0

Table 8.   Offenses Known to Law Enforcement, by Selected State and City, 2013— continued

(Number.)

State/city	Violent crime	Murder and nonnegligent manslaughter	Rape (revised definition)[1]	Robbery	Aggravated assault	Burglary	Larceny-theft	Motor vehicle theft	Arson[2]
Carney's Point Township	32	1		5	17	61	117	8	0
Carteret	49	1		24	22	86	258	24	0
Cedar Grove Township	4	0		1	3	16	64	11	0
Chatham	2	0		1	1	12	37	7	1
Chatham Township	0	0		0	0	3	36	3	0
Cherry Hill Township	123	0		41	82	268	1,866	57	0
Chesilhurst	4	1		1	2	26	28	4	0
Chester	3	0		0	2	5	18	1	0
Chesterfield Township	2	0		0	2	5	26	0	0
Chester Township	1	0		0	1	15	29	0	0
Cinnaminson Township	21	2		13	5	63	287	8	1
Clark Township	5	1		1	3	9	138	3	0
Clayton	13	0		3	10	44	132	6	0
Clementon	20	0		8	11	54	164	8	3
Cliffside Park	50	0		20	29	62	189	12	0
Clifton	175	0		57	106	358	1,060	103	1
Clinton	3	0		0	2	12	42	1	0
Clinton Township	4	0		0	4	9	44	5	0
Closter	3	0		0	3	15	34	2	0
Collingswood	26	0		12	13	110	245	24	0
Colts Neck Township	3	0		1	2	19	59	13	1
Cranbury Township	2	0		2	0	6	36	3	0
Cranford Township	4	0		4	0	26	150	11	1
Deal	2	0		1	0	36	19	8	0
Delanco Township	6	0		1	4	25	66	3	0
Delaware Township	1	0		0	1	19	11	0	0
Delran Township	16	0		13	3	41	174	8	0
Demarest	1	0		0	1	10	19	1	0
Denville Township	5	0		3	2	22	81	7	0
Deptford Township	61	1		30	26	190	1,252	47	3
Dover	28	0		15	12	71	215	11	0
Dumont	7	0		3	1	14	100	1	0
Dunellen	3	0		0	3	45	113	0	0
Eastampton Township	6	0		0	2	33	64	0	0
East Brunswick Township	30	0		9	21	118	546	16	9
East Greenwich Township	5	0		2	3	24	58	6	0
East Hanover Township	19	0		2	17	22	159	6	0
East Newark	11	0		6	5	5	14	8	0
East Orange	405	6		184	203	357	578	270	9
East Rutherford	7	0		2	5	18	129	17	0
Eatontown	26	0		10	14	60	393	6	0
Edgewater	12	0		2	9	14	190	6	0
Edgewater Park Township	16	0		10	4	56	138	18	0
Edison Township	123	2		56	57	285	854	106	18
Egg Harbor City	19	0		5	11	33	56	0	0
Egg Harbor Township	106	2		28	72	196	673	29	5
Elizabeth	999	7		554	401	793	1,861	1,001	4
Elk Township	7	0		0	7	24	53	2	1
Elmer	0	0		0	0	3	10	1	0
Elmwood Park	30	0		9	21	83	247	15	2
Elsinboro Township	0	0		0	0	4	11	0	0
Emerson	0	0		0	0	3	30	1	0
Englewood	109	2		40	66	111	308	23	1
Englewood Cliffs	2	0		2	0	6	57	1	0
Englishtown	1	0		1	0	2	26	1	0
Essex Fells	2	1		0	1	5	4	2	0
Evesham Township	25	0		4	13	87	444	17	1
Ewing Township	70	1		25	44	165	438	72	8
Fairfield Township, Essex County	11	0		4	6	18	190	20	0
Fair Haven	3	0		0	3	7	20	2	0
Fair Lawn	17	0		7	10	52	258	8	3
Fairview	21	0		11	10	40	116	10	0
Fanwood	6	0		0	6	13	60	2	0
Far Hills	0	0		0	0	2	8	0	0
Flemington	10	0		3	7	6	54	0	0
Florence Township	13	0		6	7	27	56	8	0
Florham Park	7	0		3	4	9	82	5	0
Fort Lee	28	0		12	16	36	234	16	0
Franklin	5	0		2	2	10	86	0	0
Franklin Lakes	2	0		1	1	21	48	10	0
Franklin Township, Gloucester County	12	1		2	9	95	239	10	1
Franklin Township, Hunterdon County	2	0		0	1	2	24	1	0
Franklin Township, Somerset County	79	1		42	29	373	569	59	0
Freehold	47	0		16	30	43	178	3	0
Freehold Township	30	0		10	17	52	704	14	0
Frenchtown	0	0		0	0	1	35	0	0

Table 8.   Offenses Known to Law Enforcement, by Selected State and City, 2013— continued

(Number.)

State/city	Violent crime	Murder and nonnegligent manslaughter	Rape (revised definition)[1]	Robbery	Aggravated assault	Burglary	Larceny-theft	Motor vehicle theft	Arson[2]
Galloway Township	98	2		24	63	178	411	28	2
Garfield	62	0		26	33	124	550	26	0
Garwood	5	0		1	4	7	62	1	0
Gibbsboro	4	0		0	4	10	29	1	1
Glassboro	30	0		14	14	90	325	12	0
Glen Ridge	7	0		4	3	39	108	9	1
Glen Rock	1	0		0	1	8	87	0	0
Gloucester City	29	0		13	11	107	188	6	1
Gloucester Township	190	2		35	144	320	1,049	32	8
Green Brook Township	3	0		2	1	18	99	6	1
Greenwich Township, Gloucester County	4	0		2	2	26	112	1	0
Greenwich Township, Warren County	1	0		1	0	10	100	1	0
Guttenberg	36	0		22	14	23	83	6	1
Hackensack	111	1		34	73	74	732	46	1
Hackettstown	8	0		2	5	21	100	12	0
Haddonfield	8	0		2	5	28	142	4	0
Haddon Heights	2	0		0	1	24	135	1	1
Haddon Township	19	0		11	7	79	244	13	0
Haledon	11	0		8	3	42	99	8	0
Hamburg	1	0		0	1	4	21	0	0
Hamilton Township, Atlantic County	42	0		19	22	178	824	23	10
Hamilton Township, Mercer County	189	1		78	102	448	1,283	131	1
Hammonton	8	0		1	7	47	95	9	0
Hanover Township	11	0		4	7	26	105	4	1
Harding Township	1	0		0	1	13	5	0	0
Hardyston Township	5	0		0	5	21	85	1	0
Harrington Park	0	0		0	0	1	6	0	0
Harrison	63	0		32	31	50	191	68	0
Harrison Township	3	0		1	2	48	87	6	0
Harvey Cedars	1	0		0	1	2	21	1	0
Hasbrouck Heights	3	0		3	0	8	74	1	0
Haworth	0	0		0	0	1	4	0	0
Hawthorne	4	0		1	3	60	152	9	0
Hazlet Township	7	0		6	1	22	182	7	6
Helmetta	3	0		0	1	10	24	3	0
High Bridge	4	0		0	4	9	10	0	0
Highland Park	9	0		6	3	44	167	6	0
Highlands	4	0		1	3	31	37	1	0
Hightstown	10	0		2	4	27	96	4	0
Hillsborough Township	7	0		2	4	55	135	4	2
Hillsdale	3	0		0	3	3	55	0	0
Hillside Township	91	1		53	31	147	316	102	0
Hi-Nella	5	0		0	5	2	10	1	0
Hoboken	152	1		47	98	128	780	62	0
Ho-Ho-Kus	0	0		0	0	11	5	1	0
Holland Township	0	0		0	0	12	53	0	0
Holmdel Township	8	0		2	6	28	177	7	0
Hopatcong	14	1		1	12	37	82	2	0
Hopewell	2	0		1	1	5	14	2	0
Hopewell Township	10	1		1	7	23	94	3	1
Howell Township	41	0		18	22	79	464	21	2
Independence Township	4	0		0	3	14	41	2	0
Interlaken	0	0		0	0	10	21	0	0
Irvington	815	17		492	279	448	643	522	7
Island Heights	0	0		0	0	1	7	1	0
Jackson Township	33	0		10	18	201	403	13	24
Jamesburg	7	0		5	2	22	28	1	0
Jefferson Township	6	0		2	4	36	119	2	0
Jersey City	1,655	20		717	883	1,052	3,046	738	31
Keansburg	21	0		8	13	47	181	3	2
Kearny	78	1		41	33	110	642	136	1
Kenilworth	9	0		2	3	11	125	9	0
Keyport	15	0		6	9	31	104	3	1
Kinnelon	1	1		0	0	14	43	2	0
Lacey Township	19	0		3	14	65	456	5	0
Lake Como	3	0		0	3	9	14	0	0
Lakehurst	4	0		0	3	7	29	0	0
Lakewood Township	93	2		34	52	186	768	44	6
Lambertville	3	0		1	1	12	34	2	2
Laurel Springs	1	0		1	0	19	24	1	0
Lavallette	0	0		0	0	5	42	0	0
Lawrence Township, Mercer County	47	0		28	19	94	673	36	1
Lebanon Township	1	0		0	1	11	21	3	0
Leonia	6	0		1	5	13	24	0	0
Lincoln Park	9	0		2	5	18	74	3	0

Table 8.   Offenses Known to Law Enforcement, by Selected State and City, 2013— continued

(Number.)

State/city	Violent crime	Murder and nonnegligent manslaughter	Rape (revised definition)[1]	Robbery	Aggravated assault	Burglary	Larceny-theft	Motor vehicle theft	Arson[2]
Linden	123	0		54	69	182	903	131	4
Lindenwold	122	2		50	64	200	306	27	4
Linwood	1	0		0	1	19	63	1	0
Little Egg Harbor Township	26	0		4	19	102	231	11	6
Little Falls Township	12	1		1	10	24	103	19	0
Little Ferry	9	0		2	7	21	70	13	0
Little Silver	4	0		0	4	10	66	3	0
Livingston Township	15	0		8	7	26	323	35	0
Loch Arbour	0	0		0	0	11	10	1	0
Lodi	36	0		14	22	91	309	21	1
Logan Township	7	0		1	6	23	97	15	0
Long Beach Township	2	0		0	2	43	140	2	0
Long Branch	124	5		50	63	203	603	36	2
Long Hill Township	2	0		1	1	10	38	0	0
Longport	0	0		0	0	4	2	0	0
Lopatcong Township	1	0		0	1	9	65	0	0
Lower Alloways Creek Township	3	0		0	3	6	7	0	0
Lower Township	31	0		9	18	100	355	18	2
Lumberton Township	17	0		7	10	18	374	10	2
Lyndhurst Township	17	0		7	10	28	220	28	0
Madison	4	0		1	3	21	79	3	0
Magnolia	14	1		7	5	34	55	11	1
Manalapan Township	20	0		9	11	50	229	21	1
Manasquan	3	0		1	2	34	100	0	0
Manchester Township	19	2		5	12	110	330	7	2
Mansfield Township, Burlington County	3	0		1	2	27	70	5	0
Mansfield Township, Warren County	9	0		2	4	30	152	4	1
Mantoloking	0	0		0	0	1	25	0	0
Mantua Township	11	0		5	6	61	200	8	0
Manville	10	0		3	6	35	217	15	1
Maple Shade Township	42	1		17	19	147	234	29	1
Maplewood Township	41	0		38	3	91	338	56	2
Margate City	5	0		2	3	52	152	2	2
Marlboro Township	10	0		0	9	68	239	22	3
Matawan	4	0		3	1	41	47	1	1
Maywood	6	0		4	2	18	68	4	0
Medford Lakes	1	0		0	1	2	9	0	2
Medford Township	11	0		3	5	65	195	2	5
Mendham	1	0		0	1	5	19	2	0
Mendham Township	1	0		0	1	8	20	0	0
Merchantville	7	1		2	4	13	63	4	0
Metuchen	6	0		1	4	22	154	4	0
Middlesex	6	0		4	2	27	111	2	0
Middle Township	59	0		10	39	113	465	15	3
Middletown Township	43	1		13	28	122	494	16	3
Midland Park	2	0		0	2	4	29	1	0
Millburn Township	9	1		7	1	36	416	21	0
Milltown	0	0		0	0	7	38	0	0
Millville	254	0		119	122	453	1,815	49	3
Mine Hill Township	0	0		0	0	9	19	0	1
Monmouth Beach	0	0		0	0	18	39	2	0
Monroe Township, Gloucester County	49	1		24	22	261	530	33	3
Monroe Township, Middlesex County	9	1		0	6	33	196	13	4
Montclair	73	2		33	36	195	341	35	5
Montgomery Township	3	1		0	2	26	70	7	0
Montvale	3	0		0	3	1	33	2	0
Montville Township	5	0		0	4	38	112	8	0
Moonachie	4	0		0	4	8	46	3	0
Moorestown Township	24	0		11	10	45	365	16	1
Morris Plains	3	0		1	2	6	56	0	0
Morristown	84	0		43	40	79	370	19	1
Morris Township	11	0		2	9	42	124	11	0
Mountain Lakes	0	0		0	0	6	22	4	0
Mountainside	1	0		0	0	10	36	2	0
Mount Arlington	2	0		0	2	6	35	0	0
Mount Ephraim	10	0		4	6	23	142	6	1
Mount Holly Township	38	0		19	18	44	228	11	3
Mount Laurel Township	28	0		13	7	151	558	20	3
Mount Olive Township	16	0		4	11	60	184	11	0
Mullica Township	5	0		1	4	29	43	2	0
National Park	7	0		1	6	19	36	6	0
Neptune City	19	0		8	11	38	175	6	0
Neptune Township	174	0		74	94	191	992	37	9
Netcong	7	0		0	5	13	34	2	0
Newark	3,516	112		2,433	926	2,074	3,997	2,894	34
New Brunswick	303	3		165	116	546	1,032	87	3

Table 8.   Offenses Known to Law Enforcement, by Selected State and City, 2013— continued

(Number.)

State/city	Violent crime	Murder and nonnegligent manslaughter	Rape (revised definition)[1]	Robbery	Aggravated assault	Burglary	Larceny-theft	Motor vehicle theft	Arson[2]
Newfield	1	0		0	1	9	14	1	1
New Hanover Township	0	0		0	0	1	6	0	1
New Milford	2	1		0	1	16	63	1	0
New Providence	3	0		1	1	24	87	1	0
Newton	7	0		0	7	21	84	1	1
North Arlington	12	0		4	8	47	131	19	1
North Bergen Township	102	0		43	53	135	427	76	2
North Brunswick Township	45	0		15	27	190	644	33	2
North Caldwell	1	0		0	1	11	24	3	0
Northfield	1	0		0	1	17	75	1	0
North Hanover Township	8	0		2	3	12	39	2	0
North Plainfield	53	0		20	28	121	262	25	1
Northvale	3	0		1	2	0	18	1	0
North Wildwood	11	0		1	10	28	287	1	1
Norwood	1	0		0	1	6	16	0	0
Nutley Township	20	0		6	13	58	208	19	1
Oakland	2	0		1	1	12	65	3	0
Oaklyn	6	1		1	4	21	74	2	0
Ocean City	12	0		3	6	88	346	6	0
Ocean Gate	1	0		0	1	10	28	0	0
Oceanport	6	0		3	3	41	70	2	1
Ocean Township, Monmouth County	50	0		19	29	133	588	14	3
Ocean Township, Ocean County	1	0		0	1	11	66	4	0
Ogdensburg	1	0		0	1	9	11	3	0
Old Bridge Township	47	1		18	27	151	635	46	1
Old Tappan	0	0		0	0	4	11	0	0
Oradell	2	0		0	1	3	44	2	0
Orange	377	6		266	100	269	377	225	3
Oxford Township	1	0		0	1	0	10	0	0
Palisades Park	19	0		7	12	34	78	8	0
Palmyra	25	0		12	13	47	149	9	3
Paramus	32	0		27	5	52	1,228	35	0
Park Ridge	1	0		0	0	5	22	1	0
Parsippany-Troy Hills Township	19	1		18	0	78	351	15	0
Passaic	512	2		240	269	279	726	135	2
Paterson	1,555	18		848	663	1,368	1,984	749	7
Paulsboro	27	0		14	13	43	136	8	0
Peapack and Gladstone	0	0		0	0	2	19	2	0
Pemberton	3	0		0	2	11	16	0	0
Pemberton Township	86	1		21	51	296	349	36	7
Pennington	0	0		0	0	0	5	0	0
Pennsauken Township	105	1		49	49	267	758	103	0
Penns Grove	18	0		5	12	36	97	11	1
Pennsville Township	12	0		1	10	75	283	3	0
Pequannock Township	6	0		3	3	27	90	2	0
Perth Amboy	243	1		95	137	238	663	140	3
Phillipsburg	30	1		11	12	128	234	16	3
Pine Beach	0	0		0	0	4	14	1	0
Pine Hill	46	1		10	33	91	171	12	1
Pine Valley	0	0		0	0	0	3	0	0
Piscataway Township	46	2		14	28	137	384	27	3
Pitman	7	2		3	2	20	87	2	0
Plainfield	427	9		165	244	381	807	96	15
Pleasantville	145	0		51	86	71	327	26	1
Plumsted Township	12	0		1	4	25	19	3	0
Pohatcong Township	4	0		1	3	5	205	3	1
Point Pleasant	16	0		2	13	45	167	3	0
Point Pleasant Beach	3	0		2	1	24	150	3	0
Pompton Lakes	7	0		0	7	23	93	4	0
Princeton	17	0		9	4	45	259	1	0
Prospect Park	11	1		5	4	47	73	20	0
Rahway	50	1		24	23	92	317	43	2
Ramsey	14	0		2	12	16	121	7	0
Randolph Township	4	0		3	1	30	138	4	0
Raritan	6	0		2	4	12	100	4	0
Raritan Township	4	1		1	1	29	156	4	0
Readington Township	2	0		0	2	33	126	4	0
Red Bank	19	0		10	5	28	233	3	1
Ridgefield	4	0		2	2	10	53	6	0
Ridgefield Park	5	0		0	5	16	87	11	1
Ridgewood	8	0		0	6	46	179	1	0
Ringwood	5	0		1	4	25	59	1	0
Riverdale	1	0		0	1	6	175	0	0
River Edge	1	0		0	1	14	36	3	0
Riverside Township	24	0		11	13	43	67	7	1
Riverton	4	1		1	2	21	33	2	0
River Vale Township	9	0		0	5	2	15	0	0

Table 8.   Offenses Known to Law Enforcement, by Selected State and City, 2013— continued

(Number.)

State/city	Violent crime	Murder and nonnegligent manslaughter	Rape (revised definition)[1]	Robbery	Aggravated assault	Burglary	Larceny-theft	Motor vehicle theft	Arson[2]
Robbinsville Township	6	0		1	5	32	109	1	0
Rochelle Park Township	3	0		2	1	8	46	2	0
Rockaway	5	0		1	2	6	37	4	0
Rockaway Township	11	0		9	1	48	427	11	1
Rockleigh	1	0		0	1	0	1	0	0
Roseland	1	0		0	1	8	33	7	0
Roselle	65	0		28	36	151	239	54	3
Roselle Park	8	0		1	6	28	67	9	1
Roxbury Township	7	0		2	4	48	260	7	0
Rumson	2	0		2	0	6	40	3	1
Runnemede	13	0		6	7	50	160	13	0
Rutherford	9	0		2	7	58	216	11	1
Saddle Brook Township	6	0		2	4	33	240	13	0
Saddle River	1	0		0	1	17	15	2	0
Salem	54	3		15	33	89	219	5	2
Sayreville	38	1		14	22	121	386	28	4
Scotch Plains Township	19	0		5	13	48	136	4	0
Sea Bright	1	0		0	1	3	39	1	0
Sea Girt	0	0		0	0	7	16	0	0
Sea Isle City	3	0		1	1	110	241	4	0
Seaside Heights	30	0		7	22	38	169	2	0
Seaside Park	3	0		2	1	7	26	0	0
Secaucus	18	0		7	11	38	427	41	0
Ship Bottom	1	0		0	1	5	38	2	0
Shrewsbury	3	0		1	2	7	53	4	0
Somerdale	14	0		4	8	43	287	4	2
Somers Point	28	0		4	24	47	249	5	3
Somerville	15	0		9	6	31	161	13	0
South Amboy	16	0		4	12	24	106	8	0
South Bound Brook	1	0		0	1	9	19	3	0
South Brunswick Township	21	0		8	13	90	422	28	1
South Hackensack Township	5	0		2	3	5	28	2	0
South Harrison Township	1	0		0	1	13	13	2	1
South Orange	35	0		30	4	56	234	37	0
South Plainfield	19	0		6	13	79	309	12	1
South River	28	0		9	17	41	140	7	1
South Toms River	7	0		2	4	19	60	3	1
Sparta Township	4	0		0	4	22	121	1	1
Spotswood	4	0		0	4	14	43	0	4
Springfield	12	0		6	5	38	159	14	0
Springfield Township	1	0		0	1	13	25	1	0
Spring Lake	1	0		0	1	9	60	3	0
Spring Lake Heights	1	0		0	0	4	10	0	0
Stafford Township	14	0		5	9	117	383	8	1
Stanhope	1	0		0	1	10	26	1	0
Stone Harbor	0	0		0	0	8	95	0	0
Stratford	11	0		3	8	16	96	4	0
Summit	8	0		3	4	27	175	17	1
Surf City	0	0		0	0	8	30	0	0
Swedesboro	2	0		1	1	11	21	0	1
Tavistock	0	0		0	0	0	0	0	0
Teaneck Township	49	0		22	27	113	411	17	2
Tenafly	2	0		0	2	40	53	4	0
Teterboro	1	0		0	1	2	14	1	0
Tewksbury Township	0	0		0	0	8	15	1	0
Tinton Falls	6	0		1	4	47	352	6	0
Toms River Township	74	1		48	20	527	2,192	23	9
Totowa	23	0		5	17	49	262	17	0
Trenton	1,122	37		525	547	996	909	416	20
Tuckerton	2	0		0	2	9	42	2	0
Union Beach	15	0		2	13	19	42	0	0
Union City	247	0		108	139	189	787	114	5
Union Township	92	1		60	29	151	727	130	1
Upper Saddle River	3	0		0	3	7	26	3	0
Ventnor City	12	0		6	6	162	224	5	0
Vernon Township	5	0		0	4	51	255	2	0
Verona	3	0		3	0	30	74	14	0
Vineland	208	1		84	109	594	1,681	61	3
Voorhees Township	31	0		10	20	104	428	16	4
Waldwick	1	1		0	0	12	28	0	0
Wallington	9	0		6	3	32	102	2	0
Wall Township	11	0		3	8	55	267	15	0
Wanaque	8	0		2	6	11	92	1	0
Warren Township	3	0		0	3	29	69	2	0
Washington	4	0		1	3	3	70	0	0
Washington Township, Bergen County	2	1		0	1	15	46	0	0
Washington Township, Gloucester County	23	0		16	7	246	828	29	2

Table 8.   Offenses Known to Law Enforcement, by Selected State and City, 2013— continued

(Number.)

State/city	Violent crime	Murder and nonnegligent manslaughter	Rape (revised definition)[1]	Robbery	Aggravated assault	Burglary	Larceny-theft	Motor vehicle theft	Arson[2]
Washington Township, Morris County	2	0		0	2	10	60	2	0
Washington Township, Warren County	2	0		0	2	3	37	1	0
Watchung	6	0		5	1	13	358	3	0
Waterford Township	14	0		1	11	18	79	7	1
Wayne Township	29	0		15	13	123	998	52	2
Weehawken Township	21	0		10	11	36	206	18	0
Wenonah	0	0		0	0	8	17	3	2
Westampton Township	17	0		8	6	33	179	7	1
West Amwell Township	2	0		0	2	6	9	0	0
West Caldwell Township	6	0		3	3	9	78	12	0
West Cape May	1	0		0	1	8	18	1	0
West Deptford Township	7	0		4	2	93	318	26	0
Westfield	12	0		5	3	58	181	9	0
West Long Branch	8	0		4	4	59	127	7	0
West Milford Township	24	0		3	17	98	174	5	1
West New York	161	2		58	89	135	344	39	0
West Orange	79	1		44	33	152	481	52	1
Westville	11	0		5	6	60	112	15	0
West Wildwood	3	0		1	2	6	17	0	0
West Windsor Township	17	0		9	7	37	390	14	1
Westwood	2	0		0	2	12	44	1	0
Wharton	6	0		2	4	6	83	0	0
Wildwood	90	0		30	57	147	515	9	0
Wildwood Crest	6	0		1	5	46	122	0	0
Willingboro Township	119	1		50	55	189	475	24	9
Winfield Township	0	0		0	0	5	5	1	0
Winslow Township	93	0		21	69	201	376	22	2
Woodbridge Township	135	1		66	65	296	1,622	124	7
Woodbury	45	1		20	22	109	385	13	0
Woodbury Heights	3	0		3	0	20	69	3	0
Woodcliff Lake	2	0		1	0	8	38	5	0
Woodland Park	3	0		0	3	27	124	7	0
Woodlynne	15	0		8	7	8	49	9	0
Wood-Ridge	1	0		0	1	10	42	2	0
Woodstown	7	0		2	4	9	32	2	1
Woolwich Township	1	0		0	1	17	36	0	0
Wyckoff Township	0	0		0	0	10	68	1	0
New Mexico									
Alamogordo	80	1		6	70	110	664	26	3
Albuquerque	4,325	37		1,046	2,803	7,297	20,229	3,005	83
Artesia	144	0		4	134	104	303	30	1
Aztec	26	0		0	23	40	123	12	4
Bloomfield	64	1		0	46	34	116	6	0
Bosque Farms	19	0		1	18	15	61	7	0
Carrizozo	3	0		0	3	2	9	1	0
Cimarron	7	0		0	7	9	9	0	1
Clayton	0	0		0	0	28	5	1	0
Clovis	269	1		24	215	495	1,443	89	13
Deming	148	2		10	122	216	432	23	7
Dexter	1	0		0	1	2	7	4	0
Estancia	2	0		0	2	2	17	1	0
Eunice	6	0		0	6	41	38	5	1
Farmington	291	3		43	196	297	1,285	92	12
Gallup	463	5		65	356	372	1,790	125	2
Grants	53	1		5	43	129	104	29	4
Hobbs	298	3		20	234	335	1,157	109	3
Jal	11	0		0	11	13	17	9	0
Las Cruces	332	6		74	225	724	3,454	171	6
Las Vegas	116	3		13	90	116	223	13	4
Logan	3	0		0	3	8	10	2	0
Loving	1	0		0	1	4	14	0	0
Moriarty	3	0		1	1	30	51	3	
Peralta	24	0		2	22	30	53	11	0
Questa	2	0		0	2	12	10	1	0
Raton	11	0		2	9	123	97	10	0
Red River	2	0		0	2	4	2	1	0
Santa Rosa	23	0		0	23	12	78	0	0
San Ysidro	0	0		0	0	1	1	0	0
Socorro	74	0		4	70	127	308	16	0
Sunland Park	10	0		5	1	50	96	17	1
Taos	66	0		7	56	146	336	10	0
Taos Ski Valley	1	0		0	1	2	3	0	0
Truth or Consequences	17	0		2	13	58	167	10	2
Tucumcari	26	0		5	18	95	136	4	0
New York									

Table 8.   Offenses Known to Law Enforcement, by Selected State and City, 2013— continued

(Number.)

State/city	Violent crime	Murder and nonnegligent manslaughter	Rape (revised definition)[1]	Robbery	Aggravated assault	Burglary	Larceny-theft	Motor vehicle theft	Arson[2]
Adams Village	0	0		0	0	2	10	0	0
Addison Town and Village	3	0		0	3	3	20	1	0
Akron Village	3	0		0	3	1	15	0	0
Albany	791	8		227	526	705	3,243	142	
Albion Village	23	0		4	16	53	165	5	
Alfred Village	5	0		3	2	10	36	0	
Allegany Village	3	0		0	3	0	10	0	0
Amherst Town	107	1		31	68	204	1,882	32	3
Amityville Village	9	0		4	3	16	188	6	1
Amsterdam	30	0		12	18	99	291	15	0
Arcade Village	0	0		0	0	3	35	1	0
Ardsley Village	5	0		3	2	4	28	1	0
Asharoken Village	0	0		0	0	0	2	0	0
Attica Village	2	0		0	2	0	4	1	0
Auburn	96	1		22	53	132	721	6	
Avon Village	1	0		1	0	3	20	2	
Baldwinsville Village	5	0		1	4	10	77	1	0
Ballston Spa Village	8	0		3	5	16	78	0	1
Batavia	57	0		13	37	103	454	2	
Bath Village	15	0		3	11	32	157	2	2
Bedford Town	5	0		1	4	26	127	3	
Bethlehem Town	13	0		3	10	50	388	4	
Binghamton	284	3		101	161	525	1,767	57	
Black River	0	0		0	0	2	12	0	0
Blooming Grove Town	8	0		0	7	20	72	7	
Bolivar Village	1	0		0	1	2	2	0	0
Bolton Town	2	0		0	2	4	20	0	0
Boonville Village	1	0		0	1	6	14	0	0
Brant Town	4	0		1	3	9	20	2	0
Brewster	0	0		0	0	3	10	0	0
Briarcliff Manor Village	1	0		0	1	1	10	0	0
Brighton Town	26	1		10	13	142	623	28	
Brockport Village	23	1		5	16	29	132	4	
Bronxville Village	0	0		0	0	5	39	3	0
Brownville Village	0	0		0	0	0	10	0	0
Buffalo	3,249	47		1,322	1,735	3,458	8,076	957	
Cairo Town	0	0		0	0	1	14	0	
Cambridge Village	2	0		0	2	12	31	1	
Camden Village	5	0		0	5	4	42	0	0
Camillus Town and Village	14	0		13	36	307	5	1	
Canandaigua	22	0		9	13	54	253	8	
Canastota Village	4	0		0	4	8	51	1	
Canisteo Village	3	0		1	2	3	9	0	0
Canton Village	3	0		1	2	12	80	1	
Cape Vincent Village	0	0		0	0	0	2	0	0
Carmel Town	10	0		0	8	31	158	9	1
Carroll Town	0	0		0	0	3	5	0	0
Carthage Village	1	0		0	0	12	47	1	
Cattaraugus Village	0	0		0	0	0	4	0	0
Cayuga Heights Village	1	0		1	0	12	47	0	
Cazenovia Village	0	0		0	0	5	52	1	
Central Square Village	3	0		2	1	6	45	2	0
Chatham Village	3	0		0	3	5	27	0	0
Cheektowaga Town	158	0		48	99	345	2,271	73	2
Chester Town	0	0		0	0	9	16	0	
Chittenango Village	1	0		0	1	11	53	1	
Cicero Town	12	0		2	10	45	393	2	
Clarkstown Town	65	0		17	40	99	1,388	28	
Clyde Village	4	0		3	1	16	43	1	
Cobleskill Village	5	0		3	2	14	204	0	1
Coeymans Town	39	0		0	37	13	69	4	1
Cohoes	26	0		11	14	65	163	15	
Colonie Town	63	0		31	32	186	1,753	51	10
Cooperstown Village	1	0		0	1	2	14	0	
Corning	35	0		8	24	63	349	4	0
Cornwall-on-Hudson Village	2	0		0	2	8	14	0	
Cornwall Town	1	0		0	1	10	32	0	
Cortland	18	0		3	12	88	306	4	1
Crawford Town	11	0		2	9	16	97	0	
Croton-on-Hudson Village	1	0		1	0	8	43	2	
Cuba Town	5	0		0	4	7	72	2	0
Dansville Village	2	0		1	1	24	120	8	0
Deerpark Town	7	0		2	3	52	100	0	
Delhi Village	1	0		0	1	4	30	2	
Depew Village	17	0		2	12	54	251	5	2
Deposit Village	0	0		0	0	6	8	0	0
Dewitt Town	20	0		10	10	85	618	12	0
Dexter Village	0	0		0	0	2	6	0	0

Table 8.   Offenses Known to Law Enforcement, by Selected State and City, 2013— continued

(Number.)

State/city	Violent crime	Murder and nonnegligent manslaughter	Rape (revised definition)	Robbery	Aggravated assault	Burglary	Larceny-theft	Motor vehicle theft	Arson[2]
Dobbs Ferry Village	1	0		0	1	13	89	2	0
Dolgeville Village	7	0		0	7	6	34	1	
Dryden Village	3	0		1	2	6	93	0	
Dunkirk	40	0		12	28	78	228	1	
East Aurora-Aurora Town	5	0		2	3	24	105	2	0
Eastchester Town	2	0		0	2	13	154	1	0
East Fishkill Town	9	1		1	7	18	141	6	
East Greenbush Town	12	0		4	8	36	330	7	4
East Hampton Town	20	0		1	17	56	237	7	
East Hampton Village	0	0		0	0	4	60	2	0
East Rochester Village	8	1		3	4	25	97	3	
East Syracuse Village	8	0		4	4	19	121	7	0
Eden Town	1	0		0	1	7	24	0	0
Ellenville Village	17	0		2	14	41	132	0	1
Ellicott Town	7	0		1	5	53	235	0	
Elmira	81	0		29	50	224	790	13	
Elmira Heights Village	2	0		1	1	9	78	2	0
Elmira Town	0	0		0	0	0	1	0	0
Endicott Village	46	0		13	29	138	455	11	
Evans Town	17	0		1	15	48	259	6	5
Fairport Village	5	0		0	4	13	37	3	
Fallsburg Town	22	1		0	21	65	96	1	
Fishkill Town	3	0		1	2	28	243	5	0
Floral Park Village	14	0		7	5	16	44	12	0
Florida Village	0	0		0	0	5	39	0	
Fort Plain Village	4	0		1	3	23	65	2	
Frankfort Town	0	0		0	0	22	27	1	
Frankfort Village	5	0		0	5	4	28	1	
Franklinville Village	1	0		1	0	0	32	0	0
Fredonia Village	10	0		5	3	26	182	0	
Freeport Village	152	0		76	74	168	698	67	8
Friendship Town	0	0		0	0	6	10	0	0
Fulton City	24	0		7	14	81	376	6	1
Garden City Village	10	0		4	6	33	303	10	2
Gates Town	57	0		19	34	95	922	34	
Geddes Town	7	0		2	5	21	222	8	1
Geneseo Village	6	0		3	0	7	155	0	0
Geneva	28	1		5	18	65	275	3	1
Germantown Town	0	0		0	0	2	7	0	0
Glen Cove	3	0		1	2	5	54	3	0
Glen Park Village	0	0		0	0	0	5	0	0
Glens Falls	22	0		3	17	50	288	5	
Glenville Town	13	0		2	11	57	424	11	
Gloversville	33	0		6	18	111	560	15	0
Goshen Village	2	0		1	0	2	62	0	0
Gowanda Village	5	0		0	5	11	16	2	
Granville Village	6	0		0	5	7	19	0	1
Great Neck Estates Village	0	0		0	0	6	12	2	0
Greece Town	151	0		60	82	332	1,925	46	
Greenburgh Town	48	1		16	26	55	501	22	
Greene Village	0	0		0	0	1	0	0	0
Green Island Village	2	0		1	1	7	31	4	
Greenport Town	2	0		1	1	10	201	2	
Greenwood Lake Village	2	0		0	2	3	16	2	
Groton Village	2	0		0	0	6	31	1	
Guilderland Town	12	0		5	4	48	623	1	
Hamburg Town	38	1		12	24	134	1,012	21	6
Hamburg Village	8	0		0	6	40	121	0	0
Hammondsport Village	0	0		0	0	1	9	0	0
Harrison Town	6	0		1	5	27	194	4	
Hastings-on-Hudson Village	1	0		1	0	4	75	2	0
Haverstraw Town	64	0		16	45	83	244	13	3
Hempstead Village	433	10		204	216	206	630	122	2
Herkimer Village	53	0		3	41	49	330	0	1
Highland Falls Village	3	0		0	3	8	31	0	0
Homer Village	0	0		0	0	3	29	1	0
Hoosick Falls Village	9	0		1	7	10	26	2	
Hornell	5	0		0	5	18	94	0	
Horseheads Village	2	0		0	2	20	90	0	0
Hudson	26	0		8	17	25	172	1	
Hudson Falls Village	6	0		2	4	22	90	0	
Huntington Bay Village	1	0		0	1	0	11	1	1
Hyde Park Town	18	0		4	11	42	133	5	0
Ilion Village	15	0		2	12	21	106	1	
Irondequoit Town	93	1		51	35	271	1,049	33	
Irvington Village	0	0		0	0	4	19	0	0
Jamestown	168	0		39	110	281	829	30	
Johnson City Village	69	1		20	42	111	828	10	

Table 8.   Offenses Known to Law Enforcement, by Selected State and City, 2013— continued

(Number.)

State/city	Violent crime	Murder and nonnegligent manslaughter	Rape (revised definition)[1]	Robbery	Aggravated assault	Burglary	Larceny-theft	Motor vehicle theft	Arson[2]
Johnstown	14	0		4	9	29	273	14	
Jordan Village	1	0		0	1	0	2	0	0
Kenmore Village	26	1		10	13	34	181	5	0
Kent Town	1	0		0	0	22	71	5	0
Kings Point Village	1	0		0	1	4	11	1	0
Kingston	74	1		25	44	112	565	10	1
Kirkland Town	0	0		0	0	21	81	1	
Lackawanna	89	1		11	64	100	398	35	3
Lake Placid Village	2	0		0	2	11	38	2	1
Lake Success Village	2	0		0	2	10	21	1	
Lakewood-Busti	1	0		1	0	23	316	2	
Lancaster Town	15	0		4	10	44	494	9	0
Larchmont Village	2	0		0	2	8	77	2	
Le Roy Village	11	0		3	8	17	67	0	
Lewiston Town and Village	12	0		1	11	30	96	8	
Liberty Village	21	0		2	17	43	160	3	
Little Falls	16	0		1	12	18	111	1	
Liverpool Village	2	0		1	1	6	39	1	0
Lloyd Harbor Village	0	0		0	0	2	16	0	0
Lloyd Town	6	0		0	6	20	95	3	0
Lockport	70	0		24	40	120	523	6	
Long Beach	35	0		13	21	42	277	18	
Lowville Village	2	0		0	2	7	47	4	
Lynbrook Village	12	0		3	8	18	128	18	
Lyons Village	27	0		3	19	34	142	3	
Macedon Town and Village	4	0		1	3	7	52	2	
Malone Village	4	0		2	2	28	161	3	2
Malverne Village	4	0		3	1	3	17	1	0
Mamaroneck Town	1	0		1	0	16	141	1	0
Mamaroneck Village	8	0		2	5	23	150	8	0
Manchester Village	0	0		0	0	0	0	0	0
Manlius Town	18	0		4	14	56	343	3	0
Marcellus Village	0	0		0	0	2	11	0	0
Marlborough Town	5	0		1	4	35	97	3	1
Massena Village	22	0		2	18	52	358	0	
Mechanicville	8	0		3	5	21	89	4	
Medina Village	12	0		3	9	37	100	2	
Menands Village	5	0		1	4	13	87	1	
Middleport Village	2	0		0	2	1	16	2	0
Middletown	114	1		47	60	136	683	33	4
Monroe Village	12	0		5	7	16	118	3	0
Montgomery Town	6	0		1	3	22	91	1	
Montgomery Village	2	0		0	2	3	42	0	0
Monticello Village	48	0		16	28	107	164	5	
Moravia Village	3	0		0	3	0	15	0	0
Moriah Town	7	0		0	7	3	5	1	0
Mount Hope Town	0	0		0	0	6	25	1	
Mount Kisco Village	17	0		6	10	10	98	0	0
Mount Morris Village	2	0		1	1	10	63	1	
Mount Pleasant Town	12	0		6	6	25	198	3	0
Mount Vernon	554	2		228	317	317	972	147	
Newark Village	27	0		7	17	71	261	2	
New Berlin Town	0	0		0	0	0	0	0	0
Newburgh	435	5		150	259	304	673	63	15
Newburgh Town	38	0		15	18	143	1,182	28	2
New Castle Town	2	0		0	2	13	62	2	0
New Hartford Town and Village	13	0		3	9	72	730	4	
New Paltz Town and Village	34	0		4	26	16	180	4	0
New Rochelle	175	0		81	89	150	1,172	69	
New Windsor Town	31	0		8	22	65	394	12	4
New York	52,384	335		19,170	31,767	16,606	117,931	7,434	
New York Mills Village	2	0		0	2	16	47	1	0
Niagara Falls	584	3		166	403	746	1,949	112	22
Niagara Town	13	0		2	11	48	427	14	
Niskayuna Town	13	0		5	7	51	282	8	
Nissequogue Village	0	0		0	0	1	6	1	0
North Castle Town	3	0		0	3	12	53	3	
North Greenbush Town	8	0		2	6	32	196	2	
Northport Village	6	0		1	5	11	44	4	2
North Syracuse Village	10	0		0	10	14	94	3	0
North Tonawanda	41	1		17	15	114	455	17	
Northville Village	0	0		0	0	0	1	0	0
Norwich	15	0		0	11	25	297	3	0
Ogdensburg	23	0		5	17	72	321	4	2
Ogden Town	17	0		6	9	24	176	8	
Old Brookville Village	4	0		1	3	16	28	10	0
Old Westbury Village	1	0		0	1	6	29	4	0
Olean	40	0		5	30	76	508	9	

Table 8.   Offenses Known to Law Enforcement, by Selected State and City, 2013— continued

(Number.)

State/city	Violent crime	Murder and nonnegligent manslaughter	Rape (revised definition)[1]	Robbery	Aggravated assault	Burglary	Larceny-theft	Motor vehicle theft	Arson[2]
Oneida	18	0		4	12	68	357	9	
Oneonta City	21	0		11	7	69	238	4	3
Orangetown Town	37	0		13	23	41	262	14	
Orchard Park Town	16	0		4	10	37	297	12	0
Oriskany Village	0	0		0	0	2	8	0	0
Ossining Village	36	0		21	15	46	192	5	0
Oswego City	54	1		13	37	83	533	14	
Owego Village	9	0		2	6	39	156	4	
Oxford Village	2	0		1	1	1	12	0	0
Oyster Bay Cove Village	0	0		0	0	3	16	0	0
Painted Post Village	1	0		0	1	5	66	2	1
Palmyra Village	4	0		0	4	9	31	1	
Peekskill	30	0		8	22	25	215	8	
Pelham Manor Village	2	0		1	1	14	130	3	
Pelham Village	7	0		2	4	22	149	1	
Penn Yan Village	4	0		1	2	21	89	1	0
Perry Village	3	0		0	3	14	84	1	
Piermont Village	1	0		0	0	6	13	0	
Pine Plains Town	1	0		0	1	1	9	2	0
Plattekill Town	8	0		2	5	28	77	1	
Plattsburgh City	39	0		4	32	79	396	8	
Pleasantville Village	0	0		0	0	1	21	0	0
Port Byron Village	0	0		0	0	0	0	0	0
Port Chester Village	48	0		19	27	67	483	22	0
Port Dickinson Village	0	0		0	0	0	31	0	0
Port Jervis	15	1		3	8	67	214	3	3
Portville Village	0	0		0	0	1	7	0	0
Potsdam Village	8	0		0	7	17	168	5	
Poughkeepsie	286	7		100	163	189	589	9	
Poughkeepsie Town	39	1		12	25	125	1,203	11	
Pound Ridge Town	3	0		0	3	15	18	0	
Pulaski Village	1	0		0	1	12	44	1	0
Quogue Village	0	0		0	0	13	27	1	0
Ramapo Town	57	2		9	41	88	466	13	
Red Hook Village	1	0		0	1	6	24	0	0
Rensselaer City	19	0		3	12	44	108	7	2
Rhinebeck Village	2	0		0	2	0	41	1	0
Riverhead Town	64	0		26	35	160	729	33	0
Rochester	2,107	42		918	1,055	2,587	6,855	609	132
Rockville Centre Village	22	1		11	9	30	223	18	0
Rome	47	4		23	20	157	470	35	2
Rosendale Town	1	0		0	1	16	44	0	
Rotterdam Town	33	2		16	11	109	700	20	4
Rye Brook Village	2	0		2	0	9	77	2	0
Sag Harbor Village	3	0		1	2	17	53	1	0
Salamanca	18	0		2	15	38	105	12	
Sands Point Village	0	0		0	0	4	13	1	0
Saranac Lake Village	26	1		1	23	30	115	5	
Saratoga Springs	33	1		8	21	84	550	8	
Saugerties Town	15	0		5	7	51	268	0	0
Scarsdale Village	1	0		0	1	24	153	7	
Schenectady	607	8		203	365	769	1,878	153	
Schodack Town	4	0		1	3	25	70	2	
Schoharie Village	0	0		0	0	0	0	0	0
Scotia Village	5	1		1	3	14	112	0	
Seneca Falls Town	12	0		1	11	49	238	5	
Shandaken Town	4	0		0	4	17	44	1	
Shawangunk Town	3	0		0	3	20	60	0	
Shelter Island Town	3	0		0	3	2	39	0	0
Sherburne Village	1	0		0	1	7	8	0	0
Sherrill	4	0		0	4	14	23	0	
Shortsville Village	0	0		0	0	0	0	0	0
Sidney Village	7	0		1	2	21	161	3	
Skaneateles Village	0	0		0	0	2	8	0	0
Sleepy Hollow Village	8	1		1	6	9	47	2	0
Sodus Village	0	0		0	0	2	22	0	
Solvay Village	19	0		6	13	38	142	6	0
Southampton Town	44	0		16	22	219	752	49	1
Southampton Village	3	0		1	2	9	105	4	
South Glens Falls Village	6	0		1	4	17	95	2	
Southold Town	12	0		5	6	70	271	2	
Spring Valley Village	132	2		34	87	53	335	16	
Stillwater Town	1	0		0	1	4	18	2	1
St. Johnsville Village	3	0		0	3	8	39	0	
Stony Point Town	12	0		1	11	18	83	6	
Suffern Village	9	0		1	8	11	48	1	0
Syracuse	1,192	21		400	696	1,781	4,298	394	57
Tarrytown Village	6	0		3	3	12	94	4	0

Table 8.   Offenses Known to Law Enforcement, by Selected State and City, 2013— continued

(Number.)

State/city	Violent crime	Murder and nonnegligent manslaughter	Rape (revised definition)[1]	Robbery	Aggravated assault	Burglary	Larceny-theft	Motor vehicle theft	Arson[2]
Ticonderoga Town	11	0		0	7	23	71	0	
Tonawanda	34	0		4	30	24	289	2	4
Tonawanda Town	118	1		26	86	190	882	27	1
Troy	371	1		145	211	593	1,305	87	5
Trumansburg Village	2	0		1	0	6	58	2	
Tuckahoe Village	0	0		0	0	7	27	1	
Tupper Lake Village	3	0		0	3	22	59	2	0
Tuxedo Park Village	0	0		0	0	0	0	0	0
Ulster Town	14	0		2	9	25	410	2	
Utica	361	7		102	225	449	1,997	82	
Vestal Town	16	0		6	8	39	523	9	
Walden Village	18	1		1	14	13	124	5	
Wallkill Town	40	0		16	21	91	650	26	1
Walton Village	6	0		0	5	18	50	0	
Warsaw Village	6	0		0	5	5	73	0	0
Washingtonville Village	2	0		1	1	5	51	2	0
Waterford Town and Village	4	0		0	4	6	52	1	0
Waterloo Village	11	0		3	8	23	169	2	
Watertown	109	0		16	81	169	953	43	
Watervliet	26	1		11	11	58	163	21	
Watkins Glen Village	6	0		0	6	10	80	2	
Waverly Village	5	0		1	4	9	41	4	
Webster Town and Village	21	0		3	16	101	361	7	
Weedsport Village	0	0		0	0	5	20	0	0
Wellsville Village	11	0		0	10	32	129	3	1
Westhampton Beach Village	2	0		0	2	4	37	3	0
West Seneca Town	35	1		9	24	166	710	20	0
Whitehall Village	6	0		0	6	12	49	1	
White Plains	78	1		28	46	77	1,134	21	
Whitesboro Village	4	0		0	4	14	21	1	0
Whitestown Town	0	0		0	0	13	61	3	0
Woodbury Town	3	0		2	1	9	529	3	
Woodridge Village	7	0		0	7	8	9	0	0
Woodstock Town	2	0		0	2	13	45	0	
Yonkers	1,036	6		390	615	470	1,662	236	10
Yorktown Town	15	0		2	13	45	287	2	
North Carolina									
Aberdeen	23	3		6	12	52	244	8	1
Albemarle	70	1		13	53	274	568	34	7
Apex	36	0		7	24	104	414	17	2
Archdale	8	0		2	6	79	198	20	3
Asheboro	82	1		39	34	400	1,197	45	4
Atlantic Beach	15	0		2	13	42	77	2	0
Aulander	1	0		0	1	16	5	0	0
Ayden	27	0		3	21	46	152	9	0
Banner Elk	2	0		0	2	7	17	0	0
Beaufort	16	0		3	13	59	104	6	0
Belhaven	2	0		1	1	18	17	0	0
Benson	30	0		7	21	47	139	13	1
Bethel	5	1		1	3	1	44	2	1
Beulaville	8	1		0	7	13	47	0	0
Biltmore Forest	0	0		0	0	4	9	0	0
Biscoe	3	0		1	1	16	204	5	0
Black Mountain	7	0		4	3	28	85	5	0
Blowing Rock	0	0		0	0	10	29	1	0
Boiling Spring Lakes	10	0		1	9	33	63	2	0
Boone	40	0		8	27	61	232	9	0
Brevard	10	0		0	9	63	210	10	1
Bunn	2	0		0	2	2	20	0	0
Burgaw	9	0		3	5	18	95	3	0
Burlington	362	0		100	246	546	1,977	112	4
Butner	20	0		4	15	62	154	12	6
Canton	23	0		3	19	55	183	24	1
Cape Carteret	0	0		0	0	3	16	1	0
Carolina Beach	11	0		0	10	67	181	8	0
Carrboro	53	0		16	35	175	378	21	2
Carthage	4	0		0	3	33	67	7	0
Cary	102	1		35	55	392	1,623	60	4
Catawba	2	0		0	2	6	7	0	0
Chadbourn	27	2		5	20	99	123	6	0
Chapel Hill	71	1		23	36	388	837	54	2
Charlotte-Mecklenburg	5,093	59		1,805	2,999	6,439	22,274	1,856	213
Cherryville	18	0		2	15	41	140	6	0
Claremont	7	0		0	7	13	20	0	0
Clayton	28	0		5	20	103	299	11	1
Cleveland	2	0		0	1	4	15	5	0
Clinton	62	0		16	42	121	356	23	3

Table 8.   Offenses Known to Law Enforcement, by Selected State and City, 2013— continued

(Number.)

State/city	Violent crime	Murder and nonnegligent manslaughter	Rape (revised definition)[1]	Robbery	Aggravated assault	Burglary	Larceny-theft	Motor vehicle theft	Arson[2]
Coats	4	0		0	3	28	64	4	0
Columbus	2	0		1	1	3	24	0	0
Concord	122	7		50	56	414	2,033	102	6
Cornelius	42	0		10	28	102	361	14	0
Creedmoor	10	0		3	5	27	58	0	0
Davidson	11	0		3	8	25	63	2	0
Dobson	6	0		0	5	7	36	3	1
Drexel	0	0		0	0	4	16	3	0
Duck	1	0		0	1	13	23	1	0
Eden	57	1		18	36	151	443	36	2
Edenton	39	0		9	27	66	159	6	5
Elizabeth City	109	2		25	76	241	456	26	0
Elon	2	0		1	1	27	55	3	0
Emerald Isle	12	0		0	12	104	133	3	2
Enfield	18	0		1	15	44	71	5	0
Erwin	9	0		2	7	49	93	3	0
Fairmont	22	2		8	12	77	121	7	0
Farmville	35	0		4	29	43	98	7	0
Fayetteville	1,170	25		586	494	3,279	8,351	631	49
Fletcher	7	0		3	4	52	87	8	0
Forest City	20	0		7	10	121	431	33	1
Franklin	16	0		2	14	61	227	10	1
Franklinton	7	0		0	7	18	72	6	3
Garner	52	2		24	24	169	963	46	1
Garysburg	8	0		2	6	13	19	1	0
Gastonia	510	6		150	332	752	2,873	241	19
Gibsonville	3	1		1	1	60	50	4	2
Goldsboro	283	5		67	208	571	1,670	103	2
Graham	75	0		21	49	166	383	31	3
Granite Falls	9	0		2	7	39	245	6	2
Greensboro	1,449	27		496	856	2,972	8,063	502	112
Greenville	555	7		175	353	1,157	2,573	132	10
Hamlet	49	1		9	38	123	191	7	2
Havelock	44	1		6	31	147	348	10	0
Haw River	9	0		1	8	19	30	1	0
Henderson	214	4		82	123	331	1,059	51	7
Hendersonville	53	0		18	32	112	691	47	0
Hertford	18	0		7	9	28	44	8	2
Hickory	167	3		64	92	467	1,590	151	11
Highlands	2	0		0	2	22	40	1	1
High Point	556	2		178	346	1,206	2,970	313	23
Holly Ridge	4	0		0	4	26	32	1	1
Holly Springs	23	0		4	19	58	254	6	0
Hope Mills	74	0		29	44	214	804	24	3
Hudson	3	0		0	3	27	95	6	0
Huntersville	49	0		12	33	179	733	28	3
Indian Beach	0	0		0	0	1	9	2	0
Kannapolis	87	4		25	50	290	564	63	7
Kenansville	5	0		0	4	6	21	1	0
Kernersville	86	0		19	61	165	797	52	10
Kill Devil Hills	42	0		2	37	139	172	7	2
King	13	0		0	13	56	222	4	2
Kinston	273	3		66	197	351	1,089	64	11
Kitty Hawk	3	0		0	1	22	110	3	0
Knightdale	19	3		7	8	64	396	6	2
Lake Lure	0	0		0	0	15	12	0	0
Laurel Park	1	0		1	0	0	24	0	0
Laurinburg	212	1		31	170	500	424	26	5
Leland	24	0		8	15	181	199	12	0
Lexington	85	1		33	46	214	393	29	3
Liberty	4	0		0	4	3	13	1	0
Lincolnton	52	0		8	39	71	449	12	1
Long View	25	2		4	17	93	148	18	0
Louisburg	11	0		5	5	28	70	4	1
Lumberton	383	3		127	245	737	2,196	120	3
Madison	3	0		1	2	26	74	0	0
Maiden	8	0		1	5	29	68	2	0
Manteo	7	0		1	6	13	55	1	0
Marion	30	0		4	26	217	421	18	0
Mars Hill	3	0		2	0	20	35	5	0
Matthews	58	1		21	33	87	702	34	5
Mayodan	11	1		0	10	22	236	1	0
Mebane	45	0		12	31	121	577	15	0
Mint Hill	45	0		25	20	116	274	16	5
Mocksville	11	0		5	4	44	176	2	0
Monroe	204	1		72	125	390	1,304	77	7
Mooresville	77	2		16	56	193	1,153	53	3
Morehead City	57	1		6	49	69	449	10	5

Table 8.   Offenses Known to Law Enforcement, by Selected State and City, 2013— continued

(Number.)

State/city	Violent crime	Murder and nonnegligent manslaughter	Rape (revised definition)[1]	Robbery	Aggravated assault	Burglary	Larceny-theft	Motor vehicle theft	Arson[2]
Morganton	47	0		21	20	126	347	18	0
Morrisville	12	0		7	5	70	335	15	0
Mount Airy	40	0		7	30	138	359	26	1
Mount Holly	36	1		9	26	62	186	10	1
Mount Olive	44	0		8	35	88	209	14	2
Murfreesboro	7	2		2	3	21	51	1	0
Murphy	13	0		3	9	35	82	6	0
New Bern	120	0		43	70	525	992	50	2
Newland	2	2		0	0	3	21	2	0
Newport	8	0		3	5	33	83	5	1
Newton	53	0		11	40	143	286	12	1
North Topsail Beach	2	2		0	0	25	48	2	0
North Wilkesboro	20	1		3	15	41	190	7	0
Oak Island	27	0		1	23	73	177	3	1
Oxford	86	1		27	57	235	321	18	4
Pilot Mountain	4	0		0	4	20	98	3	0
Pinebluff	0	0		0	0	7	9	0	0
Pinehurst	8	0		2	6	3	119	3	0
Pine Knoll Shores	0	0		0	0	13	16	1	0
Pineville	31	0		10	21	104	923	34	2
Pittsboro	16	0		5	11	17	74	1	0
Raeford	29	0		3	24	47	203	7	0
Raleigh	1,683	12		605	987	3,157	9,278	705	54
Ramseur	11	0		5	6	35	45	4	0
Randleman	10	0		2	6	54	378	6	0
Red Springs	27	0		15	12	150	158	20	8
Reidsville	53	0		14	37	211	675	32	3
Richlands	6	0		1	5	12	21	1	0
Rich Square	7	1		0	5	28	19	1	0
River Bend	0	0		0	0	16	22	0	0
Roanoke Rapids	92	2		23	55	239	727	23	4
Rockingham	37	0		23	9	209	729	16	10
Rockwell	2	0		1	1	8	50	1	0
Rocky Mount	599	4		154	425	992	2,179	111	10
Rolesville	4	0		1	3	35	58	1	0
Rose Hill	8	0		2	6	21	22	2	0
Rowland	4	0		2	2	23	22	1	1
Roxboro	76	0		16	55	93	385	7	1
Rutherfordton	0	0		0	0	0	139	1	0
Salisbury	262	5		78	170	475	1,236	126	4
Scotland Neck	12	1		0	11	28	42	1	0
Selma	38	0		10	26	100	180	10	3
Shallotte	20	0		4	16	78	123	9	1
Shelby	125	1		33	81	193	454	31	3
Siler City	27	0		4	20	74	241	10	0
Smithfield	71	0		23	47	138	510	23	0
Snow Hill	11	0		6	5	17	43	0	0
Southern Pines	88	3		17	67	147	400	13	1
Southern Shores	1	0		0	1	27	28	2	0
Sparta	9	0		0	8	3	36	0	0
Spencer	39	0		3	34	40	102	8	0
Spring Hope	7	0		2	5	27	16	1	0
Stallings	15	0		2	12	50	172	15	1
Stanley	5	0		3	2	36	98	5	0
Statesville	187	1		40	134	477	1,115	78	5
St. Pauls	8	1		6	1	35	44	0	2
Sunset Beach	1	0		1	0	53	44	0	0
Surf City	12	0		1	11	25	123	1	3
Sylva	21	0		4	15	51	126	7	0
Tabor City	22	0		4	18	38	104	9	2
Tarboro	53	0		11	41	79	380	6	2
Taylorsville	4	0		1	3	62	131	11	0
Thomasville	117	2		34	75	272	794	30	2
Trent Woods	3	0		0	3	31	21	1	0
Troutman	6	0		0	5	12	47	1	0
Troy	14	0		1	13	24	94	2	2
Tryon	2	0		0	2	8	34	5	0
Valdese	2	0		0	1	15	53	1	0
Vanceboro	2	0		1	1	12	39	0	0
Wadesboro	80	2		11	65	120	258	9	3
Wake Forest	43	0		11	30	98	618	15	2
Wallace	13	0		3	8	37	135	5	0
Warsaw	14	0		3	11	44	73	2	0
Waxhaw	15	0		2	12	27	130	4	0
Weaverville	3	0		1	1	23	165	5	0
Weldon	4	0		1	3	15	49	6	0
Wendell	13	0		0	12	41	121	8	0
Whispering Pines	0	0		0	0	1	42	0	0

Table 8.   Offenses Known to Law Enforcement, by Selected State and City, 2013— continued

(Number.)

State/city	Violent crime	Murder and nonnegligent manslaughter	Rape (revised definition)[1]	Robbery	Aggravated assault	Burglary	Larceny-theft	Motor vehicle theft	Arson[2]
Whitakers	6	0		1	5	10	22	1	0
Whiteville	97	2		27	68	155	449	21	3
Wilkesboro	19	0		7	9	13	301	10	1
Williamston	64	0		18	45	181	350	12	2
Wilmington	687	7		253	388	1,645	3,569	335	17
Wilson's Mills	3	0		0	3	12	18	2	0
Windsor	10	0		1	9	10	42	0	0
Wingate	20	0		3	17	36	72	7	0
Winston-Salem	1,426	15		439	892	3,883	8,359	611	72
Winterville	8	0		3	4	7	72	5	1
Woodfin	17	0		3	12	51	53	6	0
Wrightsville Beach	11	0		1	5	45	158	2	0
Yadkinville	22	0		4	18	32	93	5	3
Zebulon	31	0		9	21	50	255	5	1
North Dakota									
Belfield	0	0	0	0	0	3	14	1	0
Beulah	4	0	0	0	4	5	20	3	0
Bismarck	194	1	26	15	152	334	1,289	107	6
Bowman	1	1	0	0	0	2	18	2	0
Burlington	1	0	0	0	1	0	5	1	0
Carrington	1	0	0	1	0	2	5	1	0
Cavalier	1	0	1	0	0	5	16	1	0
Devils Lake	23	0	6	3	14	48	263	16	1
Dickinson	76	0	3	2	71	56	468	47	1
Ellendale	1	0	0	0	1	4	7	0	0
Fargo	446	3	71	58	314	701	2,342	166	13
Fessenden	0	0	0	0	0	0	0	0	1
Grafton	17	0	2	0	15	7	86	4	0
Grand Forks	144	0	30	25	89	191	1,084	68	3
Harvey	0	0	0	0	0	2	11	5	0
Jamestown	42	0	22	1	19	73	269	20	2
Kenmare	1	0	0	0	1	0	0	1	0
Killdeer	0	0	0	0	0	0	4	1	0
Lamoure	1	0	0	0	1	1	6	0	1
Lincoln	3	0	1	0	2	1	18	1	0
Lisbon	2	0	0	0	2	4	18	0	0
Mandan	57	0	17	5	35	72	501	47	3
Medora	0	0	0	0	0	0	0	0	0
Minot	122	0	14	18	90	181	708	108	12
Napoleon	0	0	0	0	0	5	6	0	0
New Town	7	0	1	1	5	5	11	3	2
Northwood	0	0	0	0	0	2	4	1	0
Oakes	2	0	1	0	1	0	2	0	1
Powers Lake	0	0	0	0	0	1	8	1	0
Rolla	2	0	0	0	2	3	11	3	0
Rugby	6	0	2	0	4	13	27	0	0
Sherwood	0	0	0	0	0	0	0	0	0
Stanley	1	0	0	0	1	1	3	7	0
Steele	0	0	0	0	0	4	2	0	0
Surrey	1	0	0	0	1	1	3	0	0
Thompson	0	0	0	0	0	0	4	0	0
Tioga	6	0	1	0	5	2	14	6	0
Valley City	14	0	1	1	12	42	113	9	1
Wahpeton	7	0	1	2	4	10	140	8	4
Watford City	12	0	3	1	8	16	65	20	0
West Fargo	44	0	10	3	31	147	336	47	2
Williston	87	1	21	8	57	78	678	203	7
Wishek	0	0	0	0	0	1	0	0	0
Ohio									
Ada	7	0	2	0	5	21	55	0	2
Akron	1,570	23	160	528	859	3,096	5,922	631	85
Albany	0	0	0	0	0	3	19	0	0
Alliance	83	1	14	12	56	237	719	22	4
Amberley Village	1	0		0	0	15	39	6	0
Amelia	1	0	0	1	0	6	25	1	1
American Township	2	0	0	1	1	12	130	5	0
Amherst	9	0	0	8	1	39	177	3	2
Arcanum	0	0	0	0	0	8	23	2	0
Ashland	14	0	10	3	1	80	433	6	6
Ashville	1	0	0	1	0	7	32	1	0
Athens	17	0	3	3	11	49	353	4	0
Aurora	9	0		3	5	24	129	5	1
Austintown	53	0	9	14	30	197	727	27	1
Bainbridge Township	3	0	0	2	1	12	254	1	1
Barberton	87	6	10	22	49	196	746	24	8
Batavia	2	0	0	2	0	14	51	0	0

Table 8.   Offenses Known to Law Enforcement, by Selected State and City, 2013— continued

(Number.)

State/city	Violent crime	Murder and nonnegligent manslaughter	Rape (revised definition)	Robbery	Aggravated assault	Burglary	Larceny-theft	Motor vehicle theft	Arson[2]
Bath Township, Summit County	2	0	0	0	2	15	127	2	0
Bazetta Township	1	0	1	0	0	33	80	6	0
Beavercreek	12	0	6	5	1	121	988	33	2
Beaver Township	5	0	2	1	2	35	94	4	0
Bedford	31	0		11	13	36	315	45	0
Bellaire	3	0	1	0	2	3	32	1	0
Bellbrook	2	0	1	1	0	9	83	1	0
Bellefontaine	45	0	10	12	23	81	492	9	1
Belpre	5	0	0	1	4	31	44	4	0
Berea	18	0	3	4	11	46	189	13	0
Bethel	4	0	0	0	4	11	83	1	3
Beverly	1	1	0	0	0	4	21	0	0
Bexley	20	0	0	13	7	111	239	12	0
Blanchester	1	0	0	1	0	7	48	3	0
Blendon Township	13	0	1	9	3	37	129	13	2
Blue Ash	7	0	1	2	4	46	334	9	0
Bluffton	1	0		0	1	13	40	0	0
Bowling Green	49	0	22	10	17	78	692	11	0
Brecksville	1	0	0	1	0	17	47	0	0
Brewster	0	0	0	0	0	4	9	0	0
Bridgeport	0	0	0	0	0	1	14	0	0
Brimfield Township	22	0		4	5	43	232	6	0
Broadview Heights	11	0	0	0	11	0	0	0	0
Brooklyn	20	0		14	6	85	556	68	0
Brookville	2	0		1	1	30	64	7	0
Brunswick	16	1	1	5	9	33	238	17	1
Brunswick Hills Township	0	0	0	0	0	25	58	4	0
Bryan	1	0	0	1	0	3	20	0	0
Burton	0	0		0	0	0	1	0	0
Cambridge	37	0		13	17	147	380	21	4
Canal Fulton	1	0	0	0	1	10	68	2	1
Canfield	2	0	1	0	1	12	60	2	0
Canton	673	11		357	233	1,218	2,597	438	11
Cardington	1	0	0	0	1	24	52	2	1
Celina	11	0	4	3	4	38	324	11	6
Centerville	19	0		2	11	73	344	18	5
Chagrin Falls	1	0		1	0	9	42	2	0
Champion Township	3	0	2	1	0	62	191	12	0
Chardon	6	0		0	6	4	99	0	0
Chillicothe	73	0	8	29	36	393	1,517	33	2
Cincinnati	2,826	70	199	1,610	947	5,467	10,488	1,276	246
Circleville	23	0	12	4	7	151	618	59	1
Clayton	5	0	0	5	0	63	126	21	0
Clearcreek Township	4	0	1	0	3	25	55	1	0
Cleveland	5,751	55	417	3,490	1,789	8,259	10,784	4,125	317
Cleveland Heights	144	1		94	44	254	1,226	76	4
Clinton Township	25	1	0	18	6	37	139	10	0
Coalton	2	1	0	1	0	7	38	1	
Coitsville Township	1	0	0	1	0	12	15	2	0
Colerain Township	87	4	5	47	31	314	1,417	46	8
Columbiana	4	0	0	0	4	14	94	2	0
Commercial Point	0	0	0	0	0	8	10	0	0
Conneaut	10	0	0	3	7	94	185	5	1
Cortland	4	0	1	2	1	16	64	0	1
Covington	1	0	0	0	1	3	31	0	1
Crestline	5	0	1	2	2	24	52	2	0
Cuyahoga Falls	69	0	13	23	33	184	1,068	35	7
Danville	0	0	0	0	0	7	24	1	0
Dayton	1,230	28	107	518	577	2,613	4,427	615	127
Deer Park	8	0		0	7	17	69	3	0
Defiance	31	1	11	3	16	86	385	2	3
Delaware	53	0		15	21	172	719	37	11
Delhi Township	17	0	3	7	7	119	536	17	1
Delphos	1	0		0	0	29	145	4	
Delta	1	0	0	1	0	8	24	1	0
Dover	14	0	6	0	8	10	45	3	0
Dublin	10	0		8	1	100	452	8	1
Eastlake	16	0		9	6	49	371	12	0
East Palestine	6	0	2	2	2	34	81	2	2
Eaton	12	0	6	2	4	72	281	16	0
Englewood	15	0	2	7	6	60	368	14	0
Evendale	8	0		0	7	10	348	6	0
Fairborn	62	3	14	23	22	211	690	24	3
Fairfax	1	0	0	1	0	8	230	1	0
Fairfield	120	1	12	37	70	174	880	46	8
Fairfield Township	25	0	2	9	14	116	814	12	2
Fairport Harbor	10	0		1	8	44	82	6	1
Findlay	75	1	12	18	44	221	1,204	27	3

Table 8. Offenses Known to Law Enforcement, by Selected State and City, 2013— continued

(Number.)

State/city	Violent crime	Murder and nonnegligent manslaughter	Rape (revised definition)	Robbery	Aggravated assault	Burglary	Larceny-theft	Motor vehicle theft	Arson[2]
Forest Park	30	0	2	27	1	87	350	31	1
Fort Recovery	0	0	0	0	0	7	4	0	0
Franklin Township	5	0	0	2	3	22	84	2	0
Fredericktown	0	0	0	0	0	9	41	1	0
Fremont	42	0		14	27	155	787	17	1
Gahanna	23	1	7	8	7	136	563	15	5
Galion	22	0	3	8	11	173	406	10	0
Gallipolis	4	0	0	1	3	31	306	4	1
Gates Mills	0	0		0	0	1	15	1	0
Georgetown	3	0	2	0	1	20	96	1	0
Germantown	1	0	0	0	1	7	34	1	0
German Township, Clark County	3	0	0	3	0	26	106	0	0
German Township, Montgomery County	0	0	0	0	0	18	31	0	0
Girard	35	0	1	3	31	80	181	10	1
Goshen Township, Mahoning County	8	0	0	0	8	30	73	7	0
Grafton	4	0	1	0	3	7	9	1	0
Grandview Heights	8	1	0	5	2	30	99	6	1
Greenfield	4	0	2	0	2	39	159	6	0
Greenhills	1	0	0	0	1	9	27	0	0
Greenville	34	0		13	15	174	362	15	5
Grove City	40	1	5	29	5	149	1,075	46	4
Groveport	3	0	0	1	2	29	127	9	0
Hamilton	378	6		189	131	1,036	2,687	202	39
Hamilton Township, Warren County	4	0	1	0	3	36	171	5	0
Harrison	3	0		1	1	23	217	5	1
Hartville	0	0	0	0	0	13	36	2	0
Heath	20	0	10	1	9	66	511	22	4
Hebron	1	0	1	0	0	6	27	0	0
Highland Heights	6	0		3	2	7	89	4	0
Hilliard	26	1		8	9	127	565	27	5
Hillsboro	9	0	4	2	3	35	269	6	0
Hinckley Township	2	0	2	0	0	23	40	1	1
Holland	8	0	0	5	3	9	246	2	0
Howland Township	22	0	2	2	18	128	373	18	0
Hubbard	5	0	1	1	3	36	93	7	1
Hubbard Township	7	0	0	1	6	58	83	4	0
Huber Heights	61	2	10	32	17	212	1,118	46	10
Hudson	3	0	0	2	1	13	114	5	2
Hunting Valley	0	0		0	0	0	0	0	0
Independence	4	0	1	1	2	16	139	0	0
Indian Hill	2	0	0	0	2	14	38	0	0
Jackson	7	0	2	2	3	17	218	9	2
Jackson Center	0	0	0	0	0	8	12	3	0
Jackson Township, Montgomery County	0	0	0	0	0	11	15	2	0
Jackson Township, Stark County	43	0	9	13	21	158	1,179	23	2
Johnstown	3	0	1	1	1	3	86	0	0
Kent	56	0	5	26	25	134	511	16	4
Kenton	13	1	2	3	7	75	271	2	0
Kettering	53	1	24	15	13	337	890	60	0
Kirtland	0	0	0	0	0	2	32	2	0
Kirtland Hills	0	0	0	0	0	0	2	0	0
Lawrence Township	9	0	4	0	5	33	43	6	0
Lebanon	20	0	7	7	6	45	348	14	0
Liberty Township	21	0	6	9	6	67	104	7	0
Lima	366	3		78	243	582	1,255	95	26
Lithopolis	0	0	0	0	0	1	5	0	0
Lockland	21	0	3	11	7	44	98	18	0
Lodi	1	0		0	1	3	48	2	
Logan	7	1	1	5	0	48	279	10	0
London	16	0	3	4	9	69	179	4	1
Lorain	304	6	30	161	107	928	1,784	79	36
Loudonville	0	0	0	0	0	7	34	1	0
Louisville	6	0	0	2	4	59	119	6	0
Loveland	7	1	4	0	2	18	107	1	1
Lowellville	0	0	0	0	0	6	8	0	0
Lyndhurst	5	0	2	0	3	0	0	0	0
Madeira	0	0	0	0	0	8	23	1	1
Mansfield	169	0	33	82	54	982	2,111	74	25
Mariemont	0	0		0	0	6	46	0	0
Marietta	19	0	5	6	8	15	164	7	0
Martins Ferry	10	0	4	3	3	10	55	2	0
Marysville	12	0	1	2	9	59	359	8	4
Mason	11	0	2	6	3	58	350	13	1
Massillon	69	0	14	31	24	249	695	31	9
Matamoras	0	0	0	0	0	6	21	0	1
Maumee	11	0	4	3	4	61	444	19	0

Table 8.   Offenses Known to Law Enforcement, by Selected State and City, 2013— continued

(Number.)

State/city	Violent crime	Murder and nonnegligent manslaughter	Rape (revised definition)[1]	Robbery	Aggravated assault	Burglary	Larceny-theft	Motor vehicle theft	Arson[2]
McArthur	0	0	0	0	0	7	19	2	0
McConnelsville	1	0	0	1	0	7	13	0	0
Medina	19	1	6	5	7	54	382	0	2
Medina Township	4	0	2	1	1	10	180	1	0
Mentor	43	0		11	12	151	868	40	4
Miamisburg	19	0	4	8	7	151	496	25	1
Miami Township, Clermont County	21	1	2	8	10	121	619	17	3
Miami Township, Montgomery County	37	1	12	5	19	130	1,057	26	2
Middlefield	4	0	0	0	4	0	46	1	0
Middleport	3	0	0	0	3	9	14	1	0
Middletown	301	0		75	187	972	2,907	95	8
Mifflin Township	13	1	1	6	5	43	73	6	1
Milford	6	0	0	1	5	45	303	3	0
Millersburg	3	0	1	1	1	7	119	4	2
Minerva Park	1	0	1	0	0	10	19	0	0
Monroe	61	0	8	5	48	91	525	11	1
Monroeville	0	0	0	0	0	4	20	2	0
Montgomery	3	0	0	1	2	15	147	2	0
Montpelier	22	0	3	2	17	32	194	2	1
Montville Township	3	0	0	2	1	14	68	0	0
Moraine	30	1	4	13	12	93	610	17	3
Moreland Hills	0	0		0	0	3	8	0	0
Mount Vernon	14	0	0	6	8	102	792	1	0
Napoleon	5	0	2	1	2	44	265	1	2
Navarre	0	0	0	0	0	8	24	3	0
Nelsonville	13	0	2	2	9	39	157	5	0
New Albany	2	0	0	0	2	24	75	0	2
Newark	67	0	18	26	23	573	1,723	74	30
New Boston	1	0	0	0	1	16	134	8	0
Newcomerstown	19	0		2	15	19	81	3	0
New Concord	1	0	0	0	1	0	4	0	0
New Franklin	5	0	2	2	1	19	49	2	0
New Lebanon	1	0	0	0	1	45	100	4	2
New Lexington	13	0	2	2	9	37	145	1	2
New London	0	0	0	0	0	5	16	0	0
New Philadelphia	8	0	1	2	5	14	269	3	0
Newtown	2	0	1	1	0	5	26	2	0
Niles	51	0	2	30	19	196	712	28	2
North Canton	12	0	2	8	2	58	280	12	1
North College Hill	24	0	0	16	8	102	292	23	0
North Ridgeville	14	0	3	5	6	76	185	5	2
Northwood	9	0	3	4	2	53	155	6	0
Norton	7	0	1	2	4	63	155	8	0
Norwalk	19	0	6	6	7	85	454	3	0
Norwood	62	0	6	37	19	296	925	40	3
Oak Harbor	3	0	1	0	2	23	26	1	0
Oak Hill	0	0	0	0	0	2	33	1	0
Oberlin	12	0	4	4	4	48	142	2	0
Obetz	4	0	0	3	1	28	114	12	0
Olmsted Falls	1	0		0	1	3	35	0	0
Olmsted Township	5	0		1	4	28	73	4	2
Ontario	7	0	2	2	3	23	632	7	0
Oregon	26	0	6	9	11	145	611	30	4
Orrville	7	0		1	2	28	94	0	0
Ottawa Hills	5	0	0	2	3	9	20	3	0
Oxford	47	0		9	35	120	445	13	7
Painesville	45	0	7	32	6	138	362	9	3
Parma Heights	17	0	5	4	8	85	340	12	4
Paulding	0	0	0	0	0	1	15	0	0
Perrysburg	5	0		1	1	30	274	11	0
Perrysville	0	0	0	0	0	3	18	0	0
Perry Township, Columbiana County	1	0	0	0	1	1	3	0	0
Perry Township, Franklin County	0	0	0	0	0	8	37	0	0
Perry Township, Montgomery County	0	0	0	0	0	12	8	5	1
Pierce Township	3	0	1	2	0	55	257	4	0
Pioneer	1	0	0	1	0	2	22	0	0
Piqua	33	0	18	14	1	213	805	23	4
Poland Township	3	0	1	0	2	20	29	2	0
Poland Village	0	0	0	0	0	0	17	0	0
Port Clinton	16	0	6	2	8	34	117	2	0
Portsmouth	89	0	9	32	48	362	1,165	51	2
Powell	2	0	0	0	2	17	64	2	1
Powhatan Point	1	0	0	0	1	1	17	0	0
Reminderville	2	0		1	1	8	14	3	0
Richfield	0	0		0	0	5	23	4	1
Richmond Heights	13	0	0	10	3	54	250	23	1

Table 8.   Offenses Known to Law Enforcement, by Selected State and City, 2013— continued

(Number.)

State/city	Violent crime	Murder and nonnegligent manslaughter	Rape (revised definition)	Robbery	Aggravated assault	Burglary	Larceny-theft	Motor vehicle theft	Arson[2]
Richwood	3	0	1	0	2	12	49	3	0
Rio Grande	1	0	0	0	1	2	4	0	0
Rittman	7	0	1	3	3	29	99	9	0
Riverside	44	1	9	20	14	186	387	46	9
Rocky Ridge	0	0		0	0	0	0	0	0
Roseville	2	0	0	0	2	2	23	1	0
Rossford	3	0	1	1	1	22	106	1	2
Russell Township	1	0		0	1	2	12	0	0
Sabina	2	0	1	1	0	23	53	2	0
Sagamore Hills	8	0		3	5	16	59	1	0
Salem	6	1	0	1	4	27	214	6	0
Salineville	2	0	1	0	1	23	15	0	0
Sandusky	78	0	5	28	45	303	819	21	3
Sebring	9	0	2	2	5	22	84	1	2
Seven Hills	5	0	0	3	2	15	32	1	0
Shaker Heights	41	0	2	34	5	234	361	49	0
Shawnee Township	0	0	0	0	0	26	131	3	2
Sheffield Lake	5	0	2	2	1	32	82	1	0
Shelby	11	0	6	4	1	80	280	5	3
Sidney	34	0	8	17	9	271	943	21	5
Silverton	17	0		3	9	40	78	16	1
Solon	7	0	2	2	3	43	201	13	2
South Bloomfield	0	0	0	0	0	9	25	4	0
South Charleston	0	0	0	0	0	7	19	2	0
South Euclid	31	0	0	22	9	149	308	15	2
South Point	8	0	0	0	8	14	38	0	0
South Russell	0	0		0	0	0	13	0	0
Spencerville	1	0	0	0	1	15	26	0	0
Springboro	11	0	4	1	6	37	154	7	0
Springdale	41	0	6	24	11	89	654	31	1
Springfield	427	6	46	208	167	1,304	2,923	236	72
Springfield Township, Hamilton County	74	4	3	44	23	254	530	57	3
Springfield Township, Mahoning County	6	0	1	0	5	35	50	3	1
Springfield Township, Summit County	23	0	4	9	10	180	900	8	3
St. Clair Township	2	0	0	1	1	0	28	0	0
Stow	23	0		3	3	91	616	3	7
Strasburg	1	0	0	0	1	3	32	1	0
Streetsboro	10	0	0	2	8	1	68	1	0
Strongsville	27	0	3	4	20	63	663	20	2
Struthers	11	0	2	1	8	34	130	3	0
Sugarcreek Township	9	0	4	0	5	24	253	2	3
Sylvania Township	15	0	0	11	4	88	479	34	0
Tallmadge	21	2		5	7	71	274	10	
Tipp City	9	0	4	3	2	37	147	5	1
Toledo	2,902	28	129	962	1,783	5,357		1,064	
Toronto	9	0	3	0	6	3	5	0	0
Trotwood	110	1	11	48	50	508	646	88	9
Troy	19	0	3	9	7	158	608	25	2
Twinsburg	9	1	3	1	4	20	104	8	0
Uhrichsville	1	0	0	0	1	24	89	3	1
Union	7	0	1	2	4	52	102	3	1
Uniontown	0	0	0	0	0	21	54	5	0
University Heights	23	0		11	9	51	223	6	0
Upper Arlington	10	0	1	7	2	87	355	3	1
Upper Sandusky	4	0	1	1	2	16	119	1	0
Urbana	20	0	4	5	11	60	319	3	5
Utica	3	0	1	0	2	12	54	5	0
Vandalia	22	0	5	11	6	71	236	32	4
Van Wert	21	1	3	1	16	81	309	2	1
Vermilion	11	0		3	6	74	61	3	1
Village of Leesburg	0	0	0	0	0	6	26	2	0
Wadsworth	18	0	8	3	7	68	387	8	0
Waite Hill	0	0	0	0	0	2	0	0	0
Walbridge	2	0	1	0	1	4	11	0	0
Walton Hills	0	0		0	0	4	21	0	
Wapakoneta	9	0	2	0	7	10	165	2	0
Warren	263	7	24	128	104	734	1,047	130	5
Warren Township	11	0	3	2	6	61	98	5	0
Washington Court House	24	0	5	10	9	156	521	5	0
Waterville	5	0	3	0	2	10	46	0	0
Wauseon	8	0	1	0	7	8	198	0	0
Waverly	0	0	0	0	0	10	97	1	0
Weathersfield	14	0	2	5	7	81	134	6	0
Wellston	12	0	3	2	7	63	186	12	0
Wells Township	3	0	1	0	2	21	40	2	0
West Alexandria	0	0	0	0	0	3	16	0	0

Table 8.   Offenses Known to Law Enforcement, by Selected State and City, 2013— continued

(Number.)

State/city	Violent crime	Murder and nonnegligent manslaughter	Rape (revised definition)[1]	Robbery	Aggravated assault	Burglary	Larceny-theft	Motor vehicle theft	Arson[2]
West Carrollton	29	2		15	5	110	248	35	
West Chester Township	43	1	10	15	17	221	1,149	29	13
Westerville	13	0	5	6	2	93	744	9	17
West Jefferson	2	0	0	1	1	15	79	9	2
West Lafayette	0	0	0	0	0	7	12	1	0
West Liberty	2	0	0	0	2	2	7	1	0
Whitehall	127	2	9	73	43	381	888	72	8
Whitehouse	3	0	2	0	1	8	12	2	0
Williamsburg	5	0	0	2	3	15	65	2	0
Willoughby	14	0		4	7	50	422	20	0
Wintersville	3	0	0	0	3	9	53	1	0
Woodlawn	12	1	0	2	9	17	94	4	3
Woodmere Village	4	0		3	1	4	31	0	0
Wooster	42	0	12	15	15	196	760	25	17
Worthington	5	0	0	2	3	123	256	5	1
Wyoming	2	0	0	0	2	54	109	8	1
Xenia	55	1	12	21	21	212	812	25	6
Yellow Springs	3	0	1	0	2	11	14	0	0
Youngstown	526	14	26	168	318	1,671	1,602	297	28
Zanesville	103	1	16	38	48	286	1,283	32	8
Oklahoma									
Achille	0	0	0	0	0	0	0	0	0
Ada	184	0		4	166	277	607	51	5
Allen	0	0	0	0	0	0	1	0	0
Altus	50	0	5	10	35	267	486	21	3
Alva	3	0	1	0	2	28	55	7	2
Anadarko	26	0	3	3	20	83	164	12	5
Antlers	9	0	1	0	8	28	37	7	0
Apache	2	0	0	0	2	11	13	1	0
Ardmore	370	0		30	316	366	1,238	77	4
Arkoma	3	0	0	0	3	1	1	2	0
Atoka	11	0	1	2	8	35	70	8	2
Bartlesville	87	2		13	61	232	596	40	7
Beaver	4	0	0	0	4	6	13	0	0
Beggs	3	0	1	0	2	10	16	1	1
Bethany	57	0		19	31	186	358	66	3
Bixby	25	0	5	3	17	56	111	20	0
Blackwell	31	1	4	2	24	57	74	3	3
Blanchard	10	0	2	0	8	43	81	2	0
Boise City	0	0	0	0	0	5	4	1	0
Boley	0	0	0	0	0	0	0	0	0
Bristow	18	0	2	0	16	63	116	15	2
Broken Arrow	147	0		32	75	409	1,490	135	9
Broken Bow	32	0		1	28	69	130	6	2
Caddo	1	0	0	0	1	1	4	1	0
Calera	0	0	0	0	0	4	12	1	0
Caney	0	0	0	0	0	2	4	0	0
Canton	0	0	0	0	0	13	3	0	0
Carnegie	6	0	0	0	6	4	0	0	0
Carney	2	0	0	0	2	7	9	0	2
Cashion	1	0	0	0	1	0	2	0	0
Catoosa	50	0		2	44	38	92	31	0
Chandler	10	1	3	1	5	21	69	4	0
Checotah	3	0	0	0	3	4	70	9	0
Chelsea	1	0	1	0	0	7	19	2	0
Cherokee	4	0	1	0	3	8	8	1	0
Chickasha	152	0		10	128	166	333	35	3
Choctaw	17	1	2	0	14	93	127	16	0
Chouteau	6	0	2	0	4	11	46	4	1
Claremore	35	0		3	24	79	405	22	1
Clayton	0	0	0	0	0	0	1	0	0
Cleveland	10	0	3	0	7	20	58	4	1
Clinton	31	0	7	1	23	49	132	21	6
Coalgate	1	0	0	0	1	1	1	0	0
Colbert	0	0	0	0	0	3	9	0	0
Collinsville	4	0	3	0	1	16	33	3	1
Comanche	2	0	0	0	2	15	19	1	1
Cordell	3	0	1	0	2	19	28	4	0
Coweta	13	0	3	0	10	29	145	15	2
Crescent	0	0	0	0	0	18	9	0	0
Cushing	16	0	2	2	12	46	141	7	1
Davenport	2	0	0	0	2	4	7	2	0
Davis	5	0	2	0	3	39	56	8	0
Del City	126	0		19	93	300	794	81	3
Depew	3	0	0	0	3	5	0	1	0
Dewar	1	0	1	0	0	3	3	0	0
Dewey	0	0	0	0	0	1	6	0	0

Table 8.   Offenses Known to Law Enforcement, by Selected State and City, 2013— continued

(Number.)

State/city	Violent crime	Murder and nonnegligent manslaughter	Rape (revised definition)[1]	Robbery	Aggravated assault	Burglary	Larceny-theft	Motor vehicle theft	Arson[2]
Dibble	0	0	0	0	0	1	0	0	0
Drumright	4	0	0	0	4	7	29	5	0
Duncan	78	1	12	19	46	308	836	45	5
Durant	168	0		10	148	277	859	39	4
Edmond	87	0		15	57	309	1,230	56	1
Elgin	0	0	0	0	0	1	4	0	0
Elk City	30	0	0	3	27	76	240	29	1
El Reno	45	0		4	32	115	307	16	7
Enid	228	3		16	185	557	1,647	90	6
Eufaula	7	0	1	4	2	32	79	9	2
Fairfax	6	0	0	0	6	11	6	1	0
Fairview	3	0	1	0	2	17	38	3	0
Fletcher	0	0	0	0	0	0	4	0	0
Forest Park	0	0	0	0	0	4	7	1	0
Fort Gibson	4	0	3	0	1	17	38	7	0
Frederick	18	0	0	1	17	32	70	3	3
Geary	7	0	0	0	7	18	26	1	1
Glenpool	69	0		4	56	45	196	7	0
Goodwell	1	0	0	0	1	15	8	1	0
Grove	33	1		0	31	30	176	6	1
Guthrie	27	0	2	3	22	70	228	16	3
Guymon	36	0		3	32	49	157	8	1
Haileyville	1	0	0	0	1	2	0	0	0
Harrah	10	0	2	0	8	52	92	22	0
Hartshorne	3	0	0	1	2	13	39	5	0
Haskell	2	1	0	0	1	2	3	1	0
Healdton	9	0	2	0	7	28	34	7	1
Heavener	9	0	3	2	4	18	45	3	1
Hennessey	1	0	0	0	1	5	28	1	0
Henryetta	10	0	1	2	7	41	70	8	0
Hinton	0	0	0	0	0	4	10	3	0
Hobart	5	0	2	1	2	65	62	6	2
Holdenville	7	1	2	0	4	16	20	10	2
Hollis	2	0	1	0	1	59	51	0	1
Hominy	14	0	1	1	12	31	44	6	0
Hooker	0	0	0	0	0	4	11	2	0
Howe	1	0	0	0	1	0	3	0	0
Hugo	3	0	0	0	3	9	9	1	0
Hulbert	0	0	0	0	0	1	2	0	0
Hydro	2	0	0	0	2	8	18	1	0
Idabel	33	0		0	28	103	250	11	0
Jay	1	0		1	0	8	56	2	0
Jones	8	0	2	0	6	11	22	1	0
Kiefer	1	0	0	0	1	8	10	3	0
Kingfisher	2	0	1	0	1	13	70	3	0
Kingston	0	0	0	0	0	1	1	0	0
Krebs	2	0	1	1	0	20	42	8	1
Lahoma	0	0	0	0	0	2	4	0	0
Lamont	0	0	0	0	0	0	1	0	0
Lawton	919	13		168	658	1,485	3,313	229	33
Lexington	3	0	1	0	2	10	32	3	3
Lindsay	25	0	1	2	22	49	59	5	2
Locust Grove	1	0	0	0	1	0	0	2	0
Lone Grove	4	0	1	0	3	26	82	7	1
Luther	0	0	0	0	0	6	4	1	0
Madill	0	0	0	0	0	9	81	2	0
Mangum	6	0	5	0	1	21	30	2	0
Mannford	3	0		0	2	3	30	1	1
Marietta	11	0	4	0	7	20	49	5	1
Marlow	8	0	0	0	8	48	103	8	1
Maysville	2	0	0	0	2	8	6	3	0
McAlester	89	1	8	16	64	241	629	62	4
McCurtain	0	0	0	0	0	0	1	0	0
McLoud	17	0	1	0	16	15	40	14	0
Medicine Park	0	0	0	0	0	0	0	0	0
Meeker	6	0	2	0	4	5	23	3	1
Miami	59	1	4	2	52	108	273	14	11
Midwest City	359	2		48	261	707	1,958	261	10
Minco	5	0	1	0	4	6	10	0	0
Moore	72	1		23	41	393	1,361	133	4
Mooreland	1	0	0	0	1	7	4	1	0
Morris	8	0	2	1	5	4	1	1	0
Mountain View	1	0	0	0	1	0	0	0	0
Muldrow	3	0	0	0	3	20	34	7	1
Muskogee	309	2	19	33	255	584	1,083	85	13
Mustang	39	0		0	37	67	357	16	3
Newcastle	8	0	1	2	5	83	210	36	0
Newkirk	3	0	1	0	2	8	18	1	0

Table 8.   Offenses Known to Law Enforcement, by Selected State and City, 2013— continued

(Number.)

State/city	Violent crime	Murder and nonnegligent manslaughter	Rape (revised definition)[1]	Robbery	Aggravated assault	Burglary	Larceny-theft	Motor vehicle theft	Arson[2]
Nichols Hills	2	0	0	0	2	17	61	7	0
Nicoma Park	2	0	0	0	2	17	31	6	0
Ninnekah	0	0	0	0	0	2	4	1	0
Noble	7	0	1	3	3	45	132	16	1
Norman	178	4		46	72	612	2,161	168	14
North Enid	0	0	0	0	0	3	0	0	0
Nowata	18	0		0	17	16	37	3	1
Oilton	4	0	0	0	4	5	3	1	0
Okemah	4	0	0	1	3	35	112	3	1
Oklahoma City	4,998	62		1,191	3,295	8,016	20,387	4,076	130
Okmulgee	45	0		4	35	96	455	27	5
Oologah	0	0	0	0	0	3	11	0	0
Owasso	56	0	4	4	48	97	540	50	1
Pauls Valley	23	0	4	1	18	49	196	8	1
Pawhuska	17	0	1	1	15	21	46	6	1
Pawnee	3	0		0	2	22	7	0	0
Perkins	7	0	1	2	4	14	37	3	0
Perry	7	0	2	0	5	34	56	3	0
Piedmont	6	0	0	0	6	10	41	6	1
Pocola	1	0	0	0	1	9	18	3	0
Ponca City	128	0		17	86	268	973	43	5
Porum	4	0	0	0	4	2	2	3	0
Poteau	39	0	2	0	37	146	379	18	2
Prague	10	0	0	0	10	33	44	6	0
Pryor	87	0		3	74	95	171	25	0
Purcell	23	0	4	2	17	78	246	21	4
Ringling	6	0	1	0	5	8	14	1	0
Roland	1	0	0	0	1	26	48	3	1
Rush Springs	1	0	1	0	0	1	2	0	0
Sallisaw	29	0	3	3	23	50	247	12	1
Sand Springs	20	0		10	5	100	561	35	2
Sapulpa	39	0	5	4	30	119	396	44	1
Sawyer	0	0	0	0	0	1	5	0	0
Sayre	6	0	0	1	5	18	26	5	2
Seiling	1	0	0	0	1	5	18	0	0
Shawnee	170	1		23	127	534	1,041	129	7
Skiatook	11	0	3	1	7	48	119	10	0
Snyder	2	0	1	0	1	2	5	0	0
South Coffeyville	0	0	0	0	0	2	4	0	0
Sparks	0	0	0	0	0	1	0	1	0
Spencer	8	0	0	2	6	64	34	11	0
Spiro	1	0	0	0	1	3	13	0	0
Stigler	10	0	3	0	7	16	90	5	2
Stilwell	14	0	3	2	9	28	154	15	4
Stonewall	0	0	0	0	0	3	1	0	0
Stratford	3	0	0	0	3	2	1	2	1
Stringtown	0	0	0	0	0	1	4	1	0
Stroud	2	0	0	0	2	24	24	7	0
Sulphur	8	0	3	0	5	31	38	3	4
Tahlequah	56	2	5	9	40	135	509	24	2
Talihina	6	0	0	0	6	3	14	5	0
Tecumseh	18	0	2	0	16	48	86	8	5
Texhoma	0	0	0	0	0	0	0	0	0
The Village	22	1		4	17	66	258	18	0
Tishomingo	5	0	3	0	2	8	28	1	2
Tonkawa	5	0	1	0	4	25	46	4	1
Tryon	3	0	0	0	3	2	0	2	0
Tulsa	3,827	60		994	2,400	5,935	12,654	2,389	154
Tushka	1	0	0	0	1	3	1	1	0
Tuttle	10	0	3	0	7	45	85	11	0
Valliant	1	0	0	0	1	3	2	2	0
Verdigris	1	0	0	0	1	12	21	2	0
Vian	4	0	1	0	3	17	31	1	1
Vinita	7	1		1	5	24	97	10	3
Wagoner	66	0		6	57	89	333	16	5
Walters	1	0	0	0	1	0	14	1	0
Warner	3	0	0	0	3	8	9	2	0
Warr Acres	54	0		17	29	101	346	55	0
Washington	3	0	0	0	3	3	0	0	0
Watonga	7	0	0	2	5	25	34	3	0
Waukomis	2	0	0	0	2	12	14	0	0
Waurika	4	0	3	0	1	5	13	5	1
Waynoka	2	0	0	0	2	0	3	1	0
Weatherford	23	0		1	16	45	201	15	0
Weleetka	7	0	1	0	6	8	12	3	0
Westville	2	0	0	0	2	18	29	0	0
Wetumka	0	0	0	0	0	2	0	0	0
Wewoka	12	0	2	0	10	15	81	3	0

Table 8.   Offenses Known to Law Enforcement, by Selected State and City, 2013— continued

(Number.)

State/city	Violent crime	Murder and nonnegligent manslaughter	Rape (revised definition)	Robbery	Aggravated assault	Burglary	Larceny-theft	Motor vehicle theft	Arson[2]
Wilburton	0	0	0	0	0	1	1	1	0
Wilson	18	0		0	18	9	17	5	2
Woodward	33	0	3	1	29	142	303	58	1
Wright City	1	0	1	0	0	2	7	0	0
Wyandotte	1	0	0	0	1	2	6	1	0
Wynnewood	1	0	1	0	0	10	9	2	0
Yale	3	0	0	0	3	4	20	1	0
Yukon	61	0	6	7	48	80	460	25	2
Oregon									
Albany	40	0		27	5	252	1,625	142	6
Amity	1	0	1	0	0	1	25	0	1
Ashland	33	0	5	7	21	76	585	13	10
Astoria	33	0		1	29	89	324	32	3
Athena	1	0	1	0	0	5	19	1	0
Aumsville	6	0	0	1	5	20	59	3	0
Baker City	27	0		2	24	68	293	9	5
Bandon	1	0		1	0	24	59	5	1
Banks	4	0		0	4	5	17	4	1
Beaverton	124	1		22	81	175	1,213	83	15
Bend	182	1	21	22	138	267	1,913	87	39
Black Butte	0	0	0	0	0	0	5	0	0
Boardman	8	0	3	0	5	22	58	4	0
Brookings	2	0		1	1	6	43	6	0
Burns	1	0		0	1	19	43	4	0
Canby	13	0		2	7	60	229	9	3
Cannon Beach	1	0		0	1	1	35	2	0
Carlton	4	0	3	0	1	3	15	0	0
Central Point	33	0	5	4	24	47	530	24	6
Clatskanie	0	0		0	0	19	28	4	0
Coburg	0	0		0	0	5	9	1	0
Columbia City	0	0	0	0	0	0	10	1	0
Condon	0	0		0	0	0	2	0	0
Coos Bay	60	1		6	50	166	745	54	3
Coquille	0	0		0	0	12	51	4	0
Cornelius	18	0		9	5	66	271	14	1
Corvallis	64	0	10	16	38	195	1,354	38	8
Cottage Grove	18	1		5	12	52	436	21	0
Dallas	41	0	6	4	31	51	254	10	2
Eagle Point	24	0	4	8	12	43	294	7	0
Enterprise	2	0		0	1	10	11	0	0
Estacada	3	0		0	3	30	74	4	0
Eugene	402	0	68	195	139	1,539	5,773	608	55
Fairview	14	1		2	7	24	193	31	4
Florence	6	0		1	3	54	308	10	2
Forest Grove	76	0		12	52	85	499	29	2
Gaston	1	0		0	1	8	20	1	0
Gearhart	0	0		0	0	4	2	0	0
Gervais	10	0	0	1	9	10	34	15	2
Gladstone	23	1		1	16	44	220	34	3
Gold Beach	0	0		0	0	6	67	2	0
Grants Pass	110	1	11	35	63	477	1,844	236	18
Gresham	611	5		275	279	920	3,123	510	26
Hermiston	18	0		9	3	96	404	75	1
Hillsboro	141	0		55	57	311	1,723	126	9
Hines	0	0		0	0	10	13	0	2
Hubbard	4	0	0	0	4	1	26	1	1
Independence	11	0	1	0	10	37	205	5	2
Jacksonville	3	0	1	0	2	4	20	1	0
John Day	1	0		0	1	5	25	2	0
Junction City	3	0		1	2	13	65	9	0
Keizer	61	0	8	7	46	112	745	50	7
King City	4	0		1	3	12	41	3	1
Klamath Falls	76	2		24	39	149	690	78	8
La Grande	28	0	4	0	24	80	315	9	1
Lake Oswego	22	0		5	11	111	480	24	13
Lakeview	10	0		1	8	7	18	6	0
Lebanon	30	0	2	11	17	117	530	54	5
Lincoln City	34	0	1	10	23	107	270	11	5
Malin	1	0		0	1	1	1	0	0
Manzanita	0	0	0	0	0	2	8	1	0
McMinnville	68	1	17	15	35	147	776	32	12
Medford	483	1	37	99	346	575	4,075	163	53
Milton-Freewater	7	0		0	4	51	244	21	9
Milwaukie	30	0		5	20	78	434	62	3
Molalla	11	0		2	7	52	207	9	3
Monmouth	13	0	1	1	11	30	196	5	1
Mount Angel	8	0	1	1	6	8	49	3	0

Table 8.   Offenses Known to Law Enforcement, by Selected State and City, 2013— continued

(Number.)

State/city	Violent crime	Murder and nonnegligent manslaughter	Rape (revised definition)[1]	Robbery	Aggravated assault	Burglary	Larceny-theft	Motor vehicle theft	Arson[2]
Newberg-Dundee	22	0	8	1	13	48	306	25	3
Newport	46	0	9	3	34	90	497	15	1
North Bend	7	0		0	4	84	407	19	4
North Plains	2	0		0	1	5	24	3	0
Ontario	65	1		12	45	118	692	22	3
Oregon City	33	1		6	18	126	827	55	0
Pendleton	54	0	15	13	26	102	655	44	1
Philomath	2	0		1	1	11	56	3	0
Phoenix	9	0	2	3	4	16	89	7	0
Pilot Rock	0	0	0	0	0	0	26	1	0
Portland	2,941	14		917	1,776	4,128	22,216	3,289	168
Prineville	24	0		1	22	45	249	1	2
Rainier	2	0		1	1	6	33	4	0
Redmond	87	0	11	15	61	157	867	43	11
Rockaway Beach	2	0	0	0	2	20	28	0	0
Rogue River	2	0	0	0	2	7	33	5	0
Salem	520	7	47	138	328	983	5,143	656	42
Scappoose	11	0		1	10	14	66	2	1
Seaside	8	0		4	2	74	465	15	1
Sherwood	8	0		2	4	31	260	10	3
Silverton	10	1	2	3	4	28	173	6	3
Springfield	98	2	14	32	50	478	2,450	270	25
Stanfield	2	0	1	0	1	6	19	4	0
Stayton	23	0	3	5	15	46	278	13	1
St. Helens	9	0		2	2	46	291	16	3
Sunriver	2	0	0	0	2	16	60	4	0
Sweet Home	10	0		4	5	82	398	21	0
Talent	7	0	2	0	5	12	115	4	1
The Dalles	14	0		6	7	141	513	38	4
Tigard	57	0		23	20	173	1,384	69	10
Tillamook	10	0	1	4	5	23	142	12	2
Toledo	16	1	2	2	11	37	103	5	0
Troutdale	22	0		9	10	64	396	49	5
Tualatin	24	0		9	8	88	658	37	3
Turner	1	1	0	0	0	7	15	2	0
Umatilla	13	0	2	0	11	25	70	12	1
Warrenton	0	0		0	0	25	134	8	0
West Linn	6	0		0	3	36	234	9	2
Wilsonville	17	0		6	5	51	374	36	2
Woodburn	82	1	7	28	46	100	586	47	7
Yamhill	0	0	0	0	0	3	13	0	0
Pennsylvania									
Abington Township, Lackawanna County	1	0	0	0	1	4	10	0	0
Abington Township, Montgomery County	63	0	5	28	30	169	952	25	4
Adamstown	0	0	0	0	0	4	12	4	0
Adams Township, Butler County	8	0	0	0	8	11	51	1	0
Adams Township, Cambria County	0	0	0	0	0	9	16	0	0
Akron	6	0	0	0	6	9	18	1	1
Alburtis	1	0	0	1	0	0	15	0	0
Aldan	2	0	1	1	0	4	82	1	0
Aleppo Township	0	0	0	0	0	0	7	0	0
Aliquippa	49	1	1	8	39	43	83	10	0
Allegheny Township, Blair County	29	0	0	0	29	11	130	3	0
Allegheny Township, Westmoreland County	4	0	0	2	2	10	90	0	0
Allentown	628	12	64	329	223	1,263	2,724	337	10
Altoona	131	2	25	29	75	259	733	43	9
Ambler	12	0	0	6	6	5	84	3	1
Ambridge	86	0	0	13	73	58	187	6	1
Amity Township	3	0	0	1	2	25	87	9	5
Annville Township	5	0	0	0	5	9	60	1	0
Armagh Township	2	0	1	0	1	2	7	0	0
Arnold	31	0	2	16	13	21	31	9	1
Ashland	4	0	0	0	4	16	40	1	2
Ashville	0	0	0	0	0	0	0	0	0
Aspinwall	0	0	0	0	0	9	37	0	0
Aston Township	7	0	0	5	2	31	216	10	3
Athens	4	0	2	0	2	2	69	1	1
Avalon	28	0	0	0	28	19	80	6	0
Avis	2	0	1	0	1	2	3	0	0
Avondale	0	0	0	0	0	1	2	0	0
Avonmore Boro	0	0	0	0	0	0	0	0	0
Baldwin Borough	22	0	2	6	14	29	110	4	0
Bally	0	0	0	0	0	0	0	0	0
Bangor	25	0	0	0	25	19	102	2	0
Beallsville	0	0	0	0	0	0	0	0	0

Table 8.   Offenses Known to Law Enforcement, by Selected State and City, 2013— continued

(Number.)

State/city	Violent crime	Murder and nonnegligent manslaughter	Rape (revised definition)	Robbery	Aggravated assault	Burglary	Larceny-theft	Motor vehicle theft	Arson[2]
Beaver Falls	51	1	2	17	31	32	364	11	1
Beaver Meadows	1	0	0	0	1	1	7	0	0
Bedford	10	0	0	0	10	6	29	1	0
Bell Acres	0	0	0	0	0	0	2	0	0
Bellevue	27	0	1	8	18	59	181	5	0
Bellwood	0	0	0	0	0	2	32	0	0
Ben Avon	2	0	0	0	2	1	35	0	0
Ben Avon Heights	0	0	0	0	0	0	7	0	0
Bensalem Township	106	0	27	58	21	198	1,738	90	13
Benton Area	0	0	0	0	0	4	16	0	0
Berlin	5	0	0	0	5	0	7	0	0
Bern Township	9	0	1	0	8	7	54	2	0
Bernville	0	0	0	0	0	0	2	0	0
Berwick	33	0	1	3	29	106	284	11	1
Bessemer	0	0	0	0	0	0	0	0	0
Bethel Park	19	0	1	2	16	33	216	7	0
Bethel Township, Armstrong County	0	0	0	0	0	0	0	0	0
Bethel Township, Berks County	5	0	0	0	5	2	18	1	0
Bethel Township, Delaware County	19	1	0	0	18	21	91	1	1
Bethlehem	183	4	27	74	78	365	1,601	44	7
Bethlehem Township	22	0	0	5	17	51	417	9	0
Biglerville	0	0	0	0	0	0	11	1	0
Birdsboro	6	0	2	2	2	8	52	2	0
Birmingham Township	1	0	0	1	0	2	19	1	0
Blair Township	1	0	0	0	1	6	25	2	0
Blakely	2	0	0	0	2	17	74	5	0
Blawnox	7	0	0	0	7	5	6	0	0
Bloomsburg Town	41	0	9	3	29	56	173	2	0
Blossburg	1	0	0	0	1	3	6	0	0
Bonneauville	1	0	0	0	1	0	5	2	0
Boswell	0	0	0	0	0	0	0	0	0
Brackenridge	2	0	0	0	2	8	60	4	0
Braddock Hills	4	0	2	0	2	3	25	0	0
Bradford	89	0	4	0	85	41	269	10	0
Bradford Township	12	0	2	1	9	5	39	5	0
Brecknock Township, Berks County	1	0	0	0	1	10	9	1	0
Brentwood	28	0	0	6	22	22	201	16	0
Briar Creek Township	1	0	0	0	1	15	53	2	0
Bridgeport	4	0	0	0	4	23	101	3	0
Bridgeville	5	0	0	0	5	11	57	1	0
Bridgewater	8	0	0	1	7	9	21	1	0
Bristol	28	0	1	17	10	55	246	9	2
Bristol Township	84	2	6	58	18	247	1,127	90	9
Brockway	10	0	0	1	9	3	48	0	0
Brookhaven	16	0	1	9	6	18	143	6	1
Brookville	5	0	2	0	3	2	79	0	1
Brownsville	10	0	0	8	2	8	34	3	0
Bryn Athyn	0	0	0	0	0	2	8	0	0
Buckingham Township	2	0	1	0	1	13	82	2	0
Buffalo Township	11	0	0	1	10	8	28	0	0
Buffalo Valley Regional	7	0	0	1	6	17	64	0	0
Burgettstown	4	0	3	0	1	11	17	1	1
Butler Township, Butler County	15	0	2	4	9	24	329	8	0
Butler Township, Luzerne County	34	0	1	0	33	35	116	1	0
Butler Township, Schuylkill County	0	0	0	0	0	10	11	1	0
Caernarvon Township, Berks County	18	0	0	0	18	12	73	4	0
California	21	0	3	7	11	18	87	2	2
Callery	0	0	0	0	0	0	0	0	0
Caln Township	71	1	1	4	65	24	295	10	0
Cambria Township	1	0	0	0	1	6	76	3	0
Cambridge Springs	1	0	0	1	0	0	6	0	0
Canton	2	0	0	0	2	7	24	2	0
Carbondale	11	0	1	4	6	42	77	12	0
Carrolltown	1	0	0	0	1	5	9	0	0
Carroll Township, Washington County	8	0	0	0	8	8	47	2	0
Carroll Township, York County	3	1	0	0	2	15	50	2	0
Carroll Valley	2	0	1	1	0	17	54	0	0
Castle Shannon	8	0	0	1	7	12	59	0	0
Catasauqua	2	0	0	0	2	15	78	10	0
Catawissa	4	0	2	1	1	7	10	0	0
Cecil Township	5	0	0	0	5	15	52	0	0
Center Township	25	0	0	3	22	30	404	1	0
Centerville	2	0	0	0	2	10	13	1	3
Central Berks Regional	13	0	2	4	7	35	105	10	3

Table 8.   Offenses Known to Law Enforcement, by Selected State and City, 2013— continued

(Number.)

State/city	Violent crime	Murder and nonnegligent manslaughter	Rape (revised definition)[1]	Robbery	Aggravated assault	Burglary	Larceny-theft	Motor vehicle theft	Arson[2]
Chalfont	0	0	0	0	0	1	18	0	0
Chambersburg	86	0	3	46	37	127	660	23	1
Charleroi Regional	51	0	3	11	37	74	265	11	5
Chartiers Township	5	0	1	0	4	16	73	2	0
Cheltenham Township	88	1	1	64	22	186	723	30	1
Cherry Tree	0	0	0	0	0	0	0	0	0
Chester	731	22	29	236	444	354	697	130	21
Chester Township	55	1	2	6	46	53	71	9	1
Chippewa Township	3	0	0	2	1	18	228	3	0
Christiana	1	0	0	0	1	9	15	1	0
Churchill	11	0	0	0	11	9	24	2	0
Clarion	5	0	1	2	2	8	54	6	1
Clarks Summit	7	0	0	0	7	9	29	0	0
Clearfield	26	0	2	4	20	17	212	4	1
Cleona	2	0	0	2	0	3	17	0	0
Clifton Heights	68	0	2	11	55	22	141	7	3
Coaldale	0	0	0	0	0	3	0	0	0
Coal Township	21	0	1	0	20	50	245	9	2
Coatesville	140	0	0	62	78	76	225	59	9
Cochranton	1	0	0	1	0	3	0	0	0
Collegeville	1	0	0	0	1	7	58	0	0
Collier Township	6	0	1	0	5	18	181	2	0
Colonial Regional	7	0	2	4	1	61	463	6	0
Columbia	24	1	2	8	13	60	154	11	3
Conemaugh Township, Cambria County	3	0	0	0	3	0	2	1	0
Conemaugh Township, Somerset County	4	0	1	1	2	18	27	0	0
Conewago Township, Adams County	6	0	4	1	1	6	82	1	0
Conewango Township	12	0	1	1	10	10	111	1	0
Conneaut Lake Regional	0	0	0	0	0	8	33	2	1
Connellsville	26	0	4	14	8	85	260	12	0
Conoy Township	2	0	0	1	1	14	14	0	0
Conshohocken	14	0	0	3	11	15	139	6	0
Conway	3	0	0	1	2	5	9	0	1
Conyngham	0	0	0	0	0	2	5	0	0
Conyngham Township, Columbia County	4	0	0	0	4	0	3	0	0
Coopersburg	4	0	0	1	3	2	16	1	0
Coplay	1	0	0	0	1	12	55	2	0
Coraopolis	43	1	1	4	37	12	112	4	0
Cornwall	1	0	0	0	1	1	3	0	0
Corry	33	0	1	1	31	59	247	2	2
Coudersport	0	0	0	0	0	1	9	0	0
Courtdale	3	0	0	1	2	2	4	1	0
Covington Township	1	0	0	0	1	11	28	1	0
Cranberry Township	17	0	3	4	10	18	409	3	1
Crescent Township	7	0	0	0	7	14	24	1	0
Cresson	3	0	0	1	2	2	16	0	0
Cresson Township	2	0	1	1	0	4	9	0	0
Croyle Township	0	0	0	0	0	1	14	1	0
Cumberland Township, Adams County	3	0	0	0	3	15	33	4	0
Cumberland Township, Greene County	18	0	0	1	17	17	148	8	2
Cumru Township	17	0	1	11	5	45	182	13	2
Curwensville	17	0	0	1	16	7	41	1	0
Dallas	0	0	0	0	0	2	8	3	0
Dallas Township	5	0	4	0	1	27	57	4	0
Dalton	1	0	0	0	1	6	14	0	0
Danville	28	0	0	0	28	7	91	1	1
Darby	466	1	87	80	298	174	304	47	5
Darby Township	53	0	0	11	42	36	240	2	1
Darlington Township	1	0	0	0	1	14	16	1	0
Decatur Township	8	1	0	0	7	9	33	3	0
Delano Township	0	0	0	0	0	0	0	0	0
Delmont	0	0	0	0	0	3	18	1	0
Derry Township, Dauphin County	35	1	1	10	23	72	386	7	4
Dickson City	25	0	0	4	21	14	230	4	1
Donora	12	0	0	1	11	13	50	1	1
Dormont	22	0	1	3	18	20	53	5	0
Douglass Township, Berks County	2	0	0	0	2	9	22	1	0
Douglass Township, Montgomery County	25	0	3	2	20	14	109	8	0
Doylestown	14	1	0	1	12	26	148	5	1
Doylestown Township	10	0	4	0	6	20	155	1	1
Dublin Borough	3	0	0	0	3	2	18	0	0
Du Bois	24	0	3	4	17	30	185	5	0
Dunbar	3	0	1	0	2	0	7	0	0

Table 8.   Offenses Known to Law Enforcement, by Selected State and City, 2013— continued

(Number.)

State/city	Violent crime	Murder and nonnegligent manslaughter	Rape (revised definition)[1]	Robbery	Aggravated assault	Burglary	Larceny-theft	Motor vehicle theft	Arson[2]
Dunmore	10	0	0	2	8	20	122	3	1
Dunnstable Township	0	0	0	0	0	6	1	0	0
Dupont	9	0	1	0	8	4	44	3	0
Duquesne	55	2	6	31	16	95	146	19	4
Duryea	4	0	1	0	3	43	92	10	0
Earl Township	2	0	1	0	1	9	36	3	0
East Berlin	0	0	0	0	0	0	0	0	0
East Bethlehem Township	5	0	0	1	4	5	34	1	0
East Brandywine Township	10	0	1	1	8	4	76	4	0
East Cocalico Township	3	0	0	0	3	28	101	11	1
East Conemaugh	0	0	0	0	0	3	15	0	0
East Coventry Township	1	0	0	0	1	7	44	0	0
East Deer Township	2	0	0	0	2	4	26	1	0
East Earl Township	1	0	1	0	0	12	70	4	0
Eastern Adams Regional	1	0	0	1	0	1	43	1	0
Eastern Pike Regional	7	0	3	1	3	14	203	3	0
East Fallowfield Township	6	1	0	1	4	35	53	5	1
East Hempfield Township	26	0	11	4	11	68	371	11	0
East Lampeter Township	19	1	0	12	6	54	740	11	2
East Lansdowne	29	0	1	7	21	20	73	3	0
East Marlborough Township	0	0	0	0	0	2	10	0	0
East Norriton Township	22	0	3	6	13	20	336	5	1
East Norwegian Township	0	0	0	0	0	0	0	1	0
Easton	96	2	14	35	45	142	542	40	7
East Penn Township	0	0	0	0	0	6	21	0	0
East Petersburg	1	0	0	1	0	5	59	1	0
East Pikeland Township	3	0	0	2	1	8	49	1	0
East Pittsburgh	57	1	2	4	50	19	47	4	0
East Rochester	4	0	0	2	2	3	41	1	0
East Taylor Township	2	0	1	0	1	8	19	0	0
Easttown Township	10	0	1	0	9	20	69	3	0
East Union Township	0	0	0	0	0	0	0	0	0
East Vincent Township	4	0	0	2	2	9	32	1	0
East Washington	15	0	0	0	15	12	36	3	0
East Whiteland Township	2	0	0	0	2	9	116	1	0
Ebensburg	7	0	1	2	4	5	36	3	1
Economy	0	0	0	0	0	11	35	3	0
Eddystone	20	0	0	5	15	14	236	4	0
Edgewood	12	0	0	4	8	5	177	3	0
Edgeworth	2	0	0	0	2	0	0	0	0
Edinboro	6	0	1	1	4	17	70	1	0
Edwardsville	44	0	1	4	39	23	227	3	1
Elizabethtown	8	0	2	2	4	22	131	2	0
Elizabeth Township	11	0	1	2	8	36	134	1	0
Elkland	0	0	0	0	0	0	12	0	0
Ellwood City	25	1	1	6	17	35	126	1	1
Emlenton Borough	0	0	0	0	0	0	1	0	0
Emmaus	7	1	1	3	2	37	167	5	0
Emporium	1	0	0	0	1	3	20	0	1
Emsworth	1	0	0	0	1	0	28	0	0
Ephrata	28	0	3	5	20	40	199	8	0
Ephrata Township	11	0	1	2	8	17	186	3	2
Erie	457	3	60	175	219	1,017	2,093	98	24
Etna	9	0	0	0	9	15	62	4	2
Everett	3	0	0	0	3	2	22	0	0
Exeter Township, Berks County	14	0	4	4	6	58	388	9	0
Fairfield	0	0	0	0	0	0	8	1	0
Fairview Township, Luzerne County	0	0	0	0	0	10	27	0	0
Fairview Township, York County	26	0	3	4	19	51	217	7	2
Falls Township, Bucks County	46	0	5	23	18	89	739	46	1
Fawn Township	3	0	0	0	3	9	18	0	0
Fayette City	0	0	0	0	0	0	3	0	0
Ferguson Township	14	0	2	2	10	28	92	2	0
Ferndale	5	0	0	1	4	1	0	0	0
Findlay Township	3	0	2	0	1	7	36	1	1
Fleetwood	5	0	0	0	5	23	68	2	0
Ford City	4	0	0	0	4	2	28	2	0
Forest City	3	0	0	0	3	4	21	0	1
Forest Hills	10	0	0	3	7	21	68	0	0
Forks Township	3	0	0	0	3	11	109	5	1
Forty Fort	5	1	1	1	2	9	49	3	0
Forward Township	1	0	0	0	1	8	45	1	1
Foster Township, McKean County	4	1	1	1	1	2	25	0	0
Foster Township, Schuylkill County	0	0	0	0	0	0	0	0	0
Fountain Hill	17	0	2	2	13	20	123	2	2
Fox Chapel	1	0	0	0	1	4	12	0	0
Frackville	10	0	2	0	8	1	17	1	0

Table 8.   Offenses Known to Law Enforcement, by Selected State and City, 2013— continued

(Number.)

State/city	Violent crime	Murder and nonnegligent manslaughter	Rape (revised definition)[1]	Robbery	Aggravated assault	Burglary	Larceny-theft	Motor vehicle theft	Arson[2]
Franconia Township	5	0	1	0	4	15	80	5	0
Franklin	8	0	1	1	6	30	146	4	1
Franklin Park	3	0	0	0	3	4	55	0	0
Franklin Township, Carbon County	11	0	2	1	8	12	37	0	0
Frazer Township	0	0	0	0	0	0	112	1	0
Freedom	9	0	1	0	8	6	35	4	0
Freeland	16	0	1	3	12	43	80	4	0
Freemansburg	3	0	1	0	2	18	64	1	0
Freeport	5	0	0	0	5	1	10	0	0
Galeton	0	0	0	0	0	3	8	0	0
Gallitzin Township	0	0	0	0	0	0	0	0	0
Geistown	0	0	0	0	0	13	31	3	0
Gettysburg	27	0	8	8	11	28	110	3	2
Gilberton	0	0	0	0	0	0	0	0	0
Girard	7	0	0	1	6	1	31	0	0
Girardville	2	0	0	0	2	1	1	0	0
Glassport	22	0	1	11	10	27	103	9	2
Granville Township	2	0	0	0	2	10	116	1	0
Great Bend	0	0	0	0	0	2	7	0	0
Greencastle	2	0	0	0	2	6	57	1	0
Greenfield Township, Blair County	1	0	0	0	1	10	84	2	0
Greensburg	26	0	4	4	18	50	282	2	1
Green Tree	14	0	0	0	14	13	55	0	2
Greenville	24	0	4	3	17	45	67	4	0
Grove City	3	0	0	0	3	18	59	1	0
Hamburg	14	0	2	2	10	15	74	4	0
Hampton Township	14	0	0	2	12	14	95	2	0
Hanover	24	1	1	8	14	36	465	4	0
Hanover Township, Luzerne County	31	0	3	9	19	66	208	19	2
Harmony Township	7	0	1	1	5	11	39	3	0
Harrisville	0	0	0	0	0	1	0	0	0
Harveys Lake	2	0	0	0	2	6	32	1	0
Hatboro	2	0	0	2	0	7	62	3	0
Hatfield Township	17	1	3	6	7	37	203	12	1
Haverford Township	27	0	1	11	15	100	603	12	0
Hazleton	83	1	2	26	54	242	358	31	5
Heidelberg	3	0	0	0	3	2	3	0	0
Heidelberg Township, Berks County	1	0	0	0	1	0	10	0	0
Hellam Township	21	0	4	0	17	14	70	7	1
Hellertown	18	0	0	1	17	15	52	0	0
Hemlock Township	1	0	0	1	0	7	95	3	0
Hempfield Township, Mercer County	6	1	1	0	4	25	137	6	0
Hermitage	38	0	5	15	18	67	488	4	1
Hickory Township	1	0	1	0	0	4	12	1	0
Highland Township	0	0	0	0	0	0	1	0	0
Highspire	9	1	0	2	6	10	66	1	0
Hilltown Township	13	1	2	2	8	40	180	2	0
Hollidaysburg	3	0	1	1	1	4	45	2	2
Homestead	43	2	2	24	15	38	179	19	0
Honesdale	20	0	1	2	17	18	98	4	0
Honey Brook	2	0	0	0	2	0	1	0	0
Horsham Township	25	0	5	5	15	37	160	9	2
Hughesville	2	0	0	1	1	2	26	0	0
Hulmeville	0	0	0	0	0	0	2	0	0
Hummelstown	1	0	0	0	1	11	51	4	0
Huntingdon	12	0	0	0	12	1	57	2	0
Independence Township, Beaver County	0	0	0	0	0	7	9	5	0
Independence Township, Washington County	0	0	0	0	0	2	6	2	0
Indiana	199	0	9	6	184	23	224	2	2
Indiana Township	4	0	1	0	3	11	39	0	0
Indian Lake	1	0	0	0	1	1	0	0	0
Ingram	0	0	0	0	0	7	20	2	0
Irwin	19	0	0	0	19	14	44	0	0
Ivyland	1	0	0	0	1	2	5	0	0
Jackson Township, Butler County	0	0	0	0	0	18	9	0	0
Jackson Township, Cambria County	2	0	0	0	2	4	5	1	0
Jamestown	0	0	0	0	0	4	8	1	0
Jeannette	7	0	0	2	5	14	63	0	1
Jefferson Hills Borough	10	0	0	2	8	21	67	3	0
Jefferson Township, Lackawanna County	5	0	1	0	4	8	9	3	0
Jefferson Township, Mercer County	2	0	0	0	2	4	11	1	0
Jefferson Township, Washington County	0	0	0	0	0	0	0	0	0

Table 8.   Offenses Known to Law Enforcement, by Selected State and City, 2013— continued

(Number.)

State/city	Violent crime	Murder and nonnegligent manslaughter	Rape (revised definition)[1]	Robbery	Aggravated assault	Burglary	Larceny-theft	Motor vehicle theft	Arson[2]
Jenkins Township	4	0	0	1	3	11	55	2	0
Jenkintown	2	0	0	0	2	5	17	0	0
Jennerstown	0	0	0	0	0	0	1	0	0
Jermyn	23	0	0	0	23	16	29	2	0
Jim Thorpe	8	0	0	1	7	11	100	2	0
Johnsonburg	8	0	0	3	5	11	40	0	1
Johnstown	129	7	2	44	76	277	497	28	7
Kenhorst	13	0	1	4	8	9	34	1	0
Kennedy Township	25	0	2	4	19	8	108	3	0
Kennett Square	11	0	1	3	7	16	72	4	0
Kidder Township	9	0	0	1	8	17	83	0	0
Kilbuck Township	0	0	0	0	0	0	6	0	0
Kingston	21	0	0	10	11	57	255	11	3
Kingston Township	10	0	0	2	8	7	43	3	1
Kittanning	7	0	0	6	1	1	18	0	1
Kline Township	0	0	0	0	0	2	27	0	0
Knox	2	0	0	0	2	3	13	0	1
Kutztown	10	0	1	6	3	24	116	8	0
Laceyville	0	0	0	0	0	0	0	0	0
Lake City	2	0	0	0	2	8	55	0	2
Lamar Township	0	0	0	0	0	5	6	0	0
Lancaster	497	5	53	249	190	441	2,165	86	19
Lancaster Township, Butler County	0	0	0	0	0	2	11	0	0
Lancaster Township, Lancaster County	20	0	5	8	7	115	365	22	1
Langhorne Manor	2	0	0	0	2	3	3	1	0
Lansdale	34	0	7	9	18	13	224	9	2
Lansdowne	33	0	4	12	17	61	175	13	2
Larksville	9	0	2	0	7	15	74	3	0
Latimore Township	0	0	0	0	0	2	18	0	0
Latrobe	27	0	1	2	24	23	167	11	2
Laureldale	6	0	1	2	3	6	21	1	0
Lawrence Park Township	6	0	0	0	6	4	29	0	0
Lawrence Township, Clearfield County	59	0	5	4	50	33	223	4	0
Lawrence Township, Tioga County	4	0	0	0	4	0	0	1	0
Lawrenceville	3	0	0	0	3	2	4	0	0
Lebanon	103	2	2	62	37	139	623	23	7
Leechburg	2	0	0	0	2	6	11	0	0
Leetsdale	6	1	0	0	5	3	39	1	0
Lehighton	11	0	0	4	7	34	118	8	2
Lehigh Township, Northampton County	5	0	1	0	4	35	103	6	1
Lehman Township	10	1	0	0	9	4	22	2	0
Lewistown	40	0	3	2	35	46	267	7	2
Liberty	1	0	0	0	1	0	15	0	0
Ligonier	5	0	0	0	5	3	14	2	0
Ligonier Township	8	0	0	1	7	4	27	1	0
Limerick Township	2	0	1	1	0	33	439	8	1
Lincoln	1	0	1	0	0	4	7	1	1
Linesville	2	0	0	0	2	2	5	0	0
Lititz	5	0	1	0	4	19	55	4	2
Little Beaver Township	0	0	0	0	0	0	0	0	0
Littlestown	9	0	0	1	8	13	75	1	0
Lock Haven	17	0	4	5	8	38	178	5	3
Locust Township	4	0	0	0	4	18	17	0	1
Logan Township	47	0	1	1	45	12	228	7	2
Loretto	0	0	0	0	0	0	0	0	0
Lower Allen Township	17	0	6	5	6	41	255	6	1
Lower Burrell	9	0	1	0	8	27	102	3	0
Lower Chichester Township	33	0	1	6	26	7	75	6	0
Lower Frederick Township	1	0	0	0	1	5	41	0	1
Lower Gwynedd Township	14	0	1	4	9	22	155	5	0
Lower Heidelberg Township	3	0	0	0	3	4	46	0	0
Lower Mahanoy Township	0	0	0	0	0	0	0	0	0
Lower Makefield Township	28	0	3	6	19	71	383	20	0
Lower Merion Township	42	0	2	25	15	257	798	35	0
Lower Milford Township	0	0	0	0	0	0	0	0	0
Lower Moreland Township	7	0	0	4	3	41	119	3	0
Lower Paxton Township	81	2	19	25	35	170	833	21	3
Lower Pottsgrove Township	25	1	2	5	17	38	256	11	0
Lower Providence Township	50	0	1	3	46	50	209	6	0
Lower Salford Township	5	0	0	0	5	17	45	1	0
Lower Saucon Township	10	1	0	0	9	20	73	2	0
Lower Southampton Township	22	1	0	9	12	58	266	11	1
Lower Swatara Township	7	1	1	2	3	14	111	4	1
Lower Windsor Township	4	0	1	0	3	11	57	10	2
Luzerne	5	0	2	0	3	15	63	2	0

Table 8.   Offenses Known to Law Enforcement, by Selected State and City, 2013— continued

(Number.)

State/city	Violent crime	Murder and nonnegligent manslaughter	Rape (revised definition)[1]	Robbery	Aggravated assault	Burglary	Larceny-theft	Motor vehicle theft	Arson[2]
Luzerne Township	1	0	0	0	1	2	27	0	0
Lykens	0	0	0	0	0	4	18	0	1
Macungie	2	0	0	0	2	4	4	1	0
Mahanoy City	10	1	2	2	5	35	94	5	2
Mahoning Township, Lawrence County	5	0	0	0	5	6	34	1	0
Main Township	0	0	0	0	0	0	0	0	0
Malvern	4	0	0	0	4	0	16	1	0
Manheim Township	26	0	5	13	8	92	721	16	3
Manor	3	0	1	0	2	9	14	1	0
Manor Township, Armstrong County	0	0	0	0	0	0	0	0	0
Manor Township, Lancaster County	11	1	2	1	7	40	200	8	1
Mansfield	1	0	0	0	1	0	4	0	0
Marcus Hook	30	0	0	0	30	3	80	3	1
Marietta	2	0	0	1	1	13	33	1	1
Marion Township, Beaver County	0	0	0	0	0	0	2	0	0
Marion Township, Berks County	0	0	0	0	0	6	4	1	0
Marlborough Township	1	0	1	0	0	4	8	1	0
Marple Township	12	0	1	5	6	34	331	7	3
Mars	1	0	1	0	0	2	10	0	0
Martinsburg	0	0	0	0	0	3	25	1	0
Masontown	4	0	0	0	4	29	67	2	0
McCandless	12	0	0	0	12	19	218	3	0
McDonald Borough	8	0	0	0	8	8	29	2	0
McKeesport	407	7	7	72	321	232	446	32	18
McKees Rocks	98	1	1	44	52	91	196	11	1
McSherrystown	1	0	0	0	1	3	12	0	0
Meadville	17	0	2	1	14	104	258	10	4
Mechanicsburg	10	0	2	6	2	24	149	2	10
Media	30	0	0	2	28	2	56	2	1
Mercer	1	0	0	1	0	7	15	0	0
Meshoppen	14	0	0	1	13	3	20	0	0
Meyersdale	0	0	0	0	0	2	4	0	0
Middleburg	1	0	0	1	0	2	40	1	1
Middlesex Township, Butler County	6	0	3	0	3	10	33	0	1
Middlesex Township, Cumberland County	9	0	1	5	3	22	169	13	0
Middletown Township	32	0	0	15	17	129	1,057	50	3
Midland	14	0	1	0	13	8	58	2	2
Midway	1	0	0	0	1	3	6	0	0
Mifflinburg	1	0	0	0	1	3	32	0	0
Mifflin County Regional	13	0	1	2	10	31	223	6	0
Milford	3	0	0	0	3	8	28	0	0
Millbourne	8	0	0	5	3	1	25	1	0
Millcreek Township, Lebanon County	2	0	1	0	1	9	41	0	1
Millersburg	3	0	0	0	3	6	44	0	0
Millersville	14	0	6	4	4	29	93	1	0
Millvale	4	0	1	3	0	18	70	0	0
Millville	0	0	0	0	0	1	6	0	0
Milton	16	0	0	2	14	19	101	1	4
Minersville	9	0	0	0	9	5	32	5	0
Mohnton	5	0	2	0	3	18	16	0	1
Monaca	10	0	0	2	8	21	110	10	0
Monessen	84	0	1	14	69	63	203	7	0
Monongahela	23	0	0	5	18	32	110	3	0
Monroeville	59	1	2	15	41	52	333	13	1
Montgomery Township	15	0	0	7	8	27	359	3	1
Montoursville	9	0	1	0	8	14	129	0	0
Montour Township	1	0	0	0	1	4	11	0	1
Montrose	7	0	1	0	6	1	9	0	0
Moon Township	14	0	2	6	6	51	229	4	0
Moore Township	4	1	0	0	3	12	60	4	0
Moosic	31	1	3	1	26	29	152	10	0
Morton	13	0	1	2	10	1	92	1	0
Moscow	4	0	0	0	4	3	14	0	0
Mount Carmel	33	0	1	2	30	32	93	1	3
Mount Carmel Township	5	0	0	0	5	3	15	3	0
Mount Gretna Borough	0	0	0	0	0	0	0	0	0
Mount Holly Springs	2	0	0	0	2	5	40	0	0
Mount Joy	10	0	1	0	9	23	123	2	0
Mount Lebanon	18	0	0	5	13	46	194	2	1
Mount Pleasant	3	0	0	1	2	8	44	1	0
Mount Pleasant Township	2	0	0	0	2	6	24	0	0
Mount Union	6	0	0	1	5	13	18	0	0
Mountville	3	0	0	2	1	9	30	0	0
Muhlenberg Township	33	0	1	21	11	70	572	24	0

Table 8.   Offenses Known to Law Enforcement, by Selected State and City, 2013— continued

(Number.)

State/city	Violent crime	Murder and nonnegligent manslaughter	Rape (revised definition)[1]	Robbery	Aggravated assault	Burglary	Larceny-theft	Motor vehicle theft	Arson[2]
Muncy	1	0	0	0	1	2	26	2	0
Muncy Township	2	0	0	0	2	4	78	0	0
Munhall	31	2	0	11	18	48	160	22	2
Murrysville	6	1	0	0	5	30	95	4	0
Myerstown	12	0	0	3	9	3	36	7	0
Nanticoke	12	0	0	7	5	72	209	9	2
Narberth	2	0	0	0	2	21	31	0	0
Nazareth	17	0	2	1	14	20	53	0	0
Nescopeck	1	0	0	0	1	9	15	1	0
Nesquehoning	11	0	1	0	10	6	70	0	1
Nether Providence Township	11	2	0	2	7	30	108	5	0
Neville Township	7	0	0	4	3	0	33	1	0
Newberry Township	9	0	2	1	6	52	212	6	1
New Bethlehem	2	0	0	0	2	1	12	0	0
New Brighton	41	0	2	16	23	59	242	1	1
New Britain	2	0	0	0	2	3	11	0	0
New Britain Township	5	0	0	3	2	10	61	2	1
New Castle	210	0	20	56	134	445	570	33	11
New Castle Township	1	0	0	0	1	0	19	0	0
New Florence	0	0	0	0	0	0	4	0	0
New Garden Township	11	0	0	5	6	26	108	9	1
New Hanover Township	4	0	0	1	3	18	61	2	0
New Holland	2	0	1	0	1	15	89	1	0
New Hope	19	0	2	0	17	13	75	1	0
New Kensington	46	0	9	18	19	51	291	17	2
New Philadelphia	3	0	0	0	3	4	0	1	0
New Sewickley Township	14	0	0	0	14	26	94	4	1
Newton Township	0	0	0	0	0	1	7	0	0
Newtown	2	0	0	0	2	3	23	0	0
Newtown Township, Bucks County	5	0	1	3	1	37	157	3	0
Newtown Township, Delaware County	6	0	0	0	6	16	104	5	0
Newville	3	0	0	0	3	10	54	0	0
Norristown	324	3	15	185	121	274	690	104	7
Northampton	7	0	3	2	2	23	125	10	2
Northampton Township	10	0	3	2	5	39	143	3	1
North Annville Township	0	0	0	0	0	2	4	0	0
North Beaver	0	0	0	0	0	1	3	1	0
North Belle Vernon	12	0	0	2	10	13	45	2	0
North Cornwall Township	9	0	1	4	4	9	187	4	0
North Coventry Township	5	1	2	0	2	24	176	5	0
Northeastern Regional	23	0	10	1	12	30	158	1	0
Northern Berks Regional	4	0	1	1	2	17	104	8	0
Northern Cambria Borough	5	0	0	1	4	15	58	3	0
Northern Lancaster County Regional	43	0	7	2	34	49	286	11	1
Northern Regional	6	1	2	0	3	19	244	5	0
Northern York Regional	73	1	5	13	54	139	802	24	12
North Franklin Township	8	0	1	6	1	18	80	9	1
North Hopewell Township	0	0	0	0	0	2	4	2	0
North Huntingdon Township	26	2	2	4	18	47	341	13	0
North Lebanon Township	22	0	0	5	17	29	326	4	0
North Londonderry Township	3	0	0	0	3	14	110	0	0
North Middleton Township	19	0	0	0	19	17	90	2	1
North Sewickley Township	11	0	0	3	8	8	45	4	1
North Strabane Township	5	0	1	0	4	24	125	4	0
Northumberland	3	0	2	0	1	11	50	3	0
North Union Township	0	0	0	0	0	0	0	0	0
North Versailles Township	34	0	1	13	20	25	131	2	0
North Wales	3	0	0	1	2	6	38	3	1
Northwest Lancaster County Regional	6	0	2	1	3	0	163	2	0
North Woodbury	0	0	0	0	0	1	11	1	0
Norwood	3	0	0	1	2	16	127	3	0
Oakland	0	0	0	0	0	0	2	1	0
Oakmont	20	0	1	2	17	17	78	1	0
O'Hara Township	0	0	0	0	0	15	55	2	0
Ohio Township	0	0	0	0	0	0	70	0	0
Oil City	13	0	3	2	8	18	133	9	1
Old Lycoming Township	5	1	0	2	2	25	97	4	0
Oley Township	0	0	0	0	0	6	10	2	0
Olyphant	3	0	0	1	2	6	20	1	1
Orwigsburg	5	0	0	0	5	4	28	2	0
Osceola Township	0	0	0	0	0	1	0	0	0
Oxford	12	0	0	2	10	24	73	8	0
Paint Township	22	0	0	0	22	29	47	3	0
Palmerton	5	0	0	0	5	18	98	4	0
Palmyra	8	0	0	3	5	18	113	3	0
Palo Alto	1	0	0	0	1	1	8	0	0

Table 8.   Offenses Known to Law Enforcement, by Selected State and City, 2013— continued

(Number.)

State/city	Violent crime	Murder and nonnegligent manslaughter	Rape (revised definition)	Robbery	Aggravated assault	Burglary	Larceny-theft	Motor vehicle theft	Arson[2]
Parkesburg	8	0	2	2	4	6	40	3	0
Parks Township	0	0	0	0	0	0	0	0	0
Patterson Township	4	0	1	1	2	22	40	3	0
Patton Township	6	0	1	4	1	16	178	1	0
Paxtang	5	0	0	4	1	6	78	2	0
Pen Argyl	13	0	0	0	13	18	38	4	0
Penbrook	6	0	0	2	4	14	36	6	0
Penn	0	0	0	0	0	1	1	0	0
Penndel	3	0	0	1	2	8	33	1	0
Penn Hills	155	3	9	45	98	273	542	46	10
Pennridge Regional	4	1	1	0	2	21	76	0	3
Penn Township, Butler County	2	0	0	0	2	2	31	2	0
Penn Township, Perry County	2	0	1	0	1	13	53	1	0
Penn Township, Westmoreland County	15	0	0	1	14	11	61	4	0
Penn Township, York County	24	0	0	3	21	17	243	4	1
Pequea Township	4	0	0	0	4	10	36	4	0
Perkasie	7	0	2	1	4	22	142	5	2
Perryopolis	3	0	1	1	1	7	9	0	0
Peters Township	9	0	1	1	7	17	97	3	0
Philadelphia	17,074	247	1,279	7,562	7,986	10,408	37,253	5,791	
Phoenixville	36	0	1	11	24	29	247	8	0
Pine Creek Township	0	0	0	0	0	3	8	0	0
Pine Grove	8	0	0	0	8	5	21	2	0
Pitcairn	35	0	1	10	24	47	101	2	0
Pittsburgh	2,259	45	78	956	1,180	2,173	7,258	616	208
Pittston	8	0	0	1	7	37	178	2	0
Plains Township	9	0	0	4	5	46	255	8	0
Pleasant Hills	1	0	0	0	1	13	97	5	0
Plymouth Township, Montgomery County	29	0	3	18	8	73	551	25	3
Pocono Mountain Regional	68	4	13	16	35	414	542	21	7
Pocono Township	11	0	0	1	10	47	192	8	0
Point Township	11	0	0	0	11	7	39	0	1
Portage	2	0	0	1	1	4	35	0	0
Portersville	0	0	0	0	0	0	0	0	0
Portland	0	0	0	0	0	0	0	0	0
Port Vue	5	1	0	0	4	7	29	0	0
Pottstown	170	2	37	63	68	219	959	42	7
Pottsville	37	1	3	10	23	53	223	15	3
Pringle	1	0	0	1	0	3	49	4	0
Prospect	0	0	0	0	0	0	0	0	0
Pulaski Township, Lawrence County	9	0	0	0	9	8	23	3	0
Punxsutawney	6	0	3	2	1	17	91	3	0
Pymatuning Township	6	0	1	0	5	43	65	11	1
Quakertown	21	0	1	1	19	31	216	6	0
Quarryville	9	0	1	1	7	7	59	0	0
Raccoon Township	2	0	0	0	2	3	12	0	0
Radnor Township	29	0	1	4	24	37	287	7	0
Rankin	22	0	0	4	18	7	11	1	2
Reading	743	11	50	328	354	1,040	1,465	294	27
Reading Township	5	0	0	0	5	4	19	0	0
Redstone Township	2	0	0	0	2	6	11	0	0
Reserve Township	2	1	0	0	1	13	47	4	3
Rice Township	1	0	0	0	1	14	23	1	0
Richland Township, Bucks County	6	0	3	1	2	28	305	6	2
Richland Township, Cambria County	16	1	1	9	5	27	610	10	0
Ridgway	1	0	0	0	1	12	76	3	1
Ridley Park	13	0	1	1	11	17	79	7	0
Ridley Township	51	0	3	17	31	51	462	43	1
Ringtown	0	0	0	0	0	2	1	0	0
Riverside	0	0	0	0	0	3	27	0	0
Roaring Brook Township	0	0	0	0	0	2	7	1	0
Roaring Spring	1	0	0	0	1	4	44	1	0
Robeson Township	6	0	0	0	6	26	49	4	0
Robinson Township, Allegheny County	26	0	1	4	21	21	325	6	0
Robinson Township, Washington County	2	0	0	0	2	7	12	1	0
Rochester	69	0	6	10	53	46	231	18	0
Rochester Township	10	0	0	1	9	2	37	3	0
Rockledge	6	0	0	1	5	2	41	1	0
Roseto	2	0	0	0	2	4	28	2	0
Ross Township	39	0	0	12	27	57	675	8	0
Royalton	0	0	0	0	0	0	0	0	0
Royersford	20	0	2	2	16	10	59	1	1
Rural Valley	0	0	0	0	0	0	0	0	0
Rush Township	4	0	3	0	1	19	106	0	0

Table 8.   Offenses Known to Law Enforcement, by Selected State and City, 2013— continued

(Number.)

State/city	Violent crime	Murder and nonnegligent manslaughter	Rape (revised definition)	Robbery	Aggravated assault	Burglary	Larceny-theft	Motor vehicle theft	Arson[2]
Ryan Township	0	0	0	0	0	2	4	0	0
Sadsbury Township, Chester County	0	0	0	0	0	5	19	2	0
Salem Township, Luzerne County	5	0	0	0	5	15	38	1	1
Salisbury Township	8	0	1	2	5	46	248	10	0
Saltsburg	0	0	0	0	0	3	14	0	0
Sandy Lake	1	0	0	0	1	0	2	0	0
Sandy Township	22	0	1	6	15	36	301	3	0
Sankertown	0	0	0	0	0	0	0	0	0
Sayre	9	0	3	0	6	26	125	2	0
Schuylkill Township, Chester County	4	0	0	0	4	13	57	0	0
Scottdale	27	0	5	0	22	8	84	2	0
Scott Township, Allegheny County	10	0	2	5	3	16	145	4	1
Scranton	166	2	18	71	75	549	1,614	114	24
Selinsgrove	79	0	1	4	74	45	136	2	1
Seward	0	0	0	0	0	1	1	0	0
Sewickley	3	0	0	1	2	6	75	1	0
Sewickley Heights	0	0	0	0	0	1	3	0	0
Shade Township	0	0	0	0	0	11	21	0	0
Shaler Township	12	1	0	5	6	66	245	3	0
Shamokin	4	0	0	1	3	9	26	1	2
Sharon Hill	61	0	2	11	48	22	164	11	0
Sharpsburg	15	0	1	1	13	17	55	2	0
Sharpsville	18	0	0	1	17	9	49	5	0
Shenandoah	17	0	0	6	11	39	136	4	3
Shillington	2	0	0	0	2	23	40	2	0
Shinglehouse	1	0	0	0	1	1	0	0	0
Shippensburg	4	1	2	1	0	6	88	0	3
Shippingport	2	0	0	0	2	0	0	0	0
Shohola Township	1	0	0	0	1	8	7	1	0
Silver Lake Township	3	0	0	0	3	7	4	1	0
Silver Spring Township	3	0	0	2	1	10	143	0	0
Sinking Spring	0	0	0	0	0	15	47	1	0
Slatington	4	0	0	1	3	15	90	4	0
Slippery Rock	7	0	0	1	6	4	33	0	0
Smethport	3	0	0	0	3	7	11	1	0
Smithton Borough	0	0	0	0	0	0	2	0	0
Solebury Township	3	0	1	1	1	20	61	1	0
Somerset	7	0	0	0	7	29	139	3	0
Souderton	18	0	1	4	13	23	78	7	1
South Abington Township	10	1	0	1	8	12	68	3	1
South Buffalo Township	1	0	0	0	1	1	15	2	0
South Centre Township	2	0	0	0	2	1	5	0	1
South Coatesville	1	0	0	0	1	0	0	0	0
South Connellsville Borough	3	0	0	0	3	1	24	0	0
Southern Regional, Lancaster County	5	0	0	1	4	8	17	0	1
Southern Regional, York County	5	0	0	1	4	27	109	2	1
South Fayette Township	5	0	1	2	2	12	64	4	1
South Greensburg	3	0	0	1	2	4	18	2	0
South Heidelberg Township	6	0	0	0	6	8	56	2	0
South Lebanon Township	7	0	0	1	6	16	104	0	1
South Londonderry Township	2	0	0	2	0	4	47	0	0
South Park Township	8	0	0	2	6	14	23	2	0
South Pymatuning Township	1	0	1	0	0	9	16	1	0
South Strabane Township	22	2	3	9	8	25	489	7	0
Southwestern Regional	12	0	1	0	11	18	99	2	0
Southwest Greensburg	7	0	0	1	6	6	18	2	0
Southwest Regional, Fayette County	10	0	0	0	10	13	27	0	0
Southwest Regional, Washington County	0	0	0	0	0	2	9	0	0
South Whitehall Township	13	0	1	2	10	88	582	13	5
South Williamsport	6	0	1	3	2	20	96	1	0
Spring City	6	0	2	0	4	9	77	1	0
Springettsbury Township	30	0	3	16	11	34	846	12	2
Springfield Township, Delaware County	10	0	1	4	5	43	579	27	0
Springfield Township, Montgomery County	13	0	0	1	12	43	154	7	0
Spring Garden Township	28	0	1	11	16	62	247	11	1
Spring Township, Berks County	19	0	1	5	13	25	245	8	3
Spring Township, Centre County	0	0	0	0	0	7	58	0	0
State College	41	0	5	13	23	101	596	10	11
St. Clair Boro	2	0	0	0	2	2	65	0	0
Steelton	26	0	2	11	13	47	145	7	1
St. Marys City	10	1	3	0	6	31	171	3	2
Stoneboro	1	0	0	0	1	1	5	0	0
Stowe Township	13	0	0	3	10	39	171	7	0

Table 8.   Offenses Known to Law Enforcement, by Selected State and City, 2013— continued

(Number.)

State/city	Violent crime	Murder and nonnegligent manslaughter	Rape (revised definition)[1]	Robbery	Aggravated assault	Burglary	Larceny-theft	Motor vehicle theft	Arson[2]
Strasburg	1	0	0	0	1	7	25	1	0
Stroud Area Regional	72	0	17	17	38	115	1,120	23	3
Sugarcreek	4	0	1	1	2	9	69	0	0
Sugarloaf Township, Luzerne County	1	0	0	0	1	5	12	0	0
Summerhill Township	1	0	1	0	0	5	21	1	0
Summit Hill	2	0	0	1	1	2	7	0	0
Summit Township	0	0	0	0	0	0	3	0	0
Susquehanna	2	0	0	0	2	3	10	0	0
Susquehanna Regional	8	0	3	0	5	23	62	0	1
Susquehanna Township, Dauphin County	46	1	4	18	23	68	284	17	0
Swatara Township	63	0	2	27	34	96	760	10	8
Swissvale	90	1	0	17	72	50	171	20	2
Swoyersville	7	0	1	1	5	29	56	1	0
Sykesville	0	0	0	0	0	0	0	0	0
Tamaqua	12	0	1	4	7	40	191	6	3
Tarentum	11	0	1	2	8	13	81	3	0
Tatamy	0	0	0	0	0	2	4	1	0
Taylor	15	0	0	4	11	19	246	9	0
Telford	14	0	6	0	8	1	36	0	0
Terre Hill	0	0	0	0	0	9	9	0	0
Throop	16	0	0	0	16	10	29	1	0
Tiadaghton Valley Regional	10	0	3	1	6	14	138	2	0
Tidioute	0	0	0	0	0	0	4	0	0
Tinicum Township, Bucks County	1	0	1	0	0	5	15	0	0
Tinicum Township, Delaware County	17	0	2	5	10	8	130	8	1
Titusville	7	0	0	3	4	16	121	0	0
Towamencin Township	14	0	1	1	12	29	94	4	2
Towanda	17	0	1	0	16	9	80	3	0
Tower City	1	0	0	0	1	0	1	0	0
Trafford	6	0	1	0	5	14	32	6	0
Trainer	21	0	1	3	17	17	58	3	1
Tredyffrin Township	16	0	3	4	9	56	164	4	0
Troy	1	0	0	0	1	9	13	0	0
Tulpehocken Township	0	0	0	0	0	3	7	0	0
Tunkhannock Township, Wyoming County	2	0	1	1	0	7	61	0	0
Turtle Creek	10	0	0	0	10	5	4	0	0
Tyrone	21	0	3	2	16	11	131	2	1
Union City	1	0	0	0	1	8	102	0	0
Uniontown	47	2	3	23	19	113	322	11	0
Union Township, Lawerence County	7	0	0	1	6	2	244	2	0
Upland	37	0	3	7	27	38	69	10	1
Upper Burrell Township	0	0	0	0	0	10	19	1	0
Upper Chichester Township	38	1	2	10	25	86	373	23	3
Upper Darby Township	450	2	20	227	201	225	1,487	140	10
Upper Dublin Township	14	0	4	4	6	25	198	11	1
Upper Gwynedd Township	11	0	4	0	7	18	61	3	1
Upper Leacock Township	2	1	0	0	1	31	94	9	0
Upper Macungine Township	10	0	2	3	5	40	262	9	1
Upper Makefield Township	3	0	0	0	3	15	42	0	0
Upper Merion Township	21	0	2	14	5	69	1,063	25	1
Upper Moreland Township	19	2	1	12	4	56	392	9	3
Upper Nazareth Township	8	0	0	0	8	5	41	0	0
Upper Perkiomen	15	0	6	2	7	21	82	8	3
Upper Pottsgrove Township	11	0	0	0	11	13	40	6	0
Upper Providence Township, Delaware County	2	0	0	0	2	10	14	1	0
Upper Providence Township, Montgomery County	9	0	0	4	5	40	240	9	0
Upper Saucon Township	4	0	2	0	2	28	168	4	0
Upper Southampton Township	8	0	0	1	7	36	160	4	0
Upper St Clair Township	5	0	0	0	5	10	108	3	0
Upper Uwchlan Township	1	0	1	0	0	10	46	1	0
Upper Yoder Township	5	0	0	0	5	5	16	0	0
Uwchlan Township	14	0	2	3	9	30	175	5	5
Valley Township	3	0	0	0	3	24	81	13	0
Vandergrft	17	0	1	2	14	4	6	1	0
Vandling	1	0	0	0	1	0	1	0	0
Vernon Township	4	0	0	0	4	4	75	0	0
Vintondale	0	0	0	0	0	0	0	0	0
Walker Township	1	0	0	0	1	0	2	0	0
Walnutport	0	0	0	0	0	0	0	0	0
Wampum	0	0	0	0	0	0	10	0	0
Warminster Township	21	1	4	9	7	50	491	14	3
Warren	46	0	5	2	39	22	196	8	2
Warrington Township	18	0	3	8	7	36	237	10	0
Warwick Township, Bucks County	19	0	4	3	12	20	112	0	1

Table 8.   Offenses Known to Law Enforcement, by Selected State and City, 2013— continued

(Number.)

State/city	Violent crime	Murder and nonnegligent manslaughter	Rape (revised definition)[1]	Robbery	Aggravated assault	Burglary	Larceny-theft	Motor vehicle theft	Arson[2]
Washington, Washington County	67	1	10	30	26	116	455	29	9
Washington Township, Fayette County	4	0	0	0	4	9	46	0	0
Washington Township, Franklin County	3	0	0	1	2	17	219	4	2
Washington Township, North-ampton County	0	0	0	0	0	21	42	1	0
Washington Township, West-moreland County	10	0	0	0	10	7	31	1	0
Watsontown	1	0	1	0	0	3	33	1	2
Waynesboro	24	1	3	11	9	40	199	3	4
Wayne Township, Lawrence County	0	0	0	0	0	4	11	1	1
Wellsboro	6	0	0	0	6	3	28	0	0
Wesleyville	3	0	1	0	2	10	83	2	1
West Brandywine Township	7	0	0	2	5	25	70	10	0
West Brownsville	0	0	0	0	0	0	23	0	0
West Caln Township	13	0	1	1	11	15	47	5	0
West Carroll Township	0	0	0	0	0	4	3	1	0
West Chester	71	1	14	28	28	90	305	21	0
West Cocalico Township	4	0	2	1	1	15	37	3	0
West Conshohocken	2	0	0	0	2	2	23	0	0
West Cornwall Township	1	0	0	1	0	0	4	0	0
West Deer Township	2	0	2	0	0	34	70	13	0
West Earl Township	6	0	3	1	2	21	42	0	0
Western Berks Regional	1	0	0	0	1	13	43	2	0
West Fallowfield Township	0	0	0	0	0	8	13	0	0
West Goshen Township	13	0	4	0	9	24	338	8	0
West Grove Borough	3	0	0	0	3	2	8	2	0
West Hempfield Township	12	0	2	2	8	27	237	5	4
West Hills Regional	5	0	0	2	3	38	52	2	1
West Homestead	12	0	0	1	11	8	19	0	0
West Kittanning	0	0	0	0	0	0	1	0	0
West Lampeter Township	4	0	0	2	2	26	130	3	0
West Lebanon Township	2	0	0	0	2	6	66	1	0
West Leechburg	0	0	0	0	0	4	5	0	0
West Mahanoy Township	0	0	0	0	0	2	21	2	1
West Manchester Township	29	0	2	6	21	40	473	12	3
West Manheim Township	10	0	1	1	8	14	48	0	0
West Mead Township	1	0	0	0	1	5	4	0	1
West Mifflin	57	1	5	19	32	87	424	16	1
West Newton	7	0	1	2	4	7	57	1	0
West Norriton Township	43	0	2	13	28	31	369	9	0
West Nottingham Township	1	0	0	1	0	3	12	1	0
West Pikeland Township	2	0	0	0	2	6	19	1	0
West Pittston	5	0	0	1	4	11	116	2	0
West Pottsgrove Township	17	0	2	10	5	11	137	3	0
West Reading	29	0	5	8	16	16	161	5	1
West Sadsbury Township	2	0	0	0	2	2	98	0	0
West Salem Township	22	0	4	2	16	35	56	4	0
Westtown-East Goshen Regional	24	0	1	2	21	25	247	8	2
West View	6	0	1	0	5	11	152	7	0
West Vincent Township	1	0	0	0	1	5	39	0	0
West Whiteland Township	8	0	1	6	1	38	441	11	0
West York	23	2	2	0	19	20	179	7	3
Whitaker Borough	0	0	0	0	0	6	12	2	0
Whitehall	11	0	0	0	11	11	37	2	0
Whitehall Township	30	1	6	16	7	157	1,171	42	3
Whitemarsh Township	12	0	1	1	10	25	159	7	1
White Oak	7	0	1	4	2	16	57	4	0
Whitpain Township	17	0	0	5	12	42	222	2	0
Wiconisco Township	1	0	0	0	1	1	4	0	0
Wilkes-Barre	208	12	30	110	56	317	969	103	6
Wilkes-Barre Township	21	0	0	12	9	16	738	10	0
Wilkins Township	6	0	0	2	4	18	96	9	1
Williamsburg	0	0	0	0	0	1	13	0	0
Williamsport	110	5	10	47	48	228	902	28	12
Willistown Township	5	0	0	2	3	10	54	1	1
Wilson	37	0	4	12	21	56	282	5	1
Wind Gap	3	0	1	0	2	4	35	4	0
Womelsdorf	2	0	0	0	2	6	27	8	0
Woodward Township	1	0	0	0	1	11	15	0	1
Wrightsville	2	0	0	0	2	5	62	0	0
Wright Township	1	0	0	0	1	7	47	4	0
Wyoming	3	0	0	1	2	15	93	3	1
Wyomissing	10	0	0	6	4	12	465	7	1
Yardley	5	0	1	2	2	3	24	1	0
Yeadon	78	0	3	40	35	72	273	32	2
York	348	12	33	174	129	486	905	90	21
York Area Regional	136	0	8	19	109	135	552	24	5

Table 8.   Offenses Known to Law Enforcement, by Selected State and City, 2013— continued

(Number.)

State/city	Violent crime	Murder and nonnegligent manslaughter	Rape (revised definition)[1]	Robbery	Aggravated assault	Burglary	Larceny-theft	Motor vehicle theft	Arson[2]
Youngsville	15	0	0	0	15	4	8	0	0
Zelienople	4	0	0	0	4	2	51	3	0
Zerbe Township	0	0	0	0	0	3	14	0	0
Rhode Island									
Barrington	3	0	1	1	1	49	162	3	1
Bristol	11	0	6	2	3	34	262	7	2
Burrillville	20	0	7	0	13	33	103	7	4
Central Falls	131	2	9	34	86	226	357	85	12
Charlestown	8	0	2	2	4	21	86	1	0
Coventry	31	0	8	2	21	99	383	14	7
Cranston	151	0	29	42	80	309	1,306	140	9
Cumberland	36	1	3	10	22	92	322	22	4
East Greenwich	6	0	1	3	2	35	132	2	1
East Providence	60	0	12	16	32	140	531	54	3
Foster	3	0	0	0	3	19	16	3	0
Glocester	3	0	1	0	2	19	29	1	0
Hopkinton	5	0	2	0	3	22	84	3	3
Jamestown	1	0	1	0	0	5	50	0	0
Johnston	26	2	8	4	12	119	399	46	7
Lincoln	22	0	2	7	13	84	335	42	2
Little Compton	0	0	0	0	0	7	18	1	0
Middletown	14	0	8	0	6	46	237	11	2
Narragansett	11	1	3	1	6	47	164	10	1
Newport	111	0	19	12	80	177	779	34	17
New Shoreham	3	0		0	3	6	14	1	0
North Kingstown	25	0	3	4	18	60	304	18	5
North Providence	47	2	10	7	28	153	338	54	2
North Smithfield	14	0	3	3	8	24	158	4	0
Pawtucket	279	5	44	71	159	619	1,356	347	15
Portsmouth	9	1	1	0	7	49	157	4	1
Providence	1,115	12	97	365	641	1,828	5,184	962	22
Richmond	5	0	1	1	3	9	45	4	0
Scituate	3	0	1	0	2	34	37	3	1
Smithfield	16	0	0	2	14	50	155	13	3
South Kingstown	21	0	7	2	12	77	210	10	1
Tiverton	21	0	5	5	11	92	174	16	0
Warren	12	0	3	4	5	50	216	14	2
Warwick	93	4	35	15	39	282	1,648	85	9
Westerly	24	0	9	2	13	74	452	12	1
West Greenwich	7	0	3	1	3	28	50	4	2
West Warwick	54	0	23	12	19	128	330	24	13
Woonsocket	241	1	41	48	151	361	777	87	15
South Carolina									
Abbeville	40	1	1	3	35	72	135	8	1
Aiken	96	1	8	32	55	215	1,206	58	4
Allendale	49	2	3	5	39	79	64	7	1
Anderson	278	2	21	43	212	510	1,767	140	10
Andrews	26	1	3	8	14	51	134	8	0
Aynor	1	0	0	0	1	0	6	1	0
Bamberg	23	0	3	2	18	28	101	5	0
Barnwell	45	2	2	12	29	124	237	4	1
Batesburg-Leesville	50	0	7	5	38	52	200	13	2
Beaufort	153	0	6	28	119	126	659	19	1
Belton	33	1	7	3	22	46	152	21	1
Bennettsville	115	1	5	11	98	95	354	5	4
Bishopville	58	1	3	4	50	43	185	14	0
Blacksburg	10	0	1	3	6	12	79	4	0
Blackville	16	1	0	1	14	25	56	8	0
Bluffton	49	0	2	13	34	61	300	18	4
Burnettown	10	0	0	0	10	7	23	4	0
Camden	97	0	6	15	76	92	356	15	1
Central	7	0	2	2	3	29	141	9	1
Chapin	9	0	0	0	9	6	29	1	0
Charleston	231	7	29	72	123	305	2,725	162	2
Cheraw	51	1	1	11	38	49	305	11	0
Chesnee	10	0	0	2	8	17	39	1	0
Chester	69	0	3	10	56	95	262	12	1
Chesterfield	7	0	0	1	6	8	42	0	0
Clemson	21	0	3	9	9	141	303	50	1
Clinton	53	1	6	7	39	84	346	13	0
Clover	148	0	1	1	146	43	101	6	0
Columbia	952	8	58	331	555	1,398	5,800	791	9
Conway	113	3	11	19	80	111	727	42	2
Cottageville	0	0	0	0	0	4	9	1	0
Coward	0	0	0	0	0	7	11	1	0
Cowpens	5	0	2	2	1	12	44	4	0

Table 8.   Offenses Known to Law Enforcement, by Selected State and City, 2013— continued

(Number.)

State/city	Violent crime	Murder and nonnegligent manslaughter	Rape (revised definition)[1]	Robbery	Aggravated assault	Burglary	Larceny-theft	Motor vehicle theft	Arson[2]
Darlington	48	0	3	6	39	50	396	13	2
Denmark	24	3	1	9	11	72	108	13	2
Dillon	107	0	17	15	75	162	651	31	4
Due West	0	0	0	0	0	1	8	1	0
Duncan	4	0	1	0	3	11	66	5	0
Easley	75	1	4	10	60	165	1,066	60	1
Edgefield	11	0	0	0	11	12	31	4	0
Edisto Beach	0	0	0	0	0	7	58	1	1
Ehrhardt	5	0	0	1	4	11	23	0	0
Elgin	15	0	2	7	6	13	63	4	0
Estill	31	2	2	7	20	45	51	1	1
Florence	293	2	29	69	193	456	2,376	104	6
Folly Beach	16	0	1	1	14	27	114	7	1
Forest Acres	72	0	5	17	50	133	446	24	0
Fort Lawn	3	0	0	1	2	7	24	1	0
Fort Mill	23	3	3	2	15	30	170	2	0
Fountain Inn	41	1	3	2	35	28	108	9	1
Gaffney	66	1	12	13	40	75	275	27	2
Gaston	5	0	1	2	2	13	67	9	0
Georgetown	111	1	6	20	84	101	395	18	2
Goose Creek	85	1	8	14	62	189	724	49	4
Great Falls	10	0	3	0	7	24	87	5	0
Greenville	455	3	35	118	299	666	2,384	211	6
Greenwood	300	9	29	31	231	336	1,127	30	7
Greer	125	0	17	19	89	140	578	50	2
Hampton	10	0	1	3	6	52	104	6	0
Hanahan	32	0	2	10	20	70	342	30	0
Hardeeville	36	0	5	8	23	51	179	16	0
Harleyville	8	0	0	0	8	24	22	3	0
Hartsville	87	2	6	18	61	120	639	33	1
Hemingway	5	0	0	2	3	9	22	0	0
Holly Hill	16	0	0	8	8	22	95	12	0
Honea Path	12	2	2	2	6	53	95	8	3
Inman	10	0	2	3	5	18	50	2	0
Irmo	53	0	0	5	48	70	256	14	1
Isle of Palms	2	0	0	0	2	28	107	5	0
Jackson	0	0	0	0	0	21	19	2	0
Johnsonville	3	0	0	2	1	8	20	1	0
Johnston	21	1	5	2	13	20	44	5	0
Kingstree	41	0	4	11	26	59	224	16	0
Lake City	68	0	9	10	49	149	420	20	1
Lake View	4	0	0	3	1	7	35	0	0
Lamar	5	0	1	1	3	7	28	1	0
Lancaster	109	2	5	18	84	153	453	13	3
Landrum	6	0	1	1	4	13	49	2	0
Latta	37	0	0	4	33	16	76	5	2
Laurens	90	0	7	16	67	72	515	14	1
Lexington	45	0	3	3	39	60	624	13	2
Liberty	9	0	1	1	7	37	79	9	0
Loris	19	0	2	2	15	24	116	4	1
Lyman	3	0	1	0	2	17	126	0	0
Lynchburg	3	0	0	1	2	6	13	0	0
Manning	58	0	0	9	49	62	335	16	0
Marion	91	2	8	22	59	168	401	26	1
Mauldin	40	0	10	8	22	75	302	33	3
McBee	1	0	0	0	1	13	22	0	0
McColl	19	0	0	3	16	20	40	1	0
McCormick	9	0	1	2	6	19	52	7	0
Moncks Corner	38	12	1	6	19	92	415	35	0
Mount Pleasant	117	0	11	16	90	169	1,195	64	7
Mullins	64	0	1	12	51	185	252	10	4
Myrtle Beach	475	2	49	186	238	608	3,497	470	18
Newberry	68	0	3	6	59	84	401	8	0
New Ellenton	8	0	1	3	4	37	44	2	0
Nichols	1	0	0	0	1	8	9	0	0
North	2	0	0	2	0	13	24	0	0
North Augusta	41	1	8	18	14	102	701	26	4
North Charleston	693	13	56	196	428	892	4,409	503	21
North Myrtle Beach	120	0	14	20	86	279	1,153	136	4
Orangeburg	99	1	5	30	63	207	598	50	1
Pacolet	9	0	2	1	6	37	73	6	0
Pageland	26	0	2	5	19	27	133	9	0
Pelion	5	0	1	1	3	2	28	1	0
Pickens	13	0	3	1	9	33	163	14	0
Port Royal	14	0	3	5	6	74	207	13	0
Prosperity	1	0	1	0	0	5	20	0	0
Ridgeland	15	3	1	8	3	35	108	7	1
Rock Hill	372	4	49	78	241	396	2,066	121	12

Table 8.   Offenses Known to Law Enforcement, by Selected State and City, 2013— continued

(Number.)

State/city	Violent crime	Murder and nonnegligent manslaughter	Rape (revised definition)[1]	Robbery	Aggravated assault	Burglary	Larceny-theft	Motor vehicle theft	Arson[2]
Salley	0	0	0	0	0	2	1	2	1
Saluda	22	0	1	2	19	20	63	3	0
Santee	13	0	2	5	6	30	96	8	0
Scranton	0	0	0	0	0	1	14	0	0
Seneca	60	0	11	6	43	55	195	11	0
Spartanburg	527	3	24	130	370	490	2,060	118	13
Springdale	9	0	1	2	6	14	95	16	1
St. George	15	1	0	3	11	18	104	9	0
St. Matthews	13	0	1	2	10	17	51	9	1
Sullivans Island	2	0	0	0	2	9	47	1	0
Summerton	10	5	0	0	5	16	34	2	0
Summerville	104	0	13	26	65	217	1,239	87	2
Sumter	387	2	13	72	300	637	1,249	128	18
Surfside Beach	19	0	2	4	13	68	174	18	2
Swansea	16	0	1	1	14	16	32	3	0
Tega Cay	2	0	0	0	2	10	115	1	0
Travelers Rest	9	0	0	1	8	19	280	10	1
Turbeville	2	1	0	0	1	7	20	1	0
Union	77	0	3	11	63	95	272	6	1
Wagener	2	0	1	1	0	18	24	4	0
Walhalla	23	0	3	1	19	33	66	4	0
Walterboro	46	1	5	11	29	63	471	14	1
Ware Shoals	25	0	7	6	12	42	108	10	1
Wellford	3	0	0	0	3	8	17	5	0
West Columbia	111	1	12	23	75	106	625	40	1
Westminster	12	0	1	1	10	17	81	5	1
West Pelzer	2	0	0	0	2	11	106	7	0
West Union	2	0	2	0	0	6	34	2	0
Whitmire	6	1	0	0	5	12	37	1	1
Williamston	23	0	2	1	20	31	140	10	0
Williston	16	0	0	2	14	39	67	6	0
Winnsboro	14	0	4	2	8	22	181	6	0
Woodruff	25	0	1	3	21	18	74	5	0
York	63	0	12	6	45	50	280	11	2
South Dakota									
Aberdeen	74	0	14	4	56	143	482	16	3
Avon	0	0	0	0	0	0	0	0	0
Belle Fourche	14	0	9	0	5	20	65	3	1
Beresford	3	0	1	1	1	2	8	3	0
Box Elder	30	0	10	0	20	77	96	9	2
Brandon	1	0	0	0	1	5	37	0	0
Brookings	9	0	1	0	8	9	62	6	0
Burke	0	0	0	0	0	0	0	0	0
Canton	2	0	0	0	2	4	14	1	0
Centerville	0	0	0	0	0	3	2	0	0
Chamberlain	18	0	2	0	16	15	76	4	0
Clark	2	0	0	0	2	5	3	0	0
Deadwood	1	0	0	1	0	2	39	3	0
Eagle Butte	0	0	0	0	0	4	3	1	1
Estelline	0	0	0	0	0	1	2	0	0
Faith	0	0	0	0	0	0	0	0	0
Flandreau	12	0	2	0	10	5	22	2	0
Freeman	0	0	0	0	0	0	0	1	0
Gettysburg	0	0	0	0	0	0	3	1	0
Hermosa	0	0	0	0	0	0	0	0	0
Hot Springs	7	0	3	0	4	2	14	6	0
Hoven	0	0	0	0	0	0	0	0	0
Huron	55	0	17	1	37	44	277	11	1
Irene	0	0	0	0	0	0	0	0	0
Jefferson	0	0	0	0	0	0	0	0	0
Kadoka	0	0	0	0	0	0	2	0	0
Kimball	0	0	0	0	0	2	1	0	0
Lead	4	0	0	0	4	1	44	3	0
Lennox	2	0	0	0	2	0	8	1	0
Leola	0	0	0	0	0	0	0	0	0
Madison	4	0	0	0	4	13	49	2	0
Martin	13	0	2	0	11	5	20	2	1
Menno	0	0	0	0	0	1	0	0	0
Miller	0	0	0	0	0	4	7	1	0
Mitchell	63	0	9	2	52	62	395	22	4
Mobridge	6	0	0	0	6	3	50	2	1
North Sioux City	0	0	0	0	0	4	37	1	0
Parkston	0	0	0	0	0	1	2	1	0
Philip	0	0	0	0	0	0	0	0	0
Pierre	31	0	13	2	16	43	357	12	0
Rapid City	398	2	63	48	285	578	1,902	149	18
Rosholt	0	0	0	0	0	0	0	0	0

Table 8. Offenses Known to Law Enforcement, by Selected State and City, 2013— continued

(Number.)

State/city	Violent crime	Murder and nonnegligent manslaughter	Rape (revised definition)[1]	Robbery	Aggravated assault	Burglary	Larceny-theft	Motor vehicle theft	Arson[2]
Scotland	0	0	0	0	0	0	0	0	0
Selby	0	0	0	0	0	2	4	0	0
Sioux Falls	636	3	138	67	428	870	3,796	264	27
Sisseton	19	0	2	2	15	11	32	3	0
Spearfish	8	0	4	0	4	48	170	13	1
Springfield	0	0	0	0	0	0	0	0	0
Sturgis	10	0	4	0	6	26	137	9	1
Summerset	1	0	0	0	1	0	0	0	0
Tea	3	0	0	0	3	9	63	6	0
Tripp	0	0	0	0	0	0	0	0	0
Tyndall	0	0	0	0	0	0	0	0	0
Vermillion	31	0	5	0	26	20	202	2	0
Viborg	0	0	0	0	0	1	0	0	0
Wagner	2	0	0	0	2	0	38	1	0
Watertown	59	1	16	3	39	108	445	30	1
Whitewood	0	0	0	0	0	0	0	0	0
Winner	6	0	2	0	4	2	12	2	0
Worthing	0	0	0	0	0	0	0	0	0
Yankton	48	0	20	2	26	57	315	15	0
Tennessee									
Adamsville	4	0	1	0	3	13	40	3	0
Alamo	10	0	2	1	7	15	53	3	0
Alcoa	61	2	4	12	43	73	350	22	2
Alexandria	2	0	0	0	2	2	9	1	0
Algood	13	0	2	0	11	20	122	2	2
Ardmore	7	0	1	0	6	3	19	2	0
Ashland City	20	0	4	2	14	27	163	10	0
Athens	161	0	13	20	128	215	840	50	2
Atoka	11	0	2	0	9	28	93	3	1
Baileyton	2	0	0	1	1	0	13	0	0
Baneberry	0	0	0	0	0	1	0	0	0
Bartlett	106	0	13	13	80	168	887	56	1
Baxter	3	0	0	0	3	11	40	1	0
Bean Station	16	2	0	4	10	24	82	6	0
Belle Meade	1	0	0	1	0	18	17	1	0
Bells	18	0	1	2	15	14	37	2	0
Benton	2	0	1	0	1	2	32	2	0
Berry Hill	3	0	0	0	3	5	36	1	0
Big Sandy	2	0	0	0	2	0	2	0	0
Blaine	0	0	0	0	0	6	6	0	0
Bluff City	5	0	0	0	5	12	38	1	0
Bolivar	35	1	0	2	32	54	195	14	0
Bradford	5	0	0	0	5	4	8	0	0
Brentwood	20	1	3	4	12	65	370	11	0
Brighton	10	0	0	0	10	9	26	4	0
Bristol	96	1	10	8	77	186	888	50	4
Brownsville	143	1	5	10	127	137	302	7	2
Bruceton	1	0	0	0	1	7	15	2	1
Burns	3	0	2	1	0	6	32	1	0
Calhoun	0	0	0	0	0	2	7	2	0
Camden	5	0	0	1	4	37	93	2	0
Carthage	6	0	0	1	5	14	29	3	0
Caryville	10	0	0	3	7	11	38	6	2
Celina	1	0	0	0	1	6	30	1	0
Centerville	9	0	0	2	7	21	48	1	0
Chapel Hill	6	0	0	0	6	3	14	3	0
Charleston	1	0	0	0	1	6	11	0	0
Chattanooga	1,692	18	64	385	1,225	2,317	8,165	986	14
Church Hill	16	0	2	1	13	23	92	2	0
Clarksburg	0	0	0	0	0	0	2	0	0
Clarksville	748	6	84	115	543	1,020	2,965	156	28
Cleveland	339	1	27	32	279	414	1,912	114	8
Clifton	1	0	0	0	1	6	2	0	0
Clinton	39	0	1	8	30	35	280	12	1
Collegedale	16	0	0	2	14	23	131	3	0
Collinwood	0	0	0	0	0	0	5	0	1
Columbia	276	0	14	38	224	302	1,084	49	8
Cookeville	143	0	16	24	103	293	1,237	65	2
Coopertown	2	0	0	0	2	16	25	4	1
Copperhill	0	0	0	0	0	1	1	0	0
Cornersville	2	0	0	0	2	5	9	1	0
Covington	114	0	8	11	95	120	420	38	1
Cowan	5	0	0	0	5	7	19	0	1
Cross Plains	5	0	0	0	5	9	26	5	0
Crossville	142	0	11	13	118	261	858	63	0
Crump	3	0	1	0	2	11	20	2	0
Cumberland City	3	0	0	0	3	8	5	0	0

Table 8.   Offenses Known to Law Enforcement, by Selected State and City, 2013— continued

(Number.)

State/city	Violent crime	Murder and nonnegligent manslaughter	Rape (revised definition)[1]	Robbery	Aggravated assault	Burglary	Larceny-theft	Motor vehicle theft	Arson[2]
Dandridge	5	0	1	1	3	15	50	4	2
Dayton	16	0	1	3	12	51	207	13	0
Decatur	3	0	0	2	1	0	44	5	0
Decaturville	2	0	0	0	2	5	8	1	0
Decherd	6	0	1	0	5	10	48	3	0
Dickson	55	1	6	8	40	120	657	31	0
Dover	3	0	0	0	3	2	15	1	0
Dresden	4	0	0	0	4	15	47	3	0
Dunlap	24	0	1	3	20	30	173	16	0
Dyer	24	0	1	0	23	9	32	2	0
Dyersburg	264	1	9	34	220	265	932	31	10
Eagleville	0	0	0	0	0	1	0	0	0
East Ridge	152	2	9	36	105	240	804	107	6
Elizabethton	42	1	0	3	38	85	584	21	0
Elkton	0	0	0	0	0	0	0	0	0
Englewood	4	0	0	0	4	4	16	3	0
Erin	10	0	1	0	9	4	13	4	0
Erwin	38	3	2	1	32	7	63	2	0
Estill Springs	10	0	2	1	7	5	31	4	0
Ethridge	6	0	0	0	6	4	15	3	0
Etowah	16	0	0	2	14	32	99	5	2
Fairview	13	0	3	1	9	18	76	8	2
Fayetteville	50	0	3	10	37	65	334	15	1
Franklin	117	0	19	20	78	90	873	25	3
Friendship	3	0	0	0	3	1	5	0	0
Gadsden	5	0	0	0	5	4	8	0	0
Gainesboro	1	0	0	0	1	4	17	0	0
Gallatin	127	2	9	7	109	72	531	26	2
Gallaway	4	0	0	0	4	7	2	2	0
Gates	1	0	0	0	1	7	2	1	0
Gatlinburg	32	0	3	7	22	95	224	12	1
Germantown	38	1	2	3	32	80	441	5	2
Gibson	0	0	0	0	0	0	6	1	0
Gleason	1	0	0	0	1	5	12	1	0
Goodlettsville	89	0	2	26	61	98	626	21	1
Gordonsville	2	0	0	0	2	10	20	2	0
Grand Junction	2	0	0	1	1	0	4	1	0
Graysville	4	0	0	1	3	6	3	1	0
Greenbrier	19	0	1	2	16	26	79	3	2
Greeneville	70	0	7	9	54	122	549	44	0
Greenfield	3	0	0	0	3	3	11	1	0
Halls	14	0	0	3	11	17	20	3	0
Harriman	40	0	2	8	30	88	228	23	2
Henderson	24	0	1	2	21	60	93	4	1
Hendersonville	91	1	3	5	82	94	645	17	3
Henning	9	0	0	1	8	24	30	1	0
Henry	0	0	0	0	0	6	9	0	0
Hohenwald	20	1	1	3	15	21	122	3	0
Hollow Rock	5	0	0	0	5	2	5	1	0
Hornbeak	0	0	0	0	0	3	0	0	0
Humboldt	131	3	10	13	105	71	272	10	5
Huntingdon	8	1	0	1	6	22	117	0	0
Huntland	5	0	0	0	5	0	5	1	0
Jacksboro	4	0	0	0	4	11	224	3	0
Jackson	925	11	40	151	723	815	2,484	156	23
Jamestown	8	0	0	0	8	12	92	2	0
Jasper	8	0	0	0	8	23	54	4	1
Jefferson City	30	0	3	1	26	42	293	12	2
Jellico	3	0	1	0	2	16	59	4	0
Johnson City	297	2	23	50	222	399	2,097	76	5
Jonesborough	8	0	0	0	8	14	62	1	0
Kenton	1	0	0	0	1	3	13	0	0
Kimball	3	0	0	0	3	4	132	11	0
Kingsport	267	0	16	31	220	381	2,151	125	10
Kingston	17	0	5	4	8	27	78	4	2
Knoxville	1,541	18	139	415	969	2,275	8,424	739	21
Lafayette	14	0	1	0	13	29	92	2	1
La Follette	52	0	7	10	35	159	389	20	2
Lake City	11	0	0	3	8	24	89	11	3
Lawrenceburg	99	0	8	3	88	143	445	18	2
Lebanon	200	2	7	19	172	149	815	41	4
Lenoir City	30	0	2	8	20	103	297	20	0
Lewisburg	83	2	4	4	73	62	220	6	2
Lexington	88	0	4	5	79	81	308	18	0
Livingston	15	0	0	0	15	11	75	3	0
Lookout Mountain	0	0	0	0	0	7	15	0	0
Loretto	2	0	0	0	2	8	15	0	0
Loudon	5	0	1	2	2	4	40	3	0

Table 8. Offenses Known to Law Enforcement, by Selected State and City, 2013— continued

(Number.)

State/city	Violent crime	Murder and nonnegligent manslaughter	Rape (revised definition)[1]	Robbery	Aggravated assault	Burglary	Larceny-theft	Motor vehicle theft	Arson[2]
Madisonville	26	0	3	3	20	34	214	20	1
Manchester	58	0	5	5	48	81	451	26	2
Martin	23	0	1	6	16	48	265	2	1
Maryville	61	0	8	7	46	142	569	23	1
Mason	19	0	0	1	18	9	19	15	1
Maury City	6	0	1	0	5	2	9	1	0
Maynardville	4	0	0	1	3	37	83	5	0
McEwen	2	0	0	0	2	3	14	1	0
McKenzie	21	0	5	1	15	89	152	9	0
Medina	4	0	0	1	3	6	18	1	0
Memphis	10,894	124	437	3,133	7,200	11,825	25,295	2,684	366
Middleton	3	0	0	0	3	3	4	0	0
Milan	42	0	3	3	36	63	199	5	1
Millersville	13	0	2	0	11	17	48	3	0
Millington	92	0	9	16	67	102	376	24	2
Minor Hill	1	0	0	0	1	0	1	0	0
Monteagle	4	0	0	0	4	3	8	0	0
Monterey	4	0	0	1	3	8	26	4	1
Morristown	162	2	11	25	124	134	1,375	74	5
Moscow	6	0	0	0	6	3	9	1	1
Mountain City	4	0	1	0	3	9	50	4	0
Mount Carmel	7	0	0	0	7	13	50	4	0
Mount Juliet	48	0	12	5	31	61	379	19	0
Mount Pleasant	59	0	0	3	56	37	83	3	0
Munford	14	0	5	1	8	35	114	1	1
Murfreesboro	705	4	54	130	517	742	3,131	178	9
Nashville	6,612	35	437	1,611	4,529	5,613	17,650	1,197	91
Newbern	26	0	0	0	26	24	67	1	0
New Johnsonville	5	0	0	0	5	4	21	1	0
New Market	0	0	0	0	0	1	8	3	0
Newport	58	0	6	6	46	92	488	27	0
New Tazewell	9	0	0	2	7	13	22	1	0
Nolensville	8	0	1	1	6	16	33	3	0
Norris	0	0	0	0	0	3	9	1	0
Oakland	8	0	1	1	6	9	50	2	0
Obion	0	0	0	0	0	1	24	2	1
Oliver Springs	15	0	2	1	12	16	75	5	0
Oneida	19	0	1	0	18	22	156	6	0
Paris	47	0	2	10	35	127	445	5	1
Parsons	4	0	0	1	3	9	19	2	0
Petersburg	0	0	0	0	0	5	6	0	0
Pigeon Forge	43	1	4	8	30	130	364	46	2
Pikeville	5	0	1	0	4	15	34	2	0
Piperton	0	0	0	0	0	1	18	0	0
Pittman Center	0	0	0	0	0	3	5	0	0
Plainview	2	0	0	0	2	14	28	1	0
Pleasant View	0	0	0	0	0	14	31	6	2
Portland	56	0	3	7	46	68	244	12	2
Powells Crossroads	0	0	0	0	0	0	0	0	0
Pulaski	60	2	5	3	50	56	273	8	0
Puryear	1	0	0	1	0	1	10	1	0
Red Bank	70	1	8	7	54	124	360	41	4
Red Boiling Springs	1	0	0	0	1	6	23	2	0
Ridgely	3	0	0	1	2	5	8	0	0
Ridgetop	1	0	0	0	1	2	14	3	0
Ripley	134	1	4	11	118	171	248	8	6
Rockwood	21	0	0	1	20	69	297	10	0
Rogersville	12	0	1	4	7	50	140	6	0
Rossville	2	0	1	0	1	0	11	0	0
Rutherford	2	0	0	0	2	2	9	0	0
Rutledge	4	0	1	1	2	13	35	1	0
Saltillo	1	0	0	0	1	3	1	0	0
Samburg	0	0	0	0	0	1	0	0	0
Savannah	35	1	1	4	29	93	386	20	1
Scotts Hill	0	0	0	0	0	0	2	1	0
Selmer	19	0	4	1	14	58	119	3	0
Sevierville	85	0	6	20	59	138	725	39	1
Sewanee	2	0	0	0	2	31	39	0	1
Sharon	0	0	0	0	0	8	18	2	0
Shelbyville	119	1	9	8	101	105	452	23	0
Signal Mountain	9	0	0	0	9	17	33	1	0
Smithville	19	0	4	1	14	43	156	8	1
Smyrna	111	0	7	14	90	114	846	36	1
Sneedville	6	0	0	0	6	14	67	1	0
Soddy-Daisy	32	0	2	3	27	59	321	23	1
South Carthage	8	0	1	1	6	4	16	1	0
South Fulton	19	0	0	2	17	22	39	6	0
Sparta	11	0	0	3	8	85	306	18	3

Table 8.   Offenses Known to Law Enforcement, by Selected State and City, 2013— continued

(Number.)

State/city	Violent crime	Murder and nonnegligent manslaughter	Rape (revised definition)[1]	Robbery	Aggravated assault	Burglary	Larceny-theft	Motor vehicle theft	Arson[2]
Spencer	0	0	0	0	0	4	5	1	0
Spring City	3	0	0	0	3	8	32	4	0
Springfield	165	3	12	18	132	97	699	29	3
Spring Hill	48	0	6	3	39	32	259	9	2
St. Joseph	0	0	0	0	0	3	13	1	2
Sunbright	0	0	0	0	0	0	5	0	0
Surgoinsville	0	0	0	0	0	3	14	0	0
Sweetwater	30	0	0	5	25	80	159	14	2
Tazewell	17	0	0	2	15	15	50	7	1
Tellico Plains	1	0	0	0	1	1	5	0	0
Tiptonville	11	0	0	2	9	31	40	3	0
Toone	1	0	0	0	1	1	0	1	0
Townsend	3	0	0	1	2	7	9	0	0
Tracy City	20	0	0	2	18	16	31	5	0
Trenton	45	1	2	5	37	34	122	1	0
Trezevant	2	0	0	0	2	7	30	0	0
Trimble	0	0	0	0	0	1	4	0	0
Troy	5	0	0	0	5	8	29	0	0
Tullahoma	73	0	1	10	62	117	450	29	2
Tusculum	0	0	0	0	0	3	6	1	0
Union City	62	0	4	10	48	106	470	15	4
Vonore	8	0	0	1	7	12	68	4	1
Wartburg	3	0	0	0	3	1	12	0	0
Wartrace	1	0	0	0	1	0	1	0	0
Watauga	0	0	0	0	0	0	1	0	0
Watertown	2	0	0	0	2	13	22	0	0
Waverly	16	0	1	1	14	16	61	0	0
Waynesboro	14	0	0	0	14	20	31	0	0
Westmoreland	7	0	1	0	6	8	34	6	0
White Bluff	7	0	1	0	6	13	36	8	0
White House	10	0	1	1	8	30	176	11	2
White Pine	3	0	0	2	1	9	82	1	0
Whiteville	14	0	0	3	11	11	26	2	1
Winchester	50	0	1	2	47	42	224	12	1
Winfield	2	0	0	1	1	3	6	0	0
Woodbury	6	0	0	1	5	20	26	3	1
Texas									
Abernathy	0	0		0	0	12	0	0	1
Abilene	477	1		125	314	1,055	3,460	254	16
Addison	51	1		11	35	129	593	62	1
Alamo	164	0		27	126	203	1,052	81	1
Alamo Heights	9	0		2	5	36	194	5	0
Alice	155	0		11	135	236	929	43	14
Allen	62	0	13	13	36	170	985	50	13
Alton	10	1		6	3	69	223	33	2
Alvarado	16	0		3	12	50	101	10	1
Alvin	53	1		15	27	117	513	38	0
Amarillo	1,286	9	214	242	821	1,816	5,643	695	50
Andrews	94	0		2	70	74	220	27	4
Angleton	58	1		6	38	86	410	16	4
Anna	7	0		1	5	46	52	5	1
Anson	4	0		0	4	15	18	0	0
Anthony	5	0		3	2	20	118	2	0
Aransas Pass	32	0		7	24	135	311	21	3
Arcola	5	0		0	5	8	10	8	0
Argyle	3	0		1	2	5	14	2	0
Arlington	1,837	18		562	1,152	3,181	10,879	940	38
Arp	0	0		0	0	0	0	0	0
Atlanta	24	0		8	13	52	184	4	0
Aubrey	6	0		1	4	10	46	1	2
Austin	3,123	26		763	2,117	6,550	32,948	2,169	105
Azle	28	0		4	21	104	346	19	2
Baird	2	0		0	2	14	13	0	0
Balch Springs	200	2		45	121	261	996	136	0
Balcones Heights	9	0		2	6	17	326	30	0
Ballinger	9	0		1	7	58	56	2	0
Bangs	0	0		0	0	2	2	2	0
Bastrop	23	0		7	14	36	426	32	3
Bay City	60	1		6	45	212	485	9	2
Bayou Vista	2	0		0	1	8	17	0	0
Baytown	285	4		126	136	916	2,373	364	14
Beaumont	1,225	16		419	731	1,922	3,987	283	40
Bedford	206	2	16	35	153	244	1,039	66	2
Bee Cave	4	0	2	0	2	5	129	4	0
Beeville	30	2		2	26	70	294	15	3
Bellaire	13	0		9	4	47	269	12	2
Bellmead	152	0		16	121	106	1,031	43	1

Table 8.   Offenses Known to Law Enforcement, by Selected State and City, 2013— continued

(Number.)

State/city	Violent crime	Murder and nonnegligent manslaughter	Rape (revised definition)[1]	Robbery	Aggravated assault	Burglary	Larceny-theft	Motor vehicle theft	Arson[2]
Bellville	13	0		1	12	26	85	4	0
Belton	67	0		6	60	152	718	8	1
Benbrook	23	1		2	19	79	390	30	1
Bertram	1	0		0	1	6	11	0	0
Beverly Hills	10	0		3	6	25	63	6	0
Big Sandy	0	0		0	0	1	3	0	0
Big Spring	147	2		19	118	308	817	51	3
Bishop	3	0		1	2	8	37	1	0
Blanco	3	0		1	2	12	30	0	0
Blue Mound	1	0		0	0	2	21	2	0
Boerne	23	0		1	19	25	319	19	0
Bogata	12	0		0	10	13	32	4	0
Bonham	22	0		2	7	61	217	4	2
Borger	134	0		2	132	141	335	43	0
Bovina	5	0		0	4	8	12	0	0
Bowie	11	0		0	6	61	242	8	5
Brady	8	0		0	8	37	87	3	0
Brazoria	16	0		2	11	15	46	6	0
Breckenridge	9	0		0	3	18	67	5	1
Brenham	68	1		10	46	88	330	12	4
Bridge City	12	0		2	7	29	85	4	0
Brookshire	20	0		3	16	25	59	7	2
Brookside Village	4	0		1	2	4	4	1	0
Brownfield	39	2		3	33	72	115	7	2
Brownsville	473	1		136	275	1,140	6,441	257	9
Brownwood	61	0		7	43	155	647	26	0
Bryan	358	2		75	250	539	1,683	89	24
Buda	9	0		3	5	17	221	14	0
Bullard	1	0		0	1	4	40	1	0
Bulverde	5	0		0	5	12	44	2	0
Burkburnett	34	0		2	26	75	228	8	0
Burleson	57	0		10	37	162	786	55	3
Burnet	26	0		2	18	30	80	8	0
Cactus	21	0		2	19	17	14	4	2
Caddo Mills	0	0		0	0	18	17	4	0
Caldwell	8	1		0	7	1	22	2	0
Calvert	5	0		0	4	8	9	1	0
Cameron	17	0		3	13	49	147	1	0
Canyon	16	0		3	12	13	95	7	1
Carrollton	185	1		73	105	706	2,048	206	10
Carthage	40	0		3	29	91	263	12	0
Castle Hills	6	0		4	2	42	284	9	0
Castroville	5	0		1	2	8	35	1	1
Cedar Hill	89	1		34	45	299	1,137	70	5
Cedar Park	69	0		8	56	113	710	28	0
Celina	7	1		0	4	17	38	1	0
Center	39	1		4	32	39	183	13	2
Chillicothe	0	0		0	0	3	5	1	1
Cibolo	16	0		3	10	44	181	8	1
Cisco	5	0		0	4	67	119	3	2
Clarksville	33	0		5	28	24	36	1	0
Cleburne	88	0	19	11	58	214	720	43	0
Cleveland	69	0		6	57	93	548	46	8
Clifton	2	0		0	2	12	26	0	
Clint	0	0		0	0	0	7	1	0
Clyde	3	0		0	3	21	36	2	1
Cockrell Hill	21	0		8	11	31	62	12	2
Coleman	10	0		0	10	94	85	4	1
College Station	379	0		37	308	432	1,750	48	0
Colleyville	9	0		4	5	39	131	4	0
Collinsville	1	0		0	1	11	8	0	0
Colorado City	34	0		1	33	43	79	3	0
Columbus	6	1		0	5	14	80	7	1
Comanche	19	0		0	18	33	102	0	0
Combes	3	0		0	2	10	20	3	0
Commerce	28	0		7	12	61	138	13	1
Conroe	216	1	29	60	126	416	1,550	105	1
Converse	124	0		9	105	69	368	23	4
Coppell	17	0		2	12	100	450	30	1
Copperas Cove	95	0		18	63	243	863	21	10
Corinth	14	0		4	7	38	179	13	0
Corpus Christi	1,939	18		390	1,384	2,595	11,519	487	46
Corrigan	6	0		0	5	14	45	3	0
Corsicana	121	1		25	72	303	879	27	2
Crandall	7	0		0	7	22	27	5	1
Crane	5	0		0	3	1	6	2	0
Crockett	25	0		3	22	56	249	5	1
Crosbyton	3	1		0	0	8	19	0	0

Table 8. Offenses Known to Law Enforcement, by Selected State and City, 2013— continued

(Number.)

State/city	Violent crime	Murder and nonnegligent manslaughter	Rape (revised definition)[1]	Robbery	Aggravated assault	Burglary	Larceny-theft	Motor vehicle theft	Arson[2]
Crowell	0	0		0	0	0	0	0	0
Crowley	14	1		4	9	89	256	15	0
Cuero	83	0		1	75	49	207	5	0
Cumby	2	0		0	2	2	2	3	1
Daingerfield	10	0		1	9	34	104	2	2
Dalhart	53	0		0	51	49	121	4	0
Dallas	8,330	143		4,202	3,442	14,516	30,374	7,384	455
Dalworthington Gardens	1	0		1	0	10	17	10	0
Danbury	1	0		0	0	4	4	0	0
Dayton	24	0		4	16	55	142	27	
Decatur	17	0		6	7	10	267	14	0
De Kalb	4	0		0	4	25	26	3	0
De Leon	4	0		0	4	16	29	1	0
Del Rio	72	0		14	58	119	632	17	2
Denison	94	4	11	15	64	145	646	53	0
Denton	338	1	93	52	192	472	2,203	102	17
Denver City	5	1		0	2	30	39	7	1
Desoto	179	5		64	96	475	1,174	78	4
Diboll	6	0		0	2	17	57	1	0
Dickinson	37	1		7	26	159	393	40	1
Dilley	6	0		1	5	30	46	5	2
Dimmitt	15	0		2	13	47	80	11	0
Donna	154	0		19	132	267	727	74	2
Double Oak	1	0		0	1	4	14	1	0
Driscoll	1	0		0	1	2	1	0	0
Dublin	2	0		0	2	24	48	3	1
Dumas	50	1		3	36	53	260	15	7
Duncanville	146	1		96	42	322	892	144	3
Eagle Pass	29	2		3	24	171	688	11	1
Early	27	0		1	23	17	48	0	0
Eastland	9	0		1	8	33	117	4	0
East Mountain	5	0		0	5	11	1	1	0
Edcouch	9	0		1	7	38	48	1	2
Edinburg	277	1		50	196	738	3,299	255	8
Edna	12	1	2	1	8	16	112	2	0
El Campo	54	0		7	40	52	269	9	1
Electra	5	0		1	3	13	20	2	0
Elgin	21	1		1	17	50	103	11	0
El Paso	2,522	10		457	1,879	1,771	12,993	794	73
Elsa	18	0		2	16	62	208	16	3
Ennis	61	0		9	51	123	578	22	5
Euless	89	0		39	46	252	1,177	139	6
Everman	26	0		3	23	55	121	9	0
Fairfield	4	0		0	4	10	18	2	0
Fair Oaks Ranch	1	0		0	1	15	13	2	0
Falfurrias	9	1		1	7	53	56	0	0
Farmers Branch	65	0		26	29	200	749	106	3
Farmersville	7	0		0	5	30	86	4	0
Farwell	3	0		1	2	1	12	1	0
Ferris	11	1		1	6	14	41	4	0
Flatonia	2	0		0	1	1	11	2	0
Florence	0	0		0	0	0	5	0	0
Floresville	13	0		0	13	38	221	14	0
Flower Mound	39	1	2	5	31	86	384	21	5
Floydada	11	0		0	10	27	31	2	0
Forney	19	0	4	2	13	91	184	33	1
Fort Stockton	58	0		3	40	68	242	6	0
Fort Worth	4,420	48	523	1,256	2,593	8,316	23,557	2,399	155
Frankston	3	0		2	1	15	31	1	0
Fredericksburg	9	0		3	6	57	195	3	0
Freeport	28	0		8	18	122	323	24	3
Freer	28	0		5	22	25	61	2	1
Friendswood	11	0		2	8	88	313	17	0
Friona	1	0		0	1	8	12	1	0
Frisco	100	0	21	22	57	374	2,075	58	15
Fulton	3	0		2	1	25	28	2	0
Gainesville	89	2		14	64	197	642	59	5
Galena Park	18	0		8	4	59	146	27	1
Galveston	236	3		93	84	439	1,707	189	6
Garden Ridge	1	0		0	1	9	20	0	0
Garland	514	6		237	218	2,053	5,671	647	30
Gatesville	22	0		3	15	39	109	13	1
Georgetown	71	1	17	7	46	93	642	32	1
Giddings	15	0		1	7	35	129	3	0
Gilmer	36	1		2	31	22	172	11	0
Gladewater	43	0		7	34	70	224	18	0
Glenn Heights	30	0		4	25	105	144	13	1
Godley	2	0		0	2	7	11	0	0

Table 8.   Offenses Known to Law Enforcement, by Selected State and City, 2013— continued

(Number.)

State/city	Violent crime	Murder and nonnegligent manslaughter	Rape (revised definition)[1]	Robbery	Aggravated assault	Burglary	Larceny-theft	Motor vehicle theft	Arson[2]
Gonzales	105	1		6	82	69	255	5	0
Gorman	3	0		0	3	18	23	2	1
Graham	18	0		2	14	79	293	14	1
Granbury	21	0		0	13	58	518	13	0
Grand Prairie	511	11		155	291	1,120	3,448	590	16
Grand Saline	2	0		0	2	21	55	0	0
Granger	1	0		0	1	2	2	0	0
Granite Shoals	7	1		0	5	16	29	9	2
Grapeland	2	0		0	2	10	16	0	0
Grapevine	88	1		20	60	182	1,270	102	2
Greenville	204	0		56	133	266	948	65	5
Gregory	2	0		1	0	9	16	3	0
Groesbeck	2	0		0	2	15	35	3	0
Groves	79	0		17	54	130	364	29	0
Gun Barrel City	12	1		0	10	50	134	15	0
Hale Center	5	0		0	5	35	26	1	1
Hallettsville	17	0		2	14	15	42	4	0
Hallsville	8	0		0	8	12	32	2	0
Haltom City	110	2		34	63	391	943	121	7
Hamlin	19	0		0	19	12	34	2	1
Harker Heights	90	0		25	57	226	687	37	1
Harlingen	264	2		59	182	496	2,012	76	11
Haskell	3	0		0	3	8	9	1	0
Hawkins	0	0		0	0	16	27	4	0
Hawley	1	0		0	1	9	6	2	0
Hearne	47	0		3	43	31	81	2	1
Heath	1	0	0	0	1	5	49	1	0
Hedwig Village	6	0		4	2	19	175	14	0
Helotes	4	0		2	1	19	94	3	0
Hemphill	1	0		0	1	5	25	4	0
Hempstead	18	0		8	10	72	134	13	0
Henderson	96	1	2	12	81	77	545	25	2
Hereford	55	0		9	40	173	283	18	2
Hewitt	14	2		1	11	30	90	7	0
Hickory Creek	7	0		2	3	2	97	9	0
Highland Park	5	0	1	3	1	33	116	11	0
Highland Village	8	0		0	8	12	99	1	0
Hill Country Village	0	0		0	0	6	32	3	0
Hillsboro	30	0		5	24	50	282	11	1
Hitchcock	29	1		4	21	82	129	23	0
Hollywood Park	0	0		0	0	13	62	1	0
Hondo	22	0		1	16	30	198	6	0
Hooks	7	1		1	4	15	22	1	0
Horizon City	13	0		4	9	59	187	20	2
Horseshoe Bay	5	0		0	4	12	57	6	0
Houston	20,993	214		9,891	10,270	23,733	73,591	13,595	708
Howe	6	0		0	5	6	10	2	0
Hubbard	0	0		0	0	4	9	2	0
Hudson	27	0		1	26	30	56	0	0
Hughes Springs	1	0		0	1	15	2	1	2
Humble	95	0		45	38	273	1,239	112	1
Huntington	4	0		0	1	15	27	2	0
Huntsville	213	0		22	169	241	798	39	0
Hurst	205	1		47	151	222	1,700	56	2
Hutchins	8	0		1	5	42	122	28	1
Hutto	8	0		2	1	28	131	5	1
Idalou	6	0		0	6	8	11	1	0
Ingleside	32	1		2	25	74	175	21	5
Ingram	5	0		0	2	10	40	2	0
Iowa Park	13	0	2	1	10	22	40	1	2
Irving	530	2		186	318	1,137	4,444	594	17
Jacksboro	13	0		1	12	38	61	3	0
Jacksonville	111	0		11	87	158	431	12	8
Jamaica Beach	0	0		0	0	1	0	0	0
Jarrell	0	0		0	0	0	10	1	0
Jasper	31	0		3	22	79	404	1	1
Jefferson	13	0		1	12	16	42	2	0
Jersey Village	38	0		9	29	44	158	16	2
Johnson City	2	0		0	2	1	9	0	0
Jones Creek	0	0		0	0	0	2	0	0
Jonestown	9	0		2	7	7	35	1	0
Joshua	15	0		0	14	25	69	8	1
Jourdanton	2	0		0	2	0	4	0	0
Junction	6	0		0	6	11	25	0	0
Karnes City	6	0		0	6	20	55	1	0
Katy	38	2	7	12	17	63	398	29	1
Kaufman	12	1		5	6	48	68	7	0
Keene	4	0		0	4	26	77	6	2

Table 8.   Offenses Known to Law Enforcement, by Selected State and City, 2013— continued

(Number.)

State/city	Violent crime	Murder and nonnegligent manslaughter	Rape (revised definition)[1]	Robbery	Aggravated assault	Burglary	Larceny-theft	Motor vehicle theft	Arson[2]
Keller	27	1		9	12	76	312	2	0
Kenedy	8	0		0	8	64	152	3	0
Kennedale	11	0		6	5	40	117	20	0
Kermit	18	0		0	18	6	19	6	0
Kerrville	48	3		8	30	90	555	24	0
Kilgore	53	2		5	37	116	510	34	2
Killeen	753	6		170	499	1,396	3,189	206	50
Kingsville	103	1		19	80	281	658	24	2
Kirby	49	3		3	42	50	118	20	2
Kirbyville	5	0		0	5	9	20	3	0
Kountze	11	0		1	10	13	32	1	0
Kress	0	0		0	0	0	2	0	0
Kyle	90	0		6	72	75	384	32	1
Lacy-Lakeview	38	0		4	26	72	161	14	2
La Feria	7	0		2	2	98	207	0	0
Lago Vista	14	1		1	11	16	69	0	0
La Grange	4	1		0	3	15	36	7	0
La Grulla	5	0		0	5	8	1	0	0
Laguna Vista	4	0		0	4	15	31	2	0
La Joya	6	0		0	6	23	4	0	0
Lake Dallas	15	0		0	14	24	106	12	1
Lake Jackson	40	1		12	18	125	445	19	2
Lakeside	7	0		1	6	12	15	2	0
Lakeview, Harris County	10	1		0	9	16	52	3	4
Lakeway	16	0		2	12	25	131	10	0
Lake Worth	14	0		8	6	124	387	16	0
La Marque	70	1		26	38	161	748	51	3
Lamesa	44	0		1	38	96	298	20	3
Lampasas	20	0		2	15	48	232	6	1
Lancaster	179	2	23	59	95	533	848	152	6
La Porte	40	0		9	19	117	433	43	7
Laredo	1,027	3		207	742	1,425	8,685	372	82
La Vernia	3	0		0	3	2	42	0	0
La Villa	0	0		0	0	13	3	1	0
Lavon	1	0		0	1	3	14	0	0
League City	96	2		22	58	386	1,476	56	1
Leander	26	0		4	20	44	277	15	2
Leon Valley	26	0		9	10	91	670	65	0
Levelland	67	0		8	46	160	362	24	1
Lewisville	243	1	48	74	120	501	1,921	299	4
Lexington	6	0		0	4	15	46	0	0
Liberty	46	1		7	28	92	447	14	1
Lindale	16	0	2	6	8	45	132	9	0
Linden	6	0		1	3	17	34	1	0
Little Elm	48	1		6	22	78	255	13	2
Littlefield	30	0		6	24	93	143	3	5
Live Oak	45	1		10	27	48	580	52	1
Livingston	43	0		7	31	37	262	10	1
Llano	0	0	0	0	0	29	43	5	1
Lockhart	45	1		5	32	91	322	12	1
Lone Star	6	0		2	3	16	43	2	0
Longview	451	5	39	152	255	630	2,542	200	11
Lorena	1	0		0	1	6	20	2	0
Lorenzo	2	0		0	2	7	1	0	0
Los Fresnos	7	0		0	4	47	106	5	1
Lubbock	1,829	5		388	1,348	2,608	8,103	846	37
Luling	29	0		5	21	18	85	5	0
Lumberton	25	0	7	4	14	46	193	5	0
Lyford	1	0		0	1	18	22	4	0
Lytle	0	0		0	0	19	153	4	2
Madisonville	17	0		2	15	23	81	9	0
Magnolia	9	0		4	5	9	31	3	0
Malakoff	13	0		0	13	19	38	5	0
Manor	15	0		0	12	22	68	5	1
Mansfield	80	1		23	40	181	812	49	0
Manvel	6	0		0	6	54	44	12	0
Marble Falls	28	0	9	4	15	40	313	9	1
Marlin	17	0		2	13	18	26	3	1
Marshall	141	3		16	104	242	792	44	8
Martindale	4	0		0	4	4	1	1	0
Mathis	25	0		0	23	44	85	6	0
McAllen	171	2		83	80	536	4,652	236	15
McGregor	7	0		1	5	14	60	2	0
McKinney	207	1	52	44	110	476	2,450	129	26
Meadows Place	7	0		4	3	23	93	10	0
Melissa	1	1		0	0	20	41	4	0
Memorial Villages	5	0		2	1	26	81	6	0
Memphis	6	0		0	5	8	15	2	0

Table 8. Offenses Known to Law Enforcement, by Selected State and City, 2013— continued

(Number.)

State/city	Violent crime	Murder and nonnegligent manslaughter	Rape (revised definition)	Robbery	Aggravated assault	Burglary	Larceny-theft	Motor vehicle theft	Arson[2]
Mercedes	106	0		13	88	132	623	41	1
Meridian	0	0		0	0	0	1	0	0
Merkel	5	0		0	5	14	18	2	0
Mesquite	402	6		204	178	1,382	4,184	766	11
Mexia	42	1		6	33	77	248	3	1
Midland	350	5		63	260	568	2,459	164	1
Midlothian	25	0		5	17	70	275	16	1
Mineola	19	0		3	16	31	154	3	0
Mineral Wells	55	0		16	34	221	610	41	2
Mission	72	0		32	36	447	2,321	177	20
Missouri City	72	0		35	32	186	889	76	0
Monahans	30	0		1	26	57	127	1	3
Mont Belvieu	9	0		1	6	12	84	25	0
Montgomery	1	0		0	1	5	10	1	0
Morgans Point Resort	2	0		0	2	14	26	0	0
Moulton	1	0		0	1	3	7	0	0
Mount Pleasant	41	0		8	33	155	486	20	7
Muleshoe	4	0		0	4	10	39	2	0
Munday	2	0		0	2	3	6	1	0
Murphy	4	0	0	1	3	11	111	0	0
Mustang Ridge	0	0		0	0	4	10	2	0
Nacogdoches	97	1		31	62	257	828	41	2
Naples	1	0		0	1	31	18	1	0
Nash	9	0		0	9	25	39	3	1
Nassau Bay	17	0		1	13	18	77	6	0
Navasota	77	0		2	74	53	143	23	2
Nederland	58	2		11	41	112	349	32	3
Needville	11	0		0	10	6	15	1	0
New Boston	9	0		1	7	53	161	7	0
New Braunfels	147	3		24	104	351	1,673	129	11
Nocona	2	0		1	0	9	13	3	0
Nolanville	22	0		1	21	21	55	0	1
Northlake	7	0		0	6	6	27	3	1
North Richland Hills	157	1		35	100	283	1,276	78	3
Oak Ridge	2	0		0	2	0	0	0	0
Odessa	1,080	2		143	879	764	3,147	463	13
O'Donnell	0	0		0	0	0	0	2	0
Olmos Park	1	0		1	0	7	41	4	0
Olney	3	0		0	3	9	30	1	2
Olton	8	0		0	8	11	10	0	0
Omaha	3	0		2	1	10	10	1	0
Onalaska	16	0		8	6	19	37	6	2
Orange	111	4		30	76	236	299	42	0
Orange Grove	1	0		0	1	5	10	0	0
Overton	7	0		0	5	21	39	1	0
Ovilla	4	0		1	3	7	25	1	1
Oyster Creek	14	1		0	13	19	27	4	0
Paducah	2	0		0	1	2	1	0	0
Palacios	4	0		3	1	66	84	7	3
Palestine	113	1		31	66	217	841	49	0
Palmer	2	0		1	1	12	16	0	0
Palmhurst	2	1		0	1	16	242	1	0
Palm Valley	0	0		0	0	4	22	1	0
Palmview	25	0		1	19	59	279	17	1
Pampa	186	1		7	178	126	552	38	2
Panhandle	5	0		0	5	3	3	1	0
Pantego	14	0		2	12	12	97	3	0
Paris	170	5		28	132	314	866	39	0
Parker	5	0		0	5	4	14	0	0
Pasadena	592	3		192	345	1,011	3,980	510	25
Pearland	152	1	34	29	88	287	1,541	100	1
Pearsall	8	0		1	7	69	177	3	2
Pecos	12	0		5	7	25	112	9	0
Penitas	36	0		2	29	34	133	7	0
Perryton	12	0		1	11	13	48	12	0
Pflugerville	59	0		7	36	92	699	31	1
Pharr	230	0		37	173	579	1,810	120	2
Pilot Point	6	0		2	3	11	21	2	0
Pittsburg	35	0		3	27	73	119	4	0
Plainview	57	0		5	45	155	697	25	2
Plano	389	3	84	106	196	944	4,730	256	16
Pleasanton	35	0		3	31	80	430	33	0
Ponder	3	1		0	2	2	18	0	0
Port Aransas	23	0		5	15	46	264	38	2
Port Arthur	359	5		121	215	726	1,537	127	14
Port Isabel	12	0		1	8	48	253	5	1
Portland	22	0		5	11	89	469	12	3
Port Neches	37	0		2	34	69	150	20	1

Table 8.   Offenses Known to Law Enforcement, by Selected State and City, 2013— continued

(Number.)

State/city	Violent crime	Murder and nonnegligent manslaughter	Rape (revised definition)[1]	Robbery	Aggravated assault	Burglary	Larceny-theft	Motor vehicle theft	Arson[2]
Poteet	13	0		2	11	43	86	10	3
Poth	12	0		0	12	7	17	2	0
Pottsboro	5	0		0	3	18	17	2	2
Premont	20	0		3	16	29	27	1	7
Presidio	1	0		0	1	9	9	1	0
Primera	2	0		0	2	12	8	2	0
Princeton	10	0		0	8	36	73	7	1
Progreso	9	0		2	6	37	42	7	1
Prosper	12	0		1	9	78	121	3	0
Queen City	9	0		0	7	22	42	1	0
Quitman	2	0		0	2	19	22	3	0
Ralls	2	0		0	2	5	2	0	0
Rancho Viejo	1	0		0	1	5	3	0	0
Ranger	9	0		1	6	12	25	5	0
Ransom Canyon	1	0		0	1	0	4	0	0
Raymondville	178	0		4	165	111	287	6	8
Red Oak	11	0		8	3	62	275	23	0
Refugio	9	0		1	7	15	41	1	0
Reno	2	0		0	2	20	41	0	0
Richardson	128	2		60	51	539	2,068	151	4
Richland Hills	5	0		1	4	54	142	23	0
Richmond	53	0		11	33	43	122	13	0
Riesel	4	0		0	4	1	9	0	0
Rio Grande City	44	0		5	37	80	382	47	1
Rio Hondo	7	0		0	7	6	38	0	0
River Oaks	8	0		2	6	48	109	6	0
Roanoke	7	0		1	6	29	108	8	0
Robinson	19	1		2	16	44	160	7	0
Robstown	15	1		3	11	102	336	17	0
Rockdale	7	1		0	6	26	122	6	0
Rockport	32	3		6	19	144	429	23	1
Rockwall	25	1	10	2	12	85	585	63	0
Rollingwood	1	0		1	0	6	13	0	0
Roma	39	0		8	31	17	70	22	6
Roman Forest	0	0		0	0	4	34	1	0
Roscoe	1	0		0	1	10	2	0	0
Rosenberg	94	1		31	51	134	495	47	0
Round Rock	149	2		37	86	297	2,086	45	6
Rowlett	82	0	16	14	52	171	689	37	3
Royse City	7	0	2	0	5	22	63	7	0
Runaway Bay	0	0		0	0	1	0	0	0
Sabinal	1	0		0	1	4	17	0	0
Sachse	14	0	3	1	10	50	169	10	0
Salado	0	0		0	0	3	28	0	0
San Angelo	263	2	54	22	185	682	2,725	185	12
San Antonio	8,828	72		2,192	5,901	14,850	58,567	6,577	315
San Augustine	6	0		1	5	4	23	3	0
San Diego	13	0		2	11	48	85	0	1
Sanger	14	0		4	8	34	123	13	1
San Juan	191	1		25	137	200	813	58	2
San Marcos	220	3		50	137	374	1,362	149	5
San Saba	7	0	1	0	6	28	33	2	1
Sansom Park Village	11	0		4	6	61	58	13	0
Santa Anna	4	0		0	2	7	14	1	0
Santa Fe	12	1		1	9	75	177	20	2
Santa Rosa	3	0		0	3	30	50	3	0
Schertz	68	0		10	46	81	483	23	0
Schulenburg	12	0		0	12	12	35	4	0
Seabrook	17	0		3	14	47	121	15	0
Seagoville	8	0		4	4	139	404	73	1
Seagraves	11	0		0	7	16	25	4	0
Sealy	35	0		5	29	50	125	4	0
Seguin	61	1		21	33	215	877	26	3
Selma	15	0		2	12	35	181	24	0
Seminole	9	0		0	5	16	74	7	0
Seven Points	6	0		0	6	18	50	3	0
Seymour	15	0		0	13	33	46	2	0
Shallowater	0	0		0	0	9	2	0	0
Shamrock	2	1		0	1	9	18	2	0
Shavano Park	3	0		0	3	12	51	1	0
Shenandoah	9	0		6	3	7	182	11	0
Sherman	120	2		21	93	312	958	46	6
Silsbee	8	0		0	8	30	169	5	4
Sinton	40	0		1	33	34	113	11	0
Slaton	16	0		2	7	28	61	1	0
Smithville	7	1		1	3	13	61	2	1
Snyder	75	1		2	62	115	350	21	0
Socorro	58	0		5	45	89	324	46	0

Table 8.   Offenses Known to Law Enforcement, by Selected State and City, 2013— continued

(Number.)

State/city	Violent crime	Murder and nonnegligent manslaughter	Rape (revised definition)[1]	Robbery	Aggravated assault	Burglary	Larceny-theft	Motor vehicle theft	Arson[2]
Somerset	3	0		1	2	17	21	6	0
Sonora	9	0		0	9	3	9	2	0
Sour Lake	5	0		1	4	7	39	2	0
South Houston	92	0		46	43	129	361	175	4
Southlake	14	1		2	11	78	365	13	1
Southmayd	4	0		1	3	10	14	4	1
South Padre Island	49	0		8	29	74	521	21	0
Southside Place	0	0		0	0	1	14	0	0
Spearman	3	1		0	0	8	23	1	0
Splendora	6	0		1	5	6	10	3	0
Springtown	16	0		0	16	17	66	3	0
Spring Valley	7	0		1	5	23	113	6	0
Spur	0	0		0	0	2	1	1	0
Stafford	94	3		45	35	93	531	79	2
Stagecoach	0	0		0	0	8	0	0	0
Stamford	16	0		1	15	40	49	6	0
Stanton	2	0		1	0	7	22	1	0
Stephenville	27	1		6	20	105	419	18	2
Stratford	3	0		0	2	5	6	0	0
Sugar Land	108	1		35	66	256	1,311	46	3
Sullivan City	3	0		1	2	16	7	0	0
Sulphur Springs	25	1		4	15	51	186	10	2
Sunrise Beach Village	0	0		0	0	1	4	0	0
Sunset Valley	3	0		3	0	1	120	0	0
Sweeny	11	0		1	10	18	38	2	1
Sweetwater	82	0	12	10	60	119	332	25	1
Taft	19	0		0	7	15	34	3	0
Tatum	7	0		0	7	17	40	1	0
Taylor	30	0		8	21	93	393	7	2
Terrell	78	6		15	54	178	423	43	4
Terrell Hills	1	0		0	1	58	25	5	0
Texarkana	329	2		71	235	470	1,725	105	27
Texas City	126	2		55	69	385	1,267	93	3
The Colony	48	0		7	35	114	407	35	6
Thorndale	2	0		0	2	7	15	1	0
Thrall	0	0		0	0	7	21	0	0
Three Rivers	25	1		0	24	19	39	2	0
Tioga	0	0		0	0	8	8	0	0
Tomball	30	0	5	9	16	64	333	24	0
Tool	7	0		0	7	13	31	3	0
Trinity	13	0		2	10	27	36	4	0
Trophy Club	9	0		2	6	12	93	4	0
Troy	4	0		0	4	18	10	1	0
Tulia	10	0		1	7	24	46	0	0
Tye	8	0		0	6	3	25	2	3
Tyler	376	5	43	53	275	825	3,111	180	10
Universal City	52	2		9	39	108	271	33	4
University Park	8	0		5	1	51	228	17	1
Uvalde	104	0		8	89	152	804	20	5
Valley Mills	1	0		0	1	10	22	0	0
Van	3	1		0	2	15	27	0	0
Van Alstyne	4	0		1	2	4	20	2	0
Venus	4	0		0	4	7	20	2	1
Vernon	37	0		2	29	86	239	21	6
Victoria	396	1	53	58	284	507	1,908	64	15
Vidor	58	0		11	47	112	361	47	0
Waco	515	4		142	311	1,508	3,751	163	42
Waelder	0	0		0	0	4	13	0	0
Wake Village	8	0		2	6	45	87	1	1
Waller	9	0		2	7	29	61	4	0
Wallis	4	0		0	4	8	10	3	1
Watauga	22	0		6	16	81	358	20	2
Waxahachie	33	2		11	20	160	832	41	3
Weatherford	7	0		1	5	83	555	22	3
Webster	46	1		21	16	82	496	61	0
Weimar	3	0		0	2	5	19	1	0
Weslaco	389	2		41	324	561	2,238	117	2
West	1	0		1	0	8	11	1	0
West Columbia	18	0		3	11	29	78	3	0
West Orange	7	0		1	6	26	274	8	0
Westover Hills	0	0		0	0	4	12	1	0
West Tawakoni	0	0		0	0	4	10	0	0
Westworth	6	0		4	2	15	160	6	0
Wharton	57	0		6	49	77	291	13	1
Whitehouse	9	0		1	4	17	53	7	0
White Oak	7	0		1	1	20	70	3	0
Whitesboro	6	0		0	5	14	46	3	0
White Settlement	24	0		8	16	98	361	38	2

Table 8.   Offenses Known to Law Enforcement, by Selected State and City, 2013— continued

(Number.)

State/city	Violent crime	Murder and nonnegligent manslaughter	Rape (revised definition)[1]	Robbery	Aggravated assault	Burglary	Larceny-theft	Motor vehicle theft	Arson[2]
Whitewright	9	0		0	6	8	25	3	0
Whitney	2	0		1	1	16	64	0	0
Wichita Falls	401	7		124	241	995	3,277	286	0
Willow Park	0	0		0	0	13	27	4	0
Wills Point	1	0		1	0	56	37	1	0
Wilmer	6	0		0	5	65	73	11	1
Windcrest	12	0		6	6	23	299	18	3
Wink	0	0		0	0	1	2	0	1
Winnsboro	8	0		1	7	36	35	3	1
Winters	4	0		1	3	10	11	1	0
Wolfforth	12	0		0	12	8	38	1	0
Woodbranch	1	0		0	1	1	16	0	0
Woodville	3	0		1	2	13	19	0	0
Woodway	8	0		2	5	20	121	2	0
Wortham	1	0		0	1	12	37	2	0
Wylie	32	1	9	3	19	75	433	18	0
Yoakum	8	0		3	5	79	79	7	0
Yorktown	12	0		0	5	21	30	1	0
Utah									
American Fork/Cedar Hills	26	1		6	16	106	674	37	1
Big Water	2	0		0	0	2	5	0	0
Blanding	18	0		0	17	14	63	2	0
Bluffdale	10	0	4	0	6	33	67	13	0
Bountiful	61	0	23	14	24		706	94	1
Brian Head	0	0		0	0	4	21	0	0
Brigham City	58	1	27	1	29	155	448	23	2
Cedar City	78	3		3	51	120	529	28	0
Centerfield	0	0		0	0	0	5	0	0
Centerville	19	0	16	1	2	29	436	23	1
Clearfield	39	0	12	4	23	99	495	36	1
Clinton	13	0	4	0	9	36	253	19	0
Cottonwood Heights	37	0		5	25	147	673	62	1
Draper	36	0	8	7	21	193	837	59	3
East Carbon	1	0		0	1	12	16	0	0
Enoch	18	0		0	18	15	45	1	2
Ephraim	1	0		0	1	15	94	3	0
Fairview	2	0		0	2	2	5	3	0
Farmington	13	0	5	0	8	39	353	24	3
Fountain Green	1	0		0	0	0	13	2	0
Grantsville	15	0	7	0	8	49	79	30	4
Harrisville	6	0		1	5	39	220	11	0
Helper	4	0	2	0	2	24	42	4	1
Hurricane	14	0	3	2	9		163	8	0
Kamas	2	0		0	1	1	15	0	0
Kanab	6	0	0	0	6	10	49	3	2
Kaysville	11	0	3	4	4	54	189	15	1
La Verkin	14	1		1	9	23	70	1	0
Layton	95	2	41	13	39	198	1,447	67	6
Lehi	32	0		4	19	147	561	55	0
Lindon	7	0	5	0	2	34	283	8	0
Logan	35	0	20	0	15	138	700	22	3
Lone Peak	2	0		1	1	55	208	14	1
Mapleton	2	0		0	0	8	92	3	0
Moab	19	0	6	0	13	25	187	16	2
Monticello	1	0		0	1	7	16	2	0
Moroni	0	0		0	0	6	5	3	0
Mount Pleasant	5	0		0	1	22	54	4	0
Naples	0	0	0	0	0	7	20	2	1
Nephi	6	0		0	5	25	120	10	0
North Ogden	9	0	8	0	1	26	179	7	0
North Park	1	0		0	0	28	151	10	0
North Salt Lake	33	0	8	8	17	63	327	52	1
Ogden	416	2	78	111	225	578	3,153	274	15
Orem	33	2	7	7	11	192	1,789	98	0
Park City	31	0	2	2	23	31	275	19	0
Parowan	5	0		0	4	14	21	3	0
Payson	9	0		0	8	71	384	22	0
Perry	13	0	1	0	12	10	71	1	0
Pleasant Grove	16	0	2	3	11	58	336	24	3
Pleasant View	2	0		1	0	34	78	9	0
Price	27	1	12	1	13	55	346	8	0
Provo	160	1	82	21	56	329	2,373	108	7
Richfield	7	0	1	1	2	31	201	6	0
Riverdale	11	0	1	2	8	34	480	24	2
Roosevelt	63	0	43	0	20	23	223	31	0
Roy	40	1	18	9	12	111	625	29	2
Salem	3	1		0	1	21	64	0	0

Table 8.   Offenses Known to Law Enforcement, by Selected State and City, 2013— continued

(Number.)

State/city	Violent crime	Murder and nonnegligent manslaughter	Rape (revised definition)	Robbery	Aggravated assault	Burglary	Larceny-theft	Motor vehicle theft	Arson[2]
Salina	5	0		0	3	17	72	2	1
Salt Lake City	1,475	7	204	422	842	2,068	9,517	1,876	34
Sandy	134	1	27	30	76	576	2,173	193	3
Santaquin/Genola	3	0		0	3	14	113	6	0
Saratoga Springs	12	0	5	0	7	24	172	5	0
Smithfield	7	0		0	6	21	29	3	0
South Jordan	28	0	8	5	15	185	993	63	1
South Ogden	24	0	9	3	12	78	242	17	0
South Salt Lake	204	2	41	45	116	213	1,138	315	5
Spanish Fork	10	1	2	2	5	87	375	12	1
Springdale	3	0		0	3	6	24	0	0
Springville	33	0		4	23	68	595	19	1
St. George	133	1	39	11	82	475	1,184	69	3
Stockton	0	0		0	0	0	0	0	0
Sunset	4	0	2	0	2	17	112	3	0
Syracuse	6	0	3	0	3	33	205	10	0
Tooele	72	0	25	12	35	261	999	77	7
Tremonton	28	0	9	1	18	29	179	8	3
Vernal	33	0	8	2	23	48	378	8	2
Washington	18	0	9	1	8	85	410	17	0
West Bountiful	17	0	13	0	4	18	109	12	0
West Valley	703	4	102	156	441	1,132	4,447	981	12
Willard	2	0	0	0	2	4	27	3	0
Woods Cross	33	0	23	1	9	46	189	36	1
Vermont									
Barre Town	2	0	0	0	2	51	107	4	0
Bennington	31	0	4	2	25	128	327	22	4
Berlin	13	0	1	1	11	13	125	5	0
Bradford	1	0	0	1	0	8	55	1	0
Brattleboro	36	0	4	7	25	98	490	18	0
Brighton	0	0	0	0	0	1	10	1	0
Bristol	2	0	0	0	2	4	31	0	0
Castleton	9	0	1	0	8	8	38	3	0
Colchester	14	0	1	2	11	75	279	0	0
Dover	1	0	0	0	1	15	71	1	0
Essex	19	1	1	8	9	111	361	9	2
Fair Haven	2	0	0	0	2	9	54	1	0
Hardwick	8	0	0	0	8	28	73	1	2
Hartford	18	1	3	3	11	37	116	7	0
Hinesburg	1	0	0	0	1	8	41	4	0
Milton	6	0	1	0	5	25	153	0	3
Morristown	1	0	0	1	0	16	85	0	0
Newport	15	0	8	1	6	38	91	3	0
Northfield	6	0	0	0	6	16	47	0	1
Norwich	0	0	0	0	0	18	29	4	0
Randolph	1	0	0	0	1	22	53	4	1
Richmond	0	0	0	0	0	23	39	1	0
Rutland	63	0	5	6	52	199	788	24	0
Shelburne	2	0	0	0	2	23	73	2	0
Springfield	20	0	1	4	15	59	224	12	1
St. Johnsbury	15	0	0	0	15	40	97	11	2
Stowe	2	0	1	0	1	8	85	1	0
Swanton	3	0	0	1	2	18	60	4	0
Vergennes	3	0	0	0	3	7	38	1	0
Waterbury	3	0	1	0	2	2	20	0	0
Weathersfield	1	0	0	0	1	16	28	2	0
Williston	5	0	1	0	4	22	253	5	2
Wilmington	3	0	0	0	3	11	24	1	0
Windsor	8	0	0	1	7	13	23	4	0
Woodstock	0	0	0	0	0	3	22	0	0
Virginia									
Abingdon	10	0	3	1	6	20	198	15	4
Alexandria	258	5	21	118	114	249	2,427	291	13
Altavista	8	0	0	2	6	4	52	0	0
Amherst	2	0	2	0	0	6	19	2	0
Appalachia	12	0	2	2	8	25	51	1	0
Ashland	26	0	1	8	17	14	221	11	1
Bedford	12	0	4	3	5	26	199	12	0
Berryville	5	0	2	1	2	7	72	1	0
Big Stone Gap	17	0	5	0	12	21	176	6	2
Blacksburg	31	0	7	4	20	91	417	15	8
Blackstone	14	0	1	6	7	14	114	1	1
Bloxom	0	0	0	0	0	1	0	0	0
Bowling Green	0	0	0	0	0	0	0	0	0
Boykins	0	0	0	0	0	1	8	1	0
Bridgewater	4	0	1	0	3	10	37	1	0

Table 8.   Offenses Known to Law Enforcement, by Selected State and City, 2013— continued

(Number.)

State/city	Violent crime	Murder and nonnegligent manslaughter	Rape (revised definition)[1]	Robbery	Aggravated assault	Burglary	Larceny-theft	Motor vehicle theft	Arson[2]
Bristol	59	0	6	7	46	61	462	20	5
Broadway	0	0	0	0	0	4	5	0	0
Brookneal	1	0	0	0	1	3	12	0	0
Buena Vista	9	1	3	0	5	1	56	1	1
Burkeville	1	0	0	0	1	0	8	1	0
Cape Charles	0	0	0	0	0	2	11	1	1
Charlottesville	211	1	20	63	127	200	1,218	53	5
Chase City	9	0	1	2	6	7	55	0	0
Chatham	0	0	0	0	0	0	9	0	0
Chesapeake	737	9	48	155	525	1,076	4,832	280	23
Chilhowie	0	0	0	0	0	4	30	2	0
Chincoteague	2	0	0	0	2	9	35	1	1
Christiansburg	30	1	13	3	13	53	478	14	2
Clarksville	3	0	0	0	3	2	16	2	0
Clifton Forge	8	0	2	0	6	9	37	4	0
Clintwood	2	0	0	0	2	3	21	1	0
Coeburn	3	0	0	0	3	23	79	3	1
Colonial Beach	8	0	3	1	4	20	57	11	0
Colonial Heights	43	1	14	13	15	49	681	18	1
Covington	7	1	0	0	6	18	85	2	1
Crewe	3	0	0	0	3	19	42	2	0
Culpeper	38	0	4	10	24	28	500	20	0
Damascus	2	0	1	0	1	3	17	0	0
Danville	150	5	20	60	65	444	1,508	84	13
Dayton	0	0	0	0	0	3	9	• 0	0
Dublin	2	0	2	0	0	5	36	5	0
Dumfries	0	0	0	0	0	21	81	11	0
Edinburg	0	0	0	0	0	3	14	0	0
Elkton	0	0	0	0	0	4	24	3	0
Emporia	24	0	2	6	16	44	187	4	2
Exmore	6	0	1	0	5	10	22	2	1
Fairfax City	26	0	3	11	12	27	346	23	0
Falls Church	24	1	4	9	10	14	194	7	0
Farmville	15	0	1	6	8	15	253	3	1
Franklin	35	0	11	12	12	97	337	12	2
Fredericksburg	114	1	3	29	81	66	1,036	32	0
Front Royal	30	0	19	7	4	40	436	25	0
Galax	12	0	0	1	11	22	249	4	1
Gate City	4	0	1	1	2	7	28	2	0
Glasgow	1	0	0	0	1	2	7	0	0
Glen Lyn	1	0	0	0	1	1	7	1	0
Gordonsville	1	0	0	1	0	0	18	1	0
Gretna	1	0	0	0	1	5	4	1	1
Grottoes	0	0	0	0	0	3	19	0	0
Grundy	0	0	0	0	0	0	8	1	0
Halifax	1	0	0	0	1	0	4	0	0
Hampton	292	22	21	120	129	722	3,525	226	23
Harrisonburg	106	1	18	16	71	206	1,126	35	1
Haymarket	0	0	0	0	0	0	23	0	0
Haysi	0	0	0	0	0	1	9	0	0
Herndon	51	0	8	18	25	27	331	8	0
Hillsville	10	0	3	2	5	6	69	7	0
Honaker	4	0	0	0	4	0	2	0	0
Hopewell	100	3	4	35	58	232	504	49	0
Hurt	0	0	0	0	0	0	2	0	0
Independence	1	0	0	1	0	0	5	0	0
Jonesville	0	0	0	0	0	0	13	0	0
Kenbridge	6	0	2	0	4	4	9	0	0
Kilmarnock	3	0	2	1	0	2	33	0	0
La Crosse	0	0	0	0	0	1	1	0	0
Lawrenceville	2	0	2	0	0	8	17	2	0
Lebanon	3	0	1	0	2	11	95	4	0
Leesburg	74	1	18	7	48	48	803	14	4
Lexington	4	0	1	1	2	6	54	2	0
Louisa	2	0	0	1	1	4	45	1	0
Luray	3	0	2	1	0	13	85	5	0
Lynchburg	330	1	36	73	220	349	1,538	87	6
Manassas	122	0	23	38	61	94	696	49	7
Manassas Park	15	0	6	3	6	23	166	14	2
Marion	25	0	4	4	17	20	180	7	0
Martinsville	56	0	2	20	34	65	408	27	2
Middleburg	0	0	0	0	0	2	8	0	0
Middletown	4	0	1	0	3	5	10	1	2
Mount Jackson	3	0	2	0	1	8	23	0	0
Narrows	4	0	2	0	2	0	4	0	0
New Market	0	0	0	0	0	3	17	1	0
Newport News	795	15	56	246	478	991	4,247	344	64
Norfolk	1,418	28	134	414	842	2,039	8,006	767	43

Table 8.   Offenses Known to Law Enforcement, by Selected State and City, 2013— continued

(Number.)

State/city	Violent crime	Murder and nonnegligent manslaughter	Rape (revised definition)[3]	Robbery	Aggravated assault	Burglary	Larceny-theft	Motor vehicle theft	Arson[2]
Norton	11	0	6	2	3	23	165	4	0
Occoquan	0	0	0	0	0	0	0	0	0
Onancock	0	0	0	0	0	4	26	0	0
Onley	0	0	0	0	0	1	5	1	0
Orange	8	0	3	1	4	11	98	3	0
Parksley	0	0	0	0	0	0	19	0	1
Pearisburg	4	0	3	0	1	4	79	2	0
Pembroke	0	0	0	0	0	6	42	0	1
Pennington Gap	5	0	1	0	4	8	41	0	1
Petersburg	163	7	9	56	91	345	671	87	3
Pocahontas	1	0	1	0	0	0	0	0	0
Poquoson	17	0	2	0	15	14	117	4	2
Portsmouth	590	12	47	177	354	1,535	3,615	205	5
Pound	2	0	0	0	2	10	18	2	0
Pulaski	27	1	10	2	14	54	295	7	0
Purcellville	2	0	0	1	1	2	34	0	1
Quantico	0	0	0	0	0	1	1	1	0
Radford	91	0	11	7	73	75	321	11	2
Rich Creek	2	0	0	0	2	0	1	0	0
Richlands	12	0	1	0	11	46	168	4	2
Richmond	1,327	37	43	624	623	1,817	5,949	938	50
Roanoke	457	9	44	142	262	628	3,636	180	21
Rocky Mount	23	0	8	0	15	9	160	4	0
Rural Retreat	0	0	0	0	0	0	9	0	0
Salem	24	2	3	12	7	74	503	27	1
Saltville	8	0	1	0	7	5	34	0	2
Shenandoah	2	0	0	0	2	16	39	0	0
Smithfield	13	0	2	2	9	17	102	9	2
South Boston	43	0	6	8	29	65	309	10	3
South Hill	16	0	2	7	7	9	116	2	0
Stanley	2	0	0	0	2	10	25	2	0
Staunton	50	1	15	5	29	71	510	17	7
Stephens City	0	0	0	0	0	7	41	3	0
St. Paul	4	0	0	0	4	9	40	1	1
Strasburg	9	0	4	0	5	6	86	0	1
Suffolk	268	7	37	64	160	500	1,980	102	24
Tappahannock	5	0	1	0	4	9	113	1	0
Tazewell	7	0	0	1	6	14	69	3	1
Timberville	0	0	0	0	0	2	4	0	0
Victoria	0	0	0	0	0	5	13	0	0
Vienna	9	0	0	2	7	29	177	3	0
Vinton	34	0	1	4	29	13	251	6	0
Virginia Beach	730	17	140	304	269	1,407	9,374	445	99
Warrenton	13	0	2	5	6	14	154	2	3
Warsaw	0	0	0	0	0	0	5	1	0
Waverly	1	0	0	0	1	6	17	1	0
Waynesboro	46	0	15	8	23	101	553	34	0
Weber City	0	0	0	0	0	2	8	1	0
West Point	2	0	0	0	2	9	26	2	0
White Stone	0	0	0	0	0	0	3	0	1
Williamsburg	22	1	4	6	11	12	171	8	0
Winchester	89	1	25	29	34	106	867	33	4
Windsor	5	0	0	0	5	4	42	1	1
Wise	7	0	2	0	5	10	66	3	1
Woodstock	16	1	1	2	12	6	99	2	0
Wytheville	10	0	2	1	7	69	159	6	0
Washington									
Aberdeen	58	0	11	13	34	208	624	112	5
Airway Heights	6	0	0	6	0	72	213	48	0
Algona	0	0	0	0	0	22	42	9	0
Anacortes	21	0	6	3	12	127	402	30	7
Arlington	37	0		11	23	198	791	135	0
Asotin	1	0	0	0	1	2	22	2	0
Auburn	293	5	34	110	144	798	2,474	672	14
Bainbridge Island	12	0	3	0	9	50	276	12	0
Battle Ground	13	0	3	1	9	58	268	25	2
Bellevue	125	1		48	56	688	3,013	248	23
Bingen	0	0	0	0	0	3	20	3	0
Black Diamond	0	0	0	0	0	11	49	7	0
Blaine	3	0	2	0	1	26	155	6	1
Bonney Lake	28	0	3	8	17	96	399	50	5
Bothell	18	0	0	4	14	173	604	69	3
Bremerton	227	1	35	55	136	452	1,354	140	13
Brewster	4	0	2	0	2	18	22	4	1
Brier	3	0	0	3	0	34	40	12	0
Buckley	1	0	1	0	0	9	138	16	5
Burien	177	0		65	75	690	1,398	524	11

Table 8.   Offenses Known to Law Enforcement, by Selected State and City, 2013— continued

(Number.)

State/city	Violent crime	Murder and nonnegligent manslaughter	Rape (revised definition)[1]	Robbery	Aggravated assault	Burglary	Larceny-theft	Motor vehicle theft	Arson[2]
Burlington	16	0	3	8	5	72	690	51	2
Camas	14	0	3	2	9	66	300	22	6
Carnation	1	0	0	0	1	15	30	0	2
Castle Rock	4	0	0	1	3	14	65	4	0
Centralia	61	0	8	18	35	155	600	43	10
Chehalis	11	0	0	3	8	36	292	13	0
Cheney	19	1	3	7	8	67	208	12	0
Chewelah	5	0	0	1	4	34	44	2	0
Clarkston	27	0	1	9	17	81	444	22	1
Cle Elum	2	0	0	0	2	37	115	11	1
Clyde Hill	2	0	0	1	1	10	14	0	0
Colfax	4	0	0	0	4	13	28	1	0
College Place	8	0	2	1	5	65	196	2	1
Colton	0	0	0	0	0	0	0	0	0
Colville	3	0	0	2	1	27	153	2	0
Connell	9	1	1	0	7	10	20	1	1
Cosmopolis	0	0	0	0	0	6	20	0	0
Coulee Dam	2	0	0	0	2	7	15	2	0
Coupeville	5	0	0	1	4	6	37	2	0
Covington	34	1		12	15	144	412	56	1
Des Moines	98	0	6	53	39	207	748	220	9
Dupont	9	0	0	0	9	16	42	1	0
Duvall	2	0	0	0	2	15	42	1	0
East Wenatchee	25	0	3	6	16	60	362	17	0
Eatonville	9	0	1	0	8	11	35	2	2
Edgewood	9	0	2	2	5	89	156	22	0
Edmonds	70	0		18	42	230	706	55	3
Ellensburg	33	0	9	7	17	113	548	30	1
Elma	4	0	0	0	4	40	91	12	0
Enumclaw	9	0	3	2	4	35	276	37	3
Ephrata	17	0	2	2	13	105	290	19	2
Everett	443	1		192	208	1,129	4,702	1,034	19
Everson	1	0	1	0	0	11	42	0	1
Federal Way	291	6	43	108	134	874	3,535	764	7
Ferndale	26	0	4	4	18	88	273	6	2
Fife	89	0	12	11	66	121	378	97	2
Fircrest	16	0	1	4	11	40	97	18	0
Forks	12	0	1	3	8	17	71	3	0
Garfield	0	0	0	0	0	0	3	1	0
Gig Harbor	22	0	6	2	14	62	382	23	2
Goldendale	8	0	0	4	4	47	109	6	0
Grand Coulee	7	0	1	1	5	24	35	9	1
Grandview	19	0	10	3	6	88	136	27	0
Granger	2	0	2	0	0	15	29	10	0
Granite Falls	9	0		0	4	5	27	82	40	1
Ilwaco	2	0	0	0	2	4	8	0	0
Issaquah	21	0	6	8	7	71	687	52	1
Kalama	7	0	5	0	2	8	32	4	0
Kelso	72	0	15	4	53	110	534	37	1
Kenmore	14	0		2	7	122	172	26	2
Kennewick	240	2	34	43	161	444	1,876	158	18
Kent	319	2	58	160	99	1,061	3,669	870	26
Kettle Falls	3	0	0	0	3	11	26	2	0
Kirkland	71	0	18	20	33	336	1,290	181	6
Kittitas	1	0	0	1	0	10	17	0	0
La Center	2	0	0	1	1	4	80	7	0
Lacey	79	0	8	22	49	236	1,165	90	1
Lake Forest Park	5	0	2	2	1	77	157	13	1
Lake Stevens	44	2	9	13	20	160	506	70	7
Lakewood	410	2	41	90	277	674	1,770	207	14
Liberty Lake	3	0	2	0	1	20	67	9	0
Long Beach	1	0	0	0	1	15	24	7	0
Longview	170	0	38	48	84	512	1,734	175	15
Lynden	9	0	1	1	7	27	97	2	1
Lynnwood	105	1		52	40	299	1,950	214	6
Mabton	0	0	0	0	0	8	24	6	0
Maple Valley	15	0		6	6	96	189	44	3
Marysville	138	1		32	93	475	1,548	365	9
Mattawa	3	0	0	0	3	9	25	14	0
McCleary	0	0	0	0	0	3	1	0	0
Medina	1	0	0	0	1	7	52	3	0
Mercer Island	8	0	2	1	5	70	281	12	1
Mill Creek	26	0	1	13	12	51	288	43	2
Milton	17	0	3	4	10	58	190	38	1
Monroe	67	1	11	7	48	92	446	79	2
Montesano	0	0	0	0	0	14	43	6	0
Morton	2	0	1	0	1	9	15	1	0
Moses Lake	103	0	19	29	55	329	1,140	106	4

Table 8.   Offenses Known to Law Enforcement, by Selected State and City, 2013— continued

(Number.)

State/city	Violent crime	Murder and nonnegligent manslaughter	Rape (revised definition)[1]	Robbery	Aggravated assault	Burglary	Larceny-theft	Motor vehicle theft	Arson[2]
Mountlake Terrace	32	0	6	9	17	137	337	73	0
Mount Vernon	89	1	15	31	42	258	1,276	128	6
Moxee	2	0	1	0	1	5	17	4	0
Mukilteo	14	0		3	7	140	350	52	3
Newcastle	12	0		6	4	65	155	16	1
Normandy Park	1	0	1	0	0	34	115	14	0
North Bend	11	0		4	4	53	170	15	1
Oak Harbor	31	0	5	4	22	113	390	23	2
Oakville	1	0	1	0	0	11	12	2	0
Ocean Shores	7	1	3	0	3	80	91	7	0
Odessa	0	0	0	0	0	1	3	0	0
Olympia	131	0	18	38	75	382	1,284	123	9
Omak	28	0	3	5	20	57	231	16	0
Oroville	1	0	1	0	0	37	72	4	0
Orting	11	0	0	5	6	32	146	14	1
Othello	47	1	3	8	35	62	236	45	2
Pacific	10	0	5	3	2	35	81	38	0
Palouse	0	0	0	0	0	2	3	0	0
Pasco	158	0	25	28	105	379	1,119	135	15
Port Angeles	94	1	18	15	60	194	634	41	2
Port Orchard	74	0	10	11	53	140	583	46	5
Port Townsend	41	0	4	1	36	67	194	11	3
Poulsbo	19	0	6	4	9	44	221	13	1
Prosser	9	0	1	0	8	18	74	16	1
Pullman	27	0	4	2	21	93	234	13	1
Puyallup	104	2	15	28	59	410	2,301	316	11
Quincy	18	0	5	1	12	108	226	35	2
Raymond	2	0	1	0	1	5	41	2	0
Reardan	1	0	0	0	1	0	3	0	0
Redmond	39	0	24	3	12	193	1,402	70	4
Renton	254	3	27	101	123	859	3,396	683	14
Republic	7	0	0	5	2	3	5	2	0
Richland	95	3	17	11	64	205	927	35	5
Ridgefield	1	0	0	1	0	8	56	2	0
Ritzville	1	0	0	0	1	17	45	2	1
Rosalia	0	0	0	0	0	0	0	0	0
Roy	1	0	0	1	0	2	13	2	0
Royal City	5	0	0	2	3	22	20	7	1
Ruston	1	0	0	0	1	3	20	1	0
Sammamish	11	0		1	6	89	175	11	2
SeaTac	172	2		66	68	380	843	347	8
Seattle	3,758	19	153	1,601	1,985	7,384	24,189	4,310	90
Sedro Woolley	18	0	4	5	9	129	502	40	1
Selah	0	0	0	0	0	31	64	6	0
Sequim	13	0	2	2	9	61	308	14	3
Shelton	36	2	5	12	17	143	526	81	2
Shoreline	80	0		24	32	426	1,070	201	19
Snohomish	23	0	0	7	16	76	268	55	3
Snoqualmie	3	0	2	0	1	17	65	8	0
Spokane	1,440	11		518	745	3,889	13,352	2,290	59
Spokane Valley	231	1		81	114	961	3,862	490	11
Springdale	1	0	0	0	1	1	0	0	0
Stanwood	9	0		2	5	28	136	24	1
Steilacoom	13	0	2	4	7	14	47	3	0
Sultan	10	0		0	10	30	93	23	0
Sumas	0	0	0	0	0	5	17	3	1
Sumner	29	0	3	10	16	127	327	63	9
Sunnyside	42	0	6	10	26	108	395	96	2
Tacoma	1,766	10	144	524	1,088	3,086	8,200	2,024	90
Tenino	1	0	0	0	1	4	30	8	0
Tieton	1	0	1	0	0	4	5	0	1
Tonasket	6	0	3	1	2	10	18	1	1
Toppenish	38	1	3	8	26	60	244	116	4
Tukwila	164	0	29	85	50	234	2,672	403	3
Tumwater	41	0	10	5	26	161	421	30	1
Twisp	1	0	0	0	1	9	16	0	0
Union Gap	11	2	1	2	6	47	323	31	1
University Place	92	0	5	34	53	162	574	58	2
Vancouver	593	2	74	146	371	1,007	3,950	976	36
Wapato	22	0	1	1	20	18	84	33	3
Warden	3	0	0	0	3	11	58	8	0
Washougal	29	0	7	5	17	53	226	32	1
Westport	0	0	0	0	0	12	36	5	0
West Richland	15	0	2	1	12	34	98	6	1
White Salmon	0	0	0	0	0	5	37	1	0
Wilbur	0	0	0	0	0	3	8	1	0
Winlock	0	0	0	0	0	12	48	1	0
Winthrop	0	0	0	0	0	2	5	0	0

Table 8.   Offenses Known to Law Enforcement, by Selected State and City, 2013— continued

(Number.)

State/city	Violent crime	Murder and nonnegligent manslaughter	Rape (revised definition)[1]	Robbery	Aggravated assault	Burglary	Larceny-theft	Motor vehicle theft	Arson[2]
Woodinville	20	1		8	3	84	252	30	3
Woodland	19	0	3	4	12	38	187	15	3
Woodway	0	0	0	0	0	6	22	0	0
Yakima	471	9	37	144	281	1,194	2,896	594	14
Yarrow Point	0	0	0	0	0	1	1	0	0
Zillah	3	0	0	0	3	11	24	8	1
West Virginia									
Alderson	0	0	0	0	0	0	10	0	0
Barboursville	1	0	1	0	0	16	270	3	0
Beech Bottom	0	0	0	0	0	0	1	0	0
Benwood	2	0	0	0	2	0	0	0	0
Bluefield	56	0	13	8	35	73	197	19	5
Bridgeport	12	0	0	0	12	18	180	3	0
Buckhannon	9	0	1	0	8	33	204	8	0
Chapmanville	2	0	0	0	2	2	34	4	0
Charles Town	10	0	0	2	8	18	51	2	1
Clearview	0	0	0	0	0	0	0	0	0
Dunbar	24	1	4	6	13	45	108	8	1
Eleanor	2	0	0	0	2	1	2	0	0
Elkins	68	0	1	5	62	52	150	3	0
Gauley Bridge	1	0	0	0	1	1	2	0	0
Glasgow	2	0	1	0	1	6	15	2	0
Glen Dale	6	0	0	0	6	5	7	1	0
Glenville	0	0	0	0	0	0	3	0	0
Grafton	3	0	0	0	3	2	7	0	0
Hamlin	15	0	0	0	15	11	20	0	0
Harpers Ferry/Bolivar	0	0	0	0	0	1	1	0	0
Harrisville	4	0	0	0	4	1	5	0	0
Hinton	3	0	0	1	2	32	36	2	1
Hurricane	3	0	3	0	0	23	132	3	0
Kenova	7	0	2	2	3	9	81	3	1
Keyser	9	0	3	1	5	11	91	0	0
Lewisburg	8	0	1	0	7	4	99	3	0
Marmet	3	0	0	3	0	6	18	1	0
Martinsburg	70	1	8	27	34	97	702	28	4
Mason	2	0	0	1	1	1	6	0	0
Milton	4	0	1	1	2	7	60	4	1
Moorefield	7	0	0	0	7	2	17	1	0
Morgantown	94	0	18	31	45	176	485	20	2
Mount Hope	0	0	0	0	0	4	4	1	0
Nitro	11	0	1	0	10	38	161	9	1
Oak Hill	27	2	2	6	17	57	186	12	4
Oceana	40	0	0	0	40	18	107	2	0
Parkersburg	127	0	21	12	94	343	982	57	26
Philippi	22	0	2	0	20	8	13	0	0
Point Pleasant	3	0	0	0	3	18	64	4	0
Princeton	60	0	0	2	58	74	253	6	2
Rainelle	0	0	0	0	0	0	0	0	0
Ravenswood	0	0	0	0	0	9	36	0	0
Reedsville	0	0	0	0	0	0	1	0	0
Ripley	3	0	0	0	3	0	5	0	1
Romney	3	0	0	0	3	0	0	0	0
Ronceverte	2	0	0	0	2	7	30	0	0
Shepherdstown	1	0	0	0	1	2	12	0	0
Shinnston	2	0	0	0	2	4	26	0	0
Sistersville	3	0	0	1	2	5	6	0	0
Sophia	1	0	0	1	0	6	38	1	0
South Charleston	80	1	2	16	61	68	439	20	0
Spencer	2	0	2	0	0	12	59	1	0
St. Albans	39	0	2	7	30	59	278	22	3
Star City	7	0	0	2	5	2	7	0	0
Summersville	22	0	0	0	22	11	101	2	0
Vienna	10	0	0	0	10	18	273	8	1
Welch	6	0	0	0	6	0	1	0	0
Wellsburg	0	0	0	0	0	16	14	2	0
West Liberty	0	0	0	0	0	0	1	0	0
Weston	2	0	0	0	2	1	6	0	0
White Hall	4	0	0	1	3	1	5	1	0
White Sulphur Springs	1	0	0	0	1	0	0	0	0
Williamson	8	1	2	4	1	7	21	0	0
Winfield	4	0	0	1	3	1	10	1	0
Wisconsin									
Adams	7	0	3	0	4	16	68	4	0
Albany	8	0	0	0	8	11	34	1	0
Algoma	1	0	1	0	0	1	81	1	0
Alma	0	0	0	0	0	0	2	0	0

Table 8. Offenses Known to Law Enforcement, by Selected State and City, 2013— continued

(Number.)

State/city	Violent crime	Murder and nonnegligent manslaughter	Rape (revised definition)[1]	Robbery	Aggravated assault	Burglary	Larceny-theft	Motor vehicle theft	Arson[2]
Altoona	8	1		1	6	17	68	0	0
Amery	11	0		0	11	6	27	3	0
Antigo	10	0		0	10	77	329	13	0
Appleton	176	1	28	14	133	186	1,088	30	15
Arcadia	3	0		1	2	2	29	2	0
Ashland	32	1		3	24	47	373	9	1
Ashwaubenon	14	0		7	2	48	684	14	0
Athens	0	0		0	0	1	6	0	0
Avoca	0	0		0	0	2	16	0	0
Bangor	3	0	1	0	2	0	11	0	0
Baraboo	25	0		3	15	46	359	5	1
Barneveld	0	0		0	0	3	13	2	0
Bayfield	1	0		0	1	4	23	0	0
Beaver Dam	8	0		1	7	104	470	1	2
Belleville	1	0	0	0	1	2	28	0	0
Beloit	129	1		36	76	320	830	45	9
Beloit Town	12	0		2	8	45	107	7	6
Berlin	3	1		2	0	5	127	3	0
Big Bend	1	0		0	1	1	24	1	0
Black River Falls	2	1		0	1	3	125	2	0
Blair	0	0		0	0	2	15	1	0
Blanchardville	1	0		0	1	2	5	0	0
Bloomer	1	0		0	1	3	20	0	0
Bloomfield	2	0		1	1	9	60	2	0
Blue Mounds	5	0		0	4	6	8	0	0
Boscobel	13	0		0	13	15	36	0	0
Brandon-Fairwater	0	0		0	0	0	1	0	0
Brillion	0	0	0	0	0	12	14	0	0
Brodhead	4	0		1	3	3	85	2	0
Brookfield	30	0		18	12	98	979	9	0
Brookfield Township	13	0		2	11	12	168	7	0
Brown Deer	15	0	0	3	12	32	340	12	2
Burlington	17	0		0	16	25	218	0	1
Butler	9	0		2	7	3	29	5	0
Caledonia	12	0		4	7	83	217	6	0
Campbellsport	0	0		0	0	1	8	0	0
Campbell Township	3	1	0	0	2	28	57	2	0
Cashton	0	0		0	0	0	0	0	0
Cedarburg	1	0		1	0	10	119	1	0
Chenequa	0	0		0	0	0	3	0	0
Chetek	4	0		0	4	7	18	0	0
Chilton	2	0	0	0	2	9	55	0	0
Chippewa Falls	26	0		1	25	22	117	8	1
Cleveland	2	0		0	2	1	13	1	0
Clinton	2	0		1	1	0	15	1	0
Clintonville	3	0		0	2	20	136	2	0
Colby-Abbotsford	1	0		0	1	5	43	2	0
Columbus	4	0		2	2	10	137	1	0
Cornell	0	0		0	0	1	44	1	0
Cottage Grove	11	0	1	1	9	10	83	2	0
Crandon	2	0		0	2	3	11	1	0
Cross Plains	0	0	0	0	0	3	20	0	0
Cuba City	2	0		0	2	2	23	0	2
Cudahy	39	0		17	12	71	361	22	0
Cumberland	13	0		0	13	9	30	1	1
Dane	0	0		0	0	0	0	0	0
Darlington	1	0		0	1	7	26	3	0
Deforest	13	0	5	0	8	5	72	1	0
Delafield	2	0		0	2	15	160	0	0
Delavan	12	0		3	7	31	270	8	0
Delavan Town	1	0		0	1	21	61	6	0
Denmark	1	0		0	1	5	7	0	0
De Pere	7	0		3	3	41	239	3	0
Dodgeville	3	0		0	3	18	39	0	0
Durand	2	0		0	2	2	5	0	0
Eagle River	4	0		0	3	18	55	4	0
East Troy	7	0		1	2	7	73	3	2
Eau Claire	123	1		14	86	235	1,287	48	7
Edgar	0	0		0	0	2	3	0	0
Edgerton	4	0		2	2	12	130	5	5
Eleva	0	0		0	0	0	2	0	0
Elkhart Lake	1	0		0	0	3	19	0	0
Elkhorn	9	0		0	8	22	117	2	0
Elk Mound	2	0		0	2	0	1	0	0
Ellsworth	6	0		0	0	14	52	0	0
Elm Grove	1	0		0	1	11	56	4	0
Elroy	2	0		0	0	12	22	0	0
Endeavor	0	0	0	0	0	0	2	0	0

Table 8.   Offenses Known to Law Enforcement, by Selected State and City, 2013— continued

(Number.)

State/city	Violent crime	Murder and nonnegligent manslaughter	Rape (revised definition)[1]	Robbery	Aggravated assault	Burglary	Larceny-theft	Motor vehicle theft	Arson[2]
Evansville	4	0		1	3	18	63	2	0
Everest	14	0		2	9	74	261	7	0
Fall Creek	0	0		0	0	0	14	0	0
Fall River	3	0		0	3	5	18	0	0
Fennimore	2	0		1	1	5	52	0	0
Fitchburg	61	0		14	42	79	348	17	0
Fond du Lac	154	1	31	11	111	126	1,021	31	5
Fontana	7	0		0	7	1	21	0	0
Fort Atkinson	12	0		3	8	28	142	4	0
Fountain City	0	0		0	0	0	42	1	0
Fox Lake	0	0		0	0	4	6	0	0
Fox Point	1	0	0	1	0	4	61	0	0
Fox Valley Metro	14	0	3	1	10	28	156	1	0
Frederic	2	0		0	2	1	8	0	0
Freedom	0	0	0	0	0	23	14	0	0
Geneva Town	2	0		0	2	19	63	0	0
Genoa City	2	0		0	0	17	30	0	0
Germantown	13	0		3	3	47	336	3	0
Gilman	0	0		0	0	2	6	0	0
Glendale	35	1		23	9	61	839	27	0
Grafton	1	0		1	0	14	153	1	0
Grand Chute	23	0	1	3	19	29	749	12	3
Grand Rapids	2	0		1	1	10	32	1	0
Grantsburg	2	0		0	2	5	18	2	0
Green Bay	500	2	52	79	367	575	2,001	98	16
Greendale	14	0		8	6	13	586	7	0
Greenfield	51	0		23	21	129	1,119	24	0
Green Lake	0	0		0	0	1	13	1	0
Hales Corners	10	0		1	7	11	125	2	0
Hartford	10	1		2	7	32	234	4	0
Hartland	6	0		0	5	13	93	3	0
Hayward	5	0	0	0	5	15	45	2	0
Hazel Green	1	0		0	1	2	5	0	0
Highland	0	0		0	0	1	6	0	0
Hobart-Lawrence	0	0		0	0	22	49	5	0
Holmen	11	0	1	0	10	21	106	4	1
Horicon	2	0		0	1	4	65	2	0
Hortonville	0	0		0	0	0	22	0	0
Hudson	12	0	2	3	7	31	389	8	1
Independence	0	0		0	0	0	1	0	0
Iron Ridge	1	0		0	1	5	8	1	0
Iron River	2	0		0	2	4	5	0	3
Jackson	5	0		2	3	10	22	2	0
Janesville	166	0		25	100	330	1,576	37	19
Jefferson	22	0		2	16	6	230	5	1
Juneau	0	0		0	0	4	46	0	0
Kaukauna	19	0	1	0	18	29	134	6	0
Kenosha	274	5		102	141	563	1,826	73	23
Kewaskum	2	0		0	2	5	23	1	0
Kewaunee	0	0	0	0	0	11	47	0	0
Kiel	4	0		0	4	6	62	3	0
Kohler	0	0		0	0	1	67	0	0
Kronenwetter	3	0		0	1	7	50	3	0
La Crosse	107	1	20	29	57	305	1,200	43	2
Ladysmith	7	0		0	7	4	79	1	0
Lake Delton	13	0		1	9	25	531	6	0
Lake Geneva	5	0		1	3	31	263	5	0
Lake Hallie	7	0		4	2	17	190	7	0
Lake Mills	3	0		0	3	5	22	0	0
Lancaster	21	0		0	20	8	39	0	0
Lodi	1	0		0	1	3	42	0	0
Lomira	1	0		0	0	7	65	0	0
Luxemburg	0	0	0	0	0	1	11	1	0
Madison	884	5	76	296	507	1,382	6,094	253	50
Manawa	3	0		1	1	6	14	0	0
Manitowoc	75	1	9	5	60	122	756	16	0
Marathon City	1	0		0	1	4	4	0	0
Marinette	8	0		1	4	38	270	16	2
Marion	4	0		0	4	6	9	0	0
Markesan	2	0		1	1	4	24	0	0
Marshall Village	4	0	1	0	3	3	30	0	0
Marshfield	12	0		3	8	49	345	6	1
Mauston	20	1		0	18	16	72	3	0
Mayville	1	0		0	0	12	67	1	0
McFarland	5	0	1	2	2	24	86	5	0
Medford	13	0		0	5	11	91	2	1
Menasha	31	0		1	29	55	362	6	1
Menomonee Falls	14	0		8	6	28	357	10	0

Table 8.   Offenses Known to Law Enforcement, by Selected State and City, 2013— continued

(Number.)

State/city	Violent crime	Murder and nonnegligent manslaughter	Rape (revised definition)	Robbery	Aggravated assault	Burglary	Larceny-theft	Motor vehicle theft	Arson[2]
Menomonie	24	0		2	19	60	370	11	1
Mequon	2	0		2	0	22	119	5	1
Merrill	29	0		0	17	39	171	7	1
Middleton	8	0		3	3	50	283	7	0
Milton	9	0		1	7	14	76	1	0
Milwaukee	8,194	104	401	3,284	4,405	6,491	16,138	4,384	293
Mineral Point	4	0		0	4	5	45	4	0
Minocqua	11	0	1	0	10	6	64	4	1
Mishicot	0	0		0	0	0	0	0	0
Monona	21	0		14	5	36	623	5	0
Monroe	17	0		1	14	24	212	9	2
Montello	0	0	0	0	0	5	23	0	0
Mosinee	2	0		0	2	16	42	3	0
Mount Horeb	5	0		0	5	17	73	0	0
Mount Pleasant	14	1		10	0	68	671	26	1
Mukwonago	5	0		1	4	6	103	4	5
Mukwonago Town	8	0		0	8	12	17	0	0
Muskego	6	0	4	0	2	37	143	10	1
Neenah	41	0		3	34	55	441	9	2
Neillsville	0	0		0	0	3	40	0	0
Neshkoro	0	0	0	0	0	0	3	1	0
New Glarus	2	0		0	1	4	32	2	0
New Holstein	7	0	0	0	7	5	58	0	0
New Lisbon	3	0		0	3	4	16	0	0
New London	7	0	1	0	6	25	138	3	1
New Richmond	15	0	0	0	15	27	179	2	0
Niagara	2	0		0	2	2	12	1	0
North Fond du Lac	7	0	0	1	6	9	59	5	0
North Hudson	0	0		0	0	7	21	0	0
North Prairie	0	0		0	0	1	13	0	0
Oak Creek	46	0		8	30	138	850	29	0
Oconomowoc	12	0		3	2	24	199	2	0
Oconomowoc Town	2	0		1	1	6	21	1	0
Oconto	10	0		2	6	14	124	4	5
Omro	4	0		0	4	5	83	4	0
Onalaska	8	0	0	0	8	26	401	2	0
Oregon	15	0	0	0	15	12	74	1	0
Osceola	16	0		0	16	4	40	1	0
Oshkosh	155	0		23	123	219	1,163	39	5
Osseo	2	0		0	2	6	38	0	0
Oxford	0	0	0	0	0	6	13	0	0
Palmyra	2	0		0	2	9	74	0	0
Park Falls	1	1		0	0	1	19	1	1
Pepin	0	0		0	0	1	21	1	0
Peshtigo	2	1		1	0	17	65	0	0
Pewaukee Village	10	0	0	1	9	20	123	1	0
Phillips	11	0		0	4	7	50	1	0
Plainfield	0	0		0	0	2	2	1	0
Platteville	5	0		0	3	32	270	2	1
Pleasant Prairie	21	0		1	14	18	280	8	0
Plover	15	0	2	1	12	24	213	0	0
Plymouth	6	0		1	5	14	152	7	0
Portage	46	1		3	22	16	40	1	0
Port Washington	0	0		0	0	8	132	7	2
Poynette	0	0		0	0	5	23	0	0
Prairie du Chien	15	0		0	12	9	178	0	0
Prescott	19	0		1	16	8	50	2	0
Princeton	1	0		1	0	0	22	2	0
Pulaski	0	0		0	0	2	25	0	1
Racine	297	1		179	96	1,211	1,704	95	9
Reedsburg	18	0		0	8	6	152	1	0
Rhinelander	23	0	5	0	18	29	197	5	0
Richland Center	2	0		0	2	19	54	1	0
Ripon	8	0	0	1	7	7	76	1	0
River Falls	29	0	9	2	18	44	253	9	1
River Hills	1	0	0	1	0	2	7	0	0
Rome Town	5	0	1	0	4	6	22	0	0
Rosendale	0	0		0	0	0	0	0	0
Rothschild	3	0		1	2	8	114	1	0
Sauk Prairie	3	0		1	0	13	63	0	1
Saukville	1	0		1	0	10	93	5	0
Seymour	9	0	1	0	8	0	17	1	0
Shawano	19	0		2	12	37	265	16	2
Sheboygan	132	1		14	97	187	1,023	31	6
Sheboygan Falls	2	0		0	2	6	124	4	1
Shiocton	0	0	0	0	0	0	11	0	0
Shorewood	30	1		14	13	32	321	24	0
Shorewood Hills	0	0	0	0	0	7	56	0	0

Table 8. Offenses Known to Law Enforcement, by Selected State and City, 2013— continued

(Number.)

State/city	Violent crime	Murder and nonnegligent manslaughter	Rape (revised definition)[1]	Robbery	Aggravated assault	Burglary	Larceny-theft	Motor vehicle theft	Arson[2]
Silver Lake	1	0		0	0	1	2	1	0
Siren	2	0	0	1	1	1	51	3	0
Slinger	1	0		1	0	7	85	1	0
South Milwaukee	41	0		15	22	46	334	19	1
Sparta	32	0		4	14	36	176	4	0
Spooner	17	0		0	13	17	50	4	0
Spring Green	0	0		0	0	2	16	0	0
Stanley	9	0		0	9	15	38	0	0
St. Croix Falls	6	0		0	6	16	79	3	0
Stevens Point	41	0		3	31	58	500	5	0
St. Francis	10	0		2	7	24	147	4	0
Stoughton	4	0		1	1	30	215	4	0
Strum	0	0		0	0	0	2	1	0
Sturgeon Bay	15	0		1	14	22	127	0	0
Sturtevant	2	0		1	0	12	41	3	0
Summit	0	0		0	0	2	20	0	0
Sun Prairie	30	1		6	17	91	680	17	3
Superior	92	1		22	47	279	1,243	100	5
Theresa	5	0		0	4	9	70	0	0
Thiensville	0	0		0	0	1	8	0	0
Tomah	24	0		1	20	19	265	6	1
Tomahawk	2	0		1	1	15	97	1	0
Town of East Troy	0	0		0	0	6	18	1	0
Town of Madison	49	0	7	10	32	41	154	17	0
Town of Menasha	19	0		1	15	32	151	7	0
Trempealeau	0	0		0	0	3	5	0	0
Twin Lakes	1	0		0	1	26	67	0	0
Two Rivers	19	0	3	1	15	42	124	7	0
Valders	0	0		0	0	0	3	1	0
Verona	6	0		2	3	12	168	1	0
Viroqua	2	0		0	2	6	62	3	0
Walworth	6	0		1	2	4	9	1	0
Washburn	3	0		0	3	5	31	0	0
Waterloo	3	0		0	2	7	30	0	0
Watertown	94	0		6	64	101	357	14	4
Waukesha	90	1		25	41	210	1,079	38	4
Waunakee	10	0		2	6	19	115	8	1
Waupaca	29	0		4	24	6	175	2	0
Waupun	10	0	4	0	6	25	104	3	1
Wausau	85	2		13	59	217	725	28	5
Wautoma	1	0		0	1	6	124	1	0
Wauwatosa	59	0		45	10	277	1,308	47	4
West Allis	196	1		104	77	631	2,128	92	15
West Bend	18	0		5	12	59	803	14	1
Westby	2	0		0	1	3	46	0	1
Westfield	0	0	0	0	0	2	8	2	0
West Milwaukee	26	0		17	8	51	543	22	0
West Salem	3	0	1	0	2	3	64	3	0
Whitefish Bay	3	0		2	0	28	162	3	0
Whitehall	4	0		0	4	2	18	0	0
Whitewater	31	0		6	20	40	197	5	1
Williams Bay	1	0		1	0	2	13	1	0
Winneconne	1	0		0	1	1	24	0	0
Wisconsin Dells	16	0		1	12	16	202	4	0
Wisconsin Rapids	10	0		0	3	97	599	16	1
Woodruff	3	0	0	0	3	2	11	0	0
Wyoming									
Afton	0	0		0	0	3	22	0	0
Buffalo	20	0		0	14	10	103	2	0
Casper	88	2		15	64	294	1,657	85	6
Cheyenne	133	1		12	108	279	1,698	88	4
Cody	14	0		2	12	33	168	3	1
Diamondville	0	0		0	0	0	0	0	0
Douglas	16	0		0	15	21	176	4	1
Evanston	7	0		3	2	26	362	8	0
Evansville	19	0		0	19	7	21	2	0
Gillette	53	2		0	45	153	821	34	8
Glenrock	1	0		0	1	6	30	0	0
Green River	56	0		1	48	28	120	8	1
Greybull	7	0		0	7	1	5	0	0
Guernsey	2	0		0	2	2	0	0	0
Hanna	1	0		0	1	1	3	3	0
Hulett	2	0		0	2	2	2	0	0
Jackson	62	0		17	36	20	199	12	0
Kemmerer	3	0		0	3	14	52	1	0
Lander	5	0		0	5	16	261	8	0
Laramie	37	1		3	23	70	562	38	2

Table 8.   Offenses Known to Law Enforcement, by Selected State and City, 2013— continued

(Number.)

State/city	Violent crime	Murder and nonnegligent manslaughter	Rape (revised definition)[1]	Robbery	Aggravated assault	Burglary	Larceny-theft	Motor vehicle theft	Arson[2]
Lusk	3	0		1	2	2	2	0	0
Mills	28	0		2	26	44	60	6	0
Moorcroft	1	0		0	1	1	30	1	0
Newcastle	8	0		0	5	16	66	2	0
Pine Bluffs	4	0		0	4	11	10	0	0
Powell	22	0		1	10	31	124	2	0
Rawlins	30	0		1	27	39	185	11	1
Riverton	45	0		5	36	41	498	24	0
Rock Springs	71	0		4	57	99	551	28	1
Saratoga	4	0		0	4	2	11	0	0
Sheridan	23	0		3	17	78	300	22	3
Sundance	0	0		0	0	2	7	2	0
Thermopolis	2	0		0	2	14	54	3	0
Torrington	18	0		0	17	33	85	3	0
Wheatland	11	0		0	11	21	85	8	0
Worland	7	0		0	7	2	45	0	0

1 The figures shown in this column for the offense of rape were reported using the revised Uniform Crime Reporting (UCR) definition of rape. See chapter notes for more detail.   2 The FBI does not publish arson data unless it receives data from either the agency or the state for all 12 months of the calendar year.

Table 9.   Offenses Known to Law Enforcement, by Selected State and University and College, 2013

(Number.)

State and university/college	Student enrollment [1]	Murder and non-negligent man-slaughter	Rape (revised definition) [2]	Robbery	Aggravated assault	Burglary	Larceny-theft	Motor vehicle theft	Arson [3]
Alabama									
Alabama A&M University	4,853	0	1	2	3	14	147	4	
Jacksonville State University	9,161	0	0	0	2	15	69	4	
Samford University	4,758	0	0	0	0	18	70	0	
Troy University	22,554	0	1	1	0	7	58	4	
Tuskegee University	3,117	0	2	4	4	30	202	3	
University of Alabama									
Huntsville	7,636	0	2	0	2	22	61	0	
Tuscaloosa	33,503	0	2	4	0	23	441	4	
University of Montevallo	3,083	0	0	0	0	6	17	0	
University of North Alabama	7,032	0	3	2	1	5	57	1	
University of South Alabama	14,636	0	1	1	1	16	118	3	
Alaska									
University of Alaska									
Anchorage	17,497	0	0	0	0	3	96	3	0
Fairbanks	9,223	0	0	3	1	3	67	3	0
Arizona									
Arizona State University, Main Campus	73,378	0		4	25	103	995	33	2
Central Arizona College	7,018	0		0	0	6	12	0	0
Northern Arizona University	25,991	0		2	10	28	214	0	3
Pima Community College	32,988	0		1	1	9	119	5	1
University of Arizona	40,223	0		7	13	29	816	12	2
Arkansas									
Arkansas State University									
Beebe	4,643	0	0	0	0	1	19	0	0
Jonesboro	13,877	0	2	0	6	18	79	0	0
Arkansas Tech University	10,950	0	1	0	1	24	75	1	0
Henderson State University	3,773	0	0	0	0	2	23	0	0
University of Arkansas									
Fayetteville	24,537	0	4	0	0	27	157	11	0
Little Rock	12,872	0	0	1	1	33	89	5	0
Medical Sciences	2,809	0	0	1	10	2	111	7	0
University of Central Arkansas	11,107	0	1	0	0	30	108	3	0
California									
Allan Hancock College	10,837	0		0	0	2	18	1	0
California State Polytechnic University									
Pomona	22,156	0		1	0	10	132	21	0
San Luis Obispo	18,679	0		1	1	2	198	15	0
California State University									
Bakersfield	8,520	0		0	2	8	55	5	0
Channel Islands	4,920	0		1	5	4	43	2	0
Chico	16,470	0		2	0	10	340	6	1
Dominguez Hills	13,933	0		1	4	9	77	1	0
East Bay	13,851	0		0	0	10	83	3	0
Fresno	22,565	0		3	0	47	323	9	0
Fullerton	37,677	0		0	4	19	169	10	0
Long Beach	36,279	0		0	2	28	190	14	0
Los Angeles	21,755	0		3	1	6	122	14	0
Monterey Bay	5,609	0		0	1	5	36	0	0
Northridge	36,164	0		1	4	23	336	12	2
Sacramento	28,539	0		1	2	10	178	2	0
San Bernardino	18,234	0		0	4	8	95	12	0
San Jose	30,448	1		6	8	19	326	10	1
San Marcos	10,610	0		0	3	9	56	1	0
Stanislaus	8,882	0		2	0	3	54	4	0
College of the Sequoias	10,947	0		0	0	20	45	2	0
Contra Costa Community College	6,899	0		7	0	28	160	23	2
Cuesta College	9,834	0		0	0	0	15	0	0
El Camino College	23,405	0		1	1	25	161	8	8
Foothill-De Anza College	38,900	0		0	0	13	35	3	0
Humboldt State University	8,116	0		0	1	5	85	2	2
Marin Community College	7,058	0		0	0	1	29	0	0
Pasadena Community College	22,859	0		4	1	6	127	2	1
Riverside Community College	17,218	0		1	1	3	88	5	0
San Bernardino Community College	17,311	0		0	0	25	82	17	1
San Diego State University	30,843	0		9	8	52	623	21	2
San Francisco State University	30,500	0		7	0	81	189	21	0
San Jose/Evergreen Community College	19,186	0		0	0	11	55	11	1
Santa Rosa Junior College	22,823	0		1	6	7	87	4	0
Solano Community College	9,772	0		0	0	0	22	2	0
Sonoma State University	9,021	0		0	1	17	137	0	1
State Center Community College District	35,367	0		11	1	21	208	28	0
University of California									

Table 9.   Offenses Known to Law Enforcement, by Selected State and University and College, 2013— continued

(Number.)

State and university/college	Student enrollment [1]	Murder and non-negligent manslaughter	Rape (revised definition) [2]	Robbery	Aggravated assault	Burglary	Larceny-theft	Motor vehicle theft	Arson [3]
Berkeley	35,893	1		18	22	65	887	17	9
Davis	32,354	0		2	4	40	608	5	2
Hastings College of Law	1,159	0		14	3	3	41	0	0
Irvine	27,479	0		1	28	48	372	16	1
Los Angeles	39,945	0		11	40	144	744	17	1
Medical Center, Sacramento		0		0	1	5	174	2	1
Merced	5,760	0		0	0	1	38	0	0
Riverside	20,947	0		6	1	16	219	7	1
San Diego	28,294	0		1	4	59	693	22	1
San Francisco	3,137	0		4	3	12	377	5	0
Santa Barbara	21,927	0		6	2	25	259	5	2
Santa Cruz	17,404	0		1	7	29	233	4	9
Ventura County Community College District	13,030	0		0	0	0	95	0	0
West Valley-Mission College	20,179	0		0	3	5	35	2	0
Colorado									
Aims Community College	4,983	0	0	1	0	4	4	0	0
Arapahoe Community College	11,806	0	0	0	0	0	9	0	0
Auraria Higher Education Center		0	0	3	0	6	201	8	0
Colorado State University, Fort Collins	30,659	0	6	2	1	12	329	4	7
Fort Lewis College	3,883	0	2	1	0	7	44	2	0
Pikes Peak Community College	15,175	0	0	0	0	1	24	1	0
Red Rocks Community College	9,031	0	0	0	0	0	10	1	0
University of Colorado									
Boulder	31,945	0	10	0	18	31	410	7	4
Colorado Springs	10,612	0	1	0	1	7	47	3	0
Denver	22,396	0	0	0	0	4	54	2	0
Health Sciences Center		0	0	0	0	23	0	0	0
University of Northern Colorado	13,070	0	1	0	1	4	129	1	1
Connecticut									
Central Connecticut State University	12,091	0	1	0	0	3	34	1	0
Eastern Connecticut State University	5,440	0	0	0	0	10	95	2	0
Southern Connecticut State University	11,117	0	3	1	0	2	54	0	0
University of Connecticut									
Health Center		0	0	0	0	0	1	0	0
Storrs, Avery Point, and Hartford		0	9	1	2	26	200	19	2
Western Connecticut State University	6,176	0	0	0	0	6	32	0	0
Yale University	11,906	0		3	0	56	255	2	0
Delaware									
Delaware State University	4,324	0	4	3	6	34	84	0	0
University of Delaware	21,856	0	0	0	2	26	182	0	1
Florida									
Edison State College	15,731	0	0	0	0	2	14	1	0
Florida A&M University	12,057	0	4	5	4	6	151	10	0
Florida Atlantic University	29,994	0	0	2	2	24	224	8	0
Florida Gulf Coast University	13,445	0	4	0	0	2	71	0	0
Florida International University	46,171	0	2	1	1	38	382	6	1
Florida State University									
Panama City		0	0	0	0	1	7	0	0
Tallahassee	40,695	0	7	5	10	51	349	10	1
New College of Florida	832	0	0	0	0	1	38	1	0
Pensacola State College	11,862	0	0	0	1	3	30	0	0
Santa Fe College	15,362	0	1	0	0	3	50	1	0
Tallahassee Community College	14,237	0	0	1	0	0	85	0	0
University of Central Florida	59,601	0	11	6	13	32	304	14	1
University of Florida	49,913	0	2	0	8	17	366	21	1
University of North Florida	16,201	0	1	1	3	7	116	1	2
University of South Florida									
St. Petersburg	4,587	0	0	1	3	0	43	5	0
Tampa	41,116	0	3	1	3	29	333	11	0
University of West Florida	12,652	0	2	0	1	19	49	2	0
Georgia									
Abraham Baldwin Agricultural College	3,233	0		0	0	0	23	0	0
Albany State University	4,275	0		0	1	1	62	0	0
Andrew College	292	0		0	0	0	1	0	0
Armstrong Atlantic State University	7,439	0		0	0	1	47	0	1
Augusta State University	6,528	0		0	0	0	14	0	0
Bainbridge College	2,942	0		0	0	3	3	0	0
Berry College	2,166	0		0	0	5	53	0	0
College of Coastal Georgia	3,156	0		0	1	1	17	0	0
Columbus State University	8,239	0		1	1	6	67	2	3
Dalton State College	5,047	0		0	0	0	7	0	0
Darton State College	6,396	0		0	1	1	49	2	0
Emory University	14,236	0		0	4	26	472	5	0

Table 9. Offenses Known to Law Enforcement, by Selected State and University and College, 2013— continued

(Number.)

State and university/college	Student enrollment [1]	Murder and non-negligent man-slaughter	Rape (revised definition) [2]	Robbery	Aggravated assault	Burglary	Larceny-theft	Motor vehicle theft	Arson [3]
Georgia College and State University	6,444	0		0	0	9	47	4	0
Georgia Gwinnett College	9,397	0		1	6	3	159	2	0
Georgia Institute of Technology	21,557	0		6	3	43	352	22	0
Georgia Military College		0		0	0	0	0	0	0
Georgia Perimeter College	23,619	1		0	0	0	110	1	
Georgia Southern University	20,574	0		1	0	6	249	4	0
Georgia Southwestern State University	2,973	0		0	4	1	25	0	0
Kennesaw State University	24,604	0		0	2	11	132	3	0
Mercer University	8,329	0		1	1	11	57	5	0
Middle Georgia College	3,104	0		0	1	5	54	0	0
Morehouse College	2,374	0		13	5	11	105	1	0
North Georgia College and State University	6,413	0		0	0	0	51	0	0
Savannah State University	4,582	1		4	3	14	159	0	
Southern Polytechnic State University	6,202	0		0	1	3	75	2	0
South Georgia College	2,226	0		0	0	1	8	0	0
Spelman College	2,145	0		6	1	13	27	0	
University of Georgia	34,519	0		5	2	35	327	5	2
University of West Georgia	11,769	0		2	2	14	164	3	0
Valdosta State University	12,515	0		4	3	25	222	1	0
Wesleyan College	715	0		0	1	0	12	1	0
West Georgia Technical College	6,645	0		0	0	0	31	0	0
Young Harris College	1,030	0		0	2	1	11	0	
Illinois									
Benedictine University, Lisle	6,516	0		0	0	5	28	0	0
Black Hawk College									
Kewannee		0		0	0	0	6	0	0
Moline	6,360	0		0	1	1	19	0	0
Chicago State University	6,107	1		1	0	0	54	2	0
College of Lake County	17,577	0		1	0	16	47	0	0
Eastern Illinois University	10,417	0		0	7	5	70	0	1
Elgin Community College	11,554	0		0	0	0	33	0	0
Harper College	14,706	0		0	0	7	18	0	0
Illinois Central College	11,125	0		0	0	1	38	0	0
Illinois State University	20,706	0		3	6	22	131	1	1
Joliet Junior College	15,589	0		0	1	0	60	0	0
Lake Land College	6,818	0		1	0	2	9	0	0
Lewis University	6,539	0		0	0	2	30	0	0
Lincoln Land Community College	7,193	0		3	0	14	0	0	0
Loyola University	15,720	0		16	0	6	146	4	0
McHenry County College	6,976	0		0	0	0	15	0	0
Moraine Valley Community College	16,650	0		0	1	0	83	0	0
Morton College	5,088	0		0	0	0	20	1	0
Northeastern Illinois University	11,149	0		0	0	1	53	1	0
Northern Illinois University	21,869	1		0	8	9	169	2	2
Northwestern University									
Chicago		0		2	1	4	45	2	0
Evanston	21,215	0		9	1	24	218	3	0
Oakton Community College	11,402	0		0	3	0	23	0	0
Parkland College	8,679	0		0	3	3	39	0	0
Rend Lake College	3,815	0		0	0	0	1	0	0
Rock Valley College	8,312	0		0	0	0	37	0	0
Southern Illinois University									
Carbondale	18,847	0		1	8	25	187	2	4
Edwardsville	14,055	0		4	5	10	112	2	0
South Suburban College	6,211	0		0	0	0	32	0	0
Southwestern Illinois College	11,938	0		0	2	0	53	2	0
University of Chicago, Cook County	15,245	0		10	4	15	321	0	0
University of Illinois									
Chicago	27,875	0		9	9	5	454	4	0
Springfield	5,048	0		0	1	1	23	0	0
Urbana	44,520	0		8	17	8	391	1	1
Western Illinois University	12,205	0		0	5	56	90	3	4
Indiana									
Ball State University	21,053	0	1	2	3	26	202	3	0
Butler University	4,712	0	3	0	1	4	153	1	0
Indiana University									
Bloomington	42,133	0		1	16	70	454	6	0
Indianapolis	30,451	0		4	6	52	231	5	1
Northwest	6,184	0		0	0	2	28	0	0
Southeast	6,904	0		0	0	1	7	0	0
Marian University	2,580	0		0	1	8	50	0	0
Purdue University	40,393	0		1	7	12	384	4	0
Iowa									
Iowa State University	30,748	0	11	1	3	13	197	5	2
University of Iowa	30,129	0	2	0	5	11	180	4	1

Table 9.   Offenses Known to Law Enforcement, by Selected State and University and College, 2013— continued

(Number.)

State and university/college	Student enrollment[1]	Murder and non-negligent manslaughter	Rape (revised definition)[2]	Robbery	Aggravated assault	Burglary	Larceny-theft	Motor vehicle theft	Arson[3]
University of Northern Iowa	12,273	0	1	0	4	8	87	1	1
Kansas									
Fort Hays State University	13,310	0	0	0	1	7	34	0	0
Kansas City, Kansas, Community College	7,479	0	0	1	1	1	39	1	0
Kansas State University	24,378	1	1	1	3	14	142	1	0
Pittsburg State University	7,289	0	0	0	0	9	80	0	0
University of Kansas									
Main Campus	27,135	0	3	0	3	22	168	5	0
Medical Center		0	0	1	3	3	169	6	0
Washburn University	7,204	0	1	0	0	9	75	2	0
Wichita State University	14,716	0	0	1	2	1	86	2	0
Kentucky									
Eastern Kentucky University	15,968	0	2	0	0	39	139	2	2
Kentucky State University	2,524	0	0	2	0	11	73	0	0
Morehead State University	11,169	0	0	1	0	18	49	0	1
Murray State University	10,832	0	4	1	1	13	81	1	7
Northern Kentucky University	15,634	0	2	0	0	6	67	0	1
University of Kentucky	28,034	0	3	4	7	43	535	16	2
University of Louisville	21,239	0	0	8	1	22	323	5	0
Western Kentucky University	21,110	0	2	2	1	39	102	1	1
Louisiana									
Delgado Community College	18,096	0		0	0	1	9	0	0
Dillard University	1,307	0		0	1	19	11	0	0
Grambling State University	5,277	0		4	5	12	79	1	0
Louisiana State University									
Baton Rouge	30,225	0		13	7	40	320	7	0
Health Sciences Center, New Orleans	2,788	0		0	0	0	0	0	0
Health Sciences Center, Shreveport	888	0		0	6	2	32	1	0
Shreveport	4,535	0		1	1	0	16	0	0
Louisiana Tech University	11,304	0		1	0	11	79	0	
Nicholls State University	6,602	0		0	0	1	17	0	0
Northwestern State University	9,447	0		1	1	19	72	0	0
Southern University and A&M College									
Baton Rouge	6,397	0		3	2	11	152	0	2
Shreveport	2,937	0		0	0	0	9	1	0
Tulane University	12,958	0		0	2	10	227	0	1
University of Louisiana									
Lafayette	16,688	0		4	5	18	158	5	
Monroe	8,548	0		5	4	2	68	0	0
University of New Orleans	10,071	0		0	0	6	44	3	
Maine									
University of Maine									
Farmington	2,179	0		0	0	2	15	0	0
Orono	10,901	0		0	0	11	163	2	11
University of Southern Maine	9,382	0		0	0	7	35	0	0
Maryland									
Bowie State University	5,421	0		2	2	16	48	0	0
Coppin State University	3,612	0		2	7	12	73	4	0
Frostburg State University	5,421	0		0	1	5	37	0	0
Hagerstown Community College	5,005	0		0	0	3	11	0	0
Morgan State University	7,952	0		7	1	32	123	2	0
Salisbury University	8,657	0		1	1	6	72	3	0
St. Mary's College	1,933	0		0	2	2	46	0	1
Towson University	21,960	0		1	0	6	110	1	0
University of Baltimore	6,558	0		0	0	2	42	0	0
University of Maryland									
Baltimore City	6,368	0		7	2	2	120	4	0
Baltimore County	13,637	0		0	1	10	86	0	0
College Park	37,248	0		3	6	52	405	18	2
Eastern Shore	4,454	0		2	1	16	70	2	0
Massachusetts									
Assumption College	2,813	0	0	0	1	5	25	0	1
Bentley College	5,647	0		3	3	20	46	0	
Boston College	14,605	0		0	0	3	128	2	
Boston University	32,603	0	5	4	11	14	312	2	0
Brandeis University	5,808	0		0	0	5	75	0	
Bridgewater State College	11,417	0	0	0	2	4	60	0	1
Bristol Community College	9,022	0		0	0	0	15	0	
Bunker Hill Community College	13,504	0		0	1	0	72	0	
Clark University	3,503	0		0	1	2	43	0	
Dean College	1,322	0		0	1	3	31	0	
Emerson College	4,531	0		0	0	7	52	0	

Table 9. Offenses Known to Law Enforcement, by Selected State and University and College, 2013— continued

(Number.)

State and university/college	Student enrollment[1]	Murder and non-negligent manslaughter	Rape (revised definition)[2]	Robbery	Aggravated assault	Burglary	Larceny-theft	Motor vehicle theft	Arson[3]
Fitchburg State College	6,889	0		0	0	4	38	0	
Framingham State College	6,506	0		0	13	8	15	0	
Hampshire College	1,461	0	1	1	0	6	53	0	0
Harvard University	28,147	0		1	3	40	498	2	
Lasell College	1,980	0		0	2	13	20	1	
Massachusetts College of Liberal Arts	1,799	0	0	1	0	7	19	0	0
Massachusetts Institute of Technology	11,189	0	0	0	1	23	326	4	0
Massasoit Community College	8,209	0	0	1	3	0	18	1	0
Merrimack College	2,694	0		1	0	5	30	0	
Mount Holyoke College	2,347	0	1	0	0	9	67	0	0
Northeastern University	27,694	0		5	10	24	372	0	
North Shore Community College	7,912	0		0	0	0	20	0	
Salem State University	9,456	0		0	6	5	61	0	
Smith College	3,212	0	1	0	0	5	74	2	0
Springfield College	3,284	0		2	0	8	19	0	
Tufts University	10,777	0	0	1	0	4	17	0	0
Medford	10,837	0	1	1	2	18	65	0	0
Suffolk		0	0	0	0	6	19	0	0
Worcester		0	0	0	0	0	7	1	0
University of Massachusetts									
Amherst	28,236	0	5	0	5	18	229	4	0
Dartmouth	9,210	0		3	15	7	135	2	
Harbor Campus, Boston	15,874	0	1	0	2	0	77	0	1
Medical Center, Worcester	1,160	1	0	1	3	0	96	2	0
Wellesley College	2,482	0		0	0	3	44	1	
Western New England College	3,802	0		0	0	5	40	1	
Westfield State University	6,081	0	8	0	0	5	38	0	1
Worcester Polytechnic Institute	5,957	0	0	1	1	2	35	0	0
Michigan									
Central Michigan University	27,626	0	1	1	1	17	88	4	0
Delta College	10,763	0	0	0	0	3	37	0	0
Eastern Michigan University	23,518	0	5	2	5	9	185	4	8
Ferris State University	14,533	0	4	0	3	8	58	0	0
Grand Rapids Community College	17,448	0	0	0	0	0	97	0	0
Grand Valley State University	24,654	0	2	0	1	4	127	0	0
Kalamazoo Valley Community College	11,052	0	0	1	0	0	36	0	2
Kirtland Community College	1,807	0	0	0	0	0	0	0	0
Macomb Community College	23,729	0	1	0	0	0	41	2	0
Michigan State University	48,783	0	12	9	4	52	625	52	1
Michigan Technological University	6,933	0	1	0	1	3	60	0	0
Mott Community College	9,968	0	0	0	2	3	62	2	1
Northern Michigan University	9,159	0	0	0	3	7	89	0	0
Oakland Community College	27,296	0	0	0	0	0	59	2	0
Oakland University	19,740	0	0	0	3	6	47	0	0
Saginaw Valley State University	10,552	0	1	0	7	9	111	0	0
University of Michigan									
Ann Arbor	43,426	0	6	6	10	25	717	5	2
Dearborn	8,790	0	1	0	0	1	24	1	0
Flint	8,289	0	0	2	1	2	57	1	0
Western Michigan University	24,598	0	8	0	7	5	130	0	0
Minnesota									
University of Minnesota									
Duluth	11,491	0	1	0	1	1	37	0	0
Morris	1,896	0	0	0	0	0	1	0	0
Twin Cities	51,853	0	1	7	4	19	430	11	2
Mississippi									
Coahoma Community College	2,305	0		1	0	2	2	0	0
Mississippi State University	20,365	0		3	1	5	163	6	0
Northeast Mississippi Community College	3,407	0		0	0	1	38	0	0
University of Mississippi									
Medical Center	2,147	0		0	0	0	108	5	0
Oxford	18,794	0		3	2	22	183	0	0
Missouri									
Lincoln University	3,205	0	0	0	6	1	27	1	1
Metropolitan Community College	20,141	0	0	0	0	1	99	4	0
Mineral Area College	3,784	0	0	0	0	0	0	0	0
Missouri Southern State University	5,417	0	2	0	3	4	26	0	0
Missouri University of Science and Technology	7,645	0	0	0	1	7	94	1	1
Missouri Western State University	6,056	0	0	0	0	12	55	1	0
Northwest Missouri State University	6,831	0	1	0	1	3	50	1	0
Southeast Missouri State University	11,601	0	3	0	1	5	38	3	0
St. Charles Community College	7,642	0	0	0	0	0	20	0	0
St. Louis Community College									
Florissant Valley		0	0	0	0	0	52	1	0

Table 9.   Offenses Known to Law Enforcement, by Selected State and University and College, 2013— continued

(Number.)

State and university/college	Student enrollment [1]	Murder and non-negligent man-slaughter	Rape (revised definition) [2]	Robbery	Aggravated assault	Burglary	Larceny-theft	Motor vehicle theft	Arson [3]
Meramec	26,603	0	0	0	1	0	29	2	0
Three Rivers Community College	4,651	0	1	0	1	8	7	0	0
Truman State University	6,237	0	1	0	0	5	59	1	0
University of Central Missouri	11,878	0	3	1	2	18	120	6	0
University of Missouri									
Columbia	34,704	0	3	2	6	13	323	2	2
Kansas City	15,990	0	0	4	1	52	70	11	0
St. Louis	16,705	0	1	2	1	4	80	1	0
Washington University	13,952	0	0	0	0	4	84	0	0
Montana									
Montana State University	14,269	0	5	0	2	4	165	4	5
University of Montana	14,946	0	1	0	1	0	6	0	0
Nebraska									
Metropolitan Community College									
Douglas County	17,376	0		0	0	0	45	0	0
Sarpy County		0		0	0	0	0	0	0
University of Nebraska									
Kearney	7,199	0		0	1	14	44	0	0
Lincoln	24,207	0		2	2	10	217	7	0
Nevada									
Truckee Meadows Community College	11,603	0		0	0	4	9	0	0
University of Nevada									
Las Vegas	27,389	0		1	3	28	179	24	2
Reno	18,227	0		1	4	18	124	5	1
New Hampshire									
University of New Hampshire	15,267	0	4	0	4	17	136	0	4
New Jersey									
Brookdale Community College	14,637	0		0	0	4	23	0	0
Essex County College	11,979	0		5	0	3	103	0	0
Kean University	15,391	0		0	1	6	115	0	0
Middlesex County College	12,898	0		0	0	0	29	1	0
Monmouth University	6,472	0		1	0	7	48	0	2
Montclair State University	18,382	0		1	3	4	124	0	0
New Jersey Institute of Technology	9,944	0		15	1	9	147	3	0
Richard Stockton College of New Jersey	8,400	0		0	0	1	36	2	0
Rowan University	12,183	0		1	3	21	84	1	0
Rutgers University									
Camden	6,343	0		2	0	4	76	0	0
Newark	12,011	0		26	1	16	113	6	0
New Brunswick	40,434	0		8	18	94	675	6	0
Stevens Institute of Technology	5,649	0		0	0	7	30	0	0
The College of New Jersey	7,270	0		0	1	6	72	0	0
University of Medicine and Dentistry, Newark	6,972	0		10	21	5	150	2	0
William Paterson University	11,423	0		1	3	0	63	1	0
New Mexico									
Eastern New Mexico University	5,804	0		0	0	4	55	2	0
New Mexico Institute of Mining and Technology	2,105	0		0	0	6	29	0	0
University of New Mexico	29,033	0		0	31	26	443	43	0
New York									
Cornell University	21,424	0		2	0	16	243	0	
Ithaca College	6,759	0		0	0	37	81	1	0
Rensselaer Polytechnic Institute	6,658	0		0	0	0	78	0	0
State University of New York									
Binghamton	15,308	0		2	1	6	167	0	
Buffalo	28,952	0		5	5	47	319	4	0
Downstate Medical Center	1,799	0		5	2	0	57	0	
Stony Brook	23,946	0		3	8	28	257	1	2
Upstate Medical Center	1,635	0		1	2	2	114	0	0
State University of New York College									
Brockport	8,271	0		1	4	9	90	3	
Buffalo	11,781	0		2	0	15	134	0	0
Cortland	7,098	0		1	0	14	40	0	
Geneseo	5,557	0		0	1	9	80	0	
New Paltz	7,655	0		0	1	3	43	1	
Oswego	7,921	0		0	1	39	111	2	
Plattsburgh	6,167	0		0	0	12	85	0	
Potsdam	4,224	0		0	0	3	50	2	
Purchase	4,240	0		0	2	7	61	0	
Technology	3,151	0		0	1	3	59	0	0
North Carolina									

Table 9.   Offenses Known to Law Enforcement, by Selected State and University and College, 2013— continued

(Number.)

State and university/college	Student enrollment[1]	Murder and nonnegligent manslaughter	Rape (revised definition)[2]	Robbery	Aggravated assault	Burglary	Larceny-theft	Motor vehicle theft	Arson[3]
Appalachian State University	17,589	0		0	0	20	59	0	1
Duke University	15,386	0		7	3	45	453	12	2
East Carolina University	26,947	0		1	1	2	224	1	0
Elon University	6,029	0		0	0	0	61	0	0
Fayetteville State University	6,060	0		3	0	23	54	4	0
Methodist University	2,359	0		0	0	6	45	0	2
North Carolina Central University	8,604	0		4	9	16	126	1	0
North Carolina School of the Arts	880	0		0	0	4	12	0	0
North Carolina State University, Raleigh	34,340	0		3	8	33	349	4	0
University of North Carolina									
Asheville	3,751	0		1	1	3	27	1	0
Chapel Hill	29,278	0		1	5	30	261	8	1
Greensboro	18,516	0		1	2	0	177	7	0
Wilmington	13,733	0		0	2	6	260	0	2
Western Carolina University	9,608	0		2	2	10	84	1	1
Winston-Salem State University	5,689	0		0	1	7	85	3	0
North Dakota									
North Dakota State College of Science	3,066	0	0	0	0	11	20	1	0
North Dakota State University	14,443	0	1	0	0	9	73	2	0
University of North Dakota	15,250	0	5	0	3	9	121	1	2
Ohio									
Bowling Green State University	17,286	0	1	2	1	13	49	0	7
Capital University	3,584	0	2	1	0	7	17	1	0
Central State University	2,152	0	0	0	1	17	80	0	0
Columbus State Community College	25,863	0	0	0	0	0	79	2	0
Cuyahoga Community College	29,701	0	0	2	0	6	125	4	0
Kent State University	28,602	0		0	0	7	167	0	3
Lakeland Community College	9,283	0	0	0	1	0	24	0	0
Miami University	17,683	0	8	0	0	32	150	1	0
Notre Dame College	2,129	0	0	0	0	2	14	0	
Ohio State University, Columbus	56,387	0	10	5	1	22	836	12	7
Ohio University	27,402	0	3	2	0	17	172	0	2
Otterbein University	2,984	0	1	0	0	3	26	0	0
Shawnee State University	4,652	0		0	0	7	55	0	0
Sinclair Community College	19,537	0	0	0	0	0	66	0	0
University of Akron	26,581	0	0	3	2	12	215	4	0
University of Cincinnati	33,347	0		4	3	11	338	0	2
University of Toledo	21,453	0	1	3	4	42	235	0	0
Wright State University	16,780	0		1	0	24	127	2	0
Youngstown State University	13,760	0		1	0	8	103	0	0
Oklahoma									
Cameron University	6,115	0		0	1	5	26	0	0
East Central University	4,819	0	0	0	0	0	19	2	0
Mid-America Christian University	2,606	0	0	0	0	0	1	1	0
Northeastern Oklahoma A&M College	2,526	0	0	0	4	16	42	1	0
Northeastern State University									
Broken Arrow		0	0	0	0	0	8	0	0
Tahlequah	8,721	0	0	0	0	1	34	1	1
Oklahoma City University	3,299	0	0	1	0	4	44	2	0
Oklahoma State University									
Main Campus	25,708	0		2	0	42	174	4	0
Okmulgee	3,936	0	1	0	1	0	16	0	0
Tulsa	457	0	0	0	0	0	7	2	0
Rogers State University	4,774	0		0	0	1	11	0	0
Seminole State College	2,185	0	0	0	0	0	6	0	0
Southeastern Oklahoma State University	4,103	0	0	0	0	10	11	0	0
Southwestern Oklahoma State University	5,106	0	1	0	0	7	18	0	0
Tulsa Community College	19,557	0		0	1	0	42	1	0
University of Central Oklahoma	17,211	0		1	0	4	72	1	0
University of Oklahoma									
Health Sciences Center	3,605	0	0	1	6	5	153	4	0
Norman	27,507	0		0	0	5	285	6	0
Oregon									
Portland State University	28,287	0		3	1	25	280	0	0
Pennsylvania									
Bloomsburg University	9,950	0	1	2	1	0	76	1	0
California University	8,608	0	1	1	2	0	33	0	0
Cheyney University	1,284	0	2	0	8	24	27	1	1
Clarion University	6,520	0	1	0	0	1	28	0	1
Dickinson College	2,386	0	2	0	2	10	72	1	0
East Stroudsburg University	6,943	0	2	1	4	5	60	0	0
Edinboro University	7,462	0	1	0	3	14	57	0	0
Elizabethtown College	1,910	0	2	0	1	1	33	0	0

Table 9. Offenses Known to Law Enforcement, by Selected State and University and College, 2013— continued

(Number.)

State and university/college	Student enrollment [1]	Murder and non-negligent man-slaughter	Rape (revised definition) [2]	Robbery	Aggravated assault	Burglary	Larceny-theft	Motor vehicle theft	Arson [3]
Indiana University	15,596	0	0	0	3	3	47	0	0
Kutztown University	9,804	0	2	2	2	1	77	0	0
Lehigh University	7,080	0	1	2	3	1	42	0	0
Lock Haven University	5,328	0	4	2	1	1	43	1	0
Mansfield University	3,131	0	0	0	0	1	29	0	0
Millersville University	8,368	0	1	0	3	6	45	0	1
Moravian College	1,910	0	0	0	3	10	32	0	0
Pennsylvania State University									
Altoona	3,863	0	1	0	1	14	33	0	0
Beaver	759	0	0	0	0	0	8	1	0
Behrend	4,149	0	0	0	0	2	33	0	0
Berks	2,747	0	0	0	0	3	13	0	0
Harrisburg	4,376	0	0	0	0	0	11	0	0
Hazelton	1,060	0	0	0	0	6	10	0	0
McKeesport	635	0	0	0	0	0	5	0	0
Mont Alto	1,107	0	1	0	1	1	6	0	0
Schuykill	867	0	0	0	0	2	12	0	0
University Park	45,783	0	9	0	20	40	453	5	9
Shippensburg University	7,724	0	4	1	2	16	41	0	0
Slippery Rock University	8,559	0	0	1	2	4	34	0	0
University of Pittsburgh									
Bradford	1,518	0	0	0	1	6	17	0	0
Johnstown	2,932	0	1	0	4	6	39	0	0
Pittsburgh	28,769	0	0	1	14	15	273	3	0
Titusville	388	0	0	0	0	0	6	0	0
West Chester University	15,411	0	0	1	1	11	66	0	0
Rhode Island									
Brown University	8,885	0	2	0	1	59	108	0	0
University of Rhode Island	16,451	0	1	2	0	19	160	2	1
South Carolina									
Benedict College	2,917	0	4	30	8	33	136	2	1
Bob Jones University	3,469	0	0	0	0	3	8	0	0
Clemson University	20,768	0	0	1	3	23	165	9	0
Coastal Carolina University	9,335	1	2	3	2	26	145	4	0
College of Charleston	11,723	0	0	0	1	2	69	2	1
Erskine College	751	0	0	0	0	0	6	0	1
Francis Marion University	4,093	0	0	0	0	1	39	1	0
Greenville Technical College	13,965	0	0	1	5	8	49	2	0
Lander University	3,049	0	0	0	0	0	21	0	0
Medical University of South Carolina	2,731	0	1	0	0	2	141	6	0
Midlands Technical College	11,949	0	0	0	0	0	28	1	0
Presbyterian College	1,403	0	0	0	1	6	24	0	
South Carolina State University	3,807	0	1	0	5	22	57	4	1
Spartanburg Methodist College	811	0	0	0	0	1	9	1	0
The Citadel	3,499	0	0	5	0	6	18	0	0
Trident Technical College	17,224	0	0	0	0	8	46	0	0
University of South Carolina									
Aiken	3,211	0	0	0	0	0	48	0	0
Columbia	31,288	0	3	2	2	18	258	36	0
Upstate	5,561	0	0	0	0	2	25	0	0
Winthrop University	6,170	0	0	0	1	5	42	0	0
South Dakota									
South Dakota State University	12,583	0	0	0	0	0	49	0	0
Tennessee									
Austin Peay State University	10,597	0	0	1	0	15	108	0	0
Christian Brothers University	1,603	0	1	0	0	1	18	0	0
Cleveland State Community College	3,640	0	0	0	0	0	3	0	0
East Tennessee State University	15,133	0	0	2	3	12	67	4	1
Middle Tennessee State University	25,394	0	3	2	9	52	170	5	0
Northeast State Community College	6,446	0	0	0	0	1	9	0	0
Roane State Community College	6,508	0	0	0	0	0	11	1	0
Southwest Tennessee Community College	12,220	0	0	3	0	2	35	0	0
Tennessee State University	8,740	0	3	8	4	31	136	3	0
Tennessee Technological University	11,469	0	0	1	4	29	73	3	0
University of Memphis	22,139	0	2	2	0	18	155	1	0
University of Tennessee									
Chattanooga	11,660	0	0	3	1	23	124	1	1
Health Science Center		0	0	0	1	3	34	0	0
Knoxville	29,833	0	4	3	2	47	340	6	0
Martin	7,743	0	0	0	1	5	30	0	0
Vanderbilt University	12,710	0	13	5	14	18	338	5	1
Volunteer State Community College	8,177	0	0	0	0	1	20	0	0
Walters State Community College	6,554	0	0	0	0	0	11	0	0

Table 9.   Offenses Known to Law Enforcement, by Selected State and University and College, 2013— continued

(Number.)

State and university/college	Student enrollment [1]	Murder and non-negligent man-slaughter	Rape (revised definition) [2]	Robbery	Aggravated assault	Burglary	Larceny-theft	Motor vehicle theft	Arson [3]
Texas									
Abilene Christian University	4,367	0		0	2	1	59	0	0
Alamo Community College District	58,007	0		1	10	27	189	11	0
Alvin Community College	5,109	0		0	0	0	7	0	0
Amarillo College	11,530	0		0	0	3	42	0	0
Angelo State University	6,888	0		0	1	8	53	1	0
Austin College	1,260	0		0	0	1	41	0	1
Baylor Health Care System		0		3	1	10	549	8	0
Baylor University, Waco	15,364	0		0	7	7	120	5	0
Brookhaven College	12,790	0		0	0	2	18	0	0
Central Texas College	22,443	0		0	1	4	17	0	0
College of the Mainland	4,010	0		0	0	0	15	1	0
El Paso Community College	32,127	0		0	1	1	75	0	0
Grayson County College	4,903	0		0	1	1	18	2	0
Hardin-Simmons University	2,301	0		0	0	0	24	1	0
Houston Community College	58,476	0		3	11	15	248	6	0
Lamar University, Beaumont	14,289	0		0	4	2	33	2	0
Laredo Community College	9,356	0		0	0	3	12	2	0
McLennan Community College	9,302	0		0	0	0	18	0	0
Midwestern State University	5,916	0		0	1	23	38	0	0
Mountain View College	9,068	0		0	1	2	39	3	0
North Lake College	11,397	0		0	0	0	20	0	0
Paris Junior College	5,513	0		1	0	5	13	0	0
Prairie View A&M University	8,336	0		3	6	22	85	8	0
Rice University	6,484	0		1	1	1	193	1	1
Richland College	19,552	0		1	0	2	51	0	0
Southern Methodist University	10,893	0		2	0	9	108	4	0
South Plains College	9,444	0		0	2	1	14	0	0
Southwestern University	1,394	0		0	0	3	11	0	0
Stephen F. Austin State University	12,999	0		0	0	13	121	0	0
St. Mary's University	3,941	0		0	0	5	52	2	0
Sul Ross State University	2,680	0		0	0	9	44	0	1
Tarleton State University	12,524	0		0	2	14	48	0	0
Texas A&M International University	7,213	0		0	1	6	30	1	0
Texas A&M University									
College Station	50,627	0		1	4	16	370	8	0
Commerce	11,871	0	2	0	1	12	54	1	0
Corpus Christi	10,508	0		0	2	13	64	0	0
Galveston	2,014	0		0	0	3	17	1	0
Kingsville	11,350	0		0	2	22	105	1	2
San Antonio		0		0	0	6	3	0	0
Texas Christian University	9,727	0		3	3	24	135	1	1
Texas Southern University	9,646	0		9	10	46	149	5	0
Texas State Technical College									
Harlingen	5,509	0		0	1	1	32	1	0
Waco	4,277	0		1	5	24	59	1	0
West Texas	810	0		0	0	0	3	0	0
Texas State University, San Marcos	34,225	0		3	2	30	262	5	3
Texas Tech University, Lubbock	32,467	0		0	5	18	279	3	2
Texas Woman's University	15,168	0		0	0	2	39	0	0
Trinity University	2,458	0		0	0	9	51	0	0
Tyler Junior College	11,374	0	0	0	0	1	65	0	0
University of Houston									
Central Campus	40,747	0		18	3	33	440	23	0
Clearlake	8,153	0		0	0	1	11	0	
Downtown Campus	13,916	0		0	1	2	77	0	0
University of Mary Hardin-Baylor	3,287	0		0	2	9	95	1	0
University of North Texas									
Denton	37,950	0		0	6	19	156	2	0
Health Science Center	1,949	0		0	0	1	16	0	0
University of Texas									
Arlington	33,239	0		6	1	18	243	4	0
Austin	52,186	0		2	1	39	405	5	0
Brownsville	13,636	0		1	0	6	63	2	0
Dallas	19,727	0		1	1	15	118	2	0
El Paso	22,749	0		1	3	24	144	3	2
Health Science Center, San Antonio	3,249	0		1	1	3	111	1	0
Health Science Center, Tyler		0		0	4	2	10	0	0
Houston	4,779	0		6	3	21	307	3	0
Medical Branch	3,012	0		1	0	2	88	3	0
Pan American	19,302	0		0	2	0	100	2	0
Permian Basin	4,021	0		0	2	2	15	0	0
San Antonio	30,474	0		2	0	12	163	4	0
Southwestern Medical School	2,424	1		1	0	2	139	11	0
Tyler	6,858	0		1	0	7	29	0	0
West Texas A&M University	7,909	0		0	2	3	47	0	0
Utah									

Table 9.   Offenses Known to Law Enforcement, by Selected State and University and College, 2013— continued

(Number.)

State and university/college	Student enrollment [1]	Murder and non-negligent man-slaughter	Rape (revised definition) [2]	Robbery	Aggravated assault	Burglary	Larceny-theft	Motor vehicle theft	Arson [3]
Brigham Young University	34,409	0	0	0	0	2	224	3	0
Snow College	4,599	0		0	0	3	25	0	0
Southern Utah University	8,297	0	0	0	0	1	25	0	1
University of Utah	32,388	0		1	12	150	513	30	1
Utah State University, Eastern		0		0	0	1	3	0	0
Utah Valley University	31,562	0		1	0	2	90	3	0
Weber State University	26,532	0		0	0	6	54	2	0
Virginia									
Christopher Newport University	5,186	0	4	1	1	1	127	0	4
College of William and Mary	8,258	0	0	0	0	32	181	2	1
Eastern Virginia Medical School	993	0	0	0	0	0	18	0	0
Emory and Henry College	945	0	0	0	0	0	0	0	0
Ferrum College	1,510	0	1	1	0	3	24	0	1
George Mason University	32,961	0	1	1	2	7	179	2	2
Hampton University	4,765	0	0	0	1	6	49	0	0
James Madison University	19,927	0	0	0	2	6	115	0	1
J. Sargeant Reynolds Community College	12,846	0	0	0	0	0	34	0	0
Longwood University	4,834	1	0	0	1	10	43	8	0
Lord Fairfax Community College	7,288	0	0	0	0	0	0	0	0
Norfolk State University	7,100	0	2	5	5	26	110	1	1
Northern Virginia Community College	51,864	0	2	0	2	0	111	1	0
Old Dominion University	24,670	0	4	7	7	36	287	6	2
Radford University	9,573	0	3	0	0	5	53	0	4
Richard Bland College	1,532	0	0	0	0	1	10	0	0
University of Mary Washington	5,093	0	1	2	0	2	14	0	0
University of Richmond	4,361	0	3	0	0	8	72	3	1
University of Virginia	23,907	0	5	0	6	60	222	22	0
University of Virginia's College at Wise	2,420	0	1	0	0	0	3	0	0
Virginia Commonwealth University	31,445	0	0	4	9	23	511	14	1
Virginia Military Institute	1,664	0	0	0	1	6	16	0	0
Virginia Polytechnic Institute and State University	31,087	0	4	1	0	68	142	2	1
Virginia State University	6,208	1	0	3	4	1	124	1	0
Virginia Western Community College	8,440	0	0	0	0	0	9	0	0
Washington									
Central Washington University	11,268	1	1	1	0	41	70	1	0
Eastern Washington University	12,587	0	2	0	2	12	62	0	1
Evergreen State College	4,509	0	3	1	0	16	93	0	0
University of Washington	43,485	0	1	5	4	65	532	14	1
Washington State University									
Pullman	27,679	0	11	1	6	28	172	5	0
Vancouver		0	0	0	0	1	8	1	0
Western Washington University	14,833	0	1	0	0	7	138	3	0
West Virginia									
Fairmong State University	4,451	0	0	2	0	5	25	2	0
Marshall University	13,708	0	0	1	10	3	58	0	0
Potomac State College	1,781	0	0	0	0	6	3	0	0
Shepherd University	4,326	0	3	1	0	3	12	0	0
West Liberty State College	2,644	0	0	1	0	8	13	1	0
West Virginia State University	1,107	0	0	0	0	1	1	0	0
West Virginia University	29,707	0	4	1	13	1	107	1	1
Wisconsin									
University of Wisconsin									
Eau Claire	11,067	0		0	4	1	58	0	0
Green Bay	6,801	0		0	0	0	17	0	0
La Crosse	10,385	0		0	0	0	0	0	0
Madison	42,269	0		1	20	50	292	3	2
Milwaukee	28,712	0		1	0	13	323	0	0
Oshkosh	13,519	0		0	0	0	48	1	1
Parkside	4,731	0		0	1	4	30	0	0
Platteville	8,668	0		0	1	2	62	2	2
River Falls	6,443	0	0	0	1	2	36	0	0
Stevens Point	9,695	0		0	0	0	78	0	0
Stout	9,283	0		0	0	3	81	1	0
Superior	2,697	0		0	0	1	11	0	0
Whitewater	12,028	0		0	0	4	49	0	0
Wyoming									
Sheridan College	4,236	0		0	0	2	6	0	0
University of Wyoming	12,903	0		1	0	15	114	3	0

Note: Caution should be exercised in making any intercampus comparisons or ranking schools because university/college crime statistics are affected by a variety of factors. These include demographic characteristics of the surrounding community, ratio of male to female students, number of on-campus residents, accessibility of the campus to outside visitors, size of enrollment, etc.   1 The student enrollment figures provided by the United States Department of Education are for the 2012 school year, the most recent available. The enrollment figures include full-time and part-time students.   2 The figures shown in this column for the offense of rape were reported using the revised Uniform Crime Reporting (UCR) definition of rape. See chapter notes for more detail.   3 A blank cell in the arson column indicates that the FBI did not receive 12 complete months of arson data for that agency.

Table 10.   Offenses Known to Law Enforcement, by Selected State Metropolitan and Nonmetropolitan Counties, 2013

(Number.)

State/county	Murder and non-negligent man-slaughter	Rape (revised definition)[1]	Robbery	Aggravated assault	Burglary	Larceny-theft	Motor vehicle theft	Arson[2]
Alabama—Metropolitan Counties								
Autauga	0	15	3	54	160	238	46	
Baldwin	0	13	27	71	250	380	44	
Bibb	0	0	0	8	65	40	18	
Blount	0	9	0	82	302	562	83	
Calhoun	0	7	5	16	183	259	11	
Chilton	1	23	1	59	228	332	44	
Elmore	0	18	6	45	269	494	20	
Etowah	2	25	3	80	261	310	36	
Geneva	1	10	1	24	87	186	23	
Hale	0	3	1	35	44	78	15	
Henry	2	4	1	20	75	61	10	
Houston	0	25	12	66	185	361	59	
Jefferson	5	81	183	436	1,908	1,664	106	31
Lawrence	2	9	5	49	142	286	31	
Limestone	0	14	5	67	263	468	56	
Lowndes	2	6	1	23	99	88	26	
Madison	1	62	30	224	630	1,418	167	
Mobile	5	48	40	131	739	1,421	227	
Montgomery	0	0	3	9	76	53	17	
Russell	3	10	1	41	122	219	34	
Tuscaloosa	6	7	26	184	461	872	113	
Alabama—Nonmetropolitan Counties								
Barbour	1	2	2	16	43	63	9	
Butler	1	6	0	28	49	85	7	
Chambers	0	0	0	4	69	45	6	
Cherokee	1	12	1	50	169	250	29	
Choctaw	0	0	0	7	19	22	1	
Clarke	0	6	4	46	62	57	16	
Cleburne	0	0	0	3	38	61	1	
Coffee	0	2	2	18	68	90	16	
Conecuh	1	4	1	22	29	54	6	
Coosa	0	2	1	10	82	119	11	
Covington	0	17	1	32	105	246	30	
Crenshaw	2	9	4	39	68	71	14	
Cullman	3	33	1	16	310	563	56	
Dale	1	9	0	24	43	107	13	
Dallas	2	9	6	43	176	305	28	
De Kalb	2	31	3	121	333	395	73	
Fayette	0	1	1	6	31	58	8	
Franklin	1	8	4	34	102	173	10	
Greene	1	1	3	30	32	48	12	
Jackson	1	33	1	65	220	298	59	
Macon	0	2	6	20	84	88	17	
Marengo	1	2	2	30	72	107	15	
Marion	1	2	0	19	59	97	12	
Monroe	0	0	1	19	50	65	6	
Pike	1	3	2	12	29	71	7	
Randolph	0	1	0	6	81	94	1	
Sumter	2	1	3	15	30	37	4	
Talladega	1	11	11	56	315	479	64	
Tallapoosa	2	10	0	9	75	103	8	
Washington	0	1	0	33	55	97	13	
Wilcox	2	2	2	23	15	56	8	
Winston	2	5	0	19	86	74	8	
Arizona—Metropolitan Counties								
Cochise	2		9	211	106	558	42	0
Coconino	1		3	83	136	269	16	28
Maricopa	18		78	925	1,231	3,471	525	58
Mohave	7		13	107	787	1,190	163	
Pima	16		153	430	2,124	6,794	688	74
Pinal	8		18	104	618	2,754		12
Yavapai	1		7	122	396	736	110	10
Yuma	6	15	4	138	557	539	83	9
Arizona—Nonmetropolitan Counties								
Apache	0		3	48	96	101	9	35
Gila	1		1	59	89	278	40	
Graham	0		0	95	50	103	19	1
La Paz	0		4	49	103	255	28	1
Navajo	0		0	50	268	190	47	4
Santa Cruz	0		1	1	78	89	35	0
Arkansas—Metropolitan Counties								
Benton	1	27	2	55	198	197	22	8

Table 10.   Offenses Known to Law Enforcement, by Selected State Metropolitan and Nonmetropolitan Counties, 2013— continued

(Number.)

State/county	Murder and non-negligent man-slaughter	Rape (revised definition)[1]	Robbery	Aggravated assault	Burglary	Larceny-theft	Motor vehicle theft	Arson[2]
Cleveland	0	0	0	1	52	44	3	2
Craighead	0	8	0	8	114	136	8	3
Crawford	1	6	2	82	91	279	34	0
Crittenden	0	6	3	131	163	254	36	4
Faulkner	1	23	1	70	347	708	124	7
Garland	2	45	17	255	826	1,076	95	0
Grant	0	2	0	18	75	111	16	0
Jefferson	2	13	1	37	210	269	58	4
Lincoln	0	0	0	6	27	22	3	0
Lonoke	1	6	2	43	72	181	86	6
Madison	0	4	2	28	61	43	3	2
Perry	0	4	0	35	73	155	5	0
Poinsett	0	2	1	1	1	97	1	0
Pulaski	0	16	28	273	885	1,149	213	17
Sebastian	0	7	1	47	99	219	16	1
Washington	1	17	1	141	191	270	31	5
Arkansas—Nonmetropolitan Counties								
Arkansas	2	2	0	12	33	88	23	0
Ashley	0	5	0	9	59	127	13	1
Baxter	1	6	0	11	180	465	25	1
Bradley	0	0	1	8	8	14	7	0
Calhoun	0	1	0	3	5	8	5	0
Carroll	0	4	0	21	51	230	21	0
Chicot	0	0	2	3	37	60	1	0
Clark	0	1	0	9	37	72	5	0
Clay	0	12	0	7	25	27	0	2
Cleburne	1	3	1	29	210	279	27	4
Columbia	0	2	2	29	39	82	14	1
Conway	0	1	0	19	74	249	25	4
Cross	0	4	0	33	69	91	12	1
Dallas	0	1	0	2	20	21	0	1
Drew	0	2	1	28	51	90	16	3
Franklin	0	4	0	24	71	139	7	3
Fulton	0	4	0	12	0	53	13	1
Greene	0	0	0	13	99	160	4	2
Hempstead	0	9	1	51	64	191	19	6
Howard	0	4	0	3	43	68	1	2
Independence	4	21	13	141	513	801	79	19
Izard	2	4	0	15	90	159	2	3
Johnson	2	9	0	11	143	55	5	2
Lawrence	0	0	0	1	13	45	1	0
Logan	2	4	0	18	119	136	21	2
Marion	1	4	1	36	72	117	2	2
Mississippi	0	4	3	29	114	254	60	1
Monroe	0	5	0	7	22	38	10	0
Newton	0	0	0	22	36	49	6	0
Ouachita	1	1	0	17	55	71	8	1
Pike	4	4	0	2	19	39	3	0
Polk	0	7	0	14	61	127	14	6
Pope	0	7	2	59	164	237	31	1
Randolph	0	1	1	17	75	170	12	6
Scott	0	2	1	8	56	50	9	1
Searcy	0	1	0	17	8	17	5	0
Sevier	0	3	1	15	71	113	19	1
St. Francis	1	2	1	10	103	240	1	2
Stone	0	4	0	24	87	129	13	3
Union	2	2	5	42	119	245	31	1
Van Buren	1	2	0	33	58	220	33	3
White	2	11	3	43	460	593	108	5
Yell	0	3	2	22	86	138	20	2
California—Metropolitan Counties								
Alameda	5		194	428	659	947	803	21
Butte	7		17	62	515	686	9	0
Contra Costa	6		118	276	838	1,288	12	18
El Dorado	2		16	166	747	1,269	50	4
Fresno	11		93	737	1,358	2,133	721	142
Imperial	1		11	173	260	433	21	8
Kern	23		409	1,633	3,859	5,044	1,738	254
Kings	4		16	139	235	303	55	9
Los Angeles	72		1,357	3,723	4,363	8,095	3,546	157
Madera	6		18	315	666	675	24	4
Marin	2		12	78	269	440	1	3
Merced	17		36	477	687	1,116	30	3
Monterey	12		46	136	482	906	24	6
Napa	0		4	30	140	229	3	3
Orange	1		23	208	261	877	103	6

Table 10.   Offenses Known to Law Enforcement, by Selected State Metropolitan and Nonmetropolitan Counties, 2013— continued

(Number.)

State/county	Murder and non-negligent man-slaughter	Rape (revised definition)[1]	Robbery	Aggravated assault	Burglary	Larceny-theft	Motor vehicle theft	Arson[2]
Placer	1		13	220	640	1,083	40	8
Riverside	20		142	500	2,405	4,192	1,189	25
Sacramento	30		1,027	1,818	4,211	7,683	117	65
San Benito	0		5	38	61	139	5	0
San Bernardino	18		133	770	2,219	2,560	1,250	71
San Diego	6		206	1,215	1,682	3,092	833	41
San Joaquin	14		144	462	1,520	2,651	160	12
San Luis Obispo	2		9	261	540	781	6	4
San Mateo	0		51	246	545	1,959	288	13
Santa Barbara	1		29	196	569	1,191	13	10
Santa Clara	3		23	150	363	951	176	0
Santa Cruz	3		35	238	740	1,118	16	15
Shasta	8		29	437	504	408	49	63
Solano	1		15	97	209	170	25	11
Sonoma	5		51	503	552	795	10	17
Stanislaus	13		106	226	1,076	1,312	63	10
Sutter	2		5	56	341	504	59	1
Tulare	18		108	495	1,180	1,613		
Ventura	3		23	84	307	648	72	18
Yolo	0		3	36	134	261	14	9
Yuba	3		24	136	457	839	7	13
California—Nonmetropolitan Counties								
Alpine	0		0	6	8	25	0	0
Amador	0		7	55	176	262	2	5
Calaveras	5		10	86	332	504	7	0
Colusa	0		1	20	92	209	7	0
Del Norte	0		16	52	161	109	2	11
Glenn	0		4	94	120	198	7	1
Humboldt	3		32	100	596	520	33	13
Inyo	0		1	39	74	107	2	1
Lake	2		29	169	373	380	6	8
Lassen	0		0	36	74	93	2	3
Mariposa	0		1	77	98	190	3	0
Mendocino	4		21	219	309	361	13	24
Modoc	1		1	31	34	48	3	2
Mono	0		0	10	20	46	2	0
Nevada	2		8	251	353	272	6	1
Plumas	1		2	75	141	227	2	2
Sierra	0		0	7	43	32	2	0
Siskiyou	0		0	23	91	85	2	0
Tehama	1		3	147	99	175	0	14
Trinity	1		5	23	46	60	0	0
Tuolumne	0		8	76	385	382	4	4
Colorado—Metropolitan Counties								
Adams	7	104	45	273	523	1,401	504	17
Arapahoe	1	29	30	165	311	808	109	32
Clear Creek	0	2	0	15	15	41	4	0
Douglas	0	45	6	75	298	970	79	15
El Paso	13	93	36	333	769	1,578	241	23
Gilpin	0	1	0	3	8	22	5	0
Jefferson	2	39	10	91	458	2,016	144	14
Larimer	1	32	7	81	179	617	39	9
Mesa	2	62	4	112	224	786	62	5
Park	1	5	1	6	21	34	4	2
Pueblo	3	6	8	33	217	943	78	7
Teller	2	3	0	5	42	44	1	1
Weld	0	15	2	104	182	414	81	8
Colorado—Nonmetropolitan Counties								
Alamosa	0	0	0	1	5	42	0	1
Archuleta	0	4	0	10	86	60	5	1
Baca	0	3	0	5	2	2	2	0
Bent	0	2	0	8	28	57	3	1
Chaffee	0	2	1	6	32	50	4	1
Cheyenne	0	1	0	0	0	7	1	0
Conejos	1	0	0	6	12	15	4	1
Costilla	0	0	0	3	10	1	2	0
Crowley	0	0	0	5	2	0	0	0
Custer	0	2	0	4	14	29	5	0
Delta	1	3	0	1	15	70	12	1
Dolores	0	0	0	1	3	5	0	0
Eagle	1	3	4	26	54	267	10	5
Fremont	0	11	0	19	65	131	13	3
Garfield	1	18	0	22	32	120	13	1
Gunnison	0	0	0	2	5	37	2	0
Hinsdale	0	1	0	0	1	4	0	0

Table 10. Offenses Known to Law Enforcement, by Selected State Metropolitan and Nonmetropolitan Counties, 2013— continued

(Number.)

State/county	Murder and non-negligent man-slaughter	Rape (revised definition)	Robbery	Aggravated assault	Burglary	Larceny-theft	Motor vehicle theft	Arson[2]
Huerfano	1	0	0	11	0	10	0	0
Jackson	0	0	0	2	1	7	0	0
Kit Carson	0	3	0	7	9	13	2	0
Lake	0	1	0	11	5	23	3	0
La Plata	0	12	1	26	63	111	8	2
Las Animas	0	1	0	5	0	1	0	0
Lincoln	0	0	0	1	5	8	1	0
Logan	0	4	0	4	45	55	7	1
Mineral	0	0	0	1	0	0	0	0
Moffat	0	0	0	0	2	6	2	0
Montezuma	0	1	1	26	39	79	9	2
Montrose	0	5	0	20	64	98	14	0
Morgan	0	3	0	14	22	111	15	1
Ouray	0	0	0	0	0	0	0	0
Pitkin	0	0	0	0	1	30	1	0
Prowers	0	0	0	3	8	28	4	0
Rio Blanco	0	0	0	3	2	24	4	0
Rio Grande	0	1	0	2	2	3	0	0
Routt	1	1	0	3	11	30	3	0
Saguache	0	3	0	7	19	30	1	0
San Juan	0	0	0	3	1	9	1	0
San Miguel	0	0	0	0	2	0	0	0
Sedgwick	0	0	0	1	4	9	0	1
Summit	1	9	1	15	28	216	14	1
Washington	0	0	0	5	16	75	5	1
Delaware—Metropolitan Counties								
New Castle County Police Department	9	101	202	671	1,529	3,736	358	5
Florida—Metropolitan Counties								
Alachua	3	45	75	411	626	1,336	84	10
Baker	0	0	4	90	98	256	14	0
Bay	4	47	52	226	488	1,749	149	5
Brevard	3	116	119	655	1,246	3,535	199	13
Broward	4	19	74	175	198	672	43	5
Charlotte	1	37	33	298	748	2,255	110	5
Citrus	5	45	65	413	631	1,911	107	21
Clay	2	54	77	431	657	2,755	124	28
Collier	12	73	107	549	989	3,301	215	20
Escambia	23	135	370	1,258	2,776	7,588	654	28
Flagler	3	20	43	144	415	1,185	58	10
Gadsden	2	6	10	90	193	214	18	3
Gilchrist	1	1	2	27	49	81	4	0
Gulf	0	4	0	66	121	159	19	0
Hernando	9	45	57	357	1,013	2,485	166	12
Highlands	2	19	41	221	722	1,483	121	7
Hillsborough	33	165	472	1,320	4,080	11,840	944	23
Indian River	2	24	29	252	476	1,378	64	5
Jefferson	0	6	1	77	45	50	8	0
Lake	1	64	39	320	876	1,787	161	8
Lee	12	94	351	766	2,527	5,344	490	29
Leon	3	26	31	338	639	1,786	84	13
Manatee	3	174	247	1,043	2,043	5,500	315	25
Marion	11	122	66	894	1,248	2,384	217	4
Martin	0	14	50	158	623	1,847	105	3
Miami-Dade	87	448	1,861	3,661	7,094	29,686	3,263	63
Nassau	1	2	6	42	257	601	44	16
Okaloosa	2	63	58	452	524	2,083	101	4
Orange	49	443	1,416	3,336	7,910	17,562	2,000	0
Osceola	2	49	74	600	1,519	3,135	176	0
Palm Beach	25	213	494	1,289	3,685	9,126	1,089	59
Pasco	20	122	197	802	2,864	6,807	528	63
Pinellas	6	123	140	747	1,422	4,050	270	22
Polk	8	73	147	1,098	2,693	4,689	540	79
Santa Rosa	3	27	13	128	474	1,135	78	8
Sarasota	3	26	91	441	1,366	4,237	191	3
Seminole	1	42	58	477	923	2,231	151	1
St. Johns	2	9	34	383	683	2,393	123	4
St. Lucie	7	18	20	253	545	1,077	92	13
Sumter	1	13	11	103	257	477	44	1
Volusia	9	72	76	471	1,390	3,076	265	29
Wakulla	0	10	4	63	102	435	23	3
Walton	3	10	4	155	283	820	70	6
Florida—Nonmetropolitan Counties								
Bradford	0	7	6	72	96	83	12	0
Calhoun	1	8	0	3	7	9	1	1
Columbia	4	9	16	251	544	638	40	7

Table 10.   Offenses Known to Law Enforcement, by Selected State Metropolitan and Nonmetropolitan Counties, 2013— continued

(Number.)

State/county	Murder and non-negligent man-slaughter	Rape (revised definition)[1]	Robbery	Aggravated assault	Burglary	Larceny-theft	Motor vehicle theft	Arson[2]
DeSoto	0	4	12	87	227	371	17	0
Dixie	1	6	5	48	185	203	9	7
Franklin	0	5	4	18	75	58	11	6
Glades	0	3	1	38	50	105	4	0
Hamilton	1	6	1	39	117	117	20	1
Hardee	1	10	2	34	139	312	23	0
Hendry	2	13	17	187	444	402	50	4
Holmes	0	1	3	57	83	130	15	0
Jackson	1	12	6	93	117	362	26	0
Lafayette	0	1	2	26	13	12	0	0
Liberty	0	0	3	9	19	33	1	0
Madison	0	4	2	98	60	147	4	2
Monroe	2	15	15	180	302	1,144	50	3
Okeechobee	3	14	17	94	314	760	28	1
Putnam	2	13	31	281	559	1,051	81	3
Suwannee	3	7	7	90	133	316	10	3
Taylor	1	12	1	60	69	82	7	0
Union	3	2	2	46	39	66	3	0
Washington	0	0	6	36	93	128	14	0
Georgia—Metropolitan Counties								
Augusta-Richmond	18		456	228	2,692	7,023	993	62
Barrow	2		7	231	312	726	66	10
Bibb	1		64	125	496	1,881	220	12
Brantley	0		7	15	188	241	9	0
Brooks	1		1	10	54	139	25	0
Burke	2		0	107	144	310	29	0
Butts	0		4	25	109	237	37	0
Carroll	2		6	78	567	895	127	4
Catoosa	0		7	71	196	685	121	
Chattahoochee	0		0	0	23	3	1	0
Cherokee	3		17	68	487	1,156	115	5
Clarke	0		0	0	0	0	0	0
Clayton	0		1	15	0	2	4	0
Clayton County Police Department	29		464	572	3,175	4,077	1,201	29
Cobb	0		0	0	0	0	0	0
Cobb County Police Department	20		419	474	2,625	7,301	846	35
Columbia	1		17	29	287	1,695	72	6
Coweta	0		24	66	450	1,057	96	5
Crawford	1		2	23	98	228	22	0
Dade	0		2	57	50	71	0	
Dawson	0		1	17	77	353	28	3
DeKalb County Police Department	60		1,846	1,262	9,227	16,524	4,006	173
Dougherty	0		0	1	3	97	3	0
Douglas	2		50	154	428	1,124	152	4
Echols	0		0	3	0	7	0	0
Effingham	2		7	16	173	51	30	
Fayette	2		9	20	242	346	29	3
Floyd	2		1	31	18	88	4	
Forsyth	0		10	85	370	1,124	48	2
Fulton	0		1	0	0	14	0	
Fulton County Police Department	18		453	365	1,641	3,306	766	7
Glynn County Police Department	4		58		574	1,746	92	2
Gwinnett County Police Department	23		652	645	3,653	9,851	1,177	49
Hall	6		26	107	643	1,420	209	6
Haralson	0		2	143	140	212	30	
Harris	0		5	9	64	183	14	0
Heard	0		1	9	43	97	23	0
Henry	0		1	12	0	207	1	0
Henry County Police Department	5		119	141	1,192	2,787	368	10
Jasper	0		0	23	37	78	3	0
Jones	0		2	9	87	300	25	1
Lamar	0		0	8	60	173	8	3
Lanier	0		1	33	47	123	2	0
Lee	0		11	79	159	707	18	1
Liberty	2		5	66	101	211	21	
Lincoln	2		0	20	42	124	7	0
Madison	0		3	31	198	428	47	9
Marion	0		0	1	9	6	2	0
McDuffie	1		6	10	106	145	29	0
McIntosh	0		8	13	86	189	13	2
Meriwether	2		5	41	116	275	22	0
Monroe	2		3	29	105	255	26	1
Morgan	0		1	7	47	114	7	
Murray	0		2	62	125	592	62	
Muscogee	1		0	0	0	0	0	0
Newton	1		37	298	825	835	178	
Oconee	0			30	71	379	15	

Table 10. Offenses Known to Law Enforcement, by Selected State Metropolitan and Nonmetropolitan Counties, 2013— continued

(Number.)

State/county	Murder and non-negligent man-slaughter	Rape (revised definition)	Robbery	Aggravated assault	Burglary	Larceny-theft	Motor vehicle theft	Arson[2]
Oglethorpe	0		0	43	87	260	7	4
Paulding	1		24	124	545	1,489	262	14
Peach	0		0	15	84	212	19	
Pickens	0		0	44	110	338	20	
Pike	0		1	6	50	188	5	0
Pulaski	0		6	37	75	127	2	
Rockdale	2		40	159	609	1,485	165	
Spalding	0		29	75	460	916	172	0
Terrell	0		1	18	29	48	5	
Twiggs	1		1	6	43	75	8	2
Walton	0		3	46	234	503	73	0
Whitfield	2		15	153	504	978	100	
Worth	0		0	30	68	145	19	
Georgia—Nonmetropolitan Counties								
Baldwin	1		8	209	203	450	22	
Banks	0		3	12	103	384	20	
Berrien	0		1	5	43	98	6	0
Bleckley	0		2	23	57	90	3	1
Bulloch	1		3	13	126	309	28	2
Camden	1		3	46	81	224	4	1
Charlton	0		0	1	19	56	11	0
Clay	0		0	0	0	0	0	
Clinch	0		1	5	25	27	6	
Coffee	1		12	41	184	551	49	6
Cook	1		0	7	49	42	8	
Crisp	0		0	8	66	282	8	0
Decatur	0		2	38	101	158	3	2
Dodge	2		5	18	151	247	13	0
Dooly	0		3	2	23	66	4	0
Early	0		1	22	36	48	6	0
Elbert	0		1	16	130	261	34	0
Emanuel	1		0	3	124	166	26	0
Fannin	1		4	29	94	187	19	8
Franklin	0		3	4	134	171	16	1
Gilmer	0		0	46	100	213	20	0
Gordon	0		3	115	218	540	40	0
Grady	0		2	38	79	128	14	
Greene	0		0	10	42	137	1	0
Habersham	0		2	33	183	253	34	0
Hancock	0		0	0	16	39	3	0
Hart	0		1	70	194	343	25	
Irwin	0		1	9	37	81	10	0
Jackson	0		4	35	135	597	52	
Jeff Davis	0		2	62	46	141	22	0
Jefferson	2		2	21	55	38	8	0
Laurens	4		3	12	193	389	15	0
Macon	0		0	0	40	41	3	0
Mitchell	2		2	24	60	156	7	0
Pierce	0		0	18	63	24	11	0
Polk	0		0	0	0	0	0	0
Polk County Police Department	0		7	29	225	383	64	4
Putnam	0		0	66	87	252	11	3
Rabun	0		1	7	57	206	8	0
Randolph	0		0	41	30	37	0	
Schley	0		1	3	9	18	1	0
Screven	0		12	42	102	147	20	
Seminole	4		1	11	24	31	2	
Stephens	0		5	21	126	297	21	0
Sumter	1		0	11	119	174	12	0
Talbot	0		1	0	21	32	4	0
Tattnall	0		3	6	75	112	19	
Taylor	1		2	12	38	48	9	6
Thomas	0		13	27	207	350	54	8
Tift	2		26	67	198	495	50	2
Toombs	0		4	14	73	84	20	
Treutlen	0		1	3	21	34	3	
Troup	1		2	8	23	63	5	
Turner	4		1	38	74	173	12	0
Union	0		7	13	118	268	18	
Upson	1		4	55	171	408	17	0
Ware	0		1	10	17	38	4	
Warren	0		1	0	8	7	3	0
Webster	0		0	0	19	27	10	0
White	0		3	19	106	109	13	
Wilcox	0		0	15	49	51	7	1
Wilkes	0		0	0	6	11	3	2
Wilkinson	0		0	4	43	36	2	

Table 10.   Offenses Known to Law Enforcement, by Selected State Metropolitan and Nonmetropolitan Counties, 2013— continued

(Number.)

State/county	Murder and non-negligent man-slaughter	Rape (revised definition)	Robbery	Aggravated assault	Burglary	Larceny-theft	Motor vehicle theft	Arson[2]
Hawaii - Metropolitan Counties								
Maui Police Department	1		97	307	948	4,314	442	87
Idaho—Metropolitan Counties								
Ada	0	55	7	135	244	584	22	9
Bannock	1	1	0	11	29	76	6	0
Boise	0	2	0	8	23	77	7	1
Bonneville	2	15	3	47	170	475	46	6
Butte	0	0	1	5	0	1	0	0
Canyon	1	14	0	76	223	256	60	5
Franklin	0	0	0	3	3	24	1	0
Gem	0	1	0	12	11	13	2	1
Jefferson	1	2	1	12	42	91	6	0
Kootenai	2	15	6	93	395	833	49	6
Nez Perce	0	0	1	10	33	81	7	0
Owyhee	0	2	0	4	24	73	13	1
Idaho—Nonmetropolitan Counties								
Adams	0	0	0	1	3	7	0	0
Bear Lake	0	1	0	0	15	36	0	0
Benewah	0	0	0	21	12	29	4	1
Bingham	0	8	0	30	71	169	30	0
Blaine	0	1	0	2	8	15	0	0
Bonner	0	5	0	34	201	176	24	3
Boundary	0	1	0	5	56	32	6	2
Camas	0	0	0	0	4	2	0	0
Caribou	0	0	0	0	83	13	1	0
Cassia	0	14	8	37	89	310	20	3
Clark	0	0	0	0	1	6	0	0
Clearwater	0	0	0	11	20	84	8	3
Custer	0	0	0	1	2	10	0	0
Elmore	1	2	0	9	11	49	4	2
Fremont	0	0	0	5	13	62	7	1
Gooding	0	0	0	14	15	27	7	0
Idaho	1	2	0	14	47	55	8	1
Jerome	0	2	0	15	33	80	20	1
Latah	0	2	0	14	68	91	8	0
Lemhi	0	1	1	5	3	19	1	0
Lewis	0	0	0	4	12	30	6	0
Lincoln	0	2	0	7	1	1	0	0
Madison	0	8	0	6	13	73	3	1
Minidoka	1	2	0	10	54	116	21	0
Oneida	3	0	0	6	14	21	2	0
Payette	0	4	1	11	34	71	8	0
Power	0	0	0	0	11	44	2	0
Shoshone	0	4	0	40	89	84	15	1
Teton	0	2	0	13	21	35	3	0
Twin Falls	1	5	2	35	71	85	10	2
Valley	0	9	0	4	22	55	2	1
Washington	0	0	0	3	16	15	2	0
Illinois—Metropolitan Counties								
Alexander	0		4	16	24	54	5	2
Bond	0		0	1	25	60	2	0
Boone	0		3	10	43	153	5	3
Champaign	1		11	73	218	374	29	8
Clinton	0		1	6	8	70	6	0
Cook	0		39	125	229	480	55	18
De Kalb	0		2	16	31	214	2	0
De Witt	1		1	6	9	26	2	0
Du Page	4		11	30	176	611	45	3
Ford	0		0	11	39	87	7	0
Grundy	0		1	12	67	110	2	2
Henry	0		0	7	11	40	3	0
Jackson	0		0	16	142	165	18	5
Jersey	0		0	4	25	79	2	0
Kane	0		3	37	127	276	15	8
Kankakee	2		4	44	152	230	26	15
Kendall	0		0	20	79	161	6	2
Lake	1		17	40	481	1,065	70	13
Macon	0		1	39	80	239	13	1
Macoupin	0		1	18	44	99	4	1
Madison	1		5	57	185	339	38	5
Marshall	0		0	6	18	17	3	0
McHenry	0		4	43	112	327	2	2
McLean	0		1	22	88	109	11	0
Menard	0		1	1	19	26	1	0

Table 10.   Offenses Known to Law Enforcement, by Selected State Metropolitan and Nonmetropolitan Counties, 2013— continued

(Number.)

State/county	Murder and non-negligent man-slaughter	Rape (revised definition)[1]	Robbery	Aggravated assault	Burglary	Larceny-theft	Motor vehicle theft	Arson[2]
Monroe	0		0	2	18	24	1	0
Peoria	0		12	68	184	495	24	7
Piatt	0		1	16	39	45	1	0
Rock Island	0		3	48	70	208	8	0
Sangamon	0		16	98	234	459	28	5
Stark	0		1	1	23	51	1	0
St. Clair	1		25	32	234	378	48	1
Tazewell	0		2	27	72	143	6	1
Will	2		29	105	409	669	57	20
Williamson	1		1	5	137	156	27	1
Winnebago	3		13	92	299	454	48	5
Woodford	0		1	1	46	81	9	0
Illinois—Nonmetropolitan Counties								
Adams	0		2	22	66	165	5	0
Brown	0		0	6	6	14	4	1
Bureau	0		1	10	39	107	7	0
Carroll	0		0	0	14	54	1	0
Cass	0		0	6	2	6	0	0
Clark	0		0	4	23	21	6	0
Clay	0		0	0	23	31	5	0
Coles	0		0	21	24	58	7	4
Cumberland	0		1	2	18	14	4	1
Douglas	0		0	7	13	28	0	0
Edgar	0		0	14	30	30	2	2
Edwards	0		0	14	18	16	0	1
Effingham	0		0	15	39	94	11	1
Fayette	0		0	3	23	77	4	0
Franklin	0		0	13	63	112	18	2
Fulton	0		1	12	44	101	6	3
Greene	0		0	6	10	15	0	1
Hancock	0		0	1	32	103	2	0
Hardin	0		0	7	6	18	0	0
Iroquois	0		0	18	84	154	4	0
Jasper	0		0	1	17	17	0	0
Jefferson	1		1	32	106	159	13	4
Jo Daviess	0		0	1	43	75	3	0
Johnson	0		0	23	7	71	0	0
Knox	0		2	16	87	146	12	1
La Salle	0		2	17	92	204	9	5
Lawrence	0		0	5	12	19	2	1
Lee	0		0	0	90	84	4	2
Livingston	1		0	13	40	172	4	110
Logan	0		0	12	77	68	5	2
Marion	0		0	12	65	118	13	1
Mason	1		0	10	23	59	0	0
Massac	0		0	7	22	45	0	2
McDonough	0		0	10	10	73	2	1
Montgomery	0		3	56	58	77	1	0
Morgan	0		2	3	41	44	2	1
Ogle	0		1	10	43	110	1	0
Perry	0		0	8	7	34	1	0
Pulaski	0		1	26	14	27	1	0
Putnam	0		0	1	5	31	0	0
Randolph	0		0	2	50	94	14	0
Saline	0		1	10	28	71	7	2
Schuyler	1		0	1	2	4	0	0
Scott	0		0	0	13	22	0	0
Shelby	0		0	7	24	48	0	3
Stephenson	0		1	6	34	149	7	0
Union	0		2	6	21	59	6	0
Wabash	0		0	4	14	31	3	0
Warren	0		0	6	26	38	2	0
Wayne	0		3	4	39	70	1	1
White	0		0	11	39	78	2	2
Whiteside	0		0	6	49	139	6	0
Indiana—Metropolitan Counties								
Bartholomew	4		2	53	107	344	50	0
Brown	0		0	0	35	48	10	1
Delaware	0		2	23	140	290	22	3
Elkhart	3	15	22	6	435	493	142	2
Floyd	1		3	2	101	404	22	0
Hancock	1		3	5	109	136	13	1
Harrison	1		2	35	91	372	25	0
Hendricks	0		7	48	224	554	69	3
Johnson	0	3	5	72	153	450	30	12
Lake	1		10	20	252	614	79	0

Table 10.   Offenses Known to Law Enforcement, by Selected State Metropolitan and Nonmetropolitan Counties, 2013— continued

(Number.)

State/county	Murder and non-negligent man-slaughter	Rape (revised definition)[1]	Robbery	Aggravated assault	Burglary	Larceny-theft	Motor vehicle theft	Arson[2]
Madison	1		4	7	162	338	24	3
Monroe	1		7	59	244	588	52	4
Scott	0		0	3	109	252	4	
Shelby	0	3	2	28	103	148	23	1
St. Joseph	2		19	72	455	870	55	
Sullivan	0		2	12	45	131	19	3
Tippecanoe	1		2	19	221	541	23	3
Vigo	0		4	11	271	601	53	5
Warrick	0		3	66	105	514	16	0
Wells	0		0	8	53	130	4	1
Indiana—Nonmetropolitan Counties								
Blackford	0		1	0	21	32	2	1
Cass	0		0	10	46	156	3	0
Clinton	0		5	7	76	159	17	1
Crawford	0		4	7	70	2	7	0
Daviess	0	1	0	6	31	50	10	1
Franklin	0		1	2	98	36	5	0
Fulton	0		0	8	39	62	16	2
Gibson	0		0	14	42	134	13	0
Grant	0		1	25	66	254	13	0
Greene	1		0	0	27	138	13	0
Henry	0		2	0	178	253	23	0
Jackson	0		1	16	92	317	22	0
Jay	0		0	12	15	75	7	0
Jennings	0		0	68	140	175	9	0
Knox	0		0	0	0	0	0	0
Kosciusko	2		6	155	170	532	48	0
LaGrange	0		1	19	62	117	15	0
Lawrence	0		1	78	134	135	10	5
Miami	0		0	8	72	111	1	3
Montgomery	0		4	68	80	203	13	0
Noble	0		0	15	74	114	15	0
Parke	1		0	2	14	31	3	1
Pike	0	0	0	20	53	177	1	
Ripley	0		1	0	60	166	10	0
Starke	1		0	5	6	20	7	2
Steuben	2		4	5	128	297	28	0
Tipton	0		1	6	28	15	8	0
Wabash	0		3	1	81	159	8	0
Iowa—Metropolitan Counties								
Bremer	0	1	0	4	17	27	0	0
Dallas	1	1	1	14	21	74	9	3
Dubuque	0	2	0	9	64	116	18	2
Grundy	0	0	0	10	16	38	2	1
Guthrie	0	1	0	3	18	15	2	0
Johnson	0	15	1	52	71	137	17	1
Linn	0	3	2	13	118	122	27	1
Madison	0	0	0	14	14	19	6	0
Mills	0	4	0	30	56	82	12	2
Plymouth	0	4	0	12	17	32	7	0
Polk	1	5	3	56	206	426	72	2
Pottawattamie	0	7	3	59	135	260	30	3
Scott	0	4	2	35	50	101	10	1
Story	0	1	2	19	60	73	13	5
Warren	0	10	0	51	75	110	23	5
Washington	0	5	0	23	32	44	5	1
Woodbury	0	2	0	19	54	75	9	2
Iowa—Nonmetropolitan Counties								
Adair	0	0	0	1	17	28	2	0
Adams	0	1	0	5	13	6	0	0
Allamakee	0	1	0	4	2	17	6	0
Appanoose	0	3	0	11	47	44	18	4
Buena Vista	0	1	0	9	27	19	0	0
Butler	0	1	0	2	9	3	1	0
Calhoun	1	0	0	5	16	34	5	0
Cass	0	0	1	5	28	36	9	0
Cedar	0	3	0	3	15	102	7	3
Cerro Gordo	0	1	0	2	44	56	12	0
Cherokee	0	0	0	3	9	20	2	0
Chickasaw	0	0	0	3	14	14	1	1
Clarke	0	2	0	4	23	29	3	0
Clay	0	0	0	7	20	15	0	3
Clayton	0	4	0	9	20	37	1	0
Clinton	0	3	2	10	28	67	9	1
Davis	0	1	0	3	3	3	4	0

Table 10.   Offenses Known to Law Enforcement, by Selected State Metropolitan and Nonmetropolitan Counties, 2013— continued

(Number.)

State/county	Murder and non-negligent man-slaughter	Rape (revised definition)[1]	Robbery	Aggravated assault	Burglary	Larceny-theft	Motor vehicle theft	Arson[2]
Delaware	0	0	0	5	8	16	3	0
Des Moines	0	1	0	15	47	100	9	2
Dickinson	1	3	0	6	8	23	0	0
Emmet	0	0	0	7	11	28	3	0
Fayette	0	0	0	7	8	39	7	0
Floyd	0	3	0	1	18	15	1	0
Greene	0	0	0	0	0	0	0	0
Hamilton	0	0	1	16	34	27	6	0
Hancock	0	1	0	2	11	13	1	0
Hardin	0	0	0	8	27	53	7	3
Henry	0	0	0	26	30	46	8	2
Howard	0	1	1	5	15	27	3	0
Humboldt	0	0	0	6	28	38	5	0
Ida	0	0	0	4	21	27	0	0
Iowa	0	1	0	9	30	58	6	0
Jasper	0	0	0	16	92	83	11	6
Jefferson	0	0	0	0	15	26	7	1
Keokuk	0	0	0	10	15	17	1	0
Kossuth	0	0	1	2	13	20	0	1
Lee	1	1	0	10	34	56	9	1
Louisa	0	2	0	4	35	21	1	0
Lucas	0	1	0	2	54	49	13	4
Marion	0	14	1	21	49	49	6	4
Marshall	0	0	0	7	36	39	13	0
Mitchell	0	0	0	0	10	9	0	0
Monona	0	3	2	7	16	57	4	1
Monroe	0	2	0	2	28	27	4	1
Muscatine	0	5	0	13	32	30	6	0
O'Brien	0	6	0	6	25	56	0	1
Osceola	0	0	0	0	0	4	1	0
Page	0	1	0	7	21	17	9	1
Palo Alto	0	0	0	14	44	24	7	1
Pocahontas	0	0	0	3	21	24	2	0
Poweshiek	0	2	0	4	9	11	3	0
Ringgold	0	0	0	0	16	22	3	0
Sac	1	2	0	8	39	40	2	0
Sioux	0	0	0	6	27	43	3	3
Tama	0	4	0	32	38	49	9	0
Taylor	0	0	0	0	8	12	2	0
Union	0	1	0	1	11	16	8	1
Van Buren	0	1	0	11	31	23	9	0
Wapello	0	0	0	9	142	69	17	2
Wayne	0	0	0	2	12	6	0	0
Webster	2	1	1	17	73	107	10	2
Winnebago	0	0	0	0	1	0	0	0
Winneshiek	0	0	0	0	1	12	0	0
Worth	1	2	0	5	29	46	9	0
Wright	0	0	0	2	4	10	1	1
Kansas—Metropolitan Counties								
Butler	1	6	1	44	200	382	42	14
Doniphan	0	0	0	6	23	24	6	0
Douglas	0	2	1	16	69	98	9	0
Harvey	0	0	0	12	30	38	5	1
Jackson	1	0	0	11	37	66	6	2
Jefferson	0	4	0	31	60	158	32	3
Johnson	1	5	0	28	61	161	25	5
Kingman	0	1	0	2	21	47	13	1
Leavenworth	1	3	3	36	121	128	29	11
Miami	0	6	1	17	92	113	14	5
Osage	0	0	0	15	47	48	11	2
Pottawatomie	0	5	2	24	64	151	20	4
Riley County Police Department	5	22	16	103	219	962	45	9
Shawnee	0	6	3	85	194	577	43	4
Sumner	1	4	1	18	63	81	12	3
Wabaunsee	0	0	0	12	33	48	3	2
Wyandotte	0	2	2	31	7	27	4	2
Kansas—Nonmetropolitan Counties								
Allen	0	0	0	2	22	48	4	2
Anderson	0	5	0	7	38	37	3	0
Barber	0	0	0	6	17	27	5	1
Barton	1	1	0	7	33	69	7	0
Bourbon	2	9	0	14	41	60	4	1
Brown	0	1	0	1	22	32	6	0
Chautauqua	0	1	0	2	9	15	2	0
Cherokee	1	5	1	33	107	129	18	3
Cheyenne	1	1	0	5	6	27	1	0

Table 10. Offenses Known to Law Enforcement, by Selected State Metropolitan and Nonmetropolitan Counties, 2013— continued

(Number.)

State/county	Murder and non-negligent man-slaughter	Rape (revised definition)[1]	Robbery	Aggravated assault	Burglary	Larceny-theft	Motor vehicle theft	Arson[2]
Clark	0	1	0	1	8	15	2	0
Clay	0	1	0	6	4	18	4	0
Cloud	0	3	0	11	33	25	4	0
Coffey	0	2	0	1	15	24	2	2
Cowley	0	2	1	21	56	81	12	0
Crawford	0	4	2	12	96	129	13	4
Dickinson	0	3	0	10	72	48	7	2
Edwards	0	1	0	4	4	18	0	0
Elk	0	0	0	2	6	12	1	0
Ellis	0	4	0	13	19	68	5	3
Ellsworth	0	0	0	2	15	21	4	0
Finney	1	4	0	20	109	159	3	2
Ford	0	3	1	18	37	49	7	0
Franklin	4	4	1	24	134	116	18	2
Geary	0	4	1	9	12	37	2	2
Gove	0	0	0	1	6	9	1	0
Grant	0	0	0	5	5	7	0	0
Gray	0	2	1	7	25	43	1	3
Greeley	0	0	0	0	1	2	0	0
Greenwood	3	0	0	15	29	47	3	0
Hamilton	0	3	1	4	14	11	0	1
Harper	0	0	0	6	11	25	2	0
Haskell	0	1	0	5	10	43	4	0
Hodgeman	0	0	0	2	5	14	0	0
Kearny	0	3	0	9	15	52	4	0
Kiowa	0	2	0	0	8	21	4	0
Labette	0	0	0	5	34	63	7	7
Lane	0	0	0	6	12	12	4	0
Lincoln	0	0	0	2	10	10	3	0
Logan	0	0	0	2	3	6	1	0
Lyon	0	1	0	6	18	94	2	7
Marion	0	0	0	4	28	26	7	0
Marshall	0	0	0	7	7	33	3	0
McPherson	0	1	0	5	41	42	5	1
Mitchell	0	1	0	6	4	7	2	0
Montgomery	0	0	1	15	58	91	16	1
Morris	0	2	0	2	17	18	1	0
Nemaha	0	1	0	7	19	21	5	0
Neosho	0	0	0	4	45	47	6	0
Ness	0	0	0	7	7	11	2	0
Norton	0	0	0	1	2	9	0	0
Osborne	0	2	0	2	14	16	2	0
Pawnee	0	0	0	2	15	21	1	0
Phillips	0	0	0	6	4	6	4	0
Pratt	0	1	0	13	33	34	8	0
Rawlins	0	0	0	0	3	7	1	0
Republic	0	0	0	1	13	35	2	0
Rice	0	2	0	7	35	24	3	0
Rooks	0	2	0	0	7	8	0	0
Rush	0	0	0	9	20	53	3	1
Russell	0	1	0	4	18	29	1	0
Saline	1	4	2	12	50	81	16	7
Scott	0	0	0	5	6	14	3	0
Seward	1	0	1	12	6	39	1	0
Stafford	0	0	0	5	9	21	1	2
Thomas	0	1	0	4	6	15	1	0
Washington	0	0	0	4	6	13	2	0
Wichita	0	0	0	4	4	9	2	0
Wilson	0	0	0	6	37	35	4	1
Woodson	0	0	0	3	16	23	2	1
Kentucky—Metropolitan Counties								
Allen	0	1	1	1	61	49	7	1
Boone	0	32	16	32	384	897	76	7
Bourbon	0	0	1	2	41	53	2	1
Boyd	0	0	1	8	35	92	3	0
Bracken	0	0	1	0	38	26	4	0
Bullitt	0	9	6	17	199	258	21	2
Butler	0	0	0	1	22	17	7	2
Campbell County Police Department	0	28	0	3	92	144	14	2
Christian	1	13	3	6	129	177	19	0
Clark	1	2	2	5	117	137	10	1
Daviess	0	6	2	7	131	352	16	3
Edmonson	0	0	0	2	25	22	6	0
Gallatin	0	0	0	1	27	44	5	0
Grant	0	1	0	1	39	65	6	1
Greenup	1	1	1	3	15	7	0	0
Hancock	0	0	0	2	4	4	2	0

Table 10.   Offenses Known to Law Enforcement, by Selected State Metropolitan and Nonmetropolitan Counties, 2013— continued

(Number.)

State/county	Murder and non-negligent man-slaughter	Rape (revised definition)[1]	Robbery	Aggravated assault	Burglary	Larceny-theft	Motor vehicle theft	Arson[2]
Hardin	1	0	0	7	39	90	6	1
Henderson	0	1	2	8	72	112	4	0
Henry	0	0	2	0	4	2	0	0
Jessamine	1	1	6	7	130	135	8	1
Kenton	0	0	0	0	0	10	2	0
Kenton County Police Department	0	3	1	9	85	94	11	0
Larue	0	0	1	1	21	18	3	0
McLean	0	0	1	0	18	16	3	0
Meade	0	1	0	8	83	67	12	1
Oldham	0	0	0	0	1	6	0	0
Oldham County Police Department	1	5	9	8	187	230	19	0
Pendleton	0	0	1	1	59	60	2	0
Scott	0	1	4	8	94	141	6	0
Shelby	0	5	2	13	140	294	26	1
Spencer	0	0	0	2	45	40	3	0
Trigg	0	1	0	5	38	40	5	0
Trimble	0	0	0	0	0	1	0	0
Warren	0	7	3	7	135	254	23	0
Woodford	0	0	0	1	1	10	0	0
Kentucky—Nonmetropolitan Counties								
Adair	0	0	1	2	27	12	5	0
Anderson	0	0	0	1	44	24	4	0
Ballard	0	2	0	2	48	72	5	1
Barren	0	2	0	7	58	39	11	1
Bath	0	0	0	0	0	1	0	0
Bell	0	1	1	9	29	51	6	3
Boyle	0	0	0	3	50	24	2	0
Breckinridge	0	1	0	1	13	13	5	0
Caldwell	0	0	0	5	14	20	4	1
Calloway	0	2	1	11	87	89	12	1
Carlisle	0	0	0	2	8	8	0	0
Carroll	0	0	0	3	8	30	1	0
Carter	0	0	1	1	30	47	8	0
Casey	0	0	1	2	44	20	5	0
Clay	0	2	0	6	26	26	7	3
Clinton	0	0	0	0	0	0	0	0
Crittenden	0	0	0	0	3	10	1	0
Cumberland	0	0	0	0	28	20	0	0
Elliott	0	0	0	1	4	5	2	0
Estill	0	0	0	2	12	13	4	0
Fleming	0	0	0	2	26	12	3	0
Floyd	0	0	1	3	14	29	14	0
Franklin	1	1	3	4	122	184	12	0
Fulton	0	0	0	4	3	16	0	0
Garrard	0	1	0	0	13	18	4	0
Graves	0	5	1	16	90	102	16	3
Grayson	0	3	0	7	58	58	9	2
Green	0	0	0	3	5	1	1	0
Harlan	0	3	0	1	11	24	2	0
Harrison	0	2	0	5	86	88	5	0
Hart	0	0	0	2	4	9	3	0
Hickman	0	0	0	0	7	5	2	0
Hopkins	0	4	3	8	95	76	19	0
Jackson County Police Department	0	0	0	1	50	30	4	0
Johnson	0	1	0	7	40	50	11	0
Knott	0	0	0	0	9	20	4	0
Knox	0	1	3	6	93	36	20	0
Laurel	1	1	11	21	171	158	38	3
Lawrence	0	2	3	2	44	34	9	2
Lee	0	0	0	0	0	6	0	0
Leslie	0	0	0	5	6	4	2	0
Letcher	0	1	0	0	28	31	1	0
Lewis	1	0	0	0	20	10	0	0
Lincoln	0	0	0	2	22	14	15	0
Livingston	0	2	0	2	36	57	9	1
Logan	0	5	1	5	59	73	4	2
Lyon	0	0	0	0	14	19	1	0
Madison	0	4	0	7	124	228	18	0
Magoffin	0	0	0	2	1	9	8	0
Marion	0	1	1	0	31	31	3	0
Marshall	2	3	1	6	95	132	15	2
Martin	0	0	0	2	19	29	10	1
Mason	0	0	2	3	73	64	7	0
McCracken	0	14	8	20	109	283	19	3
McCreary	0	0	3	2	22	41	13	0
Menifee	0	0	0	1	17	25	2	0
Mercer	0	1	2	4	41	28	6	0

Table 10.   Offenses Known to Law Enforcement, by Selected State Metropolitan and Nonmetropolitan Counties, 2013— continued

(Number.)

State/county	Murder and non-negligent man-slaughter	Rape (revised definition)[1]	Robbery	Aggravated assault	Burglary	Larceny-theft	Motor vehicle theft	Arson[2]
Metcalfe	0	1	0	2	28	28	1	0
Montgomery	1	1	6	6	193	262	17	0
Muhlenberg	0	3	1	3	27	24	3	0
Muhlenberg County Police Department	0	0	0	0	0	0	0	0
Nelson	2	3	0	5	85	109	10	2
Nicholas	0	0	0	2	6	3	0	2
Ohio	0	8	0	5	73	53	11	6
Owen	0	0	0	1	19	14	1	0
Owsley	0	0	0	1	4	12	2	0
Perry	0	0	0	2	5	11	7	1
Perry County Police Department	0	0	0	0	0	2	0	0
Pike	0	0	0	1	3	10	0	0
Powell	0	1	1	1	56	42	4	0
Pulaski	0	5	4	2	236	205	17	1
Robertson	0	0	0	0	0	1	0	0
Rockcastle	0	0	3	4	25	16	7	1
Rowan	0	0	0	3	6	28	5	0
Russell	0	0	0	1	22	26	2	0
Simpson	1	3	1	3	36	60	0	1
Taylor	1	4	1	9	86	88	7	0
Todd	0	1	0	2	48	21	2	1
Union	0	0	0	4	18	49	6	0
Washington	0	0	0	0	12	10	2	0
Wayne	0	0	0	0	40	14	4	0
Webster	0	0	0	0	1	4	2	0
Whitley	0	0	1	3	79	76	14	0
Wolfe	0	0	0	0	10	19	1	0
Louisiana—Metropolitan Counties								
Acadia	2		8	38	165	66	370	0
Ascension	8	27	48	273	631	2,104	163	1
Bossier	1	2	4	45	101	451	16	0
Caddo	0	8	4	79	207	592	46	2
Calcasieu	3	72	43	317	1,323	3,018	247	11
Cameron	0	1	0	12	23	109	3	0
De Soto	0		1	195	72	295	50	0
East Baton Rouge	14		231	131	1,522	5,360	137	
East Feliciana	1		2	32	67	100	10	0
Grant	1		0	10	68	113	4	0
Iberia	4	10	59	109	479	1,116	29	0
Iberville	0		16	267	174	491	13	0
Jefferson	43		395	1,176	2,399	9,485	789	77
Lafayette	3		57	282	504	1,208	172	14
Lafourche	7		27	57	638	1,180	60	3
Livingston	4		17	287	1,256	1,844	16	0
Ouachita	9		34	271	928	1,660	122	3
Plaquemines	2	4	1	33	72	306	9	0
Pointe Coupee	2		10	73	133	200	18	0
Rapides	4	28	16	234	588	1,250	196	7
St. Bernard	0		10	47	75	401	12	3
St. Charles	5		32	193	298	944	58	17
St. Helena	0		1	52	72	100	25	0
St. James	1	9	5	83	91	373	15	0
St. John the Baptist	13		34	19	344	794	67	2
St. Martin	0		18	88	130	192	5	
St. Tammany	0		27	176	515	1,413	151	9
Tangipahoa	8		59	552	1,167	2,092	206	12
Terrebonne	10		29	203	436	2,041	107	2
Union	0		0	40	17	31	1	0
Vermilion	2		11	80	346	490	52	
Webster	1		0	89	114	116	21	
West Baton Rouge	0		5	51	71	350	20	0
West Feliciana	0	1	2	20	26	102	9	0
Louisiana—Nonmetropolitan Counties								
Allen	1		0	38	26	186	8	
Assumption	0		5	88	90	240	38	2
Avoyelles	0		3	89	178	305	23	3
Bienville	0		4	50	63	128	17	0
Caldwell	1		0	23	84	156	9	
Catahoula	0		4	19	36	62	1	0
Claiborne	0		2	29	76	150	16	2
Concordia	1		3	42	105	175	17	0
Franklin	0		0	40	62	91	19	
Jackson	0		9	21	18	53	2	0
La Salle	0		2	34	17	47	7	0
Lincoln	0		2	39	101	208	7	
Morehouse	0	0	0	1	15	105	11	0

Table 10. Offenses Known to Law Enforcement, by Selected State Metropolitan and Nonmetropolitan Counties, 2013— continued

(Number.)

State/county	Murder and non-negligent man-slaughter	Rape (revised definition)[1]	Robbery	Aggravated assault	Burglary	Larceny-theft	Motor vehicle theft	Arson[2]
Natchitoches	2		4	44	114	433	40	0
Red River	0		1	30	16	69	7	
Richland	0		3	12	72	175	20	
Sabine	5		0	35	21	55	9	0
St. Landry	1		11	280	438	533	79	1
St. Mary	4		18	149	197	726	78	0
Vernon	1		8	67	117	542	43	3
Washington	0		6	113	156	408	39	0
West Carroll	0		0	50	41	262	19	0
Winn	0		0	12	25	55	16	
Maine—Metropolitan Counties								
Androscoggin	0		4	2	84	137	8	0
Cumberland	0		4	24	266	439	32	5
Penobscot	0		6	2	176	396	17	2
Sagadahoc	0		0	4	44	108	9	1
York	0		6	19	116	177	14	6
Maine—Nonmetropolitan Counties								
Aroostook	0		0	0	23	44	5	0
Franklin	0	8	2	2	22	47	4	0
Hancock	0		1	3	49	129	7	0
Kennebec	0	15	3	8	109	169	17	1
Knox	0		2	10	53	200	15	0
Lincoln	0		1	7	89	171	12	0
Oxford	0		1	4	118	232	5	0
Piscataquis	0		1	3	41	62	17	0
Somerset	0	9	1	10	127	242	24	2
Waldo	0		0	10	84	118	11	1
Washington	0		0	11	50	72	7	
Maryland—Metropolitan Counties								
Allegany	0		8	30	100	180	12	0
Anne Arundel	0		0	0	0	0	0	0
Baltimore County	0		0	0	0	0	0	0
Calvert	3		26	56	343	1,049	60	2
Carroll	1		12	150	306	518	34	0
Cecil	2		16	73	370	417	38	0
Charles	2		141	374	657	2,401	187	12
Frederick	4		31	171	373	1,335	76	30
Harford	5		114	306	630	1,809	79	0
Howard	0		0	0	0	0	0	0
Howard County Police Department	4		204	373	1,032	4,829	254	47
Montgomery	0		0	0	0	0	0	0
Montgomery County Police Department	8		758	787	2,586	12,104	861	119
Prince George's	0		0	111	0	0	0	0
Prince George's County Police Department	51		1,583	1,722	4,543	13,764	3,601	144
Queen Anne's	1		11	55	181	402	10	3
Somerset	0		0	5	11	25	5	0
St. Mary's	2		55	149	589	1,465	106	3
Washington	0		18	82	343	887	78	0
Wicomico	2		29	45	336	485	45	4
Worcester	0		2	15	48	157	10	0
Maryland—Nonmetropolitan Counties								
Caroline	0		6	3	113	217	11	1
Dorchester	0		1	15	45	192	6	0
Garrett	0		2	76	106	235	12	0
Kent	0		1	15	50	90	4	1
Talbot	0		0	17	72	100	5	0
Michigan—Metropolitan Counties								
Barry	0	10	0	24	97	218	19	0
Bay	2	23	4	8	101	526	30	3
Calhoun	0	19	6	51	139	262	27	2
Cass	0	21	0	23	191	275	10	3
Clinton	2	6	0	13	62	84	11	0
Eaton	0	30	19	45	211	1,012	51	7
Ingham	0	24	17	77	195	411	18	3
Jackson	0	27	8	94	166	460	29	5
Kalamazoo	1	56	32	113	474	1,234	101	10
Kent	5	113	37	190	668	1,879	102	24
Lapeer	0	20	2	31	119	213	19	1
Livingston	2	27	6	31	187	500	33	6
Macomb	1	59	37	207	438	1,457	146	6
Midland	1	23	2	28	101	261	6	4
Monroe	1	63	30	121	598	1,540	151	12
Montcalm	0	19	1	16	103	261	13	5

Table 10.   Offenses Known to Law Enforcement, by Selected State Metropolitan and Nonmetropolitan Counties, 2013— continued

(Number.)

State/county	Murder and non-negligent man-slaughter	Rape (revised definition)[3]	Robbery	Aggravated assault	Burglary	Larceny-theft	Motor vehicle theft	Arson[2]
Muskegon	1	11	3	36	160	477	30	1
Oakland	15	120	224	667	1,389	2,918	263	54
Ottawa	0	173	17	194	601	1,995	59	11
Saginaw	0	26	9	70	117	446	27	3
St. Clair	1	38	10	111	320	856	75	16
Van Buren	0	18	2	50	137	237	27	4
Washtenaw	3	62	52	360	617	1,242	152	12
Wayne	0	0	0	0	0	0	0	0
Michigan—Nonmetropolitan Counties								
Alcona	0	6	0	6	74	100	3	1
Alger	0	0	0	0	7	2	0	0
Allegan	1	26	4	66	201	416	37	3
Alpena	0	18	0	7	16	76	2	1
Antrim	0	7	3	4	66	144	12	3
Arenac	0	3	0	19	35	57	6	0
Baraga	0	0	0	2	9	20	1	0
Branch	0	8	0	6	12	39	5	0
Charlevoix	0	10	0	5	30	106	5	1
Cheboygan	0	6	1	3	24	52	1	0
Chippewa	0	3	0	5	28	74	1	0
Crawford	0	6	0	31	46	79	3	0
Delta	0	4	0	8	14	58	1	0
Emmet	0	5	0	11	18	180	5	0
Gladwin	0	9	1	21	94	115	5	0
Gogebic	0	1	0	4	19	48	1	0
Houghton	0	3	0	0	26	55	7	0
Huron	0	9	0	12	38	102	15	1
Ionia	1	19	0	13	113	197	20	6
Iosco	0	0	0	0	1	1	0	0
Iron	0	1	1	6	27	24	0	0
Isabella	0	19	7	20	113	268	17	4
Kalkaska	0	6	0	1	82	182	8	0
Keweenaw	0	0	0	2	10	29	0	0
Leelanau	0	2	0	5	10	53	1	1
Luce	0	0	0	4	11	25	2	0
Mackinac	0	0	0	11	20	42	1	0
Manistee	0	9	0	16	37	107	7	0
Marquette	0	1	0	0	27	141	6	1
Mason	1	26	0	14	164	321	11	1
Mecosta	1	20	0	181	150	387	10	4
Menominee	0	7	0	4	44	74	3	0
Missaukee	0	18	0	18	32	153	4	0
Montmorency	0	0	1	4	12	15	0	0
Oceana	1	12	0	11	85	157	9	2
Ogemaw	0	2	0	19	75	127	12	0
Osceola	0	6	0	23	49	140	6	0
Oscoda	0	4	0	32	46	83	6	0
Otsego	0	5	0	7	36	66	1	1
Presque Isle	0	4	0	3	12	15	23	0
Roscommon	1	13	0	13	28	113	9	0
Sanilac	1	14	0	39	67	99	14	1
Shiawassee	1	25	3	46	160	267	16	3
Tuscola	1	43	0	33	116	169	16	4
Wexford	0	20	1	15	56	267	16	3
Minnesota—Metropolitan Counties								
Anoka	1	30	4	27	249	978	70	8
Benton	0	11	0	11	50	130	20	3
Blue Earth	0	2	2	9	57	113	14	0
Carlton	0	2	1	10	75	173	13	2
Carver	0	17	4	21	142	563	16	2
Chisago	0	0	3	17	39	150	26	0
Clay	0	3	0	8	23	52	4	0
Dakota	0	3	1	37	60	114	6	0
Dodge	0	0	0	26	40	175	7	0
Fillmore	0	1	0	13	64	51	2	0
Hennepin	0	6	3	27	4	100	3	3
Houston	0	2	0	7	25	31	2	0
Isanti	0	3	0	11	70	182	23	1
Le Sueur	0	3	0	8	13	91	7	0
Mille Lacs	0	10	1	36	145	446	43	6
Nicollet	0	7	0	1	28	37	8	0
Olmsted	0	8	2	14	135	183	14	2
Polk	0	7	0	13	60	137	9	3
Ramsey	0	2	2	7	5	16	0	1
Scott	0	3	0	4	6	18	3	1
Sherburne	3	8	0	15	65	260	23	2

Table 10.   Offenses Known to Law Enforcement, by Selected State Metropolitan and Nonmetropolitan Counties, 2013— continued

(Number.)

State/county	Murder and non-negligent man-slaughter	Rape (revised definition)[1]	Robbery	Aggravated assault	Burglary	Larceny-theft	Motor vehicle theft	Arson[2]
Sibley	0	0	0	0	0	0	0	0
Stearns	1	10	1	11	81	255	22	1
St. Louis	1	14	6	52	309	444	66	8
Wabasha	0	0	0	7	6	48	8	0
Washington	0	6	4	22	178	603	26	3
Wright	1	10	9	45	125	1,426	59	4
Minnesota—Nonmetropolitan Counties								
Aitkin	0	17	1	21	167	260	24	1
Becker	2	6	0	6	49	95	12	1
Beltrami	1	17	0	18	99	253	17	3
Big Stone	0	1	0	2	7	26	2	0
Brown	0	0	0	0	0	6	0	0
Cass	0	50	3	23	237	883	78	1
Chippewa	0	1	0	3	3	26	1	0
Clearwater	1	6	0	18	36	59	5	0
Cook	0	0	0	4	9	148	2	0
Cottonwood	0	2	0	3	10	30	2	0
Crow Wing	0	6	1	19	233	261	29	0
Douglas	0	3	0	8	56	127	7	0
Faribault	0	0	0	2	25	25	5	1
Freeborn	0	1	0	8	20	63	11	1
Goodhue	0	4	0	5	53	150	22	0
Grant	0	0	0	5	23	41	2	0
Hubbard	1	6	0	8	77	144	6	0
Itasca	1	26	1	14	85	295	6	1
Jackson	0	1	0	5	6	63	1	0
Kanabec	0	10	1	21	84	178	20	0
Kandiyohi	1	5	0	11	47	171	11	2
Kittson	0	0	0	1	4	20	2	0
Koochiching	0	1	0	1	21	58	5	0
Lac Qui Parle	0	0	0	4	9	25	1	0
Lake	0	0	0	1	10	9	3	0
Lake of the Woods	0	0	0	2	4	11	1	0
Lincoln	0	0	0	10	2	16	0	0
Lyon	0	0	1	3	14	16	3	0
Mahnomen	0	0	2	17	21	50	6	1
Marshall	0	0	0	0	0	0	0	0
Martin	0	0	0	1	8	31	1	0
McLeod	0	2	0	8	39	63	7	0
Meeker	0	4	0	11	47	148	13	0
Morrison	1	4	0	2	52	166	18	0
Mower	0	8	2	14	69	67	10	0
Murray	0	1	0	1	7	30	2	0
Nobles	0	3	0	5	11	21	3	1
Norman	0	0	0	0	1	1	0	0
Otter Tail	1	11	0	21	173	244	24	0
Pennington	0	0	0	3	14	29	6	1
Pine	0	23	1	58	242	978	87	2
Pipestone	0	0	0	2	14	72	1	0
Pope	1	3	0	3	21	47	4	0
Red Lake	0	0	0	2	8	8	1	0
Redwood	0	0	0	5	10	16	2	1
Renville	0	1	0	1	38	71	9	0
Rice	0	4	0	6	86	125	12	0
Rock	0	0	1	72	19	57	5	0
Roseau	0	1	1	0	13	81	7	0
Steele	0	3	1	4	35	67	6	0
Stevens	0	0	0	3	10	12	4	0
Swift	0	0	0	4	4	15	2	0
Todd	1	7	1	8	80	107	3	2
Traverse	0	0	0	0	0	0	0	0
Wadena	0	3	0	5	17	35	6	2
Waseca	0	1	0	1	28	53	5	0
Watonwan	0	4	0	4	19	12	5	0
Wilkin	0	0	0	1	8	13	3	0
Winona	0	3	0	7	23	45	15	1
Yellow Medicine	0	0	0	1	12	23	1	0
Mississippi—Metropolitan Counties								
Hancock	1		5	11	143	339	51	0
Harrison	4		7	204	239	543	89	31
Jackson	1		15	55	386	892	112	11
Lamar	0		5	10	333	266	6	1
Rankin	0		4	21	122	324	49	3
Mississippi—Nonmetropolitan Counties								
Adams	0	7	5	41	182	238	16	4

Table 10.   Offenses Known to Law Enforcement, by Selected State Metropolitan and Nonmetropolitan Counties, 2013— continued

(Number.)

State/county	Murder and non-negligent man-slaughter	Rape (revised definition)	Robbery	Aggravated assault	Burglary	Larceny-theft	Motor vehicle theft	Arson[2]
Choctaw	0		0	1	36	28	0	0
Claiborne	0		2	24	96	58	27	0
Greene	2		2	7	0	7	0	0
Itawamba	0	7	0	13	80	161	23	0
Jefferson	0	2	1	17	14	19	0	0
Lauderdale	3	9	6	19	345	234	24	1
Lee	0	3	4	31	181	430	25	9
Leflore	1		7	78	128	162	17	1
Marion	3	5	6	16	144	140	7	3
Scott	4		11	83	111	111	20	0
Tippah	0		1	1	0	3	0	0
Tishomingo	0		0	3	13	0	0	0
Warren	2		6	11	76	197	25	4
Washington	1		6	13	155	256	47	0
Missouri—Metropolitan Counties								
Andrew	0	2	1	11	46	83	3	0
Bates	0	4	1	69	69	114	18	0
Bollinger	0	1	0	32	34	46	6	1
Boone	0	7	12	92	139	524	49	4
Buchanan	1	2	0	18	74	143	12	3
Caldwell	0	1	0	22	37	38	1	1
Callaway	1	5	7	63	183	383	22	2
Cape Girardeau	0	3	4	13	115	103	16	2
Cass	0	1	2	26	100	207	37	0
Christian	1	0	0	50	117	182	47	0
Clay	0	3	2	8	72	114	30	3
Clinton	0	0	1	19	9	64	12	0
Cole	1	4	3	55	66	157	14	0
Dallas	0	4	0	29	77	101	10	0
De Kalb	0	0	0	10	28	33	3	1
Franklin	1	1	1	80	143	413	33	2
Greene	1	14	9	50	471	941	119	14
Jackson	1	1	5	30	170	352	73	2
Jasper	1	2	3	107	266	340	56	9
Jefferson	0	69	11	213	444	1,632	166	20
Lafayette	1	3	0	4	41	95	22	0
Lincoln	0	0	0	40	93	129	27	2
McDonald	0	17	2	123	108	277	41	1
Moniteau	0	1	0	16	61	33	0	0
Newton	1	14	3	20	214	546	93	6
Osage	0	0	0	4	26	49	6	3
Platte	0	6	1	36	64	223	31	4
Polk	0	6	5	50	124	190	31	5
Ray	0	2	0	37	44	97	13	0
St. Charles	1	6	6	105	288	628	50	6
St. Louis County Police Department	8	113	235	687	1,769	5,432	529	37
Warren	0	17	1	47	75	125	11	4
Webster	0	5	1	15	128	106	31	5
Missouri—Nonmetropolitan Counties								
Adair	0	0	0	12	84	81	6	3
Atchison	0	0	0	0	2	3	0	0
Audrain	0	2	1	2	66	86	8	1
Barry	0	8	3	63	190	233	37	5
Barton	1	4	0	41	51	73	7	2
Benton	0	9	1	28	109	147	21	1
Butler	0	7	4	125	142	404	56	0
Camden	0	2	0	37	93	213	7	0
Carroll	0	1	0	6	25	39	1	1
Carter	0	0	0	4	23	28	5	0
Cedar	0	1	0	27	42	98	4	0
Chariton	0	0	0	17	36	57	13	1
Clark	0	0	0	10	19	17	2	0
Cooper	1	1	2	1	33	79	10	0
Crawford	2	1	0	28	90	138	11	0
Dade	0	1	0	28	16	21	16	0
Daviess	0	2	0	2	30	23	3	0
Dent	0	1	0	18	45	62	10	1
Douglas	1	0	0	22	44	69	14	1
Dunklin	0	4	1	20	45	128	9	4
Gasconade	0	2	0	18	46	65	17	0
Gentry	0	0	0	0	10	11	1	0
Grundy	0	0	0	0	31	21	3	0
Harrison	0	0	0	0	14	17	4	3
Hickory	0	0	0	1	48	53	6	0
Holt	0	0	0	5	17	46	3	0
Howard	0	0	0	1	7	42	4	0

Table 10.   Offenses Known to Law Enforcement, by Selected State Metropolitan and Nonmetropolitan Counties, 2013— continued

(Number.)

State/county	Murder and non-negligent man-slaughter	Rape (revised definition)[1]	Robbery	Aggravated assault	Burglary	Larceny-theft	Motor vehicle theft	Arson[2]
Howell	1	0	4	29	112	223	23	1
Iron	0	1	1	35	58	41	12	1
Johnson	1	0	0	14	101	197	28	0
Knox	0	0	0	0	15	22	1	0
Laclede	0	6	3	43	98	203	29	2
Lawrence	1	2	1	39	142	197	16	0
Lewis	0	1	0	4	16	37	3	0
Linn	0	0	0	9	43	39	5	1
Livingston	0	2	0	2	16	42	0	0
Macon	0	0	0	22	44	57	4	1
Madison	0	2	0	10	12	37	7	0
Maries	0	2	0	6	30	37	5	1
Marion	1	0	0	10	18	139	1	0
Mercer	0	3	0	3	21	9	2	0
Miller	1	10	1	16	79	178	20	1
Mississippi	0	0	0	7	19	31	1	0
Monroe	0	0	0	10	16	23	5	0
Montgomery	0	0	0	1	30	32	5	0
Morgan	2	4	0	30	133	124	29	0
New Madrid	0	0	0	14	14	42	5	2
Nodaway	1	0	0	20	25	51	10	0
Oregon	0	0	0	15	33	49	3	1
Ozark	3	1	0	35	56	53	5	2
Pemiscot	0	2	1	12	52	73	5	2
Perry	1	1	0	15	24	32	10	1
Pettis	2	2	1	13	73	191	15	1
Phelps	0	2	0	70	72	168	11	0
Pike	1	1	1	7	33	44	12	1
Pulaski	4	5	6	61	143	244	28	0
Putnam	0	0	0	0	7	1	0	0
Ralls	0	0	0	7	29	34	4	0
Randolph	0	0	0	9	18	61	4	0
Reynolds	0	1	1	13	19	20	3	3
Ripley	1	2	0	12	104	194	9	0
Saline	0	0	0	3	44	44	8	0
Schuyler	0	1	0	2	14	4	3	0
Scotland	0	0	0	0	12	21	4	0
Scott	0	3	3	26	35	61	6	0
Shannon	0	1	1	9	12	28	9	1
Shelby	0	1	1	1	10	21	1	0
St. Clair	0	2	0	17	33	49	10	0
Ste. Genevieve	2	2	0	21	25	67	9	1
St. Francois	2	5	3	34	142	293	65	5
Stoddard	0	0	1	22	67	116	11	0
Stone	3	11	0	110	134	257	24	1
Sullivan	0	1	0	13	39	22	1	0
Taney	0	11	0	77	120	324	59	0
Texas	3	0	1	21	107	125	19	4
Vernon	0	7	1	32	61	213	23	4
Washington	0	4	2	37	97	148	36	5
Wayne	1	2	1	19	100	109	25	1
Worth	0	0	0	0	17	19	1	0
Wright	0	0	0	10	46	71	12	2
Montana—Metropolitan Counties								
Carbon	0	0	0	6	9	35	5	0
Cascade	0	5	1	29	58	188	18	0
Missoula	0	14	1	66	89	383	39	2
Montana—Nonmetropolitan Counties								
Beaverhead	0	0	0	3	7	23	2	0
Blaine	0	0	0	4	0	6	3	0
Broadwater	0	1	0	20	6	56	8	1
Carter	0	0	0	0	1	0	0	0
Custer	0	0	0	1	1	29	1	0
Daniels	0	0	0	2	1	4	1	0
Dawson	0	0	0	7	14	72	5	0
Deer Lodge	2	5	0	12	32	146	19	0
Fallon	0	0	0	0	0	2	0	0
Fergus	0	3	0	6	24	53	7	0
Flathead	0	19	4	119	207	745	116	15
Gallatin	0	21	0	35	56	300	18	4
Garfield	0	0	0	0	0	1	2	0
Glacier	0	1	0	16	10	23	4	1
Hill	0	1	1	13	15	143	12	2
Jefferson	0	1	1	11	14	62	3	2
Judith Basin	0	0	0	2	0	8	1	0
Lake	1	9	3	61	92	134	46	1

Table 10.   Offenses Known to Law Enforcement, by Selected State Metropolitan and Nonmetropolitan Counties, 2013— continued

(Number.)

State/county	Murder and non-negligent manslaughter	Rape (revised definition)	Robbery	Aggravated assault	Burglary	Larceny-theft	Motor vehicle theft	Arson[2]
Lewis and Clark	1	14	0	37	84	282	30	6
Lincoln	0	2	0	18	23	107	7	1
Madison	0	1	0	7	5	38	5	1
McCone	0	0	0	0	0	6	2	0
Meagher	0	0	0	2	1	24	0	0
Mineral	0	0	0	1	0	0	0	0
Musselshell	0	0	0	12	11	86	5	2
Park	0	1	0	9	2	17	1	1
Phillips	0	0	0	9	13	33	6	2
Pondera	0	0	0	0	1	2	0	0
Powell	0	1	0	0	4	10	0	0
Prairie	0	0	0	0	0	1	0	0
Ravalli	0	1	0	23	27	229	3	1
Roosevelt	0	0	0	40	7	24	9	1
Sanders	0	4	0	10	10	49	6	2
Sheridan	0	2	0	11	6	43	14	1
Silver Bow	1	2	8	71	140	1,087	95	2
Stillwater	0	7	0	12	24	39	4	1
Sweet Grass	0	1	0	6	1	37	2	0
Teton	0	1	0	1	10	40	3	0
Toole	0	3	0	24	21	86	12	4
Valley	0	0	0	5	5	26	1	0
Wibaux	0	0	0	0	1	1	0	0
Nebraska—Metropolitan Counties								
Cass	0	4	0	5	27	153	16	1
Dakota	1		1	5	9	33	8	0
Dixon	0	1	0	0	26	30	7	1
Douglas	2		8	92	261	641	102	0
Hall	0	2	1	5	67	151	8	1
Hamilton	0	0	0	0	33	28	2	0
Lancaster	0		0	22	98	193	9	1
Sarpy	1	12	0	7	70	548	45	2
Nebraska—Nonmetropolitan Counties								
Adams	0	0	0	2	40	67	5	1
Antelope	0		0	3	4	9	1	0
Arthur	0		0	0	0	1	0	0
Box Butte	0		0	0	3	14	1	0
Brown	0		0	0	6	14	1	0
Buffalo	1	6	1	3	50	98	5	1
Burt	0		0	6	17	16	2	0
Butler	0	1	0	3	8	38	2	0
Cedar	0		0	0	2	33	1	0
Chase	0		0	2	10	15	2	0
Cherry	0		0	0	4	6	2	0
Cuming	0		0	0	8	12	1	0
Custer	0	0	0	0	12	48	3	0
Dawes	0		0	2	4	6	1	0
Dawson	0	3	0	4	20	56	0	0
Deuel	0	0	0	3	7	11	1	0
Dodge	0		0	5	22	88	7	0
Franklin	0		1	0	4	10	1	0
Gage	0	15	1	6	15	75	2	2
Hitchcock	0		0	3	13	8	3	0
Holt	0		0	2	0	10	0	0
Jefferson	0	3	0	2	8	30	4	0
Kearney	0	2	0	4	9	24	3	0
Keith	0	0	0	5	4	21	0	0
Lincoln	0	1	0	4	41	68	7	0
Madison	0	1	0	1	21	47	6	0
Morrill	0		0	0	0	24	1	0
Nemaha	0	3	0	3	14	36	5	0
Pawnee	0		1	0	25	24	1	0
Phelps	0	0	0	0	3	19	5	0
Pierce	0		0	5	10	15	1	0
Platte	0	1	0	2	14	82	10	1
Polk	0	0	0	0	17	40	8	0
Red Willow	0		0	2	12	17	1	0
Rock	0		0	0	1	1	0	0
Saline	0	0	0	0	38	26	9	2
Scotts Bluff	0	2	0	5	27	88	6	0
Sheridan	0		0	2	5	34	0	0
Sherman	0	0	0	1	3	9	1	0
Stanton	0		0	1	10	53	6	0
Thayer	0		0	1	24	93	2	0
Wayne	0	0	1	0	3	15	3	0
Webster	1		0	1	9	18	1	0

Table 10. Offenses Known to Law Enforcement, by Selected State Metropolitan and Nonmetropolitan Counties, 2013— continued

(Number.)

State/county	Murder and non-negligent man-slaughter	Rape (revised definition)[1]	Robbery	Aggravated assault	Burglary	Larceny-theft	Motor vehicle theft	Arson[2]
Wheeler	0		0	0	0	8	0	0
York	0	0	0	1	7	32	3	0
Nevada—Metropolitan Counties								
Carson City	4		17	112	202	654	68	6
Storey	0		2	32	32	54	2	1
Washoe	6		12	124	452	448	83	15
Nevada—Nonmetropolitan Counties								
Churchill	0		0	12	91	102	14	0
Douglas	2		11	41	143	631	41	2
Elko	0		1	14	113	105	23	0
Esmeralda	0		1	1	3	7	3	0
Eureka	0		0	8	19	13	2	0
Humboldt	0		1	50	24	29	11	0
Lander	0		0	35	59	59	9	0
Lincoln	0		0	4	1	37	7	1
Lyon	5		7	103	312	698	74	9
Nye	3		12		370	470	85	13
Pershing	0		0	30	7	23	11	1
White Pine	0		1	22	29	46	7	4
New Hampshire—Metropolitan Counties								
Rockingham	0	0	0	6	1	0	0	1
New Hampshire—Nonmetropolitan Counties								
Carroll	0	3	0	6	20	35	1	0
Cheshire	0	0	0	4	4	11	1	0
Merrimack	0	3	0	3	1	2	0	0
New Jersey—Metropolitan Counties								
Atlantic	0		0	0	0	0	0	0
Bergen	0		0	0	0	0	0	0
Bergen County Police Department	0		0	3	4	83	1	0
Burlington	0		0	0	0	0	0	0
Camden County Police Department	57		732	1,106	857	1,939	464	84
Cape May	0		0	0	0	0	0	0
Cumberland	0		0	0	0	1	0	0
Essex	0		9	7	8	17	1	0
Gloucester	0		0	0	0	0	0	0
Hudson	0		0	0	0	0	0	0
Hunterdon	0		0	0	0	0	0	0
Mercer	0		0	0	0	0	0	0
Middlesex	0		0	0	0	0	0	0
Monmouth	0		0	0	0	0	0	0
Morris	0		0	0	0	0	0	0
Ocean	0		0	0	0	0	0	0
Passaic	0		0	0	0	0	0	0
Salem	0		0	0	0	1	0	0
Somerset	0		0	0	0	0	0	0
Sussex	0		0	0	0	0	0	0
Union	0		0	0	0	0	0	0
Warren	0		0	0	0	0	0	0
New Mexico—Metropolitan Counties								
Bernalillo	8		87	519	941	1,130	230	78
Sandoval	0		4	29	83	82	17	0
San Juan	2		17	200	247	445	58	13
Valencia	3		8	306	489	491	148	13
New Mexico—Nonmetropolitan Counties								
Chaves	2		4	23	187	189	28	4
Cibola	0		0	78	46	61	10	3
Colfax	0		0	3	8	16	4	0
Curry	0		0	13	100	62	19	5
De Baca	0		0	8	8	2	5	0
Lea	3		5	35	148	367	39	1
Lincoln	0		0	15	49	59	0	0
Los Alamos	0		0	0	0	0	0	0
Luna	0		1	46	60	100	18	0
McKinley	2		4	53	104	112	16	5
Otero	0		2	50	136	164	24	0
Quay	0		0	3	5	20	3	0
Rio Arriba	3		3	35	111	61	15	0
New York—Metropolitan Counties								
Albany	0		0	5	39	99	5	
Broome	3		8	30	182	669	24	

Table 10.   Offenses Known to Law Enforcement, by Selected State Metropolitan and Nonmetropolitan Counties, 2013— continued

(Number.)

State/county	Murder and non-negligent man-slaughter	Rape (revised definition)[1]	Robbery	Aggravated assault	Burglary	Larceny-theft	Motor vehicle theft	Arson[2]
Chemung	0		5	21	58	500	7	4
Dutchess	0		7	64	137	480	6	
Erie	2		8	93	180	695	23	4
Herkimer	0		0	2	0	4	0	0
Jefferson	0		0	10	20	184	3	
Livingston	0		2	18	116	308	17	
Madison	0		0	9	58	143	4	
Monroe	2		56	88	636	2,869	100	
Nassau	12		706	633	1,737	10,558	594	
Niagara	0		22	31	234	618	52	
Oneida	1		4	24	108	280	8	
Onondaga	3		32	93	386	1,851	65	14
Ontario	0		16	30	225	829	22	0
Orleans	1		1	10	83	144	12	
Oswego	1		1	31	96	301	18	
Putnam	0		5	17	57	247	7	0
Rensselaer	0		3	21	59	146	6	0
Saratoga	0		8	47	243	905	36	
Schenectady	0		0	1	0	5	0	0
Schoharie	0		0	4	24	45	2	1
Suffolk	0		0	109	0	2	3	0
Suffolk County Police Department	27		620	930	2,979	16,551	1,051	147
Tioga	1		2	4	87	156	3	
Ulster	1		5	24	65	228	7	
Warren	0		3	10	84	579	2	
Washington	0		2	28	84	279	10	
Wayne	0		6	28	156	287	9	
Westchester Public Safety	0		1	5	3	173	2	0
Yates	0		0	5	86	181	2	0
New York—Nonmetropolitan Counties								
Cattaraugus	0		0	30	131	313	31	
Cayuga	1		0	12	62	185	1	
Chautauqua	2		6	12	239	495	0	
Chenango	2		1	6	68	273	3	
Clinton	0		0	9	0	28	2	
Columbia	0		2	12	76	234	6	
Cortland	0		3	16	77	327	1	
Delaware	0		1	15	47	113	0	
Franklin	0		0	0	0	1	0	0
Fulton	1		0	8	90	245	6	0
Genesee	0		8	15	154	428	5	
Hamilton	0		0	0	4	2	0	0
Lewis	1		0	14	50	84	4	
Montgomery	0		0	6	38	377	4	
Otsego	1		1	18	35	34	6	
Schuyler	0		1	6	14	10	2	
Seneca	1		0	3	10	74	3	
Steuben	0		1	9	42	115	2	
St. Lawrence	0		0	11	8	33	0	
Sullivan	0		3	21	113	362	12	
Wyoming	0		2	13	47	144	3	1
North Carolina—Metropolitan Counties								
Alamance	3		15	83	429	441	64	5
Alexander	0		5	33	167	228	18	3
Brunswick	2		29	96	973	1,077	87	19
Buncombe	10		25	63	897	964	152	15
Burke	1		23	82	643	798	70	2
Cabarrus	3		9	19	228	461	35	6
Caldwell	4		11	47	469	827	79	9
Catawba	3		17	101	597	727	68	4
Chatham	1		10	64	356	469	39	3
Cumberland	4		118	368	1,408	2,131	170	36
Currituck	0		3	24	116	318	15	4
Davidson	1		14	70	885	749	106	13
Davie	0		11	38	238	368	31	2
Durham	2		12	34	331	350	42	3
Edgecombe	3		11	58	300	267	24	3
Franklin	3		10	48	366	495	48	2
Gaston	0		0	6	0	0	0	0
Guilford	0		13	116	587	780	71	14
Haywood	1		4	125	445	580	54	5
Henderson	4		15	78	382	728	90	5
Iredell	0		17	105	727	836	60	17
Johnston	4		8	89	678	1,146	87	1
Lincoln	2		13	51	535	672	10	4
Madison	1		0	5	99	86	15	4

Table 10.   Offenses Known to Law Enforcement, by Selected State Metropolitan and Nonmetropolitan Counties, 2013— continued

(Number.)

State/county	Murder and non-negligent man-slaughter	Rape (revised definition)[1]	Robbery	Aggravated assault	Burglary	Larceny-theft	Motor vehicle theft	Arson[2]
Nash	9		5	40	355	239	55	7
New Hanover	1		34	107	631	1,473	96	8
Orange	0		18	19	271	199	27	1
Pamlico	0		8	35	83	212	15	2
Pender	1		4	64	217	478	36	11
Person	6		8	31	207	211	22	2
Pitt	3		34	110	485	661	45	4
Rowan	1		10	115	448	718	59	11
Stokes	1		5	111	370	494	48	4
Union	4		27	171	564	1,341	80	22
Wake	6		27	158	1,070	1,090	135	26
Yadkin	1		5	59	285	406	24	3
North Carolina—Nonmetropolitan Counties								
Anson	1		8	35	255	256	13	2
Ashe	0		0	12	151	166	9	3
Avery	0		0	20	51	106	7	2
Bertie	0		3	23	156	212	19	4
Camden	0		2	2	17	43	1	1
Carteret	1		6	68	306	501	27	4
Caswell	2		4	36	176	242	32	1
Cherokee	0		3	21	149	319	27	2
Chowan	1		1	6	48	69	9	3
Cleveland	1		13	2	461	584	26	2
Columbus	4		21	89	821	558	93	8
Dare	1		2	9	139	386	12	2
Granville	3		10	54	337	381	36	4
Halifax	2		21	71	384	404	29	7
Harnett	8		41	177	1,093	1,414	109	12
Hertford	0		9	22	172	143	24	2
Lee	5		5	26	179	365	40	1
Lenoir	0		19	76	373	447	23	2
Macon	0		4	32	196	356	20	3
Martin	0		6	36	203	190	13	1
McDowell	3		2	21	366	395	60	7
Montgomery	0		1	24	122	190	11	0
Moore	1		3	20	299	324	44	4
Northampton	0		5	24	200	174	26	2
Pasquotank	1		6	28	119	177	11	6
Perquimans	0		0	2	61	46	5	5
Polk	0		0	7	56	144	12	1
Richmond	0		24	96	515	647	41	10
Rutherford	1		9	74	509	361	68	18
Surry	0		9	69	515	600	53	11
Swain	1		0	31	105	84	8	0
Transylvania	0		1	28	125	197	14	3
Tyrrell	0		1	6	14	35	2	0
Warren	1		5	28	271	271	36	4
Washington	0		3	9	46	67	8	0
Watauga	0		0	21	41	223	19	0
Wilkes	5		12	92	517	624	51	11
Wilson	0		11	41	280	467	44	2
Yancey	1		0	9	62	47	0	0
North Dakota—Metropolitan Counties								
Burleigh	1	6	0	27	57	107	14	1
Cass	0	4	2	19	47	80	8	1
Grand Forks	1	5	0	9	33	57	7	0
Morton	0	5	0	7	7	63	9	1
Oliver	0	0	0	3	1	5	1	0
Sioux	0	0	0	0	0	0	0	0
North Dakota—Nonmetropolitan Counties								
Adams	0	0	0	1	2	6	0	0
Barnes	0	1	0	1	9	17	3	0
Benson	0	0	0	0	4	6	4	0
Billings	0	0	0	1	3	13	0	0
Bottineau	1	0	0	4	23	56	6	1
Bowman	0	0	0	1	3	0	2	0
Burke	0	1	0	0	5	10	9	0
Cavalier	0	0	0	0	1	24	3	1
Dickey	0	0	0	0	1	8	1	0
Divide	0	0	0	1	2	5	0	0
Dunn	0	0	0	3	9	17	2	0
Eddy	0	0	0	2	1	9	1	0
Emmons	0	0	0	0	15	21	2	1
Golden Valley	0	0	0	2	6	2	0	0
Grant	0	0	0	0	0	4	0	0

Table 10.   Offenses Known to Law Enforcement, by Selected State Metropolitan and Nonmetropolitan Counties, 2013— continued

(Number.)

State/county	Murder and non-negligent man-slaughter	Rape (revised definition)	Robbery	Aggravated assault	Burglary	Larceny-theft	Motor vehicle theft	Arson[2]
Griggs	0	0	0	2	0	1	0	0
Hettinger	0	0	0	1	8	13	4	0
Kidder	0	0	0	2	4	2	2	0
Lamoure	0	1	0	1	2	1	0	0
McHenry	0	0	0	0	14	24	5	0
McIntosh	0	0	0	0	1	0	0	0
McKenzie	0	2	0	18	16	59	17	3
McLean	0	3	0	9	11	69	7	2
Mercer	0	1	2	2	13	28	3	0
Mountrail	0	1	0	13	23	75	37	1
Nelson	0	1	0	2	12	11	2	0
Pembina	0	2	0	0	13	8	1	0
Pierce	0	0	0	0	11	8	0	0
Ramsey	0	0	0	1	3	17	6	0
Ransom	0	0	0	1	2	5	2	0
Renville	0	0	0	0	1	17	5	0
Richland	0	0	0	4	21	42	3	0
Rolette	0	1	2	0	2	5	2	0
Sargent	0	0	0	0	4	11	1	0
Sheridan	0	0	0	0	2	13	1	0
Slope	0	0	0	0	0	1	1	0
Stark	0	0	0	3	1	45	8	0
Steele	0	0	0	2	1	1	1	0
Stutsman	0	3	1	3	35	27	1	3
Towner	0	0	0	1	2	4	0	0
Traill	0	1	0	2	6	22	8	0
Walsh	0	0	0	8	17	61	7	1
Ward	0	1	0	20	55	97	24	2
Wells	0	0	0	1	8	6	1	1
Williams	2	4	0	29	71	236	87	2
Ohio—Metropolitan Counties								
Allen	0		7	13	240	749	36	4
Belmont	0	7	6	13	175	309	38	0
Butler	1	3	6	412	326	695	0	13
Carroll	0	1	1	46	65	183	34	2
Clark	0	8	9	25	349	923	44	6
Clermont	1	15	4	64	667	1,141	42	3
Delaware	0	7	5	19	263	716	15	1
Franklin	1	16	41	52	365	937	76	4
Fulton	1	4	0	12	85	184	8	1
Geauga	1	3	4	11	56	156	10	2
Greene	1	6	1	12	180	311	20	1
Hamilton	3		96	84	866	3,676	205	15
Jefferson	0	0	1	8	56	72	4	0
Lake	0		2	173	93	205	3	3
Lawrence	0	3	5	34	283	480	36	4
Lorain	0	13	13	16	453	431	26	3
Madison	0	5	2	5	202	343	39	3
Mahoning	0		0	0	39	115	3	0
Miami	0	13	1	4	183	317	22	6
Morrow	0	2	3	8	147	146	8	0
Perry	1	1	0	0	39	73	5	0
Pickaway	0	7	4	9	375	471	28	1
Portage	2		6	14	394	1,033	32	17
Richland	1	7	20	11	560	807	31	3
Stark	0	18	41	34	364	894	108	6
Summit	1	10	14	9	198	683	56	4
Trumbull	0	6	2	11	252	236	29	1
Warren	0	12	9	30	265	865	39	2
Ohio—Nonmetropolitan Counties								
Adams	0	2	0	8	112	169	15	2
Ashland	0	7	0	2	134	157	12	3
Ashtabula	1	4	7	28	237	749	53	2
Athens	1	8	3	4	220	350	10	3
Auglaize	0	0	1	2	51	108	10	1
Champaign	0	5	0	11	117	211	5	2
Columbiana	3	4	0	7	37	13	2	0
Coshocton	2	0	10	16	194	433	14	5
Crawford	0	1	1	5	141	171	9	0
Darke	0	4	1	5	135	210	11	0
Defiance	0	4	0	1	51	117	0	3
Erie	0	0	0	6	68	162	0	0
Fayette	0	10	4	9	194	403	15	2
Gallia	2	6	2	8	207	325	12	4
Hancock	0	2	0	3	76	120	2	1
Hardin	0	1	3	11	90	144	8	2

Table 10. Offenses Known to Law Enforcement, by Selected State Metropolitan and Nonmetropolitan Counties, 2013— continued

(Number.)

State/county	Murder and non-negligent man-slaughter	Rape (revised definition)[1]	Robbery	Aggravated assault	Burglary	Larceny-theft	Motor vehicle theft	Arson[2]
Harrison	0	0	0	0	34	37	7	0
Henry	1	4	1	9	101	136	7	3
Holmes	0	0	2	3	56	134	10	1
Knox	0	9	2	13	183	434	0	4
Logan	0	1	1	4	191	236	17	1
Marion	0	8	20	13	289	892	9	2
Meigs	3	3	1	6	100	151	17	0
Mercer	0	6	0	3	43	110	7	0
Monroe	0	1	0	2	30	35	1	0
Muskingum	1	30	8	12	295	790	64	10
Ottawa	1	0	0	0	57	282	6	0
Paulding	0	0	2	7	72	151	0	2
Pike	0	2	0	4	80	203	9	5
Preble	0	3	3	9	110	239	21	1
Putnam	2	7	1	3	40	150	1	1
Ross	0	19	17	49	472	1,060	65	13
Shelby	0	2	0	6	60	167	14	0
Tuscarawas	0	1	2	2	146	194	30	1
Van Wert	0	2	1	0	68	91	2	1
Vinton	0	1	2	12	81	108	5	0
Wayne	1	7	2	14	282	381	41	1
Oklahoma—Metropolitan Counties								
Canadian	2	1	0	5	79	81	17	5
Cleveland	0		3	33	137	168	37	5
Comanche	0	11	1	17	154	174	20	1
Cotton	0	0	0	0	18	6	0	0
Creek	0	17	2	46	165	237	62	5
Grady	1	7	0	12	126	146	24	1
Lincoln	0	6	2	19	139	164	35	8
Logan	1	2	1	15	207	198	25	1
McClain	0	4	2	5	145	176	37	2
Oklahoma	2		1	30	96	214	36	0
Okmulgee	0	1	0	5	62	73	26	6
Osage	1	5	1	17	128	195	19	6
Pawnee	1		1	14	15	44	9	2
Rogers	0		0	54	141	189	63	2
Sequoyah	0	6	2	40	142	231	20	11
Tulsa	1	25	15	161	344	391	148	11
Wagoner	1	5	2	22	115	263	42	8
Oklahoma—Nonmetropolitan Counties								
Adair	0	3	0	37	55	65	7	11
Alfalfa	0	0	0	1	9	17	1	0
Atoka	0	1	0	1	36	43	2	2
Beaver	0	0	0	1	14	39	1	1
Beckham	0	1	0	5	25	55	19	1
Blaine	0	0	0	8	18	41	4	1
Bryan	2	3	0	17	103	104	30	3
Caddo	1		1	52	102	77	13	3
Carter	2		1	22	107	164	37	2
Cherokee	0	5	4	49	261	342	59	4
Choctaw	0		2	11	60	87	7	0
Cimarron	0	0	0	0	0	2	0	0
Coal	0	0	0	1	12	23	1	2
Craig	0	0	0	1	11	14	4	1
Custer	1	0	0	7	20	51	6	0
Dewey	0	0	0	0	15	12	6	1
Ellis	0	1	0	3	18	32	4	2
Garfield	0	2	0	9	52	95	9	10
Garvin	1	6	2	13	120	141	19	4
Grant	0	0	0	0	7	12	2	0
Greer	0	0	0	0	4	4	0	0
Harmon	0	1	0	0	4	8	0	0
Harper	0	0	0	1	1	4	1	0
Haskell	0	0	0	7	19	33	9	0
Hughes	1	0	0	0	8	34	9	5
Jackson	0	2	0	6	20	36	6	2
Jefferson	0	0	1	1	6	16	3	1
Johnston	0		0	44	13	19	3	1
Kay	0		2	17	40	40	1	0
Kingfisher	0	0	0	2	27	38	9	1
Kiowa	0	2	1	1	29	33	4	1
Latimer	0	2	0	17	28	30	6	3
Love	3	0	0	5	36	41	9	0
Major	0	1	2	3	9	17	1	0
Marshall	0	2	0	14	43	58	15	1
Mayes	0	2	0	6	65	111	24	6

Table 10.   Offenses Known to Law Enforcement, by Selected State Metropolitan and Nonmetropolitan Counties, 2013— continued

(Number.)

State/county	Murder and non-negligent man-slaughter	Rape (revised definition)[1]	Robbery	Aggravated assault	Burglary	Larceny-theft	Motor vehicle theft	Arson[2]
Murray	1	5	1	20	98	108	26	5
McIntosh	0	2	0	14	19	26	3	0
Muskogee	1		13	59	114	188	48	22
Noble	0	0	0	4	22	45	5	2
Nowata	0	1	0	1	8	12	1	0
Okfuskee	0	1	0	8	52	59	12	1
Ottawa	0		1	2	48	42	30	3
Payne	2	5	4	14	109	192	23	4
Pittsburg	0	2	0	1	63	113	2	1
Pontotoc	0		0	26	86	52	18	1
Pottawatomie	1		0	26	232	313	68	2
Pushmataha	1	2	0	3	23	20	11	2
Roger Mills	0	0	0	3	4	37	2	0
Seminole	1	0	0	14	106	154	9	5
Stephens	0	4	1	12	81	159	14	2
Texas	0	1	0	1	10	40	1	0
Tillman	0	2	0	9	20	56	1	4
Washington	0		0	11	38	101	9	0
Washita	0	2	0	7	40	47	10	3
Woods	0	0	0	0	6	13	1	0
Woodward	0	4	0	7	30	48	14	2
Oregon—Metropolitan Counties								
Benton	0	1	4	25	48	167	17	7
Clackamas	2		64	64	875	3,967	447	7
Columbia	0		0	4	36	23	5	0
Deschutes	2	14	4	73	192	592	40	4
Jackson	3	15	10	109	365	996	69	14
Linn	1	7	6	332	635	92	8	
Marion	2	23	33	522	1,670	303	4	
Multnomah	0	9	48	75	585	40	0	
Polk	1	2	2	49	85	194	21	2
Washington	3	36	152	518	1,758	157	23	
Yamhill	0	14	4	16	307	421	34	4
Oregon—Nonmetropolitan Counties								
Baker	0		0	2	39	42	8	0
Clatsop	0		0	10	45	130	11	2
Coos	3		0	18	161	339	28	2
Crook	0		1	13	47	85	0	1
Curry	0		0	17	89	139	20	6
Gilliam	0		0	0	1	16	0	3
Grant	0		0	0	4	33	1	0
Harney	0		0	3	4	22	3	0
Hood River	0		3	19	35	147	12	0
Klamath	6		8	31	243	473	87	18
Lincoln	0	5	2	22	134	266	28	2
Malheur	1		0	1	28	105	7	1
Morrow	0	2	1	5	21	108	12	0
Sherman	0		0	2	8	16	5	0
Tillamook	2	1	2	8	70	147	20	3
Umatilla	1	7	2	18	120	263	64	2
Union	0	3	0	3	33	106	17	2
Wasco	0		1	6	53	97	10	1
Wheeler	0	0	0	7	7	11	0	0
Pennsylvania—Metropolitan Counties								
Allegheny County Police Department	0	19	0	91	0	102	12	134
Beaver	0	0	0	0	0	0	0	0
Berks	0	0	0	4	0	0	0	0
Blair	0	0	0	0	0	0	0	0
Butler	0	0	0	0	0	0	0	0
Centre	0	0	0	0	0	0	0	0
Cumberland	0	0	0	0	0	0	0	0
Erie	0	0	0	7	0	2	0	0
Franklin	0	0	0	0	0	0	0	0
Lancaster	0	0	0	2	0	0	0	0
Lycoming	0	0	0	0	0	0	0	0
Mercer	0	0	0	1	0	0	0	0
Monroe	0	0	0	0	0	0	0	0
Montgomery	0	0	0	0	0	0	0	0
Northampton	0	0	0	0	0	0	0	0
Westmoreland	0	0	0	0	0	0	0	0
York	0	0	0	4	0	0	0	0
Pennsylvania—Nonmetropolitan Counties								
Bedford	0	0	0	0	0	0	0	0
Bradford	0	0	0	0	0	0	0	0

Table 10.   Offenses Known to Law Enforcement, by Selected State Metropolitan and Nonmetropolitan Counties, 2013— continued

(Number.)

State/county	Murder and non-negligent man-slaughter	Rape (revised definition)[1]	Robbery	Aggravated assault	Burglary	Larceny-theft	Motor vehicle theft	Arson[2]
Elk	0	0	0	1	0	0	0	0
Greene	0	0	0	0	0	0	0	0
Indiana	0	0	0	0	0	0	0	0
Jefferson	0	0	0	0	0	0	0	0
Schuylkill	0	0	0	0	0	0	0	0
Snyder	0	0	0	0	0	0	0	0
Tioga	0	0	0	0	0	0	0	0
Union	0	0	0	0	0	0	0	0
Warren	0	0	0	0	0	0	0	0
Wayne	0	0	0	0	0	0	0	0
South Carolina—Metropolitan Counties								
Aiken	5	52	49	279	1,150	1,949	363	5
Anderson	8	63	142	590	2,169	4,776	672	23
Beaufort	2	59	62	540	851	2,211	178	13
Berkeley	5	33	69	287	1,110	2,007	357	13
Calhoun	0	0	4	44	135	215	40	1
Charleston	6	24	49	416	612	1,125	173	13
Chester	5	12	12	66	230	399	27	6
Darlington	5	19	18	215	682	1,285	149	7
Dorchester	6	22	32	236	579	1,238	201	4
Edgefield	0	1	0	5	100	174	31	0
Fairfield	2	5	11	98	188	379	45	1
Florence	2	20	39	151	648	1,442	208	1
Greenville	21	236	321	1,596	3,050	7,177	895	73
Horry County Police Department	6	129	133	687	1,558	4,348	609	33
Lancaster	6	18	31	228	656	1,425	84	6
Laurens	3	30	12	214	487	758	104	7
Lexington	5	50	79	375	1,018	3,135	402	13
Pickens	3	27	16	185	671	1,106	216	5
Richland	17	129	265	1,587	2,014	5,709	1,020	24
Saluda	2	1	2	53	73	175	24	3
Spartanburg	1	97	131	474	1,606	3,424	408	45
Sumter	5	38	36	263	745	1,023	127	14
Union	5	9	3	48	177	368	18	7
York	2	32	36	318	602	1,546	120	22
South Carolina—Nonmetropolitan Counties								
Abbeville	3	2	0	26	165	287	13	4
Allendale	1	1	0	6	24	19	5	0
Bamberg	0	0	0	38	61	128	27	2
Barnwell	1	11	6	45	116	224	29	3
Chesterfield	3	12	5	84	333	559	58	5
Clarendon	6	10	26	64	319	491	64	3
Colleton	5	21	14	163	280	626	89	15
Dillon	2	8	20	142	248	491	62	6
Georgetown	1	8	14	107	371	667	81	9
Greenwood	8	17	17	144	320	1,091	48	3
Hampton	2	7	4	54	126	187	21	0
Lee	0	3	2	53	146	207	38	8
Marion	1	7	8	65	313	378	37	2
Marlboro	0	11	8	114	240	404	40	2
McCormick	0	0	1	17	31	54	8	1
Newberry	4	5	3	46	83	233	11	1
Oconee	7	44	8	257	499	1,077	87	10
Orangeburg	4	33	49	319	1,080	1,861	443	20
South Dakota—Metropolitan Counties								
Custer	0	0	0	7	20	75	5	1
Lincoln	0	9	0	8	88	114	16	1
McCook	0	1	0	0	13	45	1	0
Meade	0	1	0	7	2	7	1	0
Minnehaha	0	8	1	28	135	155	18	0
Pennington	0	26	2	35	108	225	13	1
Turner	0	3	0	3	13	27	9	0
Union	0	3	0	1	13	41	3	3
South Dakota—Nonmetropolitan Counties								
Aurora	0	0	0	4	9	13	0	0
Beadle	0	0	0	2	9	19	1	0
Bennett	1	0	0	8	1	1	0	0
Bon Homme	0	0	0	0	2	1	0	0
Brookings	0	2	0	5	8	50	6	1
Brown	0	2	0	3	9	21	4	0
Butte	0	0	0	3	7	44	3	0
Charles Mix	0	3	0	11	23	21	6	1
Clark	0	0	0	0	2	2	0	0
Clay	0	1	1	2	16	35	4	0

Table 10. Offenses Known to Law Enforcement, by Selected State Metropolitan and Nonmetropolitan Counties, 2013— continued

(Number.)

State/county	Murder and non-negligent man-slaughter	Rape (revised definition)[1]	Robbery	Aggravated assault	Burglary	Larceny-theft	Motor vehicle theft	Arson[2]
Codington	0	0	1	7	32	38	1	0
Corson	0	0	0	1	9	8	1	0
Davison	0	0	0	2	3	5	4	1
Deuel	0	0	1	2	5	10	3	0
Dewey	0	0	0	1	3	0	1	0
Douglas	0	0	0	0	2	0	0	0
Edmunds	0	0	0	0	0	0	0	0
Faulk	0	0	0	0	0	6	0	0
Hamlin	0	0	1	1	19	12	0	0
Hand	0	1	0	0	1	3	0	0
Hanson	0	0	0	2	1	2	1	0
Harding	0	0	0	1	1	3	0	0
Hughes	0	2	0	0	6	10	4	0
Hutchinson	0	0	0	0	5	5	1	0
Jerauld	0	0	0	0	1	0	0	0
Lawrence	0	0	0	8	9	164	1	0
Marshall	0	0	0	11	9	29	1	1
McPherson	0	0	0	0	1	0	0	0
Mellette	0	1	0	2	3	5	0	0
Miner	0	0	0	1	2	1	0	0
Moody	0	0	0	1	3	32	3	0
Perkins	0	0	0	2	6	5	1	0
Potter	0	0	0	1	0	0	0	0
Roberts	0	1	1	9	8	2	1	0
Spink	0	1	0	1	7	35	1	0
Stanley	0	0	0	0	9	0	0	0
Sully	0	0	0	0	2	1	1	0
Walworth	0	0	0	1	0	0	0	0
Yankton	0	0	0	0	29	37	3	0
Ziebach	0	0	0	0	0	0	0	0
Tennessee—Metropolitan Counties								
Anderson	0	9	6	49	278	357	45	10
Blount	3	28	23	210	519	788	83	5
Bradley	0	7	3	146	322	538	76	0
Campbell	0	4	2	31	204	218	32	8
Cannon	0	0	0	17	62	45	12	1
Carter	0	4	4	75	259	382	29	6
Cheatham	1	10	6	70	186	402	56	4
Chester	0	4	1	17	40	78	17	0
Crockett	0	2	0	35	29	93	9	0
Dickson	0	8	6	107	216	291	27	6
Fayette	0	1	5	62	70	216	32	0
Grainger	1	0	0	9	92	155	14	1
Hamblen	0	2	6	53	182	374	35	5
Hamilton	1	15	8	196	522	995	122	2
Hickman	2	4	1	63	126	128	16	0
Jefferson	0	19	4	84	274	459	41	2
Knox	2	20	75	377	1,300	3,652	307	32
Loudon	0	4	5	27	135	236	23	2
Macon	0	3	0	76	30	123	16	0
Madison	0	7	11	140	280	397	43	4
Marion	0	0	6	69	93	171	37	0
Maury	1	16	6	123	162	340	46	4
Montgomery	2	11	7	95	160	478	45	4
Morgan	1	3	1	38	91	256	27	1
Polk	0	2	2	17	88	170	41	0
Roane	0	4	6	61	180	291	21	0
Robertson	3	7	0	69	86	134	22	2
Rutherford	1	15	10	225	328	716	73	6
Sequatchie	0	6	1	32	48	91	21	2
Shelby	3	42	75	387	889	1,928	147	14
Smith	0	7	2	22	82	119	11	1
Sullivan	1	32	4	304	370	780	64	20
Sumner	1	10	7	74	198	360	33	2
Tipton	2	11	9	160	156	452	54	8
Unicoi	0	1	0	28	19	94	5	1
Union	1	1	3	43	155	201	26	5
Washington	1	16	10	132	353	488	45	5
Williamson	0	6	1	70	132	291	26	3
Wilson	0	6	4	92	243	530	73	4
Tennessee—Nonmetropolitan Counties								
Bedford	0	5	0	42	85	185	11	0
Benton	0	2	0	23	36	65	10	1
Bledsoe	0	0	0	8	15	39	16	0
Carroll	0	2	0	15	113	76	18	0
Claiborne	0	4	7	104	253	243	35	7

Table 10.   Offenses Known to Law Enforcement, by Selected State Metropolitan and Nonmetropolitan Counties, 2013— continued

(Number.)

State/county	Murder and non-negligent man-slaughter	Rape (revised definition)[1]	Robbery	Aggravated assault	Burglary	Larceny-theft	Motor vehicle theft	Arson[2]
Clay	0	0	0	8	24	31	1	0
Cocke	0	4	11	150	292	309	48	13
Coffee	2	6	3	49	111	220	39	3
Cumberland	5	2	4	56	324	425	93	4
Decatur	1	4	0	42	67	120	22	0
DeKalb	0	1	1	9	85	169	24	1
Dyer	0	3	0	46	46	103	12	0
Fentress	0	3	2	21	117	171	13	1
Franklin	1	6	4	39	43	167	26	3
Gibson	3	3	1	50	108	138	15	0
Giles	0	5	0	28	98	102	17	1
Greene	1	9	12	104	360	542	84	13
Grundy	0	3	1	67	152	83	37	9
Hancock	1	0	0	6	30	44	8	1
Hardeman	0	7	9	55	176	162	28	1
Haywood	1	0	3	21	65	110	18	1
Henderson	0	6	0	52	141	239	17	6
Henry	1	7	3	38	141	261	35	0
Houston	0	3	0	16	24	32	6	0
Humphreys	0	0	0	20	62	95	8	1
Jackson	1	0	0	23	56	78	12	1
Johnson	1	8	3	76	90	103	25	3
Lauderdale	2	5	0	44	81	158	23	4
Lawrence	1	5	3	120	222	289	39	10
Lewis	2	4	2	29	36	70	8	3
Lincoln	3	3	2	73	146	217	33	1
Marshall	0	2	1	21	34	63	11	2
McMinn	0	4	3	81	231	450	66	9
McNairy	0	2	2	57	75	196	26	2
Meigs	0	4	2	38	85	146	37	2
Monroe	2	1	3	114	298	456	54	4
Moore	0	3	0	3	15	68	4	0
Obion	0	2	0	18	66	101	15	1
Overton	1	3	1	32	107	108	16	5
Perry	0	0	1	28	22	60	11	0
Putnam	1	3	5	99	239	462	38	2
Rhea	1	4	3	56	97	165	19	4
Scott	1	3	0	39	81	147	17	3
Sevier	1	13	9	78	671	885	97	0
Stewart	0	4	0	37	62	82	10	0
Van Buren	0	0	0	11	13	66	5	5
Warren	0	2	5	30	167	243	62	1
Wayne	0	1	0	20	16	26	13	0
Weakley	3	1	1	40	66	70	10	1
White	0	0	1	44	101	303	27	4
Texas—Metropolitan Counties								
Aransas	0		3	15	163	182	16	1
Archer	0		1	6	17	41	9	0
Armstrong	0		0	4	4	30	1	2
Austin	0		0	18	42	67	14	1
Bandera	0		1	15	82	147	30	0
Bastrop	4		12	150	263	414	80	5
Bell	5		8	47	210	476	23	12
Bexar	19		84	289	1,777	3,960	362	68
Bowie	1		0	74	297	470	71	9
Brazoria	2		31	131	550	853	70	5
Brazos	0		3	35	146	259	30	2
Burleson	1		1	10	72	63	5	0
Caldwell	1		2	40	64	118	20	0
Callahan	0		0	1	28	35	8	0
Cameron	3		14	76	523	916	71	4
Carson	0		0	4	11	21	5	0
Chambers	1		7	46	193	339	64	1
Clay	0		0	4	52	31	13	3
Collin	0	8	3	58	317	247	44	1
Comal	2		6	121	273	514	51	2
Coryell	0		0	2	47	61	7	0
Crosby	1		0	1	2	5	0	0
Dallas	0		1	32	73	177	19	11
Denton	2		7	45	228	421	54	2
Ector	1		36	60	401	1,299	187	0
Ellis	4		2	27	189	318	34	1
El Paso	2		25	141	349	736	95	8
Falls	0		0	2	22	21	3	1
Fort Bend	6		147	627	1,313	2,367	207	15
Galveston	3		27	35	327	543	61	13
Goliad	1	0	0	7	55	57	3	2

Table 10.   Offenses Known to Law Enforcement, by Selected State Metropolitan and Nonmetropolitan Counties, 2013— continued

(Number.)

State/county	Murder and non-negligent man-slaughter	Rape (revised definition)[1]	Robbery	Aggravated assault	Burglary	Larceny-theft	Motor vehicle theft	Arson[2]
Grayson	1		4	66	186	355	53	0
Gregg	1		6	61	190	319	32	7
Guadalupe	0		2	47	236	358	14	12
Hardin	2		0	29	125	185	40	0
Harris	106		3,260	4,942	13,447	31,501	5,781	241
Hays	1		10	137	231	261	26	2
Hidalgo	14		126	245	2,321	3,109	300	33
Hood	2		1	47	129	297	31	5
Hudspeth	0		0	1	7	18	0	0
Hunt	0		4	89	342	490	99	0
Irion	0		0	1	7	27	1	1
Jefferson	5		2	22	176	298	34	4
Johnson	0		5	66	293	642	61	12
Jones	0		0	0	27	59	4	0
Kaufman	2	33	10	80	407	469	97	0
Kendall	0		0	4	68	136	15	0
Lampasas	1		1	2	27	86	4	2
Liberty	0		10	164	326	548	138	7
Lynn	0		0	0	22	13	1	0
Martin	0		0	2	9	46	7	0
McLennan	0	23	4	42	224	324	62	6
Medina	0		1	13	61	87	8	0
Midland	1		4	49	190	451	86	1
Montgomery	5		110	346	1,681	3,677	472	13
Nueces	0		4	59	111	129	20	2
Oldham	0		1	0	8	16	2	0
Orange	0		5	76	247	346	58	1
Parker	4		2	53	325	585	80	0
Potter	0		1	13	54	138	13	0
Randall	0		3	24	83	143	19	1
Robertson	1		0	1	38	95	12	0
Rockwall	0	5	2	20	32	70	8	0
Rusk	0	6	3	63	249	266	40	2
San Patricio	1		2	28	140	190	19	0
Smith	3		17	166	665	1,056	146	20
Somervell	0		1	9	31	56	5	0
Tarrant	1		14	85	370	716	61	9
Taylor	0		2	16	84	72	9	2
Tom Green	3		2	10	114	189	10	2
Travis	9		35	432	974	2,068	164	37
Victoria	1	17	3	60	155	347	41	0
Waller	1		3	20	83	148	25	0
Webb	1		4	87	99	163	16	1
Wichita	0		3	38	51	92	14	4
Williamson	1		7	95	303	789	60	5
Wise	1		3	57	150	253	37	10
Texas—Nonmetropolitan Counties								
Anderson	0		3	47	211	208	43	18
Andrews	0		0	8	38	54	6	0
Angelina	2		4	97	345	443	38	1
Baylor	0		0	2	15	4	2	0
Bee	0		0	26	25	56	6	3
Blanco	0		0	14	27	43	11	1
Borden	0		0	2	5	8	3	0
Bosque	0		1	1	55	67	6	0
Brewster	0		1	3	6	13	2	1
Briscoe	0		0	1	8	9	1	1
Brooks	0		1	2	11	14	0	0
Brown	0		0	13	79	108	4	1
Burnet	4		0	21	83	190	27	2
Calhoun	0		0	15	67	81	1	0
Camp	0		0	5	80	98	12	0
Cass	1		3	41	223	232	50	4
Castro	0		0	1	21	34	2	0
Cherokee	0		9	59	167	340	62	1
Childress	0		0	3	1	7	0	0
Cochran	0		0	6	37	70	4	1
Coke	0		0	1	15	2	3	0
Collingsworth	0		0	0	0	0	0	0
Colorado	1		2	13	38	95	14	0
Comanche	1		0	1	33	62	7	0
Concho	1		0	3	3	4	3	0
Cottle	0		0	0	0	0	0	0
Crane	0		0	0	7	17	2	0
Culberson	0		0	3	7	4	1	0
Dallam	0		0	0	5	7	2	0
Dawson	1		1	0	8	32	7	0

Table 10.   Offenses Known to Law Enforcement, by Selected State Metropolitan and Nonmetropolitan Counties, 2013— continued

(Number.)

State/county	Murder and non-negligent man-slaughter	Rape (revised definition)	Robbery	Aggravated assault	Burglary	Larceny-theft	Motor vehicle theft	Arson[2]
Deaf Smith	0		0	6	38	29	8	1
Delta	0		1	0	44	33	5	0
DeWitt	0	2	0	14	69	62	12	0
Dickens	0		0	3	1	3	1	0
Dimmit	0		1	44	130	262	21	1
Donley	0		1	4	20	18	1	0
Duval	0		0	51	54	78	18	0
Eastland	0		0	1	21	30	7	0
Edwards	0		0	4	14	27	2	1
Erath	3		0	11	45	59	10	0
Fannin	0		0	16	52	64	12	0
Fayette	1		1	9	63	89	5	0
Fisher	0		0	17	34	50	9	1
Floyd	0		1	1	22	27	2	0
Foard	0		0	3	1	3	0	0
Franklin	0		0	5	45	45	9	0
Freestone	0		2	12	67	58	13	2
Frio	0		1	3	18	40	4	0
Gaines	3		1	3	39	81	7	3
Garza	0		0	3	17	31	0	0
Gillespie	1		0	3	29	75	2	0
Glasscock	0		0	0	6	2	1	0
Gonzales	0		1	16	45	109	6	0
Gray	1		0	4	22	53	13	1
Grimes	0		6	16	88	140	22	0
Hale	0		0	7	32	62	0	0
Hall	0		0	2	2	6	0	0
Hamilton	0		2	13	56	88	6	3
Hansford	0		0	1	4	10	0	0
Hardeman	0		1	0	63	55	3	0
Harrison	0		0	55	166	257	15	2
Hartley	0		0	0	5	11	0	0
Haskell	0		0	3	10	14	9	1
Hemphill	0		0	4	17	56	3	0
Henderson	0		6	144	506	513	123	10
Hill	1		4	28	147	195	14	4
Hockley	0		1	20	33	67	9	1
Hopkins	0		1	13	52	56	12	3
Houston	0		0	7	82	97	21	1
Howard	1		0	29	57	117	16	1
Hutchinson	0		1	18	45	76	4	0
Jack	0		0	8	50	35	4	1
Jackson	2	0	0	1	12	28	6	0
Jasper	1		1	55	158	267	10	2
Jeff Davis	0		0	3	9	7	1	0
Jim Hogg	0		0	3	13	9	1	0
Jim Wells	3		0	55	209	174	34	5
Karnes	1		0	1	42	92	8	0
Kenedy	0		0	0	4	3	2	0
Kent	0		0	2	5	6	0	0
Kerr	1		0	16	107	186	17	0
Kimble	0		0	0	9	6	0	0
King	0		0	0	2	0	0	0
Kinney	0		0	1	2	0	1	0
Knox	0		0	0	8	14	3	0
Lamar	1		1	27	134	201	14	0
Lamb	0		1	2	36	72	8	0
La Salle	0		0	6	3	41	0	0
Lavaca	0	2	0	3	63	34	3	0
Lee	0		1	8	48	75	9	0
Leon	0		0	21	80	141	19	0
Limestone	0		2	8	110	160	10	6
Lipscomb	0		0	6	8	15	0	0
Live Oak	0		0	10	58	113	10	0
Llano	0		2	11	98	182	6	0
Loving	0		0	3	1	6	0	0
Marion	0		5	39	133	146	16	3
Mason	0		0	1	8	32	1	0
Matagorda	0		4	44	91	154	21	1
Maverick	0		3	61	137	294	11	1
McCulloch	0		0	1	14	27	0	0
McMullen	0		0	6	7	27	0	0
Menard	0		0	0	0	4	1	0
Milam	0		1	16	76	81	6	2
Mills	0		0	7	6	16	3	0
Mitchell	0		0	3	9	20	5	0
Montague	0		0	17	63	109	10	0
Moore	0		0	5	20	50	7	0

Table 10. Offenses Known to Law Enforcement, by Selected State Metropolitan and Nonmetropolitan Counties, 2013— continued

(Number.)

State/county	Murder and non-negligent man-slaughter	Rape (revised definition)[1]	Robbery	Aggravated assault	Burglary	Larceny-theft	Motor vehicle theft	Arson[2]
Morris	0		2	20	43	38	6	0
Motley	0		0	1	3	7	1	0
Nacogdoches	0		1	63	224	272	59	1
Navarro	5		0	30	201	257	8	1
Nolan	0		0	2	27	34	7	1
Palo Pinto	0		0	10	82	72	18	0
Panola	0		4	22	118	197	30	1
Parmer	0		0	0	9	22	0	1
Pecos	0		1	0	23	51	2	0
Polk	1	26	4	50	226	311	42	2
Presidio	0		0	3	0	0	0	0
Rains	0		0	18	76	111	10	0
Reagan	0		0	0	1	1	0	0
Real	0		0	0	4	10	2	0
Red River	0		0	6	46	77	8	0
Reeves	0		1	12	13	69	10	0
Refugio	1		0	5	10	27	0	0
Roberts	0		0	0	4	14	1	0
Runnels	0		0	0	1	33	0	0
Sabine	0		0	25	66	60	6	0
San Augustine	0		0	7	35	47	5	1
San Jacinto	2		11	52	237	346	74	2
San Saba	0		0	0	10	14	3	1
Schleicher	0		0	0	8	6	1	0
Scurry	1		0	14	32	72	9	0
Shackelford	0		1	3	5	11	2	0
Shelby	0		1	47	111	150	17	3
Sherman	0		0	2	1	8	1	0
Starr	1		9	92	126	136	36	1
Stephens	0		0	6	14	20	2	1
Sterling	0		0	3	0	9	0	0
Stonewall	0		0	2	7	5	4	0
Sutton	0		0	0	0	0	0	0
Swisher	1		0	3	3	16	0	0
Terrell	0		0	0	2	7	0	1
Terry	0		0	4	24	34	3	0
Throckmorton	0		0	2	8	10	2	0
Titus	0		0	30	104	118	11	4
Trinity	0		0	20	111	96	12	3
Upton	0		0	0	1	16	2	0
Uvalde	1		1	13	52	86	7	0
Val Verde	0		2	9	36	80	1	0
Walker	3		5	25	145	164	33	1
Ward	0		0	28	35	145	15	0
Washington	0		4	30	58	102	12	0
Wheeler	0		0	5	20	44	13	0
Wilbarger	0		0	2	17	19	1	2
Willacy	0		1	25	68	153	9	1
Winkler	0		1	5	4	43	5	0
Wood	1		1	29	347	352	25	1
Young	0		0	5	34	48	5	1
Utah—Metropolitan Counties								
Box Elder	0		1	0	45	142	12	0
Cache	1		0	10	53	222	10	1
Davis	2	6	0	6	49	143	13	0
Juab	0		0	1	13	53	9	0
Salt Lake County Unified Police Department	6	131	218	530	1,959	8,528	1,261	44
Tooele	0	5	1	11	73	87	38	5
Utah	0	22	0	15	32	232	17	3
Washington	0	2	0	9	45	86	11	1
Weber	0	15	9	17	186	655	55	6
Utah—Nonmetropolitan Counties								
Beaver	0		0	6	4	18	3	0
Carbon	0	3	0	12	53	149	3	0
Daggett	0	0	0	0	2	12	0	0
Duchesne	0	2	3	23	56	186	22	5
Emery	0	3	0	7	24	121	16	0
Grand	1		3	2	27	50	3	0
Iron	0		5	28	57	92	9	0
Kane	0	1	0	10	7	17	1	0
Millard	0	3	0	30	32	169	6	0
Piute	0		0	5	9	8	1	0
Rich	0		0	3	14	23	0	1
San Juan	0		1	11	24	46	7	0
Sanpete	0		0	6	23	89	9	0
Sevier	0		1	14	48	135	12	0

Table 10.   Offenses Known to Law Enforcement, by Selected State Metropolitan and Nonmetropolitan Counties, 2013— continued

(Number.)

State/county	Murder and non-negligent man-slaughter	Rape (revised definition)[1]	Robbery	Aggravated assault	Burglary	Larceny-theft	Motor vehicle theft	Arson[2]
Summit	1	5	20	30	353	27	3
Uintah	2	8	0	28	53	150	21	1
Vermont—Metropolitan Counties								
Chittenden	0	0	0	0	0	0	0	0
Franklin	0	3	1	6	16	23	2	0
Grand Isle	0	0	0	2	40	47	4	0
Vermont—Nonmetropolitan Counties								
Addison	0	8	0	0	0	0	1	0
Bennington	0	0	0	0	2	3	0	0
Caledonia	0	0	0	0	0	1	0	0
Essex	0	1	0	1	17	14	0	0
Lamoille	0	0	1	7	36	84	2	1
Orange	0	4	0	0	7	23	0	0
Rutland	0	0	0	3	9	85	1	0
Windham	0	1	0	0	5	33	0	1
Virginia—Metropolitan Counties								
Albemarle County Police Department	1	43	24	58	242	1,392	43	6
Amelia	0	3	1	4	35	69	13	2
Amherst	1	9	2	20	49	298	25	1
Appomattox	0	4	0	4	19	82	6	0
Arlington County Police Department	0	39	125	198	236	3,406	156	3
Bedford	0	12	2	13	175	429	49	7
Botetourt	1	3	3	9	36	207	17	2
Buckingham	1	8	5	15	45	92	23	2
Campbell	3	16	7	41	104	541	24	1
Caroline	0	9	5	17	102	247	1	4
Charles City	0	1	0	4	5	16	1	0
Chesterfield County Police Department	9	74	144	171	1,356	4,734	226	51
Clarke	0	0	1	2	23	96	6	4
Craig	0	0	0	6	1	5	2	0
Culpeper	0	3	3	30	47	141	19	4
Dinwiddie	4	12	6	32	104	262	19	2
Fauquier	2	13	10	27	99	435	21	6
Floyd	0	3	0	7	31	93	8	1
Fluvanna	1	4	2	14	42	145	11	3
Franklin	4	8	1	47	106	365	48	3
Frederick	1	28	12	28	210	1,053	78	4
Giles	0	2	1	4	18	78	4	1
Gloucester	0	11	6	22	92	557	22	4
Goochland	0	0	1	3	35	127	4	1
Greene	0	5	1	10	45	219	5	2
Hanover	1	13	10	69	85	874	47	5
Henrico County Police Department	13	32	200	341	1,091	6,255	362	30
Isle of Wight	1	4	3	22	83	198	13	1
James City County Police Department	1	19	9	29	132	748	30	8
King William	0	1	2	3	18	63	7	0
Loudoun	4	63	36	113	223	2,357	98	31
Mathews	1	1	1	0	31	64	3	1
Montgomery	0	9	1	24	83	262	23	3
Nelson	0	4	2	10	41	136	14	1
New Kent	0	8	1	13	48	137	6	1
Powhatan	0	5	1	13	47	175	10	0
Prince George County Police Department	0	10	9	23	73	290	11	2
Prince William County Police Department	6	72	241	364	686	5,467	315	13
Pulaski	0	9	1	49	64	476	10	1
Rappahannock	0	0	0	1	0	0	0	0
Roanoke County Police Department	0	27	10	77	233	1,006	33	3
Rockingham	0	15	1	38	122	252	8	4
Scott	0	8	6	13	74	206	15	2
Spotsylvania	6	35	49	157	264	1,810	100	2
Stafford	4	39	28	106	173	1,791	73	9
Sussex	0	5	4	2	25	68	12	0
Warren	0	11	5	4	61	232	24	2
Washington	2	23	3	24	143	690	16	4
York	1	24	11	44	152	1,093	34	9
Virginia—Nonmetropolitan Counties								
Accomack	3	8	6	13	119	271	25	0
Alleghany	2	3	0	7	49	97	2	3
Bath	0	0	1	0	6	27	1	0
Bland	0	0	0	2	23	39	1	1
Brunswick	0	4	0	8	48	46	10	1
Buchanan	0	11	1	30	115	276	30	6
Carroll	2	7	1	18	90	230	20	4
Cumberland	0	3	2	9	17	33	4	0

Table 10. Offenses Known to Law Enforcement, by Selected State Metropolitan and Nonmetropolitan Counties, 2013— continued

(Number.)

State/county	Murder and non-negligent man-slaughter	Rape (revised definition)[1]	Robbery	Aggravated assault	Burglary	Larceny-theft	Motor vehicle theft	Arson[2]
Dickenson	0	4	1	15	43	101	8	2
Essex	1	1	1	13	56	36	7	0
Grayson	2	4	1	6	48	100	9	1
Greensville	1	1	1	9	26	57	6	1
Halifax	0	15	3	22	96	251	25	3
Henry	4	13	21	133	414	854	91	3
Highland	0	0	0	1	0	7	0	0
King and Queen	0	5	0	10	14	44	4	0
King George	0	9	5	15	58	298	24	0
Lancaster	0	1	0	9	0	3	0	1
Louisa	0	14	3	25	81	404	28	7
Lunenburg	1	1	0	6	29	42	0	0
Madison	1	4	3	4	18	95	4	1
Mecklenburg	2	22	3	25	114	163	11	1
Middlesex	2	1	1	6	20	76	3	1
Northampton	2	3	2	2	46	73	10	0
Northumberland	0	2	3	16	32	74	6	2
Nottoway	0	1	1	2	13	52	5	0
Orange	0	6	3	2	33	228	14	2
Page	0	6	1	4	57	148	14	1
Patrick	0	2	3	13	87	169	19	2
Pittsylvania	0	18	4	26	194	301	21	13
Prince Edward	2	9	1	11	39	78	9	2
Richmond	0	0	1	5	17	36	7	1
Rockbridge	0	2	2	10	60	190	9	1
Russell	3	10	2	15	93	188	7	3
Shenandoah	1	8	4	17	75	172	4	1
Smyth	0	7	0	13	47	232	5	3
Southampton	0	6	2	15	113	167	16	1
Surry	2	4	1	3	36	34	1	0
Tazewell	0	10	0	18	109	406	17	4
Westmoreland	0	5	3	16	35	117	14	2
Wise	0	22	6	19	110	382	36	4
Wythe	0	4	4	17	14	111	7	1
Washington—Metropolitan Counties								
Asotin	0	2	3	20	46	131	10	0
Benton	2	5	4	42	153	290	47	2
Chelan	0	4	3	35	147	307	32	0
Clark	1	26	39	179	910	2,040	440	33
Columbia	0	1	0	2	54	156	3	0
Cowlitz	1	40	4	45	229	310	53	2
Douglas	0	2	2	11	139	243	37	0
Franklin	1	3	1	19	50	129	12	7
King	4	113	194	2,105	2,498	688	42	
Kitsap	1	62	35	263	1,213	2,585	286	22
Pend Oreille	1	4	0	12	143	250	41	2
Pierce	10	93	182	690	3,263	5,523	1,108	59
Skagit	3	10	17	77	595	744	89	11
Skamania	0	6	0	13	27	71	8	0
Spokane	4		41	94	963	2,451	374	10
Stevens	2	13	3	12	218	241	46	2
Thurston	3	31	33	177	1,102	1,256	197	12
Walla Walla	0	5	1	6	130	230	17	3
Whatcom	0		12	115	417	828	85	10
Yakima	4	11	23	70	678	717	209	11
Washington—Nonmetropolitan Counties								
Adams	2	5	1	16	119	157	34	2
Clallam	0	12	4	50	303	523	48	2
Ferry	0	5	0	3	25	16	2	1
Garfield	0	0	0	3	7	40	4	1
Grant	1	20	11	63	434	873	155	10
Grays Harbor	0	3	2	29	242	232	52	
Island	0	10	3	22	315	431	26	4
Jefferson	0	10	0	19	90	250	22	4
Kittitas	0	2	1	11	131	183	26	2
Klickitat	1	0	0	7	54	22	17	
Lewis	1	10	1	47	265	315	31	3
Lincoln	0	2	0	7	48	80	9	2
Mason	1	13	7	61	550	613	110	6
Okanogan	5	4	3	22	155	223	35	3
Pacific	0	2	1	25	161	144	16	0
Wahkiakum	0	0	0	3	9	17	2	0
Whitman	0	4	2	8	22	37	4	2
West Virginia—Metropolitan Counties								
Boone	0	0	0	10	26	48	10	1

Table 10. Offenses Known to Law Enforcement, by Selected State Metropolitan and Nonmetropolitan Counties, 2013— continued

(Number.)

State/county	Murder and non-negligent man-slaughter	Rape (revised definition)	Robbery	Aggravated assault	Burglary	Larceny-theft	Motor vehicle theft	Arson[2]
Brooke	0	2	2	2	45	46	9	0
Fayette	0	13	7	47	140	188	18	7
Hampshire	0	2	0	59	50	28	2	0
Hancock	0	4	1	5	30	28	6	2
Jefferson	0	7	4	18	51	259	5	0
Marshall	0	3	1	34	70	81	11	0
Mineral	0	1	0	10	7	11	4	1
Monongalia	1	7	3	80	74	262	23	1
Ohio	0	4	1	23	81	191	9	0
Preston	0	3	1	38	39	66	14	1
Putnam	0	3	1	99	56	219	22	1
Wayne	0	1	3	30	67	78	3	1
Wirt	0	0	0	6	15	17	2	1
Wood	0	11	0	86	135	160	18	3
West Virginia—Nonmetropolitan Counties								
Braxton	0	1	0	9	18	41	2	0
Grant	0	0	0	3	7	6	0	0
Greenbrier	0	0	1	4	22	62	7	0
Hardy	0	1	0	8	2	4	0	0
Harrison	1	2	8	51	81	141	15	5
Jackson	0	2	0	65	21	36	1	1
Lewis	0	1	0	0	22	42	1	0
Logan	0	0	0	84	18	42	8	1
Marion	0	2	1	82	40	21	3	2
Mason	1	1	0	5	0	101	15	1
McDowell	3	1	2	14	40	31	9	3
Mingo	0	0	0	6	0	0	1	0
Monroe	0	0	0	5	27	50	0	0
Morgan	1	4	1	18	19	28	1	1
Nicholas	1	2	3	113	41	120	5	0
Pleasants	0	3	0	2	4	15	2	1
Randolph	1	0	0	37	19	31	2	0
Ritchie	1	0	0	4	10	13	0	0
Roane	2	1	0	15	0	55	6	0
Summers	0	0	0	0	0	0	0	0
Taylor	0	0	0	0	5	9	2	0
Tyler	1	2	0	8	10	33	0	1
Upshur	0	0	0	0	16	36	2	0
Wetzel	0	0	0	2	2	10	0	0
Wyoming	0	1	1	76	77	105	7	1
Wisconsin—Metropolitan Counties								
Brown	0		11	64	190	885	26	0
Calumet	0	0	0	11	37	67	6	0
Chippewa	0	9	1	4	93	235	18	1
Columbia	2	13	0	19	89	191	17	1
Dane	2	7	9	25	197	523	36	0
Douglas	0		3	4	172	176	20	0
Eau Claire	0		2	9	71	141	6	0
Fond du Lac	0	8	4	16	99	158	8	8
Green	0		0	7	34	85	6	0
Iowa	0	4	0	6	17	54	7	0
Kenosha	0		2	23	127	375	31	4
Kewaunee	0	2	0	3	37	53	5	0
La Crosse	0	0	0	12	26	106	12	0
Marathon	0		1	14	130	296	10	2
Milwaukee	0	3	10	12	9	146	26	2
Outagamie	0	5	1	17	92	207	11	2
Ozaukee	0		1	12	49	130	12	0
Pierce	0		0	11	64	113	4	0
Racine	0		3	7	77	329	16	0
Rock	1		2	30	160	172	20	2
Sheboygan	0		4	12	50	355	19	4
St. Croix	1	2	1	20	97	225	22	1
Washington	0		8	25	96	285	21	1
Waukesha	0		9	34	125	409	24	0
Winnebago	0		1	16	65	167	6	0
Wisconsin—Nonmetropolitan Counties								
Adams	1		2	33	169	284	18	1
Ashland	0		0	14	16	22	3	0
Barron	0	0	1	0	47	81	10	2
Bayfield	2		1	17	74	60	3	0
Buffalo	0		0	0	3	34	6	0
Burnett	0	1	2	20	435	173	17	3
Clark	2	0	1	12	71	97	16	5
Dodge	0	1	1	15	82	137	12	0

Table 10.   Offenses Known to Law Enforcement, by Selected State Metropolitan and Nonmetropolitan Counties, 2013— continued

(Number.)

State/county	Murder and non-negligent man-slaughter	Rape (revised definition)[1]	Robbery	Aggravated assault	Burglary	Larceny-theft	Motor vehicle theft	Arson[2]
Door	0	2	1	6	37	94	2	1
Dunn	0		0	20	48	97	21	1
Florence	0		0	9	27	54	5	0
Forest	0		0	16	32	97	4	0
Grant	0	4	1	24	88	101	10	0
Green Lake	0		0	3	19	66	7	0
Iron	0		1	6	18	33	2	0
Jackson	0		5	5	14	99	12	0
Jefferson	0		3	29	73	249	13	5
Juneau	0	5	2	26	87	186	9	0
Lafayette	3		0	3	17	90	11	0
Langlade	0		0	6	71	107	10	0
Lincoln	1	1	0	9	58	65	5	1
Manitowoc	0	2	0	11	56	94	10	3
Marinette	1		2	6	185	164	13	2
Marquette	0	3	1	0	38	80	6	0
Menominee	0		0	4	16	15	2	0
Monroe	0	2	0	7	41	141	12	1
Oneida	0	3	0	25	57	123	6	0
Pepin	0		0	2	15	18	3	1
Polk	0		2	67	92	172	18	0
Portage	0	3	0	18	98	119	13	1
Price	0	1	0	12	13	78	6	1
Richland	0		0	0	35	0	4	0
Rusk	0	3	0	10	27	56	6	1
Sauk	0	13	0	5	85	341	15	1
Sawyer	1	2	0	20	61	125	16	0
Shawano	0		0	6	116	205	21	0
Taylor	0		0	11	30	73	11	1
Trempealeau	0		0	5	22	61	10	0
Vernon	0		0	16	59	88	5	0
Vilas	0	4	0	6	43	98	9	0
Walworth	0		0	4	50	163	17	1
Washburn	0	2	1	8	93	167	4	0
Waupaca	0		0	3	129	280	26	1
Waushara	0		1	7	43	180	9	3
Wood	0		1	3	69	103	7	0
Wyoming—Metropolitan Counties								
Laramie	0		1	52	151	361	28	2
Natrona	1		0	29	32	141	18	0
Wyoming—Nonmetropolitan Counties								
Albany	0		0	6	7	45	3	0
Big Horn	0		0	0	8	14	2	0
Campbell	0		1	18	51	148	21	0
Carbon	0		0	7	6	71	1	0
Converse	0		0	4	4	45	4	0
Crook	0		0	0	8	25	3	0
Fremont	5		0	18	51	142	8	0
Goshen	0		0	12	25	40	2	0
Hot Springs	0		0	2	3	21	4	0
Johnson	0		0	1	3	30	2	0
Lincoln	0		1	3	14	70	1	1
Niobrara	0		0	0	2	3	0	1
Park	3		0	30	17	52	2	0
Platte	0		0	2	16	17	3	0
Sheridan	0		0	1	7	30	2	1
Sublette	0		0	13	13	101	5	0
Sweetwater	0		0	18	25	73	13	3
Uinta	0		0	0	3	62	3	0
Washakie	0		0	1	0	3	0	0
Weston	0		0	2	6	3	3	0

Note: The data shown in this table do not reflect county totals but are the number of offenses reported by the sheriff's office or county police department.   1 The figures shown in this column for the offense of rape were reported using the revised Uniform Crime Reporting (UCR) definition of rape. See chapter notes for more detail.   2 The figures shown in this column for the offense of rape were reported using the legacy Uniform Crime Reporting (UCR) definition of rape. See chapter notes for more detail.

Table 11.   Offenses Known to Law Enforcement, by Selected State, Tribal, and Other Agencies, 2013

(Number.)

State/other agency unit/office	Murder and non-negligent man-slaughter	Rape (revised definition)[1]	Robbery	Aggravated as-sault	Burglary	Larceny-theft	Motor vehicle theft	Arson[2]
Alabama								
State Agency								
State Fire Marshal	0		6	0	48	238	12	0
Tribal Agency								
Poarch Creek Tribal	0		6	0	48	238	12	0
Alaska								
State Agency								
Alaska State Troopers	18	367	21	773	972	1,633	396	33
Other Agencies								
Anchorage International Airport	0	0	0	0	0	116	7	0
Fairbanks International Airport	0	0	0	1	0	6	2	0
Arizona								
State Agency								
Arizona Department of Public Safety	0		3	18	5	56	0	2
Tribal Agencies								
Ak-Chin Tribal	0		1	0	0	3	2	0
Cocopah Tribal	0		0	4	11	28	2	0
Colorado River Agency	0		0	0	0	0	0	0
Colorado River Tribal	4		0	13	81	3	23	1
Fort Apache Agency	3		0	10	0	0	0	4
Fort McDowell Tribal	0		3	6	4	22	9	0
Fort Mojave Tribal	0		0	36	17	80	10	2
Gila River Indian Community	3		21	179	103	272	106	11
Hopi Tribal	0		0	21	0	12	3	0
Hualapai Tribal	0		0	55	29	4	1	4
Kaibab Paiute Tribal	0		0	1	0	0	0	0
Navajo Nation	8		27	210	982	1,146	747	328
Pascua Yaqui Tribal	0		4	15	54	166	19	4
Quechan Tribal	0		1	9	4	22	3	0
Salt River Tribal	0		10	28	83	405	53	2
San Carlos Agency	7		0	8	0	0	0	8
San Carlos Apache	3		10	277	113	217	11	21
Tohono O'odham Nation	8		21	125	110	69	77	35
Tonto Apache Tribal	0		0	3	5	0	0	0
Truxton Canon Agency	0		0	8	1	0	0	0
White Mountain Apache Tribal	1		1	103	313	478	29	1
Yavapai-Apache Nation	1		0	8	5	18	0	0
Yavapai-Prescott Tribal	0		1	0	9	65	1	1
Other Agencies								
Tucson Airport Authority	0		1	0	5	61	16	0
California								
State Agencies								
Atascadero State Hospital	0		0	278	0	5	0	0
California State Fair	0		0	0	0	48	0	0
Coalinga State Hospital	0		0	54	1	16	0	1
Department of Parks and Recreation								
Angeles	0		0	0	14	1	0	0
Bay Area	0		0	0	0	8	1	0
Calaveras County	0		0	0	1	0	0	0
Capital	0		0	2	2	4	1	0
Channel Coast	0		0	0	2	26	0	0
Colorado	0		0	0	0	0	0	0
Four Rivers District	0		0	1	0	8	0	0
Gold Fields District	0		0	1	4	45	4	0
Hollister Hills	0		0	0	1	0	1	0
Hungry Valley	0		0	0	0	0	1	0
Inland Empire	0		0	2	2	4	0	0
Marin County	0		0	0	3	0	0	0
Mendocino Headquarters	0		0	5	0	12	0	1
Monterey County	0		0	0	26	24	1	0
North Coast Redwoods	0		0	2	0	18	1	0
Northern Buttes	0		0	0	1	26	0	1
Oceano Dunes	0		0	1	8	43	3	0
Ocotillo Wells	0		0	0	0	0	0	0
Orange Coast	0		0	0	13	36	0	0
Russian River	0		0	1	3	19	0	0
San Diego Coast	0		2	1	16	38	1	0
San Joaquin	0		0	3	1	0	1	0
San Luis Obispo Coast	0		0	0	0	8	0	0
Santa Cruz Mountains	0		1	3	4	64	3	1
Sierra	0		0	0	2	8	0	0
Silverado	0		0	0	0	1	0	0
Tehachapi District	0		0	1	6	5	0	0

Table 11. Offenses Known to Law Enforcement, by Selected State, Tribal, and Other Agencies, 2013— continued

(Number.)

State/other agency unit/office	Murder and non-negligent man-slaughter	Rape (revised definition)[1]	Robbery	Aggravated as-sault	Burglary	Larceny-theft	Motor vehicle theft	Arson[2]
Twin Cities	0		0	0	0	0	0	0
Fairview Developmental Center	0		0	21	4	8	0	0
Highway Patrol								
Alameda County	0		0	0	0	50	193	0
Alpine County	0		0	0	0	0	0	0
Amador County	0		0	0	0	0	20	0
Butte County	0		0	0	1	52	237	0
Calaveras County	0		0	0	0	9	170	0
Colusa County	0		0	4	0	3	19	0
Contra Costa County	0		0	1	0	4	869	0
Del Norte County	0		0	0	0	0	115	0
El Dorado County	0		0	1	2	150	175	0
Fresno County	0		0	0	0	31	211	0
Glenn County	0		0	0	0	3	32	0
Humboldt County	0		0	0	1	39	255	0
Imperial County	0		0	0	0	10	52	0
Inyo County	0		0	0	0	5	12	0
Kern County	0		0	4	2	16	224	0
Kings County	0		0	0	0	0	53	0
Lake County	0		0	1	0	16	96	0
Lassen County	0		0	1	1	5	13	0
Los Angeles County	0		1	27	11	634	569	0
Madera County	0		0	1	3	31	227	0
Marin County	0		0	1	0	23	100	0
Mariposa County	0		0	0	0	4	11	0
Mendocino County	0		0	3	0	22	118	0
Merced County	0		0	1	1	103	548	0
Modoc County	0		0	0	0	3	9	0
Mono County	0		0	1	0	0	1	0
Monterey County	0		1	2	0	45	381	0
Napa County	0		0	0	0	14	61	0
Nevada County	0		0	0	0	23	80	0
Orange County	0		0	3	0	18	30	0
Placer County	0		0	1	0	59	147	0
Plumas County	0		0	2	0	8	12	0
Riverside County	0		0	5	25	11	77	0
Sacramento County	0		1	3	8	849	3,103	0
San Benito County	0		0	0	0	0	14	0
San Bernardino County	0		0	3	0	14	28	0
San Diego County	0		1	8	4	35	66	0
San Francisco County	0		1	0	0	3	13	0
San Joaquin County	0		0	2	0	131	721	0
San Luis Obispo County	0		0	0	0	12	159	0
San Mateo County	0		0	1	0	5	7	0
Santa Barbara County	0		0	1	1	39	148	0
Santa Clara County	0		0	0	0	11	87	0
Santa Cruz County	0		0	0	0	103	468	0
Shasta County	0		0	0	2	41	385	0
Sierra County	0		0	0	0	0	0	0
Siskiyou County	0		0	1	1	7	33	0
Solano County	0		0	1	0	0	69	0
Sonoma County	0		0	1	0	74	205	0
Stanislaus County	0		0	2	1	75	892	0
Sutter County	0		0	0	0	2	52	0
Tehama County	0		0	0	3	8	151	0
Trinity County	0		0	0	2	3	28	0
Tulare County	0		0	1	0	79	557	0
Tuolumne County	0		0	0	0	74	78	0
Ventura County	0		0	0	0	0	34	0
Yolo County	0		0	0	0	0	49	0
Yuba County	0		0	0	0	14	236	0
Lanterman State Hospital	0		0	0	1	0	0	0
Napa State Hospital	0		0	53	1	3	0	0
Patton State Hospital	1		1	130	0	10	0	0
Porterville Developmental Center	0		0	10	0	19	0	0
Sonoma Developmental Center	0		0	48	0	1	0	0
Tribal Agencies								
Hoopa Valley Tribal	0		7	125	52	126	7	3
Sycuan Tribal	0		2	3	10	46	18	0
Tule River Tribal	0		1	53	12	20	11	0
Yurok Tribal	1		1	15	21	28	9	6
Other Agencies								
East Bay Municipal Utility	0		0	0	3	15	3	0
East Bay Regional Parks								
Alameda County	0		2	0	3	129	10	3
Contra Costa County	0		3	3	6	176	6	1
Fontana Unified School District	0		8	20	25	57	0	6

Table 11. Offenses Known to Law Enforcement, by Selected State, Tribal, and Other Agencies, 2013— continued

(Number.)

State/other agency unit/office	Murder and non-negligent manslaughter	Rape (revised definition)	Robbery	Aggravated assault	Burglary	Larceny-theft	Motor vehicle theft	Arson[2]
Los Angeles County Metropolitan Transportation Authority	0		0	1	3	28	0	0
Los Angeles Transportation Services Bureau	0		407	280	16	1,008	107	5
Monterey Peninsula Airport	0		0	0	15	6	2	0
Port of San Diego Harbor	0		8	21	54	513	5	8
San Bernardino Unified School District	0		68	13	185	281	24	6
San Francisco Bay Area Rapid Transit								
Alameda County	1		128	26	12	1,405	339	4
Contra Costa County	1		24	20	9	562	169	2
San Francisco County	0		50	16	2	366	0	0
San Mateo County	0		7	7	1	171	15	0
Santa Clara Transit District	0		25	14	2	68	17	0
Shasta County Marshal	0		0	0	0	0	0	0
Stockton Unified School District	0		15	25	107	312	3	5
Twin Rivers Unified School District	0		5	14	97	62	4	0
Union Pacific Railroad								
Alameda County	0		0	1	78	17	0	1
Amador County	0		0	0	0	0	0	0
Butte County	0		0	0	0	2	0	0
Calaveras County	0		0	0	0	0	0	0
Colusa County	0		0	0	0	0	0	0
Contra Costa County	0		0	0	1	5	0	0
El Dorado County	0		0	0	0	0	0	0
Fresno County	0		0	0	1	6	0	0
Glenn County	0		0	0	0	0	0	0
Humboldt County	0		0	0	0	0	0	0
Imperial County	0		0	0	2	2	0	0
Inyo County	0		0	0	0	0	0	0
Kern County	0		0	0	6	2	0	1
Kings County	0		0	0	0	0	0	0
Lassen County	0		0	0	0	4	0	0
Los Angeles County	0		0	3	313	135	0	2
Madera County	0		0	0	0	1	0	0
Marin County	0		0	0	0	0	0	0
Mendocino County	0		0	0	0	0	0	0
Merced County	0		0	0	1	2	0	0
Modoc County	0		0	0	0	0	0	0
Monterey County	0		0	0	0	0	0	0
Napa County	0		0	0	0	0	0	0
Nevada County	0		0	0	0	1	0	0
Orange County	0		0	0	0	2	0	0
Placer County	0		0	0	6	15	0	1
Plumas County	0		0	0	0	0	0	0
Riverside County	0		0	2	4	20	0	1
Sacramento County	0		0	0	2	14	0	1
San Benito County	0		0	0	0	1	0	0
San Bernardino County	0		0	2	8	35	0	1
San Francisco County	0		0	0	1	0	0	0
San Joaquin County	0		0	0	122	27	0	0
San Luis Obispo County	0		0	0	0	0	0	0
San Mateo County	0		0	0	0	0	0	0
Santa Barbara County	0		0	0	0	2	0	0
Santa Clara County	0		0	0	0	14	0	0
Santa Cruz County	0		0	0	0	0	0	0
Shasta County	0		0	1	0	10	0	0
Sierra County	0		0	0	0	0	0	0
Siskiyou County	0		0	0	0	0	0	0
Solano County	0		0	0	1	2	0	0
Sonoma County	0		0	0	0	0	0	0
Stanislaus County	0		0	0	1	7	0	0
Sutter County	0		0	0	0	0	0	1
Tehama County	0		0	0	0	2	0	0
Trinity County	0		0	0	0	0	0	0
Tulare County	0		0	0	0	0	0	0
Ventura County	0		0	0	0	2	0	0
Yolo County	0		0	1	0	6	0	0
Yuba County	0		0	0	2	0	0	0
Colorado								
State Agencies								
Colorado Bureau of Investigation	0	0	0	0	0	1	0	
Colorado Mental Health Institute	0	0	0	2	0	1	0	0
Colorado State Patrol	0	0	0	25	2	12	8	0
Tribal Agencies								
Southern Ute Tribal	1		0	3	4	4	5	0
Ute Mountain Tribal	0		2	16	3	3	10	0
Other Agencies								

Table 11.   Offenses Known to Law Enforcement, by Selected State, Tribal, and Other Agencies, 2013— continued

(Number.)

State/other agency unit/office	Murder and non-negligent man-slaughter	Rape (revised definition)[1]	Robbery	Aggravated as-sault	Burglary	Larceny-theft	Motor vehicle theft	Arson[2]
All Crimes Enforcement Team	0	0	0	0	0	0	0	0
Delta Montrose Drug Task Force	0	0	0	0	0	0	0	0
Southwest Drug Task Force	0	0	0	0	0	0	0	
Connecticut								
State Agencies								
Connecticut State Police	6	82	53	272	1,267	2,713	412	55
State Capitol Police	0	0	0	0	1	1	1	0
Tribal Agencies								
Mashantucket Pequot Tribal	0		0	14	0	28	2	0
Mohegan Tribal	0		3	2	0	144	1	1
Other Agency								
Metropolitan Transportation Authority		0	3	80	79	0	0	0
Delaware								
State Agencies								
Environmental Control	0	0	0	0	0	5	0	0
Park Rangers	0	0	0	1	11	72	0	0
River and Bay Authority	0	0	0	0	4	7	2	0
State Capitol Police	0	0	0	0	0	19	1	0
State Fire Marshal	0	0	0	14	10	0	0	143
State Police Headquarters	0	1	0	1	0	1	0	0
State Police								
Kent County	3	50	45	223	476	1,031	72	2
New Castle County	3	28	234	219	532	4,784	164	1
Sussex County	3	81	55	435	1,501	2,365	150	2
District of Columbia								
Other Agency: Metro Transit Police	0	2	418	106	2	1,425	87	2
Florida								
State Agencies								
Capitol Police	0	0	0	0	0	14	0	0
Department of Corrections, Office of the Inspector General								
Baker County	0	0	0	0	0	0	0	0
Dixie County	0	0	0	0	0	0	0	0
Gulf County	0	0	0	0	0	0	0	0
Marion County	0	0	0	0	0	0	0	0
Martin County	0	0	0	0	0	0	0	0
Polk County	0	0	0	0	0	0	0	0
Taylor County	0	0	0	0	0	0	0	0
Department of Insurance								
Broward County	0	0	0	0	0	0	0	0
Duval County	0	0	0	0	0	0	0	0
Escambia County	0	0	0	0	0	0	0	0
Hillsborough County	0	0	0	0	0	0	0	0
Lee County	0	0	0	0	0	0	0	0
Miami-Dade County	0	0	0	0	0	0	0	0
Orange County	0	0	0	0	0	0	0	0
Palm Beach County	0	0	0	0	0	0	0	0
Pinellas County	0	0	0	0	0	0	0	0
Department of Law Enforcement								
Duval County, Jacksonville	0	0	0	0	0	0	0	0
Escambia County, Pensacola	0	0	0	1	0	0	0	0
Hillsborough County, Tampa	0	1	0	0	0	2	0	0
Lee County, Fort Myers	0	0	0	0	0	0	0	0
Leon County, Tallahassee	0	0	0	0	0	0	5	0
Miami-Dade County, Miami	0	0	0	0	0	0	0	0
Orange County, Orlando	0	0	0	0	0	0	0	0
Division of Alcoholic Beverages and Tobacco								
Alachua County	0	0	0	0	0	0	0	0
Baker County	0	0	0	0	0	0	0	0
Bay County	0	0	0	0	0	0	0	0
Bradford County	0	0	0	0	0	0	0	0
Brevard County	0	0	0	0	0	0	0	0
Broward County	0	0	0	0	0	0	0	0
Calhoun County	0	0	0	0	0	0	0	0
Charlotte County	0	0	0	0	0	0	0	0
Citrus County	0	0	0	0	0	0	0	0
Clay County	0	0	0	0	0	0	0	0
Collier County	0	0	0	0	0	0	0	0
Columbia County	0	0	0	0	0	0	0	0
DeSoto County	0	0	0	0	0	0	0	0
Dixie County	0	0	0	0	0	0	0	0
Duval County	0	0	0	0	0	0	0	0
Escambia County	0	0	0	0	0	0	0	0

Table 11.   Offenses Known to Law Enforcement, by Selected State, Tribal, and Other Agencies, 2013— continued

(Number.)

State/other agency unit/office	Murder and non-negligent man-slaughter	Rape (revised definition)[1]	Robbery	Aggravated as-sault	Burglary	Larceny-theft	Motor vehicle theft	Arson[2]
Flagler County	0	0	0	0	0	0	0	0
Franklin County	0	0	0	0	0	0	0	0
Gadsden County	0	0	0	0	0	0	0	0
Gilchrist County	0	0	0	0	0	0	0	0
Glades County	0	0	0	0	0	0	0	0
Gulf County	0	0	0	0	0	0	0	0
Hamilton County	0	0	0	0	0	0	0	0
Hardee County	0	0	0	0	0	0	0	0
Hendry County	0	0	0	0	0	0	0	0
Hernando County	0	0	0	0	0	0	0	0
Highlands County	0	0	0	0	0	0	0	0
Hillsborough County	0	0	0	0	0	0	0	0
Holmes County	0	0	0	0	0	0	0	0
Indian River County	0	0	0	0	0	0	0	0
Jackson County	0	0	0	0	0	0	0	0
Jefferson County	0	0	0	0	0	0	0	0
Lafayette County	0	0	0	0	0	0	0	0
Lake County	0	0	0	0	0	0	0	0
Lee County	0	0	0	0	0	0	0	0
Leon County	0	0	0	0	0	0	0	0
Levy County	0	0	0	0	0	0	0	0
Liberty County	0	0	0	0	0	0	0	0
Madison County	0	0	0	0	0	0	0	0
Manatee County	0	0	0	0	0	0	0	0
Marion County	0	0	0	0	0	0	0	0
Martin County	0	0	0	0	0	0	0	0
Miami-Dade County	0	0	0	0	0	0	0	0
Monroe County	0	0	0	0	0	0	0	0
Nassau County	0	0	0	0	0	0	0	0
Okaloosa County	0	0	0	0	0	0	0	0
Okeechobee County	0	0	0	0	0	0	0	0
Orange County	0	0	0	0	0	0	0	0
Osceola County	0	0	0	0	0	0	0	0
Palm Beach County	0	0	0	0	0	0	0	0
Pasco County	0	0	0	0	0	0	0	0
Pinellas County	0	0	0	0	0	0	0	0
Polk County	0	0	0	0	0	0	0	0
Putnam County	0	0	0	0	0	0	0	0
Santa Rosa County	0	0	0	0	0	0	0	0
Sarasota County	0	0	0	0	0	0	0	0
Seminole County	0	0	0	0	0	0	0	0
St. Johns County	0	0	0	0	0	0	0	0
St. Lucie County	0	0	0	0	0	0	0	0
Sumter County	0	0	0	0	0	0	0	0
Suwannee County	0	0	0	0	0	0	0	0
Taylor County	0	0	0	0	0	0	0	0
Union County	0	0	0	0	0	0	0	0
Volusia County	0	0	0	0	0	0	0	0
Wakulla County	0	0	0	0	0	0	0	0
Walton County	0	0	0	0	0	0	0	0
Washington County	0	0	0	0	0	0	0	0
Florida Game Commission								
Alachua County	0	0	0	0	0	0	0	0
Baker County	0	0	0	0	0	0	0	0
Bay County	0	0	0	0	0	0	0	0
Bradford County	0	0	0	0	0	0	0	0
Brevard County	0	0	0	0	0	0	0	0
Broward County	0	0	0	0	0	0	0	0
Calhoun County	0	0	0	0	0	0	0	0
Charlotte County	0	0	0	0	0	0	0	0
Citrus County	0	0	0	0	0	0	0	0
Clay County	0	0	0	0	0	0	0	0
Collier County	0	0	0	0	0	0	0	0
Columbia County	0	0	0	0	0	0	0	0
DeSoto County	0	0	0	0	0	0	0	0
Dixie County	0	0	0	0	0	0	0	0
Duval County	0	0	0	0	0	0	0	0
Escambia County	0	0	0	0	0	0	0	0
Flagler County	0	0	0	0	0	0	0	0
Franklin County	0	0	0	0	0	0	0	0
Gadsden County	0	0	0	0	0	0	0	0
Gilchrist County	0	0	0	0	0	0	0	0
Glades County	0	0	0	0	0	0	0	0
Gulf County	0	0	0	0	0	0	0	0
Hamilton County	0	0	0	0	0	0	0	0
Hardee County	0	0	0	0	0	0	0	0
Hendry County	0	0	0	0	0	0	0	0
Hernando County	0	0	0	0	0	0	0	0

Table 11.   Offenses Known to Law Enforcement, by Selected State, Tribal, and Other Agencies, 2013— continued

(Number.)

State/other agency unit/office	Murder and non-negligent man-slaughter	Rape (revised definition)[1]	Robbery	Aggravated as-sault	Burglary	Larceny-theft	Motor vehicle theft	Arson[2]
Highlands County	0	0	0	0	0	0	0	0
Hillsborough County	0	0	0	0	0	0	0	0
Holmes County	0	0	0	0	0	0	0	0
Indian River County	0	0	0	0	0	0	0	0
Jackson County	0	0	0	0	0	0	0	0
Jefferson County	0	0	0	0	0	0	0	0
Lafayette County	0	0	0	0	0	0	0	0
Lake County	0	0	0	0	0	0	0	0
Lee County	0	0	0	0	0	0	0	0
Leon County	0	0	0	0	0	0	0	0
Levy County	0	0	0	0	0	0	0	0
Liberty County	0	0	0	0	0	0	0	0
Madison County	0	0	0	0	0	0	0	0
Manatee County	0	0	0	0	0	0	0	0
Marion County	0	0	0	0	0	0	0	0
Martin County	0	0	0	0	0	0	0	0
Miami-Dade County	0	0	0	0	0	0	0	0
Monroe County	0	0	0	0	0	0	0	0
Nassau County	0	0	0	0	0	0	0	0
Okaloosa County	0	0	0	0	0	0	0	0
Okeechobee County	0	0	0	0	0	0	0	0
Orange County	0	0	0	0	0	0	0	0
Osceola County	0	0	0	0	0	0	0	0
Palm Beach County	0	0	0	0	0	0	0	0
Pasco County	0	0	0	0	0	0	0	0
Pinellas County	0	0	0	0	0	0	0	0
Polk County	0	0	0	0	0	0	0	0
Putnam County	0	0	0	0	0	0	0	0
Santa Rosa County	0	0	0	0	0	0	0	0
Sarasota County	0	0	0	0	0	0	0	0
Seminole County	0	0	0	0	0	0	0	0
St. Johns County	0	0	0	0	0	0	0	0
St. Lucie County	0	0	0	0	0	0	0	0
Sumter County	0	0	0	0	0	0	0	0
Suwannee County	0	0	0	0	0	0	0	0
Taylor County	0	0	0	0	0	0	0	0
Union County	0	0	0	0	0	0	0	0
Volusia County	0	0	0	0	0	0	0	0
Wakulla County	0	0	0	0	0	0	0	0
Walton County	0	0	0	0	0	0	0	0
Washington County	0	0	0	0	0	0	0	0
Highway Patrol								
Alachua County	0	0	0	5	0	1	0	0
Baker County	0	0	0	0	0	1	1	0
Bay County	0	0	0	0	0	0	0	0
Bradford County	0	0	0	0	0	0	0	0
Brevard County	0	0	0	0	0	0	1	0
Broward County	0	0	0	11	0	37	2	0
Calhoun County	0	0	0	0	0	0	0	0
Charlotte County	0	0	0	0	0	0	0	0
Citrus County	0	0	0	0	0	0	0	0
Clay County	0	0	0	0	0	0	0	0
Collier County	0	0	0	1	0	0	3	0
Columbia County	0	0	0	0	0	19	5	0
DeSoto County	0	0	0	0	0	0	0	0
Dixie County	0	0	0	0	0	0	0	0
Duval County	0	0	0	0	0	7	1	0
Escambia County	0	0	0	0	0	0	0	0
Flagler County	0	0	0	0	0	38	0	0
Franklin County	0	0	0	0	0	0	0	0
Gadsden County	0	0	0	1	0	1	0	0
Gilchrist County	0	0	0	0	0	0	0	0
Glades County	0	0	0	0	0	0	0	0
Gulf County	0	0	0	0	0	0	0	0
Hamilton County	0	0	0	0	0	2	0	0
Hardee County	0	0	0	0	0	0	0	0
Hendry County	0	0	0	0	0	0	0	0
Hernando County	0	0	0	0	0	0	0	0
Highlands County	0	0	0	0	0	0	0	0
Hillsborough County	0	0	0	11	0	4	2	0
Holmes County	0	0	0	0	0	0	0	0
Indian River County	0	0	0	1	0	0	0	0
Jackson County	0	0	0	0	0	0	0	0
Jefferson County	0	0	0	0	0	0	0	0
Lafayette County	0	0	0	0	0	0	0	0
Lake County	0	0	0	1	0	0	0	0
Lee County	0	0	0	3	0	3	2	0
Leon County	0	0	0	1	0	1	0	0

Table 11.   Offenses Known to Law Enforcement, by Selected State, Tribal, and Other Agencies, 2013— continued

(Number.)

State/other agency unit/office	Murder and non-negligent man-slaughter	Rape (revised definition)	Robbery	Aggravated as-sault	Burglary	Larceny-theft	Motor vehicle theft	Arson[2]
Levy County	0	0	0	0	0	0	0	0
Liberty County	0	0	0	0	0	0	0	0
Madison County	0	0	0	2	0	2	0	0
Manatee County	0	0	0	0	0	0	0	0
Marion County	0	0	0	0	0	2	0	0
Martin County	0	0	0	2	0	0	0	0
Miami-Dade County	0	0	0	6	0	2	1	0
Monroe County	0	0	0	0	0	1	0	0
Nassau County	0	0	0	0	0	0	0	0
Okaloosa County	0	0	0	0	0	1	0	0
Okeechobee County	0	0	0	3	0	17	0	0
Orange County	0	0	0	3	0	0	0	0
Osceola County	0	0	0	2	0	8	4	0
Palm Beach County	0	0	0	13	0	5	3	0
Pasco County	0	0	0	1	0	0	2	0
Pinellas County	0	0	0	1	0	0	0	0
Polk County	0	0	0	2	0	2	0	0
Putnam County	0	0	0	0	0	0	0	0
Santa Rosa County	0	0	0	0	0	0	0	0
Sarasota County	0	0	0	1	0	0	2	0
Seminole County	0	0	0	1	0	0	1	0
St. Johns County	0	0	0	0	0	1	0	0
St. Lucie County	0	0	0	3	0	1	0	0
Sumter County	0	0	0	0	0	2	0	0
Suwannee County	0	0	0	0	0	0	3	0
Taylor County	0	0	0	0	0	0	0	0
Union County	0	0	0	0	0	0	0	0
Volusia County	0	0	0	2	0	0	0	0
Wakulla County	0	0	0	0	0	0	0	0
Walton County	0	0	0	0	0	0	0	0
Washington County	0	0	0	1	0	1	0	0
State Treasurer's Office, Division of Insurance Fraud	0	0	0	0	0	0	0	0
Tribal Agencies								
Miccosukee Tribal	0		1	16	20	97	12	1
Seminole Tribal	0		22	28	25	612	45	0
Other Agencies								
Duval County Schools	0	11	20	59	121	438	11	4
Florida School for the Deaf and Blind	0	1	0	0	0	1	0	0
Fort Lauderdale Airport	0	0	0	0	1	269	13	0
Jacksonville Aviation Authority	0	0	0	0	1	18	15	0
Lee County Port Authority	0	0	0	0	0	75	10	0
Melbourne International Airport	0	0	0	0	0	0	3	0
Miami-Dade County Public Schools	0	7	75	93	336	1,150	20	6
Northwest Florida Beaches International Airport	0	0	0	0	0	5	0	0
Palm Beach County School District	2	1	12	109	43	922	8	5
Port Canaveral	0	0	0	3	4	41	0	0
Port Everglades	0	3	0	6	1	58	2	0
Sarasota-Manatee Airport Authority	0	0	0	1	0	4	1	0
St. Petersburg-Clearwater International Airport	0	0	0	0	0	6	1	0
Tampa International Airport	0	0	0	4	0	145	12	0
Volusia County Beach Management	0	1	0	14	2	155	4	0
Georgia								
State Agencies								
Georgia Department of Public Safety	0		0	0	0	0	0	0
Georgia Department of Transportation, Office of Investigations	0		0	0	0	1	0	0
Georgia Forestry Commission	0		0	0	0	0	0	93
Georgia Public Safety Training Center	0		0	0	0	0	0	0
Georgia World Congress	0		5	8	2	120	0	0
Ports Authority, Savannah	0		0	0	0	12	0	0
State Board of Workers Compensation, Fraud Investigation Division	0		0	0	0	0	0	0
Other Agencies								
Cherokee County Board of Education	0		0	4	3	119	0	
Cherokee County Marshal	0		0	0	0	0	0	0
Decatur County Schools	0		0	1	0	0	0	0
DeKalb County School System	0		52	20	70	538	16	
Fayette County Marshal	0		0	0	0	0	0	0
Fulton County Marshal	0		0	2	0	9	0	
Fulton County School System	0		1	6	10	121	11	0
Glynn County School System	0		0	0	12	62	0	0
Gwinnett County Public Schools	0		7	2	1	245	3	0
Hartsfield-Jackson Atlanta International Airport	0		1	3	2	301	44	0

Table 11.   Offenses Known to Law Enforcement, by Selected State, Tribal, and Other Agencies, 2013— continued

(Number.)

State/other agency unit/office	Murder and non-negligent man-slaughter	Rape (revised definition)[1]	Robbery	Aggravated as-sault	Burglary	Larceny-theft	Motor vehicle theft	Arson[2]
Metropolitan Atlanta Rapid Transit Authority	0		57	75	2	316	80	4
Muscogee City Marshal	0		0	0	0	0	0	0
Richmond County Marshal	0		0	0	0	0	0	0
Savannah Fire and Emergency Services, Arson Unit	0		0	0	0	0	0	37
Stone Mountain Park	0		0	0	0	45	3	0
Washington County Board of Education	0		0	0	0	0	0	0
Idaho								
State Agency								
Idaho State Police	1	8	0	17	3	2	9	0
Illinois								
State Agencies								
Illinois Department of Natural Resources	0		0	0	0	3	0	0
Illinois State Police	29		25	79	41	148	582	6
Secretary of State Police	0		0	1	1	15	0	0
Other Agencies								
Alton & Southern Railway								
Belt Railway	0		0	0	0	11	0	1
Canadian National Railway	0		0	0	0	1	0	0
Canton Park District	0		0	1	2	106	0	0
Capitol Airport Authority	0		0	0	0	0	0	1
Chicago Fire Department, Arson Investigations	0		0	0	0	0	0	0
Cook County Forest Preserve	0		0	0	0	0	0	508
Decatur Park District	0		6	1	4	68	7	1
Du Page County Forest Preserve	0		1	5	5	29	3	2
Fon du Lac Park District	0		1	0	0	21	0	0
Fox Valley Park District	0		0	0	0	0	0	0
Indiana Harbor Belt Railroad	0		7	4	0	75	1	0
Kane County Forest Preserve	0		0	0	1	3	0	0
McHenry County Conservation District	0		0	0	0	12	0	0
Naperville Park District	0		0	1	1	2	1	1
Rockford Park District	0		0	0	0	14	0	1
Round Lake Park District	0		18	27	23	50	2	0
Terminal Railroad Association	0		0	1	0	1	0	0
	0		0	0	3	9	1	0
Indiana								
State Agencies								
Indiana State Excise Police	0		0	4	0	13	0	0
Northern Indiana Commuter Transportation District	0		0	0	0	15	5	0
State Police								
Allen County	0		0	6	1	20	3	
Bartholomew County	0		0	0	0	7	3	0
Benton County	0		0	0	0	0	0	
Boone County	0		0	0	0	3	1	
Brown County	0		0	2	0	2	0	
Carroll County	0		2	1	1	6	3	
Cass County	0		0	0	2	5	1	0
Clark County	0		0	15	10	22	8	0
Clay County	0		0	2	2	9	0	
Clinton County	0		0	0	0	7	0	0
Crawford County	0		0	1	4	12	0	1
Daviess County	0		1	2	0	10	1	
Dearborn County	0		0	2	3	9	8	0
Decatur County	0		0	0	0	7	0	0
De Kalb County	1		0	0	0	2	0	
Delaware County	0		0	0	2	8	0	0
Dubois County	0		0	0	1	9	1	0
Elkhart County	0		0	0	0	9	1	0
Fayette County	0		0	1	2	3	0	
Floyd County	0		0	4	1	4	3	0
Fountain County	0		0	0	1	5	0	
Franklin County	0		1	1	5	5	2	0
Fulton County	0		0	2	2	3	1	0
Gibson County	0		0	6	3	14	1	0
Grant County	1		0	0	2	1	1	0
Greene County	0		0	5	3	9	3	0
Hamilton County	0		0	0	0	6	2	
Hancock County	0		0	0	0	5	3	0
Harrison County	1		0	2	5	22	3	0
Hendricks County	0		0	1	0	12	1	0
Henry County	1		0	0	1	8	0	0
Howard County	0		0	1	1	5	0	0
Huntington County	0		0	0	1	2	1	

Table 11. Offenses Known to Law Enforcement, by Selected State, Tribal, and Other Agencies, 2013— continued

(Number.)

State/other agency unit/office	Murder and non-negligent man-slaughter	Rape (revised definition)[1]	Robbery	Aggravated as-sault	Burglary	Larceny-theft	Motor vehicle theft	Arson[2]
Jackson County	0		0	1	3	8	2	0
Jasper County	0		0	0	0	3	2	
Jay County	0		0	0	1	5	0	
Jefferson County	0		1	0	6	10	1	
Jennings County	0		0	2	4	5	1	0
Johnson County	0		0	4	0	2	3	0
Knox County	0		0	3	0	14	1	0
Kosciusko County	0		0	3	0	7	1	0
LaGrange County	0		0	2	7	15	2	
Lake County	2		1	4	0	21	22	0
La Porte County	0		1	5	0	7	4	0
Lawrence County	0		0	1	7	8	2	0
Madison County	0		0	1	4	19	2	0
Marion County	0		4	8	3	119	133	0
Marshall County	0		0	2	2	9	0	0
Martin County	0		0	6	3	3	0	0
Miami County	0		0	4	3	17	2	0
Monroe County	0		0	0	5	15	6	0
Montgomery County	0		0	9	1	3	0	0
Morgan County	0		0	4	1	7	7	0
Newton County	0		0	1	0	1	0	
Noble County	0		0	0	3	5	0	0
Orange County	0		0	3	3	9	0	0
Owen County	0		0	1	5	8	0	0
Parke County	0		0	3	1	4	0	
Perry County	0		0	2	0	7	0	0
Pike County	1		0	6	2	9	0	
Porter County	0		1	1	1	12	6	0
Posey County	0		0	1	0	7	1	
Pulaski County	0		0	2	0	3	0	
Putnam County	0		0	3	2	18	2	0
Ripley County	0		0	2	20	32	6	0
Rush County	0		0	0	1	0	0	
Scott County	0		0	3	0	9	4	0
Shelby County	0		0	2	1	2	1	0
Spencer County	0		1	1	1	3	1	0
Starke County	0		0	1	0	2	0	0
Steuben County	1		0	3	2	13	2	0
St. Joseph County	0		0	0	1	13	2	0
Sullivan County	0		1	4	0	8	1	1
Switzerland County	0		0	1	2	4	0	
Tippecanoe County	0		0	4	0	21	2	0
Tipton County	0		1	0	3	5	1	
Union County	0		0	1	0	2	0	
Vanderburgh County	0		0	4	0	18	0	0
Vermillion County	0		0	0	2	3	0	0
Vigo County	1		0	1	9	24	8	0
Wabash County	0		0	0	0	4	1	
Warren County	0		0	0	0	1	0	
Warrick County	0		0	1	2	6	0	
Washington County	0		0	3	1	8	1	0
Wayne County	1		0	3	2	9	1	0
Wells County	0		0	0	2	3	0	
White County	3		1	3	1	7	0	
Whitley County	0		0	1	1	5	3	0
Other Agencies								
Indianapolis International Airport	0		0	0	0	39	6	0
Kansas								
State Agencies								
Kansas Alcoholic Beverage Control	0	0	0	0	0	0	0	0
Kansas Department of Wildlife and Parks	0	1	0	6	0	22	1	0
Kansas Highway Patrol	1	0	0	31	2	47	18	0
Kansas Lottery Security Division	0	0	0	0	0	0	0	0
Tribal Agencies								
Potawatomi Tribal	0	0	0	5	2	47	3	0
Other Agencies								
Shawnee Mission Public Schools Unified School District	0	0	0	0	0	16	0	0
Goddard	0	0	0	0	0	31	0	0
Seaman	0	0	0	0	0	0	0	1
Kentucky								
State Agencies								
Alcohol Beverage Control	0	0	0	0	0	2	0	0
Kentucky Fairgrounds Security	0	0	0	0	0	5	0	0
Kentucky Horse Park	0	0	0	0	1	38	0	0

Table 11.   Offenses Known to Law Enforcement, by Selected State, Tribal, and Other Agencies, 2013— continued

(Number.)

State/other agency unit/office	Murder and non-negligent man-slaughter	Rape (revised definition)[1]	Robbery	Aggravated as-sault	Burglary	Larceny-theft	Motor vehicle theft	Arson[2]
Motor Vehicle Enforcement	0	0	0	1	1	15	10	0
State Police								
Ashland	4	26	4	16	85	120	20	4
Bowling Green	0	32	4	19	71	58	15	11
Campbellsburg	1	17	3	15	80	60	12	2
Cannabis Suppression Section	0	0	0	0	0	0	0	0
Columbia	7	56	1	23	96	49	7	20
Drug Enforcement Area 2	0	0	0	0	0	8	0	0
Dry Ridge	0	30	5	17	172	141	23	14
Electronic Crimes	0	0	0	0	0	0	0	0
Elizabethtown	5	36	7	13	101	121	18	1
Frankfort	1	24	2	7	66	79	7	5
Harlan	6	30	9	22	141	154	26	5
Hazard	8	18	11	39	155	121	45	4
Henderson	0	10	0	6	36	56	7	2
London	1	33	6	20	140	143	36	17
Madisonville	3	16	0	7	63	64	14	19
Mayfield	0	29	4	29	68	92	10	6
Morehead	4	50	4	20	182	116	25	8
Pikeville	4	30	38	52	251	200	113	8
Richmond	5	37	5	25	200	192	31	10
Special Investigations	0	0	0	0	0	0	2	0
West Drug Enforcement Branch	0	0	0	0	0	1	0	0
Unlawful Narcotics Investigation, Treatment and Education	0	0	0	0	0	1	0	0
Other Agencies								
Barren County Drug Task Force	0	0	0	0	1	1	0	1
Buffalo Trace-Gateway Narcotics Task Force	0	0	0	0	0	0	0	0
Cincinnati-Northern Kentucky International Airport	0	0	0	0	1	65	0	0
Fayette County Schools	0	1	2	3	13	192	0	2
FIVCO Area Drug Task Force	0	0	0	0	0	2	0	0
Greater Hardin County Narcotics Task Force	0	0	0	1	0	2	0	0
Jefferson County Board of Education	0	0	0	14	36	48	0	1
Lee County Constable, District	0	0	0	0	1	0	2	0
Lexington Bluegrass Airport	0	0	1	0	0	11	32	0
McCracken County Public Schools	0	0	0	0	0	3	0	0
Montgomery County School District	0	0	0	0	0	4	0	0
Northern Kentucky Narcotics Enforcement Unit	0	0	0	1	0	0	0	0
Pennyrile Narcotics Task Force	0	0	0	0	0	5	0	0
South Central Kentucky Drug Task Force	0	0	0	0	0	4	1	0
Warren County Constable, District	0	0	0	0	0	2	0	0
Louisiana								
State Agency								
Tensas Basin Levee District	0		0	0	0	0	0	0
Tribal Agencies								
Chitimacha Tribal	0		0	2	4	42	4	0
Coushatta Tribal	0		0	0	7	200	3	0
Tunica-Biloxi Tribal	0		0	8	0	117	2	0
Maine								
State Agencies								
Drug Enforcement Agency								
Androscoggin County	0		0	0	0	0	0	0
Aroostook County	0		0	0	0	0	0	0
Cumberland County	0		0	0	0	1	0	0
Franklin County	0		0	0	0	0	0	0
Hancock County	0		0	0	0	0	0	0
Kennebec County	0		0	0	0	0	0	0
Knox County	0		0	0	0	0	0	0
Lincoln County	0		0	0	0	0	0	0
Oxford County	0		0	0	0	0	0	0
Penobscot County	0		0	0	0	1	0	0
Piscataquis County	0		0	0	0	0	0	0
Sagadahoc County	0		0	0	0	0	0	0
Somerset County	0		0	0	0	0	0	0
Waldo County	0		0	0	0	0	0	0
Washington County	0		0	0	0	0	0	0
York County	0		0	0	0	0	0	0
State Police								
Androscoggin County	1		1	3	36	65	8	3
Aroostook County	4		0	8	125	136	7	4
Cumberland County	1		0	3	14	24	5	0
Franklin County	0		0	6	32	37	2	0
Hancock County	1		0	8	84	103	8	0

Table 11. Offenses Known to Law Enforcement, by Selected State, Tribal, and Other Agencies, 2013— continued

(Number.)

State/other agency unit/office	Murder and non-negligent man-slaughter	Rape (revised definition)[1]	Robbery	Aggravated as-sault	Burglary	Larceny-theft	Motor vehicle theft	Arson[2]
Kennebec County	1		1	9	98	200	12	2
Knox County	1		0	0	0	3	0	0
Lincoln County	0		0	1	1	0	0	0
Oxford County	0		1	8	66	100	8	0
Penobscot County	2		2	10	107	178	11	2
Piscataquis County	0		0	0	3	1	0	0
Sagadahoc County	0		0	1	1	1	1	0
Somerset County	1		1	4	32	124	8	0
Waldo County	0		0	2	24	81	10	0
Washington County	0		0	11	57	64	8	0
York County	0		0	26	101	118	11	0
State Police Computer Crimes Task Force								
Androscoggin County	0		0	0	0	0	0	0
Aroostook County	0		0	0	0	0	0	0
Cumberland County	0		0	0	0	0	0	0
Franklin County	0		0	0	0	0	0	0
Hancock County	0		0	0	0	0	0	0
Kennebec County	0		0	0	0	0	0	0
Knox County	0		0	0	0	0	0	0
Lincoln County	0		0	0	0	0	0	0
Oxford County	0		0	0	0	0	0	0
Penobscot County	0		0	0	0	0	0	0
Piscataquis County	0		0	0	0	0	0	0
Sagadahoc County	0		0	0	0	0	0	0
Somerset County	0		0	0	0	0	0	0
Waldo County	0		0	0	0	0	0	0
Washington County	0		0	0	0	0	0	0
York County	0		0	0	0	0	0	0
Tribal Agencies								
Passamaquoddy Indian Township	0		0	2	6	25	2	4
Passamaquoddy Pleasant Point Tribal	0		0	3	7	0	0	4
Penobscot Nation	0		0	4	14	21	2	2
Maryland								
State Agencies								
Comptroller of the Treasury, Field Enforcement Division	0		0	0	0	0	0	0
Department of Public Safety and Correctional Services, Internal Investigations Unit	0		0	506	0	5	0	0
General Services								
Annapolis, Anne Arundel County	0		0	0	0	19	0	0
Baltimore City	0		3	0	1	23	0	0
Maryland State Police Statewide	0		0	1	0	2	0	0
Natural Resources Police	0		1	4	24	225	0	16
Springfield Hospital	0		0	0	0	6	0	0
State Fire Marshal	0		0	0	0	0	0	0
State Police								
Allegany County	3		7	16	76	408	13	9
Anne Arundel County	1		0	5	4	29	9	0
Baltimore City	0		0	1	0	0	0	0
Baltimore County	0		0	12	3	39	11	1
Calvert County	1		1	6	38	141	4	10
Caroline County	0		0	5	53	58	6	1
Carroll County	1		5	36	83	332	14	2
Cecil County	3		24	87	204	486	28	12
Charles County	1		0	0	0	3	0	16
Dorchester County	0		4	3	31	35	5	1
Frederick County	0		10	40	97	283	12	4
Garrett County	0		2	44	65	105	11	3
Harford County	0		22	23	40	228	15	14
Howard County	1		0	3	0	11	0	4
Kent County	0		1	11	11	19	1	0
Montgomery County	0		0	2	0	19	3	0
Prince George's County	0		1	8	0	20	21	0
Queen Anne's County	1		6	31	45	123	10	3
Somerset County	2		3	17	59	99	3	9
St. Mary's County	1		7	20	49	219	13	11
Talbot County	1		0	5	41	44	3	0
Washington County	1		3	30	52	142	14	62
Wicomico County	1		7	41	118	154	14	11
Worcester County	0		1	18	58	119	8	4
Transit Administration	0		0	0	0	0	0	0
Transportation Authority	0		0	5	2	175	25	0
Other Agencies								
Maryland-National Capital Park Police								
Montgomery County	0		17	4	13	168	2	1

Table 11. Offenses Known to Law Enforcement, by Selected State, Tribal, and Other Agencies, 2013— continued

(Number.)

State/other agency unit/office	Murder and non-negligent man-slaughter	Rape (revised definition)	Robbery	Aggravated as-sault	Burglary	Larceny-theft	Motor vehicle theft	Arson[2]
Prince George's County	1		45	26	8	237	4	0
Massachusetts								
State Agencies								
Division of Law Enforcement, Environmental Police	0	0	1	5	7	9	1	1
Massachusetts Bay Transportation Authority								
Bristol County	0		0	0	0	9	12	
Essex County	0		1	1	0	18	1	
Middlesex County	0		10	5	3	106	3	
Norfolk County	0		6	11	1	85	1	
Plymouth County	0		0	1	0	17	1	
Suffolk County	1		171	92	5	286	3	0
Worcester County	0		0	0	1	4	1	
State Police								
Hampshire County	0		0	6	0	0	0	
Tribal Agency								
Wampanoag Tribe of Gay Head	0		0	0	0	0	0	0
Michigan								
State Agencies								
State Police								
Alcona County	0	4	0	0	1	4	0	0
Alger County	0	4	1	7	21	28	1	1
Allegan County	1	39	1	42	127	201	25	2
Alpena County	0	11	1	12	28	96	5	0
Antrim County	0	7	0	0	8	13	0	0
Arenac County	0	2	0	2	4	10	1	1
Baraga County	0	5	1	5	11	15	0	1
Barry County	0	11	2	27	58	94	11	3
Bay County	0	26	2	19	78	145	20	1
Benzie County	1	3	0	1	5	4	0	0
Berrien County	0	18	2	24	62	131	9	2
Branch County	0	27	1	22	59	114	16	3
Calhoun County	0	21	0	26	65	93	13	2
Cass County	0	2	0	6	11	24	2	0
Charlevoix County	0	5	0	0	4	6	2	0
Cheboygan County	0	5	0	8	15	22	4	0
Chippewa County	1	9	0	17	31	58	6	1
Clare County	0	14	1	2	33	26	2	1
Clinton County	0	8	0	3	4	11	0	0
Crawford County	0	6	0	1	3	7	1	0
Delta County	0	6	0	17	27	54	4	2
Dickinson County	0	9	0	1	13	31	6	0
Eaton County	0	9	0	3	18	73	7	2
Emmet County	0	15	0	3	16	88	3	1
Genesee County	1	29	4	45	58	78	17	3
Gladwin County	0	14	0	11	11	14	0	2
Gogebic County	1	1	0	2	4	27	0	1
Grand Traverse County	0	9	1	7	17	52	5	0
Gratiot County	0	7	0	19	23	53	5	0
Hillsdale County	0	12	1	12	48	57	11	3
Houghton County	0	6	0	8	19	50	2	0
Huron County	1	0	0	3	3	6	1	0
Ingham County	0	7	1	7	47	39	2	0
Ionia County	2	15	0	22	60	109	8	2
Iosco County	0	11	0	26	63	75	3	6
Iron County	0	3	0	1	19	19	1	0
Isabella County	0	8	2	10	38	112	9	3
Jackson County	0	30	3	37	71	147	15	2
Kalamazoo County	0	9	1	13	19	31	3	0
Kalkaska County	0	4	0	9	23	39	2	0
Kent County	0	8	0	2	0	28	1	0
Lake County	0	6	0	0	12	9	2	0
Lapeer County	0	16	0	18	34	60	4	1
Leelanau County	0	1	0	0	1	4	0	0
Lenawee County	2	38	0	42	41	69	7	0
Livingston County	1	27	1	37	82	224	23	0
Luce County	0	9	0	11	29	34	4	0
Mackinac County	0	7	0	5	19	17	1	1
Macomb County	1	13	0	14	60	70	7	1
Manistee County	1	7	0	8	36	64	7	0
Marquette County	0	14	2	13	51	108	8	2
Mason County	2	8	0	1	14	42	0	1
Mecosta County	0	8	0	4	25	66	4	0
Menominee County	0	1	0	3	18	24	3	0
Midland County	0	10	0	1	0	1	2	1
Missaukee County	0	3	0	1	4	10	1	0

Table 11.   Offenses Known to Law Enforcement, by Selected State, Tribal, and Other Agencies, 2013— continued

(Number.)

State/other agency unit/office	Murder and non-negligent man-slaughter	Rape (revised definition)	Robbery	Aggravated as-sault	Burglary	Larceny-theft	Motor vehicle theft	Arson[2]
Monroe County	3	10	4	28	52	141	16	3
Montcalm County	0	37	0	35	101	143	15	2
Montmorency County	0	1	0	2	8	2	0	1
Muskegon County	2	27	0	20	66	138	13	2
Newaygo County	1	25	1	19	93	129	9	1
Oakland County	0	17	3	20	87	138	16	1
Oceana County	0	8	0	7	29	44	0	2
Ogemaw County	0	20	2	5	48	57	7	4
Ontonagon County	0	2	0	2	10	14	3	0
Osceola County	0	12	0	4	28	34	2	2
Oscoda County	0	1	0	2	3	3	1	0
Otsego County	0	11	0	9	34	63	6	1
Ottawa County	0	4	0	4	1	2	0	1
Presque Isle County	0	1	0	1	6	4	1	0
Roscommon County	0	6	1	18	39	75	4	1
Saginaw County	7	23	7	41	55	80	15	21
Sanilac County	0	8	0	6	23	37	3	0
Schoolcraft County	0	4	0	4	21	37	3	0
Shiawassee County	0	5	0	8	38	75	6	0
St. Clair County	0	8	0	6	44	54	10	2
St. Joseph County	0	12	1	23	81	100	17	0
Tuscola County	0	13	0	20	41	44	3	1
Van Buren County	2	24	0	38	114	135	18	2
Washtenaw County	0	15	0	29	46	68	20	3
Wayne County	6	19	10	41	2	255	41	1
Wexford County	0	16	1	13	40	142	7	0
Tribal Agencies								
Bay Mills Tribal	0		0	2	0	13	0	3
Grand Traverse Tribal	1		0	4	3	16	0	0
Keweenaw Bay Tribal	0		0	1	0	18	0	0
Lac Vieux Desert Tribal	0		0	6	2	19	1	4
Little River Band of Ottawa Indians	0	0	0	0	0	31	0	0
Nottawaseppi Huron Band of Pota-watomi	0	0	0	5	2	52	0	1
Pokagon Tribal	0		0	8	3	123	1	0
Saginaw Chippewa Tribal	0		3	12	32	94	18	0
Sault Ste. Marie Tribal	0		0	3	4	59	1	2
Other Agencies								
Bishop International Airport	0	0	0	0	0	1	6	0
Gerald R. Ford International Airport	0	0	0	0	0	11	6	0
Huron-Clinton Metropolitan Author-ity								
Hudson Metropark	0	0	0	0	1	0	0	0
Kensington Metropark	0	0	0	1	0	6	0	0
Lower Huron Metropark	0	0	0	1	0	21	0	0
Stony Creek Metropark	0	0	0	1	0	21	1	0
Wayne County Airport	0	0	0	4	1	125	81	0
Minnesota								
State Agencies								
Capitol Security, St. Paul	0	0	0	0	0	16	1	0
Minnesota State Patrol	0	0	0	0	0	0	0	0
State Patrol								
Brainerd	0	0	0	0	0	0	0	0
Detroit Lakes	0	0	0	0	0	0	0	0
Duluth	0	0	0	0	0	0	1	0
Golden Valley	0	0	0	0	0	0	0	0
Mankato	0	0	0	0	0	0	0	0
Marshall	0	0	0	0	0	0	0	0
Oakdale	0	0	0	0	0	0	0	0
Rochester	0	0	0	0	0	0	0	0
St. Cloud	0	0	0	0	0	0	0	0
Thief River Falls	0	0	0	0	0	0	0	0
Virginia	0	0	0	0	0	0	0	0
Tribal Agencies								
Fond du Lac Tribal	0	1	0	7	8	85	4	0
Lower Sioux Tribal	0		5	9	3	34	8	3
Mille Lacs Tribal	0	0	0	23	9	41	5	6
Nett Lake Tribal	0		0	5	9	16	5	0
Red Lake Agency	1		8	91	93	313	38	18
Upper Sioux Community	0	0	0	0	0	0	0	0
White Earth Tribal	0		0	17	65	142	23	2
Other Agencies								
Minneapolis-St. Paul International Airport	0	0	0	5	1	263	52	0
Three Rivers Park District	0	1	0	2	0	59	0	1
Mississippi								
State Agency								

Table 11. Offenses Known to Law Enforcement, by Selected State, Tribal, and Other Agencies, 2013— continued

(Number.)

State/other agency unit/office	Murder and non-negligent man-slaughter	Rape (revised definition)[1]	Robbery	Aggravated assault	Burglary	Larceny-theft	Motor vehicle theft	Arson[2]
State Capitol Police	0		0	0	9	18	5	0
Tribal Agency								
Choctaw Tribal	0		0	72	83	64	99	7
Other Agencies								
Singing River Health System	0		0	0	1	0	0	0
Missouri								
State Agencies								
Capitol Police	0	0	0	0	0	17	2	1
Department of Conservation	0	0	0	0	0	0	0	0
Department of Social Services, State Technical Assistance	0	0	0	1	0	0	0	0
Division of Alcohol and Tobacco Control	0	0	0	0	0	0	0	0
Gaming Commission, Enforcement Division	0	0	2	8	0	293	3	0
State Fire Marshal	0	0	0	0	0	0	0	220
State Highway Patrol								
Jefferson City	0	0	0	5	3	42	13	0
Kirkwood	1	0	0	5	1	2	3	0
Lee's Summit	2	0	1	5	0	10	14	0
Macon	3	1	2	8	2	7	3	0
Poplar Bluff	0	2	0	4	3	9	11	0
Rolla	1	1	0	3	0	4	2	1
Springfield	0	0	0	9	0	45	15	0
St. Joseph	0	3	0	12	0	10	16	0
Willow Springs	0	0	0	8	1	1	5	0
State Park Rangers	0	0	0	0	7	95	0	0
Other Agencies								
Clay County Drug Task Force	0	0	0	0	0	0	0	0
Clay County Park Authority	0	0	0	0	0	7	0	0
Jackson County Drug Task Force	0	0	0	0	0	0	0	0
Jackson County Park Rangers	0	0	0	0	0	0	0	0
Lambert-St. Louis International Airport	0	0	0	3	0	194	2	0
Platte County Multi-Jurisdictional Enforcement Group	0	0	0	0	0	0	0	0
Springfield-Branson Airport	0	0	0	1	0	10	1	0
St. Charles County Park Rangers	0	0	0	0	0	0	0	0
St. Peters Ranger Division	0	0	0	0	1	15	0	0
Western Missouri Cyber Crimes Task Force	0	0	0	0	0	0	0	0
Montana								
Tribal Agencies								
Blackfeet Agency	2		5	40	48	12	87	3
Crow Agency	1		0	19	18	30	2	1
Fort Belknap Tribal	0		0	14	1	36	1	1
Fort Peck Assiniboine and Sioux Tribes	0		2	41	63	69	23	2
Northern Cheyenne Agency	2		2	22	10	4	6	0
Rocky Boys Tribal	1		1	33	45	35	5	6
Nebraska								
State Agencies								
Nebraska State Patrol	0		0	2	0	6	0	0
State Patrol								
Adams County	0		0	0	0	1	0	0
Antelope County	0		0	0	1	1	0	0
Arthur County	0		0	0	0	0	0	0
Banner County	0		0	0	0	1	0	0
Blaine County	0		0	0	0	0	0	0
Boone County	0		0	0	0	0	0	0
Box Butte County	0		0	0	0	0	0	0
Boyd County	0		0	0	0	0	0	0
Brown County	0		0	0	0	0	0	0
Buffalo County	0		0	2	0	1	1	0
Burt County	0		0	0	0	0	0	0
Butler County	0		0	0	2	2	0	0
Cass County	0		0	0	0	3	2	0
Cedar County	0		0	0	0	0	0	0
Chase County	0		0	0	0	1	0	0
Cherry County	0		0	0	0	0	0	0
Cheyenne County	0		0	0	0	3	0	0
Clay County	0		0	0	0	0	0	0
Colfax County	0		0	0	0	0	0	0
Cuming County	0		0	0	0	0	0	0
Custer County	0		0	0	0	0	0	0
Dakota County	0		0	0	0	0	0	0
Dawes County	0		0	0	0	0	0	0
Dawson County	0		0	0	0	0	0	0

Table 11.   Offenses Known to Law Enforcement, by Selected State, Tribal, and Other Agencies, 2013— continued

(Number.)

State/other agency unit/office	Murder and non-negligent man-slaughter	Rape (revised definition)[1]	Robbery	Aggravated as-sault	Burglary	Larceny-theft	Motor vehicle theft	Arson[2]
Deuel County	0		0	0	0	0	0	0
Dixon County	0		0	0	0	0	0	0
Dodge County	0		0	0	0	0	0	0
Douglas County	0		0	0	0	4	1	0
Dundy County	0		0	0	0	0	0	0
Fillmore County	0		0	0	0	0	0	0
Franklin County	0		0	0	1	0	0	0
Frontier County	0		0	0	0	0	0	0
Furnas County	0		0	0	1	0	0	0
Gage County	0		0	0	0	0	0	0
Garden County	0		0	1	0	0	0	0
Garfield County	0		0	0	0	0	0	0
Gosper County	0		0	0	0	0	0	0
Grant County	0		0	0	0	0	0	0
Greeley County	0		0	0	0	0	0	0
Hall County	0		0	1	1	4	0	0
Hamilton County	0		0	0	0	0	0	0
Harlan County	0		0	0	0	0	0	0
Hayes County	0		0	0	0	0	0	0
Hitchcock County	0		0	0	2	0	0	0
Holt County	0		0	0	0	0	0	0
Hooker County	0		0	0	0	0	0	0
Howard County	0		0	0	0	0	1	0
Jefferson County	0		0	0	0	0	1	0
Johnson County	0		0	0	0	0	0	0
Kearney County	0		0	0	0	0	0	0
Keith County	0		0	0	0	0	0	0
Keya Paha County	0		0	0	0	0	0	0
Kimball County	0		0	0	0	0	0	0
Knox County	0		0	0	0	0	0	0
Lancaster County	0		0	0	0	6	0	0
Lincoln County	0		0	1	1	1	1	1
Logan County	0		0	0	0	0	0	0
Loup County	0		0	0	0	0	0	0
Madison County	0		0	0	2	1	0	0
McPherson County	0		0	0	0	0	0	0
Merrick County	0		0	0	0	1	0	0
Morrill County	0		0	0	0	1	0	0
Nance County	0		0	0	0	0	0	0
Nemaha County	0		0	0	0	0	0	0
Nuckolls County	0		0	0	0	0	0	0
Otoe County	0		0	0	0	0	0	0
Pawnee County	0		1	0	0	0	0	0
Perkins County	0		0	0	0	0	0	0
Phelps County	0		0	0	0	0	0	0
Pierce County	0		0	1	0	1	0	0
Platte County	0		0	0	0	0	0	0
Polk County	0		0	0	0	0	0	0
Red Willow County	0		0	0	0	1	0	0
Richardson County	0		0	0	0	0	0	0
Rock County	0		0	0	0	0	0	0
Saline County	0		0	0	0	0	0	0
Sarpy County	0		0	1	0	2	0	0
Saunders County	0		0	1	0	3	0	0
Scotts Bluff County	0		0	1	0	1	0	0
Seward County	0		0	0	0	1	0	0
Sheridan County	0		0	1	0	0	0	0
Sherman County	0		0	0	0	0	0	0
Sioux County	0		0	0	0	0	0	0
Stanton County	0		0	0	0	0	0	0
Thayer County	0		0	0	0	0	0	0
Thomas County	0		0	0	0	1	0	0
Thurston County	0		0	0	0	0	0	0
Valley County	0		0	0	0	1	0	0
Washington County	0		0	0	0	0	0	0
Wayne County	0		0	0	4	0	0	0
Webster County	0		0	0	0	0	0	0
Wheeler County	0		0	0	0	0	0	0
York County	0		0	0	0	0	1	0
Tribal Agencies								
Santee Tribal	0		1	34	10	11	1	0
Winnebago Tribal	0		0	35	10	9	5	4
Nevada								
Tribal Agencies								
Duckwater Tribal	0		0	0	0	1	0	0
Eastern Nevada Agency	0		0	7	6	15	2	0
Ely Shoshone Tribal	0		0	0	3	2	0	0

Table 11.   Offenses Known to Law Enforcement, by Selected State, Tribal, and Other Agencies, 2013— continued

(Number.)

State/other agency unit/office	Murder and non-negligent man-slaughter	Rape (revised definition)[1]	Robbery	Aggravated as-sault	Burglary	Larceny-theft	Motor vehicle theft	Arson[2]
Fallon Tribal	0		1	3	3	16	1	0
Las Vegas Paiute Tribal	0		0	1	2	35	1	1
Lovelock Paiute Tribal	0		0	0	2	3	0	3
Moapa Tribal	0		2	3	3	10	2	8
Pyramid Lake Tribal	0		0	13	10	14	3	0
Reno-Sparks Indian Colony	1		0	3	2	236	1	0
South Fork Band Tribal	1		0	0	0	0	0	0
Walker River Tribal	0		0	10	18	4	5	1
Washoe Tribal	0		0	27	38	34	3	4
Western Nevada Agency	1		0	5	3	0	1	2
Western Shoshone Tribal	0		0	8	12	8	3	0
Yerington Paiute Tribal	0		0	3	6	3	3	0
Yomba Shoshone Tribal	0		0	7	1	0	0	0
Other Agencies								
Clark County School District	0		17	112	191	895	22	16
Washoe County School District	0		1	8	16	170	0	0
New Jersey								
State Agencies								
New Jersey Transit Police	0		69	15	13	384	19	2
Palisades Interstate Parkway	0		0	0	1	4	0	0
Port Authority of New York and New Jersey	0		11	35	7	416	29	0
State Police								
Bergen County	0		2	2	6	59	9	2
Hunterdon County	1		3	9	45	120	13	1
Other Agencies								
Park Police								
Union County	0		6	21	5	8	0	0
Prosecutor								
Atlantic County	0		0	0	0	0	0	0
Bergen County	0		0	0	0	0	0	0
Burlington County	0		0	0	0	0	0	0
Camden County	0		0	0	0	0	0	0
Cape May County	0		0	0	0	0	0	0
Cumberland County	0		0	0	0	0	0	0
Essex County	0		0	0	0	0	0	0
Hudson County	0		0	0	0	0	0	0
Hunterdon County	0		0	0	0	0	0	0
Mercer County	0		0	0	0	0	0	0
Middlesex County	0		0	0	0	0	0	0
Monmouth County	0		0	0	0	0	0	0
Morris County	0		0	0	0	0	0	0
Ocean County	0		0	0	0	0	0	0
Passaic County	0		0	0	0	0	0	0
Salem County	0		0	0	0	0	0	0
Somerset County	0		0	0	0	0	0	0
Sussex County	0		0	0	0	0	0	0
Union County	0		0	0	0	0	0	0
Warren County	0		0	0	0	0	0	0
New Mexico								
Tribal Agencies								
Isleta Tribal	0		0	65	35	115	12	1
Jemez Pueblo	0		0	19	12	6	1	1
Jicarilla Apache Tribal	0		0	0	0	0	0	0
Laguna Tribal	0		0	85	6	62	12	0
Mescalero Tribal	0		0	10	6	4	2	0
Northern Pueblos Agency	0		0	4	11	1	6	0
Ohkay Owingeh Tribal	0		1	9	6	16	2	0
Pojoaque Tribal	0		5	1	19	39	8	0
Ramah Navajo Tribal	0		0	3	0	0	1	0
Santa Ana Tribal	0		0	1	6	37	6	1
Santa Clara Pueblo	0		2	19	12	5	4	1
Southern Pueblos Agency	0		0	1	8	0	2	0
Taos Pueblo	0		0	8	2	1	2	0
Tesuque Pueblo	0		0	2	0	5	1	0
Zuni Tribal	0		1	37	2	0	1	0
New York								
State Agencies								
State Park								
New York City Region	0		5	1	0	105	0	
Niagara Region	0		2	0	4	58	2	
State Police								
Albany County	0		0	5	17	159	2	0
Allegany County	0		0	15	124	211	9	3
Broome County	0		3	28	156	448	19	4

Table 11.   Offenses Known to Law Enforcement, by Selected State, Tribal, and Other Agencies, 2013— continued

(Number.)

State/other agency unit/office	Murder and non-negligent man-slaughter	Rape (revised definition)[1]	Robbery	Aggravated as-sault	Burglary	Larceny-theft	Motor vehicle theft	Arson[2]
Cattaraugus County	0		3	11	58	277	10	1
Cayuga County	0		1	9	71	157	3	2
Chautauqua County	0		1	14	66	211	11	0
Chemung County	0		2	33	40	211	5	2
Chenango County	0		2	10	58	107	6	2
Clinton County	3		5	35	169	742	29	5
Columbia County	0		6	18	86	173	5	1
Cortland County	0		2	2	28	89	6	0
Delaware County	2		3	16	80	147	11	3
Dutchess County	3		10	66	131	424	23	3
Erie County	0		2	16	46	287	18	
Essex County	0		2	12	82	148	16	3
Franklin County	0		0	19	99	269	17	3
Fulton County	0		1	2	32	85	4	0
Genesee County	0		0	3	17	95	1	0
Greene County	1		2	26	146	239	23	7
Hamilton County	0		0	1	11	26	0	0
Herkimer County	4		1	21	126	164	11	3
Jefferson County	0		0	16	122	562	32	6
Lewis County	0		0	6	38	66	6	0
Livingston County	0		1	9	12	36	4	0
Madison County	1		0	8	48	123	7	2
Monroe County	0		1	0	1	66	8	0
Montgomery County	0		0	0	18	78	6	
Nassau County	1		0	0	0	4	1	0
New York County	0		0	2	0	44	0	0
Niagara County	0		6	4	18	171	6	0
Oneida County	1		2	43	145	401	30	4
Onondaga County	1		6	17	135	579	35	4
Ontario County	0		1	8	40	170	2	4
Orange County	4		15	36	112	754	18	4
Orleans County	0		0	6	15	27	3	0
Oswego County	0		4	23	196	462	35	7
Otsego County	0		1	12	67	277	4	1
Putnam County	0		3	4	18	66	6	0
Rensselaer County	2		0	17	113	344	21	1
Saratoga County	0		12	28	101	561	8	7
Schenectady County	0		0	2	6	97	4	0
Schoharie County	0		1	6	70	95	5	0
Schuyler County	0		0	1	9	16	2	0
Seneca County	1		1	25	42	106	0	1
Steuben County	1		0	30	94	284	13	9
St. Lawrence County	1		3	34	174	397	25	5
Suffolk County	0		6	5	11	31	6	
Sullivan County	0		1	36	148	228	19	3
Tioga County	0		0	2	28	68	14	0
Tompkins County	0		3	11	57	184	8	0
Ulster County	1		6	58	128	344	23	1
Warren County	0		1	6	19	186	1	0
Washington County	0		2	4	45	105	10	1
Wayne County	2		7	23	169	321	17	3
Westchester County	0		8	33	77	279	11	0
Wyoming County	0		0	13	13	36	2	1
Tribal Agencies								
Oneida Indian Nation	0		0	7	6	282	2	0
St. Regis Tribal	0		0	0	28	74	17	29
Other Agencies								
New York City Department of Environmental Protection Police								
Delaware County	0		0	0	0	0	0	0
Westchester County	0		0	0	0	2	0	0
New York City Metropolitan Transportation Authority	1		39	21	9	595	7	
Onondaga County Parks	0		0	0	4	60	0	0
Suffolk County Parks	0		0	0	1	35	0	0
North Carolina								
State Agencies								
North Carolina Highway Patrol	0		0	0	0	0	0	0
State Park Rangers								
Chimney Rock	0		0	0	0	0	0	0
Elk Knob	0		0	0	0	0	0	0
Fort Fisher	0		0	0	0	0	0	0
Fort Macon	0		0	0	0	0	0	0
Hanging Rock	0		0	0	0	0	0	0
Haw River	0		0	0	0	0	0	0
New River-Mount Jefferson	0		0	0	0	0	0	0
Tribal Agency								
Cherokee Tribal	2		4	86	126	512	26	6

Table 11. Offenses Known to Law Enforcement, by Selected State, Tribal, and Other Agencies, 2013— continued
(Number.)

State/other agency unit/office	Murder and non-negligent man-slaughter	Rape (revised definition)	Robbery	Aggravated assault	Burglary	Larceny-theft	Motor vehicle theft	Arson[2]
Other Agencies								
Pitt County Memorial Hospital	0		2	4	1	67	0	0
Raleigh-Durham International Airport	0		1	0	0	73	7	0
Triad Alcohol Beverage Control Law Enforcement	0		0	1	0	10	0	0
North Dakota								
State Agencies								
North Dakota Highway Patrol	0	0	0	2	0	2	2	0
Tribal Agencies								
Standing Rock Agency	1		2	171	88	98	42	10
Turtle Mountain Agency	2		3	74	117	334	101	54
Ohio								
State Agencies								
Ohio Investigative Unit	0	0	0	0	0	0	0	0
Ohio State Highway Patrol	3	56	13	342	14	242	66	3
Other Agencies								
Hamilton County Park District	0	0	0	0	1	57	0	1
Holden Arboretum	0		0	0	0	1	0	0
Lake Metroparks	0		0	0	0	12	0	0
Medina County Park District	0		0	0	0	0	0	
Robinson Memorial Hospital	0		1	0	0	7	0	0
Toledo Fire Department, Fire Investigation Unit	0		0	0	0	0	0	368
Oklahoma								
State Agencies								
Capitol Park Police	0		0	0	0	5	1	0
Department of Agriculture, Forestry Service	0	0	0	0	4	34	0	16
Grand River Dam Authority, Lake Patrol	0	0	0	0	3	0	0	0
Tribal Agencies								
Absentee Shawnee Tribal	0		0	4	19	15	8	0
Anadarko Agency	0		0	4	13	26	6	1
Cherokee Nation	0		1	3	9	10	7	3
Chickasaw Nation	0		4	53	75	570	58	0
Choctaw Nation	1		0	0	31	305	6	0
Citizen Potawatomi Nation	0		2	4	15	176	12	0
Comanche Nation	0	0	1	4	8	52	1	0
Concho Agency	0		0	5	1	5	2	2
Eastern Shawnee Tribal	0		0	0	0	25	1	0
Iowa Tribal	0		0	0	0	4	0	0
Kaw Tribal	0		0	0	0	1	0	0
Kickapoo Tribal	0		1	8	17	24	9	1
Miami Agency	0		0	2	6	17	10	0
Miami Tribal	0		0	0	0	1	0	0
Muscogee Nation Tribal	0		2	8	14	63	15	1
Osage Nation	0		2	10	27	79	18	2
Otoe-Missouria Tribal	0		0	2	3	9	3	0
Pawnee Agency	1		0	2	1	2	0	0
Pawnee Tribal	0		0	1	0	7	0	0
Ponca Tribal	0		0	4	11	7	4	0
Quapaw Tribal	0		1	2	6	59	5	0
Sac and Fox Tribal	0		0	2	13	11	1	0
Seminole Nation Lighthorse	0		0	0	1	12	0	0
Tonkawa Tribal	0	0	0	1	1	6	0	0
Wyandotte Nation	0	0	0	0	0	8	0	0
Other Agencies								
Jenks Public Schools	0		0	5	0	3	0	0
McAlester Public Schools	0	0	0	0	0	1	0	0
Norman Public Schools	0	0	0	0	3	19	0	0
Putnam City Campus	0	0	2	4	5	38	0	0
Oregon								
State Agency								
State Police								
Baker County	0		0	0	0	3	1	0
Benton County	0		0	1	3	57	3	0
Clackamas County	0		0	1	0	5	5	0
Clatsop County	0		0	0	0	0	0	0
Columbia County	0		0	0	0	0	1	0
Coos County	0		0	1	0	0	1	1
Crook County	0		0	1	0	1	0	0
Curry County	0		1	0	0	4	3	0
Deschutes County	0		0	0	0	6	3	0
Douglas County	0		0	4	0	5	2	0
Gilliam County	0		0	0	0	1	0	0

Table 11.   Offenses Known to Law Enforcement, by Selected State, Tribal, and Other Agencies, 2013— continued

(Number.)

State/other agency unit/office	Murder and non-negligent man-slaughter	Rape (revised definition)[1]	Robbery	Aggravated as-sault	Burglary	Larceny-theft	Motor vehicle theft	Arson[2]
Grant County	0		0	0	0	0	0	0
Harney County	0		0	1	0	0	0	0
Hood River County	0		0	1	0	2	0	0
Jackson County	0		0	0	0	2	3	0
Jefferson County	0		0	0	0	2	0	0
Josephine County	2		2	6	1	3	7	2
Klamath County	0		0	2	0	7	3	1
Lake County	0		0	0	0	0	0	0
Lane County	0		0	2	5	10	3	1
Lincoln County	0		0	0	0	0	0	0
Linn County	0		0	1	0	3	2	0
Malheur County	1		0	1	0	1	0	0
Marion County	1		0	6	2	13	4	0
Morrow County	0		0	0	0	0	0	0
Multnomah County	0		1	0	0	0	1	0
Polk County	0		0	1	0	0	0	0
Sherman County	0		0	0	0	0	0	0
Tillamook County	0		0	3	0	0	0	0
Umatilla County	0		1	1	0	2	2	0
Union County	0		0	0	0	3	3	0
Wallowa County	0		0	0	0	0	1	0
Wasco County	0		0	1	0	1	1	0
Washington County	0		0	0	0	2	1	0
Wheeler County	0		0	0	0	0	0	0
Yamhill County	0		0	0	0	0	1	0
Tribal Agencies								
Burns Paiute Tribal	0		0	4	4	5	2	1
Columbia River Inter-Tribal Fisher-ies Enforcement	0		0	14	12	43	13	0
Grand Ronde Tribal	0	1	0	0	1	46	2	0
Other Agencies								
Blue Mountain Enforcement Nar-cotics Team, Morrow County								
Morrow County	0	0	0	0	0	0	0	0
Umatilla County	0	0	0	0	0	0	0	0
Port of Portland	0		1	0	4	394	56	0
Pennsylvania								
State Agencies								
Bureau of Forestry								
Adams County	0	0	0	0	0	0	0	0
Allegheny County	0	0	0	0	0	0	0	0
Armstrong County	0	0	0	0	0	0	0	0
Beaver County	0	0	0	0	0	0	0	0
Bedford County	0	0	0	0	0	0	0	1
Berks County	0	0	0	0	0	0	0	1
Blair County	0	0	0	0	0	0	0	0
Bucks County	0	0	0	0	0	0	0	0
Butler County	0	0	0	0	0	0	0	0
Centre County	0	0	0	0	0	0	0	0
Crawford County	0	0	0	0	0	0	0	0
Cumberland County	0	0	0	0	0	0	0	0
Dauphin County	0	0	0	0	0	0	0	0
Delaware County	0	0	0	0	0	0	0	0
Erie County	0	0	0	0	0	0	0	0
Forest County	0	0	0	0	0	0	0	0
Fulton County	0	0	0	0	0	0	0	0
Greene County	0	0	0	0	0	0	0	0
Indiana County	0	0	0	0	0	0	0	0
Jefferson County	0	0	0	0	0	0	0	0
Juniata County	0	0	0	0	0	0	0	0
Lancaster County	0	0	0	0	0	0	0	0
Lebanon County	0	0	0	0	0	0	0	0
Lycoming County	0	0	0	0	0	0	0	0
McKean County	0	0	0	0	0	0	0	0
Mercer County	0	0	0	0	0	0	0	0
Mifflin County	0	0	0	0	0	0	0	0
Montgomery County	0	0	0	0	0	0	0	0
Montour County	0	0	0	0	0	0	0	0
Perry County	0	0	0	0	0	0	0	0
Potter County	0	0	0	0	0	0	0	0
Snyder County	0	0	0	0	0	0	0	0
Somerset County	0	0	0	0	0	0	0	0
Sullivan County	0	0	0	0	0	0	0	0
Susquehanna County	0	0	0	0	0	0	0	0
Union County	0	0	0	0	0	0	0	0
Warren County	0	0	0	0	0	0	0	0
Washington County	0	0	0	0	0	0	0	0
Wayne County	0	0	0	0	0	0	0	0

Table 11.   Offenses Known to Law Enforcement, by Selected State, Tribal, and Other Agencies, 2013— continued

(Number.)

State/other agency unit/office	Murder and non-negligent man-slaughter	Rape (revised definition)[1]	Robbery	Aggravated assault	Burglary	Larceny-theft	Motor vehicle theft	Arson[2]
Bureau of Narcotics								
Adams County	0	0	0	0	0	0	0	0
Allegheny County	0	0	0	0	0	0	0	0
Armstrong County	0	0	0	0	0	0	0	0
Beaver County	0	0	0	0	0	0	0	0
Bedford County	0	0	0	0	0	0	0	0
Berks County	0	0	0	0	0	0	0	0
Blair County	0	0	0	0	0	0	0	0
Bucks County	0	0	0	0	0	0	0	0
Butler County	0	0	0	0	0	0	0	0
Cambria County	0	0	0	0	0	0	0	0
Cameron County	0	0	0	0	0	0	0	0
Carbon County	0	0	0	0	0	0	0	0
Centre County	0	0	0	0	0	0	0	0
Clarion County	0	0	0	0	0	0	0	0
Clearfield County	0	0	0	0	0	0	0	0
Clinton County	0	0	0	0	0	0	0	0
Crawford County	0	0	0	0	0	0	0	0
Cumberland County	0	0	0	0	0	0	0	0
Dauphin County	0	0	0	0	0	0	0	0
Elk County	0	0	0	0	0	0	0	0
Erie County	0	0	0	0	0	0	0	0
Fayette County	0	0	0	0	0	0	0	0
Forest County	0	0	0	0	0	0	0	0
Franklin County	0	0	0	0	0	0	0	0
Fulton County	0	0	0	0	0	0	0	0
Greene County	0	0	0	0	0	0	0	0
Huntingdon County	0	0	0	0	0	0	0	0
Indiana County	0	0	0	0	0	0	0	0
Jefferson County	0	0	0	0	0	0	0	0
Juniata County	0	0	0	0	0	0	0	0
Lancaster County	0	0	0	0	0	0	0	0
Lawrence County	0	0	0	0	0	0	0	0
Lebanon County	0	0	0	0	0	0	0	0
Lehigh County	0	0	0	0	0	0	0	0
Lycoming County	0	0	0	0	0	0	0	0
McKean County	0	0	0	0	0	0	0	0
Mercer County	0	0	0	0	0	0	0	0
Mifflin County	0	0	0	0	0	0	0	0
Monroe County	0	0	0	0	0	0	0	0
Montgomery County	0	0	0	0	0	0	0	0
Montour County	0	0	0	0	0	0	0	0
Northampton County	0	0	0	0	0	0	0	0
Northumberland County	0	0	0	0	0	0	0	0
Perry County	0	0	0	0	0	0	0	0
Potter County	0	0	0	0	0	0	0	0
Schuylkill County	0	0	0	0	0	0	0	0
Snyder County	0	0	0	0	0	0	0	0
Somerset County	0	0	0	0	0	0	0	0
Tioga County	0	0	0	0	0	0	0	0
Union County	0	0	0	0	0	0	0	0
Venango County	0	0	0	0	0	0	0	0
Warren County	0	0	0	0	0	0	0	0
Washington County	0	0	0	0	0	0	0	0
Westmoreland County	0	0	0	0	0	0	0	0
York County	0	0	0	0	0	0	0	0
Pennsylvania Fish and Boat Commission	0	0	0	0	0	2	0	0
State Park Rangers								
Beltzville	0	0	0	1	0	8	0	0
Ben Rush	0	0	0	0	0	0	0	0
Black Moshannon	0	0	0	0	4	0	0	0
Caledonia	0	0	0	0	0	1	0	0
Codorus	0	0	0	0	0	11	0	0
Colonel Denning	0	0	0	0	0	0	0	0
Delaware Canal	0	1	0	0	0	3	0	1
Evansburg	0	0	0	0	0	0	0	0
Fort Washington	0	0	0	0	0	0	0	0
Frances Slocum	0	0	0	1	0	2	0	0
French Creek	0	0	0	0	0	0	0	0
Greenwood Furnace	0	0	0	0	0	0	0	0
Guifford Pinchot	0	1	0	0	2	3	0	0
Hickory Run	0	0	0	1	0	10	0	0
Keystone	0	0	0	0	0	2	0	0
Kings Gap Environmental Education Center	0	0	0	0	0	0	0	0
Kooser	0	0	0	0	0	0	0	0
Lackawanna	0	0	0	0	0	0	0	0
Laurel Hill	0	0	0	0	0	5	0	0

Table 11.　Offenses Known to Law Enforcement, by Selected State, Tribal, and Other Agencies, 2013— continued

(Number.)

State/other agency unit/office	Murder and non-negligent man-slaughter	Rape (revised definition)[1]	Robbery	Aggravated as-sault	Burglary	Larceny-theft	Motor vehicle theft	Arson[2]
Laurel Ridge	0	0	0	0	0	1	0	0
Linn Run	0	0	0	0	0	1	0	0
Little Buffalo	0	0	0	0	0	1	0	0
Marsh Creek	0	0	0	0	0	0	0	0
Maurice K. Goddard	0	0	0	0	0	0	0	0
Neshaminy	0	0	0	2	0	3	2	0
Nockamixon	0	0	0	0	0	0	0	0
Ohiopyle	0	0	0	1	4	5	0	0
Oil Creek	0	0	0	0	0	0	0	0
Pine Grove Furnace	0	0	0	0	0	0	0	0
Presque Isle	0	0	0	0	0	29	1	0
Prince Gallitzin	0	0	0	0	0	0	0	0
Pymatuning	0	0	0	0	1	35	0	0
Raccoon	0	0	0	0	1	6	0	0
Ricketts Glen	0	0	0	0	0	0	0	0
Ridley Creek	0	0	0	0	0	4	0	0
Tobyhanna	0	0	0	0	0	0	0	0
Tuscarora	0	0	0	0	0	2	0	0
Tyler	0	0	0	0	0	3	0	0
White Clay	0	0	0	0	0	0	0	0
Worlds End	0	0	0	0	0	1	0	0
State Police, Bureau of Criminal Investigation								
Adams County	0	0	0	0	0	0	0	0
Allegheny County	0	1	0	0	0	14	3	0
Armstrong County	0	0	0	0	0	0	2	0
Beaver County	0	0	0	0	0	8	2	0
Bedford County	0	0	0	0	0	0	0	0
Berks County	0	0	0	0	0	0	0	0
Blair County	0	0	0	0	0	0	0	0
Bradford County	0	0	0	0	0	0	0	0
Bucks County	0	0	0	0	0	0	0	0
Butler County	0	0	0	0	0	5	1	0
Cambria County	0	0	0	0	0	1	0	0
Cameron County	0	0	0	0	0	0	0	0
Carbon County	0	0	0	0	0	0	0	0
Centre County	0	0	0	0	0	1	0	0
Chester County	0	0	0	0	0	0	0	0
Clarion County	0	0	0	0	0	0	0	0
Clearfield County	0	0	0	0	0	0	0	0
Clinton County	0	0	0	0	0	0	0	0
Columbia County	0	0	0	0	0	0	0	0
Crawford County	0	0	0	0	0	0	0	0
Cumberland County	0	0	0	0	0	0	0	0
Dauphin County	0	0	0	0	0	2	0	0
Delaware County	0	0	0	0	0	0	0	0
Elk County	0	0	0	0	0	0	0	0
Erie County	0	0	0	0	0	0	0	0
Fayette County	0	0	0	0	1	0	1	0
Forest County	0	0	0	0	0	0	0	0
Franklin County	0	0	0	0	0	0	0	0
Fulton County	0	0	0	0	0	0	0	0
Greene County	0	0	0	0	1	0	0	0
Huntingdon County	0	0	0	0	0	0	0	0
Indiana County	0	0	0	0	0	1	0	0
Jefferson County	0	0	0	0	0	0	0	0
Juniata County	0	0	0	0	0	0	0	0
Lackawanna County	0	1	0	0	0	0	0	0
Lancaster County	0	0	0	0	0	0	0	0
Lawrence County	0	0	0	0	0	1	0	0
Lebanon County	0	0	0	0	0	0	0	0
Lehigh County	0	0	0	0	0	0	0	0
Luzerne County	0	0	0	0	0	0	0	0
Lycoming County	0	0	0	0	0	0	0	0
McKean County	0	0	0	0	0	0	0	0
Mercer County	0	0	0	0	0	0	1	0
Mifflin County	0	0	0	0	0	0	0	0
Monroe County	0	0	0	0	0	0	0	0
Montgomery County	0	0	0	0	0	0	0	0
Montour County	0	0	0	0	0	0	0	0
Northampton County	0	0	0	0	0	0	0	0
Northumberland County	0	0	0	0	0	0	0	0
Perry County	0	0	0	0	0	0	0	0
Philadelphia County	0	0	0	0	0	0	0	0
Pike County	0	0	0	0	0	0	0	0
Potter County	0	0	0	0	0	0	0	0
Schuylkill County	0	0	0	0	0	0	0	0
Snyder County	0	0	0	0	0	0	0	0

Table 11.   Offenses Known to Law Enforcement, by Selected State, Tribal, and Other Agencies, 2013— continued

(Number.)

State/other agency unit/office	Murder and non-negligent man-slaughter	Rape (revised definition)[1]	Robbery	Aggravated as-sault	Burglary	Larceny-theft	Motor vehicle theft	Arson[2]
Somerset County	0	0	0	0	0	0	0	0
Sullivan County	0	0	0	0	0	0	0	0
Susquehanna County	0	0	0	0	0	0	0	0
Tioga County	0	0	0	0	0	0	0	0
Union County	0	0	0	0	0	0	0	0
Venango County	0	0	0	0	0	0	0	0
Warren County	0	0	0	0	0	1	0	0
Washington County	0	0	0	0	0	2	0	0
Wayne County	0	0	0	0	0	0	0	0
Westmoreland County	0	0	0	0	0	1	0	0
Wyoming County	0	0	0	0	0	0	0	0
York County	0	0	0	0	0	1	0	0
State Police								
Adams County	0	12	5	25	192	465	26	1
Allegheny County	0	1	1	28	1	358	1	0
Armstrong County	0	6	9	29	114	219	17	1
Beaver County	0	1	2	26	69	76	9	3
Bedford County	0	15	7	48	155	269	24	9
Berks County	0	16	8	65	255	421	40	10
Blair County	0	1	0	25	55	126	9	2
Bradford County	2	35	4	33	186	276	25	3
Bucks County	0	4	11	20	67	318	12	2
Butler County	1	16	1	28	177	408	28	6
Cambria County	4	7	3	25	90	122	28	5
Cameron County	0	2	0	3	21	18	1	1
Carbon County	0	3	1	28	135	157	9	1
Centre County	0	20	4	30	108	347	9	2
Chester County	0	27	19	72	491	946	43	4
Clarion County	3	27	2	18	115	294	21	8
Clearfield County	3	20	3	27	132	277	15	8
Clinton County	0	6	0	4	80	241	7	0
Columbia County	1	2	1	43	54	134	6	0
Crawford County	1	8	3	20	235	402	21	6
Cumberland County	0	5	3	20	186	535	29	6
Delaware County	0	4	22	30	138	902	24	3
Elizabethville	3	26	9	108	241	595	38	15
Elk County	3	7	0	4	48	187	7	0
Erie County	1	18	32	57	349	1,222	41	5
Fayette County	3	33	45	83	685	1,461	92	38
Franklin County	3	28	22	58	332	1,129	55	9
Fulton County	0	5	2	21	54	146	4	0
Greene County	0	7	12	23	107	272	37	0
Huntingdon County	2	15	2	32	185	279	18	6
Indiana County	4	22	12	27	201	539	18	8
Jefferson County	2	11	0	27	122	175	29	5
Juniata County	0	5	1	16	55	175	6	4
Lackawanna County	1	7	6	25	84	78	18	20
Lancaster County	0	13	14	32	298	439	36	3
Lawrence County	3	6	4	11	110	172	18	4
Lebanon County	0	8	13	38	110	280	17	2
Lehigh County	1	13	10	45	244	712	30	16
Luzerne County	1	16	20	108	273	837	44	24
Lycoming County	0	15	5	31	228	429	19	1
McKean County	0	4	1	4	30	72	9	0
Mercer County	0	4	5	19	115	193	17	5
Mifflin County	1	5	1	15	39	87	6	1
Monroe County	4	18	22	403	510	920	49	6
Montour County	0	1	0	32	46	62	5	0
Northampton County	0	0	2	8	95	295	16	1
Northumberland County	1	12	4	20	105	187	8	1
Perry County	0	43	11	55	190	416	18	9
Philadelphia County	0	0	2	12	0	6	0	0
Pike County	2	13	6	42	367	334	30	19
Potter County	0	9	1	10	89	70	6	3
Schuylkill County	0	11	14	86	174	552	36	9
Skippack	1	6	7	66	150	556	17	5
Snyder County	1	3	3	7	61	256	3	0
Somerset County	3	16	4	21	191	332	19	5
Sullivan County	0	2	0	3	31	50	2	1
Susquehanna County	1	19	3	11	118	198	22	4
Tioga County	2	10	3	25	159	249	19	3
Tionesta	2	4	0	12	45	44	2	0
Union County	0	8	0	25	74	210	5	0
Venango County	0	10	0	12	90	266	13	0
Warren County	0	9	2	15	71	153	10	7
Washington County	1	13	10	65	240	515	38	13
Wayne County	1	20	5	19	226	391	27	11
Westmoreland County	5	24	51	134	416	1,270	63	8

Table 11.   Offenses Known to Law Enforcement, by Selected State, Tribal, and Other Agencies, 2013— continued

(Number.)

State/other agency unit/office	Murder and non-negligent manslaughter	Rape (revised definition)[1]	Robbery	Aggravated assault	Burglary	Larceny-theft	Motor vehicle theft	Arson[2]
Wyoming County	3	11	2	19	72	220	14	2
York County	2	21	12	105	167	484	33	6
Other Agencies								
Allegheny County District Attorney, Criminal Investigation Division	0	0	9	1	2	43	1	0
Allegheny County Housing Authority	2	0	0	8	7	33	0	0
Allegheny County Port Authority	0	0	15	78	0	75	1	1
County Detective								
Beaver County	0	0	0	2	1	5	0	0
Berks County	0	0	0	115	1	3	0	0
Bucks County	1	0	0	1	0	10	0	0
Clarion County	0	0	0	2	0	0	0	0
Cumberland County	0	1	0	2	0	2	0	0
Dauphin County	0	2	0	8	0	29	1	0
Lancaster County	0	0	0	0	0	0	0	0
Lehigh County	0	0	2	0	4	0	85	0
Luzerne County	0	0	0	2	0	3	0	0
McKean County	0	0	0	0	1	10	0	0
Monroe County	0	0	0	6	0	14	0	0
Montgomery County	0	1	0	6	0	9	0	2
Montour County	0	0	0	0	0	0	0	0
Schuylkill County	0	0	0	1	0	2	0	0
Westmoreland County	0	0	0	6	0	76	0	0
Wyoming County	0	1	0	4	0	4	0	0
York County	0	2	0	5	0	2	1	0
Delaware County District Attorney, Criminal Investigation Division	0	2	0	3	0	4	0	0
Delaware County Park	0	1	0	17	2	138	0	0
Erie Municipal Airport Authority	0	0	0	0	0	0	0	0
Fort Indiantown Gap	0	0	0	0	3	8	3	0
Harrisburg International Airport	0	0	0	1	0	6	4	0
Lehigh Valley International Airport	0	0	0	1	0	2	5	0
Westmoreland County Park	0	0	0	1	0	14	0	0
Rhode Island								
State Agencies								
Department of Environmental Management	0	0	0	2	2	39	0	1
Rhode Island State Airport	0	0	0	0	1	19	16	0
Rhode Island State Police Headquarters	0	15	0	12	1	29	26	1
State Police								
Chepachet	0	8	1	1	1	16	8	0
Hope Valley	0	2	0	0	7	32	9	2
Lincoln	0	2	1	4	5	45	20	1
Portsmouth	0	0	0	0	0	2	0	1
Wickford	0	2	2	5	5	28	4	0
Tribal Agency								
Narragansett Tribal	0		0	0	0	0	0	0
South Carolina								
State Agencies								
Bureau of Protective Services	0	0	0	0	6	19	0	0
Department of Mental Health	0	0	0	1	0	23	0	0
Highway Patrol								
Abbeville County	0	0	0	0	0	0	0	0
Aiken County	0	0	0	0	0	0	0	0
Anderson County	0	0	0	0	0	1	2	0
Bamberg County	0	0	0	0	0	0	0	0
Barnwell County	0	0	0	0	0	0	0	0
Beaufort County	0	0	0	0	0	0	0	0
Berkeley County	0	0	0	0	0	1	0	0
Calhoun County	0	0	0	0	0	0	1	0
Charleston County	0	0	0	0	0	0	0	0
Cherokee County	0	0	0	0	0	0	0	0
Chester County	0	0	0	0	0	0	0	0
Chesterfield County	0	0	0	1	0	0	0	0
Clarendon County	0	0	0	0	0	0	0	0
Colleton County	0	0	0	0	0	0	0	0
Darlington County	0	0	0	0	0	0	0	0
Dillon County	0	0	0	0	0	0	0	0
Dorchester County	0	0	0	0	0	0	1	0
Edgefield County	0	0	0	0	0	0	0	0
Fairfield County	0	0	0	0	0	0	0	0
Florence County	0	0	0	0	0	0	0	0
Georgetown County	0	0	0	0	0	0	0	0
Greenville County	0	0	0	0	0	0	0	0
Greenwood County	0	0	0	0	0	0	0	0
Hampton County	0	0	0	0	0	0	1	0

Table 11.   Offenses Known to Law Enforcement, by Selected State, Tribal, and Other Agencies, 2013— continued

(Number.)

State/other agency unit/office	Murder and non-negligent man-slaughter	Rape (revised definition)	Robbery	Aggravated assault	Burglary	Larceny-theft	Motor vehicle theft	Arson[2]
Horry County	0	0	0	1	0	1	0	0
Jasper County	0	0	0	0	0	0	0	0
Kershaw County	0	0	0	0	0	0	0	0
Lancaster County	0	0	0	0	0	0	0	0
Laurens County	0	0	0	0	0	0	0	0
Lee County	0	0	0	0	0	0	0	0
Lexington County	0	0	0	0	0	0	1	0
Marion County	0	0	0	0	0	0	0	0
Newberry County	0	0	0	0	0	0	0	0
Oconee County	0	0	0	1	0	0	0	0
Orangeburg County	0	0	0	0	0	0	0	0
Pickens County	0	0	0	0	0	0	0	0
Richland County	0	0	0	0	0	2	0	0
Saluda County	0	0	0	0	0	0	0	0
Spartanburg County	0	0	0	0	0	0	0	0
Sumter County	0	0	0	0	0	0	0	0
Union County	0	0	0	0	0	0	0	0
Williamsburg County	0	0	0	0	0	0	0	0
York County	0	0	0	0	0	0	0	0
South Carolina School for the Deaf and Blind	0	0	0	0	0	0	0	0
State Transport Police								
Anderson County	0	0	0	0	0	0	0	0
Other Agencies								
15th Circuit Drug Enforcement Unit	0	0	0	0	0	0	0	0
Charleston County Aviation Authority	0	0	0	0	0	25	2	0
Greenville Hospital	0	0	0	1	2	109	2	0
Greenville-Spartanburg International Airport	0	0	0	1	0	14	1	0
Lexington County Medical Center	1	0	1	0	0	47	0	0
South Dakota								
State Agency								
Division of Criminal Investigation	5	8	2	9	2	7	0	1
Highway Patrol	0	0	0	4	0	4	11	0
Tribal Agencies								
Cheyenne River Tribal	1		4	14	8	9	6	5
Crow Creek Tribal	0		0	52	25	46	14	2
Flandreau Tribal	0		0	2	2	4	0	0
Lower Brule Tribal	0		0	51	74	110	13	37
Oglala Sioux Tribal	3		6	35	29	131	33	8
Rosebud Tribal	1		1	410	186	368	59	19
Sisseton-Wahpeton Tribal	0		0	18	34	146	37	4
Yankton Tribal	1		1	48	14	4	3	0
Tennessee								
State Agencies								
Alcoholic Beverage Commission	0	0	0	0	0	0	0	0
Department of Correction, Internal Affairs	0	1	0	9	0	2	0	0
Department of Safety	0	0	0	30	0	16	7	0
State Fire Marshal	0	0	0	0	0	0	0	20
State Park Rangers								
Bicentennial Capitol Mall	0	1	0	0	0	0	0	0
Big Hill Pond	0	0	0	0	0	0	0	0
Big Ridge	0	0	0	0	0	1	0	0
Bledsoe Creek	0	0	0	0	0	0	0	0
Booker T. Washington	0	0	0	0	0	0	0	0
Burgess Falls Natural Area	0	0	0	0	0	0	0	0
Cedars of Lebanon	0	0	0	0	0	0	0	0
Chickasaw	0	0	0	0	1	1	0	0
Cove Lake	0	0	0	0	0	0	0	0
Cumberland Mountain	0	0	0	0	0	0	0	0
Cumberland Trail	0	0	0	0	0	3	0	0
Cummins Falls	0	0	0	0	0	0	0	0
David Crockett	0	0	0	2	0	0	0	0
Davy Crockett Birthplace	0	0	0	0	0	1	0	0
Dunbar Cave Natural Area	0	0	0	0	0	0	0	0
Edgar Evins	0	0	0	0	0	0	0	0
Fall Creek Falls	0	0	0	0	0	7	0	0
Fort Loudon State Historic Park	0	0	0	0	0	0	0	0
Fort Pillow State Historic Park	0	0	0	0	0	0	0	0
Frozen Head Natural Area	0	0	0	0	0	2	0	0
Harpeth Scenic Rivers	0	0	0	0	0	14	0	0
Harrison Bay	0	0	0	0	2	17	0	0
Henry Horton	0	0	0	0	0	4	0	0
Hiwassee/Ocoee State Scenic Rivers	0	0	0	0	0	1	0	0
Indian Mountain	0	0	0	0	0	0	0	0

Table 11. Offenses Known to Law Enforcement, by Selected State, Tribal, and Other Agencies, 2013— continued

(Number.)

State/other agency unit/office	Murder and non-negligent manslaughter	Rape (revised definition)	Robbery	Aggravated assault	Burglary	Larceny-theft	Motor vehicle theft	Arson[2]
Johnsonville State Historic Park	0	0	0	0	0	0	0	0
Long Hunter	0	0	0	0	0	6	0	0
Meeman-Shelby Forest	0	0	0	0	0	4	0	1
Montgomery Bell	0	0	0	0	0	7	0	0
Mousetail Landing	0	0	0	0	0	1	0	0
Natchez Trace	0	0	0	0	0	0	0	0
Nathan Bedford Forrest	0	0	0	0	0	3	0	0
Norris Dam	0	0	0	0	0	3	0	0
Old Stone Fort State Archaeological Park	0	0	0	0	0	0	0	0
Panther Creek	0	0	0	0	0	0	0	0
Paris Landing	0	0	0	0	0	1	0	0
Pickett	0	0	0	0	0	2	0	0
Pickwick Landing	0	0	0	0	0	6	0	0
Pinson Mounds State Archaeological Park	0	0	0	0	0	0	0	0
Radnor Lake Natural Area	0	0	0	0	0	0	0	0
Red Clay State Historic Park	0	0	0	0	0	0	0	0
Reelfoot Lake	0	0	0	0	0	0	0	0
Roan Mountain	0	0	0	0	0	0	0	0
Rock Island	0	0	0	0	0	0	0	0
Sgt. Alvin C. York	0	0	0	0	0	0	0	0
South Cumberland Recreation Area	0	0	0	0	0	9	0	2
Standing Stone	0	0	0	0	0	0	0	0
Sycamore Shoals State Historic Park	0	0	0	0	0	0	0	0
Tim's Ford	0	0	0	2	0	2	0	0
T.O. Fuller	0	0	0	0	0	3	0	0
Warrior's Path	0	0	0	1	0	0	0	0
TennCare Office of Inspector General	0	0	0	0	0	0	0	0
Tennessee Bureau of Investigation	0	0	0	3	0	4	1	0
Tennessee Department of Revenue, Special Investigations Unit	0	0	0	0	0	0	0	0
Wildlife Resources Agency								
Region 1	0	0	0	0	0	0	0	0
Region 2	0	0	0	0	0	0	0	0
Region 3	0	0	0	0	0	0	0	0
Region 4	0	0	0	0	0	0	0	0
Other Agencies								
Chattanooga Housing Authority	0	0	0	1	0	0	0	1
Chattanooga Metropolitan Airport	0	0	0	0	0	1	0	0
Dickson Parks and Recreation	0	0	0	0	0	1	0	0
Drug Task Force								
1st Judicial District	0	0	0	0	0	0	0	0
2nd Judicial District	0	0	0	0	0	0	0	0
3rd Judicial District	0	0	0	0	0	0	0	0
4th Judicial District	0	0	0	0	0	0	0	0
5th Judicial District	0	0	0	0	0	0	0	0
7th Judicial District	0	0	0	0	0	0	0	0
8th Judicial District	0	0	0	0	0	0	0	0
9th Judicial District	0	0	0	0	0	0	0	0
10th Judicial District	0	0	0	0	0	1	0	0
12th Judicial District	0	0	0	0	0	0	0	0
14th Judicial District	0	0	0	0	0	0	0	0
15th Judicial District	0	0	0	0	0	0	0	0
17th Judicial District	0	0	0	0	1	0	0	0
18th Judicial District	0	0	0	0	0	0	0	0
19th Judicial District	0	0	0	1	0	2	0	0
21st Judicial District	0	0	0	0	0	2	0	0
22nd Judicial District	0	0	0	0	0	0	0	0
23rd Judicial District	0	0	0	0	0	1	0	0
24th Judicial District	0	0	0	0	0	1	0	0
25th Judicial District	0	0	0	0	0	0	0	0
27th Judicial District	0	0	0	4	0	0	0	0
31st Judicial District	0	0	0	0	0	0	0	0
Knoxville Metropolitan Airport	0	1	0	0	0	12	0	0
Memphis International Airport	0	0	0	2	3	139	12	0
Metropolitan Nashville Park Police	0	1	4	3	6	168	1	0
Nashville International Airport	0	0	0	1	1	42	5	0
Tri-Cities Regional Airport	0	0	0	0	0	2	0	0
West Tennessee Violent Crime Task Force	1	0	0	2	0	0	0	0
Texas								
Tribal Agency								
Ysleta Del Sur Pueblo Tribal	0		0	66	10	57	0	0
Other Agencies								
Amarillo International Airport	0		0	0	0	0	0	0
Dallas-Fort Worth International Airport	0	0	0	5	5	332	15	0

Table 11.   Offenses Known to Law Enforcement, by Selected State, Tribal, and Other Agencies, 2013— continued

(Number.)

State/other agency unit/office	Murder and non-negligent manslaughter	Rape (revised definition)[1]	Robbery	Aggravated assault	Burglary	Larceny-theft	Motor vehicle theft	Arson[2]
Hospital District								
Dallas County	0		4	21	11	430	0	0
Tarrant County	0		1	0	2	151	2	0
Houston Metropolitan Transit Authority	0		0	0	0	42	4	0
Independent School District								
Aldine	0		8	0	8	98	3	1
Alvin	0		0	8	5	51	0	0
Angleton	0		0	2	3	12	0	0
Austin	0		5	9	25	758	3	4
Barbers Hill	0		0	0	0	12	0	0
Cedar Hill	0		0	0	2	69	0	0
Columbia-Brazoria	0		0	3	6	19	1	0
Conroe	0		0	7	4	217	0	1
East Central	0	0	0	0	0	0	0	0
Ector County	0		0	25	11	90	2	0
El Paso	0		1	15	31	274	0	1
Floresville	0		0	0	0	13	0	0
Fort Bend	0		3	5	17	457	0	0
Judson	0		0	0	0	2	0	0
Killeen	0		2	3	8	93	0	1
Klein	0		1	1	1	29	1	1
Lyford	0		0	0	0	6	0	0
Mexia	0		0	1	3	6	0	0
Midland	0		0	10	1	25	0	0
Pasadena	0		2	2	14	113	9	2
Pflugerville	0		0	5	2	89	1	1
Raymondville	0		0	0	2	6	0	1
Rio Grande City	0		0	2	0	54	2	0
Sealy	0		0	0	0	9	0	0
Socorro	0		0	19	3	73	0	0
Spring Branch	0		1	1	10	65	1	1
Taft	0		0	0	1	0	0	0
United	0		0	8	3	62	0	2
Port of Brownsville	0		0	1	5	32	0	0
Port of Houston Authority	0		0	0	0	25	1	0
Utah								
State Agencies								
Parks and Recreation	0	0	0	2	2	13	1	1
Utah Highway Patrol	4	1	0	37	2	163	23	0
Wildlife Resources	0	0	0	1	0	6	1	0
Tribal Agency								
Goshute Tribal	0		0	0	1	0	0	0
Uintah and Ouray Tribal	0		0	11	7	0	4	0
Other Agencies								
Cache-Rich Drug Task Force	0	0	0	0	2	2	0	1
Davis Metropolitan Narcotics Strike Force	0	0	0	0	0	0	0	0
Granite School District	0		0	3	9	122	4	6
Utah County Attorney, Investigations Division	0		0	0	0	0	0	0
Utah County Major Crime Task Force	0		0	0	0	11	0	0
Utah Transit Authority	0	1	4	5	1	1,615	54	0
Vermont								
State Agencies								
Attorney General	0	0	0	0	0	1	0	0
Department of Motor Vehicles	0	0	0	0	0	2	0	0
State Police								
Bradford	0	0	2	6	82	95	12	3
Brattleboro	0	1	0	5	82	74	5	0
Derby	1	8	1	18	130	204	15	0
Middlesex	0	0	0	0	91	144	0	1
New Haven	0	3	0	15	141	165	20	1
Rockingham	0	4	2	5	78	77	8	3
Royalton	0	0	1	3	66	77	5	0
Shaftsbury	0	3	0	11	94	71	9	3
St. Albans	1	10	1	18	93	206	32	4
St. Johnsbury	3	6	1	22	150	198	8	8
Vermont State Police	0	0	0	0	1	0	0	0
Vermont State Police Headquarters, Bureau of Criminal Investigations	0	0	0	0	0	0	0	0
Virginia								
State Agencies								
Alcoholic Beverage Control Commission	0	0	0	0	0	37	0	0
Central State Hospital	0	0	0	1	0	10	0	0

Table 11.   Offenses Known to Law Enforcement, by Selected State, Tribal, and Other Agencies, 2013— continued

(Number.)

State/other agency unit/office	Murder and non-negligent man-slaughter	Rape (revised definition)[1]	Robbery	Aggravated as-sault	Burglary	Larceny-theft	Motor vehicle theft	Arson[2]
Department of Conservation and Recreation	0	0	0	0	2	40	0	0
Department of Game and Inland Fisheries, Enforcement Division	0	0	0	1	0	9	2	0
Department of Motor Vehicles	0	0	0	0	0	7	20	0
State Police								
Accomack County	0	0	0	2	0	8	2	50
Alleghany County	0	0	0	1	0	5	0	0
Amherst County	0	0	0	1	1	1	0	0
Appomattox County	0	0	0	0	0	0	0	0
Augusta County	1	0	0	1	0	1	0	0
Bath County	0	0	0	1	0	0	0	0
Bedford County	0	0	0	2	2	0	1	0
Botetourt County	0	0	0	0	0	1	1	1
Buchanan County	0	0	0	1	4	18	5	6
Buckingham County	0	0	0	0	0	3	0	0
Campbell County	0	0	0	1	0	2	0	0
Caroline County	0	0	0	4	2	15	11	1
Charlotte County	0	0	0	0	0	1	0	0
Chesapeake	0	0	0	0	0	3	1	0
Chesterfield County	0	0	1	11	0	4	1	0
Craig County	0	2	0	0	0	1	3	0
Culpeper County	0	0	0	0	0	4	0	0
Danville	0	0	0	0	0	0	0	1
Dickenson County	0	0	0	4	3	4	1	0
Dinwiddie County	0	0	0	1	0	0	0	0
Fairfax County	0	0	0	12	0	10	1	0
Fauquier County	0	0	0	0	0	7	1	0
Floyd County	0	0	0	1	0	1	0	0
Franklin County	0	0	0	1	0	1	3	1
Frederick County	0	0	0	1	1	4	4	0
Fredericksburg	0	0	0	3	0	1	0	0
Gloucester County	1	0	0	0	0	0	0	0
Goochland County	0	0	0	0	0	1	0	0
Greene County	0	0	0	0	0	1	0	0
Greensville County	0	0	0	6	0	0	0	0
Halifax County	0	0	0	1	0	1	3	0
Hampton	0	0	0	4	0	3	2	0
Hanover County	0	0	0	5	0	0	2	0
Harrisonburg	0	0	0	0	0	2	3	0
Henrico County	1	0	0	4	0	6	2	0
Henry County	0	0	0	2	0	1	1	1
Hopewell	0	0	0	0	0	0	0	0
Isle of Wight County	0	0	0	0	1	1	0	0
King George County	0	0	0	2	1	0	0	0
Loudoun County	0	0	0	0	0	2	1	0
Louisa County	0	0	0	0	2	3	0	1
Lunenburg County	0	1	0	0	0	2	1	0
Lynchburg	0	0	0	0	0	1	0	0
Mathews County	0	0	0	0	0	1	0	1
Mecklenburg County	0	0	0	3	0	5	1	0
Montgomery County	0	1	0	2	0	2	0	0
New Kent County	0	0	0	11	0	3	0	0
Newport News	0	0	0	3	0	0	4	5
Norfolk	0	0	0	0	0	0	3	0
Northampton County	0	0	0	0	0	0	1	0
Nottoway County	0	0	0	5	1	3	2	0
Orange County	0	0	0	0	0	1	0	0
Page County	0	0	0	3	0	22	0	0
Petersburg	0	0	0	2	0	4	2	0
Pittsylvania County	1	0	0	6	0	14	18	1
Portsmouth	0	0	0	0	0	1	3	0
Prince Edward County	0	0	0	0	0	0	0	0
Prince William County	0	0	0	18	1	4	2	0
Pulaski County	0	0	0	0	0	5	1	0
Richmond	0	1	0	5	0	2	6	0
Roanoke	0	0	0	0	0	7	0	1
Roanoke County	0	1	0	2	1	3	1	1
Rockbridge County	0	0	0	0	0	3	0	2
Rockingham County	0	0	0	0	1	10	8	0
Shenandoah County	0	0	0	1	0	2	2	0
Smyth County	0	0	0	2	2	8	1	0
Southampton County	0	0	0	0	0	0	0	0
Spotsylvania County	0	0	0	0	0	1	0	0
Stafford County	0	0	0	0	0	1	1	0
Tazewell County	0	0	0	0	0	11	1	2
Virginia Beach	2	0	0	1	0	2	10	0
Warren County	0	0	0	0	0	2	0	0
Washington County	0	0	0	0	2	1	0	0

Table 11.   Offenses Known to Law Enforcement, by Selected State, Tribal, and Other Agencies, 2013— continued

(Number.)

State/other agency unit/office	Murder and non-negligent man-slaughter	Rape (revised definition)[1]	Robbery	Aggravated as-sault	Burglary	Larceny-theft	Motor vehicle theft	Arson[2]
Winchester	0	0	0	1	0	0	0	0
Wise County	0	0	0	2	0	2	3	0
Wythe County	0	0	0	1	0	8	1	0
Virginia State Capitol	0	0	0	0	0	30	0	0
Other Agencies								
Norfolk Airport Authority	0	0	0	0	0	35	1	0
Port Authority, Norfolk	0	0	0	0	0	1	0	0
Reagan National Airport	0	0	0	3	1	351	51	0
Richmond International Airport	0	0	0	0	0	13	9	0
Washington								
State Agency								
State Gambling Commission, Enforcement Unit	0	0	0	0	0	13	9	0
State Insurance Commissioner, Special Investigations Unit	0	0	0	0	0	5	0	0
Washington State Patrol	0	0	0	0	0	0	0	0
Tribal Agencies								
Chehalis Tribal	0		2	0	22	92	18	3
Kalispel Tribal	0		0	34	8	70	14	0
Lower Elwha Tribal	0		0	2	36	0	1	0
Lummi Tribal	0	15	1	26	77	179	22	2
Makah Tribal	0		0	9	7	17	0	1
Swinomish Tribal	0	2	0	0	14	45	0	0
Tulalip Tribal	0		15	55	103	762	68	5
Other Agency								
Port of Seattle	0	1	2	26	16	806	86	0
Skagit County Interlocal Drug Enforcement Unit	0	0	0	0	0	0	0	0
West Virginia								
State Agencies								
Division of Natural Resources								
Barbour County	0	0	0	0	0	0	0	0
Berkeley County	0	0	0	0	0	0	0	0
Boone County	0	0	0	0	0	0	0	0
Brooke County	0	0	0	0	0	0	0	0
Cabell County	0	0	0	0	0	0	0	0
Calhoun County	0	0	0	0	0	0	0	0
Doddridge County	0	0	0	0	0	0	0	0
Fayette County	0	0	0	0	0	0	0	0
Gilmer County	0	0	0	0	0	0	0	0
Grant County	0	0	0	0	0	0	0	0
Greenbrier County	0	0	0	0	0	0	0	0
Hampshire County	0	0	0	0	0	0	0	0
Hancock County	0	0	0	0	0	0	0	0
Hardy County	0	0	0	0	0	0	0	0
Harrison County	0	0	0	0	0	0	0	0
Jackson County	0	0	0	0	0	0	0	0
Jefferson County	0	0	0	0	0	0	0	0
Kanawha County	0	0	0	0	0	0	0	0
Lincoln County	0	0	0	0	0	0	0	0
Logan County	0	0	0	0	0	0	0	0
Marion County	0	0	0	0	0	0	0	0
Marshall County	0	0	0	0	0	0	0	0
Mason County	0	0	0	0	0	0	0	0
McDowell County	0	0	0	0	0	0	0	0
Mercer County	0	0	0	0	0	0	0	0
Mineral County	0	0	0	0	0	0	0	0
Mingo County	0	0	0	0	0	0	0	0
Monongalia County	0	0	0	0	0	0	0	0
Monroe County	0	0	0	0	0	0	0	0
Morgan County	0	0	0	0	0	0	0	0
Ohio County	0	0	0	0	0	0	0	0
Pendleton County	0	0	0	0	0	0	0	0
Pleasants County	0	0	0	0	0	0	0	0
Preston County	0	0	0	0	0	0	0	0
Putnam County	0	0	0	0	0	0	0	0
Raleigh County	0	0	0	0	0	0	0	0
Ritchie County	0	0	0	0	0	0	0	0
Roane County	0	0	0	0	0	0	0	0
Summers County	0	0	0	0	0	0	0	0
Taylor County	0	0	0	0	0	0	0	0
Tucker County	0	0	0	0	0	0	0	0
Tyler County	0	0	0	0	0	0	0	0
Wayne County	0	0	0	0	0	0	0	0
Wetzel County	0	0	0	0	0	0	0	0
Wirt County	0	0	0	0	0	0	0	0
Wood County	0	0	0	0	0	0	0	0

Table 11.   Offenses Known to Law Enforcement, by Selected State, Tribal, and Other Agencies, 2013— continued

(Number.)

State/other agency unit/office	Murder and non-negligent man-slaughter	Rape (revised definition)	Robbery	Aggravated as-sault	Burglary	Larceny-theft	Motor vehicle theft	Arson[2]
Wyoming County	0	0	0	0	0	0	0	0
State Police								
Beckley	0	1	5	16	64	193	15	1
Berkeley Springs	0	1	0	7	38	51	4	1
Bridgeport	0	3	0	10	35	102	18	1
Buckhannon	0	0	0	8	21	56	5	2
Clay	1	2	1	12	24	27	3	1
Elizabeth	0	3	1	5	26	26	2	0
Elkins	0	9	0	15	61	137	11	1
Fairmont	0	4	1	8	16	40	5	0
Franklin	1	3	0	3	13	21	2	0
Gauley Bridge	0	0	1	6	11	22	3	1
Gilbert	0	0	0	2	7	13	0	0
Glenville	0	0	0	6	10	25	6	0
Grafton	0	0	0	0	0	4	0	0
Grantsville	0	0	0	7	12	19	6	1
Hamlin	0	9	1	19	45	159	30	2
Harrisville	1	0	0	5	10	27	3	0
Hinton	0	2	0	1	25	29	4	0
Hundred	0	0	0	3	18	13	3	0
Internet Crimes Against Children Unit	0	14	0	13	0	0	0	0
Jesse	0	1	1	5	12	27	2	0
Kearneysville	0	2	1	23	52	141	20	0
Keyser	0	2	2	19	53	104	11	1
Kingwood	0	1	0	7	41	96	8	1
Lewisburg	0	0	0	5	11	55	1	0
Logan	3	6	7	55	100	242	45	3
Madison	0	5	0	15	52	117	17	1
Marlinton	0	2	0	6	25	33	3	3
Martinsburg	0	9	11	30	151	436	51	2
Moorefield	0	4	0	11	17	16	3	0
Morgantown	0	14	6	24	130	379	28	2
Moundsville	0	3	1	2	2	18	1	0
New Cumberland	0	1	0	1	1	15	0	1
Oak Hill	1	7	1	13	42	78	10	2
Paden City	0	3	0	8	12	20	4	0
Parkersburg	0	1	0	10	35	60	6	0
Parsons	0	0	0	7	9	15	1	0
Petersburg	0	3	0	4	16	21	5	0
Philippi	0	7	0	2	19	14	1	0
Point Pleasant	0	3	1	6	12	37	6	0
Princeton	0	1	3	13	65	258	14	1
Quincy	0	3	0	6	11	88	6	1
Rainelle	0	1	0	0	15	41	3	0
Richwood	0	0	0	3	5	8	2	0
Ripley	2	2	0	2	36	45	7	0
Romney	1	5	0	10	25	61	4	1
South Charleston	0	4	2	23	49	303	29	2
Spencer	0	3	0	6	13	28	5	0
St. Marys	0	1	0	4	6	9	4	0
Summersville	0	2	0	3	8	33	3	1
Sutton	0	2	0	6	19	29	5	1
Union	1	2	0	7	18	27	5	1
Upperglade	0	1	0	27	8	16	1	0
Wayne	1	3	0	14	87	201	21	1
Welch	1	7	1	21	58	93	13	4
Wellsburg	0	2	0	8	2	8	0	0
Weston	0	2	0	22	18	94	2	0
West Union	1	4	0	2	2	27	5	0
Wheeling	0	3	0	1	1	27	0	0
Whitesville	0	0	1	2	10	33	0	0
Williamson	0	4	1	50	58	112	20	3
Winfield	0	5	3	6	34	142	12	0
State Police, Bureau of Criminal Investigation								
Beckley	0	0	0	0	0	0	0	0
Bluefield	0	0	0	0	0	0	0	0
Buckhannon	0	0	0	0	0	0	0	0
Charleston	0	1	0	0	0	3	0	0
Fairmont	0	0	0	0	0	0	0	0
State Police, Parkway Authority								
Fayette County	0	0	0	0	0	1	0	0
Kanawha County	0	0	0	0	0	2	0	0
Mercer County	0	0	0	0	0	0	0	0
Raleigh County	0	0	0	0	0	5	1	0
Other Agencies								
Central West Virginia Drug Task Force	0	0	0	1	0	0	0	0

Table 11. Offenses Known to Law Enforcement, by Selected State, Tribal, and Other Agencies, 2013— continued

(Number.)

State/other agency unit/office	Murder and non-negligent manslaughter	Rape (revised definition)[1]	Robbery	Aggravated assault	Burglary	Larceny-theft	Motor vehicle theft	Arson[2]
Eastern Panhandle Drug and Violent Crime Task Force	0	0	0	0	0	2	0	0
Greenbrier County Drug and Violent Crime Task Force	0	0	0	0	0	0	0	0
Hancock/Brooke/Weirton Drug Task Force	0	0	0	0	0	0	0	0
Harrison County Drug and Violent Crime Task Force	0	0	0	0	0	0	0	0
Huntington Drug and Violent Crime Task Force	0	0	0	0	1	0	0	0
Kanawha County Parks and Recreation	0	0	0	0	0	2	0	0
Logan County Drug and Violent Crime Task Force	0	0	0	0	0	0	0	0
Metropolitan Drug Enforcement Network Team	0	0	0	0	0	0	0	0
Ohio Valley Drug and Violent Crime Task Force	0	0	0	1	0	0	0	0
Parkersburg Narcotics and Violent Crime Task Force	0	0	0	0	0	0	0	0
Potomac Highlands Drug and Violent Crime Task Force	0	0	0	0	0	0	0	0
Three Rivers Drug and Violent Crime Task Force	0	0	0	0	0	0	0	0
Wisconsin								
State Agencies								
Capitol Police	0		0	0	0	80	0	0
Department of Natural Resources	0		0	0	0	0	0	0
Wisconsin State Patrol	0		0	0	0	0	0	0
Tribal Agencies								
Lac du Flambeau Tribal		9	52	240	187	5	1	0
Menominee Tribal		6	33	93	72	9	0	2
Oneida Tribal	3		9	64	48	2	2	1
St. Croix Tribal		0	5	70	49	7	0	0
Stockbridge Munsee Tribal	0		0	65	41	7	0	1
		1	0	87	62	6	1	
Wyoming								
Tribal Agency								
Wind River Agency	1		0	37	11	42	24	9
Puerto Rico and Other Outlying Areas								
Guam	9		145	400	1,620	2,521	378	9
Puerto Rico	883		6,016	2,395	13,961	29,360	5,530	
Virgin Islands								
St. Croix	18		103	212	571	563	114	58
St. Thomas	15		128	576	564	727	112	44
Federal Agencies								
National Institutes of Health	0		0	0	1	48	0	0
United States Department of the Interior								
Bureau of Indian Affairs[3]	79		309	4,200	5,461	14,643	2,816	801
Bureau of Land Management	2		1	11	34	607	25	87
Bureau of Reclamation	0		0	1	4	3	0	0
Fish and Wildlife Service	6		2	17	21	79	13	7
National Park Service	11		41	141	322	3,085	80	53

1 The figures shown in this column for the offense of rape were reported using the revised Uniform Crime Reporting (UCR) definition of rape. See chapter notes for more detail.   2 The FBI does not publish arson data unless it receives data from either the agency or the state for all 12 months of the calendar year.

Table 12.   Crime Trends, by Population Group, 2012–2013

(Number, percent change.)

Population group	Murder and non-negligent man-slaughter	Forcible rape[1]	Robbery	Aggravated assault	Burglary	Larceny-theft	Motor vehicle theft	Arson	Estimated population, 2013
Total, All Agencies									
2012	14,349	65,733	345,758	719,432	1,992,895	5,816,991	697,980	51,126	
2013	13,716	62,034	335,428	683,971	1,820,544	5,665,392	674,292	44,245	299,269,511
Percent change	-4.4	-5.6	-3.0	-4.9	-8.6	-2.6	-3.4	-13.5	
Total, Cities									
2012	11,198	50,003	303,475	554,542	1,460,169	4,655,398	556,242	38,974	
2013	10,511	47,606	294,292	525,185	1,335,527	4,557,867	541,485	33,432	202,966,923
Percent change	-6.1	-4.8	-3.0	-5.3	-8.5	-2.1	-2.7	-14.2	
Group I (250,000 and over)									
2012	5,897	15,715	167,168	228,105	493,768	1,401,823	259,570	12,945	
2013	5,356	15,522	162,815	219,295	454,980	1,395,583	247,312	12,150	57,394,814
Percent change	-9.2	-1.2	-2.6	-3.9	-7.9	-0.4	-4.7	-6.1	
1,000,000 and over (Group I subset)									
2012	2,255	5,254	74,843	83,655	166,197	523,397	93,657	3,547	
2013	1,930	5,356	71,478	82,488	151,503	521,708	86,932	3,612	25,735,804
Percent change	-14.4	+1.9	-4.5	-1.4	-8.8	-0.3	-7.2	+1.8	
500,000 to 999,999 (Group I subset)									
2012	1,929	5,833	48,874	81,803	177,258	481,094	88,656	4,772	
2013	1,786	5,848	48,375	78,207	164,283	482,351	86,649	4,466	16,780,477
Percent change	-7.4	+0.3	-1.0	-4.4	-7.3	+0.3	-2.3	-6.4	
250,000 to 499,999 (Group I subset)									
2012	1,713	4,628	43,451	62,647	150,313	397,332	77,257	4,626	
2013	1,640	4,318	42,962	58,600	139,194	391,524	73,731	4,072	14,878,533
Percent change	-4.3	-6.7	-1.1	-6.5	-7.4	-1.5	-4.6	-12.0	
Group II (100,000 to 249,999)									
2012	1,788	8,812	50,456	93,088	268,959	793,349	105,319	6,540	
2013	1,806	7,951	48,590	87,061	246,360	778,577	106,005	5,603	32,029,761
Percent change	+1.0	-9.8	-3.7	-6.5	-8.4	-1.9	+0.7	-14.3	
Group III (50,000 to 99,999)									
2012	1,162	7,351	34,531	73,136	215,072	687,344	74,981	5,584	
2013	1,171	6,972	33,264	68,626	194,902	673,912	73,705	4,599	32,516,218
Percent change	+0.8	-5.2	-3.7	-6.2	-9.4	-2.0	-1.7	-17.6	
Group IV (25,000 to 49,999)									
2012	920	6,370	23,082	55,528	172,406	616,275	47,444	4,538	
2013	865	6,035	22,462	51,079	158,056	601,616	46,603	3,489	28,988,979
Percent change	-6.0	-5.3	-2.7	-8.0	-8.3	-2.4	-1.8	-23.1	
Group V (10,000 to 24,999)									
2012	826	6,011	17,517	53,405	169,750	608,579	39,301	3,809	
2013	713	5,587	17,065	50,633	153,632	586,929	38,394	3,212	28,865,002
Percent change	-13.7	-7.1	-2.6	-5.2	-9.5	-3.6	-2.3	-15.7	
Group VI (under 10,000)									
2012	605	5,744	10,721	51,280	140,214	548,028	29,627	5,558	
2013	600	5,539	10,096	48,491	127,597	521,250	29,466	4,379	23,172,149
Percent change	-0.8	-3.6	-5.8	-5.4	-9.0	-4.9	-0.5	-21.2	
Metropolitan Counties									
2012	2,337	11,357	39,349	130,619	405,229	938,019	118,438	9,151	
2013	2,386	10,425	38,507	126,000	369,194	901,047	110,596	8,153	71,774,379
Percent change	+2.1	-8.2	-2.1	-3.5	-8.9	-3.9	-6.6	-10.9	
Nonmetropolitan Counties [2]									
2012	814	4,373	2,934	34,271	127,497	223,574	23,300	3,001	
2013	819	4,003	2,629	32,786	115,823	206,478	22,211	2,660	24,528,209
Percent change	+0.6	-8.5	-10.4	-4.3	-9.2	-7.6	-4.7	-11.4	
Suburban Areas [3]									
2012	3,773	21,495	75,543	225,296	709,426	2,112,377	202,042	17,202	
2013	3,692	20,220	73,494	214,640	642,401	2,030,729	192,167	14,556	131,056,632
Percent change	-2.1	-5.9	-2.7	-4.7	-9.4	-3.9	-4.9	-15.4	

1 The rape figures in this table are based on the legacy Uniform Crime Reporting (UCR) definition of rape. The rape figures shown for 2012 and 2013 include converted National Incident-Based Reporting System rape data and those states/agencies that reported the legacy UCR definition of rape for both years.   2 Includes state police agencies that report aggregately for the entire state.   3 Suburban areas include law enforcement agencies in cities with less than 50,000 inhabitants and county law enforcement agencies that are within a Metropolitan Statistical Area. Suburban areas exclude all metropolitan agencies associated with a principal city. The agencies associated with suburban areas also appear in other groups within this table.

Table 13.   Crime Trends, by Suburban and Nonsuburban Cities,[1] by Population Group, 2012–2013

(Number, percent change.)

Population group	Violent crime	Murder and non-negligent man-slaughter	Forcible rape[2]	Robbery	Aggravated assault	Property crime	Burglary	Larceny-theft	Motor vehicle theft	Ar-son
Suburban Cities										
2012	142,445	1,436	10,138	36,194	94,677	1,562,159	304,197	1,174,358	83,604	8,051
2013	134,728	1,306	9,795	34,987	88,640	1,484,460	273,207	1,129,682	81,571	6,403
Percent change	-5.4	-9.1	-3.4	-3.3	-6.4	-5.0	-10.2	-3.8	-2.4	-20.5
Group IV (25,000 to 49,999)										
2012	55,251	565	3,842	15,895	34,949	565,264	113,398	416,770	35,096	2,771
2013	51,991	568	3,674	15,336	32,413	543,497	102,567	406,411	34,519	2,060
Percent change	-5.9	+0.5	-4.4	-3.5	-7.3	-3.9	-9.6	-2.5	-1.6	-25.7
Group V (10,000 to 24,999)										
2012	48,978	557	3,505	12,758	32,158	544,968	110,079	405,185	29,704	2,503
2013	46,384	451	3,259	12,451	30,223	515,202	98,259	388,411	28,532	2,062
Percent change	-5.3	-19.0	-7.0	-2.4	-6.0	-5.5	-10.7	-4.1	-3.9	-17.6
Group VI (under 10,000)										
2012	38,216	314	2,791	7,541	27,570	451,927	80,720	352,403	18,804	2,777
2013	36,353	287	2,862	7,200	26,004	425,761	72,381	334,860	18,520	2,281
Percent change	-4.9	-8.6	+2.5	-4.5	-5.7	-5.8	-10.3	-5.0	-1.5	-17.9
Nonsuburban Cities										
2012	89,564	915	7,987	15,126	65,536	809,465	178,173	598,524	32,768	5,854
2013	84,437	872	7,366	14,636	61,563	779,083	166,078	580,113	32,892	4,677
Percent change	-5.7	-4.7	-7.8	-3.2	-6.1	-3.8	-6.8	-3.1	+0.4	-20.1
Group IV (25,000 to 49,999)										
2012	30,649	355	2,528	7,187	20,579	270,861	59,008	199,505	12,348	1,767
2013	28,450	297	2,361	7,126	18,666	262,778	55,489	195,205	12,084	1,429
Percent change	-7.2	-16.3	-6.6	-0.8	-9.3	-3.0	-6.0	-2.2	-2.1	-19.1
Group V (10,000 to 24,999)										
2012	28,781	269	2,506	4,759	21,247	272,662	59,671	203,394	9,597	1,306
2013	27,614	262	2,328	4,614	20,410	263,753	55,373	198,518	9,862	1,150
Percent change	-4.1	-2.6	-7.1	-3.0	-3.9	-3.3	-7.2	-2.4	+2.8	-11.9
Group VI (under 10,000)										
2012	30,134	291	2,953	3,180	23,710	265,942	59,494	195,625	10,823	2,781
2013	28,373	313	2,677	2,896	22,487	252,552	55,216	186,390	10,946	2,098
Percent change	-5.8	+7.6	-9.3	-8.9	-5.2	-5.0	-7.2	-4.7	+1.1	-24.6

1 Suburban cities include law enforcement agencies in cities with less than 50,000 inhabitants that are within a Metropolitan Statistical Area. Suburban cities exclude all metropolitan agencies associated with a principal city. Nonsuburban cities include law enforcement agencies in cities with less than 50,000 inhabitants that are not associated with a Metropolitan Statistical Area.   2 The rape figures in this table are based on the legacy Uniform Crime Reporting (UCR) definition of rape. The rape figures shown for 2012 and 2013 include converted National Incident-Based Reporting System rape data and those states/agencies that reported the legacy UCR definition of rape for both years.

Table 14.   Crime Trends, by Metropolitan and Nonmetropolitan Counties,[1] by Population Group, 2012–2013

(Number, percent change.)

Population group and range	Violent crime	Arson	Number of agencies	Estimated population, 2013	Murder and nonnegligent manslaughter	Forcible rape[2]	Robbery	Aggravated assault	Property crime	Burglary	Larceny-theft	Motor vehicle theft
Metropolitan Counties												
100,000 and over												
2012	123,238	5,426			1,516	5,930	31,810	83,982	937,921	248,881	613,142	75,898
2013	119,377	4,791	167	42,999,902	1,481	5,605	31,191	81,100	891,399	227,693	594,118	69,588
Percent change	-3.1	-11.7			-2.3	-5.5	-1.9	-3.4	-5.0	-8.5	-3.1	-8.3
25,000 to 99,999												
2012	44,281	2,426			611	3,928	5,595	34,147	394,752	124,622	246,719	23,411
2013	42,841	2,147	454	23,785,185	681	3,532	5,507	33,121	368,405	112,967	232,785	22,653
Percent change	-3.3	-11.5			+11.5	-10.1	-1.6	-3.0	-6.7	-9.4	-5.6	-3.2
Under 25,000												
2012	15,907	1,281			208	1,454	1,934	12,311	126,260	30,946	76,268	19,046
2013	14,828	1,206	1,209	4,734,722	224	1,247	1,796	11,561	118,654	27,839	72,551	18,264
Percent change	-6.8	-5.9			+7.7	-14.2	-7.1	-6.1	-6.0	-10.0	-4.9	-4.1
Nonmetropolitan Counties												
25,000 and over												
2012	16,185	957			269	1,388	1,437	13,091	156,705	53,998	94,149	8,558
2013	15,668	915	263	9,888,909	271	1,376	1,254	12,767	144,640	49,082	87,311	8,247
Percent change	-3.2	-4.4			+0.7	-0.9	-12.7	-2.5	-7.7	-9.1	-7.3	-3.6
10,000 to 24,999												
2012	14,761	996			276	1,332	846	12,307	128,635	43,843	77,180	7,612
2013	13,565	879	577	9,301,274	272	1,216	814	11,263	118,419	39,947	71,549	6,923
Percent change	-8.1	-11.7			-1.4	-8.7	-3.8	-8.5	-7.9	-8.9	-7.3	-9.1
Under 10,000												
2012	8,299	704			162	1,111	339	6,687	64,692	20,210	39,297	5,185
2013	8,119	581	1,352	4,283,698	174	1,013	309	6,623	61,552	19,359	36,900	5,293
Percent change	-2.2	-17.5			+7.4	-8.8	-8.8	-1.0	-4.9	-4.2	-6.1	+2.1

1 Metropolitan counties include sheriffs and county law enforcement agencies associated with a Metropolitan Statistical Area. Nonmetropolitan counties include sheriffs and county law enforcement agencies that are not associated with a Metropolitan Statistical Area. The offenses from state police agencies are not included in this table.   2 The rape figures in this table are based on the legacy Uniform Crime Reporting (UCR) definition of rape. The rape figures shown for 2012 and 2013 include converted National Incident-Based Reporting System rape data and those states/agencies that reported the legacy UCR definition of rape for both years.

Table 15.   Crime Trends, Additional Information About Selected Offenses, by Population Group, 2012–2013

(Number, percent change.)

Population group	Forcible rape[1]		Robbery			
	Rape by force	Assault to rape-attempts	Firearm	Knife or cutting instrument	Other weapon	Strong-arm
Total, All Agencies						
2012	57,904	4,034	125,366	23,532	26,784	129,662
2013	54,785	3,778	122,266	22,553	26,448	126,341
Percent change	-5.4	-6.3	-2.5	-4.2	-1.3	-2.6
Total, Cities						
2012	43,629	3,203	106,720	20,385	22,654	113,730
2013	41,711	2,929	103,978	19,645	22,452	110,844
Percent change	-4.4	-8.6	-2.6	-3.6	-0.9	-2.5
250,000 and over						
2012	13,218	1,335	58,514	9,577	9,899	55,041
2013	13,167	1,243	57,387	9,296	10,213	54,475
Percent change	-0.4	-6.9	-1.9	-2.9	+3.2	-1.0
1,000,000 and over						
2012	3,628	464	17,072	3,471	3,225	17,398
2013	3,751	493	16,905	3,284	3,339	16,965
Percent change	+3.4	+6.3	-1.0	-5.4	+3.5	-2.5
500,000 to 999,999						
2012	5,345	488	22,034	3,573	3,751	19,516
2013	5,438	410	21,055	3,559	3,985	19,776
Percent change	+1.7	-16.0	-4.4	-0.4	+6.2	+1.3
250,000 to 499,999						
2012	4,245	383	19,408	2,533	2,923	18,127
2013	3,978	340	19,427	2,453	2,889	17,734
Percent change	-6.3	-11.2	+0.1	-3.2	-1.2	-2.2
100,000 to 249,999						
2012	8,002	529	19,654	3,820	4,488	20,524
2013	7,281	404	18,660	3,787	4,358	19,830
Percent change	-9.0	-23.6	-5.1	-0.9	-2.9	-3.4
50,000 to 99,999						
2012	6,660	358	11,381	2,972	3,435	15,641
2013	6,319	354	11,106	2,746	3,164	15,144
Percent change	-5.1	-1.1	-2.4	-7.6	-7.9	-3.2
25,000 to 49,999						
2012	5,532	289	7,516	1,861	2,224	10,308
2013	5,286	266	7,501	1,782	2,124	9,859
Percent change	-4.4	-8.0	-0.2	-4.2	-4.5	-4.4
10,000 to 24,999						
2012	5,209	272	6,074	1,254	1,680	7,249
2013	4,837	236	5,975	1,259	1,652	6,910
Percent change	-7.1	-13.2	-1.6	+0.4	-1.7	-4.7
under 10,000						
2012	5,008	420	3,581	901	928	4,967
2013	4,821	426	3,349	775	941	4,626
Percent change	-3.7	+1.4	-6.5	-14.0	+1.4	-6.9
Metropolitan Counties						
2012	10,219	612	17,496	2,848	3,758	14,838
2013	9,379	631	17,171	2,654	3,661	14,602
Percent change	-8.2	+3.1	-1.9	-6.8	-2.6	-1.6
Nonmetropolitan Counties						
2012	4,056	219	1,150	299	372	1,094
2013	3,695	218	1,117	254	335	895
Percent change	-8.9	-0.5	-2.9	-15.1	-9.9	-18.2
Suburban Areas[2]						
2012	18,768	1,178	29,464	5,612	6,988	30,719
2013	17,774	1,090	28,896	5,254	6,868	29,581
Percent change	-5.3	-7.5	-1.9	-6.4	-1.7	-3.7

Table 15.   Crime Trends, Additional Information About Selected Offenses, by Population Group, 2012–2013

(Number, percent change.)

Population group	Aggravated assault				Burglary			Motor vehicle theft		
	Firearm	Knife or cutting instrument	Other weapon	Hands, fists, feet, etc.	Forcible entry	Unlawful entry	Attempted forcible entry	Autos	Trucks and buses	Other vehicles
Total, All Agencies										
2012	146,045	125,595	218,469	180,637	1,133,013	642,852	121,877	489,915	100,562	72,193
2013	139,931	120,063	205,112	169,644	1,032,491	595,997	110,688	474,529	98,265	70,768
Percent change	-4.2	-4.4	-6.1	-6.1	-8.9	-7.3	-9.2	-3.1	-2.3	-2.0
Total, Cities										
2012	114,571	99,625	164,323	129,365	819,460	462,161	94,108	396,405	77,287	49,010
2013	109,162	95,137	153,573	120,988	749,353	428,701	85,643	387,342	76,870	48,709
Percent change	-4.7	-4.5	-6.5	-6.5	-8.6	-7.2	-9.0	-2.3	-0.5	-0.6
250,000 and over										
2012	57,698	39,067	66,720	32,632	300,481	120,250	28,858	174,383	42,469	16,975
2013	54,464	37,830	62,733	31,536	276,762	114,318	26,312	167,759	41,535	17,267
Percent change	-5.6	-3.2	-6.0	-3.4	-7.9	-4.9	-8.8	-3.8	-2.2	+1.7
1,000,000 and over										
2012	14,265	11,624	18,405	8,150	86,764	31,529	6,521	43,313	19,048	6,105
2013	13,948	11,271	17,054	8,448	81,336	29,260	6,526	42,058	17,903	6,901
Percent change	-2.2	-3.0	-7.3	+3.7	-6.3	-7.2	+0.1	-2.9	-6.0	+13.0
500,000 to 999,999										
2012	23,217	16,169	29,034	13,383	118,496	45,928	12,834	68,922	13,803	5,931
2013	22,425	15,684	27,420	12,678	108,789	44,393	11,101	66,462	14,136	6,051
Percent change	-3.4	-3.0	-5.6	-5.3	-8.2	-3.3	-13.5	-3.6	+2.4	+2.0
250,000 to 499,999										
2012	20,216	11,274	19,281	11,099	95,221	42,793	9,503	62,148	9,618	4,939
2013	18,091	10,875	18,259	10,410	86,637	40,665	8,685	59,239	9,496	4,315
Percent change	-10.5	-3.5	-5.3	-6.2	-9.0	-5.0	-8.6	-4.7	-1.3	-12.6
100,000 to 249,999										
2012	20,359	18,779	29,724	19,758	150,106	89,054	18,806	78,674	14,523	10,085
2013	19,678	17,728	27,501	18,139	139,320	80,824	17,350	79,024	14,225	10,287
Percent change	-3.3	-5.6	-7.5	-8.2	-7.2	-9.2	-7.7	+0.4	-2.1	+2.0
50,000 to 99,999										
2012	13,777	14,076	23,069	19,994	119,402	74,184	14,810	57,504	8,700	7,528
2013	12,626	13,340	21,484	18,864	107,508	68,112	13,351	55,844	9,368	7,215
Percent change	-8.4	-5.2	-6.9	-5.7	-10.0	-8.2	-9.9	-2.9	+7.7	-4.2
25,000 to 49,999										
2012	8,685	10,422	16,639	16,444	91,429	61,232	11,694	35,362	4,518	5,832
2013	8,431	9,851	15,449	14,277	83,224	57,458	10,490	34,957	4,587	5,510
Percent change	-2.9	-5.5	-7.2	-13.2	-9.0	-6.2	-10.3	-1.1	+1.5	-5.5
10,000 to 24,999										
2012	8,115	9,197	15,393	18,195	87,304	62,354	10,485	28,737	4,110	4,550
2013	8,084	8,698	14,438	17,263	78,429	57,186	9,774	28,071	4,204	4,354
Percent change	-0.4	-5.4	-6.2	-5.1	-10.2	-8.3	-6.8	-2.3	+2.3	-4.3
under 10,000										
2012	5,937	8,084	12,778	22,342	70,738	55,087	9,455	21,745	2,967	4,040
2013	5,879	7,690	11,968	20,909	64,110	50,803	8,366	21,687	2,951	4,076
Percent change	-1.0	-4.9	-6.3	-6.4	-9.4	-7.8	-11.5	-0.3	-0.5	+0.9
Metropolitan Counties										
2012	25,468	21,326	44,373	38,002	238,034	135,613	22,947	78,949	19,588	18,374
2013	25,013	20,490	41,972	36,202	214,641	126,102	20,833	73,596	17,877	17,196
Percent change	-1.8	-3.9	-5.4	-4.7	-9.8	-7.0	-9.2	-6.8	-8.7	-6.4
Nonmetropolitan Counties										
2012	6,006	4,644	9,773	13,270	75,519	45,078	4,822	14,561	3,687	4,809
2013	5,756	4,436	9,567	12,454	68,497	41,194	4,212	13,591	3,518	4,863
Percent change	-4.2	-4.5	-2.1	-6.1	-9.3	-8.6	-12.7	-6.7	-4.6	+1.1
Suburban Areas [2]										
2012	38,494	37,086	71,518	71,224	393,188	246,078	44,158	140,831	28,076	27,773
2013	37,835	35,377	67,086	66,878	354,490	226,330	39,680	134,176	26,452	26,151
Percent change	-1.7	-4.6	-6.2	-6.1	-9.8	-8.0	-10.1	-4.7	-5.8	-5.8

Table 15.   Crime Trends, Additional Information About Selected Offenses, by Population Group, 2012–2013

(Number, percent change.)

Population group	Arson			Number of agencies	Estimated population, 2013
	Structure	Mobile	Other		
Total, All Agencies					
2012	22,052	10,970	14,985		
2013	18,896	9,834	12,904	14,540	277,860,576
Percent change	-14.3	-10.4	-13.9		
Total, Cities					
2012	16,690	8,022	11,669		
2013	14,163	7,032	10,096	10,448	183,948,238
Percent change	-15.1	-12.3	-13.5		
250,000 and over					
2012	5,800	3,460	3,451		
2013	5,281	3,142	3,444	74	46,027,577
Percent change	-8.9	-9.2	-0.2		
1,000,000 and over					
2012	1,274	1,077	1,196		
2013	1,293	1,010	1,291	8	14,619,124
Percent change	+1.5	-6.2	+7.9		
500,000 to 999,999					
2012	2,362	1,297	975		
2013	2,210	1,132	962	24	16,780,477
Percent change	-6.4	-12.7	-1.3		
250,000 to 499,999					
2012	2,164	1,086	1,280		
2013	1,778	1,000	1,191	42	14,627,976
Percent change	-17.8	-7.9	-7.0		
100,000 to 249,999					
2012	2,713	1,421	1,951		
2013	2,299	1,341	1,681	208	30,980,768
Percent change	-15.3	-5.6	-13.8		
50,000 to 99,999					
2012	2,501	1,074	1,686		
2013	1,978	864	1,531	450	31,117,040
Percent change	-20.9	-19.6	-9.2		
25,000 to 49,999					
2012	1,807	767	1,545		
2013	1,382	585	1,210	783	27,051,566
Percent change	-23.5	-23.7	-21.7		
10,000 to 24,999					
2012	1,671	647	1,141		
2013	1,447	610	882	1,688	26,781,028
Percent change	-13.4	-5.7	-22.7		
under 10,000					
2012	2,198	653	1,895		
2013	1,776	490	1,348	7,245	21,990,259
Percent change	-19.2	-25.0	-28.9		
Metropolitan Counties					
2012	3,832	2,372	2,629		
2013	3,407	2,250	2,248	1,792	70,048,493
Percent change	-11.1	-5.1	-14.5		
Nonmetropolitan Counties					
2012	1,530	576	687		
2013	1,326	552	560	2,300	23,863,845
Percent change	-13.3	-4.2	-18.5		
Suburban Areas [2]					
2012	6,897	3,571	5,106		
2013	5,910	3,207	4,100	7,890	125,037,901
Percent change	-14.3	-10.2	-19.7		

1 The rape figures in this table are based on the legacy Uniform Crime Reporting (UCR) definition of rape. The rape figures shown for 2012 and 2013 include converted National Incident-Based Reporting System rape data and those states/agencies that reported the legacy UCR definition of rape for both years.   2 Suburban areas include law enforcement agencies in cities with less than 50,000 inhabitants and county law enforcement agencies that are within a Metropolitan Statistical Area. Suburban areas exclude all metropolitan agencies associated with a principal city. The agencies associated with suburban areas also appear in other groups within this table.

Table 16. Rate: Number of Violent Crimes Per 100,000 Population, by Population Group, 2013

(Number, rate.)

Population group	Violent crime		Murder and nonnegligent manslaughter		Rape (revised definition)[1]		Rape (legacy definition)[2]		Robbery		Aggravated assault	
	Number of offenses known	Rate	Number of offenses known	Rate	Number of offenses known	Rate	Number of offenses known	Rate	Number of offenses known	Rate	Number of offenses known	Rate
Total, All Agencies	1,114,351	382.1	13,483	4.6	53,621	39.8	36,209	23.1	329,441	112.9	681,597	233.7
Total, Cities	895,791	449.7	10,346	5.2	37,637	44.0	28,923	25.4	290,331	145.7	528,554	265.3
Group I (250,000 and over)	415,673	734.7	5,282	9.3	10,086	65.7	11,824	28.7	160,525	283.7	227,956	402.9
1,000,000 and over (Group I subset)	172,961	672.1	1,930	7.5	1,279	82.3	6,035	25.0	71,478	277.7	92,239	358.4
500,000 to 999,999 (Group I subset)	132,681	831.1	1,712	10.7	4,584	65.3	3,183	35.6	46,085	288.7	77,117	483.1
250,000 to 499,999 (Group I subset)	110,031	739.5	1,640	11.0	4,223	62.3	2,606	32.2	42,962	288.8	58,600	393.9
Group II (100,000 to 249,999)	147,135	462.9	1,781	5.6	6,540	50.5	4,531	24.1	48,035	151.1	86,248	271.3
Group III (50,000 to 99,999)	111,639	346.2	1,169	3.6	5,909	40.4	3,625	20.6	33,087	102.6	67,849	210.4
Group IV (25,000 to 49,999)	80,625	283.3	827	2.9	5,138	36.3	3,037	21.2	22,060	77.5	49,563	174.1
Group V (10,000 to 24,999)	75,568	268.7	701	2.5	5,331	35.2	2,873	22.1	16,795	59.7	49,868	177.3
Group VI (under 10,000)	65,151	296.0	586	2.7	4,633	34.8	3,033	34.8	9,829	44.7	47,070	213.8
Metropolitan Counties	176,598	256.1	2,337	3.4	10,858	31.7	5,717	16.5	36,566	53.0	121,120	175.7
Nonmetropolitan Counties [3]	41,962	178.5	800	3.4	5,126	34.1	1,569	18.5	2,544	10.8	31,923	135.8
Suburban Areas [4]	312,722	247.0	3,609	2.9	19,718	30.8	11,018	17.6	70,836	55.9	207,541	163.9

1 The figures shown in this column for the offense of rape were reported using the revised Uniform Crime Reporting (UCR) definition of rape. See chapter notes for more detail.   2 The figures shown in this column for the offense of rape were reported using the legacy Uniform Crime Reporting (UCR) definition of rape. See chapter notes for more detail.   3 Includes state police agencies that report aggregately for the entire state.   4 Suburban areas include law enforcement agencies in cities with less than 50,000 inhabitants and county law enforcement agencies that are within a Metropolitan Statistical Area. Suburban areas exclude all metropolitan agencies associated with a principal city. The agencies associated with suburban areas also appear in other groups within this table.

Table 16A.   Rate: Number of Property Crimes Per 100,000 Population, by Population Group, 2013

(Number, rate.)

Population group	Property crime		Burglary		Larceny-theft		Motor vehicle theft		Number of agencies	Estimated population, 2013
	Number of offenses known	Rate	Number of offenses known	Rate	Number of offenses known	Rate	Number of offenses known	Rate		
Total, All Agencies	8,033,404	2,754.2	1,781,179	610.7	5,586,992	1,915.5	665,233	228.1	14,439	291,676,240
Total, Cities	6,368,265	3,196.7	1,311,054	658.1	4,522,141	2,270.0	535,070	268.6	10,444	199,216,695
Group I (250,000 and over)	2,086,616	3,688.0	443,718	784.3	1,398,837	2,472.4	244,061	431.4	76	56,578,450
1,000,000 and over (Group I subset)	760,143	2,953.6	151,503	588.7	521,708	2,027.2	86,932	337.8	10	25,735,804
500,000 to 999,999 (Group I subset)	722,024	4,522.8	153,021	958.5	485,605	3,041.9	83,398	522.4	23	15,964,113
250,000 to 499,999 (Group I subset)	604,449	4,062.6	139,194	935.5	391,524	2,631.5	73,731	495.6	43	14,878,533
Group II (100,000 to 249,999)	1,121,035	3,526.7	243,270	765.3	772,410	2,430.0	105,355	331.4	214	31,786,896
Group III (50,000 to 99,999)	935,283	2,900.3	193,189	599.1	668,768	2,073.8	73,326	227.4	467	32,247,892
Group IV (25,000 to 49,999)	794,193	2,790.2	155,391	545.9	592,993	2,083.3	45,809	160.9	825	28,464,143
Group V (10,000 to 24,999)	767,121	2,727.3	151,190	537.5	578,075	2,055.2	37,856	134.6	1,765	28,127,503
Group VI (under 10,000)	664,017	3,016.6	124,296	564.7	511,058	2,321.7	28,663	130.2	7,097	22,011,811
Metropolitan Counties	1,330,333	1,929.3	357,567	518.6	864,293	1,253.4	108,473	157.3	1,741	68,954,749
Nonmetropolitan Counties[1]	334,806	1,424.4	112,558	478.9	200,558	853.3	21,690	92.3	2,254	23,504,796
Suburban Areas[2]	2,791,140	2,204.6	626,125	494.5	1,976,444	1,561.1	188,571	148.9	7,921	126,607,539

1 Includes state police agencies that report aggregately for the entire state.   2 Suburban areas include law enforcement agencies in cities with less than 50,000 inhabitants and county law enforcement agencies that are within a Metropolitan Statistical Area. Suburban areas exclude all metropolitan agencies associated with a principal city. The agencies associated with suburban areas also appear in other groups within this table.

Table 17.   Rate: Number of Violent Crimes Per 100,000 Inhabitants, by Suburban and Nonsuburban Cities,[1] by Population Group, 2013

(Number, rate.)

Population group	Violent crime		Murder and nonnegligent manslaughter		Rape (revised definition)[2]		Rape (legacy definition)[3]		Robbery		Aggravated assault	
	Number of offenses known	Rate	Number of offenses known	Rate	Number of offenses known	Rate	Number of offenses known	Rate	Number of offenses known	Rate	Number of offenses known	Rate
Total, Suburban Cities	136,124	236.1	1,272	2.2	8,860	29.7	5,301	19.0	34,270	59.4	86,421	149.9
Group IV (25,000 to 49,999)	51,962	233.7	544	2.4	3,054	29.1	1,997	17.0	15,029	67.6	31,338	140.9
Group V (10,000 to 24,999)	47,444	220.0	444	2.1	3,220	28.7	1,744	16.8	12,238	56.7	29,798	138.1
Group VI (under 10,000)	36,718	265.2	284	2.1	2,586	32.0	1,560	27.1	7,003	50.6	25,285	182.6
Total, Nonsuburban Cities	85,220	406.8	842	4.0	6,242	48.9	3,642	44.5	14,414	68.8	60,080	286.8
Group IV (25,000 to 49,999)	28,663	460.3	283	4.5	2,084	57.0	1,040	40.4	7,031	112.9	18,225	292.7
Group V (10,000 to 24,999)	28,124	428.9	257	3.9	2,111	54.0	1,129	42.6	4,557	69.5	20,070	306.1
Group VI (under 10,000)	28,433	348.2	302	3.7	2,047	39.3	1,473	49.7	2,826	34.6	21,785	266.8

1 Suburban cities include law enforcement agencies in cities with less than 50,000 inhabitants that are within a Metropolitan Statistical Area. Suburban cities exclude all metropolitan agencies associated with a principal city. Nonsuburban cities include law enforcement agencies in cities with less than 50,000 inhabitants that are not associated with a Metropolitan Statistical Area.   2 The figures shown in this column for the offense of rape were reported using the revised Uniform Crime Reporting (UCR) definition of rape. See chapter notes for more detail.   3 The figures shown in this column for the offense of rape were reported using the legacy Uniform Crime Reporting (UCR) definition of rape. See chapter notes for more detail.

Table 17A.   Rate: Number of Property Crimes Per 100,000 Inhabitants, by Suburban and Nonsuburban Cities,[1] by Population Group, 2013

(Number, rate.)

Population group	Property crime		Burglary		Larceny-theft		Motor vehicle theft		Number of agencies	Estimated population, 2013
	Number of offenses known	Rate	Number of offenses known	Rate	Number of offenses known	Rate	Number of offenses known	Rate		
Total, Suburban Cities	1,460,807	2,533.8	268,558	465.8	1,112,151	1,929.0	80,098	138.9	6,180	57,652,790
25,000 to 49,999	537,600	2,417.6	101,332	455.7	402,292	1,809.1	33,976	152.8	649	22,236,736
10,000 to 24,999	506,939	2,350.2	96,703	448.3	382,131	1,771.6	28,105	130.3	1,340	21,570,172
under 10,000	416,268	3,006.4	70,523	509.3	327,728	2,367.0	18,017	130.1	4,191	13,845,882
Total, Nonsuburban Cities	764,524	3,649.2	162,319	774.8	569,975	2,720.6	32,230	153.8	3,507	20,950,667
25,000 to 49,999	256,593	4,120.4	54,059	868.1	190,701	3,062.3	11,833	190.0	176	6,227,407
10,000 to 24,999	260,182	3,967.8	54,487	830.9	195,944	2,988.2	9,751	148.7	425	6,557,331
under 10,000	247,749	3,033.9	53,773	658.5	183,330	2,245.1	10,646	130.4	2,906	8,165,929

1 Suburban cities include law enforcement agencies in cities with less than 50,000 inhabitants that are within a Metropolitan Statistical Area. Suburban cities exclude all metropolitan agencies associated with a principal city. Nonsuburban cities include law enforcement agencies in cities with less than 50,000 inhabitants that are not associated with a Metropolitan Statistical Area.

Table 18.   Rate: Number of Violent Crimes Per 100,000 Inhabitants, by Metropolitan and Nonmetropolitan Counties,[1] by Population Group, 2013

(Number, rate.)

Population group	Violent crime		Murder and nonnegligent manslaughter		Rape (revised definition)[2]		Rape (legacy definition)[3]		Robbery		Aggravated assault	
	Number of offenses known	Rate	Number of offenses known	Rate	Number of offenses known	Rate	Number of offenses known	Rate	Number of offenses known	Rate	Number of offenses known	Rate
Metropolitan Counties												
100,000 and over	117,863	282.9	1,457	3.5	6,227	33.0	3,456	15.2	29,329	70.4	77,394	185.8
25,000 to 99,999	42,886	190.4	654	2.9	3,304	26.7	1,657	16.3	5,303	23.5	31,968	142.0
Under 25,000	15,849	331.9	226	4.7	1,327	43.5	604	35.0	1,934	40.5	11,758	246.3
Nonmetropolitan Counties												
25,000 and over	16,075	171.6	266	2.8	1,607	29.7	636	16.1	1,210	12.9	12,356	131.9
10,000 to 24,999	14,053	155.5	269	3.0	1,340	23.1	584	18.0	801	8.9	11,059	122.4
Under 10,000	8,384	207.3	169	4.2	1,124	39.3	342	28.9	292	7.2	6,457	159.7

1 Metropolitan counties include sheriffs and county law enforcement agencies associated with a Metropolitan Statistical Area. Nonmetropolitan counties include sheriffs and county law enforcement agencies that are not associated with a Metropolitan Statistical Area. The offenses from state police agencies are not included in this table.   2 The figures shown in this column for the offense of rape were reported using the revised Uniform Crime Reporting (UCR) definition of rape. See chapter notes for more detail.   3 The figures shown in this column for the offense of rape were reported using the legacy Uniform Crime Reporting (UCR) definition of rape. See chapter notes for more detail.

Table 18A.   Rate: Number of Property Crimes Per 100,000 Inhabitants, by Metropolitan and Nonmetropolitan Counties,[1] by Population Group, 2013

Population group	Property crime		Burglary		Larceny-theft		Motor vehicle theft		Number of agencies	Estimated population, 2013
	Number of offenses known	Rate	Number of offenses known	Rate	Number of offenses known	Rate	Number of offenses known	Rate		
Metropolitan Counties										
100,000 and over	858,047	2,059.0	221,931	532.7	568,073	1,363.6	68,043	163.3	165	41,660,407
25,000 to 99,999	352,908	1,567.1	107,618	477.9	223,157	990.9	22,133	98.3	431	22,519,533
Under 25,000	119,378	2,500.2	28,018	586.8	73,063	1,530.2	18,297	383.2	1,145	4,774,809
Nonmetropolitan Counties										
25,000 and over	139,520	1,489.3	47,371	505.6	84,151	898.2	7,998	85.4	251	9,368,448
10,000 to 24,999	115,849	1,281.8	39,226	434.0	69,835	772.7	6,788	75.1	563	9,037,791
Under 10,000	60,206	1,488.7	18,959	468.8	36,027	890.8	5,220	129.1	1,276	4,044,229

1 Metropolitan counties include sheriffs and county law enforcement agencies associated with a Metropolitan Statistical Area. Nonmetropolitan counties include sheriffs and county law enforcement agencies that are not associated with a Metropolitan Statistical Area. The offenses from state police agencies are not included in this table.

Table 19.   Rate: Number of Crimes Per 100,000 Inhabitants, Additional Information About Selected Offenses, by Population Group, 2013

(Number, rate.)

Population group	Rape (revised definition)[1]		Robbery			Aggravated assault				Burglary		
	Rape by force	Assault to rape-attempts	Firearm	Knife or cutting instrument	Other weapon	Strong-arm	Firearm	Knife or cutting instrument	Other weapon	Hands, fists, feet, etc.	Forcible entry	Unlawful entry
Total, All Agencies												
Number of offenses known	51,003	2,525	124,885	23,652	27,711	136,213	142,324	126,221	212,470	178,348	1,022,551	592,856
Rate	37.9	1.9	44.7	8.5	9.9	48.7	50.9	45.2	76.0	63.8	365.9	212.1
Total, Cities												
Number of offenses known	35,626	1,918	107,340	20,933	23,879	121,469	111,985	102,144	162,863	131,072	746,385	428,936
Rate	41.9	2.3	56.8	11.1	12.6	64.3	59.3	54.1	86.2	69.4	395.1	227.0
Group I (250,000 and over)												
Number of offenses known	9,401	685	60,683	10,686	11,741	65,600	57,488	45,264	72,102	43,351	279,180	117,941
Rate	61.2	4.5	112.7	19.8	21.8	121.8	106.7	84.0	133.9	80.5	518.4	219.0
1,000,000 and over (Group I subset)												
Number of offenses known	1,163	116	20,927	4,785	5,007	28,944	17,166	18,780	26,318	20,224	88,966	34,938
Rate	74.9	7.5	90.9	20.8	21.8	125.8	74.6	81.6	114.4	87.9	386.6	151.8
500,000 to 999,999 (Group I subset)												
Number of offenses known	4,265	319	20,014	3,433	3,804	18,834	22,030	15,471	27,121	12,495	101,250	41,658
Rate	60.8	4.5	125.4	21.5	23.8	118.0	138.0	96.9	169.9	78.3	634.2	260.9
250,000 to 499,999 (Group I subset)												
Number of offenses known	3,973	250	19,742	2,468	2,930	17,822	18,292	11,013	18,663	10,632	88,964	41,345
Rate	58.6	3.7	132.7	16.6	19.7	119.8	122.9	74.0	125.4	71.5	597.9	277.9
Group II (100,000 to 249,999)												
Number of offenses known	6,236	225	19,038	3,760	4,337	19,695	19,915	17,724	28,026	18,013	139,239	80,403
Rate	49.4	1.8	62.2	12.3	14.2	64.3	65.0	57.9	91.5	58.8	454.6	262.5
Group III (50,000 to 99,999)												
Number of offenses known	5,655	240	11,047	2,728	3,157	15,049	12,498	13,269	21,383	18,554	106,156	67,638
Rate	38.8	1.6	35.9	8.9	10.3	48.9	40.6	43.1	69.5	60.3	344.8	219.7
Group IV (25,000 to 49,999)												
Number of offenses known	4,919	219	7,425	1,759	2,111	9,810	8,275	9,727	15,326	14,109	82,071	56,739
Rate	34.8	1.5	27.9	6.6	7.9	36.9	31.1	36.5	57.6	53.0	308.4	213.2
Group V (10,000 to 24,999)												
Number of offenses known	5,042	289	5,890	1,244	1,612	6,810	8,003	8,618	14,283	16,915	77,203	56,395
Rate	33.3	1.9	22.5	4.8	6.2	26.1	30.6	33.0	54.7	64.7	295.5	215.8
Group VI (under 10,000)												
Number of offenses known	4,373	260	3,257	756	921	4,505	5,806	7,542	11,743	20,130	62,536	49,820
Rate	32.9	2.0	15.6	3.6	4.4	21.5	27.8	36.1	56.2	96.3	299.1	238.3
Metropolitan Counties												
Number of offenses known	10,439	419	16,447	2,474	3,506	13,893	24,656	19,763	40,256	35,208	209,467	123,895
Rate	30.5	1.2	24.3	3.7	5.2	20.5	36.4	29.2	59.5	52.0	309.6	183.1
Nonmetropolitan Counties												
Number of offenses known	4,938	188	1,098	245	326	851	5,683	4,314	9,351	12,068	66,699	40,025
Rate	32.9	1.3	4.8	1.1	1.4	3.7	24.8	18.8	40.8	52.7	291.3	174.8
Suburban Areas [3]												
Number of offenses known	18,859	859	27,980	5,044	6,683	28,687	37,394	34,529	65,143	65,277	347,375	222,847
Rate	29.4	1.3	23.1	4.2	5.5	23.7	30.9	28.5	53.7	53.9	286.6	183.9

Table 19.   Rate: Number of Crimes Per 100,000 Inhabitants, Additional Information About Selected Offenses, by Population Group, 2013

(Number, rate.)

Population group	Motor vehicle theft				Number of agencies	Estimated population, 2013
	Attempted forcible entry	Autos	Trucks and buses	Other vehicles		
Total, All Agencies						
Number of offenses known	111,067	476,012	97,938	70,594	13,786	279,478,151
Rate	39.7	170.3	35.0	25.3		
Total, Cities						
Number of offenses known	87,047	390,346	76,762	48,700	9,886	188,924,303
Rate	46.1	206.6	40.6	25.8		
Group I (250,000 and over)						
Number of offenses known	28,822	172,001	41,683	17,741	75	53,857,896
Rate	53.5	319.4	77.4	32.9		
1,000,000 and over (Group I subset)						
Number of offenses known	9,824	48,504	17,985	7,807	9	23,015,250
Rate	42.7	210.7	78.1	33.9		
500,000 to 999,999 (Group I subset)						
Number of offenses known	10,113	63,755	14,080	5,563	23	15,964,113
Rate	63.3	399.4	88.2	34.8		
250,000 to 499,999 (Group I subset)						
Number of offenses known	8,885	59,742	9,618	4,371	43	14,878,533
Rate	59.7	401.5	64.6	29.4		
Group II (100,000 to 249,999)						
Number of offenses known	17,015	79,459	14,162	10,170	206	30,629,341
Rate	55.6	259.4	46.2	33.2		
Group III (50,000 to 99,999)						
Number of offenses known	13,222	55,447	9,326	7,129	445	30,788,690
Rate	42.9	180.1	30.3	23.2		
Group IV (25,000 to 49,999)						
Number of offenses known	10,529	34,595	4,539	5,448	770	26,613,840
Rate	39.6	130.0	17.1	20.5		
Group V (10,000 to 24,999)						
Number of offenses known	9,547	27,738	4,147	4,269	1,646	26,129,364
Rate	36.5	106.2	15.9	16.3		
Group VI (under 10,000)						
Number of offenses known	7,912	21,106	2,905	3,943	6,744	20,905,172
Rate	37.8	101.0	13.9	18.9		
Metropolitan Counties						
Number of offenses known	19,961	72,351	17,748	17,154	1,698	67,654,800
Rate	29.5	106.9	26.2	25.4		
Nonmetropolitan Counties						
Number of offenses known	4,059	13,315	3,428	4,740	2,202	22,899,048
Rate	17.7	58.1	15.0	20.7		
Suburban Areas [3]						
Number of offenses known	38,508	132,153	26,219	25,933	7,494	121,209,213
Rate	31.8	109.0	21.6	21.4		

1 The figures shown in this column for the offense of rape were reported using the revised Uniform Crime Reporting (UCR) definition of rape. See chapter notes for more detail.   2 The figures shown in this column for the offense of rape were reported using the legacy Uniform Crime Reporting (UCR) definition of rape. See chapter notes for more detail.   3 Suburban areas include law enforcement agencies in cities with less than 50,000 inhabitants and county law enforcement agencies that are within a Metropolitan Statistical Area. Suburban areas exclude all metropolitan agencies associated with a principal city. The agencies associated with suburban areas also appear in other groups within this table.

Table 20.   Murder, by Selected State, Territory, and Type of Weapon, 2013

(Number.)

State/territory	Total murders[1]	Total firearms	Handguns	Rifles	Shotguns	Firearms (type unknown)	Knives or cutting instruments	Other weapons	Hands, fists, feet, etc.[2]
Alabama[3]	2	1	1	0	0	0	1	0	0
Alaska	34	12	5	3	1	3	5	13	4
Arizona	304	184	133	11	11	29	56	55	9
Arkansas	154	110	53	5	5	47	22	17	5
California	1,745	1,224	805	29	48	342	238	191	92
Colorado	174	88	46	5	3	34	34	39	13
Connecticut	86	60	34	0	0	26	12	5	9
Delaware	39	33	22	1	0	10	4	2	0
District of Columbia	103	81	30	1	1	49	12	5	5
Georgia	534	411	348	11	10	42	40	74	9
Hawaii	9	6	1	2	2	1	2	1	0
Idaho	26	15	10	1	0	4	2	5	4
Illinois[3]	433	364	352	3	2	7	41	19	9
Indiana	311	238	149	6	7	76	19	41	13
Iowa	42	18	8	1	1	8	13	6	5
Kansas	112	78	39	9	5	25	8	16	10
Kentucky	165	111	82	10	6	13	23	22	9
Louisiana	453	356	298	8	9	41	34	40	23
Maine	24	12	3	2	1	6	5	2	5
Maryland	379	268	263	0	4	1	57	29	25
Massachusetts	135	78	35	2	0	41	25	25	7
Michigan	625	440	203	16	23	198	43	106	36
Minnesota	110	60	53	0	4	3	17	24	9
Mississippi	142	110	80	3	8	19	9	14	9
Missouri	371	273	137	14	6	116	41	45	12
Montana	15	9	5	0	1	3	3	2	1
Nebraska	57	39	11	2	0	26	8	7	3
Nevada	157	87	26	0	3	58	24	36	10
New Hampshire	21	5	3	0	0	2	6	5	5
New Jersey	401	291	229	0	2	60	53	37	20
New Mexico	106	59	46	5	2	6	19	20	8
New York	648	362	290	4	19	49	136	113	37
North Carolina	452	315	204	27	8	76	50	55	32
North Dakota	11	4	0	2	0	2	4	3	0
Ohio	434	309	208	3	4	94	37	69	19
Oklahoma	191	127	108	6	8	5	24	24	16
Oregon	78	43	15	0	4	24	12	18	5
Pennsylvania	594	440	328	20	22	70	52	74	28
Rhode Island	31	18	3	0	1	14	5	6	2
South Carolina	296	224	126	9	13	76	20	33	19
South Dakota	12	3	0	0	1	2	1	4	4
Tennessee	327	223	152	11	9	51	18	67	19
Texas	1,133	760	530	34	30	166	164	129	80
Utah	49	31	25	2	1	3	6	7	5
Vermont	9	5	1	2	1	1	0	1	3
Virginia	315	225	126	3	6	90	30	40	20
Washington	155	86	47	0	7	32	29	27	13
West Virginia	54	30	17	3	3	7	2	20	2
Wisconsin	157	103	72	6	6	19	18	24	12
Wyoming	15	9	6	3	0	0	2	4	0
Guam	9	2	1	0	0	1	4	1	2
Virgin Islands	14	14	13	0	0	1	0	0	0

1 Total number of murders for which supplemental homicide data were received.   2 Pushed is included in hands, fists, feet, etc.   3 Limited supplemental homicide data were received.

Table 21. Robbery, by State and Type of Weapon, 2013

(Number.)

State	Total robberies[1]	Firearms	Knives or cutting instruments	Other weapons	Strong-arm	Agency count	Population
Alabama	4,012	2,494	185	388	945	259	3,913,139
Alaska	623	139	55	58	371	32	730,730
Arizona	6,544	2,535	659	722	2,628	107	6,368,698
Arkansas	1,996	1,030	124	150	692	222	2,616,509
California	53,632	16,282	4,641	5,091	27,618	736	38,324,460
Colorado	3,088	1,162	278	373	1,275	203	5,038,948
Connecticut	3,530	1,148	351	271	1,760	104	3,596,080
Delaware	1,226	513	105	97	511	45	922,919
District of Columbia	4,078	1,545	304	243	1,986	2	646,449
Florida	23,064	9,371	1,392	2,073	10,228	613	19,325,547
Georgia	11,862	6,998	423	1,191	3,250	442	8,945,359
Hawaii	97	10	5	22	60	1	159,652
Idaho	214	55	34	32	93	107	1,606,277
Illinois[2]	394	194	24	33	143	1	150,209
Indiana	6,624	3,353	368	564	2,339	252	4,870,182
Iowa	864	261	74	111	418	197	2,712,559
Kansas	1,309	610	98	125	476	240	2,633,420
Kentucky	3,220	1,463	221	294	1,242	371	4,318,520
Louisiana	5,392	2,736	211	409	2,036	190	4,401,455
Maine	335	75	40	39	181	183	1,328,302
Maryland	8,000	3,316	785	475	3,424	152	4,589,319
Massachusetts	6,608	1,779	1,193	749	2,887	326	6,459,273
Michigan	9,917	4,729	495	783	3,910	540	9,184,659
Minnesota	3,674	1,122	252	502	1,798	331	5,419,634
Mississippi	1,665	1,089	70	135	371	67	1,420,332
Missouri	5,480	2,642	315	423	2,100	602	6,000,253
Montana	199	67	13	30	89	95	926,356
Nebraska	1,026	466	72	74	414	204	1,654,880
Nevada	5,170	1,846	448	542	2,334	49	2,742,647
New Hampshire	625	162	104	76	283	148	1,174,048
New Jersey	11,956	4,565	858	680	5,853	543	8,517,242
New Mexico	1,483	630	216	122	515	71	1,425,916
New York	27,127	6,451	2,330	2,306	16,040	483	19,154,951
North Carolina	7,696	3,912	578	661	2,545	312	7,971,054
North Dakota	156	44	29	19	64	100	714,526
Ohio	10,879	4,293	513	1,026	5,047	438	8,343,740
Oklahoma	2,996	1,303	250	234	1,209	344	3,696,802
Oregon	2,125	411	245	225	1,244	181	3,383,136
Pennsylvania	14,019	5,726	956	906	6,431	1,210	11,828,225
Rhode Island	684	225	89	95	275	49	1,051,511
South Carolina	3,893	2,101	244	320	1,228	259	4,566,990
South Dakota	155	36	23	34	62	119	763,020
Tennessee	7,248	3,945	417	784	2,102	449	6,292,929
Texas	31,504	15,804	2,433	2,542	10,725	946	25,752,157
Utah	1,165	318	147	151	549	123	2,615,082
Vermont	48	16	8	6	18	60	448,429
Virginia	4,134	2,225	249	378	1,282	351	7,051,789
Washington	5,600	1,190	471	668	3,271	239	6,460,793
West Virginia	240	93	28	43	76	241	1,108,044
Wisconsin	4,811	2,377	222	427	1,785	386	5,588,661
Wyoming	74	28	7	9	30	61	562,339

1 The number of robberies from agencies that submitted 12 months of data in 2013 for which breakdowns by type of weapon were included.   2 Limited data were received.

Table 22.   Aggravated Assault, by State and Type of Weapon, 2013

(Number.)

State	Total aggravated assaults[1]	Firearms	Knives or cutting instruments	Other weapons	Personal weapons	Agency count	Population
Alabama	12,045	2,272	1,798	6,163	1,812	259	3,913,139
Alaska	3,105	550	630	825	1,100	32	730,730
Arizona	16,855	3,942	2,938	4,977	4,998	107	6,368,698
Arkansas	8,490	2,471	1,226	1,657	3,136	222	2,616,509
California	89,005	15,616	14,522	30,029	28,838	736	38,324,460
Colorado	9,738	2,542	2,394	2,449	2,353	203	5,038,948
Connecticut	4,869	631	1,046	1,771	1,421	104	3,596,080
Delaware	2,899	743	687	1,129	340	45	922,919
District of Columbia	3,830	858	1,274	1,205	493	2	646,449
Florida	60,648	13,613	11,177	22,020	13,838	613	19,325,547
Georgia	18,847	5,719	3,288	5,070	4,770	442	8,945,359
Hawaii	307	0	27	139	141	1	159,652
Idaho	2,510	396	480	800	834	107	1,606,277
Illinois[2]	1,507	766	196	266	279	1	150,209
Indiana	11,874	2,024	1,424	3,689	4,737	252	4,870,182
Iowa	5,308	550	906	1,008	2,844	197	2,712,559
Kansas	6,809	1,971	1,536	2,080	1,222	240	2,633,420
Kentucky	4,152	912	765	1,515	960	371	4,318,520
Louisiana	15,435	3,847	2,406	4,500	4,682	190	4,401,455
Maine	910	39	174	255	442	183	1,328,302
Maryland	12,051	1,691	3,199	4,000	3,161	152	4,589,319
Massachusetts	17,652	2,016	4,350	8,219	3,067	326	6,459,273
Michigan	25,978	7,658	5,288	8,843	4,189	540	9,184,659
Minnesota	6,870	1,257	1,302	1,831	2,480	331	5,419,634
Mississippi	2,487	771	316	594	806	67	1,420,332
Missouri	17,981	5,185	2,406	4,984	5,406	602	6,000,253
Montana	1,776	240	251	568	717	95	926,356
Nebraska	2,858	635	496	1,005	722	204	1,654,880
Nevada	9,786	1,666	1,915	4,061	2,144	49	2,742,647
New Hampshire	1,341	217	304	307	513	148	1,174,048
New Jersey	11,797	2,265	2,535	3,635	3,362	543	8,517,242
New Mexico	6,538	1,361	1,157	2,039	1,981	71	1,425,916
New York	45,807	5,328	12,247	13,014	15,218	483	19,154,951
North Carolina	17,421	6,127	3,289	4,244	3,761	312	7,971,054
North Dakota	1,398	30	165	274	929	100	714,526
Ohio	11,693	2,897	2,084	4,289	2,423	438	8,343,740
Oklahoma	11,425	1,950	2,013	4,077	3,385	344	3,696,802
Oregon	4,946	598	928	1,740	1,680	181	3,383,136
Pennsylvania	22,227	4,452	3,249	5,270	9,256	1,210	11,828,225
Rhode Island	1,550	398	363	492	297	49	1,051,511
South Carolina	17,258	5,749	3,168	4,726	3,615	259	4,566,990
South Dakota	1,919	190	438	532	759	119	763,020
Tennessee	27,748	8,295	5,374	10,115	3,964	449	6,292,929
Texas	63,987	15,053	14,435	21,462	13,037	946	25,752,157
Utah	3,397	604	909	1,147	737	123	2,615,082
Vermont	363	62	74	67	160	60	448,429
Virginia	8,514	1,970	1,729	2,477	2,338	351	7,051,789
Washington	10,871	1,631	1,749	3,992	3,499	239	6,460,793
West Virginia	2,497	392	289	646	1,170	241	1,108,044
Wisconsin	9,195	2,087	1,150	2,025	3,933	386	5,588,661
Wyoming	889	87	155	248	399	61	562,339

1 The number of aggravated assaults from agencies that submitted 12 months of data in 2013 for which breakdowns by type of weapon were included.   2 Limited data were received.

Table 23.   Offense Analysis, Number and Percent Change, 2012–2013

(Number, percent, dollars; 14,230 agencies; 2013 estimated population 289,935,142.)

Classification	Number of offenses, 2013	Percent change from 2012	Percent distribution[1]	Average value (dollars)
Murder	12,404	-3.9	NA	
Rape (Revised Definition) [2]	53,949	NA	NA	
Rape (Legacy Definition) [3]	31,824	NA	NA	
Robbery	301,235	-2.3	100.0	$1,170
By location				
Street/highway	127,880	-3.1	42.5	853
Commercial house	39,944	-0.9	13.3	1,808
Gas or service station	7,292	-1.1	2.4	830
Convenience store	14,929	-3.0	5.0	1,171
Residence	50,081	-3.5	16.6	1,480
Bank	5,684	-0.9	1.9	3,542
Miscellaneous	55,425	-0.2	18.4	961
Burglary	1,743,560	-8.2	100.0	2,322
By location				
Residence (dwelling)	1,289,030	-9.1	73.9	2,315
Residence, night	356,993	-9.4	20.5	1,736
Residence, day	682,770	-9.3	39.2	2,521
Residence, unknown	249,267	-8.1	14.3	2,577
Nonresidence (store, office, etc.)	454,530	-5.7	26.1	2,344
Nonresidence, night	185,922	-6.5	10.7	2,356
Nonresidence, day	165,482	-5.1	9.5	1,957
Nonresidence, unknown	103,126	-5.4	5.9	2,945
Larceny-theft (except motor vehicle theft)	5,392,153	-2.4	100.0	1,259
By type				
Pocket-picking	29,047	+1.1	0.5	514
Purse-snatching	23,171	-1.6	0.4	467
Shoplifting	1,074,188	+4.3	19.9	207
From motor vehicles (except accessories)	1,259,348	-5.0	23.4	937
Motor vehicle accessories	393,385	-6.4	7.3	556
Bicycles	190,703	-4.5	3.5	420
From buildings	662,964	-2.5	12.3	1,384
From coin-operated machines	14,248	-6.4	0.3	448
All others	1,745,099	-3.2	32.4	2,372
By value				
Over $200	2,525,685	-2.3	46.8	2,625
$50 to $200	1,202,569	-3.6	22.3	104
Under $50	1,663,899	-1.7	30.9	21
Motor Vehicle Theft	652,288	-0.3	NA	5,972

NA = Not available.   1 Because of rounding, the percentages may not add to 100.0.   2 The figures shown in this column for the offense of rape were reported using the revised Uniform Crime Reporting (UCR) definition of rape. See chapter notes for more detail.   3 The figures shown in this column for the offense of rape were reported using the legacy Uniform Crime Reporting (UCR) definition of rape. See chapter notes for more detail.

Table 24.   Property Stolen and Recovered, by Type and Value, 2013

(Dollars, percent; 13,658 agencies; 2013 estimated population 281,066,647.)

Type of property	Value of property (dollars)		Percent recovered
	Stolen	Recovered	
Total	$10,087,916,015	$2,503,262,060	19.2
Currency, notes, etc.	2,013,267,402	28,453,259	1.4
Jewelry and precious metals	1,743,673,506	88,475,237	5.1
Clothing and furs	304,670,804	33,542,000	11.0
Locally stolen motor vehicles	3,937,054,674	2,159,429,364	54.8
Office equipment	846,233,329	32,167,043	3.8
Televisions, radios, stereos, etc.	665,750,318	32,632,767	4.9
Firearms	154,826,891	13,693,638	8.8
Household goods	422,439,091	114,868,752	27.2
Consumable goods	231,420,776	14,425,417	6.2
Livestock	16,367,591	1,303,936	8.0
Miscellaneous	4,406,114,070	313,240,430	7.1

SECTION III

OFFENSES CLEARED

OFFENSES CLEARED

Figure 3.1 Percent of Crime Cleared by Arrest or Exceptional Means

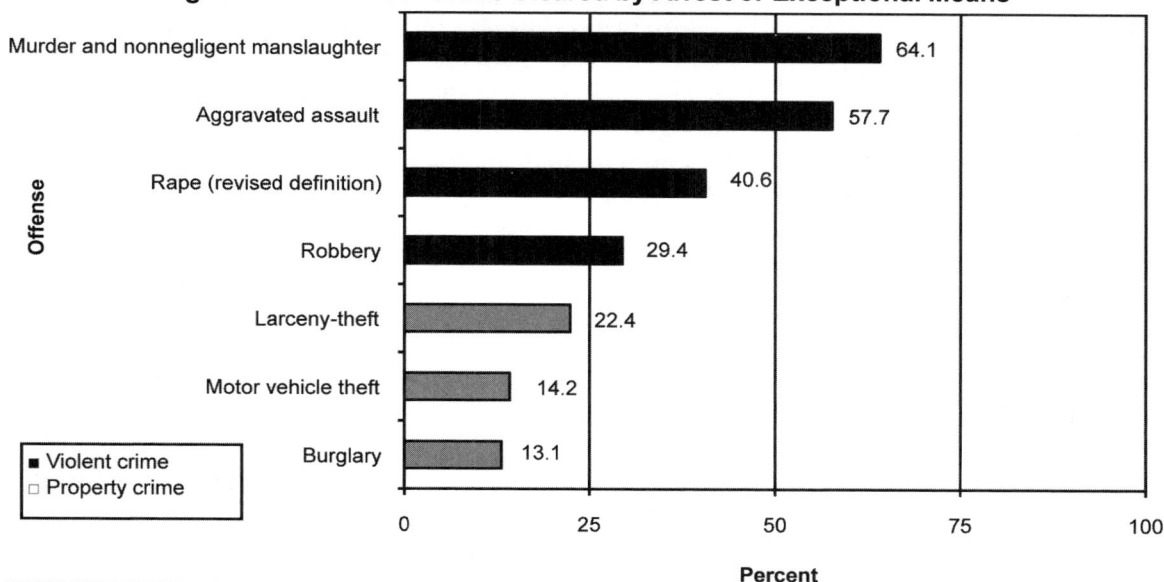

Law enforcement agencies that report crime to the Federal Bureau of Investigation (FBI) can clear, or "close," offenses in one of two ways: by arrest or by exceptional means. However, the administrative closing of a case by a local law enforcement agency does not necessarily mean that the agency can clear an offense for Uniform Crime Reporting (UCR) purposes. To clear an offense within the program's guidelines, the reporting agency must adhere to certain criteria, which are outlined in this section. (**Note : The UCR program does not distinguish between offenses cleared by arrest and those cleared by exceptional means in its data presentations. The distinction is made solely for the purpose of a definition and not for data collection and publication.) See Appendix I for information on the UCR program's statistical methodology.**

Important Note: Rape Data

In 2013, the FBI UCR Program initiated the collection of rape data within the Summary Reporting System under a revised definition. The definition changed to the revised UCR definition below.

- Legacy UCR definition of rape: The carnal knowledge of a female forcibly and against her will.

- Revised UCR definition of rape: Penetration, no matter how slight, of the vagina or anus with any body part or object, or oral penetration by a sex organ of another person, without the consent of the victim.

For more information, please see http://www.fbi.gov/about-us/cjis/ucr/crime-in-the-u.s/2013/crime-in-the-u.s.-2013/rape-addendum/rape_addendum_final.

Cleared by Arrest

In the UCR program, a law enforcement agency reports that an offense is cleared by arrest, or solved for crime reporting purposes, when at least one person is arrested, charged with the commission of the offense, and turned over to the court for prosecution (whether following arrest, court summons, or police notice). To qualify as a clearance, all of these conditions must be met.

In its calculations, the UCR program counts the number of offenses that are cleared, not the number of arrestees. Therefore, the arrest of one person may clear several crimes, and the arrest of many persons may clear only one offense. In addition, some clearances recorded by an agency during a particular calendar year, such as 2013, may pertain to offenses that occurred in previous years.

Cleared by Exceptional Means

In certain situations, elements beyond law enforcement's control prevent the agency from arresting and formally charging the offender. When this occurs, the agency can clear the offense exceptionally. There are four UCR program requirements that law enforcement must meet in order to clear an offense by exceptional means. The agency must have:

- Identified the offender

305

- Gathered enough evidence to support an arrest, make a charge, and turn over the offender to the court for prosecution

- Identified the offender's exact location so that the suspect could be taken into custody immediately

- Encountered a circumstance outside the control of law enforcement that prohibits the agency from arresting, charging, and prosecuting the offender

Examples of exceptional clearances include, but are not limited to, the death of the offender (e.g., suicide or justifiably killed by a law enforcement officer or a citizen), the victim's refusal to cooperate with the prosecution after the offender has been identified, or the denial of extradition because the offender committed a crime in another jurisdiction and is being prosecuted for that offense. In the UCR program, the recovery of property does not clear an offense.

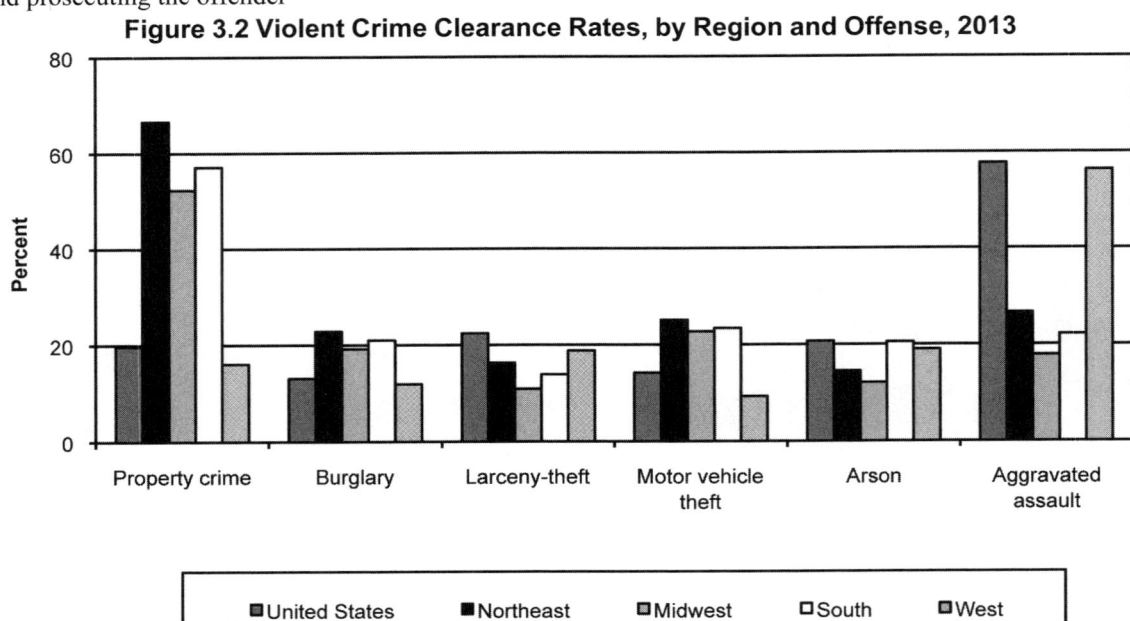

Figure 3.2 Violent Crime Clearance Rates, by Region and Offense, 2013

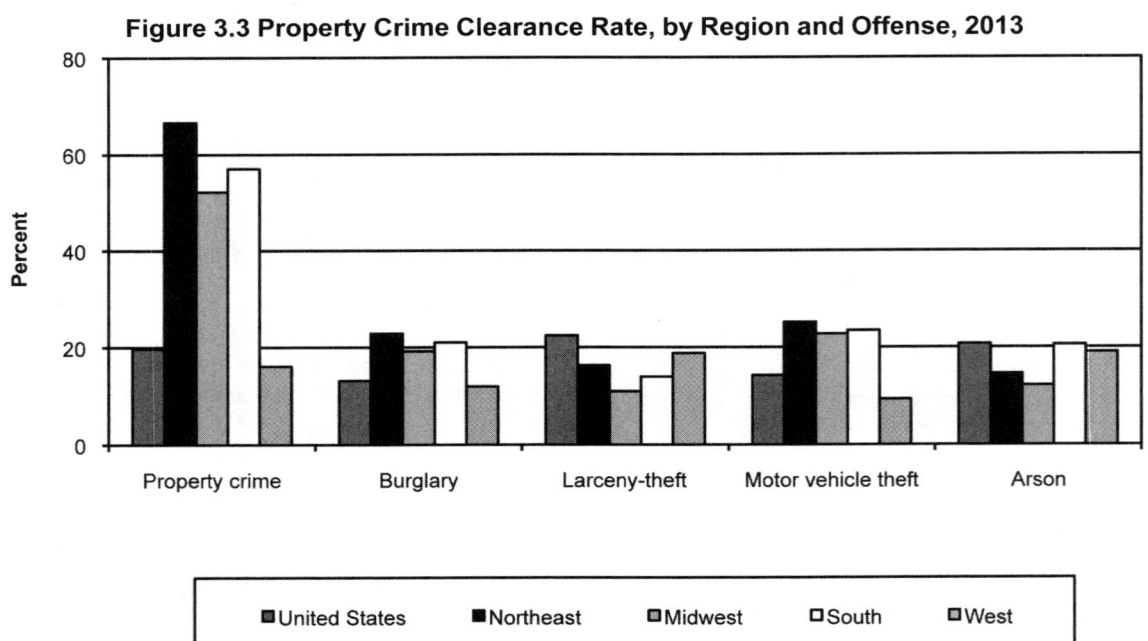

Figure 3.3 Property Crime Clearance Rate, by Region and Offense, 2013

National Clearances

A review of the data for 2013 revealed law enforcement agencies in the United States cleared 48.1 percent of violent crimes (murder, rape, robbery, and aggravated assault) and 19.7 percent of property crimes (burglary, larceny-theft, and motor vehicle theft) brought to their attention. In addition, law enforcement cleared 20.7 percent of arson offenses, which are reported in a slightly different manner than the other property crimes. (Table 25) More details concerning this offense are furnished in the arson text in this section.

As in most years, law enforcement agencies cleared a higher percentage of violent crimes than property crimes in 2013. As a rule, clearance rates generally rise due to the more vigorous investigative efforts put forth for violent crimes. In addition, violent crimes more often involve victims and/or witnesses who are able to identify the perpetrators. Clearance rates for arson crimes, however, rose from 2012.

A breakdown of the clearances for violent crimes for 2013 revealed that the nation's law enforcement agencies cleared 64.1 percent of murder offenses (an increase from 2012), 57.7 percent of aggravated assault offenses, 40.0 percent of rape offenses (legacy definition), and 29.4 percent of robbery offenses. (Table 25)

For property crime offenses in 2013, law enforcement agencies throughout the nation collectively 13.1 percent of burglary offenses, 22.4 percent of larceny-theft offenses, and 14.2 percent of motor vehicle theft offenses (up more than two percentage points from 2012). (Table 25)

Regional Clearances

The UCR program divides the nation into four regions: the Northeast, the Midwest, the South, and the West. (See Appendix III for further details.) A review of clearance data for 2013 by region showed that agencies in the Northeast cleared the greatest proportion of their violent crime offenses (53.6 percent). Law enforcement agencies in the South cleared 48.9 percent of their violent crimes, while agencies in the West and Midwest cleared 46.4 percent and 42.7 percent of their violent crimes, respectively. (Table 26)

For murder and nonnegligent manslaughter in 2013, the South cleared 67.9 percent of offenses, closely followed by the West (67.7 percent). The Northeast cleared 61.7 percent and the Midwest cleared 51.7 percent of these offenses. Rape (revised definition) offenses were cleared 46.9 percent of the time in the South, 42.9 percent of the time in the Northeast, 35.2 percent of the time in the West, and 34.8 percent of the time in the Midwest. For robbery, the Northeast had the highest clearance rate, at 33.5 percent. The Northeast also had the highest proportion of clearances for aggravated assault (66.6 percent). (Table 26)

Clearance data for 2013 showed that, among the regions, law enforcement agencies in the Northeast cleared the highest percentage of their property crimes (22.8 percent). Agencies in the South and Midwest cleared 21.0 percent and 19.2 percent, respectively. Agencies in the West cleared 16.1 percent of their property crimes. (Table 26)

Agencies in the Northeast cleared the highest percentage of burglary offenses at 16.3 percent, followed by the South at 13.9 percent, the West at 11.9 percent, and the Midwest at 10.9 percent. For larceny-theft, the Northeast (25.1 percent) was followed by the South at 23.4 percent, the Midwest at 22.7 percent, and the West at 18.8 percent. The South cleared the highest proportion of motor vehicle thefts at 20.5 percent, followed by the Northeast at 14.5 percent. The Northeast cleared the greatest percentage of arson offenses (26.6 percent), followed by the South (22.1 percent). (Table 26)

Clearances by Population Groups

The UCR program uses the following population group designations in its data presentations: cities (grouped according to population size) and counties (classified as either metropolitan or nonmetropolitan counties). A breakdown of these classifications is furnished in Appendix III.

CITIES

In 2013, the clearance data collected showed that law enforcement agencies in the nation's cities cleared 46.3 percent of their violent crime offenses. Among the city population groups, agencies in the smallest cities, those with fewer than 10,000 inhabitants, cleared the greatest proportion of their violent crime offenses (56.2 percent), and law enforcement in cities with 250,000 to 499,999 inhabitants cleared the smallest proportion of their violent crime offenses (38.7 percent). (Table 25)

The clearance data for murder showed that among the city population groups, cities with populations of 1,000,000 or more inhabitants cleared the greatest percentage of their murders (79.2 percent). Law enforcement agencies in cities with 250,000 to 499,999 inhabitants cleared the lowest percentage of their murders (57.2 percent). For rape (revised definition), cities with 1,000,000 or more inhabitants cleared the largest percentage of offenses at 70.4 percent, while cities with 25,000 to 49,999 inhabitants cleared the lowest percentage of offenses at 34.0 percent. Cities with under 10,000 inhabitants cleared the greatest percentage of their robbery offenses at 37.0 percent, and cities with 250,000 to 499,999 inhabitants cleared the lowest proportion of their robbery offenses at 23.7 percent. For aggravated assault, cities with fewer than 10,000 inhabitants cleared the highest proportion of offenses (63.3 percent); cities with 500,000 to 999,999 inhabitants cleared the lowest percentage of offenses (47.4 percent). (Table 25)

In 2013, agencies in the nation's cities collectively cleared 19.7 percent of their property crime offenses. Law enforcement in cities with 10,000 to 24,999 inhabitants cleared the highest proportion of the property crimes (36.2 percent) brought to their attention; cities with 1,000,000 or more inhabitants cleared the smallest proportion of their property crimes (14.7 percent). (Table 25)

Law enforcement agencies in cities cleared 12.7 percent of burglaries, 22.8 percent of larceny-thefts, 11.3 percent of motor vehicle thefts, and 19.8 percent of arsons in 2013. For burglaries, cities with fewer than 10,000 inhabitants cleared the largest percentage of their offenses at 17.3 percent, while cities with 500,000 to 999,999 inhabitants cleared the smallest percentage of their offenses at 9.5 percent. Cities with 10,000 to 24,999 inhabitants cleared the greatest percentage of their larceny-theft offenses (29.4 percent), and cities with 500,000 to 999,999 inhabitants cleared the lowest proportion of larceny-theft offenses (15.9 percent). For motor vehicle theft, cities with fewer than 10,000 inhabitants cleared the highest percentages of their offenses at 23.4 percent. Cities with 10,000 to 24,999 inhabitants cleared the greatest percentage of their arson offenses, at 23.7 percent. (Table 25)

METROPOLITAN AND NONMETROPOLITAN COUNTIES

In 2013, law enforcement agencies in metropolitan counties cleared 54.3 percent of their violent crime offenses. Of the violent crimes made known to law enforcement agencies in metropolitan counties, murder offenses had the highest proportion of clearance (65.7 percent), followed by aggravated assaults (62.3 percent), rapes (revised definition, 48.6 percent), and robberies (32.3 percent). Law enforcement agencies in metropolitan counties cleared 19.6 percent of their total property crimes, 13.8 percent of burglaries, 21.1 percent of larceny-thefts, 25.9 percent of motor vehicle thefts, and 22.9 percent of their arsons. (Table 25)

Like their counterparts in metropolitan counties, nonmetropolitan counties collectively cleared a greater proportion of their violent crimes than did the nation as a whole in 2013. Nonmetropolitan counties cleared 59.0 percent of their violent crime offenses and 18.7 percent of property crimes. Of the violent crimes known to them, law enforcement in nonmetropolitan counties had the highest number of clearances for murder (73.9 percent), with 47.5 percent of rapes (revised definition), 41.9 percent of robberies, and 62.7 percent of aggravated assaults being cleared. Agencies in nonmetropolitan counties reported clearing 15.8 percent of their burglaries, 19.9 percent of their larceny-thefts, 23.6 percent of their motor vehicle thefts, and 24.8 percent of their arsons. (Table 25)

Clearances by Classification Group and Type

For rape (revised definition), by classification group and type, law enforcement agencies cleared 37.5 percent of assault-to-rape attempts and 38.9 percent of rapes by force in 2013. Cleared robbery offenses included 33.4 percent of offenses involving strong-arm tactics, 33.4 percent of offenses involving knives or other cutting instruments, 31.0 percent of offenses involving other weapons, and 23.2 percent of offenses involving firearms. For aggravated assaults, agencies cleared 64.8 percent of offenses involving knives or other cutting instruments; 63.8 percent of offenses involving hands, feet, fists, etc.; 57.7 percent of offenses involving other weapons; and 42.2 percent of offenses involving firearms. (Table 27)

For property crime clearances grouped by classification and type, data showed that the highest percentage of burglary clearances in the nation in 2013 (14.6 percent) were of offenses that involved unlawful entry of structures. Law enforcement agencies cleared 11.8 percent of burglaries involving forcible entry and 11.7 percent of attempted forcible entry offenses. For motor vehicle theft, agencies cleared 14.2 percent of motor vehicle theft offenses involving automobiles and 9.6 percent of motor vehicle theft offenses involving trucks and buses. (Table 27)

In 2013, 24.2 percent of structural arson offenses were cleared by arrest or exceptional means, while 10.7 percent of mobile arson offenses and 21.9 percent of other arson crimes were cleared. (Table 27)

CLEARANCES AND JUVENILES

When an offender under 18 years of age is cited to appear in juvenile court or before other juvenile authorities, the UCR program considers the incident for which the juvenile is being held responsible to be cleared by arrest, although a physical arrest may not have occurred. In addition, according to program definitions, clearances that include both adult and juvenile offenders are classified as clearances for crimes committed by adults. Therefore, the juvenile clearance data are limited to those clearances involving juveniles only, and the figures in this publication should not be used to present a definitive picture of juvenile involvement in crime.

Of the clearances for violent crimes that were reported in the nation in 2013, 8.8 percent involved only juveniles, unchanged from 2012 and down from 9.5 percent in 2011. In the nation's cities, collectively, 8.9 percent of violent crime clearances involved only juveniles (also unchanged since 2012), with juveniles in cities exclusively involved in 3.6 percent of murder clearances, 15.9 percent of rape (revised definition) clearances, 13.3 percent of robbery clearances, and 7.4 percent of aggravated assault clearances. Of the nation's city population groups, cities with 500,000 to 999,999 inhabitants had the highest percentage of overall clearances for violent crime only involving juveniles (9.5 percent); cities with 1,000,000 or more inhabitants and cities with 250,000 to 499,999 inhabitants had the lowest percentages (each at 8.6 percent). (Table 28)

Law enforcement agencies in metropolitan counties reported that 9.0 percent of their violent crime clearances—including 3.5 percent of their murder clearances, 21.0 percent of their rape (revised definition) clearances, 12.1 percent of their robbery clearances, and 7.9 percent of their aggravated assault clearances—involved only juveniles. Agencies in nonmetropolitan counties reported that 6.8 percent of their clearances for violent crime involved only juveniles, including 3.2 percent of their murder clearances, 15.9 percent of their rape (revised definition) clearances, 4.6 percent of their robbery clearances, and 5.7 percent of their aggravated assault clearances. (Table 28)

In 2013, 10.8 percent of clearances for property crime involved only juveniles, a decrease of nearly two percentage points since 2012. In cities collectively, 11.2 percent of the clearances for property crime, 10.5 percent of clearances for burglary, 11.4 percent of clearances for larceny-theft, 10.5 percent of clearances for motor vehicle theft, and 29.8 percent of clearances for arson involved juveniles only. Among the population groups labeled city, the percentages of clearances involving only juveniles for overall property crime ranged from a low of 9.2 percent in cities fewer than 10,000 inhabitants to a high of 12.8 percent in cities with populations of 100,000 to 249,999. (Table 28)

Metropolitan counties reported that 9.4 percent of all property crime clearances, 8.9 percent of burglary clearances, 10.3 percent of larceny-theft clearances, 5.2 percent of motor vehicle theft clearances, and 25.7 percent of arson clearances involved persons under 18 years of age. In nonmetropolitan counties, 75 percent of property crime clearances, 7.6 percent of burglary clearances, 7.2 percent of larceny-theft clearances, 9.4 percent of motor vehicle theft clearances, and 15.0 percent of arson clearances involved juveniles exclusively. In suburban areas, 28.3 percent of arson clearances involved only juveniles. (Table 28)

Table 25.   Number and Percent of Offenses Cleared by Arrest or Exceptional Means, by Population Group, 2013

(Number, percent.)

Population group	Violent crime	Murder and nonnegligent manslaughter	Rape (revised definition)[1]	Robbery	Aggravated assault	Property crime	Burglary	Larceny-theft	Motor vehicle theft	Arson[2]
Total, All Agencies										
Offenses known	1,093,431	13,075	54,598	319,047	672,440	7,946,255	1,774,472	5,515,119	656,664	43,356
Percent cleared by arrest	48.1	64.1	40.6	29.4	57.7	19.7	13.1	22.4	14.2	20.7
Total Cities										
Offenses known	868,659	9,911	38,571	277,919	515,331	6,232,236	1,292,660	4,415,748	523,828	32,770
Percent cleared by arrest	46.3	62.9	37.4	29.0	56.2	19.7	12.7	22.8	11.3	19.8
Group I (250,000 and over)										
Offenses known	397,038	4,942	10,656	151,000	219,295	2,029,407	437,205	1,357,526	234,676	12,231
Percent cleared by arrest	42.2	63.0	43.7	26.8	52.4	14.7	10.0	17.3	8.2	15.1
1,000,000 and over (Group I subset)										
Offenses known	150,302	1,516	1,279	59,663	82,488	664,235	133,728	456,211	74,296	3,612
Percent cleared by arrest	47.8	79.2	70.4	30.8	59.4	15.2	10.2	17.9	7.6	11.4
500,000 to 999,999 (Group I subset)										
Offenses known	136,705	1,786	5,154	48,375	78,207	760,723	164,283	509,791	86,649	4,466
Percent cleared by arrest	38.9	57.2	40.4	24.6	47.4	13.7	9.5	15.9	8.1	16.5
250,000 to 499,999 (Group I subset)										
Offenses known	110,031	1,640	4,223	42,962	58,600	604,449	139,194	391,524	73,731	4,153
Percent cleared by arrest	38.7	54.5	39.5	23.7	49.3	15.5	10.5	18.5	8.9	16.8
Group II (100,000 to 249,999)										
Offenses known	145,118	1,769	6,540	47,667	84,807	1,110,662	242,061	763,346	105,255	5,435
Percent cleared by arrest	45.2	61.3	34.2	28.9	54.8	18.2	11.8	21.2	10.7	19.9
Group III (50,000 to 99,999)										
Offenses known	109,378	1,147	5,982	32,246	66,634	915,000	189,633	652,727	72,640	4,466
Percent cleared by arrest	48.3	57.5	36.7	31.1	58.1	20.9	13.1	24.3	11.3	21.1
Group IV (25,000 to 49,999)										
Offenses known	77,991	781	5,195	21,246	48,084	767,427	151,007	571,330	45,090	3,227
Percent cleared by arrest	50.2	65.2	34.0	33.4	59.8	24.0	14.3	27.3	15.4	23.7
Group V (10,000 to 24,999)										
Offenses known	73,203	678	5,409	15,868	48,798	740,642	146,430	557,404	36,808	3,068
Percent cleared by arrest	54.2	69.0	36.0	35.9	62.5	26.2	15.9	29.4	18.3	27.1
Group VI (under 10,000)										
Offenses known	65,931	594	4,789	9,892	47,713	669,098	126,324	513,415	29,359	4,280
Percent cleared by arrest	56.2	67.0	34.2	37.0	63.3	23.8	17.3	25.4	23.4	23.5
Metropolitan Counties										
Offenses known	181,930	2,343	10,809	38,492	124,504	1,372,177	366,639	894,885	110,653	8,072
Percent cleared by arrest	54.3	65.7	48.6	31.3	62.3	19.6	13.8	21.1	25.9	22.9
Nonmetropolitan Counties										
Offenses known	42,842	821	5,218	2,636	32,605	341,842	115,173	204,486	22,183	2,577
Percent cleared by arrest	59.0	73.9	47.5	41.9	62.7	18.7	15.8	19.9	23.6	24.8
Suburban Areas[3]										
Offenses known	313,927	3,545	19,824	71,201	208,988	2,785,562	628,062	1,968,162	189,338	14,076
Percent cleared by arrest	54.1	65.2	42.5	32.9	62.9	21.8	14.7	24.1	22.0	24.1

1 The figures shown in this column for the offense of rape were reported using the revised Uniform Crime Reporting (UCR) definition of rape. See chapter notes for more detail.   2 Not all agencies submit reports for arson to the FBI. As a result, the number of reports the FBI uses to compute the percent of offenses cleared for arson is less than the number it uses to compute the percent of offenses cleared for all other offenses.   3 Suburban area includes law enforcement agencies in cities with less than 50,000 inhabitants and county law enforcement agencies that are within a Metropolitan Statistical Area. Suburban area excludes all metropolitan agencies associated with a principal city. The agencies associated with suburban areas also appear in other groups within this table.

Table 26.   Number and Percent of Offenses Cleared by Arrest or Exceptional Means, by Region and Geographic Division, 2013

(Number, percent.)

Geographic region/division	Violent crime	Murder and non-negligent man-slaughter	Rape (revised definition)[1]	Robbery	Aggravated assault	Property crime	Burglary	Larceny-theft	Motor vehicle theft	Arson[2]
Total, All Agencies										
Offenses known	1,093,431	13,075	54,598	319,047	672,440	7,946,255	1,774,472	5,515,119	656,664	43,356
Percent cleared by arrest	48.1	64.1	40.6	29.4	57.7	19.7	13.1	22.4	14.2	20.7
Northeast										
Offenses known	186,289	1,921	7,261	65,237	107,622	1,070,663	202,634	806,176	61,853	4,656
Percent cleared by arrest	53.6	61.7	42.9	33.5	66.6	22.8	16.3	25.1	14.5	26.6
New England										
Offenses known	43,381	305	3,588	11,840	26,810	297,296	61,880	215,959	19,457	1,378
Percent cleared by arrest	48.4	59.7	27.6	26.9	59.6	18.0	12.8	20.1	11.2	25.4
Middle Atlantic										
Offenses known	142,908	1,616	3,673	53,397	80,812	773,367	140,754	590,217	42,396	3,278
Percent cleared by arrest	55.2	62.1	57.9	34.9	68.9	24.7	17.9	26.9	16.0	27.1
Midwest										
Offenses known	177,502	2,291	18,232	47,954	106,328	1,346,215	305,039	937,543	103,633	9,576
Percent cleared by arrest	42.7	51.7	34.8	23.9	52.3	19.2	10.9	22.7	12.1	17.8
East North Central										
Offenses known	112,755	1,573	11,157	35,257	62,783	804,943	198,113	544,471	62,359	6,157
Percent cleared by arrest	37.5	44.6	32.3	21.7	47.1	17.5	10.0	21.1	10.1	15.4
West North Central										
Offenses known	64,747	718	7,075	12,697	43,545	541,272	106,926	393,072	41,274	3,419
Percent cleared by arrest	51.7	67.4	38.7	30.2	59.9	21.8	12.4	25.0	15.1	22.0
South										
Offenses known	462,284	5,932	21,018	125,257	296,214	3,467,593	817,650	2,418,222	231,721	15,590
Percent cleared by arrest	48.9	67.9	46.9	29.7	57.1	21.0	13.9	23.4	20.5	22.1
South Atlantic										
Offenses known	235,606	3,075	11,933	66,976	149,004	1,738,947	402,439	1,224,665	111,843	7,218
Percent cleared by arrest	51.8	68.3	53.2	32.4	60.2	23.1	16.3	24.9	27.2	26.0
East South Central										
Offenses known	70,652	910	5,677	16,260	47,264	500,316	128,241	342,354	29,721	2,703
Percent cleared by arrest	48.4	68.5	43.3	30.3	55.0	22.3	13.8	25.5	21.3	19.6
West South Central										
Offenses known	156,026	1,947	3,408	42,021	99,946	1,228,330	286,970	851,203	90,157	5,669
Percent cleared by arrest	44.8	67.0	31.1	25.3	53.3	17.5	10.5	20.4	11.8	18.2
West										
Offenses known	267,356	2,931	8,087	80,599	162,276	2,061,784	449,149	1,353,178	259,457	13,534
Percent cleared by arrest	46.4	67.7	35.2	28.9	56.3	16.1	11.9	18.8	9.3	19.0
Mountain										
Offenses known	81,980	913	5,071	18,164	53,202	646,172	136,733	454,766	54,673	3,943
Percent cleared by arrest	46.3	71.1	81.3	28.0	54.9	19.7	10.7	23.3	12.0	22.6
Pacific										
Offenses known	185,376	2,018	3,016	62,435	109,074	1,415,612	312,416	898,412	204,784	9,591
Percent cleared by arrest	46.5	66.1	35.5	29.2	57.0	14.5	12.4	16.5	8.6	17.6

1 The figures shown in this column for the offense of rape were reported using the revised Uniform Crime Reporting (UCR) definition of rape. See chapter notes for more detail.   2 Not all agencies submit reports for arson to the FBI. As a result, the number of reports the FBI uses to compute the percent of offenses cleared for arson is less than the number it uses to compute the percent of offenses cleared for all other offenses.

Table 27.   Number and Percent of Offenses Cleared by Arrest or Exceptional Means, Additional Information About Selected Offenses, by Population Group, 2013

(Number, percent.)

Population group	Rape (revised definition)[1] Rape by force	Rape (revised definition)[1] Assault to rape-attempts	Rape (legacy definition)[2] Rape by force	Rape (legacy definition)[2] Assault to rape-attempts	Robbery Firearm	Robbery Knife or cutting instrument	Robbery Other weapon	Robbery Strong-arm	Aggravated assault Firearm	Aggravated assault Knife or cutting instrument	Aggravated assault Other weapon	Aggravated assault Hands, fists, feet, etc.
Total, All Agencies												
Offenses known	45,683	2,301	31,349	2,914	118,186	22,773	26,211	128,764	131,053	117,355	194,762	169,273
Percent cleared by arrest	38.9	37.5	39.9	41.3	23.2	33.4	31.0	33.4	42.2	64.8	57.7	63.8
Total Cities												
Offenses known	33,312	1,814	24,609	2,310	102,818	20,300	22,834	116,173	105,480	96,666	152,865	126,715
Percent cleared by arrest	36.3	38.6	39.9	41.8	23.3	33.0	30.9	33.1	38.2	64.2	56.6	64.4
Group I (250,000 and over)												
Offenses known	9,221	683	9,973	1,172	59,298	10,539	11,583	64,787	55,019	43,617	69,566	42,243
Percent cleared by arrest	41.7	41.6	39.1	42.1	21.1	30.5	28.2	31.3	34.2	63.5	53.6	63.0
1,000,000 and over (Group I subset)												
Offenses known	1,163	116	4,659	697	20,927	4,785	5,007	28,944	17,166	18,780	26,318	20,224
Percent cleared by arrest	69.1	83.6	43.3	42.3	23.0	33.2	31.1	36.0	37.7	67.9	59.1	70.4
500,000 to 999,999 (Group I subset)												
Offenses known	4,367	335	2,960	223	20,195	3,482	3,845	19,429	21,056	15,054	26,366	12,454
Percent cleared by arrest	38.7	30.4	36.3	37.2	20.8	27.4	26.0	27.7	32.9	58.4	47.8	56.6
250,000 to 499,999 (Group I subset)												
Offenses known	3,691	232	2,354	252	18,176	2,272	2,731	16,414	16,797	9,783	16,882	9,565
Percent cleared by arrest	36.7	36.6	34.5	45.6	19.3	29.8	26.1	27.4	32.2	63.0	54.2	55.5
Group II (100,000 to 249,999)												
Offenses known	5,459	190	4,061	274	17,863	3,584	4,063	18,106	18,489	16,285	25,379	16,684
Percent cleared by arrest	33.0	32.1	45.6	39.8	24.3	32.6	32.0	32.2	37.4	62.9	56.6	62.7
Group III (50,000 to 99,999)												
Offenses known	5,030	206	3,139	230	10,019	2,557	2,794	13,423	11,224	12,169	18,861	17,559
Percent cleared by arrest	36.0	42.2	36.5	47.4	25.1	33.6	32.8	34.1	39.5	63.4	59.8	64.9
Group IV (25,000 to 49,999)												
Offenses known	4,493	196	2,519	166	6,830	1,675	1,967	8,931	7,501	8,991	13,931	13,146
Percent cleared by arrest	32.7	41.8	37.1	38.6	27.1	36.3	33.3	37.2	47.5	64.4	59.3	64.4
Group V (10,000 to 24,999)												
Offenses known	4,769	273	2,303	147	5,546	1,188	1,488	6,401	7,423	8,057	13,307	16,363
Percent cleared by arrest	35.3	39.2	42.4	42.2	29.9	41.8	36.8	41.2	47.3	69.1	62.5	66.2
Group VI (under 10,000)												
Offenses known	4,340	266	2,614	321	3,262	757	939	4,525	5,824	7,547	11,821	20,720
Percent cleared by arrest	33.9	30.1	38.3	39.9	31.9	44.8	37.9	38.9	53.3	66.2	59.0	67.1
Metropolitan Counties												
Offenses known	7,492	300	5,329	453	14,311	2,226	3,057	11,738	20,034	16,507	32,833	30,596
Percent cleared by arrest	44.8	36.3	39.7	39.7	22.1	36.2	31.0	35.7	57.7	67.8	61.2	63.2
Nonmetropolitan Counties												
Offenses known	4,879	187	1,411	151	1,057	247	320	853	5,539	4,182	9,064	11,962
Percent cleared by arrest	47.9	28.3	41.2	38.4	35.8	47.4	38.1	46.3	62.2	67.3	62.9	59.3
Suburban Areas												
Offenses known	15,241	711	9,586	775	24,990	4,657	5,981	25,392	31,442	30,049	55,553	59,355
Percent cleared by arrest	39.4	37.6	40.8	39.1	24.7	38.2	33.4	37.7	55.1	68.2	61.9	65.5

Table 27. Number and Percent of Offenses Cleared by Arrest or Exceptional Means, Additional Information About Selected Offenses, by Population Group, 2013

(Number, percent.)

Population group	Burglary			Motor vehicle theft			Arson			Number of agencies	Estimated population, 2013
	Forcible entry	Unlawful entry	Attempted forcible entry	Autos	Trucks and buses	Other vehicles	Structure	Mobile	Other		
Total, All Agencies											
Offenses known	972,967	561,037	103,013	464,533	90,884	66,463	18,435	9,699	12,712	14,331	269,287,716
Percent cleared by arrest	11.8	14.6	11.7	14.2	9.6	17.9	24.2	10.7	21.9		
Total Cities											
Offenses known	722,131	411,717	81,820	383,825	72,459	46,581	14,078	6,976	10,005	10,479	184,209,392
Percent cleared by arrest	11.3	14.6	11.9	11.7	8.7	9.8	23.2	9.5	21.6		
Group I (250,000 and over)											
Offenses known	275,536	116,359	28,813	171,513	40,589	17,510	5,199	3,119	3,400	72	52,805,569
Percent cleared by arrest	9.0	11.8	11.2	8.6	6.0	7.5	19.2	5.5	17.5		
1,000,000 and over (Group I subset)											
Offenses known	88,966	34,938	9,824	48,504	17,985	7,807	1,293	1,010	1,291	9	23,015,250
Percent cleared by arrest	9.0	11.9	14.9	9.0	4.4	6.2	19.5	3.9	9.5		
500,000 to 999,999 (Group I subset)											
Offenses known	103,323	42,984	10,907	65,709	13,504	5,859	2,142	1,131	934	23	15,934,732
Percent cleared by arrest	8.3	11.7	9.3	8.1	6.5	9.0	18.8	6.8	23.4		
250,000 to 499,999 (Group I subset)											
Offenses known	83,247	38,437	8,082	57,300	9,100	3,844	1,764	978	1,175	40	13,855,587
Percent cleared by arrest	9.7	11.8	9.4	8.9	8.1	8.0	19.5	5.8	21.6		
Group II (100,000 to 249,999)											
Offenses known	132,276	74,339	15,136	76,906	12,614	9,504	2,164	1,287	1,645	192	28,691,848
Percent cleared by arrest	10.6	13.5	9.8	10.6	10.9	9.0	22.7	10.3	22.9		
Group III (50,000 to 99,999)											
Offenses known	98,682	62,619	11,402	53,320	8,613	6,397	1,878	837	1,505	420	29,118,053
Percent cleared by arrest	11.3	15.3	14.5	11.6	10.3	7.6	24.4	9.4	23.0		
Group IV (25,000 to 49,999)											
Offenses known	77,080	54,077	8,974	33,352	3,946	5,098	1,301	555	1,156	745	25,674,031
Percent cleared by arrest	12.6	15.2	10.7	16.0	12.2	11.7	28.6	13.2	22.4		
Group V (10,000 to 24,999)											
Offenses known	74,851	54,156	9,198	27,051	3,868	4,097	1,415	598	876	1,634	25,893,377
Percent cleared by arrest	15.1	17.3	13.7	19.2	16.4	14.0	28.4	15.6	32.0		
Group VI (under 10,000)											
Offenses known	63,706	50,167	8,297	21,683	2,829	3,975	2,121	580	1,423	7,416	22,026,514
Percent cleared by arrest	16.5	18.4	14.3	24.8	18.8	18.0	25.6	19.7	21.2		
Metropolitan Counties											
Offenses known	183,476	109,409	16,982	67,183	14,979	15,104	3,028	2,162	2,125	1,657	61,501,709
Percent cleared by arrest	12.5	14.4	10.5	25.5	11.8	44.0	28.0	12.8	22.3		
Nonmetropolitan Counties											
Offenses known	67,360	39,911	4,211	13,525	3,446	4,778	1,329	561	582	2,195	23,576,615
Percent cleared by arrest	15.5	15.8	12.2	27.0	19.4	15.2	25.7	17.6	25.9		
Suburban Areas											
Offenses known	313,914	203,666	34,326	125,439	22,499	23,446	5,755	3,163	4,011	7,711	114,428,508
Percent cleared by arrest	13.4	15.7	11.3	21.6	12.4	33.3	27.8	13.6	25.1		

1 The figures shown in this column for the offense of rape were reported using the revised Uniform Crime Reporting (UCR) definition of rape. See chapter notes for more detail.   2 The figures shown in this column for the offense of rape were reported using the legacy Uniform Crime Reporting (UCR) definition of rape. See chapter notes for more detail.

Table 28.   Number of Offenses Cleared by Arrest or Exceptional Means and Percent Involving Persons Under 18 Years of Age, by Population Group, 2013

(Number, percent.)

Population group	Violent crime	Murder and non-negligent man-slaughter	Rape (revised definition)[1]	Robbery	Aggravated assault	Property crime	Burglary	Larceny-theft	Motor vehicle theft	Arson[2]
Total, All Agencies										
Offenses known	477,735	7,761	18,646	86,094	351,547	1,429,145	208,967	1,133,743	86,435	8,490
Percent under 18 years	8.8	3.6	16.9	13.1	7.4	10.8	9.9	11.1	8.9	27.9
Total Cities										
Offenses known	375,727	5,896	12,789	75,979	270,314	1,150,297	151,232	943,231	55,834	6,238
Percent under 18 years	8.9	3.6	15.9	13.3	7.4	11.2	10.5	11.4	10.5	29.8
Group I (250,000 and over)	161,223	3,002	4,133	39,286	110,405	285,722	41,668	225,484	18,570	1,800
Offenses known	8.9	3.5	15.4	15.2	6.7	11.2	11.2	11.2	11.3	30.3
Percent under 18 years										
1,000,000 and over (Group I subset)										
Offenses known	71,801	1,200	901	18,377	49,009	101,185	13,650	81,889	5,646	413
Percent under 18 years	8.6	2.7	18.0	15.6	6.1	9.9	9.6	10.0	8.7	26.6
500,000 to 999,999 (Group I subset)										
Offenses known	50,807	970	1,791	11,525	35,365	98,101	14,643	76,709	6,749	723
Percent under 18 years	9.5	3.1	16.5	16.1	7.3	11.9	12.8	11.6	13.8	31.3
250,000 to 499,999 (Group I subset)										
Offenses known	38,615	832	1,441	9,384	26,031	86,436	13,375	66,886	6,175	664
Percent under 18 years	8.6	5.0	12.3	13.2	6.8	12.0	10.9	12.2	11.1	31.5
Group II (100,000 to 249,999)										
Offenses known	59,153	995	1,866	12,560	41,799	182,420	25,447	146,686	10,287	1,023
Percent under 18 years	8.7	5.0	16.2	12.0	7.5	12.8	12.2	13.1	10.8	27.9
Group III (50,000 to 99,999)										
Offenses known	47,460	598	1,899	8,871	34,838	174,742	22,361	144,834	7,547	903
Percent under 18 years	8.8	3.5	14.7	12.6	7.5	12.7	10.2	13.2	10.9	33.1
Group IV (25,000 to 49,999)										
Offenses known	35,534	476	1,552	6,429	26,079	170,020	18,868	144,740	6,412	726
Percent under 18 years	9.0	2.9	17.5	10.3	8.2	10.8	9.7	11.1	9.1	31.5
Group V (10,000 to 24,999)										
Offenses known	36,831	444	1,789	5,338	28,222	183,186	21,925	154,871	6,390	799
Percent under 18 years	9.2	3.6	18.1	9.0	8.7	10.3	9.1	10.5	9.7	30.7
Group VI (under 10,000)										
Offenses known	35,526	381	1,550	3,495	28,971	154,207	20,963	126,616	6,628	987
Percent under 18 years	8.7	2.6	14.5	11.4	8.0	9.2	9.6	9.1	9.0	25.6
Metropolitan Counties										
Offenses known	78,325	1,280	3,468	9,103	62,176	217,766	40,476	151,736	25,554	1,633
Percent under 18 years	9.0	3.5	21.0	12.1	7.9	9.4	8.9	10.3	5.2	25.7
Nonmetropolitan Counties										
Offenses known	23,683	585	2,389	1,012	19,057	61,082	17,259	38,776	5,047	619
Percent under 18 years	6.8	3.2	15.9	4.6	5.7	7.5	7.6	7.2	9.4	15.0
Suburban Areas [3]										
Offenses known	143,079	1,998	6,268	19,526	111,074	532,615	77,841	417,021	37,753	3,113
Percent under 18 years	9.3	3.3	19.5	11.5	8.4	9.8	9.2	10.2	6.4	28.3

1 The figures shown in this column for the offense of rape were reported using the revised Uniform Crime Reporting (UCR) definition of rape. See chapter notes for more detail.   2 Not all agencies submit reports for arson to the FBI. As a result, the number of reports the FBI uses to compute the percent of offenses cleared for arson is less than the number it uses to compute the percent of offenses cleared for all other offenses.   3 Suburban area includes law enforcement agencies in cities with less than 50,000 inhabitants and county law enforcement agencies that are within a Metropolitan Statistical Area. Suburban area excludes all metropolitan agencies associated with a principal city. The agencies associated with suburban areas also appear in other groups within this table.

SECTION IV

PERSONS ARRESTED

PERSONS ARRESTED

Figure 4.1 Percent Change in the Number of Persons Arrested, by Offense, 2004–2013

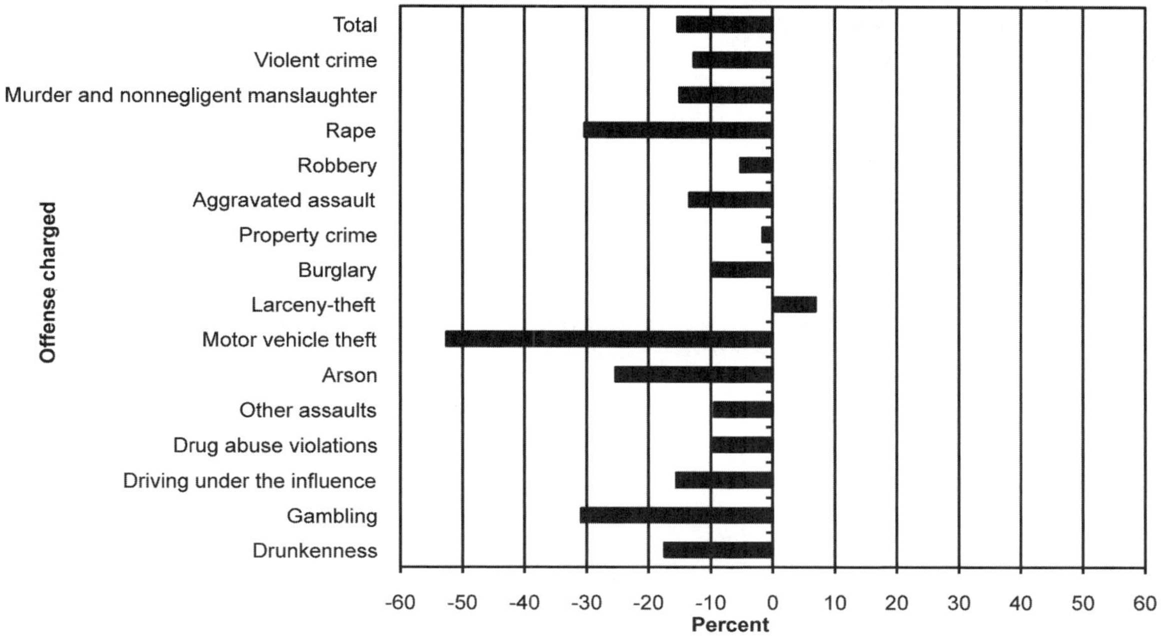

In the Uniform Crime Reporting (UCR) program, one arrest is counted for each separate instance in which an individual is arrested, cited, or summoned for criminal acts in Part I and Part II crimes. (See Appendix I for additional information concerning Part I and Part II crimes.) One person may be arrested multiple times during the year; as a result, the arrest figures in this section should not be taken as the total number of individuals arrested. Instead, it provides the number of *arrest occurrences* reported by law enforcement. Information regarding the UCR program's statistical methodology and table construction can be found in Appendix I.

Important Note: Rape Data

In 2013, the FBI UCR Program initiated the collection of rape data within the Summary Reporting System under a revised definition. The definition changed to the revised UCR definition below.

- Legacy UCR definition of rape: The carnal knowledge of a female forcibly and against her will.

- Revised UCR definition of rape: Penetration, no matter how slight, of the vagina or anus with any body part or object, or oral penetration by a sex organ of another person, without the consent of the victim.

For more information, please see http://www.fbi.gov/about-us/cjis/ucr/crime-in-the-u.s/2013/crime-in-the-u.s.-2013/rape-addendum/rape_addendum_final.

Data Collection: Juveniles

The UCR Program considers a juvenile to be an individual under 18 years of age regardless of state definition. The program does not collect data regarding police contact with a juvenile who has not committed an offense, nor does it collect data on situations in which police take a juvenile into custody for his or her protection, e.g., neglect cases.

National Volume, Trends, and Rates

VOLUME

The FBI estimated that 11,302,102 arrests occurred in 2013 for all offenses (except traffic violations). Of these arrests, 480,360 were for violent crimes and 1,559,284 were for property crimes. UCR does not collect data for traffic violations. Of the total violent crimes in 2013, aggravated assaults accounted for 74.7 percent of the violent crime total, or 358,860 incidents. Robbery had the next highest proportion with just under 20.0 percent, or 94,406 incidents; followed by rape at 3.5 percent (16,863 incidents) and murder and non-negligent manslaughter, at 2.1 percent (10,231 incidents). Of the estimated arrests for property crimes in 2013, 1,231,580 (79.0 percent) were for larceny-theft, 252,629 (16.2 percent) were for burglary, 64,566 (4.1 percent) were for motor vehicle theft, and 10,509 (0.6 percent) were for arson. Outside of these categories, the most frequent identifiable arrests made in 2013 were for drug abuse violations (estimated at 1,501,043 arrests). These arrests comprised 13.3 percent of the total number of all arrests. (Table 29)

A comparison of arrest figures from 2012 to 2013 revealed a 2.0 percent decrease. Arrests for violent crimes decreased 1.8 percent and arrests for property crimes increased 0.3 percent over this time period. An examination of the 5-year and 10-year arrest trends showed that the total number of arrests in 2013 fell 12.3 percent from the 2009 total. Arrests for violent crimes showed an 12.2 percent decrease from 2009 to 2013 and property crimes showed a 2.4 percent decrease. In the 10-year trend data (2004 to 2013), the number of arrests decreased 15.3 percent. For violent crimes, the number of arrests fell 12.7 percent, while arrests for property crimes decreased 1.6 percent. (Tables 32, 34, and 36)

TRENDS

The number of adults arrested for violent crime (arrestees age 18 years and over) decreased 3.4 percent from 2012 to 2013, decreased 10.6 percent from 2009 to 2013, and decreased 10.1 percent from 2004 to 2013. The number of juveniles arrested for violent crime (arrestees under 18 years of age) decreased 8.6 percent from 2012 to 2013, decreased 36.0 percent from 2009 to 2013, and decreased 45.7 percent from 2004 to 2013. (Tables 32, 34, and 36)

The trend data for murder and nonnegligent manslaughter showed that the number of arrests for this offense decreased 0.3 percent from 2012 to 2013, decreased 12.2 percent from 2009 to 2013, and decreased 15.0 percent from 2004 to 2013. The number of adults arrested for murder decreased 3.4 percent from 2012 to 2013, decreased 9.6 percent from 2009 to 2013, and fell 14.2 percent from 2004 to 2013. The number of juveniles arrested for murder rose 14.1 percent from 2012 to 2013, decreased 37.0 percent from 2009 to 2013, and fell 23.5 percent from 2004 to 2013. (Tables 32, 34, and 36)

For rape (based on the legacy definition), the trend data showed that arrests decreased 5.4 percent from 2012 to 2013, with adult arrests decreasing 5.7 percent and juvenile arrests dropping 3.5 percent. The 5-year trend data showed that arrests decreased 17.6 percent from 2009 to 2013; adult arrests decreased 17.1 percent and juvenile arrests declined 20.8 percent during this period. The 10-year trend data showed that rape arrests dropped 30.3 percent from 2004 to 2013, with adult arrests falling 28.7 percent and juvenile arrests falling 38.5 percent. (Tables 32, 34, and 36)

For robbery, the data showed that arrests decreased 2.2 percent from 2012 to 2013, with adult arrests decreasing 1.8 percent and juvenile arrests falling 3.6 percent. The 5-year trend data showed that total robbery arrests fell 20.4 percent from 2009 to 2013; adult arrests decreased 15.4 percent and juvenile arrests dropped 35.3 percent during this period. The 10-year trend data showed that arrests fell 5.2 percent from 2004 to 2013, with adult arrests dropping 1.5 percent and juvenile arrests falling by 17.4 percent. (Tables 32, 34, and 36)

The aggravated assault trend data showed that the number of arrests for this offense fell 4.4 percent from 2012 to 2013, dropped 12.4 percent from 2009 to 2013, and fell 13.4 percent from 2004 to 2013. The number of adults arrested for aggravated assault decreased 3.7 percent from 2012 to 2013,

declined 9.2 percent from 2009 to 2013, and decreased 8.4 percent from 2004 to 2013. The number of juveniles arrested for aggravated assault dropped 12.2 percent from 2012 to 2013, fell 37.4 percent from 2009 to 2013, and dropped 46.1 percent from 2004 to 2013. (Tables 32, 34, and 36)

The 2-year, 5-year, and 10-year trend data showed that the number of arrests for property crime decreased 2.9 percent from 2012 to 2013, decreased 7.1 percent from 2009 to 2013, and decreased 1.6 percent from 2004 to 2013. The number of adults arrested for property crime offenses (arrestees age 18 years and over) decreased 0.2 percent from 2012 to 2013, increased 3.3 percent from 2009 to 2013, and increased 14.5 percent from 2004 to 2013. The number of juveniles arrested for property crime (arrestees under 18 years of age) decreased 15.0 percent from 2012 to 2013, decreased 39.4 percent from 2009 to 2013, and decreased 43.7 percent from 2004 to 2013. (Tables 32, 34, and 36)

The trend data for burglary showed that the number of arrests for this offense decreased 8.6 percent from 2012 to 2013, decreased 13.5 percent from 2009 to 2013, and decreased 9.6 percent from 2004 to 2013. The number of adults arrested for burglary fell 6.5 percent from 2012 to 2013, fell 4.5 percent from 2009 to 2013, and rose 3.4 percent from 2004 to 2013. The number of juveniles arrested for burglary decreased 17.6 percent from 2012 to 2013, decreased 40.1 percent from 2009 to 2013, and fell 43.8 percent from 2004 to 2013. (Tables 32, 34, and 36)

For larceny-theft, the 2-year trend data showed that arrests fell 1.7 percent from 2012 to 2013, with adult arrests increasing 1.1 percent and juvenile arrests decreasing 14.6 percent. The 5-year trend data showed that total larceny-theft arrests decreased 5.1 percent from 2009 to 2013; adult arrests increased 5.7 percent, while juvenile arrests dropped by 39.6 percent during this period. The 10-year trend data showed that larceny-theft arrests rose 6.9 percent from 2004 to 2013, with adult arrests increasing 25.0 percent and juvenile arrests falling 40.9 percent. (Tables 32, 34, and 36)

For motor vehicle theft, the 2-year trend data showed that arrests fell 1.0 percent from 2012 to 2013, with adult arrests increasing 0.8 percent and juvenile arrests decreasing 9.1 percent. The 5-year trend data showed that total motor vehicle theft arrests dropped 15.5 percent from 2009 to 2013; juvenile arrests fell by 38.1 percent and adult arrests dropped 8.1 percent during this period. The 10-year trend data showed that arrests dropped 52.6 percent from 2004 to 2013, with adult arrests falling 47.3 percent and juvenile arrests dropping by 67.7 percent. (Tables 32, 34, and 36)

The arson trend data showed that the number of arrests for this offense decreased 2.0 percent from 2012 to 2013, fell 5.8 percent from 2009 to 2013, and fell 25.3 percent from 2004 to 2013. The number of adults arrested for arson rose 6.8 percent from 2012 to 2013, increased 8.1 percent from 2009 to 2013, and fell 1.7 percent from 2004 to 2013. The number of juveniles arrested for arson dropped 15.3 percent from 2012 to 2013, dropped 23.6 percent from 2009 to 2013, and dropped 48.4 percent from 2004 to 2013. (Tables 32, 34, and 36)

RATES

The rate of arrests was estimated at 3,690.5 arrests per 100,000 inhabitants in 2013. The arrest rate for violent crime was 159.8 arrests per 100,000 inhabitants, and the arrest rate for property crime was 513.2 arrests per 100,000 inhabitants. Law enforcement agencies throughout the nation reported 3.4 murder arrests, 5.5 rape arrests, 32.0 robbery arrests, and 118.8 aggravated assault arrests per 100,000 inhabitants in 2013. Rates for all violent crimes were down from the 2012 rates. Law enforcement agencies throughout the nation reported 513.2 property crime arrests, 82.9 burglary arrests, 405.5 larceny-theft arrests, 21.4 motor vehicle theft arrests, and 3.4 arson arrests per 100,000 inhabitants in 2013. Rates for property crimes were also down from the 2012 rates. (Table 30)

Figure 4.2 Arrest Distribution, Violent Crime, by Age, 2013

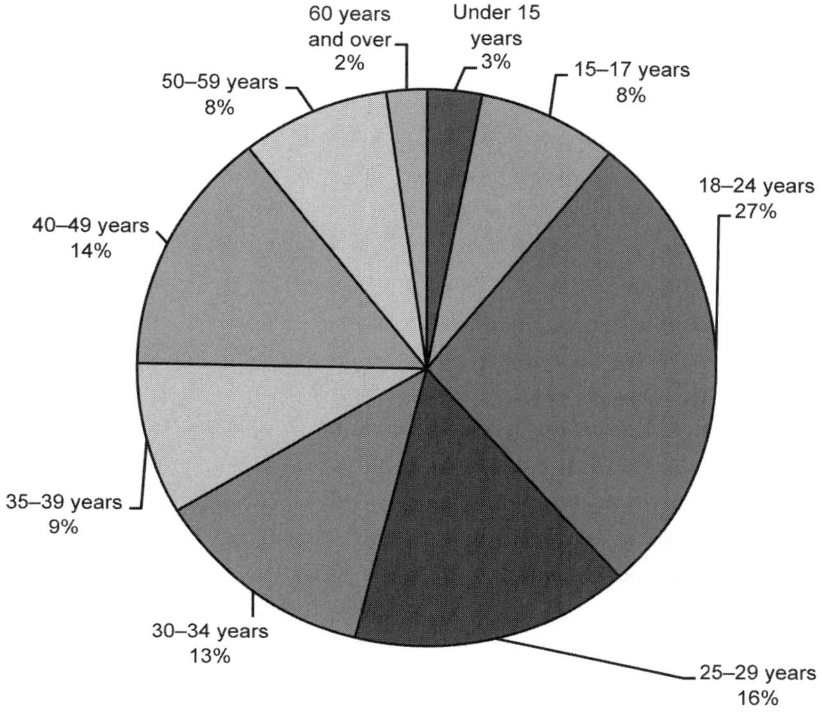

By Age, Sex, and Race

Law enforcement agencies that contributed arrest data to the UCR program reported information on the age, sex, and race of the persons they arrested. According to the data for 2013, adults accounted for 90.3 percent of arrestees nationally. (Table 38)

A review of arrest data by age from 2012 to 2013 showed that arrests of adults decreased 3.7 percent during this period, with a 3.4 percent drop in arrests for violent crime and a 0.2 percent drop in arrests for property crimes. The arrest total for juveniles (those under 18 years of age) decreased 15.5 percent from 2012 to 2013. Over the 2-year period, arrests of juveniles for violent crimes fell 8.6 percent; juvenile arrests for property crimes decreased 15.0 percent. (Table 36)

By sex, males accounted for 73.5 percent of all persons arrested in 2013. Males represented 79.9 percent of arrestees for violent crime, 88.3 percent of arrestees for murder, 98.1 percent of arrestees for rape, 86.6 percent for robbery, and 77.0 percent for aggravated assault. Females accounted for 20.1 percent of violent crime arrestees, 11.7 percent of murder arrestees, 1.9 percent of rape arrestees, 13.4 percent of robbery arrestees, and 23.0 percent of aggravated assault arrestees. (Table 42)

Most arrestees for property crime in 2013 (84.3 percent) were over 18 years of age. By sex, males accounted for 62.2 percent of arrestees for property crime, 83.0 percent of arrestees for burglary, 56.9 percent of arrestees for larceny-theft, 80.1 percent of arrestees for motor vehicle theft, and 80.3 percent of arrestees for arson. Females accounted for 37.8 percent of property crime arrestees. Of the four property crimes, larceny-theft had the highest proportion of female arrestees at 43.1 percent. (Tables 38 and 42)

In 2013, 68.9 percent of all persons arrested were White, 28.3 percent were Black, and the remaining 1.6 percent were of other races (American Indian or Alaskan Native, Asian, and Native Hawaiian or Pacific Islander). Of all arrestees for violent crimes, 58.4 percent were White, 38.7 percent were Black, and 2.9 percent were of other races. For murder, 45.3 percent of arrestees were White, 52.2 percent were Black, and 2.5 percent were of other races. For rape (an aggregate total of the revised and legacy definitions), 66.2 percent of arrestees were White, 31.3 percent were Black, and 2.5 percent of arrestees were of other races. For robbery, 41.9 percent of arrestees were White, 56.4 percent of arrestees were Black, and 1.7 percent of arrestees were of other races. For aggravated assault, 62.9 percent of arrestees were White, 33.9 percent of arrestees were Black, and 3.2 percent were of other races. (Table 43)

Of all arrestees for property crimes in 2013, 68.2 percent were White, 29.0 percent were Black, and 2.8 percent were of other races. For burglary, 67.5 percent of arrestees were White, 30.4 percent were Black, and 2.1 percent were of other races. For larceny-theft, 68.3 percent of arrestees were White, 28.7 percent were Black, and 3.0 percent were of other races. For motor vehicle theft, 66.7 percent of arrestees were White, 30.5 percent of arrestees were Black, and 2.8 percent were of other

races. For arson, 74.1 percent of arrestees were White, 23.0 percent of arrestees were Black, and 2.9 percent were of other races. (Table 43)

Outside of the scope of violent and property crimes, White adults were most commonly arrested for drug abuse violations (815,181 arrests) and driving under the influence (766,440 arrests). Black adults were most frequently arrested for drug abuse violations (365,785 arrests) and other assaults (283,357 arrests). (Table 43)

Figure 4.3 Arrest Distribution, Property Crime, by Age, 2013

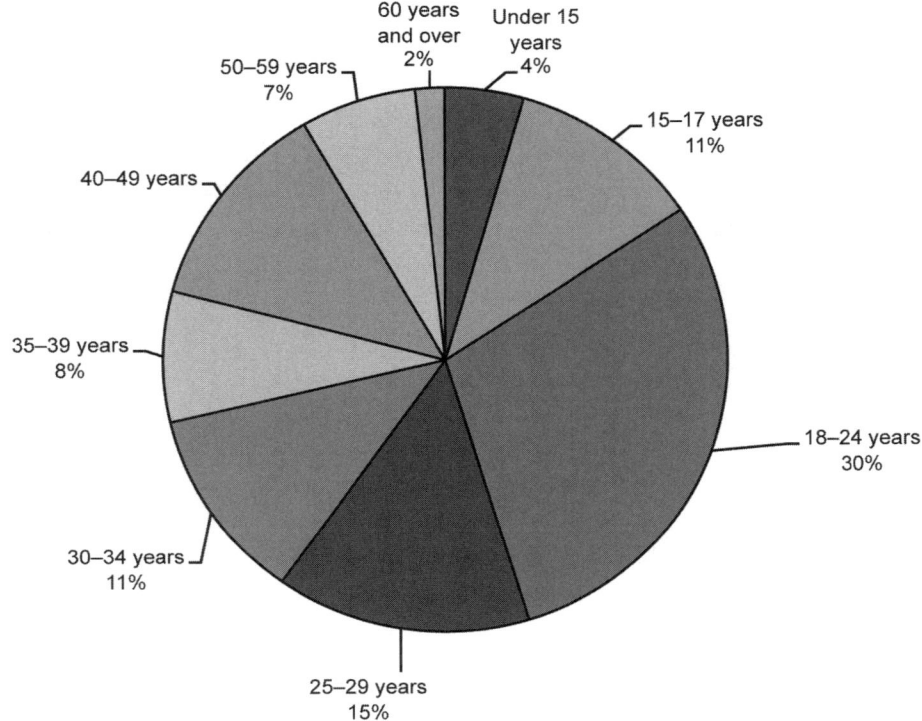

Regional Arrest Rates

The UCR program divides the United States into four regions: the Northeast, the Midwest, the South, and the West. (Appendix III provides more information about the regions.) Law enforcement agencies in the Northeast had an overall arrest rate of 3,084.1 arrests per 100,000 inhabitants, below the national rate (3,690.5 arrests per 100,000 inhabitants). In this region, the arrest rate for violent crimes was 140.2 arrests per 100,000 inhabitants, and for property crime, the arrest rate was 457.0 arrests per 100,000 inhabitants. In the Midwest, law enforcement agencies reported an arrest rate of 3,647.2 arrests per 100,000 inhabitants. The arrest rate for violent crimes was 128.4 and the arrest rate for property crime was 513.1. Law enforcement agencies in the South, the nation's most populous region, reported an arrest rate of 4,096.9 per 100,000 inhabitants. Arrests for violent crime occurred at a rate of 148.3 arrests per 100,000 residents, and for property crime, the arrest rate was 576.6 arrests per 100,000 inhabitants. In the West, law enforcement agencies reported an overall arrest rate

of 3.718.7 arrests per 100,000 inhabitants. The region's violent crime arrest rate was 210.0, the highest of the regions, while its property crime arrest rate was 471.7. (Table 30)

The regional murder arrest rates were 2.4 in the Northeast, 3.1 in the Midwest, 4.2 in the South, and 3.3 in the West. For rape (the aggregate of the revised and legacy definitions), the regional arrest rates were 5.6 in the Northeast, 6.2 in the Midwest, 5.5 in the South, and 5.1 in the West. Regional arrest rates for robbery were 36.4 in the Northeast, 27.9 in the Midwest, 30.0 in the South, and 34.7 in the West. For aggravated assault, the regional arrest rates were 95.8 in the Northeast, 91.2 in the Midwest, 108.6 in the South, and 166.9 in the West. (Table 30)

The regional burglary arrest rates were 68.3 in the Northeast, 61.1 in the Midwest, 86.4 in the South, and 103.9 in the West. For larceny-theft, the regional arrest rates were 370.6 in the Northeast, 426.5 in the Midwest, 470.3 in the South, and 332.9 in the West. Regional arrest rates for motor vehicle theft were 14.4 in the Northeast, 22.5 in the Midwest, 16.9 in the

South, and 30.8 in the West. For arson, the regional arrest rates were 3.4 in the Northeast, 3.7 in the Midwest, 3.0 in the South, and 4.1 in the West. (Table 30)

Population Groups: Trends and Rates

The national UCR program aggregates data by various population groups, which include cities, metropolitan counties, and nonmetropolitan counties. Definitions of these groups can be found in Appendix III. The total number of arrests in U.S. cities fell 5.3 percent from 2012 to 2013. The number of arrests for violent crimes declined 4.1 percent and arrests for property crimes decreased 2.3 percent during the 2-year time frame. (Table 44)

In 2013, law enforcement agencies in cities collectively recorded an arrest rate of 3,981.9 arrests per 100,000 inhabitants. The nation's smallest cities, those with fewer than 10,000 inhabitants, had the highest arrest rate among the city population groups with 5,035.7 arrests per 100,000 inhabitants. Law enforcement agencies in cities with 50,000 to 99,999 inhabitants recorded the lowest rate, 3,613.4. In the nation's metropolitan counties, law enforcement agencies reported an arrest rate of 2,971.2 per 100,000 inhabitants. Agencies in nonmetropolitan counties reported an arrest rate of 3,330.8. (Table 31)

By population group, law enforcement agencies in the nation's cities collectively reported 181.3 violent crime arrests per 100,000 inhabitants in 2013. In the city population groups, cities with 250,000 or more inhabitants reported the highest violent crime arrest rate (259.8) and cities with 10,000 to 24,999 inhabitants reported the lowest violent crime arrest rate (132.0). Cities reported an overall murder arrest rate of 3.7 per 100,000 inhabitants; cities with 250,000 or more inhabitants had the highest murder arrest rate (6.5) and cities with under 10,000 inhabitants had the lowest murder arrest rate (1.9). The collective city rape arrest rate (an aggregate derived from the revised and legacy definitions) was 5.9 per 100,000 inhabitants, with the highest rate in cities with 250,000 or more inhabitants (7.7) and the lowest rate in cities with 25,000 to 49,999 inhabitants (4.8). The overall robbery arrest rate for cities was 40.3 per 100,000 inhabitants; cities with 250,000 or more inhabitants had the highest robbery arrest rate (69.3) and cities with fewer than 10,000 inhabitants had the lowest robbery arrest rate (18.3). For aggravated assault, the collective city arrest rate was 131.4 per 100,000 inhabitants, with the greatest arrest rate in cities with 250,000 or more inhabitants (176.2) and the lowest arrest rate in cities with 10,000 to 24,999 inhabitants (107.7). (Table 31)

Agencies in metropolitan counties reported a violent crime arrest rate of 121.4 per 100,000 inhabitants, with arrest rates of 2.8 for murder, 4.3 for rape, 17.3 for robbery, and 97.0 for aggravated assault. Agencies in nonmetropolitan counties reported arrest rates of 94.1 for violent crime, 3.0 for murder, 5.7 for rape, 6.6 for robbery, and 78.8 for aggravated assault. (Table 31)

By population group, law enforcement agencies in the nation's cities collectively reported 614.1 property crime arrests per 100,000 inhabitants in 2013. In the city population groups, cities with 10,000 to 24,999 inhabitants reported the highest property crime arrest rate (665.8) and cities with 250,000 or more inhabitants reported the lowest property crime arrest rate (558.1). Cities reported an overall burglary arrest rate of 89.1 per 100,000 inhabitants; cities with 100,000 to 249,999 inhabitants had the highest burglary arrest rate (103.3) and cities with 25,000 to 49,999 inhabitants had the lowest burglary arrest rate (75.9). The collective city larceny-theft arrest rate was 497.9 per 100,000 inhabitants, with the highest rate in cities with 10,000 to 24,999 inhabitants (568.0) and the lowest rate in cities with 250,000 or more inhabitants (429.5). The overall motor vehicle theft arrest rate for cities was 23.2 per 100,000 inhabitants; cities with 250,000 or more inhabitants had the highest motor vehicle theft arrest rate (32.6), and cities with 25,000 to 49,999 inhabitants had the lowest motor vehicle theft arrest rate (15.7). For arson, the collective city arrest rate was 3.9 per 100,000 inhabitants, with the greatest arrest rate in cities with 100,000 to 249,999 inhabitants (5.5) and the lowest arrest rate in cities with more than 250,000 inhabitants, 25,000 to 49,999 inhabitants, and 10,000 to 24,999 inhabitants (all with rates of 3.3). (Table 31)

Agencies in metropolitan counties reported a property crime arrest rate of 317.4 per 100,000 inhabitants, with arrest rates of 68.3 for burglary, 228.9 for larceny-theft, 17.8 for motor vehicle theft, and 2.4 for arson. Agencies in nonmetropolitan counties reported arrest rates of 244.9 for property crime, 73.6 for burglary, 152.2 for larceny-theft, 16.6 for motor vehicle theft, and 2.5 for arson. (Table 31)

In suburban areas, the rates per 100,000 inhabitants for violent crime and property crime were 122.7 and 457.7, respectively. The rate for murder was 2.3; for rape, 4.5; for robbery, 20.6; and for aggravated assault, 95.2. Specific property crime rates included 70.8 for burglary, 367.3 for larceny-theft, 16.6 for motor vehicle theft, and 2.9 for arson. (Table 31)

Community Types

In 2013, law enforcement agencies in the nation's cities reported that 89.3 percent of arrests in their jurisdictions were of adults and 10.7 percent of arrests were of juveniles. Adults accounted for 88.1 percent of arrestees for violent crimes, while juveniles accounted for 11.9 percent of these arrests. Adults made up 83.5 percent of the arrestees for property crimes, and juveniles accounted for the remaining 16.5 percent. Of all arrests in the nation's cities in 2013, 39.1 percent were of individuals under 25 years of age. In metropolitan counties, 34.3 percent of arrests were of individuals under 25 years of age. In nonmetropolitan counties, 30.1 percent of persons arrested were of individuals under 25 years of age. (Tables 46, 47, 53, and 59)

Males accounted for 73.2 percent and females accounted for 26.8 percent of arrestees in the nation's cities in 2013. In metropolitan counties, males comprised 74.0 percent of arrestees, and in nonmetropolitan counties, males represented 74.7 percent of all arrestees. (Tables 48, 54, and 60)

By race, 66.5 percent of arrestees in the nation's cities in 2013 were White, 30.7 percent were Black, and 2.8 percent were of other races (American Indian or Alaska Native and Asian or

Pacific Islander). Whites accounted for 72.7 percent of arrestees in metropolitan counties in 2013, Blacks made up 25.1 percent of arrestees, and persons of other races made up 2.2 percent of the total. In nonmetropolitan counties, Whites made up 83.4 percent of arrestees, Blacks accounted for 13.4 percent of arrestees, and other races made up 3.2 percent of the total. (Tables 49, 55, and 61)

Table 29.   Estimated Number of Arrests, 2013

(Number.)

Offense	Arrests
Total [1]	11,302,102
Violent crime [2]	480,360
Murder and nonnegligent manslaughter	10,231
Rape[3]	16,863
Robbery	94,406
Aggravated assault	358,860
Property crime [2]	1,559,284
Burglary	252,629
Larceny-theft	1,231,580
Motor vehicle theft	64,566
Arson	10,509
Other assaults	1,097,741
Forgery and counterfeiting	60,969
Fraud	143,528
Embezzlement	15,730
Stolen property; buying, receiving, possessing	92,691
Vandalism	201,168
Weapons; carrying, possessing, etc.	137,779
Prostitution and commercialized vice	48,620
Sex offenses (except forcible rape and prostitution)	57,925
Drug abuse violations	1,501,043
Gambling	6,024
Offenses against the family and children	101,247
Driving under the influence	1,166,824
Liquor laws	354,872
Drunkenness	443,527
Disorderly conduct	467,993
Vagrancy	25,755
All other offenses	3,282,651
Suspicion	1,096
Curfew and loitering law violations	56,371

1 Does not include suspicion.   2 Violent crimes are offenses of murder and nonnegligent manslaughter, forcible rape, robbery, and aggravated assault. Property crimes are offenses of burglary, larceny-theft, motor vehicle theft, and arson.   3 The rape figures in this table are an aggregate total of the data submitted using both the revised and legacy Uniform Crime Reporting definitions.

Table 30.   Number and Rate of Arrests, by Geographic Region, 2013

(Number, rate per 100,000 inhabitants.)

Offense charged	United States total		Northeast		Midwest		South		West	
	Total	Rate	Total	Rate	Total	Rate	Total	Rate	Total	Rate
TOTAL [1]	9,069,148	3,690.5	1,385,990	3,084.1	1,782,251	3,647.2	3,451,627	4,096.9	2,449,280	3,618.6
Murder and nonnegligent manslaughter	8,401	3.4	1,085	2.4	1,534	3.1	3,543	4.2	2,239	3.3
Rape [2]	13,617	5.5	2,508	5.6	3,039	6.2	4,640	5.5	3,430	5.1
Robbery	78,753	32.0	16,362	36.4	13,619	27.9	25,284	30.0	23,488	34.7
Aggravated assault	292,007	118.8	43,042	95.8	44,551	91.2	91,462	108.6	112,952	166.9
Burglary	203,709	82.9	30,704	68.3	29,870	61.1	72,817	86.4	70,318	103.9
Larceny-theft	996,495	405.5	166,563	370.6	208,393	426.5	396,236	470.3	225,303	332.9
Motor vehicle theft	52,507	21.4	6,449	14.4	11,002	22.5	14,202	16.9	20,854	30.8
Arson	8,413	3.4	1,661	3.7	1,449	3.0	2,499	3.0	2,804	4.1
Violent crime [3]	392,778	159.8	62,997	140.2	62,743	128.4	124,929	148.3	142,109	210.0
Property crime [3]	1,261,124	513.2	205,377	457.0	250,714	513.1	485,754	576.6	319,279	471.7
Other assaults	885,822	360.5	154,677	344.2	179,959	368.3	354,542	420.8	196,644	290.5
Forgery and counterfeiting	48,826	19.9	8,618	19.2	7,724	15.8	21,402	25.4	11,082	16.4
Fraud	113,510	46.2	20,009	44.5	20,524	42.0	56,662	67.3	16,315	24.1
Embezzlement	12,664	5.2	1,361	3.0	2,199	4.5	6,895	8.2	2,209	3.3
Stolen property; buying, receiving, possessing	74,792	30.4	13,316	29.6	12,860	26.3	20,190	24.0	28,426	42.0
Vandalism	162,068	66.0	35,778	79.6	33,184	67.9	42,556	50.5	50,550	74.7
Weapons; carrying, possessing, etc.	112,673	45.9	14,548	32.4	22,958	47.0	38,275	45.4	36,892	54.5
Prostitution and commercialized vice	42,110	17.1	5,616	12.5	6,224	12.7	13,807	16.4	16,463	24.3
Sex offenses (except forcible rape and prostitution)	46,832	19.1	7,089	15.8	9,335	19.1	14,015	16.6	16,393	24.2
Drug abuse violations	1,209,661	492.2	200,571	446.3	226,385	463.3	455,503	540.7	327,202	483.4
Gambling	5,089	2.1	415	0.9	2,520	5.2	1,639	1.9	515	0.8
Offenses against the family and children	78,812	32.1	16,781	37.3	15,882	32.5	35,164	41.7	10,985	16.2
Driving under the influence	918,462	373.8	130,652	290.7	191,485	391.9	294,813	349.9	301,512	445.5
Liquor laws	280,860	114.3	34,048	75.8	95,990	196.4	71,999	85.5	78,823	116.5
Drunkenness	358,036	145.7	33,501	74.5	22,166	45.4	203,825	241.9	98,544	145.6
Disorderly conduct	375,142	152.7	90,572	201.5	116,902	239.2	112,756	133.8	54,912	81.1
Vagrancy	21,633	8.8	1,648	3.7	3,658	7.5	5,329	6.3	10,998	16.2
All other offenses (except traffic)	2,620,320	1,066.3	330,170	734.7	489,841	1,002.4	1,081,380	1,283.5	718,929	1,062.2
Suspicion	844	0.3	58	0.1	190	0.4	555	0.7	41	0.1
Curfew and loitering law violations	47,934	19.5	18,246	40.6	8,998	18.4	10,192	12.1	10,498	15.5

1 Does not include suspicion.   2 The rape figures in this table are an aggregate total of the data submitted using both the revised and legacy Uniform Crime Reporting definitions.   3 Violent crimes are offenses of murder and nonnegligent manslaughter, revised and legacy rape, robbery, and aggravated assault. Property crimes are offenses of burglary, larceny-theft, motor vehicle theft, and arson.

Table 31. Number and Rate of Arrests, by Population Group and Area[1], 2013

(Number, rate per 100,000 inhabitants.)

Offense charged	Total		Total cities		250,000 and over		100,000 to 249,999 population		50,000 to 99,999 population		25,000 to 49,999 population		10,000 to 24,999 population	
	Total	Rate	Total	Rate	Total	Rate	Total	Rate	Total	Rate	Total	Rate	Total	Rate
Total [2]	9,069,148	3,690.5	6,663,998	3,981.9	1,790,769	4,032.1	1,007,570	3,799.1	1,015,895	3,613.4	921,571	3,669.6	967,480	4,011.8
Violent crime [3]	392,778	159.8	303,405	181.3	115,377	259.8	51,298	193.4	45,994	163.6	33,340	132.8	31,838	132.0
Murder and nonnegligent manslaughter	8,401	3.4	6,167	3.7	2,893	6.5	1,073	4.0	767	2.7	566	2.3	510	2.1
Rape[4]	13,617	5.5	9,956	5.9	3,436	7.7	1,367	5.2	1,465	5.2	1,194	4.8	1,341	5.6
Robbery	78,753	32.0	67,460	40.3	30,787	69.3	11,109	41.9	9,552	34.0	6,849	27.3	5,664	23.5
Aggravated assault	292,007	118.8	219,822	131.4	78,261	176.2	37,749	142.3	34,210	121.7	24,731	98.5	24,323	100.9
Property crime [3]	1,261,124	513.2	1,027,716	614.1	247,849	558.1	163,473	616.4	171,794	611.1	162,941	648.8	160,573	665.8
Burglary	203,709	82.9	149,031	89.1	41,146	92.6	27,384	103.3	26,131	92.9	19,069	75.9	19,019	78.9
Larceny-theft	996,495	405.5	833,302	497.9	190,742	429.5	127,400	480.4	138,899	494.0	139,078	553.8	136,967	568.0
Motor vehicle theft	52,507	21.4	38,841	23.2	14,484	32.6	7,238	27.3	5,701	20.3	3,970	15.8	3,781	15.7
Arson	8,413	3.4	6,542	3.9	1,477	3.3	1,451	5.5	1,063	3.8	824	3.3	806	3.3
Other assaults	885,822	360.5	666,195	398.1	192,868	434.3	105,694	398.5	104,566	371.9	91,501	364.3	90,034	373.3
Forgery and counterfeiting	48,826	19.9	35,960	21.5	8,738	19.7	5,275	19.9	5,620	20.0	5,334	21.2	5,775	23.9
Fraud	113,510	46.2	75,435	45.1	15,282	34.4	9,951	37.5	11,579	41.2	12,116	48.2	12,356	51.2
Embezzlement	12,664	5.2	9,682	5.8	2,172	4.9	1,632	6.2	1,599	5.7	1,606	6.4	1,602	6.6
Stolen property; buying, receiving, possessing	74,792	30.4	55,382	33.1	14,169	31.9	8,918	33.6	10,627	37.8	8,607	34.3	7,611	31.6
Vandalism	162,068	66.0	124,734	74.5	33,186	74.7	18,734	70.6	19,832	70.5	18,296	72.9	17,677	73.3
Weapons; carrying, possessing, etc.	112,673	45.9	87,816	52.5	35,012	78.8	13,773	51.9	12,086	43.0	9,217	36.7	8,352	34.6
Prostitution and commercialized vice	42,110	17.1	38,619	23.1	27,641	62.2	4,699	17.7	2,560	9.1	1,938	7.7	1,123	4.7
Sex offenses (except forcible rape and prostitution)	46,832	19.1	33,349	19.9	11,587	26.1	4,831	18.2	4,857	17.3	4,249	16.9	3,962	16.4
Drug abuse violations	1,209,661	492.2	880,503	526.1	276,253	622.0	131,482	495.8	134,791	479.4	112,495	447.9	110,404	457.8
Gambling	5,089	2.1	4,225	2.5	3,124	7.0	278	1.0	169	0.6	94	0.4	169	0.7
Offenses against the family and children	78,812	32.1	37,350	22.3	5,980	13.5	7,414	28.0	4,813	17.1	6,506	25.9	6,127	25.4
Driving under the influence	918,462	373.8	532,729	318.3	118,787	267.5	72,207	272.3	78,312	278.5	76,851	306.0	88,885	368.6
Liquor laws	280,860	114.3	224,739	134.3	45,157	101.7	24,628	92.9	28,760	102.3	29,378	117.0	36,982	153.4
Drunkenness	358,036	145.7	307,420	183.7	63,810	143.7	55,929	210.9	54,872	195.2	41,468	165.1	44,714	185.4
Disorderly conduct	375,142	152.7	313,717	187.5	70,434	158.6	38,451	145.0	45,243	160.9	45,544	181.4	54,137	224.5
Vagrancy	21,633	8.8	19,376	11.6	8,651	19.5	2,528	9.5	3,998	14.2	2,052	8.2	969	4.0
All other offenses (except traffic)	2,620,320	1,066.3	1,840,531	1,099.8	467,801	1,053.3	282,728	1,066.0	269,527	958.7	254,622	1,013.9	280,702	1,164.0
Suspicion	844	0.3	484	0.3	0	0.0	0	0.0	164	0.6	107	0.4	80	0.3
Curfew and loitering law violations	47,934	19.5	45,115	27.0	26,891	60.5	3,647	13.8	4,296	15.3	3,416	13.6	3,488	14.5

Table 31.   Number and Rate of Arrests, by Population Group and Area[1], 2013

(Number, rate per 100,000 inhabitants.)

Offense charged	under 10,000 population		Metropolitan counties		Nonmetropolitan counties		Suburban areas	
	Total	Rate	Total	Rate	Total	Rate	Total	Rate
Total [2]	960,713	5,035.7	1,699,763	2,971.2	705,387	3,330.8	3,757,710	3,379.9
Violent crime [3]	25,558	134.0	69,443	121.4	19,930	94.1	136,378	122.7
Murder and nonnegligent manslaughter	358	1.9	1,609	2.8	625	3.0	2,583	2.3
Rape[4]	1,153	6.0	2,448	4.3	1,213	5.7	4,987	4.5
Robbery	3,499	18.3	9,895	17.3	1,398	6.6	22,956	20.6
Aggravated assault	20,548	107.7	55,491	97.0	16,694	78.8	105,852	95.2
Property crime [3]	121,086	634.7	181,553	317.4	51,855	244.9	508,808	457.7
Burglary	16,282	85.3	39,089	68.3	15,589	73.6	78,750	70.8
Larceny-theft	100,216	525.3	130,963	228.9	32,230	152.2	408,402	367.3
Motor vehicle theft	3,667	19.2	10,155	17.8	3,511	16.6	18,458	16.6
Arson	921	4.8	1,346	2.4	525	2.5	3,198	2.9
Other assaults	81,532	427.4	161,057	281.5	58,570	276.6	346,497	311.7
Forgery and counterfeiting	5,218	27.4	9,949	17.4	2,917	13.8	21,671	19.5
Fraud	14,151	74.2	26,370	46.1	11,705	55.3	53,643	48.2
Embezzlement	1,071	5.6	2,410	4.2	572	2.7	5,443	4.9
Stolen property; buying, receiving, possessing	5,450	28.6	15,187	26.5	4,223	19.9	32,653	29.4
Vandalism	17,009	89.2	28,264	49.4	9,070	42.8	66,003	59.4
Weapons; carrying, possessing, etc.	9,376	49.1	18,544	32.4	6,313	29.8	38,920	35.0
Prostitution and commercialized vice	658	3.4	3,338	5.8	153	0.7	6,612	5.9
Sex offenses (except forcible rape and prostitution)	3,863	20.2	9,740	17.0	3,743	17.7	18,565	16.7
Drug abuse violations	115,078	603.2	238,806	417.4	90,352	426.6	495,730	445.9
Gambling	391	2.0	724	1.3	140	0.7	996	0.9
Offenses against the family and children	6,510	34.1	31,135	54.4	10,327	48.8	43,365	39.0
Driving under the influence	97,687	512.0	228,201	398.9	157,532	743.9	422,322	379.9
Liquor laws	59,834	313.6	35,940	62.8	20,181	95.3	119,823	107.8
Drunkenness	46,627	244.4	34,999	61.2	15,617	73.7	125,344	112.7
Disorderly conduct	59,908	314.0	43,338	75.8	18,087	85.4	157,241	141.4
Vagrancy	1,178	6.2	2,026	3.5	231	1.1	5,398	4.9
All other offenses (except traffic)	285,151	1,494.7	556,178	972.2	223,611	1,055.9	1,142,346	1,027.5
Suspicion	133	0.7	44	0.1	316	1.5	290	0.3
Curfew and loitering law violations	3,377	17.7	2,561	4.5	258	1.2	9,952	9.0

1 Suburban areas include law enforcement agencies in cities with less than 50,000 inhabitants and county law enforcement agencies that are within a Metropolitan Statistical Area. Suburban areas exclude all metropolitan agencies associated with a principal city. The agencies associated with suburban areas also appear in other groups within this table.   2 Does not include suspicion.   3 Violent crimes are offenses of murder and nonnegligent manslaughter, forcible rape, robbery, and aggravated assault. Property crimes are offenses of burglary, larceny-theft, motor vehicle theft, and arson.   4 The rape figures in this table are an aggregate total of the data submitted using both the revised and legacy Uniform Crime Reporting definitions.

Table 32.   Ten-Year Arrest Trends, 2004 and 2013

(Number, percent change; 7,858 agencies; 2013 estimated population 192,473,854; 2004 estimated population 178,805,123.)

Offense charged	Number of persons arrested								
	Total, all ages			Under 18 years of age			18 years of age and over		
	2004	2013	Percent change	2004	2013	Percent change	2004	2013	Percent change
Total [1]	8,402,488	7,120,525	-15.3	1,226,865	666,263	-45.7	7,175,623	6,454,262	-10.1
Violent crime [2]	358,066	312,739	-12.7	53,905	33,667	-37.5	304,161	279,072	-8.2
Murder and nonnegligent manslaughter	7,872	6,695	-15.0	643	492	-23.5	7,229	6,203	-14.2
Rape[3]	15,019	10,471	-30.3	2,414	1,484	-38.5	12,605	8,987	-28.7
Robbery	64,349	61,019	-5.2	14,936	12,340	-17.4	49,413	48,679	-1.5
Aggravated assault	270,826	234,554	-13.4	35,912	19,351	-46.1	234,914	215,203	-8.4
Property crime [2]	998,816	983,307	-1.6	275,169	154,838	-43.7	723,647	828,469	+14.5
Burglary	180,617	163,261	-9.6	49,721	27,960	-43.8	130,896	135,301	+3.4
Larceny-theft	721,769	771,869	+6.9	198,071	117,141	-40.9	523,698	654,728	+25.0
Motor vehicle theft	87,337	41,385	-52.6	22,784	7,367	-67.7	64,553	34,018	-47.3
Arson	9,093	6,792	-25.3	4,593	2,370	-48.4	4,500	4,422	-1.7
Other assaults	769,970	696,659	-9.5	148,743	91,436	-38.5	621,227	605,223	-2.6
Forgery and counterfeiting	71,993	37,884	-47.4	2,988	649	-78.3	69,005	37,235	-46.0
Fraud	196,788	88,245	-55.2	4,622	2,755	-40.4	192,166	85,490	-55.5
Embezzlement	11,995	10,202	-14.9	698	233	-66.6	11,297	9,969	-11.8
Stolen property; buying, receiving, possessing	78,027	58,443	-25.1	13,879	6,354	-54.2	64,148	52,089	-18.8
Vandalism	160,941	128,589	-20.1	61,262	29,676	-51.6	99,679	98,913	-0.8
Weapons; carrying, possessing, etc.	110,697	91,150	-17.7	25,478	12,771	-49.9	85,219	78,379	-8.0
Prostitution and commercialized vice	55,369	35,562	-35.8	1,157	550	-52.5	54,212	35,012	-35.4
Sex offenses (except forcible rape and prostitution)	54,292	35,604	-34.4	10,923	6,249	-42.8	43,369	29,355	-32.3
Drug abuse violations	1,080,301	976,882	-9.6	118,392	75,767	-36.0	961,909	901,115	-6.3
Gambling	6,365	4,400	-30.9	1,099	569	-48.2	5,266	3,831	-27.3
Offenses against the family and children	73,249	60,479	-17.4	3,608	1,668	-53.8	69,641	58,811	-15.6
Driving under the influence	840,325	710,351	-15.5	11,212	4,315	-61.5	829,113	706,036	-14.8
Liquor laws	343,782	206,285	-40.0	71,976	34,283	-52.4	271,806	172,002	-36.7
Drunkenness	363,978	300,708	-17.4	11,117	5,107	-54.1	352,861	295,601	-16.2
Disorderly conduct	364,859	258,950	-29.0	110,374	53,471	-51.6	254,485	205,479	-19.3
Vagrancy	23,137	18,154	-21.5	3,138	545	-82.6	19,999	17,609	-12.0
All other offenses (except traffic)	2,372,952	2,080,548	-12.3	230,539	125,976	-45.4	2,142,413	1,954,572	-8.8
Suspicion	4,249	399	-90.6	535	38	-92.9	3,714	361	-90.3
Curfew and loitering law violations	66,586	25,384	-61.9	66,586	25,384	-61.9	NA	NA	NA

NA = Not available.   1 Does not include suspicion.   2 Violent crimes are offenses of murder and nonnegligent manslaughter, forcible rape, robbery, and aggravated assault. Property crimes are offenses of burglary, larceny-theft, motor vehicle theft, and arson.   3 The rape figures in this table are based on the legacy definition of rape only. The rape figures shown include converted National Incident-Based Reporting System rape data and those states/agencies that reported the legacy definition of rape for both years.

Table 33.　Ten-Year Arrest Trends, by Age and Sex, 2004 and 2013

(Number, percent change; 7,858 agencies; 2013 estimated population 192,473,854; 2004 estimated population 178,805,123.)

Offense charged	Male						Female					
	Total			Under 18			Total			Under 18		
	2004	2013	Percent change	2004	2013	Percent change	2004	2013	Percent change	2004	2013	Percent change
Total [1]	6,428,484	5,249,466	-18.3	880,360	474,379	-46.1	1,974,004	1,871,059	-5.2	346,505	191,884	-44.6
Violent crime [2]	294,024	250,096	-14.9	44,135	27,489	-37.7	64,042	62,643	-2.2	9,770	6,178	-36.8
Murder and nonnegligent manslaughter	6,976	5,899	-15.4	579	426	-26.4	896	796	-11.2	64	66	+3.1
Rape [3]	14,804	10,303	-30.4	2,350	1,431	-39.1	215	168	-21.9	64	53	-17.2
Robbery	57,297	52,850	-7.8	13,493	11,146	-17.4	7,052	8,169	+15.8	1,443	1,194	-17.3
Aggravated assault	214,947	181,044	-15.8	27,713	14,486	-47.7	55,879	53,510	-4.2	8,199	4,865	-40.7
Property crime [2]	677,366	612,072	-9.6	181,361	102,042	-43.7	321,450	371,235	+15.5	93,808	52,796	-43.7
Burglary	153,657	134,520	-12.5	43,716	24,592	-43.7	26,960	28,741	+6.6	6,005	3,368	-43.9
Larceny-theft	443,937	438,967	-1.1	114,914	69,383	-39.6	277,832	332,902	+19.8	83,157	47,758	-42.6
Motor vehicle theft	72,175	33,139	-54.1	18,772	6,058	-67.7	15,162	8,246	-45.6	4,012	1,309	-67.4
Arson	7,597	5,446	-28.3	3,959	2,009	-49.3	1,496	1,346	-10.0	634	361	-43.1
Other assaults	579,814	502,938	-13.3	98,809	57,829	-41.5	190,156	193,721	+1.9	49,934	33,607	-32.7
Forgery and counterfeiting	43,282	23,763	-45.1	1,965	462	-76.5	28,711	14,121	-50.8	1,023	187	-81.7
Fraud	105,222	52,978	-49.7	2,919	1,838	-37.0	91,566	35,267	-61.5	1,703	917	-46.2
Embezzlement	5,892	5,195	-11.8	424	161	-62.0	6,103	5,007	-18.0	274	72	-73.7
Stolen property; buying, receiving, possessing	63,803	45,940	-28.0	11,674	5,361	-54.1	14,224	12,503	-12.1	2,205	993	-55.0
Vandalism	133,903	102,840	-23.2	52,463	25,044	-52.3	27,038	25,749	-4.8	8,799	4,632	-47.4
Weapons; carrying, possessing, etc.	101,813	83,516	-18.0	22,772	11,539	-49.3	8,884	7,634	-14.1	2,706	1,232	-54.5
Prostitution and commercialized vice	17,110	11,124	-35.0	311	104	-66.6	38,259	24,438	-36.1	846	446	-47.3
Sex offenses (except forcible rape and prostitution)	49,501	32,947	-33.4	9,896	5,601	-43.4	4,791	2,657	-44.5	1,027	648	-36.9
Drug abuse violations	875,292	772,299	-11.8	97,947	62,043	-36.7	205,009	204,583	-0.2	20,445	13,724	-32.9
Gambling	5,914	3,873	-34.5	1,073	545	-49.2	451	527	+16.9	26	24	-7.7
Offenses against the family and children	55,810	44,894	-19.6	2,269	1,034	-54.4	17,439	15,585	-10.6	1,339	634	-52.7
Driving under the influence	684,615	536,202	-21.7	8,862	3,283	-63.0	155,710	174,149	+11.8	2,350	1,032	-56.1
Liquor laws	256,914	148,148	-42.3	46,834	21,047	-55.1	86,868	58,137	-33.1	25,142	13,236	-47.4
Drunkenness	310,471	245,802	-20.8	8,558	3,754	-56.1	53,507	54,906	+2.6	2,559	1,353	-47.1
Disorderly conduct	270,910	188,386	-30.5	74,220	35,078	-52.7	93,949	70,564	-24.9	36,154	18,393	-49.1
Vagrancy	18,567	14,289	-23.0	2,221	419	-81.1	4,570	3,865	-15.4	917	126	-86.3
All other offenses (except traffic)	1,833,436	1,554,858	-15.2	166,822	92,400	-44.6	539,516	525,690	-2.6	63,717	33,576	-47.3
Suspicion	3,362	300	-91.1	380	31	-91.8	887	99	-88.8	155	7	-95.5
Curfew and loitering law violations	44,825	17,306	-61.4	44,825	17,306	-61.4	21,761	8,078	-62.9	21,761	8,078	-62.9

1 Does not include suspicion.　2 Violent crimes are offenses of murder and nonnegligent manslaughter, forcible rape, robbery, and aggravated assault. Property crimes are offenses of burglary, larceny-theft, motor vehicle theft, and arson.　3 The rape figures in this table are based on the legacy definition of rape only. The rape figures shown include converted National Incident-Based Reporting System rape data and those states/agencies that reported the legacy definition of rape for both years.

Table 34.   Five-Year Arrest Trends, by Age, 2009 and 2013

(Number, percent change; 9,006 agencies; 2013 estimated population 208,385,233; 2009 estimated population 202,066,342.)

Offense charged	Number of persons arrested								
	Total, all ages			Under 18 years of age			18 years of age and over		
	2009	2013	Percent change	2009	2013	Percent change	2009	2013	Percent change
Total [1]	8,987,695	7,645,953	-14.9	1,170,810	714,767	-39.0	7,816,885	6,931,186	-11.3
Violent crime [2]	388,215	332,699	-14.3	56,148	35,912	-36.0	332,067	296,787	-10.6
Murder and nonnegligent manslaughter	7,960	6,985	-12.2	775	488	-37.0	7,185	6,497	-9.6
Rape[3]	13,454	11,084	-17.6	1,981	1,568	-20.8	11,473	9,516	-17.1
Robbery	82,311	65,501	-20.4	20,650	13,357	-35.3	61,661	52,144	-15.4
Aggravated assault	284,490	249,129	-12.4	32,742	20,499	-37.4	251,748	228,630	-9.2
Property crime [2]	1,130,971	1,050,696	-7.1	274,728	166,462	-39.4	856,243	884,234	+3.3
Burglary	200,533	173,551	-13.5	50,386	30,172	-40.1	150,147	143,379	-4.5
Larceny-theft	870,506	825,754	-5.1	208,114	125,764	-39.6	662,392	699,990	+5.7
Motor vehicle theft	52,321	44,222	-15.5	12,887	7,973	-38.1	39,434	36,249	-8.1
Arson	7,611	7,169	-5.8	3,341	2,553	-23.6	4,270	4,616	+8.1
Other assaults	854,893	745,943	-12.7	139,981	97,560	-30.3	714,912	648,383	-9.3
Forgery and counterfeiting	56,413	40,832	-27.6	1,380	696	-49.6	55,033	40,136	-27.1
Fraud	141,665	94,707	-33.1	4,249	2,992	-29.6	137,416	91,715	-33.3
Embezzlement	12,806	10,974	-14.3	431	254	-41.1	12,375	10,720	-13.4
Stolen property; buying, receiving, possessing	64,669	63,393	-2.0	11,245	7,006	-37.7	53,424	56,387	+5.5
Vandalism	178,743	137,270	-23.2	60,233	31,563	-47.6	118,510	105,707	-10.8
Weapons; carrying, possessing, etc.	113,050	96,595	-14.6	22,762	13,750	-39.6	90,288	82,845	-8.2
Prostitution and commercialized vice	49,815	37,062	-25.6	972	599	-38.4	48,843	36,463	-25.3
Sex offenses (except forcible rape and prostitution)	49,751	38,769	-22.1	8,534	6,889	-19.3	41,217	31,880	-22.7
Drug abuse violations	1,123,327	1,039,812	-7.4	114,584	80,428	-29.8	1,008,743	959,384	-4.9
Gambling	7,332	4,573	-37.6	1,344	601	-55.3	5,988	3,972	-33.7
Offenses against the family and children	73,707	67,026	-9.1	2,988	1,869	-37.4	70,719	65,157	-7.9
Driving under the influence	947,140	758,220	-19.9	8,756	4,759	-45.6	938,384	753,461	-19.7
Liquor laws	352,403	223,265	-36.6	68,657	37,615	-45.2	283,746	185,650	-34.6
Drunkenness	428,847	323,238	-24.6	10,275	5,479	-46.7	418,572	317,759	-24.1
Disorderly conduct	390,891	287,933	-26.3	102,000	58,014	-43.1	288,891	229,919	-20.4
Vagrancy	23,715	19,000	-19.9	1,909	564	-70.5	21,806	18,436	-15.5
All other offenses (except traffic)	2,539,389	2,247,266	-11.5	219,681	135,075	-38.5	2,319,708	2,112,191	-8.9
Suspicion	1,191	566	-52.5	152	45	-70.4	1,039	521	-49.9
Curfew and loitering law violations	59,953	26,680	-55.5	59,953	26,680	-55.5	NA	NA	NA

NA = Not available.   1 Does not include suspicion.   2 Violent crimes are offenses of murder and nonnegligent manslaughter, forcible rape, robbery, and aggravated assault. Property crimes are offenses of burglary, larceny-theft, motor vehicle theft, and arson.   3 The rape figures in this table are based on the legacy definition of rape only. The rape figures shown include converted National Incident-Based Reporting System rape data and those states/agencies that reported the legacy definition of rape for both years.

Table 35. Five-Year Arrest Trends, by Age and Sex, 2009 and 2013

(Number, percent change; 9,006 agencies; 2013 estimated population 208,385,233; 2009 estimated population 202,066,342.)

Offense charged	Male						Female					
	Total			Under 18			Total			Under 18		
	2009	2013	Percent change	2009	2013	Percent change	2009	2013	Percent change	2009	2013	Percent change
Total [1]	6,746,292	5,622,476	-16.7	831,433	508,424	-38.8	2,241,403	2,023,477	-9.7	339,377	206,343	-39.2
Violent crime [2]	315,042	266,036	-15.6	46,050	29,358	-36.2	73,173	66,663	-8.9	10,098	6,554	-35.1
Murder and nonnegligent manslaughter	7,107	6,179	-13.1	716	441	-38.4	853	806	-5.5	59	47	-20.3
Rape[3]	13,280	10,894	-18.0	1,944	1,509	-22.4	174	190	+9.2	37	59	+59.5
Robbery	72,529	56,818	-21.7	18,550	12,061	-35.0	9,782	8,683	-11.2	2,100	1,296	-38.3
Aggravated assault	222,126	192,145	-13.5	24,840	15,347	-38.2	62,364	56,984	-8.6	7,902	5,152	-34.8
Property crime [2]	708,334	653,040	-7.8	170,775	109,611	-35.8	422,637	397,656	-5.9	103,953	56,851	-45.3
Burglary	168,916	143,044	-15.3	44,183	26,574	-39.9	31,617	30,507	-3.5	6,203	3,598	-42.0
Larceny-theft	490,227	468,890	-4.4	113,018	74,325	-34.2	380,279	356,864	-6.2	95,096	51,439	-45.9
Motor vehicle theft	42,836	35,356	-17.5	10,642	6,548	-38.5	9,485	8,866	-6.5	2,245	1,425	-36.5
Arson	6,355	5,750	-9.5	2,932	2,164	-26.2	1,256	1,419	+13.0	409	389	-4.9
Other assaults	631,877	538,086	-14.8	92,013	61,846	-32.8	223,016	207,857	-6.8	47,968	35,714	-25.5
Forgery and counterfeiting	35,347	25,523	-27.8	968	488	-49.6	21,066	15,309	-27.3	412	208	-49.5
Fraud	80,476	57,044	-29.1	2,756	2,009	-27.1	61,189	37,663	-38.4	1,493	983	-34.2
Embezzlement	6,215	5,625	-9.5	248	174	-29.8	6,591	5,349	-18.8	183	80	-56.3
Stolen property; buying, receiving, possessing	52,427	49,767	-5.1	9,473	5,884	-37.9	12,242	13,626	+11.3	1,772	1,122	-36.7
Vandalism	146,700	109,573	-25.3	52,068	26,605	-48.9	32,043	27,697	-13.6	8,165	4,958	-39.3
Weapons; carrying, possessing, etc.	104,002	88,258	-15.1	20,540	12,408	-39.6	9,048	8,337	-7.9	2,222	1,342	-39.6
Prostitution and commercialized vice	14,924	11,682	-21.7	192	110	-42.7	34,891	25,380	-27.3	780	489	-37.3
Sex offenses (except forcible rape and prostitution)	45,042	35,714	-20.7	7,578	6,116	-19.3	4,709	3,055	-35.1	956	773	-19.1
Drug abuse violations	912,831	819,978	-10.2	96,719	65,766	-32.0	210,496	219,834	+4.4	17,865	14,662	-17.9
Gambling	6,586	3,959	-39.9	1,308	557	-57.4	746	614	-17.7	36	44	+22.2
Offenses against the family and children	55,377	49,813	-10.0	1,900	1,161	-38.9	18,330	17,213	-6.1	1,088	708	-34.9
Driving under the influence	732,962	569,663	-22.3	6,548	3,605	-44.9	214,178	188,557	-12.0	2,208	1,154	-47.7
Liquor laws	252,354	159,956	-36.6	42,452	23,107	-45.6	100,049	63,309	-36.7	26,205	14,508	-44.6
Drunkenness	358,625	263,451	-26.5	7,675	4,010	-47.8	70,222	59,787	-14.9	2,600	1,469	-43.5
Disorderly conduct	286,868	209,038	-27.1	67,878	38,009	-44.0	104,023	78,895	-24.2	34,122	20,005	-41.4
Vagrancy	18,380	14,992	-18.4	1,340	436	-67.5	5,335	4,008	-24.9	569	128	-77.5
All other offenses (except traffic)	1,941,259	1,673,160	-13.8	162,288	99,046	-39.0	598,130	574,106	-4.0	57,393	36,029	-37.2
Suspicion	875	439	-49.8	121	37	-69.4	316	127	-59.8	31	8	-74.2
Curfew and loitering law violations	40,664	18,118	-55.4	40,664	18,118	-55.4	19,289	8,562	-55.6	19,289	8,562	-55.6

1 Does not include suspicion.   2 Violent crimes are offenses of murder and nonnegligent manslaughter, forcible rape, robbery, and aggravated assault. Property crimes are offenses of burglary, larceny-theft, motor vehicle theft, and arson.   3 The rape figures in this table are based on the legacy definition of rape only. The rape figures shown include converted National Incident-Based Reporting System rape data and those states/agencies that reported the legacy definition of rape for both years.

Table 36. Current Year Over Previous Year Arrest Trends, 2012–2013

(Number, percent change; 9,412 agencies; 2013 estimated population 210,277,851; 2012 estimated population 208,777,994.)

Offense charged	Number of persons arrested											
	Total, all ages			Under 15 years of age			Under 18 years of age			18 years of age and over		
	2012	2013	Percent change	2012	2013	Percent change	2012	2013	Percent change	2012	2013	Percent change
Total [1]	8,026,954	7,634,314	-4.9	229,577	194,429	-15.3	831,366	702,779	-15.5	7,195,588	6,931,535	-3.7
Violent crime [2]	343,222	329,703	-3.9	10,306	9,402	-8.8	36,905	33,713	-8.6	306,317	295,990	-3.4
Murder and nonnegligent manslaughter	6,763	6,742	-0.3	47	63	+34.0	425	485	+14.1	6,338	6,257	-1.3
Rape[3]	11,598	10,967	-5.4	607	572	-5.8	1,607	1,550	-3.5	9,991	9,417	-5.7
Robbery	64,030	62,646	-2.2	2,349	2,325	-1.0	12,408	11,957	-3.6	51,622	50,689	-1.8
Aggravated assault	260,831	249,348	-4.4	7,303	6,442	-11.8	22,465	19,721	-12.2	238,366	229,627	-3.7
Property crime [2]	1,077,394	1,046,585	-2.9	54,898	45,810	-16.6	192,669	163,822	-15.0	884,725	882,763	-0.2
Burglary	190,916	174,506	-8.6	9,941	8,029	-19.2	36,067	29,715	-17.6	154,849	144,791	-6.5
Larceny-theft	837,404	823,575	-1.7	41,740	34,860	-16.5	146,223	124,844	-14.6	691,181	698,731	+1.1
Motor vehicle theft	42,081	41,650	-1.0	1,567	1,542	-1.6	7,598	6,907	-9.1	34,483	34,743	+0.8
Arson	6,993	6,854	-2.0	1,650	1,379	-16.4	2,781	2,356	-15.3	4,212	4,498	+6.8
Other assaults	782,502	738,781	-5.6	42,078	37,691	-10.4	108,705	96,475	-11.3	673,797	642,306	-4.7
Forgery and counterfeiting	44,624	41,367	-7.3	132	76	-42.4	943	703	-25.5	43,681	40,664	-6.9
Fraud	105,634	98,335	-6.9	573	588	+2.6	3,222	3,070	-4.7	102,412	95,265	-7.0
Embezzlement	11,254	11,349	+0.8	20	26	+30.0	285	260	-8.8	10,969	11,089	+1.1
Stolen property; buying, receiving, possessing	67,623	64,789	-4.2	1,957	1,620	-17.2	8,778	7,122	-18.9	58,845	57,667	-2.0
Vandalism	147,291	133,943	-9.1	14,785	11,648	-21.2	38,254	30,820	-19.4	109,037	103,123	-5.4
Weapons; carrying, possessing, etc.	96,930	93,839	-3.2	5,354	4,520	-15.6	15,528	13,329	-14.2	81,402	80,510	-1.1
Prostitution and commercialized vice	35,645	34,792	-2.4	38	55	+44.7	567	576	+1.6	35,078	34,216	-2.5
Sex offenses (except forcible rape and prostitution)	44,170	38,599	-12.6	3,957	3,368	-14.9	8,003	6,915	-13.6	36,167	31,684	-12.4
Drug abuse violations	991,032	1,005,019	+1.4	15,051	13,387	-11.1	86,818	76,568	-11.8	904,214	928,451	+2.7
Gambling	2,815	2,493	-11.4	33	41	+24.2	262	183	-30.2	2,553	2,310	-9.5
Offenses against the family and children	71,847	69,387	-3.4	717	610	-14.9	2,282	1,894	-17.0	69,565	67,493	-3.0
Driving under the influence	849,335	782,603	-7.9	106	105	-0.9	5,921	4,873	-17.7	843,414	777,730	-7.8
Liquor laws	273,305	226,501	-17.1	4,759	3,632	-23.7	48,790	37,592	-23.0	224,515	188,909	-15.9
Drunkenness	363,894	322,556	-11.4	832	650	-21.9	7,132	5,467	-23.3	356,762	317,089	-11.1
Disorderly conduct	315,394	280,353	-11.1	27,576	22,575	-18.1	70,723	56,989	-19.4	244,671	223,364	-8.7
Vagrancy	19,376	19,141	-1.2	267	145	-45.7	985	590	-40.1	18,391	18,551	+0.9
All other offenses (except traffic)	2,349,757	2,267,608	-3.5	37,642	31,759	-15.6	160,684	135,247	-15.8	2,189,073	2,132,361	-2.6
Suspicion	909	537	-40.9	29	16	-44.8	130	44	-66.2	779	493	-36.7
Curfew and loitering law violations	33,910	26,571	-21.6	8,496	6,721	-20.9	33,910	26,571	-21.6	NA	NA	NA

NA = Not available.   1 Does not include suspicion.   2 Violent crimes are offenses of murder and nonnegligent manslaughter, forcible rape, robbery, and aggravated assault. Property crimes are offenses of burglary, larceny-theft, motor vehicle theft, and arson.   3 The rape figures in this table are based on the legacy definition of rape only. The rape figures shown include converted National Incident-Based Reporting System rape data and those states/agencies that reported the legacy definition of rape for both years.

Table 37.   Current Year Over Previous Year Arrest Trends, by Age and Sex, 2012–2013

(Number, percent change; 9,412 agencies; 2013 estimated population 210,277,851; 2012 estimated population 208,777,994.)

Offense charged	Male Total			Male Under 18			Female Total			Female Under 18		
	2012	2013	Percent change	2012	2013	Percent change	2012	2013	Percent change	2012	2013	Percent change
Total [1]	5,910,106	5,595,287	-5.3	585,914	497,197	-15.1	2,116,848	2,039,027	-3.7	245,452	205,582	-16.2
Violent crime [2]	274,183	262,735	-4.2	29,909	27,402	-8.4	69,039	66,968	-3.0	6,996	6,311	-9.8
Murder and nonnegligent manslaughter	5,981	5,917	-1.1	382	419	+9.7	782	825	+5.5	43	66	+53.5
Rape[3]	11,474	10,781	-6.0	1,581	1,489	-5.8	124	186	+50.0	26	61	+134.6
Robbery	55,510	54,138	-2.5	11,109	10,808	-2.7	8,520	8,508	-0.1	1,299	1,149	-11.5
Aggravated assault	201,218	191,899	-4.6	16,837	14,686	-12.8	59,613	57,449	-3.6	5,628	5,035	-10.5
Property crime [2]	670,056	647,624	-3.3	124,778	107,312	-14.0	407,338	398,961	-2.1	67,891	56,510	-16.8
Burglary	158,335	143,419	-9.4	31,596	26,091	-17.4	32,581	31,087	-4.6	4,471	3,624	-18.9
Larceny-theft	472,040	465,455	-1.4	84,440	73,538	-12.9	365,364	358,120	-2.0	61,783	51,306	-17.0
Motor vehicle theft	33,934	33,190	-2.2	6,376	5,628	-11.7	8,147	8,460	+3.8	1,222	1,279	+4.7
Arson	5,747	5,560	-3.3	2,366	2,055	-13.1	1,246	1,294	+3.9	415	301	-27.5
Other assaults	564,734	532,074	-5.8	68,837	61,358	-10.9	217,768	206,707	-5.1	39,868	35,117	-11.9
Forgery and counterfeiting	27,898	25,794	-7.5	653	497	-23.9	16,726	15,573	-6.9	290	206	-29.0
Fraud	62,652	59,104	-5.7	2,167	2,068	-4.6	42,982	39,231	-8.7	1,055	1,002	-5.0
Embezzlement	5,747	5,831	+1.5	173	177	+2.3	5,507	5,518	+0.2	112	83	-25.9
Stolen property; buying, receiving, possessing	53,933	50,854	-5.7	7,363	5,980	-18.8	13,690	13,935	+1.8	1,415	1,142	-19.3
Vandalism	117,482	106,845	-9.1	32,073	25,933	-19.1	29,809	27,098	-9.1	6,181	4,887	-20.9
Weapons; carrying, possessing, etc.	88,821	85,631	-3.6	14,090	11,999	-14.8	8,109	8,208	+1.2	1,438	1,330	-7.5
Prostitution and commercialized vice	11,631	11,391	-2.1	118	105	-11.0	24,014	23,401	-2.6	449	471	+4.9
Sex offenses (except forcible rape and prostitution)	40,584	35,546	-12.4	7,165	6,133	-14.4	3,586	3,053	-14.9	838	782	-6.7
Drug abuse violations	783,403	787,654	+0.5	71,397	62,087	-13.0	207,629	217,365	+4.7	15,421	14,481	-6.1
Gambling	2,235	1,913	-14.4	227	156	-31.3	580	580	0.0	35	27	-22.9
Offenses against the family and children	53,609	51,643	-3.7	1,434	1,170	-18.4	18,238	17,744	-2.7	848	724	-14.6
Driving under the influence	639,413	587,451	-8.1	4,393	3,680	-16.2	209,922	195,152	-7.0	1,528	1,193	-21.9
Liquor laws	194,088	162,004	-16.5	29,586	23,037	-22.1	79,217	64,497	-18.6	19,204	14,555	-24.2
Drunkenness	297,247	262,655	-11.6	5,173	4,001	-22.7	66,647	59,901	-10.1	1,959	1,466	-25.2
Disorderly conduct	225,365	201,151	-10.7	45,265	36,884	-18.5	90,029	79,202	-12.0	25,458	20,105	-21.0
Vagrancy	15,298	15,089	-1.4	751	447	-40.5	4,078	4,052	-0.6	234	143	-38.9
All other offenses (except traffic)	1,758,673	1,684,250	-4.2	117,308	98,723	-15.8	591,084	583,358	-1.3	43,376	36,524	-15.8
Suspicion	698	431	-38.3	101	40	-60.4	211	106	-49.8	29	4	-86.2
Curfew and loitering law violations	23,054	18,048	-21.7	23,054	18,048	-21.7	10,856	8,523	-21.5	10,856	8,523	-21.5

1 Does not include suspicion.   2 Violent crimes are offenses of murder and nonnegligent manslaughter, forcible rape, robbery, and aggravated assault. Property crimes are offenses of burglary, larceny-theft, motor vehicle theft, and arson.   3 The rape figures in this table are based on the legacy definition of rape only. The rape figures shown include converted National Incident-Based Reporting System rape data and those states/agencies that reported the legacy definition of rape for both years.

Table 38.   Arrests, Distribution by Age, 2013

(Number, percent; 11,951 agencies; 2013 estimated population 245,741,701.)

Offense charged	All ages	Under 15	Under 18	18 and over	Under 10	10–12	13–14	15	16	17	18	19	20
Total	9,069,992	244,688	875,262	8,194,730	6,394	53,316	184,978	165,481	209,804	255,289	334,841	371,156	376,711
Total percent distribution[1]	100.0	2.7	9.7	90.3	0.1	0.6	2.0	1.8	2.3	2.8	3.7	4.1	4.2
Violent crime [2]	392,778	12,291	43,651	349,127	274	2,706	9,311	8,441	10,698	12,221	14,482	15,612	15,896
Violent crime percent distribution[1]	100.0	3.1	11.1	88.9	0.1	0.7	2.4	2.1	2.7	3.1	3.7	4.0	4.0
Murder and nonnegligent manslaughter	8,401	71	614	7,787	0	9	62	91	163	289	440	480	565
Rape[3]	13,617	790	2,089	11,528	17	205	568	369	413	517	580	607	596
Robbery	78,753	3,209	15,932	62,821	14	412	2,783	3,268	4,397	5,058	5,920	5,443	4,959
Aggravated assault	292,007	8,221	25,016	266,991	243	2,080	5,898	4,713	5,725	6,357	7,542	9,082	9,776
Property crime [2]	1,261,124	56,138	198,599	1,062,525	1,122	12,087	42,929	38,326	48,553	55,582	65,189	60,699	55,654
Property crime percent distribution[1]	100.0	4.5	15.7	84.3	0.1	1.0	3.4	3.0	3.8	4.4	5.2	4.8	4.4
Burglary	203,709	9,509	34,760	168,949	241	1,945	7,323	6,792	8,669	9,790	11,827	11,094	10,065
Larceny-theft	996,495	42,806	151,427	845,068	692	9,380	32,734	28,896	36,858	42,867	50,282	46,851	43,092
Motor vehicle theft	52,507	2,140	9,469	43,038	19	223	1,898	2,145	2,620	2,564	2,810	2,488	2,228
Arson	8,413	1,683	2,943	5,470	170	539	974	493	406	361	270	266	269
Other assaults	885,822	46,365	118,253	767,569	1,415	12,238	32,712	22,928	24,818	24,142	23,071	25,144	27,541
Forgery and counterfeiting	48,826	94	850	47,976	3	20	71	90	189	477	1,277	1,745	2,032
Fraud	113,510	697	3,542	109,968	10	140	547	539	918	1,388	2,368	3,262	3,845
Embezzlement	12,664	35	318	12,346	1	6	28	27	78	178	506	748	774
Stolen property; buying, receiving, possessing	74,792	1,953	8,388	66,404	19	281	1,653	1,699	2,187	2,549	3,623	3,582	3,487
Vandalism	162,068	14,326	37,678	124,390	689	4,129	9,508	7,145	7,843	8,364	8,128	7,612	7,090
Weapons; carrying, possessing, etc.	112,673	5,673	16,683	95,990	320	1,516	3,837	3,007	3,627	4,376	5,444	5,435	5,267
Prostitution and commercialized vice	42,110	61	655	41,455	1	5	55	80	180	334	1,202	1,722	1,843
Sex offenses (except forcible rape and prostitution)	46,832	4,145	8,389	38,443	149	1,188	2,808	1,461	1,391	1,392	1,568	1,493	1,446
Drug abuse violations	1,209,661	16,075	94,187	1,115,474	85	2,209	13,781	15,648	24,490	37,974	61,494	66,235	64,345
Gambling	5,089	104	615	4,474	0	14	90	87	170	254	254	268	269
Offenses against the family and children	78,812	741	2,224	76,588	39	156	546	504	439	540	950	1,140	1,421
Driving under the influence	918,462	117	5,963	912,499	11	9	97	249	1,320	4,277	13,087	19,543	24,754
Liquor laws	280,860	4,562	48,126	232,734	35	316	4,211	7,192	13,456	22,916	43,972	48,601	41,435
Drunkenness	358,036	696	5,902	352,134	18	56	622	932	1,389	2,885	7,376	9,117	9,506
Disorderly conduct	375,142	29,362	76,318	298,824	651	6,734	21,977	15,680	15,812	15,464	13,371	13,079	12,988
Vagrancy	21,633	176	733	20,900	3	28	145	158	175	224	659	728	670
All other offenses (except traffic)	2,620,320	36,882	156,079	2,464,241	1,173	6,560	29,149	30,491	39,573	49,133	66,783	85,363	96,414
Suspicion	844	83	175	669	9	20	54	32	37	23	37	28	34
Curfew and loitering law violations	47,934	14,112	47,934	NA	367	2,898	10,847	10,765	12,461	10,596	NA	NA	NA

Table 38. Arrests, Distribution by Age, 2013

(Number, percent; 11,951 agencies; 2013 estimated population 245,741,701.)

Offense charged	21	22	23	24	25–29	30–34	35–39	40–44	45–49	50–54	55–59	60–64	65 and over
Total	377,447	371,177	358,242	337,984	1,430,952	1,156,177	810,769	699,790	603,569	486,501	272,335	122,664	84,415
Total percent distribution[1]	4.2	4.1	3.9	3.7	15.8	12.7	8.9	7.7	6.7	5.4	3.0	1.4	0.9
Violent crime [2]	16,646	16,004	15,541	14,551	62,666	50,587	34,917	29,307	24,808	19,170	10,310	4,765	3,865
Violent crime percent distribution[1]	4.2	4.1	4.0	3.7	16.0	12.9	8.9	7.5	6.3	4.9	2.6	1.2	1.0
Murder and nonnegligent manslaughter	539	477	439	360	1,422	952	572	464	377	317	158	97	128
Rape[3]	574	486	442	403	1,661	1,657	1,231	1,075	795	615	378	212	216
Robbery	4,383	3,897	3,471	2,965	10,976	7,283	4,372	3,537	2,720	1,787	766	229	113
Aggravated assault	11,150	11,144	11,189	10,823	48,607	40,695	28,742	24,231	20,916	16,451	9,008	4,227	3,408
Property crime [2]	51,907	49,488	46,333	43,335	183,851	145,108	98,517	85,435	72,015	54,534	29,095	12,457	8,908
Property crime percent distribution[1]	4.1	3.9	3.7	3.4	14.6	11.5	7.8	6.8	5.7	4.3	2.3	1.0	0.7
Burglary	9,300	8,823	8,131	7,520	30,938	23,328	14,749	11,980	9,593	6,797	3,186	1,082	536
Larceny-theft	40,151	38,385	36,006	33,759	143,866	114,257	78,899	69,734	59,567	45,908	25,055	11,066	8,190
Motor vehicle theft	2,221	2,081	1,984	1,860	8,154	6,768	4,376	3,262	2,422	1,461	631	197	95
Arson	235	199	212	196	893	755	493	459	433	368	223	112	87
Other assaults	32,206	32,685	32,382	30,889	136,313	115,864	84,266	73,313	61,047	47,281	25,333	11,143	9,091
Forgery and counterfeiting	1,907	2,007	2,116	2,115	9,551	8,081	5,643	4,407	3,288	2,152	1,045	417	193
Fraud	3,887	4,053	4,240	4,192	19,250	17,616	13,438	11,741	9,056	6,430	3,620	1,643	1,327
Embezzlement	728	654	580	530	2,055	1,642	1,202	1,057	788	584	268	149	81
Stolen property; buying, receiving, possessing	3,307	3,192	3,165	2,978	12,596	10,440	6,779	5,223	3,693	2,580	1,075	433	251
Vandalism	7,402	6,917	6,258	5,705	22,411	16,386	10,646	8,708	6,969	5,300	2,661	1,220	977
Weapons; carrying, possessing, etc.	5,428	5,442	5,035	4,597	18,173	13,625	8,357	6,152	4,813	3,794	2,270	1,163	995
Prostitution and commercialized vice	1,990	2,027	1,913	1,874	7,410	5,785	4,161	4,042	3,290	2,256	1,055	489	396
Sex offenses (except forcible rape and prostitution)	1,310	1,340	1,276	1,131	5,053	4,701	3,987	3,632	3,462	3,073	2,118	1,326	1,527
Drug abuse violations	61,524	58,989	55,457	51,148	205,771	157,451	100,040	79,587	65,380	49,239	25,159	9,592	4,063
Gambling	247	246	184	175	670	431	323	292	295	277	231	149	163
Offenses against the family and children	1,855	2,101	2,386	2,543	13,884	14,923	11,752	9,402	6,685	4,300	2,045	707	494
Driving under the influence	39,725	42,165	42,350	40,106	167,636	128,832	93,720	83,940	74,392	64,915	40,487	21,230	15,617
Liquor laws	7,043	5,107	4,215	3,528	13,392	11,113	9,039	10,039	11,395	11,526	7,253	3,280	1,796
Drunkenness	15,302	14,273	13,403	12,055	52,315	44,698	34,133	34,677	37,016	34,590	20,659	8,727	4,287
Disorderly conduct	17,125	15,269	13,841	12,623	48,627	37,777	27,060	24,154	22,893	20,038	11,293	4,999	3,687
Vagrancy	713	592	555	597	2,416	2,355	1,817	2,017	2,367	2,545	1,726	787	356
All other offenses (except traffic)	107,144	108,581	106,968	103,278	446,800	368,665	260,912	222,627	189,884	151,889	84,613	37,985	26,335
Suspicion	51	45	44	34	112	97	60	38	33	28	19	3	6
Curfew and loitering law violations	NA	NA	NA	NA	NA	NA	NA	NA	NA	NA	NA	NA	NA

NA = Not available.   1 Because of rounding, the percentages may not sum to 100 percent. assault. Property crimes are offenses of burglary, larceny-theft, motor vehicle theft, and arson. Uniform Crime Reporting definitions. 2 Violent crimes are offenses of murder and nonnegligent manslaughter, forcible rape, robbery, and aggravated 3 The rape figures in this table are an aggregate total of the data submitted using both the revised and legacy

Table 39.   Male Arrests, Distribution by Age, 2013

(Number, percent; 11,951 agencies; 2013 estimated population 245,741,701.)

Offense charged	All ages	Under 15	Under 18	18 and over	Under 10	10–12	13–14	15	16	17	18	19	20
Total	6,662,833	170,601	622,630	6,040,203	5,246	38,471	126,884	115,270	149,571	187,188	248,770	274,746	277,523
Total percent distribution[1]	100.0	2.6	9.3	90.7	0.1	0.6	1.9	1.7	2.2	2.8	3.7	4.1	4.2
Violent crime [2]	313,751	9,618	35,488	278,263	234	2,151	7,233	6,769	8,768	10,333	12,229	12,898	12,958
Violent crime percent distribution[1]	100.0	3.1	11.3	88.7	0.1	0.7	2.3	2.2	2.8	3.3	3.9	4.1	4.1
Murder and nonnegligent manslaughter	7,415	53	541	6,874	0	8	45	79	143	266	409	441	531
Rape[3]	13,362	751	2,014	11,348	17	198	536	355	399	509	571	598	582
Robbery	68,239	2,852	14,403	53,836	13	372	2,467	2,918	3,974	4,659	5,311	4,863	4,371
Aggravated assault	224,735	5,962	18,530	206,205	204	1,573	4,185	3,417	4,252	4,899	5,938	6,996	7,474
Property crime [2]	785,022	37,964	130,836	654,186	882	8,312	28,770	25,520	31,601	35,751	42,210	38,402	35,020
Property crime percent distribution[1]	100.0	4.8	16.7	83.3	0.1	1.1	3.7	3.3	4.0	4.6	5.4	4.9	4.5
Burglary	169,018	8,363	30,740	138,278	206	1,712	6,445	5,967	7,754	8,656	10,498	9,582	8,616
Larceny-theft	567,174	26,484	89,780	477,394	515	5,954	20,015	17,392	21,331	24,573	29,057	26,517	24,354
Motor vehicle theft	42,078	1,684	7,825	34,253	15	178	1,491	1,748	2,173	2,220	2,413	2,082	1,825
Arson	6,752	1,433	2,491	4,261	146	468	819	413	343	302	242	221	225
Other assaults	639,502	29,535	75,173	564,329	1,180	8,349	20,006	13,979	15,770	15,889	15,601	17,169	19,026
Forgery and counterfeiting	30,570	70	607	29,963	3	11	56	70	133	334	801	1,153	1,253
Fraud	68,270	517	2,390	65,880	9	109	399	363	615	895	1,576	2,140	2,428
Embezzlement	6,536	27	207	6,329	1	6	20	19	54	107	271	403	400
Stolen property; buying, receiving, possessing	58,734	1,600	7,034	51,700	15	218	1,367	1,385	1,848	2,201	3,021	2,959	2,824
Vandalism	129,202	12,068	31,727	97,475	602	3,488	7,978	6,007	6,599	7,053	6,790	6,306	5,684
Weapons; carrying, possessing, etc.	102,864	4,937	14,944	87,920	284	1,305	3,348	2,674	3,284	4,049	5,089	5,077	4,918
Prostitution and commercialized vice	13,818	19	132	13,686	1	3	15	13	32	68	184	240	329
Sex offenses (except forcible rape and prostitution)	43,193	3,678	7,433	35,760	129	1,053	2,496	1,256	1,229	1,270	1,450	1,394	1,350
Drug abuse violations	953,984	12,397	77,022	876,962	72	1,733	10,592	12,540	20,238	31,847	50,956	54,391	52,251
Gambling	4,349	86	570	3,779	0	10	76	82	163	239	244	250	252
Offenses against the family and children	57,806	447	1,366	56,440	27	101	319	299	257	363	655	760	940
Driving under the influence	689,383	84	4,496	684,887	10	6	68	188	992	3,232	9,985	14,831	18,582
Liquor laws	199,751	2,386	29,321	170,430	21	173	2,192	4,007	8,185	14,743	29,325	33,441	28,879
Drunkenness	291,223	432	4,313	286,910	14	31	387	640	1,007	2,234	5,613	7,227	7,513
Disorderly conduct	270,299	18,677	49,973	220,326	532	4,447	13,698	9,979	10,475	10,842	9,783	9,531	9,445
Vagrancy	17,114	120	569	16,545	2	16	102	124	147	178	512	491	463
All other offenses (except traffic)	1,952,465	25,806	114,554	1,837,911	913	4,767	20,126	21,785	29,198	37,765	52,443	65,659	72,987
Suspicion	647	57	125	522	7	12	38	26	26	16	32	24	21
Curfew and loitering law violations	34,350	10,076	34,350	NA	308	2,170	7,598	7,545	8,950	7,779	NA	NA	NA

Table 39.   Male Arrests, Distribution by Age, 2013

(Number, percent; 11,951 agencies; 2013 estimated population 245,741,701.)

Offense charged	21	22	23	24	25–29	30–34	35–39	40–44	45–49	50–54	55–59	60–64	65 and over
Total	278,716	272,085	262,079	245,700	1,037,667	838,557	587,109	510,154	449,365	373,989	216,968	99,194	67,581
Total percent distribution[1]	4.2	4.1	3.9	3.7	15.6	12.6	8.8	7.7	6.7	5.6	3.3	1.5	1.0
Violent crime[2]	13,332	12,702	12,340	11,530	49,305	39,797	27,312	23,074	19,441	15,316	8,607	4,052	3,370
Violent crime percent distribution[1]	4.2	4.0	3.9	3.7	15.7	12.7	8.7	7.4	6.2	4.9	2.7	1.3	1.1
Murder and nonnegligent manslaughter	480	436	391	324	1,241	827	494	390	312	265	134	87	112
Rape[3]	563	476	437	395	1,638	1,627	1,199	1,060	787	610	378	212	215
Robbery	3,843	3,365	2,965	2,521	9,215	6,013	3,620	2,957	2,290	1,524	674	202	102
Aggravated assault	8,446	8,425	8,547	8,290	37,211	31,330	21,999	18,667	16,052	12,917	7,421	3,551	2,941
Property crime[2]	32,597	30,632	28,484	26,348	110,354	86,745	58,670	52,547	45,726	35,208	18,565	7,617	5,061
Property crime percent distribution[1]	4.2	3.9	3.6	3.4	14.1	11.1	7.5	6.7	5.8	4.5	2.4	1.0	0.6
Burglary	7,856	7,252	6,671	6,096	24,925	18,370	11,634	9,489	7,765	5,582	2,619	896	427
Larceny-theft	22,764	21,580	20,110	18,650	78,489	62,586	43,210	40,104	35,677	28,109	15,235	6,467	4,485
Motor vehicle theft	1,797	1,645	1,541	1,445	6,247	5,220	3,447	2,610	1,964	1,228	540	168	81
Arson	180	155	162	157	693	569	379	344	320	289	171	86	68
Other assaults	22,575	22,949	23,126	22,091	99,690	86,162	62,733	54,749	45,979	36,225	19,990	8,919	7,345
Forgery and counterfeiting	1,198	1,321	1,318	1,264	5,767	4,898	3,414	2,661	2,162	1,520	768	328	137
Fraud	2,431	2,530	2,598	2,585	11,402	9,942	7,552	6,836	5,521	4,109	2,295	1,083	852
Embezzlement	376	350	281	298	1,096	809	596	508	404	283	128	85	41
Stolen property; buying, receiving, possessing	2,628	2,485	2,422	2,231	9,442	7,820	5,131	4,118	2,968	2,159	906	370	216
Vandalism	5,892	5,429	4,869	4,409	17,255	12,647	8,173	6,683	5,380	4,088	2,100	994	776
Weapons; carrying, possessing, etc.	5,059	5,027	4,646	4,214	16,609	12,360	7,542	5,527	4,316	3,461	2,056	1,083	936
Prostitution and commercialized vice	369	407	423	491	2,275	2,053	1,681	1,514	1,251	1,053	665	396	355
Sex offenses (except forcible rape and prostitution)	1,196	1,229	1,181	1,017	4,620	4,295	3,636	3,385	3,230	2,936	2,045	1,290	1,506
Drug abuse violations	49,571	46,836	43,887	40,183	159,899	121,495	76,725	60,044	49,759	38,545	20,689	8,209	3,522
Gambling	229	217	173	160	606	371	260	213	201	208	156	107	132
Offenses against the family and children	1,210	1,375	1,561	1,673	9,540	10,651	8,935	7,486	5,468	3,495	1,744	571	376
Driving under the influence	28,864	30,583	31,058	29,776	125,786	97,505	70,755	62,129	54,746	48,703	31,671	17,083	12,830
Liquor laws	5,288	3,874	3,250	2,676	10,358	8,673	6,964	7,841	9,152	9,766	6,387	2,966	1,590
Drunkenness	12,309	11,515	10,990	9,869	42,384	36,035	27,189	27,545	30,019	28,968	17,930	7,905	3,899
Disorderly conduct	12,682	11,306	10,223	9,219	35,440	27,425	19,313	17,297	16,950	15,539	9,081	4,080	3,012
Vagrancy	530	468	437	454	1,885	1,815	1,343	1,611	1,925	2,118	1,542	624	327
All other offenses (except traffic)	80,343	80,813	78,777	75,186	323,865	266,980	189,145	164,359	144,738	120,267	69,626	31,431	21,292
Suspicion	37	37	35	26	89	79	40	27	29	22	17	1	6
Curfew and loitering law violations	NA	NA	NA	NA	NA	NA	NA	NA	NA	NA	NA	NA	NA

NA = Not available.   1 Because of rounding, the percentages may not sum to 100 percent.   2 Violent crimes are offenses of murder and nonnegligent manslaughter, forcible rape, robbery, and aggravated assault. Property crimes are offenses of burglary, larceny-theft, motor vehicle theft, and arson.   3 The rape figures in this table are an aggregate total of the data submitted using both the revised and legacy Uniform Crime Reporting definitions.

Table 40. Female Arrests, Distribution by Age, 2013

(Number, percent; 11,951 agencies; 2013 estimated population 245,741,701.)

Offense charged	All ages	Under 15	Under 18	18 and over	Under 10	10–12	13–14	15	16	17	18	19	20
Total	2,407,159	74,087	252,632	2,154,527	1,148	14,845	58,094	50,211	60,233	68,101	86,071	96,410	99,188
Total percent distribution[1]	100.0	3.1	10.5	89.5	*	0.6	2.4	2.1	2.5	2.8	3.6	4.0	4.1
Violent crime [2]	79,027	2,673	8,163	70,864	40	555	2,078	1,672	1,930	1,888	2,253	2,714	2,938
Violent crime percent distribution[1]	100.0	3.4	10.3	89.7	0.1	0.7	2.6	2.1	2.4	2.4	2.9	3.4	3.7
Murder and nonnegligent manslaughter	986	18	73	913	0	1	17	12	20	23	31	39	34
Rape[3]	255	39	75	180	0	7	32	14	14	8	9	9	14
Robbery	10,514	357	1,529	8,985	1	40	316	350	423	399	609	580	588
Aggravated assault	67,272	2,259	6,486	60,786	39	507	1,713	1,296	1,473	1,458	1,604	2,086	2,302
Property crime [2]	476,102	18,174	67,763	408,339	240	3,775	14,159	12,806	16,952	19,831	22,979	22,297	20,634
Property crime percent distribution[1]	100.0	3.8	14.2	85.8	0.1	0.8	3.0	2.7	3.6	4.2	4.8	4.7	4.3
Burglary	34,691	1,146	4,020	30,671	35	233	878	825	915	1,134	1,329	1,512	1,449
Larceny-theft	429,321	16,322	61,647	367,674	177	3,426	12,719	11,504	15,527	18,294	21,225	20,334	18,738
Motor vehicle theft	10,429	456	1,644	8,785	4	45	407	397	447	344	397	406	403
Arson	1,661	250	452	1,209	24	71	155	80	63	59	28	45	44
Other assaults	246,320	16,830	43,080	203,240	235	3,889	12,706	8,949	9,048	8,253	7,470	7,975	8,515
Forgery and counterfeiting	18,256	24	243	18,013	0	9	15	20	56	143	476	592	779
Fraud	45,240	180	1,152	44,088	1	31	148	176	303	493	792	1,122	1,417
Embezzlement	6,128	8	111	6,017	0	0	8	8	24	71	235	345	374
Stolen property; buying, receiving, possessing	16,058	353	1,354	14,704	4	63	286	314	339	348	602	623	663
Vandalism	32,866	2,258	5,951	26,915	87	641	1,530	1,138	1,244	1,311	1,338	1,306	1,406
Weapons; carrying, possessing, etc.	9,809	736	1,739	8,070	36	211	489	333	343	327	355	358	349
Prostitution and commercialized vice	28,292	42	523	27,769	0	2	40	67	148	266	1,018	1,482	1,514
Sex offenses (except forcible rape and prostitution)	3,639	467	956	2,683	20	135	312	205	162	122	118	99	96
Drug abuse violations	255,677	3,678	17,165	238,512	13	476	3,189	3,108	4,252	6,127	10,538	11,844	12,094
Gambling	740	18	45	695	0	4	14	5	7	15	10	18	17
Offenses against the family and children	21,006	294	858	20,148	12	55	227	205	182	177	295	380	481
Driving under the influence	229,079	33	1,467	227,612	1	3	29	61	328	1,045	3,102	4,712	6,172
Liquor laws	81,109	2,176	18,805	62,304	14	143	2,019	3,185	5,271	8,173	14,647	15,160	12,556
Drunkenness	66,813	264	1,589	65,224	4	25	235	292	382	651	1,763	1,890	1,993
Disorderly conduct	104,843	10,685	26,345	78,498	119	2,287	8,279	5,701	5,337	4,622	3,588	3,548	3,543
Vagrancy	4,519	56	164	4,355	1	12	43	34	28	46	147	237	207
All other offenses (except traffic)	667,855	11,076	41,525	626,330	260	1,793	9,023	8,706	10,375	11,368	14,340	19,704	23,427
Suspicion	197	26	50	147	2	8	16	6	11	7	5	4	13
Curfew and loitering law violations	13,584	4,036	13,584	NA	59	728	3,249	3,220	3,511	2,817	NA	NA	NA

Table 40.   Female Arrests, Distribution by Age, 2013

(Number, percent; 11,951 agencies; 2013 estimated population 245,741,701.)

Offense charged	21	22	23	24	25–29	30–34	35–39	40–44	45–49	50–54	55–59	60–64	65 and over
Total	98,731	99,092	96,163	92,284	393,285	317,620	223,660	189,636	154,204	112,512	55,367	23,470	16,834
Total percent distribution[1]	4.1	4.1	4.0	3.8	16.3	13.2	9.3	7.9	6.4	4.7	2.3	1.0	0.7
Violent crime [2]	3,314	3,302	3,201	3,021	13,361	10,790	7,605	6,233	5,367	3,854	1,703	713	495
Violent crime percent distribution[1]	4.2	4.2	4.1	3.8	16.9	13.7	9.6	7.9	6.8	4.9	2.2	0.9	0.6
Murder and nonnegligent manslaughter	59	41	48	36	181	125	78	74	65	52	24	10	16
Rape[3]	11	10	5	8	23	30	32	15	8	5	0	0	1
Robbery	540	532	506	444	1,761	1,270	752	580	430	263	92	27	11
Aggravated assault	2,704	2,719	2,642	2,533	11,396	9,365	6,743	5,564	4,864	3,534	1,587	676	467
Property crime [2]	19,310	18,856	17,849	16,987	73,497	58,363	39,847	32,888	26,289	19,326	10,530	4,840	3,847
Property crime percent distribution[1]	4.1	4.0	3.7	3.6	15.4	12.3	8.4	6.9	5.5	4.1	2.2	1.0	0.8
Burglary	1,444	1,571	1,460	1,424	6,013	4,958	3,115	2,491	1,828	1,215	567	186	109
Larceny-theft	17,387	16,805	15,896	15,109	65,377	51,671	35,689	29,630	23,890	17,799	9,820	4,599	3,705
Motor vehicle theft	424	436	443	415	1,907	1,548	929	652	458	233	91	29	14
Arson	55	44	50	39	200	186	114	115	113	79	52	26	19
Other assaults	9,631	9,736	9,256	8,798	36,623	29,702	21,533	18,564	15,068	11,056	5,343	2,224	1,746
Forgery and counterfeiting	709	686	798	851	3,784	3,183	2,229	1,746	1,126	632	277	89	56
Fraud	1,456	1,523	1,642	1,607	7,848	7,674	5,886	4,905	3,535	2,321	1,325	560	475
Embezzlement	352	304	299	232	959	833	606	549	384	301	140	64	40
Stolen property; buying, receiving, possessing	679	707	743	747	3,154	2,620	1,648	1,105	725	421	169	63	35
Vandalism	1,510	1,488	1,389	1,296	5,156	3,739	2,473	2,025	1,589	1,212	561	226	201
Weapons; carrying, possessing, etc.	369	415	389	383	1,564	1,265	815	625	497	333	214	80	59
Prostitution and commercialized vice	1,621	1,620	1,490	1,383	5,135	3,732	2,480	2,528	2,039	1,203	390	93	41
Sex offenses (except forcible rape and prostitution)	114	111	95	114	433	406	351	247	232	137	73	36	21
Drug abuse violations	11,953	12,153	11,570	10,965	45,872	35,956	23,315	19,543	15,621	10,694	4,470	1,383	541
Gambling	18	29	11	15	64	60	63	79	94	69	75	42	31
Offenses against the family and children	645	726	825	870	4,344	4,272	2,817	1,916	1,217	805	301	136	118
Driving under the influence	10,861	11,582	11,292	10,330	41,850	31,327	22,965	21,811	19,646	16,212	8,816	4,147	2,787
Liquor laws	1,755	1,233	965	852	3,034	2,440	2,075	2,198	2,243	1,760	866	314	206
Drunkenness	2,993	2,758	2,413	2,186	9,931	8,663	6,944	7,132	6,997	5,622	2,729	822	388
Disorderly conduct	4,443	3,963	3,618	3,404	13,187	10,352	7,747	6,857	5,943	4,499	2,212	919	675
Vagrancy	183	124	118	143	531	540	474	406	442	427	184	163	29
All other offenses (except traffic)	26,801	27,768	28,191	28,092	122,935	101,685	71,767	58,268	45,146	31,622	14,987	6,554	5,043
Suspicion	14	8	9	8	23	18	20	11	4	6	2	2	0
Curfew and loitering law violations	NA	NA	NA	NA	NA	NA	NA	NA	NA	NA	NA	NA	NA

* = Less than one-tenth of one percent.   NA = Not available.   1 Because of rounding, the percentages may not sum to 100 percent.   2 Violent crimes are offenses of murder and nonnegligent manslaughter, forcible rape, robbery, and aggravated assault. Property crimes are offenses of burglary, larceny-theft, motor vehicle theft, and arson.   3 The rape figures in this table are an aggregate total of the data submitted using both the revised and legacy Uniform Crime Reporting definitions.

Table 41.   Arrests of Persons Under 15, 18, 21, and 25 Years of Age, 2013

(Number, percent; 11,951 agencies; 2013 estimated population 245,741,701.)

Offense charged	Total, all ages	Number of persons arrested				Percent of total all ages			
		Under 15	Under 18	Under 21	Under 25	Under 15	Under 18	Under 21	Under 25
Total	9,069,992	244,688	875,262	1,957,970	3,402,820	2.7	9.7	21.6	37.5
Violent crime [1]	392,778	12,291	43,651	89,641	152,383	3.1	11.1	22.8	38.8
Murder and nonnegligent manslaughter	8,401	71	614	2,099	3,914	0.8	7.3	25.0	46.6
Rape[2]	13,617	790	2,089	3,872	5,777	5.8	15.3	28.4	42.4
Robbery	78,753	3,209	15,932	32,254	46,970	4.1	20.2	41.0	59.6
Aggravated assault	292,007	8,221	25,016	51,416	95,722	2.8	8.6	17.6	32.8
Property crime [1]	1,261,124	56,138	198,599	380,141	571,204	4.5	15.7	30.1	45.3
Burglary	203,709	9,509	34,760	67,746	101,520	4.7	17.1	33.3	49.8
Larceny-theft	996,495	42,806	151,427	291,652	439,953	4.3	15.2	29.3	44.2
Motor vehicle theft	52,507	2,140	9,469	16,995	25,141	4.1	18.0	32.4	47.9
Arson	8,413	1,683	2,943	3,748	4,590	20.0	35.0	44.6	54.6
Other assaults	885,822	46,365	118,253	194,009	322,171	5.2	13.3	21.9	36.4
Forgery and counterfeiting	48,826	94	850	5,904	14,049	0.2	1.7	12.1	28.8
Fraud	113,510	697	3,542	13,017	29,389	0.6	3.1	11.5	25.9
Embezzlement	12,664	35	318	2,346	4,838	0.3	2.5	18.5	38.2
Stolen property; buying, receiving, possessing	74,792	1,953	8,388	19,080	31,722	2.6	11.2	25.5	42.4
Vandalism	162,068	14,326	37,678	60,508	86,790	8.8	23.2	37.3	53.6
Weapons; carrying, possessing, etc.	112,673	5,673	16,683	32,829	53,331	5.0	14.8	29.1	47.3
Prostitution and commercialized vice	42,110	61	655	5,422	13,226	0.1	1.6	12.9	31.4
Sex offenses (except forcible rape and prostitution)	46,832	4,145	8,389	12,896	17,953	8.9	17.9	27.5	38.3
Drug abuse violations	1,209,661	16,075	94,187	286,261	513,379	1.3	7.8	23.7	42.4
Gambling	5,089	104	615	1,406	2,258	2.0	12.1	27.6	44.4
Offenses against the family and children	78,812	741	2,224	5,735	14,620	0.9	2.8	7.3	18.6
Driving under the influence	918,462	117	5,963	63,347	227,693	*	0.6	6.9	24.8
Liquor laws	280,860	4,562	48,126	182,134	202,027	1.6	17.1	64.8	71.9
Drunkenness	358,036	696	5,902	31,901	86,934	0.2	1.6	8.9	24.3
Disorderly conduct	375,142	29,362	76,318	115,756	174,614	7.8	20.3	30.9	46.5
Vagrancy	21,633	176	733	2,790	5,247	0.8	3.4	12.9	24.3
All other offenses (except traffic)	2,620,320	36,882	156,079	404,639	830,610	1.4	6.0	15.4	31.7
Suspicion	844	83	175	274	448	9.8	20.7	32.5	53.1
Curfew and loitering law violations	47,934	14,112	47,934	47,934	47,934	29.4	100.0	100.0	100.0

* = Less than one-tenth of one percent.   1 Violent crimes in this table are offenses of murder and nonnegligent manslaughter, rape (revised and legacy definitions), robbery, and aggravated assault. Property crimes are offenses of burglary, larceny-theft, motor vehicle theft, and arson.   2 The rape figures in this table are an aggregate total of the data submitted using both the revised and legacy Uniform Crime Reporting definitions.

Table 42.   Arrests, Distribution by Sex, 2013

(Number, percent; 11,951 agencies; 2013 estimated population 245,741,701.)

Offense charged	Number of persons arrested			Percent male	Percent female	Percent distribution[1]		
	Total	Male	Female			Total	Male	Female
Total	9,069,992	6,662,833	2,407,159	73.5	26.5	100.0	100.0	100.0
Violent crime [2]	392,778	313,751	79,027	79.9	20.1	4.3	4.7	3.3
Murder and nonnegligent manslaughter	8,401	7,415	986	88.3	11.7	0.1	0.1	*
Rape[3]	13,617	13,362	255	98.1	1.9	0.2	0.2	*
Robbery	78,753	68,239	10,514	86.6	13.4	0.9	1.0	0.4
Aggravated assault	292,007	224,735	67,272	77.0	23.0	3.2	3.4	2.8
Property crime [2]	1,261,124	785,022	476,102	62.2	37.8	13.9	11.8	19.8
Burglary	203,709	169,018	34,691	83.0	17.0	2.2	2.5	1.4
Larceny-theft	996,495	567,174	429,321	56.9	43.1	11.0	8.5	17.8
Motor vehicle theft	52,507	42,078	10,429	80.1	19.9	0.6	0.6	0.4
Arson	8,413	6,752	1,661	80.3	19.7	0.1	0.1	0.1
Other assaults	885,822	639,502	246,320	72.2	27.8	9.8	9.6	10.2
Forgery and counterfeiting	48,826	30,570	18,256	62.6	37.4	0.5	0.5	0.8
Fraud	113,510	68,270	45,240	60.1	39.9	1.3	1.0	1.9
Embezzlement	12,664	6,536	6,128	51.6	48.4	0.1	0.1	0.3
Stolen property; buying, receiving, possessing	74,792	58,734	16,058	78.5	21.5	0.8	0.9	0.7
Vandalism	162,068	129,202	32,866	79.7	20.3	1.8	1.9	1.4
Weapons; carrying, possessing, etc.	112,673	102,864	9,809	91.3	8.7	1.2	1.5	0.4
Prostitution and commercialized vice	42,110	13,818	28,292	32.8	67.2	0.5	0.2	1.2
Sex offenses (except forcible rape and prostitution)	46,832	43,193	3,639	92.2	7.8	0.5	0.6	0.2
Drug abuse violations	1,209,661	953,984	255,677	78.9	21.1	13.3	14.3	10.6
Gambling	5,089	4,349	740	85.5	14.5	0.1	0.1	*
Offenses against the family and children	78,812	57,806	21,006	73.3	26.7	0.9	0.9	0.9
Driving under the influence	918,462	689,383	229,079	75.1	24.9	10.1	10.3	9.5
Liquor laws	280,860	199,751	81,109	71.1	28.9	3.1	3.0	3.4
Drunkenness	358,036	291,223	66,813	81.3	18.7	3.9	4.4	2.8
Disorderly conduct	375,142	270,299	104,843	72.1	27.9	4.1	4.1	4.4
Vagrancy	21,633	17,114	4,519	79.1	20.9	0.2	0.3	0.2
All other offenses (except traffic)	2,620,320	1,952,465	667,855	74.5	25.5	28.9	29.3	27.7
Suspicion	844	647	197	76.7	23.3	*	*	*
Curfew and loitering law violations	47,934	34,350	13,584	71.7	28.3	0.5	0.5	0.6

* = Less than one-tenth of 1 percent   1 Because of rounding, the percentages may not sum to 100.   2 Violent crimes in this table are offenses of murder and nonnegligent manslaughter, rape (revised and legacy definitions), robbery, and aggravated assault. Property crimes are offenses of burglary, larceny-theft, motor vehicle theft, and arson.   3 The rape figures in this table are an aggregate total of the data submitted using both the revised and legacy Uniform Crime Reporting definitions.

Table 43.   Arrests, Distribution by Race, 2013

(Number, percent; 11,951 agencies; 2013 estimated population 245,741,701.)

Offense charged	Total arrests					Percent distribution[1]				
	Total	White	Black	American Indian or Alaskan Native	Asian	Total	White	Black	American Indian or Alaskan Native	Asian
Total	9,014,635	6,214,197	2,549,655	140,290	105,109	100.0	68.9	28.3	1.6	1.2
Violent crime [2]	391,467	228,782	151,627	5,193	5,346	100.0	58.4	38.7	1.3	1.4
Murder and nonnegligent manslaughter	8,383	3,799	4,379	98	101	100.0	45.3	52.2	1.2	1.2
Rape[3]	13,515	8,946	4,229	160	173	100.0	66.2	31.3	1.2	1.3
Robbery	78,538	32,945	44,271	579	649	100.0	41.9	56.4	0.7	0.8
Aggravated assault	291,031	183,092	98,748	4,356	4,423	100.0	62.9	33.9	1.5	1.5
Property crime [2]	1,254,696	855,225	363,952	19,183	15,633	100.0	68.2	29.0	1.5	1.2
Burglary	203,089	136,990	61,709	1,966	2,196	100.0	67.5	30.4	1.0	1.1
Larceny-theft	990,936	677,173	284,358	16,402	12,605	100.0	68.3	28.7	1.7	1.3
Motor vehicle theft	52,307	34,864	15,960	685	725	100.0	66.7	30.5	1.3	1.4
Arson	8,364	6,198	1,925	130	107	100.0	74.1	23.0	1.6	1.3
Other assaults	881,086	573,546	283,357	14,041	9,717	100.0	65.1	32.2	1.6	1.1
Forgery and counterfeiting	48,581	31,208	16,375	288	677	100.0	64.2	33.7	0.6	1.4
Fraud	112,920	74,682	35,958	1,145	1,094	100.0	66.1	31.8	1.0	1.0
Embezzlement	12,574	7,882	4,386	87	207	100.0	62.7	34.9	0.7	1.6
Stolen property; buying, receiving, possessing	74,541	50,237	22,687	684	862	100.0	67.4	30.4	0.9	1.2
Vandalism	161,078	113,842	42,566	2,951	1,638	100.0	70.7	26.4	1.8	1.0
Weapons; carrying, possessing, etc.	112,228	65,317	44,671	888	1,251	100.0	58.2	39.8	0.8	1.1
Prostitution and commercialized vice	41,946	22,666	17,378	386	1,492	100.0	54.0	41.4	0.9	3.6
Sex offenses (except forcible rape and prostitution)	46,553	33,695	11,462	622	744	100.0	72.4	24.6	1.3	1.6
Drug abuse violations	1,204,162	815,181	365,785	9,408	12,930	100.0	67.7	30.4	0.8	1.1
Gambling	5,055	1,433	3,362	27	226	100.0	28.3	66.5	0.5	4.5
Offenses against the family and children	78,465	51,017	25,519	1,414	511	100.0	65.0	32.5	1.8	0.7
Driving under the influence	910,470	766,440	113,928	12,575	16,831	100.0	84.2	12.5	1.4	1.8
Liquor laws	277,444	222,201	40,665	10,861	3,672	100.0	80.1	14.7	3.9	1.3
Drunkenness	356,427	288,146	56,885	7,399	3,550	100.0	80.8	16.0	2.1	1.0
Disorderly conduct	372,202	231,604	129,782	7,982	2,775	100.0	62.2	34.9	2.1	0.7
Vagrancy	21,354	13,732	6,802	581	222	100.0	64.3	31.9	2.7	1.0
All other offenses (except traffic)	2,602,939	1,741,855	790,854	43,953	25,090	100.0	66.9	30.4	1.7	1.0
Suspicion	825	499	303	12	11	100.0	60.5	36.7	1.5	1.3
Curfew and loitering law violations	47,622	25,007	21,351	610	630	100.0	52.5	44.8	1.3	1.3

Table 43. Arrests, Distribution by Race, 2013

(Number, percent; 11,951 agencies; 2013 estimated population 245,741,701.)

Offense charged	Arrests under 18					Percent distribution[1]				
	Total	White	Black	American Indian or Alaskan Native	Asian	Total	White	Black	American Indian or Alaskan Native	Asian
Total	868,693	547,395	298,425	12,601	9,716	100.0	63.0	34.4	1.5	1.1
Violent crime [2]	43,495	19,479	23,195	389	386	100.0	44.8	53.3	0.9	0.9
Murder and nonnegligent manslaughter	613	263	333	10	6	100.0	42.9	54.3	1.6	1.0
Rape[3]	2,065	1,316	709	21	18	100.0	63.7	34.3	1.0	0.9
Robbery	15,903	4,356	11,351	63	111	100.0	27.4	71.4	0.4	0.7
Aggravated assault	24,914	13,544	10,802	295	251	100.0	54.4	43.4	1.2	1.0
Property crime [2]	197,179	117,801	73,443	2,877	2,929	100.0	59.7	37.2	1.5	1.5
Burglary	34,610	19,948	13,913	331	385	100.0	57.6	40.2	1.0	1.1
Larceny-theft	150,213	90,606	54,725	2,368	2,431	100.0	60.3	36.4	1.6	1.6
Motor vehicle theft	9,428	5,090	4,111	135	81	100.0	54.0	43.6	1.4	0.9
Arson	2,928	2,157	694	43	32	100.0	73.7	23.7	1.5	1.1
Other assaults	117,546	67,130	47,948	1,459	937	100.0	57.1	40.8	1.2	0.8
Forgery and counterfeiting	847	521	302	6	17	100.0	61.5	35.7	0.7	2.0
Fraud	3,517	2,045	1,352	71	49	100.0	58.1	38.4	2.0	1.4
Embezzlement	316	191	110	8	7	100.0	60.4	34.8	2.5	2.2
Stolen property; buying, receiving, possessing	8,349	4,222	3,952	81	85	100.0	50.6	47.3	1.0	1.0
Vandalism	37,364	27,564	8,968	511	304	100.0	73.8	24.0	1.4	0.8
Weapons; carrying, possessing, etc.	16,598	9,867	6,322	139	246	100.0	59.4	38.1	0.8	1.5
Prostitution and commercialized vice	654	242	405	4	3	100.0	37.0	61.9	0.6	0.5
Sex offenses (except forcible rape and prostitution)	8,298	5,925	2,202	65	102	100.0	71.4	26.5	0.8	1.2
Drug abuse violations	93,579	68,322	22,819	1,234	1,161	100.0	73.0	24.4	1.3	1.2
Gambling	622	59	556	0	7	100.0	9.5	89.4	0.0	1.1
Offenses against the family and children	2,210	1,462	648	88	12	100.0	66.2	29.3	4.0	0.5
Driving under the influence	5,908	5,395	313	112	85	100.0	91.3	5.3	1.9	1.4
Liquor laws	47,594	41,710	3,554	1,713	603	100.0	87.6	7.5	3.6	1.3
Drunkenness	5,863	5,081	549	141	81	100.0	86.7	9.4	2.4	1.4
Disorderly conduct	75,705	40,394	33,859	894	526	100.0	53.4	44.7	1.2	0.7
Vagrancy	729	509	214	2	3	100.0	69.8	29.4	0.3	0.4
All other offenses (except traffic)	154,523	104,323	46,334	2,197	1,543	100.0	67.5	30.0	1.4	1.0
Suspicion	175	146	29	0	0	100.0	83.4	16.6	0.0	0.0
Curfew and loitering law violations	47,622	25,007	21,351	610	630	100.0	52.5	44.8	1.3	1.3

Table 43.   Arrests, Distribution by Race, 2013

(Number, percent; 11,951 agencies; 2013 estimated population 245,741,701.)

Offense charged	Arrests 18 and over					Percent distribution[1]				
	Total	White	Black	American Indian or Alaskan Native	Asian	Total	White	Black	American Indian or Alaskan Native	Asian
Total	8,145,942	5,666,802	2,251,230	127,689	95,393	100.0	69.6	27.6	1.6	1.2
Violent crime [2]	347,972	209,303	128,432	4,804	4,960	100.0	60.1	36.9	1.4	1.4
Murder and nonnegligent manslaughter	7,770	3,536	4,046	88	95	100.0	45.5	52.1	1.1	1.2
Rape[3]	11,450	7,630	3,520	139	155	100.0	66.6	30.7	1.2	1.4
Robbery	62,635	28,589	32,920	516	538	100.0	45.6	52.6	0.8	0.9
Aggravated assault	266,117	169,548	87,946	4,061	4,172	100.0	63.7	33.0	1.5	1.6
Property crime [2]	1,057,517	737,424	290,509	16,306	12,704	100.0	69.7	27.5	1.5	1.2
Burglary	168,479	117,042	47,796	1,635	1,811	100.0	69.5	28.4	1.0	1.1
Larceny-theft	840,723	586,567	229,633	14,034	10,174	100.0	69.8	27.3	1.7	1.2
Motor vehicle theft	42,879	29,774	11,849	550	644	100.0	69.4	27.6	1.3	1.5
Arson	5,436	4,041	1,231	87	75	100.0	74.3	22.6	1.6	1.4
Other assaults	763,540	506,416	235,409	12,582	8,780	100.0	66.3	30.8	1.6	1.1
Forgery and counterfeiting	47,734	30,687	16,073	282	660	100.0	64.3	33.7	0.6	1.4
Fraud	109,403	72,637	34,606	1,074	1,045	100.0	66.4	31.6	1.0	1.0
Embezzlement	12,258	7,691	4,276	79	200	100.0	62.7	34.9	0.6	1.6
Stolen property; buying, receiving, possessing	66,192	46,015	18,735	603	777	100.0	69.5	28.3	0.9	1.2
Vandalism	123,714	86,278	33,598	2,440	1,334	100.0	69.7	27.2	2.0	1.1
Weapons; carrying, possessing, etc.	95,630	55,450	38,349	749	1,005	100.0	58.0	40.1	0.8	1.1
Prostitution and commercialized vice	41,292	22,424	16,973	382	1,489	100.0	54.3	41.1	0.9	3.6
Sex offenses (except forcible rape and prostitution)	38,255	27,770	9,260	557	642	100.0	72.6	24.2	1.5	1.7
Drug abuse violations	1,110,583	746,859	342,966	8,174	11,769	100.0	67.2	30.9	0.7	1.1
Gambling	4,433	1,374	2,806	27	219	100.0	31.0	63.3	0.6	4.9
Offenses against the family and children	76,255	49,555	24,871	1,326	499	100.0	65.0	32.6	1.7	0.7
Driving under the influence	904,562	761,045	113,615	12,463	16,746	100.0	84.1	12.6	1.4	1.9
Liquor laws	229,850	180,491	37,111	9,148	3,069	100.0	78.5	16.1	4.0	1.3
Drunkenness	350,564	283,065	56,336	7,258	3,469	100.0	80.7	16.1	2.1	1.0
Disorderly conduct	296,497	191,210	95,923	7,088	2,249	100.0	64.5	32.4	2.4	0.8
Vagrancy	20,625	13,223	6,588	579	219	100.0	64.1	31.9	2.8	1.1
All other offenses (except traffic)	2,448,416	1,637,532	744,520	41,756	23,547	100.0	66.9	30.4	1.7	1.0
Suspicion	650	353	274	12	11	100.0	54.3	42.2	1.8	1.7
Curfew and loitering law violations	NA	NA	NA	NA	NA	NA	NA	NA	NA	NA

* = Less than one-tenth of one percent.   NA = Not available.   1 Because of rounding, the percentages may not sum to 100. rape, robbery, and aggravated assault. Property crimes are offenses of burglary, larceny-theft, motor vehicle theft, and arson.   both the revised and legacy Uniform Crime Reporting definitions.   2 Violent crimes are offenses of murder and nonnegligent manslaughter, forcible   3 The rape figures in this table are an aggregate total of the data submitted using

Table 44.   Arrest Trends, Cities, 2012–2013

(Number, percent change; 6,662 agencies; 2013 estimated population 139,725,629; 2012 estimated population 138,602,589.)

Offense charged	Number of persons arrested								
	Total, all ages			Under 18 years of age			18 years of age and over		
	2012	2013	Percent change	2012	2013	Percent change	2012	2013	Percent change
Total [1]	5,768,189	5,460,008	-5.3	663,531	559,471	-15.7	5,104,658	4,900,537	-4.0
Violent crime [2]	258,238	247,553	-4.1	29,448	26,913	-8.6	228,790	220,640	-3.6
Murder and nonnegligent manslaughter	4,742	4,664	-1.6	328	371	+13.1	4,414	4,293	-2.7
Rape[3]	8,334	7,828	-6.1	1,181	1,133	-4.1	7,153	6,695	-6.4
Robbery	53,132	52,125	-1.9	10,703	10,361	-3.2	42,429	41,764	-1.6
Aggravated assault	192,030	182,936	-4.7	17,236	15,048	-12.7	174,794	167,888	-4.0
Property crime [2]	856,747	837,268	-2.3	161,196	137,962	-14.4	695,551	699,306	+0.5
Burglary	136,727	126,076	-7.8	27,972	23,515	-15.9	108,755	102,561	-5.7
Larceny-theft	685,262	676,603	-1.3	125,233	107,288	-14.3	560,029	569,315	+1.7
Motor vehicle theft	29,611	29,386	-0.8	5,721	5,264	-8.0	23,890	24,122	+1.0
Arson	5,147	5,203	+1.1	2,270	1,895	-16.5	2,877	3,308	+15.0
Other assaults	578,176	546,622	-5.5	81,240	71,693	-11.8	496,936	474,929	-4.4
Forgery and counterfeiting	32,133	29,882	-7.0	687	515	-25.0	31,446	29,367	-6.6
Fraud	67,341	63,952	-5.0	2,523	2,403	-4.8	64,818	61,549	-5.0
Embezzlement	8,601	8,636	+0.4	237	227	-4.2	8,364	8,409	+0.5
Stolen property; buying, receiving, possessing	48,620	47,163	-3.0	7,021	5,804	-17.3	41,599	41,359	-0.6
Vandalism	111,569	100,835	-9.6	29,868	23,924	-19.9	81,701	76,911	-5.9
Weapons; carrying, possessing, etc.	73,405	70,904	-3.4	12,504	10,669	-14.7	60,901	60,235	-1.1
Prostitution and commercialized vice	33,041	31,505	-4.6	501	510	+1.8	32,540	30,995	-4.7
Sex offenses (except forcible rape and prostitution)	30,766	27,008	-12.2	5,589	4,880	-12.7	25,177	22,128	-12.1
Drug abuse violations	703,653	707,837	+0.6	66,567	58,665	-11.9	637,086	649,172	+1.9
Gambling	1,962	1,681	-14.3	207	138	-33.3	1,755	1,543	-12.1
Offenses against the family and children	32,590	30,996	-4.9	1,667	1,310	-21.4	30,923	29,686	-4.0
Driving under the influence	484,521	442,554	-8.7	3,814	3,120	-18.2	480,707	439,434	-8.6
Liquor laws	215,940	177,885	-17.6	35,766	27,177	-24.0	180,174	150,708	-16.4
Drunkenness	310,747	273,925	-11.8	6,131	4,732	-22.8	304,616	269,193	-11.6
Disorderly conduct	259,388	227,911	-12.1	58,589	46,191	-21.2	200,799	181,720	-9.5
Vagrancy	16,591	16,917	+2.0	731	477	-34.7	15,860	16,440	+3.7
All other offenses (except traffic)	1,613,999	1,544,776	-4.3	129,084	107,963	-16.4	1,484,915	1,436,813	-3.2
Suspicion	708	399	-43.6	124	37	-70.2	584	362	-38.0
Curfew and loitering law violations	30,161	24,198	-19.8	30,161	24,198	-19.8	NA	NA	NA

NA = Not available.   1 Does not include suspicion.   2 Violent crimes are offenses of murder and nonnegligent manslaughter, forcible rape, robbery, and aggravated assault. Property crimes are offenses of burglary, larceny-theft, motor vehicle theft, and arson.   3 The rape figures in this table are based on the legacy definition of rape only. The rape figures shown include converted National Incident-Based Reporting System rape data and those states/agencies that reported the legacy definition of rape for both years.

Table 45.   Arrest Trends, Cities, by Age and Sex, 2012–2013

(Number, percent change; 6,662 agencies; 2013 estimated population 139,725,629; 2012 estimated population 138,602,589.)

Offense charged	Male						Female					
	Total			Under 18			Total			Under 18		
	2012	2013	Percent change	2012	2013	Percent change	2012	2013	Percent change	2012	2013	Percent change
Total [1]	4,226,004	3,982,894	-5.8	464,491	393,802	-15.2	1,542,185	1,477,114	-4.2	199,040	165,669	-16.8
Violent crime [2]	205,534	196,669	-4.3	23,902	21,975	-8.1	52,704	50,884	-3.5	5,546	4,938	-11.0
Murder and nonnegligent manslaughter	4,216	4,127	-2.1	295	322	+9.2	526	537	+2.1	33	49	+48.5
Rape[3]	8,253	7,712	-6.6	1,160	1,089	-6.1	81	116	+43.2	21	44	+109.5
Robbery	46,069	45,171	-1.9	9,562	9,364	-2.1	7,063	6,954	-1.5	1,141	997	-12.6
Aggravated assault	146,996	139,659	-5.0	12,885	11,200	-13.1	45,034	43,277	-3.9	4,351	3,848	-11.6
Property crime [2]	519,458	507,271	-2.3	101,821	88,554	-13.0	337,289	329,997	-2.2	59,375	49,408	-16.8
Burglary	112,908	103,205	-8.6	24,252	20,516	-15.4	23,819	22,871	-4.0	3,720	2,999	-19.4
Larceny-theft	378,457	376,392	-0.5	70,846	62,092	-12.4	306,805	300,211	-2.1	54,387	45,196	-16.9
Motor vehicle theft	23,903	23,474	-1.8	4,801	4,284	-10.8	5,708	5,912	+3.6	920	980	+6.5
Arson	4,190	4,200	+0.2	1,922	1,662	-13.5	957	1,003	+4.8	348	233	-33.0
Other assaults	416,122	392,821	-5.6	51,014	45,408	-11.0	162,054	153,801	-5.1	30,226	26,285	-13.0
Forgery and counterfeiting	19,982	18,572	-7.1	484	357	-26.2	12,151	11,310	-6.9	203	158	-22.2
Fraud	40,964	39,394	-3.8	1,703	1,597	-6.2	26,377	24,558	-6.9	820	806	-1.7
Embezzlement	4,373	4,416	+1.0	138	153	+10.9	4,228	4,220	-0.2	99	74	-25.3
Stolen property; buying, receiving, possessing	38,759	37,063	-4.4	5,930	4,916	-17.1	9,861	10,100	+2.4	1,091	888	-18.6
Vandalism	88,955	80,272	-9.8	25,163	20,179	-19.8	22,614	20,563	-9.1	4,705	3,745	-20.4
Weapons; carrying, possessing, etc.	67,473	65,030	-3.6	11,419	9,691	-15.1	5,932	5,874	-1.0	1,085	978	-9.9
Prostitution and commercialized vice	10,587	9,943	-6.1	103	88	-14.6	22,454	21,562	-4.0	398	422	+6.0
Sex offenses (except forcible rape and prostitution)	28,121	24,774	-11.9	4,945	4,293	-13.2	2,645	2,234	-15.5	644	587	-8.9
Drug abuse violations	560,469	558,356	-0.4	54,714	47,670	-12.9	143,184	149,481	+4.4	11,853	10,995	-7.2
Gambling	1,627	1,358	-16.5	195	133	-31.8	335	323	-3.6	12	5	-58.3
Offenses against the family and children	21,649	20,443	-5.6	1,051	799	-24.0	10,941	10,553	-3.5	616	511	-17.0
Driving under the influence	363,456	330,789	-9.0	2,849	2,359	-17.2	121,065	111,765	-7.7	965	761	-21.1
Liquor laws	154,566	128,617	-16.8	21,859	16,781	-23.2	61,374	49,268	-19.7	13,907	10,396	-25.2
Drunkenness	254,721	223,950	-12.1	4,438	3,474	-21.7	56,026	49,975	-10.8	1,693	1,258	-25.7
Disorderly conduct	185,574	163,729	-11.8	37,507	29,844	-20.4	73,814	64,182	-13.0	21,082	16,347	-22.5
Vagrancy	13,227	13,425	+1.5	579	363	-37.3	3,364	3,492	+3.8	152	114	-25.0
All other offenses (except traffic)	1,209,801	1,149,489	-5.0	94,091	78,655	-16.4	404,198	395,287	-2.2	34,993	29,308	-16.2
Suspicion	553	320	-42.1	97	34	-64.9	155	79	-49.0	27	3	-88.9
Curfew and loitering law violations	20,586	16,513	-19.8	20,586	16,513	-19.8	9,575	7,685	-19.7	9,575	7,685	-19.7

1 Does not include suspicion.   2 Violent crimes are offenses of murder and nonnegligent manslaughter, forcible rape, robbery, and aggravated assault. Property crimes are offenses of burglary, larceny-theft, motor vehicle theft, and arson.   3 The rape figures in this table are based on the legacy definition of rape only. The rape figures shown include converted National Incident-Based Reporting System rape data and those states/agencies that reported the legacy definition of rape for both years.

Table 46.   Arrests, Cities, Distribution by Age, 2013

(Number, percent; 8,659 agencies; 2013 estimated population 167,355,619.)

Offense charged	All ages	Under 15	Under 18	18 and over	Under 10	10–12	13–14	15	16	17	18	19	20
Total	6,664,482	202,913	714,152	5,950,330	4,950	43,991	153,972	137,781	170,672	202,786	259,014	283,902	283,806
Total percent distribution[1]	100.0	3.0	10.7	89.3	0.1	0.7	2.3	2.1	2.6	3.0	3.9	4.3	4.3
Violent crime [2]	303,405	10,097	36,072	267,333	207	2,160	7,730	7,087	8,831	10,057	11,646	12,455	12,549
Violent crime percent distribution[1]	100.0	3.3	11.9	88.1	0.1	0.7	2.5	2.3	2.9	3.3	3.8	4.1	4.1
Murder and nonnegligent manslaughter	6,167	55	490	5,677		1	54	73	135	227	342	371	462
Rape[3]	9,956	581	1,543	8,413	7	147	427	278	303	381	400	433	422
Robbery	67,460	2,928	14,234	53,226	12	379	2,537	2,957	3,887	4,462	5,084	4,656	4,189
Aggravated assault	219,822	6,533	19,805	200,017	188	1,633	4,712	3,779	4,506	4,987	5,820	6,995	7,476
Property crime [2]	1,027,716	48,775	169,882	857,834	943	10,544	37,288	33,135	41,467	46,505	53,129	49,527	45,156
Property crime percent distribution[1]	100.0	4.7	16.5	83.5	0.1	1.0	3.6	3.2	4.0	4.5	5.2	4.8	4.4
Burglary	149,031	7,815	27,835	121,196	201	1,617	5,997	5,614	6,919	7,487	8,700	7,992	7,218
Larceny-theft	833,302	37,802	131,989	701,313	589	8,282	28,931	25,371	32,095	36,721	42,119	39,407	36,068
Motor vehicle theft	38,841	1,746	7,620	31,221	13	189	1,544	1,743	2,117	2,014	2,109	1,928	1,672
Arson	6,542	1,412	2,438	4,104	140	456	816	407	336	283	201	200	198
Other assaults	666,195	35,716	90,015	576,180	994	9,393	25,329	17,664	18,614	18,021	17,597	19,481	21,454
Forgery and counterfeiting	35,960	76	645	35,315	2	15	59	66	144	359	1,021	1,358	1,529
Fraud	75,435	541	2,821	72,614	8	113	420	427	746	1,107	1,806	2,457	2,855
Embezzlement	9,682	28	271	9,411	1	5	22	22	67	154	397	629	620
Stolen property; buying, receiving, possessing	55,382	1,676	6,946	48,436	18	246	1,412	1,421	1,792	2,057	2,839	2,753	2,698
Vandalism	124,734	11,634	29,751	94,983	508	3,409	7,717	5,688	5,992	6,437	6,273	5,780	5,377
Weapons; carrying, possessing, etc.	87,816	4,468	13,793	74,023	175	1,118	3,175	2,561	3,107	3,657	4,509	4,502	4,388
Prostitution and commercialized vice	38,619	54	578	38,041	1	3	50	72	162	290	1,096	1,569	1,701
Sex offenses (except forcible rape and prostitution)	33,349	2,972	6,001	27,348	87	864	2,021	1,049	993	987	1,075	1,011	980
Drug abuse violations	880,503	13,128	74,373	806,130	63	1,819	11,246	12,703	19,366	29,176	46,260	49,161	47,073
Gambling	4,225	91	569	3,656		12	79	82	161	235	234	243	245
Offenses against the family and children	37,350	522	1,569	35,781	31	116	375	377	312	358	650	783	933
Driving under the influence	532,729	86	3,870	528,859	7	7	72	169	867	2,748	7,734	11,694	14,660
Liquor laws	224,739	3,615	35,719	189,020	27	260	3,328	5,531	9,876	16,697	34,675	38,686	32,688
Drunkenness	307,420	588	5,127	302,293	17	46	525	808	1,201	2,530	6,254	7,780	8,005
Disorderly conduct	313,717	24,714	63,953	249,764	514	5,673	18,527	13,294	13,241	12,704	11,371	11,201	11,229
Vagrancy	19,376	152	617	18,759	3	25	124	130	147	188	602	665	609
All other offenses (except traffic)	1,840,531	30,564	126,412	1,714,119	991	5,368	24,205	25,379	31,950	38,519	49,819	62,144	69,035
Suspicion	484	18	53	431	4	14	12	13	10	27	23	22
Curfew and loitering law violations	45,115	13,398	45,115	NA	353	2,791	10,254	10,104	11,623	9,990	NA	NA	NA

Table 46.   Arrests, Cities, Distribution by Age, 2013

(Number, percent; 8,659 agencies; 2013 estimated population 167,355,619.)

Offense charged	21	22	23	24	25–29	30–34	35–39	40–44	45–49	50–54	55–59	60–64	65 and over
Total	282,460	274,764	262,453	246,480	1,029,252	820,928	570,659	496,382	435,042	356,056	200,765	89,424	58,943
Total percent distribution[1]	4.2	4.1	3.9	3.7	15.4	12.3	8.6	7.4	6.5	5.3	3.0	1.3	0.9
Violent crime [2]	13,174	12,656	12,236	11,396	48,533	38,430	26,350	21,850	18,452	14,134	7,563	3,388	2,521
Violent crime percent distribution[1]	4.3	4.2	4.0	3.8	16.0	12.7	8.7	7.2	6.1	4.7	2.5	1.1	0.8
Murder and nonnegligent manslaughter	431	376	318	270	1,059	681	407	316	230	195	92	63	64
Rape[3]	425	359	344	320	1,239	1,210	903	802	565	460	279	125	127
Robbery	3,687	3,287	2,929	2,514	9,219	6,111	3,744	3,038	2,319	1,517	654	188	90
Aggravated assault	8,631	8,634	8,645	8,292	37,016	30,428	21,296	17,694	15,338	11,962	6,538	3,012	2,240
Property crime [2]	41,913	39,656	37,062	34,800	146,666	115,804	79,008	69,179	58,919	45,121	24,229	10,350	7,315
Property crime percent distribution[1]	4.1	3.9	3.6	3.4	14.3	11.3	7.7	6.7	5.7	4.4	2.4	1.0	0.7
Burglary	6,689	6,239	5,818	5,357	21,517	16,357	10,545	8,763	7,234	5,180	2,432	780	375
Larceny-theft	33,355	31,729	29,610	27,919	118,552	94,065	64,995	57,800	49,677	38,653	21,195	9,349	6,820
Motor vehicle theft	1,688	1,533	1,476	1,384	5,917	4,813	3,092	2,274	1,681	1,015	439	136	64
Arson	181	155	158	140	680	569	376	342	327	273	163	85	56
Other assaults	25,422	25,628	25,290	23,985	104,735	86,933	61,874	53,144	44,293	34,342	18,236	7,790	5,976
Forgery and counterfeiting	1,438	1,510	1,527	1,585	6,998	6,002	4,076	3,178	2,404	1,523	749	287	130
Fraud	2,864	2,954	2,940	2,953	13,210	11,480	8,475	7,192	5,535	3,976	2,239	988	690
Embezzlement	589	515	465	433	1,590	1,236	883	752	573	397	186	101	45
Stolen property; buying, receiving, possessing	2,484	2,376	2,379	2,198	9,216	7,565	4,771	3,656	2,584	1,773	719	276	149
Vandalism	5,818	5,436	4,889	4,504	17,294	12,458	7,986	6,556	5,124	4,002	2,000	845	641
Weapons; carrying, possessing, etc.	4,391	4,410	3,970	3,671	14,146	10,424	6,197	4,403	3,406	2,612	1,576	788	630
Prostitution and commercialized vice	1,825	1,886	1,773	1,710	6,795	5,311	3,818	3,722	3,005	2,076	962	436	356
Sex offenses (except forcible rape and prostitution)	919	953	902	819	3,630	3,323	2,854	2,606	2,512	2,257	1,539	965	1,003
Drug abuse violations	44,906	42,790	40,109	36,902	147,346	112,551	71,257	57,278	47,365	35,506	18,053	6,799	2,774
Gambling	233	226	173	158	573	342	243	215	210	196	146	107	112
Offenses against the family and children	1,143	1,222	1,387	1,365	6,946	6,689	4,850	3,693	2,662	1,879	931	353	295
Driving under the influence	24,147	25,262	25,239	23,673	98,361	74,729	53,734	47,839	41,907	36,387	22,751	11,970	8,772
Liquor laws	5,715	4,131	3,367	2,822	10,759	9,084	7,489	8,553	9,947	10,197	6,482	2,913	1,512
Drunkenness	13,383	12,341	11,548	10,314	44,777	37,986	28,819	29,659	31,898	30,194	18,067	7,637	3,631
Disorderly conduct	14,953	13,170	11,859	10,770	40,897	31,337	22,075	19,676	18,632	16,367	9,267	4,076	2,884
Vagrancy	626	503	477	503	2,062	2,031	1,618	1,830	2,166	2,348	1,646	736	337
All other offenses (except traffic)	76,480	77,112	74,832	71,894	304,643	247,155	174,247	151,382	133,428	110,751	63,415	28,616	19,166
Suspicion	37	27	29	25	75	58	35	19	20	18	9	3	4
Curfew and loitering law violations	NA	NA	NA	NA	NA	NA	NA	NA	NA	NA	NA	NA	NA

NA = Not available.   1 Because of rounding, the percentages may not sum to 100.   2 Violent crimes are offenses of murder and nonnegligent manslaughter, forcible rape, robbery, and aggravated assault. Property crimes are offenses of burglary, larceny-theft, motor vehicle theft, and arson.   3 The rape figures in this table are an aggregate total of the data submitted using both the revised and legacy Uniform Crime Reporting definitions.

Table 47.   Arrests, Cities, Persons under 15, 18, 21, and 25 Years of Age, 2013

(Number, percent; 8,659 agencies; 2013 estimated population 167,355,619.)

Offense charged	Total, all ages	Number of persons arrested				Percent of total of all ages			
		Under 15	Under 18	Under 21	Under 25	Under 15	Under 18	Under 21	Under 25
Total	6,664,482	202,913	714,152	1,540,874	2,607,031	3.0	10.7	23.1	39.1
Violent crime [1]	303,405	10,097	36,072	72,722	122,184	3.3	11.9	24.0	40.3
Murder and nonnegligent manslaughter	6,167	55	490	1,665	3,060	0.9	7.9	27.0	49.6
Rape [2]	9,956	581	1,543	2,798	4,246	5.8	15.5	28.1	42.6
Robbery	67,460	2,928	14,234	28,163	40,580	4.3	21.1	41.7	60.2
Aggravated assault	219,822	6,533	19,805	40,096	74,298	3.0	9.0	18.2	33.8
Property crime [1]	1,027,716	48,775	169,882	317,694	471,125	4.7	16.5	30.9	45.8
Burglary	149,031	7,815	27,835	51,745	75,848	5.2	18.7	34.7	50.9
Larceny-theft	833,302	37,802	131,989	249,583	372,196	4.5	15.8	30.0	44.7
Motor vehicle theft	38,841	1,746	7,620	13,329	19,410	4.5	19.6	34.3	50.0
Arson	6,542	1,412	2,438	3,037	3,671	21.6	37.3	46.4	56.1
Other assaults	666,195	35,716	90,015	148,547	248,872	5.4	13.5	22.3	37.4
Forgery and counterfeiting	35,960	76	645	4,553	10,613	0.2	1.8	12.7	29.5
Fraud	75,435	541	2,821	9,939	21,650	0.7	3.7	13.2	28.7
Embezzlement	9,682	28	271	1,917	3,919	0.3	2.8	19.8	40.5
Stolen property; buying, receiving, possessing	55,382	1,676	6,946	15,236	24,673	3.0	12.5	27.5	44.6
Vandalism	124,734	11,634	29,751	47,181	67,828	9.3	23.9	37.8	54.4
Weapons; carrying, possessing, etc.	87,816	4,468	13,793	27,192	43,634	5.1	15.7	31.0	49.7
Prostitution and commercialized vice	38,619	54	578	4,944	12,138	0.1	1.5	12.8	31.4
Sex offenses (except forcible rape and prostitution)	33,349	2,972	6,001	9,067	12,660	8.9	18.0	27.2	38.0
Drug abuse violations	880,503	13,128	74,373	216,867	381,574	1.5	8.4	24.6	43.3
Gambling	4,225	91	569	1,291	2,081	2.2	13.5	30.6	49.3
Offenses against the family and children	37,350	522	1,569	3,935	9,052	1.4	4.2	10.5	24.2
Driving under the influence	532,729	86	3,870	37,958	136,279	*	0.7	7.1	25.6
Liquor laws	224,739	3,615	35,719	141,768	157,803	1.6	15.9	63.1	70.2
Drunkenness	307,420	588	5,127	27,166	74,752	0.2	1.7	8.8	24.3
Disorderly conduct	313,717	24,714	63,953	97,754	148,506	7.9	20.4	31.2	47.3
Vagrancy	19,376	152	617	2,493	4,602	0.8	3.2	12.9	23.8
All other offenses (except traffic)	1,840,531	30,564	126,412	307,410	607,728	1.7	6.9	16.7	33.0
Suspicion	484	18	53	125	243	3.7	11.0	25.8	50.2
Curfew and loitering law violations	45,115	13,398	45,115	45,115	45,115	29.7	100.0	100.0	100.0

* = Less than one-tenth of one percent.   1 Violent crimes are offenses of murder and nonnegligent manslaughter, forcible rape, robbery, and aggravated assault. Property crimes are offenses of burglary, larceny-theft, motor vehicle theft, and arson.   2 The rape figures in this table are an aggregate total of the data submitted using both the revised and legacy Uniform Crime Reporting definitions.

Table 48.   Arrests, Cities, Distribution by Sex, 2013

(Number, percent; 8,659 agencies; 2013 estimated population 167,355,619.)

Offense charged	Number of persons arrested			Percent male	Percent female	Percent distribution[1]		
	Total	Male	Female			Total	Male	Female
Total	6,664,482	4,878,172	1,786,310	73.2	26.8	100.0	100.0	100.0
Violent crime [2]	303,405	241,803	61,602	79.7	20.3	4.6	5.0	3.4
Murder and nonnegligent manslaughter	6,167	5,485	682	88.9	11.1	0.1	0.1	0.0
Rape[3]	9,956	9,783	173	98.3	1.7	0.1	0.2	0.0
Robbery	67,460	58,612	8,848	86.9	13.1	1.0	1.2	0.5
Aggravated assault	219,822	167,923	51,899	76.4	23.6	3.3	3.4	2.9
Property crime [2]	1,027,716	627,889	399,827	61.1	38.9	15.4	12.9	22.4
Burglary	149,031	123,490	25,541	82.9	17.1	2.2	2.5	1.4
Larceny-theft	833,302	467,977	365,325	56.2	43.8	12.5	9.6	20.5
Motor vehicle theft	38,841	31,206	7,635	80.3	19.7	0.6	0.6	0.4
Arson	6,542	5,216	1,326	79.7	20.3	0.1	0.1	0.1
Other assaults	666,195	480,392	185,803	72.1	27.9	10.0	9.8	10.4
Forgery and counterfeiting	35,960	22,483	13,477	62.5	37.5	0.5	0.5	0.8
Fraud	75,435	46,327	29,108	61.4	38.6	1.1	0.9	1.6
Embezzlement	9,682	4,953	4,729	51.2	48.8	0.1	0.1	0.3
Stolen property; buying, receiving, possessing	55,382	43,532	11,850	78.6	21.4	0.8	0.9	0.7
Vandalism	124,734	99,178	25,556	79.5	20.5	1.9	2.0	1.4
Weapons; carrying, possessing, etc.	87,816	80,532	7,284	91.7	8.3	1.3	1.7	0.4
Prostitution and commercialized vice	38,619	12,317	26,302	31.9	68.1	0.6	0.3	1.5
Sex offenses (except forcible rape and prostitution)	33,349	30,674	2,675	92.0	8.0	0.5	0.6	0.1
Drug abuse violations	880,503	700,334	180,169	79.5	20.5	13.2	14.4	10.1
Gambling	4,225	3,755	470	88.9	11.1	0.1	0.1	0.0
Offenses against the family and children	37,350	24,228	13,122	64.9	35.1	0.6	0.5	0.7
Driving under the influence	532,729	398,105	134,624	74.7	25.3	8.0	8.2	7.5
Liquor laws	224,739	161,323	63,416	71.8	28.2	3.4	3.3	3.6
Drunkenness	307,420	250,955	56,465	81.6	18.4	4.6	5.1	3.2
Disorderly conduct	313,717	226,291	87,426	72.1	27.9	4.7	4.6	4.9
Vagrancy	19,376	15,427	3,949	79.6	20.4	0.3	0.3	0.2
All other offenses (except traffic)	1,840,531	1,374,769	465,762	74.7	25.3	27.6	28.2	26.1
Suspicion	484	377	107	77.9	22.1	0.0	0.0	0.0
Curfew and loitering law violations	45,115	32,528	12,587	72.1	27.9	0.7	0.7	0.7

1 Because of rounding, the percentages may not sum to 100.   2 Violent crimes are offenses of murder and nonnegligent manslaughter, forcible rape, robbery, and aggravated assault. Property crimes are offenses of burglary, larceny-theft, motor vehicle theft, and arson.   3 The rape figures in this table are an aggregate total of the data submitted using both the revised and legacy Uniform Crime Reporting definitions.

Table 49.   Arrests, Cities, Distribution by Race, 2013

(Number, percent; 8,659 agencies; 2013 estimated population 167,355,619.)

Offense charged	Total arrests						Percent distribution[1]					
	Total	White	Black	American Indian or Alaskan Native	Asian	Native Hawaiian or Other Pacific Islander	Total	White	Black	American Indian or Alaskan Native	Asian	Native Hawaiian or Other Pacific Islander
Total	6,626,283	4,403,180	2,031,290	108,604	79,265	3,944	100.0	66.5	30.7	1.6	1.2	0.1
Violent crime [2]	302,398	166,936	126,725	3,840	4,473	424	100.0	55.2	41.9	1.3	1.5	0.1
Murder and nonnegligent manslaughter	6,154	2,455	3,568	50	76	5	100.0	39.9	58.0	0.8	1.2	0.1
Rape[3]	9,885	6,081	3,538	119	143	4	100.0	61.5	35.8	1.2	1.4	*
Robbery	67,293	27,540	38,644	479	547	83	100.0	40.9	57.4	0.7	0.8	0.1
Aggravated assault	219,066	130,860	80,975	3,192	3,707	332	100.0	59.7	37.0	1.5	1.7	0.2
Property crime [2]	1,022,221	685,085	306,526	16,834	13,201	575	100.0	67.0	30.0	1.6	1.3	0.1
Burglary	148,586	94,619	50,570	1,367	1,835	195	100.0	63.7	34.0	0.9	1.2	0.1
Larceny-theft	828,443	561,672	240,846	14,878	10,719	328	100.0	67.8	29.1	1.8	1.3	*
Motor vehicle theft	38,688	24,094	13,481	490	573	50	100.0	62.3	34.8	1.3	1.5	0.1
Arson	6,504	4,700	1,629	99	74	2	100.0	72.3	25.0	1.5	1.1	*
Other assaults	662,359	409,753	233,085	11,237	7,946	338	100.0	61.9	35.2	1.7	1.2	0.1
Forgery and counterfeiting	35,793	22,695	12,341	225	506	26	100.0	63.4	34.5	0.6	1.4	0.1
Fraud	75,023	47,215	26,182	791	804	31	100.0	62.9	34.9	1.1	1.1	*
Embezzlement	9,602	5,919	3,414	72	186	11	100.0	61.6	35.6	0.7	1.9	0.1
Stolen property; buying, receiving, possessing	55,198	35,971	17,930	512	724	61	100.0	65.2	32.5	0.9	1.3	0.1
Vandalism	123,929	85,003	35,074	2,437	1,349	66	100.0	68.6	28.3	2.0	1.1	0.1
Weapons; carrying, possessing, etc.	87,487	48,246	37,484	647	1,036	74	100.0	55.1	42.8	0.7	1.2	0.1
Prostitution and commercialized vice	38,475	20,622	16,215	354	1,264	20	100.0	53.6	42.1	0.9	3.3	0.1
Sex offenses (except forcible rape and prostitution)	33,140	22,632	9,362	502	620	24	100.0	68.3	28.2	1.5	1.9	0.1
Drug abuse violations	877,391	567,508	292,828	6,703	9,705	647	100.0	64.7	33.4	0.8	1.1	0.1
Gambling	4,194	946	3,130	15	102	1	100.0	22.6	74.6	0.4	2.4	*
Offenses against the family and children	37,128	24,999	10,830	940	357	2	100.0	67.3	29.2	2.5	1.0	*
Driving under the influence	529,575	442,466	69,654	7,678	9,389	388	100.0	83.6	13.2	1.4	1.8	0.1
Liquor laws	222,143	173,041	36,333	9,708	3,023	38	100.0	77.9	16.4	4.4	1.4	*
Drunkenness	305,956	244,399	51,549	6,476	3,143	389	100.0	79.9	16.8	2.1	1.0	0.1
Disorderly conduct	311,144	189,740	112,150	6,827	2,378	49	100.0	61.0	36.0	2.2	0.8	*
Vagrancy	19,086	12,040	6,276	551	204	15	100.0	63.1	32.9	2.9	1.1	0.1
All other offenses (except traffic)	1,828,736	1,174,589	603,360	31,666	18,367	754	100.0	64.2	33.0	1.7	1.0	*
Suspicion	464	233	209	11	11	0	100.0	50.2	45.0	2.4	2.4	0.0
Curfew and loitering law violations	44,841	23,142	20,633	578	477	11	100.0	51.6	46.0	1.3	1.1	*

Table 49.   Arrests, Cities, Distribution by Race, 2013

(Number, percent; 8,659 agencies; 2013 estimated population 167,355,619.)

Offense charged	Arrests under 18					Percent distribution				
	White	Black	American Indian or Alaskan Native	Asian	Native Hawaiian or Other Pacific Islander	White	Black	American Indian or Alaskan Native	Asian	Native Hawaiian or Other Pacific Islander
Total	437,876	251,934	10,374	8,065	482	61.8	35.5	1.5	1.1	0.1
Violent crime [2]	15,387	19,899	294	331	42	42.8	55.3	0.8	0.9	0.1
Murder and nonnegligent manslaughter	200	281	2	6	1	40.8	57.3	0.4	1.2	0.2
Rape[3]	900	591	20	15	1	58.9	38.7	1.3	1.0	0.1
Robbery	3,872	10,171	52	94	19	27.3	71.6	0.4	0.7	0.1
Aggravated assault	10,415	8,856	220	216	21	52.8	44.9	1.1	1.1	0.1
Property crime [2]	99,908	63,442	2,598	2,570	120	59.2	37.6	1.5	1.5	0.1
Burglary	15,244	11,857	252	331	32	55.0	42.8	0.9	1.2	0.1
Larceny-theft	79,140	47,339	2,198	2,149	77	60.5	36.2	1.7	1.6	0.1
Motor vehicle theft	3,752	3,654	108	66	10	49.4	48.1	1.4	0.9	0.1
Arson	1,772	592	40	24	1	73.0	24.4	1.6	1.0	*
Other assaults	49,893	37,601	1,131	760	64	55.8	42.0	1.3	0.8	0.1
Forgery and counterfeiting	395	230	6	10	1	61.5	35.8	0.9	1.6	0.2
Fraud	1,562	1,132	61	44	0	55.8	40.4	2.2	1.6	0.0
Embezzlement	158	96	8	7	0	58.7	35.7	3.0	2.6	0.0
Stolen property; buying, receiving, possessing	3,421	3,343	67	77	8	49.5	48.3	1.0	1.1	0.1
Vandalism	21,507	7,309	420	258	13	72.9	24.8	1.4	0.9	*
Weapons; carrying, possessing, etc.	8,022	5,359	105	214	21	58.5	39.1	0.8	1.6	0.2
Prostitution and commercialized vice	201	370	3	3	0	34.8	64.1	0.5	0.5	0.0
Sex offenses (except forcible rape and prostitution)	4,080	1,711	54	85	4	68.8	28.8	0.9	1.4	0.1
Drug abuse violations	53,028	18,994	967	889	26	71.8	25.7	1.3	1.2	*
Gambling	30	545	0	1	0	5.2	94.6	0.0	0.2	0.0
Offenses against the family and children	961	508	79	9	0	61.7	32.6	5.1	0.6	0.0
Driving under the influence	3,477	227	76	59	1	90.5	5.9	2.0	1.5	*
Liquor laws	30,446	2,938	1,485	474	12	86.1	8.3	4.2	1.3	*
Drunkenness	4,389	483	133	77	11	86.2	9.5	2.6	1.5	0.2
Disorderly conduct	34,080	28,087	729	463	32	53.8	44.3	1.2	0.7	0.1
Vagrancy	423	187	2	2	1	68.8	30.4	0.3	0.3	0.2
All other offenses (except traffic)	83,337	38,816	1,578	1,255	115	66.6	31.0	1.3	1.0	0.1
Suspicion	29	24	0	0	0	54.7	45.3	0.0	0.0	0.0
Curfew and loitering law violations	23,142	20,633	578	477	11	51.6	46.0	1.3	1.1	*

Table 49.   Arrests, Cities, Distribution by Race, 2013

(Number, percent; 8,659 agencies; 2013 estimated population 167,355,619.)

Offense charged	Arrests 18 and over					Percent distribution[1]					
	White	Black	American Indian or Alaskan Native	Asian	Native Hawaiian or Other Pacific Islander	Total	White	Black	American Indian or Alaskan Native	Asian	Native Hawaiian or Other Pacific Islander
Total	3,965,304	1,779,356	98,230	71,200	3,462	100.0	67.0	30.1	1.7	1.2	0.1
Violent crime [2]	151,549	106,826	3,546	4,142	382	100.0	56.9	40.1	1.3	1.6	0.1
Murder and nonnegligent manslaughter	2,255	3,287	48	70	4	100.0	39.8	58.0	0.8	1.2	0.1
Rape[3]	5,181	2,947	99	128	3	100.0	62.0	35.3	1.2	1.5	*
Robbery	23,668	28,473	427	453	64	100.0	44.6	53.6	0.8	0.9	0.1
Aggravated assault	120,445	72,119	2,972	3,491	311	100.0	60.4	36.2	1.5	1.8	0.2
Property crime [2]	585,177	243,084	14,236	10,631	455	100.0	68.6	28.5	1.7	1.2	0.1
Burglary	79,375	38,713	1,115	1,504	163	100.0	65.7	32.0	0.9	1.2	0.1
Larceny-theft	482,532	193,507	12,680	8,570	251	100.0	69.2	27.7	1.8	1.2	*
Motor vehicle theft	20,342	9,827	382	507	40	100.0	65.4	31.6	1.2	1.6	0.1
Arson	2,928	1,037	59	50	1	100.0	71.9	25.4	1.4	1.2	*
Other assaults	359,860	195,484	10,106	7,186	274	100.0	62.8	34.1	1.8	1.3	*
Forgery and counterfeiting	22,300	12,111	219	496	25	100.0	63.4	34.5	0.6	1.4	0.1
Fraud	45,653	25,050	730	760	31	100.0	63.2	34.7	1.0	1.1	*
Embezzlement	5,761	3,318	64	179	11	100.0	61.7	35.6	0.7	1.9	0.1
Stolen property; buying, receiving, possessing	32,550	14,587	445	647	53	100.0	67.4	30.2	0.9	1.3	0.1
Vandalism	63,496	27,765	2,017	1,091	53	100.0	67.2	29.4	2.1	1.2	0.1
Weapons; carrying, possessing, etc.	40,224	32,125	542	822	53	100.0	54.5	43.5	0.7	1.1	0.1
Prostitution and commercialized vice	20,421	15,845	351	1,261	20	100.0	53.9	41.8	0.9	3.3	0.1
Sex offenses (except forcible rape and prostitution)	18,552	7,651	448	535	20	100.0	68.2	28.1	1.6	2.0	0.1
Drug abuse violations	514,480	273,834	5,736	8,816	621	100.0	64.0	34.1	0.7	1.1	0.1
Gambling	916	2,585	15	101	1	100.0	25.3	71.4	0.4	2.8	*
Offenses against the family and children	24,038	10,322	861	348	2	100.0	67.6	29.0	2.4	1.0	*
Driving under the influence	438,989	69,427	7,602	9,330	387	100.0	83.5	13.2	1.4	1.8	0.1
Liquor laws	142,595	33,395	8,223	2,549	26	100.0	76.3	17.9	4.4	1.4	*
Drunkenness	240,010	51,066	6,343	3,066	378	100.0	79.8	17.0	2.1	1.0	0.1
Disorderly conduct	155,660	84,063	6,098	1,915	17	100.0	62.8	33.9	2.5	0.8	*
Vagrancy	11,617	6,089	549	202	14	100.0	62.9	33.0	3.0	1.1	0.1
All other offenses (except traffic)	1,091,252	564,544	30,088	17,112	639	100.0	64.1	33.1	1.8	1.0	*
Suspicion	204	185	11	11	0	100.0	49.6	45.0	2.7	2.7	0.0
Curfew and loitering law violations	NA	NA	NA	NA	NA	NA	NA	NA	NA	NA	NA

* = Less than one-tenth of one percent.   NA = Not available.   1 Because of rounding, the percentages may not sum to 100.   2 Violent crimes are offenses of murder and nonnegligent manslaughter, forcible rape, robbery, and aggravated assault. Property crimes are offenses of burglary, larceny-theft, motor vehicle theft, and arson.   3 The rape figures in this table are an aggregate total of the data submitted using both the revised and legacy Uniform Crime Reporting definitions.

Table 50.   Arrest Trends, Metropolitan Counties, 2012–2013

(Number, percent change; 1,130 agencies; 2013 estimated population 52,484,326; 2012 estimated population 51,967,607.)

Offense charged	Number of persons arrested								
	Total, all ages			Under 18 years of age			18 years of age and over		
	2012	2013	Percent change	2012	2013	Percent change	2012	2013	Percent change
Total [1]	1,610,965	1,558,656	-3.2	134,294	114,957	-14.4	1,476,671	1,443,699	-2.2
Violent crime [2]	66,922	64,792	-3.2	6,336	5,749	-9.3	60,586	59,043	-2.5
Murder and nonnegligent man-slaughter	1,473	1,538	+4.4	74	80	+8.1	1,399	1,458	+4.2
Rape[3]	2,288	2,160	-5.6	319	303	-5.0	1,969	1,857	-5.7
Robbery	9,558	9,254	-3.2	1,601	1,501	-6.2	7,957	7,753	-2.6
Aggravated assault	53,603	51,840	-3.3	4,342	3,865	-11.0	49,261	47,975	-2.6
Property crime [2]	171,879	165,226	-3.9	25,740	21,590	-16.1	146,139	143,636	-1.7
Burglary	38,983	35,195	-9.7	6,164	4,783	-22.4	32,819	30,412	-7.3
Larceny-theft	122,351	119,535	-2.3	17,844	15,213	-14.7	104,507	104,322	-0.2
Motor vehicle theft	9,282	9,296	+0.2	1,340	1,237	-7.7	7,942	8,059	+1.5
Arson	1,263	1,200	-5.0	392	357	-8.9	871	843	-3.2
Other assaults	150,113	142,782	-4.9	22,555	20,314	-9.9	127,558	122,468	-4.0
Forgery and counterfeiting	9,896	9,042	-8.6	222	164	-26.1	9,674	8,878	-8.2
Fraud	26,477	24,080	-9.1	563	522	-7.3	25,914	23,558	-9.1
Embezzlement	2,136	2,230	+4.4	43	28	-34.9	2,093	2,202	+5.2
Stolen property; buying, receiving, possessing	15,216	14,074	-7.5	1,516	1,120	-26.1	13,700	12,954	-5.4
Vandalism	26,881	25,350	-5.7	6,543	5,444	-16.8	20,338	19,906	-2.1
Weapons; carrying, possessing, etc.	17,951	17,340	-3.4	2,627	2,320	-11.7	15,324	15,020	-2.0
Prostitution and commercialized vice	2,474	3,148	+27.2	58	59	+1.7	2,416	3,089	+27.9
Sex offenses (except forcible rape and prostitution)	9,830	8,609	-12.4	1,761	1,518	-13.8	8,069	7,091	-12.1
Drug abuse violations	213,899	219,526	+2.6	16,816	14,738	-12.4	197,083	204,788	+3.9
Gambling	714	708	-0.8	47	42	-10.6	667	666	-0.1
Offenses against the family and children	29,484	29,059	-1.4	467	436	-6.6	29,017	28,623	-1.4
Driving under the influence	216,262	202,767	-6.2	1,241	1,006	-18.9	215,021	201,761	-6.2
Liquor laws	36,937	31,526	-14.6	8,926	7,112	-20.3	28,011	24,414	-12.8
Drunkenness	36,539	33,708	-7.7	747	538	-28.0	35,792	33,170	-7.3
Disorderly conduct	40,342	37,227	-7.7	9,632	8,529	-11.5	30,710	28,698	-6.6
Vagrancy	2,593	1,998	-22.9	240	106	-55.8	2,353	1,892	-19.6
All other offenses (except traffic)	530,977	523,336	-1.4	24,771	21,494	-13.2	506,206	501,842	-0.9
Suspicion	187	42	-77.5	3	6	+100.0	184	36	-80.4
Curfew and loitering law violations	3,443	2,128	-38.2	3,443	2,128	-38.2	NA	NA	NA

NA = Not available.   1 Does not include suspicion.   2 Violent crimes in this table are offenses of murder and nonnegligent manslaughter, rape (legacy definition), robbery, and aggravated assault. Property crimes are offenses of burglary, larceny-theft, motor vehicle theft, and arson.   3 The rape figures in this table are based on the legacy definition of rape only. The rape figures shown include converted National Incident-Based Reporting System rape data and those states/agencies that reported the legacy definition of rape for both years.

Table 51.   Arrest Trends, Metropolitan Counties, by Age and Sex, 2012–2013

(Number, percent change; 1,130 agencies; 2013 estimated population 52,484,326; 2012 estimated population 51,967,607.)

Offense charged	Male						Female					
	Total			Under 18			Total			Under 18		
	2012	2013	Percent change	2012	2013	Percent change	2012	2013	Percent change	2012	2013	Percent change
Total [1]	1,197,700	1,152,561	-3.8	96,924	82,815	-14.6	413,265	406,095	-1.7	37,370	32,142	-14.0
Violent crime [2]	53,852	52,019	-3.4	5,086	4,576	-10.0	13,070	12,773	-2.3	1,250	1,173	-6.2
Murder and nonnegligent manslaughter	1,301	1,333	+2.5	65	69	+6.2	172	205	+19.2	9	11	+22.2
Rape[3]	2,262	2,126	-6.0	314	295	-6.1	26	34	+30.8	5	8	+60.0
Robbery	8,302	7,886	-5.0	1,454	1,357	-6.7	1,256	1,368	+8.9	147	144	-2.0
Aggravated assault	41,987	40,674	-3.1	3,253	2,855	-12.2	11,616	11,166	-3.9	1,089	1,010	-7.3
Property crime [2]	114,494	108,498	-5.2	18,354	15,391	-16.1	57,385	56,728	-1.1	7,386	6,199	-16.1
Burglary	32,697	29,191	-10.7	5,590	4,302	-23.0	6,286	6,004	-4.5	574	481	-16.2
Larceny-theft	73,310	70,950	-3.2	11,297	9,768	-13.5	49,041	48,585	-0.9	6,547	5,445	-16.8
Motor vehicle theft	7,440	7,370	-0.9	1,129	1,012	-10.4	1,842	1,926	+4.6	211	225	+6.6
Arson	1,047	987	-5.7	338	309	-8.6	216	213	-1.4	54	48	-11.1
Other assaults	108,705	102,968	-5.3	14,528	13,005	-10.5	41,408	39,814	-3.8	8,027	7,309	-8.9
Forgery and counterfeiting	6,362	5,748	-9.7	143	127	-11.2	3,534	3,294	-6.8	79	37	-53.2
Fraud	15,412	14,191	-7.9	376	381	+1.3	11,065	9,889	-10.6	187	141	-24.6
Embezzlement	1,114	1,175	+5.5	32	22	-31.3	1,022	1,055	+3.2	11	6	-45.5
Stolen property; buying, receiving, possessing	12,160	11,040	-9.2	1,244	919	-26.1	3,056	3,034	-0.7	272	201	-26.1
Vandalism	21,335	20,262	-5.0	5,359	4,522	-15.6	5,546	5,088	-8.3	1,184	922	-22.1
Weapons; carrying, possessing, etc.	16,227	15,519	-4.4	2,320	2,007	-13.5	1,724	1,821	+5.6	307	313	+2.0
Prostitution and commercialized vice	976	1,379	+41.3	9	16	+77.8	1,498	1,769	+18.1	49	43	-12.2
Sex offenses (except forcible rape and prostitution)	9,123	7,998	-12.3	1,630	1,373	-15.8	707	611	-13.6	131	145	+10.7
Drug abuse violations	166,781	170,251	+2.1	13,956	11,951	-14.4	47,118	49,275	+4.6	2,860	2,787	-2.6
Gambling	501	488	-2.6	28	21	-25.0	213	220	+3.3	19	21	+10.5
Offenses against the family and children	24,333	23,813	-2.1	286	285	-0.3	5,151	5,246	+1.8	181	151	-16.6
Driving under the influence	162,195	151,749	-6.4	901	740	-17.9	54,067	51,018	-5.6	340	266	-21.8
Liquor laws	25,306	21,396	-15.5	5,296	4,292	-19.0	11,631	10,130	-12.9	3,630	2,820	-22.3
Drunkenness	29,720	27,208	-8.5	544	389	-28.5	6,819	6,500	-4.7	203	149	-26.6
Disorderly conduct	28,461	26,400	-7.2	6,100	5,497	-9.9	11,881	10,827	-8.9	3,532	3,032	-14.2
Vagrancy	1,934	1,481	-23.4	167	77	-53.9	659	517	-21.5	73	29	-60.3
All other offenses (except traffic)	396,427	387,590	-2.2	18,283	15,836	-13.4	134,550	135,746	+0.9	6,488	5,658	-12.8
Suspicion	132	32	-75.8	1	5	+400.0	55	10	-81.8	2	1	-50.0
Curfew and loitering law violations	2,282	1,388	-39.2	2,282	1,388	-39.2	1,161	740	-36.3	1,161	740	-36.3

1 Does not include suspicion.   2 Violent crimes are offenses of murder and nonnegligent manslaughter, forcible rape, robbery, and aggravated assault. Property crimes are offenses of burglary, larceny-theft, motor vehicle theft, and arson.   3 The rape figures in this table are based on the legacy definition rape only. The rape figures shown include converted National Incident-Based Reporting System rape data and those states/agencies that reported the legacy definition of rape for both years.

Table 52.   Arrests, Metropolitan Counties, Distribution by Age, 2013

(Number, percent; 1,374 agencies; 2013 estimated population 57,208,460.)

Offense charged	All ages	Under 15	Under 18	18 and over	Under 10	10–12	13–14	15	16	17	18	19	20
Total	1,699,811	33,904	127,586	1,572,225	1,065	7,459	25,380	22,458	30,970	40,254	55,293	62,736	66,449
Total percent distribution[1]	100.0	2.0	7.5	92.5	0.1	0.4	1.5	1.3	1.8	2.4	3.3	3.7	3.9
Violent crime [2]	69,447	1,866	6,342	63,105	55	470	1,341	1,166	1,551	1,759	2,287	2,497	2,710
Violent crime percent distribution[1]	100.0	2.7	9.1	90.9	0.1	0.7	1.9	1.7	2.2	2.5	3.3	3.6	3.9
Murder and nonnegligent manslaughter	1,609	5	84	1,525	0	1	4	13	20	46	75	81	80
Rape[3]	2,452	154	390	2,062	11	48	95	65	73	98	101	99	117
Robbery	9,895	271	1,595	8,300	2	28	241	298	477	549	762	692	685
Aggravated assault	55,491	1,436	4,273	51,218	42	393	1,001	790	981	1,066	1,349	1,625	1,828
Property crime [2]	181,553	6,073	23,679	157,874	119	1,216	4,738	4,382	5,868	7,356	9,504	8,794	8,134
Property crime percent distribution[1]	100.0	3.3	13.0	87.0	0.1	0.7	2.6	2.4	3.2	4.1	5.2	4.8	4.5
Burglary	39,089	1,283	5,253	33,836	21	241	1,021	942	1,312	1,716	2,232	2,253	2,002
Larceny-theft	130,963	4,283	16,667	114,296	72	890	3,321	3,084	4,127	5,173	6,682	6,071	5,660
Motor vehicle theft	10,155	288	1,367	8,788	2	19	267	288	383	408	542	432	424
Arson	1,346	219	392	954	24	66	129	68	46	59	48	38	48
Other assaults	161,057	8,807	22,833	138,224	346	2,332	6,129	4,301	4,949	4,776	4,019	4,224	4,572
Forgery and counterfeiting	9,949	17	179	9,770	1	5	11	24	37	101	201	335	409
Fraud	26,370	119	563	25,807	2	21	96	89	142	213	433	599	732
Embezzlement	2,410	6	37	2,373	0	1	5	4	7	20	102	106	136
Stolen property; buying, receiving, possessing	15,187	233	1,209	13,978	0	29	204	241	332	403	631	669	628
Vandalism	28,264	2,065	6,164	22,100	112	542	1,411	1,170	1,450	1,479	1,419	1,419	1,330
Weapons; carrying, possessing, etc.	18,544	1,056	2,489	16,055	124	349	583	392	443	598	759	749	710
Prostitution and commercialized vice	3,338	4	67	3,271	0	0	4	7	15	41	103	142	136
Sex offenses (except forcible rape and prostitution)	9,740	880	1,757	7,983	44	244	592	307	310	260	311	343	328
Drug abuse violations	238,806	2,482	16,138	222,668	21	346	2,115	2,449	4,205	7,002	11,506	12,726	12,765
Gambling	724	13	42	682	0	2	11	5	7	17	18	21	19
Offenses against the family and children	31,135	139	461	30,674	3	18	118	91	96	135	208	247	335
Driving under the influence	228,201	15	1,199	227,002	2	1	12	47	244	893	3,079	4,504	5,972
Liquor laws	35,940	674	8,390	27,550	7	37	630	1,098	2,386	4,232	6,094	6,283	5,523
Drunkenness	34,999	85	559	34,440	0	7	78	84	142	248	799	945	1,051
Disorderly conduct	43,338	3,698	9,730	33,608	90	811	2,797	1,929	2,059	2,044	1,470	1,362	1,246
Vagrancy	2,026	22	108	1,918	0	3	19	25	28	33	53	56	57
All other offenses (except traffic)	556,178	4,987	23,071	533,107	122	924	3,941	4,052	5,937	8,095	12,296	16,715	19,653
Suspicion	44	6	8	36	3	0	3	0	0	2	1	0	3
Curfew and loitering law violations	2,561	657	2,561	NA	14	101	542	595	762	547	NA	NA	NA

Table 52.   Arrests, Metropolitan Counties, Distribution by Age, 2013

(Number, percent; 1,374 agencies; 2013 estimated population 57,208,460.)

Offense charged	21	22	23	24	25–29	30–34	35–39	40–44	45–49	50–54	55–59	60–64	65 and over
Total	67,944	69,102	68,646	65,410	284,305	233,689	165,396	140,952	117,004	89,486	48,147	21,685	15,981
Total percent distribution[1]	4.0	4.1	4.0	3.8	16.7	13.7	9.7	8.3	6.9	5.3	2.8	1.3	0.9
Violent crime [2]	2,764	2,677	2,632	2,465	11,009	9,286	6,477	5,591	4,846	3,814	2,049	1,044	957
Violent crime percent distribution[1]	4.0	3.9	3.8	3.5	15.9	13.4	9.3	8.1	7.0	5.5	3.0	1.5	1.4
Murder and nonnegligent manslaughter	84	80	88	67	259	186	113	109	103	88	44	24	44
Rape[3]	102	89	73	50	279	308	217	186	151	110	68	55	57
Robbery	609	524	479	390	1,490	988	541	416	338	239	93	36	18
Aggravated assault	1,969	1,984	1,992	1,958	8,981	7,804	5,606	4,880	4,254	3,377	1,844	929	838
Property crime [2]	7,834	7,563	7,210	6,504	28,295	22,300	14,582	12,547	10,414	7,489	3,858	1,636	1,210
Property crime percent distribution[1]	4.3	4.2	4.0	3.6	15.6	12.3	8.0	6.9	5.7	4.1	2.1	0.9	0.7
Burglary	1,879	1,825	1,647	1,557	6,656	4,924	2,868	2,269	1,723	1,160	535	199	107
Larceny-theft	5,520	5,279	5,154	4,541	19,843	15,819	10,703	9,450	8,051	5,936	3,139	1,379	1,069
Motor vehicle theft	400	430	367	359	1,643	1,423	933	742	562	331	137	44	19
Arson	35	29	42	47	153	134	78	86	78	62	47	14	15
Other assaults	4,965	5,230	5,195	5,118	22,938	20,898	16,018	14,458	12,011	9,219	4,957	2,338	2,064
Forgery and counterfeiting	381	409	453	424	1,963	1,535	1,194	950	658	478	234	101	45
Fraud	746	775	932	899	4,281	4,175	3,381	3,035	2,496	1,658	876	418	371
Embezzlement	116	128	93	83	381	311	239	242	172	135	67	34	28
Stolen property; buying, receiving, possessing	646	621	616	604	2,673	2,193	1,567	1,194	873	622	265	116	60
Vandalism	1,191	1,140	1,032	920	3,830	2,869	1,963	1,640	1,407	962	473	283	222
Weapons; carrying, possessing, etc.	801	770	840	714	3,026	2,300	1,524	1,229	930	793	457	235	218
Prostitution and commercialized vice	164	138	138	155	591	450	333	307	273	167	87	51	36
Sex offenses (except forcible rape and prostitution)	288	283	274	235	1,042	1,001	822	742	654	618	409	257	376
Drug abuse violations	12,112	11,870	11,234	10,406	42,071	31,999	20,325	15,748	12,807	9,651	4,867	1,805	776
Gambling	11	16	10	14	75	76	67	62	71	69	72	37	44
Offenses against the family and children	498	622	722	881	5,095	6,166	5,152	4,381	3,159	1,924	890	266	128
Driving under the influence	9,617	10,470	10,802	10,407	43,540	32,555	23,460	20,688	18,320	15,644	9,623	4,830	3,491
Liquor laws	771	575	498	440	1,650	1,259	964	904	908	826	478	218	159
Drunkenness	1,391	1,402	1,337	1,266	5,280	4,552	3,516	3,358	3,512	3,026	1,811	753	441
Disorderly conduct	1,532	1,451	1,343	1,289	5,223	4,431	3,300	2,959	2,900	2,585	1,397	618	502
Vagrancy	80	78	68	84	314	286	176	164	181	185	71	49	16
All other offenses (except traffic)	22,035	22,881	23,216	22,501	101,018	85,044	60,334	50,750	40,411	29,617	15,203	6,596	4,837
Suspicion	1	3	1	1	10	3	2	3	1	4	3	0	0
Curfew and loitering law violations	NA	NA	NA	NA	NA	NA	NA	NA	NA	NA	NA	NA	NA

NA = Not available.   1 Because of rounding, the percentages may not sum to 100. Property crimes are offenses of burglary, larceny-theft, motor vehicle theft, and arson. Crime Reporting definitions.   2 Violent crimes are offenses of murder and nonnegligent manslaughter, forcible rape, robbery, and aggravated assault.   3 The rape figures in this table are an aggregate total of the data submitted using both the revised and legacy Uniform Crime Reporting definitions.

Table 53.   Arrests, Metropolitan Counties, Persons Under 15, 18, 21, and 25 Years of Age, 2013

(Number, percent; 1,374 agencies; 2013 estimated population 57,208,191.)

Offense charged	Total, all ages	Number of persons arrested				Percent of total all ages			
		Under 15	Under 18	Under 21	Under 25	Under 15	Under 18	Under 21	Under 25
Total	1,699,807	33,900	127,582	312,060	583,162	2.0	7.5	18.4	34.3
Violent crime [1]	69,443	1,862	6,338	13,832	24,370	2.7	9.1	19.9	35.1
Murder and nonnegligent man-slaughter	1,609	5	84	320	639	0.3	5.2	19.9	39.7
Rape [2]	2,448	150	386	703	1,017	6.1	15.8	28.7	41.5
Robbery	9,895	271	1,595	3,734	5,736	2.7	16.1	37.7	58.0
Aggravated assault	55,491	1,436	4,273	9,075	16,978	2.6	7.7	16.4	30.6
Property crime [1]	181,553	6,073	23,679	50,111	79,222	3.3	13.0	27.6	43.6
Burglary	39,089	1,283	5,253	11,740	18,648	3.3	13.4	30.0	47.7
Larceny-theft	130,963	4,283	16,667	35,080	55,574	3.3	12.7	26.8	42.4
Motor vehicle theft	10,155	288	1,367	2,765	4,321	2.8	13.5	27.2	42.6
Arson	1,346	219	392	526	679	16.3	29.1	39.1	50.4
Other assaults	161,057	8,807	22,833	35,648	56,156	5.5	14.2	22.1	34.9
Forgery and counterfeiting	9,949	17	179	1,124	2,791	0.2	1.8	11.3	28.1
Fraud	26,370	119	563	2,327	5,679	0.5	2.1	8.8	21.5
Embezzlement	2,410	6	37	381	801	0.2	1.5	15.8	33.2
Stolen property; buying, receiving, possessing	15,187	233	1,209	3,137	5,624	1.5	8.0	20.7	37.0
Vandalism	28,264	2,065	6,164	10,332	14,615	7.3	21.8	36.6	51.7
Weapons; carrying, possessing, etc.	18,544	1,056	2,489	4,707	7,832	5.7	13.4	25.4	42.2
Prostitution and commercialized vice	3,338	4	67	448	1,043	0.1	2.0	13.4	31.2
Sex offenses (except forcible rape and prostitution)	9,740	880	1,757	2,739	3,819	9.0	18.0	28.1	39.2
Drug abuse violations	238,806	2,482	16,138	53,135	98,757	1.0	6.8	22.3	41.4
Gambling	724	13	42	100	151	1.8	5.8	13.8	20.9
Offenses against the family and children	31,135	139	461	1,251	3,974	0.4	1.5	4.0	12.8
Driving under the influence	228,201	15	1,199	14,754	56,050	*	0.5	6.5	24.6
Liquor laws	35,940	674	8,390	26,290	28,574	1.9	23.3	73.1	79.5
Drunkenness	34,999	85	559	3,354	8,750	0.2	1.6	9.6	25.0
Disorderly conduct	43,338	3,698	9,730	13,808	19,423	8.5	22.5	31.9	44.8
Vagrancy	2,026	22	108	274	584	1.1	5.3	13.5	28.8
All other offenses (except traffic)	556,178	4,987	23,071	71,735	162,368	0.9	4.1	12.9	29.2
Suspicion	44	6	8	12	18	13.6	18.2	27.3	40.9
Curfew and loitering law violations	2,561	657	2,561	2,561	2,561	25.7	100.0	100.0	100.0

* = Less than one-tenth of one percent.   1 Violent crimes are offenses of murder and nonnegligent manslaughter, forcible rape, robbery, and aggravated assault. Property crimes are offenses of burglary, larceny-theft, motor vehicle theft, and arson.   2 The rape figures in this table are an aggregate total of the data submitted using both the revised and legacy Uniform Crime Reporting definitions.

Table 54.   Arrests, Metropolitan Counties, Distribution by Sex, 2013

(Number, percent; 1,374 agencies; 2013 estimated population 57,208,460.)

Offense charged	Number of persons arrested			Percent male	Percent female	Percent distribution[1]		
	Total	Male	Female			Total	Male	Female
Total	1,699,807	1,257,336	442,471	74.0	26.0	100.0	100.0	100.0
Violent crime [2]	69,443	55,766	13,677	80.3	19.7	4.1	4.4	3.1
Murder and nonnegligent manslaughter	1,609	1,398	211	86.9	13.1	0.1	0.1	*
Rape[3]	2,448	2,410	38	98.4	1.6	0.1	0.2	*
Robbery	9,895	8,437	1,458	85.3	14.7	0.6	0.7	0.3
Aggravated assault	55,491	43,521	11,970	78.4	21.6	3.3	3.5	2.7
Property crime [2]	181,553	119,670	61,883	65.9	34.1	10.7	9.5	14.0
Burglary	39,089	32,490	6,599	83.1	16.9	2.3	2.6	1.5
Larceny-theft	130,963	78,006	52,957	59.6	40.4	7.7	6.2	12.0
Motor vehicle theft	10,155	8,075	2,080	79.5	20.5	0.6	0.6	0.5
Arson	1,346	1,099	247	81.6	18.4	0.1	0.1	0.1
Other assaults	161,057	116,194	44,863	72.1	27.9	9.5	9.2	10.1
Forgery and counterfeiting	9,949	6,344	3,605	63.8	36.2	0.6	0.5	0.8
Fraud	26,370	15,594	10,776	59.1	40.9	1.6	1.2	2.4
Embezzlement	2,410	1,291	1,119	53.6	46.4	0.1	0.1	0.3
Stolen property; buying, receiving, possessing	15,187	11,924	3,263	78.5	21.5	0.9	0.9	0.7
Vandalism	28,264	22,614	5,650	80.0	20.0	1.7	1.8	1.3
Weapons; carrying, possessing, etc.	18,544	16,596	1,948	89.5	10.5	1.1	1.3	0.4
Prostitution and commercialized vice	3,338	1,425	1,913	42.7	57.3	0.2	0.1	0.4
Sex offenses (except forcible rape and prostitution)	9,740	9,028	712	92.7	7.3	0.6	0.7	0.2
Drug abuse violations	238,806	185,131	53,675	77.5	22.5	14.0	14.7	12.1
Gambling	724	501	223	69.2	30.8	*	*	0.1
Offenses against the family and children	31,135	25,484	5,651	81.9	18.1	1.8	2.0	1.3
Driving under the influence	228,201	170,929	57,272	74.9	25.1	13.4	13.6	12.9
Liquor laws	35,940	24,308	11,632	67.6	32.4	2.1	1.9	2.6
Drunkenness	34,999	28,200	6,799	80.6	19.4	2.1	2.2	1.5
Disorderly conduct	43,338	30,834	12,504	71.1	28.9	2.5	2.5	2.8
Vagrancy	2,026	1,500	526	74.0	26.0	0.1	0.1	0.1
All other offenses (except traffic)	556,178	412,302	143,876	74.1	25.9	32.7	32.8	32.5
Suspicion	44	32	12	72.7	27.3	*	*	*
Curfew and loitering law violations	2,561	1,669	892	65.2	34.8	0.2	0.1	0.2

* = Less than one-tenth of one percent.   1 Because of rounding, the percentages may not sum to 100.   2 Violent crimes are offenses of murder and nonnegligent manslaughter, forcible rape, robbery, and aggravated assault. Property crimes are offenses of burglary, larceny-theft, motor vehicle theft, and arson.   3 The rape figures in this table are an aggregate total of the data submitted using both the revised and legacy Uniform Crime Reporting definitions.

Table 55.   Arrests, Metropolitan Counties, Distribution by Race, 2013

(Number, percent; 1,374 agencies; 2013 estimated population 57,208,460.)

Offense charged	Total arrests						Percent distribution[1]					
	Total	White	Black	American Indian or Alaskan Native	Asian	Native Hawaiian or Other Pacific Islander	Total	White	Black	American Indian or Alaskan Native	Asian	Native Hawaiian or Other Pacific Islander
Total	1,693,094	1,230,918	425,496	13,587	21,751	1,342	100.0	72.7	25.1	0.8	1.3	0.1
Violent crime [2]	69,266	46,279	21,551	542	808	86	100.0	66.8	31.1	0.8	1.2	0.1
Murder and nonnegligent manslaughter	1,607	929	647	10	20	1	100.0	57.8	40.3	0.6	1.2	0.1
Rape[3]	2,433	1,818	576	13	24	2	100.0	74.7	23.7	0.5	1.0	0.1
Robbery	9,856	4,574	5,134	39	99	10	100.0	46.4	52.1	0.4	1.0	0.1
Aggravated assault	55,370	38,958	15,194	480	665	73	100.0	70.4	27.4	0.9	1.2	0.1
Property crime [2]	180,974	126,590	50,960	982	2,318	124	100.0	69.9	28.2	0.5	1.3	0.1
Burglary	38,997	29,270	9,172	183	342	30	100.0	75.1	23.5	0.5	0.9	0.1
Larceny-theft	130,507	88,508	39,426	707	1,796	70	100.0	67.8	30.2	0.5	1.4	0.1
Motor vehicle theft	10,130	7,758	2,126	76	148	22	100.0	76.6	21.0	0.8	1.5	0.2
Arson	1,340	1,054	236	16	32	2	100.0	78.7	17.6	1.2	2.4	0.1
Other assaults	160,541	115,504	42,191	1,140	1,621	85	100.0	71.9	26.3	0.7	1.0	0.1
Forgery and counterfeiting	9,908	6,201	3,532	33	137	5	100.0	62.6	35.6	0.3	1.4	0.1
Fraud	26,284	17,971	7,896	157	256	4	100.0	68.4	30.0	0.6	1.0	*
Embezzlement	2,404	1,468	905	9	21	1	100.0	61.1	37.6	0.4	0.9	*
Stolen property; buying, receiving, possessing	15,152	10,861	4,084	75	125	7	100.0	71.7	27.0	0.5	0.8	*
Vandalism	28,150	21,214	6,414	249	261	12	100.0	75.4	22.8	0.9	0.9	*
Weapons; carrying, possessing, etc.	18,484	12,258	5,939	74	186	27	100.0	66.3	32.1	0.4	1.0	0.1
Prostitution and commercialized vice	3,318	1,916	1,146	29	223	4	100.0	57.7	34.5	0.9	6.7	0.1
Sex offenses (except forcible rape and prostitution)	9,696	7,771	1,746	66	110	3	100.0	80.1	18.0	0.7	1.1	*
Drug abuse violations	237,935	174,210	59,636	1,204	2,693	192	100.0	73.2	25.1	0.5	1.1	0.1
Gambling	721	393	193	7	122	6	100.0	54.5	26.8	1.0	16.9	0.8
Offenses against the family and children	31,065	18,290	12,465	174	135	1	100.0	58.9	40.1	0.6	0.4	*
Driving under the influence	227,077	191,702	28,277	1,358	5,441	299	100.0	84.4	12.5	0.6	2.4	0.1
Liquor laws	35,568	31,091	3,419	529	523	6	100.0	87.4	9.6	1.5	1.5	*
Drunkenness	34,919	29,924	4,228	355	369	43	100.0	85.7	12.1	1.0	1.1	0.1
Disorderly conduct	43,164	27,607	14,851	355	345	6	100.0	64.0	34.4	0.8	0.8	*
Vagrancy	2,024	1,537	455	12	18	2	100.0	75.9	22.5	0.6	0.9	0.1
All other offenses (except traffic)	553,863	386,456	154,885	6,220	5,886	416	100.0	69.8	28.0	1.1	1.1	0.1
Suspicion	43	36	7	0	0	0	100.0	83.7	16.3	0.0	0.0	0.0
Curfew and loitering law violations	2,538	1,639	716	17	153	13	100.0	64.6	28.2	0.7	6.0	0.5

Table 55.   Arrests, Metropolitan Counties, Distribution by Race, 2013

(Number, percent; 1,374 agencies; 2013 estimated population 57,208,460.)

Offense charged	Arrests under 18						Percent distribution[1]					
	Total	White	Black	American Indian or Alaskan Native	Asian	Native Hawaiian or Other Pacific Islander	Total	White	Black	American Indian or Alaskan Native	Asian	Native Hawaiian or Other Pacific Islander
Total	126,905	82,454	41,851	999	1,529	72	100.0	65.0	33.0	0.8	1.2	C.1
Violent crime [2]	6,315	3,182	3,031	47	51	4	100.0	50.4	48.0	0.7	0.8	0.1
Murder and nonnegligent manslaughter	83	40	43	0	0	0	100.0	48.2	51.8	0.0	0.0	0.0
Rape[3]	380	269	107	1	3	0	100.0	70.8	28.2	0.3	0.8	0.0
Robbery	1,592	436	1,129	7	17	3	100.0	27.4	70.9	0.4	1.1	0.2
Aggravated assault	4,260	2,437	1,752	39	31	1	100.0	57.2	41.1	0.9	0.7	*
Property crime [2]	23,564	13,808	9,282	115	350	9	100.0	58.6	39.4	0.5	1.5	*
Burglary	5,239	3,390	1,780	19	49	1	100.0	64.7	34.0	0.4	0.9	*
Larceny-theft	16,577	9,203	7,005	85	278	6	100.0	55.5	42.3	0.5	1.7	*
Motor vehicle theft	1,360	927	408	9	15	1	100.0	68.2	30.0	0.7	1.1	0.1
Arson	388	288	89	2	8	1	100.0	74.2	22.9	0.5	2.1	0.3
Other assaults	22,743	13,162	9,273	143	157	8	100.0	57.9	40.8	0.6	0.7	*
Forgery and counterfeiting	179	100	72	0	7	0	100.0	55.9	40.2	0.0	3.9	0.0
Fraud	561	361	194	2	4	0	100.0	64.3	34.6	0.4	0.7	0.0
Embezzlement	37	24	13	0	0	0	100.0	64.9	35.1	0.0	0.0	0.0
Stolen property; buying, receiving, possessing	1,201	634	554	4	8	1	100.0	52.8	46.1	0.3	0.7	0.1
Vandalism	6,125	4,579	1,463	43	37	3	100.0	74.8	23.9	0.7	0.6	*
Weapons; carrying, possessing, etc.	2,478	1,559	877	8	31	3	100.0	62.9	35.4	0.3	1.3	0.1
Prostitution and commercialized vice	67	32	35	0	0	0	100.0	47.8	52.2	0.0	0.0	0.0
Sex offenses (except forcible rape and prostitution)	1,739	1,293	426	5	15	0	100.0	74.4	24.5	0.3	0.9	0.0
Drug abuse violations	16,059	12,137	3,499	154	253	16	100.0	75.6	21.8	1.0	1.6	0.1
Gambling	42	27	9	0	6	0	100.0	64.3	21.4	0.0	14.3	0.0
Offenses against the family and children	461	325	127	6	3	0	100.0	70.5	27.5	1.3	0.7	0.0
Driving under the influence	1,188	1,103	60	6	17	2	100.0	92.8	5.1	0.5	1.4	0.2
Liquor laws	8,297	7,547	536	96	116	2	100.0	91.0	6.5	1.2	1.4	*
Drunkenness	555	495	55	1	4	0	100.0	89.2	9.9	0.2	0.7	0.0
Disorderly conduct	9,703	4,609	4,982	53	59	0	100.0	47.5	51.3	0.5	0.6	0.0
Vagrancy	108	80	27	0	1	0	100.0	74.1	25.0	0.0	0.9	0.0
All other offenses (except traffic)	22,937	15,754	6,616	299	257	11	100.0	68.7	28.8	1.3	1.1	*
Suspicion	8	4	4	0	0	0	100.0	50.0	50.0	0.0	0.0	0.0
Curfew and loitering law violations	2,538	1,639	716	17	153	13	100.0	64.6	28.2	0.7	6.0	0.5

Table 55.   Arrests, Metropolitan Counties, Distribution by Race, 2013

(Number, percent; 1,374 agencies; 2013 estimated population 57,208,460.)

Offense charged	Arrests 18 and over						Percent distribution[1]					
	Total	White	Black	American Indian or Alaskan Native	Asian	Native Hawaiian or Other Pacific Islander	Total	White	Black	American Indian or Alaskan Native	Asian	Native Hawaiian or Other Pacific Islander
Total	1,566,189	1,148,464	383,645	12,588	20,222	1,270	100.0	73.3	24.5	0.8	1.3	0.1
Violent crime [2]	62,951	43,097	18,520	495	757	82	100.0	68.5	29.4	0.8	1.2	0.1
Murder and nonnegligent manslaughter	1,524	889	604	10	20	1	100.0	58.3	39.6	0.7	1.3	0.1
Rape[3]	2,053	1,549	469	12	21	2	100.0	75.5	22.8	0.6	1.0	0.1
Robbery	8,264	4,138	4,005	32	82	7	100.0	50.1	48.5	0.4	1.0	0.1
Aggravated assault	51,110	36,521	13,442	441	634	72	100.0	71.5	26.3	0.9	1.2	0.1
Property crime [2]	157,410	112,782	41,678	867	1,968	115	100.0	71.6	26.5	0.6	1.3	0.1
Burglary	33,758	25,880	7,392	164	293	29	100.0	76.7	21.9	0.5	0.9	0.1
Larceny-theft	113,930	79,305	32,421	622	1,518	64	100.0	69.6	28.5	0.5	1.3	0.1
Motor vehicle theft	8,770	6,831	1,718	67	133	21	100.0	77.9	19.6	0.8	1.5	0.2
Arson	952	766	147	14	24	1	100.0	80.5	15.4	1.5	2.5	0.1
Other assaults	137,798	102,342	32,918	997	1,464	77	100.0	74.3	23.9	0.7	1.1	0.1
Forgery and counterfeiting	9,729	6,101	3,460	33	130	5	100.0	62.7	35.6	0.3	1.3	0.1
Fraud	25,723	17,610	7,702	155	252	4	100.0	68.5	29.9	0.6	1.0	*
Embezzlement	2,367	1,444	892	9	21	1	100.0	61.0	37.7	0.4	0.9	*
Stolen property; buying, receiving, possessing	13,951	10,227	3,530	71	117	6	100.0	73.3	25.3	0.5	0.8	*
Vandalism	22,025	16,635	4,951	206	224	9	100.0	75.5	22.5	0.9	1.0	*
Weapons; carrying, possessing, etc.	16,006	10,699	5,062	66	155	24	100.0	66.8	31.6	0.4	1.0	0.1
Prostitution and commercialized vice	3,251	1,884	1,111	29	223	4	100.0	58.0	34.2	0.9	6.9	0.1
Sex offenses (except forcible rape and prostitution)	7,957	6,478	1,320	61	95	3	100.0	81.4	16.6	0.8	1.2	*
Drug abuse violations	221,876	162,073	56,137	1,050	2,440	176	100.0	73.0	25.3	0.5	1.1	0.1
Gambling	679	366	184	7	116	6	100.0	53.9	27.1	1.0	17.1	0.9
Offenses against the family and children	30,604	17,965	12,338	168	132	1	100.0	58.7	40.3	0.5	0.4	*
Driving under the influence	225,889	190,599	28,217	1,352	5,424	297	100.0	84.4	12.5	0.6	2.4	0.1
Liquor laws	27,271	23,544	2,883	433	407	4	100.0	86.3	10.6	1.6	1.5	*
Drunkenness	34,364	29,429	4,173	354	365	43	100.0	85.6	12.1	1.0	1.1	0.1
Disorderly conduct	33,461	22,998	9,869	302	286	6	100.0	68.7	29.5	0.9	0.9	*
Vagrancy	1,916	1,457	428	12	17	2	100.0	76.0	22.3	0.6	0.9	0.1
All other offenses (except traffic)	530,926	370,702	148,269	5,921	5,629	405	100.0	69.8	27.9	1.1	1.1	0.1
Suspicion	35	32	3	0	0	0	100.0	91.4	8.6	0.0	0.0	0.0
Curfew and loitering law violations	NA	NA	NA	NA	NA	NA	NA	NA	NA	NA	NA	NA

* = Less than one-tenth of one percent.   NA = Not available.   1 Because of rounding, the percentages may not sum to 100.   2 Violent crimes are offenses of murder and nonnegligent manslaughter, forcible rape, robbery, and aggravated assault. Property crimes are offenses of burglary, larceny-theft, motor vehicle theft, and arson.   3 The rape figures in this table are an aggregate total of the data submitted using both the revised and legacy Uniform Crime Reporting definitions.

Table 56. Arrest Trends, Nonmetropolitan Counties, 2012–2013

(Number, percent change; 1,620 agencies; 2013 estimated population 18,067,896; 2012 estimated population 18,207,798.)

Offense charged	Number of persons arrested								
	Total, all ages			Under 18 years of age			18 years of age and over		
	2012	2013	Percent change	2012	2013	Percent change	2012	2013	Percent change
Total [1]	647,800	615,650	-5.0	33,541	28,351	-15.5	614,259	587,299	-4.4
Violent crime [2]	18,062	17,358	-3.9	1,121	1,051	-6.2	16,941	16,307	-3.7
Murder and nonnegligent manslaughter	548	540	-1.5	23	34	+47.8	525	506	-3.6
Rape[3]	976	979	+0.3	107	114	+6.5	869	865	-0.5
Robbery	1,340	1,267	-5.4	104	95	-8.7	1,236	1,172	-5.2
Aggravated assault	15,198	14,572	-4.1	887	808	-8.9	14,311	13,764	-3.8
Property crime [2]	48,768	44,091	-9.6	5,733	4,270	-25.5	43,035	39,821	-7.5
Burglary	15,206	13,235	-13.0	1,931	1,417	-26.6	13,275	11,818	-11.0
Larceny-theft	29,791	27,437	-7.9	3,146	2,343	-25.5	26,645	25,094	-5.8
Motor vehicle theft	3,188	2,968	-6.9	537	406	-24.4	2,651	2,562	-3.4
Arson	583	451	-22.6	119	104	-12.6	464	347	-25.2
Other assaults	54,213	49,377	-8.9	4,910	4,468	-9.0	49,303	44,909	-8.9
Forgery and counterfeiting	2,595	2,443	-5.9	34	24	-29.4	2,561	2,419	-5.5
Fraud	11,816	10,303	-12.8	136	145	+6.6	11,680	10,158	-13.0
Embezzlement	517	483	-6.6	5	5	0.0	512	478	-6.6
Stolen property; buying, receiving, possessing	3,787	3,552	-6.2	241	198	-17.8	3,546	3,354	-5.4
Vandalism	8,841	7,758	-12.2	1,843	1,452	-21.2	6,998	6,306	-9.9
Weapons; carrying, possessing, etc.	5,574	5,595	+0.4	397	340	-14.4	5,177	5,255	+1.5
Prostitution and commercialized vice	130	139	+6.9	8	7	-12.5	122	132	+8.2
Sex offenses (except forcible rape and prostitution)	3,574	2,982	-16.6	653	517	-20.8	2,921	2,465	-15.6
Drug abuse violations	73,480	77,656	+5.7	3,435	3,165	-7.9	70,045	74,491	+6.3
Gambling	139	104	-25.2	8	3	-62.5	131	101	-22.9
Offenses against the family and children	9,773	9,332	-4.5	148	148	0.0	9,625	9,184	-4.6
Driving under the influence	148,552	137,282	-7.6	866	747	-13.7	147,686	136,535	-7.6
Liquor laws	20,428	17,090	-16.3	4,098	3,303	-19.4	16,330	13,787	-15.6
Drunkenness	16,608	14,923	-10.1	254	197	-22.4	16,354	14,726	-10.0
Disorderly conduct	15,664	15,215	-2.9	2,502	2,269	-9.3	13,162	12,946	-1.6
Vagrancy	192	226	+17.7	14	7	-50.0	178	219	+23.0
All other offenses (except traffic)	204,781	199,496	-2.6	6,829	5,790	-15.2	197,952	193,706	-2.1
Suspicion	14	96	+585.7	3	1	-66.7	11	95	+763.6
Curfew and loitering law violations	306	245	-19.9	306	245	-19.9	NA	NA	NA

NA = Not available.   1 Does not include suspicion.   2 Violent crimes are offenses of murder and nonnegligent manslaughter, forcible rape, robbery, and aggravated assault. Property crimes are offenses of burglary, larceny-theft, motor vehicle theft, and arson.   3 The rape figures in this table are based on the legacy definition of rape only. The rape figures shown include converted National Incident-Based Reporting System rape data and those states/agencies that reported the legacy definition of rape for both years.

Table 57.   Arrest Trends, Nonmetropolitan Counties, by Age and Sex, 2012–2013

(Number, percent; 1,620 agencies; 2013 estimated population 18,067,896; 2012 estimated population 18,207,798.)

Offense charged	Male						Female					
	Total			Under 18			Total			Under 18		
	2012	2013	Percent change	2012	2013	Percent change	2012	2013	Percent change	2012	2013	Percent change
Total [1]	486,402	459,832	-5.5	24,499	20,580	-16.0	161,398	155,818	-3.5	9,042	7,771	-14.1
Violent crime [2]	14,797	14,047	-5.1	921	851	-7.6	3,265	3,311	+1.4	200	200	0.0
Murder and nonnegligent manslaughter	464	457	-1.5	22	28	+27.3	84	83	-1.2	1	6	+500.0
Rape [3]	959	943	-1.7	107	105	-1.9	17	36	+111.8	0	9	
Robbery	1,139	1,081	-5.1	93	87	-6.5	201	186	-7.5	11	8	-27.3
Aggravated assault	12,235	11,566	-5.5	699	631	-9.7	2,963	3,006	+1.5	188	177	-5.9
Property crime [2]	36,104	31,855	-11.8	4,603	3,367	-26.9	12,664	12,236	-3.4	1,130	903	-20.1
Burglary	12,730	11,023	-13.4	1,754	1,273	-27.4	2,476	2,212	-10.7	177	144	-18.6
Larceny-theft	20,273	18,113	-10.7	2,297	1,678	-26.9	9,518	9,324	-2.0	849	665	-21.7
Motor vehicle theft	2,591	2,346	-9.5	446	332	-25.6	597	622	+4.2	91	74	-18.7
Arson	510	373	-26.9	106	84	-20.8	73	78	+6.8	13	20	+53.8
Other assaults	39,907	36,285	-9.1	3,295	2,945	-10.6	14,306	13,092	-8.5	1,615	1,523	-5.7
Forgery and counterfeiting	1,554	1,474	-5.1	26	13	-50.0	1,041	969	-6.9	8	11	37.5
Fraud	6,276	5,519	-12.1	88	90	+2.3	5,540	4,784	-13.6	48	55	+14.6
Embezzlement	260	240	-7.7	3	2	-33.3	257	243	-5.4	2	3	+50.0
Stolen property; buying, receiving, possessing	3,014	2,751	-8.7	189	145	-23.3	773	801	+3.6	52	53	+1.9
Vandalism	7,192	6,311	-12.2	1,551	1,232	-20.6	1,649	1,447	-12.2	292	220	-24.7
Weapons; carrying, possessing, etc.	5,121	5,082	-0.8	351	301	-14.2	453	513	+13.2	46	39	-15.2
Prostitution and commercialized vice	68	69	+1.5	6	1	-83.3	62	70	+12.9	2	6	+200.0
Sex offenses (except forcible rape and prostitution)	3,340	2,774	-16.9	590	467	-20.8	234	208	-11.1	63	50	-20.6
Drug abuse violations	56,153	59,047	+5.2	2,727	2,466	-9.6	17,327	18,609	+7.4	708	699	-1.3
Gambling	107	67	-37.4	4	2	-50.0	32	37	+15.6	4	1	-75.0
Offenses against the family and children	7,627	7,387	-3.1	97	86	-11.3	2,146	1,945	-9.4	51	62	+21.6
Driving under the influence	113,762	104,913	-7.8	643	581	-9.6	34,790	32,369	-7.0	223	166	-25.6
Liquor laws	14,216	11,991	-15.7	2,431	1,964	-19.2	6,212	5,099	-17.9	1,667	1,339	-19.7
Drunkenness	12,806	11,497	-10.2	191	138	-27.7	3,802	3,426	-9.9	63	59	-6.3
Disorderly conduct	11,330	11,022	-2.7	1,658	1,543	-6.9	4,334	4,193	-3.3	844	726	-14.0
Vagrancy	137	183	+33.6	5	7	+40.0	55	43	-21.8	9	0	-100.0
All other offenses (except traffic)	152,445	147,171	-3.5	4,934	4,232	-14.2	52,336	52,325	*	1,895	1,558	-17.8
Suspicion	13	79	+507.7	3	1	-66.7	1	17	+1,600.0	0	0	
Curfew and loitering law violations	186	147	-21.0	186	147	-21.0	120	98	-18.3	120	98	-18.3

* = Less than one-tenth of one percent.   1 Does not include suspicion.   2 Violent crimes are offenses of murder and nonnegligent manslaughter, forcible rape, robbery, and aggravated assault. Property crimes are offenses of burglary, larceny-theft, motor vehicle theft, and arson.   3 The rape figures in this table are based on the legacy definition of rape only. The rape figures shown include converted National Incident-Based Reporting System rape data and those states/agencies that reported the legacy definition of rape for both years.

Table 58.   Arrests, Nonmetropolitan Counties, Distribution by Age, 2013

(Number, percent; 1,918 agencies; 2013 estimated population 21,177,622.)

Offense charged	Total, all ages	Ages-under 15	Ages-under 18	Ages 18 and over	Under 10	10–12	13–14	15	16	17	18	19	20
Total	705,703	7,875	33,528	672,175	383	1,866	5,626	5,242	8,162	12,249	20,534	24,518	26,456
Total percent distribution[1]	100.0	1.1	4.8	95.2	0.1	0.3	0.8	0.7	1.2	1.7	2.9	3.5	3.7
Violent crime [2]	19,930	332	1,241	18,689	16	76	240	188	316	405	549	660	637
Violent crime percent distribution[1]	100.0	1.7	6.2	93.8	0.1	0.4	1.2	0.9	1.6	2.0	2.8	3.3	3.2
Murder and nonnegligent manslaughter	625	11	40	585	0	7	4	5	8	16	23	28	23
Rape[3]	1,213	59	160	1,053	3	10	46	26	37	38	79	75	57
Robbery	1,398	10	103	1,295	0	5	5	13	33	47	74	95	85
Aggravated assault	16,694	252	938	15,756	13	54	185	144	238	304	373	462	472
Property crime [2]	51,855	1,290	5,038	46,817	60	327	903	809	1,218	1,721	2,556	2,378	2,364
Property crime percent distribution[1]	100.0	2.5	9.7	90.3	0.1	0.6	1.7	1.6	2.3	3.3	4.9	4.6	4.6
Burglary	15,589	411	1,672	13,917	19	87	305	236	438	587	895	849	845
Larceny-theft	32,230	721	2,771	29,459	31	208	482	441	636	973	1,481	1,373	1,364
Motor vehicle theft	3,511	106	482	3,029	4	15	87	114	120	142	159	128	132
Arson	525	52	113	412	6	17	29	18	24	19	21	28	23
Other assaults	58,570	1,842	5,405	53,165	75	513	1,254	963	1,255	1,345	1,455	1,439	1,515
Forgery and counterfeiting	2,917	1	26	2,891	0	0	1	0	8	17	55	52	94
Fraud	11,705	37	158	11,547	0	6	31	23	30	68	129	206	258
Embezzlement	572	1	10	562	0	0	1	1	4	4	7	13	18
Stolen property; buying, receiving, possessing	4,223	44	233	3,990	1	6	37	37	63	89	153	160	161
Vandalism	9,070	627	1,763	7,307	69	178	380	287	401	448	436	413	383
Weapons; carrying, possessing, etc.	6,313	149	401	5,912	21	49	79	54	77	121	176	184	169
Prostitution and commercialized vice	153	3	10	143	0	2	1	1	3	3	3	11	6
Sex offenses (except forcible rape and prostitution)	3,743	293	631	3,112	18	80	195	105	88	145	182	139	138
Drug abuse violations	90,352	465	3,676	86,676	1	44	420	496	919	1,796	3,728	4,348	4,507
Gambling	140	0	4	136	0	0	0	0	2	2	2	4	5
Offenses against the family and children	10,327	80	194	10,133	5	22	53	36	31	47	92	110	153
Driving under the influence	157,532	16	894	156,638	2	1	13	33	209	636	2,274	3,345	4,122
Liquor laws	20,181	273	4,017	16,164	1	19	253	563	1,194	1,987	3,203	3,632	3,224
Drunkenness	15,617	23	216	15,401	1	3	19	40	46	107	323	392	450
Disorderly conduct	18,087	950	2,635	15,452	47	250	653	457	512	716	530	516	513
Vagrancy	231	2	8	223	0	0	2	3	0	3	4	7	4
All other offenses (except traffic)	223,611	1,331	6,596	217,015	60	268	1,003	1,060	1,686	2,519	4,668	6,504	7,726
Suspicion	316	59	114	202	6	16	37	20	24	11	9	5	9
Curfew and loitering law violations	258	57	258	NA	0	6	51	66	76	59	NA	NA	NA

Table 58.   Arrests, Nonmetropolitan Counties, Distribution by Age, 2013

(Number, percent; 1,918 agencies; 2013 estimated population 21,177,622.)

Offense charged	21	22	23	24	25–29	30–34	35–39	40–44	45–49	50–54	55–59	60–64	65 and over
Total	27,043	27,311	27,143	26,094	117,395	101,560	74,714	62,456	51,523	40,959	23,423	11,555	9,491
Total percent distribution[1]	3.8	3.9	3.8	3.7	16.6	14.4	10.6	8.9	7.3	5.8	3.3	1.6	1.3
Violent crime [2]	708	671	673	690	3,124	2,871	2,090	1,866	1,510	1,222	698	333	387
Violent crime percent distribution[1]	3.6	3.4	3.4	3.5	15.7	14.4	10.5	9.4	7.6	6.1	3.5	1.7	1.9
Murder and nonnegligent manslaughter	24	21	33	23	104	85	52	39	44	34	22	10	20
Rape[3]	47	38	25	33	143	139	111	87	79	45	31	32	32
Robbery	87	86	63	61	267	184	87	83	63	31	19	5	5
Aggravated assault	550	526	552	573	2,610	2,463	1,840	1,657	1,324	1,112	626	286	330
Property crime [2]	2,160	2,269	2,061	2,031	8,890	7,004	4,927	3,709	2,682	1,924	1,008	471	383
Property crime percent distribution[1]	4.2	4.4	4.0	3.9	17.1	13.5	9.5	7.2	5.2	3.7	1.9	0.9	0.7
Burglary	732	759	666	606	2,765	2,047	1,336	948	636	457	219	103	54
Larceny-theft	1,276	1,377	1,242	1,299	5,471	4,373	3,201	2,484	1,839	1,319	721	338	301
Motor vehicle theft	133	118	141	117	594	532	351	246	179	115	55	17	12
Arson	19	15	12	9	60	52	39	31	28	33	13	13	16
Other assaults	1,819	1,827	1,897	1,786	8,640	8,033	6,374	5,711	4,743	3,720	2,140	1,015	1,051
Forgery and counterfeiting	88	88	136	106	590	544	373	279	226	151	62	29	18
Fraud	277	324	368	340	1,759	1,961	1,582	1,514	1,025	796	505	237	266
Embezzlement	23	11	22	14	84	95	80	63	43	52	15	14	8
Stolen property; buying, receiving, possessing	177	195	170	176	707	682	441	373	236	185	91	41	42
Vandalism	393	341	337	281	1,287	1,059	697	512	438	336	188	92	114
Weapons; carrying, possessing, etc.	236	262	225	212	1,001	901	636	520	477	389	237	140	147
Prostitution and commercialized vice	1	3	2	9	24	24	10	13	12	13	6	2	4
Sex offenses (except forcible rape and prostitution)	103	104	100	77	381	377	311	284	296	198	170	104	148
Drug abuse violations	4,506	4,329	4,114	3,840	16,354	12,901	8,458	6,561	5,208	4,082	2,239	988	513
Gambling	3	4	1	3	22	13	13	15	14	12	13	5	7
Offenses against the family and children	214	257	277	297	1,843	2,068	1,750	1,328	864	497	224	88	71
Driving under the influence	5,961	6,433	6,309	6,026	25,735	21,548	16,526	15,413	14,165	12,884	8,113	4,430	3,354
Liquor laws	557	401	350	266	983	770	586	582	540	503	293	149	125
Drunkenness	528	530	518	475	2,258	2,160	1,798	1,660	1,606	1,370	781	337	215
Disorderly conduct	640	648	639	564	2,507	2,009	1,685	1,519	1,361	1,086	629	305	301
Vagrancy	7	11	10	10	40	38	23	23	20	12	9	2	3
All other offenses (except traffic)	8,629	8,588	8,920	8,883	41,139	36,466	26,331	20,495	16,045	11,521	5,995	2,773	2,332
Suspicion	13	15	14	8	27	36	23	16	12	6	7	0	2
Curfew and loitering law violations	NA	NA	NA	NA	NA	NA	NA	NA	NA	NA	NA	NA	NA

NA = Not available.   1 Because of rounding, the percentages may not sum to 100.   2 Violent crimes are offenses of murder and nonnegligent manslaughter, forcible rape, robbery, and aggravated assault.
Property crimes are offenses of burglary, larceny-theft, motor vehicle theft, and arson.   3 The rape figures in this table are an aggregate total of the data submitted using both the revised and legacy Uniform Crime Reporting definitions.

Table 59.   Arrests, Nonmetropolitan Counties, Persons under 15, 18, 21, and 25 Years of Age, 2013

(Number, percent;1,918 agencies; 2013 estimated population 21,177,622.)

Offense charged	Total, all ages	Number of persons arrested				Percent of total all ages			
		Under 15	Under 18	Under 21	Under 25	Under 15	Under 18	Under 21	Under 25
Total	705,703	7,875	33,528	105,036	212,627	1.1	4.8	14.9	30.1
Violent crime [1]	19,930	332	1,241	3,087	5,829	1.7	6.2	15.5	29.2
Murder and nonnegligent man-slaughter	625	11	40	114	215	1.8	6.4	18.2	34.4
Rape[2]	1,213	59	160	371	514	4.9	13.2	30.6	42.4
Robbery	1,398	10	103	357	654	0.7	7.4	25.5	46.8
Aggravated assault	16,694	252	938	2,245	4,446	1.5	5.6	13.4	26.6
Property crime [1]	51,855	1,290	5,038	12,336	20,857	2.5	9.7	23.8	40.2
Burglary	15,589	411	1,672	4,261	7,024	2.6	10.7	27.3	45.1
Larceny-theft	32,230	721	2,771	6,989	12,183	2.2	8.6	21.7	37.8
Motor vehicle theft	3,511	106	482	901	1,410	3.0	13.7	25.7	40.2
Arson	525	52	113	185	240	9.9	21.5	35.2	45.7
Other assaults	58,570	1,842	5,405	9,814	17,143	3.1	9.2	16.8	29.3
Forgery and counterfeiting	2,917	1	26	227	645	*	0.9	7.8	22.1
Fraud	11,705	37	158	751	2,060	0.3	1.3	6.4	17.6
Embezzlement	572	1	10	48	118	0.2	1.7	8.4	20.6
Stolen property; buying, receiving, possessing	4,223	44	233	707	1,425	1.0	5.5	16.7	33.7
Vandalism	9,070	627	1,763	2,995	4,347	6.9	19.4	33.0	47.9
Weapons; carrying, possessing, etc.	6,313	149	401	930	1,865	2.4	6.4	14.7	29.5
Prostitution and commercialized vice	153	3	10	30	45	2.0	6.5	19.6	29.4
Sex offenses (except forcible rape and prostitution)	3,743	293	631	1,090	1,474	7.8	16.9	29.1	39.4
Drug abuse violations	90,352	465	3,676	16,259	33,048	0.5	4.1	18.0	36.6
Gambling	140	0	4	15	26	*	2.9	10.7	18.6
Offenses against the family and children	10,327	80	194	549	1,594	0.8	1.9	5.3	15.4
Driving under the influence	157,532	16	894	10,635	35,364	*	0.6	6.8	22.4
Liquor laws	20,181	273	4,017	14,076	15,650	1.4	19.9	69.7	77.5
Drunkenness	15,617	23	216	1,381	3,432	0.1	1.4	8.8	22.0
Disorderly conduct	18,087	950	2,635	4,194	6,685	5.3	14.6	23.2	37.0
Vagrancy	231	2	8	23	61	0.9	3.5	10.0	26.4
All other offenses (except traffic)	223,611	1,331	6,596	25,494	60,514	0.6	2.9	11.4	27.1
Suspicion	316	59	114	137	187	18.7	36.1	43.4	59.2
Curfew and loitering law violations	258	57	258	258	258	22.1	100.0	100.0	100.0

* = Less than one-tenth of one percent.   1 Violent crimes are offenses of murder and nonnegligent manslaughter, forcible rape, robbery, and aggravated assault. Property crimes are offenses of burglary, larceny-theft, motor vehicle theft, and arson.   2 The rape figures in this table are an aggregate total of the data submitted using both the revised and legacy Uniform Crime Reporting definitions.

Table 60. Arrests, Nonmetropolitan Counties, Distribution by Sex, 2013

(Number, percent; 1,918 agencies; 2013 estimated population 21,177,622.)

Offense charged	Number of persons arrested			Percent male	Percent female	Percent distribution[1]		
	Total	Male	Female			Total	Male	Female
Total	705,703	527,325	178,378	74.7	25.3	100.0	100.0	100.0
Violent crime [2]	19,930	16,182	3,748	81.2	18.8	2.8	3.1	2.1
Murder and nonnegligent manslaughter	625	532	93	85.1	14.9	0.1	0.1	0.1
Rape[3]	1,213	1,169	44	96.4	3.6	0.2	0.2	*
Robbery	1,398	1,190	208	85.1	14.9	0.2	0.2	0.1
Aggravated assault	16,694	13,291	3,403	79.6	20.4	2.4	2.5	1.9
Property crime [2]	51,855	37,463	14,392	72.2	27.8	7.3	7.1	8.1
Burglary	15,589	13,038	2,551	83.6	16.4	2.2	2.5	1.4
Larceny-theft	32,230	21,191	11,039	65.7	34.3	4.6	4.0	6.2
Motor vehicle theft	3,511	2,797	714	79.7	20.3	0.5	0.5	0.4
Arson	525	437	88	83.2	16.8	0.1	0.1	*
Other assaults	58,570	42,916	15,654	73.3	26.7	8.3	8.1	8.8
Forgery and counterfeiting	2,917	1,743	1,174	59.8	40.2	0.4	0.3	0.7
Fraud	11,705	6,349	5,356	54.2	45.8	1.7	1.2	3.0
Embezzlement	572	292	280	51.0	49.0	0.1	0.1	0.2
Stolen property; buying, receiving, possessing	4,223	3,278	945	77.6	22.4	0.6	0.6	0.5
Vandalism	9,070	7,410	1,660	81.7	18.3	1.3	1.4	0.9
Weapons; carrying, possessing, etc.	6,313	5,736	577	90.9	9.1	0.9	1.1	0.3
Prostitution and commercialized vice	153	76	77	49.7	50.3	*	*	*
Sex offenses (except forcible rape and prostitution)	3,743	3,491	252	93.3	6.7	0.5	0.7	0.1
Drug abuse violations	90,352	68,519	21,833	75.8	24.2	12.8	13.0	12.2
Gambling	140	93	47	66.4	33.6	*	*	*
Offenses against the family and children	10,327	8,094	2,233	78.4	21.6	1.5	1.5	1.3
Driving under the influence	157,532	120,349	37,183	76.4	23.6	22.3	22.8	20.8
Liquor laws	20,181	14,120	6,061	70.0	30.0	2.9	2.7	3.4
Drunkenness	15,617	12,068	3,549	77.3	22.7	2.2	2.3	2.0
Disorderly conduct	18,087	13,174	4,913	72.8	27.2	2.6	2.5	2.8
Vagrancy	231	187	44	81.0	19.0	*	*	*
All other offenses (except traffic)	223,611	165,394	58,217	74.0	26.0	31.7	31.4	32.6
Suspicion	316	238	78	75.3	24.7	*	*	*
Curfew and loitering law violations	258	153	105	59.3	40.7	*	*	0.1

* = Less than one-tenth of 1 percent.   1 Because of rounding, the percentages may not sum to 100.   2 Violent crimes are offenses of murder and nonnegligent manslaughter, forcible rape, robbery, and aggravated assault. Property crimes are offenses of burglary, larceny-theft, motor vehicle theft, and arson.   3 The rape figures in this table are an aggregate total of the data submitted using both the revised and legacy Uniform Crime Reporting definitions.

Table 61.   Arrests, Nonmetropolitan Counties, Distribution by Race, 2013

(Number, percent; 1,918 agencies; 2013 estimated population 21,177,622.)

Offense charged	Total arrests						Percent distribution[1]					
	Total	White	Black	American Indian or Alaskan Native	Asian	Native Hawaiian or Other Pacific Islander	Total	White	Black	American Indian or Alaskan Native	Asian	Native Hawaiian or Other Pacific Islander
Total	695,258	580,099	92,869	18,099	4,093	98	100.0	83.4	13.4	2.6	0.6	*
Violent crime [2]	19,803	15,567	3,351	811	65	9	100.0	78.6	16.9	4.1	0.3	*
Murder and nonnegligent manslaughter	622	415	164	38	5	0	100.0	66.7	26.4	6.1	0.8	0.0
Rape[3]	1,197	1,047	115	28	6	1	100.0	87.5	9.6	2.3	0.5	0.1
Robbery	1,389	831	493	61	3	1	100.0	59.8	35.5	4.4	0.2	0.1
Aggravated assault	16,595	13,274	2,579	684	51	7	100.0	80.0	15.5	4.1	0.3	*
Property crime [2]	51,501	43,550	6,466	1,367	114	4	100.0	84.6	12.6	2.7	0.2	*
Burglary	15,506	13,101	1,967	416	19	3	100.0	84.5	12.7	2.7	0.1	*
Larceny-theft	31,986	26,993	4,086	817	90	0	100.0	84.4	12.8	2.6	0.3	0.0
Motor vehicle theft	3,489	3,012	353	119	4	1	100.0	86.3	10.1	3.4	0.1	*
Arson	520	444	60	15	1	0	100.0	85.4	11.5	2.9	0.2	0.0
Other assaults	58,186	48,289	8,081	1,664	150	2	100.0	83.0	13.9	2.9	0.3	*
Forgery and counterfeiting	2,880	2,312	502	30	34	2	100.0	80.3	17.4	1.0	1.2	0.1
Fraud	11,613	9,496	1,880	197	34	6	100.0	81.8	16.2	1.7	0.3	0.1
Embezzlement	568	495	67	6	0	0	100.0	87.1	11.8	1.1	0.0	0.0
Stolen property; buying, receiving, possessing	4,191	3,405	673	97	13	3	100.0	81.2	16.1	2.3	0.3	0.1
Vandalism	8,999	7,625	1,078	265	28	3	100.0	84.7	12.0	2.9	0.3	*
Weapons; carrying, possessing, etc.	6,257	4,813	1,248	167	29	0	100.0	76.9	19.9	2.7	0.5	0.0
Prostitution and commercialized vice	153	128	17	3	5	0	100.0	83.7	11.1	2.0	3.3	0.0
Sex offenses (except forcible rape and prostitution)	3,717	3,292	354	54	14	3	100.0	88.6	9.5	1.5	0.4	0.1
Drug abuse violations	88,836	73,463	13,321	1,501	532	19	100.0	82.7	15.0	1.7	0.6	*
Gambling	140	94	39	5	2	0	100.0	67.1	27.9	3.6	1.4	0.0
Offenses against the family and children	10,272	7,728	2,224	300	19	1	100.0	75.2	21.7	2.9	0.2	*
Driving under the influence	153,818	132,272	15,997	3,539	2,001	9	100.0	86.0	10.4	2.3	1.3	*
Liquor laws	19,733	18,069	913	624	126	1	100.0	91.6	4.6	3.2	0.6	*
Drunkenness	15,552	13,823	1,108	568	38	15	100.0	88.9	7.1	3.7	0.2	0.1
Disorderly conduct	17,894	14,257	2,781	800	52	4	100.0	79.7	15.5	4.5	0.3	*
Vagrancy	244	155	71	18	0	0	100.0	63.5	29.1	7.4	0.0	0.0
All other offenses (except traffic)	220,340	180,810	32,609	6,067	837	17	100.0	82.1	14.8	2.8	0.4	*
Suspicion	318	230	87	1	0	0	100.0	72.3	27.4	0.3	0.0	0.0
Curfew and loitering law violations	243	226	2	15	0	0	100.0	93.0	0.8	6.2	0.0	0.0

Table 61.   Arrests, Nonmetropolitan Counties, Distribution by Race, 2013

(Number, percent; 1,918 agencies; 2013 estimated population 21,177,622.)

Offense charged	Arrests under 18						Percent distribution[1]					
	Total	White	Black	American Indian or Alaskan Native	Asian	Native Hawaiian or Other Pacific Islander	Total	White	Black	American Indian or Alaskan Native	Asian	Native Hawaiian or Other Pacific Islander
Total	33,057	27,065	4,640	1,228	122	2	100.0	81.9	14.0	3.7	0.4	*
Violent crime [2]	1,227	910	265	48	4	0	100.0	74.2	21.6	3.9	0.3	0.0
Murder and nonnegligent manslaughter	40	23	9	8	0	0	100.0	57.5	22.5	20.0	0.0	0.0
Rape[3]	158	147	11	0	0	0	100.0	93.0	7.0	0.0	0.0	0.0
Robbery	103	48	51	4	0	0	100.0	46.6	49.5	3.9	0.0	0.0
Aggravated assault	926	692	194	36	4	0	100.0	74.7	21.0	3.9	0.4	0.0
Property crime [2]	4,977	4,085	719	164	9	0	100.0	82.1	14.4	3.3	0.2	0.0
Burglary	1,655	1,314	276	60	5	0	100.0	79.4	16.7	3.6	0.3	0.0
Larceny-theft	2,733	2,263	381	85	4	0	100.0	82.8	13.9	3.1	0.1	0.0
Motor vehicle theft	478	411	49	18	0	0	100.0	86.0	10.3	3.8	0.0	0.0
Arson	111	97	13	1	0	0	100.0	87.4	11.7	0.9	0.0	0.0
Other assaults	5,354	4,075	1,074	185	20	0	100.0	76.1	20.1	3.5	0.4	0.0
Forgery and counterfeiting	26	26	0	0	0	0	100.0	100.0	0.0	0.0	0.0	0.0
Fraud	157	122	26	8	1	0	100.0	77.7	16.6	5.1	0.6	0.0
Embezzlement	10	9	1	0	0	0	100.0	90.0	10.0	0.0	0.0	0.0
Stolen property; buying, receiving, possessing	232	167	55	10	0	0	100.0	72.0	23.7	4.3	0.0	0.0
Vandalism	1,732	1,478	196	48	9	1	100.0	85.3	11.3	2.8	0.5	0.1
Weapons; carrying, possessing, etc.	399	286	86	26	1	0	100.0	71.7	21.6	6.5	0.3	0.0
Prostitution and commercialized vice	10	9	0	1	0	0	100.0	90.0	0.0	10.0	0.0	0.0
Sex offenses (except forcible rape and prostitution)	625	552	65	6	2	0	100.0	88.3	10.4	1.0	0.3	0.0
Drug abuse violations	3,616	3,157	326	113	19	1	100.0	87.3	9.0	3.1	0.5	*
Gambling	4	2	2	0	0	0	100.0	50.0	50.0	0.0	0.0	0.0
Offenses against the family and children	192	176	13	3	0	0	100.0	91.7	6.8	1.6	0.0	0.0
Driving under the influence	880	815	26	30	9	0	100.0	92.6	3.0	3.4	1.0	0.0
Liquor laws	3,942	3,717	80	132	13	0	100.0	94.3	2.0	3.3	0.3	0.0
Drunkenness	215	197	11	7	0	0	100.0	91.6	5.1	3.3	0.0	0.0
Disorderly conduct	2,611	1,705	790	112	4	0	100.0	65.3	30.3	4.3	0.2	0.0
Vagrancy	6	6	0	0	0	0	100.0	100.0	0.0	0.0	0.0	0.0
All other offenses (except traffic)	6,485	5,232	902	320	31	0	100.0	80.7	13.9	4.9	0.5	0.0
Suspicion	114	113	1	0	0	0	100.0	99.1	0.9	0.0	0.0	0.0
Curfew and loitering law violations	243	226	2	15	0	0	100.0	93.0	0.8	6.2	0.0	0.0

Table 61.   Arrests, Nonmetropolitan Counties, Distribution by Race, 2013

(Number, percent; 1,918 agencies; 2013 estimated population 21,177,622.)

Offense charged	Arrests 18 and over						Percent distribution[1]					
	Total	White	Black	American Indian or Alaskan Native	Asian	Native Hawaiian or Other Pacific Islander	Total	White	Black	American Indian or Alaskan Native	Asian	Native Hawaiian or Other Pacific Islander
Total	662,201	553,034	88,229	16,871	3,971	96	100.0	83.5	13.3	2.5	0.6	*
Violent crime [2]	18,576	14,657	3,086	763	61	9	100.0	78.9	16.6	4.1	0.3	*
Murder and nonnegligent manslaughter	582	392	155	30	5	0	100.0	67.4	26.6	5.2	0.9	0.0
Rape[3]	1,039	900	104	28	6	1	100.0	86.6	10.0	2.7	0.6	0.1
Robbery	1,286	783	442	57	3	1	100.0	60.9	34.4	4.4	0.2	0.1
Aggravated assault	15,669	12,582	2,385	648	47	7	100.0	80.3	15.2	4.1	0.3	*
Property crime [2]	46,524	39,465	5,747	1,203	105	4	100.0	84.8	12.4	2.6	0.2	*
Burglary	13,851	11,787	1,691	356	14	3	100.0	85.1	12.2	2.6	0.1	*
Larceny-theft	29,253	24,730	3,705	732	86	0	100.0	84.5	12.7	2.5	0.3	0.0
Motor vehicle theft	3,011	2,601	304	101	4	1	100.0	86.4	10.1	3.4	0.1	*
Arson	409	347	47	14	1	0	100.0	84.8	11.5	3.4	0.2	0.0
Other assaults	52,832	44,214	7,007	1,479	130	2	100.0	83.7	13.3	2.8	0.2	*
Forgery and counterfeiting	2,854	2,286	502	30	34	2	100.0	80.1	17.6	1.1	1.2	0.1
Fraud	11,456	9,374	1,854	189	33	6	100.0	81.8	16.2	1.6	0.3	0.1
Embezzlement	558	486	66	6	0	0	100.0	87.1	11.8	1.1	0.0	0.0
Stolen property; buying, receiving, possessing	3,959	3,238	618	87	13	3	100.0	81.8	15.6	2.2	0.3	0.1
Vandalism	7,267	6,147	882	217	19	2	100.0	84.6	12.1	3.0	0.3	*
Weapons; carrying, possessing, etc.	5,858	4,527	1,162	141	28	0	100.0	77.3	19.8	2.4	0.5	0.0
Prostitution and commercialized vice	143	119	17	2	5	0	100.0	83.2	11.9	1.4	3.5	0.0
Sex offenses (except forcible rape and prostitution)	3,092	2,740	289	48	12	3	100.0	88.6	9.3	1.6	0.4	0.1
Drug abuse violations	85,220	70,306	12,995	1,388	513	18	100.0	82.5	15.2	1.6	0.6	*
Gambling	136	92	37	5	2	0	100.0	67.6	27.2	3.7	1.5	0.0
Offenses against the family and children	10,080	7,552	2,211	297	19	1	100.0	74.9	21.9	2.9	0.2	*
Driving under the influence	152,938	131,457	15,971	3,509	1,992	9	100.0	86.0	10.4	2.3	1.3	*
Liquor laws	15,791	14,352	833	492	113	1	100.0	90.9	5.3	3.1	0.7	*
Drunkenness	15,337	13,626	1,097	561	38	15	100.0	88.8	7.2	3.7	0.2	0.1
Disorderly conduct	15,283	12,552	1,991	688	48	4	100.0	82.1	13.0	4.5	0.3	*
Vagrancy	238	149	71	18	0	0	100.0	62.6	29.8	7.6	0.0	0.0
All other offenses (except traffic)	213,855	175,578	31,707	5,747	806	17	100.0	82.1	14.8	2.7	0.4	*
Suspicion	204	117	86	1	0	0	100.0	57.4	42.2	0.5	0.0	0.0
Curfew and loitering law violations	NA	NA	NA	NA	NA	NA	NA	NA	NA	NA	NA	NA

NA = Not available.   * = Less than one-tenth of one percent.   1 Because of rounding, the percentages may not sum to 100.   2 Violent crimes are offenses of murder and nonnegligent manslaughter, forcible rape, robbery, and aggravated assault. Property crimes are offenses of burglary, larceny-theft, motor vehicle theft, and arson.   3 The rape figures in this table are an aggregate total of the data submitted using both the revised and legacy Uniform Crime Reporting definitions.

Table 61A.   Arrests, Nonmetropolitan Counties, Distribution by Ethnicity, 2013

(Number, percent; 1,918 agencies; 2013 estimated population 21,177,622.)

Offense charged	Total arrests			Percent distribution[1]			Arrests under 18		
	Total[2]	Hispanic or Latino	Not Hispanic or Latino	Total[2]	Hispanic or Latino	Not Hispanic or Latino	Total[2]	Hispanic or Latino	Not Hispanic or Latino
Total	347,942	23,118	324,824	100.0	6.6	93.4	17,116	1,353	15,763
Violent crime [3]	10,139	681	9,458	100.0	6.7	93.3	649	38	611
Murder and nonnegligent manslaughter	336	14	322	100.0	4.2	95.8	15	1	14
Rape[4]	902	66	836	100.0	7.3	92.7	148	8	140
Robbery	627	30	597	100.0	4.8	95.2	39	1	38
Aggravated assault	8,274	571	7,703	100.0	6.9	93.1	447	28	419
Property crime [3]	24,632	866	23,766	100.0	3.5	96.5	2,508	189	2,319
Burglary	7,621	235	7,386	100.0	3.1	96.9	752	40	712
Larceny-theft	14,791	505	14,286	100.0	3.4	96.6	1,422	112	1,310
Motor vehicle theft	1,949	118	1,831	100.0	6.1	93.9	280	34	246
Arson	271	8	263	100.0	3.0	97.0	54	3	51
Other assaults	31,940	1,453	30,487	100.0	4.5	95.5	2,745	168	2,577
Forgery and counterfeiting	1,331	124	1,207	100.0	9.3	90.7	25	3	22
Fraud	5,728	209	5,519	100.0	3.6	96.4	46	5	41
Embezzlement	339	8	331	100.0	2.4	97.6	6	0	6
Stolen property; buying, receiving, possessing	2,007	131	1,876	100.0	6.5	93.5	108	22	86
Vandalism	4,964	298	4,666	100.0	6.0	94.0	1,026	53	973
Weapons; carrying, possessing, etc.	2,686	158	2,528	100.0	5.9	94.1	154	9	145
Prostitution and commercialized vice	76	2	74	100.0	2.6	97.4	2	0	2
Sex offenses (except forcible rape and prostitution)	1,457	112	1,345	100.0	7.7	92.3	260	16	244
Drug abuse violations	40,662	2,705	37,957	100.0	6.7	93.3	1,709	171	1,538
Gambling	51	4	47	100.0	7.8	92.2	2	1	1
Offenses against the family and children	4,578	237	4,341	100.0	5.2	94.8	81	5	76
Driving under the influence	59,931	5,083	54,848	100.0	8.5	91.5	434	54	380
Liquor laws	10,805	848	9,957	100.0	7.8	92.2	2,410	183	2,227
Drunkenness	11,029	634	10,395	100.0	5.7	94.3	141	17	124
Disorderly conduct	9,778	389	9,389	100.0	4.0	96.0	1,272	46	1,226
Vagrancy	51	0	51	100.0	0.0	100.0	4	0	4
All other offenses (except traffic)	125,535	9,166	116,369	100.0	7.3	92.7	3,384	364	3,020
Suspicion	73	1	72	100.0	1.4	98.6	0	0	0
Curfew and loitering law violations	150	9	141	100.0	6.0	94.0	150	9	141

Table 61A.   Arrests, Nonmetropolitan Counties, Distribution by Ethnicity, 2013

(Number, percent; 1,918 agencies; 2013 estimated population 21,177,622.)

Offense charged	Percent distribution[1]			Arrests 18 and over			Percent distribution[1]		
	Total[2]	Hispanic or Latino	Not Hispanic or Latino	Total[2]	Hispanic or Latino	Not Hispanic or Latino	Total[2]	Hispanic or Latino	Not Hispanic or Latino
Total	100.0	7.9	92.1	330,826	21,765	309,061	100.0	6.6	93.4
Violent crime [3]	100.0	5.9	94.1	9,490	643	8,847	100.0	6.8	93.2
Murder and nonnegligent manslaughter	100.0	6.7	93.3	321	13	308	100.0	4.0	96.0
Rape[4]	100.0	5.4	94.6	754	58	696	100.0	7.7	92.3
Robbery	100.0	2.6	97.4	588	29	559	100.0	4.9	95.1
Aggravated assault	100.0	6.3	93.7	7,827	543	7,284	100.0	6.9	93.1
Property crime [3]	100.0	7.5	92.5	22,124	677	21,447	100.0	3.1	96.9
Burglary	100.0	5.3	94.7	6,869	195	6,674	100.0	2.8	97.2
Larceny-theft	100.0	7.9	92.1	13,369	393	12,976	100.0	2.9	97.1
Motor vehicle theft	100.0	12.1	87.9	1,669	84	1,585	100.0	5.0	95.0
Arson	100.0	5.6	94.4	217	5	212	100.0	2.3	97.7
Other assaults	100.0	6.1	93.9	29,195	1,285	27,910	100.0	4.4	95.6
Forgery and counterfeiting	100.0	12.0	88.0	1,306	121	1,185	100.0	9.3	90.7
Fraud	100.0	10.9	89.1	5,682	204	5,478	100.0	3.6	96.4
Embezzlement	100.0	0.0	100.0	333	8	325	100.0	2.4	97.6
Stolen property; buying, receiving, possessing	100.0	20.4	79.6	1,899	109	1,790	100.0	5.7	94.3
Vandalism	100.0	5.2	94.8	3,938	245	3,693	100.0	6.2	93.8
Weapons; carrying, possessing, etc.	100.0	5.8	94.2	2,532	149	2,383	100.0	5.9	94.1
Prostitution and commercialized vice	100.0	0.0	100.0	74	2	72	100.0	2.7	97.3
Sex offenses (except forcible rape and prostitution)	100.0	6.2	93.8	1,197	96	1,101	100.0	8.0	92.0
Drug abuse violations	100.0	10.0	90.0	38,953	2,534	36,419	100.0	6.5	93.5
Gambling	100.0	50.0	50.0	49	3	46	100.0	6.1	93.9
Offenses against the family and children	100.0	6.2	93.8	4,497	232	4,265	100.0	5.2	94.8
Driving under the influence	100.0	12.4	87.6	59,497	5,029	54,468	100.0	8.5	91.5
Liquor laws	100.0	7.6	92.4	8,395	665	7,730	100.0	7.9	92.1
Drunkenness	100.0	12.1	87.9	10,888	617	10,271	100.0	5.7	94.3
Disorderly conduct	100.0	3.6	96.4	8,506	343	8,163	100.0	4.0	96.0
Vagrancy	100.0	0.0	100.0	47	0	47	100.0	0.0	100.0
All other offenses (except traffic)	100.0	10.8	89.2	122,151	8,802	113,349	100.0	7.2	92.8
Suspicion				73	1	72	100.0	1.4	98.6
Curfew and loitering law violations	100.0	6.0	94.0	NA	NA	NA	NA	NA	NA

NA = Not available.   1 Because of rounding, the percentages may not sum to 100.   2 The ethnicity totals are representative of those agencies that provided ethnicity breakdowns. Not all agencies provide ethnicity data; therefore, the race and ethnicity totals will not be equal.   3 Violent crimes are offenses of murder and nonnegligent manslaughter, forcible rape, robbery, and aggravated assault. Property crimes are offenses of burglary, larceny-theft, motor vehicle theft, and arson.   4 The rape figures in this table are an aggregate total of the data submitted using both the revised and legacy Uniform Crime Reporting definitions.

Table 62.   Arrest Trends, Suburban Areas,[1] 2012–2013

(Number, percent change; 4,928 agencies; 2013 estimated population 91,923,343; 2012 estimated population 91,089,328.)

| Offense charged | Number of persons arrested | | | | | | | | |
| | Total, all ages | | | Under 18 years of age | | | 18 years of age and over | | |
	2012	2013	Percent change	2012	2013	Percent change	2012	2013	Percent change
Total [2]	3,133,889	3,004,029	-4.1	318,198	269,056	-15.4	2,815,691	2,734,973	-2.9
Violent crime [3]	115,861	111,083	-4.1	12,331	11,244	-8.8	103,530	99,839	-3.6
Murder and nonnegligent manslaughter	2,157	2,188	+1.4	127	161	+26.8	2,030	2,027	-0.1
Rape[4]	4,084	3,877	-5.1	618	597	-3.4	3,466	3,280	-5.4
Robbery	18,788	18,160	-3.3	3,336	3,104	-7.0	15,452	15,056	-2.6
Aggravated assault	90,832	86,858	-4.4	8,250	7,382	-10.5	82,582	79,476	-3.8
Property crime [3]	400,472	388,346	-3.0	65,752	55,842	-15.1	334,720	332,504	-0.7
Burglary	71,312	64,265	-9.9	12,452	10,025	-19.5	58,860	54,240	-7.8
Larceny-theft	310,989	306,199	-1.5	49,606	42,577	-14.2	261,383	263,622	+0.9
Motor vehicle theft	15,426	15,328	-0.6	2,528	2,341	-7.4	12,898	12,987	+0.7
Arson	2,745	2,554	-7.0	1,166	899	-22.9	1,579	1,655	+4.8
Other assaults	289,547	273,353	-5.6	45,007	39,689	-11.8	244,540	233,664	-4.4
Forgery and counterfeiting	18,958	17,279	-8.9	452	340	-24.8	18,506	16,939	-8.5
Fraud	46,191	43,003	-6.9	1,315	1,244	-5.4	44,876	41,759	-6.9
Embezzlement	4,208	4,432	+5.3	81	92	+13.6	4,127	4,340	+5.2
Stolen property; buying, receiving, possessing	28,394	26,719	-5.9	3,429	2,701	-21.2	24,965	24,018	-3.8
Vandalism	56,083	51,099	-8.9	15,134	12,341	-18.5	40,949	38,758	-5.4
Weapons; carrying, possessing, etc.	33,392	32,615	-2.3	5,694	4,906	-13.8	27,698	27,709	*
Prostitution and commercialized vice	4,350	5,297	+21.8	94	100	+6.4	4,256	5,197	+22.1
Sex offenses (except forcible rape and prostitution)	16,803	14,680	-12.6	3,242	2,830	-12.7	13,561	11,850	-12.6
Drug abuse violations	401,378	409,235	+2.0	39,209	34,355	-12.4	362,169	374,880	+3.5
Gambling	971	914	-5.9	77	61	-20.8	894	853	-4.6
Offenses against the family and children	38,745	37,677	-2.8	934	863	-7.6	37,811	36,814	-2.6
Driving under the influence	366,838	341,319	-7.0	2,576	2,121	-17.7	364,262	339,198	-6.9
Liquor laws	105,212	87,108	-17.2	21,612	16,883	-21.9	83,600	70,225	-16.0
Drunkenness	106,811	97,487	-8.7	2,841	2,130	-25.0	103,970	95,357	-8.3
Disorderly conduct	114,523	101,873	-11.0	27,259	22,276	-18.3	87,264	79,597	-8.8
Vagrancy	4,391	3,840	-12.5	358	209	-41.6	4,033	3,631	-10.0
All other offenses (except traffic)	971,088	949,834	-2.2	61,128	51,993	-14.9	909,960	897,841	-1.3
Suspicion	440	231	-47.5	102	28	-72.5	338	203	-39.9
Curfew and loitering law violations	9,673	6,836	-29.3	9,673	6,836	-29.3	NA	NA	NA

NA = Not available.   * = Less than one-tenth of 1 percent.   1 Suburban areas include law enforcement agencies in cities with less than 50,000 inhabitants and county law enforcement agencies that are within a Metropolitan Statistical Area. Suburban areas exclude all metropolitan agencies associated with a principal city.   2 Does not include suspicion.   3 Violent crimes are offenses of murder and nonnegligent manslaughter, forcible rape, robbery, and aggravated assault. Property crimes are offenses of burglary, larceny-theft, motor vehicle theft, and arson.   4 The rape figures in this table are based on the legacy definition of rape only. The rape figures shown include converted National Incident-Based Reporting System rape data and those states/agencies that reported the legacy definition of rape for both years.

Table 63.   Arrest Trends, Suburban Areas[1], by Age and Sex, 2012–2013

(Number, percent change; [4,928 agencies; 2013 estimated population 91,923,343; 2012 estimated population 91,089,328.)

Offense charged	Male						Female					
	Total			Under 18			Total			Under 18		
	2012	2013	Percent change	2012	2013	Percent change	2012	2013	Percent change	2012	2013	Percent change
Total [2]	2,303,679	2,197,889	-4.6	227,493	193,003	-15.2	830,210	806,140	-2.9	90,705	76,053	-16.2
Violent crime [3]	93,165	89,041	-4.4	9,971	9,054	-9.2	22,696	22,042	-2.9	2,360	2,190	-7.2
Murder and nonnegligent manslaughter	1,903	1,892	-0.6	110	124	+12.7	254	296	+16.5	17	37	+117.6
Rape[4]	4,032	3,811	-5.5	605	571	-5.6	52	66	+26.9	13	26	+100.0
Robbery	16,267	15,573	-4.3	3,025	2,814	-7.0	2,521	2,587	+2.6	311	290	-6.8
Aggravated assault	70,963	67,765	-4.5	6,231	5,545	-11.0	19,869	19,093	-3.9	2,019	1,837	-9.0
Property crime [3]	252,858	242,729	-4.0	44,304	37,845	-14.6	147,614	145,617	-1.4	21,448	17,997	-16.1
Burglary	59,705	53,318	-10.7	11,081	8,893	-19.7	11,607	10,947	-5.7	1,371	1,132	-17.4
Larceny-theft	178,580	175,140	-1.9	30,126	26,245	-12.9	132,409	131,059	-1.0	19,480	16,332	-16.2
Motor vehicle theft	12,318	12,156	-1.3	2,128	1,907	-10.4	3,108	3,172	+2.1	400	434	+8.5
Arson	2,255	2,115	-6.2	969	800	-17.4	490	439	-10.4	197	99	-49.7
Other assaults	208,115	196,154	-5.7	28,880	25,649	-11.2	81,432	77,199	-5.2	16,127	14,040	-12.9
Forgery and counterfeiting	11,972	10,859	-9.3	296	245	-17.2	6,986	6,420	-8.1	156	95	-39.1
Fraud	27,206	25,676	-5.6	893	856	-4.1	18,985	17,327	-8.7	422	388	-8.1
Embezzlement	2,154	2,272	+5.5	59	68	+15.3	2,054	2,160	+5.2	22	24	+9.1
Stolen property; buying, receiving, possessing	22,517	20,805	-7.6	2,828	2,258	-20.2	5,877	5,914	+0.6	601	443	-26.3
Vandalism	45,112	41,073	-9.0	12,666	10,398	-17.9	10,971	10,026	-8.6	2,468	1,943	-21.3
Weapons; carrying, possessing, etc.	30,322	29,368	-3.1	5,106	4,341	-15.0	3,070	3,247	+5.8	588	565	-3.9
Prostitution and commercialized vice	1,726	2,185	+26.6	30	35	+16.7	2,624	3,112	+18.6	64	65	+1.6
Sex offenses (except forcible rape and prostitution)	15,585	13,611	-12.7	2,934	2,531	-13.7	1,218	1,069	-12.2	308	299	-2.9
Drug abuse violations	314,684	318,453	+1.2	32,354	27,893	-13.8	86,694	90,782	+4.7	6,855	6,462	-5.7
Gambling	703	650	-7.5	55	39	-29.1	268	264	-1.5	22	22	0.0
Offenses against the family and children	30,671	29,660	-3.3	583	565	-3.1	8,074	8,017	-0.7	351	298	-15.1
Driving under the influence	274,046	254,022	-7.3	1,896	1,581	-16.6	92,792	87,297	-5.9	680	540	-20.6
Liquor laws	73,197	60,511	-17.3	13,191	10,372	-21.4	32,015	26,597	-16.9	8,421	6,511	-22.7
Drunkenness	85,710	78,117	-8.9	2,030	1,544	-23.9	21,101	19,370	-8.2	811	586	-27.7
Disorderly conduct	81,851	73,029	-10.8	17,856	14,748	-17.4	32,672	28,844	-11.7	9,403	7,528	-19.9
Vagrancy	3,401	3,001	-11.8	268	165	-38.4	990	839	-15.3	90	44	-51.1
All other offenses (except traffic)	722,242	702,059	-2.8	44,851	38,202	-14.8	248,846	247,775	-0.4	16,277	13,791	-15.3
Suspicion	335	187	-44.2	77	26	-66.2	105	44	-58.1	25	2	-92.0
Curfew and loitering law violations	6,442	4,614	-28.4	6,442	4,614	-28.4	3,231	2,222	-31.2	3,231	2,222	-31.2

1 Suburban areas include law enforcement agencies in cities with less than 50,000 inhabitants and county law enforcement agencies that are within a Metropolitan Statistical Area. Suburban areas exclude all metropolitan agencies associated with a principal city.   2 Does not include suspicion.   3 Violent crimes are offenses of murder and nonnegligent manslaughter, forcible rape, robbery, and aggravated assault. Property crimes are offenses of burglary, larceny-theft, motor vehicle theft, and arson.   4 The rape figures in this table are based on the legacy definition of rape only. The rape figures shown include converted National Incident-Based Reporting System rape data and those states/agencies that reported the legacy definition of rape for both years.

Table 64.   Arrests, Suburban Areas,[1] Distribution by Age, 2013

(Number, percent; 6,631 agencies; 2013 estimated population 111,178,219.)

Offense charged	All ages	Under 15	Under 18	18 and over	Under 10	10–12	13–14	15	16	17	18	19	20
Total	3,758,000	95,666	349,531	3,408,469	2,713	20,936	72,017	63,763	82,966	107,136	149,386	161,781	161,245
Total percent distribution[2]	100.0	2.5	9.3	90.7	0.1	0.6	1.9	1.7	2.2	2.9	4.0	4.3	4.3
Violent crime [3]	136,378	4,376	14,681	121,697	107	1,031	3,238	2,733	3,496	4,076	4,967	5,310	5,481
Violent crime percent distribution[2]	100.0	3.2	10.8	89.2	0.1	0.8	2.4	2.0	2.6	3.0	3.6	3.9	4.0
Murder and nonnegligent manslaughter	2,583	26	188	2,395	0	2	24	33	49	80	128	133	149
Rape[4]	4,987	315	864	4,123	13	78	224	142	186	221	222	235	230
Robbery	22,956	734	3,952	19,004	2	76	656	763	1,118	1,337	1,799	1,646	1,538
Aggravated assault	105,852	3,301	9,677	96,175	92	875	2,334	1,795	2,143	2,438	2,818	3,296	3,564
Property crime [3]	508,808	20,250	73,847	434,961	386	4,324	15,540	13,907	17,781	21,909	26,440	24,592	22,609
Property crime percent distribution[2]	100.0	4.0	14.5	85.5	0.1	0.8	3.1	2.7	3.5	4.3	5.2	4.8	4.4
Burglary	78,750	3,281	12,301	66,449	85	664	2,532	2,332	3,048	3,640	4,532	4,399	3,878
Larceny-theft	408,402	15,662	57,529	350,873	236	3,389	12,037	10,743	13,802	17,322	20,793	19,284	17,830
Motor vehicle theft	18,458	660	2,871	15,587	5	63	592	621	789	801	984	809	773
Arson	3,198	647	1,146	2,052	60	208	379	211	142	146	131	100	128
Other assaults	346,497	19,516	49,823	296,674	667	5,188	13,661	9,559	10,528	10,220	9,284	9,729	10,565
Forgery and counterfeiting	21,671	42	424	21,247	1	12	29	49	95	238	575	863	939
Fraud	53,643	289	1,559	52,084	8	56	225	242	398	630	1,159	1,505	1,793
Embezzlement	5,443	21	137	5,306	1	5	15	7	26	83	244	298	315
Stolen property; buying, receiving, possessing	32,653	794	3,455	29,198	7	104	683	705	862	1,094	1,588	1,535	1,534
Vandalism	66,003	5,911	16,051	49,952	271	1,676	3,964	3,050	3,420	3,670	3,628	3,371	3,009
Weapons; carrying, possessing, etc.	38,920	2,380	6,113	32,807	190	690	1,500	1,039	1,188	1,506	1,876	1,714	1,654
Prostitution and commercialized vice	6,612	12	126	6,486	0	1	11	15	28	71	200	256	284
Sex offenses (except forcible rape and prostitution)	18,565	1,749	3,665	14,900	80	456	1,213	667	636	613	692	649	616
Drug abuse violations	495,730	6,881	42,068	453,662	39	941	5,901	6,574	10,876	17,737	29,824	30,944	28,563
Gambling	996	18	74	922	0	3	15	8	20	28	23	28	26
Offenses against the family and children	43,365	331	1,040	42,325	16	57	258	214	213	282	415	498	655
Driving under the influence	422,322	38	2,778	419,544	3	1	34	105	574	2,061	6,057	8,809	11,388
Liquor laws	119,823	2,036	23,655	96,168	11	117	1,908	3,343	6,559	11,717	23,109	23,791	18,885
Drunkenness	125,344	293	2,438	122,906	5	29	259	367	614	1,164	3,275	3,780	3,788
Disorderly conduct	157,241	12,663	33,361	123,880	301	2,917	9,445	6,776	6,878	7,044	6,168	5,802	5,518
Vagrancy	5,398	68	287	5,111	0	9	59	58	75	86	181	167	191
All other offenses (except traffic)	1,142,346	15,264	63,958	1,078,388	594	2,938	11,732	11,981	15,858	20,855	29,671	38,131	43,416
Suspicion	290	14	39	251	3	3	8	9	7	9	10	9	16
Curfew and loitering law violations	9,952	2,720	9,952	NA	23	378	2,319	2,355	2,834	2,043	NA	NA	NA

Table 64.   Arrests, Suburban Areas,[1] Distribution by Age, 2013

(Number, percent; 6,631 agencies; 2013 estimated population 111,178,219.)

Offense charged	21	22	23	24	25–29	30–34	35–39	40–44	45–49	50–54	55–59	60–64	65 and over
Total	157,783	154,623	150,499	142,360	599,562	481,857	336,224	289,213	244,449	191,470	105,261	47,385	35,371
Total percent distribution[2]	4.2	4.1	4.0	3.8	16.0	12.8	8.9	7.7	6.5	5.1	2.8	1.3	0.9
Violent crime[3]	5,561	5,391	5,231	4,960	21,282	17,508	12,313	10,509	8,981	6,998	3,730	1,851	1,624
Violent crime percent distribution[2]	4.1	4.0	3.8	3.6	15.6	12.8	9.0	7.7	6.6	5.1	2.7	1.4	1.2
Murder and nonnegligent manslaughter	151	126	139	107	404	274	185	171	145	128	59	37	59
Rape[4]	212	188	157	125	562	589	433	381	282	208	125	79	95
Robbery	1,366	1,160	1,080	923	3,285	2,201	1,300	1,042	781	537	228	84	34
Aggravated assault	3,832	3,917	3,855	3,805	17,031	14,444	10,395	8,915	7,773	6,125	3,318	1,651	1,436
Property crime[3]	21,613	20,387	19,461	18,161	76,953	60,606	40,176	34,466	28,623	21,335	11,098	4,740	3,701
Property crime percent distribution[2]	4.2	4.0	3.8	3.6	15.1	11.9	7.9	6.8	5.6	4.2	2.2	0.9	0.7
Burglary	3,746	3,539	3,249	3,132	12,798	9,409	5,667	4,507	3,523	2,388	1,087	382	213
Larceny-theft	17,037	16,030	15,436	14,265	60,908	48,464	32,707	28,522	23,989	18,245	9,693	4,247	3,423
Motor vehicle theft	756	756	689	675	2,916	2,451	1,637	1,267	953	573	232	76	40
Arson	74	62	87	89	331	282	165	170	158	129	86	35	25
Other assaults	11,719	11,805	11,792	11,406	50,021	44,161	33,151	29,900	25,007	19,138	10,320	4,617	4,059
Forgery and counterfeiting	819	920	946	935	4,249	3,469	2,410	2,018	1,380	935	490	203	96
Fraud	1,784	1,784	1,965	1,949	9,036	8,306	6,384	5,662	4,499	3,155	1,695	787	621
Embezzlement	296	290	238	205	863	692	486	507	355	274	128	69	46
Stolen property; buying, receiving, possessing	1,422	1,353	1,380	1,314	5,603	4,510	2,976	2,352	1,654	1,153	519	199	106
Vandalism	2,970	2,742	2,374	2,226	8,580	6,321	4,254	3,502	2,807	2,095	1,082	554	437
Weapons; carrying, possessing, etc.	1,780	1,735	1,700	1,477	6,068	4,497	2,893	2,249	1,801	1,502	915	495	451
Prostitution and commercialized vice	316	303	264	295	1,153	871	657	617	520	367	191	111	81
Sex offenses (except forcible rape and prostitution)	548	572	550	452	1,981	1,794	1,476	1,338	1,242	1,106	736	490	658
Drug abuse violations	26,341	24,867	23,448	21,215	83,785	61,671	38,421	29,502	23,808	17,674	8,909	3,243	1,447
Gambling	17	26	14	22	95	98	88	86	99	90	99	54	57
Offenses against the family and children	884	999	1,123	1,308	7,256	8,318	6,687	5,604	4,110	2,588	1,213	410	257
Driving under the influence	18,344	19,374	19,693	18,805	77,369	58,305	42,249	38,810	34,682	30,224	18,858	9,562	7,015
Liquor laws	2,817	1,922	1,593	1,324	4,843	3,777	2,844	2,792	2,880	2,724	1,579	741	547
Drunkenness	5,757	5,249	4,704	4,235	18,173	15,294	11,862	11,644	12,480	11,374	6,827	2,902	1,562
Disorderly conduct	6,974	6,176	5,614	5,108	19,750	15,465	10,988	10,169	9,575	8,271	4,511	2,098	1,693
Vagrancy	218	197	187	189	743	678	463	426	519	505	265	123	59
All other offenses (except traffic)	47,585	48,512	48,208	46,759	201,715	165,484	115,423	97,051	79,414	59,944	32,088	14,135	10,852
Suspicion	18	19	14	15	44	32	23	9	13	18	8	1	2
Curfew and loitering law violations	NA	NA	NA	NA	NA	NA	NA	NA	NA	NA	NA	NA	NA

NA = Not available.   1 Suburban areas include law enforcement agencies in cities with less than 50,000 inhabitants and county law enforcement agencies that are within a Metropolitan Statistical Area. Suburban areas exclude all metropolitan agencies associated with a principal city.   2 Because of rounding, the percentages may not sum to 100.   3 Violent crimes are offenses of murder and nonnegligent manslaughter, forcible rape, robbery, and aggravated assault. Property crimes are offenses of burglary, larceny-theft, motor vehicle theft, and arson.   4 The rape figures in this table are an aggregate total of the data submitted using both the revised and legacy Uniform Crime Reporting definitions.

Table 65.   Arrests, Suburban Areas,[1] Persons under 15, 18, 21, and 25 Years of Age, 2013

(Number, percent; 6,631 agencies; 2013 estimated population 111,178,219.)

Offense charged	Total, all ages	Number of persons arrested				Percent of total all ages			
		Under 15	Under 18	Under 21	Under 25	Under 15	Under 18	Under 21	Under 25
Total	3,758,000	95,666	349,531	821,943	1,427,208	2.5	9.3	21.9	38.0
Violent crime [2]	136,378	4,376	14,681	30,439	51,582	3.2	10.8	22.3	37.8
Murder and nonnegligent man-slaughter	2,583	26	188	598	1,121	1.0	7.3	23.2	43.4
Rape[3]	4,987	315	864	1,551	2,233	6.3	17.3	31.1	44.8
Robbery	22,956	734	3,952	8,935	13,464	3.2	17.2	38.9	58.7
Aggravated assault	105,852	3,301	9,677	19,355	34,764	3.1	9.1	18.3	32.8
Property crime [2]	508,808	20,250	73,847	147,488	227,110	4.0	14.5	29.0	44.6
Burglary	78,750	3,281	12,301	25,110	38,776	4.2	15.6	31.9	49.2
Larceny-theft	408,402	15,662	57,529	115,436	178,204	3.8	14.1	28.3	43.6
Motor vehicle theft	18,458	660	2,871	5,437	8,313	3.6	15.6	29.5	45.0
Arson	3,198	647	1,146	1,505	1,817	20.2	35.8	47.1	56.8
Other assaults	346,497	19,516	49,823	79,401	126,123	5.6	14.4	22.9	36.4
Forgery and counterfeiting	21,671	42	424	2,801	6,421	0.2	2.0	12.9	29.6
Fraud	53,643	289	1,559	6,016	13,498	0.5	2.9	11.2	25.2
Embezzlement	5,443	21	137	994	2,023	0.4	2.5	18.3	37.2
Stolen property; buying, receiving, possessing	32,653	794	3,455	8,112	13,581	2.4	10.6	24.8	41.6
Vandalism	66,003	5,911	16,051	26,059	36,371	9.0	24.3	39.5	55.1
Weapons; carrying, possessing, etc.	38,920	2,380	6,113	11,357	18,049	6.1	15.7	29.2	46.4
Prostitution and commercialized vice	6,612	12	126	866	2,044	0.2	1.9	13.1	30.9
Sex offenses (except forcible rape and prostitution)	18,565	1,749	3,665	5,622	7,744	9.4	19.7	30.3	41.7
Drug abuse violations	495,730	6,881	42,068	131,399	227,270	1.4	8.5	26.5	45.8
Gambling	996	18	74	151	230	1.8	7.4	15.2	23.1
Offenses against the family and children	43,365	331	1,040	2,608	6,922	0.8	2.4	6.0	16.0
Driving under the influence	422,322	38	2,778	29,032	105,248	*	0.7	6.9	24.9
Liquor laws	119,823	2,036	23,655	89,440	97,096	1.7	19.7	74.6	81.0
Drunkenness	125,344	293	2,438	13,281	33,226	0.2	1.9	10.6	26.5
Disorderly conduct	157,241	12,663	33,361	50,849	74,721	8.1	21.2	32.3	47.5
Vagrancy	5,398	68	287	826	1,617	1.3	5.3	15.3	30.0
All other offenses (except traffic)	1,142,346	15,264	63,958	175,176	366,240	1.3	5.6	15.3	32.1
Suspicion	290	14	39	74	140	4.8	13.4	25.5	48.3
Curfew and loitering law violations	9,952	2,720	9,952	9,952	9,952	27.3	100.0	100.0	100.0

* = Less than one-tenth of one percent.   1 Suburban areas include law enforcement agencies in cities with less than 50,000 inhabitants and county law enforcement agencies that are within a Metropolitan Statistical Area. Suburban areas exclude all metropolitan agencies associated with a principal city.   2 Violent crimes are offenses of murder and nonnegligent manslaughter, forcible rape, robbery, and aggravated assault. Property crimes are offenses of burglary, larceny-theft, motor vehicle theft, and arson.   3 The rape figures in this table are an aggregate total of the data submitted using both the revised and legacy Uniform Crime Reporting definitions.

Table 66. Arrests, Suburban Areas,[1] Distribution by Sex, 2013

(Number, percent; 6,631 agencies; 2013 estimated population 111,178,218)

Offense charged	Number of persons arrested			Percent male	Percent female	Percent distribution[2]		
	Total	Male	Female			Total	Male	Female
Total	3,758,000	2,738,028	1,019,972	72.9	27.1	100.0	100.0	100.0
Violent crime [3]	136,378	109,093	27,285	80.0	20.0	3.6	4.0	2.7
Murder and nonnegligent manslaughter	2,583	2,241	342	86.8	13.2	0.1	0.1	*
Rape[4]	4,987	4,900	87	98.3	1.7	0.1	0.2	*
Robbery	22,956	19,754	3,202	86.1	13.9	0.6	0.7	0.3
Aggravated assault	105,852	82,198	23,654	77.7	22.3	2.8	3.0	2.3
Property crime [3]	508,808	315,589	193,219	62.0	38.0	13.5	11.5	18.9
Burglary	78,750	65,788	12,962	83.5	16.5	2.1	2.4	1.3
Larceny-theft	408,402	232,491	175,911	56.9	43.1	10.9	8.5	17.2
Motor vehicle theft	18,458	14,673	3,785	79.5	20.5	0.5	0.5	0.4
Arson	3,198	2,637	561	82.5	17.5	0.1	0.1	0.1
Other assaults	346,497	248,904	97,593	71.8	28.2	9.2	9.1	9.6
Forgery and counterfeiting	21,671	13,576	8,095	62.6	37.4	0.6	0.5	0.8
Fraud	53,643	32,019	21,624	59.7	40.3	1.4	1.2	2.1
Embezzlement	5,443	2,796	2,647	51.4	48.6	0.1	0.1	0.3
Stolen property; buying, receiving, possessing	32,653	25,380	7,273	77.7	22.3	0.9	0.9	0.7
Vandalism	66,003	52,929	13,074	80.2	19.8	1.8	1.9	1.3
Weapons; carrying, possessing, etc.	38,920	35,051	3,869	90.1	9.9	1.0	1.3	0.4
Prostitution and commercialized vice	6,612	2,632	3,980	39.8	60.2	0.2	0.1	0.4
Sex offenses (except forcible rape and prostitution)	18,565	17,175	1,390	92.5	7.5	0.5	0.6	0.1
Drug abuse violations	495,730	385,521	110,209	77.8	22.2	13.2	14.1	10.8
Gambling	996	715	281	71.8	28.2	*	*	*
Offenses against the family and children	43,365	33,534	9,831	77.3	22.7	1.2	1.2	1.0
Driving under the influence	422,322	313,922	108,400	74.3	25.7	11.2	11.5	10.6
Liquor laws	119,823	82,960	36,863	69.2	30.8	3.2	3.0	3.6
Drunkenness	125,344	100,589	24,755	80.3	19.7	3.3	3.7	2.4
Disorderly conduct	157,241	112,167	45,074	71.3	28.7	4.2	4.1	4.4
Vagrancy	5,398	4,229	1,169	78.3	21.7	0.1	0.2	0.1
All other offenses (except traffic)	1,142,346	842,341	300,005	73.7	26.3	30.4	30.8	29.4
Suspicion	290	233	57	80.3	19.7	*	*	*
Curfew and loitering law violations	9,952	6,673	3,279	67.1	32.9	0.3	0.2	0.3

* = Less than one-tenth of one percent. 1 Suburban areas include law enforcement agencies in cities with less than 50,000 inhabitants and county law enforcement agencies that are within a Metropolitan Statistical Area. Suburban areas exclude all metropolitan agencies associated with a principal city. 2 Because of rounding, the percentages may not sum to 100. 3 Violent crimes are offenses of murder and nonnegligent manslaughter, forcible rape, robbery, and aggravated assault. Property crimes are offenses of burglary, larceny-theft, motor vehicle theft, and arson. 4 The rape figures in this table are an aggregate total of the data submitted using both the revised and legacy Uniform Crime Reporting definitions.

Table 67.   Arrests, Suburban Areas,[1] Distribution by Race, 2013

(Number, percent; 6,631 agencies; 2013 estimated population 111,178,219.)

Offense charged	Total arrests						Percent distribution					
	Total	White	Black	American Indian or Alaskan Native	Asian	Native Hawaiian or Other Pacific Islander	Total	White	Black	American Indian or Alaskan Native	Asian	Native Hawaiian or Other Pacific Islander
Total	3,740,366	2,730,821	930,245	33,913	43,181	2,206	100.0	73.0	24.9	0.9	1.2	0.1
Violent crime [3]	135,943	88,812	44,327	1,120	1,528	156	100.0	65.3	32.6	0.8	1.1	0.1
Murder and nonnegligent manslaughter	2,580	1,363	1,164	17	35	1	100.0	52.8	45.1	0.7	1.4	*
Rape[4]	4,948	3,610	1,244	28	64	2	100.0	73.0	25.1	0.6	1.3	*
Robbery	22,880	10,933	11,633	104	185	25	100.0	47.8	50.8	0.5	0.8	0.1
Aggravated assault	105,535	72,906	30,286	971	1,244	128	100.0	69.1	28.7	0.9	1.2	0.1
Property crime [3]	506,197	358,714	137,211	4,380	5,652	240	100.0	70.9	27.1	0.9	1.1	*
Burglary	78,543	57,783	19,549	439	693	79	100.0	73.6	24.9	0.6	0.9	0.1
Larceny-theft	406,063	284,669	112,825	3,759	4,679	131	100.0	70.1	27.8	0.9	1.2	*
Motor vehicle theft	18,406	13,746	4,252	155	225	28	100.0	74.7	23.1	0.8	1.2	0.2
Arson	3,185	2,516	585	27	55	2	100.0	79.0	18.4	0.8	1.7	0.1
Other assaults	344,925	246,223	92,206	2,817	3,526	153	100.0	71.4	26.7	0.8	1.0	*
Forgery and counterfeiting	21,576	13,822	7,389	78	278	9	100.0	64.1	34.2	0.4	1.3	*
Fraud	53,388	35,888	16,719	257	515	9	100.0	67.2	31.3	0.5	1.0	*
Embezzlement	5,415	3,432	1,886	37	57	3	100.0	63.4	34.8	0.7	1.1	0.1
Stolen property; buying, receiving, possessing	32,565	22,806	9,244	173	321	21	100.0	70.0	28.4	0.5	1.0	0.1
Vandalism	65,644	49,673	14,822	563	564	22	100.0	75.7	22.6	0.9	0.9	*
Weapons; carrying, possessing, etc.	38,784	25,744	12,461	167	373	39	100.0	66.4	32.1	0.4	1.0	0.1
Prostitution and commercialized vice	6,582	3,979	2,138	49	412	4	100.0	60.5	32.5	0.7	6.3	0.1
Sex offenses (except forcible rape and prostitution)	18,463	14,399	3,631	154	266	13	100.0	78.0	19.7	0.8	1.4	0.1
Drug abuse violations	493,689	363,351	122,119	2,568	5,333	318	100.0	73.6	24.7	0.5	1.1	0.1
Gambling	999	525	315	7	146	6	100.0	52.6	31.5	0.7	14.6	0.6
Offenses against the family and children	43,212	27,660	14,857	454	239	2	100.0	64.0	34.4	1.1	0.6	*
Driving under the influence	420,105	357,301	50,825	3,179	8,413	387	100.0	85.1	12.1	0.8	2.0	0.1
Liquor laws	118,543	101,042	13,220	2,368	1,888	25	100.0	85.2	11.2	2.0	1.6	*
Drunkenness	124,856	105,995	16,353	1,232	1,152	124	100.0	84.9	13.1	1.0	0.9	0.1
Disorderly conduct	156,354	106,409	47,262	1,425	1,226	32	100.0	68.1	30.2	0.9	0.8	*
Vagrancy	5,390	3,776	1,533	25	48	8	100.0	70.1	28.4	0.5	0.9	0.1
All other offenses (except traffic)	1,137,609	793,888	319,251	12,810	11,039	621	100.0	69.8	28.1	1.1	1.0	0.1
Suspicion	270	148	114	1	7	0	100.0	54.8	42.2	0.4	2.6	0.0
Curfew and loitering law violations	9,857	7,234	2,362	49	198	14	100.0	73.4	24.0	0.5	2.0	0.1

Table 67.   Arrests, Suburban Areas,[1] Distribution by Race, 2013

(Number, percent; 6,631 agencies; 2013 estimated population 111,178,219.)

Offense charged	Arrests under 18						Percent distribution					
	Total	White	Black	American Indian or Alaskan Native	Asian	Native Hawaiian or Other Pacific Islander	Total	White	Black	American Indian or Alaskan Native	Asian	Native Hawaiian or Other Pacific Islander
Total	347,374	237,623	102,938	2,761	3,808	244	100.0	68.4	29.6	0.8	1.1	0.1
Violent crime [3]	14,623	7,563	6,823	106	121	10	100.0	51.7	46.7	0.7	0.8	0.1
Murder and nonnegligent manslaughter	187	70	114	0	3	0	100.0	37.4	61.0	0.0	1.6	0.0
Rape[4]	853	582	259	6	6	0	100.0	68.2	30.4	0.7	0.7	0.0
Robbery	3,940	1,216	2,672	18	28	6	100.0	30.9	67.8	0.5	0.7	0.2
Aggravated assault	9,643	5,695	3,778	82	84	4	100.0	59.1	39.2	0.9	0.9	*
Property crime [3]	73,330	45,075	26,659	572	990	34	100.0	61.5	36.4	0.8	1.4	*
Burglary	12,259	7,949	4,113	58	128	11	100.0	64.8	33.6	0.5	1.0	0.1
Larceny-theft	57,075	34,327	21,420	487	820	21	100.0	60.1	37.5	0.9	1.4	*
Motor vehicle theft	2,855	1,922	889	19	24	1	100.0	67.3	31.1	0.7	0.8	*
Arson	1,141	877	237	8	18	1	100.0	76.9	20.8	0.7	1.6	0.1
Other assaults	49,564	30,466	18,343	348	376	31	100.0	61.5	37.0	0.7	0.8	0.1
Forgery and counterfeiting	424	266	148	1	9	0	100.0	62.7	34.9	0.2	2.1	0.0
Fraud	1,544	929	596	7	12	0	100.0	60.2	38.6	0.5	0.8	0.0
Embezzlement	136	80	47	6	3	0	100.0	58.8	34.6	4.4	2.2	0.0
Stolen property; buying, receiving, possessing	3,437	1,837	1,553	16	28	3	100.0	53.4	45.2	0.5	0.8	0.1
Vandalism	15,932	12,297	3,434	97	97	7	100.0	77.2	21.6	0.6	0.6	*
Weapons; carrying, possessing, etc.	6,086	4,073	1,903	26	75	9	100.0	66.9	31.3	0.4	1.2	0.1
Prostitution and commercialized vice	126	67	58	1	0	0	100.0	53.2	46.0	0.8	0.0	0.0
Sex offenses (except forcible rape and prostitution)	3,628	2,724	841	19	40	4	100.0	75.1	23.2	0.5	1.1	0.1
Drug abuse violations	41,829	32,953	7,911	372	568	25	100.0	78.8	18.9	0.9	1.4	0.1
Gambling	85	37	41	0	7	0	100.0	43.5	48.2	0.0	8.2	0.0
Offenses against the family and children	1,036	758	253	17	8	0	100.0	73.2	24.4	1.6	0.8	0.0
Driving under the influence	2,764	2,570	134	19	39	2	100.0	93.0	4.8	0.7	1.4	0.1
Liquor laws	23,428	21,043	1,764	298	316	7	100.0	89.8	7.5	1.3	1.3	*
Drunkenness	2,418	2,150	217	27	22	2	100.0	88.9	9.0	1.1	0.9	0.1
Disorderly conduct	33,234	18,942	13,841	184	248	19	100.0	57.0	41.6	0.6	0.7	0.1
Vagrancy	287	211	74	0	1	1	100.0	73.5	25.8	0.0	0.3	0.3
All other offenses (except traffic)	63,567	46,325	15,920	596	650	76	100.0	72.9	25.0	0.9	1.0	0.1
Suspicion	39	23	16	0	0	0	100.0	59.0	41.0	0.0	0.0	0.0
Curfew and loitering law violations	9,857	7,234	2,362	49	198	14	100.0	73.4	24.0	0.5	2.0	0.1

Table 67.   Arrests, Suburban Areas,[1] Distribution by Race, 2013

(Number, percent; 6,631 agencies; 2013 estimated population 111,178,219.)

Offense charged	Arrests 18 and over						Percent distribution					
	Total	White	Black	American Indian or Alaskan Native	Asian	Native Hawaiian or Other Pacific Islander	Total	White	Black	American Indian or Alaskan Native	Asian	Native Hawaiian or Other Pacific Islander
Total	3,392,992	2,493,198	827,307	31,152	39,373	1,962	100.0	73.5	24.4	0.9	1.2	0.1
Violent crime [3]	121,320	81,249	37,504	1,014	1,407	146	100.0	67.0	30.9	0.8	1.2	0.1
Murder and nonnegligent manslaughter	2,393	1,293	1,050	17	32	1	100.0	54.0	43.9	0.7	1.3	*
Rape[4]	4,095	3,028	985	22	58	2	100.0	73.9	24.1	0.5	1.4	*
Robbery	18,940	9,717	8,961	86	157	19	100.0	51.3	47.3	0.5	0.8	0.1
Aggravated assault	95,892	67,211	26,508	889	1,160	124	100.0	70.1	27.6	0.9	1.2	0.1
Property crime [3]	432,867	313,639	110,552	3,808	4,662	206	100.0	72.5	25.5	0.9	1.1	*
Burglary	66,284	49,834	15,436	381	565	68	100.0	75.2	23.3	0.6	0.9	0.1
Larceny-theft	348,988	250,342	91,405	3,272	3,859	110	100.0	71.7	26.2	0.9	1.1	*
Motor vehicle theft	15,551	11,824	3,363	136	201	27	100.0	76.0	21.6	0.9	1.3	0.2
Arson	2,044	1,639	348	19	37	1	100.0	80.2	17.0	0.9	1.8	*
Other assaults	295,361	215,757	73,863	2,469	3,150	122	100.0	73.0	25.0	0.8	1.1	*
Forgery and counterfeiting	21,152	13,556	7,241	77	269	9	100.0	64.1	34.2	0.4	1.3	*
Fraud	51,844	34,959	16,123	250	503	9	100.0	67.4	31.1	0.5	1.0	*
Embezzlement	5,279	3,352	1,839	31	54	3	100.0	63.5	34.8	0.6	1.0	0.1
Stolen property; buying, receiving, possessing	29,128	20,969	7,691	157	293	18	100.0	72.0	26.4	0.5	1.0	0.1
Vandalism	49,712	37,376	11,388	466	467	15	100.0	75.2	22.9	0.9	0.9	*
Weapons; carrying, possessing, etc.	32,698	21,671	10,558	141	298	30	100.0	66.3	32.3	0.4	0.9	0.1
Prostitution and commercialized vice	6,456	3,912	2,080	48	412	4	100.0	60.6	32.2	0.7	6.4	0.1
Sex offenses (except forcible rape and prostitution)	14,835	11,675	2,790	135	226	9	100.0	78.7	18.8	0.9	1.5	0.1
Drug abuse violations	451,860	330,398	114,208	2,196	4,765	293	100.0	73.1	25.3	0.5	1.1	0.1
Gambling	914	488	274	7	139	6	100.0	53.4	30.0	0.8	15.2	0.7
Offenses against the family and children	42,176	26,902	14,604	437	231	2	100.0	63.8	34.6	1.0	0.5	*
Driving under the influence	417,341	354,731	50,691	3,160	8,374	385	100.0	85.0	12.1	0.8	2.0	0.1
Liquor laws	95,115	79,999	11,456	2,070	1,572	18	100.0	84.1	12.0	2.2	1.7	*
Drunkenness	122,438	103,845	16,136	1,205	1,130	122	100.0	84.8	13.2	1.0	0.9	0.1
Disorderly conduct	123,120	87,467	33,421	1,241	978	13	100.0	71.0	27.1	1.0	0.8	*
Vagrancy	5,103	3,565	1,459	25	47	7	100.0	69.9	28.6	0.5	0.9	0.1
All other offenses (except traffic)	1,074,042	747,563	303,331	12,214	10,389	545	100.0	69.6	28.2	1.1	1.0	0.1
Suspicion	231	125	98	1	7	0	100.0	54.1	42.4	0.4	3.0	0.0
Curfew and loitering law violations	NA	NA	NA	NA	NA	NA	NA	NA	NA	NA	NA	NA

NA = Not available.   * = Less than one-tenth of one percent.   1 Suburban areas include law enforcement agencies in cities with less than 50,000 inhabitants and county law enforcement agencies that are within a Metropolitan Statistical Area. Suburban areas exclude all metropolitan agencies associated with a principal city.   2 Because of rounding, the percentages may not sum to 100.   3 Violent crimes are offenses of murder and nonnegligent manslaughter, forcible rape, robbery, and aggravated assault. Property crimes are offenses of burglary, larceny-theft, motor vehicle theft, and arson.   4 The rape figures in this table are an aggregate total of the data submitted using both the revised and legacy Uniform Crime Reporting definitions.

Table 67A.   Arrests, Suburban Areas,[1] Distribution by Ethnicity, 2013

(Number, percent; 6,631 agencies; 2013 estimated population 111,178,219.)

Offense charged	Total arrests			Percent distribution			Arrests under 18		
	Total[3]	Hispanic or Latino	Not Hispanic or Latino	Total[3]	Hispanic or Latino	Not Hispanic or Latino	Total[3]	Hispanic or Latino	Not Hispanic or Latino
Total	2,177,192	307,874	1,869,318	100.0	14.1	85.9	192,131	30,627	161,504
Violent crime [4]	83,226	16,664	66,562	100.0	20.0	80.0	8,197	1,561	6,636
Murder and nonnegligent manslaughter	1,583	351	1,232	100.0	22.2	77.8	69	14	55
Rape[5]	3,899	711	3,188	100.0	18.2	81.8	774	90	684
Robbery	12,074	1,966	10,108	100.0	16.3	83.7	1,918	354	1,564
Aggravated assault	65,670	13,636	52,034	100.0	20.8	79.2	5,436	1,103	4,333
Property crime [4]	278,258	30,028	248,230	100.0	10.8	89.2	39,946	6,247	33,699
Burglary	48,494	7,201	41,293	100.0	14.8	85.2	7,140	1,538	5,602
Larceny-theft	215,980	19,814	196,166	100.0	9.2	90.8	30,489	4,156	26,333
Motor vehicle theft	12,040	2,829	9,211	100.0	23.5	76.5	1,664	467	1,197
Arson	1,744	184	1,560	100.0	10.6	89.4	653	86	567
Other assaults	196,975	23,024	173,951	100.0	11.7	88.3	26,875	3,807	23,068
Forgery and counterfeiting	12,316	1,613	10,703	100.0	13.1	86.9	217	28	189
Fraud	30,944	2,413	28,531	100.0	7.8	92.2	864	113	751
Embezzlement	3,690	297	3,393	100.0	8.0	92.0	94	14	80
Stolen property; buying, receiving, possessing	19,196	3,754	15,442	100.0	19.6	80.4	1,837	455	1,382
Vandalism	37,364	4,844	32,520	100.0	13.0	87.0	10,275	1,702	8,573
Weapons; carrying, possessing, etc.	21,272	4,705	16,567	100.0	22.1	77.9	3,355	903	2,452
Prostitution and commercialized vice	3,038	422	2,616	100.0	13.9	86.1	50	6	44
Sex offenses (except forcible rape and prostitution)	8,830	2,181	6,649	100.0	24.7	75.3	1,577	324	1,253
Drug abuse violations	269,652	44,383	225,269	100.0	16.5	83.5	21,440	3,738	17,702
Gambling	396	25	371	100.0	6.3	93.7	12	0	12
Offenses against the family and children	24,722	1,168	23,554	100.0	4.7	95.3	577	40	537
Driving under the influence	284,056	59,718	224,338	100.0	21.0	79.0	1,748	284	1,464
Liquor laws	74,732	6,956	67,776	100.0	9.3	90.7	14,885	1,563	13,322
Drunkenness	108,316	15,394	92,922	100.0	14.2	85.8	1,780	424	1,356
Disorderly conduct	97,019	7,376	89,643	100.0	7.6	92.4	17,967	2,598	15,369
Vagrancy	2,415	264	2,151	100.0	10.9	89.1	129	35	94
All other offenses (except traffic)	615,776	81,932	533,844	100.0	13.3	86.7	35,331	6,075	29,256
Suspicion	33	3	30	100.0	9.1	90.9	9	0	9
Curfew and loitering law violations	4,966	710	4,256	100.0	14.3	85.7	4,966	710	4,256

Table 67A.   Arrests, Suburban Areas,[1] Distribution by Ethnicity, 2013

(Number, percent; 6,631 agencies; 2013 estimated population 111,178,219.)

Offense charged	Percent distribution			Arrests 18 and over			Percent distribution[1]		
	Total[3]	Hispanic or Latino	Not Hispanic or Latino	Total[3]	Hispanic or Latino	Not Hispanic or Latino	Total[3]	Hispanic or Latino	Not Hispanic or Latino
Total	100.0	15.9	84.1	1,985,061	277,247	1,707,814	100.0	14.0	86.0
Violent crime [4]	100.0	19.0	81.0	75,029	15,103	59,926	100.0	20.1	79.9
Murder and nonnegligent manslaughter	100.0	20.3	79.7	1,514	337	1,177	100.0	22.3	77.7
Rape[5]	100.0	11.6	88.4	3,125	621	2,504	100.0	19.9	80.1
Robbery	100.0	18.5	81.5	10,156	1,612	8,544	100.0	15.9	84.1
Aggravated assault	100.0	20.3	79.7	60,234	12,533	47,701	100.0	20.8	79.2
Property crime [4]	100.0	15.6	84.4	238,312	23,781	214,531	100.0	10.0	90.0
Burglary	100.0	21.5	78.5	41,354	5,663	35,691	100.0	13.7	86.3
Larceny-theft	100.0	13.6	86.4	185,491	15,658	169,833	100.0	8.4	91.6
Motor vehicle theft	100.0	28.1	71.9	10,376	2,362	8,014	100.0	22.8	77.2
Arson	100.0	13.2	86.8	1,091	98	993	100.0	9.0	91.0
Other assaults	100.0	14.2	85.8	170,100	19,217	150,883	100.0	11.3	88.7
Forgery and counterfeiting	100.0	12.9	87.1	12,099	1,585	10,514	100.0	13.1	86.9
Fraud	100.0	13.1	86.9	30,080	2,300	27,780	100.0	7.6	92.4
Embezzlement	100.0	14.9	85.1	3,596	283	3,313	100.0	7.9	92.1
Stolen property; buying, receiving, possessing	100.0	24.8	75.2	17,359	3,299	14,060	100.0	19.0	81.0
Vandalism	100.0	16.6	83.4	27,089	3,142	23,947	100.0	11.6	88.4
Weapons; carrying, possessing, etc.	100.0	26.9	73.1	17,917	3,802	14,115	100.0	21.2	78.8
Prostitution and commercialized vice	100.0	12.0	88.0	2,988	416	2,572	100.0	13.9	86.1
Sex offenses (except forcible rape and prostitution)	100.0	20.5	79.5	7,253	1,857	5,396	100.0	25.6	74.4
Drug abuse violations	100.0	17.4	82.6	248,212	40,645	207,567	100.0	16.4	83.6
Gambling	100.0	0.0	100.0	384	25	359	100.0	6.5	93.5
Offenses against the family and children	100.0	6.9	93.1	24,145	1,128	23,017	100.0	4.7	95.3
Driving under the influence	100.0	16.2	83.8	282,308	59,434	222,874	100.0	21.1	78.9
Liquor laws	100.0	10.5	89.5	59,847	5,393	54,454	100.0	9.0	91.0
Drunkenness	100.0	23.8	76.2	106,536	14,970	91,566	100.0	14.1	85.9
Disorderly conduct	100.0	14.5	85.5	79,052	4,778	74,274	100.0	6.0	94.0
Vagrancy	100.0	27.1	72.9	2,286	229	2,057	100.0	10.0	90.0
All other offenses (except traffic)	100.0	17.2	82.8	580,445	75,857	504,588	100.0	13.1	86.9
Suspicion	100.0	0.0	100.0	24	3	21	100.0	12.5	87.5
Curfew and loitering law violations	100.0	14.3	85.7	NA	NA	NA	NA	NA	NA

NA = Not available.   1 Suburban areas include law enforcement agencies in cities with less than 50,000 inhabitants and county law enforcement agencies that are within a Metropolitan Statistical Area. Suburban areas exclude all metropolitan agencies associated with a principal city.   2 Because of rounding, the percentages may not sum to 100.   3 The ethnicity totals are representative of those agencies that provided ethnicity breakdowns. Not all agencies provide ethnicity data; therefore, the race and ethnicity totals will not be equal.   4 Violent crimes are offenses of murder and nonnegligent manslaughter, forcible rape, robbery, and aggravated assault. Property crimes are offenses of burglary, larceny-theft, motor vehicle theft, and arson.   5 The rape figures in this table are an aggregate total of the data submitted using both the revised and legacy Uniform Crime Reporting definitions.

Table 68.   Police Disposition of Juvenile Offenders Taken into Custody, 2013

(Number, percent.)

Population group	Total[1]	Handled within department and released	Referred to juvenile court jurisdiction	Referred to welfare agency	Referred to other police agency	Referred to criminal or adult court	Number of agencies	Estimated population, 2013
Total Agencies								
Number	319,768	72,298	216,734	2,201	2,853	25,682	4,615	114,586,923
Percent[2]	100.0	22.6	67.8	0.7	0.9	8.0		
Total Cities								
Number	261,313	62,753	175,952	1,702	2,343	18,563	3,457	81,378,251
Percent[2]	100.0	24.0	67.3	0.7	0.9	7.1		
250,000 and over								
Number	80,074	26,636	50,817	376	472	1,773	34	22,601,402
Percent[2]	100.0	33.3	63.5	0.5	0.6	2.2		
100,000 to 249,999								
Number	36,187	6,679	28,209	261	365	673	88	13,025,823
Percent[2]	100.0	18.5	78.0	0.7	1.0	1.9		
50,000 to 99,999								
Number	45,987	9,736	32,032	295	476	3,448	221	15,275,315
Percent[2]	100.0	21.2	69.7	0.6	1.0	7.5		
25,000 to 49,999								
Number	32,297	6,675	21,536	243	499	3,344	337	11,685,288
Percent[2]	100.0	20.7	66.7	0.8	1.5	10.4		
10,000 to 24,999								
Number	36,905	6,992	24,417	280	354	4,862	702	11,263,958
Percent[2]	100.0	18.9	66.2	0.8	1.0	13.2		
under 10,000								
Number	29,863	6,035	18,941	247	177	4,463	2,075	7,526,465
Percent[2]	100.0	20.2	63.4	0.8	0.6	14.9		
Metropolitan Counties								
Number	49,467	8,270	34,762	367	369	5,699	646	26,278,991
Percent[2]	100.0	16.7	70.3	0.7	0.7	11.5		
Nonmetropolitan Counties								
Number	8,988	1,275	6,020	132	141	1,420	512	6,929,681
Percent[2]	100.0	14.2	67.0	1.5	1.6	15.8		
Suburban Areas [3]								
Number	142,304	28,483	94,497	1,166	1,459	16,699	3,088	59,923,884
Percent[2]	100.0	20.0	66.4	0.8	1.0	11.7		

1 Includes all offenses except traffic and neglect cases.   2 Because of rounding, the percentages may not sum to 100.   3 Suburban areas include law enforcement agencies in cities with less than 50,000 inhabitants and county law enforcement agencies that are within a Metropolitan Statistical Area. Suburban areas exclude all metropolitan agencies associated with a principal city. The agencies associated with suburban areas also appear in other groups within this table.

Table 69.   Arrests, by State, 2013

(Number)

State	Total, all classes[1]	Violent crime[2]	Property crime[2]	Murder and nonnegligent manslaughter	Rape[3]	Robbery	Aggravated assault	Burglary	Larceny-theft	Motor vehicle theft	Arson
Alabama											
Under 18	175	6	102	0	0	3	3	2	99	1	0
Total, all ages	2,119	26	684	2	2	12	10	11	670	2	1
Alaska											
Under 18	2,211	138	730	8	15	13	102	38	649	33	10
Total, all ages	29,568	1,638	4,006	22	106	222	1,288	264	3,461	215	66
Arizona											
Under 18	29,861	955	6,755	20	32	270	633	959	5,413	304	79
Total, all ages	279,551	9,493	42,399	253	265	1,815	7,160	4,302	36,258	1,623	216
Arkansas											
Under 18	9,197	302	2,516	4	34	78	186	473	1,981	54	8
Total, all ages	138,054	4,013	16,631	95	211	650	3,057	2,762	13,443	369	57
California											
Under 18	94,067	8,170	21,758	108	116	3,103	4,843	7,559	12,323	1,505	371
Total, all ages	1,212,801	101,342	139,624	1,425	1,600	15,930	82,387	50,390	74,234	13,909	1,091
Colorado											
Under 18	26,158	539	5,673	7	39	132	361	456	4,853	276	88
Total, all ages	230,910	5,691	28,833	120	333	1,000	4,238	2,425	24,873	1,340	195
Connecticut											
Under 18	8,960	457	1,959	4	28	205	220	262	1,353	164	180
Total, all ages	95,685	3,562	15,338	48	178	1,117	2,219	2,065	12,300	574	399
Delaware											
Under 18	4,113	340	910	0	15	113	212	140	740	20	10
Total, all ages	37,321	2,175	7,407	9	64	511	1,591	991	6,295	93	28
District of Columbia											
Under 18	369	36	40	0	0	27	9	0	39	1	0
Total, all ages	6,154	108	99	0	0	77	31	0	94	5	0
Florida											
Under 18	72,304	4,663	20,479	38	295	1,674	2,656	5,750	13,374	1,284	71
Total, all ages	904,135	40,567	122,990	662	1,842	7,940	30,123	22,822	94,392	5,452	324
Georgia											
Under 18	32,285	1,510	8,661	91	50	585	784	1,828	6,361	419	53
Total, all ages	323,435	12,146	49,993	455	346	2,714	8,631	7,258	40,956	1,579	200
Hawaii											
Under 18	740	25	117	0	5	7	13	18	83	13	3
Total, all ages	9,556	300	1,350	1	19	57	223	225	972	144	9
Idaho											
Under 18	8,633	153	1,819	0	16	13	124	253	1,454	76	36
Total, all ages	61,668	1,519	6,690	19	86	107	1,307	1,026	5,422	182	60
Illinois											
Under 18	20,391	2,073	3,825	40	0	1,117	916	637	2,298	880	10
Total, all ages	120,760	6,076	16,792	363	9	2,541	3,163	1,932	12,315	2,487	58
Indiana											
Under 18	15,960	806	4,251	11	31	213	551	529	3,390	287	45
Total, all ages	129,146	6,138	21,723	158	167	1,059	4,754	2,523	18,047	1,042	111
Iowa											
Under 18	12,888	488	3,820	2	27	85	374	470	3,132	148	70
Total, all ages	101,402	4,055	15,466	32	102	348	3,573	1,790	13,079	457	140
Kansas											
Under 18	5,784	186	1,368	3	26	19	138	138	1,156	57	17
Total, all ages	78,182	2,145	7,209	63	130	206	1,746	867	5,904	383	55
Kentucky											
Under 18	6,364	339	2,351	6	17	170	146	460	1,723	84	84
Total, all ages	178,212	3,687	22,506	129	187	1,275	2,096	3,669	18,060	607	170
Louisiana											
Under 18	16,666	1,122	4,274	11	65	179	867	854	3,150	234	36
Total, all ages	149,789	8,563	28,322	205	263	954	7,141	4,353	23,026	843	100
Maine											
Under 18	4,492	76	1,166	0	16	20	40	183	913	50	20
Total, all ages	49,548	808	7,749	17	82	177	532	1,095	6,358	250	46
Maryland											
Under 18	15,429	1,172	3,797	10	24	617	521	771	2,547	376	103
Total, all ages	168,692	6,925	20,773	166	207	2,156	4,396	4,206	15,382	926	259
Massachusetts											
Under 18	9,366	1,028	1,789	3	17	245	763	419	1,265	65	40
Total, all ages	135,362	10,512	19,719	50	270	1,573	8,619	3,363	15,672	560	124
Michigan											
Under 18	21,241	1,317	6,003	8	87	453	769	980	4,601	340	82
Total, all ages	251,825	11,591	32,025	247	627	2,104	8,613	4,885	25,344	1,547	249
Minnesota											
Under 18	25,554	877	6,154	7	91	344	435	449	5,484	180	41
Total, all ages	158,799	5,636	28,649	91	564	1,196	3,785	2,638	24,895	1,015	101
Mississippi											

Table 69.   Arrests, by State, 2013— continued

(Number)

State	Total, all classes[1]	Violent crime[2]	Property crime[2]	Murder and nonnegligent manslaughter	Rape[3]	Robbery	Aggravated assault	Burglary	Larceny-theft	Motor vehicle theft	Ar-son
Under 18	5,549	131	1,407	10	13	59	49	227	1,122	50	8
Total, all ages	72,824	1,404	8,978	95	86	325	898	1,245	7,394	263	76
Missouri											
Under 18	23,652	1,002	5,802	14	99	369	520	734	4,764	240	64
Total, all ages	276,973	9,234	40,261	238	232	1,938	6,826	5,119	33,284	1,659	199
Montana											
Under 18	5,152	61	1,165	0	3	2	56	86	1,026	47	6
Total, all ages	30,089	837	4,785	15	36	63	723	311	4,251	209	14
Nebraska											
Under 18	9,858	167	2,477	0	20	59	88	175	2,195	68	39
Total, all ages	69,957	1,912	9,981	42	156	270	1,444	753	8,839	325	64
Nevada											
Under 18	10,509	610	2,170	4	29	160	417	386	1,640	114	30
Total, all ages	122,498	6,200	13,930	117	202	1,517	4,364	2,668	10,380	744	138
New Hampshire											
Under 18	4,736	92	671	0	7	29	56	69	579	11	12
Total, all ages	44,554	871	5,222	8	52	241	570	470	4,637	85	30
New Jersey											
Under 18	21,459	1,748	3,723	16	40	920	772	780	2,728	122	93
Total, all ages	302,955	10,871	31,093	232	289	3,557	6,793	5,566	24,643	666	218
New Mexico											
Under 18	4,951	223	1,806	16	12	10	185	156	1,448	32	170
Total, all ages	65,526	3,149	10,782	71	93	226	2,759	1,182	8,740	217	643
New York											
Under 18	26,195	1,817	7,370	32	43	867	875	1,352	5,562	343	113
Total, all ages	300,442	12,902	59,628	254	354	3,605	8,689	7,872	49,635	1,794	327
North Carolina											
Under 18	28,760	1,487	7,729	39	48	597	803	2,028	5,468	145	88
Total, all ages	395,015	17,148	62,371	567	411	3,876	12,294	14,163	46,754	1,137	317
North Dakota											
Under 18	4,003	38	672	0	7	2	29	50	579	34	9
Total, all ages	30,642	585	2,947	8	32	44	501	218	2,556	157	16
Ohio											
Under 18	23,051	878	4,801	6	48	458	366	776	3,736	183	106
Total, all ages	224,248	6,589	35,489	134	368	2,191	3,896	4,972	29,585	705	227
Oklahoma											
Under 18	11,971	460	3,438	11	24	133	292	505	2,742	93	98
Total, all ages	125,534	4,908	18,620	156	207	658	3,887	2,361	15,517	517	225
Oregon											
Under 18	7,042	151	1,613	0	6	28	117	158	1,327	73	55
Total, all ages	54,323	1,648	9,446	29	53	288	1,278	960	7,816	567	103
Pennsylvania											
Under 18	61,442	3,414	8,045	17	242	1,175	1,980	1,262	6,255	381	147
Total, all ages	413,486	22,113	61,049	460	1,152	5,873	14,628	9,280	48,997	2,328	444
Rhode Island											
Under 18	3,083	108	623	0	12	42	54	130	455	22	16
Total, all ages	30,598	848	3,590	10	72	188	578	707	2,707	132	44
South Carolina											
Under 18	15,418	656	4,277	33	62	187	374	729	3,413	103	32
Total, all ages	181,016	7,607	30,727	295	347	1,320	5,645	4,460	25,399	726	142
South Dakota											
Under 18	4,868	66	892	1	2	1	62	93	733	55	11
Total, all ages	35,061	780	3,301	12	33	35	700	357	2,763	161	20
Tennessee											
Under 18	28,585	1,705	5,878	13	80	433	1,179	1,060	4,510	265	43
Total, all ages	371,938	17,896	45,903	361	353	2,189	14,993	6,715	37,063	1,927	198
Texas											
Under 18	85,922	3,491	20,849	30	194	1,217	2,050	3,362	16,599	727	161
Total, all ages	931,814	29,631	128,617	648	1,572	6,642	20,769	15,671	108,288	4,167	491
Utah											
Under 18	17,991	257	4,062	1	46	50	160	241	3,684	100	37
Total, all ages	131,389	2,064	18,253	33	164	371	1,496	1,103	16,721	365	64
Vermont											
Under 18											
Total, all ages	779	34	144	0	8	4	22	21	99	16	8
	13,418	510	1,989	6	59	31	414	286	1,614	60	29
Virginia											
Under 18	21,995	604	4,490	10	32	279	283	651	3,642	123	74
Total, all ages	321,040	6,858	37,223	331	326	1,754	4,447	4,074	32,079	867	203
Washington											
Under 18	16,939	903	5,049	8	80	304	511	798	4,006	197	48
Total, all ages	189,806	7,699	36,129	121	436	1,868	5,274	5,231	29,491	1,232	175
West Virginia											
Under 18	1,463	54	346	2	5	6	41	41	296	6	3

Table 69.   Arrests, by State, 2013— continued

(Number)

State	Total, all classes[1]	Violent crime[2]	Property crime[2]	Murder and nonnegligent manslaughter	Rape[3]	Robbery	Aggravated assault	Burglary	Larceny-theft	Motor vehicle theft	Ar-son
Total, all ages	49,225	1,834	6,900	29	58	171	1,576	878	5,816	174	32
Wisconsin											
Under 18	55,187	1,344	8,546	6	167	528	643	975	7,164	325	82
Total, all ages	305,446	8,002	36,871	146	619	1,687	5,550	3,816	31,782	1,064	209
Wyoming											
Under 18	3,798	35	716	2	9	2	22	37	648	27	4
Total, all ages	31,636	529	3,052	13	37	24	455	231	2,684	107	30

Table 69.   Arrests, by State, 2013

(Number)

State	Forgery and counterfeiting	Fraud	Embezzlement	Stolen property; buying, receiving, possessing	Vandalism	Weapons; carrying, possessing, etc.	Prostitution and commercialized vice	Sex offenses (except forcible rape and prostitution)	Drug abuse violations	Gambling
Alabama										
Under 18	0	0	0	3	0	2	0	0	16	0
Total, all ages	7	15	17	30	6	27	4	0	325	0
Alaska										
Under 18	3	9	10	8	108	22	1	22	240	0
Total, all ages	49	172	87	32	776	234	647	219	1,475	0
Arizona										
Under 18	24	83	10	91	2,187	221	8	310	3,917	0
Total, all ages	1,519	2,287	201	1,257	11,283	2,637	743	1,688	30,962	1
Arkansas										
Under 18	8	28	1	86	253	124	4	52	830	0
Total, all ages	804	1,584	27	1,022	1,308	997	198	192	11,391	39
California										
Under 18	80	241	8	1,806	4,959	4,211	205	1,356	9,284	10
Total, all ages	5,598	6,722	1,053	19,613	17,445	25,676	10,260	10,286	217,520	389
Colorado										
Under 18	10	82	1	56	1,136	303	13	191	3,056	0
Total, all ages	648	1,758	89	646	5,141	1,841	314	687	12,370	3
Connecticut										
Under 18	8	40	6	40	375	161	0	94	724	1
Total, all ages	574	1,018	185	318	1,936	1,030	221	427	9,137	14
Delaware										
Under 18	2	54	0	52	175	77	0	40	486	0
Total, all ages	386	1,795	196	394	907	332	100	188	6,250	3
District of Columbia										
Under 18	0	0	0	3	10	26	0	0	20	0
Total, all ages	10	2	1	8	28	67	3	0	323	0
Florida										
Under 18	42	433	13	175	1,363	808	28	184	7,994	5
Total, all ages	2,527	13,988	950	2,794	6,680	5,088	3,755	2,663	126,137	303
Georgia										
Under 18	69	241	8	441	571	613	25	461	2,986	5
Total, all ages	3,790	5,334	518	3,355	3,667	3,392	1,176	3,564	44,539	211
Hawaii										
Under 18	0	1	0	0	10	6	0	5	157	0
Total, all ages	10	5	0	0	80	112	6	40	1,087	70
Idaho										
Under 18	6	22	2	33	325	119	1	74	911	0
Total, all ages	169	373	52	250	981	437	14	266	7,591	32
Illinois										
Under 18	3	11	0	14	822	770	8	42	3,984	369
Total, all ages	188	202	1	72	3,096	3,438	1,424	562	35,001	2,019
Indiana										
Under 18	11	49	4	114	606	201	6	188	1,100	0
Total, all ages	755	1,047	145	710	1,464	1,437	725	1,057	12,470	74
Iowa										
Under 18	14	35	9	37	720	143	2	68	982	0
Total, all ages	566	724	72	244	2,069	711	113	224	9,182	4
Kansas										
Under 18	4	21	19	38	319	47	4	63	815	0
Total, all ages	370	940	202	380	2,002	594	245	246	8,130	3
Kentucky										
Under 18	18	10	6	163	165	94	3	54	697	2
Total, all ages	1,051	1,063	428	1,902	1,096	1,007	298	418	21,830	15
Louisiana										
Under 18	14	18	1	148	502	266	14	129	1,603	47
Total, all ages	659	1,643	158	1,273	2,758	1,815	529	760	20,727	83
Maine										
Under 18	5	9	0	19	286	17	0	52	501	0
Total, all ages	271	669	43	187	1,255	304	49	222	5,608	7
Maryland										
Under 18	26	29	4	9	586	309	2	88	2,406	11
Total, all ages	536	1,041	191	95	2,222	2,384	759	578	34,006	88
Massachusetts										
Under 18	16	24	1	163	461	161	1	53	382	0
Total, all ages	597	1,490	133	1,351	2,864	1,384	923	450	11,206	15
Michigan										
Under 18	18	257	16	202	619	410	5	160	2,434	5
Total, all ages	603	4,326	1,010	1,614	2,831	4,035	295	837	34,128	71
Minnesota										
Under 18	26	136	4	351	1,016	421	6	161	2,693	2
Total, all ages	984	2,145	25	1,895	3,213	1,736	721	1,201	19,056	33

Table 69.   Arrests, by State, 2013— continued

(Number)

State	Forgery and counterfeiting	Fraud	Embezzlement	Stolen prop- erty; buying, receiving, possessing	Vandalism	Weapons; car- rying, possess- ing, etc.	Prostitution and commercialized vice	Sex offenses (except forcible rape and pros- titution)	Drug abuse violations	Gambling
Mississippi										
Under 18	2	34	1	49	103	95	3	13	424	6
Total, all ages	374	954	437	480	673	705	149	187	8,037	81
Missouri										
Under 18	26	45	13	297	1,011	349	5	366	2,583	2
Total, all ages	1,554	2,601	299	2,488	4,637	3,050	222	1,509	35,131	192
Montana										
Under 18	2	9	3	5	281	16	0	15	359	0
Total, all ages	64	207	38	33	921	86	7	79	1,958	0
Nebraska										
Under 18	9	68	9	123	652	100	0	121	1,224	0
Total, all ages	385	1,348	82	639	2,103	956	164	502	10,366	6
Nevada										
Under 18	0	29	5	100	478	141	103	64	922	4
Total, all ages	727	1,416	393	1,358	1,586	1,560	3,550	1,080	11,207	10
New Hampshire										
Under 18	9	22	4	76	317	7	0	45	558	3
Total, all ages	282	899	47	736	1,242	96	48	164	4,270	18
New Jersey										
Under 18	29	67	6	460	850	661	18	224	4,022	32
Total, all ages	1,255	2,956	271	3,073	3,980	3,969	1,147	1,180	50,775	143
New Mexico										
Under 18	2	12	5	36	145	63	4	22	566	2
Total, all ages	176	366	165	676	891	402	265	119	4,773	7
New York										
Under 18	57	229	5	568	2,479	406	22	390	3,805	16
Total, all ages	2,952	5,444	90	4,661	15,131	3,248	1,158	2,191	61,633	117
North Carolina										
Under 18	30	298	16	402	1,101	1,044	14	145	2,435	2
Total, all ages	2,114	13,751	1,291	3,933	6,579	6,120	715	1,394	35,470	197
North Dakota										
Under 18	1	11	7	32	159	17	0	26	346	0
Total, all ages	77	377	36	141	453	333	43	77	3,345	2
Ohio										
Under 18	15	123	3	426	1,058	306	6	176	1,742	0
Total, all ages	1,141	2,376	39	3,072	3,684	2,781	1,710	680	28,612	16
Oklahoma										
Under 18	4	45	31	258	286	188	5	29	1,295	0
Total, all ages	612	1,666	436	2,571	1,241	2,148	320	498	16,946	11
Oregon										
Under 18	2	34	0	35	609	62	0	60	1,128	0
Total, all ages	330	901	19	290	2,080	847	49	338	10,009	0
Pennsylvania										
Under 18	55	168	26	283	2,216	1,151	24	481	4,076	7
Total, all ages	2,509	6,765	441	2,441	8,089	4,153	1,995	2,304	54,452	100
Rhode Island										
Under 18	0	17	1	37	205	89	0	26	168	0
Total, all ages	120	497	101	372	953	342	66	114	2,240	1
South Carolina										
Under 18	11	69	3	184	507	437	6	87	2,079	0
Total, all ages	1,508	4,692	364	2,251	3,018	2,033	473	453	28,838	102
South Dakota										
Under 18	0	42	5	32	181	43	1	17	813	0
Total, all ages	95	649	29	102	517	179	67	69	5,382	7
Tennessee										
Under 18	54	137	8	61	1,246	499	4	163	2,780	52
Total, all ages	1,940	7,165	727	701	4,399	3,351	1,507	799	46,923	344
Texas										
Under 18	89	274	21	105	2,547	717	89	639	12,304	15
Total, all ages	5,302	9,102	439	840	9,678	10,042	6,597	3,799	133,711	402
Utah										
Under 18	13	58	3	142	974	220	8	347	1,716	0
Total, all ages	729	977	26	1,068	3,161	1,114	177	850	13,377	3
Vermont										
Under 18										
Total, all ages	1	2	0	9	64	12	0	1	67	0
	58	271	50	177	328	22	9	37	1,250	0
Virginia										
Under 18	35	133	16	129	840	301	3	203	2,537	2
Total, all ages	1,990	6,151	1,520	978	4,255	3,501	862	1,031	39,536	58
Washington										
Under 18	12	20	2	220	1,087	264	6	149	1,881	0
Total, all ages	1,005	931	78	3,139	5,645	1,855	399	602	11,346	0

Table 69.   Arrests, by State, 2013— continued

(Number)

State	Forgery and counterfeiting	Fraud	Embezzlement	Stolen property; buying, receiving, possessing	Vandalism	Weapons; carrying, possessing, etc.	Prostitution and commercialized vice	Sex offenses (except forcible rape and prostitution)	Drug abuse violations	Gambling
West Virginia										
Under 18	0	10	1	6	60	18	1	14	162	0
Total, all ages	319	704	145	357	721	354	117	154	6,651	5
Wisconsin										
Under 18	26	173	14	427	1,846	726	23	885	3,495	20
Total, all ages	1,006	3,789	259	1,503	7,115	3,708	495	2,371	25,582	93
Wyoming										
Under 18	1	13	0	9	165	27	2	18	476	0
Total, all ages	58	200	8	64	560	91	32	139	3,527	0

Table 69.   Arrests, by State, 2013

(Number)

State	Offenses against the family and children	Driving under the influence	Liquor laws	Drunkenness[4]	Disorderly conduct	Vagrancy	All other offenses (except traffic)	Suspicion	Curfew and loitering law violations	Number of agencies	Estimated population, 2013
Alabama											
Under 18	0	1	11	1	8	0	8	0	0	1	84,139
Total, all ages	1	259	16	132	21	4	312	0	0		
Alaska											
Under 18	1	29	287	11	22	0	302	0	6	31	473,660
Total, all ages	224	2,689	1,385	100	939	607	10,693	0	6		
Arizona											
Under 18	200	291	3,266	0	1,769	10	3,860	0	1,890	86	6,466,774
Total, all ages	2,247	31,662	17,822	0	15,533	481	79,003	0	1,890		
Arkansas											
Under 18	1	67	333	95	864	0	1,932	0	243	230	2,746,564
Total, all ages	314	7,811	2,355	8,628	3,292	565	65,618	0	243		
California											
Under 18	4	598	2,267	1,699	4,078	175	18,057	0	3,883	685	38,284,824
Total, all ages	266	161,055	14,029	90,812	7,205	7,193	295,305	0	3,883		
Colorado											
Under 18	64	290	2,159	48	2,305	0	7,362	0	1,236	203	5,107,902
Total, all ages	3,183	28,723	13,377	238	10,359	367	99,945	0	1,236		
Connecticut											
Under 18	28	44	86	0	1,484	0	1,212	0	11	99	3,410,076
Total, all ages	1,284	8,207	377	6	10,032	16	25,301	0	11		
Delaware											
Under 18	2	1	160	9	301	0	376	0	52	46	923,312
Total, all ages	267	325	1,336	530	1,782	571	5,101	0	52		
District of Columbia											
Under 18	0	0	5	0	20	0	155	0	1	1	
Total, all ages	0	10	860	66	57	33	4,243	0	1		
Florida											
Under 18	0	230	1,061	0	0	0	23,853	0	0	614	19,487,611
Total, all ages	0	41,994	25,229	0	0	0	425,913	0	0		
Georgia											
Under 18	163	162	800	48	3,771	63	6,371	5	675	387	8,998,583
Total, all ages	3,634	25,912	7,649	2,657	23,724	1,133	94,916	84	675		
Hawaii											
Under 18	0	8	28	0	11	0	147	0	188	1	159,652
Total, all ages	11	998	133	0	139	0	4,458	0	188		
Idaho											
Under 18	8	89	760	112	298	0	2,742	0	338	107	1,606,277
Total, all ages	733	8,109	3,158	511	2,006	9	23,230	0	338		
Illinois											
Under 18	6	13	133	0	2,727	0	2,490	0	162	2	2,870,763
Total, all ages	311	3,868	614	0	11,639	44	17,685	0	162		
Indiana											
Under 18	70	68	1,434	107	1,124	18	2,347	123	317	138	3,817,113
Total, all ages	936	12,295	7,230	7,454	4,278	121	35,090	139	317		
Iowa											
Under 18	3	97	966	162	1,478	0	1,766	0	406	198	2,780,814
Total, all ages	1,279	9,825	5,181	11,256	5,515	38	25,870	0	406		
Kansas											
Under 18	10	83	627	4	252	0	992	0	0	238	2,068,879
Total, all ages	250	9,730	4,660	355	2,337	0	27,719	0	0		
Kentucky											
Under 18	3	69	42	98	284	7	944	0	2	369	4,315,933
Total, all ages	4,891	21,946	260	17,041	4,715	212	62,669	0	2		
Louisiana											
Under 18	40	34	103	35	2,168	47	2,610	16	138	138	3,114,237
Total, all ages	1,077	6,182	1,650	3,118	7,929	417	43,979	54	138		
Maine											
Under 18	4	51	727	2	135	0	753	0	50	179	1,326,033
Total, all ages	93	5,826	3,631	16	1,663	7	15,208	0	50		
Maryland											
Under 18	15	71	590	2	647	13	2,517	16	209	146	3,899,502
Total, all ages	1,828	14,793	3,265	80	3,930	269	56,212	288	209		
Massachusetts											
Under 18	62	57	639	201	712	1	1,733	6	0	318	6,411,005
Total, all ages	1,648	8,381	3,664	7,256	6,522	16	35,755	58	0		
Michigan											
Under 18	4	244	1,957	12	754	0	3,425	0	419	534	9,198,477
Total, all ages	3,578	27,643	12,941	367	7,326	269	79,464	0	419		
Minnesota											
Under 18	11	203	2,786	0	2,604	23	3,345	0	2,150	326	5,419,634
Total, all ages	685	21,206	14,072	0	10,832	323	29,357	0	2,150		

Table 69.   Arrests, by State, 2013— continued

(Number)

State	Offenses against the family and children	Driving under the influence	Liquor laws	Drunkenness[4]	Disorderly conduct	Vagrancy	All other offenses (except traffic)	Suspicion	Curfew and loitering law violations	Number of agencies	Estimated population, 2013
Mississippi											
Under 18	248	51	72	39	870	3	1,080	5	159	61	1,289,404
Total, all ages	2,684	7,764	864	4,197	4,606	140	22,602	129	159		
Missouri											
Under 18	52	202	1,412	25	1,663	5	3,934	0	1,126	368	5,567,717
Total, all ages	3,156	23,950	8,090	586	11,253	400	100,474	0	1,126		
Montana											
Under 18	56	69	868	0	531	0	753	0	490	91	970,435
Total, all ages	288	4,300	2,876	0	3,272	24	6,363	0	490		
Nebraska											
Under 18	12	126	1,072	0	631	2	1,447	0	137	198	1,659,743
Total, all ages	1,248	9,193	7,177	0	2,724	52	13,749	0	137		
Nevada											
Under 18	31	50	1,013	67	206	5	1,959	0	864	31	2,543,547
Total, all ages	925	8,841	5,968	175	1,495	2,073	45,192	2	864		
New Hampshire											
Under 18	1	36	604	212	178	0	1,077	0	17	148	1,174,048
Total, all ages	175	3,700	3,410	3,263	1,191	72	13,355	0	17		
New Jersey											
Under 18	108	153	1,053	0	1,868	25	3,344	0	1,000	482	8,585,551
Total, all ages	11,168	23,765	3,753	0	13,653	233	116,439	0	1,000		
New Mexico											
Under 18	18	34	203	1	134	0	1,072	0	0	50	1,349,565
Total, all ages	782	6,352	2,404	79	1,762	0	25,569	0	0		
New York											
Under 18	36	170	502	0	1,126	11	3,467	0	0	435	10,496,474
Total, all ages	342	29,977	2,893	0	9,750	798	53,135	0	0		
North Carolina											
Under 18	60	318	962	0	2,613	0	4,628	0	0	306	8,759,566
Total, all ages	7,462	41,247	7,877	0	10,608	269	127,599	0	0		
North Dakota											
Under 18	53	38	661	2	655	0	811	0	88	98	714,526
Total, all ages	133	7,077	3,985	338	1,848	6	6,375	0	88		
Ohio											
Under 18	161	94	904	15	1,567	20	5,529	3	492	416	8,369,913
Total, all ages	1,532	33,808	7,208	1,722	13,498	35	48,940	51	492		
Oklahoma											
Under 18	74	108	210	438	675	0	2,230	0	1,239	319	3,707,079
Total, all ages	666	13,244	1,590	16,713	2,419	6	31,361	0	1,239		
Oregon											
Under 18	5	35	879	0	323	0	997	0	391	106	1,451,298
Total, all ages	252	6,699	3,452	0	3,282	1	9,446	0	391		
Pennsylvania											
Under 18	35	380	3,691	232	9,731	49	4,390	0	17,143	1,148	11,907,015
Total, all ages	1,717	45,744	15,432	22,919	44,251	505	56,227	0	17,143		
Rhode Island											
Under 18	66	16	56	1	597	0	546	0	25	48	1,051,511
Total, all ages	102	2,576	645	38	2,767	1	11,212	0	25		
South Carolina											
Under 18	17	99	532	74	2,139	0	1,749	0	24	261	4,599,031
Total, all ages	1,480	18,919	7,855	9,519	14,052	581	26,847	0	24		
South Dakota											
Under 18	123	80	1,058	3	243	0	702	5	167	112	777,314
Total, all ages	329	6,328	4,242	85	2,038	290	6,863	0	167		
Tennessee											
Under 18	57	118	782	237	2,476	0	5,371	0	1,870	454	6,413,655
Total, all ages	3,146	26,276	7,191	17,612	9,598	26	142,087	0	1,870		
Texas											
Under 18	91	456	2,690	1,583	7,322	134	15,610	0	4,087	889	25,561,086
Total, all ages	5,003	78,352	17,120	92,767	20,602	906	275,472	0	4,087		
Utah											
Under 18	19	85	1,168	137	1,303	29	4,983	0	936	124	2,782,447
Total, all ages	1,423	9,038	6,930	4,076	4,361	55	52,454	0	936		
Vermont											
Under 18											
Total, all ages	5	16	84	2	66	0	129	0	0	67	577,603
	252	2,476	243	3	743	0	3,538	0	0		
Virginia											
Under 18	45	104	1,316	159	769	0	5,230	0	1,457	355	8,250,187
Total, all ages	2,628	25,813	10,353	28,325	4,536	186	108,073	0	1,457		
Washington											
Under 18	19	190	1,324	3	303	11	2,140	0	7	228	5,937,459
Total, all ages	448	29,153	4,586	30	3,533	134	57,333	0	7		

Table 69.   Arrests, by State, 2013— continued

(Number)

State	Offenses against the family and children	Driving under the influence	Liquor laws	Drunkenness[4]	Disorderly conduct	Vagrancy	All other offenses (except traffic)	Suspicion	Curfew and loitering law violations	Number of agencies	Estimated population, 2013
West Virginia											
Under 18	0	21	99	6	26	0	392	0	36	252	1,587,813
Total, all ages	83	5,960	1,758	2,440	885	11	14,289	0	36		
Wisconsin											
Under 18	127	295	4,164	0	10,344	57	16,211	0	3,534	382	5,621,676
Total, all ages	2,445	26,562	20,590	3	43,614	2,080	98,255	0	3,534		
Wyoming											
Under 18	6	49	581	20	143	25	852	1	269	59	551,885
Total, all ages	203	3,893	2,703	2,523	1,026	54	9,938	39	269		

NOTE: Because the number of agencies submitting arrest data varies from year to year, users are cautioned about making direct comparisons between 2013 arrest totals and those published in previous years' editions of Crime in the United States. Further, arrest figures may vary widely from state to state because some Part II crimes are not considered crimes in some states.   1 Does not include traffic arrests.   2 Violent crimes are offenses of murder and nonnegligent manslaughter, forcible rape, robbery, and aggravated assault. Property crimes are offenses of burglary, larceny-theft, motor vehicle theft, and arson.   3 The rape figures in this table are an aggregate total of the data submitted using both the revised and legacy Uniform Crime Reporting definitions.   4 Drunkenness is not considered a crime in some states; therefore, the figures vary widely from state to state.

SECTION V

LAW ENFORCEMENT PERSONNEL

LAW ENFORCEMENT PERSONNEL

Figure 5.1 Average Number of Officers and Employees in Cities, by Region, 2013

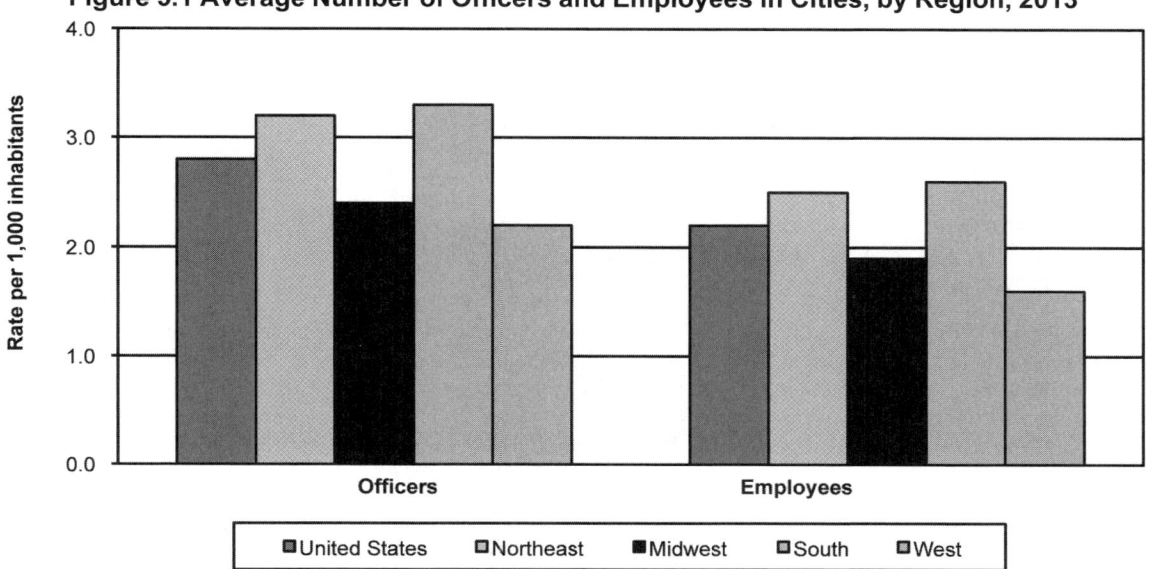

The Uniform Crime Reporting (UCR) program defines law enforcement officers as individuals who ordinarily carry a firearm and a badge, have full arrest powers, and are paid from government funds set aside specifically for sworn law enforcement representatives. Because of law enforcement's varied service requirements and functions, as well as the distinct demographic traits and characteristics of jurisdictions, readers should use caution when comparing staffing levels between agencies based on police employment data from the UCR program. In addition, the data presented here reflect existing staff levels and should not be interpreted as preferred officer strengths recommended by the Federal Bureau of Investigation (FBI). Also, readers should note that the totals given for sworn officers for any particular agency reflect both patrol officers on the street and officers assigned to various other duties, such as administrative and investigative positions and assignments to special teams.

Each year, law enforcement agencies across the United States report the total number of sworn law enforcement officers and civilians in their agencies as of October 31 to the UCR program. Civilian employees include personnel such as clerks, radio dispatchers, meter attendants, stenographers, jailers, correctional officers, and mechanics, (provided that they are full-time employees of the agency).

This section of Crime in the United States presents those data as the number and rate of law enforcement officers and civilian employees throughout the United States. In 2013, 626,942 sworn officers and 275,468 civilians provided law enforcement services to more than 268 million people nationwide. These law enforcement personnel were employed by 13,051 state, city, university/college, metropolitan/ nonmetropolitan county, and other designated law enforcement agencies. Of the slightly less than 1 million law enforcement employees, 73.4 percent were male. (Table 74)

The data in this section are broken down by geographic region and division, population group, state, city, university/college, metropolitan/nonmetropolitan county, and other law enforcement agency groups. (Information about geographic regions and divisions and population groups can be found in Appendix III.) UCR program staff compute the rate of sworn officers and law enforcement employees by taking the number of employees (sworn officers only or in combination with civilians), dividing by the population for which the agency provides law enforcement service, and multiplying by 1,000.

- Tables 70 and 71 present the number and rate of law enforcement personnel per 1,000 inhabitants collectively employed by agencies, broken down by geographic region and division by population group

- Tables 72 and 73 provide a count of law enforcement agencies by population group, based on the employment rate ranges for sworn officer and civilian employees per 1,000 inhabitants

- Table 74 provides the number of total officers, the percentage of male and female sworn officers, and the civilian employees by population group

- Table 75 lists the percentage of full-time civilian law enforcement employees by population group

- Table 76 breaks down by state the number of sworn law enforcement officers and civilians employed by state law enforcement agencies

- Table 77 provides the number of total officers, the percentage of male and female sworn officers, and the civilian employees by state

- Tables 78 to 80 list the number of law enforcement employees for cities, universities and colleges, and metropolitan and nonmetropolitan counties

- Table 81 supplies employee data for those law enforcement agencies that serve selected transit systems, parks and forests, schools and school districts, hospitals, etc., in the nation

The demographic traits and characteristics of a jurisdiction affect its requirements for law enforcement service. For instance, a village between two large cities may require more law enforcement than a community of the same size with no urban center nearby. A town with legal gambling may have different law enforcement needs than a town near a military base. A city largely made up of college students may have different law enforcement needs than a city whose residents are mainly retirees.

Similarly, the functions of law enforcement agencies are diverse. Employees of these agencies patrol local streets and major highways, protect citizens in the nation's smallest towns and largest cities, and conduct investigations on offenses at the local and state levels. State police in one area may enforce traffic laws on state highways and interstates; in another area, they may be responsible for investigating violent crimes. Sheriff's departments may collect tax monies, serve as the enforcement authority for local and state courts, administer jail facilities, or carry out some combination of these duties. This has an impact on an agency's staffing levels.

Because of the differing service requirements and functions, care should be taken when drawing comparisons between and among the staffing levels of law enforcement agencies. The data in this section are not intended as recommended or preferred officer strength; they should be used merely as guides. Adequate staffing levels can be determined only after careful study of the conditions that affect the service requirements in a particular jurisdiction.

Rate

The UCR program computes these rates by taking the number of employees, dividing by the population of the agency's jurisdiction, and multiplying by 1,000.

An examination of the 2013 law enforcement employee data by population group showed that the nation's cities had a collective rate of 2.8 law enforcement employees per 1,000 inhabitants. Cities with fewer than 10,000 inhabitants had the highest rate of law enforcement employees, with a rate of 4,5 per 1,000 inhabitants. Cities with 50,000 to 99,999 inhabitants had the lowest rate of law enforcement employees (2.1 per 1,000 in population). The nation's largest cities, those with 250,000 or more inhabitants, averaged 3.4 law enforcement employees for every 1,000 inhabitants. (Table 70) These rates are either static or do not significantly differentiate from their 2012 levels.

Sworn Personnel

An analysis of the 2013 data showed that law enforcement agencies in the cities in the Northeast and the South had the highest rate of sworn officers—at rates of 2.5 and 2.6 per 1,000 inhabitants, respectively, followed by the Midwest (1.9), and the West (1.6). (Table 71)

By population group in 2013, there were 2.2 sworn officers for each 1,000 resident population. This rate remained static from 2012 to 2013. Cities with fewer than 10,000 inhabitants had the highest rate at 3.5 sworn officers per 1,000 inhabitants. The nation's largest cities, those with 250,000 or more inhabitants, averaged 2.6 officers per 1,000 inhabitants, the same as in 2012. (Table 71)

Males accounted for 88.4 percent of all full-time sworn law enforcement officers in 2013, three-tenths of a percentage point more than in 2012. Cities with populations of 1 million and over employed the highest percentage (17.0 percent) of full-time female officers. Of the city population groups, cities with populations of 10,000 to 24,999 inhabitants employed the highest percentage (92.1 percent) of male officers. In metropolitan counties, 87.1 percent of officers were male, and in nonmetropolitan counties, 92.6 percent of officers were male. (Table 74)

Civilian Employees

Civilian employees provide a myriad of services to the nation's law enforcement and criminal justice agencies. Among other duties, they dispatch officers, provide administrative and record keeping support, and query local, state, and national databases.

In 2013, 39.3 percent of all law enforcement employees in the nation were civilians. Male employees accounted for 60.7 percent of all full-time civilian law enforcement employees in 2013. In cities, civilians made up 32.1 percent of law enforcement agencies employees. Civilians made up 44.9 percent of law enforcement employees in metropolitan counties, 42.5 percent of law enforcement employees in nonmetropolitan counties, and 42.9 percent of law enforcement employees in suburban areas. (Table 74)

Table 70.   Full-Time Law Enforcement Employees,[1] by Region and Geographic Division and Population Group, 2013

(Number, rate per 1,000 inhabitants)

Region/geographic division	Total	250,000 and over population	100,000 to 249,999 population	50,000 to 99,999 population	25,000 to 49,999 population	10,000 to 24,999 population	under 10,000 population	Total city agencies	City population, 2013, estimated
Total									
Number of employees	503,227	175,797	63,410	57,806	53,525	58,127	94,562	9,894	179,802,240
Average number of employees per 1,000 inhabitants	2.8	3.4	2.2	2.1	2.2	2.3	4.5		
Northeast									
Number of employees	141,190	63,599	8,446	14,450	17,059	18,043	19,593	2,511	43,905,307
Average number of employees per 1,000 inhabitants	3.2	5.4	3.0	2.3	2.2	2.1	3.1		
New England									
Number of employees	33,950	2,704	4,426	6,086	6,841	7,168	6,725	796	13,004,141
Average number of employees per 1,000 inhabitants	2.6	4.2	3.0	2.3	2.2	2.2	3.7		
Middle Atlantic									
Number of employees	107,240	60,895	4,020	8,364	10,218	10,875	12,868	1,715	30,901,166
Average number of employees per 1,000 inhabitants	3.5	5.5	2.9	2.3	2.2	2.0	2.8		
Midwest									
Number of employees	79,766	19,889	8,195	10,919	10,402	13,049	17,312	2,418	33,568,819
Average number of employees per 1,000 inhabitants	2.4	3.1	2.1	1.8	1.9	2.0	3.2		
East North Central									
Number of employees	48,115	13,024	4,469	6,838	7,149	7,671	8,964	1,247	20,345,551
Average number of employees per 1,000 inhabitants	2.4	3.1	2.2	1.9	1.9	2.0	3.1		
West North Central									
Number of employees	31,651	6,865	3,726	4,081	3,253	5,378	8,348	1,171	13,223,268
Average number of employees per 1,000 inhabitants	2.4	3.2	2.1	1.7	1.9	2.1	3.3		
South									
Number of employees	175,764	45,570	27,180	18,377	17,870	20,793	45,974	3,683	53,170,268
Average number of employees per 1,000 inhabitants	3.3	3.1	2.6	2.6	2.6	2.9	6.5		
South Atlantic									
Number of employees	88,525	22,199	14,801	9,662	9,002	9,930	22,931	1,644	23,704,335
Average number of employees per 1,000 inhabitants	3.7	4.0	2.8	2.8	2.8	3.1	7.8		
East South Central									
Number of employees	31,430	7,256	4,641	2,517	3,576	4,321	9,119	824	9,149,063
Average number of employees per 1,000 inhabitants	3.4	2.9	3.3	2.8	2.6	3.1	5.8		
West South Central									
Number of employees	55,809	16,115	7,738	6,198	5,292	6,542	13,924	1,215	20,316,870
Average number of employees per 1,000 inhabitants	2.7	2.5	2.1	2.2	2.4	2.5	5.5		
West									
Number of employees	106,507	46,739	19,589	14,060	8,194	6,242	11,683	1,282	49,157,846
Average number of employees per 1,000 inhabitants	2.2	2.5	1.7	1.7	1.7	2.0	5.1		
Mountain									
Number of employees	35,556	14,983	6,750	3,675	2,953	2,108	5,087	519	14,532,260
Average number of employees per 1,000 inhabitants	2.4	2.6	1.9	2.0	1.9	2.3	4.7		
Pacific									
Number of employees	70,951	31,756	12,839	10,385	5,241	4,134	6,596	763	34,625,586
Average number of employees per 1,000 inhabitants	2.0	2.4	1.6	1.6	1.7	1.9	5.4		

1 Full-time law enforcement employees include civilians.

Table 71. Full-Time Law Enforcement Officers, by Region and Geographic Division, and Population Group, 2013

(Number, rate per 1,000 inhabitants.)

Region/geographic division	Total	250,000 and over population	100,000 to 249,999 population	50,000 to 99,999 population	25,000 to 49,999 population	10,000 to 24,999 population	under 10,000 population	Total city agencies	City population, 2013, estimated
Total									
Number of officers	389,934	133,309	48,284	44,972	42,624	47,120	73,625	9,894	179,802,240
Average number of officers per 1,000 inhabitants	2.2	2.6	1.7	1.6	1.7	1.8	3.5		
Northeast									
Number of officers	111,953	46,840	7,165	12,023	14,343	15,317	16,265	2,511	43,905,307
Average number of officers per 1,000 inhabitants	2.5	4.0	2.5	1.9	1.8	1.7	2.5		
New England									
Number of officers	28,083	2,131	3,808	5,208	5,722	5,818	5,396	796	13,004,141
Average number of officers per 1,000 inhabitants	2.2	3.3	2.6	1.9	1.8	1.8	3.0		
Middle Atlantic									
Number of officers	83,870	44,709	3,357	6,815	8,621	9,499	10,869	1,715	30,901,166
Average number of officers per 1,000 inhabitants	2.7	4.0	2.5	1.9	1.8	1.7	2.4		
Midwest									
Number of officers	65,308	16,190	6,756	8,888	8,287	10,706	14,481	2,418	33,568,819
Average number of officers per 1,000 inhabitants	1.9	2.5	1.7	1.5	1.5	1.7	2.7		
East North Central									
Number of officers	39,878	11,017	3,749	5,587	5,755	6,315	7,455	1,247	20,345,551
Average number of officers per 1,000 inhabitants	2.0	2.6	1.8	1.6	1.5	1.7	2.6		
West North Central									
Number of officers	25,430	5,173	3,007	3,301	2,532	4,391	7,026	1,171	13,223,268
Average number of officers per 1,000 inhabitants	1.9	2.4	1.7	1.4	1.5	1.7	2.7		
South									
Number of officers	135,928	36,010	20,666	14,103	14,065	16,308	34,776	3,683	53,170,268
Average number of officers per 1,000 inhabitants	2.6	2.5	2.0	2.0	2.1	2.3	4.9		
South Atlantic									
Number of officers	68,956	17,098	11,439	7,514	7,184	8,023	17,698	1,644	23,704,335
Average number of officers per 1,000 inhabitants	2.9	3.1	2.2	2.2	2.3	2.5	6.0		
East South Central									
Number of officers	24,843	5,965	3,486	1,971	2,884	3,379	7,158	824	9,149,063
Average number of officers per 1,000 inhabitants	2.7	2.4	2.5	2.2	2.1	2.4	4.5		
West South Central									
Number of officers	42,129	12,947	5,741	4,618	3,997	4,906	9,920	1,215	20,316,870
Average number of officers per 1,000 inhabitants	2.1	2.0	1.6	1.7	1.8	1.9	3.9		
West									
Number of officers	76,745	34,269	13,697	9,958	5,929	4,789	8,103	1,282	49,157,846
Average number of officers per 1,000 inhabitants	1.6	1.8	1.2	1.2	1.3	1.5	3.5		
Mountain									
Number of officers	24,845	10,128	4,794	2,590	2,172	1,642	3,519	519	14,532,260
Average number of officers per 1,000 inhabitants	1.7	1.8	1.4	1.4	1.4	1.8	3.2		
Pacific									
Number of officers	51,900	24,141	8,903	7,368	3,757	3,147	4,584	763	34,625,586
Average number of officers per 1,000 inhabitants	1.5	1.8	1.1	1.1	1.2	1.4	3.7		

Table 72.   Full-Time Law Enforcement Employees,[1] Range in Rate, by Population Group, 2013

(Number, rate per 1,000 inhabitants.)

Rate range	Total cities[2]	Group I	Group II	Group III	Group IV	Group V	Group VI
Total Cities							
Number	8,844	73	193	405	719	1,597	5,857
Percent[3]	100.0	100.0	100.0	100.0	100.0	100.0	100.0
0.1–0.5							
Number	104	0	0	0	1	5	98
Percent	1.2	0.0	0.0	0.0	0.1	0.3	1.7
0.6–1.0							
Number	484	0	2	10	20	50	402
Percent	5.5	0.0	1.0	2.5	2.8	3.1	6.9
1.1–1.5							
Number	1,185	4	42	86	128	228	697
Percent	13.4	5.5	21.8	21.2	17.8	14.3	11.9
1.6–2.0							
Number	1,794	12	53	122	202	392	1,013
Percent	20.3	16.4	27.5	30.1	28.1	24.5	17.3
2.1–2.5							
Number	1,666	21	42	102	195	400	906
Percent	18.8	28.8	21.8	25.2	27.1	25.0	15.5
2.6–3.0							
Number	1,167	9	28	51	97	259	723
Percent	13.2	12.3	14.5	12.6	13.5	16.2	12.3
3.1–3.5							
Number	777	9	18	18	39	133	560
Percent	8.8	12.3	9.3	4.4	5.4	8.3	9.6
3.6–4.0							
Number	474	6	2	9	25	66	366
Percent	5.4	8.2	1.0	2.2	3.5	4.1	6.2
4.1–4.5							
Number	314	5	5	4	4	29	267
Percent	3.6	6.8	2.6	1.0	0.6	1.8	4.6
4.6–5.0							
Number	213	2	0	1	4	15	191
Percent	2.4	2.7	0.0	0.2	0.6	0.9	3.3
5.1 and over							
Number	666	5	1	2	4	20	634
Percent	7.5	6.8	0.5	0.5	0.6	1.3	10.8

Note: Group I: 250,000 and over population. Group II: 100,000 to 249,999 population. Group III: 50,000 to 99,999 population. Group IV: 25,000 to 49,999 population. Group V: 10,000 to 24,999 population. Group VI: under 10,000 population.   1 Full-time law enforcement employees include civilians.   2 The number of agencies used to compile these figures differs from other tables that include data about law enforcement employees because agencies with no resident population are excluded from this table. These agencies include those associated with universities and colleges (see Table 79) and other agencies (see Table 81), as well as some state agencies that have concurrent jurisdiction with other local law enforcement.   3 Because of rounding, the percentages may not sum to 100.

Table 73.   Full-Time Law Enforcement Officers, Range in Rate, by Population Group, 2013

(Number, rate per 1,000 inhabitants.)

Rate range	Total cities[1]	Group I	Group II	Group III	Group IV	Group V	Group VI
Total Cities							
Number	8,844	73	193	405	719	1,597	5,857
Percent[2]	100.0	100.0	100.0	100.0	100.0	100.0	100.0
0.1–0.5							
Number	116	0	0	0	5	5	106
Percent	1.3	0.0	0.0	0.0	0.7	0.3	1.8
0.6–1.0							
Number	719	4	30	60	66	100	459
Percent	8.1	5.5	15.5	14.8	9.2	6.3	7.8
1.1–1.5							
Number	1,825	13	69	141	248	435	919
Percent	20.6	17.8	35.8	34.8	34.5	27.2	15.7
1.6–2.0							
Number	2,220	25	48	131	232	547	1,237
Percent	25.1	34.2	24.9	32.3	32.3	34.3	21.1
2.1–2.5							
Number	1,472	9	30	48	102	297	986
Percent	16.6	12.3	15.5	11.9	14.2	18.6	16.8
2.6–3.0							
Number	935	8	7	16	50	128	726
Percent	10.6	11.0	3.6	4.0	7.0	8.0	12.4
3.1–3.5							
Number	527	6	7	6	11	45	452
Percent	6.0	8.2	3.6	1.5	1.5	2.8	7.7
3.6–4.0							
Number	295	3	2	1	2	24	263
Percent	3.3	4.1	1.0	0.2	0.3	1.5	4.5
4.1–4.5							
Number	201	4	0	2	0	10	185
Percent	2.3	5.5	0.0	0.5	0.0	0.6	3.2
4.6–5.0							
Number	115	0	0	0	0	2	113
Percent	1.3	0.0	0.0	0.0	0.0	0.1	1.9
5.1 and over							
Number	419	1	0	0	3	4	411
Percent	4.7	1.4	0.0	0.0	0.4	0.3	7.0

Note: Group I: 250,000 and over population. Group II: 100,000 to 249,999 population. Group III: 50,000 to 99,999 population. Group IV: 25,000 to 49,999 population. Group V: 10,000 to 24,999 population. Group VI: under 10,000 population.   1 The number of agencies used to compile these figures differs from other tables that include data about law enforcement employees because agencies with no resident population are excluded from this table. These agencies include those associated with universities and colleges (see Table 79) and other agencies (see Table 81), as well as some state agencies that have concurrent jurisdiction with other local law enforcement.   2 Because of rounding, the percentages may not sum to 100.

Table 74.   Full-Time Law Enforcement Employees, by Population Group, Percent Male and Female, 2013

(Number, percent.)

Population group	Total law enforcement employees (number)	Law enforcement employees (percent)		Total officers (number)	Officers (percent)		Civilians (number)	Civilians (percent)		Agencies (number)	Population, 2013, estimated
		Male	Female		Male	Female		Male	Female		
Total Agencies	902,410	73.4	26.6	626,942	88.4	11.6	275,468	39.3	60.7	13,051	268,684,780
Total Cities	503,227	75.6	24.4	389,934	88.3	11.7	113,293	32.1	67.9	9,894	179,802,240
Group I (250,000 and over)	175,797	72.0	28.0	133,309	84.0	16.0	42,488	34.3	65.7	73	51,744,651
1,000,000 and over (Group I subset)	87,468	70.1	29.9	64,168	83.0	17.0	23,300	34.5	65.5	8	20,834,644
500,000 to 999,999 (Group I subset)	49,447	75.5	24.5	39,168	85.1	14.9	10,279	38.7	61.3	23	16,417,960
250,000 to 499,999 (Group I subset)	38,882	72.0	28.0	29,973	84.8	15.2	8,909	28.8	71.2	42	14,492,047
Group II (100,000 to 249,999)	63,410	73.3	26.7	48,284	88.1	11.9	15,126	26.0	74.0	193	28,587,514
Group III (50,000 to 99,999)	57,806	76.8	23.2	44,972	90.4	9.6	12,834	29.2	70.8	405	27,923,876
Group IV (25,000 to 49,999)	53,525	78.1	21.9	42,624	90.8	9.2	10,901	28.1	71.9	719	24,881,626
Group V (10,000 to 24,999)	58,127	79.7	20.3	47,120	92.1	7.9	11,007	26.8	73.2	1,597	25,483,611
Group VI (under 10,000)	94,562	79.4	20.6	73,625	90.8	9.2	20,937	39.0	61.0	6,907	21,180,962
Metropolitan Counties	287,561	70.2	29.8	172,044	87.1	12.9	115,517	44.9	55.1	1,256	66,747,452
Nonmetropolitan Counties	111,622	71.6	28.4	64,964	92.6	7.4	46,658	42.5	57.5	1,901	22,135,088
Suburban Areas [1]	434,810	73.2	26.8	287,855	88.6	11.4	146,955	42.9	57.1	6,969	117,915,697

1 Suburban areas include law enforcement agencies in cities with less than 50,000 inhabitants and county law enforcement agencies that are within a Metropolitan Statistical Area. Suburban areas exclude all metropolitan agencies associated with a principal city. The agencies associated with suburban areas also appear in other groups within this table.

Table 75. Full-Time Civilian Law Enforcement Employees, by Population Group, 2013

(Number, percent.)

Population group	Civilian employees (percent)	Agencies (number)	Population, 2013, estimated
Total Agencies	30.5	13,051	268,684,780
Total Cities	22.5	9,894	179,802,240
Group I (250,000 and over)	24.2	73	51,744,651
1,000,000 and over (Group I subset)	26.6	8	20,834,644
500,000 to 999,999 (Group I subset)	20.8	23	16,417,960
250,000 to 499,999 (Group I subset)	22.9	42	14,492,047
Group II (100,000 to 249,999)	23.9	193	28,587,5`4
Group III (50,000 to 99,999)	22.2	405	27,923,876
Group IV (25,000 to 49,999)	20.4	719	24,881,626
Group V (10,000 to 24,999)	18.9	1,597	25,483,611
Group VI (under 10,000)	22.1	6,907	21,180,962
Metropolitan Counties	40.2	1,256	66,747,452
Nonmetropolitan Counties	41.8	1,901	22,135,088
Suburban Areas [1]	33.8	6,969	117,915,697

1Suburban areas include law enforcement agencies in cities with less than 50,000 inhabitants and county law enforcement agencies that are within a Metropolitan Statistical Area. Suburban areas exclude all metropolitan agencies associated with a principal city. The agencies associated with suburban areas also appear in other groups within this table.

Table 76.   Full-Time State Law Enforcement Employees, by Selected State, 2013

(Number.)

State/agency	Law enforcement employees	Officers		Civilians	
		Male	Female	Male	Female
Alabama [1]					
Other state agencies	258	197	7	16	38
Alaska					
State Troopers	643	435	19	51	138
Arizona					
Department of Public Safety	1,899	1,051	45	337	466
Arkansas [1]					
Other state agencies	31	29	0	0	2
California					
Highway Patrol	10,623	6,724	512	1,454	1,933
Other state agencies[2]	1,275	938	198	38	101
Colorado					
State Patrol	932	620	49	57	206
Other state agencies	295	51	5	82	157
Connecticut					
State Police	1,661	1,040	89	251	281
Other state agencies	37	27	1	7	2
Delaware					
State Police	924	608	75	102	139
Other state agencies	668	296	103	58	211
Florida					
Highway Patrol	2,335	1,637	209	157	332
Other state agencies	3,304	1,450	216	539	1,099
Georgia [1]					
Other state agencies	1,077	312	84	226	455
Idaho					
State Police	463	246	14	50	153
Illinois					
State Police	2,910	1,570	180	459	701
Other state agencies	221	110	9	65	37
Indiana					
State Police	1,780	1,172	56	233	319
Other state agencies	8	7	0	0	1
Iowa					
Department of Public Safety	896	559	34	150	153
Kansas					
Highway Patrol	768	468	19	113	168
Other state agencies	500	296	17	62	125
Kentucky					
State Police	1,687	953	23	336	375
Other state agencies	366	298	7	38	23
Louisiana					
State Police	1,722	1,095	69	179	379
Maine					
State Police	440	287	24	59	70
Other state agencies[2]	48	20	2	19	7
Maryland					
State Police	2,184	1,377	107	342	358
Other state agencies	1,646	873	135	317	321
Massachusetts					
State Police	2,609	1,970	139	195	305
Other state agencies	336	286	35	6	9
Michigan					
State Police	2,530	1,505	181	356	488
Minnesota					
State Patrol	740	482	55	103	100

Table 76.   Full-Time State Law Enforcement Employees, by Selected State, 2013— continued

(Number.)

State/agency	Law enforcement employees	Officers		Civilians	
		Male	Female	Male	Female
Other state agencies	60	11	2	39	8
Mississippi [1]					
Other state agencies	74	57	3	2	12
Missouri					
State Highway Patrol	2,269	1,110	58	497	604
Other state agencies	451	396	33	0	22
Montana					
Highway Patrol	278	213	10	15	40
Other state agencies	24	16	0	2	6
Nebraska					
State Patrol	696	427	25	83	161
Nevada					
Highway Patrol	558	399	46	46	67
New Hampshire					
State Police	508	302	31	58	117
New Jersey					
State Police	3,704	2,352	105	590	657
Other state agencies[2]	29	26	0	1	2
New York					
State Police	5,489	4,205	399	357	528
Other state agencies	187	160	14	3	10
North Carolina					
Highway Patrol	2,125	1,558	46	313	208
Other state agencies	1,078	682	117	104	175
North Dakota					
Highway Patrol	194	140	9	13	32
Ohio					
Highway Patrol	2,421	1,466	142	402	411
Other state agencies	397	318	23	17	39
Oklahoma					
Department of Public Safety	1,400	765	20	272	343
Other state agencies	120	51	7	50	12
Oregon					
State Police	745	563	43	48	91
Other state agencies	92	68	12	0	12
Pennsylvania					
State Police	6,073	3,957	211	910	995
Other state agencies	379	289	19	44	27
Rhode Island					
State Police	273	206	21	28	18
Other state agencies	86	64	4	11	7
South Carolina					
Highway Patrol	1,010	805	29	51	125
Other state agencies[2]	1,148	698	139	96	215
South Dakota					
Highway Patrol	244	158	3	52	31
Other state agencies	167	46	4	40	77
Tennessee					
Department of Safety	1,655	779	36	258	582
Other state agencies	1,168	650	148	139	231
Texas					
Department of Public Safety	9,178	3,280	214	1,925	3,759
Utah [1]					
Other state agencies	54	48	5	0	1
Vermont					
State Police	447	246	30	72	99
Other state agencies	120	88	6	9	17

Table 76.   Full-Time State Law Enforcement Employees, by Selected State, 2013— continued

(Number.)

State/agency	Law enforcement employees	Officers		Civilians	
		Male	Female	Male	Female
Virginia					
State Police	2,750	1,914	111	245	480
Other state agencies	757	486	60	80	131
Washington					
State Patrol	2,204	966	87	577	574
Other state agencies	141	59	22	16	44
West Virginia					
State Police	1,046	645	20	145	236
Other state agencies	209	165	0	17	27
Wisconsin					
State Patrol	623	414	49	72	88
Other state agencies	376	283	55	17	21
Wyoming					
Highway Patrol	327	177	8	61	81

Note: Caution should be used when comparing data from one state to another. The responsibilities of the various state police, highway patrol, and department of public safety agencies range from full law enforcement duties to traffic patrol only, which can affect the data for the level of employment for agencies as well as the ratio of sworn officers to civilians employed. Any valid comparison must take these factors and the other identified variables affecting crime into consideration.   1 Police Employee data were not received from the State Police/Highway Patrol/Department of Public Safety for the state.   2 The total employee count includes employees from agencies that are not represented in other law enforcement employee tables.

Table 77.   Full-Time Law Enforcement Employees, by State, 2013

(Number.)

State	Total law enforcement employees	Total officers		Total civilians		Total agencies	Population, 2013, estimated
		Male	Female	Male	Female		
Alabama	14,173	8,773	719	1,718	2,963	296	4,255,554
Alaska	1,937	1,202	110	187	438	36	732,933
Arizona	21,192	10,702	1,253	4,343	4,894	96	6,452,958
Arkansas	9,250	5,402	491	1,321	2,036	275	2,931,406
California	117,322	66,880	10,032	14,813	25,597	460	32,855,611
Colorado	17,441	10,389	1,592	1,803	3,657	236	5,250,935
Connecticut	10,349	7,716	801	778	1,054	102	3,596,080
Delaware	3,168	2,021	318	318	511	54	924,670
District of Columbia	5,065	3,546	1,033	201	285	2	646,449
Florida	67,816	36,331	6,015	9,096	16,374	345	17,707,637
Georgia	29,070	18,027	3,471	2,408	5,164	384	7,874,446
Hawaii	3,658	2,612	274	244	528	4	1,404,054
Idaho	4,272	2,547	160	297	1,268	108	1,611,052
Illinois	14,563	8,606	814	2,473	2,670	262	4,224,723
Indiana	9,693	6,509	545	1,223	1,416	111	3,577,585
Iowa	7,747	4,635	400	1,070	1,642	228	2,940,917
Kansas	9,249	5,619	555	1,254	1,821	299	2,335,161
Kentucky	9,120	6,632	460	783	1,245	306	3,664,515
Louisiana	10,987	6,635	1,593	840	1,919	54	1,876,708
Maine	2,806	2,095	148	218	345	132	1,327,738
Maryland	22,726	15,092	2,220	2,276	3,138	153	5,927,650
Massachusetts	19,650	14,915	1,378	1,385	1,972	331	6,491,295
Michigan	22,669	14,716	2,193	2,713	3,047	621	9,839,233
Minnesota	13,348	7,699	1,044	1,997	2,608	316	5,336,155
Mississippi	4,609	2,595	308	653	1,053	66	1,213,729
Missouri	20,093	13,010	1,390	2,204	3,489	561	5,938,974
Montana	2,542	1,575	109	328	530	98	965,672
Nebraska	4,915	3,126	371	416	1,002	152	1,817,308
Nevada	8,812	4,852	507	1,277	2,176	36	2,790,136
New Hampshire	3,432	2,396	216	241	579	155	1,206,956
New Jersey	31,931	22,309	2,151	3,038	4,433	479	7,966,491
New Mexico	511	320	33	64	94	28	164,145
New York	78,497	50,474	8,054	7,085	12,884	361	17,856,511
North Carolina	33,505	20,630	2,628	4,831	5,416	514	9,732,673
North Dakota	1,992	1,310	161	169	352	104	722,555
Ohio	16,934	11,695	1,452	1,288	2,499	212	5,370,790
Oklahoma	12,216	7,224	617	2,005	2,370	324	3,849,983
Oregon	9,787	5,391	568	1,695	2,133	215	3,894,070
Pennsylvania	30,082	22,699	2,579	1,800	3,004	1,030	9,796,604
Rhode Island	3,056	2,251	183	277	345	48	1,051,511
South Carolina	15,050	10,115	1,406	1,261	2,268	362	4,716,123
South Dakota	2,652	1,429	100	494	629	131	840,617
Tennessee	26,564	15,002	1,593	4,702	5,267	452	6,489,858
Texas	78,457	41,008	5,051	14,068	18,330	982	22,415,430
Utah	4,776	2,981	255	674	866	101	2,156,475
Vermont	1,575	1,051	107	155	262	87	624,228
Virginia	23,766	16,550	2,206	1,316	3,694	283	8,258,885
Washington	14,609	9,358	983	1,598	2,670	256	6,954,564
West Virginia	4,496	3,413	121	358	604	351	1,840,871
Wisconsin	17,989	10,826	1,678	2,218	3,267	389	5,698,086
Wyoming	2,291	1,415	190	195	491	63	566,020

Table 78.   Full-Time Law Enforcement Employees, by Selected State and City, 2013

(Number.)

State/city	Population	Total law enforcement employees	Total officers	Total civilians
ALABAMA				
Abbeville	2,645	19	12	7
Adamsville	4,481	33	19	14
Alabaster	31,170	81	65	16
Albertville	21,636	63	43	20
Anniston	22,648	125	86	39
Arab	8,295	35	24	11
Ardmore	1,304	11	7	4
Arley	353	3	2	1
Ashford	2,177	9	5	4
Ashland	1,926	9	5	4
Athens	23,972	56	46	10
Atmore	10,099	31	27	4
Attalla	5,999	28	22	6
Auburn	57,970	114	108	6
Bayou La Batre	2,647	19	14	5
Berry	1,124	2	2	0
Birmingham	212,001	1,126	836	290
Blountsville	1,697	4	4	0
Boaz	9,709	30	20	10
Brent	4,894	5	5	0
Brewton	5,331	32	25	7
Bridgeport	2,389	11	7	4
Brighton	2,911	10	5	5
Brilliant	892	2	2	0
Brookside	1,355	4	4	0
Brundidge	2,073	14	9	5
Butler	1,850	7	7	0
Calera	12,726	35	28	7
Camp Hill	995	6	6	0
Carbon Hill	1,988	7	5	2
Carrollton	1,002	2	2	0
Cedar Bluff	1,814	4	4	0
Centre	3,603	13	12	1
Centreville	2,708	6	6	0
Chatom	1,245	6	6	0
Cherokee	1,034	5	2	3
Citronelle	3,881	11	8	3
Clanton	8,682	32	30	2
Clayton	2,967	3	3	0
Cleveland	1,320	1	1	0
Clio	1,612	3	3	0
Coaling	1,677	3	3	0
Collinsville	1,978	8	4	4
Columbiana	4,219	12	9	3
Cottonwood	1,295	3	3	0
Courtland	607	4	4	0
Creola	1,924	11	7	4
Crossville	1,850	5	5	0
Cullman	14,881	69	49	20
Dadeville	3,186	15	14	1
Daleville	5,260	23	17	6
Daphne	23,204	73	48	25
Dauphin Island	1,236	25	11	14
Decatur	56,091	158	134	24
Demopolis	7,240	30	24	6
Dora	1,992	11	7	4
Dothan	67,811	231	158	73
Douglas	762	3	3	0
East Brewton	2,437	8	4	4
Eclectic	1,015	9	5	4
Elba	3,955	24	15	9
Elberta	1,595	9	8	1
Enterprise	28,145	65	49	16
Eufaula	12,896	49	36	13
Fairfield	11,003	42	30	12
Fairhope	16,847	54	35	19
Falkville	1,281	6	6	0
Fayette	4,530	10	10	0
Flomaton	1,423	14	7	7
Florala	1,988	7	7	0
Florence	39,481	136	109	27
Foley	15,615	89	61	28
Fort Deposit	1,274	4	4	0
Fort Payne	14,103	37	30	7
Frisco City	1,272	2	2	0
Fyffe	1,025	4	4	0
Gardendale	13,830	38	28	10

Table 78.   Full-Time Law Enforcement Employees, by Selected State and City, 2013— continued

(Number.)

State/city	Population	Total law enforcement employees	Total officers	Total civilians
Geneva	4,501	12	11	1
Georgiana	1,666	10	7	3
Geraldine	900	6	5	1
Glencoe	5,222	8	7	1
Gordo	1,712	4	4	0
Grant	915	1	1	0
Greensboro	2,418	15	11	4
Greenville	7,820	37	32	5
Gulf Shores	10,233	60	43	17
Guntersville	8,388	46	33	13
Haleyville	4,086	16	12	4
Hamilton	6,546	15	13	2
Hammondville	485	1	1	0
Hanceville	3,173	13	10	3
Hartford	2,653	13	8	5
Hartselle	14,563	37	29	8
Headland	4,694	15	11	4
Heflin	3,449	12	11	1
Helena	17,306	24	21	3
Henagar	2,343	9	5	4
Hokes Bluff	4,361	7	7	0
Hollywood	990	3	2	1
Homewood	25,299	105	73	32
Hoover	84,139	220	158	62
Hueytown	15,956	45	36	9
Huntsville	184,738	477	377	100
Ider	718	4	3	1
Irondale	12,452	40	32	8
Jackson	5,038	25	19	6
Jacksonville	12,385	37	27	10
Jasper	14,185	66	51	15
Kinsey	2,228	2	2	0
Lake View	2,064	3	2	1
Lanett	6,424	23	21	2
Leeds	11,914	34	27	7
Leesburg	1,020	3	3	0
Leighton	724	2	2	0
Lineville	2,283	12	8	4
Littleville	1,003	4	4	0
Loxley	1,694	20	14	6
Madison	45,540	104	77	27
Maplesville	706	5	5	0
Margaret	4,484	2	2	0
Marion	3,544	7	6	1
McIntosh	228	8	8	0
Midfield	5,310	16	12	4
Midland City	2,476	7	4	3
Millbrook	15,042	40	30	10
Millry	527	5	4	1
Mobile	250,557	782	521	261
Monroeville	6,327	22	16	6
Montevallo	6,503	16	12	4
Montgomery	205,087	687	515	172
Morris	1,897	5	4	1
Moulton	3,397	11	11	0
Mountain Brook	20,354	68	51	17
Mount Vernon	1,561	10	8	2
Munford	1,275	1	1	0
Muscle Shoals	13,431	42	33	9
Napier Field	353	1	1	0
New Brockton	1,166	1	1	0
New Hope	2,799	5	5	0
New Site	762	2	2	0
Newton	1,509	4	4	0
Northport	24,308	77	58	19
Notasulga	906	5	2	3
Odenville	3,642	9	8	1
Oneonta	6,661	20	19	1
Opelika	28,302	103	83	20
Opp	6,698	29	23	6
Owens Crossroads	1,766	8	6	2
Oxford	21,261	58	50	8
Ozark	14,897	37	31	6
Parrish	974	14	7	7
Pelham	22,199	81	65	16
Pell City	13,263	36	33	3
Phenix City	37,266	110	88	22
Piedmont	4,777	16	12	4
Pleasant Grove	10,463	23	18	5

Table 78.   Full-Time Law Enforcement Employees, by Selected State and City, 2013— continued

(Number.)

State/city	Population	Total law enforcement employees	Total officers	Total civilians
Powell	955	2	2	0
Prattville	35,154	87	79	8
Priceville	2,878	5	5	0
Prichard	22,350	52	33	19
Rainbow City	9,683	34	23	11
Rainsville	4,989	15	11	4
Reform	1,666	5	5	0
Riverside	2,269	3	3	0
Robertsdale	5,629	25	13	12
Rockford	452	2	1	1
Rogersville	1,248	5	5	0
Russellville	9,844	25	22	3
Samson	1,940	7	6	1
Saraland	13,505	55	38	17
Sardis City	1,755	4	4	0
Satsuma	6,125	22	16	6
Scottsboro	14,791	70	46	24
Section	766	2	2	0
Sheffield	9,012	33	28	5
Silverhill	736	6	6	0
Skyline	847	4	2	2
Slocomb	1,993	5	4	1
Snead	845	4	4	0
Somerville	728	3	3	0
Southside	8,513	19	13	6
Springville	4,175	10	10	0
Steele	1,060	3	3	0
Stevenson	2,022	9	5	4
St. Florian	418	3	2	1
Sulligent	1,879	7	7	0
Sumiton	2,461	20	12	8
Summerdale	938	5	5	0
Sylvania	1,858	3	3	0
Tallassee	4,830	23	17	6
Tarrant	6,323	26	22	4
Taylor	2,425	2	2	0
Thomaston	400	1	1	0
Thomasville	4,068	26	21	5
Town Creek	1,080	3	3	0
Triana	499	2	2	0
Trinity	2,148	7	7	0
Troy	18,329	73	52	21
Trussville	20,235	68	55	13
Tuscaloosa	94,126	361	285	76
Tuscumbia	8,398	28	21	7
Tuskegee	9,341	38	25	13
Valley	9,468	29	28	1
Valley Head	554	2	1	1
Vernon	1,940	7	7	0
Vestavia Hills	34,103	83	81	2
Wadley	739	4	4	0
Walnut Grove	697	1	1	0
Warrior	3,230	15	10	5
Weaver	3,079	11	8	3
Wedowee	810	8	8	0
Winfield	4,672	12	11	1
Woodstock	1,446	4	4	0
York	2,436	10	6	4
ALASKA				
Anchorage	299,455	479	344	135
Bethel	6,463	22	14	8
Bristol Bay Borough	985	10	4	6
Cordova	2,273	13	6	7
Craig	1,263	10	4	6
Dillingham	2,438	19	8	11
Fairbanks	32,505	51	48	3
Haines	2,561	8	3	5
Homer	5,309	23	12	11
Hoonah	747	6	3	3
Juneau	32,946	82	45	37
Kenai	7,422	27	18	9
Ketchikan	8,305	36	24	12
Kodiak	6,564	39	17	22
Kotzebue	3,375	17	7	10
Nome	3,805	14	8	6
North Pole	2,236	15	14	1
North Slope Borough	9,674	67	40	27
Palmer	6,453	29	13	16

Table 78.   Full-Time Law Enforcement Employees, by Selected State and City, 2013— continued

(Number.)

State/city	Population	Total law enforcement employees	Total officers	Total civilians
Petersburg	2,981	15	9	6
Sand Point	972	4	3	1
Seldovia	264	1	1	0
Seward	2,749	17	10	7
Sitka	9,093	27	14	13
Skagway	956	10	4	6
Soldotna	4,418	15	13	2
Unalaska	4,340	28	12	16
Valdez	4,032	11	11	0
Wasilla	8,645	42	21	21
Whittier	220	4	4	0
Wrangell	2,414	14	7	7
ARIZONA				
Apache Junction	36,626	85	56	29
Avondale	78,905	159	108	51
Benson	5,077	23	14	9
Bisbee	5,463	19	14	5
Buckeye	55,710	122	86	36
Bullhead City	39,577	113	71	42
Camp Verde	10,942	29	18	11
Casa Grande	50,058	106	73	33
Chandler	248,718	474	322	152
Chino Valley	10,850	29	23	6
Clarkdale	4,090	11	8	3
Clifton	3,499	12	6	6
Colorado City	4,831	9	5	4
Coolidge	11,820	44	32	12
Cottonwood	11,285	49	34	15
Douglas	17,223	44	30	14
Eagar	5,034	9	5	4
El Mirage	32,837	55	41	14
Eloy	17,602	37	30	7
Flagstaff	67,963	158	110	48
Florence	26,682	45	30	15
Fredonia	1,318	3	3	0
Gilbert	225,232	334	226	108
Glendale	234,006	490	383	107
Globe	7,414	28	20	8
Goodyear	71,048	124	93	31
Hayden	996	8	7	1
Holbrook	4,988	15	13	2
Huachuca City	1,811	11	6	5
Jerome	444	5	5	0
Kearny	2,010	8	4	4
Kingman	28,400	69	54	15
Lake Havasu City	52,891	115	77	38
Mammoth	1,473	5	3	2
Maricopa	44,871	64	56	8
Mesa	456,155	1,141	765	376
Miami	1,793	10	7	3
Nogales	20,736	74	56	18
Oro Valley	41,493	125	97	28
Page	7,330	27	18	9
Parker	3,011	15	12	3
Patagonia	903	3	3	0
Payson	15,192	38	27	11
Peoria	161,641	273	179	94
Phoenix	1,502,139	3,905	2,890	1,015
Pima	2,427	4	4	0
Pinetop-Lakeside	4,266	24	16	8
Prescott	40,752	115	70	45
Prescott Valley	39,209	71	58	13
Quartzsite	3,648	9	8	1
Safford	9,471	24	20	4
Sahuarita	26,535	48	41	7
San Luis	28,231	49	32	17
Scottsdale	225,523	651	410	241
Sedona	10,036	32	22	10
Show Low	10,732	40	29	11
Sierra Vista	46,728	93	68	25
Snowflake-Taylor	9,651	22	14	8
Somerton	15,014	28	19	9
South Tucson	5,694	30	26	4
Springerville	2,009	8	6	2
St. Johns	3,584	5	3	2
Superior	2,898	7	5	2
Surprise	122,497	177	129	48
Tempe	168,501	483	345	138

Table 78.   Full-Time Law Enforcement Employees, by Selected State and City, 2013— continued

(Number.)

State/city	Population	Total law enforcement employees	Total officers	Total civilians
Thatcher	4,999	12	11	1
Tolleson	6,754	40	30	10
Tombstone	1,349	9	5	4
Tucson	525,486	1,268	983	285
Wellton	2,920	5	4	1
Wickenburg	6,583	21	13	8
Willcox	3,678	18	9	9
Williams	3,019	17	9	8
Winslow	9,326	29	20	9
Yuma	96,014	251	171	80
ARKANSAS				
Alma	5,484	19	11	8
Arkadelphia	10,829	29	23	6
Arkansas City	346	1	1	0
Ashdown	4,616	13	11	2
Ash Flat	1,069	3	3	0
Atkins	3,036	7	6	1
Augusta	2,149	6	6	0
Austin	2,701	3	3	0
Bald Knob	2,931	11	7	4
Barling	4,733	10	10	0
Bay	1,825	3	3	0
Bearden	930	2	2	0
Beebe	7,744	20	13	7
Bella Vista	27,606	37	26	11
Benton	32,548	76	57	19
Bentonville	39,132	95	67	28
Berryville	5,417	13	11	2
Blytheville	15,220	51	36	15
Bono	2,153	5	5	0
Booneville	3,922	12	8	4
Bradford	768	3	3	0
Brinkley	3,024	14	10	4
Bryant	19,366	53	42	11
Bull Shoals	1,975	4	4	0
Cabot	24,695	51	40	11
Caddo Valley	622	5	4	1
Camden	11,726	39	24	15
Cammack Village	760	4	4	0
Caraway	1,279	2	2	0
Carlisle	2,210	9	5	4
Cave City	1,881	3	3	0
Cave Springs	2,060	6	5	1
Centerton	10,377	15	14	1
Charleston	2,532	4	4	0
Cherokee Village	4,613	9	8	1
Clarendon	1,576	4	4	0
Clarksville	9,319	24	20	4
Clinton	2,561	9	8	1
Conway	64,060	160	115	45
Corning	3,254	12	8	4
Cotter	954	2	2	0
Crossett	5,383	25	15	10
Danville	2,370	5	5	0
Dardanelle	4,672	15	10	5
Decatur	1,766	5	5	0
De Queen	6,636	16	13	3
Dermott	2,775	11	5	6
Des Arc	1,657	4	4	0
De Valls Bluff	591	2	2	0
De Witt	3,259	15	9	6
Diaz	1,274	2	2	0
Dierks	1,126	3	3	0
Dover	1,393	4	4	0
Dumas	4,481	20	11	9
Earle	2,342	5	3	2
Elkins	2,794	6	6	0
England	2,806	13	9	4
Etowah	342	1	1	0
Eudora	2,169	4	4	0
Eureka Springs	2,075	17	11	6
Fairfield Bay	2,295	15	6	9
Farmington	6,230	11	10	1
Fayetteville	77,900	161	115	46
Flippin	1,343	6	6	0
Fordyce	4,218	14	9	5
Forrest City	15,184	42	31	11
Fort Smith	87,821	210	163	47

Table 78.   Full-Time Law Enforcement Employees, by Selected State and City, 2013— continued

(Number.)

State/city	Population	Total law enforcement employees	Total officers	Total civilians
Gassville	2,048	4	4	0
Gentry	3,341	10	8	2
Glenwood	2,218	1	1	0
Gosnell	3,455	8	8	0
Gravette	2,409	10	9	1
Greenbrier	5,082	14	9	5
Green Forest	2,768	10	8	2
Greenland	1,312	4	4	0
Greenwood	9,223	21	20	1
Greers Ferry	881	3	3	0
Gurdon	2,184	6	4	2
Guy	724	3	2	1
Hamburg	2,828	6	5	1
Hampton	1,306	5	4	1
Hardy	763	3	3	0
Harrisburg	2,317	4	4	0
Harrison	13,234	39	28	11
Hazen	1,412	7	5	2
Heber Springs	7,146	24	16	8
Helena-West Helena	11,591	34	20	14
Highland	1,031	3	3	0
Hope	10,020	33	24	9
Hot Springs	35,551	129	102	27
Hoxie	2,690	5	4	1
Huntsville	2,375	8	7	1
Jacksonville	28,739	93	78	15
Johnson	3,498	12	12	0
Jonesboro	71,114	163	153	10
Judsonia	2,055	4	3	1
Kensett	1,682	3	3	0
Lake City	2,199	4	4	0
Lakeview	727	2	2	0
Lake Village	2,482	14	9	5
Leachville	1,941	4	4	0
Lepanto	1,861	8	4	4
Lewisville	1,244	2	2	0
Lincoln	2,345	6	6	0
Little Flock	2,699	5	5	0
Little Rock	197,399	675	557	118
Lonoke	4,244	16	11	5
Lowell	7,832	23	15	8
Luxora	1,147	2	2	0
Madison	746	3	2	1
Magnolia	11,682	23	20	3
Malvern	10,981	24	21	3
Mammoth Spring	979	2	2	0
Marianna	4,035	35	20	15
Marion	12,258	29	25	4
Marked Tree	2,526	9	5	4
Marmaduke	1,147	4	4	0
Marvell	1,112	6	3	3
Maumelle	17,686	41	31	10
Mayflower	2,336	7	6	1
McCrory	1,673	5	5	0
McGehee	4,024	29	12	17
McRae	691	3	2	1
Mena	5,721	14	13	1
Mineral Springs	1,200	3	3	0
Monette	1,502	3	3	0
Monticello	9,830	28	21	7
Morrilton	6,789	25	22	3
Mountain Home	12,246	33	26	7
Mountain View	2,838	10	9	1
Mulberry	1,634	3	3	0
Murfreesboro	1,635	3	3	0
Nashville	4,607	17	16	1
Newport	7,658	23	16	7
North Little Rock	65,398	227	191	36
Ola	1,257	4	3	1
Osceola	7,494	34	20	14
Ozark	3,653	10	8	2
Pangburn	607	2	2	0
Paragould	27,294	54	45	9
Paris	3,457	15	9	6
Parkin	1,079	2	1	1
Pea Ridge	5,006	11	11	0
Perryville	1,448	3	3	0
Piggott	3,751	8	7	1
Pine Bluff	46,399	181	152	29

Table 78.   Full-Time Law Enforcement Employees, by Selected State and City, 2013— continued

(Number.)

State/city	Population	Total law enforcement employees	Total officers	Total civilians
Plainview	602	1	1	0
Plummerville	822	4	4	0
Pocahontas	6,592	16	15	1
Pottsville	3,064	6	5	1
Prairie Grove	4,737	11	11	0
Prescott	3,260	11	10	1
Quitman	752	4	4	0
Ravenden	454	2	2	0
Redfield	1,428	6	5	1
Rison	1,329	3	3	0
Rockport	752	6	4	2
Rogers	59,787	133	95	38
Rose Bud	487	3	2	1
Russellville	28,760	59	53	6
Salem	1,650	3	3	0
Searcy	23,720	65	47	18
Sheridan	4,834	30	14	16
Sherwood	29,900	87	61	26
Siloam Springs	15,873	46	32	14
Smackover	1,817	5	4	1
Springdale	73,939	175	129	46
Stamps	1,635	3	3	0
Star City	2,206	6	5	1
Stuttgart	9,263	28	20	8
Swifton	773	1	1	0
Texarkana	30,074	108	84	24
Trumann	7,163	25	18	7
Tuckerman	1,798	7	6	1
Van Buren	23,063	58	44	14
Vilonia	4,202	9	9	0
Waldron	3,516	10	9	1
Walnut Ridge	4,714	9	7	2
Ward	4,454	11	9	2
Warren	5,947	21	14	7
Weiner	699	1	1	0
West Fork	2,426	6	5	1
West Memphis	25,500	101	78	23
White Hall	5,381	17	15	2
Wynne	8,323	19	17	2
CALIFORNIA				
Alameda	76,206	111	81	30
Albany	19,104	29	24	5
Alhambra	84,710	126	83	43
Alturas	2,681	7	6	1
Anaheim	345,320	518	361	157
Anderson	10,098	21	15	6
Antioch	106,447	107	83	24
Arcadia	57,855	94	66	28
Arcata	17,805	39	26	13
Arroyo Grande	17,634	34	24	10
Arvin	20,390	26	19	7
Atascadero	28,938	37	28	9
Atherton	7,278	24	18	6
Atwater	28,906	37	29	8
Auburn	13,779	26	19	7
Avenal	14,712	18	16	2
Azusa	47,754	84	57	27
Bakersfield	361,859	488	339	149
Baldwin Park	76,745	89	64	25
Banning	30,503	39	27	12
Barstow	23,144	53	36	17
Bear Valley	5,328	17	7	10
Beaumont	40,208	67	50	17
Bell	35,928	36	25	11
Bell Gardens	42,980	67	50	17
Belmont	26,697	45	32	13
Belvedere	2,120	9	8	1
Benicia	27,558	47	33	14
Berkeley	116,217	261	167	94
Beverly Hills	34,780	165	117	48
Bishop	3,861	18	12	6
Blythe	20,629	33	22	11
Brawley	25,753	46	31	15
Brea	40,600	91	58	33
Brentwood	54,301	75	59	16
Brisbane	4,429	13	11	2
Broadmoor	4,301	11	10	1
Buena Park	82,632	119	84	35

Table 78. Full-Time Law Enforcement Employees, by Selected State and City, 2013— continued

(Number.)

State/city	Population	Total law enforcement employees	Total officers	Total civilians
Burbank	104,727	233	148	85
Burlingame	29,936	55	37	18
Calexico	39,527	53	35	18
California City	13,339	27	19	8
Calipatria	8,061	4	4	0
Calistoga	5,223	13	9	4
Campbell	40,549	65	41	24
Capitola	10,038	29	21	8
Carlsbad	110,505	159	112	47
Carmel	3,833	21	14	7
Cathedral City	53,064	71	46	25
Central Marin	34,105	54	42	12
Ceres	45,876	66	51	15
Chico	88,226	135	83	52
Chino	80,704	142	92	50
Chowchilla	17,696	22	16	6
Chula Vista	255,073	289	202	87
Citrus Heights	85,337	133	89	44
City of Angels	3,729	8	7	1
Claremont	35,623	59	36	23
Clayton	11,439	13	11	2
Clearlake	14,951	29	21	8
Cloverdale	8,718	20	13	7
Clovis	99,483	148	93	55
Coalinga	16,398	30	20	10
Colma	1,481	23	17	6
Colton	53,403	69	44	25
Colusa	5,957	10	9	1
Concord	125,464	196	148	48
Corcoran	23,290	31	21	10
Corning	7,631	22	14	8
Corona	160,159	211	150	61
Coronado	23,183	60	41	19
Costa Mesa	112,538	193	117	76
Cotati	7,388	16	10	6
Covina	48,524	83	54	29
Crescent City	7,333	13	11	2
Culver City	39,452	145	101	44
Cypress	49,067	70	51	19
Daly City	104,536	146	104	42
Davis	66,126	91	58	33
Delano	52,210	66	44	22
Del Rey Oaks	1,673	6	6	0
Desert Hot Springs	27,936	33	28	5
Dinuba	23,440	45	35	10
Dixon	18,743	27	22	5
Dos Palos	5,071	11	7	4
Downey	113,222	148	109	39
East Palo Alto	29,086	45	32	13
El Cajon	102,012	184	119	65
El Centro	43,249	69	47	22
El Cerrito	24,184	50	43	7
Elk Grove	160,925	198	123	75
El Monte	115,591	157	115	42
El Segundo	16,911	82	61	21
Emeryville	10,415	51	35	16
Escalon	7,304	9	8	1
Escondido	148,650	198	150	48
Etna	721	3	2	1
Eureka	26,881	76	48	28
Exeter	10,506	20	18	2
Fairfax	7,563	16	11	5
Fairfield	108,425	172	111	61
Farmersville	10,786	15	14	1
Ferndale	1,364	5	5	0
Firebaugh	8,062	15	11	4
Folsom	73,782	91	65	26
Fontana	203,427	261	169	92
Fort Bragg	7,245	20	15	5
Fortuna	11,803	24	15	9
Foster City	32,652	48	36	12
Fountain Valley	56,805	78	60	18
Fowler	6,038	13	12	1
Fremont	224,475	267	169	98
Fresno	508,876	900	701	199
Fullerton	139,676	199	135	64
Galt	24,553	42	31	11
Gardena	59,703	117	90	27
Garden Grove	175,469	216	154	62

Table 78.   Full-Time Law Enforcement Employees, by Selected State and City, 2013— continued

(Number.)

State/city	Population	Total law enforcement employees	Total officers	Total civilians
Gilroy	51,240	87	58	29
Glendale	195,366	349	241	108
Glendora	50,893	81	49	32
Gonzales	8,428	14	12	2
Grass Valley	12,792	25	21	4
Greenfield	16,922	17	14	3
Gridley	6,563	19	14	5
Grover Beach	13,398	24	16	8
Guadalupe	7,205	13	11	2
Gustine	5,655	11	9	2
Hanford	54,425	77	51	26
Hawthorne	86,132	132	96	36
Hayward	150,955	289	179	110
Healdsburg	11,483	23	15	8
Hemet	81,698	81	58	23
Hercules	24,831	24	21	3
Hermosa Beach	19,858	57	32	25
Hillsborough	11,245	30	23	7
Hollister	36,414	29	24	5
Huntington Beach	195,842	310	193	117
Huntington Park	58,852	104	64	40
Huron	6,812	11	9	2
Imperial	15,943	20	18	2
Indio	80,243	92	59	33
Inglewood	111,672	230	162	68
Ione	7,160	5	5	0
Irvine	235,830	281	194	87
Irwindale	1,440	31	23	8
Jackson	4,549	9	8	1
Kensington	5,230	10	10	0
Kerman	14,543	22	19	3
King City	13,260	19	16	3
Kingsburg	11,651	15	10	5
Laguna Beach	23,313	78	44	34
La Habra	61,740	102	67	35
Lakeport	4,674	10	9	1
Lake Shastina	2,482	4	3	1
La Mesa	58,482	93	66	27
La Palma	15,950	30	23	7
La Verne	31,439	58	40	18
Lemoore	24,802	36	29	7
Lincoln	44,831	26	19	7
Lindsay	13,208	22	19	3
Livermore	84,350	127	85	42
Livingston	13,683	25	17	8
Lodi	63,639	100	70	30
Lompoc	43,581	68	46	22
Long Beach	469,665	1,117	775	342
Los Alamitos	11,735	27	23	4
Los Altos	30,225	43	28	15
Los Angeles	3,878,725	12,616	9,843	2,773
Los Banos	36,965	55	36	19
Los Gatos	30,351	56	38	18
Madera	62,973	76	56	20
Mammoth Lakes	8,258	14	11	3
Manhattan Beach	35,930	97	62	35
Manteca	72,261	84	61	23
Marina	20,426	38	30	8
Martinez	36,910	47	35	12
Marysville	12,168	28	18	10
McFarland	12,288	17	14	3
Mendota	11,472	13	11	2
Menlo Park	33,146	66	46	20
Merced	81,329	111	80	31
Mill Valley	14,239	26	21	5
Milpitas	69,522	100	78	22
Modesto	204,252	292	217	75
Monrovia	37,071	74	45	29
Montclair	37,785	68	50	18
Montebello	63,566	106	71	35
Monterey	29,338	63	49	14
Monterey Park	61,152	97	67	30
Moraga	16,664	13	12	1
Morgan Hill	39,907	52	35	17
Morro Bay	10,412	22	17	5
Mountain View	77,399	141	93	48
Mount Shasta	3,309	10	7	3
Murrieta	107,768	126	85	41
Napa	78,761	110	68	42

Table 78.   Full-Time Law Enforcement Employees, by Selected State and City, 2013— continued

(Number.)

State/city	Population	Total law enforcement employees	Total officers	Total civilians
National City	59,637	106	79	27
Nevada City	3,039	11	10	1
Newark	43,950	75	54	21
Newman	10,691	15	12	3
Newport Beach	87,639	211	135	76
Novato	53,735	76	59	17
Oakdale	21,340	27	19	8
Oakland	403,887	895	639	256
Oceanside	172,525	280	200	80
Ontario	168,144	340	230	110
Orange	140,304	212	152	60
Orange Cove	9,750	13	11	2
Orland	7,420	11	9	2
Oroville	15,581	36	23	13
Oxnard	202,594	378	227	151
Pacifica	38,494	37	33	4
Pacific Grove	15,518	24	18	6
Palm Springs	46,282	119	86	33
Palo Alto	66,964	144	87	57
Palos Verdes Estates	13,658	36	24	12
Paradise	26,222	28	19	9
Parlier	14,856	13	11	2
Pasadena	139,003	326	226	100
Paso Robles	30,795	46	33	13
Petaluma	59,224	81	61	20
Piedmont	10,963	28	20	8
Pinole	18,848	39	27	12
Pismo Beach	7,824	34	23	11
Pittsburg	66,387	87	69	18
Placentia	52,002	63	47	16
Placerville	10,339	26	17	9
Pleasant Hill	34,044	55	39	16
Pleasanton	72,975	113	81	32
Pomona	151,366	255	157	98
Porterville	55,267	90	61	29
Port Hueneme	21,910	30	22	8
Red Bluff	14,170	33	24	9
Redding	91,035	130	98	32
Redlands	70,282	115	79	36
Redondo Beach	67,993	143	88	55
Redwood City	79,707	123	94	29
Reedley	25,018	41	26	15
Rialto	102,520	130	94	36
Richmond	107,341	286	186	100
Ridgecrest	28,537	46	30	16
Rio Dell	3,368	5	5	0
Rio Vista	7,622	12	11	1
Ripon	14,802	32	23	9
Riverside	316,423	520	367	153
Rocklin	59,621	78	52	26
Rohnert Park	41,326	69	49	20
Roseville	126,236	186	122	64
Ross	2,447	8	8	0
Sacramento	478,182	880	612	268
Salinas	155,742	187	141	46
San Bernardino	214,322	400	246	154
San Bruno	42,495	61	45	16
Sand City	344	8	7	1
San Diego	1,349,306	2,511	1,875	636
San Fernando	23,955	45	31	14
San Francisco	833,863	2,577	2,150	427
San Gabriel	40,287	65	52	13
Sanger	24,649	37	32	5
San Jose	992,143	1,424	1,077	347
San Leandro	87,490	125	89	36
San Luis Obispo	46,095	83	59	24
San Marino	13,308	35	28	7
San Mateo	100,440	143	107	36
San Pablo	29,893	72	52	20
San Rafael	58,725	84	62	22
San Ramon	74,434	73	58	15
Santa Ana	332,848	565	317	248
Santa Barbara	90,006	207	140	67
Santa Clara	120,150	195	133	62
Santa Cruz	62,517	109	88	21
Santa Maria	102,051	143	94	49
Santa Monica	92,488	378	202	176
Santa Paula	30,159	36	27	9
Santa Rosa	171,564	231	161	70

Table 78.   Full-Time Law Enforcement Employees, by Selected State and City, 2013— continued

(Number.)

State/city	Population	Total law enforcement employees	Total officers	Total civilians
Sausalito	7,066	23	18	5
Scotts Valley	11,694	27	20	7
Seal Beach	24,798	48	31	17
Seaside	34,147	42	35	7
Sebastopol	7,570	19	14	5
Selma	23,935	39	32	7
Shafter	17,139	29	20	9
Sierra Madre	11,048	17	14	3
Signal Hill	11,240	47	34	13
Simi Valley	126,215	173	122	51
Soledad	26,637	17	14	3
Sonora	4,774	20	13	7
South Gate	95,591	111	69	42
South Lake Tahoe	21,243	56	37	19
South Pasadena	25,937	47	33	14
South San Francisco	66,157	112	80	32
Stallion Springs	2,562	3	3	0
St. Helena	5,934	16	11	5
Stockton	299,796	524	351	173
Suisun City	28,805	32	21	11
Sunnyvale	148,160	270	196	74
Susanville	16,270	16	15	1
Sutter Creek	2,445	6	6	0
Taft	8,839	21	16	5
Tehachapi	13,607	17	15	2
Tiburon	9,133	16	13	3
Torrance	147,534	352	222	130
Tracy	85,174	116	80	36
Truckee	16,146	36	24	12
Tulare	61,424	110	74	36
Tulelake	987	2	2	0
Turlock	70,075	108	73	35
Tustin	78,836	134	87	47
Ukiah	15,874	42	28	14
Union City	72,480	95	73	22
Upland	75,640	87	68	19
Vacaville	94,347	146	92	54
Vallejo	118,336	109	82	27
Ventura	108,204	167	130	37
Vernon	115	52	42	10
Visalia	127,824	201	135	66
Walnut Creek	66,149	109	75	34
Watsonville	52,076	81	66	15
Weed	2,927	14	9	5
West Covina	107,867	146	90	56
Westminster	91,885	119	85	34
Westmorland	2,279	5	5	0
West Sacramento	49,751	88	65	23
Wheatland	3,522	9	8	1
Whittier	86,450	170	120	50
Williams	5,176	12	10	2
Willits	4,832	18	12	6
Willows	6,122	9	8	1
Winters	6,992	10	8	2
Woodlake	7,417	10	9	1
Woodland	56,523	73	58	15
Yreka	7,639	20	14	6
Yuba City	65,133	81	58	23
COLORADO				
Alamosa	9,489	28	24	4
Arvada	110,792	222	161	61
Aspen	6,685	37	27	10
Ault	1,565	10	9	1
Aurora	343,484	806	675	131
Avon	6,336	17	16	1
Basalt	3,818	11	9	2
Bayfield	2,459	8	8	0
Berthoud	5,316	8	7	1
Black Hawk	119	28	19	9
Boulder	102,828	260	172	88
Breckenridge	4,568	27	20	7
Brighton	35,024	76	56	20
Broomfield	59,424	193	108	85
Brush	5,529	14	11	3
Buena Vista	2,678	9	7	2
Burlington	3,939	7	6	1
Calhan	802	3	3	0
Campo	109	3	2	1

Table 78.   Full-Time Law Enforcement Employees, by Selected State and City, 2013— continued

(Number.)

State/city	Population	Total law enforcement employees	Total officers	Total civilians
Canon City	16,474	47	34	13
Carbondale	6,522	15	13	2
Castle Rock	52,309	88	65	23
Cedaredge	2,192	8	6	2
Centennial	104,771	153	119	34
Center	2,281	11	6	5
Central City	675	7	7	0
Cherry Hills Village	6,297	26	22	4
Collbran	706	1	1	0
Colorado Springs	436,108	979	649	330
Columbine Valley	1,315	6	6	0
Commerce City	49,200	118	92	26
Cortez	8,470	47	27	20
Craig	8,909	30	23	7
Crested Butte	1,510	8	7	1
Cripple Creek	1,179	15	7	8
Dacono	4,373	11	9	2
De Beque	502	3	3	0
Del Norte	1,675	6	5	1
Delta	8,799	19	16	3
Denver	648,981	1,662	1,395	267
Dillon	906	8	7	1
Durango	17,303	59	51	8
Eagle	6,466	11	9	2
Eaton	4,575	9	8	1
Edgewater	5,241	16	14	2
Elizabeth	1,366	6	5	1
Empire	279	1	1	0
Englewood	31,454	95	71	24
Erie	19,627	24	22	2
Estes Park	6,064	29	19	10
Evans	19,893	33	31	2
Fairplay	667	3	3	0
Federal Heights	11,894	37	24	13
Firestone	11,128	23	19	4
Florence	3,888	19	9	10
Fort Collins	150,066	287	194	93
Fort Lupton	7,649	14	11	3
Fort Morgan	11,487	29	24	5
Fountain	27,163	64	42	22
Fowler	1,167	2	2	0
Fraser/Winter Park	2,064	10	9	1
Frederick	9,639	20	17	3
Frisco	2,740	15	12	3
Fruita	12,723	19	16	3
Georgetown	1,019	3	3	0
Gilcrest	1,066	2	2	0
Glendale	4,502	33	24	9
Glenwood Springs	9,715	30	24	6
Golden	19,334	60	43	17
Granby	1,733	7	6	1
Grand Junction	60,167	200	109	91
Greeley	96,111	192	145	47
Green Mountain Falls	667	1	1	0
Greenwood Village	14,614	91	65	26
Gunnison	5,884	26	13	13
Haxtun	926	2	2	0
Hayden	1,780	5	4	1
Holyoke	2,254	4	4	0
Hotchkiss	917	3	3	0
Hugo	725	3	2	1
Idaho Springs	1,683	8	7	1
Ignacio	709	7	7	0
Johnstown	11,437	18	17	1
Kersey	1,500	4	4	0
Kiowa	717	3	2	1
Kremmling	1,366	4	4	0
Lafayette	26,145	48	40	8
La Junta	7,023	18	12	6
Lakeside	8	6	5	1
Lakewood	146,298	410	264	146
Lamar	7,801	29	16	13
La Salle	2,017	6	6	0
La Veta	773	2	2	0
Leadville	2,596	9	7	2
Limon	1,864	6	5	1
Littleton	44,375	91	65	26
Lochbuie	5,336	6	6	0
Log Lane Village	879	1	1	0

Table 78.   Full-Time Law Enforcement Employees, by Selected State and City, 2013— continued

(Number.)

State/city	Population	Total law enforcement employees	Total officers	Total civilians
Lone Tree	12,056	52	45	7
Longmont	89,434	177	133	44
Louisville	19,291	35	30	5
Loveland	71,325	129	90	39
Mancos	1,343	3	3	0
Manitou Springs	5,220	15	12	3
Manzanola	426	3	2	1
Meeker	2,528	5	5	0
Milliken	5,839	10	9	1
Minturn	1,025	4	3	1
Monte Vista	4,423	12	10	2
Montrose	18,918	53	38	15
Monument	5,800	15	12	3
Morrison	434	7	6	1
Mountain View	513	7	7	0
Mountain Village	1,360	8	5	3
Mount Crested Butte	799	7	6	1
Nederland	1,488	4	3	1
New Castle	4,571	8	7	1
Northglenn	37,232	72	59	13
Oak Creek	870	2	2	0
Olathe	1,799	3	3	0
Ouray	1,016	3	3	0
Pagosa Springs	1,710	8	7	1
Palisade	2,649	9	8	1
Palmer Lake	2,537	1	1	0
Paonia	1,417	5	5	0
Parachute	1,100	5	5	0
Parker	47,748	99	63	36
Platteville	2,577	7	7	0
Pueblo	108,062	259	184	75
Rangely	2,479	10	5	5
Ridgway	932	3	3	0
Rifle	9,306	22	21	1
Rocky Ford	3,906	10	9	1
Salida	5,346	17	15	2
Sheridan	5,880	37	31	6
Silt	2,991	7	7	0
Silverthorne	3,921	18	15	3
Simla	619	2	2	0
Snowmass Village	2,851	13	9	4
South Fork	375	4	2	2
Springfield	1,438	3	3	0
Steamboat Springs	12,008	38	24	14
Sterling	14,690	25	20	5
Stratton	673	1	1	0
Telluride	2,313	13	9	4
Thornton	125,775	216	158	58
Timnath	1,436	2	2	0
Trinidad	8,689	32	24	8
Vail	5,241	66	32	34
Walsenburg	2,960	12	10	2
Walsh	538	1	1	0
Westminster	110,093	245	176	69
Wheat Ridge	30,882	101	74	27
Wiggins	910	4	2	2
Windsor	20,094	25	21	4
Woodland Park	7,185	29	20	9
Wray	2,373	8	7	1
Yuma	3,563	7	6	1
CONNECTICUT				
Ansonia	19,128	55	47	8
Avon	18,325	37	29	8
Berlin	20,657	54	41	13
Bethel	19,338	49	37	12
Bloomfield	20,637	60	48	12
Branford	28,021	68	56	12
Bridgeport	147,076	467	411	56
Bristol	60,642	139	113	26
Brookfield	16,884	44	34	10
Canton	10,369	20	15	5
Cheshire	29,310	54	42	12
Clinton	13,179	34	24	10
Coventry	12,419	20	15	5
Cromwell	14,290	35	26	9
Danbury	83,363	149	144	5
Darien	21,229	59	51	8
Derby	12,806	38	36	2

Table 78.   Full-Time Law Enforcement Employees, by Selected State and City, 2013— continued

(Number.)

State/city	Population	Total law enforcement employees	Total officers	Total civilians
East Hampton	12,934	16	14	2
East Hartford	51,275	153	117	36
East Haven	29,166	51	48	3
Easton	7,636	16	14	2
East Windsor	11,455	32	25	7
Enfield	44,661	113	91	22
Fairfield	60,772	110	104	6
Farmington	25,587	57	41	16
Glastonbury	34,782	73	57	16
Granby	11,326	19	15	4
Greenwich	62,576	177	152	25
Groton	9,359	35	28	7
Groton Long Point	519	5	5	0
Groton Town	29,946	69	65	4
Guilford	22,409	45	37	8
Hamden	60,829	128	103	25
Hartford	124,927	488	455	33
Madison	18,294	39	28	11
Manchester	58,304	143	112	31
Meriden	60,558	127	117	10
Middlebury	7,570	14	10	4
Middletown	47,221	113	99	14
Milford	53,041	126	114	12
Monroe	19,889	53	42	11
Naugatuck	31,744	71	59	12
New Britain	73,134	167	156	11
New Canaan	20,224	49	43	6
New Haven	131,071	435	385	50
Newington	30,612	64	52	12
New London	27,738	83	68	15
New Milford	27,743	62	49	13
Newtown	28,188	49	45	4
North Branford	14,369	27	22	5
North Haven	24,013	55	47	8
Norwalk	87,590	216	177	39
Norwich	40,485	104	88	16
Old Saybrook	10,239	31	25	6
Orange	13,926	53	42	11
Plainfield	15,224	19	15	4
Plainville	17,850	42	35	7
Plymouth	12,043	31	25	6
Portland	9,463	12	11	1
Putnam	9,461	18	15	3
Redding	9,341	23	17	6
Ridgefield	25,168	47	42	5
Rocky Hill	19,731	43	35	8
Seymour	16,568	39	37	2
Shelton	40,475	62	53	9
Simsbury	23,651	46	36	10
Southington	43,542	84	67	17
South Windsor	25,871	53	41	12
Stamford	125,876	332	283	49
Stonington	18,561	46	34	12
Stratford	52,285	103	96	7
Suffield	15,908	25	19	6
Thomaston	7,758	29	16	13
Torrington	35,634	91	82	9
Trumbull	36,665	84	74	10
Vernon	29,104	63	50	13
Wallingford	45,185	92	68	24
Waterbury	109,763	337	279	58
Waterford	19,541	52	45	7
Watertown	22,183	49	38	11
West Hartford	63,276	151	129	22
West Haven	55,349	134	124	10
Weston	10,402	15	14	1
Westport	27,279	77	64	13
Wethersfield	26,722	57	46	11
Willimantic	17,839	47	43	4
Wilton	18,803	48	44	4
Winchester	11,019	22	18	4
Windsor	29,154	61	49	12
Windsor Locks	12,560	30	22	8
Wolcott	16,735	33	24	9
Woodbridge	8,954	33	25	8
DELAWARE				
Bethany Beach	1,111	10	9	1
Blades	1,293	3	3	0

Table 78.   Full-Time Law Enforcement Employees, by Selected State and City, 2013— continued

(Number.)

State/city	Population	Total law enforcement employees	Total officers	Total civilians
Bridgeville	2,138	8	8	0
Camden	3,516	8	7	1
Cheswold	1,432	3	3	0
Clayton	3,035	9	8	1
Dagsboro	838	4	4	0
Delaware City	1,719	3	3	0
Delmar	1,655	15	14	1
Dewey Beach	352	10	8	2
Dover	37,402	121	93	28
Ellendale	393	1	1	0
Elsmere	6,165	13	12	1
Felton	1,351	4	4	0
Fenwick Island	395	6	6	0
Frankford	887	2	2	0
Georgetown	6,689	16	14	2
Greenwood	1,017	4	3	1
Harrington	3,697	11	10	1
Laurel	3,873	15	14	1
Lewes	2,869	14	13	1
Middletown	19,658	33	29	4
Milford	9,872	39	31	8
Millsboro	4,018	15	14	1
Milton	2,687	8	7	1
Newark	32,674	82	67	15
New Castle	5,388	18	16	2
Newport	1,064	7	7	0
Ocean View	1,972	8	7	1
Rehoboth Beach	1,387	26	16	10
Seaford	7,241	37	26	11
Selbyville	2,281	7	6	1
Smyrna	10,900	29	22	7
South Bethany	471	6	6	0
Wilmington	71,460	380	317	63
Wyoming	1,400	3	3	0
DISTRICT OF COLUMBIA				
Washington	646,449	4,403	3,976	427
FLORIDA				
Alachua	9,338	27	20	7
Altamonte Springs	42,040	117	102	15
Altha	536	1	1	0
Apalachicola	2,269	8	7	1
Apopka	45,397	126	90	36
Arcadia	7,615	19	14	5
Atlantic Beach	12,933	36	25	11
Atlantis	2,064	17	12	5
Auburndale	14,048	43	35	8
Aventura	37,357	120	83	37
Bal Harbour Village	2,623	28	21	7
Bartow	17,781	60	37	23
Bay Harbor Islands	5,881	27	21	6
Belleair	3,904	15	14	1
Belle Isle	6,371	17	15	2
Belleview	4,532	12	10	2
Biscayne Park	3,192	12	11	1
Blountstown	2,527	12	8	4
Boca Raton	88,749	285	191	94
Bonifay	2,766	7	6	1
Bowling Green	2,902	7	7	0
Boynton Beach	70,692	213	154	59
Bradenton	51,023	143	120	23
Bradenton Beach	1,196	10	10	0
Brooksville	7,705	29	26	3
Bunnell	2,740	12	10	2
Cape Coral	163,461	309	221	88
Carrabelle	2,872	5	5	0
Casselberry	26,518	61	51	10
Cedar Key	696	4	4	0
Center Hill	983	2	2	0
Chattahoochee	3,055	10	9	1
Chiefland	2,219	11	9	2
Chipley	3,572	12	11	1
Clearwater	108,908	325	230	95
Clermont	29,620	60	55	5
Clewiston	6,999	24	17	7
Cocoa	17,238	87	68	19
Cocoa Beach	11,268	51	33	18
Coconut Creek	55,659	117	89	28

Table 78.   Full-Time Law Enforcement Employees, by Selected State and City, 2013— continued

(Number.)

State/city	Population	Total law enforcement employees	Total officers	Total civilians
Coleman	797	1	1	0
Coral Springs	126,608	300	203	97
Crescent City	1,554	8	7	1
Crestview	22,818	54	42	12
Cross City	1,697	5	5	0
Cutler Bay	42,831	53	49	4
Dade City	6,529	32	23	9
Davenport	3,006	9	8	1
Davie	96,581	230	171	59
Daytona Beach	62,381	247	205	42
Daytona Beach Shores	4,260	36	29	7
De Funiak Springs	5,584	28	20	8
Deland	27,575	75	59	16
Delray Beach	62,887	214	151	63
Doral	48,896	123	91	32
Dunnellon	1,750	10	9	1
Eatonville	2,252	15	13	2
Edgewater	20,820	35	29	6
Edgewood	2,664	15	12	3
El Portal	2,411	7	7	0
Eustis	19,001	55	43	12
Fellsmere	5,314	9	8	1
Fernandina Beach	11,770	40	30	10
Flagler Beach	4,611	18	15	3
Florida City	12,132	45	35	10
Fort Lauderdale	172,398	658	491	167
Fort Myers	66,835	243	173	70
Fort Pierce	42,866	145	110	35
Fort Walton Beach	20,568	52	41	11
Fruitland Park	4,208	13	13	0
Gainesville	126,589	355	294	61
Golden Beach	956	23	20	3
Graceville	2,215	9	7	2
Greenacres City	38,735	63	45	18
Green Cove Springs	6,994	24	19	5
Gretna	1,420	7	7	0
Groveland	9,325	31	24	7
Gulf Breeze	6,044	25	17	8
Gulf Stream	812	11	11	0
Haines City	21,154	58	50	8
Hallandale	38,710	134	98	36
Hampton	491	1	1	0
Havana	1,705	14	10	4
Hialeah Gardens	22,728	55	37	18
Highland Beach	3,642	15	14	1
High Springs	5,545	18	12	6
Hillsboro Beach	1,957	18	14	4
Holly Hill	11,619	30	25	5
Hollywood	146,643	426	294	132
Homestead	64,024	142	105	37
Howey-in-the-Hills	1,127	5	5	0
Indialantic	2,735	16	11	5
Indian Creek Village	90	16	10	6
Indian Harbour Beach	8,256	26	19	7
Indian River Shores	3,989	14	12	2
Indian Shores	1,432	13	11	2
Interlachen	1,373	4	4	0
Jacksonville	845,745	2,914	1,581	1,333
Jacksonville Beach	21,783	77	57	20
Jasper	4,450	8	7	1
Jennings	876	2	2	0
Juno Beach	3,268	17	15	2
Jupiter	57,826	132	109	23
Jupiter Inlet Colony	417	5	5	0
Kenneth City	5,001	13	12	1
Key Biscayne	12,891	39	31	8
Key Colony Beach	819	5	5	0
Key West	25,185	117	92	25
Kissimmee	64,617	191	127	64
Lady Lake	14,148	33	28	5
Lake Alfred	5,148	15	10	5
Lake City	12,115	55	39	16
Lake Clarke Shores	3,472	12	11	1
Lake Hamilton	1,276	7	6	1
Lake Helen	2,619	6	5	1
Lakeland	100,725	310	207	103
Lake Mary	14,836	56	40	16
Lake Placid	2,125	9	7	2
Lake Wales	14,854	50	43	7

Table 78. Full-Time Law Enforcement Employees, by Selected State and City, 2013— continued

(Number.)

State/city	Population	Total law enforcement employees	Total officers	Total civilians
Lantana	10,689	34	27	7
Largo	77,913	174	134	40
Lauderhill	69,798	123	111	12
Leesburg	20,910	94	71	23
Lighthouse Point	10,831	40	31	9
Live Oak	6,941	21	17	4
Longwood	13,781	41	35	6
Lynn Haven	19,112	37	27	10
Maitland	16,527	52	46	6
Manalapan	434	14	11	3
Marco Island	16,942	42	36	6
Margate	55,576	140	105	35
Marianna	9,706	25	18	7
Mascotte	5,211	13	12	1
Medley	862	46	37	9
Melbourne	77,277	211	158	53
Melbourne Beach	3,116	10	9	1
Melbourne Village	666	5	5	0
Mexico Beach	1,098	7	6	1
Miami	418,394	1,428	1,066	362
Miami Beach	91,433	505	373	132
Miami Gardens	111,870	263	212	51
Miami Lakes	30,713	48	45	3
Miami Shores	10,694	43	35	8
Miami Springs	14,361	54	43	11
Milton	9,234	24	17	7
Miramar	130,926	265	197	68
Monticello	2,431	60	21	39
Mount Dora	12,795	47	32	15
Naples	20,292	93	67	26
Neptune Beach	7,137	26	19	7
New Port Richey	14,944	49	37	12
New Smyrna Beach	23,007	55	43	12
Niceville	13,880	27	22	5
North Bay Village	7,431	33	26	7
North Miami	61,120	150	114	36
North Miami Beach	43,417	124	89	35
North Palm Beach	12,352	42	30	12
North Port	58,699	126	99	27
Oakland	2,697	10	9	1
Ocala	57,144	233	163	70
Ocean Ridge	1,840	19	14	5
Ocoee	39,201	91	80	11
Opa Locka	15,848	64	55	9
Orange City	10,804	24	20	4
Orange Park	8,478	29	22	7
Orlando	253,238	940	718	222
Ormond Beach	38,442	85	65	20
Oviedo	35,889	68	61	7
Palatka	10,446	38	32	6
Palm Bay	104,391	233	153	80
Palm Beach	8,589	88	58	30
Palm Beach Gardens	50,333	153	107	46
Palm Beach Shores	1,177	13	9	4
Palmetto	12,911	48	35	13
Palmetto Bay	24,418	46	42	4
Palm Springs	20,489	52	38	14
Panama City	36,358	127	91	36
Panama City Beach	11,890	69	53	16
Parker	4,416	10	9	1
Pembroke Pines	162,064	293	234	59
Pensacola	52,454	200	154	46
Perry	7,000	24	22	2
Pinellas Park	49,884	121	102	19
Plantation	88,929	228	151	77
Plant City	36,278	81	64	17
Ponce Inlet	3,049	13	11	2
Port Orange	56,850	100	85	15
Port Richey	2,670	20	12	8
Port St. Joe	3,394	6	6	0
Port St. Lucie	169,877	283	219	64
Punta Gorda	16,942	47	32	15
Quincy	7,758	30	23	7
Riviera Beach	33,326	142	100	42
Rockledge	25,558	63	46	17
Sanford	54,972	146	126	20
Sanibel	6,827	38	24	14
Satellite Beach	10,290	30	21	9
Sea Ranch Lakes	702	12	7	5

Table 78.   Full-Time Law Enforcement Employees, by Selected State and City, 2013— continued

(Number.)

State/city	Population	Total law enforcement employees	Total officers	Total civilians
Sebastian	22,502	54	35	19
Sebring	10,318	38	32	6
Sewall's Point	2,055	10	9	1
Shalimar	773	3	3	0
South Daytona	12,231	36	28	8
South Miami	12,142	53	47	6
South Palm Beach	1,203	7	7	0
Springfield	9,089	21	15	6
Starke	5,394	19	18	1
St. Augustine	13,536	60	47	13
St. Augustine Beach	6,490	18	16	2
St. Cloud	40,213	111	76	35
St. Petersburg	247,084	728	533	195
Stuart	15,920	60	40	20
Sunny Isles Beach	21,735	61	50	11
Sunrise	90,274	219	169	50
Surfside	5,980	39	28	11
Tallahassee	188,714	424	355	69
Tampa	351,314	1,205	952	253
Tarpon Springs	23,720	60	47	13
Tavares	14,337	28	25	3
Temple Terrace	25,379	66	48	18
Tequesta	5,804	22	16	6
Titusville	43,989	114	86	28
Treasure Island	6,746	22	19	3
Trenton	1,983	3	2	1
Umatilla	3,554	7	6	1
Valparaiso	5,138	16	12	4
Venice	21,151	55	43	12
Vero Beach	15,621	68	49	19
Village of Pinecrest	19,092	69	49	20
Virginia Gardens	2,471	7	6	1
Waldo	1,025	7	6	1
Wauchula	4,918	17	13	4
Webster	840	3	3	0
Welaka	688	1	1	0
West Melbourne	19,418	43	35	8
West Miami	6,254	22	18	4
West Palm Beach	102,510	349	261	88
Wildwood	6,793	31	24	7
Williston	2,728	19	11	8
Wilton Manors	12,110	41	30	11
Windermere	2,619	13	12	1
Winter Garden	37,819	85	69	16
Winter Haven	35,325	112	82	30
Winter Park	29,259	105	78	27
Winter Springs	33,624	78	65	13
Zephyrhills	14,023	37	24	13
GEORGIA				
Abbeville	2,888	7	4	3
Adairsville	4,686	15	13	2
Adel	5,240	20	17	3
Adrian	656	1	1	0
Alapaha	646	1	1	0
Alma	3,529	12	10	2
Americus	16,190	44	37	7
Arcade	1,752	3	3	0
Ashburn	3,814	17	16	1
Athens-Clarke County	120,122	298	235	63
Atlanta	451,020	2,294	1,855	439
Attapulgus	441	1	1	0
Auburn	7,061	21	16	5
Austell	6,820	30	24	6
Avondale Estates	2,789	12	12	0
Baldwin	3,289	9	6	3
Ball Ground	1,484	2	2	0
Barnesville	6,489	20	18	2
Blackshear	3,499	13	11	2
Blairsville	549	8	7	1
Boston	1,318	4	4	0
Bowdon	2,042	8	6	2
Braselton	7,973	15	14	1
Bremen	6,203	21	19	2
Brookhaven	49,173	64	57	7
Brunswick	15,709	70	65	5
Buchanan	1,162	10	9	1
Butler	1,899	8	6	2
Byron	4,772	23	19	4

Table 78.   Full-Time Law Enforcement Employees, by Selected State and City, 2013— continued

(Number.)

State/city	Population	Total law enforcement employees	Total officers	Total civilians
Cairo	9,875	27	24	3
Calhoun	15,866	49	42	7
Camilla	5,033	21	18	3
Canton	24,042	41	37	4
Carrollton	25,164	74	62	12
Cartersville	19,835	62	51	11
Cedartown	9,779	34	31	3
Centerville	7,644	20	17	3
Chamblee	15,886	68	50	18
Chatsworth	4,284	14	13	1
Chickamauga	3,125	6	6	0
Claxton	2,643	9	8	1
Cleveland	3,739	13	12	1
Cochran	4,782	15	14	1
College Park	14,871	103	78	25
Colquitt	1,932	11	9	2
Columbus	201,165	552	454	98
Commerce	6,476	25	20	5
Conyers	15,465	83	63	20
Coolidge	525	2	2	0
Covington	13,416	64	54	10
Cumming	5,562	23	15	8
Dallas	12,194	25	18	7
Dalton	33,475	96	82	14
Danielsville	563	2	2	0
Decatur	20,001	54	41	13
Dillard	340	3	3	0
Doerun	785	5	4	1
Donalsonville	2,822	10	9	1
Douglas	11,892	43	36	7
Douglasville	31,347	117	91	26
Duluth	28,350	73	56	17
Dunwoody	47,531	56	47	9
East Dublin	2,398	8	8	0
East Ellijay	539	13	8	5
Eastman	5,295	16	14	2
East Point	36,172	156	114	42
Eatonton	6,483	21	14	7
Elberton	4,476	23	20	3
Ellaville	1,808	6	6	0
Emerson	1,486	8	6	2
Ephesus	420	1	1	0
Eton	902	3	3	0
Fairburn	13,938	43	35	8
Fayetteville	16,216	43	41	2
Fitzgerald	9,034	34	27	7
Flowery Branch	6,117	14	13	1
Folkston	5,646	6	5	1
Forest Park	19,007	100	80	20
Forsyth	3,960	20	15	5
Fort Oglethorpe	9,504	32	30	2
Fort Valley	9,688	34	29	5
Franklin Springs	1,025	8	8	0
Gainesville	35,111	106	95	11
Garden City	8,968	50	39	11
Glennville	5,210	22	12	10
Gordon	2,044	13	8	5
Grantville	3,113	11	10	1
Greensboro	3,371	22	18	4
Greenville	854	5	4	1
Griffin	23,313	101	89	12
Grovetown	12,525	29	24	5
Hahira	2,877	8	7	1
Hampton	7,133	19	17	2
Hapeville	6,799	44	27	17
Harlem	2,811	12	8	4
Hazlehurst	4,279	18	14	4
Helen	520	10	9	1
Helena	3,147	3	3	0
Hiawassee	870	4	4	0
Hinesville	35,311	101	82	19
Hoboken	533	2	1	1
Hogansville	3,105	18	13	5
Holly Springs	9,807	20	20	0
Homerville	2,413	10	9	1
Jefferson	9,638	26	23	3
Jesup	10,289	29	27	2
Johns Creek	84,093	71	62	9
Jonesboro	4,530	29	23	6

Table 78.   Full-Time Law Enforcement Employees, by Selected State and City, 2013— continued

(Number.)

State/city	Population	Total law enforcement employees	Total officers	Total civilians
Kingsland	16,393	41	38	3
Lafayette	7,062	23	21	2
LaGrange	30,723	92	78	14
Lakeland	3,402	22	20	2
Lake Park	755	3	3	0
Lavonia	2,121	15	15	0
Lawrenceville	29,821	90	68	22
Lilburn	12,455	35	30	5
Lincolnton	1,491	5	5	0
Loganville	10,699	29	26	3
Lookout Mountain	1,577	7	7	0
Ludowici	1,941	9	6	3
Lumber City	1,266	1	1	0
Manchester	4,069	17	12	5
Marietta	58,893	164	128	36
Marshallville	1,382	2	2	0
Maysville	1,795	3	3	0
McDonough	22,713	48	42	6
McIntyre	650	5	5	0
McRae	5,588	9	8	1
Meigs	1,035	3	3	0
Metter	4,184	13	12	1
Midville	267	1	1	0
Midway	2,152	7	6	1
Milledgeville	19,927	65	44	21
Milton	35,751	36	32	4
Montezuma	3,318	13	11	2
Morrow	6,948	47	32	15
Mountain City	1,078	3	3	0
Nashville	4,993	16	13	3
Newnan	34,453	87	71	16
Nicholls	3,438	3	2	1
Norcross	15,834	55	40	15
Norman Park	976	2	2	0
Oakwood	4,126	16	14	2
Omega	1,260	5	5	0
Oxford	2,180	4	4	0
Palmetto	4,775	19	17	2
Patterson	735	1	1	0
Peachtree City	34,706	68	63	5
Pelham	3,853	13	12	1
Pine Mountain	1,332	9	8	1
Pooler	21,069	44	38	6
Porterdale	1,446	7	7	0
Port Wentworth	6,338	26	22	4
Powder Springs	14,350	30	27	3
Quitman	3,607	18	16	2
Register	179	3	2	1
Remerton	1,158	9	8	1
Reynolds	1,037	5	5	0
Richmond Hill	10,841	39	32	7
Ringgold	3,665	9	9	0
Riverdale	15,610	60	47	13
Rochelle	1,133	8	6	2
Rockmart	4,125	18	16	2
Rossville	4,033	11	10	1
Sandersville	5,807	20	18	2
Sardis	985	5	5	0
Savannah-Chatham Metropolitan	235,200	776	563	213
Senoia	3,669	15	13	2
Shiloh	445	2	1	1
Smyrna	53,080	137	94	43
Snellville	19,260	56	44	12
Social Circle	4,288	12	11	1
Sparks	1,987	4	4	0
Sparta	1,314	13	7	6
Springfield	2,798	7	6	1
Statesboro	30,201	74	61	13
Statham	2,443	8	8	0
Stillmore	528	2	1	1
Stone Mountain	5,984	16	16	0
Summerville	4,449	15	13	2
Suwanee	16,539	46	37	9
Swainsboro	7,707	25	23	2
Sylvania	2,540	13	11	2
Sylvester	6,322	25	22	3
Talbotton	891	5	1	4
Tallapoosa	3,100	12	11	1
Tallulah Falls	169	3	2	1

Table 78.   Full-Time Law Enforcement Employees, by Selected State and City, 2013— continued

(Number.)

State/city	Population	Total law enforcement employees	Total officers	Total civilians
Tennille	1,518	8	7	1
Thomasville	18,451	63	56	7
Thunderbolt	2,625	11	9	2
Tifton	16,781	49	41	8
Tignall	521	2	1	1
Toccoa	8,379	32	30	2
Trion	1,796	10	9	1
Tybee Island	3,091	29	21	8
Tyrone	6,997	17	16	1
Union City	20,826	71	53	18
Union Point	1,639	7	7	0
Valdosta	58,483	163	138	25
Vidalia	10,652	37	28	9
Vienna	3,792	8	7	1
Villa Rica	14,307	43	35	8
Warm Springs	406	2	2	0
Warner Robins	71,614	140	95	45
Washington	3,967	14	14	0
Watkinsville	2,896	7	7	0
Waverly Hall	737	3	3	0
Waycross	14,206	71	60	11
Waynesboro	5,793	29	20	9
Whigham	481	4	3	1
Willacoochee	1,366	6	5	1
Winder	14,291	47	42	5
Winterville	1,137	2	2	0
Woodstock	25,515	58	49	9
Wrens	2,096	7	7	0
Zebulon	1,151	7	6	1
HAWAII				
Honolulu	984,683	2,433	1,956	477
IDAHO				
Aberdeen	1,959	7	4	3
American Falls	4,404	9	7	2
Bellevue	2,269	4	4	0
Blackfoot	11,826	30	27	3
Boise	214,330	366	280	86
Bonners Ferry	2,586	5	5	0
Buhl	4,183	8	7	1
Caldwell	48,069	77	63	14
Cascade	893	5	4	1
Chubbuck	14,224	31	17	14
Coeur d'Alene	46,023	85	69	16
Cottonwood	926	1	1	0
Emmett	6,509	13	12	1
Filer	2,575	5	5	0
Fruitland	4,734	11	9	2
Garden City	11,342	34	26	8
Gooding	3,502	5	5	0
Grangeville	3,153	6	6	0
Hagerman	862	1	1	0
Hailey	7,915	13	12	1
Heyburn	3,134	7	6	1
Homedale	2,606	5	5	0
Idaho City	460	1	1	0
Idaho Falls	58,188	128	85	43
Jerome	11,059	23	20	3
Kamiah	1,323	3	3	0
Kellogg	2,109	8	7	1
Ketchum	2,670	14	10	4
Kimberly	3,351	8	7	1
Lewiston	32,093	68	46	22
McCall	2,851	14	12	2
Meridian	82,064	106	83	23
Montpelier	2,520	6	4	2
Moscow	24,714	42	34	8
Mountain Home	13,644	34	29	5
Nampa	84,634	154	105	49
Orofino	3,098	7	6	1
Osburn	1,542	2	2	0
Parma	2,030	4	4	0
Payette	7,442	14	12	2
Pinehurst	1,616	2	2	0
Pocatello	54,935	130	91	39
Ponderay	1,110	7	7	0
Post Falls	28,959	69	42	27
Preston	5,128	7	6	1

Table 78.   Full-Time Law Enforcement Employees, by Selected State and City, 2013— continued

(Number.)

State/city	Population	Total law enforcement employees	Total officers	Total civilians
Priest River	1,706	6	4	2
Rathdrum	7,078	15	12	3
Rexburg	26,298	37	29	8
Rigby	4,031	8	7	1
Rupert	5,500	13	12	1
Salmon	3,020	7	6	1
Sandpoint	7,412	21	18	3
Shelley	4,408	7	7	0
Shoshone	1,488	5	5	0
Soda Springs	2,946	8	7	1
Spirit Lake	2,016	6	5	1
St. Anthony	3,446	5	5	0
St. Maries	2,335	5	5	0
Sun Valley	1,391	10	9	1
Twin Falls	45,378	98	68	30
Weiser	5,399	15	12	3
Wendell	2,740	3	3	0
Wilder	1,568	3	3	0
ILLINOIS				
Algonquin	29,980	56	46	10
Alton	27,277	82	61	21
Aviston	2,059	1	1	0
Bannockburn	1,577	7	7	0
Barrington	10,356	27	23	4
Batavia	26,401	46	40	6
Belleville	43,527	91	75	16
Berkeley	5,237	18	14	4
Berwyn	56,838	147	108	39
Bloomingdale	22,301	55	45	10
Bourbonnais	18,623	30	24	6
Bradley	15,860	45	33	12
Braidwood	6,214	16	15	1
Buffalo Grove	41,774	75	64	11
Bull Valley	1,062	2	2	0
Burnham	4,239	12	9	3
Burr Ridge	10,737	29	26	3
Byron	3,697	8	7	1
Cairo	2,608	10	5	5
Canton	14,461	32	23	9
Carlinville	5,828	16	11	5
Carrollton	2,409	6	6	0
Cary	18,090	30	27	3
Central City	1,147	3	3	0
Champaign	82,966	146	122	24
Channahon	12,604	24	22	2
Chenoa	3,250	3	3	0
Chester	8,448	10	7	3
Chicago Ridge	14,463	33	28	5
Chillicothe	6,135	13	9	4
Cicero	84,204	179	154	25
Clayton	702	1	1	0
Colfax	1,062	1	1	0
Country Club Hills	16,954	50	33	17
Countryside	5,982	27	24	3
Crete	8,278	19	17	2
Crystal Lake	40,383	74	63	11
Danville	32,532	77	66	11
Deerfield	18,283	54	40	14
De Pue	1,778	3	3	0
De Soto	1,591	3	2	1
Des Plaines	58,975	111	91	20
Dixon	15,304	32	28	4
Downers Grove	49,558	107	74	33
Du Quoin	5,993	13	9	4
Dwight	4,206	9	8	1
Earlville	1,673	3	3	0
East Alton	6,181	15	10	5
East Carondelet	482	1	1	0
Easton	308	1	1	0
East Peoria	23,458	64	48	16
Edwardsville	24,511	55	41	14
Effingham	12,633	34	21	13
Elburn	5,689	8	7	1
Elgin	110,454	222	180	42
Elizabeth	757	1	1	0
Elk Grove Village	33,414	101	85	16
Elmwood Park	24,998	41	35	6
Erie	1,576	3	3	0

Table 78.   Full-Time Law Enforcement Employees, by Selected State and City, 2013— continued

(Number.)

State/city	Population	Total law enforcement employees	Total officers	Total civilians
Eureka	5,360	6	6	0
Evanston	75,709	224	165	59
Fairfield	5,068	16	12	4
Fairmont City	2,573	8	7	1
Fairmount	630	1	1	0
Farmington	2,405	5	5	0
Findlay	669	1	1	0
Fisher	1,924	2	2	0
Forest Park	14,233	54	38	16
Galena	3,392	11	10	1
Genoa	5,185	7	6	1
Georgetown	3,424	4	4	0
Gibson City	3,388	9	7	2
Gifford	975	1	1	0
Gilberts	7,484	8	8	0
Gillespie	3,247	9	6	3
Gilman	1,780	2	2	0
Glendale Heights	34,630	71	48	23
Glenview	45,125	72	69	3
Glenwood	9,060	29	26	3
Godfrey	17,894	16	15	1
Grafton	661	2	2	0
Granite City	29,447	73	58	15
Greenfield	1,034	3	3	0
Hampton	1,863	4	4	0
Hanover Park	38,499	82	60	22
Harvard	9,326	21	16	5
Hazel Crest	14,208	36	30	6
Henry	2,379	3	3	0
Herrin	12,751	25	18	7
Hinsdale	17,222	27	25	2
Hodgkins	1,896	23	21	2
Homer	1,197	1	1	0
Homewood	19,445	41	36	5
Hopedale	869	1	1	0
Island Lake	8,027	13	13	0
Jerome	1,650	6	6	0
Joliet	148,462	323	256	67
Kankakee	27,286	77	69	8
Kewanee	12,739	30	22	8
Kildeer	3,974	8	7	1
La Grange	15,718	37	27	10
Lake in the Hills	29,133	55	37	18
Lakemoor	6,047	14	12	2
Lake Villa	8,798	18	17	1
Lake Zurich	19,999	51	34	17
La Salle	9,448	30	24	6
Leland	961	1	1	0
Leland Grove	1,574	5	5	0
Lindenhurst	14,470	17	15	2
Lovington	1,122	1	1	0
Lyons	10,781	32	25	7
Maple Park	1,312	1	1	0
Marengo	7,572	15	13	2
Marine	945	1	1	0
Marseilles	5,056	10	9	1
Martinsville	1,155	2	2	0
Matteson	19,188	44	39	5
Mattoon	18,297	41	37	4
Maywood	24,184	66	52	14
McHenry	26,761	59	45	14
Melrose Park	25,559	85	74	11
Mendota	7,409	20	15	5
Minooka	11,149	20	17	3
Morris	13,882	29	26	3
Morton Grove	23,516	58	45	13
Mount Morris	2,937	5	4	1
Mount Prospect	54,600	103	84	19
Mount Pulaski	1,540	2	2	0
Mount Vernon	15,203	53	39	14
Mundelein	31,291	70	51	19
Murphysboro	7,866	23	16	7
New Lenox	24,805	41	37	4
Newton	2,808	8	7	1
O'Fallon	29,388	59	43	16
Oak Lawn	57,083	122	106	16
Oakwood	1,568	1	1	0
Okawville	1,418	3	3	0
Onarga	1,329	1	1	0

Table 78.   Full-Time Law Enforcement Employees, by Selected State and City, 2013— continued

(Number.)

State/city	Population	Total law enforcement employees	Total officers	Total civilians
Oquawka	1,308	2	2	0
Oregon	3,641	9	8	1
Orland Park	57,578	121	96	25
Oswego	32,057	58	49	9
Palestine	1,337	3	2	1
Palos Hills	17,646	33	30	3
Paris	8,612	21	15	6
Park Forest	22,052	48	41	7
Park Ridge	37,788	64	54	10
Paxton	4,441	7	7	0
Pekin	34,085	64	56	8
Pinckneyville	5,582	8	7	1
Pittsfield	4,529	6	6	0
Plainfield	40,639	67	51	16
Polo	2,300	4	4	0
Pontoon Beach	5,732	20	14	6
Posen	6,028	17	15	2
Princeton	7,484	19	16	3
Quincy	40,841	88	75	13
Raleigh	352	1	1	0
Rankin	550	1	1	0
Red Bud	3,613	6	6	0
Richmond	1,905	2	2	0
Ridge Farm	869	1	1	0
Riverdale	13,625	40	36	4
Riverside	8,908	24	19	5
Riverton	3,480	8	8	0
Riverwoods	3,656	7	7	0
Rockdale	1,973	4	4	0
Rock Island	38,893	110	83	27
Roodhouse	1,759	4	4	0
Round Lake Heights	2,728	5	5	0
Schiller Park	11,876	39	32	7
Sherman	4,396	6	6	0
Shorewood	16,387	28	24	4
Smithton	3,757	7	7	0
South Barrington	4,683	21	18	3
South Beloit	7,804	15	14	1
South Elgin	22,295	33	29	4
South Holland	22,178	51	48	3
Springfield	117,351	278	239	39
Spring Grove	5,758	11	9	2
St. Charles	33,433	61	51	10
Steger	9,595	22	13	9
Stockton	1,832	5	4	1
Streator	13,514	31	24	7
Sugar Grove	9,142	12	12	0
Summit	11,579	34	28	6
Sycamore	17,469	33	30	3
Thornton	2,347	12	10	2
Tilton	2,674	4	4	0
Urbana	41,598	66	54	12
Vernon Hills	25,860	72	41	31
Wamac	1,165	2	2	0
Warrensburg	1,197	2	2	0
Watseka	5,172	9	9	0
Westville	3,162	4	4	0
Wheeling	38,027	83	61	22
Wood Dale	13,953	51	35	16
Woodhull	803	1	1	0
Wood River	10,442	24	18	6
Woodstock	25,164	51	37	14
Yorkville	17,657	29	26	3
INDIANA				
Albion	2,344	7	6	1
Anderson	55,367	122	107	15
Angola	8,587	21	17	4
Auburn	12,802	24	23	1
Bargersville	6,341	12	11	1
Batesville	6,489	17	12	5
Bedford	13,400	39	30	9
Beech Grove	14,384	34	31	3
Bloomington	82,415	127	95	32
Bremen	4,597	16	12	4
Brownsburg	22,908	46	38	8
Carmel	84,880	135	111	24
Charlestown	7,781	20	15	5
Chesterfield	2,508	6	6	0

Table 78.   Full-Time Law Enforcement Employees, by Selected State and City, 2013— continued

(Number.)

State/city	Population	Total law enforcement employees	Total officers	Total civilians
Chesterton	13,238	26	22	4
Clinton	4,810	6	5	1
Columbia City	8,850	19	18	1
Crawfordsville	16,055	36	32	4
Danville	9,151	14	12	2
Delphi	2,887	7	7	0
Edinburgh	4,509	16	11	5
Elwood	8,492	20	17	3
Evansville	120,284	317	286	31
Fort Wayne	254,820	461	429	32
Frankfort	16,235	33	30	3
Franklin	24,034	56	41	15
Gary	78,819	269	220	49
Greenwood	53,208	78	58	20
Hagerstown	1,764	5	5	0
Hammond	79,329	240	207	33
Hartford City	6,053	12	11	1
Indianapolis	850,220	1,749	1,539	210
Jasper	15,195	30	21	9
Jeffersonville	45,846	88	75	13
Lake Station	12,335	28	25	3
La Porte	22,112	48	42	6
Lawrenceburg	5,012	24	20	4
Ligonier	4,385	11	10	1
Linton	5,359	14	10	4
Mooresville	9,490	28	22	6
Muncie	70,059	109	103	6
Munster	23,349	47	39	8
Nappanee	6,694	17	15	2
New Haven	15,575	27	19	8
North Judson	1,759	4	4	0
North Liberty	1,890	3	3	0
North Manchester	5,987	15	11	4
North Vernon	6,640	20	18	2
Oakland City	2,425	4	4	0
Peru	11,219	29	27	2
Portage	36,862	68	61	7
Porter	4,883	14	11	3
Portland	6,278	17	13	4
Rushville	6,204	16	11	5
Scottsburg	6,614	14	14	0
Seymour	18,655	57	40	17
Shelbyville	19,159	62	49	13
South Bend	100,711	322	252	70
South Whitley	1,728	5	5	0
Tell City	7,228	20	12	8
Terre Haute	61,215	138	129	9
Tipton	4,983	14	12	2
Valparaiso	32,090	56	51	5
Warsaw	13,897	43	36	7
Waterloo	2,240	6	6	0
Westfield	32,698	45	40	5
West Lafayette	30,687	64	46	18
Whitestown	3,778	14	14	0
Winona Lake	4,934	5	5	0
Zionsville	24,433	26	25	1
IOWA				
Adel	3,990	10	9	1
Albia	3,829	7	6	1
Algona	5,495	14	10	4
Altoona	15,683	26	24	2
Ames	61,193	75	53	22
Anamosa	5,653	8	7	1
Ankeny	50,194	56	48	8
Atlantic	6,977	13	12	1
Audubon	2,070	3	3	0
Belle Plaine	2,499	4	4	0
Belmond	2,340	5	5	0
Bloomfield	2,591	6	6	0
Blue Grass	1,590	2	2	0
Boone	12,515	17	16	1
Burlington	25,677	54	41	13
Camanche	4,422	8	8	0
Carlisle	3,939	7	6	1
Carroll	9,988	15	14	1
Cedar Falls	40,213	43	42	1
Cedar Rapids	128,642	269	204	65
Centerville	5,444	16	11	5

Table 78.   Full-Time Law Enforcement Employees, by Selected State and City, 2013— continued

(Number.)

State/city	Population	Total law enforcement employees	Total officers	Total civilians
Chariton	4,243	6	5	1
Charles City	7,471	21	14	7
Cherokee	5,149	9	8	1
Clarinda	5,455	14	10	4
Clarion	2,772	7	6	1
Clear Lake	7,731	21	15	6
Clinton	26,572	45	39	6
Coralville	19,949	36	33	3
Council Bluffs	62,021	131	112	19
Cresco	3,894	7	7	0
Creston	7,890	18	11	7
Davenport	101,834	190	164	26
Decorah	8,103	19	12	7
Denison	8,411	18	13	5
Des Moines	207,391	475	366	109
De Witt	5,273	11	10	1
Dubuque	58,313	107	102	5
Dyersville	4,093	6	6	0
Eagle Grove	3,496	7	7	0
Eldridge	5,979	9	8	1
Emmetsburg	3,820	7	6	1
Estherville	6,179	12	12	0
Evansdale	4,754	8	7	1
Fairfield	9,488	19	13	6
Forest City	3,967	8	8	0
Fort Dodge	24,632	43	40	3
Fort Madison	11,012	20	18	2
Garner	3,082	5	5	0
Glenwood	5,220	11	10	1
Grinnell	9,090	17	15	2
Grundy Center	2,719	4	4	0
Hampton	4,378	11	7	4
Harlan	5,079	9	8	1
Hawarden	2,548	4	4	0
Hiawatha	7,173	14	14	0
Humboldt	4,644	6	6	0
Independence	5,969	11	10	1
Indianola	14,993	21	19	2
Iowa City	70,855	104	82	22
Iowa Falls	5,117	14	10	4
Jefferson	4,233	7	7	0
Johnston	19,175	26	24	2
Keokuk	10,720	28	24	4
Knoxville	7,297	16	14	2
Le Mars	9,788	15	14	1
Leon	1,896	3	3	0
Lisbon	2,172	2	2	0
Manchester	5,103	15	10	5
Maquoketa	6,066	17	11	6
Marengo	2,485	4	4	0
Marion	36,181	50	41	9
Marshalltown	27,722	61	43	18
Mason City	27,747	50	45	5
Monticello	3,795	7	6	1
Mount Pleasant	8,768	16	14	2
Mount Vernon	4,609	6	6	0
Muscatine	23,027	45	42	3
New Hampton	3,542	6	6	0
New London	1,883	3	3	0
Newton	15,064	26	21	5
North Liberty	14,821	16	15	1
Oelwein	6,350	15	10	5
Ogden	2,020	3	3	0
Onawa	2,929	6	6	0
Orange City	6,187	7	7	0
Osage	3,626	6	5	1
Osceola	5,064	12	11	1
Oskaloosa	11,570	18	16	2
Ottumwa	24,738	49	40	9
Pella	10,418	21	15	6
Perry	8,065	19	12	7
Pleasant Hill	9,072	18	16	2
Polk City	3,830	6	6	0
Prairie City	1,672	1	1	0
Red Oak	5,614	12	10	2
Rock Rapids	2,609	1	1	0
Rock Valley	3,518	5	5	0
Sac City	2,166	4	4	0
Sergeant Bluff	4,280	9	8	1

Table 78.   Full-Time Law Enforcement Employees, by Selected State and City, 2013— continued

(Number.)

State/city	Population	Total law enforcement employees	Total officers	Total civilians
Sheldon	5,096	7	7	0
Shenandoah	5,084	12	9	3
Sigourney	2,043	3	3	0
Sioux Center	7,263	7	7	0
Sioux City	82,676	142	120	22
Spencer	11,186	27	19	8
Spirit Lake	4,955	10	9	1
St. Ansgar	1,121	1	1	0
Storm Lake	10,812	23	19	4
Story City	3,424	5	5	0
Tipton	3,196	6	6	0
Toledo	2,257	5	5	0
Urbandale	41,499	52	47	5
Vinton	5,187	8	8	0
Washington	7,346	12	11	1
Waterloo	68,255	137	125	12
Waukee	16,633	18	16	2
Waukon	3,861	7	7	0
Waverly	10,089	17	16	1
Webster City	7,830	15	11	4
West Branch	2,334	3	3	0
West Burlington	3,027	9	9	0
West Des Moines	60,068	80	66	14
West Liberty	3,729	7	6	1
West Union	2,487	4	4	0
Williamsburg	3,076	6	6	0
Wilton	2,810	4	4	0
Windsor Heights	4,880	13	11	2
Winterset	5,174	8	8	0
KANSAS				
Abilene	6,743	19	16	3
Altamont	1,066	3	3	0
Andover	12,188	30	23	7
Anthony	2,203	7	6	1
Argonia	496	1	1	0
Arkansas City	12,322	30	24	6
Arma	1,482	4	4	0
Atchison	10,940	25	23	2
Attica	610	1	1	0
Atwood	1,215	2	2	0
Augusta	9,197	31	21	10
Baldwin City	4,527	10	9	1
Basehor	4,828	12	10	2
Bel Aire	6,857	9	8	1
Belle Plaine	1,628	5	5	0
Belleville	1,928	5	5	0
Beloit	3,832	8	8	0
Benton	871	2	2	0
Blue Rapids	998	1	1	0
Buhler	1,347	3	3	0
Burlingame	911	2	2	0
Burlington	2,645	9	7	2
Burrton	899	2	2	0
Caldwell	1,036	3	3	0
Caney	2,135	9	5	4
Canton	748	1	1	0
Carbondale	1,413	4	3	1
Cawker City	464	1	1	0
Cedar Vale	557	1	1	0
Chanute	9,176	22	20	2
Chapman	1,423	3	3	0
Chase	463	1	1	0
Cheney	2,127	5	5	0
Cherokee	719	1	1	0
Claflin	639	1	1	0
Clay Center	4,306	9	7	2
Clearwater	2,491	7	6	1
Coffeyville	9,902	33	25	8
Colby	5,403	18	12	6
Colwich	1,335	2	2	0
Concordia	5,296	18	11	7
Council Grove	2,154	7	6	1
Derby	23,104	56	46	10
Dodge City	28,265	58	42	16
Eastborough	773	7	7	0
Edwardsville	4,387	17	16	1
El Dorado	12,859	26	24	2
Elkhart	2,143	3	3	0

Table 78.   Full-Time Law Enforcement Employees, by Selected State and City, 2013— continued

(Number.)

State/city	Population	Total law enforcement employees	Total officers	Total civilians
Ellinwood	2,116	5	5	0
Ellis	2,105	5	5	0
Ellsworth	3,113	7	6	1
Elwood	1,203	5	5	0
Emporia	24,981	64	43	21
Enterprise	847	1	1	0
Erie	1,116	4	3	1
Eudora	6,196	10	9	1
Fairway	3,957	10	8	2
Florence	447	1	1	0
Fort Scott	7,887	26	18	8
Fredonia	2,371	7	6	1
Frontenac	3,466	11	8	3
Garden City	27,047	89	57	32
Garden Plain	866	3	3	0
Gardner	20,708	25	23	2
Garnett	3,297	8	8	0
Girard	2,798	7	6	1
Goddard	4,572	12	11	1
Goodland	4,584	9	8	1
Grandview Plaza	1,809	6	6	0
Great Bend	15,896	35	30	5
Halstead	2,093	6	6	0
Hays	21,156	39	32	7
Haysville	10,988	28	25	3
Herington	2,481	8	7	1
Hesston	3,749	7	6	1
Hiawatha	3,120	9	8	1
Highland	1,009	2	2	0
Hill City	1,456	4	4	0
Hillsboro	2,904	5	5	0
Hoisington	2,686	6	6	0
Holcomb	2,124	4	3	1
Holton	3,292	7	7	0
Holyrood	445	1	1	0
Horton	1,743	10	6	4
Howard	637	1	1	0
Hoxie	1,189	2	2	0
Hugoton	3,931	7	5	2
Humboldt	1,958	5	4	1
Hutchinson	41,909	105	67	38
Independence	9,165	26	19	7
Inman	1,392	3	3	0
Iola	5,697	17	16	1
Junction City	26,491	61	42	19
Kansas City	147,618	467	377	90
Kechi	1,973	4	3	1
Kingman	3,169	7	7	0
La Cygne	1,109	2	2	0
La Harpe	576	1	1	0
Lansing	11,688	18	17	1
Larned	4,012	7	7	0
Lawrence	90,034	178	145	33
Leavenworth	35,965	76	54	22
Leawood	32,748	83	60	23
Lenexa	49,777	121	82	39
Lewis	437	1	1	0
Liberal	21,261	47	33	14
Lindsborg	3,468	7	6	1
Little River	543	1	1	0
Louisburg	4,268	8	8	0
Lyndon	1,035	1	1	0
Lyons	3,729	7	6	1
Maize	3,787	9	8	1
Marion	1,862	5	5	0
Marysville	3,296	9	8	1
McLouth	860	2	2	0
McPherson	13,245	37	31	6
Meade	1,627	3	3	0
Medicine Lodge	2,008	6	6	0
Merriam	11,228	34	29	5
Minneapolis	2,019	4	4	0
Mission	9,511	30	28	2
Mission Hills	3,584	3	3	0
Moran	548	1	1	0
Mound City	676	1	1	0
Moundridge	1,741	3	3	0
Mount Hope	818	2	2	0
Mulberry	519	1	1	0

Table 78. Full-Time Law Enforcement Employees, by Selected State and City, 2013— continued

(Number.)

State/city	Population	Total law enforcement employees	Total officers	Total civilians
Mulvane	6,307	20	14	6
Neodesha	2,378	8	7	1
Newton	19,196	36	31	5
North Newton	1,784	2	2	0
Norton	2,863	6	6	0
Oberlin	1,716	4	4	0
Olathe	131,342	191	164	27
Onaga	708	1	1	0
Osawatomie	4,368	17	11	6
Osborne	1,411	3	3	0
Oswego	1,796	5	5	0
Ottawa	12,546	31	26	5
Overland Park	180,555	293	247	46
Oxford	1,020	2	2	0
Paola	5,529	22	16	6
Park City	7,475	17	16	1
Parsons	10,278	32	23	9
Peabody	1,162	2	2	0
Plainville	1,920	5	5	0
Pleasanton	1,170	2	2	0
Prairie Village	21,870	59	46	13
Protection	521	1	1	0
Quinter	930	1	1	0
Roeland Park	6,843	17	15	2
Rose Hill	3,931	11	9	2
Rossville	1,149	2	2	0
Russell	4,471	9	8	1
Salina	48,120	103	74	29
Scott City	3,814	12	7	5
Sedan	1,084	2	2	0
Sedgwick	1,702	2	2	0
Seneca	1,990	5	5	0
Shawnee	64,060	106	86	20
Silver Lake	1,440	2	2	0
Smith Center	1,622	3	3	0
South Hutchinson	2,498	10	8	2
Spearville	810	1	1	0
Spring Hill	5,665	14	12	2
Stafford	1,015	4	4	0
Sterling	2,283	5	5	0
St. John	1,257	3	3	0
St. Marys	2,664	5	5	0
Stockton	1,343	5	5	0
Tonganoxie	5,138	11	10	1
Topeka	128,009	357	295	62
Troy	989	1	1	0
Udall	748	3	3	0
Valley Center	7,009	14	13	1
Victoria	1,237	2	2	0
Wa Keeney	1,852	5	5	0
Wakefield	989	1	1	0
Waterville	664	1	1	0
Wathena	1,348	1	1	0
Wellington	7,945	20	17	3
Wellsville	1,840	5	4	1
Westwood	2,071	8	7	1
Winfield	12,372	26	23	3
Yates Center	1,400	3	3	0
KENTUCKY				
Adairville	840	1	1	0
Albany	2,032	7	7	0
Alexandria	8,683	16	14	2
Anchorage	2,391	13	9	4
Ashland	21,432	52	48	4
Auburn	1,330	2	2	0
Audubon Park	1,496	4	4	0
Augusta	1,189	3	3	0
Barbourville	3,139	15	14	1
Bardstown	12,916	28	27	1
Beattyville	1,269	4	4	0
Beaver Dam	3,527	6	6	0
Bellefonte	876	4	4	0
Bellevue	5,918	11	10	1
Benham	484	2	2	0
Benton	4,407	8	8	0
Berea	14,331	34	32	2
Booneville	80	1	1	0
Bowling Green	61,130	152	113	39

Table 78.   Full-Time Law Enforcement Employees, by Selected State and City, 2013— continued

(Number.)

State/city	Population	Total law enforcement employees	Total officers	Total civilians
Burkesville	1,526	10	6	4
Burnside	828	4	4	0
Butler	594	1	1	0
Cadiz	2,624	10	9	1
Calvert City	2,540	7	6	1
Campbellsville	10,804	38	22	16
Caneyville	618	1	1	0
Carrollton	3,966	11	10	1
Catlettsburg	1,829	8	8	0
Cave City	2,283	6	6	0
Central City	5,891	12	12	0
Clarkson	886	1	1	0
Clay City	1,062	2	2	0
Clinton	1,342	4	4	0
Cloverport	1,159	1	1	0
Cold Spring	6,194	11	10	1
Columbia	4,490	14	12	2
Corbin	7,257	30	22	8
Covington	40,766	120	105	15
Cumberland	2,151	7	7	0
Cynthiana	6,305	15	14	1
Danville	16,388	45	33	12
Dawson Springs	2,753	5	4	1
Dayton	5,368	10	9	1
Eddyville	2,578	4	4	0
Edgewood	8,679	14	14	0
Elizabethtown	29,470	62	46	16
Elkton	2,211	6	6	0
Elsmere	8,478	15	14	1
Eminence	2,478	6	6	0
Erlanger	18,432	52	40	12
Ferguson	948	1	1	0
Flatwoods	7,412	12	11	1
Fleming-Neon	746	2	2	0
Florence	31,434	65	61	4
Fort Thomas	16,227	23	22	1
Franklin	8,581	25	24	1
Fulton	2,310	8	8	0
Georgetown	30,611	54	51	3
Glasgow	14,117	38	34	4
Graymoor-Devondale	2,914	1	1	0
Grayson	4,082	11	11	0
Greenville	4,415	9	9	0
Guthrie	1,442	4	4	0
Hardinsburg	2,343	5	5	0
Harlan	1,677	12	11	1
Harrodsburg	8,301	27	17	10
Hartford	2,712	6	6	0
Hawesville	1,000	1	1	0
Hazard	5,455	29	21	8
Henderson	28,952	76	55	21
Highland Heights	6,938	12	11	1
Hodgenville	3,228	5	5	0
Hollow Creek	795	1	1	0
Hopkinsville	33,253	99	70	29
Hyden	361	1	1	0
Independence	25,937	33	31	2
Indian Hills	2,918	7	7	0
Inez	702	1	1	0
Irvine	2,431	6	6	0
Irvington	1,193	4	4	0
Jackson	2,168	11	8	3
Jamestown	1,790	5	5	0
Jeffersontown	27,017	61	50	11
Jenkins	2,131	3	3	0
Junction City	2,217	3	3	0
La Center	1,022	1	1	0
Lakeside Park-Crestview Hills	5,881	12	11	1
Lancaster	3,429	10	10	0
Lawrenceburg	11,080	23	14	9
Lebanon	5,649	24	17	7
Lebanon Junction	1,861	4	4	0
Leitchfield	6,814	16	15	1
Lewisburg	801	1	1	0
Lexington	308,712	665	557	108
Liberty	2,196	5	5	0
London	6,067	37	34	3
Louisa	2,465	4	4	0
Louisville Metro	671,120	1,441	1,200	241

Table 78.   Full-Time Law Enforcement Employees, by Selected State and City, 2013— continued

(Number.)

State/city	Population	Total law enforcement employees	Total officers	Total civilians
Ludlow	4,536	10	9	1
Lynnview	928	3	3	0
Madisonville	19,761	55	44	11
Manchester	1,425	11	11	0
Marion	3,021	8	5	3
Martin	620	6	5	1
Maysville	9,024	31	24	7
Meadow Vale	748	1	1	0
Monticello	6,189	10	9	1
Morehead	6,864	25	17	8
Mount Sterling	7,023	23	21	2
Mount Vernon	2,469	8	8	0
Mount Washington	9,377	15	14	1
Muldraugh	1,092	4	4	0
Murray	18,048	44	37	7
Newport	15,425	43	40	3
Nicholasville	28,497	65	57	8
Oak Grove	7,638	19	15	4
Olive Hill	1,574	6	6	0
Owensboro	58,304	139	101	38
Owingsville	1,553	4	4	0
Paintsville	4,123	11	10	1
Paris	9,752	28	25	3
Park Hills	2,993	5	5	0
Pewee Valley	1,486	1	1	0
Pikeville	6,870	28	21	7
Pineville	1,834	8	8	0
Pioneer Village	496	5	4	1
Pippa Passes	532	6	2	4
Powderly	736	2	2	0
Prestonsburg	3,210	16	16	0
Princeton	6,293	17	16	1
Prospect	4,818	9	8	1
Providence	3,171	6	6	0
Raceland	2,377	6	6	0
Radcliff	23,177	51	40	11
Ravenna	595	2	2	0
Richmond	32,333	68	57	11
Russell	3,319	12	12	0
Russell Springs	2,455	9	8	1
Russellville	6,949	20	19	1
Salyersville	1,831	4	4	0
Scottsville	4,310	21	13	8
Sebree	1,594	1	1	0
Shelbyville	14,743	24	23	1
Shepherdsville	11,534	25	23	2
Shively	15,511	32	27	5
Simpsonville	2,608	5	5	0
Smiths Grove	723	1	1	0
South Shore	1,115	1	1	0
Springfield	2,577	15	8	7
Stanton	2,697	7	7	0
Sturgis	1,888	4	4	0
Taylor Mill	6,670	11	10	1
Taylorsville	782	4	4	0
Tompkinsville	2,311	11	9	2
Uniontown	983	2	2	0
Vanceburg	1,466	6	6	0
Versailles	8,881	36	35	1
Villa Hills	7,362	6	6	0
Vine Grove	5,298	6	6	0
Wayland	419	1	1	0
West Buechel	1,255	8	8	0
West Point	766	4	4	0
Whitesburg	2,060	7	5	2
Wilder	3,045	7	7	0
Williamsburg	5,258	12	12	0
Wilmore	3,804	8	7	1
Winchester	18,478	48	33	15
LOUISIANA				
Basile	1,802	13	8	5
Bernice	1,644	5	5	0
Blanchard	2,922	6	5	1
Bogalusa	11,998	55	35	20
Clinton	1,619	16	7	9
Denham Springs	10,102	41	33	8
De Quincy	3,165	11	11	0
Gonzales	10,301	42	39	3

Table 78.   Full-Time Law Enforcement Employees, by Selected State and City, 2013— continued

(Number.)

State/city	Population	Total law enforcement employees	Total officers	Total civilians
Greenwood	3,268	11	10	1
Gretna	17,760	142	95	47
Hammond	20,162	107	81	26
Houma	33,717	92	78	14
Kenner	66,854	240	177	63
Lake Arthur	2,728	10	6	4
Livonia	1,439	9	9	0
Mandeville	12,162	45	32	13
Montgomery	706	1	1	0
New Orleans	377,022	1,442	1,210	232
Olla	1,392	3	3	0
Patterson	6,079	30	30	0
Ruston	21,969	51	39	12
Vinton	3,191	11	7	4
Walker	6,172	22	18	4
Westlake	4,571	21	21	0
Westwego	8,521	40	38	2
Zachary	15,749	44	43	1
MAINE				
Ashland	1,277	2	2	0
Auburn	22,948	59	52	7
Augusta	18,893	55	40	15
Baileyville	1,487	3	3	0
Bangor	32,744	87	74	13
Bar Harbor	5,275	17	13	4
Bath	8,384	22	18	4
Belfast	6,654	14	13	1
Berwick	7,529	12	11	1
Biddeford	21,324	68	46	22
Boothbay Harbor	2,135	8	7	1
Brewer	9,376	20	19	1
Bridgton	5,308	9	8	1
Brownville	1,225	2	2	0
Brunswick	20,354	49	33	16
Bucksport	4,937	11	7	4
Buxton	8,103	14	7	7
Calais	3,054	9	8	1
Camden	4,848	12	10	2
Cape Elizabeth	9,104	14	13	1
Caribou	8,012	16	15	1
Carrabassett Valley	780	2	2	0
Clinton	3,425	2	2	0
Cumberland	7,353	12	11	1
Damariscotta	2,204	4	4	0
Dexter	3,856	5	5	0
Dixfield	2,504	5	5	0
Dover-Foxcroft	4,110	5	5	0
East Millinocket	3,027	4	4	0
Eastport	1,302	4	4	0
Eliot	6,257	8	7	1
Ellsworth	7,853	20	16	4
Fairfield	6,657	9	8	1
Falmouth	11,468	26	17	9
Farmington	7,657	14	13	1
Fort Fairfield	3,412	3	3	0
Fort Kent	4,055	8	4	4
Freeport	8,094	15	13	2
Fryeburg	3,407	6	6	0
Gardiner	5,731	13	12	1
Gorham	16,764	25	23	2
Gouldsboro	1,733	2	2	0
Greenville	1,624	3	2	1
Hallowell	2,362	3	3	0
Hampden	7,275	11	10	1
Holden	3,094	3	3	0
Houlton	6,046	18	14	4
Islesboro	568	1	1	0
Jay	4,827	8	7	1
Kennebunk	11,023	21	19	2
Kennebunkport	3,517	16	12	4
Kittery	9,540	25	19	6
Lewiston	36,422	92	81	11
Limestone	2,269	3	3	0
Lincoln	5,094	7	6	1
Lisbon	8,923	18	13	5
Livermore Falls	3,161	6	6	0
Machias	2,173	4	4	0
Madawaska	3,957	6	5	1

Table 78. Full-Time Law Enforcement Employees, by Selected State and City, 2013— continued

(Number.)

State/city	Population	Total law enforcement employees	Total officers	Total civilians
Madison	4,776	7	6	1
Mechanic Falls	3,013	5	5	0
Mexico	2,633	5	5	0
Milbridge	1,340	2	2	0
Millinocket	4,430	5	5	0
Milo	2,295	3	3	0
Monmouth	4,105	4	4	0
Mount Desert	2,059	11	7	4
Newport	3,250	7	7	0
North Berwick	4,620	9	8	1
Norway	4,970	9	8	1
Oakland	6,253	11	10	1
Ogunquit	905	11	9	2
Old Orchard Beach	8,681	22	20	2
Old Town	7,736	15	14	1
Orono	10,663	14	13	1
Oxford	4,075	7	6	1
Paris	5,140	8	7	1
Phippsburg	2,230	1	1	0
Pittsfield	4,162	6	6	0
Portland	66,256	216	159	57
Presque Isle	9,483	21	16	5
Rangeley	1,176	3	3	0
Richmond	3,388	5	5	0
Rockland	7,205	21	18	3
Rockport	3,314	7	6	1
Rumford	5,738	9	9	0
Sabattus	5,060	8	7	1
Saco	18,848	48	34	14
Sanford	20,913	43	39	4
Scarborough	19,252	54	37	17
Searsport	2,618	3	3	0
Skowhegan	8,537	15	14	1
South Berwick	7,275	12	8	4
South Portland	25,126	61	54	7
Southwest Harbor	1,765	9	5	4
Swan's Island	331	1	1	0
Thomaston	2,776	5	5	0
Topsham	8,728	13	12	1
Van Buren	2,125	3	3	0
Veazie	1,895	4	4	0
Waldoboro	5,016	8	7	1
Washburn	1,651	1	1	0
Waterville	15,897	41	31	10
Wells	9,803	29	21	8
Westbrook	17,647	40	38	2
Wilton	4,066	6	6	0
Windham	17,363	29	25	4
Winslow	7,704	10	9	1
Winthrop	6,051	14	8	6
Wiscasset	3,673	3	3	0
Yarmouth	8,460	14	13	1
York	12,695	35	25	10
MARYLAND				
Aberdeen	15,039	48	40	8
Annapolis	38,649	151	115	36
Baltimore	622,671	3,220	2,829	391
Baltimore City Sheriff		188	161	27
Bel Air	10,314	44	31	13
Berlin	4,589	18	13	5
Berwyn Heights	3,198	8	7	1
Bladensburg	9,381	23	17	6
Boonsboro	3,457	4	4	0
Bowie	56,483	62	57	5
Brentwood	3,116	3	2	1
Brunswick	6,078	13	11	2
Cambridge	12,530	56	45	11
Capitol Heights	4,455	10	9	1
Centreville	4,503	12	11	1
Chestertown	5,406	13	12	1
Cheverly	6,325	16	12	4
Chevy Chase Village	2,024	16	10	6
Colmar Manor	1,436	5	4	1
Cottage City	1,339	7	5	2
Crisfield	2,656	14	11	3
Cumberland	20,495	56	51	5
Delmar	3,047	15	14	1
Denton	4,357	13	12	1

Table 78.   Full-Time Law Enforcement Employees, by Selected State and City, 2013— continued

(Number.)

State/city	Population	Total law enforcement employees	Total officers	Total civilians
District Heights	5,982	11	10	1
Easton	16,721	62	47	15
Edmonston	1,483	9	7	2
Elkton	15,629	46	40	6
Fairmount Heights	1,532	2	2	0
Federalsburg	2,683	9	8	1
Forest Heights	2,504	7	5	2
Frederick	66,709	173	133	40
Frostburg	8,740	19	15	4
Fruitland	5,158	21	20	1
Glenarden	6,163	14	12	2
Greenbelt	23,680	68	53	15
Greensboro	1,888	3	3	0
Hagerstown	40,866	109	96	13
Hampstead	6,336	9	8	1
Hancock	1,562	4	3	1
Havre de Grace	13,530	46	37	9
Hurlock	2,060	11	10	1
Hyattsville	17,955	47	35	12
Landover Hills	1,776	6	5	1
La Plata	9,032	17	16	1
Laurel	25,675	83	64	19
Luke	64	1	1	0
Manchester	4,806	5	5	0
Morningside	2,049	8	6	2
Mount Rainier	8,268	19	15	4
New Carrollton	12,456	23	17	6
North East	3,685	10	9	1
Oakland	1,896	3	3	0
Ocean City	7,086	125	98	27
Ocean Pines	12,024	18	14	4
Oxford	638	3	3	0
Perryville	4,401	13	12	1
Pocomoke City	4,163	23	16	7
Princess Anne	3,302	14	12	2
Ridgely	1,608	5	5	0
Rising Sun	2,874	6	6	0
Riverdale Park	7,126	29	19	10
Rock Hall	1,321	4	4	0
Salisbury	31,517	113	87	26
Seat Pleasant	4,653	14	12	2
Smithsburg	2,989	5	4	1
Snow Hill	2,112	7	6	1
St. Michaels	1,017	9	8	1
Sykesville	4,453	6	5	1
Takoma Park	17,349	55	39	16
Taneytown	6,730	15	14	1
Thurmont	6,405	14	12	2
Trappe	1,064	1	1	0
University Park	2,603	9	8	1
Upper Marlboro	639	3	3	0
Westminster	18,632	56	43	13
MASSACHUSETTS				
Abington	16,121	25	19	6
Acton	22,871	45	35	10
Acushnet	10,362	19	17	2
Adams	8,352	20	16	4
Agawam	28,659	58	49	9
Amesbury	16,655	37	31	6
Amherst	39,127	49	47	2
Andover	34,529	72	53	19
Aquinnah	321	4	4	0
Arlington	44,098	79	64	15
Ashburnham	6,166	10	10	0
Ashby	3,169	8	5	3
Ashfield	1,740	1	1	0
Ashland	17,162	28	21	7
Auburn	16,361	47	36	11
Avon	4,406	17	13	4
Ayer	7,788	23	18	5
Barnstable	44,837	130	115	15
Barre	5,453	9	8	1
Becket	1,778	3	3	0
Bedford	13,947	37	28	9
Belchertown	14,744	23	18	5
Bellingham	16,619	34	27	7
Belmont	25,421	57	40	17
Berkley	6,543	6	6	0

Table 78.   Full-Time Law Enforcement Employees, by Selected State and City, 2013— continued

(Number.)

State/city	Population	Total law enforcement employees	Total officers	Total civilians
Berlin	2,921	11	7	4
Bernardston	2,136	3	3	0
Beverly	40,592	67	63	4
Billerica	41,926	74	60	14
Blackstone	9,094	20	17	3
Blandford	1,242	2	1	1
Bolton	5,060	14	9	5
Boston	643,799	2,704	2,131	573
Bourne	19,875	50	43	7
Boxborough	5,151	16	11	5
Boxford	8,145	13	13	0
Braintree	36,496	88	72	16
Brewster	9,825	26	20	6
Bridgewater	27,034	37	35	2
Brockton	94,448	201	180	21
Brookline	59,382	143	131	12
Buckland	1,902	2	2	0
Burlington	25,435	68	60	8
Cambridge	107,282	304	267	37
Canton	22,100	44	44	0
Carlisle	5,029	15	10	5
Carver	11,552	20	15	5
Charlton	13,195	22	18	4
Chelmsford	34,862	68	54	14
Chelsea	37,454	106	97	9
Cheshire	3,214	1	1	0
Chicopee	55,566	134	130	4
Chilmark	911	5	5	0
Clinton	13,721	31	27	4
Cohasset	8,450	16	15	1
Concord	19,437	44	35	9
Dalton	6,725	12	11	1
Danvers	27,263	53	41	12
Dartmouth	34,562	79	62	17
Dedham	25,094	57	55	2
Deerfield	5,120	8	8	0
Dennis	14,173	49	41	8
Dighton	7,194	10	10	0
Douglas	8,628	19	15	4
Dover	5,778	16	16	0
Dracut	30,533	43	37	6
Dudley	11,619	15	12	3
Dunstable	3,350	9	8	1
Duxbury	15,244	28	26	2
East Bridgewater	14,044	24	20	4
East Brookfield	2,192	4	4	0
Eastham	4,956	22	16	6
Easthampton	15,997	32	26	6
East Longmeadow	15,946	27	26	1
Easton	23,420	42	32	10
Egremont	1,225	2	2	0
Erving	1,803	5	5	0
Essex	3,618	8	7	1
Everett	42,966	98	91	7
Fairhaven	15,951	38	32	6
Fall River	89,220	277	224	53
Falmouth	31,592	60	54	6
Fitchburg	40,521	90	72	18
Foxborough	17,195	42	33	9
Framingham	70,753	126	118	8
Franklin	32,633	56	44	12
Freetown	8,996	18	18	0
Gardner	20,341	44	32	12
Georgetown	8,457	15	11	4
Gill	1,503	2	2	0
Gloucester	29,383	63	58	5
Grafton	18,182	22	18	4
Granby	6,297	13	10	3
Granville	1,616	1	1	0
Greenfield	17,598	35	31	4
Groton	11,164	24	18	6
Groveland	6,917	12	9	3
Halifax	7,574	12	11	1
Hamilton	8,122	19	13	6
Hampden	5,161	16	11	5
Hanover	14,275	38	28	10
Hanson	10,342	26	21	5
Hardwick	3,005	4	4	0
Harvard	6,548	13	10	3

Table 78.   Full-Time Law Enforcement Employees, by Selected State and City, 2013— continued

(Number.)

State/city	Population	Total law enforcement employees	Total officers	Total civilians
Harwich	12,299	40	33	7
Hatfield	3,275	3	3	0
Haverhill	62,249	101	88	13
Hingham	22,687	52	50	2
Holbrook	10,959	21	20	1
Holden	17,775	27	20	7
Holland	2,488	2	2	0
Holliston	14,199	26	21	5
Holyoke	40,215	135	116	19
Hopedale	5,952	16	12	4
Hopkinton	15,689	29	20	9
Hubbardston	4,448	7	7	0
Hudson	19,659	42	31	11
Hull	10,331	25	24	1
Ipswich	13,699	29	24	5
Kingston	12,791	29	22	7
Lakeville	10,939	20	16	4
Lancaster	7,943	12	11	1
Lanesboro	3,047	7	7	0
Lawrence	77,812	133	116	17
Lee	5,883	11	10	1
Leicester	11,183	22	17	5
Lenox	4,993	11	10	1
Leominster	41,175	81	67	14
Leverett	1,871	2	2	0
Lexington	32,632	63	48	15
Lincoln	6,563	19	13	6
Longmeadow	15,844	33	27	6
Lowell	109,449	304	230	74
Ludlow	21,214	38	32	6
Lunenburg	11,149	12	12	0
Lynn	91,769	202	183	19
Lynnfield	11,900	22	17	5
Malden	60,816	115	104	11
Manchester-by-the-Sea	5,255	18	14	4
Mansfield	23,552	34	34	0
Marblehead	20,209	37	28	9
Marion	4,923	15	15	0
Marlborough	39,531	77	65	12
Marshfield	25,581	43	40	3
Mashpee	14,041	47	36	11
Maynard	10,393	22	21	1
Medfield	12,309	20	17	3
Medford	57,428	105	103	2
Medway	12,929	21	20	1
Melrose	27,648	31	31	0
Mendon	5,902	18	14	4
Merrimac	6,590	10	7	3
Methuen	48,363	105	89	16
Middleboro	23,547	42	38	4
Middleton	9,394	14	13	1
Milford	28,312	55	45	10
Millbury	13,355	22	17	5
Millville	3,209	6	5	1
Milton	27,269	61	48	13
Monson	8,716	17	12	5
Montague	8,418	20	15	5
Monterey	953	2	2	0
Nahant	3,461	13	12	1
Nantucket	10,378	46	33	13
Natick	34,085	67	55	12
Needham	29,544	56	48	8
New Bedford	95,156	302	261	41
New Braintree	1,026	1	1	0
Newbury	6,821	11	11	0
Newburyport	17,773	36	30	6
Newton	86,867	173	131	42
Norfolk	11,663	18	16	2
North Adams	13,516	29	24	5
Northampton	28,581	60	55	5
North Andover	28,667	51	39	12
North Attleboro	28,913	52	39	13
Northborough	14,878	25	18	7
Northbridge	16,026	27	19	8
North Brookfield	4,695	6	6	0
Northfield	3,035	3	3	0
North Reading	15,406	30	29	1
Norton	19,414	30	29	1
Norwell	10,622	31	23	8

Table 78.   Full-Time Law Enforcement Employees, by Selected State and City, 2013— continued

(Number.)

State/city	Population	Total law enforcement employees	Total officers	Total civilians
Norwood	28,906	68	57	11
Oak Bluffs	4,679	17	15	2
Orange	7,818	11	10	1
Orleans	5,892	23	17	6
Oxford	13,828	25	20	5
Palmer	12,155	27	21	6
Paxton	4,884	19	17	2
Peabody	52,178	75	60	15
Pelham	1,321	1	1	0
Pembroke	18,040	30	28	2
Pepperell	11,920	17	16	1
Petersham	1,243	2	2	0
Phillipston	1,701	2	2	0
Pittsfield	43,992	102	87	15
Plainville	8,512	19	14	5
Plymouth	57,893	118	103	15
Plympton	2,852	8	8	0
Princeton	3,452	9	6	3
Provincetown	2,983	27	20	7
Quincy	93,490	219	192	27
Randolph	33,583	60	59	1
Raynham	13,580	35	26	9
Reading	25,398	56	42	14
Rehoboth	11,809	28	23	5
Revere	53,777	100	91	9
Rochester	5,367	10	10	0
Rockland	17,656	39	32	7
Rockport	7,116	17	15	2
Rowley	6,015	15	11	4
Rutland	8,272	10	9	1
Salem	42,468	101	90	11
Salisbury	8,490	18	14	4
Sandwich	20,713	35	34	1
Saugus	27,628	74	58	16
Scituate	18,230	33	29	4
Seekonk	14,102	36	34	2
Sharon	17,935	34	30	4
Sheffield	3,225	6	6	0
Shelburne	1,900	3	3	0
Sherborn	4,236	14	14	0
Shirley	7,649	14	9	5
Shrewsbury	36,315	55	43	12
Somerset	18,340	35	29	6
Somerville	77,768	139	125	14
South Hadley	17,794	31	26	5
Southborough	9,908	20	15	5
Southbridge	16,870	37	34	3
Southwick	9,597	23	17	6
Spencer	11,801	21	17	4
Springfield	153,586	500	442	58
Sterling	7,895	17	12	5
Stockbridge	1,966	6	6	0
Stoneham	21,763	40	33	7
Stoughton	28,186	61	56	5
Stow	6,949	15	11	4
Sturbridge	9,399	23	18	5
Sudbury	18,312	37	28	9
Sunderland	3,705	5	5	0
Sutton	9,137	20	16	4
Swampscott	13,995	33	32	1
Swansea	16,099	37	31	6
Taunton	56,264	109	104	5
Tewksbury	29,953	71	57	14
Topsfield	6,351	12	11	1
Truro	2,016	15	10	5
Tyngsboro	12,183	29	23	6
Upton	7,690	17	12	5
Uxbridge	13,629	22	17	5
Wakefield	25,838	44	43	1
Walpole	24,771	44	38	6
Waltham	62,446	167	140	27
Wareham	22,567	57	46	11
Warren	5,158	10	7	3
Warwick	779	2	2	0
Watertown	33,254	78	65	13
Wayland	13,411	30	22	8
Webster	16,871	35	31	4
Wellesley	29,053	61	40	21
Wellfleet	2,747	19	14	5

Table 78.   Full-Time Law Enforcement Employees, by Selected State and City, 2013— continued

(Number.)

State/city	Population	Total law enforcement employees	Total officers	Total civilians
Wenham	5,045	11	10	1
Westborough	18,563	35	29	6
West Boylston	7,821	14	13	1
West Bridgewater	6,966	21	20	1
West Brookfield	3,749	5	4	1
Westfield	41,493	84	80	4
Westford	23,196	54	43	11
Westminster	7,377	18	13	5
West Newbury	4,419	9	8	1
Weston	11,893	30	25	5
Westport	15,735	34	29	5
West Springfield	28,647	92	83	9
Westwood	14,850	34	26	8
Weymouth	55,432	106	89	17
Whately	1,510	2	2	0
Whitman	14,682	27	26	1
Wilbraham	14,375	26	26	0
Williamsburg	2,474	2	2	0
Williamstown	7,682	16	12	4
Wilmington	23,187	50	48	2
Winchendon	10,551	18	13	5
Winchester	22,082	46	38	8
Winthrop	18,131	33	32	1
Woburn	39,284	82	76	6
Worcester	183,454	477	429	48
Wrentham	11,195	21	19	2
Yarmouth	23,736	74	61	13
MICHIGAN				
Adrian	20,759	28	25	3
Adrian Township	6,199	2	2	0
Akron	394	1	1	0
Albion	8,524	19	19	0
Allegan	5,055	10	9	1
Allen Park	27,601	37	35	2
Alma	9,256	16	15	1
Almont	2,678	6	6	0
Alpena	10,299	18	16	2
Ann Arbor	116,799	145	118	27
Argentine Township	6,755	6	5	1
Armada	1,728	2	2	0
Auburn Hills	21,680	62	48	14
Au Gres	861	1	1	0
Augusta	899	3	3	0
Bad Axe	3,052	7	7	0
Bancroft	526	1	1	0
Bangor	1,857	3	3	0
Baraga	2,019	2	2	0
Baroda-Lake Township	3,824	3	2	1
Barry Township	3,372	4	4	0
Bath Township	11,761	13	12	1
Battle Creek	61,032	117	101	16
Bay City	34,395	56	52	4
Belding	5,751	9	8	1
Bellaire	1,078	2	2	0
Belleville	3,900	9	7	2
Bellevue	1,275	2	2	0
Benton Harbor	10,039	18	17	1
Benton Township	14,578	28	23	5
Berkley	15,173	32	27	5
Berrien Springs-Oronoko Township	9,170	11	9	2
Beverly Hills	10,399	24	23	1
Big Rapids	10,735	18	17	1
Birch Run	1,525	6	5	1
Birmingham	20,544	39	30	9
Blackman Township	38,115	34	33	1
Blissfield	3,276	5	5	0
Bloomfield Hills	3,952	28	25	3
Bloomfield Township	41,791	91	72	19
Boyne City	3,757	8	7	1
Breckenridge	1,308	1	1	0
Bridgeport Township	10,341	7	6	1
Bridgman	2,275	4	4	0
Brighton	7,586	18	17	1
Bronson	2,340	4	4	0
Brown City	1,292	2	2	0
Brownstown Township	30,388	43	34	9
Buchanan	4,419	9	8	1
Buena Vista Township	8,500	15	14	1

Table 78.   Full-Time Law Enforcement Employees, by Selected State and City, 2013— continued

(Number.)

State/city	Population	Total law enforcement employees	Total officers	Total civilians
Burr Oak	820	1	1	0
Burton	29,263	32	29	3
Byron	562	1	1	0
Cadillac	10,239	17	15	2
Calumet	716	1	1	0
Cambridge Township	5,663	4	3	1
Canton Township	88,958	110	76	34
Capac	1,848	1	1	0
Carleton	2,324	4	3	1
Caro	4,135	7	7	0
Carrollton Township	5,997	7	6	1
Carson City	1,089	3	3	0
Caseville	756	2	2	0
Cass City	2,372	4	4	0
Cassopolis	1,760	5	5	0
Cedar Springs	3,565	7	7	0
Center Line	8,251	21	17	4
Central Lake	945	8	8	0
Charlevoix	2,524	8	7	1
Charlotte	9,046	17	16	1
Cheboygan	4,789	8	8	0
Chelsea	5,056	12	8	4
Chesterfield Township	43,784	50	38	12
Chikaming Township	3,088	5	5	0
Chocolay Township	6,029	5	4	1
Clare	3,095	8	7	1
Clawson	11,984	19	17	2
Clayton Township	7,322	4	4	0
Clay Township	8,891	16	12	4
Clinton	2,293	4	4	0
Clinton Township	98,071	92	80	12
Clio	2,580	4	4	0
Coldwater	10,876	18	17	1
Coleman	1,231	2	2	0
Coloma Township	6,475	10	8	2
Colon	1,157	3	3	0
Columbia Township	7,415	6	6	0
Concord	1,049	1	1	0
Constantine	2,052	4	4	0
Corunna	3,410	4	3	1
Covert Township	2,833	6	6	0
Croswell	2,379	5	5	0
Crystal Falls	1,431	2	2	0
Davison	5,050	8	7	1
Davison Township	19,212	19	17	2
Dearborn	96,012	209	182	27
Dearborn Heights	56,583	98	80	18
Decatur	1,778	5	5	0
Denton Township	5,434	4	4	0
Detroit	699,889	2,632	2,356	276
Dewitt	4,587	7	6	1
Dewitt Township	14,494	15	15	0
Dowagiac	5,840	15	14	1
Dryden Township	4,771	4	4	0
Dundee	3,926	12	12	0
Durand	3,350	4	4	0
East Grand Rapids	11,100	30	28	2
East Jordan	2,358	4	4	0
East Lansing	48,506	70	57	13
Eastpointe	32,402	40	37	3
Eaton Rapids	5,199	8	7	1
Ecorse	9,294	20	18	2
Elk Rapids	1,629	5	5	0
Elkton	790	2	2	0
Elsie	969	1	1	0
Emmett Township	11,648	16	14	2
Erie Township	4,458	2	2	0
Escanaba	12,531	40	29	11
Essexville	3,436	8	8	0
Evart	1,877	4	4	0
Fair Haven Township	1,076	8	7	1
Farmington	10,514	24	22	2
Farmington Hills	81,084	135	104	31
Fennville	1,396	1	1	0
Fenton	11,493	16	14	2
Ferndale	20,104	48	41	7
Flat Rock	9,772	17	17	0
Flint	99,941	150	122	28
Flint Township	31,182	37	34	3

Table 78.   Full-Time Law Enforcement Employees, by Selected State and City, 2013— continued

(Number.)

State/city	Population	Total law enforcement employees	Total officers	Total civilians
Flushing	8,204	10	10	0
Forsyth Township	6,278	9	8	1
Fowlerville	2,910	6	5	1
Frankenmuth	4,925	7	7	0
Frankfort	1,281	2	2	0
Franklin	3,194	10	10	0
Fraser	14,529	47	36	11
Fremont	4,034	8	7	1
Frost Township	1,037	1	1	0
Fruitport	1,090	10	9	1
Gagetown	380	1	1	0
Galesburg	2,035	2	2	0
Garden City	27,110	31	29	2
Gaylord	3,615	10	9	1
Genesee Township	20,977	14	12	2
Gerrish Township	2,942	7	7	0
Gibraltar	4,564	9	8	1
Gladstone	4,915	9	9	0
Gladwin	2,907	4	4	0
Grand Beach	271	4	4	0
Grand Blanc	8,105	20	17	3
Grand Blanc Township	36,793	43	38	5
Grand Haven	10,731	34	31	3
Grand Ledge	7,772	15	15	0
Grand Rapids	191,213	353	282	71
Grandville	15,669	25	23	2
Grant	882	1	1	0
Grayling	1,872	6	6	0
Green Oak Township	17,977	16	14	2
Greenville	8,423	20	16	4
Grosse Ile Township	10,194	24	17	7
Grosse Pointe	5,300	23	23	0
Grosse Pointe Farms	9,271	39	32	7
Grosse Pointe Park	11,287	42	36	6
Grosse Pointe Shores	2,948	14	14	0
Grosse Pointe Woods	15,760	36	32	4
Hamburg Township	21,455	17	16	1
Hampton Township	9,555	11	10	1
Hamtramck	22,017	28	27	1
Hancock	4,614	7	7	0
Harbor Beach	1,659	4	4	0
Harbor Springs	1,204	6	5	1
Harper Woods	13,922	33	29	4
Hart	2,103	4	4	0
Hartford	2,633	5	5	0
Hastings	7,288	14	12	2
Hazel Park	16,642	37	33	4
Hesperia	945	1	1	0
Highland Park	11,591	5	5	0
Hillsdale	8,188	16	14	2
Holland	33,354	65	57	8
Holly	6,150	10	10	0
Homer	1,641	3	3	0
Home Township	1,335	1	1	0
Hopkins	607	1	1	0
Houghton	7,699	8	7	1
Howard City	1,786	3	3	0
Howell	9,514	18	16	2
Hudson	2,263	2	2	0
Huntington Woods	6,305	18	17	1
Huron Township	15,607	14	12	2
Imlay City	3,586	8	8	0
Inkster	24,850	26	25	1
Ionia	11,434	17	15	2
Iron Mountain	7,641	13	13	0
Iron River	2,951	4	4	0
Ironwood	5,202	11	10	1
Ishpeming	6,582	10	9	1
Ishpeming Township	3,579	1	1	0
Jackson	33,378	59	46	13
Jonesville	2,231	4	4	0
Kalamazoo	75,352	255	209	46
Kalamazoo Township	24,153	39	31	8
Kalkaska	2,017	3	2	1
Keego Harbor	3,013	12	12	0
Kentwood	50,016	80	69	11
Kingsford	5,153	17	17	0
Kingston	432	1	1	0
Kinross Township	7,821	2	2	0

Table 78.   Full-Time Law Enforcement Employees, by Selected State and City, 2013— continued

(Number.)

State/city	Population	Total law enforcement employees	Total officers	Total civilians
Laingsburg	1,262	1	1	0
Lake Angelus	295	1	1	0
Lake Linden	1,001	1	1	0
Lake Odessa	2,017	4	4	0
Lake Orion	3,052	6	4	2
Lakeview	1,003	2	2	0
L'Anse	1,949	4	4	0
Lansing	113,907	214	185	29
Lansing Township	8,087	15	14	1
Lapeer	8,819	22	20	2
Lathrup Village	4,128	8	8	0
Laurium	1,962	4	4	0
Lawton	1,870	5	5	0
Lennon	500	1	1	0
Leslie	1,844	3	3	0
Lexington	1,143	3	3	0
Lincoln Park	37,295	48	41	7
Lincoln Township	14,618	12	11	1
Linden	3,897	5	5	0
Litchfield	1,355	3	3	0
Livonia	95,220	156	122	34
Lowell	3,858	7	5	2
Ludington	8,035	15	14	1
Luna Pier	1,417	3	3	0
Mackinac Island	494	5	4	1
Mackinaw City	808	7	7	0
Madison Heights	30,080	55	43	12
Madison Township	8,567	3	3	0
Mancelona	1,379	4	2	2
Manistee	6,158	12	12	0
Manistique	3,031	8	8	0
Manton	1,292	1	1	0
Marenisco Township	1,730	1	1	0
Marine City	4,153	3	3	0
Marlette	1,828	4	4	0
Marquette	21,590	39	34	5
Marshall	7,050	13	13	0
Marysville	9,763	15	13	2
Mason	8,246	13	12	1
Mattawan	1,971	4	4	0
Mayville	928	10	10	0
Melvindale	10,473	25	23	2
Memphis	1,178	1	1	0
Mendon	858	1	1	0
Menominee	8,476	16	15	1
Meridian Township	40,609	41	37	4
Metamora Township	4,238	4	4	0
Michiana	182	3	3	0
Midland	42,072	49	47	2
Milan	5,875	12	9	3
Milford	16,170	23	18	5
Millington	1,046	1	1	0
Monroe	20,474	45	39	6
Montague	2,338	5	5	0
Montrose Township	7,706	9	8	1
Morenci	2,190	2	2	0
Morrice	899	2	2	0
Mount Morris	3,012	7	5	2
Mount Morris Township	20,990	30	27	3
Mount Pleasant	26,238	35	29	6
Mundy Township	14,781	17	14	3
Munising	2,325	4	4	0
Muskegon	36,658	85	76	9
Muskegon Heights	10,768	18	16	2
Muskegon Township	17,693	15	14	1
Napoleon Township	6,771	2	2	0
Nashville	1,622	2	2	0
Negaunee	4,650	7	6	1
Newaygo	1,961	4	4	0
New Baltimore	12,148	17	16	1
New Buffalo	1,877	8	7	1
Niles	11,471	25	17	8
North Branch	1,029	2	2	0
Northfield Township	8,387	11	10	1
North Muskegon	3,756	7	7	0
Northville	5,992	13	13	0
Northville Township	28,734	41	30	11
Norton Shores	23,834	29	27	2
Norway	2,853	4	4	0

Table 78.   Full-Time Law Enforcement Employees, by Selected State and City, 2013— continued

(Number.)

State/city	Population	Total law enforcement employees	Total officers	Total civilians
Novi	57,469	84	63	21
Oakley	285	1	1	0
Oak Park	29,684	57	46	11
Olivet	1,610	2	2	0
Ontwa Township-Edwardsburg	6,585	7	7	0
Orchard Lake	2,424	9	8	1
Oscoda Township	6,819	12	11	1
Otisville	840	1	1	0
Otsego	3,953	7	6	1
Ovid	1,608	2	2	0
Owosso	14,745	21	19	2
Oxford	3,476	16	10	6
Paw Paw	3,470	9	8	1
Pentwater	849	3	3	0
Perry	2,104	4	4	0
Petoskey	5,722	19	18	1
Pigeon	1,177	1	1	0
Pinckney	2,461	4	4	0
Pinconning	1,288	1	1	0
Pittsfield Township	36,091	49	38	11
Plainwell	3,798	8	7	1
Pleasant Ridge	2,550	6	6	0
Plymouth	8,949	16	15	1
Plymouth Township	27,076	40	26	14
Portage	47,387	69	52	17
Port Austin	647	1	1	0
Port Huron	29,542	57	48	9
Portland	3,891	6	6	0
Potterville	2,613	2	2	0
Prairieville Township	3,388	3	3	0
Raisin Township	7,468	6	5	1
Reading	1,063	1	1	0
Redford Township	47,432	69	57	12
Reed City	2,396	4	4	0
Reese	1,421	2	2	0
Richfield Township, Genesee County	8,523	11	9	2
Richfield Township, Roscommon County	3,663	7	6	1
Richland	768	2	2	0
Richland Township, Saginaw County	4,089	3	3	0
Richmond	5,741	11	9	2
River Rouge	7,723	21	19	2
Riverview	12,267	25	24	1
Rochester	12,947	27	21	6
Rockford	5,894	11	10	1
Rockwood	3,221	7	7	0
Rogers City	2,764	6	6	0
Romeo	3,597	11	8	3
Romulus	23,483	54	43	11
Roosevelt Park	3,800	5	5	0
Rose City	645	1	1	0
Roseville	47,327	65	62	3
Royal Oak	58,804	82	69	13
Saginaw	50,580	63	55	8
Saginaw Township	40,636	48	43	5
Saline	9,028	16	12	4
Sand Lake	512	1	1	0
Sandusky	2,624	4	4	0
Saugatuck-Douglas	2,173	9	8	1
Sault Ste. Marie	14,203	26	24	2
Schoolcraft	1,548	3	3	0
Scottville	1,215	1	1	0
Sebewaing	1,715	3	3	0
Shelby	2,040	3	3	0
Shelby Township	75,347	87	69	18
Shepherd	1,525	2	2	0
Somerset Township	4,582	1	1	0
Southfield	72,755	150	124	26
Southgate	29,459	44	40	4
South Haven	4,355	21	19	2
South Lyon	11,552	17	16	1
South Rockwood	1,660	2	2	0
Sparta	4,224	5	5	0
Spaulding Township	2,112	1	1	0
Spring Arbor Township	8,276	2	2	0
Springfield	5,210	13	12	1
Spring Lake-Ferrysburg	5,311	10	9	1
Springport Township	2,160	2	2	0
Standish	1,461	1	1	0

Table 78.   Full-Time Law Enforcement Employees, by Selected State and City, 2013— continued

(Number.)

State/city	Population	Total law enforcement employees	Total officers	Total civilians
Stanton	1,409	1	1	0
St. Charles	2,021	2	2	0
St. Clair	5,375	9	9	0
St. Clair Shores	59,754	89	84	5
Sterling Heights	130,634	186	147	39
St. Ignace	2,454	4	3	1
St. Johns	7,906	11	10	1
St. Joseph	8,293	19	17	2
St. Joseph Township	9,953	11	10	1
St. Louis	7,416	7	6	1
Stockbridge	1,222	2	2	0
Sturgis	10,850	23	18	5
Sumpter Township	9,310	14	12	2
Suttons Bay	616	1	1	0
Swartz Creek	5,646	7	6	1
Sylvan Lake	1,749	2	2	0
Tawas	4,526	6	5	1
Taylor	61,836	90	70	20
Tecumseh	8,401	14	12	2
Thetford Township	6,872	2	2	0
Thomas Township	11,846	7	7	0
Three Oaks	1,599	1	1	0
Three Rivers	7,712	18	16	2
Tittabawassee Township	9,849	5	4	1
Traverse City	14,989	29	28	1
Trenton	18,483	33	32	1
Troy	82,608	138	91	47
Tuscarora Township	2,996	8	7	1
Ubly	836	1	1	0
Unadilla Township	3,402	2	2	0
Union City	1,591	4	4	0
Utica	4,765	16	12	4
Van Buren Township	28,282	50	38	12
Vassar	2,635	3	3	0
Vernon	760	1	1	0
Vicksburg	2,993	6	6	0
Walker	24,158	38	34	4
Walled Lake	7,101	7	6	1
Warren	134,167	236	198	38
Waterford Township	72,949	63	50	13
Waterloo Township	2,841	2	2	0
Watervliet	1,716	1	1	0
Wayland	4,074	8	7	1
Wayne	17,232	28	28	0
West Bloomfield Township	65,840	95	73	22
West Branch	2,110	5	4	1
Westland	82,554	103	77	26
White Cloud	1,387	2	2	0
Whitehall	2,683	8	8	0
White Lake Township	30,585	35	25	10
White Pigeon	1,508	4	4	0
Williamston	3,836	6	5	1
Wixom	13,744	20	17	3
Wolverine Lake	4,370	5	5	0
Woodhaven	12,652	29	27	2
Wyandotte	25,378	44	33	11
Wyoming	73,786	98	84	14
Yale	1,909	3	3	0
Ypsilanti	19,677	27	23	4
Zeeland	5,575	10	9	1
Zilwaukee	1,629	2	2	0
MINNESOTA				
Albany	2,599	5	4	1
Albert Lea	17,867	35	25	10
Alexandria	11,716	25	21	4
Annandale	3,317	4	4	0
Anoka	17,270	33	27	6
Appleton	1,368	3	3	0
Apple Valley	50,262	52	43	9
Austin	24,823	34	31	3
Avon	1,414	3	3	0
Babbitt	1,467	4	4	0
Baxter	7,719	15	14	1
Bayport	3,649	6	5	1
Becker	4,622	6	5	1
Belgrade	752	2	2	0
Belle Plaine	6,848	10	8	2
Bemidji	13,805	34	32	2

Table 78.   Full-Time Law Enforcement Employees, by Selected State and City, 2013— continued

(Number.)

State/city	Population	Total law enforcement employees	Total officers	Total civilians
Benson	3,142	8	7	1
Big Lake	10,296	13	11	2
Blackduck	795	2	2	0
Blaine	60,093	76	59	17
Blooming Prairie	1,962	3	3	0
Bloomington	87,057	140	111	29
Blue Earth	3,264	5	5	0
Brainerd	13,493	29	23	6
Breckenridge	3,388	7	7	0
Brooklyn Center	30,814	60	48	12
Brooklyn Park	78,353	132	104	28
Brownton	741	1	1	0
Buffalo	15,802	20	17	3
Burnsville	61,371	88	74	14
Caledonia	2,807	5	4	1
Cambridge	8,244	15	14	1
Canby	1,729	5	5	0
Cannon Falls	4,080	9	8	1
Centennial Lakes	10,812	18	16	2
Champlin	23,881	29	24	5
Chaska	24,158	27	24	3
Chisholm	5,042	12	11	1
Cloquet	12,005	21	19	2
Cold Spring	5,455	8	7	1
Columbia Heights	19,715	32	27	5
Coon Rapids	62,056	70	62	8
Corcoran	5,539	8	7	1
Cottage Grove	35,339	45	39	6
Crookston	7,827	15	13	2
Crosby	2,369	8	7	1
Crystal	22,642	34	29	5
Dawson	1,495	3	3	0
Dayton	4,885	6	5	1
Deephaven	3,742	8	7	1
Detroit Lakes	8,887	16	14	2
Dilworth	4,111	6	5	1
Duluth	86,211	178	153	25
Eagan	65,052	80	69	11
Eagle Lake	2,573	2	2	0
East Grand Forks	8,528	23	20	3
Echo	269	1	1	0
Eden Prairie	62,714	92	68	24
Edina	49,405	73	50	23
Elk River	23,351	40	31	9
Elmore	645	1	1	0
Ely	3,432	8	7	1
Eveleth	3,691	11	10	1
Fairmont	10,400	18	15	3
Faribault	23,405	36	31	5
Farmington	22,190	29	25	4
Fergus Falls	13,244	28	23	5
Floodwood	528	4	3	1
Forest Lake	19,140	29	26	3
Fridley	27,775	43	38	5
Gilbert	1,794	7	7	0
Glencoe	5,532	9	8	1
Glenwood	2,518	3	3	0
Golden Valley	20,904	40	30	10
Goodview	3,996	4	4	0
Grand Rapids	10,934	22	19	3
Granite Falls	2,790	4	4	0
Hallock	962	1	1	0
Hastings	22,365	32	29	3
Hermantown	9,660	18	15	3
Hibbing	16,267	30	26	4
Hokah	566	1	1	0
Hopkins	18,108	36	27	9
Houston	978	2	2	0
Hoyt Lakes	2,002	5	5	0
Hutchinson	13,857	29	20	9
International Falls	6,336	12	11	1
Inver Grove Heights	34,294	39	34	5
Isanti	5,417	9	8	1
Janesville	2,267	2	2	0
Jordan	5,955	10	8	2
Kasson	6,023	8	8	0
Kimball	761	4	4	0
La Crescent	4,802	8	7	1
Lake City	4,988	12	10	2

Table 78.   Full-Time Law Enforcement Employees, by Selected State and City, 2013— continued

(Number.)

State/city	Population	Total law enforcement employees	Total officers	Total civilians
Lake Crystal	2,557	3	3	0
Lakefield	1,686	3	3	0
Lakes Area	9,302	14	12	2
Lakeville	57,758	59	51	8
Lester Prairie	1,683	3	3	0
Le Sueur	4,021	8	7	1
Lewiston	1,589	2	2	0
Lino Lakes	20,910	26	24	2
Litchfield	6,653	10	9	1
Little Falls	8,266	15	13	2
Long Prairie	3,392	5	5	0
Mankato	40,360	60	50	10
Maple Grove	65,318	77	65	12
Mapleton	1,766	3	3	0
Maplewood	39,765	52	47	5
Marshall	13,370	26	20	6
Medina	5,093	11	10	1
Melrose	3,603	5	4	1
Mendota Heights	11,158	18	17	1
Milaca	2,882	12	11	1
Minneapolis	396,206	977	844	133
Minnetonka	51,573	72	55	17
Minnetrista	9,119	12	10	2
Montevideo	5,201	11	10	1
Montgomery	2,926	5	4	1
Moorhead	39,322	67	53	14
Moose Lake	2,798	4	4	0
Morris	5,276	10	8	2
Mounds View	12,486	21	19	2
Mountain Lake	2,075	4	4	0
New Brighton	21,995	31	27	4
New Hope	20,852	38	31	7
Newport	3,457	7	7	0
New Prague	7,457	11	9	2
New Richland	1,209	1	1	0
New Ulm	13,185	25	22	3
North Branch	9,966	12	10	2
Northfield	20,675	25	20	5
North Mankato	13,357	14	13	1
North St. Paul	11,767	19	17	2
Oakdale	27,820	39	29	10
Oak Park Heights	4,655	11	10	1
Olivia	2,418	5	5	0
Orono	21,190	31	27	4
Ortonville	1,858	3	3	0
Osakis	1,710	3	3	0
Osseo	2,484	6	5	1
Owatonna	25,377	38	35	3
Park Rapids	3,673	11	10	1
Paynesville	2,429	4	4	0
Plainview	3,292	5	5	0
Plymouth	73,684	78	69	9
Princeton	4,653	13	11	2
Prior Lake	24,056	26	24	2
Proctor	3,053	7	6	1
Ramsey	24,186	26	22	4
Red Wing	16,489	32	27	5
Redwood Falls	5,152	12	10	2
Richfield	36,367	52	42	10
Robbinsdale	14,363	27	23	4
Rochester	109,675	189	133	56
Rogers	11,782	19	16	3
Roseau	2,603	6	5	1
Rosemount	22,579	25	22	3
Roseville	34,991	55	47	8
Sartell	16,258	18	17	1
Sauk Centre	4,325	7	6	1
Sauk Rapids	13,008	13	12	1
Savage	28,285	39	32	7
Shakopee	39,214	55	46	9
Silver Bay	1,861	4	4	0
Silver Lake	815	2	2	0
Slayton	2,095	4	4	0
Sleepy Eye	3,501	6	6	0
South Lake Minnetonka	11,992	16	14	2
South St. Paul	20,484	28	26	2
Springfield	2,102	4	4	0
Spring Grove	1,304	2	2	0
Spring Lake Park	6,458	13	11	2

Table 78.   Full-Time Law Enforcement Employees, by Selected State and City, 2013— continued

(Number.)

State/city	Population	Total law enforcement employees	Total officers	Total civilians
St. Anthony	8,445	26	23	3
Staples	2,916	6	5	1
St. Charles	3,688	5	5	0
St. Cloud	65,977	121	100	21
St. Francis	6,274	12	10	2
Stillwater	18,631	24	20	4
St. James	4,580	8	7	1
St. Joseph	6,671	9	8	1
St. Louis Park	46,723	65	51	14
St. Paul	294,690	752	587	165
St. Paul Park	5,335	9	9	0
St. Peter	11,506	19	14	5
Thief River Falls	8,686	16	14	2
Tracy	2,135	5	4	1
Two Harbors	3,676	9	8	1
Virginia	8,625	16	16	0
Wabasha	2,497	6	5	1
Wadena	4,092	7	6	1
Waite Park	6,683	18	15	3
Warroad	1,768	6	5	1
Waseca	9,443	15	14	1
Wayzata	3,805	13	12	1
Wells	2,275	4	4	0
West Hennepin	5,458	12	10	2
West St. Paul	19,761	33	30	3
Wheaton	1,368	4	4	0
White Bear Lake	24,472	35	28	7
Willmar	19,691	36	32	4
Windom	4,594	10	9	1
Winnebago	1,394	3	3	0
Winona	28,077	40	36	4
Winsted	2,299	4	4	0
Woodbury	65,259	78	68	10
Worthington	12,903	33	23	10
Wyoming	7,690	10	9	1
Zumbrota	3,305	4	4	0
MISSISSIPPI				
Aberdeen	5,473	21	16	5
Ackerman	1,461	5	5	0
Amory	7,167	26	19	7
Batesville	7,417	48	37	11
Bay St. Louis	10,591	26	22	4
Biloxi	44,744	171	123	48
Brandon	22,326	48	38	10
Byhalia	1,270	14	9	5
Byram	11,795	37	25	12
Carthage	5,018	18	14	4
Columbia	6,430	28	21	7
Columbus	23,377	84	72	12
D'Iberville	10,123	34	32	2
Flowood	8,249	64	49	15
Fulton	3,984	10	10	0
Gautier	18,532	45	35	10
Greenville	33,119	109	92	17
Greenwood	16,112	75	57	18
Hollandale	2,629	11	7	4
Horn Lake	26,670	73	57	16
Indianola	10,443	32	25	7
Iuka	3,015	12	9	3
Jackson	176,039	725	442	283
Kosciusko	7,190	21	21	0
Long Beach	15,467	51	37	14
Madison	25,044	96	76	20
Magee	4,401	15	11	4
Meridian	40,748	109	90	19
Olive Branch	34,827	94	71	23
Pascagoula	22,217	101	65	36
Pass Christian	5,020	21	19	2
Petal	10,902	31	25	6
Ridgeland	24,319	92	65	27
Ripley	5,332	12	11	1
Ruleville	2,915	12	8	4
Southaven	50,801	134	112	22
Starkville	24,519	62	51	11
West Point	11,179	31	27	4
MISSOURI				
Adrian	1,633	3	3	0

Table 78.   Full-Time Law Enforcement Employees, by Selected State and City, 2013— continued

(Number.)

State/city	Population	Total law enforcement employees	Total officers	Total civilians
Advance	1,341	3	3	0
Alton	882	1	1	0
Anderson	1,999	4	4	0
Appleton City	1,081	4	4	0
Arbyrd	504	1	1	0
Archie	1,187	4	4	0
Arnold	21,070	60	49	11
Ashland	3,844	7	6	1
Aurora	7,474	22	15	7
Ava	2,970	15	9	6
Ballwin	30,452	63	51	12
Battlefield	5,783	6	6	0
Bella Villa	726	5	5	0
Belle	1,531	3	3	0
Bellefontaine Neighbors	10,819	36	34	2
Bel-Nor	1,490	6	6	0
Bel-Ridge	2,726	19	14	5
Belton	23,273	62	41	21
Berkeley	8,946	47	37	10
Bernie	1,938	9	5	4
Bertrand	815	1	1	0
Bethany	3,168	5	5	0
Beverly Hills	570	6	4	2
Billings	1,060	4	4	0
Birch Tree	664	2	2	0
Bismarck	1,506	3	3	0
Bloomfield	1,901	5	5	0
Blue Springs	53,131	129	94	35
Bolivar	10,408	23	19	4
Bonne Terre	7,088	10	10	0
Boonville	8,301	28	21	7
Bourbon	1,644	9	8	1
Bowling Green	5,534	15	11	4
Branson	10,918	58	42	16
Branson West	458	6	6	0
Braymer	849	1	1	0
Breckenridge Hills	4,724	17	16	1
Brentwood	8,030	35	27	8
Bridgeton	11,657	67	49	18
Brookfield	4,403	18	11	7
Brunswick	831	1	1	0
Bucklin	451	1	1	0
Buckner	3,070	9	8	1
Buffalo	3,100	7	6	1
Butler	4,137	14	10	4
Butterfield Village	464	1	1	0
Byrnes Mill	2,785	6	6	0
Cabool	2,126	10	6	4
California	4,327	7	6	1
Calverton Park	1,290	7	7	0
Camdenton	3,810	20	16	4
Cameron	9,867	24	16	8
Campbell	1,982	4	4	0
Canton	2,377	5	4	1
Cape Girardeau	38,716	92	74	18
Cardwell	708	2	2	0
Carl Junction	7,390	17	12	5
Carrollton	3,663	8	8	0
Carterville	1,823	6	6	0
Carthage	13,988	36	27	9
Caruthersville	6,107	19	18	1
Cassville	3,255	11	11	0
Center	513	1	1	0
Centralia	4,169	13	8	5
Chaffee	2,948	10	6	4
Charlack	1,362	7	7	0
Charleston	5,907	18	12	6
Chesterfield	47,744	96	86	10
Chillicothe	9,419	24	17	7
Clarkton	1,276	3	3	0
Claycomo	1,462	8	8	0
Clayton	15,901	63	53	10
Clever	2,343	5	5	0
Clinton	9,054	24	23	1
Cole Camp	1,111	3	3	0
Columbia	114,587	185	152	33
Concordia	2,406	6	6	0
Conway	777	1	1	0
Cottleville	3,682	11	11	0

Table 78.   Full-Time Law Enforcement Employees, by Selected State and City, 2013— continued

(Number.)

State/city	Population	Total law enforcement employees	Total officers	Total civilians
Country Club Hills	1,266	12	12	0
Country Club Village	2,477	2	2	0
Crane	1,410	3	3	0
Crestwood	11,931	31	25	6
Creve Coeur	17,862	51	47	4
Crocker	1,120	5	4	1
Crystal City	4,821	23	17	6
Cuba	3,390	13	12	1
Delta	440	1	1	0
Desloge	4,960	10	10	0
De Soto	6,460	20	15	5
Des Peres	8,434	49	41	8
Dexter	7,882	23	17	6
Diamond	929	3	2	1
Dixon	1,573	5	4	1
Doniphan	1,992	12	8	4
Doolittle	615	2	2	0
Drexel	960	2	2	0
Duenweg	1,088	3	3	0
Duquesne	1,706	6	6	0
East Prairie	3,205	11	7	4
Edina	1,155	3	2	1
Edmundson	837	11	10	1
Eldon	4,589	12	11	1
El Dorado Springs	3,520	11	7	4
Ellington	995	3	3	0
Ellisville	9,146	21	20	1
Ellsinore	453	1	1	0
Elsberry	1,953	3	3	0
Eminence	587	1	1	0
Emma	233	1	1	0
Essex	464	1	1	0
Eureka	10,450	26	22	4
Excelsior Springs	11,346	35	24	11
Exeter	767	1	1	0
Fair Play	467	1	1	0
Farmington	17,506	34	26	8
Fayette	2,718	7	7	0
Ferguson	21,115	65	54	11
Ferrelview	462	1	1	0
Festus	11,782	36	25	11
Flordell Hills	819	12	12	0
Florissant	52,289	110	89	21
Foley	164	3	3	0
Fordland	795	2	2	0
Foristell	505	8	7	1
Forsyth	2,285	8	7	1
Fredericktown	4,101	11	9	2
Freeman	480	1	1	0
Frontenac	3,516	22	21	1
Fulton	12,713	35	28	7
Galena	422	1	1	0
Gallatin	1,730	1	1	0
Garden City	1,637	4	4	0
Gerald	1,324	4	4	0
Gideon	1,047	3	3	0
Gladstone	26,083	67	48	19
Glasgow	1,102	3	3	0
Glendale	5,920	14	11	3
Glen Echo Park	160	6	4	2
Goodman	1,244	2	2	0
Gower	1,498	3	3	0
Grain Valley	13,081	28	22	6
Granby	2,170	4	4	0
Grandview	24,630	65	53	12
Greenfield	1,299	3	3	0
Greenville	490	2	2	0
Greenwood	5,331	11	10	1
Hallsville	1,544	2	2	0
Hamilton	1,722	5	4	1
Hannibal	17,784	47	37	10
Hardin	551	1	1	0
Harrisonville	9,999	30	23	7
Hartville	606	2	2	0
Hawk Point	673	1	1	0
Hayti	2,890	10	9	1
Hayti Heights	613	4	2	2
Hazelwood	25,670	82	68	14
Herculaneum	3,756	13	12	1

Table 78.   Full-Time Law Enforcement Employees, by Selected State and City, 2013— continued

(Number.)

State/city	Population	Total law enforcement employees	Total officers	Total civilians
Hermann	2,380	11	6	5
Higginsville	4,730	15	9	6
Highlandville	916	2	2	0
Hillsboro	2,949	7	7	0
Hillsdale	1,513	17	16	1
Holcomb	630	2	2	0
Holden	2,333	7	6	1
Hollister	4,415	19	13	6
Holt	457	1	1	0
Holts Summit	3,401	10	9	1
Hornersville	658	3	2	1
Houston	2,083	6	6	0
Howardville	370	2	1	1
Humansville	1,039	1	1	0
Hurley	173	1	1	0
Iberia	736	2	2	0
Independence	117,381	282	201	81
Indian Point	521	2	2	0
Iron Mountain Lake	718	2	2	0
Ironton	1,416	3	3	0
Jackson	14,307	31	22	9
Jasper	898	1	1	0
Jefferson City	43,193	120	83	37
Jennings	14,752	35	35	0
Jonesburg	744	1	1	0
Joplin	49,272	117	92	25
Kahoka	2,039	3	3	0
Kansas City	465,514	1,937	1,367	570
Kearney	8,977	16	15	1
Kennett	10,897	27	23	4
Kimberling City	2,325	7	6	1
King City	1,024	1	1	0
Kirksville	17,529	29	26	3
Knob Noster	2,804	12	7	5
Ladue	8,548	33	27	6
La Grange	932	9	8	1
Lake Lotawana	1,956	6	6	0
Lake Ozark	1,623	18	12	6
Lakeshire	1,427	4	4	0
Lake St. Louis	14,733	38	30	8
Lake Tapawingo	728	2	2	0
Lake Winnebago	1,129	5	5	0
Lamar	4,511	12	10	2
La Monte	1,141	2	2	0
La Plata	1,359	3	3	0
Lathrop	2,042	4	4	0
Laurie	920	5	5	0
Lawson	2,418	6	5	1
Leadington	410	6	5	1
Leadwood	1,246	5	5	0
Lee's Summit	92,765	189	134	55
Liberty	30,000	53	37	16
Licking	3,061	5	5	0
Lincoln	1,183	3	3	0
Linn Creek	243	4	3	1
Lone Jack	1,069	6	6	0
Louisiana	3,322	12	7	5
Lowry City	617	2	2	0
Macon	5,507	14	12	2
Malden	4,248	17	13	4
Manchester	18,187	41	38	3
Mansfield	1,280	4	4	0
Maplewood	8,009	33	31	2
Marble Hill	1,502	4	4	0
Marceline	2,171	9	6	3
Marionville	2,207	4	4	0
Marshall	13,019	35	26	9
Marshfield	6,696	12	11	1
Marston	487	1	1	0
Marthasville	1,129	1	1	0
Maryland Heights	27,439	97	79	18
Maryville	12,027	26	20	6
Matthews	643	2	2	0
Maysville	1,123	1	1	0
Memphis	1,846	3	3	0
Merriam Woods	1,754	3	3	0
Mexico	11,564	36	34	2
Milan	1,893	5	5	0
Miller	694	1	1	0

Table 78.   Full-Time Law Enforcement Employees, by Selected State and City, 2013— continued

(Number.)

State/city	Population	Total law enforcement employees	Total officers	Total civilians
Miner	977	11	7	4
Miramiguoa	119	1	1	0
Moberly	13,979	37	27	10
Moline Acres	2,435	13	12	1
Monett	8,927	28	20	8
Monroe City	2,474	7	7	0
Montgomery City	2,779	6	6	0
Morehouse	937	2	2	0
Morley	691	2	1	1
Moscow Mills	2,540	5	5	0
Mound City	1,084	2	2	0
Mountain Grove	4,741	16	12	4
Mountain View	2,715	9	8	1
Mount Vernon	4,549	10	10	0
Neosho	12,213	20	19	1
Nevada	8,110	23	19	4
Newburg	458	2	2	0
New Florence	745	2	2	0
New Franklin	1,087	2	1	1
New Haven	2,096	6	6	0
New London	983	1	1	0
New Madrid	3,028	8	8	0
Nixa	20,110	30	25	5
Noel	1,820	3	3	0
Norborne	683	1	1	0
Normandy	4,988	28	28	0
North Kansas City	4,310	45	34	11
Northwoods	4,202	14	12	2
Oak Grove	7,865	15	14	1
Odessa	5,221	11	10	1
O'Fallon	82,672	146	113	33
Old Monroe	278	1	1	0
Olivette	7,800	24	22	2
Oran	1,280	1	1	0
Oregon	801	1	1	0
Orrick	816	3	3	0
Osage Beach	4,366	38	25	13
Osceola	905	3	3	0
Overland	15,990	63	47	16
Owensville	2,619	9	8	1
Ozark	18,487	34	30	4
Pacific	7,039	25	18	7
Pagedale	3,302	19	17	2
Palmyra	3,610	8	7	1
Park Hills	8,733	14	13	1
Parkville	5,843	18	17	1
Parma	672	3	3	0
Peculiar	4,852	9	8	1
Perry	705	1	1	0
Perryville	8,270	27	23	4
Pevely	5,574	18	13	5
Piedmont	1,961	7	7	0
Pierce City	1,281	3	3	0
Pilot Knob	720	2	2	0
Pine Lawn	3,257	26	22	4
Pineville	785	5	5	0
Platte City	4,809	13	11	2
Platte Woods	397	2	2	0
Plattsburg	2,281	6	6	0
Pleasant Hill	8,193	19	13	6
Pleasant Hope	611	4	1	3
Pleasant Valley	3,031	13	9	4
Polo	547	1	1	0
Poplar Bluff	17,216	55	44	11
Portageville	3,140	16	10	6
Potosi	2,658	11	10	1
Purcell	393	1	1	0
Purdy	1,092	2	2	0
Puxico	870	2	2	0
Qulin	458	1	1	0
Randolph	53	2	2	0
Raymore	19,643	42	29	13
Raytown	29,501	73	53	20
Reeds Spring	900	2	2	0
Republic	15,569	27	22	5
Rich Hill	1,351	3	3	0
Richland	1,888	6	5	1
Richmond	5,648	12	10	2
Richmond Heights	8,555	42	41	1

Table 78.   Full-Time Law Enforcement Employees, by Selected State and City, 2013— continued

(Number.)

State/city	Population	Total law enforcement employees	Total officers	Total civilians
Riverside	3,032	31	23	8
Riverview	2,840	10	10	0
Rockaway Beach	847	2	2	0
Rock Hill	4,637	11	10	1
Rock Port	1,271	3	3	0
Rogersville	3,266	8	7	1
Rolla	19,839	56	37	19
Salem	4,966	18	13	5
Salisbury	1,565	5	4	1
Sarcoxie	1,284	3	3	0
Savannah	5,113	6	6	0
Scott City	4,541	17	12	5
Sedalia	21,494	58	45	13
Seligman	840	2	2	0
Senath	1,762	4	2	2
Seneca	2,408	6	6	0
Seymour	1,928	5	5	0
Shelbina	1,658	8	8	0
Shrewsbury	6,239	20	18	2
Sikeston	16,328	74	58	16
Silex	257	1	1	0
Slater	1,851	5	4	1
Southwest City	957	3	3	0
Sparta	1,783	4	4	0
Springfield	163,062	387	316	71
St. Ann	12,966	49	39	10
St. Charles	66,628	151	110	41
St. Clair	4,694	16	14	2
Steele	2,175	6	6	0
Steelville	1,698	6	6	0
Ste. Genevieve	4,286	10	9	1
Stewartsville	753	1	1	0
St. James	4,149	9	8	1
St. John	6,487	25	23	2
St. Joseph	77,347	161	113	48
St. Louis	318,563	1,842	1,287	555
St. Marys	347	1	1	0
Stover	1,063	3	3	0
St. Peters	54,503	110	86	24
Strafford	2,372	7	7	0
St. Robert	4,615	33	22	11
Sturgeon	901	2	2	0
Sugar Creek	3,339	23	17	6
Sullivan	7,067	24	16	8
Summersville	499	2	2	0
Sunset Hills	8,522	31	25	6
Sweet Springs	1,481	4	4	0
Tarkio	1,522	3	3	0
Terre du Lac	2,340	6	6	0
Thayer	2,260	11	7	4
Tipton	3,204	3	3	0
Town and Country	10,881	29	28	1
Trenton	6,048	19	12	7
Trimble	630	1	1	0
Troy	11,049	26	24	2
Union	10,506	24	22	2
Unionville	1,835	4	4	0
University City	35,186	89	70	19
Urbana	419	2	2	0
Van Buren	826	1	1	0
Vandalia	4,060	7	6	1
Velda City	1,411	7	7	0
Velda Village Hills	1,052	6	4	2
Verona	612	1	1	0
Versailles	2,414	9	9	0
Viburnum	674	2	2	0
Vienna	596	2	2	0
Vinita Park	1,880	14	13	1
Walnut Grove	713	2	2	0
Warrensburg	19,958	35	32	3
Warrenton	8,015	22	19	3
Warsaw	2,121	7	7	0
Warson Woods	1,955	7	6	1
Washington	13,898	31	28	3
Waverly	834	1	1	0
Waynesville	5,207	12	11	1
Weatherby Lake	1,790	5	5	0
Webb City	10,777	26	21	5
Webster Groves	23,078	49	47	2

Table 78.   Full-Time Law Enforcement Employees, by Selected State and City, 2013— continued

(Number.)

State/city	Population	Total law enforcement employees	Total officers	Total civilians
Wellston	2,351	18	13	5
Wellsville	1,176	4	4	0
Wentzville	31,820	78	59	19
Weston	1,704	4	4	0
West Plains	12,345	33	28	5
Wheaton	693	2	2	0
Willard	5,440	11	10	1
Willow Springs	2,177	7	6	1
Winfield	1,413	7	6	1
Winona	1,311	4	4	0
Woodson Terrace	4,064	19	17	2
Wright City	3,376	10	9	1
MONTANA				
Baker	1,857	5	5	0
Belgrade	7,610	18	15	3
Billings	107,802	161	139	22
Boulder	1,187	3	3	0
Bozeman	39,167	68	61	7
Bridger	714	2	2	0
Chinook	1,257	4	4	0
Colstrip	2,370	11	6	5
Columbia Falls	4,721	10	9	1
Columbus	1,957	5	4	1
Conrad	2,581	5	5	0
Cut Bank	2,990	6	5	1
Deer Lodge	3,122	6	5	1
Dillon	4,223	9	8	1
East Helena	2,052	5	5	0
Ennis	859	1	1	0
Eureka	1,120	3	3	0
Fort Benton	1,495	4	4	0
Glasgow	3,342	12	9	3
Glendive	5,264	14	9	5
Great Falls	58,940	129	85	44
Hamilton	4,555	16	15	1
Havre	9,672	26	20	6
Helena	29,411	73	51	22
Hot Springs	556	3	3	0
Joliet	635	1	1	0
Kalispell	20,665	42	34	8
Laurel	6,998	17	13	4
Libby	2,703	6	6	0
Livingston	7,062	14	14	0
Manhattan	1,559	3	3	0
Miles City	8,624	16	16	0
Missoula	68,877	125	102	23
Plains	1,081	3	3	0
Polson	4,614	15	13	2
Red Lodge	2,163	7	7	0
Ronan City	1,923	3	3	0
Sidney	6,191	13	12	1
Stevensville	1,883	2	2	0
Thompson Falls	1,347	4	4	0
Troy	966	2	2	0
West Yellowstone	1,320	12	6	6
Whitefish	6,496	17	15	2
Wolf Point	2,770	8	6	2
NEBRASKA				
Albion	1,612	3	3	0
Alliance	8,510	22	16	6
Ashland	2,502	6	5	1
Aurora	4,397	8	7	1
Bayard	1,157	4	4	0
Beatrice	12,055	31	21	10
Bellevue	53,023	109	94	15
Bennington	1,476	4	2	2
Blair	7,978	18	15	3
Bridgeport	1,501	3	3	0
Broken Bow	3,464	7	6	1
Central City	2,908	6	5	1
Chadron	5,845	20	14	6
Columbus	22,624	52	36	16
Cozad	3,929	7	7	0
Crete	7,238	16	11	5
Emerson	827	2	2	0
Fairbury	3,914	7	6	1
Falls City	4,294	12	8	4

Table 78.   Full-Time Law Enforcement Employees, by Selected State and City, 2013— continued

(Number.)

State/city	Population	Total law enforcement employees	Total officers	Total civilians
Fremont	26,098	39	35	4
Gering	8,480	17	14	3
Gordon	1,552	5	4	1
Gothenburg	3,557	7	6	1
Grand Island	50,441	98	84	14
Hastings	25,012	52	38	14
Holdrege	5,548	16	10	6
Imperial	2,140	4	4	0
Kearney	32,113	66	53	13
Kimball	2,455	7	6	1
La Vista	17,790	38	33	5
Lexington	10,204	20	18	2
Lincoln	267,565	456	321	135
Madison	2,424	4	4	0
McCook	7,639	21	16	5
Milford	2,177	4	4	0
Minden	2,972	5	5	0
Mitchell	1,698	4	4	0
Nebraska City	7,269	14	13	1
Neligh	1,561	3	3	0
Norfolk	24,362	58	38	20
North Platte	24,551	64	40	24
Ogallala	4,620	11	10	1
Omaha	425,076	901	767	134
O'Neill	3,677	8	7	1
Ord	2,100	3	3	0
Papillion	21,274	43	39	4
Pierce	1,738	3	3	0
Plattsmouth	6,422	17	14	3
Ralston	7,662	15	13	2
Schuyler	6,303	10	8	2
Scottsbluff	15,057	34	29	5
Scribner	853	1	1	0
Seward	7,063	13	11	2
Sidney	6,831	16	14	2
South Sioux City	13,407	28	27	1
St. Paul	2,335	4	4	0
Superior	1,925	4	4	0
Valentine	2,768	6	5	1
Valley	1,994	4	4	0
Wahoo	4,493	6	6	0
Wayne	5,656	11	6	5
West Point	3,329	7	6	1
Wilber	1,912	4	4	0
Wymore	1,400	3	3	0
York	7,875	21	15	6
NEVADA				
Boulder City	15,219	44	30	14
Carlin	2,457	8	6	2
Elko	19,748	44	39	5
Fallon	8,411	30	20	10
Henderson	268,237	554	327	227
Las Vegas Metropolitan Police Department	1,500,455	4,668	2,444	2,224
Lovelock	1,898	6	5	1
Mesquite	16,321	50	28	22
North Las Vegas	225,632	425	268	157
Reno	232,561	353	297	56
Sparks	92,768	146	104	42
West Wendover	4,540	21	13	8
Winnemucca	7,827	26	22	4
Yerington	2,997	6	6	0
NEW HAMPSHIRE				
Alexandria	1,604	2	2	0
Alstead	1,938	2	2	0
Alton	5,290	14	12	2
Amherst	11,274	18	17	1
Antrim	2,631	7	5	2
Ashland	2,056	7	5	2
Atkinson	6,812	6	6	0
Auburn	5,132	9	7	2
Barnstead	4,616	2	2	0
Barrington	8,728	11	10	1
Bartlett	2,762	5	4	1
Bedford	21,645	45	33	12
Belmont	7,329	18	15	3
Bennington	1,466	2	2	0

Table 78.　Full-Time Law Enforcement Employees, by Selected State and City, 2013— continued

(Number.)

State/city	Population	Total law enforcement employees	Total officers	Total civilians
Berlin	9,652	30	22	8
Bethlehem	2,527	7	7	0
Boscawen	3,960	7	6	1
Bow	7,633	18	13	5
Bradford	1,653	2	2	0
Brentwood	4,620	5	5	0
Bristol	3,037	10	9	1
Campton	3,302	7	6	1
Candia	3,929	8	7	1
Canterbury	2,374	3	3	0
Carroll	750	4	4	0
Center Harbor	1,099	3	3	0
Charlestown	4,974	8	5	3
Chester	4,875	7	6	1
Claremont	12,990	31	25	6
Colebrook	2,221	6	6	0
Concord	42,615	89	78	11
Conway	10,056	32	22	10
Danville	4,490	5	4	1
Deerfield	4,362	8	7	1
Deering	1,908	2	2	0
Derry	33,296	68	54	14
Dover	30,287	63	46	17
Dublin	1,580	4	3	1
Dunbarton	2,797	3	3	0
Durham	15,311	20	18	2
East Kingston	2,386	4	3	1
Effingham	1,461	2	2	0
Enfield	4,546	8	7	1
Epping	6,633	15	14	1
Epsom	4,620	6	5	1
Exeter	14,487	34	24	10
Farmington	6,799	16	14	2
Fitzwilliam	2,383	2	2	0
Franconia	1,104	3	3	0
Franklin	8,451	27	19	8
Freedom	1,483	3	3	0
Fremont	4,363	4	3	1
Gilford	7,147	20	14	6
Gilmanton	3,784	6	5	1
Goffstown	17,721	43	29	14
Gorham	2,725	10	7	3
Grantham	2,943	5	4	1
Greenland	3,690	7	7	0
Hampstead	8,568	8	8	0
Hampton	15,067	43	34	9
Hampton Falls	2,294	4	4	0
Hancock	1,647	3	3	0
Hanover	11,195	32	20	12
Haverhill	4,641	8	7	1
Henniker	4,838	9	8	1
Hillsborough	5,995	19	13	6
Hinsdale	3,996	8	7	1
Hooksett	13,582	33	22	11
Hopkinton	5,599	7	7	0
Hudson	24,591	62	45	17
Jaffrey	5,417	12	11	1
Keene	23,236	55	43	12
Kingston	6,075	9	8	1
Laconia	16,109	49	39	10
Lancaster	3,373	6	5	1
Lebanon	13,598	43	33	10
Lee	4,345	8	7	1
Lincoln	1,651	16	10	6
Lisbon	1,579	4	4	0
Litchfield	8,344	13	11	2
Littleton	5,930	11	9	2
Londonderry	24,338	74	59	15
Loudon	5,337	7	6	1
Madison	2,513	4	3	1
Manchester	110,411	278	217	61
Marlborough	2,054	3	3	0
Meredith	6,305	18	14	4
Merrimack	25,553	52	38	14
Middleton	1,778	4	4	0
Milford	15,162	31	26	5
Milton	4,603	8	7	1
Mont Vernon	2,427	2	2	0
Moultonborough	4,022	11	10	1

Table 78.   Full-Time Law Enforcement Employees, by Selected State and City, 2013— continued

(Number.)

State/city	Population	Total law enforcement employees	Total officers	Total civilians
Nashua	87,052	240	177	63
New Boston	5,384	7	6	1
Newbury	2,110	4	4	0
New Durham	2,652	6	5	1
Newfields	1,691	4	4	0
New Hampton	2,195	6	6	0
Newington	755	11	10	1
New Ipswich	5,134	6	5	1
New London	4,409	8	7	1
Newmarket	8,950	20	13	7
Newport	6,380	15	10	5
Newton	4,747	7	5	2
Northfield	4,829	8	7	1
North Hampton	4,359	13	12	1
Northumberland	2,210	4	4	0
Northwood	4,295	9	8	1
Nottingham	4,895	7	6	1
Orford	1,233	2	2	0
Ossipee	4,296	10	9	1
Pelham	13,034	28	21	7
Pembroke	7,126	13	11	2
Peterborough	6,383	13	11	2
Pittsfield	4,091	8	8	0
Plaistow	7,620	26	18	8
Plymouth	7,041	16	10	6
Portsmouth	21,453	78	61	17
Raymond	10,256	25	17	8
Rindge	5,998	9	8	1
Rochester	29,849	67	54	13
Rollinsford	2,517	4	4	0
Rye	5,297	10	9	1
Salem	28,882	76	61	15
Sanbornton	2,970	7	6	1
Sandown	6,183	7	7	0
Sandwich	1,316	2	2	0
Seabrook	8,805	33	26	7
Somersworth	11,751	30	23	7
South Hampton	818	1	1	0
Strafford	4,021	5	5	0
Stratham	7,337	11	10	1
Sugar Hill	564	2	2	0
Sunapee	3,330	5	5	0
Thornton	2,482	4	3	1
Tilton	3,623	19	17	2
Troy	2,139	6	6	0
Wakefield	5,018	12	11	1
Warner	2,843	5	4	1
Washington	1,109	1	1	0
Waterville Valley	246	7	6	1
Weare	8,901	10	9	1
Webster	1,877	3	3	0
Wilton	3,670	8	7	1
Winchester	4,302	9	8	1
Windham	14,092	26	19	7
Wolfeboro	6,236	18	13	5
Woodstock	1,354	5	5	0
NEW JERSEY				
Aberdeen Township	18,150	40	34	6
Absecon	8,380	30	25	5
Allenhurst	493	13	10	3
Allentown	1,812	5	5	0
Alpine	1,958	12	12	0
Andover Township	6,273	17	12	5
Asbury Park	15,779	88	84	4
Atlantic City	39,482	373	312	61
Atlantic Highlands	4,352	15	14	1
Avalon	1,309	30	22	8
Avon-by-the-Sea	1,916	11	11	0
Barnegat Township	21,544	52	41	11
Barrington	6,880	14	13	1
Bay Head	987	9	8	1
Bayonne	64,950	274	175	99
Beach Haven	1,178	14	12	2
Beachwood	11,110	19	17	2
Bedminster Township	8,213	17	15	2
Belleville	36,229	209	100	109
Belmar	5,735	24	17	7
Belvidere	2,619	7	6	1

Table 78.   Full-Time Law Enforcement Employees, by Selected State and City, 2013— continued

(Number.)

State/city	Population	Total law enforcement employees	Total officers	Total civilians
Bergenfield	27,125	55	44	11
Berkeley Heights Township	13,452	31	25	6
Berlin	7,623	18	17	1
Berlin Township	5,449	18	17	1
Bernards Township	26,880	43	37	6
Bernardsville	7,764	24	18	6
Blairstown Township	5,839	6	4	2
Bloomfield	47,710	136	123	13
Bloomingdale	7,706	19	18	1
Bogota	8,294	21	16	5
Boonton	8,501	25	20	5
Boonton Township	4,442	13	13	0
Bordentown	3,913	13	11	2
Bordentown Township	11,357	23	21	2
Bound Brook	10,791	29	24	5
Bradley Beach	4,298	20	16	4
Branchburg Township	14,551	26	26	0
Brick Township	75,371	187	130	57
Bridgeton	25,280	72	62	10
Bridgewater Township	45,009	82	68	14
Brielle	4,785	14	14	0
Brigantine	9,411	44	33	11
Brooklawn	1,948	7	7	0
Buena	4,554	9	7	2
Burlington	9,865	34	31	3
Burlington Township	22,750	48	40	8
Butler	7,611	17	16	1
Caldwell	7,876	22	22	0
Califon	1,047	30	27	3
Cape May	3,559	27	22	5
Carlstadt	6,388	25	23	2
Carney's Point Township	8,029	22	17	5
Carteret	24,484	62	53	9
Cedar Grove Township	12,648	29	28	1
Chatham	9,105	23	19	4
Chatham Township	10,681	21	19	2
Cherry Hill Township	71,145	160	132	28
Chesterfield Township	7,518	10	9	1
Chester Township	7,940	16	15	1
Cinnaminson Township	16,686	23	23	0
Clark Township	15,021	52	41	11
Clayton	8,188	17	16	1
Clementon	5,013	12	11	1
Cliffside Park	23,991	49	43	6
Clifton	85,022	173	145	28
Clinton	2,654	9	9	0
Clinton Township	13,010	24	23	1
Closter	8,548	18	18	0
Collingswood	13,875	26	22	4
Colts Neck Township	10,075	21	20	1
Cranbury Township	3,900	18	17	1
Cranford Township	23,165	57	44	13
Cresskill	8,690	26	22	4
Deal	744	21	17	4
Delanco Township	4,737	9	8	1
Delaware Township	4,476	8	7	1
Delran Township	16,862	34	30	4
Demarest	5,001	12	12	0
Denville Township	16,829	42	32	10
Deptford Township	30,492	66	61	5
Dover	18,352	37	31	6
Dumont	17,718	40	32	8
Dunellen	7,461	15	15	0
Eastampton Township	6,103	15	14	1
East Brunswick Township	48,073	108	82	26
East Hanover Township	11,350	37	33	4
East Newark	2,456	8	8	0
East Orange	64,425	298	236	62
East Rutherford	9,010	39	39	0
East Windsor Township	27,564	53	41	12
Eatontown	12,405	45	36	9
Edgewater	12,143	35	28	7
Edgewater Park Township	8,860	10	9	1
Edison Township	101,316	209	160	49
Egg Harbor City	4,316	15	14	1
Egg Harbor Township	43,709	115	87	28
Elizabeth	127,067	415	317	98
Elk Township	4,254	12	11	1
Elmer	1,381	2	2	0

Table 78.   Full-Time Law Enforcement Employees, by Selected State and City, 2013— continued

(Number.)

State/city	Population	Total law enforcement employees	Total officers	Total civilians
Elmwood Park	20,077	40	35	5
Emerson	7,814	21	18	3
Englewood	27,782	101	79	22
Englishtown	1,929	7	7	0
Essex Fells	2,210	13	13	0
Evesham Township	45,798	77	69	8
Ewing Township	36,449	85	68	17
Fairfield Township, Essex County	7,517	37	35	2
Fair Haven	6,075	13	13	0
Fair Lawn	33,015	62	56	6
Fairview	14,358	36	31	5
Fanwood	7,447	18	17	1
Far Hills	924	6	6	0
Flemington	4,653	14	14	0
Florence Township	12,397	28	26	2
Florham Park	11,913	38	33	5
Franklin	4,915	12	12	0
Franklin Lakes	10,746	26	21	5
Franklin Township, Somerset County	63,829	117	99	18
Freehold	12,108	32	29	3
Freehold Township	36,048	66	62	4
Frenchtown	1,347	5	4	1
Galloway Township	37,304	69	47	22
Garfield	31,035	65	57	8
Garwood	4,621	19	15	4
Gibbsboro	2,262	6	6	0
Glassboro	19,038	49	45	4
Glen Ridge	7,626	27	22	5
Glen Rock	11,877	22	21	1
Gloucester Township	64,440	140	120	20
Green Brook Township	7,240	26	21	5
Greenwich Township, Gloucester County	4,901	20	18	2
Greenwich Township, Warren County	5,582	10	9	1
Guttenberg	11,431	24	23	1
Hackensack	44,180	166	113	53
Hackettstown	9,779	19	17	2
Haddonfield	11,590	23	21	2
Haddon Heights	7,665	16	15	1
Haddon Township	14,732	25	23	2
Haledon	8,627	20	19	1
Hamburg	3,186	9	7	2
Hamilton Township, Atlantic County	26,788	70	54	16
Hamilton Township, Mercer County	88,993	203	168	35
Hammonton	14,737	33	27	6
Hanover Township	13,951	35	28	7
Harding Township	3,892	10	9	1
Hardyston Township	8,049	27	21	6
Harrington Park	4,859	11	11	0
Harrison	13,975	49	38	11
Harrison Township	12,616	19	18	1
Harvey Cedars	344	8	8	0
Hasbrouck Heights	11,983	28	27	1
Haworth	3,413	12	11	1
Hawthorne	18,945	34	30	4
Hazlet Township	20,193	46	39	7
Helmetta	2,199	7	7	0
High Bridge	3,560	7	7	0
Highland Park	14,420	33	27	6
Highlands	4,969	16	13	3
Hightstown	5,572	18	12	6
Hillsborough Township	39,037	65	50	15
Hillsdale	10,400	20	16	4
Hillside Township	21,689	77	65	12
Hi-Nella	867	12	12	0
Hoboken	52,771	138	121	17
Ho-Ho-Kus	4,166	19	15	4
Holmdel Township	16,657	46	38	8
Hopatcong	14,857	32	24	8
Hopewell Township	17,304	38	30	8
Howell Township	51,100	93	78	15
Independence Township	5,604	9	8	1
Interlaken	821	22	18	4
Jackson Township	55,817	99	80	19
Jamesburg	5,985	17	13	4
Jefferson Township	21,516	45	38	7
Jersey City	256,886	929	770	159
Keansburg	9,981	41	34	7
Kearny	41,677	108	101	7

Table 78. Full-Time Law Enforcement Employees, by Selected State and City, 2013— continued

(Number.)

State/city	Population	Total law enforcement employees	Total officers	Total civilians
Kenilworth	8,069	28	24	4
Keyport	7,228	19	15	4
Lacey Township	27,865	5	3	2
Lake Como	1,730	10	10	0
Lakehurst	2,666	11	10	1
Lakewood Township	92,664	150	120	30
Lambertville	3,815	13	11	2
Laurel Springs	1,901	5	5	0
Lavallette	1,877	16	12	4
Lawrence Township, Mercer County	33,172	60	56	4
Lebanon Township	6,439	10	9	1
Leonia	9,055	18	17	1
Lincoln Park	10,522	29	23	6
Linden	41,041	140	108	32
Lindenwold	17,863	40	37	3
Linwood	7,089	17	16	1
Little Egg Harbor Township	20,412	45	37	8
Little Silver	5,988	19	16	3
Livingston Township	29,621	83	68	15
Lodi	24,462	44	41	3
Logan Township	6,019	20	19	1
Long Branch	30,602	95	77	18
Long Hill Township	8,796	25	23	2
Longport	885	13	13	0
Lopatcong Township	8,085	15	14	1
Lower Alloways Creek Township	1,746	13	11	2
Lower Township	22,467	55	42	13
Lumberton Township	12,516	18	16	2
Lyndhurst Township	21,477	50	46	4
Madison	16,216	32	26	6
Magnolia	4,363	11	11	0
Mahwah Township	26,292	59	51	8
Manalapan Township	39,313	57	53	4
Manasquan	5,860	21	17	4
Mansfield Township, Burlington County	8,652	13	12	1
Mansfield Township, Warren County	7,551	13	12	1
Mantoloking	297	9	8	1
Mantua Township	15,097	28	26	2
Manville	10,412	27	24	3
Maple Shade Township	19,291	38	34	4
Maplewood Township	24,230	71	60	11
Marlboro Township	40,190	88	65	23
Matawan	8,745	20	19	1
Maywood	9,613	25	21	4
Medford Lakes	4,196	9	8	1
Medford Township	23,285	32	28	4
Mendham	5,029	12	11	1
Mendham Township	5,908	16	14	2
Merchantville	3,824	15	13	2
Metuchen	13,748	35	29	6
Middlesex	13,787	25	24	1
Middle Township	18,861	49	44	5
Middletown Township	66,246	131	104	27
Midland Park	7,268	15	14	1
Millburn Township	20,177	65	54	11
Milltown	6,972	18	14	4
Millville	28,661	80	69	11
Monmouth Beach	3,280	9	9	0
Monroe Township, Middlesex County	41,356	62	46	16
Montclair	37,962	124	104	20
Montgomery Township	22,467	36	30	6
Montvale	8,004	23	22	1
Montville Township	21,757	42	37	5
Moonachie	2,747	20	17	3
Moorestown Township	20,706	38	33	5
Morris Plains	5,773	18	16	2
Morristown	18,552	59	55	4
Morris Township	22,640	47	42	5
Mountain Lakes	4,311	14	13	1
Mountainside	6,815	28	23	5
Mount Arlington	5,324	15	14	1
Mount Ephraim	4,678	13	12	1
Mount Holly Township	9,316	21	20	1
Mount Laurel Township	41,839	62	56	6
Mount Olive Township	28,611	57	48	9
Mullica Township	6,202	14	13	1
Neptune City	4,830	19	18	1
Neptune Township	27,856	155	145	10

Table 78.   Full-Time Law Enforcement Employees, by Selected State and City, 2013— continued

(Number.)

State/city	Population	Total law enforcement employees	Total officers	Total civilians
Netcong	3,279	9	9	0
Newark	278,246	1,276	1,007	269
New Brunswick	56,542	170	137	33
Newfield	1,538	5	5	0
New Hanover Township	8,011	4	3	1
New Milford	16,577	34	32	2
New Providence	12,463	28	23	5
Newton	7,812	42	22	20
North Arlington	15,597	35	28	7
North Bergen Township	62,436	132	116	16
North Brunswick Township	41,425	93	76	17
North Caldwell	6,403	20	15	5
North Hanover Township	7,738	10	9	1
North Plainfield	22,030	51	45	6
Northvale	4,919	13	13	0
North Wildwood	3,973	29	21	8
Norwood	5,855	15	14	1
Oakland	12,927	28	22	6
Oaklyn	4,023	13	12	1
Ocean City	11,473	71	58	13
Ocean Gate	2,027	8	7	1
Oceanport	5,833	15	14	1
Ocean Township, Monmouth County	27,180	65	57	8
Ocean Township, Ocean County	8,565	29	22	7
Ogdensburg	2,365	7	7	0
Old Bridge Township	66,528	111	86	25
Old Tappan	5,882	14	13	1
Oradell	8,126	21	20	1
Orange	30,952	122	104	18
Palmyra	7,412	17	16	1
Park Ridge	8,948	17	17	0
Parsippany-Troy Hills Township	53,851	108	91	17
Passaic	70,445	179	152	27
Paterson	145,082	466	365	101
Paulsboro	6,034	18	17	1
Peapack and Gladstone	2,570	9	8	1
Pemberton	1,392	5	5	0
Pemberton Township	27,949	42	38	4
Pennington	2,585	5	4	1
Pennsauken Township	35,788	94	78	16
Pennsville Township	13,183	23	21	2
Pequannock Township	15,580	36	31	5
Phillipsburg	14,619	37	36	1
Pine Beach	2,138	7	6	1
Pine Hill	10,704	23	20	3
Piscataway Township	58,259	102	84	18
Pitman	8,930	15	14	1
Plainfield	50,433	164	143	21
Plainsboro Township	23,256	45	36	9
Pohatcong Township	3,291	13	12	1
Point Pleasant	18,458	39	32	7
Point Pleasant Beach	4,678	28	22	6
Pompton Lakes	11,163	21	18	3
Princeton	28,688	68	52	16
Prospect Park	5,903	15	15	0
Rahway	27,930	82	73	9
Ramsey	14,826	39	32	7
Randolph Township	25,969	36	30	6
Raritan	7,352	17	16	1
Raritan Township	21,849	30	27	3
Readington Township	15,910	25	23	2
Red Bank	12,174	44	37	7
Ridgefield	11,340	30	28	2
Ridgefield Park	12,923	36	29	7
Ridgewood	25,315	45	41	4
Ringwood	12,383	23	19	4
Riverdale	4,025	19	15	4
River Edge	11,517	24	21	3
Riverside Township	8,063	14	14	0
Riverton	2,798	5	5	0
River Vale Township	9,885	22	20	2
Robbinsville Township	14,046	37	28	9
Rockaway	6,500	15	14	1
Rockaway Township	24,444	65	53	12
Roselle	21,388	73	60	13
Roselle Park	13,593	42	34	8
Roxbury Township	23,599	43	40	3
Rumson	7,021	20	16	4
Rutherford	18,291	40	38	2

Table 78.   Full-Time Law Enforcement Employees, by Selected State and City, 2013— continued

(Number.)

State/city	Population	Total law enforcement employees	Total officers	Total civilians
Saddle Brook Township	14,152	28	25	3
Saddle River	3,190	22	17	5
Salem	5,175	22	20	2
Sayreville	44,174	101	87	14
Scotch Plains Township	23,914	49	44	5
Sea Bright	1,381	12	11	1
Sea Girt	1,796	11	11	0
Sea Isle City	2,093	32	22	10
Seaside Heights	2,892	35	27	8
Seaside Park	1,589	14	13	1
Ship Bottom	1,159	12	11	1
Shrewsbury	3,941	20	15	5
Somerdale	5,276	14	13	1
Somers Point	10,806	36	31	5
Somerville	12,174	33	30	3
South Amboy	8,753	28	23	5
South Bound Brook	4,889	13	12	1
South Brunswick Township	44,575	102	73	29
South Harrison Township	3,202	5	5	0
South Orange	16,297	52	47	5
South Plainfield	23,789	63	49	14
South River	16,198	39	29	10
South Toms River	3,698	11	10	1
Sparta Township	19,494	40	28	12
Spotswood	8,459	24	20	4
Springfield	17,238	46	42	4
Springfield Township	3,414	10	9	1
Spring Lake	2,992	13	13	0
Spring Lake Heights	4,680	12	12	0
Stafford Township	27,063	69	50	19
Stanhope	3,529	10	9	1
Stratford	6,982	16	15	1
Summit	21,973	55	46	9
Surf City	1,207	10	10	0
Swedesboro	2,911	18	17	1
Teaneck Township	40,245	107	92	15
Tenafly	14,696	40	34	6
Tewksbury Township	5,854	9	8	1
Tinton Falls	17,849	39	38	1
Toms River Township	92,332	180	152	28
Totowa	10,985	31	27	4
Trenton	84,439	311	237	74
Tuckerton	3,369	10	10	0
Union Beach	6,198	16	12	4
Union City	68,254	180	153	27
Union Township	57,335	184	130	54
Upper Saddle River	8,321	21	17	4
Ventnor City	10,604	49	38	11
Verona	13,429	30	28	2
Vineland	60,863	165	139	26
Voorhees Township	29,284	52	45	7
Waldwick	9,936	22	17	5
Wall Township	26,051	81	66	15
Warren Township	15,841	36	29	7
Washington Township, Bergen County	9,271	19	19	0
Washington Township, Gloucester County	48,110	79	72	7
Washington Township, Morris County	18,782	30	27	3
Washington Township, Warren County	6,493	30	29	1
Watchung	5,844	37	30	7
Waterford Township	10,747	21	20	1
Wayne Township	54,917	142	117	25
Weehawken Township	12,937	55	46	9
Wenonah	2,263	7	7	0
Westampton Township	8,796	24	22	2
West Caldwell Township	10,878	31	25	6
West Deptford Township	21,497	40	37	3
Westfield	30,770	65	53	12
West Milford Township	26,095	56	49	7
West New York	52,102	108	98	10
West Orange	46,794	103	90	13
Westville	4,247	16	15	1
West Wildwood	589	7	7	0
West Windsor Township	28,557	61	49	12
Westwood	11,056	30	25	5
Wharton	6,593	21	20	1
Wildwood	5,228	38	30	8
Wildwood Crest	3,222	24	18	6

Table 78.   Full-Time Law Enforcement Employees, by Selected State and City, 2013— continued

(Number.)

State/city	Population	Total law enforcement employees	Total officers	Total civilians
Willingboro Township	31,914	75	64	11
Winfield Township	1,489	8	8	0
Winslow Township	39,212	85	70	15
Woodbridge Township	100,568	254	191	63
Woodbury	10,073	30	28	2
Woodbury Heights	3,026	8	7	1
Woodcliff Lake	5,864	19	18	1
Woodland Park	12,636	28	25	3
Woodlynne	2,967	8	8	0
Wood-Ridge	8,632	25	21	4
Woodstown	3,519	10	8	2
Woolwich Township	11,167	18	17	1
Wyckoff Township	16,949	29	23	6
NEW MEXICO				
Artesia	11,376	37	23	14
Aztec	6,654	18	16	2
Deming	14,770	35	33	2
Dexter	1,274	4	4	0
Estancia	1,625	6	5	1
Eunice	3,019	16	10	6
Jal	2,114	12	5	7
Logan	996	4	4	0
Loving	1,410	4	4	0
Raton	6,521	23	14	9
Red River	475	11	4	7
Santa Clara	1,683	7	5	2
Santa Rosa	2,786	13	7	6
San Ysidro	195	1	1	0
Taos Ski Valley	69	3	3	0
NEW YORK				
Addison Town and Village	2,577	3	3	0
Akron Village	2,846	1	1	0
Albany	97,956	436	332	104
Alfred Village	4,089	6	6	0
Allegany Village	1,781	2	2	0
Amherst Town	118,296	182	152	30
Amity Town and Belmont Village	2,242	1	1	0
Amityville Village	9,519	24	23	1
Amsterdam	18,182	41	39	2
Arcade Village	2,053	6	6	0
Ardsley Village	4,523	19	19	0
Asharoken Village	658	3	3	0
Attica Village	2,522	5	5	0
Auburn	27,270	71	66	5
Baldwinsville Village	7,473	12	11	1
Ballston Spa Village	5,418	6	6	0
Batavia	15,374	33	30	3
Bath Village	5,733	12	10	2
Beacon	15,278	31	29	2
Bedford Town	17,627	42	37	5
Boonville Village	2,054	3	3	0
Brant Town	2,065	1	1	0
Brewster	2,358	15	15	0
Briarcliff Manor Village	7,976	19	19	0
Brockport Village	8,284	12	11	1
Bronxville Village	6,390	23	21	2
Buchanan Village	2,259	6	6	0
Buffalo	258,789	916	741	175
Cairo Town	6,577	1	1	0
Caledonia Village	2,151	3	3	0
Cambridge Village	1,854	6	6	0
Camden Village	2,219	2	2	0
Camillus Town and Village	24,165	25	23	2
Canajoharie Village	2,178	4	4	0
Canisteo Village	2,246	1	1	0
Carmel Town	34,462	38	33	5
Carthage Village	3,862	4	4	0
Catskill Village	3,971	19	18	1
Cazenovia Village	2,732	5	4	1
Cheektowaga Town	78,361	167	129	38
Chester Town	7,990	14	14	0
Clarkstown Town	80,705	187	163	24
Clayton Village	2,063	3	3	0
Clifton Springs Village	2,117	1	1	0
Cobleskill Village	4,503	11	11	0
Coeymans Town	7,458	9	6	3
Cohoes	16,179	37	33	4

Table 78.   Full-Time Law Enforcement Employees, by Selected State and City, 2013— continued

(Number.)

State/city	Population	Total law enforcement employees	Total officers	Total civilians
Colonie Town	78,215	147	107	40
Corning	11,087	23	19	4
Cornwall Town	9,543	10	7	3
Cortland	19,331	46	43	3
Crawford Town	9,264	10	8	2
Croton-on-Hudson Village	8,180	22	20	2
Cuba Town	3,209	4	4	0
Dansville Village	4,605	5	5	0
Deerpark Town	7,827	3	3	0
Delhi Village	2,985	5	5	0
Depew Village	15,189	35	29	6
Deposit Village	1,628	1	1	0
Dewitt Town	22,681	37	35	2
Dolgeville Village	2,191	2	2	0
Dryden Village	1,913	6	6	0
East Aurora-Aurora Town	13,774	19	15	4
Eastchester Town	19,800	47	45	2
East Fishkill Town	29,315	40	32	8
East Greenbush Town	16,470	34	25	9
East Hampton Town	19,674	85	63	22
East Hampton Village	1,104	28	23	5
East Rochester Village	6,596	9	8	1
East Syracuse Village	3,036	7	6	1
Eden Town	7,684	5	4	1
Ellicottville	1,601	3	3	0
Elmira	28,921	89	77	12
Elmira Heights Village	4,079	9	9	0
Elmira Town	5,948	4	4	0
Elmsford Village	4,735	18	18	0
Evans Town	16,292	28	22	6
Fairport Village	5,335	11	10	1
Fallsburg Town	12,109	20	20	0
Floral Park Village	15,926	47	34	13
Fort Edward Village	3,318	5	5	0
Fort Plain Village	2,265	4	4	0
Frankfort Village	2,579	3	3	0
Franklinville Village	1,702	2	2	0
Fredonia Village	10,988	18	14	4
Freeport Village	43,214	103	87	16
Garden City Village	22,596	63	50	13
Gates Town	28,468	36	31	5
Geddes Town	10,442	15	13	2
Geneseo Village	7,891	7	7	0
Geneva	13,194	40	35	5
Glen Cove	27,134	53	49	4
Glens Falls	14,582	32	30	2
Glenville Town	21,839	36	22	14
Gloversville	15,315	31	29	2
Gouverneur Village	3,902	8	6	2
Granville Village	2,498	5	5	0
Great Neck Estates Village	2,794	16	13	3
Greece Town	96,667	104	98	6
Greenburgh Town	44,787	144	115	29
Greene Village	1,553	1	1	0
Greenwood Lake Village	3,118	9	8	1
Groton Village	2,381	1	1	0
Guilderland Town	33,805	44	34	10
Hamburg Town	45,535	77	60	17
Hamburg Village	9,517	14	13	1
Harrison Town	27,876	65	59	6
Haverstraw Town	37,196	77	70	7
Hempstead Village	55,198	148	121	27
Herkimer Village	7,693	20	20	0
Highland Falls Village	3,847	12	9	3
Homer Village	3,270	5	5	0
Hornell	8,481	24	23	1
Horseheads Village	6,701	10	10	0
Hudson	6,676	29	25	4
Hudson Falls Village	7,187	14	14	0
Huntington Bay Village	1,428	4	4	0
Ilion Village	8,002	19	17	2
Inlet Town	329	3	2	1
Interlaken Village	605	1	1	0
Irondequoit Town	51,506	60	49	11
Irvington Village	6,530	23	22	1
Jamestown	30,658	70	60	10
Johnson City Village	14,866	37	32	5
Kenmore Village	15,256	24	24	0
Kensington Village	1,174	6	6	0

Table 78.   Full-Time Law Enforcement Employees, by Selected State and City, 2013— continued

(Number.)

State/city	Population	Total law enforcement employees	Total officers	Total civilians
Kent Town	13,381	25	20	5
Kings Point Village	5,042	24	22	2
Kingston	23,665	79	74	5
Kirkland Town	8,296	7	6	1
Lake Placid Village	2,491	14	11	3
Lake Success Village	3,009	24	21	3
Lakewood-Busti	7,280	10	9	1
Lancaster Town	36,369	64	49	15
Le Roy Village	4,354	7	7	0
Lewisboro Town	12,614	3	3	0
Lewiston Town and Village	16,175	11	10	1
Little Falls	4,912	10	9	1
Liverpool Village	2,311	6	5	1
Lloyd Harbor Village	3,683	13	12	1
Lloyd Town	10,751	12	10	2
Lockport	20,904	52	49	3
Lowville Village	3,457	6	6	0
Lynbrook Village	19,528	58	50	8
Lyons Village	3,543	10	8	2
Macedon Town and Village	9,132	7	6	1
Malone Village	5,881	14	14	0
Malverne Village	8,542	24	24	0
Mamaroneck Town	12,146	38	37	1
Mamaroneck Village	19,164	54	49	5
Marlborough Town	8,769	8	6	2
Massena Village	10,808	26	21	5
Maybrook Village	2,951	4	4	0
Mechanicville	5,213	12	11	1
Medina Village	5,953	12	11	1
Menands Village	3,991	14	11	3
Middleport Village	1,813	3	3	0
Mohawk Village	2,714	4	4	0
Monroe Village	8,544	22	18	4
Montgomery Village	4,188	4	4	0
Moriah Town	3,628	2	2	0
Mount Hope Town	7,112	4	4	0
Mount Kisco Village	11,028	31	29	2
Mount Morris Village	2,912	5	5	0
Mount Pleasant Town	26,564	46	39	7
Newark Village	8,978	18	17	1
Newburgh	28,571	85	74	11
Newburgh Town	30,984	56	46	10
New Castle Town	17,864	38	36	2
New Hartford Town and Village	20,355	22	19	3
New Paltz Town and Village	14,248	24	20	4
New Rochelle	78,800	210	154	56
New Windsor Town	25,767	49	40	9
New York	8,396,126	49,526	34,822	14,704
Niagara Falls	49,574	173	152	21
Niagara Town	8,241	6	5	1
Niskayuna Town	22,097	38	27	11
North Greenbush Town	12,137	18	16	2
Northport Village	7,411	21	17	4
North Syracuse Village	6,964	11	10	1
Norwich	7,049	19	19	0
Ogdensburg	11,072	30	25	5
Old Brookville Village	2,171	34	26	8
Old Westbury Village	4,625	30	25	5
Oneida	11,220	27	23	4
Oneonta City	13,825	30	25	5
Orangetown Town	37,438	92	83	9
Ossining Village	25,314	63	55	8
Oswego City	18,139	55	50	5
Owego Village	3,818	9	8	1
Oxford Village	1,433	1	1	0
Oyster Bay Cove Village	4,233	14	14	0
Painted Post Village	2,116	2	2	0
Palmyra Village	3,475	6	6	0
Peekskill	23,908	63	54	9
Pelham Manor Village	5,558	27	26	1
Pelham Village	6,982	28	25	3
Penn Yan Village	5,123	13	12	1
Perry Village	3,633	4	4	0
Plattsburgh City	19,672	56	48	8
Pleasantville Village	7,100	20	20	0
Port Chester Village	29,328	60	58	2
Port Dickinson Village	1,602	5	4	1
Port Jervis	8,689	32	31	1
Port Washington	19,036	66	58	8

Table 78.   Full-Time Law Enforcement Employees, by Selected State and City, 2013— continued

(Number.)

State/city	Population	Total law enforcement employees	Total officers	Total civilians
Potsdam Village	9,613	17	13	4
Poughkeepsie	30,778	124	91	33
Poughkeepsie Town	43,866	89	79	10
Quogue Village	977	14	13	1
Ramapo Town	87,204	129	107	22
Rensselaer City	9,517	33	27	6
Riverhead Town	33,789	99	83	16
Rochester	210,562	866	735	131
Rockville Centre Village	24,129	60	51	9
Rome	32,557	77	75	2
Rosendale Town	6,026	3	2	1
Rye	15,910	40	35	5
Rye Brook Village	9,480	28	27	1
Sag Harbor Village	2,279	12	11	1
Sands Point Village	2,715	20	20	0
Saranac Lake Village	5,369	12	12	0
Saratoga Springs	27,081	81	67	14
Saugerties Town	19,318	27	22	5
Scarsdale Village	17,564	47	42	5
Schenectady	66,041	192	148	44
Scotia Village	7,700	14	13	1
Seneca Falls Town	2,362	14	12	2
Shandaken Town	3,043	4	4	0
Shawangunk Town	14,205	6	6	0
Sidney Village	3,805	8	8	0
Skaneateles Village	2,450	2	2	0
Sleepy Hollow Village	9,996	24	24	0
Solvay Village	6,487	15	13	2
Southampton Town	50,603	117	89	28
Southampton Village	3,161	44	29	15
South Glens Falls Village	3,640	6	6	0
South Nyack Village	3,579	6	6	0
Southold Town	19,963	67	52	15
Spring Valley Village	32,288	66	58	8
St. Johnsville Village	1,691	1	1	0
Stony Point Town	15,307	24	23	1
Suffern Village	10,886	27	23	4
Syracuse	143,834	508	440	68
Tarrytown Village	11,449	37	33	4
Ticonderoga Town	4,982	7	7	0
Tonawanda	14,987	34	28	6
Tonawanda Town	58,082	151	102	49
Troy	49,898	139	127	12
Trumansburg Village	1,820	15	15	0
Tuckahoe Village	6,578	26	23	3
Tupper Lake Village	3,642	9	9	0
Tuxedo Town	2,986	15	12	3
Utica	61,686	171	155	16
Vernon Village	1,160	1	1	0
Vestal Town	27,980	36	33	3
Wallkill Town	27,940	32	31	1
Walton Village	3,012	5	4	1
Wappingers Falls Village	5,476	5	2	3
Warsaw Village	3,453	5	5	0
Warwick Town	18,332	37	32	5
Washingtonville Village	5,828	15	13	2
Waterford Town and Village	8,392	14	10	4
Waterloo Village	5,175	9	8	1
Watertown	28,179	67	63	4
Watervliet	10,245	26	25	1
Watkins Glen Village	1,862	4	4	0
Waverly Village	4,337	11	10	1
Wayland Village	1,842	1	1	0
West Seneca Town	44,821	83	69	14
Whitehall Village	2,604	4	4	0
White Plains	57,559	200	190	10
Whitesboro Village	3,733	6	6	0
Whitestown Town	9,141	7	7	0
Windham Town	1,683	1	1	0
Woodbury Town	10,685	23	19	4
Woodstock Town	5,931	10	10	0
Yonkers	199,134	694	616	78
Yorktown Town	36,643	63	55	8
Yorkville Village	2,660	4	4	0
NORTH CAROLINA				
Aberdeen	6,760	29	27	2
Ahoskie	4,988	19	14	5
Albemarle	15,946	55	49	6

Table 78.   Full-Time Law Enforcement Employees, by Selected State and City, 2013— continued

(Number.)

State/city	Population	Total law enforcement employees	Total officers	Total civilians
Andrews	1,743	5	5	0
Angier	4,635	12	12	0
Apex	41,356	76	61	15
Archdale	11,524	30	25	5
Asheboro	25,665	82	75	7
Asheville	86,445	249	213	36
Atlantic Beach	1,491	18	17	1
Aurora	518	2	2	0
Ayden	5,065	22	18	4
Badin	1,979	5	5	0
Bailey	572	2	2	0
Bakersville	454	1	1	0
Bald Head Island	163	15	14	1
Banner Elk	1,117	10	9	1
Beaufort	4,107	16	15	1
Beech Mountain	319	13	9	4
Belhaven	1,624	12	8	4
Belmont	10,319	40	32	8
Benson	3,452	14	13	1
Bethel	1,625	5	5	0
Beulaville	1,346	5	5	0
Biltmore Forest	1,393	15	14	1
Biscoe	1,694	10	9	1
Black Creek	774	2	2	0
Black Mountain	8,012	22	18	4
Bladenboro	1,735	6	6	0
Blowing Rock	1,234	11	10	1
Boiling Spring Lakes	5,546	10	10	0
Boiling Springs	4,610	9	9	0
Bolton	682	2	1	1
Boone	17,998	43	34	9
Boonville	1,215	5	5	0
Brevard	7,536	30	23	7
Broadway	1,280	4	4	0
Brookford	378	1	1	0
Bryson City	1,446	8	7	1
Bunn	350	3	3	0
Burgaw	4,005	13	13	0
Burlington	51,401	167	124	43
Burnsville	1,667	8	8	0
Butner	7,661	37	31	6
Cameron	293	1	1	0
Candor	838	5	5	0
Canton	4,164	18	13	5
Cape Carteret	1,928	6	6	0
Carolina Beach	5,937	28	27	1
Carrboro	20,709	39	37	2
Carthage	2,321	11	10	1
Cary	148,905	222	184	38
Caswell Beach	404	4	4	0
Catawba	605	1	1	0
Chadbourn	1,835	9	8	1
Chapel Hill	58,744	131	105	26
Charlotte-Mecklenburg[1]	837,638	1,979	1,587	392
Cherryville	5,818	19	14	5
China Grove	4,154	12	12	0
Chocowinity	812	3	3	0
Claremont	1,355	9	8	1
Clayton	17,315	46	42	4
Cleveland	870	5	5	0
Clinton	8,774	33	29	4
Clyde	1,222	3	3	0
Coats	2,318	6	6	0
Columbus	983	7	7	0
Concord	82,899	181	156	25
Conover	8,168	30	28	2
Conway	800	1	1	0
Cooleemee	965	3	3	0
Cornelius	26,683	69	53	16
Cramerton	4,212	13	13	0
Creedmoor	4,254	16	12	4
Dallas	4,537	16	12	4
Davidson	11,657	18	17	1
Denton	1,645	7	6	1
Dobson	1,586	6	6	0
Drexel	1,863	5	5	0
Duck	375	10	9	1
Dunn	9,672	49	34	15
Durham	242,865	621	517	104

Table 78.   Full-Time Law Enforcement Employees, by Selected State and City, 2013— continued

(Number.)

State/city	Population	Total law enforcement employees	Total officers	Total civilians
East Bend	604	2	2	0
East Spencer	1,533	6	6	0
Eden	15,282	52	44	8
Edenton	4,994	19	17	2
Elizabeth City	18,395	69	55	14
Elizabethtown	3,603	14	13	1
Elkin	4,024	21	17	4
Elon	9,627	16	15	1
Emerald Isle	3,669	19	16	3
Enfield	2,485	11	10	1
Erwin	4,620	13	12	1
Fair Bluff	936	4	4	0
Fairmont	2,714	13	11	2
Farmville	4,767	19	14	5
Fayetteville	202,524	540	362	178
Fletcher	7,320	16	15	1
Forest City	7,394	33	31	2
Four Oaks	1,980	6	6	0
Foxfire Village	936	2	2	0
Franklin	3,894	18	18	0
Franklinton	2,060	9	9	0
Fremont	1,277	4	4	0
Fuquay-Varina	20,562	37	32	5
Garner	27,021	69	63	6
Garysburg	1,012	2	2	0
Gaston	1,105	3	3	0
Gastonia	73,049	192	170	22
Gibsonville	6,632	15	14	1
Glen Alpine	1,512	3	3	0
Goldsboro	37,230	113	102	11
Graham	14,270	39	36	3
Granite Falls	4,647	16	13	3
Granite Quarry	2,935	8	8	0
Greensboro	279,343	808	666	142
Greenville	88,018	228	177	51
Grifton	2,682	7	7	0
Hamlet	6,625	24	20	4
Havelock	20,765	33	26	7
Haw River	2,344	8	8	0
Henderson	15,309	58	50	8
Hendersonville	13,342	51	39	12
Hertford	2,175	8	7	1
Hickory	40,109	147	112	35
Highlands	923	11	10	1
High Point	107,261	251	216	35
Hillsborough	6,329	26	26	0
Holden Beach	598	8	8	0
Holly Ridge	1,654	10	9	1
Holly Springs	27,557	55	43	12
Hope Mills	15,699	40	35	5
Hot Springs	555	1	1	0
Hudson	3,720	12	11	1
Huntersville	50,162	87	77	10
Indian Beach	114	4	4	0
Jackson	494	1	1	0
Jacksonville	68,709	153	122	31
Jefferson	1,589	3	3	0
Jonesville	2,266	11	10	1
Kannapolis	44,150	102	79	23
Kenansville	885	4	4	0
Kenly	1,394	8	8	0
Kernersville	23,553	82	63	19
Kill Devil Hills	6,869	33	27	6
King	6,860	21	18	3
Kings Mountain	10,646	39	32	7
Kinston	21,619	74	64	10
Kitty Hawk	3,348	17	15	2
Knightdale	13,153	26	25	1
Kure Beach	2,078	11	10	1
Lake Lure	1,190	10	9	1
Lake Royale	2,589	6	6	0
Lake Waccamaw	1,482	5	5	0
Landis	3,090	11	11	0
Laurel Park	2,243	7	7	0
Laurinburg	15,740	44	38	6
Leland	15,535	29	27	2
Lenoir	17,926	66	50	16
Lexington	18,939	69	61	8
Liberty	2,672	11	10	1

Table 78.   Full-Time Law Enforcement Employees, by Selected State and City, 2013— continued

(Number.)

State/city	Population	Total law enforcement employees	Total officers	Total civilians
Lilesville	519	1	1	0
Lillington	3,391	13	12	1
Lincolnton	10,686	37	32	5
Littleton	661	2	2	0
Locust	2,948	13	12	1
Long View	4,867	17	17	0
Louisburg	3,426	12	11	1
Lowell	3,563	9	9	0
Lumberton	21,828	90	80	10
Madison	2,214	14	13	1
Maggie Valley	1,137	11	10	1
Magnolia	970	2	2	0
Maiden	3,340	15	14	1
Manteo	1,353	9	8	1
Marion	7,945	25	24	1
Marshall	867	2	2	0
Mars Hill	2,061	5	5	0
Marshville	2,513	8	8	0
Matthews	29,178	69	57	12
Maxton	2,470	13	9	4
Mayodan	2,471	15	12	3
Maysville	1,036	3	3	0
Mebane	13,129	33	26	7
Middlesex	822	4	4	0
Mint Hill	24,350	37	34	3
Misenheimer	670	5	5	0
Mocksville	5,097	20	19	1
Monroe	33,895	94	82	12
Montreat	673	4	4	0
Mooresville	33,676	95	73	22
Morehead City	9,159	44	38	6
Morganton	16,852	93	63	30
Morrisville	21,229	32	31	1
Mount Airy	10,450	54	41	13
Mount Gilead	1,181	8	8	0
Mount Holly	13,814	38	30	8
Mount Olive	4,672	16	15	1
Murfreesboro	2,807	15	10	5
Murphy	1,592	9	7	2
Nags Head	2,827	23	21	2
Nashville	5,382	17	16	1
Navassa	1,536	2	2	0
New Bern	30,514	106	76	30
Newland	683	5	5	0
Newport	4,778	9	9	0
Newton	12,980	43	34	9
Norlina	1,088	4	4	0
North Topsail Beach	735	12	11	1
North Wilkesboro	4,256	25	24	1
Northwest	762	1	1	0
Norwood	2,386	7	6	1
Oakboro	1,865	6	6	0
Oak Island	7,064	22	21	1
Ocean Isle Beach	572	13	13	0
Old Fort	908	3	3	0
Oxford	8,607	38	32	6
Parkton	443	2	2	0
Pembroke	3,027	16	12	4
Pikeville	690	2	2	0
Pilot Mountain	1,477	9	8	1
Pinebluff	1,382	4	4	0
Pinehurst	15,100	28	23	5
Pine Knoll Shores	1,344	7	7	0
Pine Level	1,774	5	5	0
Pinetops	1,355	9	6	3
Pineville	8,027	46	35	11
Pink Hill	548	2	2	0
Pittsboro	3,933	12	12	0
Plymouth	3,711	10	9	1
Polkton	3,317	1	1	0
Princeton	1,246	4	4	0
Raeford	4,894	18	17	1
Raleigh	428,993	870	773	97
Ramseur	1,703	5	5	0
Randleman	4,144	13	13	0
Ranlo	3,468	7	7	0
Red Springs	3,469	17	17	0
Reidsville	14,286	54	49	5
Richlands	1,643	6	6	0

Table 78.   Full-Time Law Enforcement Employees, by Selected State and City, 2013— continued

(Number.)

State/city	Population	Total law enforcement employees	Total officers	Total civilians
Rich Square	926	2	2	0
River Bend	3,175	6	6	0
Roanoke Rapids	15,686	39	35	4
Robbins	1,140	5	5	0
Robersonville	1,447	8	8	0
Rockingham	9,480	38	33	5
Rockwell	2,112	5	5	0
Rocky Mount	57,021	193	146	47
Rolesville	4,424	13	12	1
Rose Hill	1,687	4	4	0
Rowland	1,052	7	6	1
Roxboro	8,310	37	33	4
Rutherfordton	4,206	15	14	1
Salisbury	33,626	83	76	7
Saluda	699	4	4	0
Sanford	29,390	104	83	21
Scotland Neck	2,021	8	7	1
Selma	6,217	25	23	2
Seven Devils	196	6	6	0
Shallotte	3,837	14	13	1
Sharpsburg	2,029	8	8	0
Shelby	20,261	82	69	13
Siler City	8,243	26	21	5
Smithfield	11,451	43	41	2
Snow Hill	1,592	4	4	0
Southern Pines	12,846	42	33	9
Southern Shores	2,782	12	11	1
Southport	3,085	11	11	0
Sparta	1,724	6	6	0
Spencer	3,262	13	12	1
Spindale	4,296	12	12	0
Spring Hope	1,325	4	4	0
Spring Lake	13,639	30	27	3
Spruce Pine	2,149	12	12	0
Stallings	14,544	25	22	3
Stanfield	1,487	4	4	0
Stanley	3,599	10	9	1
Stantonsburg	789	4	4	0
Star	873	3	3	0
Statesville	25,199	96	77	19
Stoneville	1,045	5	5	0
St. Pauls	2,440	18	13	5
Sugar Mountain	196	5	5	0
Sunset Beach	3,669	14	14	0
Surf City	2,005	21	18	3
Swansboro	2,924	10	9	1
Sylva	2,744	15	15	0
Tabor City	3,969	10	9	1
Tarboro	11,297	34	28	6
Taylorsville	2,067	11	11	0
Thomasville	26,866	73	67	6
Topsail Beach	388	8	7	1
Trent Woods	4,230	5	5	0
Troutman	2,446	15	15	0
Troy	3,488	12	11	1
Tryon	1,615	10	8	2
Valdese	4,493	12	11	1
Vanceboro	1,015	2	2	0
Vass	726	3	3	0
Wadesboro	5,673	29	24	5
Wagram	823	2	2	0
Wake Forest	33,852	72	59	13
Wallace	4,015	18	14	4
Walnut Creek	854	2	2	0
Warrenton	840	5	4	1
Warsaw	3,172	15	13	2
Washington	9,761	43	33	10
Waxhaw	10,481	22	20	2
Waynesville	9,776	42	34	8
Weaverville	3,814	15	14	1
Weldon	1,621	8	8	0
Wendell	6,248	15	14	1
West Jefferson	1,291	8	8	0
Whispering Pines	3,045	9	8	1
Whitakers	739	2	2	0
White Lake	793	6	6	0
Whiteville	5,466	25	22	3
Wilkesboro	3,431	23	21	2
Williamston	5,390	21	20	1

Table 78.   Full-Time Law Enforcement Employees, by Selected State and City, 2013— continued

(Number.)

State/city	Population	Total law enforcement employees	Total officers	Total civilians
Wilmington	110,985	319	255	64
Wilson	49,737	134	119	15
Wilson's Mills	2,374	5	5	0
Windsor	3,564	9	9	0
Wingate	3,702	6	6	0
Winston-Salem	235,811	693	544	149
Winterville	9,539	19	18	1
Woodfin	6,178	14	14	0
Woodland	771	2	2	0
Wrightsville Beach	2,551	26	24	2
Yadkinville	2,949	14	13	1
Youngsville	1,177	11	10	1
Zebulon	4,664	21	20	1
NORTH DAKOTA				
Belfield	856	4	3	1
Beulah	3,149	6	5	1
Bismarck	65,850	126	99	27
Bowman	1,687	3	3	0
Burlington	1,054	3	3	0
Cando	1,164	3	3	0
Carrington	2,108	10	5	5
Cavalier	1,268	4	4	0
Devils Lake	7,260	18	16	2
Dickinson	20,347	57	38	19
Ellendale	1,388	2	2	0
Fargo	111,101	162	143	19
Fessenden	486	1	1	0
Grafton	4,326	11	10	1
Grand Forks	53,625	97	82	15
Harvey	1,827	4	3	1
Hazen	2,423	4	4	0
Hillsboro	1,602	2	2	0
Jamestown	15,286	33	29	4
Kenmare	1,050	3	3	0
Killdeer	841	3	3	0
Lamoure	895	1	1	0
Lincoln	2,898	2	2	0
Lisbon	2,149	3	3	0
Mandan	19,168	36	30	6
Medora	139	2	2	0
Minot	44,635	97	72	25
Napoleon	757	1	1	0
New Town	2,362	4	3	1
Northwood	918	2	2	0
Oakes	1,840	3	3	0
Powers Lake	314	1	1	0
Rolla	1,333	4	4	0
Rugby	2,972	5	5	0
Scranton	285	1	1	0
Sherwood	254	1	1	0
Stanley	1,949	5	5	0
Steele	708	1	1	0
Surrey	1,042	2	2	0
Thompson	1,002	1	1	0
Tioga	1,247	7	6	1
Valley City	6,580	14	13	1
Wahpeton	7,812	16	14	2
Watford City	2,793	11	10	1
West Fargo	28,018	49	39	10
Williston	19,949	52	38	14
Wishek	974	2	2	0
OHIO				
Ada	5,755	11	8	3
Akron	198,405	454	412	42
Alliance	22,144	55	41	14
American Township	12,318	1	1	0
Arcanum	2,098	3	3	0
Ashland	20,306	33	26	7
Athens	23,721	38	25	13
Aurora	15,457	36	28	8
Austintown	36,192	49	37	12
Bainbridge Township	11,454	26	18	8
Bath Township, Summit County	9,724	28	21	7
Beaver Township	6,606	15	11	4
Bedford	12,858	42	31	11
Bedford Heights	10,608	36	28	8
Bellbrook	7,061	13	12	1

Table 78.   Full-Time Law Enforcement Employees, by Selected State and City, 2013— continued

(Number.)

State/city	Population	Total law enforcement employees	Total officers	Total civilians
Bellefontaine	13,147	30	23	7
Bellville	1,887	4	4	0
Belpre	6,429	14	10	4
Berea	18,939	34	28	6
Blue Ash	12,105	38	32	6
Bluffton	4,000	6	6	0
Bowling Green	31,844	55	41	14
Cambridge	10,534	31	25	6
Celina	10,392	18	13	5
Champion Township	9,480	9	8	1
Cincinnati	296,491	1,083	961	122
Clearcreek Township	14,642	14	14	0
Cleveland	389,181	1,727	1,476	251
Cleveland Heights	46,309	120	103	17
Clyde	6,281	17	13	4
Columbiana	6,315	15	11	4
Columbus	816,364	2,181	1,862	319
Conneaut	12,895	20	15	5
Covington	2,596	6	5	1
Cuyahoga Falls	49,133	72	69	3
Danville	1,021	2	2	0
Dayton	141,167	413	347	66
Defiance	16,790	29	26	3
Delaware	36,260	58	51	7
Delphos	7,097	14	11	3
Dennison	2,634	2	2	0
Dublin	43,387	90	64	26
Eastlake	18,423	35	24	11
Englewood	13,455	26	20	6
Evendale	2,762	21	19	2
Fairborn	32,820	56	42	14
Fairfield	42,677	77	58	19
Fairfield Township	21,781	19	18	1
Fairlawn	7,376	30	20	10
Findlay	41,660	71	54	17
Forest Park	18,672	41	35	6
Fort Recovery	1,422	2	2	0
Franklin	11,831	29	22	7
Gahanna	34,011	67	52	15
Gates Mills	2,256	11	10	1
Grafton	5,716	4	4	0
Green Springs	1,343	2	2	0
Groveport	5,598	22	21	1
Hamilton	62,268	128	108	20
Hartville	2,944	11	11	0
Highland Heights	8,277	31	24	7
Hinckley Township	7,777	11	10	1
Holland	1,758	9	9	0
Hudson	22,340	35	29	6
Indian Hill	5,789	24	19	5
Jackson Township, Mahoning County	2,078	5	5	0
Jamestown	2,019	3	3	0
Kalida	1,553	1	1	0
Kettering	55,907	112	79	33
Kirtland	6,851	13	9	4
Lakewood	51,167	112	91	21
Lancaster	38,902	80	63	17
Lexington	4,751	12	8	4
Lodi	2,778	5	4	1
Lordstown	3,363	13	9	4
Louisville	9,143	11	10	1
Loveland	12,236	17	16	1
Mansfield	46,832	106	76	30
Marblehead	899	3	3	0
Mariemont	3,379	11	10	1
Marietta	14,013	37	31	6
Mason	31,204	46	41	5
Maumee	14,081	56	42	14
Mentor-on-the-Lake	7,434	9	8	1
Middletown	48,691	107	76	31
Milan	1,352	4	2	2
Milford	6,671	17	15	2
Millersburg	3,084	10	9	1
Monroe	15,284	25	20	5
Moreland Hills	3,302	15	14	1
Napoleon	8,663	20	15	5
Navarre	1,937	5	5	0
New Albany	8,772	21	15	6
Newark	47,702	87	70	17

Table 78.   Full-Time Law Enforcement Employees, by Selected State and City, 2013— continued

(Number.)

State/city	Population	Total law enforcement employees	Total officers	Total civilians
New Boston	2,227	15	11	4
New Bremen	2,979	6	6	0
New Franklin	14,232	19	13	6
New Lexington	4,749	7	5	2
New London	2,426	5	5	0
New Washington	938	1	1	0
North Canton	17,380	31	23	8
Oberlin	8,305	23	17	6
Olmsted Falls	8,910	14	10	4
Ontario	6,137	25	21	4
Orange Village	3,287	15	14	1
Oregon	20,188	57	44	13
Orrville	8,400	20	15	5
Oxford Township	2,123	13	13	0
Painesville	19,655	36	33	3
Parma Heights	20,395	40	33	7
Perrysburg	21,279	46	33	13
Perry Township, Montgomery County	3,347	3	3	0
Pickerington	18,812	39	27	12
Plain City	4,219	7	7	0
Portsmouth	20,322	41	38	3
Powell	12,093	19	17	2
Reynoldsburg	36,472	68	54	14
Rittman	6,505	11	8	3
Roseville	1,854	2	2	0
Russells Point	1,365	3	3	0
Russell Township	5,216	10	9	1
Sagamore Hills	10,988	14	10	4
Salem	12,115	20	20	0
Seaman	930	2	2	0
Sebring	4,337	9	5	4
Sharonville	13,510	45	37	8
Shawnee Township	12,247	17	11	6
Sidney	20,980	45	35	10
Silver Lake	2,509	8	8	0
Solon	23,105	74	47	27
South Russell	3,825	9	9	0
Springboro	17,711	28	25	3
Springdale	11,192	40	33	7
Springfield	60,012	143	129	14
Springfield Township, Hamilton County	36,330	47	41	6
Springfield Township, Mahoning County	6,583	8	8	0
Springfield Township, Summit County	17,630	25	22	3
St. Henry	2,480	2	2	0
Stow	34,625	45	37	8
Streetsboro	16,115	36	28	8
Strongsville	44,583	105	68	37
Struthers	10,522	19	15	4
Sugarcreek Township	8,187	18	17	1
Tallmadge	17,501	26	23	3
Toledo	283,035	642	532	110
Trenton	12,196	19	14	5
Union	6,393	5	5	0
Vandalia	15,181	39	30	9
Van Wert	10,852	28	20	8
Wadsworth	21,758	37	28	9
Waite Hill	470	5	5	0
Walbridge	3,065	5	5	0
Wapakoneta	9,812	19	14	5
Warren Township	5,450	6	6	0
Washington Court House	14,083	23	18	5
Weathersfield	8,241	9	8	1
Wellington	4,813	9	6	3
West Alexandria	1,355	3	3	0
West Carrollton	13,079	28	22	6
West Chester Township	59,435	105	84	21
Westerville	37,363	89	73	16
Whitehall	18,480	60	47	13
Williamsburg	2,514	5	5	0
Willoughby	22,374	58	43	15
Wilmington	12,439	21	19	2
Yellow Springs	3,539	11	8	3
Youngstown	64,938	186	149	37
Zanesville	25,378	87	51	36
OKLAHOMA				
Achille	501	3	2	1
Ada	17,170	37	34	3

Table 78.   Full-Time Law Enforcement Employees, by Selected State and City, 2013— continued

(Number.)

State/city	Population	Total law enforcement employees	Total officers	Total civilians
Allen	937	2	2	0
Altus	19,634	55	43	12
Alva	4,901	11	9	2
Anadarko	6,843	20	15	5
Antlers	2,335	10	5	5
Apache	1,447	9	4	5
Ardmore	24,793	65	47	18
Arkoma	1,945	5	2	3
Atoka	3,098	16	15	1
Bartlesville	36,389	80	58	22
Beaver	1,492	3	3	0
Beggs	1,255	8	4	4
Bethany	19,529	39	30	9
Bixby	23,122	33	25	8
Blackwell	6,952	23	16	7
Blanchard	8,016	15	10	5
Boise City	1,203	2	2	0
Boley	1,188	1	1	0
Bristow	4,239	12	8	4
Broken Arrow	102,956	184	130	54
Broken Bow	4,155	18	13	5
Caddo	1,027	3	3	0
Calera	2,205	10	9	1
Caney	201	4	3	1
Canton	614	3	3	0
Carnegie	1,720	5	3	2
Carney	644	3	3	0
Cashion	812	5	4	1
Catoosa	7,168	15	14	1
Chandler	3,093	11	7	4
Checotah	3,393	14	10	4
Chelsea	1,967	6	3	3
Cherokee	1,501	8	4	4
Chickasha	16,201	35	27	8
Choctaw	11,768	15	14	1
Chouteau	2,111	9	8	1
Claremore	18,953	53	37	16
Clayton	786	6	2	4
Cleveland	3,224	7	7	0
Clinton	9,423	26	18	8
Coalgate	1,981	4	4	0
Colbert	1,161	5	4	1
Collinsville	5,952	15	10	5
Comanche	1,645	5	5	0
Cordell	2,903	11	6	5
Coweta	9,559	21	14	7
Crescent	1,483	9	4	5
Cushing	7,860	20	14	6
Davenport	804	2	2	0
Davis	2,736	11	10	1
Del City	21,959	46	33	13
Depew	480	2	2	0
Dewar	882	1	1	0
Dewey	3,508	12	11	1
Dibble	826	2	2	0
Drumright	2,909	6	6	0
Duncan	23,234	60	45	15
Durant	16,585	40	37	3
Edmond	85,974	142	113	29
Elgin	2,617	8	8	0
Elk City	12,463	37	24	13
El Reno	17,743	43	30	13
Enid	49,965	108	87	21
Eufaula	2,919	16	12	4
Fairfax	1,373	6	3	3
Fairview	2,653	8	5	3
Fletcher	1,194	1	1	0
Forest Park	1,044	4	4	0
Fort Gibson	4,123	10	10	0
Frederick	3,825	11	10	1
Geary	1,289	10	5	5
Glenpool	11,588	25	18	7
Goodwell	1,339	4	4	0
Grove	6,684	28	20	8
Guthrie	10,752	27	20	7
Guymon	12,066	29	20	9
Haileyville	785	3	3	0
Harrah	5,498	9	9	0
Hartshorne	2,041	5	5	0

Table 78.   Full-Time Law Enforcement Employees, by Selected State and City, 2013— continued

(Number.)

State/city	Population	Total law enforcement employees	Total officers	Total civilians
Haskell	1,989	6	6	0
Healdton	2,786	10	6	4
Heavener	3,377	12	8	4
Hennessey	2,127	8	4	4
Henryetta	5,814	17	12	5
Hinton	3,216	5	5	0
Hobart	3,678	13	7	6
Holdenville	5,763	14	8	6
Hollis	2,045	9	5	4
Hominy	3,558	9	4	5
Hooker	2,016	3	3	0
Howe	797	1	1	0
Hugo	5,304	17	15	2
Hulbert	604	4	4	0
Hydro	967	2	2	0
Idabel	7,015	26	20	6
Jay	2,480	15	9	6
Jenks	18,357	22	16	6
Jones	2,834	5	5	0
Kiefer	1,848	4	4	0
Kingfisher	4,644	13	11	2
Kingston	1,615	8	8	0
Krebs	1,983	8	6	2
Lahoma	620	2	2	0
Lawton	98,548	231	159	72
Lexington	2,209	9	6	3
Lindsay	2,788	15	9	6
Locust Grove	1,416	8	4	4
Lone Grove	5,163	10	7	3
Luther	1,396	7	6	1
Madill	3,809	12	11	1
Mangum	2,897	11	6	5
Mannford	3,089	9	7	2
Marietta	2,661	8	6	2
Marlow	4,618	15	10	5
Maysville	1,214	6	4	2
McAlester	18,277	56	40	16
McCurtain	526	1	1	0
McLoud	4,110	13	8	5
Medicine Park	423	2	2	0
Meeker	1,144	5	5	0
Miami	13,794	41	32	9
Midwest City	56,590	125	92	33
Minco	1,649	3	3	0
Moore	58,628	98	82	16
Mooreland	1,225	2	2	0
Morris	1,457	3	3	0
Mountain View	780	2	2	0
Muldrow	3,313	15	10	5
Muskogee	38,884	96	87	9
Mustang	18,895	28	21	7
Newcastle	8,479	17	16	1
Newkirk	2,267	4	4	0
Nichols Hills	3,836	21	16	5
Nicoma Park	2,458	6	6	0
Ninnekah	1,023	3	3	0
Noble	6,702	16	11	5
Norman	116,970	216	163	53
North Enid	886	3	3	0
Nowata	3,761	9	6	3
Oilton	1,020	4	4	0
Okemah	3,331	12	8	4
Oklahoma City	605,034	1,326	1,007	319
Okmulgee	12,345	27	21	6
Oologah	1,188	3	3	0
Owasso	31,973	65	47	18
Pauls Valley	6,080	21	14	7
Pawhuska	3,567	12	8	4
Pawnee	2,163	4	4	0
Perkins	2,854	9	8	1
Perry	5,079	16	10	6
Piedmont	6,384	11	9	2
Pocola	4,011	10	6	4
Ponca City	24,858	74	54	20
Porum	721	2	2	0
Poteau	8,529	30	23	7
Prague	2,396	9	5	4
Pryor	9,496	32	23	9
Purcell	5,965	22	19	3

Table 78.   Full-Time Law Enforcement Employees, by Selected State and City, 2013— continued

(Number.)

State/city	Population	Total law enforcement employees	Total officers	Total civilians
Ringling	1,019	2	2	0
Roland	3,277	8	5	3
Rush Springs	1,238	4	4	0
Sallisaw	8,586	30	22	8
Sand Springs	19,180	43	32	11
Sapulpa	20,857	54	44	10
Sawyer	320	1	1	0
Sayre	4,556	14	8	6
Seiling	850	2	2	0
Seminole	7,498	17	13	4
Shawnee	30,886	79	57	22
Skiatook	7,751	23	18	5
Snyder	1,367	3	3	0
South Coffeyville	786	3	3	0
Spencer	4,007	8	7	1
Spiro	2,161	4	4	0
Stigler	2,744	13	9	4
Stillwater	46,834	109	72	37
Stilwell	3,988	18	13	5
Stonewall	475	2	2	0
Stratford	1,508	4	4	0
Stringtown	401	2	2	0
Stroud	2,688	12	8	4
Sulphur	5,018	13	12	1
Tahlequah	16,509	42	34	8
Talihina	1,112	9	5	4
Tecumseh	6,580	13	12	1
Texhoma	980	1	1	0
The Village	9,188	26	21	5
Tishomingo	3,064	8	7	1
Tonkawa	3,150	14	9	5
Tryon	488	1	1	0
Tulsa	394,498	873	780	93
Tushka	306	3	3	0
Tuttle	6,284	16	11	5
Valliant	751	5	4	1
Verdigris	4,161	5	4	1
Vian	1,411	3	3	0
Vinita	5,578	21	15	6
Wagoner	8,573	20	15	5
Walters	2,568	4	4	0
Warner	1,631	3	3	0
Warr Acres	10,360	31	26	5
Washington	625	2	2	0
Watonga	2,987	5	4	1
Waukomis	1,313	2	2	0
Waurika	2,018	3	3	0
Waynoka	917	4	4	0
Weatherford	11,529	31	20	11
Weleetka	1,005	8	5	3
Westville	1,586	11	6	5
Wetumka	1,250	4	4	0
Wewoka	3,454	10	9	1
Wilburton	2,804	7	6	1
Wilson	1,730	4	4	0
Woodward	12,402	38	28	10
Wright City	757	2	2	0
Wyandotte	338	10	9	1
Wynnewood	2,187	6	5	1
Yale	1,227	6	3	3
Yukon	24,570	64	44	20
OREGON				
Albany	51,645	82	57	25
Amity	1,624	2	2	0
Ashland	20,455	33	26	7
Astoria	9,543	25	17	8
Athena	1,144	2	2	0
Aumsville	3,738	7	6	1
Baker City	9,660	14	14	0
Bandon	3,039	7	6	1
Beaverton	93,551	173	137	36
Bend	79,926	108	85	23
Black Butte		7	6	1
Boardman	3,369	10	9	1
Brookings	6,313	20	13	7
Burns	2,706	3	3	0
Canby	16,031	28	23	5
Cannon Beach	1,692	9	8	1

Table 78. Full-Time Law Enforcement Employees, by Selected State and City, 2013— continued

(Number.)

State/city	Population	Total law enforcement employees	Total officers	Total civilians
Carlton	2,022	3	2	1
Central Point	17,485	30	24	6
Clatskanie	1,726	6	5	1
Coburg	1,043	4	3	1
Columbia City	1,938	3	3	0
Condon	722	2	1	1
Coos Bay	15,816	37	24	13
Coquille	3,826	8	7	1
Cornelius	12,231	14	13	1
Corvallis	55,218	91	53	38
Cottage Grove	9,795	26	17	9
Dallas	14,803	18	16	2
Eagle Point	8,669	12	11	1
Enterprise	1,870	4	4	0
Eugene	158,499	335	196	139
Fairview	9,225	17	15	2
Florence	8,489	22	14	8
Forest Grove	22,239	32	28	4
Gearhart	1,485	3	3	0
Gervais	2,573	6	5	1
Gladstone	11,699	19	16	3
Gold Beach	2,239	7	6	1
Grants Pass	34,865	77	50	27
Gresham	109,965	152	121	31
Hermiston	17,214	34	25	9
Hillsboro	96,313	180	131	49
Hines	1,508	3	3	0
Hood River	7,336	14	12	2
Hubbard	3,203	12	11	1
Independence	8,661	15	12	3
Jacksonville	2,813	6	5	1
John Day	1,702	10	4	6
Junction City	5,605	16	10	6
Keizer	37,018	44	37	7
King City	3,389	5	5	0
Klamath Falls	21,043	41	36	5
La Grande	13,034	32	18	14
Lake Oswego	37,428	69	42	27
Lakeview	2,252	5	5	0
Lebanon	15,810	35	25	10
Lincoln City	7,976	36	25	11
Madras	6,377	10	9	1
Malin	791	1	1	0
Manzanita	607	4	4	0
McMinnville	32,642	44	37	7
Medford	76,949	137	101	36
Merrill	827	2	1	1
Milton-Freewater	7,126	17	11	6
Milwaukie	20,480	40	37	3
Molalla	8,282	13	11	2
Monmouth	9,792	15	13	2
Mount Angel	3,405	6	5	1
Myrtle Creek	3,422	8	7	1
Myrtle Point	2,483	5	5	0
Newberg-Dundee	25,647	48	35	13
Newport	10,029	24	19	5
North Bend	9,605	23	16	7
North Plains	2,033	2	2	0
Nyssa	3,192	9	8	1
Oakridge	3,207	6	5	1
Ontario	11,069	30	21	9
Oregon City	33,025	49	42	7
Pendleton	16,902	24	21	3
Philomath	4,598	10	9	1
Phoenix	4,600	10	8	2
Pilot Rock	1,518	3	3	0
Portland	609,136	1,156	938	218
Port Orford	1,126	3	3	0
Prineville	9,161	28	18	10
Rainier	1,887	6	5	1
Redmond	27,153	38	29	9
Reedsport	4,098	18	9	9
Rockaway Beach	1,313	4	4	0
Rogue River	2,173	5	4	1
Roseburg	21,890	39	35	4
Salem	158,234	302	187	115
Sandy	9,978	19	15	4
Scappoose	6,677	10	9	1
Seaside	6,475	28	19	9

Table 78.   Full-Time Law Enforcement Employees, by Selected State and City, 2013— continued

(Number.)

State/city	Population	Total law enforcement employees	Total officers	Total civilians
Sherwood	18,932	25	22	3
Silverton	9,380	18	16	2
Springfield	60,024	82	66	16
Stanfield	2,058	5	5	0
Stayton	7,733	15	13	2
St. Helens	12,917	15	14	1
Sunriver		11	10	1
Sutherlin	7,747	17	15	2
Sweet Home	9,035	22	15	7
Talent	6,191	10	8	2
The Dalles	13,831	26	23	3
Tigard	50,311	86	68	18
Tillamook	4,932	10	8	2
Toledo	3,461	15	9	6
Troutdale	16,566	27	23	4
Tualatin	26,925	47	39	8
Turner	1,896	2	2	0
Umatilla	7,040	12	10	2
Vernonia	2,139	4	4	0
Warrenton	5,146	10	9	1
West Linn	25,744	35	31	4
Weston	670	2	2	0
Winston	5,343	8	7	1
Woodburn	24,263	40	32	8
Yamhill	1,040	3	3	0
PENNSYLVANIA				
Abington Township, Lackawanna County	1,750	3	3	0
Abington Township, Montgomery County	55,559	112	91	21
Adams Township, Butler County	12,582	7	7	0
Adams Township, Cambria County	5,868	3	3	0
Akron	3,918	4	4	0
Albion	1,499	2	2	0
Alburtis	2,390	4	4	0
Aldan	4,150	5	5	0
Aleppo Township	1,918	15	12	3
Aliquippa	9,323	18	17	1
Allegheny Township, Blair County	6,726	8	7	1
Allegheny Township, Westmoreland County	8,332	9	8	1
Allentown	119,277	234	211	23
Altoona	46,103	72	64	8
Ambler	6,514	16	14	2
Ambridge	6,963	13	13	0
Amity Township	12,744	13	12	1
Annville Township	4,852	7	5	2
Archbald	7,111	5	5	0
Armagh Township	3,854	1	1	0
Arnold	5,076	12	12	0
Ashland	2,778	2	2	0
Ashley	2,776	2	2	0
Aspinwall	2,796	7	6	1
Aston Township	16,873	18	16	2
Athens	3,356	4	4	0
Athens Township	5,243	10	9	1
Austin	569	1	1	0
Avalon	4,692	7	6	1
Avoca	2,665	2	2	0
Avonmore Boro	992	1	1	0
Baden	4,090	4	4	0
Baldwin Borough	19,810	26	25	1
Baldwin Township	1,984	5	5	0
Bally	1,107	2	2	0
Bangor	5,241	10	9	1
Barrett Township	4,149	5	5	0
Beaver	4,473	10	9	1
Beaver Falls	8,720	19	18	1
Bedford	2,778	5	5	0
Bedminster Township	6,969	7	6	1
Bell Acres	1,404	3	3	0
Bellefonte	6,353	12	10	2
Bellevue	8,347	18	15	3
Bellwood	1,809	1	1	0
Ben Avon	1,773	15	12	3
Ben Avon Heights	374	15	12	3
Bensalem Township	60,516	129	100	29
Berlin	2,065	2	2	0
Bern Township	6,877	12	12	0

Table 78.   Full-Time Law Enforcement Employees, by Selected State and City, 2013— continued

(Number.)

State/city	Population	Total law enforcement employees	Total officers	Total civilians
Berwick	10,326	15	14	1
Bethel Park	32,392	44	38	6
Bethel Township, Berks County	4,125	2	2	0
Bethlehem	75,135	175	149	26
Bethlehem Township	23,873	33	32	1
Biglerville	1,206	2	2	0
Birdsboro	5,162	8	8	0
Birmingham Township	4,241	4	4	0
Blairsville	3,411	3	3	0
Blair Township	4,573	4	4	0
Blakely	6,545	4	4	0
Blawnox	1,433	3	3	0
Bloomsburg Town	14,563	20	16	4
Bonneauville	1,805	1	1	0
Boyertown	4,047	7	6	1
Brackenridge	3,249	4	4	0
Braddock Hills	1,876	2	2	0
Bradford	8,660	18	18	0
Bradford Township	4,834	5	5	0
Branch Township	1,818	1	1	0
Brecknock Township, Berks County	4,614	5	5	0
Brentwood	9,613	15	13	2
Briar Creek Township	3,020	4	4	0
Bridgeport	4,574	7	6	1
Bridgeville	5,140	9	8	1
Bridgewater	702	3	3	0
Brighton Township	8,243	6	6	0
Bristol	9,674	12	10	2
Bristol Township	54,456	68	58	10
Brockway	2,048	2	2	0
Brookhaven	8,049	8	7	1
Brookville	3,878	7	6	1
Brownsville	2,309	2	2	0
Bryn Athyn	1,402	5	5	0
Buckingham Township	20,396	23	21	2
Buffalo Township	7,314	5	5	0
Buffalo Valley Regional	12,144	16	15	1
Bushkill Township	8,344	17	15	2
Butler	13,577	24	23	1
Butler Township, Butler County	17,095	22	20	2
Butler Township, Luzerne County	9,427	9	8	1
Butler Township, Schuykill County	5,850	4	4	0
Caernarvon Township, Berks County	4,030	9	8	1
California	7,267	8	7	1
Caln Township	14,090	19	18	1
Cambria Township	6,025	3	3	0
Cambridge Springs	2,383	3	3	0
Camp Hill	7,864	11	10	1
Canonsburg	8,982	17	17	0
Canton	1,998	3	3	0
Carbondale	8,869	9	9	0
Carlisle	18,928	37	32	5
Carnegie	7,958	14	12	2
Carrolltown	836	2	2	0
Carroll Township, Washington County	5,621	2	2	0
Carroll Township, York County	6,074	10	10	0
Carroll Valley	3,896	4	3	1
Castle Shannon	8,301	13	12	1
Catasauqua	6,510	9	8	1
Catawissa	1,527	3	3	0
Cecil Township	11,683	16	15	1
Center Township	11,775	15	14	1
Centerville	3,236	3	3	0
Central Berks Regional	9,493	15	14	1
Chalfont	4,066	8	7	1
Chambersburg	20,381	36	34	2
Charleroi Regional	6,756	7	7	0
Chartiers Township	7,938	12	12	0
Cheltenham Township	36,903	82	74	8
Chester	34,037	113	103	10
Chester Township	4,132	11	10	1
Cheswick	1,740	1	1	0
Chippewa Township	8,152	9	8	1
Churchill	3,007	10	10	0
Clairton	6,761	8	8	0
Clarion	5,117	9	8	1
Clarks Summit	6,588	6	5	1
Clearfield	6,108	9	7	2
Cleona	2,119	4	4	0

Table 78.   Full-Time Law Enforcement Employees, by Selected State and City, 2013— continued

(Number.)

State/city	Population	Total law enforcement employees	Total officers	Total civilians
Clifton Heights	6,654	11	10	1
Coaldale	2,238	1	1	0
Coal Township	10,417	13	12	1
Coatesville	13,144	30	26	4
Cochranton	1,114	2	2	0
Colebrookdale District	6,037	11	9	2
Collegeville	5,161	8	8	0
Collier Township	7,543	15	14	1
Collingdale	8,782	9	8	1
Colonial Regional	19,575	26	24	2
Columbia	10,375	19	16	3
Conemaugh Township, Cambria County	1,966	2	2	0
Conemaugh Township, Somerset County	7,175	7	6	1
Conewago Township, Adams County	7,099	10	9	1
Conewango Township	3,495	4	4	0
Confluence	763	1	1	0
Conneaut Lake Regional	3,538	4	3	1
Connellsville	7,567	16	15	1
Conoy Township	3,391	16	14	2
Conshohocken	7,875	21	19	2
Conway	2,164	4	4	0
Conyngham	1,907	2	2	0
Coopersburg	2,406	7	7	0
Coplay	3,228	4	4	0
Coraopolis	5,661	14	10	4
Cornwall	4,188	7	6	1
Corry	6,546	14	12	2
Covington Township	2,330	3	3	0
Crafton	6,401	9	9	0
Cranberry Township	29,062	34	28	6
Crescent Township	2,643	3	3	0
Cresson	1,668	10	10	0
Cresson Township	4,278	6	5	1
Croyle Township	2,304	1	1	0
Cumberland Township, Adams County	6,169	6	6	0
Cumberland Township, Greene County	6,493	4	4	0
Cumru Township	15,222	22	22	0
Curwensville	2,499	2	2	0
Dale	1,203	2	2	0
Dallas	2,808	4	4	0
Dallas Township	9,075	8	8	0
Dalton	1,233	1	1	0
Danville	4,648	8	6	2
Darby	10,680	18	17	1
Darby Township	9,274	15	14	1
Decatur Township	4,519	2	2	0
Delmont	2,652	4	4	0
Derry	2,644	3	3	0
Derry Township, Dauphin County	24,838	46	39	7
Dickson City	6,061	6	6	0
Donegal Township	2,467	1	1	0
Donora	4,735	6	6	0
Dormont	8,573	14	13	1
Douglass Township, Berks County	3,337	3	3	0
Douglass Township, Montgomery County	10,345	12	11	1
Downingtown	7,932	19	16	3
Doylestown	8,361	20	15	5
Doylestown Township	17,575	22	20	2
Dublin Borough	2,155	2	2	0
Du Bois	7,685	13	13	0
Duboistown	1,205	1	1	0
Dunbar	1,029	1	1	0
Duncansville	1,226	2	2	0
Dunmore	14,074	18	18	0
Duquesne	5,555	15	14	1
Duryea	4,936	2	2	0
East Bangor	1,432	1	1	0
East Berlin	1,521	1	1	0
East Bethlehem Township	2,331	1	1	0
East Brandywine Township	7,461	13	12	1
East Cocalico Township	10,399	22	20	2
East Coventry Township	6,765	8	7	1
East Deer Township	1,494	1	1	0
East Earl Township	6,659	9	9	0
Eastern Adams Regional	7,315	5	5	0
Eastern Pike Regional	4,715	10	9	1

Table 78.   Full-Time Law Enforcement Employees, by Selected State and City, 2013— continued

(Number.)

State/city	Population	Total law enforcement employees	Total officers	Total civilians
East Fallowfield Township	7,549	7	7	0
East Hempfield Township	23,935	38	34	4
East Lampeter Township	16,780	38	35	3
East Lansdowne	2,661	5	3	2
East Marlborough Township	7,196	1	1	0
East McKeesport	2,709	3	3	0
East Norriton Township	14,107	30	27	3
Easton	27,001	67	62	5
East Pennsboro Township	20,886	20	19	1
East Penn Township	2,859	2	2	0
East Pikeland Township	7,300	8	7	1
East Pittsburgh	1,818	1	1	0
East Taylor Township	2,661	1	1	0
Easttown Township	10,564	14	13	1
East Vincent Township	6,858	7	7	0
East Washington	2,218	1	1	0
East Whiteland Township	10,654	20	17	3
Ebensburg	3,279	3	3	0
Economy	9,107	12	11	1
Eddystone	2,410	8	7	1
Edgewood	3,107	9	9	0
Edgeworth	1,682	7	4	3
Edinboro	6,450	8	8	0
Edwardsville	4,798	13	12	1
Elizabeth	2,001	2	2	0
Elizabethtown	11,562	18	16	2
Elizabeth Township	13,298	12	12	0
Elkland	1,835	2	2	0
Ellwood City	7,739	12	10	2
Emmaus	11,338	20	18	2
Emporium	1,995	2	2	0
Emsworth	2,447	15	12	3
Ephrata	13,541	31	27	4
Erie	100,814	192	170	22
Etna	3,440	8	7	1
Evans City	1,808	2	2	0
Everett	1,786	3	3	0
Exeter	5,638	4	4	0
Exeter Township, Berks County	25,749	32	30	2
Exeter Township, Luzerne County	2,381	7	7	0
Fairview Township, Luzerne County	4,525	5	5	0
Fairview Township, York County	16,915	18	16	2
Falls Township, Bucks County	34,234	60	53	7
Fawn Township	2,380	2	2	0
Ferguson Township	17,807	23	21	2
Ferndale	1,592	1	1	0
Findlay Township	5,201	24	17	7
Fleetwood	4,086	6	6	0
Folcroft	6,612	11	10	1
Ford City	2,938	3	3	0
Forest City	1,859	2	2	0
Forest Hills	6,510	9	9	0
Forks Township	15,131	21	20	1
Forty Fort	4,186	5	5	0
Forward Township	3,375	5	5	0
Foster Township, McKean County	4,287	4	4	0
Fountain Hill	4,631	8	7	1
Fox Chapel	5,415	10	10	0
Frackville	3,757	2	2	0
Franconia Township	13,245	17	15	2
Franklin	6,415	23	17	6
Franklin Park	14,027	14	13	1
Franklin Township, Beaver County	4,041	1	1	0
Franklin Township, Carbon County	4,236	4	4	0
Frazer Township	1,155	2	2	0
Freedom Township	3,466	3	3	0
Freeland	3,509	3	3	0
Freemansburg	2,624	4	3	1
Freeport	1,785	2	2	0
Galeton	1,157	1	1	0
Gallitzin	1,880	6	6	0
Geistown	2,410	1	1	0
Gettysburg	7,653	16	13	3
Gilpin Township	2,479	1	1	0
Girard	3,068	3	3	0
Glassport	4,466	5	5	0
Glenolden	7,158	11	10	1
Granville Township	5,108	9	7	2
Greencastle	4,025	6	5	1

Table 78.   Full-Time Law Enforcement Employees, by Selected State and City, 2013— continued

(Number.)

State/city	Population	Total law enforcement employees	Total officers	Total civilians
Greenfield Township, Blair County	4,165	4	4	0
Greenfield Township, Lackawanna County	2,098	1	1	0
Greensburg	14,689	38	28	10
Green Tree	4,431	11	10	1
Greenville	5,890	10	9	1
Grove City	8,206	12	11	1
Hamburg	4,283	6	5	1
Hampden Township	28,360	27	26	1
Hampton Township	18,478	19	18	1
Hanover	15,362	28	25	3
Hanover Township, Luzerne County	11,075	16	15	1
Harmar Township	3,007	8	8	0
Harmony Township	3,157	4	4	0
Harrisburg	49,203	230	179	51
Harrison Township	10,471	21	18	3
Harveys Lake	2,800	3	3	0
Hastings	2,274	1	1	0
Hatboro	7,387	17	14	3
Hatfield Township	20,890	30	26	4
Haverford Township	48,717	82	70	12
Hazleton	25,191	41	38	3
Hegins Township	3,501	2	2	0
Heidelberg	1,246	3	3	0
Heidelberg Township, Berks County	1,738	1	1	0
Hellam Township	8,691	10	8	2
Hellertown	5,857	11	10	1
Hemlock Township	2,246	6	6	0
Hempfield Township, Mercer County	3,777	6	5	1
Hermitage	16,163	32	29	3
Highspire	2,384	6	6	0
Hilltown Township	15,199	20	17	3
Hollidaysburg	5,836	10	8	2
Homer City	1,682	2	2	0
Homestead	3,152	14	13	1
Honesdale	4,294	9	9	0
Honey Brook	1,749	1	1	0
Hooversville	632	1	1	0
Hopewell Township	12,595	15	14	1
Horsham Township	26,397	47	40	7
Hughestown	1,397	1	1	0
Hughesville	2,150	2	2	0
Hummelstown	4,517	8	7	1
Huntingdon	7,068	11	11	0
Independence Township, Beaver County	2,487	2	2	0
Indiana	13,942	24	22	2
Indiana Township	7,324	10	10	0
Ingram	3,319	4	4	0
Irwin	3,921	3	3	0
Ivyland	1,041	2	2	0
Jackson Township, Butler County	3,643	10	8	2
Jackson Township, Cambria County	4,297	2	2	0
Jackson Township, Luzerne County	4,615	3	3	0
Jeannette	9,493	17	14	3
Jefferson Hills Borough	11,102	16	15	1
Jefferson Township, Mercer County	1,862	2	2	0
Jefferson Township, Washington County	1,168	1	1	0
Jenkins Township	4,477	3	3	0
Jenkintown	4,449	13	11	2
Jermyn	2,165	1	1	0
Jessup	4,653	5	2	3
Jim Thorpe	4,734	7	6	1
Johnsonburg	2,435	3	3	0
Johnstown	21,954	41	38	3
Kane	3,681	5	5	0
Kennedy Township	7,848	12	10	2
Kennett Square	6,126	13	10	3
Kennett Township	7,885	2	2	0
Kidder Township	1,947	6	6	0
Kilbuck Township	702	15	12	3
Kingston	13,117	20	19	1
Kingston Township	7,035	11	11	0
Kiskiminetas Township	4,738	1	1	0
Kittanning	3,966	9	8	1
Kline Township	1,422	2	1	1
Knox	1,141	3	3	0
Koppel	754	2	2	0
Kulpmont	2,898	1	1	0

Table 78.   Full-Time Law Enforcement Employees, by Selected State and City, 2013— continued

(Number.)

State/city	Population	Total law enforcement employees	Total officers	Total civilians
Kutztown	5,003	13	11	2
Laflin Borough	1,486	3	3	0
Lake City	3,020	3	3	0
Lancaster	59,370	165	143	22
Lancaster Township, Butler County	2,534	1	1	0
Langhorne Borough	1,616	1	1	0
Lansdale	16,395	32	25	7
Lansdowne	10,621	18	15	3
Lansford	3,876	6	6	0
Larksville	4,463	4	4	0
Latimore Township	2,582	1	1	0
Latrobe	8,204	12	12	0
Laureldale	3,905	5	5	0
Lawrence Park Township	3,933	9	8	1
Lawrence Township, Clearfield County	7,583	8	7	1
Lebanon	25,583	45	41	4
Leechburg	2,110	3	3	0
Leetsdale	1,214	4	4	0
Leet Township	1,631	4	4	0
Lehighton	5,417	9	8	1
Lehigh Township, Northampton County	10,482	13	12	1
Lehman Township	3,518	2	2	0
Lewistown	8,370	13	11	2
Liberty	2,549	1	1	0
Liberty Township, Adams County	1,240	1	1	0
Ligonier	1,547	2	2	0
Ligonier Township	6,541	4	4	0
Limerick Township	18,619	23	21	2
Lincoln	1,073	2	2	0
Lititz	9,389	16	13	3
Littlestown	4,434	9	8	1
Lock Haven	9,806	13	13	0
Locust Township	2,540	4	2	2
Logan Township	12,340	18	16	2
Lower Allen Township	18,040	21	19	2
Lower Burrell	11,605	16	15	1
Lower Chichester Township	3,470	5	5	0
Lower Frederick Township	4,883	3	3	0
Lower Gwynedd Township	11,546	17	16	1
Lower Heidelberg Township	5,630	10	9	1
Lower Makefield Township	32,667	42	38	4
Lower Merion Township	58,226	149	133	16
Lower Milford Township	3,832	2	2	0
Lower Moreland Township	13,122	28	23	5
Lower Paxton Township	47,692	58	52	6
Lower Pottsgrove Township	12,156	18	16	2
Lower Providence Township	25,672	31	31	0
Lower Salford Township	15,319	19	17	2
Lower Saucon Township	10,803	17	15	2
Lower Southampton Township	19,027	33	30	3
Lower Swatara Township	8,331	12	11	1
Lower Windsor Township	7,404	10	9	1
Luzerne Township	5,981	1	1	0
Lykens	1,771	1	1	0
Macungie	3,114	5	5	0
Mahanoy City	4,106	4	4	0
Mahanoy Township	3,246	1	1	0
Mahoning Township, Carbon County	4,279	4	4	0
Mahoning Township, Lawrence County	3,014	3	3	0
Mahoning Township, Montour County	4,212	7	6	1
Malvern	3,041	6	5	1
Manheim	4,861	16	15	1
Manheim Township	38,857	79	63	16
Manor	3,282	2	2	0
Manor Township, Lancaster County	20,106	18	16	2
Mansfield	3,629	5	5	0
Marcus Hook	2,394	6	5	1
Marietta	2,589	17	15	2
Marion Township, Beaver County	912	2	2	0
Marlborough Township	3,288	3	3	0
Marple Township	23,554	34	29	5
Mars	1,681	1	1	0
Martinsburg	1,946	2	2	0
Marysville	2,516	2	2	0
Masontown	3,419	5	5	0
Mayfield	1,795	1	1	0
McAdoo	2,257	3	3	0

Table 78.   Full-Time Law Enforcement Employees, by Selected State and City, 2013— continued

(Number.)

State/city	Population	Total law enforcement employees	Total officers	Total civilians
McCandless	28,792	31	29	2
McKeesport	21,456	55	52	3
McKees Rocks	6,086	12	11	1
McSherrystown	3,036	4	4	0
Meadville	13,227	28	22	6
Mechanicsburg	8,962	15	14	1
Media	5,337	24	16	8
Mercer	1,967	4	4	0
Mercersburg	1,555	2	2	0
Meshoppen	1,479	2	2	0
Meyersdale	2,135	2	2	0
Middleburg	1,290	3	2	1
Middlesex Township, Butler County	5,448	4	4	0
Middlesex Township, Cumberland County	7,235	10	9	1
Middletown	8,866	21	16	5
Middletown Township	45,526	59	53	6
Midland	2,600	6	5	1
Mifflin	642	1	1	0
Mifflinburg	3,518	10	9	1
Mifflin County Regional	16,944	12	12	0
Milford	1,002	2	2	0
Millbourne	1,163	1	1	0
Millcreek Township, Erie County	54,268	71	60	11
Millcreek Township, Lebanon County	5,513	2	2	0
Millersburg	2,539	5	4	1
Millersville	8,327	13	11	2
Millvale	3,733	3	3	0
Milton	7,024	9	8	1
Minersville	4,313	5	5	0
Mohnton	3,047	4	4	0
Monaca	5,743	9	9	0
Monessen	7,596	12	12	0
Monongahela	4,254	9	7	2
Monroeville	28,401	52	45	7
Montgomery	1,583	1	1	0
Montgomery Township	25,675	45	36	9
Montoursville	4,631	6	5	1
Montour Township	1,331	3	3	0
Montrose	1,571	1	1	0
Moon Township	24,987	35	29	6
Moore Township	9,247	11	10	1
Moosic	5,741	10	10	0
Morris-Cooper Regional	5,609	1	1	0
Morrisville	8,692	12	11	1
Morton	2,679	5	4	1
Moscow	2,022	3	3	0
Mount Carmel	5,841	8	8	0
Mount Carmel Township	3,124	6	6	0
Mount Holly Springs	2,029	3	3	0
Mount Joy	7,984	14	13	1
Mount Lebanon	33,093	53	44	9
Mount Oliver	3,392	8	8	0
Mount Pleasant	4,446	3	3	0
Mount Pleasant Township	3,533	4	4	0
Mount Union	2,411	5	5	0
Muhlenberg Township	19,867	31	29	2
Muncy	2,480	7	3	4
Muncy Township	1,115	2	2	0
Munhall	11,373	25	21	4
Murrysville	20,262	25	20	5
Myerstown	3,112	3	2	1
Nanticoke	10,406	14	13	1
Nanty Glo	2,669	1	1	0
Narberth	4,299	4	4	0
Nazareth	5,713	4	3	1
Neshannock Township	9,474	7	7	0
Nesquehoning	3,308	4	4	0
Nether Providence Township	13,758	15	14	1
Neville Township	1,080	15	12	3
Newberry Township	15,361	18	16	2
New Bethlehem	2,835	6	6	0
New Brighton	9,145	9	7	2
New Britain	3,147	6	5	1
New Britain Township	11,075	13	12	1
New Castle	22,729	37	34	3
New Cumberland	7,253	9	8	1
New Garden Township	12,109	12	11	1
New Hanover Township	11,943	10	9	1

Table 78.   Full-Time Law Enforcement Employees, by Selected State and City, 2013— continued

(Number.)

State/city	Population	Total law enforcement employees	Total officers	Total civilians
New Holland	5,416	15	14	1
New Hope	2,522	11	9	2
New Kensington	12,916	22	22	0
New Philadelphia	1,072	1	1	0
Newport Township	5,481	1	1	0
New Sewickley Township	7,526	8	8	0
Newton Township	2,865	1	1	0
Newtown	2,240	5	5	0
Newtown Township, Bucks County	22,596	32	28	4
Newtown Township, Delaware County	12,292	18	16	2
Newville	1,326	3	3	0
New Wilmington	2,468	5	5	0
Norristown	34,453	80	65	15
Northampton	9,937	14	12	2
Northampton Township	39,772	49	43	6
North Annville Township	2,423	1	1	0
North Belle Vernon	1,936	2	2	0
North Braddock	4,844	3	3	0
North Catasauqua	2,838	5	5	0
North Cornwall Township	7,734	10	9	1
North Coventry Township	7,942	13	12	1
North East, Erie County	4,248	7	7	0
Northeastern Regional	11,477	13	11	2
Northern Berks Regional	12,954	14	13	1
Northern Cambria Borough	3,741	2	2	0
Northern Lancaster County Regional	33,488	27	26	1
Northern Regional	32,008	31	29	2
Northern York Regional	67,657	53	49	4
North Fayette Township	14,093	25	20	5
North Franklin Township	4,590	7	6	1
North Hopewell Township	2,799	2	2	0
North Huntingdon Township	30,787	36	29	7
North Londonderry Township	8,243	10	9	1
North Middleton Township	11,314	10	9	1
North Sewickley Township	5,629	1	1	0
North Strabane Township	13,833	20	19	1
Northumberland	3,780	5	5	0
North Versailles Township	12,383	25	22	3
North Wales	3,239	5	4	1
Northwest Lancaster County Regional	18,776	17	15	2
Norwood	5,891	8	7	1
Oakmont	6,406	7	7	0
O'Hara Township	8,453	16	15	1
Ohio Township	5,917	15	12	3
Ohioville	3,514	2	2	0
Oil City	10,320	23	18	5
Old Forge	8,281	3	3	0
Old Lycoming Township	5,049	10	9	1
Oley Township	3,673	3	3	0
Oliver Township	1,922	1	1	0
Olyphant	5,199	3	3	0
Orangeville Area	1,746	1	1	0
Orwigsburg	3,053	4	4	0
Oxford	5,129	12	11	1
Paint Township	5,237	5	4	1
Palmerton	5,362	9	8	1
Palmer Township	20,845	35	32	3
Palmyra	7,449	9	8	1
Palo Alto	1,020	1	1	0
Parkesburg	3,638	10	9	1
Parkside	2,325	3	3	0
Parks Township	2,707	2	2	0
Patterson Township	2,999	3	3	0
Patton	1,726	2	2	0
Patton Township	15,513	20	18	2
Paxtang	1,550	3	3	0
Pen Argyl	3,570	5	5	0
Penbrook	2,985	8	8	0
Penndel	2,232	1	1	0
Penn Hills	42,295	54	51	3
Pennridge Regional	11,039	11	10	1
Penn Township, Butler County	5,055	4	3	1
Penn Township, Perry County	3,187	2	2	0
Penn Township, Westmoreland County	19,870	23	21	2
Penn Township, York County	15,688	24	22	2
Pequea Township	4,626	8	8	0
Perkasie	8,527	18	16	2
Perryopolis	1,767	2	2	0

Table 78.   Full-Time Law Enforcement Employees, by Selected State and City, 2013— continued

(Number.)

State/city	Population	Total law enforcement employees	Total officers	Total civilians
Peters Township	21,730	23	21	2
Philadelphia	1,553,153	7,325	6,508	817
Phoenixville	16,531	29	28	1
Pine Creek Township	3,275	2	2	0
Pine Grove	2,160	3	3	0
Pitcairn	3,284	4	3	1
Pittsburgh	307,632	923	861	62
Pittston	7,710	7	7	0
Plainfield Township	6,156	12	12	0
Plains Township	9,929	19	18	1
Pleasant Hills	8,294	20	18	2
Plum	27,476	28	26	2
Plumstead Township	12,688	17	15	2
Plymouth	5,917	4	4	0
Plymouth Township, Montgomery County	16,647	51	44	7
Pocono Mountain Regional	38,878	43	38	5
Pocono Township	10,951	18	17	1
Point Township	3,749	5	5	0
Polk	807	2	2	0
Portage	2,573	2	2	0
Port Allegany	2,130	3	3	0
Port Carbon	1,855	2	2	0
Port Vue	3,787	3	3	0
Pottstown	22,509	49	39	10
Pottsville	14,070	24	23	1
Pringle	976	20	19	1
Prospect Park	6,474	9	9	0
Pulaski Township, Lawrence County	3,370	2	2	0
Punxsutawney	5,883	12	9	3
Pymatuning Township	3,238	5	5	0
Quakertown	8,950	20	18	2
Quarryville	2,657	4	4	0
Raccoon Township	3,049	4	4	0
Radnor Township	31,527	57	47	10
Ralpho Township	4,351	6	6	0
Rankin	2,118	1	1	0
Reading	88,107	188	164	24
Reading Township	5,794	3	3	0
Redstone Township	5,516	2	2	0
Reilly Township	717	1	1	0
Reserve Township	3,330	5	5	0
Reynoldsville	2,720	2	2	0
Rice Township	3,533	5	5	0
Richland Township, Bucks County	13,135	14	12	2
Richland Township, Cambria County	12,581	22	21	1
Ridgway	3,987	6	5	1
Ridley Park	7,007	15	10	5
Ridley Township	30,994	37	32	5
Riverside	1,933	3	3	0
Roaring Brook Township	1,966	1	1	0
Roaring Spring	2,574	3	3	0
Robeson Township	7,326	6	5	1
Robinson Township, Allegheny County	13,586	29	27	2
Rochester	3,613	7	6	1
Rochester Township	2,780	4	4	0
Rockledge	2,552	4	4	0
Ross Township	31,140	45	43	2
Rostraver Township	11,268	15	14	1
Royersford	4,787	8	7	1
Rush Township	3,384	3	3	0
Sadsbury Township, Chester County	3,762	2	2	0
Salem Township, Luzerne County	4,252	4	4	0
Salisbury Township	13,672	19	17	2
Sandy Lake	651	1	1	0
Sandy Township	10,633	11	10	1
Saxton	718	1	1	0
Sayre	6,583	14	14	0
Schuylkill Haven	5,337	8	8	0
Schuylkill Township, Chester County	8,542	13	11	2
Scottdale	4,312	7	7	0
Scott Township, Allegheny County	17,015	22	21	1
Scott Township, Columbia County	5,088	6	6	0
Scott Township, Lackawanna County	4,944	4	4	0
Scranton	75,732	170	150	20
Selinsgrove	5,560	7	6	1
Sewickley	4,363	8	7	1
Shade Township	2,715	1	1	0
Shaler Township	28,781	26	26	0

Table 78.   Full-Time Law Enforcement Employees, by Selected State and City, 2013— continued

(Number.)

State/city	Population	Total law enforcement employees	Total officers	Total civilians
Shamokin	7,303	13	12	1
Shamokin Dam	1,680	3	3	0
Sharon	13,750	27	26	1
Sharon Hill	5,696	10	9	1
Sharpsburg	3,438	6	6	0
Sharpsville	4,330	6	5	1
Shenandoah	4,976	4	4	0
Shenango Township, Lawrence County	7,403	7	7	0
Shillington	5,257	8	7	1
Shinglehouse	1,130	1	1	0
Shippensburg	5,496	10	9	1
Shippingport	214	2	2	0
Shiremanstown	1,565	2	2	0
Shohola Township	2,413	1	1	0
Silver Lake Township	1,689	1	1	0
Silver Spring Township	14,743	18	16	2
Sinking Spring	4,005	7	6	1
Slatington	4,272	6	6	0
Slippery Rock	3,676	4	4	0
Smithton Borough	391	1	1	0
Smith Township	4,450	3	3	0
Solebury Township	8,701	16	14	2
Somerset	6,154	8	7	1
Souderton	6,647	5	4	1
South Abington Township	9,162	12	11	1
South Beaver Township	2,703	4	4	0
South Buffalo Township	2,635	2	2	0
South Centre Township	4,216	4	4	0
South Coatesville	1,409	2	2	0
South Connellsville Borough	1,952	2	2	0
Southern Regional Lancaster County	3,812	8	8	0
Southern Regional York County	10,658	11	10	1
South Fayette Township	15,079	18	17	1
South Fork	903	1	1	0
South Greensburg	2,087	2	2	0
South Heidelberg Township	7,354	7	7	0
South Lebanon Township	9,614	8	7	1
South Londonderry Township	7,213	7	6	1
South Park Township	13,528	17	16	1
South Pymatuning Township	2,651	2	2	0
South Strabane Township	9,564	17	16	1
Southwestern Regional	17,544	14	13	1
Southwest Greensburg	2,117	2	2	0
Southwest Mercer County Regional	10,197	21	20	1
Southwest Regional, Fayette County	1,619	5	4	1
South Whitehall Township	19,578	40	37	3
South Williamsport	6,399	9	7	2
Spring City	3,335	4	3	1
Springdale	3,402	2	2	0
Springdale Township	1,635	4	4	0
Springettsbury Township	26,716	35	32	3
Springfield Township, Bucks County	5,050	4	4	0
Springfield Township, Delaware County	24,267	35	30	5
Springfield Township, Montgomery County	19,500	30	28	2
Spring Garden Township	12,944	22	19	3
Spring Township, Berks County	27,450	29	28	1
Spring Township, Centre County	7,664	8	7	1
State College	56,612	71	60	11
St. Clair Boro	2,952	6	6	0
Steelton	5,951	14	12	2
Stewartstown	2,392	5	4	1
St. Marys City	12,874	14	13	1
Stoneboro	1,031	1	1	0
Stonycreek Township	2,778	3	3	0
Stowe Township	6,347	7	7	0
Strasburg	2,847	4	4	0
Stroud Area Regional	34,404	56	49	7
Sugarcreek	5,219	5	4	1
Sugarloaf Township, Luzerne County	4,240	4	4	0
Summerhill Township	2,421	2	2	0
Summit Hill	3,002	6	4	2
Sunbury	9,819	14	13	1
Susquehanna Regional	8,049	17	15	2
Susquehanna Township, Dauphin County	24,443	43	41	2
Swarthmore	6,189	9	9	0
Swatara Township	23,857	52	49	3
Sweden Township	880	1	1	0

Table 78.   Full-Time Law Enforcement Employees, by Selected State and City, 2013— continued

(Number.)

State/city	Population	Total law enforcement employees	Total officers	Total civilians
Swissvale	8,962	15	15	0
Swoyersville	5,050	5	5	0
Sykesville	1,142	1	1	0
Tamaqua	6,972	8	7	1
Tarentum	4,518	8	7	1
Tatamy	1,142	1	1	0
Taylor	6,252	7	7	0
Telford	4,880	6	5	1
Throop	4,100	6	6	0
Tiadaghton Valley Regional	6,693	11	10	1
Tidioute	675	1	1	0
Tilden Township	3,603	3	3	0
Tinicum Township, Bucks County	3,982	5	5	0
Tinicum Township, Delaware County	4,096	18	16	2
Titusville	5,470	11	10	1
Towamencin Township	18,117	31	26	5
Towanda	2,900	6	6	0
Trafford	3,193	4	4	0
Trainer	1,846	4	4	0
Tredyffrin Township	29,492	46	40	6
Troy	1,312	2	2	0
Tullytown	1,869	7	6	1
Tulpehocken Township	3,275	3	3	0
Tunkhannock	1,797	4	4	0
Tunkhannock Township, Wyoming County	6,297	5	5	0
Turtle Creek	5,331	6	5	1
Tyrone	5,444	14	11	3
Union City	3,274	4	3	1
Uniontown	10,190	21	20	1
Union Township, Lawrence County	5,088	4	4	0
Upland	3,246	6	5	1
Upper Allen Township	18,496	21	20	1
Upper Burrell Township	2,302	2	2	0
Upper Chichester Township	16,929	22	21	1
Upper Darby Township	82,771	145	126	19
Upper Dublin Township	26,262	46	40	6
Upper Gwynedd Township	15,848	24	21	3
Upper Macungine Township	21,972	30	28	2
Upper Makefield Township	8,273	16	15	1
Upper Merion Township	28,585	82	66	16
Upper Moreland Township	24,149	40	34	6
Upper Nazareth Township	6,388	9	8	1
Upper Perkiomen	6,831	10	9	1
Upper Pottsgrove Township	5,387	9	8	1
Upper Providence Township, Delaware County	10,310	14	13	1
Upper Providence Township, Montgomery County	21,699	27	25	2
Upper Saucon Township	15,606	21	20	1
Upper Southampton Township	15,199	25	22	3
Upper St. Clair Township	19,319	33	26	7
Upper Uwchlan Township	11,494	11	11	0
Upper Yoder Township	5,340	13	13	0
Uwchlan Township	18,401	23	22	1
Valley Township	7,300	5	5	0
Vandergrift	5,120	8	8	0
Vandling	747	2	2	0
Vernon Township	5,544	2	2	0
Verona	2,468	4	3	1
Versailles	1,509	3	3	0
Walnutport	2,064	3	3	0
Warminster Township	32,802	50	45	5
Warren	9,477	21	15	6
Warrington Township	23,565	33	29	4
Warwick Township, Bucks County	14,625	19	17	2
Washington, Washington County	13,905	33	31	2
Washington Township, Fayette County	3,838	2	2	0
Washington Township, Franklin County	14,261	16	14	2
Washington Township, Northampton County	5,155	5	5	0
Washington Township, Westmoreland County	7,354	7	7	0
Watsontown	2,368	5	5	0
Waynesboro	10,650	20	18	2
Waynesburg	4,106	9	8	1
Weatherly	2,495	4	4	0
Wellsboro	3,300	7	7	0
Wesleyville	3,296	11	10	1
West Brandywine Township	7,446	5	5	0

Table 78.   Full-Time Law Enforcement Employees, by Selected State and City, 2013— continued

(Number.)

State/city	Population	Total law enforcement employees	Total officers	Total civilians
West Caln Township	9,081	2	2	0
West Chester	18,988	60	47	13
West Conshohocken	1,333	10	9	1
West Deer Township	11,880	12	11	1
West Earl Township	7,981	5	5	0
Western Berks Regional	4,561	6	5	1
West Fallowfield Township	2,584	2	2	0
Westfield	1,074	2	2	0
West Goshen Township	22,970	31	27	4
West Grove Borough	2,867	2	2	0
West Hazleton	4,567	4	3	1
West Hempfield Township	16,337	23	20	3
West Hills Regional	10,649	12	11	1
West Homestead	1,940	8	6	2
West Lampeter Township	15,465	16	15	1
West Mahanoy Township	2,837	3	3	0
West Manchester Township	18,831	31	28	3
West Manheim Township	7,990	8	8	0
West Mead Township	5,164	2	2	0
West Mifflin	20,276	40	34	6
West Newton	2,591	2	2	0
West Norriton Township	15,781	31	27	4
West Penn Township	4,415	3	3	0
West Pikeland Township	4,072	4	4	0
West Pittston	4,840	3	3	0
West Pottsgrove Township	3,890	10	9	1
West Reading	4,201	13	11	2
West Sadsbury Township	2,472	4	4	0
West Shore Regional	7,691	12	10	2
Westtown-East Goshen Regional	32,201	29	26	3
West View	6,755	12	8	4
West Vincent Township	4,856	6	5	1
West Whiteland Township	18,452	26	24	2
West York	4,578	12	12	0
Whitehall	13,936	25	20	5
Whitehall Township	27,215	49	43	6
White Haven Borough	1,125	2	2	0
Whitemarsh Township	17,495	41	35	6
White Oak	7,857	11	10	1
Whitpain Township	19,152	37	29	8
Wiconisco Township	1,201	1	1	0
Wilkes-Barre	41,166	79	75	4
Wilkes-Barre Township	2,959	14	13	1
Wilkinsburg	15,900	25	21	4
Wilkins Township	6,359	12	12	0
Williamsburg	1,244	1	1	0
Williamsport	29,536	53	49	4
Willistown Township	10,600	19	17	2
Wilson	7,844	13	12	1
Wind Gap	2,724	4	4	0
Womelsdorf	2,818	4	4	0
Wrightsville	2,293	4	4	0
Wright Township	5,676	6	6	0
Wyoming	3,055	3	3	0
Wyomissing	10,479	24	23	1
Yardley	2,455	2	2	0
Yeadon	11,509	14	13	1
York	43,841	118	105	13
York Area Regional	60,995	50	45	5
Youngsville	1,686	2	2	0
Zelienople	3,771	10	9	1
RHODE ISLAND				
Barrington	16,286	31	24	7
Bristol	22,160	48	38	10
Burrillville	16,141	27	20	7
Central Falls	19,404	45	37	8
Charlestown	7,770	25	20	5
Coventry	34,971	71	56	15
Cranston	80,718	170	141	29
Cumberland	34,028	55	44	11
East Greenwich	13,104	41	33	8
East Providence	47,200	108	91	17
Foster	4,660	14	10	4
Glocester	9,858	19	14	5
Hopkinton	8,112	19	14	5
Jamestown	5,442	18	14	4
Johnston	29,068	81	67	14
Lincoln	21,334	42	36	6

Table 78.   Full-Time Law Enforcement Employees, by Selected State and City, 2013— continued

(Number.)

State/city	Population	Total law enforcement employees	Total officers	Total civilians
Little Compton	3,474	13	10	3
Middletown	16,037	40	35	5
Narragansett	15,668	47	35	12
Newport	23,874	95	80	15
New Shoreham	1,040	4	4	0
North Kingstown	26,156	53	42	11
North Providence	32,234	79	62	17
North Smithfield	12,138	27	25	2
Pawtucket	71,305	176	135	41
Portsmouth	17,300	34	32	2
Providence	178,887	504	410	94
Richmond	7,598	17	14	3
Scituate	10,443	24	17	7
Smithfield	21,490	55	40	15
South Kingstown	30,309	70	52	18
Tiverton	15,792	40	30	10
Warren	10,557	28	22	6
Warwick	81,789	216	165	51
Westerly	22,629	61	47	14
West Greenwich	6,085	17	12	5
West Warwick	28,817	63	50	13
Woonsocket	41,057	99	84	15
SOUTH CAROLINA				
Abbeville	5,163	19	18	1
Aiken	29,965	111	85	26
Allendale	3,272	8	8	0
Anderson	26,812	129	94	35
Atlantic Beach	351	3	1	2
Aynor	613	5	5	0
Bamberg	3,556	12	10	2
Barnwell	4,657	17	15	2
Batesburg-Leesville	5,408	27	22	5
Beaufort	12,918	48	44	4
Belton	4,222	13	13	0
Bennettsville	8,809	37	33	4
Bishopville	3,336	11	9	2
Blacksburg	1,866	12	11	1
Blackville	2,344	7	6	1
Bluffton	13,047	38	35	3
Bonneau	507	5	3	2
Bowman	954	5	4	1
Branchville	1,009	3	3	0
Briarcliffe Acres	488	1	1	0
Burnettown	2,734	2	2	0
Calhoun Falls	1,972	5	5	0
Camden	6,923	31	29	2
Campobello	511	5	5	0
Cayce	12,726	63	52	11
Central	5,153	10	9	1
Chapin	1,506	6	6	0
Charleston	127,206	549	433	116
Cheraw	5,767	30	28	2
Chesnee	886	5	5	0
Chester	5,489	25	22	3
Chesterfield	1,446	5	4	1
Clemson	14,136	36	27	9
Clinton	8,479	39	35	4
Clover	5,342	22	17	5
Columbia	132,240	443	374	69
Conway	19,121	58	54	4
Cottageville	746	6	5	1
Coward	752	1	1	0
Darlington	6,200	29	26	3
Denmark	3,475	11	9	2
Dillon	6,627	27	25	2
Due West	1,237	5	5	0
Duncan	3,253	16	15	1
Easley	20,115	55	43	12
Edgefield	4,670	8	8	0
Edisto Beach	411	7	7	0
Ehrhardt	538	4	3	1
Elgin	1,350	7	6	1
Elloree	691	4	3	1
Estill	1,996	8	6	2
Eutawville	313	3	3	0
Fairfax	1,906	7	6	1
Florence	37,611	135	121	14
Folly Beach	2,702	22	17	5

Table 78.   Full-Time Law Enforcement Employees, by Selected State and City, 2013— continued

(Number.)

State/city	Population	Total law enforcement employees	Total officers	Total civilians
Forest Acres	10,516	33	26	7
Fort Lawn	871	3	3	0
Fort Mill	11,530	39	35	4
Fountain Inn	7,975	32	24	8
Gaffney	12,675	43	40	3
Gaston	1,662	2	2	0
Georgetown	9,072	36	32	4
Goose Creek	39,425	89	64	25
Great Falls	1,936	6	6	0
Greeleyville	421	2	2	0
Greenville	61,185	239	191	48
Greenwood	23,334	58	52	6
Greer	26,955	70	52	18
Hampton	2,740	11	11	0
Hanahan	19,538	36	28	8
Hardeeville	4,064	20	18	2
Harleyville	696	4	4	0
Hartsville	7,877	35	32	3
Hemingway	442	3	3	0
Holly Hill	1,259	6	6	0
Inman	2,392	10	8	2
Irmo	11,616	26	23	3
Isle of Palms	4,283	24	19	5
Iva	1,244	11	8	3
Jackson	1,738	4	4	0
Jamestown	76	5	4	1
Johnsonville	1,498	6	5	1
Johnston	2,286	7	7	0
Jonesville	879	2	2	0
Kingstree	3,239	13	12	1
Lake City	6,726	18	17	1
Lake View	792	4	4	0
Lamar	978	4	4	0
Lancaster	8,824	48	38	10
Landrum	2,433	10	9	1
Lane	490	1	1	0
Latta	1,349	10	10	0
Laurens	9,068	31	26	5
Lexington	19,547	51	48	3
Liberty	3,255	16	11	5
Loris	2,486	11	9	2
Lyman	3,318	9	7	2
Lynchburg	355	3	3	0
Manning	4,034	19	18	1
Marion	6,813	21	19	2
Mauldin	24,099	56	46	10
Mayesville	733	1	1	0
McBee	857	2	2	0
McColl	2,086	7	6	1
McCormick	2,720	7	7	0
Moncks Corner	8,913	28	25	3
Mount Pleasant	73,198	167	141	26
Mullins	4,574	26	23	3
Myrtle Beach	28,663	272	193	79
Newberry	10,246	37	33	4
New Ellenton	2,094	5	5	0
Nichols	362	3	3	0
Ninety Six	2,003	5	5	0
North	753	3	3	0
North Augusta	22,033	78	58	20
North Charleston	103,324	431	338	93
North Myrtle Beach	14,672	93	67	26
Olanta	569	2	2	0
Orangeburg	13,826	88	66	22
Pacolet	2,279	5	5	0
Pageland	2,716	17	12	5
Pamplico	1,238	3	3	0
Pawleys Island	103	6	5	1
Pelion	689	2	2	0
Perry	237	1	1	0
Pickens	3,148	13	13	0
Pine Ridge	2,147	2	2	0
Port Royal	11,446	22	21	1
Prosperity	1,185	2	2	0
Ridgeland	4,072	13	12	1
Ridgeville	1,991	1	1	0
Rock Hill	68,617	176	134	42
Salem	135	2	2	0
Santee	952	8	8	0

Table 78.   Full-Time Law Enforcement Employees, by Selected State and City, 2013— continued

(Number.)

State/city	Population	Total law enforcement employees	Total officers	Total civilians
Scranton	903	1	1	0
Seneca	8,096	46	36	10
Simpsonville	19,315	49	38	11
Society Hill	555	4	3	1
South Congaree	2,380	7	6	1
Spartanburg	37,522	137	118	19
Springdale	2,698	7	7	0
Springfield	514	2	2	0
St. Matthews	1,971	7	6	1
Sullivans Island	1,858	9	8	1
Summerton	972	5	5	0
Summerville	45,210	104	84	20
Sumter	40,928	150	106	44
Surfside Beach	4,061	27	21	6
Swansea	858	3	3	0
Tega Cay	8,028	23	21	2
Travelers Rest	4,803	21	15	6
Union	8,124	33	31	2
Wagener	812	5	5	0
Walhalla	4,243	15	14	1
Walterboro	5,281	43	29	14
Ware Shoals	2,162	7	7	0
Wellford	2,427	8	8	0
West Columbia	15,715	63	52	11
Westminster	2,433	11	11	0
West Pelzer	883	4	4	0
West Union	292	2	2	0
Whitmire	1,439	2	2	0
Williamston	4,008	16	15	1
Williston	3,067	9	8	1
Winnsboro	3,428	20	20	0
Woodruff	4,122	12	11	1
Yemassee	1,008	7	6	1
York	7,927	34	27	7
SOUTH DAKOTA				
Aberdeen	26,999	50	42	8
Alcester	809	1	1	0
Avon	581	1	1	0
Belle Fourche	5,676	12	11	1
Beresford	2,049	4	4	0
Box Elder	9,079	12	11	1
Brandon	9,393	12	11	1
Brookings	22,741	45	31	14
Burke	605	1	1	0
Canton	3,268	5	5	0
Centerville	887	1	1	0
Chamberlain	2,405	6	6	0
Clark	1,045	1	1	0
Deadwood	1,260	15	12	3
Eagle Butte	1,363	2	2	0
Elk Point	1,998	4	4	0
Estelline	757	1	1	0
Faith	420	1	1	0
Flandreau	2,311	9	8	1
Gettysburg	1,180	2	2	0
Gregory	1,282	3	3	0
Groton	1,491	4	4	0
Hot Springs	3,541	8	6	2
Hoven	409	1	1	0
Huron	12,956	32	26	6
Jefferson	547	1	1	0
Kadoka	695	1	1	0
Kimball	707	1	1	0
Lead	3,076	6	5	1
Lennox	2,229	4	4	0
Leola	449	1	1	0
Madison	6,904	11	10	1
Martin	1,071	4	4	0
Menno	587	1	1	0
Milbank	3,288	7	7	0
Miller	1,460	4	4	0
Mitchell	15,555	37	25	12
Mobridge	3,478	14	7	7
North Sioux City	2,550	8	7	1
Parkston	1,471	3	3	0
Philip	782	2	2	0
Pierre	13,996	32	27	5
Platte	1,244	2	2	0

Table 78.   Full-Time Law Enforcement Employees, by Selected State and City, 2013— continued

(Number.)

State/city	Population	Total law enforcement employees	Total officers	Total civilians
Rapid City	70,406	146	113	33
Selby	640	1	1	0
Sioux Falls	161,754	279	245	34
Sisseton	2,505	7	7	0
Spearfish	10,778	29	20	9
Springfield	1,979	2	2	0
Sturgis	6,652	18	16	2
Summerset	1,923	3	3	0
Tea	4,459	6	6	0
Tripp	625	1	1	0
Tyndall	1,054	2	2	0
Vermillion	10,892	21	19	2
Viborg	773	1	1	0
Wagner	1,575	5	5	0
Watertown	21,900	54	35	19
Webster	1,839	5	5	0
Whitewood	934	3	3	0
Winner	2,821	10	10	0
Yankton	14,561	36	25	11
TENNESSEE				
Adamsville	2,235	7	6	1
Alamo	2,461	4	4	0
Alcoa	8,605	47	39	8
Alexandria	975	3	3	0
Algood	3,517	14	14	0
Ardmore	1,206	11	7	4
Ashland City	4,637	16	14	2
Athens	13,504	32	30	2
Atoka	8,821	19	18	1
Baileyton	430	2	2	0
Bartlett	56,360	142	110	32
Baxter	1,389	5	5	0
Bean Station	2,972	9	8	1
Belle Meade	2,999	23	16	7
Bells	2,451	4	4	0
Benton	1,330	7	6	1
Berry Hill	551	19	14	5
Big Sandy	549	1	1	0
Blaine	1,860	3	1	2
Bluff City	1,748	9	9	0
Bolivar	5,231	21	20	1
Bradford	1,030	5	4	1
Brentwood	39,635	71	55	16
Brighton	2,960	6	6	0
Bristol	26,660	84	64	20
Brownsville	9,886	34	30	4
Bruceton	1,454	4	4	0
Burns	1,469	1	1	0
Calhoun	493	2	2	0
Camden	3,634	20	13	7
Carthage	2,271	12	8	4
Caryville	2,270	5	5	0
Celina	1,494	8	6	2
Centerville	3,531	22	13	9
Chapel Hill	1,450	5	5	0
Charleston	664	3	3	0
Chattanooga	172,286	525	432	93
Church Hill	6,727	11	10	1
Clarksville	145,599	332	268	64
Cleveland	42,735	100	88	12
Clifton	2,697	5	5	0
Clinton	9,881	29	27	2
Collegedale	9,468	23	23	0
Collierville	46,726	136	99	37
Collinwood	995	5	5	0
Columbia	34,952	95	88	7
Cookeville	31,174	85	66	19
Coopertown	4,310	4	3	1
Copperhill	340	3	3	0
Cornersville	1,194	7	4	3
Covington	9,076	33	32	1
Cowan	1,705	5	5	0
Cross Plains	1,724	2	2	0
Crossville	11,199	46	42	4
Crump	1,417	2	2	0
Cumberland City	306	2	2	0
Dandridge	2,862	11	10	1
Dayton	7,351	19	18	1

Table 78.   Full-Time Law Enforcement Employees, by Selected State and City, 2013— continued

(Number.)

State/city	Population	Total law enforcement employees	Total officers	Total civilians
Decatur	1,570	5	5	0
Decaturville	862	1	1	0
Decherd	2,451	10	9	1
Dickson	14,920	52	48	4
Dover	1,420	6	6	0
Dresden	2,954	10	9	1
Dunlap	5,005	12	11	1
Dyer	2,300	7	6	1
Dyersburg	17,013	66	58	8
Eagleville	620	2	2	0
East Ridge	21,386	39	35	4
Elizabethton	14,220	43	39	4
Elkton	569	1	1	0
Englewood	1,533	5	5	0
Erin	1,323	5	4	1
Erwin	6,038	13	13	0
Estill Springs	2,017	6	6	0
Etowah	3,489	11	10	1
Fairview	8,059	24	24	0
Fayetteville	7,155	24	23	1
Franklin	67,465	144	122	22
Friendship	672	1	1	0
Gadsden	468	1	1	0
Gainesboro	946	6	5	1
Gallatin	31,961	93	70	23
Gallaway	668	2	2	0
Gates	644	1	1	0
Gatlinburg	4,074	51	41	10
Germantown	39,631	111	87	24
Gibson	384	3	3	0
Gleason	1,419	5	5	0
Goodlettsville	16,570	53	40	13
Gordonsville	1,198	6	6	0
Grand Junction	312	4	4	0
Graysville	1,512	4	4	0
Greenbrier	6,586	16	15	1
Greeneville	15,015	53	51	2
Greenfield	2,151	8	7	1
Halls	2,223	8	8	0
Harriman	6,240	19	18	1
Henderson	6,396	15	15	0
Hendersonville	53,617	121	94	27
Henning	935	3	3	0
Henry	463	2	2	0
Hohenwald	3,659	18	12	6
Hollow Rock	707	1	1	0
Hornbeak	417	1	1	0
Humboldt	8,458	30	24	6
Huntingdon	3,967	16	12	4
Huntland	850	9	7	2
Jacksboro	2,002	6	6	0
Jackson	67,371	272	226	46
Jamestown	1,952	9	9	0
Jasper	3,277	8	8	0
Jefferson City	8,213	23	21	2
Jellico	2,309	6	5	1
Johnson City	64,928	168	139	29
Jonesborough	5,163	21	17	4
Kenton	1,251	4	4	0
Kimball	1,405	9	9	0
Kingsport	51,496	161	111	50
Kingston	5,850	13	12	1
Kingston Springs	2,767	7	6	1
Knoxville	183,249	497	393	104
Lafayette	4,756	23	16	7
La Follette	7,256	28	20	8
Lake City	1,777	10	7	3
La Vergne	34,143	72	54	18
Lawrenceburg	10,445	39	35	4
Lebanon	28,208	89	73	16
Lenoir City	8,945	25	24	1
Lewisburg	11,242	41	30	11
Lexington	7,844	32	27	5
Livingston	4,082	22	18	4
Lookout Mountain	1,866	20	16	4
Loretto	1,727	4	4	0
Loudon	5,710	16	15	1
Madisonville	4,784	18	15	3
Manchester	10,258	40	34	6

Table 78.   Full-Time Law Enforcement Employees, by Selected State and City, 2013— continued

(Number.)

State/city	Population	Total law enforcement employees	Total officers	Total civilians
Martin	11,404	37	28	9
Maryville	28,009	56	50	6
Mason	1,611	5	5	0
Maynardville	2,382	4	4	0
McEwen	1,696	5	5	0
McKenzie	5,406	21	17	4
McMinnville	13,595	37	33	4
Medina	3,920	11	11	0
Memphis	657,691	2,694	2,319	375
Middleton	686	4	4	0
Milan	7,789	27	21	6
Millersville	6,596	16	12	4
Millington	10,500	43	30	13
Minor Hill	528	2	2	0
Monteagle	1,172	6	6	0
Monterey	2,829	7	7	0
Morristown	29,300	91	84	7
Moscow	547	4	3	1
Mountain City	2,504	8	8	0
Mount Carmel	5,422	8	7	1
Mount Juliet	27,542	56	43	13
Mount Pleasant	4,583	20	14	6
Munford	6,036	15	14	1
Murfreesboro	115,587	272	223	49
Nashville	635,673	1,674	1,368	306
Newbern	3,332	17	11	6
New Hope	1,075	1	1	0
New Johnsonville	1,899	4	4	0
New Market	1,362	3	3	0
Newport	6,912	28	24	4
New Tazewell	2,974	9	9	0
Niota	718	2	2	0
Nolensville	6,164	8	8	0
Norris	1,643	7	7	0
Oakland	6,976	18	16	2
Oak Ridge	29,319	77	61	16
Obion	1,092	4	4	0
Oliver Springs	3,250	14	10	4
Oneida	3,740	17	12	5
Paris	10,168	37	26	11
Parsons	2,343	6	6	0
Petersburg	544	1	1	0
Pigeon Forge	6,023	63	51	12
Pikeville	1,599	3	3	0
Piperton	1,498	6	6	0
Pittman Center	536	3	3	0
Plainview	2,094	1	1	0
Pleasant View	4,208	5	5	0
Portland	11,944	34	26	8
Powells Crossroads	1,321	1	1	0
Pulaski	7,717	27	25	2
Puryear	672	1	1	0
Red Bank	11,865	25	23	2
Red Boiling Springs	1,119	5	5	0
Ridgely	1,734	4	4	0
Ridgetop	1,942	6	6	0
Ripley	8,373	31	25	6
Rockwood	5,475	17	15	2
Rogersville	4,389	17	13	4
Rossville	679	6	6	0
Rutherford	1,129	4	3	1
Rutledge	1,130	5	5	0
Savannah	6,987	20	18	2
Scotts Hill	989	1	1	0
Selmer	4,544	19	17	2
Sevierville	15,883	71	56	15
Sewanee	2,366	13	9	4
Sharon	930	1	1	0
Shelbyville	20,669	50	41	9
Signal Mountain	7,751	15	14	1
Smithville	4,592	13	12	1
Smyrna	42,240	87	65	22
Soddy-Daisy	13,004	32	27	5
Somerville	3,142	11	11	0
South Carthage	1,311	4	4	0
South Fulton	2,298	7	6	1
South Pittsburg	3,098	9	9	0
Sparta	5,088	16	15	1
Spencer	1,633	2	2	0

Table 78.   Full-Time Law Enforcement Employees, by Selected State and City, 2013— continued

(Number.)

State/city	Population	Total law enforcement employees	Total officers	Total civilians
Spring City	2,000	8	8	0
Springfield	16,598	59	38	21
Spring Hill	31,807	44	41	3
Sunbright	551	3	3	0
Surgoinsville	1,786	2	2	0
Sweetwater	5,870	20	19	1
Tazewell	2,185	6	6	0
Tellico Plains	893	5	5	0
Tiptonville	4,392	7	7	0
Townsend	450	4	4	0
Tracy City	1,473	5	5	0
Trenton	4,195	24	18	6
Trimble	630	1	1	0
Troy	1,342	4	4	0
Tullahoma	18,773	42	37	5
Tusculum	2,677	2	2	0
Union City	10,738	39	31	8
Vonore	1,484	9	9	0
Wartburg	912	5	5	0
Wartrace	649	2	1	1
Watauga	452	1	1	0
Watertown	1,490	6	6	0
Waverly	4,139	13	12	1
Waynesboro	2,435	7	7	0
Westmoreland	2,254	12	9	3
White Bluff	3,318	5	5	0
White House	10,679	23	20	3
White Pine	2,227	9	8	1
Whiteville	4,580	6	6	0
Whitwell	1,702	5	5	0
Winchester	8,410	25	23	2
Winfield	965	1	1	0
Woodbury	2,709	9	8	1
TEXAS				
Abernathy	2,821	4	4	0
Abilene	119,401	238	170	68
Addison	15,961	88	64	24
Alamo	18,876	37	27	10
Alamo Heights	7,443	34	22	12
Alice	19,673	52	39	13
Allen	91,289	169	117	52
Alpine	5,985	18	9	9
Alton	14,756	21	15	6
Alvarado	3,813	16	15	1
Alvin	25,110	72	49	23
Amarillo	196,577	389	339	50
Andrews	12,529	28	19	9
Angleton	19,016	48	36	12
Anna	8,634	13	12	1
Anson	2,332	7	5	2
Anthony	5,201	19	18	1
Aransas Pass	8,316	31	21	10
Archer City	1,740	1	1	0
Arcola	1,663	4	4	0
Argyle	3,554	8	7	1
Arlington	378,765	807	624	183
Arp	986	4	4	0
Athens	12,886	29	23	6
Atlanta	5,575	16	12	4
Aubrey	2,730	6	6	0
Austin	859,180	2,233	1,675	558
Azle	11,304	32	24	8
Baird	1,492	2	2	0
Balch Springs	25,186	57	39	18
Balcones Heights	2,840	24	19	5
Ballinger	3,738	8	7	1
Bangs	1,586	3	3	0
Bastrop	7,447	22	18	4
Bay City	17,429	58	37	21
Baytown	73,709	199	149	50
Beaumont	118,177	299	253	46
Bedford	48,513	135	79	56
Beeville	13,181	30	23	7
Bellaire	17,617	51	35	16
Bellmead	9,950	25	18	7
Bellville	4,136	11	10	1
Belton	19,734	42	30	12
Benbrook	22,157	41	32	9

Table 78.   Full-Time Law Enforcement Employees, by Selected State and City, 2013— continued

(Number.)

State/city	Population	Total law enforcement employees	Total officers	Total civilians
Bertram	1,359	4	4	0
Beverly Hills	2,006	10	7	3
Big Sandy	1,368	5	5	0
Big Spring	27,640	49	41	8
Bishop	3,174	11	6	5
Blanco	1,800	6	5	1
Blue Mound	2,466	12	8	4
Boerne	11,857	48	32	16
Bogata	1,136	4	4	0
Bonham	10,050	27	19	8
Borger	13,034	43	28	15
Bovina	1,841	2	2	0
Bowie	5,163	21	15	6
Brackettville	1,686	1	1	0
Brady	5,560	15	9	6
Brazoria	3,054	11	7	4
Breckenridge	5,638	16	10	6
Bremond	926	2	2	0
Brenham	16,268	40	35	5
Bridge City	7,926	20	15	5
Bridgeport	6,121	22	15	7
Brookshire	4,784	18	13	5
Brookside Village	1,548	4	4	0
Brownfield	9,636	24	19	5
Brownsville	181,590	349	244	105
Brownwood	18,873	56	35	21
Bruceville-Eddy	1,494	5	5	0
Bryan	78,578	171	138	33
Buda	10,098	14	13	1
Bullard	2,638	10	9	1
Bulverde	4,783	15	14	1
Burkburnett	10,829	25	19	6
Burleson	39,714	77	58	19
Burnet	6,075	16	15	1
Cactus	3,241	8	7	1
Caddo Mills	1,375	4	4	0
Caldwell	4,175	12	11	1
Calvert	1,177	4	4	0
Cameron	5,367	15	10	5
Canyon	14,026	25	22	3
Carrollton	127,459	194	155	39
Carthage	6,918	23	17	6
Castle Hills	4,273	29	22	7
Castroville	2,754	9	8	1
Cedar Hill	46,918	86	67	19
Cedar Park	59,948	111	80	31
Celina	6,786	10	9	1
Center	5,328	26	19	7
Chillicothe	697	1	1	0
Cibolo	21,690	32	26	6
Cisco	3,837	11	9	2
Cleburne	29,327	67	51	16
Cleveland	7,635	27	17	10
Clifton	3,411	8	7	1
Clint	923	1	1	0
Clyde	3,706	10	9	1
Cockrell Hill	4,317	21	15	6
Coleman	4,544	15	8	7
College Station	98,919	187	127	60
Colleyville	24,289	43	35	8
Collinsville	1,631	3	3	0
Colorado City	4,084	11	6	5
Columbus	3,611	12	11	1
Comanche	4,234	11	10	1
Combes	3,035	8	8	0
Commerce	8,267	20	15	5
Conroe	62,962	154	109	45
Converse	20,115	45	32	13
Coppell	40,449	72	58	14
Copperas Cove	33,780	71	50	21
Corinth	20,692	35	31	4
Corpus Christi	314,523	667	449	218
Corrigan	1,559	13	10	3
Corsicana	23,940	53	43	10
Crandall	3,016	13	13	0
Crane	3,563	13	8	5
Crockett	6,595	20	17	3
Crosbyton	1,758	3	3	0
Crowell	921	1	1	0

Table 78.   Full-Time Law Enforcement Employees, by Selected State and City, 2013— continued

(Number.)

State/city	Population	Total law enforcement employees	Total officers	Total civilians
Crowley	13,804	39	29	10
Crystal City	7,366	11	7	4
Cuero	7,011	18	16	2
Cumby	789	5	5	0
Daingerfield	2,513	9	8	1
Dalhart	8,340	18	15	3
Dallas	1,255,015	4,028	3,474	554
Dalworthington Gardens	2,337	18	11	7
Danbury	1,730	1	1	0
Dayton	7,361	26	17	9
Decatur	6,244	26	21	5
Deer Park	33,295	79	57	22
De Kalb	1,663	5	5	0
De Leon	2,205	5	5	0
Del Rio	35,499	69	48	21
Denison	22,652	54	45	9
Denton	123,260	206	153	53
Denver City	4,625	11	6	5
DeSoto	51,703	97	67	30
Devine	4,464	13	9	4
Diboll	5,390	19	13	6
Dickinson	19,204	42	30	12
Dilley	4,023	7	6	1
Dimmitt	4,500	9	7	2
Donna	16,320	37	28	9
Double Oak	2,993	7	7	0
Driscoll	751	5	4	1
Dublin	3,710	12	8	4
Dumas	15,074	29	23	6
Duncanville	39,811	70	58	12
Eagle Lake	3,588	9	8	1
Early	2,785	9	7	2
Eastland	3,912	11	9	2
East Mountain	801	2	2	0
Edcouch	3,213	11	9	2
Edgewood	1,429	2	2	0
Edinburg	82,271	171	125	46
Edna	5,598	10	8	2
El Campo	11,525	39	27	12
Electra	2,762	3	2	1
Elgin	8,259	24	17	7
El Paso	679,700	1,281	1,069	212
Elsa	6,493	16	15	1
Ennis	18,679	40	34	6
Euless	53,236	130	88	42
Everman	6,276	18	13	5
Fairfield	2,874	13	9	4
Fair Oaks Ranch	6,437	16	15	1
Falfurrias	4,919	16	15	1
Farmers Branch	29,609	105	73	32
Farmersville	3,448	11	9	2
Farwell	1,347	2	2	0
Ferris	2,498	13	9	4
Flatonia	1,398	5	5	0
Florence	1,213	2	2	0
Floresville	6,882	17	15	2
Flower Mound	68,835	122	84	38
Floydada	2,991	6	6	0
Forest Hill	12,712	26	20	6
Forney	16,257	36	24	12
Fort Stockton	8,357	32	22	10
Frankston	1,229	7	6	1
Fredericksburg	10,768	35	31	4
Freeport	12,090	44	30	14
Freer	2,769	12	7	5
Friendswood	37,226	71	57	14
Friona	4,066	10	6	4
Frisco	131,769	214	148	66
Fulton	1,417	1	1	0
Gainesville	16,089	53	39	14
Galena Park	11,097	23	18	5
Galveston	48,067	176	140	36
Ganado	2,036	3	3	0
Garden Ridge	3,573	14	13	1
Garland	235,683	443	317	126
Gatesville	16,072	25	17	8
Georgetown	53,844	112	71	41
Giddings	4,912	15	10	5
Gilmer	5,104	18	14	4

Table 78.   Full-Time Law Enforcement Employees, by Selected State and City, 2013— continued

(Number.)

State/city	Population	Total law enforcement employees	Total officers	Total civilians
Gladewater	6,503	23	17	6
Glenn Heights	11,853	24	15	9
Godley	1,035	6	6	0
Gonzales	7,324	28	21	7
Gorman	1,071	2	2	0
Graham	8,773	25	23	2
Granbury	8,464	37	31	6
Grand Prairie	183,822	332	221	111
Grand Saline	3,114	6	6	0
Granger	1,501	2	2	0
Granite Shoals	4,945	8	8	0
Grapevine	49,075	127	91	36
Greenville	25,895	74	56	18
Gregory	1,914	4	4	0
Groesbeck	4,348	9	9	0
Groves	15,725	22	21	1
Gun Barrel City	5,785	20	14	6
Hale Center	2,246	3	3	0
Hallettsville	2,592	8	7	1
Hallsville	3,924	5	5	0
Haltom City	43,676	79	70	9
Hamlin	2,037	7	4	3
Harker Heights	28,125	57	43	14
Harlingen	65,885	171	131	40
Haskell	3,323	2	2	0
Hawkins	1,282	4	4	0
Hawley	610	1	1	0
Hearne	4,443	18	12	6
Heath	7,733	18	17	1
Hedwig Village	2,643	23	17	6
Helotes	8,054	21	19	2
Hemphill	1,200	3	3	0
Hempstead	6,187	20	17	3
Henderson	13,837	41	33	8
Hereford	15,327	29	22	7
Hewitt	13,944	32	23	9
Hickory Creek	3,493	11	11	0
Hidalgo	11,863	38	26	12
Highland Park	8,900	70	55	15
Highland Village	15,754	38	27	11
Hill Country Village	1,016	13	13	0
Hillsboro	8,377	30	23	7
Hitchcock	7,250	24	18	6
Holliday	1,700	3	3	0
Hollywood Park	3,168	11	10	1
Hondo	8,925	19	16	3
Hooks	2,731	7	7	0
Horizon City	19,439	27	20	7
Horseshoe Bay	3,334	19	17	2
Howe	2,602	5	5	0
Hubbard	1,416	5	5	0
Hudson	4,750	6	5	1
Hughes Springs	1,727	4	4	0
Humble	15,473	75	55	20
Huntington	2,102	5	5	0
Huntsville	39,990	61	53	8
Hurst	38,456	118	75	43
Hutchins	5,439	22	17	5
Hutto	19,513	28	24	4
Idalou	2,264	5	5	0
Ingleside	9,541	24	17	7
Ingram	1,805	7	7	0
Iowa Park	6,408	17	11	6
Irving	228,367	473	329	144
Italy	1,872	7	6	1
Itasca	1,638	6	6	0
Jacinto City	10,772	24	19	5
Jacksboro	4,487	10	9	1
Jacksonville	14,816	35	26	9
Jamaica Beach	1,006	5	5	0
Jarrell	1,051	2	2	0
Jasper	7,702	27	21	6
Jefferson	2,057	7	6	1
Jersey Village	7,845	30	28	2
Johnson City	1,733	4	4	0
Jones Creek	2,067	4	4	0
Jonestown	2,024	8	7	1
Joshua	5,966	11	10	1
Jourdanton	4,111	9	9	0

Table 78.   Full-Time Law Enforcement Employees, by Selected State and City, 2013— continued

(Number.)

State/city	Population	Total law enforcement employees	Total officers	Total civilians
Junction	2,539	5	5	0
Karnes City	3,201	9	8	1
Katy	14,837	61	47	14
Kaufman	6,865	23	16	7
Keene	6,071	19	13	6
Keller	42,644	82	48	34
Kemah	1,912	21	16	5
Kenedy	3,423	11	10	1
Kennedale	7,156	21	19	2
Kerens	1,562	6	6	0
Kermit	5,956	20	13	7
Kerrville	22,484	61	47	14
Kilgore	13,938	48	37	11
Killeen	136,539	318	235	83
Kingsville	26,198	66	50	16
Kirby	8,288	20	14	6
Kountze	2,088	7	6	1
Kyle	31,732	53	37	16
Lacy-Lakeview	6,566	24	16	8
La Feria	7,340	17	13	4
Lago Vista	6,550	23	16	7
La Grange	4,656	10	10	0
La Grulla	1,639	7	5	2
Laguna Vista	3,179	7	7	0
La Joya	4,153	17	12	5
Lake Dallas	7,390	22	14	8
Lake Jackson	27,273	58	43	15
Lakeside	1,357	3	3	0
Lakeview, Harrison County	6,413	17	13	4
Lakeway	12,815	39	29	10
Lake Worth	4,710	34	25	9
La Marque	14,976	34	25	9
Lamesa	9,136	23	17	6
Lampasas	6,899	29	19	10
Lancaster	38,209	57	46	11
La Porte	34,671	106	75	31
La Vernia	1,137	6	6	0
La Villa	1,978	9	7	2
Lavon	2,318	7	7	0
League City	89,596	149	107	42
Leander	30,657	52	38	14
Leonard	1,969	4	4	0
Leon Valley	10,833	30	23	7
Levelland	13,681	37	26	11
Lewisville	100,710	208	148	60
Lexington	1,170	5	5	0
Liberty	8,857	26	16	10
Lindale	5,257	21	15	6
Linden	1,964	6	5	1
Littlefield	6,368	12	10	2
Live Oak	14,541	44	31	13
Livingston	5,207	25	18	7
Llano	3,249	8	7	1
Lockhart	12,971	34	23	11
Lometa	882	1	1	0
Lone Star	1,553	5	5	0
Longview	81,273	219	160	59
Lorena	1,709	6	5	1
Lorenzo	1,180	1	1	0
Los Fresnos	5,800	23	16	7
Lott	739	4	4	0
Lubbock	237,875	547	399	148
Lufkin	36,315	92	72	20
Luling	5,612	25	16	9
Lumberton	12,081	20	17	3
Lyford	2,611	3	3	0
Lytle	2,665	8	7	1
Madisonville	4,452	14	12	2
Magnolia	1,490	15	13	2
Malakoff	2,327	6	6	0
Manor	6,137	16	14	2
Manvel	6,381	14	10	4
Marble Falls	6,095	31	18	13
Marlin	5,847	15	11	4
Marshall	25,169	65	47	18
Martindale	1,145	3	3	0
Mathis	4,989	16	11	5
McAllen	136,169	404	266	138
McGregor	5,036	18	11	7

Table 78.   Full-Time Law Enforcement Employees, by Selected State and City, 2013— continued

(Number.)

State/city	Population	Total law enforcement employees	Total officers	Total civilians
McKinney	146,869	213	165	48
Meadows Place	4,721	16	15	1
Melissa	5,839	10	9	1
Memorial Villages	11,660	41	32	9
Memphis	2,232	4	4	0
Mercedes	16,480	36	31	5
Meridian	1,484	1	1	0
Merkel	2,608	4	4	0
Mexia	7,544	26	16	10
Midland	122,259	227	176	51
Midlothian	19,425	51	37	14
Milford	728	3	3	0
Mineola	4,485	18	12	6
Mineral Wells	16,717	36	27	9
Mission	81,360	185	141	44
Missouri City	69,487	116	93	23
Monahans	7,163	18	12	6
Mont Belvieu	4,366	16	11	5
Montgomery	670	7	7	0
Morgans Point Resort	4,257	8	7	1
Moulton	898	2	2	0
Mount Pleasant	16,101	38	25	13
Muleshoe	5,121	12	8	4
Munday	1,331	2	2	0
Murphy	19,347	35	22	13
Mustang Ridge	939	4	4	0
Nacogdoches	34,413	85	62	23
Nash	3,076	9	8	1
Nassau Bay	4,092	13	12	1
Navasota	7,239	31	23	8
Nederland	17,464	36	23	13
Needville	2,879	5	5	0
New Boston	4,507	14	10	4
New Braunfels	61,651	123	97	26
New Deal	800	1	1	0
Nixon	2,418	6	5	1
Nocona	2,996	9	5	4
Nolanville	4,483	5	5	0
Northeast	3,255	7	6	1
Northlake	1,897	8	8	0
North Richland Hills	65,899	175	106	69
Oak Ridge	168	1	1	0
Odessa	108,265	191	140	51
O'Donnell	809	1	1	0
Olmos Park	2,314	13	13	0
Olney	3,221	8	6	2
Omaha	1,012	2	2	0
Onalaska	1,724	6	6	0
Orange	19,057	56	41	15
Orange Grove	1,357	6	6	0
Overton	2,580	10	7	3
Ovilla	3,535	10	9	1
Oyster Creek	1,124	10	6	4
Paducah	1,164	8	2	6
Palacios	4,666	15	10	5
Palestine	18,458	42	27	15
Palmer	2,023	10	9	1
Palmhurst	2,698	15	10	5
Palm Valley	1,311	5	5	0
Palmview	5,625	26	20	6
Pampa	18,471	28	26	2
Panhandle	2,438	4	4	0
Pantego	2,483	17	12	5
Paris	25,048	82	60	22
Parker	4,205	6	6	0
Pasadena	153,195	341	256	85
Pearland	98,183	187	145	42
Pearsall	9,488	17	16	1
Pecos	8,786	39	17	22
Penitas	4,693	17	12	5
Perryton	9,392	21	13	8
Pflugerville	53,007	104	76	28
Pharr	73,932	179	126	53
Pilot Point	4,017	9	8	1
Pinehurst	2,087	8	6	2
Pittsburg	4,514	12	10	2
Plainview	22,225	39	32	7
Plano	275,795	569	347	222
Point Comfort	738	1	1	0

Table 78.   Full-Time Law Enforcement Employees, by Selected State and City, 2013— continued

(Number.)

State/city	Population	Total law enforcement employees	Total officers	Total civilians
Ponder	1,463	2	2	0
Port Aransas	3,726	26	18	8
Port Arthur	54,032	158	121	37
Port Isabel	5,055	27	21	6
Portland	15,572	33	24	9
Port Lavaca	12,329	26	20	6
Port Neches	12,773	19	16	3
Poteet	3,375	8	7	1
Poth	1,993	4	4	0
Pottsboro	2,190	8	7	1
Premont	2,722	6	6	0
Presidio	4,204	6	5	1
Primera	4,146	9	8	1
Princeton	7,684	13	12	1
Progreso	5,776	7	7	0
Prosper	12,501	20	14	6
Queen City	1,464	6	6	0
Ralls	1,966	2	2	0
Rancho Viejo	2,486	8	8	0
Ranger	2,456	4	4	0
Ransom Canyon	1,114	3	3	0
Raymondville	11,164	22	14	8
Refugio	2,828	10	9	1
Reno	3,261	5	4	1
Richardson	104,577	236	146	90
Richland Hills	8,012	21	17	4
Richmond	11,841	40	29	11
Richwood	3,646	8	8	0
Riesel	1,018	3	3	0
Rio Grande City	13,971	37	29	8
Rio Hondo	2,429	5	5	0
River Oaks	7,620	24	18	6
Roanoke	6,644	38	29	9
Robinson	11,237	29	20	9
Robstown	11,665	32	24	8
Rockdale	5,391	17	11	6
Rockport	9,256	25	23	2
Rockwall	40,622	90	71	19
Rollingwood	1,529	7	7	0
Roma	9,900	29	23	6
Roman Forest	1,820	8	8	0
Roscoe	1,298	1	1	0
Rosebud	1,400	4	4	0
Rose City	511	1	1	0
Rosenberg	32,059	86	66	20
Rowlett	58,177	107	70	37
Royse City	10,132	17	15	2
Runaway Bay	1,352	4	4	0
Rusk	5,613	12	11	1
Sabinal	1,692	4	4	0
Sachse	21,986	42	30	12
Saginaw	21,208	44	37	7
Salado	2,159	6	6	0
San Angelo	96,661	199	167	32
San Antonio	1,399,725	2,889	2,312	577
San Augustine	2,081	8	7	1
San Benito	24,555	51	43	8
San Diego	4,437	7	7	0
Sanger	7,226	14	13	1
San Juan	35,588	56	45	11
San Marcos	51,786	139	101	38
San Saba	3,086	2	2	0
Sansom Park Village	4,804	16	12	4
Santa Anna	1,067	3	3	0
Santa Fe	12,565	29	22	7
Santa Rosa	2,895	4	4	0
Schertz	35,882	74	53	21
Schulenburg	2,872	9	8	1
Seabrook	12,580	41	32	9
Seagoville	15,652	29	22	7
Seagraves	2,581	4	3	1
Sealy	6,163	20	18	2
Seguin	26,635	71	51	20
Selma	7,747	31	29	2
Seminole	6,877	12	10	2
Seven Points	1,456	11	7	4
Seymour	2,636	6	5	1
Shallowater	2,516	5	5	0
Shamrock	2,008	8	3	5

Table 78.   Full-Time Law Enforcement Employees, by Selected State and City, 2013— continued

(Number.)

State/city	Population	Total law enforcement employees	Total officers	Total civilians
Shavano Park	3,274	17	16	1
Shenandoah	2,478	23	22	1
Sherman	39,377	84	59	25
Silsbee	6,662	21	16	5
Sinton	5,698	12	11	1
Slaton	6,112	16	10	6
Smithville	3,865	14	9	5
Snyder	11,459	20	18	2
Socorro	32,891	37	25	12
Somerset	1,703	3	3	0
Somerville	1,375	5	5	0
Sonora	2,866	7	5	2
Sour Lake	1,782	7	6	1
South Houston	17,445	39	29	10
South Padre Island	2,919	38	31	7
Southside Place	1,775	9	5	4
Spearman	3,292	4	4	0
Splendora	1,667	8	8	0
Springtown	2,698	16	11	5
Spring Valley	4,009	21	16	5
Spur	1,239	1	1	0
Stafford	18,034	64	47	17
Stagecoach	561	3	3	0
Stamford	2,999	8	7	1
Stanton	2,651	4	4	0
Stephenville	18,595	50	38	12
Stratford	2,069	5	4	1
Sullivan City	4,122	13	9	4
Sulphur Springs	15,613	39	28	11
Sunray	1,960	1	1	0
Sunrise Beach Village	692	4	4	0
Sunset Valley	696	13	13	0
Surfside Beach	500	6	6	0
Sweeny	3,739	7	7	0
Sweetwater	10,604	27	22	5
Taft	3,053	10	8	2
Tahoka	2,589	4	4	0
Taylor	16,317	35	26	9
Teague	3,504	8	7	1
Temple	69,937	162	134	28
Terrell	16,233	53	36	17
Terrell Hills	5,061	16	15	1
Texarkana	37,467	103	90	13
Texas City	45,793	111	85	26
The Colony	39,903	81	52	29
Thorndale	1,293	2	2	0
Thrall	899	2	2	0
Three Rivers	1,887	10	9	1
Timpson	1,189	5	5	0
Tolar	715	1	1	0
Tomball	11,029	55	42	13
Tom Bean	1,037	4	4	0
Tool	2,264	10	6	4
Trenton	643	3	2	1
Trinity	2,636	11	6	5
Trophy Club	10,173	20	18	2
Troup	1,914	9	8	1
Troy	1,723	5	5	0
Tulia	4,964	15	8	7
Tye	1,248	4	4	0
Tyler	100,033	242	191	51
Universal City	19,344	39	29	10
University Park	24,031	50	37	13
Uvalde	16,218	47	34	13
Valley Mills	1,187	2	2	0
Valley View	768	2	2	0
Van	2,644	7	7	0
Van Alstyne	3,088	12	7	5
Venus	3,105	6	6	0
Vernon	10,703	31	21	10
Victoria	64,979	137	104	33
Vidor	10,984	29	23	6
Waco	127,570	324	248	76
Waelder	1,085	4	4	0
Wake Village	5,446	10	9	1
Waller	2,375	12	11	1
Wallis	1,269	2	2	0
Watauga	24,210	45	36	9
Waxahachie	31,530	76	59	17

Table 78.   Full-Time Law Enforcement Employees, by Selected State and City, 2013— continued

(Number.)

State/city	Population	Total law enforcement employees	Total officers	Total civilians
Weatherford	26,702	75	58	17
Webster	11,116	63	48	15
Weimar	2,128	9	8	1
Weslaco	37,248	78	57	21
West	2,836	8	8	0
West Columbia	3,907	17	10	7
West Lake Hills	3,309	20	14	6
West Orange	3,463	11	9	2
Westover Hills	708	14	10	4
West Tawakoni	1,605	3	3	0
West University Place	15,357	32	21	11
Westworth	2,554	19	14	5
Wharton	8,767	33	23	10
Whitehouse	7,919	16	15	1
White Oak	6,447	19	15	4
Whitesboro	3,823	13	8	5
White Settlement	16,703	47	33	14
Whitewright	1,607	5	5	0
Whitney	2,108	7	6	1
Wichita Falls	104,514	275	192	83
Willis	5,949	16	14	2
Willow Park	4,248	17	12	5
Wills Point	3,504	12	11	1
Wilmer	3,805	15	11	4
Windcrest	5,617	30	22	8
Wink	980	1	1	0
Winnsboro	3,250	13	9	4
Wolfforth	3,983	11	10	1
Woodbranch	1,344	5	3	2
Woodville	2,531	10	9	1
Woodway	8,626	40	26	14
Wortham	1,044	3	3	0
Wylie	45,138	51	46	5
Yoakum	5,927	16	10	6
Yorktown	2,133	5	5	0
UTAH				
Alta	391	8	4	4
American Fork/Cedar Hills	37,544	40	33	7
Big Water	471	1	1	0
Blanding	3,543	5	5	0
Bountiful	42,976	52	36	16
Brigham City	18,217	29	25	4
Cedar City	29,180	42	34	8
Centerfield	1,373	1	1	0
Clearfield	30,433	45	32	13
Clinton	20,903	17	16	1
Cottonwood Heights	34,208	42	36	6
East Carbon	1,269	4	4	0
Enoch	6,049	7	5	2
Ephraim	6,145	5	5	0
Fairview	1,253	1	1	0
Farmington	21,582	18	15	3
Fountain Green	1,078	1	1	0
Garland	2,345	4	4	0
Grantsville	9,530	14	12	2
Harrisville	5,870	10	9	1
Helper	2,185	6	6	0
Hildale	2,976	9	5	4
Hurricane	14,558	22	20	2
Kamas	1,926	2	2	0
Kanab	4,438	7	7	0
Kaysville	28,575	24	22	2
La Verkin	4,174	4	4	0
Layton	69,044	107	74	33
Lindon	10,550	16	15	1
Logan	49,049	89	60	29
Mantua	668	1	1	0
Mapleton	8,583	9	8	1
Moab	5,096	20	15	5
Moroni	1,430	1	1	0
Mount Pleasant	3,282	4	4	0
Naples	1,928	14	7	7
Nephi	5,452	11	9	2
North Ogden	17,915	21	18	3
North Salt Lake	16,815	25	20	5
Ogden	84,045	160	131	29
Park City	7,957	51	39	12
Parowan	2,837	5	4	1

Table 78.   Full-Time Law Enforcement Employees, by Selected State and City, 2013— continued

(Number.)

State/city	Population	Total law enforcement employees	Total officers	Total civilians
Payson	19,120	20	18	2
Perry	4,471	5	5	0
Pleasant Grove	34,796	34	26	8
Pleasant View	8,446	9	8	1
Price	8,589	40	17	23
Provo	116,937	146	102	44
Riverdale	8,595	22	19	3
Roosevelt	6,404	12	11	1
Roy	37,810	45	37	8
Salem	6,867	10	9	1
Sandy	89,943	147	111	36
Santa Clara/Ivins	13,680	15	13	2
South Jordan	57,593	54	47	7
South Ogden	16,792	25	22	3
South Salt Lake	24,595	69	58	11
Spanish Fork	36,690	32	28	4
Springville	30,940	39	28	11
Sunset	5,137	8	8	0
Tooele	32,241	38	33	5
Tremonton	7,824	12	10	2
Vernal	10,099	23	20	3
Washington	21,616	22	20	2
West Bountiful	5,345	10	9	1
West Jordan	109,831	142	106	36
West Valley	133,373	223	180	43
Willard	1,737	2	2	0
Woods Cross	10,343	15	13	2
VERMONT				
Barre	8,938	24	18	6
Barre Town	7,932	8	7	1
Bellows Falls	3,076	9	8	1
Bennington	15,492	32	25	7
Berlin	2,867	8	7	1
Bradford	2,777	1	1	0
Brandon	3,905	8	7	1
Brattleboro	11,784	40	27	13
Bristol	3,871	3	3	0
Burlington	42,235	127	94	33
Castleton	4,649	4	4	0
Chester	3,104	5	4	1
Colchester	17,288	36	28	8
Dover	1,110	6	5	1
Essex	20,199	33	27	6
Fair Haven	2,681	4	4	0
Hardwick	2,957	8	7	1
Hartford	9,804	22	21	1
Hinesburg	4,475	5	5	0
Ludlow	1,940	9	5	4
Lyndonville	1,203	3	3	0
Manchester	4,323	12	8	4
Middlebury	8,473	15	13	2
Milton	10,577	16	15	1
Montpelier	7,764	24	16	8
Morristown	5,369	11	11	0
Newport	4,513	13	11	2
Northfield	6,175	7	6	1
Norwich	3,387	5	4	1
Pittsford	2,929	1	1	0
Randolph	4,757	5	5	0
Richmond	4,094	5	5	0
Royalton	2,767	1	1	0
Rutland	16,137	43	33	10
Rutland Town	4,034	3	3	0
Shelburne	7,551	18	12	6
South Burlington	18,549	48	40	8
Springfield	9,259	21	16	5
St. Albans	6,888	32	22	10
St. Johnsbury	7,590	15	9	6
Stowe	4,413	11	11	0
Swanton	6,440	7	6	1
Thetford	2,603	3	3	0
Vergennes	2,580	6	6	0
Vernon	2,187	5	4	1
Waterbury	5,112	2	2	0
Weathersfield	2,806	2	2	0
Williston	9,042	18	15	3
Wilmington	1,846	6	5	1
Windsor	3,483	11	10	1

Table 78.   Full-Time Law Enforcement Employees, by Selected State and City, 2013— continued

(Number.)

State/city	Population	Total law enforcement employees	Total officers	Total civilians
Winhall	760	7	6	1
Winooski	7,229	19	14	5
Woodstock	3,003	9	6	3
VIRGINIA				
Abingdon	8,186	28	26	2
Alexandria	148,519	402	307	95
Altavista	3,486	13	12	1
Amherst	2,223	5	5	0
Appalachia	1,728	5	5	0
Ashland	7,310	27	24	3
Bedford	5,894	26	23	3
Berryville	4,290	10	9	1
Big Stone Gap	5,568	17	15	2
Blacksburg	42,603	77	63	14
Blackstone	3,574	15	11	4
Bloxom	390	1	1	0
Bluefield	5,339	22	17	5
Boykins	554	1	1	0
Bridgewater	5,817	9	9	0
Bristol	17,641	72	52	20
Broadway	3,766	4	4	0
Brookneal	1,121	1	1	0
Buena Vista	6,747	16	14	2
Burkeville	424	1	1	0
Cape Charles	996	5	5	0
Cedar Bluff	1,106	3	3	0
Charlottesville	44,187	139	113	26
Chase City	2,328	9	8	1
Chatham	1,494	3	3	0
Chesapeake	230,577	516	384	132
Chilhowie	1,750	6	6	0
Chincoteague	2,949	14	10	4
Christiansburg	21,581	73	57	16
Clarksville	1,129	8	7	1
Clifton Forge	3,876	12	10	2
Clintwood	1,374	4	4	0
Coeburn	2,117	6	6	0
Colonial Beach	3,554	12	11	1
Colonial Heights	17,553	54	50	4
Covington	5,725	25	17	8
Crewe	2,295	6	5	1
Culpeper	16,703	50	42	8
Damascus	815	5	5	0
Danville	43,133	135	126	9
Dayton	1,558	9	8	1
Dublin	2,512	10	9	1
Dumfries	5,194	9	7	2
Edinburg	1,058	2	2	0
Elkton	2,776	7	6	1
Emporia	5,693	36	26	10
Exmore	1,446	5	5	0
Fairfax City	23,801	84	67	17
Falls Church	13,517	44	32	12
Farmville	8,142	27	26	1
Franklin	8,520	40	27	13
Fredericksburg	28,411	99	71	28
Front Royal	14,730	44	36	8
Galax	6,870	38	24	14
Gate City	1,996	3	3	0
Glade Spring	1,456	3	3	0
Glasgow	1,138	1	1	0
Glen Lyn	112	1	1	0
Gordonsville	1,539	7	6	1
Gretna	1,245	4	4	0
Grottoes	2,723	6	6	0
Grundy	1,008	6	6	0
Halifax	1,301	4	4	0
Hampton	136,949	385	277	108
Harrisonburg	51,767	105	89	16
Haymarket	1,949	7	6	1
Haysi	490	2	2	0
Herndon	24,561	70	55	15
Hillsville	2,702	14	13	1
Honaker	1,416	3	3	0
Hopewell	22,305	80	63	17
Hurt	1,281	2	2	0
Independence	924	2	2	0
Jonesville	1,030	2	2	0

Table 78.   Full-Time Law Enforcement Employees, by Selected State and City, 2013— continued

(Number.)

State/city	Population	Total law enforcement employees	Total officers	Total civilians
Kenbridge	1,231	4	4	0
Kilmarnock	1,464	4	4	0
La Crosse	600	1	1	0
Lawrenceville	1,259	6	6	0
Lebanon	3,384	12	11	1
Leesburg	46,951	100	84	16
Lexington	6,995	19	17	2
Louisa	1,571	5	5	0
Luray	4,862	14	12	2
Lynchburg	77,757	193	169	24
Manassas	41,512	123	97	26
Manassas Park	16,332	44	32	12
Marion	5,838	20	18	2
Martinsville	13,771	49	44	5
Middleburg	739	6	6	0
Middletown	1,307	2	2	0
Mount Jackson	2,024	5	5	0
Narrows	1,976	5	5	0
New Market	2,185	5	5	0
Newport News	181,074	559	426	133
Norfolk	247,303	857	763	94
Norton	4,108	24	16	8
Occoquan	987	1	1	0
Onancock	1,263	5	5	0
Onley	519	3	3	0
Orange	4,841	17	15	2
Parksley	848	3	3	0
Pearisburg	2,699	7	7	0
Pembroke	1,097	2	2	0
Pennington Gap	1,864	5	5	0
Petersburg	31,847	139	105	34
Poquoson	12,108	24	23	1
Portsmouth	97,018	343	247	96
Pound	1,026	4	4	0
Pulaski	8,978	35	26	9
Purcellville	8,474	15	14	1
Quantico	523	1	1	0
Radford	16,810	48	36	12
Remington	612	1	1	0
Rich Creek	755	1	1	0
Richlands	5,652	24	17	7
Richmond	212,830	866	703	163
Roanoke	97,927	296	252	44
Rocky Mount	4,827	22	20	2
Rural Retreat	1,487	1	1	0
Salem	25,066	89	61	28
Saltville	2,043	7	7	0
Shenandoah	2,350	6	5	1
Smithfield	8,141	24	20	4
South Boston	8,048	31	28	3
South Hill	4,592	22	20	2
Stanley	1,672	4	4	0
Staunton	24,007	66	51	15
Stephens City	1,888	4	4	0
St. Paul	960	6	6	0
Strasburg	6,516	20	18	2
Suffolk	85,475	225	175	50
Tappahannock	2,398	11	10	1
Tazewell	4,507	16	15	1
Timberville	2,569	4	4	0
Victoria	1,687	6	5	1
Vienna	16,335	51	40	11
Vinton	8,104	25	23	2
Virginia Beach	450,687	955	782	173
Warrenton	9,860	22	20	2
Warsaw	1,493	4	3	1
Waverly	2,114	13	7	6
Waynesboro	21,175	54	44	10
Weber City	1,285	5	5	0
West Point	3,311	10	9	1
White Stone	346	2	2	0
Williamsburg	15,565	40	37	3
Winchester	27,163	99	74	25
Windsor	2,631	6	6	0
Wise	3,251	13	12	1
Woodstock	5,193	17	16	1
Wytheville	8,194	38	27	11

WASHINGTON

Table 78.   Full-Time Law Enforcement Employees, by Selected State and City, 2013— continued

(Number.)

State/city	Population	Total law enforcement employees	Total officers	Total civilians
Aberdeen	16,408	48	36	12
Airway Heights	6,441	15	14	1
Algona	3,123	8	7	1
Anacortes	15,980	30	24	6
Arlington	18,425	28	24	4
Asotin	1,276	2	2	0
Auburn	74,565	117	99	18
Bainbridge Island	23,326	23	19	4
Battle Ground	18,146	24	21	3
Bellevue	127,678	209	170	39
Bellingham	82,645	154	107	47
Black Diamond	4,304	8	7	1
Blaine	4,875	12	10	2
Bonney Lake	18,156	36	27	9
Bothell	35,007	81	56	25
Bremerton	39,754	71	58	13
Brewster	2,356	7	6	1
Brier	6,303	8	7	1
Buckley	4,927	11	9	2
Burien	49,822	70	51	19
Burlington	8,492	29	24	5
Camas	20,848	27	25	2
Castle Rock	1,984	6	5	1
Centralia	16,549	36	31	5
Chehalis	7,312	21	17	4
Cheney	11,117	20	14	6
Chewelah	2,606	6	5	1
Clarkston	7,295	15	14	1
Cle Elum	2,798	8	7	1
Clyde Hill	3,146	8	7	1
Colfax	2,860	5	5	0
College Place	8,913	14	11	3
Colville	4,674	11	10	1
Connell	5,913	6	6	0
Cosmopolis	1,605	5	4	1
Coulee Dam	1,096	3	3	0
Coupeville	1,875	2	2	0
Covington	18,526	21	16	5
Des Moines	30,684	42	32	10
Dupont	8,999	8	6	2
Duvall	7,342	14	13	1
East Wenatchee	13,509	24	21	3
Eatonville	2,826	4	4	0
Edgewood	9,542	6	6	0
Edmonds	40,615	59	50	9
Ellensburg	18,367	37	28	9
Elma	3,033	8	7	1
Enumclaw	11,431	30	18	12
Ephrata	7,986	18	14	4
Everett	105,129	222	183	39
Everson	2,570	6	5	1
Federal Way	92,741	146	119	27
Ferndale	12,173	20	18	2
Fife	9,380	48	30	18
Fircrest	6,609	10	9	1
Forks	3,744	13	6	7
Gig Harbor	7,699	18	16	2
Goldendale	3,446	10	9	1
Grand Coulee	1,046	8	8	0
Grandview	11,048	23	17	6
Granger	3,313	7	7	0
Granite Falls	3,435	6	5	1
Hoquiam	8,472	24	18	6
Issaquah	33,365	61	33	28
Kalama	2,316	5	5	0
Kelso	11,802	27	23	4
Kenmore	21,531	20	16	4
Kennewick	76,508	107	93	14
Kent	124,359	182	138	44
Kettle Falls	1,596	4	3	1
Kirkland	51,288	132	97	35
Kittitas	1,443	3	3	0
La Center	3,071	10	8	2
Lacey	44,298	61	52	9
Lake Forest Park	13,088	21	18	3
Lake Stevens	29,388	27	22	5
Lakewood	59,057	115	97	18
Langley	1,047	3	3	0
Liberty Lake	7,979	11	10	1

Table 78.   Full-Time Law Enforcement Employees, by Selected State and City, 2013— continued

(Number.)

State/city	Population	Total law enforcement employees	Total officers	Total civilians
Long Beach	1,344	7	6	1
Longview	36,374	67	56	11
Lynden	12,808	19	15	4
Lynnwood	36,396	98	67	31
Mabton	2,328	3	3	0
Maple Valley	24,644	23	19	4
Marysville	63,153	67	57	10
Mattawa	4,532	5	4	1
McCleary	1,609	4	4	0
Medina	3,096	8	7	1
Mercer Island	23,969	34	30	4
Mill Creek	18,806	29	24	5
Milton	7,076	14	13	1
Monroe	17,562	41	30	11
Montesano	3,881	10	8	2
Morton	1,126	2	2	0
Moses Lake	21,410	40	32	8
Mountlake Terrace	20,286	34	26	8
Mount Vernon	32,450	56	44	12
Moxee	3,598	5	5	0
Mukilteo	20,707	32	28	4
Napavine	1,766	2	2	0
Newcastle	10,928	11	9	2
Normandy Park	6,556	13	10	3
North Bend	6,094	9	7	2
Oak Harbor	22,288	38	32	6
Ocean Shores	5,632	13	11	2
Odessa	880	2	2	0
Olympia	48,046	85	59	26
Omak	4,801	12	10	2
Oroville	1,674	6	5	1
Orting	6,913	10	10	0
Othello	7,577	20	14	6
Pacific	6,911	12	10	2
Palouse	1,028	3	3	0
Pasco	67,099	82	71	11
Pe Ell	632	1	1	0
Port Angeles	19,053	59	32	27
Port Orchard	11,818	25	23	2
Port Townsend	9,112	17	15	2
Poulsbo	9,429	19	16	3
Prosser	5,817	13	12	1
Pullman	31,895	39	26	13
Puyallup	38,532	75	53	22
Quincy	7,085	20	16	4
Raymond	2,793	7	6	1
Reardan	565	1	1	0
Redmond	57,263	122	83	39
Renton	96,657	143	115	28
Republic	1,105	4	3	1
Richland	52,465	67	56	11
Ridgefield	5,426	9	8	1
Ritzville	1,679	4	4	0
Roy	803	2	2	0
Royal City	2,219	3	3	0
Ruston	766	3	3	0
Sammamish	49,805	32	26	6
SeaTac	27,896	58	43	15
Seattle	642,814	1,864	1,294	570
Sedro Woolley	10,652	17	14	3
Selah	7,376	15	14	1
Sequim	6,626	22	19	3
Shelton	9,780	21	18	3
Shoreline	54,762	69	52	17
Snohomish	9,323	20	17	3
Snoqualmie	11,890	21	18	3
Soap Lake	1,557	3	3	0
South Bend	1,602	5	4	1
Spokane	209,524	365	280	85
Spokane Valley	90,835	99	98	1
Springdale	278	1	1	0
Stanwood	6,476	13	11	2
Steilacoom	6,099	8	7	1
Sumas	1,340	6	6	0
Sumner	9,575	22	18	4
Sunnyside	16,099	42	27	15
Tacoma	203,226	370	334	36
Tenino	1,700	2	2	0
Tieton	1,200	2	2	0

Table 78.   Full-Time Law Enforcement Employees, by Selected State and City, 2013— continued

(Number.)

State/city	Population	Total law enforcement employees	Total officers	Total civilians
Toledo	725	2	2	0
Tonasket	1,022	5	4	1
Toppenish	9,029	23	17	6
Tukwila	19,765	86	70	16
Tumwater	18,343	31	26	5
Twisp	946	2	2	0
Union Gap	6,059	19	16	3
University Place	31,708	18	16	2
Vancouver	166,535	209	187	22
Walla Walla	31,889	69	41	28
Wapato	5,067	17	11	6
Warden	2,759	5	4	1
Washougal	14,733	23	18	5
Wenatchee	32,677	45	36	9
Westport	2,042	9	7	2
West Richland	12,905	16	14	2
White Salmon	2,269	5	4	1
Wilbur	856	2	2	0
Winlock	1,326	2	2	0
Winthrop	409	3	3	0
Woodinville	11,325	18	14	4
Woodland	5,535	12	10	2
Yakima	93,589	182	141	41
Yelm	7,211	14	12	2
Zillah	3,051	8	7	1
WEST VIRGINIA				
Alderson	1,184	3	2	1
Anawalt	217	1	1	0
Anmoore	770	2	2	0
Ansted	1,406	3	2	1
Athens	1,051	1	1	0
Barboursville	4,099	20	18	2
Beckley	17,593	69	49	20
Belington	1,920	3	3	0
Belle	1,243	4	4	0
Benwood	1,389	6	6	0
Berkeley Springs	614	3	2	1
Bethlehem	2,471	4	4	0
Bluefield	10,517	24	19	5
Bradshaw	321	1	1	0
Bramwell	369	1	1	0
Bridgeport	8,425	33	30	3
Buckhannon	5,649	10	9	1
Burnsville	501	1	1	0
Cameron	925	3	3	0
Capon Bridge	354	2	2	0
Cedar Grove	982	5	4	1
Ceredo	1,402	9	6	3
Chapmanville	1,264	5	5	0
Charleston	50,919	182	158	24
Charles Town	5,421	16	15	1
Chesapeake	1,537	3	3	0
Chester	2,543	7	6	1
Clarksburg	16,389	48	44	4
Clendenin	1,213	4	4	0
Danville	682	2	2	0
Davy	402	1	1	0
Delbarton	562	3	3	0
Dunbar	7,834	16	14	2
Eleanor	1,559	2	2	0
Elkins	7,183	13	10	3
Fairmont	18,740	40	35	5
Fairview	412	1	1	0
Farmington	379	1	1	0
Fayetteville	2,888	9	9	0
Follansbee	2,949	7	7	0
Fort Gay	687	3	3	0
Gary	928	2	2	0
Gassaway	899	1	1	0
Gauley Bridge	609	1	1	0
Gilbert	432	4	4	0
Glasgow	894	3	3	0
Glen Dale	1,494	11	6	5
Glenville	1,553	3	3	0
Grafton	5,183	7	6	1
Grantsville	555	2	2	0
Grant Town	614	1	1	0
Granville	1,903	12	11	1

Table 78.   Full-Time Law Enforcement Employees, by Selected State and City, 2013— continued

(Number.)

State/city	Population	Total law enforcement employees	Total officers	Total civilians
Hamlin	1,136	5	5	0
Handley	342	1	1	0
Harpers Ferry/Bolivar	1,339	5	4	1
Harrisville	1,819	1	1	0
Henderson	269	1	1	0
Hinton	2,604	7	6	1
Hundred	296	12	8	4
Huntington	49,172	110	102	8
Hurricane	6,382	18	16	2
Iaeger	289	1	1	0
Kenova	3,119	6	6	0
Kermit	389	1	1	0
Keyser	5,307	14	9	5
Kimball	186	1	1	0
Kingwood	2,960	2	2	0
Lewisburg	3,981	14	12	2
Logan	1,727	9	8	1
Lumberport	880	2	2	0
Mabscott	1,398	2	2	0
Madison	3,046	8	6	2
Man	737	2	2	0
Mannington	2,071	4	4	0
Marmet	1,489	5	5	0
Martinsburg	17,589	61	48	13
Mason	956	4	3	1
Masontown	550	1	1	0
Matewan	475	2	2	0
Matoaka	222	1	1	0
McMechen	1,883	3	3	0
Milton	2,525	5	5	0
Monongah	1,052	1	1	0
Montgomery	1,628	6	5	1
Moorefield	2,492	9	8	1
Morgantown	31,406	77	66	11
Moundsville	9,130	22	18	4
Mount Hope	1,398	6	5	1
Mullens	1,521	3	3	0
New Cumberland	1,082	3	2	1
New Haven	1,538	4	3	1
New Martinsville	5,345	15	11	4
Nitro	7,137	17	16	1
Northfork	406	1	1	0
Nutter Fort	1,580	6	6	0
Oak Hill	7,709	15	14	1
Oceana	1,355	5	5	0
Paden City	2,577	6	4	2
Parkersburg	31,207	73	65	8
Parsons	1,424	1	1	0
Paw Paw	498	2	2	0
Petersburg	2,418	2	2	0
Philippi	2,944	6	6	0
Piedmont	857	1	1	0
Pineville	650	3	3	0
Point Pleasant	4,300	10	9	1
Pratt	594	1	1	0
Princeton	6,474	23	19	4
Rainelle	1,492	3	2	1
Ranson	4,684	14	13	1
Ravenswood	3,852	10	9	1
Reedsville	600	2	1	1
Rhodell	173	2	1	1
Richwood	2,036	3	3	0
Ridgeley	660	2	2	0
Ripley	3,249	8	7	1
Rivesville	943	2	2	0
Romney	1,806	4	3	1
Ronceverte	1,778	6	6	0
Salem	1,570	1	1	0
Shepherdstown	2,149	6	5	1
Shinnston	2,192	7	7	0
Sistersville	1,357	4	4	0
Smithers	807	4	3	1
Sophia	1,336	3	3	0
South Charleston	13,308	43	41	2
Spencer	2,238	4	4	0
St. Albans	10,952	24	23	1
Star City	1,904	6	5	1
St. Marys	1,847	6	6	0
Stonewood	1,784	2	2	0

Table 78.   Full-Time Law Enforcement Employees, by Selected State and City, 2013— continued

(Number.)

State/city	Population	Total law enforcement employees	Total officers	Total civilians
Summersville	3,569	18	17	1
Sutton	982	1	1	0
Sylvester	159	1	1	0
Terra Alta	1,494	2	1	1
Triadelphia	794	1	1	0
Vienna	10,664	21	18	3
War	808	2	2	0
Wardensville	274	2	2	0
Webster Springs	759	2	2	0
Weirton	19,435	39	36	3
Welch	2,303	8	7	1
Wellsburg	2,760	6	6	0
West Logan	416	1	1	0
Weston	4,076	8	6	2
Westover	4,135	7	7	0
West Union	821	1	1	0
Wheeling	28,127	84	81	3
White Hall	660	3	3	0
White Sulphur Springs	2,467	6	5	1
Whitesville	498	3	3	0
Williamson	3,069	10	8	2
Williamstown	2,912	7	6	1
Winfield	2,339	5	4	1
WISCONSIN				
Adams	1,924	6	5	1
Albany	1,015	6	3	3
Algoma	3,143	4	4	0
Altoona	7,018	12	11	1
Amery	2,859	7	6	1
Antigo	7,988	18	15	3
Appleton	73,141	133	108	25
Arcadia	2,950	3	3	0
Ashland	8,097	20	19	1
Ashwaubenon	17,145	57	51	6
Athens	1,100	1	1	0
Bangor	1,494	3	3	0
Baraboo	12,047	33	27	6
Barneveld	1,238	1	1	0
Barron	3,391	6	6	0
Bayfield	488	3	3	0
Bayside	4,418	35	13	22
Beaver Dam	16,326	35	30	5
Belleville	2,436	4	4	0
Beloit	36,817	81	68	13
Beloit Town	7,665	11	9	2
Berlin	5,519	13	12	1
Big Bend	1,299	3	3	0
Black River Falls	3,571	7	6	1
Blanchardville	826	2	1	1
Bloomer	3,544	6	5	1
Bloomfield	6,319	7	7	0
Blue Mounds	892	2	2	0
Boscobel	3,216	6	6	0
Brandon-Fairwater	1,234	1	1	0
Brillion	3,193	8	7	1
Brodhead	3,270	12	8	4
Brookfield	37,996	79	62	17
Brookfield Township	6,126	14	13	1
Brown Deer	12,114	34	31	3
Burlington	10,502	26	20	6
Butler	1,838	7	6	1
Caledonia	24,681	32	29	3
Campbellsport	1,988	2	1	1
Campbell Township	4,419	5	5	0
Cashton	1,094	2	2	0
Cedarburg	11,446	27	19	8
Chenequa	598	9	8	1
Chetek	2,203	6	5	1
Chilton	3,975	6	6	0
Chippewa Falls	13,676	27	23	4
Cleveland	1,497	2	1	1
Clinton	2,138	5	5	0
Clintonville	4,485	15	11	4
Colby-Abbotsford	4,117	7	6	1
Columbus	5,017	12	11	1
Coon Valley	785	1	1	0
Cornell	1,473	2	2	0
Cottage Grove	6,478	12	11	1

Table 78.   Full-Time Law Enforcement Employees, by Selected State and City, 2013— continued

(Number.)

State/city	Population	Total law enforcement employees	Total officers	Total civilians
Crandon	1,914	4	3	1
Cross Plains	3,671	6	5	1
Cuba City	2,066	4	3	1
Cudahy	18,362	41	31	10
Cumberland	2,156	4	4	0
Dane	1,067	3	2	1
Darlington	2,439	5	5	0
Deforest	9,349	20	17	3
Delafield	7,149	16	14	2
Delavan	10,092	27	22	5
Delavan Town	5,335	11	10	1
De Pere	24,314	39	35	4
Dodgeville	4,691	11	10	1
Durand	1,896	3	3	0
Eagle River	1,365	6	6	0
Eagle Village	1,953	3	3	0
East Troy	4,322	7	7	0
Eau Claire	67,309	134	98	36
Edgar	1,474	1	1	0
Edgerton	5,515	11	10	1
Eleva	682	1	1	0
Elkhart Lake	959	3	3	0
Elkhorn	10,084	18	15	3
Ellsworth	3,211	4	4	0
Elm Grove	5,942	24	17	7
Elroy	1,424	3	3	0
Evansville	5,094	10	9	1
Everest	17,093	28	25	3
Fall Creek	1,339	2	2	0
Fennimore	2,516	5	5	0
Fitchburg	26,122	56	44	12
Fond du Lac	43,042	76	70	6
Fontana	1,700	7	6	1
Fort Atkinson	12,493	26	19	7
Fountain City	837	1	1	0
Fox Lake	1,500	3	3	0
Fox Point	6,744	18	17	1
Fox Valley Metro	20,474	33	30	3
Franklin	36,283	72	58	14
Frederic	1,111	1	1	0
Freedom	5,963	2	2	0
Geneva Town	5,045	7	6	1
Germantown	19,796	42	32	10
Gillett	1,355	4	4	0
Gilman	408	2	1	1
Glendale	12,947	47	43	4
Grafton	11,519	30	23	7
Grand Chute	21,616	33	29	4
Grand Rapids	7,634	4	4	0
Grantsburg	1,316	3	3	0
Green Bay	105,107	223	186	37
Greendale	14,417	38	29	9
Greenfield	37,171	73	53	20
Green Lake	970	6	3	3
Hales Corners	7,762	19	16	3
Hartford	14,248	29	25	4
Hartland	9,196	18	16	2
Hayward	2,311	9	8	1
Hazel Green	1,254	1	1	0
Highland	853	1	1	0
Hillsboro	1,436	4	2	2
Hobart-Lawrence	11,587	6	5	1
Holmen	9,395	11	10	1
Horicon	3,615	8	7	1
Hortonville	2,713	5	4	1
Hudson	13,123	24	21	3
Hurley	1,550	7	6	1
Independence	1,348	3	3	0
Iron Ridge	917	1	1	0
Iron River	1,135	2	2	0
Jackson	6,773	12	11	1
Janesville	63,603	114	101	13
Jefferson	7,979	17	14	3
Juneau	2,775	5	4	1
Kaukauna	15,766	25	24	1
Kendall	471	1	1	0
Kenosha	100,418	210	199	11
Kewaskum	4,044	8	7	1
Kewaunee	2,940	6	6	0

Table 78.   Full-Time Law Enforcement Employees, by Selected State and City, 2013— continued

(Number.)

State/city	Population	Total law enforcement employees	Total officers	Total civilians
Kiel	3,684	8	7	1
Kohler	2,103	8	7	1
Kronenwetter	7,353	7	6	1
La Crosse	51,741	110	92	18
Ladysmith	3,248	10	9	1
Lake Delton	2,932	22	20	2
Lake Geneva	7,731	32	22	10
Lake Hallie	6,561	9	8	1
Lake Mills	5,808	12	10	2
Lancaster	3,813	7	7	0
Lodi	3,047	6	5	1
Lomira	2,401	4	3	1
Luxemburg	2,589	2	2	0
Madison	242,523	573	462	111
Manawa	1,336	7	7	0
Manitowoc	33,288	68	59	9
Maple Bluff	1,352	6	6	0
Marathon City	1,528	2	2	0
Marinette	10,834	27	23	4
Marion	1,239	6	3	3
Markesan	1,458	4	4	0
Marshall Village	3,961	7	6	1
Marshfield	18,900	47	39	8
Mauston	4,428	17	8	9
Mayville	5,076	8	7	1
McFarland	8,116	16	14	2
Medford	4,286	10	9	1
Menasha	17,565	40	31	9
Menomonee Falls	35,859	74	55	19
Menomonie	16,250	32	26	6
Mequon	23,264	44	36	8
Merrill	9,427	25	22	3
Middleton	18,384	46	36	10
Milton	5,551	13	11	2
Milwaukee	600,805	2,549	1,862	687
Mineral Point	2,495	5	5	0
Minocqua	4,440	16	11	5
Mishicot	1,424	1	1	0
Mondovi	2,690	4	4	0
Monona	7,763	24	19	5
Monroe	10,785	35	26	9
Montello	1,457	3	2	1
Mosinee	3,980	8	7	1
Mount Horeb	7,359	13	11	2
Mount Pleasant	26,179	49	43	6
Mukwonago	7,452	21	14	7
Mukwonago Town	8,065	12	6	6
Muskego	24,489	45	36	9
Neenah	25,850	50	40	10
Neillsville	2,411	6	5	1
New Berlin	39,741	79	67	12
New Glarus	2,176	4	4	0
New Holstein	3,257	7	6	1
New Lisbon	2,510	4	4	0
New London	7,226	19	17	2
New Richmond	8,480	16	15	1
Niagara	1,610	4	4	0
North Fond du Lac	4,934	11	9	2
North Hudson	3,789	5	4	1
Oak Creek	35,046	73	57	16
Oconomowoc	15,926	29	23	6
Oconomowoc Town	8,565	12	11	1
Oconto	4,505	9	8	1
Oconto Falls	2,843	5	5	0
Omro	3,563	7	6	1
Onalaska	18,408	30	27	3
Oregon	9,666	18	16	2
Osceola	2,503	6	5	1
Oshkosh	66,848	115	98	17
Osseo	1,716	4	4	0
Palmyra	1,790	3	3	0
Park Falls	2,376	8	7	1
Pepin	807	2	1	1
Peshtigo	3,481	7	6	1
Pewaukee Village	8,217	20	18	2
Phillips	1,425	5	5	0
Plainfield	853	2	2	0
Platteville	11,310	26	20	6
Plover	12,281	22	19	3

Table 78.   Full-Time Law Enforcement Employees, by Selected State and City, 2013— continued

(Number.)

State/city	Population	Total law enforcement employees	Total officers	Total civilians
Plymouth	8,382	16	16	0
Portage	10,168	26	22	4
Port Washington	11,404	24	19	5
Poynette	2,502	5	4	1
Prairie du Chien	5,829	13	12	1
Prescott	4,178	9	8	1
Princeton	1,199	3	3	0
Pulaski	3,565	13	6	7
Racine	78,141	233	200	33
Reedsburg	9,497	26	19	7
Rhinelander	7,612	20	17	3
Rice Lake	8,333	17	16	1
Richland Center	5,097	13	11	2
Ripon	7,711	20	14	6
River Falls	15,227	24	22	2
River Hills	1,611	12	12	0
Rome Town	2,704	7	6	1
Rosendale	1,055	1	1	0
Rothschild	5,263	11	9	2
Sauk Prairie	4,561	15	13	2
Saukville	4,516	12	10	2
Seymour	3,441	6	6	0
Shawano	9,157	21	19	2
Sheboygan	48,791	111	81	30
Sheboygan Falls	7,761	15	14	1
Shiocton	920	2	1	1
Shorewood	13,206	30	25	5
Shorewood Hills	1,613	8	6	2
Silver Lake	2,431	8	4	4
Siren	793	2	2	0
Slinger	5,127	10	9	1
Somerset	2,663	6	5	1
South Milwaukee	21,263	39	33	6
Sparta	9,623	20	18	2
Spencer	1,929	3	3	0
Spooner	2,640	7	6	1
Spring Green	1,625	4	3	1
Stanley	3,640	4	4	0
St. Croix Falls	2,104	5	5	0
Stevens Point	26,764	50	43	7
St. Francis	9,597	26	21	5
Stoughton	13,031	26	21	5
Sturgeon Bay	9,094	20	20	0
Sturtevant	6,975	10	9	1
Summit	4,711	8	8	0
Sun Prairie	30,729	70	51	19
Superior	26,737	61	56	5
Theresa	1,237	2	2	0
Thiensville	3,224	7	6	1
Three Lakes	2,120	5	5	0
Tomah	9,355	21	19	2
Tomahawk	3,321	9	8	1
Town of East Troy	4,077	7	6	1
Town of Madison	6,521	16	14	2
Town of Menasha	18,872	31	26	5
Trempealeau	1,614	2	2	0
Twin Lakes	6,039	17	13	4
Two Rivers	11,499	28	25	3
Valders	952	1	1	0
Verona	11,408	21	19	2
Viroqua	4,411	11	9	2
Walworth	2,824	7	6	1
Washburn	2,101	5	5	0
Waterloo	3,370	9	8	1
Watertown	23,995	52	38	14
Waukesha	70,988	152	118	34
Waunakee	12,829	19	17	2
Waupaca	6,036	14	13	1
Waupun	11,279	18	17	1
Wausau	39,176	77	70	7
Wautoma	2,216	6	5	1
Wauwatosa	47,273	111	88	23
West Allis	60,830	146	122	24
West Bend	31,666	71	54	17
Westby	2,271	3	3	0
Westfield	1,234	3	3	0
West Milwaukee	4,225	24	19	5
West Salem	4,914	8	7	1
Whitefish Bay	14,145	27	24	3

Table 78.   Full-Time Law Enforcement Employees, by Selected State and City, 2013— continued

(Number.)

State/city	Population	Total law enforcement employees	Total officers	Total civilians
Whitehall	1,583	4	4	0
Whitewater	14,541	34	23	11
Williams Bay	2,616	8	7	1
Winneconne	2,395	6	5	1
Wisconsin Dells	2,695	20	15	5
Wisconsin Rapids	18,170	41	36	5
Woodruff	809	6	5	1
WYOMING				
Afton	1,906	3	3	0
Basin	1,294	3	3	0
Buffalo	4,639	22	13	9
Casper	58,688	146	98	48
Cheyenne	62,149	129	106	23
Cody	9,736	24	21	3
Diamondville	724	4	3	1
Douglas	6,335	22	14	8
Evanston	12,228	37	31	6
Evansville	2,897	12	10	2
Gillette	31,884	83	53	30
Glenrock	2,587	12	7	5
Green River	12,933	31	26	5
Greybull	1,855	6	5	1
Guernsey	1,178	4	4	0
Hanna	823	1	1	0
Hulett	393	1	1	0
Jackson	9,918	32	24	8
Kemmerer	2,631	7	7	0
Lander	7,733	22	21	1
Laramie	31,940	77	49	28
Lovell	2,387	10	6	4
Lusk	1,548	6	5	1
Mills	3,486	15	12	3
Moorcroft	1,026	4	3	1
Newcastle	3,465	16	8	8
Pine Bluffs	1,152	7	3	4
Powell	6,304	22	16	6
Rawlins	9,081	30	19	11
Riverton	11,057	38	28	10
Rock Springs	24,405	64	52	12
Saratoga	1,656	10	5	5
Sheridan	17,776	43	28	15
Sundance	1,221	3	3	0
Thermopolis	3,023	13	7	6
Torrington	6,797	24	17	7
Wheatland	3,644	11	10	1
Worland	5,441	12	11	1

1 The employee data presented in this table for Charlotte-Mecklenburg represent only Charlotte-Mecklenburg Police Department and exclude Mecklenburg County Sheriff's Office.

Table 79.   Full-Time Law Enforcement Employees, by Selected State and University or College, 2013

(Number.)

State and university/college	Student enrollment[1]	Law enforcement employees	Officers	Civilians
ALABAMA				
Alabama A&M University	4,853	36	16	20
Alabama State University	5,816	42	31	11
Auburn University, Montgomery	5,005	17	10	7
Bishop State Community College	3,791	13	10	3
Calhoun Community College	11,177	8	7	1
Faulkner State Community College	4,400	5	5	0
Jacksonville State University	9,161	19	14	5
Jefferson State Community College	8,878	11	9	2
Northwest-Shoals Community College	3,717	4	4	0
Samford University	4,758	18	14	4
Troy University	22,554	27	17	10
Tuskegee University	3,117	35	17	18
University of Alabama				
Birmingham	17,999	160	88	72
Huntsville	7,636	25	18	7
Tuscaloosa	33,503	84	71	13
University of Montevallo	3,083	19	9	10
University of North Alabama	7,032	14	12	2
University of South Alabama	14,636	36	28	8
Wallace Community College				
Dothan	4,581	3	3	0
Selma	1,790	5	3	2
ALASKA				
University of Alaska				
Anchorage	17,497	24	16	8
Fairbanks	9,223	15	9	6
ARIZONA				
Arizona State University, Main Campus	73,378	126	71	55
Central Arizona College	7,018	9	6	3
Northern Arizona University	25,991	30	19	11
Pima Community College	32,988	53	29	24
University of Arizona	40,223	122	67	55
Yavapai College	8,283	8	7	1
ARKANSAS				
Arkansas State University				
Beebe	4,643	5	4	1
Jonesboro	13,877	24	20	4
Arkansas Tech University	10,950	17	15	2
Henderson State University	3,773	9	8	1
Northwest Arkansas Community College	8,341	17	14	3
Southern Arkansas University	3,330	5	5	0
Southern Arkansas University Tech	1,817	4	4	0
University of Arkansas				
Fayetteville	24,537	40	33	7
Little Rock	12,872	33	21	12
Medical Sciences	2,809	51	36	15
Monticello	3,945	9	8	1
Pine Bluff	2,828	18	8	10
University of Central Arkansas	11,107	37	27	10
CALIFORNIA				
Allan Hancock College	10,837	11	4	7
California State Polytechnic University				
Pomona	22,156	26	17	9
San Luis Obispo	18,679	32	15	17
California State University				
Bakersfield	8,520	15	11	4
Channel Islands	4,920	26	15	11
Chico	16,470	27	16	11
Dominguez Hills	13,933	25	18	7
East Bay	13,851	23	13	10
Fresno	22,565	30	21	9
Fullerton	37,677	39	27	12
Long Beach	36,279	36	23	13
Los Angeles	21,755	29	16	13
Monterey Bay	5,609	20	14	6
Northridge	36,164	35	22	13
Sacramento	28,539	36	23	13
San Bernardino	18,234	25	14	11
San Jose	30,448	69	30	39
San Marcos	10,610	30	14	16
Stanislaus	8,882	20	11	9

Table 79.   Full-Time Law Enforcement Employees, by Selected State and University or College, 2013— continued

(Number.)

State and university/college	Student enrollment[1]	Law enforcement employees	Officers	Civilians
College of the Sequoias	10,947	8	7	1
Contra Costa Community College	6,899	34	23	11
Cuesta College	9,834	11	6	5
El Camino College	23,405	33	25	8
Foothill-De Anza College	38,900	16	10	6
Humboldt State University	8,116	19	12	7
Marin Community College	7,058	8	7	1
Pasadena Community College	22,859	16	10	6
Riverside Community College	17,218	29	23	6
San Bernardino Community College	17,311	14	8	6
San Diego State University	30,843	47	23	24
San Francisco State University	30,500	54	29	25
San Jose/Evergreen Community College	19,186	10	3	7
Santa Rosa Junior College	22,823	25	13	12
Solano Community College	9,772	2	1	1
Sonoma State University	9,021	21	12	9
State Center Community College District	35,367	18	14	4
University of California				
Berkeley	35,893	147	65	82
Davis	32,354	89	45	44
Hastings College of Law	1,159	12	12	0
Irvine	27,479	47	33	14
Los Angeles	39,945	94	56	38
Merced	5,760	25	12	13
Riverside	20,947	42	29	13
San Diego	28,294	65	33	32
San Francisco	3,137	117	47	70
Santa Barbara	21,927	48	32	16
Santa Cruz	17,404	23	13	10
Ventura County Community College District	13,030	15	14	1
West Valley-Mission College	20,179	15	9	6
COLORADO				
Adams State University	3,290	5	4	1
Arapahoe Community College	11,806	16	9	7
Auraria Higher Education Center[2]		40	29	11
Colorado School of Mines	5,721	8	7	1
Colorado State University, Fort Collins	30,659	45	33	12
Fort Lewis College	3,883	10	8	2
Pikes Peak Community College	15,175	20	18	2
Red Rocks Community College	9,031	6	3	3
University of Colorado				
Boulder	31,945	66	37	29
Colorado Springs	10,612	28	16	12
Denver	22,396	61	26	35
Health Sciences Center[2]		57	25	32
University of Northern Colorado	13,070	21	14	7
CONNECTICUT				
Central Connecticut State University	12,091	27	21	6
Eastern Connecticut State University	5,440	24	17	7
Southern Connecticut State University	11,117	31	25	6
University of Connecticut				
Health Center[2]		34	14	20
Storrs, Avery Point, and Hartford[2]		87	70	17
Western Connecticut State University	6,176	22	15	7
Yale University	11,906	100	84	16
DELAWARE				
Delaware State University	4,324	34	16	18
University of Delaware	21,856	75	47	28
FLORIDA				
Edison State College	15,731	19	10	9
Florida A&M University	12,057	37	29	8
Florida Atlantic University	29,994	52	34	18
Florida Gulf Coast University	13,445	21	15	6
Florida International University	46,171	84	58	26
Florida State University				
Panama City[2]		6	5	1
Tallahassee	40,695	81	63	18
New College of Florida	832	18	12	6
Pensacola State College	11,862	14	8	6
Santa Fe College	15,362	20	16	4
Tallahassee Community College	14,237	25	12	13
University of Central Florida	59,601	95	60	35

Table 79.   Full-Time Law Enforcement Employees, by Selected State and University or College, 2013— continued

(Number.)

State and university/college	Student enrollment[1]	Law enforcement employees	Officers	Civilians
University of Florida	49,913	122	81	41
University of North Florida	16,201	33	25	8
University of South Florida				
St. Petersburg	4,587	20	14	6
Tampa	41,116	57	42	15
University of West Florida	12,652	30	21	9
GEORGIA				
Abraham Baldwin Agricultural College	3,233	13	13	0
Albany State University	4,275	32	17	15
Andrew College	292	3	3	0
Armstrong Atlantic State University	7,439	29	20	9
Augusta Technical College	4,339	2	2	0
Bainbridge College	2,942	9	5	4
Berry College	2,166	18	12	6
Clark Atlanta University	3,419	44	15	29
Dalton State College	5,047	16	13	3
Darton State College	6,396	12	11	1
Emory University	14,236	69	49	20
Fort Valley State University	3,568	34	12	22
Georgia College and State University	6,444	22	15	7
Georgia Gwinnett College	9,397	25	20	5
Georgia Institute of Technology	21,557	96	73	23
Georgia Military College[2]		5	3	2
Georgia Perimeter College	23,619	127	45	82
Georgia Regents University	2,506	59	42	17
Georgia Southern University	20,574	46	36	10
Georgia Southwestern State University	2,973	10	9	1
Georgia State University	32,087	151	66	85
Gordon State College	4,171	11	10	1
Gwinnett Technical College	6,682	2	1	1
Kennesaw State University	24,604	69	37	32
Mercer University	8,329	31	22	9
Middle Georgia College	3,104	15	14	1
North Georgia College and State University	6,413	39	31	8
Piedmont College	2,464	3	3	0
Southern Crescent Technical College	5,543	4	3	1
Southern Polytechnic State University	6,202	13	11	2
South Georgia College	2,226	11	7	4
Spelman College	2,145	27	17	10
University of Georgia	34,519	107	85	22
University of West Georgia	11,769	38	27	11
Valdosta State University	12,515	31	23	8
Wesleyan College	715	5	5	0
West Georgia Technical College	6,645	6	6	0
Young Harris College	1,030	4	4	0
ILLINOIS				
Illinois Central College	11,125	21	8	13
Illinois State University	20,706	31	24	7
Joliet Junior College	15,589	23	14	9
Lewis University	6,539	17	9	8
Parkland College	8,679	17	11	6
Rend Lake College	3,815	5	5	0
Southern Illinois University				
Carbondale	18,847	56	37	19
Edwardsville	14,055	56	38	18
School of Medicine[2]		16	7	9
University of Illinois, Springfield	5,048	22	15	7
INDIANA				
Butler University	4,712	28	20	8
Indiana State University	12,114	34	24	10
Indiana University, Southeast	6,904	14	11	3
Marian University	2,580	13	8	5
Purdue University	40,393	55	39	16
IOWA				
Iowa State University	30,748	44	34	10
University of Iowa	30,129	70	41	29
University of Northern Iowa	12,273	25	17	8
KANSAS				
Emporia State University	5,867	9	8	1
Kansas City, Kansas, Community College	7,479	17	16	1
Kansas State University	24,378	40	21	19
Pittsburg State University	7,289	15	13	2

Table 79.   Full-Time Law Enforcement Employees, by Selected State and University or College, 2013— continued

(Number.)

State and university/college	Student enrollment[1]	Law enforcement employees	Officers	Civilians
University of Kansas, Main Campus	27,135	56	27	29
Washburn University	7,204	19	14	5
Wichita State University	14,716	38	25	13
KENTUCKY				
Eastern Kentucky University	15,968	28	21	7
Kentucky State University	2,524	12	8	4
Morehead State University	11,169	25	15	10
Murray State University	10,832	20	15	5
Northern Kentucky University	15,634	22	16	6
University of Louisville	21,239	48	38	10
LOUISIANA				
Delgado Community College	18,096	41	27	14
Louisiana State University				
Baton Rouge	30,225	69	59	10
Health Sciences Center, Shreveport	888	43	30	13
McNeese State University	8,584	13	8	5
Tulane University	12,958	125	82	43
University of New Orleans	10,071	27	27	0
MAINE				
University of Maine				
Farmington	2,179	4	4	0
Orono	10,901	27	19	8
University of Southern Maine	9,382	19	11	8
MARYLAND				
Bowie State University	5,421	27	13	14
Coppin State University	3,612	31	21	10
Frostburg State University	5,421	21	17	4
Hagerstown Community College	5,005	1	1	0
Morgan State University	7,952	56	37	19
Salisbury University	8,657	28	14	14
St. Mary's College	1,933	13	1	12
Towson University	21,960	59	39	20
University of Baltimore	6,558	37	17	20
University of Maryland				
Baltimore City	6,368	142	49	93
Baltimore County	13,637	42	25	17
College Park	37,248	132	87	45
Eastern Shore	4,454	18	14	4
MASSACHUSETTS				
Amherst College	1,817	16	12	4
Assumption College	2,813	28	18	10
Bentley University	5,647	32	21	11
Boston College	14,605	75	53	22
Boston University	32,603	69	53	16
Brandeis University	5,808	29	21	8
Bridgewater State University	11,417	26	21	5
Bristol Community College	9,022	10	6	4
Bunker Hill Community College	13,504	14	13	1
Clark University	3,503	13	11	2
Dean College	1,322	36	32	4
Emerson College	4,531	20	16	4
Fitchburg State University	6,889	18	15	3
Framingham State University	6,506	18	15	3
Hampshire College	1,461	16	12	4
Holyoke Community College	7,164	12	12	0
Lasell College	1,980	34	22	12
Massachusetts College of Art	2,326	30	9	21
Massachusetts College of Liberal Arts	1,799	13	9	4
Massachusetts Institute of Technology	11,189	57	54	3
Massasoit Community College	8,209	16	14	2
Merrimack College	2,694	16	11	5
Mount Holyoke College	2,347	20	14	6
Northeastern University	27,694	89	56	33
North Shore Community College	7,912	25	23	2
Quinsigamond Community College	8,991	14	13	1
Salem State University	9,456	26	22	4
Smith College	3,212	18	14	4
Springfield College	3,284	42	15	27
Tufts University, Medford	10,837	72	40	32
University of Massachusetts				
Amherst	28,236	76	57	19
Dartmouth	9,210	37	24	13
Harbor Campus, Boston	15,874	40	30	10

Table 79.   Full-Time Law Enforcement Employees, by Selected State and University or College, 2013— continued

(Number.)

State and university/college	Student enrollment[1]	Law enforcement employees	Officers	Civilians
Wellesley College	2,482	19	14	5
Wentworth Institute of Technology	4,152	21	14	7
Western New England University	3,802	28	18	10
Westfield State University	6,081	25	19	6
Worcester Polytechnic Institute	5,957	23	17	6
MICHIGAN				
Central Michigan University	27,626	29	22	7
Delta College	10,763	10	7	3
Eastern Michigan University	23,518	41	31	10
Ferris State University	14,533	18	14	4
Grand Rapids Community College	17,448	16	12	4
Grand Valley State University	24,654	20	16	4
Kalamazoo Valley Community College	11,052	8	5	3
Kellogg Community College	6,002	1	1	0
Kirtland Community College	1,807	1	1	0
Lansing Community College	19,082	15	12	3
Macomb Community College	23,729	34	30	4
Michigan State University	48,783	108	75	33
Michigan Technological University	6,933	15	12	3
Mott Community College	9,968	13	9	4
Northern Michigan University	9,159	26	20	6
Oakland Community College	27,296	24	23	1
Oakland University	19,740	27	22	5
Saginaw Valley State University	10,552	13	11	2
University of Michigan				
Ann Arbor	43,426	71	52	19
Dearborn	8,790	26	9	17
Flint	8,289	28	15	13
Western Michigan University	24,598	65	30	35
MINNESOTA				
University of Minnesota				
Duluth	11,491	12	10	2
Morris	1,896	5	3	2
Twin Cities	51,853	63	50	13
MISSISSIPPI				
Coahoma Community College	2,305	10	9	1
Jackson State University	8,819	69	42	27
Mississippi State University	20,365	44	35	9
Northeast Mississippi Community College	3,407	8	8	0
University of Mississippi				
Medical Center	2,147	80	61	19
Oxford	18,794	48	32	16
MISSOURI				
Lincoln University	3,205	15	12	3
Metropolitan Community College	20,141	48	35	13
Mineral Area College	3,784	9	8	1
Missouri Southern State University	5,417	8	7	1
Missouri University of Science and Technology	7,645	19	12	7
Missouri Western State University	6,056	12	10	2
Northwest Missouri State University	6,831	14	12	2
Southeast Missouri State University	11,601	25	17	8
St. Charles Community College	7,642	11	9	2
St. Louis Community College				
Florissant Valley[2]		11	9	2
Meramec	26,603	12	9	3
Three Rivers Community College	4,651	6	5	1
Truman State University	6,237	9	8	1
University of Central Missouri	11,878	22	19	3
University of Missouri				
Columbia	34,704	52	34	18
Kansas City	15,990	41	26	15
St. Louis	16,705	29	23	6
Washington University	13,952	50	29	21
MONTANA				
Montana State University	14,269	34	18	16
NEBRASKA				
Metropolitan Community College	17,376	22	18	4
University of Nebraska				
Kearney	7,199	12	9	3
Lincoln	24,207	60	31	29
Truckee Meadows Community College	11,603	10	7	3

Table 79.   Full-Time Law Enforcement Employees, by Selected State and University or College, 2013— continued

(Number.)

State and university/college	Student enrollment[1]	Law enforcement employees	Officers	Civilians
University of Nevada				
Las Vegas	27,389	49	33	16
Reno	18,227	21	16	5
NEW HAMPSHIRE				
University of New Hampshire	15,267	32	19	13
NEW JERSEY				
Brookdale Community College	14,637	11	11	0
Essex County College	11,979	46	11	35
Kean University	15,391	51	25	26
Middlesex County College	12,898	15	10	5
Monmouth University	6,472	34	17	17
Montclair State University	18,382	46	35	11
New Jersey Institute of Technology	9,944	65	30	35
Princeton University	7,975	90	29	61
Richard Stockton College of New Jersey	8,400	27	17	10
Rowan University	12,183	92	34	58
Rutgers University				
Camden	6,343	73	20	53
Newark	12,011	31	25	6
New Brunswick	40,434	108	60	48
Stevens Institute of Technology	5,649	22	18	4
The College of New Jersey	7,270	26	16	10
William Paterson University	11,423	44	30	14
NEW MEXICO				
Eastern New Mexico University	5,804	9	8	1
New Mexico Institute of Mining and Technology	2,105	24	9	15
New Mexico State University	17,651	32	19	13
University of New Mexico	29,033	1	1	0
NEW YORK				
Cornell University	21,424	75	52	23
Ithaca College	6,759	39	21	18
State University of New York				
Albany	17,312	61	40	21
Binghamton	15,308	45	31	14
Buffalo	28,952	35	33	2
Stony Brook	23,946	146	66	80
Upstate Medical Center	1,635	112	14	98
State University of New York Agricultural and Technical College				
Alfred	3,528	17	12	5
Canton	3,780	10	9	1
Farmingdale	7,889	23	16	7
Morrisville	3,095	13	11	2
State University of New York College				
Brockport	8,271	17	15	2
Buffalo	11,781	35	33	2
Environmental Science and Forestry	2,255	10	9	1
Fredonia	5,521	16	15	1
Geneseo	5,557	19	15	4
New Paltz	7,655	27	23	4
Old Westbury	4,422	23	19	4
Oneonta	6,041	27	17	10
Optometry	336	17	6	11
Plattsburgh	6,167	23	16	7
Potsdam	4,224	14	12	2
Purchase	4,240	31	26	5
Technology	3,151	14	11	3
NORTH CAROLINA				
Appalachian State University	17,589	41	25	16
Beaufort County Community College	1,964	2	2	0
Belmont Abbey College	1,706	5	4	1
Davidson College	1,790	9	7	2
Duke University	15,386	156	57	99
East Carolina University	26,947	67	53	14
Elizabeth City State University	2,878	16	7	9
Elon University	6,029	21	15	6
Fayetteville State University	6,060	33	15	18
Methodist University	2,359	9	8	1
North Carolina Agricultural and Technical State University	10,636	25	21	4
North Carolina Central University	8,604	57	27	30
North Carolina School of the Arts	880	17	12	5
North Carolina State University, Raleigh	34,340	54	40	14

Table 79.   Full-Time Law Enforcement Employees, by Selected State and University or College, 2013— continued

(Number.)

State and university/college	Student enrollment[1]	Law enforcement employees	Officers	Civilians
Queens University	2,394	14	7	7
Saint Augustine's University	1,442	24	7	17
University of North Carolina				
Asheville	3,751	21	14	7
Chapel Hill	29,278	98	50	48
Charlotte	26,232	55	45	10
Greensboro	18,516	50	31	19
Pembroke	6,269	18	14	4
Wilmington	13,733	45	29	16
Wake Forest University	7,432	44	22	22
Western Carolina University	9,608	20	20	0
Winston-Salem State University	5,689	32	15	17
NORTH DAKOTA				
North Dakota State College of Science	3,066	4	3	1
North Dakota State University	14,443	24	15	9
University of North Dakota	15,250	19	16	3
OHIO				
Cuyahoga Community College	29,701	33	25	8
Kent State University	28,602	41	30	11
Lakeland Community College	9,283	14	10	4
Miami University	17,683	32	23	9
Ohio State University				
Columbus	56,387	53	46	7
Mansfield	1,265	5	1	4
Marion	1,273	1	1	0
Newark	2,390	5	1	4
Wooster	612	5	5	0
Ohio University	27,402	31	24	7
Shawnee State University	4,652	9	7	2
University of Cincinnati	33,347	103	47	56
University of Toledo	21,453	45	37	8
Wright State University	16,780	26	20	6
OKLAHOMA				
Cameron University	6,115	13	13	0
East Central University	4,819	5	5	0
Mid-America Christian University	2,606	5	5	0
Northeastern Oklahoma A&M College	2,526	9	8	1
Northeastern State University				
Broken Arrow[2]		7	7	0
Tahlequah	8,721	18	14	4
Oklahoma City University	3,299	18	13	5
Oklahoma State University				
Main Campus	25,708	44	33	11
Okmulgee	3,936	6	6	0
Tulsa	457	9	7	2
Rogers State University	4,774	8	8	0
Seminole State College	2,185	2	2	0
Southeastern Oklahoma State University	4,103	8	7	1
Southwestern Oklahoma State University	5,106	7	6	1
Tulsa Community College	19,557	32	25	7
University of Central Oklahoma	17,211	24	17	7
University of Oklahoma				
Health Sciences Center	3,605	61	43	18
Norman	27,507	70	39	31
PENNSYLVANIA				
Bloomsburg University	9,950	22	16	6
California University	8,608	21	17	4
Cheyney University	1,284	20	12	8
Clarion University	6,520	16	11	5
Dickinson College	2,386	20	14	6
East Stroudsburg University	6,943	19	17	2
Edinboro University	7,462	15	14	1
Indiana University	15,596	30	22	8
Kutztown University	9,804	19	15	4
Lehigh University	7,080	31	22	9
Lock Haven University	5,328	13	11	2
Mansfield University	3,131	12	9	3
Millersville University	8,368	18	16	2
Moravian College	1,910	14	11	3
Pennsylvania State University				
Altoona	3,863	10	8	2
Beaver	759	6	6	0
Behrend	4,149	11	7	4

Table 79.   Full-Time Law Enforcement Employees, by Selected State and University or College, 2013— continued

(Number.)

State and university/college	Student enrollment[1]	Law enforcement employees	Officers	Civilians
Berks	2,747	9	8	1
Harrisburg	4,376	8	7	1
Hazleton	1,060	5	5	0
McKeesport	635	5	5	0
Mont Alto	1,107	5	5	0
Schuylkill	867	5	5	0
University Park	45,783	76	45	31
Shippensburg University	7,724	19	16	3
Slippery Rock University	8,559	20	16	4
University of Pittsburgh				
Bradford	1,518	7	6	1
Greensburg	1,723	9	8	1
Johnstown	2,932	14	13	1
Pittsburgh	28,769	154	93	61
Titusville	388	7	6	1
West Chester University	15,411	22	21	1
RHODE ISLAND				
Brown University	8,885	90	51	39
University of Rhode Island	16,451	31	26	5
SOUTH CAROLINA				
Benedict College	2,917	25	22	3
Bob Jones University	3,469	4	4	0
Clemson University	20,768	40	30	10
Coastal Carolina University	9,335	76	30	46
College of Charleston	11,723	43	32	11
Columbia College	1,257	14	13	1
Denmark Technical College	2,003	11	5	6
Erskine College	751	2	2	0
Francis Marion University	4,093	15	13	2
Furman University	2,915	19	14	5
Lander University	3,049	15	13	2
Medical University of South Carolina	2,731	81	60	21
Midlands Technical College	11,949	6	6	0
Orangeburg-Calhoun Technical College	3,004	5	4	1
South Carolina State University	3,807	27	15	12
Spartanburg Methodist College	811	5	4	1
The Citadel	3,499	17	16	1
Trident Technical College	17,224	29	25	4
University of South Carolina				
Aiken	3,211	8	7	1
Columbia	31,288	87	69	18
Upstate	5,561	16	15	1
Winthrop University	6,170	23	16	7
SOUTH DAKOTA				
South Dakota State University	12,583	18	13	5
TENNESSEE				
Austin Peay State University	10,597	27	16	11
Christian Brothers University	1,603	16	8	8
Cleveland State Community College	3,640	2	2	0
East Tennessee State University	15,133	27	20	7
Jackson State Community College	4,494	3	2	1
Middle Tennessee State University	25,394	48	40	8
Northeast State Community College	6,446	7	7	0
Roane State Community College	6,508	8	6	2
Southwest Tennessee Community College	12,220	26	14	12
Tennessee Technological University	11,469	21	14	7
Tennessee State University	8,740	37	22	15
University of Memphis	22,139	41	37	4
University of Tennessee				
Chattanooga	11,660	25	14	11
Health Science Center[2]		55	26	29
Knoxville	29,833	79	51	28
Martin	7,743	16	12	4
Vanderbilt University	12,710	166	86	80
Volunteer State Community College	8,177	9	7	2
Walters State Community College	6,554	10	8	2
TEXAS				
Abilene Christian University	4,367	15	14	1
Alamo Community College District	58,007	83	62	21
Alvin Community College	5,109	12	10	2
Amarillo College	11,530	14	12	2
Angelo State University	6,888	16	12	4
Austin College	1,260	8	7	1

Table 79.   Full-Time Law Enforcement Employees, by Selected State and University or College, 2013— continued

(Number.)

State and university/college	Student enrollment[1]	Law enforcement employees	Officers	Civilians
Baylor Health Care System[2]		152	51	101
Baylor University, Waco	15,364	36	27	9
Brookhaven College	12,790	29	17	12
Central Texas College	22,443	8	7	1
College of the Mainland	4,010	8	7	1
Eastfield College	14,178	22	21	1
El Paso Community College	32,127	38	33	5
Grayson College	4,903	4	3	1
Hardin-Simmons University	2,301	8	7	1
Houston Baptist University	2,589	13	11	2
Houston Community College	58,476	100	64	36
Lamar University, Beaumont	14,289	46	29	17
Laredo Community College	9,356	23	21	2
McLennan Community College	9,302	15	8	7
Midwestern State University	5,916	15	10	5
Mountain View College	9,068	13	13	0
North Lake College	11,397	23	22	1
Paris Junior College	5,513	4	4	0
Prairie View A&M University	8,336	37	17	20
Rice University	6,484	56	28	28
Richland College	19,552	21	21	0
Southern Methodist University	10,893	34	26	8
South Plains College	9,444	6	6	0
Southwestern University	1,394	7	6	1
Stephen F. Austin State University	12,999	49	27	22
St. Mary's University	3,941	21	17	4
Sul Ross State University	2,680	9	7	2
Tarleton State University	12,524	17	16	1
Texas A&M International University	7,213	28	19	9
Texas A&M University				
College Station	50,627	121	62	59
Commerce	11,871	30	20	10
Corpus Christi	10,508	27	15	12
Galveston	2,014	9	8	1
Kingsville	11,350	19	14	5
San Antonio[2]		13	11	2
Texas Southern University	9,646	65	32	33
Texas State Technical College				
Harlingen	5,509	14	10	4
Waco	4,277	16	14	2
West Texas	810	5	5	0
Texas State University, San Marcos	34,225	43	36	7
Texas Tech University, Lubbock	32,467	83	49	34
Texas Woman's University	15,168	39	17	22
Tyler Junior College	11,374	21	19	2
University of Houston				
Central Campus	40,747	131	42	89
Downtown Campus	13,916	30	17	13
University of Mary Hardin-Baylor	3,287	11	9	2
University of North Texas				
Denton	37,950	74	40	34
Health Science Center	1,949	21	9	12
University of Texas				
Arlington	33,239	123	38	85
Austin	52,186	153	62	91
Brownsville	13,636	33	10	23
Dallas	19,727	52	21	31
El Paso	22,749	55	23	32
Health Science Center, San Antonio	3,249	103	36	67
Health Science Center, Tyler[2]		17	8	9
Houston	4,779	342	89	253
Medical Branch	3,012	97	55	42
Pan American	19,302	41	19	22
Permian Basin	4,021	19	11	8
San Antonio	30,474	104	45	59
Southwestern Medical School	2,424	130	39	91
Tyler	6,858	25	12	13
West Texas A&M University	7,909	18	14	4
UTAH				
Snow College	4,599	2	2	0
University of Utah	32,388	113	32	81
Utah State University				
Eastern[2]		2	1	1
Logan	28,786	17	11	6
Utah Valley University	31,562	11	9	2
Weber State University	26,532	12	11	1

Table 79.   Full-Time Law Enforcement Employees, by Selected State and University or College, 2013— continued

(Number.)

State and university/college	Student enrollment[1]	Law enforcement employees	Officers	Civilians
VERMONT				
University of Vermont	13,098	33	21	12
VIRGINIA				
Christopher Newport University	5,186	24	19	5
College of William and Mary	8,258	27	21	6
Eastern Virginia Medical School	993	49	20	29
Emory and Henry College	945	4	2	2
Ferrum College	1,510	9	9	0
George Mason University	32,961	67	45	22
Hampton University	4,765	54	31	23
James Madison University	19,927	41	31	10
J. Sargeant Reynolds Community College	12,846	23	14	9
Longwood University	4,834	22	15	7
Lord Fairfax Community College	7,288	2	2	0
Norfolk State University	7,100	36	21	15
Northern Virginia Community College	51,864	60	48	12
Old Dominion University	24,670	54	46	8
Radford University	9,573	30	20	10
Richard Bland College	1,532	4	4	0
Thomas Nelson Community College	10,942	13	9	4
University of Mary Washington	5,093	22	16	6
University of Richmond	4,361	33	20	13
University of Virginia	23,907	123	50	73
University of Virginia's College at Wise	2,420	10	9	1
Virginia Commonwealth University	31,445	126	84	42
Virginia Military Institute	1,664	10	9	1
Virginia Polytechnic Institute and State University	31,087	69	49	20
Virginia State University	6,208	35	20	15
Virginia Western Community College	8,440	9	9	0
WASHINGTON				
Central Washington University	11,268	14	13	1
Eastern Washington University	12,587	14	13	1
Evergreen State College	4,509	17	8	9
University of Washington, Pullman	43,485	82	44	38
Washington State University				
Pullman	27,679	22	17	5
Vancouver[2]		4	3	1
Western Washington University	14,833	21	15	6
WEST VIRGINIA				
Bluefield State College	1,935	2	2	0
Concord University	2,834	8	6	2
Fairmont State University	4,451	10	7	3
Glenville State College	1,898	3	3	0
Marshall University	13,708	23	22	1
Potomac State College	1,781	5	4	1
Shepherd University	4,326	10	9	1
West Liberty University	2,804	5	5	0
West Virginia State University	2,644	6	5	1
West Virginia Tech	1,107	7	6	1
West Virginia University	29,707	61	49	12
WISCONSIN				
University of Wisconsin				
Eau Claire	11,067	12	11	1
Green Bay	6,801	13	10	3
La Crosse	10,385	16	11	5
Madison	42,269	126	67	59
Milwaukee	28,712	55	43	12
Oshkosh	13,519	13	11	2
Parkside	4,731	12	8	4
Platteville	8,668	9	8	1
River Falls	6,443	10	7	3
Stevens Point	9,695	8	3	5
Stout	9,283	9	8	1
Superior	2,697	7	2	5
Whitewater	12,028	16	14	2
WYOMING				
Northern Wyoming Community College District	4,236	6	4	2
University of Wyoming	12,903	25	14	11

1 The student enrollment figures provided by the United States Department of Education are for the 2012 school year, the most recent available. The enrollment figures include full-time and part-time students.
2 Student enrollment figures were not available.

Table 80.   Full-Time Law Enforcement Employees, by Selected State Metropolitan and Nonmetropolitan Counties, 2013

(Number.)

State/county	Law enforcement employees	Officers	Civilians
ALABAMA			
Metropolitan Counties			
Autauga	63	25	38
Baldwin	283	102	181
Bibb	10	9	1
Blount	52	48	4
Calhoun	55	50	5
Chilton	58	30	28
Colbert	53	31	22
Elmore	102	50	52
Etowah	155	60	95
Geneva	28	12	16
Hale	12	10	2
Henry	17	13	4
Houston	166	64	102
Jefferson	550	436	114
Lauderdale	43	38	5
Lawrence	52	31	21
Lee	160	70	90
Limestone	106	44	62
Lowndes	34	13	21
Madison	346	113	233
Mobile	484	162	322
Montgomery	175	125	50
Pickens	33	9	24
Russell	114	40	74
St. Clair	50	43	7
Tuscaloosa	172	99	73
Walker	80	30	50
Nonmetropolitan Counties			
Barbour	34	14	20
Bullock	18	6	12
Butler	13	11	2
Cherokee	44	23	21
Choctaw	13	6	7
Clarke	39	12	27
Cleburne	26	10	16
Coffee	2	2	0
Covington	28	25	3
Crenshaw	9	7	2
Cullman	133	74	59
Dale	43	21	22
Dallas	51	25	26
De Kalb	86	34	52
Escambia	63	26	37
Fayette	19	11	8
Greene	31	11	20
Jackson	82	33	49
Marengo	27	11	16
Marshall	84	42	42
Perry	18	8	10
Pike	31	17	14
Sumter	24	7	17
Talladega	102	37	65
Tallapoosa	55	23	32
Wilcox	28	8	20
Winston	31	12	19
ARIZONA			
Metropolitan Counties			
Cochise	164	75	89
Maricopa	3,373	659	2,714
Mohave	266	91	175
Pima	1,466	519	947
Pinal	550	206	344
Yavapai	176	125	51
Yuma	328	84	244
Nonmetropolitan Counties			
Apache	73	29	44
Gila	136	44	92
Graham	80	23	57
Greenlee	39	15	24
La Paz	86	30	56
Santa Cruz	50	38	12

Table 80.   Full-Time Law Enforcement Employees, by Selected State Metropolitan and Nonmetropolitan Counties, 2013— continued

(Number.)

State/county	Law enforcement employees	Officers	Civilians
ARKANSAS			
Metropolitan Counties			
Benton	225	146	79
Cleveland	13	8	5
Craighead	116	38	78
Crawford	65	32	33
Crittenden	152	44	108
Faulkner	157	52	105
Garland	129	106	23
Grant	18	15	3
Jefferson	158	47	111
Lincoln	23	10	13
Little River	24	8	16
Lonoke	59	27	32
Madison	17	9	8
Miller	69	25	44
Perry	20	10	10
Poinsett	44	13	31
Pulaski	498	127	371
Saline	94	42	52
Sebastian	139	33	106
Washington	296	163	133
Nonmetropolitan Counties			
Arkansas	11	10	1
Ashley	46	19	27
Baxter	53	33	20
Boone	55	25	30
Bradley	5	4	1
Calhoun	11	5	6
Carroll	21	18	3
Chicot	8	7	1
Clark	27	13	14
Clay	23	9	14
Cleburne	40	23	17
Columbia	38	20	18
Conway	38	19	19
Cross	39	16	23
Dallas	25	6	19
Desha	8	7	1
Drew	23	10	13
Franklin	20	8	12
Fulton	18	6	12
Greene	52	18	34
Hempstead	50	17	33
Hot Spring	27	25	2
Howard	24	12	12
Independence	78	51	27
Izard	34	20	14
Jackson	23	13	10
Johnson	35	14	21
Lafayette	24	8	16
Lawrence	23	12	11
Lee	10	5	5
Logan	25	12	13
Marion	20	18	2
Mississippi	87	33	54
Monroe	14	3	11
Montgomery	19	11	8
Nevada	16	5	11
Newton	12	7	5
Ouachita	42	17	25
Phillips	24	18	6
Pike	21	8	13
Polk	24	12	12
Pope	38	33	5
Prairie	17	7	10
Randolph	28	10	18
Scott	28	8	20
Searcy	12	6	6
Sevier	32	15	17
Sharp	28	12	16
St. Francis	41	18	23
Stone	19	9	10
Union	59	27	32
Van Buren	38	23	15
White	100	51	49
Woodruff	15	7	8
Yell	27	14	13

Table 80.   Full-Time Law Enforcement Employees, by Selected State Metropolitan and Nonmetropolitan Counties, 2013— continued

(Number.)

State/county	Law enforcement employees	Officers	Civilians
CALIFORNIA			
Metropolitan Counties			
Alameda	1,599	938	661
Butte	299	109	190
Contra Costa	965	654	311
El Dorado	339	156	183
Fresno	1,005	813	192
Imperial	268	182	86
Kern	1,239	942	297
Kings	251	79	172
Los Angeles	16,704	9,186	7,518
Madera	103	71	32
Marin	293	195	98
Merced	225	106	119
Monterey	382	281	101
Napa	133	104	29
Orange	3,663	1,901	1,762
Placer	459	234	225
Riverside	3,897	2,053	1,844
Sacramento	1,850	1,177	673
San Benito	39	17	22
San Bernardino	3,228	1,742	1,486
San Diego	3,954	2,361	1,593
San Francisco	1,012	841	171
San Joaquin	700	276	424
San Luis Obispo	381	153	228
San Mateo	619	320	299
Santa Barbara	606	429	177
Santa Clara	1,572	1,115	457
Santa Cruz	304	135	169
Shasta	220	142	78
Solano	418	109	309
Sonoma	581	228	353
Stanislaus	535	402	133
Sutter	128	105	23
Tulare	729	532	197
Ventura	1,227	757	470
Yolo	242	84	158
Yuba	165	124	41
Nonmetropolitan Counties			
Alpine	18	15	3
Amador	86	42	44
Calaveras	97	55	42
Colusa	67	33	34
Del Norte	53	24	29
Glenn	60	25	35
Humboldt	213	169	44
Inyo	53	34	19
Lake	147	51	96
Lassen	74	55	19
Mariposa	65	52	13
Mendocino	157	120	37
Modoc	28	13	15
Mono	57	28	29
Nevada	160	63	97
Plumas	58	30	28
Sierra	16	10	6
Siskiyou	93	74	19
Tehama	114	81	33
Trinity	40	32	8
Tuolumne	125	61	64
COLORADO			
Metropolitan Counties			
Adams	534	363	171
Arapahoe	511	334	177
Boulder	385	214	171
Clear Creek	63	28	35
Douglas	442	290	152
Elbert	38	31	7
El Paso	780	477	303
Gilpin	51	31	20
Jefferson	784	532	252
Larimer	364	173	191
Mesa	214	97	117
Park	48	42	6
Pueblo	327	245	82

Table 80.   Full-Time Law Enforcement Employees, by Selected State Metropolitan and Nonmetropolitan Counties, 2013— continued

(Number.)

State/county	Law enforcement employees	Officers	Civilians
Teller	75	28	47
Weld	342	265	77
Nonmetropolitan Counties			
Alamosa	41	28	13
Archuleta	31	17	14
Baca	11	4	7
Bent	21	12	9
Chaffee	51	18	33
Cheyenne	6	2	4
Conejos	18	7	11
Costilla	11	6	5
Crowley	17	10	7
Custer	18	8	10
Delta	70	38	32
Dolores	6	4	2
Eagle	65	38	27
Fremont	78	72	6
Garfield	131	97	34
Grand	50	22	28
Gunnison	30	13	17
Hinsdale	5	4	1
Huerfano	24	11	13
Jackson	11	4	7
Kiowa	7	6	1
Kit Carson	29	7	22
Lake	17	10	7
La Plata	135	105	30
Las Animas	37	15	22
Lincoln	24	13	11
Logan	47	24	23
Mineral	4	3	1
Moffat	36	33	3
Montezuma	71	28	43
Montrose	108	49	59
Morgan	55	46	9
Otero	22	20	2
Ouray	7	7	0
Phillips	5	4	1
Pitkin	60	25	35
Rio Blanco	32	13	19
Rio Grande	37	19	18
Routt	50	23	27
Saguache	14	7	7
San Juan	4	3	1
San Miguel	36	17	19
Sedgwick	10	5	5
Summit	71	53	18
Washington	43	33	10
Yuma	18	17	1
DELAWARE			
Metropolitan Counties			
New Castle County Police Department	460	353	107
FLORIDA			
Metropolitan Counties			
Alachua	498	285	213
Baker	145	47	98
Bay	279	213	66
Brevard	1,186	546	640
Broward	2,950	1,506	1,444
Charlotte	367	256	111
Citrus	416	211	205
Clay	527	254	273
Collier	872	555	317
Escambia	641	405	236
Flagler	232	171	61
Gadsden	68	48	20
Gilchrist	53	27	26
Gulf	38	27	11
Hernando	511	325	186
Highlands	315	135	180
Hillsborough	3,215	1,228	1,987
Indian River	447	301	146
Jefferson	60	21	39
Lake	431	272	159
Lee	911	556	355
Leon	398	241	157

Table 80. Full-Time Law Enforcement Employees, by Selected State Metropolitan and Nonmetropolitan Counties, 2013— continued

(Number.)

State/county	Law enforcement employees	Officers	Civilians
Manatee	1,056	481	575
Marion	733	323	410
Martin	394	237	157
Miami-Dade	3,917	2,762	1,155
Nassau	211	146	65
Okaloosa	342	253	89
Orange	1,804	1,219	585
Osceola	594	382	212
Palm Beach	3,265	1,462	1,803
Pasco	848	538	310
Pinellas	1,419	777	642
Sarasota	931	392	539
Seminole	1,156	429	727
St. Johns	381	264	117
St. Lucie	617	253	364
Sumter	262	181	81
Volusia	756	449	307
Wakulla	81	52	29
Walton	241	166	75
Nonmetropolitan Counties			
Bradford	58	37	21
Calhoun	32	17	15
Columbia	162	87	75
DeSoto	112	62	50
Franklin	63	49	14
Glades	121	84	37
Hamilton	61	18	43
Hardee	98	50	48
Hendry	141	70	71
Holmes	35	23	12
Jackson	81	62	19
Lafayette	29	12	17
Levy	135	60	75
Madison	40	36	4
Monroe	495	194	301
Okeechobee	100	67	33
Putnam	172	107	65
Suwannee	105	61	44
Taylor	66	27	39
Union	20	14	6
Washington	75	56	19
GEORGIA			
Metropolitan Counties			
Augusta-Richmond	710	639	71
Barrow	184	128	56
Bartow	257	222	35
Bibb	342	278	64
Brantley	49	18	31
Brooks	51	22	29
Bryan	73	45	28
Butts	82	46	36
Carroll	186	106	80
Catoosa	131	66	65
Chattahoochee	12	7	5
Cherokee	409	345	64
Clarke	168	145	23
Clayton	378	262	116
Clayton County Police Department	405	352	53
Cobb	710	449	261
Cobb County Police Department	633	566	67
Coweta	238	154	84
Dade	43	26	17
Dawson	106	60	46
DeKalb	754	581	173
DeKalb County Police Department	1,151	901	250
Dougherty	234	108	126
Dougherty County Police Department	50	44	6
Douglas	315	281	34
Echols	9	8	1
Effingham	136	78	58
Fayette	215	141	74
Floyd	137	89	48
Floyd County Police Department	78	73	5
Forsyth	325	245	80
Fulton	978	748	230
Glynn County Police Department	127	112	15
Gwinnett County Police Department	958	696	262

Table 80.   Full-Time Law Enforcement Employees, by Selected State Metropolitan and Nonmetropolitan Counties, 2013— continued

(Number.)

State/county	Law enforcement employees	Officers	Civilians
Harris	51	49	2
Heard	42	23	19
Henry	269	250	19
Henry County Police Department	240	209	31
Houston	313	113	200
Jasper	26	15	11
Jones	77	48	29
Lee	79	49	30
Lincoln	34	25	9
Lowndes	236	140	96
Marion	12	12	0
McDuffie	36	18	18
McIntosh	65	42	23
Meriwether	51	28	23
Monroe	95	58	37
Murray	88	57	31
Oconee	88	56	32
Oglethorpe	48	20	28
Paulding	266	230	36
Peach	62	31	31
Pulaski	46	25	21
Spalding	185	98	87
Twiggs	44	24	20
Walton	189	172	17
Worth	34	25	9
Nonmetropolitan Counties			
Ben Hill	62	58	4
Bleckley	42	13	29
Camden	117	67	50
Clinch	19	11	8
Coffee	112	51	61
Cook	50	46	4
Decatur	36	31	5
Dodge	49	20	29
Dooly	75	34	41
Early	51	24	27
Elbert	55	54	1
Emanuel	33	31	2
Fannin	44	42	2
Franklin	60	32	28
Gilmer	96	76	20
Gordon	119	74	45
Habersham	45	41	4
Hancock	51	33	18
Hart	43	27	16
Irwin	21	13	8
Jackson	169	106	63
Jefferson	45	42	3
Laurens	101	59	42
Miller	19	9	10
Mitchell	51	21	30
Pierce	40	39	1
Polk	70	32	38
Polk County Police Department	42	39	3
Putnam	74	41	33
Rabun	53	51	2
Randolph	25	14	11
Schley	8	4	4
Seminole	31	16	15
Stephens	68	35	33
Stewart	10	4	6
Talbot	14	10	4
Thomas	76	41	35
Tift	109	59	50
Treutlen	21	11	10
Troup	79	69	10
Turner	32	16	16
Union	42	38	4
Ware	124	44	80
Warren	14	7	7
Wayne	54	29	25
Webster	5	4	1
White	75	43	32
Wilcox	15	8	7
Wilkes	27	14	13
Wilkinson	28	16	12

Table 80.   Full-Time Law Enforcement Employees, by Selected State Metropolitan and Nonmetropolitan Counties, 2013— continued

(Number.)

State/county	Law enforcement employees	Officers	Civilians
HAWAII			
Metropolitan Counties			
Maui Police Department	462	353	109
Hawaii Police Department	571	435	136
Nonmetropolitan Counties			
Kauai Police Department	192	142	50
IDAHO			
Metropolitan Counties			
Ada	446	139	307
Bannock	66	42	24
Boise	21	11	10
Bonneville	107	65	42
Butte	10	4	6
Canyon	202	106	96
Franklin	14	10	4
Gem	24	13	11
Jefferson	32	19	13
Kootenai	157	92	65
Nez Perce	41	22	19
Owyhee	21	14	7
Nonmetropolitan Counties			
Adams	17	10	7
Bear Lake	12	6	6
Benewah	16	8	8
Bingham	53	35	18
Blaine	25	18	7
Bonner	56	39	17
Boundary	20	10	10
Camas	6	4	2
Caribou	14	7	7
Cassia	54	35	19
Clark	7	3	4
Clearwater	22	15	7
Custer	15	7	8
Elmore	44	22	22
Fremont	27	18	9
Gooding	17	12	5
Idaho	31	20	11
Jerome	23	19	4
Latah	39	26	13
Lemhi	10	9	1
Lewis	10	5	5
Lincoln	9	6	3
Madison	35	22	13
Minidoka	29	18	11
Oneida	13	8	5
Payette	31	16	15
Power	17	9	8
Shoshone	35	15	20
Teton	18	10	8
Twin Falls	69	43	26
Valley	28	16	12
Washington	15	9	6
ILLINOIS			
Metropolitan Counties			
Champaign	59	54	5
De Witt	33	15	18
Ford	27	7	20
Grundy	47	31	16
Jackson	82	27	55
Kane	249	86	163
Kankakee	218	57	161
Kendall	115	53	62
Lake	509	196	313
Macon	134	63	71
Macoupin	48	18	30
Madison	162	80	82
Marshall	18	8	10
McLean	132	53	79
Mercer	36	12	24
Monroe	35	15	20
Rock Island	154	64	90
Sangamon	191	61	130
Tazewell	113	39	74

Table 80.   Full-Time Law Enforcement Employees, by Selected State Metropolitan and Nonmetropolitan Counties, 2013— continued

(Number.)

State/county	Law enforcement employees	Officers	Civilians
Vermilion	44	39	5
Will	598	231	367
Williamson	88	36	52
Winnebago	336	103	233
Nonmetropolitan Counties			
Brown	8	7	1
Clay	16	10	6
Coles	48	24	24
Cumberland	16	6	10
Edgar	17	7	10
Effingham	54	18	36
Fayette	29	11	18
Fulton	40	22	18
Greene	13	6	7
Hardin	7	4	3
Iroquois	24	13	11
Jo Daviess	37	18	19
La Salle	117	40	77
Mason	21	9	12
Massac	26	11	15
McDonough	25	13	12
Morgan	31	14	17
Ogle	69	28	41
Perry	35	13	22
Pike	25	13	12
Scott	6	2	4
Union	13	12	1
INDIANA			
Metropolitan Counties			
Bartholomew	94	40	54
Brown	40	14	26
Delaware	105	41	64
Elkhart	170	62	108
Floyd	101	29	72
Harrison	24	21	3
Hendricks	103	45	58
Johnson	156	115	41
La Porte	156	59	97
Monroe	59	35	24
Newton	37	15	22
Posey	42	12	30
Shelby	86	29	57
Vigo	124	70	54
Warrick	79	38	41
Nonmetropolitan Counties			
Blackford	28	9	19
Cass	59	18	41
Clinton	57	19	38
Crawford	16	7	9
Daviess	63	19	44
Franklin	42	13	29
Gibson	42	17	25
Greene	42	17	25
Henry	59	28	31
Jay	49	11	38
LaGrange	54	18	36
Martin	18	7	11
Montgomery	70	21	49
Parke	51	20	31
Ripley	27	11	16
Steuben	55	21	34
Tipton	31	13	18
Wabash	36	16	20
IOWA			
Metropolitan Counties			
Benton	29	12	17
Black Hawk	131	99	32
Bremer	30	11	19
Dallas	50	23	27
Dubuque	89	76	13
Grundy	16	12	4
Guthrie	10	6	4
Harrison	12	11	1
Johnson	89	67	22
Jones	24	10	14

Table 80.   Full-Time Law Enforcement Employees, by Selected State Metropolitan and Nonmetropolitan Counties, 2013— continued

(Number.)

State/county	Law enforcement employees	Officers	Civilians
Linn	185	119	66
Madison	16	7	9
Mills	20	11	9
Plymouth	29	10	19
Polk	477	127	350
Scott	154	43	111
Story	83	31	52
Warren	33	23	10
Washington	30	17	13
Woodbury	107	36	71
Nonmetropolitan Counties			
Adair	14	5	9
Adams	11	6	5
Allamakee	15	8	7
Appanoose	14	7	7
Audubon	8	4	4
Boone	28	11	17
Buchanan	30	13	17
Buena Vista	33	13	20
Butler	20	11	9
Calhoun	11	6	5
Carroll	15	9	6
Cass	11	8	3
Cedar	36	12	24
Cerro Gordo	71	20	51
Cherokee	18	5	13
Chickasaw	15	8	7
Clarke	18	6	12
Clay	24	10	14
Clinton	42	24	18
Crawford	13	10	3
Davis	12	5	7
Decatur	11	6	5
Delaware	17	13	4
Des Moines	48	20	28
Dickinson	20	9	11
Emmet	17	8	9
Fayette	35	10	25
Floyd	18	11	7
Franklin	10	8	2
Fremont	18	8	10
Greene	16	7	9
Hamilton	28	10	18
Hancock	10	7	3
Hardin	28	10	18
Henry	28	11	17
Howard	14	7	7
Humboldt	14	8	6
Ida	15	7	8
Iowa	27	12	15
Jackson	17	10	7
Jasper	43	13	30
Jefferson	30	10	20
Keokuk	11	6	5
Kossuth	24	9	15
Lee	34	15	19
Louisa	26	10	16
Lucas	12	4	8
Lyon	24	10	14
Mahaska	25	9	16
Marion	35	13	22
Marshall	55	19	36
Mitchell	13	6	7
Monona	18	8	10
Monroe	19	5	14
Montgomery	19	8	11
Muscatine	26	22	4
O'Brien	28	9	19
Osceola	11	7	4
Page	14	8	6
Palo Alto	15	8	7
Pocahontas	17	7	10
Poweshiek	25	11	14
Ringgold	13	6	7
Sac	19	8	11
Shelby	15	9	6
Sioux	39	14	25
Tama	22	13	9

Table 80.   Full-Time Law Enforcement Employees, by Selected State Metropolitan and Nonmetropolitan Counties, 2013— continued

(Number.)

State/county	Law enforcement employees	Officers	Civilians
Union	12	6	6
Van Buren	11	5	6
Wapello	38	10	28
Wayne	15	6	9
Webster	31	16	15
Winneshiek	23	10	13
Worth	24	12	12
Wright	20	8	12
KANSAS			
Metropolitan Counties			
Butler	106	60	46
Douglas	136	79	57
Harvey	39	19	20
Jackson	38	15	23
Jefferson	39	23	16
Johnson	598	465	133
Kingman	20	7	13
Leavenworth	75	55	20
Linn	21	10	11
Miami	41	23	18
Pottawatomie	39	28	11
Riley County Police Department	204	104	100
Sedgwick	505	179	326
Shawnee	188	107	81
Sumner	60	25	35
Wabaunsee	21	7	14
Nonmetropolitan Counties			
Allen	21	8	13
Anderson	30	10	20
Atchison	28	13	15
Bourbon	10	8	2
Brown	23	16	7
Chase	10	5	5
Chautauqua	17	8	9
Cherokee	50	23	27
Cheyenne	5	4	1
Clark	11	6	5
Clay	20	8	12
Cloud	22	8	14
Coffey	34	12	22
Cowley	49	25	24
Crawford	66	29	37
Decatur	3	3	0
Dickinson	31	19	12
Edwards	10	6	4
Elk	9	4	5
Ellsworth	14	7	7
Finney	91	37	54
Franklin	62	27	35
Geary	87	34	53
Gove	5	4	1
Graham	7	3	4
Grant	16	7	9
Gray	17	10	7
Greeley	7	3	4
Greenwood	23	13	10
Hamilton	12	6	6
Haskell	16	11	5
Hodgeman	8	4	4
Jewell	10	6	4
Kearny	21	13	8
Kiowa	18	8	10
Lincoln	8	8	0
Logan	4	3	1
Lyon	85	25	60
Marion	14	8	6
Marshall	19	10	9
McPherson	34	16	18
Meade	17	5	12
Mitchell	20	8	12
Morris	12	7	5
Morton	10	6	4
Nemaha	18	8	10
Neosho	39	17	22
Ness	12	7	5
Norton	10	5	5
Ottawa	18	5	13

Table 80.   Full-Time Law Enforcement Employees, by Selected State Metropolitan and Nonmetropolitan Counties, 2013— continued

(Number.)

State/county	Law enforcement employees	Officers	Civilians
Pawnee	15	8	7
Pratt	14	7	7
Rawlins	8	3	5
Reno	75	50	25
Republic	12	8	4
Rice	7	6	1
Rooks	10	5	5
Rush	12	7	5
Russell	18	11	7
Saline	93	47	46
Scott	9	4	5
Seward	50	16	34
Sheridan	8	3	5
Sherman	11	5	6
Smith	5	5	0
Stafford	9	4	5
Stanton	13	5	8
Thomas	13	4	9
Trego	4	3	1
Wallace	7	3	4
Washington	13	5	8
Wichita	9	4	5
Woodson	13	8	5
KENTUCKY			
Metropolitan Counties			
Allen	16	14	2
Boone	138	131	7
Bourbon	8	7	1
Boyd	35	31	4
Bullitt	54	49	5
Butler	9	6	3
Campbell County Police Department	29	28	1
Clark	17	13	4
Daviess	43	38	5
Edmonson	8	6	2
Grant	14	12	2
Greenup	18	15	3
Henry	8	7	1
Jefferson	253	204	49
Kenton	31	21	10
Kenton County Police Department	33	31	2
Larue	7	6	1
McLean	8	7	1
Meade	14	11	3
Oldham	20	18	2
Pendleton	7	6	1
Scott	33	31	2
Shelby	25	23	2
Trigg	12	9	3
Warren	82	37	45
Woodford	13	9	4
Nonmetropolitan Counties			
Adair	8	6	2
Anderson	17	15	2
Ballard	13	11	2
Barren	21	16	5
Bath	5	4	1
Bell	23	9	14
Boyle	11	10	1
Breathitt	5	2	3
Breckinridge	14	11	3
Caldwell	11	9	2
Calloway	27	13	14
Carlisle	3	2	1
Carroll	4	3	1
Carter	10	7	3
Casey	8	6	2
Clinton	5	4	1
Crittenden	5	4	1
Cumberland	5	4	1
Elliott	4	2	2
Estill	5	4	1
Fleming	8	7	1
Franklin	28	25	3
Fulton	5	4	1
Garrard	9	8	1
Graves	17	14	3

Table 80.   Full-Time Law Enforcement Employees, by Selected State Metropolitan and Nonmetropolitan Counties, 2013— continued

(Number.)

State/county	Law enforcement employees	Officers	Civilians
Grayson	11	8	3
Green	4	4	0
Harrison	10	10	0
Hart	13	9	4
Hickman	3	3	0
Johnson	15	12	3
Knott	10	7	3
Laurel	38	25	13
Lawrence	11	9	2
Lee	2	1	1
Letcher	11	5	6
Lewis	6	4	2
Lincoln	9	7	2
Logan	20	19	1
Lyon	5	5	0
Madison	30	22	8
Marion	9	7	2
Marshall	24	22	2
Mason	14	12	2
McCracken	43	37	6
McCreary	7	6	1
Mercer	10	9	1
Metcalfe	5	4	1
Monroe	4	3	1
Muhlenberg	16	14	2
Nelson	31	24	7
Nicholas	3	2	1
Ohio	27	14	13
Owen	7	5	2
Owsley	3	3	0
Perry	21	11	10
Perry County Police Department	1	1	0
Pike	21	9	12
Rockcastle	4	3	1
Rowan	12	7	5
Taylor	13	10	3
Todd	7	4	3
Union	10	9	1
Washington	8	6	2
Wayne	12	9	3
Webster	8	6	2
Whitley	21	15	6
Wolfe	5	4	1
LOUISIANA			
Metropolitan Counties			
Ascension	300	259	41
Bossier	377	318	59
Caddo	669	439	230
Calcasieu	832	600	232
Cameron	71	63	8
Iberia	302	214	88
Jefferson	1,423	979	444
Livingston	252	252	0
Plaquemines	186	186	0
Pointe Coupee	186	186	0
St. Charles	384	269	115
St. Helena	51	31	20
St. James	101	77	24
St. Tammany	710	442	268
West Feliciana	72	72	0
Nonmetropolitan Counties			
Assumption	104	62	42
Avoyelles	158	158	0
Claiborne	99	38	61
Jefferson Davis	71	57	14
Madison	78	78	0
Sabine	11	10	1
MAINE			
Metropolitan Counties			
Androscoggin	29	19	10
Cumberland	71	60	11
Penobscot	34	29	5
Sagadahoc	21	19	2
York	31	27	4
Nonmetropolitan Counties			

Table 80.   Full-Time Law Enforcement Employees, by Selected State Metropolitan and Nonmetropolitan Counties, 2013— continued

(Number.)

State/county	Law enforcement employees	Officers	Civilians
Aroostook	21	15	6
Franklin	34	22	12
Hancock	18	16	2
Kennebec	24	21	3
Knox	21	20	1
Lincoln	26	24	2
Oxford	28	26	2
Piscataquis	17	7	10
Somerset	17	15	2
Waldo	20	18	2
Washington	11	10	1
MARYLAND			
Metropolitan Counties			
Allegany	30	28	2
Anne Arundel	95	69	26
Anne Arundel County Police Department	884	673	211
Baltimore County	91	78	13
Baltimore County Police Department	2,078	1,827	251
Calvert	145	121	24
Carroll	142	108	34
Cecil	93	81	12
Charles	431	295	136
Frederick	231	168	63
Harford	373	283	90
Howard	67	48	19
Howard County Police Department	637	459	178
Montgomery	166	136	30
Montgomery County Police Department	1,806	1,337	469
Prince George's	317	226	91
Prince George's County Police Department	1,946	1,701	245
Queen Anne's	65	60	5
Somerset	24	21	3
St. Mary's	264	132	132
Washington	241	92	149
Wicomico	106	85	21
Worcester	59	48	11
Nonmetropolitan Counties			
Caroline	32	27	5
Dorchester	40	36	4
Garrett	53	29	24
Kent	23	20	3
Talbot	31	28	3
MICHIGAN			
Metropolitan Counties			
Barry	53	30	23
Bay	76	36	40
Berrien	155	71	84
Calhoun	173	86	87
Cass	70	33	37
Clinton	59	25	34
Eaton	131	67	64
Genesee	237	122	115
Ingham	175	96	79
Jackson	137	57	80
Kalamazoo	216	157	59
Kent	511	192	319
Lapeer	77	46	31
Livingston	70	64	6
Macomb	471	234	237
Midland	61	61	0
Monroe	157	68	89
Montcalm	51	24	27
Muskegon	113	47	66
Oakland	980	811	169
Ottawa	225	128	97
Saginaw	128	66	62
St. Clair	184	76	108
Van Buren	92	58	34
Washtenaw	305	124	181
Wayne	817	722	95
Nonmetropolitan Counties			
Alcona	18	14	4
Alger	11	8	3
Allegan	99	53	46
Alpena	24	12	12

Table 80.   Full-Time Law Enforcement Employees, by Selected State Metropolitan and Nonmetropolitan Counties, 2013— continued

(Number.)

State/county	Law enforcement employees	Officers	Civilians
Antrim	38	30	8
Arenac	22	14	8
Baraga	13	6	7
Benzie	14	13	1
Branch	38	33	5
Charlevoix	35	19	16
Chippewa	20	15	5
Clare	40	34	6
Crawford	25	24	1
Delta	32	18	14
Dickinson	29	12	17
Emmet	46	24	22
Gladwin	40	16	24
Gogebic	22	15	7
Grand Traverse	125	67	58
Gratiot	38	22	16
Hillsdale	36	26	10
Houghton	29	28	1
Huron	21	21	0
Ionia	45	22	23
Iosco	23	4	19
Iron	11	9	2
Isabella	46	20	26
Kalkaska	35	16	19
Keweenaw	8	6	2
Lake	66	16	50
Leelanau	38	19	19
Lenawee	99	40	59
Luce	4	3	1
Mackinac	23	10	13
Manistee	17	15	2
Marquette	56	23	33
Mason	40	37	3
Mecosta	47	22	25
Menominee	32	15	17
Missaukee	2	1	1
Montmorency	29	15	14
Newaygo	68	25	43
Oceana	33	20	13
Ogemaw	17	15	2
Ontonagon	9	9	0
Osceola	21	18	3
Oscoda	16	11	5
Otsego	23	10	13
Presque Isle	12	12	0
Roscommon	52	31	21
Sanilac	62	25	37
Schoolcraft	10	3	7
Shiawassee	69	34	35
St. Joseph	53	26	27
Tuscola	43	23	20
Wexford	56	23	33
MINNESOTA			
Metropolitan Counties			
Anoka	248	128	120
Benton	70	24	46
Blue Earth	84	25	59
Carlton	45	27	18
Carver	144	74	70
Chisago	77	40	37
Clay	67	32	35
Dakota	150	73	77
Dodge	33	22	11
Fillmore	32	19	13
Hennepin	750	337	413
Houston	27	13	14
Isanti	55	20	35
Le Sueur	31	17	14
Mille Lacs	72	28	44
Nicollet	46	18	28
Olmsted	157	64	93
Polk	23	19	4
Ramsey	389	214	175
Scott	121	40	81
Sherburne	256	81	175
Sibley	21	11	10
Stearns	181	64	117
St. Louis	238	98	140

Table 80.   Full-Time Law Enforcement Employees, by Selected State Metropolitan and Nonmetropolitan Counties, 2013— continued

(Number.)

State/county	Law enforcement employees	Officers	Civilians
Wabasha	29	17	12
Washington	230	93	137
Wright	231	137	94
Nonmetropolitan Counties			
Aitkin	49	18	31
Becker	54	19	35
Beltrami	63	29	34
Big Stone	8	5	3
Brown	35	9	26
Cass	67	38	29
Chippewa	18	8	10
Clearwater	22	9	13
Cook	20	13	7
Cottonwood	20	9	11
Crow Wing	123	39	84
Douglas	75	27	48
Faribault	25	10	15
Freeborn	65	22	43
Goodhue	99	39	60
Grant	11	6	5
Hubbard	43	16	27
Itasca	71	36	35
Jackson	27	14	13
Kanabec	46	18	28
Kandiyohi	100	33	67
Kittson	10	5	5
Koochiching	18	10	8
Lac Qui Parle	7	7	0
Lake	29	17	12
Lake of the Woods	11	5	6
Lincoln	12	6	6
Lyon	50	16	34
Mahnomen	19	12	7
Marshall	23	13	10
Martin	28	12	16
McLeod	57	23	34
Meeker	44	20	24
Morrison	48	17	31
Mower	69	22	47
Murray	15	9	6
Nobles	34	12	22
Norman	8	5	3
Otter Tail	76	32	44
Pennington	27	7	20
Pine	78	33	45
Pipestone	21	11	10
Pope	17	8	9
Red Lake	10	6	4
Redwood	23	12	11
Renville	29	13	16
Rice	51	25	26
Rock	15	10	5
Roseau	19	8	11
Steele	24	19	5
Stevens	14	6	8
Swift	16	9	7
Todd	29	14	15
Traverse	12	5	7
Wadena	21	9	12
Waseca	27	11	16
Watonwan	14	7	7
Wilkin	16	6	10
Winona	59	20	39
Yellow Medicine	21	10	11
MISSISSIPPI			
Metropolitan Counties			
Hinds	440	117	323
Hancock	68	60	8
Lamar	77	39	38
Rankin	193	83	110
Tunica	129	78	51
Nonmetropolitan Counties			
Adams	67	34	33
Claiborne	24	11	13
Clay	39	12	27
Franklin	8	4	4

Table 80.   Full-Time Law Enforcement Employees, by Selected State Metropolitan and Nonmetropolitan Counties, 2013— continued

(Number.)

State/county	Law enforcement employees	Officers	Civilians
Itawamba	23	12	11
Jefferson	58	9	49
Jones	90	45	45
Kemper	17	11	6
Lee	126	44	82
Marion	20	17	3
Panola	77	39	38
Pike	65	34	31
Prentiss	33	15	18
Warren	59	37	22
Washington	51	37	14
MISSOURI			
Metropolitan Counties			
Andrew	27	17	10
Bates	48	21	27
Bollinger	15	10	5
Boone	71	58	13
Buchanan	107	76	31
Caldwell	15	9	6
Callaway	25	22	3
Cape Girardeau	72	43	29
Cass	91	72	19
Christian	76	54	22
Clay	179	115	64
Clinton	21	15	6
Cole	52	42	10
Dallas	17	14	3
De Kalb	12	6	6
Franklin	127	104	23
Greene	310	164	146
Jackson	125	91	34
Jasper	131	92	39
Jefferson	216	145	71
Lafayette	41	38	3
Lincoln	79	46	33
McDonald	28	23	5
Moniteau	24	10	14
Newton	67	34	33
Osage	13	10	3
Platte	125	86	39
Polk	29	18	11
Ray	31	14	17
St. Charles	226	154	72
St. Louis County Police Department	1,066	819	247
Warren	57	37	20
Webster	24	14	10
Nonmetropolitan Counties			
Adair	23	11	12
Atchison	10	5	5
Audrain	40	31	9
Barry	34	20	14
Benton	23	16	7
Butler	40	17	23
Camden	107	68	39
Carroll	9	8	1
Carter	9	5	4
Cedar	21	11	10
Chariton	14	10	4
Clark	12	6	6
Cooper	9	8	1
Crawford	36	24	12
Dade	7	6	1
Daviess	6	5	1
Dent	17	13	4
Douglas	9	5	4
Dunklin	17	10	7
Gasconade	13	12	1
Gentry	5	5	0
Grundy	15	5	10
Harrison	16	5	11
Henry	37	23	14
Hickory	15	10	5
Holt	8	5	3
Howard	11	6	5
Howell	31	24	7
Iron	14	8	6
Johnson	65	40	25

Table 80.   Full-Time Law Enforcement Employees, by Selected State Metropolitan and Nonmetropolitan Counties, 2013— continued

(Number.)

State/county	Law enforcement employees	Officers	Civilians
Knox	4	3	1
Laclede	25	24	1
Lawrence	38	28	10
Lewis	11	6	5
Linn	7	6	1
Livingston	8	8	0
Macon	14	12	2
Maries	10	9	1
Marion	38	16	22
Mercer	8	3	5
Miller	35	16	19
Mississippi	39	9	30
Monroe	8	7	1
Montgomery	17	15	2
Morgan	44	27	17
New Madrid	27	11	16
Nodaway	13	11	2
Oregon	10	6	4
Ozark	16	9	7
Pemiscot	37	14	23
Perry	36	24	12
Pettis	43	19	24
Phelps	62	22	40
Pike	30	11	19
Pulaski	26	15	11
Putnam	4	3	1
Ralls	9	8	1
Randolph	33	16	17
Reynolds	10	9	1
Ripley	9	8	1
Saline	34	21	13
Schuyler	8	3	5
Scotland	5	2	3
Scott	44	21	23
Shannon	7	3	4
Shelby	10	5	5
St. Clair	65	20	45
Ste. Genevieve	52	38	14
St. Francois	67	55	12
Stoddard	24	12	12
Stone	64	50	14
Sullivan	5	4	1
Taney	53	38	15
Texas	25	9	16
Vernon	26	17	9
Washington	30	20	10
Wayne	18	7	11
Worth	4	3	1
Wright	13	6	7
MONTANA			
Metropolitan Counties			
Carbon	16	9	7
Cascade	52	33	19
Golden Valley	2	2	0
Missoula	161	47	114
Yellowstone	130	46	84
Nonmetropolitan Counties			
Blaine	12	7	5
Broadwater	22	9	13
Carter	3	3	0
Chouteau	20	10	10
Custer	8	6	2
Daniels	5	2	3
Dawson	12	6	6
Deer Lodge	19	19	0
Fallon	11	4	7
Fergus	21	9	12
Flathead	110	54	56
Gallatin	63	52	11
Garfield	2	2	0
Glacier	20	13	7
Granite	11	5	6
Hill	18	12	6
Jefferson	20	12	8
Judith Basin	6	5	1
Lake	37	23	14
Lewis and Clark	76	44	32

Table 80.   Full-Time Law Enforcement Employees, by Selected State Metropolitan and Nonmetropolitan Counties, 2013— continued

(Number.)

State/county	Law enforcement employees	Officers	Civilians
Liberty	10	4	6
Madison	21	10	11
McCone	6	4	2
Meagher	8	4	4
Mineral	13	8	5
Musselshell	8	7	1
Park	21	13	8
Phillips	11	7	4
Pondera	9	8	1
Powder River	6	2	4
Powell	10	5	5
Prairie	3	3	0
Ravalli	70	29	41
Richland	17	8	9
Roosevelt	17	14	3
Rosebud	18	12	6
Sanders	23	11	12
Sheridan	7	6	1
Silver Bow	95	48	47
Stillwater	15	9	6
Sweet Grass	13	7	6
Teton	12	9	3
Treasure	2	2	0
Valley	12	7	5
Wheatland	7	6	1
Wibaux	2	2	0
NEBRASKA			
Metropolitan Counties			
Cass	36	20	16
Dakota	17	15	2
Dixon	14	7	7
Douglas	196	123	73
Hall	39	31	8
Hamilton	21	9	12
Howard	12	5	7
Lancaster	100	82	18
Merrick	11	7	4
Sarpy	198	130	68
Saunders	20	11	9
Nonmetropolitan Counties			
Adams	31	18	13
Antelope	13	4	9
Arthur	1	1	0
Banner	1	1	0
Boone	13	5	8
Box Butte	17	5	12
Boyd	3	3	0
Brown	9	5	4
Buffalo	45	26	19
Burt	4	4	0
Butler	24	10	14
Cedar	5	5	0
Chase	8	4	4
Cheyenne	19	10	9
Clay	10	6	4
Colfax	17	8	9
Cuming	6	5	1
Custer	7	6	1
Dawes	13	7	6
Dawson	67	33	34
Deuel	5	4	1
Dodge	24	21	3
Dundy	8	4	4
Fillmore	11	6	5
Franklin	7	3	4
Frontier	7	4	3
Furnas	13	7	6
Gage	17	14	3
Garden	10	4	6
Gosper	5	4	1
Greeley	3	2	1
Harlan	8	4	4
Hayes	1	1	0
Hitchcock	8	4	4
Holt	12	5	7
Hooker	2	2	0
Jefferson	16	8	8

Table 80.   Full-Time Law Enforcement Employees, by Selected State Metropolitan and Nonmetropolitan Counties, 2013— continued

(Number.)

State/county	Law enforcement employees	Officers	Civilians
Johnson	12	6	6
Keith	13	6	7
Keya Paha	1	1	0
Lincoln	61	24	37
Logan	2	2	0
Loup	1	1	0
Madison	56	31	25
McPherson	1	1	0
Morrill	9	4	5
Nance	11	7	4
Nemaha	10	9	1
Nuckolls	7	4	3
Otoe	25	14	11
Pawnee	5	4	1
Perkins	9	4	5
Phelps	8	6	2
Pierce	7	4	3
Platte	69	21	48
Polk	12	7	5
Red Willow	8	7	1
Richardson	10	6	4
Rock	7	3	4
Saline	14	14	0
Scotts Bluff	23	17	6
Sheridan	7	6	1
Sherman	6	5	1
Stanton	8	7	1
Thayer	11	7	4
Thomas	1	1	0
Thurston	16	8	8
Valley	9	4	5
Wayne	6	5	1
Webster	9	6	3
Wheeler	1	1	0
York	24	10	14
NEVADA			
Metropolitan Counties			
Carson City	125	92	33
Storey	23	22	1
Washoe	680	416	264
Nonmetropolitan Counties			
Churchill	44	36	8
Douglas	114	101	13
Elko	72	56	16
Esmeralda	49	10	39
Eureka	21	13	8
Humboldt	54	36	18
Lander	29	19	10
Lincoln	31	26	5
Lyon	98	72	26
Mineral	22	16	6
Nye	136	99	37
Pershing	20	13	7
White Pine	32	27	5
NEW HAMPSHIRE			
Metropolitan Counties			
Rockingham	49	25	24
Nonmetropolitan Counties			
Carroll	25	13	12
Cheshire	22	10	12
Merrimack	33	20	13
NEW JERSEY			
Metropolitan Counties			
Atlantic	131	107	24
Bergen County Police Department	180	88	92
Burlington	85	70	15
Camden County Police Department	441	418	23
Cape May	163	132	31
Cumberland	61	55	6
Essex	397	303	94
Gloucester	102	86	16
Hudson	322	234	88
Mercer	185	148	37
Middlesex	225	187	38

Table 80.   Full-Time Law Enforcement Employees, by Selected State Metropolitan and Nonmetropolitan Counties, 2013— continued

(Number.)

State/county	Law enforcement employees	Officers	Civilians
Monmouth	589	424	165
Morris	113	82	31
Ocean	247	131	116
Salem	202	164	38
Somerset	206	167	39
Union	202	162	40
Warren	22	18	4
NEW MEXICO			
Nonmetropolitan Counties			
Cibola	23	17	6
Curry	26	17	9
Hidalgo	11	9	2
Lincoln	27	18	9
Luna	39	34	5
Otero	65	47	18
Quay	8	7	1
Socorro	13	7	6
Taos	39	22	17
NEW YORK			
Metropolitan Counties			
Albany	165	120	45
Chemung	47	43	4
Dutchess	128	98	30
Erie	180	140	40
Herkimer	14	4	10
Jefferson	50	41	9
Livingston	72	48	24
Monroe	330	273	57
Nassau	2,977	2,200	777
Niagara	145	107	38
Oneida	106	85	21
Orleans	40	27	13
Oswego	82	66	16
Putnam	96	79	17
Rensselaer	39	33	6
Saratoga	152	110	42
Schenectady	16	10	6
Schoharie	28	16	12
Suffolk	381	263	118
Suffolk County Police Department	2,906	2,352	554
Tioga	52	33	19
Tompkins	47	41	6
Ulster	59	56	3
Washington	46	35	11
Wayne	61	53	8
Westchester Public Safety	337	266	71
Yates	47	25	22
Nonmetropolitan Counties			
Allegany	46	27	19
Cattaraugus	90	68	22
Cayuga	43	39	4
Chautauqua	107	60	47
Chenango	37	23	14
Clinton	24	24	0
Cortland	37	34	3
Delaware	30	17	13
Fulton	38	24	14
Genesee	77	48	29
Hamilton	6	5	1
Lewis	28	18	10
Montgomery	97	76	21
Otsego	18	16	2
Schuyler	20	17	3
Seneca	42	30	12
St. Lawrence	34	33	1
NORTH CAROLINA			
Metropolitan Counties			
Alamance	277	121	156
Alexander	75	39	36
Brunswick	250	156	94
Buncombe	392	247	145
Burke	114	86	28
Cabarrus	324	187	137
Caldwell	106	66	40
Catawba	188	139	49

Table 80.   Full-Time Law Enforcement Employees, by Selected State Metropolitan and Nonmetropolitan Counties, 2013— continued

(Number.)

State/county	Law enforcement employees	Officers	Civilians
Chatham	112	83	29
Craven	129	72	57
Cumberland	588	300	288
Currituck	101	64	37
Davidson	190	126	64
Davie	82	51	31
Durham	453	175	278
Edgecombe	131	50	81
Forsyth	486	203	283
Franklin	103	65	38
Gaston	214	124	90
Gaston County Police Department	220	126	94
Gates	13	12	1
Guilford	630	255	375
Haywood	94	52	42
Henderson	195	135	60
Hoke	111	59	52
Iredell	240	172	68
Johnston	184	106	78
Jones	26	16	10
Lincoln	155	103	52
Madison	43	24	19
Mecklenburg[1]	1,183	313	870
Nash	132	76	56
New Hanover	455	337	118
Orange	139	105	34
Pamlico	40	19	21
Pender	109	63	46
Person	84	46	38
Pitt	280	125	155
Randolph	219	163	56
Rockingham	143	97	46
Rowan	189	127	62
Stokes	67	47	20
Union	262	187	75
Wake	926	372	554
Wayne	151	90	61
Yadkin	65	31	34
Nonmetropolitan Counties			
Alleghany	26	10	16
Anson	62	32	30
Ashe	62	31	31
Avery	49	26	23
Beaufort	86	52	34
Bertie	38	25	13
Bladen	71	46	25
Camden	20	18	2
Carteret	86	50	36
Caswell	54	36	18
Cherokee	64	26	38
Chowan	36	16	20
Clay	43	16	27
Cleveland	164	90	74
Columbus	111	71	40
Dare	142	62	80
Duplin	98	73	25
Graham	18	16	2
Granville	102	51	51
Greene	49	23	26
Halifax	90	62	28
Harnett	220	121	99
Hertford	29	23	6
Hyde	20	15	5
Jackson	72	48	24
Lee	97	60	37
Lenoir	131	67	64
Macon	70	50	20
Martin	37	35	2
McDowell	62	42	20
Mitchell	18	17	1
Montgomery	55	30	25
Moore	123	75	48
Northampton	52	28	24
Pasquotank	48	42	6
Perquimans	15	12	3
Polk	40	30	10
Richmond	89	53	36
Robeson	233	133	100

Table 80.   Full-Time Law Enforcement Employees, by Selected State Metropolitan and Nonmetropolitan Counties, 2013— continued

(Number.)

State/county	Law enforcement employees	Officers	Civilians
Rutherford	128	77	51
Sampson	124	95	29
Scotland	65	37	28
Stanly	86	50	36
Surry	100	71	29
Swain	47	25	22
Transylvania	75	58	17
Tyrrell	16	10	6
Vance	65	37	28
Warren	65	37	28
Washington	45	21	24
Watauga	45	42	3
Wilkes	116	72	44
Wilson	138	86	52
Yancey	36	21	15
NORTH DAKOTA			
Metropolitan Counties			
Burleigh	95	49	46
Cass	151	98	53
Grand Forks	38	31	7
Morton	41	24	17
Oliver	5	4	1
Sioux	1	1	0
Nonmetropolitan Counties			
Adams	5	4	1
Barnes	8	7	1
Benson	4	4	0
Billings	5	5	0
Bottineau	14	10	4
Bowman	5	4	1
Burke	8	7	1
Cavalier	11	5	6
Dickey	5	4	1
Divide	8	8	0
Dunn	14	13	1
Eddy	6	6	0
Emmons	6	5	1
Foster	3	3	0
Golden Valley	6	5	1
Grant	4	4	0
Griggs	5	4	1
Hettinger	4	4	0
Kidder	4	3	1
Lamoure	5	4	1
Logan	2	2	0
McHenry	7	7	0
McIntosh	3	3	0
McKenzie	26	14	12
McLean	36	20	16
Mercer	27	15	12
Mountrail	22	11	11
Nelson	6	5	1
Pembina	12	7	5
Pierce	7	3	4
Ramsey	7	6	1
Ransom	5	4	1
Renville	6	6	0
Richland	25	13	12
Rolette	18	9	9
Sargent	5	4	1
Sheridan	2	2	0
Slope	1	1	0
Stark	25	21	4
Steele	4	3	1
Stutsman	11	9	2
Towner	3	3	0
Traill	13	8	5
Walsh	16	10	6
Ward	60	27	33
Wells	3	3	0
Williams	59	33	26
OHIO			
Metropolitan Counties			
Allen	146	68	78
Carroll	27	20	7
Delaware	204	90	114

Table 80. Full-Time Law Enforcement Employees, by Selected State Metropolitan and Nonmetropolitan Counties, 2013— continued

(Number.)

State/county	Law enforcement employees	Officers	Civilians
Licking	190	99	91
Mahoning	232	218	14
Morrow	40	22	18
Pickaway	87	32	55
Stark	232	124	108
Union	53	34	19
Nonmetropolitan Counties			
Ashland	67	39	28
Ashtabula	70	31	39
Coshocton	52	41	11
Crawford	60	23	37
Fayette	38	23	15
Holmes	50	35	15
Knox	59	53	6
Mercer	56	24	32
Monroe	21	14	7
Morgan	14	9	5
Muskingum	106	70	36
Ottawa	61	41	20
Putnam	50	29	21
Washington	83	44	39
OKLAHOMA			
Metropolitan Counties			
Canadian	90	55	35
Cleveland	188	72	116
Comanche	40	29	11
Cotton	10	4	6
Creek	39	34	5
Grady	22	20	2
Le Flore	20	14	6
Lincoln	36	15	21
Logan	35	24	11
McClain	29	19	10
Oklahoma	720	254	466
Okmulgee	14	13	1
Osage	85	46	39
Pawnee	26	10	16
Rogers	43	37	6
Sequoyah	44	18	26
Tulsa	589	276	313
Wagoner	53	27	26
Nonmetropolitan Counties			
Adair	11	11	0
Alfalfa	10	5	5
Atoka	24	9	15
Beaver	12	7	5
Beckham	40	14	26
Blaine	17	8	9
Bryan	19	16	3
Caddo	38	18	20
Carter	58	19	39
Cherokee	32	23	9
Choctaw	15	6	9
Cimarron	10	4	6
Coal	9	9	0
Craig	25	10	15
Custer	40	13	27
Delaware	37	17	20
Dewey	14	7	7
Ellis	17	7	10
Garfield	66	25	41
Garvin	33	22	11
Grant	10	5	5
Greer	6	2	4
Harmon	4	3	1
Harper	8	5	3
Haskell	20	8	12
Hughes	13	6	7
Jackson	37	14	23
Jefferson	34	5	29
Johnston	29	8	21
Kay	22	15	7
Kingfisher	17	8	9
Kiowa	13	2	11
Latimer	16	8	8
Love	21	8	13

Table 80.   Full-Time Law Enforcement Employees, by Selected State Metropolitan and Nonmetropolitan Counties, 2013— continued

(Number.)

State/county	Law enforcement employees	Officers	Civilians
Major	11	5	6
Marshall	25	7	18
Mayes	49	22	27
McCurtain	20	15	5
McIntosh	47	12	35
Murray	10	10	0
Muskogee	107	43	64
Noble	21	6	15
Nowata	19	7	12
Okfuskee	16	5	11
Ottawa	39	14	25
Payne	95	38	57
Pittsburg	83	17	66
Pontotoc	41	15	26
Pottawatomie	27	23	4
Pushmataha	14	7	7
Roger Mills	12	7	5
Seminole	39	17	22
Stephens	65	20	45
Texas	40	13	27
Tillman	28	4	24
Washington	56	29	27
Washita	30	9	21
Woods	7	6	1
Woodward	35	11	24
OREGON			
Metropolitan Counties			
Benton	78	64	14
Clackamas	437	225	212
Columbia	14	11	3
Deschutes	210	82	128
Jackson	166	108	58
Josephine	38	8	30
Lane	269	58	211
Linn	165	50	115
Marion	339	91	248
Multnomah	746	116	630
Polk	52	18	34
Washington	539	237	302
Yamhill	96	45	51
Nonmetropolitan Counties			
Baker	24	11	13
Clatsop	52	25	27
Coos	91	28	63
Crook	29	17	12
Curry	34	12	22
Douglas	144	112	32
Gilliam	7	6	1
Grant	17	5	12
Harney	20	14	6
Hood River	27	16	11
Jefferson	34	15	19
Klamath	68	27	41
Lake	21	8	13
Lincoln	87	27	60
Malheur	62	19	43
Morrow	29	14	15
Sherman	9	8	1
Tillamook	55	26	29
Umatilla	74	49	25
Union	32	16	16
Wallowa	13	7	6
Wasco	29	16	13
Wheeler	4	3	1
PENNSYLVANIA			
Metropolitan Counties			
Adams	13	11	2
Allegheny	187	155	32
Allegheny County Police Department	253	200	53
Beaver	33	25	8
Berks	109	95	14
Blair	29	25	4
Bucks	69	52	17
Butler	23	20	3
Centre	17	14	3
Cumberland	34	28	6

Table 80.   Full-Time Law Enforcement Employees, by Selected State Metropolitan and Nonmetropolitan Counties, 2013— continued

(Number.)

State/county	Law enforcement employees	Officers	Civilians
Erie	44	37	7
Franklin	22	18	4
Lancaster	61	52	9
Lycoming	17	12	5
Mercer	19	16	3
Monroe	43	22	21
Montgomery	128	106	22
Northampton	57	53	4
Pike	21	17	4
Washington	29	26	3
Westmoreland	61	53	8
Wyoming	4	3	1
York	122	112	10
Nonmetropolitan Counties			
Bedford	10	8	2
Bradford	11	9	2
Clarion	11	8	3
Clearfield	12	8	4
Elk	6	5	1
Greene	6	5	1
Indiana	19	16	3
Jefferson	8	7	1
Lawrence	18	14	4
Northumberland	8	6	2
Schuylkill	19	15	4
Snyder	5	5	0
Tioga	9	7	2
Union	9	8	1
Warren	11	9	2
Wayne	15	12	3
SOUTH CAROLINA			
Metropolitan Counties			
Aiken	233	131	102
Anderson	376	227	149
Beaufort	261	235	26
Berkeley	203	132	71
Calhoun	30	28	2
Charleston	772	266	506
Chester	99	54	45
Darlington	129	71	58
Dorchester	174	136	38
Edgefield	65	38	27
Fairfield	53	48	5
Florence	227	188	39
Greenville	513	425	88
Horry County Police Department	247	228	19
Jasper	36	31	5
Kershaw	68	60	8
Lancaster	131	112	19
Laurens	137	130	7
Lexington	419	262	157
Pickens	134	112	22
Richland	576	535	41
Saluda	10	9	1
Spartanburg	336	307	29
Sumter	140	124	16
Union	34	31	3
York	349	181	168
Nonmetropolitan Counties			
Abbeville	32	30	2
Allendale	15	13	2
Bamberg	16	13	3
Barnwell	41	26	15
Cherokee	59	50	9
Clarendon	47	43	4
Colleton	125	60	65
Dillon	47	43	4
Georgetown	153	94	59
Greenwood	119	67	52
Hampton	34	31	3
Lee	29	25	4
Marion	42	39	3
Marlboro	31	26	5
McCormick	20	15	5
Newberry	85	47	38
Oconee	145	85	60

Table 80.   Full-Time Law Enforcement Employees, by Selected State Metropolitan and Nonmetropolitan Counties, 2013— continued

(Number.)

State/county	Law enforcement employees	Officers	Civilians
Orangeburg	108	89	19
Williamsburg	39	35	4
SOUTH DAKOTA			
Metropolitan Counties			
Custer	12	11	1
Lincoln	18	16	2
McCook	7	6	1
Meade	54	17	37
Minnehaha	209	77	132
Pennington	332	82	250
Turner	10	8	2
Union	33	8	25
Nonmetropolitan Counties			
Aurora	4	3	1
Beadle	28	6	22
Bennett	4	3	1
Bon Homme	8	3	5
Brookings	21	13	8
Brown	50	16	34
Brule	9	4	5
Buffalo	1	1	0
Butte	15	4	11
Campbell	2	2	0
Charles Mix	20	6	14
Clark	3	3	0
Clay	11	7	4
Codington	27	9	18
Corson	5	4	1
Davison	7	5	2
Day	6	3	3
Deuel	7	3	4
Dewey	4	3	1
Douglas	3	3	0
Edmunds	7	4	3
Fall River	8	6	2
Faulk	9	4	5
Grant	10	4	6
Gregory	3	2	1
Haakon	2	2	0
Hamlin	5	4	1
Hand	3	2	1
Hanson	2	2	0
Harding	3	2	1
Hughes	47	6	41
Hutchinson	3	3	0
Hyde	2	2	0
Jackson	2	2	0
Jerauld	4	3	1
Jones	2	2	0
Kingsbury	6	5	1
Lake	12	5	7
Lawrence	38	13	25
Lyman	5	4	1
Marshall	11	6	5
McPherson	2	2	0
Mellette	4	4	0
Miner	4	3	1
Moody	8	4	4
Perkins	7	6	1
Potter	3	2	1
Roberts	34	6	28
Sanborn	3	3	0
Shannon	1	1	0
Spink	12	7	5
Stanley	6	5	1
Sully	3	3	0
Todd	2	1	1
Tripp	4	4	0
Walworth	3	3	0
Yankton	30	13	17
Ziebach	2	2	0
TENNESSEE			
Metropolitan Counties			
Anderson	169	60	109
Blount	261	136	125
Bradley	200	97	103

Table 80.   Full-Time Law Enforcement Employees, by Selected State Metropolitan and Nonmetropolitan Counties, 2013— continued

(Number.)

State/county	Law enforcement employees	Officers	Civilians
Campbell	70	38	32
Cannon	37	17	20
Carter	111	49	62
Cheatham	71	37	34
Chester	39	13	26
Crockett	33	15	18
Dickson	147	65	82
Fayette	87	40	47
Grainger	45	22	23
Hamblen	87	33	54
Hamilton	369	158	211
Hartsville-Trousdale	42	19	23
Hawkins	104	60	44
Hickman	37	18	19
Jefferson	101	49	52
Knox	1,117	458	659
Loudon	82	49	33
Macon	59	30	29
Madison	231	78	153
Marion	47	20	27
Maury	152	83	69
Montgomery	336	90	246
Morgan	45	20	25
Polk	51	19	32
Roane	63	33	30
Robertson	151	44	107
Rutherford	417	210	207
Sequatchie	43	22	21
Shelby	1,913	583	1,330
Smith	58	26	32
Sullivan	255	114	141
Sumner	274	87	187
Tipton	97	55	42
Unicoi	42	30	12
Union	42	25	17
Washington	215	96	119
Williamson	252	147	105
Wilson	255	102	153
Nonmetropolitan Counties			
Bedford	80	35	45
Benton	60	19	41
Bledsoe	38	13	25
Carroll	61	24	37
Claiborne	93	35	58
Clay	24	16	8
Cocke	69	37	32
Coffee	89	44	45
Cumberland	106	46	60
Decatur	33	16	17
DeKalb	46	25	21
Dyer	80	32	48
Fentress	36	22	14
Franklin	48	41	7
Gibson	64	28	36
Giles	65	29	36
Greene	153	59	94
Grundy	33	14	19
Hancock	32	12	20
Hardeman	69	26	43
Hardin	47	22	25
Haywood	51	23	28
Henderson	68	30	38
Henry	63	32	31
Houston	23	12	11
Humphreys	35	20	15
Jackson	45	14	31
Johnson	46	16	30
Lake	18	7	11
Lauderdale	71	22	49
Lawrence	87	43	44
Lewis	32	16	16
Lincoln	63	27	36
Marshall	51	25	26
McMinn	74	33	41
McNairy	37	18	19
Meigs	32	16	16
Monroe	72	43	29
Moore	28	14	14

Table 80.   Full-Time Law Enforcement Employees, by Selected State Metropolitan and Nonmetropolitan Counties, 2013— continued

(Number.)

State/county	Law enforcement employees	Officers	Civilians
Obion	62	26	36
Overton	54	21	33
Perry	36	16	20
Pickett	15	9	6
Putnam	138	64	74
Rhea	54	53	1
Scott	68	30	38
Sevier	228	99	129
Stewart	43	20	23
Van Buren	17	9	8
Warren	82	40	42
Wayne	45	15	30
Weakley	42	21	21
White	65	29	36
TEXAS			
Metropolitan Counties			
Aransas	69	25	44
Archer	18	9	9
Armstrong	8	4	4
Atascosa	84	31	53
Austin	63	42	21
Bandera	66	31	35
Bastrop	194	75	119
Bell	259	91	168
Bexar	1,688	537	1,151
Brazoria	349	168	181
Brazos	226	102	124
Burleson	34	13	21
Caldwell	107	29	78
Callahan	13	5	8
Cameron	510	123	387
Carson	21	7	14
Chambers	90	44	46
Clay	23	11	12
Collin	475	162	313
Comal	255	126	129
Coryell	66	27	39
Crosby	15	6	9
Denton	594	242	352
Ector	218	93	125
Ellis	216	79	137
El Paso	1,096	251	845
Falls	21	7	14
Fort Bend	754	574	180
Goliad	26	13	13
Grayson	127	60	67
Gregg	254	106	148
Guadalupe	212	86	126
Hardin	69	32	37
Harris	3,986	2,144	1,842
Hays	293	130	163
Hidalgo	762	265	497
Hood	134	52	82
Hudspeth	41	16	25
Hunt	132	43	89
Irion	9	4	5
Jefferson	394	165	229
Johnson	123	92	31
Jones	22	8	14
Kaufman	242	87	155
Kendall	76	48	28
Lampasas	35	18	17
Liberty	75	54	21
Lubbock	472	192	280
Lynn	21	7	14
Martin	9	5	4
McLennan	335	124	211
Medina	64	27	37
Midland	185	69	116
Montgomery	722	406	316
Nueces	282	72	210
Oldham	11	6	5
Parker	117	85	32
Potter	214	100	114
Randall	181	76	105
Robertson	32	14	18
Rockwall	116	40	76
Rusk	73	35	38

Table 80.   Full-Time Law Enforcement Employees, by Selected State Metropolitan and Nonmetropolitan Counties, 2013— continued

(Number.)

State/county	Law enforcement employees	Officers	Civilians
San Patricio	108	48	60
Smith	307	178	129
Somervell	41	20	21
Tarrant	1,397	470	927
Taylor	207	91	116
Tom Green	165	61	104
Travis	1,605	334	1,271
Victoria	192	106	86
Waller	73	54	19
Webb	303	245	58
Wichita	209	61	148
Williamson	493	207	286
Wilson	73	30	43
Wise	141	60	81
Nonmetropolitan Counties			
Anderson	82	35	47
Andrews	37	14	23
Angelina	115	46	69
Bailey	19	5	14
Baylor	8	3	5
Bee	41	19	22
Blanco	26	10	16
Borden	3	2	1
Bosque	37	18	19
Brewster	24	13	11
Briscoe	2	2	0
Brooks	28	8	20
Brown	65	26	39
Burnet	61	45	16
Calhoun	63	24	39
Camp	17	7	10
Cass	46	21	25
Castro	19	8	11
Cherokee	75	32	43
Childress	22	5	17
Cochran	13	7	6
Coke	6	5	1
Coleman	12	5	7
Collingsworth	10	5	5
Colorado	47	20	27
Comanche	35	11	24
Cottle	1	1	0
Crane	11	6	5
Culberson	10	6	4
Dallam	6	5	1
Dawson	19	7	12
Deaf Smith	36	12	24
Delta	22	11	11
Dewitt	45	19	26
Dickens	7	4	3
Dimmit	58	29	29
Donley	9	6	3
Duval	38	15	23
Eastland	30	11	19
Edwards	11	5	6
Erath	61	21	40
Fannin	25	18	7
Fayette	45	25	20
Fisher	9	5	4
Floyd	11	7	4
Foard	3	2	1
Franklin	19	9	10
Freestone	33	15	18
Frio	40	18	22
Gaines	26	14	12
Garza	33	8	25
Gillespie	41	28	13
Glasscock	5	4	1
Gonzales	50	19	31
Gray	41	14	27
Grimes	52	25	27
Hale	69	21	48
Hall	10	4	6
Hamilton	22	10	12
Hansford	12	7	5
Hardeman	12	7	5
Harrison	107	58	49
Hartley	5	5	0

Table 80.   Full-Time Law Enforcement Employees, by Selected State Metropolitan and Nonmetropolitan Counties, 2013— continued

(Number.)

State/county	Law enforcement employees	Officers	Civilians
Haskell	10	4	6
Hemphill	17	9	8
Henderson	148	82	66
Hill	75	31	44
Hockley	27	10	17
Hopkins	58	25	33
Houston	46	20	26
Howard	51	17	34
Hutchinson	33	13	20
Jack	29	11	18
Jackson	34	14	20
Jasper	50	21	29
Jeff Davis	7	4	3
Jim Hogg	39	16	23
Jim Wells	68	31	37
Karnes	28	18	10
Kenedy	18	11	7
Kent	10	3	7
Kerr	95	47	48
Kimble	13	9	4
King	2	2	0
Kinney	27	17	10
Kleberg	88	22	66
Knox	9	3	6
Lamar	75	26	49
Lamb	32	13	19
La Salle	35	24	11
Lavaca	31	13	18
Lee	40	13	27
Leon	42	23	19
Limestone	89	22	67
Lipscomb	11	7	4
Live Oak	44	13	31
Llano	56	33	23
Loving	4	3	1
Madison	22	11	11
Marion	11	10	1
Mason	10	5	5
Matagorda	76	35	41
Maverick	81	31	50
McCulloch	13	7	6
McMullen	13	11	2
Menard	10	5	5
Milam	57	18	39
Mills	11	7	4
Mitchell	20	5	15
Montague	27	14	13
Moore	40	15	25
Morris	22	9	13
Motley	4	4	0
Nacogdoches	81	42	39
Navarro	121	58	63
Nolan	31	12	19
Ochiltree	19	8	11
Palo Pinto	54	27	27
Panola	59	27	32
Parmer	19	6	13
Pecos	38	23	15
Polk	99	51	48
Presidio	26	7	19
Rains	25	10	15
Reagan	20	12	8
Real	8	4	4
Red River	27	12	15
Refugio	45	17	28
Roberts	5	4	1
Runnels	26	6	20
Sabine	18	9	9
San Augustine	19	8	11
San Jacinto	58	23	35
San Saba	9	4	5
Schleicher	11	5	6
Scurry	42	10	32
Shackelford	15	5	10
Shelby	31	14	17
Sherman	9	4	5
Starr	112	55	57
Stephens	27	8	19
Sterling	6	5	1

Table 80.   Full-Time Law Enforcement Employees, by Selected State Metropolitan and Nonmetropolitan Counties, 2013— continued

(Number.)

State/county	Law enforcement employees	Officers	Civilians
Stonewall	9	3	6
Sutton	13	4	9
Swisher	8	2	6
Terrell	15	7	8
Terry	32	10	22
Throckmorton	6	2	4
Titus	59	27	32
Trinity	17	11	6
Upton	18	9	9
Uvalde	64	17	47
Val Verde	63	41	22
Van Zandt	74	31	43
Walker	68	33	35
Ward	32	14	18
Washington	55	30	25
Wharton	72	42	30
Wheeler	17	10	7
Wilbarger	18	7	11
Willacy	46	16	30
Winkler	21	9	12
Wood	62	27	35
Yoakum	20	9	11
Young	35	11	24
Zapata	91	36	55
Zavala	21	18	3
UTAH			
Metropolitan Counties			
Box Elder	77	26	51
Cache	139	85	54
Davis	322	141	181
Salt Lake County Unified Police Department	547	405	142
Tooele	85	30	55
Utah	361	270	91
Washington	157	44	113
Weber	72	72	0
Nonmetropolitan Counties			
Beaver	75	27	48
Daggett	26	20	6
Emery	40	34	6
Garfield	28	7	21
Grand	44	18	26
Iron	76	39	37
Kane	44	19	25
Millard	51	44	7
Piute	4	4	0
Rich	10	4	6
San Juan	29	26	3
Sanpete	51	18	33
Uintah	70	22	48
Wasatch	47	25	22
Wayne	5	5	0
VERMONT			
Metropolitan Counties			
Chittenden	24	18	6
Franklin	14	12	2
Grand Isle	6	4	2
Nonmetropolitan Counties			
Addison	4	4	0
Bennington	10	7	3
Caledonia	9	8	1
Essex	3	3	0
Lamoille	24	12	12
Orange	11	11	0
Orleans	8	6	2
Rutland	22	18	4
Washington	13	11	2
Windham	17	11	6
Windsor	14	11	3
VIRGINIA			
Metropolitan Counties			
Albemarle County Police Department	149	121	28
Amelia	27	17	10
Amherst	50	46	4
Appomattox	22	21	1

Table 80.   Full-Time Law Enforcement Employees, by Selected State Metropolitan and Nonmetropolitan Counties, 2013— continued

(Number.)

State/county	Law enforcement employees	Officers	Civilians
Arlington County Police Department	420	352	68
Augusta	77	66	11
Bedford	91	83	8
Botetourt	114	93	21
Buckingham	24	17	7
Campbell	68	59	9
Caroline	71	50	21
Charles City	18	11	7
Chesterfield County Police Department	589	485	104
Clarke	28	16	12
Craig	14	9	5
Culpeper	99	83	16
Dinwiddie	41	38	3
Fairfax County Police Department	1,598	1,327	271
Fauquier	161	119	42
Floyd	29	19	10
Fluvanna	43	30	13
Franklin	77	70	7
Frederick	126	111	15
Giles	39	28	11
Gloucester	96	80	16
Goochland	41	31	10
Greene	24	21	3
Hanover	229	213	16
Henrico County Police Department	777	606	171
Isle of Wight	50	47	3
James City County Police Department	97	91	6
King William	32	21	11
Loudoun	622	511	111
Mathews	18	11	7
Montgomery	123	108	15
Nelson	23	18	5
New Kent	44	32	12
Powhatan	56	40	16
Prince George County Police Department	75	54	21
Prince William County Police Department	695	565	130
Pulaski	57	47	10
Rappahannock	26	25	1
Roanoke County Police Department	156	142	14
Rockingham	69	53	16
Scott	32	25	7
Spotsylvania	211	167	44
Stafford	238	170	68
Sussex	43	38	5
Warren	99	51	48
Washington	80	59	21
York	94	86	8
Nonmetropolitan Counties			
Accomack	69	58	11
Alleghany	62	43	19
Bath	12	12	0
Bland	16	10	6
Brunswick	38	25	13
Buchanan	47	34	13
Carroll	41	35	6
Charlotte	35	33	2
Cumberland	22	16	6
Dickenson	30	20	10
Essex	19	13	6
Grayson	29	23	6
Greensville	35	22	13
Halifax	38	31	7
Henry	128	115	13
Highland	12	7	5
King and Queen	17	10	7
King George	42	28	14
Lancaster	35	29	6
Lee	35	35	0
Louisa	63	48	15
Lunenburg	21	14	7
Madison	33	20	13
Mecklenburg	52	50	2
Middlesex	22	16	6
Northampton	83	66	17
Northumberland	33	22	11
Nottoway	25	14	11
Orange	46	37	9
Page	59	47	12

Table 80.   Full-Time Law Enforcement Employees, by Selected State Metropolitan and Nonmetropolitan Counties, 2013— continued

(Number.)

State/county	Law enforcement employees	Officers	Civilians
Patrick	67	51	16
Pittsylvania	131	114	17
Prince Edward	30	23	7
Richmond	22	13	9
Rockbridge	42	34	8
Russell	50	33	17
Shenandoah	82	73	9
Smyth	43	43	0
Southampton	80	65	15
Surry	22	12	10
Tazewell	63	44	19
Westmoreland	37	23	14
Wise	61	45	16
Wythe	47	39	8
WASHINGTON			
Metropolitan Counties			
Asotin	13	11	2
Benton	204	168	36
Chelan	72	58	14
Clark	207	131	76
Columbia	10	9	1
Cowlitz	48	42	6
Douglas	34	27	7
Franklin	27	25	2
King	286	195	91
Kitsap	145	115	30
Pend Oreille	41	16	25
Pierce	354	297	57
Skagit	102	48	54
Skamania	21	17	4
Snohomish	335	266	69
Spokane	173	118	55
Stevens	30	26	4
Thurston	108	86	22
Walla Walla	56	27	29
Whatcom	180	81	99
Yakima	87	54	33
Nonmetropolitan Counties			
Adams	32	14	18
Clallam	42	35	7
Ferry	25	8	17
Garfield	14	7	7
Grant	76	49	27
Grays Harbor	69	57	12
Island	58	33	25
Jefferson	27	22	5
Kittitas	70	34	36
Klickitat	38	19	19
Lewis	52	36	16
Lincoln	26	14	12
Mason	96	47	49
Okanogan	34	29	5
Pacific	47	18	29
San Juan	32	20	12
Wahkiakum	17	6	11
Whitman	22	18	4
WEST VIRGINIA			
Metropolitan Counties			
Berkeley	87	57	30
Boone	30	23	7
Brooke	28	16	12
Cabell	49	42	7
Clay	5	5	0
Fayette	38	31	7
Hampshire	25	17	8
Hancock	30	26	4
Jefferson	35	28	7
Kanawha	124	104	20
Lincoln	7	7	0
Marshall	31	28	3
Mineral	14	12	2
Monongalia	71	37	34
Ohio	35	33	2
Preston	27	16	11
Putnam	48	37	11
Raleigh	66	44	22

Table 80. Full-Time Law Enforcement Employees, by Selected State Metropolitan and Nonmetropolitan Counties, 2013— continued

(Number.)

State/county	Law enforcement employees	Officers	Civilians
Wayne	24	20	4
Wirt	5	3	2
Wood	54	38	16
Nonmetropolitan Counties			
Barbour	13	9	4
Braxton	10	8	2
Calhoun	1	1	0
Doddridge	6	6	0
Gilmer	5	5	0
Grant	8	8	0
Greenbrier	34	29	5
Hardy	11	9	2
Harrison	46	45	1
Jackson	22	15	7
Lewis	18	14	4
Logan	20	18	2
Marion	46	35	11
Mason	21	15	6
McDowell	15	14	1
Mercer	34	27	7
Mingo	23	20	3
Monroe	8	7	1
Morgan	12	11	1
Nicholas	30	26	4
Pendleton	3	3	0
Pleasants	7	6	1
Pocahontas	16	10	6
Randolph	14	13	1
Ritchie	10	7	3
Roane	11	6	5
Summers	11	6	5
Taylor	15	7	8
Tucker	4	4	0
Tyler	7	7	0
Upshur	10	9	1
Webster	10	5	5
Wetzel	8	8	0
Wyoming	27	21	6
WISCONSIN			
Metropolitan Counties			
Brown	318	155	163
Calumet	50	23	27
Chippewa	66	53	13
Columbia	99	40	59
Dane	547	403	144
Douglas	77	35	42
Eau Claire	108	40	68
Fond du Lac	121	56	65
Green	54	28	26
Iowa	23	21	2
Kenosha	325	115	210
Kewaunee	36	36	0
La Crosse	110	41	69
Marathon	175	64	111
Milwaukee	635	299	336
Oconto	56	26	30
Outagamie	192	74	118
Ozaukee	95	74	21
Pierce	46	44	2
Racine	212	131	81
Rock	200	96	104
Sheboygan	168	71	97
St. Croix	85	77	8
Washington	166	69	97
Waukesha	330	160	170
Winnebago	189	131	58
Nonmetropolitan Counties			
Adams	65	28	37
Barron	66	26	40
Bayfield	36	20	16
Buffalo	22	10	12
Burnett	30	14	16
Clark	48	43	5
Crawford	30	29	1
Dodge	167	73	94
Door	63	50	13

Table 80.   Full-Time Law Enforcement Employees, by Selected State Metropolitan and Nonmetropolitan Counties, 2013— continued

(Number.)

State/county	Law enforcement employees	Officers	Civilians
Dunn	54	25	29
Florence	15	10	5
Forest	40	18	22
Grant	48	27	21
Green Lake	30	17	13
Iron	18	11	7
Jackson	47	21	26
Jefferson	120	96	24
Juneau	54	43	11
Lafayette	17	16	1
Langlade	34	16	18
Lincoln	63	29	34
Manitowoc	87	59	28
Marinette	61	30	31
Marquette	37	37	0
Menominee	11	10	1
Monroe	38	36	2
Oneida	84	36	48
Pepin	11	10	1
Polk	71	27	44
Portage	99	47	52
Price	24	14	10
Richland	29	29	0
Rusk	31	28	3
Sauk	141	45	96
Sawyer	46	24	22
Shawano	109	38	71
Taylor	38	18	20
Trempealeau	52	24	28
Vernon	29	26	3
Vilas	70	34	36
Walworth	201	82	119
Washburn	17	14	3
Waupaca	97	47	50
Waushara	53	25	28
Wood	70	43	27
WYOMING			
Metropolitan Counties			
Laramie	167	124	43
Natrona	162	120	42
Nonmetropolitan Counties			
Albany	45	42	3
Big Horn	11	10	1
Campbell	61	46	15
Carbon	27	16	11
Converse	42	33	9
Crook	20	9	11
Fremont	4	3	1
Goshen	36	23	13
Hot Springs	8	6	2
Johnson	30	29	1
Lincoln	34	21	13
Niobrara	15	4	11
Park	29	19	10
Platte	11	9	2
Sheridan	25	19	6
Sublette	39	34	5
Sweetwater	95	67	28
Uinta	51	21	30
Washakie	8	7	1
Weston	7	7	0

1 The employee data presented in this table for Mecklenburg represent only Mecklenburg County Sheriff's Office employees and exclude Charlotte-Mecklenburg Police Department employees.

Table 81.   Full-Time Law Enforcement Employees, by Selected State and Agency, 2013

(Number.)

State/agency	Law enforcement employees	Officers	Civilians
ALABAMA			
State Agencies			
Alabama Alcoholic Beverage Control Board	144	115	29
Alabama Conservation Department Marine Police	75	56	19
Alabama Criminal Justice Information Center, Investigative Unit	8	8	0
Alabama Department of Mental Health	3	2	1
State Fire Marshal	28	23	5
Tribal Agencies			
Poarch Creek Tribal	56	49	7
Other Agencies			
Huntsville International Airport	20	19	1
Trussville Fire Department, Fire and Explosion Investigation Unit	2	2	0
ALASKA			
Other Agencies			
Anchorage International Airport	66	64	2
Fairbanks International Airport	34	28	6
ARIZONA			
Other Agencies			
Tucson Airport Authority	46	22	24
ARKANSAS			
State Agencies			
Camp Robinson	9	9	0
State Capitol Police	22	20	2
CALIFORNIA			
State Agencies			
Atascadero State Hospital	132	118	14
California State Fair	6	2	4
Coalinga State Hospital	235	220	15
Department of Parks and Recreation, Capital	594	546	48
Fairview Developmental Center	17	13	4
Lanterman State Hospital	12	9	3
Napa State Hospital	117	105	12
Patton State Hospital	70	53	17
Porterville Developmental Center	52	47	5
Sonoma Developmental Center	22	10	12
Other Agencies			
East Bay Regional Parks, Alameda County	80	56	24
Fontana Unified School District	64	17	47
Monterey Peninsula Airport	6	6	0
Port of San Diego Harbor	151	124	27
San Bernardino Unified School District	77	22	55
San Francisco Bay Area Rapid Transit, Contra Costa County	261	175	86
Shasta County Marshal	22	18	4
Stockton Unified School District	27	21	6
Twin Rivers Unified School District	25	20	5
COLORADO			
State Agencies			
Colorado Bureau of Investigation	218	40	178
Colorado Mental Health Institute	77	16	61
Other Agencies			
All Crimes Enforcement Team	3	3	0
CONNECTICUT			
State Agencies			
State Capitol Police	37	28	9
Other Agencies			
Metropolitan Transportation Authority	746	679	67
DELAWARE			
State Agencies			
Attorney General			
Kent County	69	42	27
New Castle County	286	148	138
Sussex County	51	25	26
Division of Alcohol and Tobacco Enforcement	20	16	4
Environmental Control	15	11	4

Table 81.   Full-Time Law Enforcement Employees, by Selected State and Agency, 2013— continued

(Number.)

State/agency	Law enforcement employees	Officers	Civilians
Fish and Wildlife	28	24	4
Park Rangers	20	20	0
River and Bay Authority	57	44	13
State Capitol Police	71	49	22
State Fire Marshal	51	20	31
Other Agencies			
Amtrak Police	19	19	0
Wilmington Fire Department	10	9	1
DISTRICT OF COLUMBIA			
Other Agencies			
Metro Transit Police	662	603	59
FLORIDA			
State Agencies			
Capitol Police	103	80	23
Department of Insurance, Pinellas County	174	135	39
Department of Law Enforcement, Leon County, Tallahassee	1,718	439	1,279
Division of Alcoholic Beverages and Tobacco, Leon County	173	104	69
Florida Game Commission, Leon County	962	773	189
State Treasurer's Office, Division of Insurance Fraud	174	135	39
Tribal Agencies			
Miccosukee Tribal	46	31	15
Seminole Tribal	219	139	80
Other Agencies			
Duval County Schools	89	79	10
Florida School for the Deaf and Blind	16	10	6
Jacksonville Aviation Authority	51	36	15
Lee County Port Authority	73	46	27
Melbourne International Airport	12	11	1
Miami-Dade County Public Schools	206	168	38
Northwest Florida Beaches International Airport	21	15	6
Palm Beach County School District	209	158	51
Port Canaveral	59	30	29
Tampa International Airport	170	56	114
Volusia County Beach Management	47	43	4
GEORGIA			
State Agencies			
Georgia Bureau of Investigation, Headquarters	707	235	472
Georgia Department of Transportation, Office of Investigations	3	3	0
Georgia Forestry Commission	4	4	0
Georgia Public Safety Training Center	153	38	115
Georgia World Congress	89	34	55
Ports Authority, Savannah	113	76	37
State Board of Workers Compensation, Fraud Investigation Division	8	6	2
Other Agencies			
Chatham County Board of Education	47	38	9
Cherokee County Board of Education	13	11	2
Cherokee County Marshal	15	8	7
Cobb County Board of Education	42	40	2
Fulton County Marshal	69	54	15
Fulton County School System	64	62	2
Glynn County School System	17	17	0
Gwinnett County Public Schools	32	28	4
Hartsfield-Jackson Atlanta International Airport	174	156	18
Metropolitan Atlanta Rapid Transit Authority	364	311	53
Muscogee City Marshal	21	19	2
Savannah Fire and Emergency Services, Arson Unit	2	2	0
Stone Mountain Park	24	20	4
Washington County Board of Education	6	6	0
ILLINOIS			
State Agencies			
Secretary of State Police	221	119	102
Other Agencies			
Cook County Forest Preserve	112	106	6
DuPage County Forest Preserve	30	25	5
Indiana Harbor Belt Railroad	11	11	0
Round Lake Park District	1	1	0

Table 81.   Full-Time Law Enforcement Employees, by Selected State and Agency, 2013— continued

(Number.)

State/agency	Law enforcement employees	Officers	Civilians
INDIANA			
State Agencies			
Northern Indiana Commuter Transportation District	8	7	1
Other Agencies			
Indianapolis International Airport	44	43	1
KANSAS			
State Agencies			
Kansas Bureau of Investigation	249	72	177
Kansas Department of Wildlife and Parks	181	179	2
Kansas Lottery Security Division	7	4	3
Kansas Racing Commission, Security Division	45	41	4
Securities Office, Investigation Section	5	5	0
State Fire Marshal	13	12	1
Other Agencies			
Blue Valley School District	8	8	0
Johnson County Park	19	18	1
Metropolitan Topeka Airport Authority	21	17	4
Shawnee Mission Public Schools	8	8	0
Topeka Fire Department, Arson Investigation	4	3	1
Unified School District			
Auburn-Washburn	1	1	0
Bluestem	1	1	0
Goddard	6	5	1
Maize	4	4	0
Seaman	1	1	0
Shawnee Heights	1	1	0
KENTUCKY			
State Agencies			
Alcohol Beverage Control	32	28	4
Fish and Wildlife Enforcement	149	140	9
Kentucky Horse Park	8	8	0
Motor Vehicle Enforcement	161	115	46
Unlawful Narcotics Investigation, Treatment and Education	16	14	2
Other Agencies			
Adair County Constable, District 6	1	1	0
Barren County Drug Task Force	7	6	1
Cincinnati-Northern Kentucky International Airport	68	49	19
Fayette County Schools	32	28	4
Graves County Schools	1	1	0
Jefferson County Board of Education	27	20	7
Lake Cumberland Area Drug Enforcement Task Force	4	3	1
Louisville Regional Airport Authority	44	37	7
McCracken County Public Schools	7	7	0
Montgomery County School District	5	5	0
Northern Kentucky Narcotics Enforcement Unit	3	2	1
Pennyrile Narcotics Task Force	6	5	1
South Central Kentucky Drug Task Force	1	1	0
MARYLAND			
State Agencies			
Comptroller of the Treasury, Field Enforcement Division	54	26	28
Department of Public Safety and Correctional Services, Internal Investigations Unit	38	18	20
General Services			
Annapolis, Anne Arundel County	69	28	41
Baltimore City	100	36	64
Natural Resources Police	511	236	275
Springfield Hospital	44	6	38
State Fire Marshal	69	42	27
Transit Administration	172	154	18
Transportation Authority	589	462	127
Other Agencies			
Maryland-National Capital Park Police			
Montgomery County	94	77	17
Prince George's County	134	109	25
MASSACHUSETTS			
State Agencies			
Division of Law Enforcement, Environmental Police	87	84	3
Massachusetts Bay Transportation Authority	249	237	12

Table 81.   Full-Time Law Enforcement Employees, by Selected State and Agency, 2013— continued

(Number.)

State/agency	Law enforcement employees	Officers	Civilians
Other Agencies			
Beth Israel Deaconess Medical Center	59	14	45
MICHIGAN			
Other Agencies			
Bishop International Airport	8	7	1
Capitol Region Airport Authority	11	11	0
Genesee County Parks and Recreation	3	3	0
Gerald R. Ford International Airport	19	18	1
Huron-Clinton Metropolitan Authority			
Hudson Mills Metropark	3	3	0
Kensington Metropark	11	10	1
Lower Huron Metropark	3	3	0
Stony Creek Metropark	9	9	0
Wayne County Airport	110	98	12
MINNESOTA			
State Agencies			
Capitol Security, St. Paul	60	13	47
Tribal Agencies			
Upper Sioux Community	7	7	0
Other Agencies			
Minneapolis-St. Paul International Airport	130	75	55
Three Rivers Park District	33	21	12
MISSISSIPPI			
State Agencies			
State Capitol Police	74	60	14
Other Agencies			
Singing River Health System	14	13	1
MISSOURI			
State Agencies			
Capitol Police	32	29	3
Department of Conservation	203	195	8
Department of Social Services, State Technical Assistance Team	13	9	4
Division of Alcohol and Tobacco Control	14	13	1
Gaming Commission, Enforcement Division	125	122	3
State Fire Marshal	22	20	2
State Park Rangers	42	41	1
Other Agencies			
Clay County Drug Task Force	4	4	0
Clay County Park Authority	8	8	0
Jackson County Drug Task Force	20	16	4
Jackson County Park Rangers	22	20	2
Springfield-Branson Airport	8	8	0
St. Charles County Park Rangers	11	11	0
St. Peters Ranger Division	5	5	0
MONTANA			
State Agencies			
Gambling Investigations Bureau	24	18	6
NEVADA			
Other Agencies			
Clark County School District	201	158	43
Washoe County School District	42	37	5
NEW JERSEY			
State Agencies			
Palisades Interstate Parkway	29	26	3
Other Agencies			
Park Police			
Morris County	30	29	1
Union County	87	69	18
Prosecutor			
Atlantic County	172	78	94
Camden County	238	156	82
Cape May County	84	40	44
Cumberland County	106	37	69
Gloucester County	95	35	60
Mercer County	165	54	111

Table 81.   Full-Time Law Enforcement Employees, by Selected State and Agency, 2013— continued

(Number.)

State/agency	Law enforcement employees	Officers	Civilians
Middlesex County	182	65	117
Monmouth County	270	76	194
Morris County	148	61	87
Ocean County	164	72	92
Passaic County	186	76	110
Salem County	45	18	27
Somerset County	110	45	65
Sussex County	51	32	19
Union County	157	70	87
Warren County	61	22	39
NEW YORK			
State Agencies			
State Park			
Allegany Region	14	12	2
Central Region	19	15	4
Finger Lakes Region	16	14	2
Genesee Region	13	12	1
Long Island Region	59	58	1
Niagara Region	23	22	1
Saratoga/Capital Region	17	16	1
Taconic Region	11	11	0
Thousand Island Region	15	14	1
Other Agencies			
New York City Department of Environmental Protection Police, Ulster County	224	210	14
New York City Metropolitan Transportation Authority	746	679	67
Onondaga County Parks	1	1	0
Suffolk County Parks	35	35	0
NORTH CAROLINA			
State Agencies			
Department of Health and Human Resources	6	6	0
Department of Wildlife	229	208	21
Division of Alcohol Law Enforcement	111	97	14
Division of Marine Fisheries	63	53	10
North Carolina Arboretum	3	3	0
North Carolina State Bureau of Investigation	363	223	140
State Capitol Police	67	45	22
State Fairgrounds	7	2	5
State Park Rangers			
Carolina Beach	6	4	2
Chimney Rock	5	3	2
Cliffs of the Neuse	8	4	4
Crowders Mountain	6	5	1
Dismal Swamp	2	1	1
Elk Knob	3	3	0
Eno River	8	5	3
Falls Lake Recreation Area	13	11	2
Fort Fisher	2	2	0
Fort Macon	5	5	0
Goose Creek	9	4	5
Gorges	9	3	6
Grandfather Mountain	5	3	2
Hammocks Beach	4	4	0
Hanging Rock	9	5	4
Haw River	1	1	0
Jockey's Ridge	6	5	1
Jones Lake	4	3	1
Jordan Lake State Recreation Area	17	14	3
Kerr Lake	14	12	2
Lake James	9	5	4
Lake Norman	3	3	0
Lake Waccamaw	6	3	3
Lumber River	7	6	1
Mayo River	3	2	1
Medoc Mountain	6	3	3
Merchants Millpond	2	2	0
Morrow Mountain	6	4	2
Mount Mitchell	2	1	1
New River-Mount Jefferson	6	6	0
Pettigrew	3	2	1
Pilot Mountain	4	4	0
Raven Rock	5	3	2
Singletary Lake	3	2	1
South Mountains	5	5	0
Stone Mountain	10	6	4
Weymouth Woods/Sandhills Nature Preserve	2	2	0

Table 81.   Full-Time Law Enforcement Employees, by Selected State and Agency, 2013— continued

(Number.)

State/agency	Law enforcement employees	Officers	Civilians
William B. Umstead	11	6	5
Tribal Agencies			
Cherokee Tribal	68	62	6
Other Agencies			
Asheville Regional Airport	18	13	5
Beaufort County Alcohol Beverage Control Enforcement	1	1	0
Durham County Alcohol Beverage Control Law Enforcement Office	2	2	0
Nash County Alcohol Beverage Control Enforcement	1	1	0
Piedmont Triad International Airport	32	21	11
Pitt County Memorial Hospital	54	51	3
Raleigh-Durham International Airport	29	27	2
Triad Alcohol Beverage Control Law Enforcement	5	4	1
WakeMed Campus Police	65	40	25
Wilmington International Airport	13	9	4
OHIO			
State Agencies			
Ohio Department of Natural Resources	397	341	56
Other Agencies			
Cleveland Metropolitan Park District	80	70	10
Hamilton County Park District	35	32	3
Lake Metroparks	14	12	2
Port Columbus International Airport	54	40	14
Preservation Parks of Delaware County	5	5	0
OKLAHOMA			
State Agencies			
Capitol Park Police	84	35	49
Department of Agriculture, Forestry Service Law Enforcement Section	13	10	3
Grand River Dam Authority, Lake Patrol	23	13	10
Other Agencies			
Jenks Public Schools	9	8	1
McAlester Public Schools	1	1	0
Norman Public Schools	4	4	0
Putnam City Campus	14	9	5
OREGON			
State Agencies			
Liquor Commission			
Benton County	2	2	0
Clackamas County	6	6	0
Clatsop County	2	1	1
Columbia County	1	1	0
Coos County	2	1	1
Crook County	1	1	0
Deschutes County	3	2	1
Douglas County	2	1	1
Harney County	1	1	0
Hood River County	1	1	0
Jackson County	3	2	1
Jefferson County	1	1	0
Josephine County	1	1	0
Klamath County	1	1	0
Lane County	6	5	1
Lincoln County	2	1	1
Marion County	3	2	1
Multnomah County	15	11	4
Polk County	1	1	0
Tillamook County	1	1	0
Umatilla County	2	2	0
Washington County	33	33	0
Wheeler County	1	1	0
Yamhill County	1	1	0
Other Agencies			
Blue Mountain Enforcement Narcotics Team			
Morrow County	6	5	1
Umatilla County	9	8	1
Port of Portland	66	49	17
PENNSYLVANIA			
State Agencies			

Table 81.   Full-Time Law Enforcement Employees, by Selected State and Agency, 2013— continued

(Number.)

State/agency	Law enforcement employees	Officers	Civilians
Pennsylvania Fish and Boat Commission	93	85	8
State Capitol Police	141	132	9
State Park Rangers			
Beltzville	2	2	0
Ben Rush	1	1	0
Black Moshannon	2	2	0
Caledonia	1	1	0
Codorus	11	2	9
Delaware Canal	5	5	0
Evansburg	3	3	0
Fort Washington	1	1	0
Frances Slocum	2	2	0
French Creek	2	2	0
Guifford Pinchot	5	3	2
Hickory Run	5	5	0
Kings Gap Environmental Education Center	1	1	0
Kooser	5	5	0
Lackawanna	3	2	1
Laurel Hill	5	5	0
Laurel Ridge	5	5	0
Linn Run	1	1	0
Little Buffalo	2	2	0
Marsh Creek	2	2	0
Neshaminy	6	1	5
Nockamixon	1	1	0
Ohiopyle	13	5	8
Pine Grove Furnace	2	2	0
Presque Isle	5	5	0
Prince Gallitzin	17	4	13
Promised Land	1	1	0
Pymatuning	3	3	0
Raccoon	11	3	8
Ricketts Glen	4	4	0
Ridley Creek	4	4	0
Tobyhanna	1	1	0
Tuscarora	1	1	0
Tyler	4	1	3
White Clay	1	1	0
Worlds End	7	2	5
Other Agencies			
Allegheny County District Attorney, Criminal Investigation Division	30	26	4
Allegheny County Housing Authority	9	8	1
Allegheny County Port Authority	50	40	10
County Detective			
Beaver County	8	8	0
Berks County	35	32	3
Bucks County	17	14	3
Butler County	4	4	0
Chester County	23	20	3
Cumberland County	8	6	2
Dauphin County	12	10	2
Erie County	9	8	1
Lackawanna County	13	13	0
Lancaster County	15	13	2
Lebanon County	7	5	2
Lehigh County	37	17	20
Luzerne County	10	10	0
McKean County	8	2	6
Monroe County	6	5	1
Montgomery County	63	39	24
Montour County	1	1	0
Pike County	3	3	0
Schuylkill County	6	6	0
Wayne County	1	1	0
Westmoreland County	58	14	44
Wyoming County	5	5	0
York County	10	9	1
Delaware County District Attorney, Criminal Investigation Division	41	34	7
Delaware County Park	56	55	1
Erie Municipal Airport Authority	10	9	1
Fort Indiantown Gap	25	14	11
Harrisburg International Airport	14	6	8
Lehigh Valley International Airport	8	7	1
Washington County Alternative Education	1	1	0
Westmoreland County Park	25	24	1
Wyoming Area School District	1	1	0

Table 81. Full-Time Law Enforcement Employees, by Selected State and Agency, 2013— continued

(Number.)

State/agency	Law enforcement employees	Officers	Civilians
RHODE ISLAND			
State Agencies			
Department of Environmental Management	42	33	9
Rhode Island State Airport	44	35	9
SOUTH CAROLINA			
State Agencies			
Bureau of Protective Services	68	62	6
Department of Natural Resources			
Abbeville County	3	3	0
Aiken County	5	5	0
Allendale County	3	3	0
Anderson County	4	4	0
Bamberg County	2	2	0
Barnwell County	4	4	0
Beaufort County	6	6	0
Berkeley County	7	7	0
Calhoun County	3	3	0
Charleston County	19	17	2
Cherokee County	4	4	0
Chester County	2	2	0
Chesterfield County	3	3	0
Clarendon County	5	5	0
Colleton County	3	3	0
Darlington County	2	2	0
Dillon County	2	2	0
Dorchester County	5	5	0
Edgefield County	3	3	0
Fairfield County	3	3	0
Florence County	10	8	2
Georgetown County	5	5	0
Greenville County	4	4	0
Greenwood County	4	4	0
Hampton County	3	3	0
Horry County	4	4	0
Jasper County	2	2	0
Kershaw County	4	4	0
Lancaster County	2	2	0
Laurens County	3	3	0
Lee County	2	2	0
Lexington County	6	6	0
Marion County	2	2	0
Marlboro County	3	3	0
McCormick County	3	3	0
Newberry County	4	4	0
Oconee County	4	4	0
Orangeburg County	4	4	0
Pickens County	9	7	2
Richland County	67	48	19
Saluda County	3	3	0
Spartanburg County	5	5	0
Sumter County	3	3	0
Union County	3	3	0
Williamsburg County	4	4	0
York County	5	4	1
Department of Public Safety, Illegal Immigration Enforcement Unit	8	7	1
Employment Security Commission	4	4	0
Forestry Commission			
Anderson County	1	1	0
Bamberg County	1	1	0
Barnwell County	1	1	0
Beaufort County	1	1	0
Berkeley County	1	1	0
Charleston County	1	1	0
Chesterfield County	4	4	0
Clarendon County	1	1	0
Colleton County	1	1	0
Darlington County	1	1	0
Fairfield County	1	1	0
Florence County	2	2	0
Hampton County	1	1	0
Horry County	1	1	0
Kershaw County	2	2	0
Lexington County	4	4	0
Oconee County	1	1	0
Orangeburg County	1	1	0
Pickens County	2	2	0
Richland County	2	1	1

Table 81.   Full-Time Law Enforcement Employees, by Selected State and Agency, 2013— continued

(Number.)

State/agency	Law enforcement employees	Officers	Civilians
Spartanburg County	1	1	0
Sumter County	2	2	0
Williamsburg County	2	2	0
York County	1	1	0
South Carolina Division of Public Railways	1	1	0
State Museum	1	1	0
State Ports Authority	63	29	34
State Transport Police			
Aiken County	4	4	0
Bamberg County	15	15	0
Charleston County	4	4	0
Dorchester County	20	17	3
Edgefield County	7	7	0
Florence County	6	6	0
Greenville County	19	15	4
Lexington County	1	1	0
Richland County	51	28	23
York County	10	10	0
Other Agencies			
15th Circuit Drug Enforcement Unit	4	3	1
Charleston County Aviation Authority	46	29	17
Columbia Metropolitan Airport	18	18	0
Greenville Hospital	16	15	1
Greenville-Spartanburg International Airport	20	19	1
Lexington County Medical Center	47	18	29
SOUTH DAKOTA			
State Agencies			
Division of Criminal Investigation	167	50	117
TENNESSEE			
State Agencies			
Alcoholic Beverage Commission	67	34	33
Department of Correction, internal Affairs	82	23	59
State Fire Marshal	28	23	5
State Park Rangers			
Bicentennial Capitol Mall	6	6	0
Big Hill Pond	2	2	0
Big Ridge	4	4	0
Bledsoe Creek	2	2	0
Booker T. Washington	3	3	0
Burgess Falls Natural Area	3	3	0
Cedars of Lebanon	4	4	0
Chickasaw	4	4	0
Cove Lake	4	4	0
Cumberland Mountain	4	4	0
Cumberland Trail	7	7	0
Cummins Falls	2	2	0
David Crockett	4	4	0
Davy Crockett Birthplace	3	3	0
Dunbar Cave Natural Area	2	2	0
Edgar Evins	4	4	0
Fall Creek Falls	9	9	0
Fort Loudon State Historic Park	4	4	0
Fort Pillow State Historic Park	2	2	0
Frozen Head Natural Area	4	4	0
Harpeth Scenic Rivers	3	3	0
Harrison Bay	5	5	0
Henry Horton	6	5	1
Hiwassee/Ocoee State Scenic Rivers	6	6	0
Indian Mountain	2	2	0
Johnsonville State Historic Park	2	2	0
Long Hunter	4	4	0
Meeman-Shelby Forest	5	5	0
Montgomery Bell	6	6	0
Mousetail Landing	2	2	0
Natchez Trace	5	5	0
Nathan Bedford Forrest	3	3	0
Norris Dam	4	4	0
Old Stone Fort State Archaeological Park	3	3	0
Panther Creek	3	3	0
Paris Landing	5	5	0
Pickett	4	4	0
Pickwick Landing	5	5	0
Pinson Mounds State Archaeological Park	2	2	0
Radnor Lake Natural Area	5	5	0
Red Clay State Historic Park	2	2	0
Reelfoot Lake	4	4	0

Table 81.   Full-Time Law Enforcement Employees, by Selected State and Agency, 2013— continued

(Number.)

State/agency	Law enforcement employees	Officers	Civilians
Roan Mountain	4	4	0
Rock Island	4	4	0
Sgt. Alvin C. York	2	2	0
South Cumberland Recreation Area	5	5	0
Standing Stone	3	3	0
Sycamore Shoals State Historic Park	2	2	0
Tim's Ford	5	5	0
T.O. Fuller	3	3	0
Warrior's Path	5	5	0
TennCare Office of Inspector General	44	17	27
Tennessee Bureau of Investigation	498	293	205
Tennessee Department of Revenue, Special Investigations Unit	47	28	19
Wildlife Resources Agency			
Region 1	46	42	4
Region 2	64	55	9
Region 3	48	44	4
Region 4	48	44	4
Other Agencies			
Chattanooga Housing Authority	6	5	1
Chattanooga Metropolitan Airport	11	10	1
Dickson Parks and Recreation	10	1	9
Drug Task Force			
3rd Judicial District	4	3	1
4th Judicial District	3	2	1
7th Judicial District	1	1	0
8th Judicial District	4	3	1
9th Judicial District	2	2	0
10th Judicial District	10	9	1
12th Judicial District	1	1	0
14th Judicial District	1	1	0
15th Judicial District	5	4	1
17th Judicial District	5	5	0
18th Judicial District	3	3	0
19th Judicial District	9	8	1
21st Judicial District	9	7	2
22nd Judicial District	2	2	0
23rd Judicial District	8	6	2
24th Judicial District	2	1	1
25th Judicial District	2	2	0
27th Judicial District	4	3	1
Knoxville Metropolitan Airport	44	27	17
Memphis International Airport	64	50	14
Metropolitan Nashville Park Police	20	20	0
Nashville International Airport	69	54	15
Smyrna/Rutherford County Airport Authority	4	4	0
Tri-Cities Regional Airport	15	14	1
West Tennessee Violent Crime Task Force	8	7	1
TEXAS			
Other Agencies			
Amarillo International Airport	13	13	0
Dallas-Fort Worth International Airport	186	167	19
Hospital District			
Dallas County	119	70	49
Tarrant County	58	40	18
Houston Metropolitan Transit Authority	210	179	31
Independent School District			
Aldine	57	49	8
Alvin	22	19	3
Angleton	8	7	1
Austin	103	75	28
Barbers Hill	5	4	1
Bay City	8	7	1
Cedar Hill	30	7	23
Columbia-Brazoria	3	3	0
Conroe	72	55	17
Ector County	31	28	3
Edinburg	114	77	37
El Paso	48	39	9
Fort Bend	59	47	12
Hallsville	6	6	0
Judson	20	19	1
Katy	52	41	11
Killeen	18	18	0
Laredo	95	26	69
Lyford	3	3	0
Midland	17	15	2

Table 81.   Full-Time Law Enforcement Employees, by Selected State and Agency, 2013— continued

(Number.)

State/agency	Law enforcement employees	Officers	Civilians
Pasadena	40	32	8
Pflugerville	20	20	0
Raymondville	3	3	0
Rio Grande City	14	14	0
Sealy	3	3	0
Socorro	37	30	7
Spring	51	45	6
Spring Branch	37	29	8
Taft	2	2	0
United	170	53	117
Port of Brownsville	19	9	10
Port of Houston Authority	56	48	8
UTAH			
State Agencies			
Parks and Recreation	54	53	1
Other Agencies			
Granite School District	24	15	9
Utah County Attorney, Investigations Division	8	6	2
VERMONT			
State Agencies			
Attorney General	4	4	0
Department of Liquor Control, Division of En-forcement and Licensing	22	16	6
Department of Motor Vehicles	42	28	14
Fish and Wildlife Department	42	40	2
Secretary of State, Investigations Unit	10	6	4
VIRGINIA			
State Agencies			
Alcoholic Beverage Control Commission	162	125	37
Central State Hospital	17	16	1
Department of Conservation and Recreation	226	97	129
Department of Game and Inland Fisheries, Enforcement Division	179	164	15
Department of Motor Vehicles	84	69	15
Virginia State Capitol	89	75	14
Other Agencies			
Norfolk Airport Authority	44	37	7
Port Authority, Norfolk	38	27	11
Regan National Airport	313	212	101
Richmond International Airport	37	28	9
WASHINGTON			
State Agencies			
State Gambling Commission, Enforcement Unit	133	76	57
State Insurance Commissioner, Special Investi-gations Unit	8	5	3
Tribal Agencies			
Chehalis Tribal	10	9	1
Colville Tribal	43	30	13
Kalispel Tribal	14	12	2
La Push Tribal	5	5	0
Lower Elwha Tribal	4	3	1
Lummi Tribal	26	24	2
Makah Tribal	16	8	8
Nisqually Tribal	14	10	4
Nooksack Tribal	10	9	1
Port Gamble S'Klallam Tribal	10	10	0
Puyallup Tribal	37	27	10
Quinault Indian Nation	21	11	10
Sauk-Suiattle Tribal	3	2	1
Shoalwater Bay Tribal	5	5	0
Skokomish Tribal	10	8	2
Spokane Agency	20	13	7
Squaxin Island Tribal	14	12	2
Stillaguamish Tribal	10	10	0
Suquamish Tribal	21	18	3
Swinomish Tribal	19	15	4
Tulalip Tribal	45	26	19
Upper Skagit Tribal	7	6	1
Yakama Nation	36	26	10
Other Agencies			
Port of Seattle	124	95	29

Table 81.   Full-Time Law Enforcement Employees, by Selected State and Agency, 2013— continued

(Number.)

State/agency	Law enforcement employees	Officers	Civilians
WEST VIRGINIA			
State Agencies			
Capitol Protective Services	33	12	21
Division of Natural Resources			
Barbour County	2	2	0
Berkeley County	1	1	0
Boone County	1	1	0
Braxton County	2	2	0
Brooke County	1	1	0
Cabell County	3	3	0
Calhoun County	1	1	0
Clay County	1	1	0
Doddridge County	1	1	0
Fayette County	3	3	0
Gilmer County	1	1	0
Grant County	2	2	0
Greenbrier County	3	3	0
Hampshire County	6	5	1
Hancock County	1	1	0
Hardy County	2	2	0
Harrison County	2	2	0
Jackson County	2	2	0
Jefferson County	2	2	0
Kanawha County	10	7	3
Lewis County	3	3	0
Lincoln County	2	2	0
Logan County	2	2	0
Marion County	5	5	0
Marshall County	2	2	0
Mason County	1	1	0
McDowell County	1	1	0
Mercer County	3	3	0
Mineral County	2	2	0
Mingo County	1	1	0
Monongalia County	2	2	0
Monroe County	1	1	0
Nicholas County	1	1	0
Ohio County	1	1	0
Pendleton County	1	1	0
Pleasants County	1	1	0
Pocahontas County	2	2	0
Preston County	2	2	0
Putnam County	7	6	1
Raleigh County	4	3	1
Randolph County	2	2	0
Roane County	1	1	0
Summers County	3	3	0
Taylor County	2	2	0
Tucker County	1	1	0
Upshur County	6	5	1
Wayne County	2	2	0
Webster County	2	2	0
Wetzel County	1	1	0
Wirt County	1	1	0
Wood County	7	6	1
Wyoming County	1	1	0
State Fire Marshal, Kanawha County	56	41	15
Other Agencies			
Central West Virginia Drug Task Force	2	2	0
Eastern Panhandle Drug and Violent Crime Task Force	11	10	1
Greenbrier County Drug and Violent Crime Task Force	4	3	1
Hancock/Brooke/Weirton Drug Task Force	6	6	0
Harrison County Drug and Violent Crime Task Force	7	7	0
Huntington Drug and Violent Crime Task Force	3	2	1
Kanawha County Parks and Recreation	3	3	0
Logan County Drug and Violent Crime Task Force	5	4	1
Metropolitan Drug Enforcement Network Team	19	18	1
Ohio Valley Drug and Violent Crime Task Force	5	5	0
Parkersburg Narcotics and Violent Crime Task Force	5	5	0
Potomac Highlands Drug and Violent Crime Task Force	3	3	0
Southern Regional Drug and Violent Crime Task Force	9	8	1
Three Rivers Drug and Violent Crime Task Force	2	2	0

Table 81.   Full-Time Law Enforcement Employees, by Selected State and Agency, 2013— continued

(Number.)

State/agency	Law enforcement employees	Officers	Civilians
WISCONSIN			
State Agencies			
Capitol Police	50	40	10
Department of Natural Resources	326	298	28
Tribal Agencies			
Lac du Flambeau Tribal	13	10	3
Menominee Tribal	40	24	16
Oneida Tribal	28	20	8
St. Croix Tribal	19	11	8
PUERTO RICO AND OUTLYING AREAS			
Puerto Rico	15,334	14,629	705
Virgin Islands			
St. Croix	271	196	75
St. Thomas	291	204	87
FEDERAL AGENCIES			
National Institutes of Health	118	93	25
United States Department of the Interior			
Bureau of Indian Affairs[1]	730	349	381
Bureau of Land Management	318	303	15
Bureau of Reclamation	114	23	91
Fish and Wildlife Service	578	575	3
National Park Service	2,140	2,039	101

1 Tribal figures represented throughout Table 81 may be included in the aggregated totals listed under the Bureau of Indian Affairs data.

SECTION VI

HATE CRIMES

HATE CRIMES

Figure 6.1 Percent Distribution of Single-Bias Hate Crime Incidents, 2013

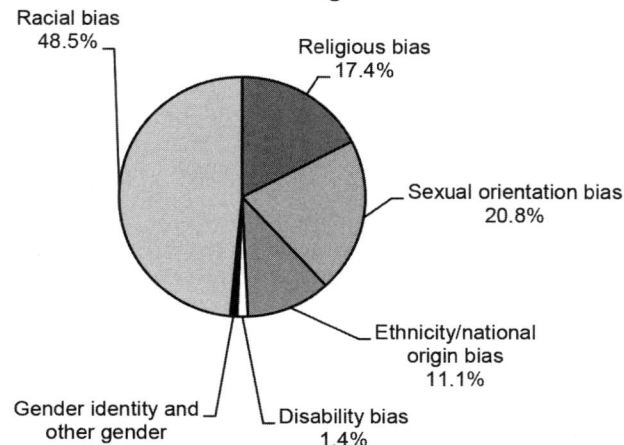

Racial bias
48.5%

Religious bias
17.4%

Sexual orientation bias
20.8%

Ethnicity/national
origin bias
11.1%

Gender identity and
other gender
0.9%

Disability bias
1.4%

The Federal Bureau of Investigation (FBI) began the procedures for implementing, collecting, and managing hate crime data after Congress passed the Hate Crime Statistics Act in 1990. This act required the collection of data "about crimes that manifest evidence of prejudice based on race, religion, sexual orientation, or ethnicity." In 1994, the Hate Crime Statistics Act was amended to include bias against persons with disabilities. The Church Arson Prevention Act, which was signed into law in July 1996, removed the sunset clause from the original statute and mandated that the collection of hate crime data become a permanent part of the UCR program. In 2009, Congress further amended the Hate Crime Statistics Act by passing the Matthew Shepard and James Byrd, Jr., Hate Crime Prevention Act. The amendment includes the collection of data for crimes motivated by bias against a particular gender and gender identity, as well as for crimes committed by, and crimes directed against, juveniles.

Definitions

Hate crimes include any crime motivated by bias against race, religion, sexual orientation, ethnicity/national origin, and/or disability. Because motivation is subjective, it is sometimes difficult to know with certainty whether a crime resulted from the offender's bias. Moreover, the presence of bias alone does not necessarily mean that a crime can be considered a hate crime. Only when law enforcement investigation reveals sufficient evidence to lead a reasonable and prudent person to conclude that the offender's actions were motivated, in whole or in part, by his or her bias should an incident be reported as a hate crime.

Data Collection

The UCR (Uniform Crime Reporting) program collects data about both single-bias and multiple-bias hate crimes. A single-bias incident is defined as an incident in which one or more offense types are motivated by the same bias. A multiple-bias incident is defined as an incident in which more than one offense type occurs and at least two offense types are motivated by different biases.

A table with selected places in the United States that did not report hate crimes in 2013 is available at http://www.fbi.gov/about-us/cjis/ucr/hate-crime/2013/tables/14tabledatadecpdf/table_14_hate_crime_zero_data_submitted _per_quarter_by_state_and_agency_2013.xls/view .

Important Note: Rape

In 2013, the FBI UCR Program initiated the collection of rape data under a revised definition and removed the term "forcible" from the offense name. The UCR Program now defines rape as follows:

- **Rape (revised):** Penetration, no matter how slight, of the vagina or anus with any body part or object, or oral penetration by a sex organ of another person, without the consent of the victim. This includes the offenses of rape, sodomy, and sexual assault with an object.

- **Rape (legacy):** The carnal knowledge of a female forcibly and against her will.

The offenses of fondling, incest, and statutory rape are included in the Crimes Against Persons, Other category.

CRIMES AGAINST PERSONS, PROPERTY, OR SOCIETY

The UCR program's data collection guidelines stipulate that a hate crime may involve multiple offenses, victims, and offenders within one incident; therefore, the Hate Crime Statistics program is incident-based. According to UCR counting guidelines:

- One offense is counted for each victim in crimes against persons

- One offense is counted for each offense type in crimes against property

- One offense is counted for each offense type in crimes against society

VICTIMS

In the UCR program, the victim of a hate crime may be an individual, a business, an institution, or society as a whole.

OFFENDERS

According to the UCR program, the term known offender does not imply that the suspect's identity is known; rather, the term indicates that some aspect of the suspect was identified, thus distinguishing the suspect from an unknown offender. Law enforcement agencies specify the number of offenders, and when possible, the race of the offender or offenders as a group.

RACE/ETHNICITY

The UCR program uses the following racial designations in its Hate Crime Statistics program: White; Black; American Indian or Alaskan Native; Asian; Native Hawaiian or Other Pacific Islander; and Multiple Races, Group. In addition, the UCR program uses the ethnic designations of Hispanic or Latino and Not Hispanic or Latino.

Agencies that participated in the Hate Crime Statistics program in 2013 represented more than 295 million inhabitants, or 93.2 percent of the nation's population. Their jurisdictions covered 49 states, the District of Columbia, Guam, and the U.S. Virgin Islands. The law enforcement agencies that voluntarily participate in the Hate Crime Statistics program collect details about an offender's bias motivation associated with 11 offense types already being reported to the UCR program: murder and nonnegligent manslaughter, rape, aggravated assault, simple assault, and intimidation (crimes against persons); and robbery, burglary, larceny-theft, motor vehicle theft, arson, and destruction/damage/vandalism (crimes against property). The law enforcement agencies that participate in the UCR program via the National Incident-Based Reporting System (NIBRS) collect data about additional offenses for crimes against persons and crimes against property. These data appear in the category of other. These agencies also collect hate crime data for the category called crimes against society, which includes drug or narcotic offenses, gambling offenses, prostitution offenses, and weapon law violations.

National Volume and Percent Distribution

In 2013, 1,826 law enforcement agencies reported 5,928 hate crime incidents involving 6,933 offenses. Of these, 6,921 were single-bias offenses. An analysis of the single-bias incidents revealed that 48.5 percent were racially motivated, 17.4 percent were motivated by religious bias, 20.8 percent resulted from sexual-orientation bias, 11.1 percent were based on an ethnicity/national origin bias, 0.9 percent were motivated by gender and gender-identity bias, and 1.4 percent were prompted by a disability bias. (Table 82)

The majority of the 3,407 hate crime offenses that were racially motivated resulted from an anti-Black bias (66.4 percent) followed by an anti-White basis (21.4 percent). Bias against people of more than one race accounted for 3.2 percent of offenses, while anti-Asian bias accounted for 4.6 percent of racially motivated offenses, anti–Native Hawaiian and Other Pacific Islander accounted for 0.1 percent of these offenses, and anti–American Indian or Alaska Native bias accounted for 4.3 percent of these offenses. (Table 82)

Hate crimes motivated by religious bias accounted for 1,163 offenses reported by law enforcement. A breakdown of these offenses revealed 59.2 percent were motivated by anti-Jewish bias, 14.2 percent by anti-Islamic (Muslim) bias, 4.4 percent were anti–multiple religions or groups, 6.4 percent had an anti-Catholic bias, 3.6 percent were anti-Protestant, 0.6 percent were anti-atheism/agnoticism/etc., and the remainder, 11.6 percent, of offenses were based on a bias against other religions—those not specified. (Table 82)

In 2013, more hate crimes (1,402) were committed on the basis of sexual orientation bias than on religious bias. Of the offenses based on sexual orientation, 22.6 percent were classified as having an anti–lesbian, gay, bisexual, or transgender (mixed group) bias; 60.6 percent were classified as having an anti–male homosexual bias; 13.2 percent had an anti–female homosexual basis; 1.9 percent had an anti-bisexual bias; and 1.7 percent had an anti-heterosexual bias. (Table 82)

The majority of the 794 offenses that were committed on the perceived ethnicity or national origin of the victim had an anti–Hispanic or Latino basis (52.6 percent). The remaining 47.4 percent were based on bias against another ethnicity or national origin. (Table 82)

Other hate crime offenses were committed based on disability. The majority (75.0 percent) were classified as anti-mental disability, with the rest (25.0 percent) classified as anti–physical disability. (Table 82)

Of the 33 gender identity bias offenses reported, 25 were anti-transgender and 8 were anti–gender nonconforming. Of the 30 gender bias offenses reported, 25 were anti-female and 5 were anti-male. (Table 82)

Figure 6.2 Hates Crimes, by Type of Victim, 2013

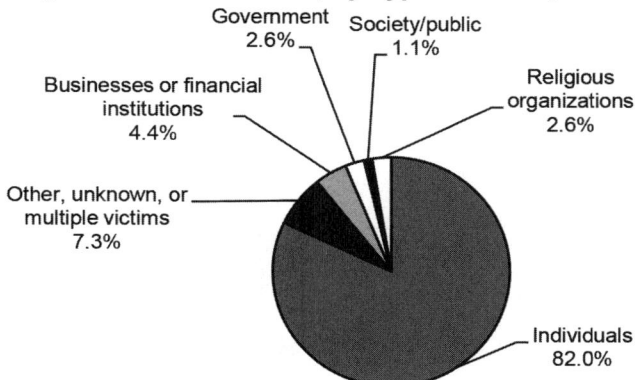

Crimes Against Persons

Law enforcement agencies reported 4,430 hate crime offenses against persons in 2013, up from 3,258 offenses in 2012. Approximately 43.5 percent involved intimidation, 38.8 percent involved simple assault, and 16.6 percent involved aggravated assault. In addition, there were 5 murders and 21 rapes. (Table 83)

Crimes Against Property

In 2013, hate crime offences against property totaled 2,424. Approximately 73.6 percent of offenses involved destruction/damage or vandalism. The remaining 25.2 percent of crimes against property consisted of robbery, burglary, larceny-theft, motor vehicle theft, arson, and other crimes. (Table 83)

Table 82.   Incidents, Offenses, Victims,[1] and Known Offenders,[2] by Bias Motivation, 2013

(Number.)

Bias motivation	Incidents	Offenses	Victims	Known offenders
Total	5,928	6,933	7,242	5,814
Single-Bias Incidents	5,922	6,921	7,230	5,808
Race	2,871	3,407	3,563	2,733
Anti-White	653	728	754	680
Anti-Black or African American	1,856	2,263	2,371	1,747
Anti-American Indian or Alaska Native	129	146	159	108
Anti-Asian	135	158	164	130
Anti-Native Hawaiian or Other Pacific Islander	3	3	3	7
Anti-Multiple races, group	95	109	112	61
Religion	1,031	1,163	1,223	682
Anti-Jewish	625	689	737	393
Anti-Catholic	70	74	75	72
Anti-Protestant	35	42	47	17
Anti-Islamic (Muslim)	135	165	167	127
Anti-other religion	117	135	137	44
Anti-multiple religions, group	42	51	53	25
Anti-atheism/agnosticism/etc.	7	7	7	4
Sexual orientation	1,233	1,402	1,461	1,514
Anti-gay (male)	750	849	890	975
Anti-lesbian	160	185	191	174
Anti-lesbian, gay, bisexual, or transgender (mixed group)	277	317	329	324
Anti-heterosexual	21	24	24	20
Anti-bisexual	25	27	27	21
Ethnicity	655	794	821	743
Anti-Hispanic or Latino	331	418	432	418
Anti-Not Hispanic or Latino[3]	324	376	389	325
Disability	83	92	99	77
Anti-physical	22	23	24	23
Anti-mental	61	69	75	54
Gender	18	30	30	20
Anti-male	5	5	5	7
Anti-female	13	25	25	13
Gender Identity	31	33	33	39
Anti-transgender	23	25	25	30
Anti-gender nonconforming	8	8	8	9
Multiple-Bias Incidents [4]	6	12	12	6

1 The term victim may refer to a person, business, institution, or society as a whole.   2 The term known offender does not imply that the identity of the suspect is known, but only that an attribute of the suspect has been identified, which distinguishes him/her from an unknown offender.   3 The term anti-not Hispanic or Latino does not imply the victim was targeted because he/she was not of Hispanic origin, but it refers to other or unspecified ethnic biases that are not Hispanic or Latino.   4 A multiple-bias incident is an incident in which one or more offense types are motivated by two or more biases.

Table 83.   Incidents, Offenses, Victims, and Known Offenders, by Offense Type, 2013

(Number.)

Offense type	Incidents[1]	Offenses	Victims[2]	Known offenders[3]
Total	5,928	6,933	7,242	5,814
Crimes against persons	3,607	4,430	4,430	4,440
Murder and nonnegligent manslaughter	5	5	5	5
Rape (revised definition)[4]	15	15	15	15
Rape (legacy definition)[5]	6	6	6	10
Aggravated assault	588	734	734	882
Simple assault	1,441	1,720	1,720	2,013
Intimidation	1,528	1,925	1,925	1,494
Other[6]	24	25	25	21
Crimes against property	2,424	2,424	2,733	1,527
Robbery	126	126	145	261
Burglary	174	174	202	164
Larceny-theft	225	225	246	168
Motor vehicle theft	20	20	21	9
Arson	36	36	40	21
Destruction/damage/vandalism	1,783	1,783	2,011	862
Other[6]	60	60	68	42
Crimes against society [6]	79	79	79	102

1 The actual number of incidents is 5,928. However, the column figures will not add to the total because incidents may include more than one offense type, and these are counted in each appropriate offense type category.   2 The term victim may refer to a person, business, institution, or society as a whole.   3 The term known offender does not imply that the identity of the suspect is known, but only that an attribute of the suspect has been identified, which distinguishes him/her from an unknown offender. The actual number of known offenders is 5,814. However, the column figures will not add to the total because some offenders are responsible for more than one offense type, and are, therefore, counted more than once in this table.   4 The figures shown in this row for the offense of rape include only those reported by law enforcement agencies that used the revised Uniform Crime Reporting (UCR) definition of rape.   5 The figures shown in this row for the offense of rape include only those reported by law enforcement agencies that used the legacy UCR definition of rape.   6 Includes additional offenses collected in the National Incident-Based Reporting System.

Table 84.   Offenses, Known Offender's Race, by Offense Type, 2013

(Number.)

Offense type	Total offenses	Known offender's race						
		White	Black or African American	American Indian or Alaska Native	Asian	Native Hawaiian or Other Pacific Islander	Group of multiple races	Unknown race
Total	6,933	2,962	1,092	50	41	2	199	787
Crimes against persons:	4,430	2,471	926	37	36	2	170	328
Murder and nonnegligent manslaughter	5	4	0	0	0	0	0	1
Rape (revised definition)[1]	15	7	6	0	0	0	0	1
Rape (legacy definition)[2]	6	4	1	0	0	0	0	1
Aggravated assault	734	443	188	7	2	0	32	31
Simple assault	1,720	845	451	25	19	2	119	177
Intimidation	1,925	1,153	276	5	15	0	19	115
Other[3]	25	15	4	0	0	0	0	2
Crimes against property:	2,424	435	157	10	5	0	25	456
Robbery	126	48	54	1	1	0	1	9
Burglary	174	42	14	1	1	0	14	20
Larceny-theft	225	61	29	0	0	0	2	32
Motor vehicle theft	20	1	3	1	0	0	0	2
Arson	36	8	1	0	0	0	0	10
Destruction/damage/vandalism	1,783	251	52	6	3	0	8	373
Other[3]	60	24	4	1	0	0	0	10
Crimes against society [3]	**79**	**56**	**9**	**3**	**0**	**0**	**4**	**3**

1 The figures shown in this row for the offense of rape include only those reported by law enforcement agencies that used the revised Uniform Crime Reporting (UCR) definition of rape. See the data declaration for further explanation.   2 The figures shown in this row for the offense of rape include only those reported by law enforcement agencies that used the legacy UCR definition of rape. See the data declaration for further explanation.   3 Includes additional offenses collected in the National Incident-Based Reporting System. See Methodology.

Table 85.   Offenses, Offense Type, by Bias Motivation, 2013

(Number.)

Bias motivation	Total offenses	Crimes against persons						Crimes against property							Crimes against society[2]
		Murder and nonnegligent manslaughter	Rape (revised definition)[1]	Aggravated assault	Simple assault	Intimidation	Other[2]	Robbery	Burglary	Larceny-theft	Motor vehicle theft	Arson	Destruction/damage/vandalism	Other[2]	
Total	6,933	5	15	734	1,720	1,925	25	126	174	225	20	36	1,783	60	79
Single-Bias Incidents	6,921	5	15	733	1,717	1,922	25	125	174	225	20	36	1,779	60	79
Race	3,407	2	7	398	750	1,087	15	54	91	126	11	17	759	36	54
Anti-White	728	1	6	79	194	155	9	24	32	75	6	4	98	17	28
Anti-Black or African American	2,263	1	0	288	478	829	2	23	36	16	1	11	557	7	14
Anti-American Indian or Alaska Native	146	0	0	11	16	26	1	3	16	27	4	0	22	10	10
Anti-Asian	158	0	1	15	43	43	2	4	6	5	0	2	34	2	1
Anti-Native Hawaiian or Other Pacific Islander	3	0	0	1	1	1	0	0	0	0	0	0	0	0	0
Anti-Multiple races, group	109	0	0	4	18	33	1	0	1	3	0	0	48	0	1
Religion	1,163	0	1	23	134	255	1	3	29	38	1	17	649	6	5
Anti-Jewish	689	0	0	5	72	152	0	1	6	11	0	4	437	1	0
Anti-Catholic	74	0	0	0	6	11	0	0	6	9	0	3	36	1	2
Anti-Protestant	42	0	0	0	0	3	0	0	6	5	0	3	24	1	0
Anti-Islamic (Muslim)	165	0	0	17	41	53	0	2	2	2	0	1	43	2	1
Anti-other religion	135	0	1	1	11	26	1	0	5	4	1	5	78	1	1
Anti-multiple religions, group	51	0	0	0	3	10	0	0	3	6	0	1	27	0	1
Anti-atheism/agnosticism/etc.	7	0	0	0	1	0	0	0	1	1	0	0	4	0	0
Sexual orientation	1,402	2	3	193	547	318	1	47	30	17	3	2	223	8	4
Anti-gay (male)	849	2	0	120	359	188	0	30	23	4	0	2	115	6	0
Anti-lesbian	185	0	0	24	66	56	0	3	0	3	0	0	28	1	0
Anti-lesbian, gay, bisexual, or transgender (mixed group)	317	0	1	47	111	58	0	13	3	4	2	0	76	1	1
Anti-heterosexual	24	0	1	0	6	6	1	0	3	2	0	0	2	0	3
Anti-bisexual	27	0	1	2	5	10	0	1	1	4	1	0	2	0	0
Ethnicity	794	1	1	103	241	235	6	15	18	23	3	0	132	7	9
Anti-Hispanic or Latino	418	1	1	79	118	128	0	11	9	7	1	0	55	4	4
Anti-Not Hispanic or Latino[3]	376	0	0	24	123	107	6	4	9	16	2	0	77	3	5
Disability	92	0	1	6	16	21	2	3	5	17	1	0	11	3	6
Anti-physical	23	0	1	1	5	5	0	2	0	6	0	0	2	1	0
Anti-mental	69	0	0	5	11	16	2	1	5	11	1	0	9	2	6
Gender	30	0	2	2	19	2	0	0	0	2	1	0	1	0	1
Anti-male	5	0	0	1	1	0	0	0	0	1	1	0	1	0	0
Anti-female	25	0	2	1	18	2	0	0	0	1	0	0	0	0	1
Gender Identity	33	0	0	8	10	4	0	3	1	2	0	0	4	0	0
Anti-transgender	25	0	0	8	7	4	0	3	1	0	0	0	2	0	0
Anti-gender non-conforming	8	0	0	0	3	0	0	0	0	2	0	0	2	0	0
Multiple-Bias Incidents[4]	12	0	0	1	3	3	0	1	0	0	0	0	4	0	0

1 The figures shown in this column for the offense of rape include only those reported by law enforcement agencies that used the revised Uniform Crime Reporting (UCR) definition of rape.   2 Includes additional offenses collected in the National Incident-Based Reporting System.   3 The term anti-not Hispanic or Latino does not imply the victim was targeted because he/she was not of Hispanic origin, but it refers to other or unspecified ethnic biases that are not Hispanic or Latino.   4 A multiple-bias incident is an incident in which one or more offense types are motivated by two or more biases.

Table 86.   Offenses, Known Offender's Race, by Bias Motivation, 2013

(Number.)

Bias motivation	Total offenses	Known offender's race							Known offender's ethnicity[1]				Unknown offender
		White	Black or African American	American Indian or Alaska Native	Asian	Native Hawaiian or Other Pacific Islander	Group of multiple races	Unknown race	Hispanic or Latino	Not Hispanic or Latino	Group of multiple ethnicities	Unknown ethnicity	
Total	6,933	2,963	1,091	50	41	2	199	787	13	173	12	98	1,800
Single-Bias Incidents	6,921	2,955	1,089	50	41	2	199	787	13	173	12	98	1,798
Race	3,407	1,667	446	33	22	1	77	266	5	66	9	35	895
Anti-White	728	176	299	14	4	1	15	43	0	16	3	10	176
Anti-Black or African American	2,263	1,336	85	9	14	0	58	175	4	46	2	19	586
Anti-American Indian or Alaska Native	146	47	31	7	3	0	0	14	0	0	2	4	44
Anti-Asian	158	69	23	0	1	0	3	15	1	3	1	1	47
Anti-Native Hawaiian or Other Pacific Islander	3	2	0	0	0	0	1	0	0	0	0	0	0
Anti-Multiple races, group	109	37	8	3	0	0	0	19	0	1	1	1	42
Religion	1,163	297	68	1	0	0	22	306	1	4	1	9	469
Anti-Jewish	689	143	35	0	0	0	4	236	0	2	0	7	271
Anti-Catholic	74	25	0	0	0	0	2	24	1	1	0	0	23
Anti-Protestant	42	8	0	0	0	0	0	9	0	1	0	0	25
Anti-Islamic (Muslim)	165	67	20	0	0	0	16	17	0	0	1	1	45
Anti-other religion	135	39	4	1	0	0	0	13	0	0	0	0	78
Anti-multiple religions, group	51	15	7	0	0	0	0	6	0	0	0	1	23
Anti-atheism/agnosticism/etc.	7	0	2	0	0	0	0	1	0	0	0	0	4
Sexual orientation	1,402	564	329	7	11	0	75	149	6	36	0	32	267
Anti-gay (male)	849	334	208	4	9	0	51	95	2	19	0	25	148
Anti-lesbian	185	81	41	2	1	0	10	18	0	6	0	3	32
Anti-lesbian, gay, bisexual, or transgender (mixed group)	317	126	73	0	1	0	14	29	3	8	0	2	74
Anti-heterosexual	24	10	3	0	0	0	0	5	0	1	0	2	6
Anti-bisexual	27	13	4	1	0	0	0	2	1	2	0	0	7
Ethnicity	794	365	203	8	3	1	20	53	1	52	2	15	141
Anti-Hispanic or Latino	418	220	97	4	2	1	14	12	1	13	2	2	68
Anti-Not Hispanic or Latino[2]	376	145	106	4	1	0	6	41	0	39	0	13	73
Disability	92	32	21	1	5	0	4	8	0	4	0	0	21
Anti-physical	23	10	7	0	0	0	1	1	0	0	0	0	4
Anti-mental	69	22	14	1	5	0	3	7	0	4	0	0	17
Gender	30	22	4	0	0	0	0	3	0	1	0	2	1
Anti-male	5	2	1	0	0	0	0	2	0	0	0	2	
Anti-female	25	20	3	0	0	0	0	1	0	1	0	0	1
Gender Identity	33	8	18	0	0	0	1	2	0	10	0	5	4
Anti-transgender	25	4	17	0	0	0	0	0	0	9	0	5	4
Anti-gender nonconforming	8	4	1	0	0	0	1	2	0	1	0	0	0
Multiple-Bias Incidents[3]	12	8	2	0	0	0	0	0	0	0	0	0	2

1 The total number of offenses by the known offender's ethnicity do not equal the total number of offenses by the known offender's race because not all law enforcement agencies that report offender race data also report offender ethnicity data.   2 The term anti-not Hispanic or Latino does not imply the victim was targeted because he/she was not of Hispanic origin, but it refers to other or unspecified ethnic biases that are not Hispanic or Latino.   3 In a multiple-bias incident, two conditions must be met: (a) more than one offense type must occur in the incident and (b) at least two offense types must be motivated by different biases.

Table 87.   Offenses, Victim Type, by Offense Type, 2013

(Number.)

Offense type	Total offenses	Victim type					
		Individual	Business/financial institution	Government	Religious organiza-tion	Society/ public[1]	Other/ unknown/ multiple
Total	6,933	5,682	307	177	180	79	508
Crimes against persons[2]	4,430	4,430	NA	NA	NA	NA	NA
Crimes against property	2,424	1,252	307	177	180	0	508
Robbery	126	120	1	0	0	0	5
Burglary	174	116	15	0	16	0	27
Larceny-theft	225	145	56	3	8	0	13
Motor vehicle theft	20	17	2	0	0	0	1
Arson	36	16	0	0	9	0	11
Destruction/ dam-age/vandalism	1,783	796	220	172	147	0	448
Other[2]	60	42	13	2	0	0	3
Crimes against society[2]	79	NA	NA	NA	NA	79	NA

NA = Not available.   1 The victim type society/public is collected only in the National Incident-Based Reporting System (NIBRS).   2 Includes additional offenses collected in the NIBRS.

Table 88.   Victims, Offense Type, by Bias Motivation, 2013

(Number.)

Bias motivation	Total victims	Crimes against persons						
		Murder and nonnegligent manslaughter	Rape (revised definition)[1]	Rape (legacy definition)[2]	Aggravated assault	Simple assault	Intimidation	Other[3]
Total	7,242	5	15	6	734	1,720	1,925	25
Single-Bias Incidents	7,230	5	15	6	733	1,717	1,922	25
Race	3,563	2	7	0	398	750	1,087	15
Anti-White	754	1	6	0	79	194	155	9
Anti-Black or African American	2,371	1	0	0	288	478	829	2
Anti-American Indian or Alaska Native	159	0	0	0	11	16	26	1
Anti-Asian	164	0	1	0	15	43	43	2
Anti-Native Hawaiian or Other Pacific Islander	3	0	0	0	1	1	1	0
Anti-Multiple races, group	112	0	0	0	4	18	33	1
Religion	1,223	0	1	1	23	134	255	1
Anti-Jewish	737	0	0	0	5	72	152	0
Anti-Catholic	75	0	0	0	0	6	11	0
Anti-Protestant	47	0	0	0	0	0	3	0
Anti-Islamic (Muslim)	167	0	0	1	17	41	53	0
Anti-other religion	137	0	1	0	1	11	26	1
Anti-multiple religions, group	53	0	0	0	0	3	10	0
Anti-atheism/agnosticism/etc.	7	0	0	0	0	1	0	0
Sexual orientation	1,461	2	3	4	193	547	318	1
Anti-gay (male)	890	2	0	0	120	359	188	0
Anti-lesbian	191	0	0	4	24	66	56	0
Anti-lesbian, gay, bisexual, or transgender (mixed group)	329	0	1	0	47	111	58	0
Anti-heterosexual	24	0	1	0	0	6	6	1
Anti-bisexual	27	0	1	0	2	5	10	0
Ethnicity	821	1	1	0	103	241	235	6
Anti-Hispanic or Latino	432	1	1	0	79	118	128	0
Anti-Not Hispanic or Latino[4]	389	0	0	0	24	123	107	6
Disability	99	0	1	0	6	16	21	2
Anti-physical	24	0	1	0	1	5	5	0
Anti-mental	75	0	0	0	5	11	16	2
Gender	30	0	2	0	2	19	2	0
Anti-male	5	0	0	0	1	1	0	0
Anti-female	25	0	2	0	1	18	2	0
Gender Identity	33	0	0	1	8	10	4	0
Anti-transgender	25	0	0	0	8	7	4	0
Anti-gender nonconforming	8	0	0	1	0	3	0	0
Multiple-Bias Incidents [5]	12	0	0	0	1	3	3	0
Individual Victim Age Total [6]	2,801							
Individual victims 18 and over	2,352							
Individual victims under 18	449							

Table 88.   Victims, Offense Type, by Bias Motivation, 2013

(Number.)

Bias motivation	Crimes against property							Crimes against society[5]
	Robbery	Burglary	Larceny-theft	Motor vehicle theft	Arson	Destruction/ damage/ vandalism	Other[3]	
Total	145	202	246	21	40	2,011	68	79
Single-Bias Incidents	144	202	246	21	40	2,007	68	79
Race	60	110	138	12	20	867	43	54
Anti-White	25	36	79	6	4	111	21	28
Anti-Black or African American	25	49	21	1	11	645	7	14
Anti-American Indian or Alaska Native	6	17	30	5	0	24	13	10
Anti-Asian	4	6	5	0	5	37	2	1
Anti-Native Hawaiian or Other Pacific Islander	0	0	0	0	0	0	0	0
Anti-Multiple races, group	0	2	3	0	0	50	0	1
Religion	4	32	40	1	18	702	6	5
Anti-Jewish	1	7	12	0	4	483	1	0
Anti-Catholic	0	6	9	0	3	37	1	2
Anti-Protestant	0	8	5	0	3	27	1	0
Anti-Islamic (Muslim)	3	2	2	0	1	44	2	1
Anti-other religion	0	5	4	1	6	79	1	1
Anti-multiple religions, group	0	3	7	0	1	28	0	1
Anti-atheism/agnosticism/etc.	0	1	1	0	0	4	0	0
Sexual orientation	56	33	18	3	2	269	8	4
Anti-gay (male)	37	26	4	0	2	146	6	0
Anti-lesbian	3	0	4	0	0	33	1	0
Anti-lesbian, gay, bisexual, or transgender (mixed group)	15	3	4	2	0	86	1	1
Anti-heterosexual	0	3	2	0	0	2	0	3
Anti-bisexual	1	1	4	1	0	2	0	0
Ethnicity	17	20	24	3	0	153	8	9
Anti-Hispanic or Latino	13	9	7	1	0	67	4	4
Anti-Not Hispanic or Latino[4]	4	11	17	2	0	86	4	5
Disability	4	6	22	1	0	11	3	6
Anti-physical	3	0	6	0	0	2	1	0
Anti-mental	1	6	16	1	0	9	2	6
Gender	0	0	2	1	0	1	0	1
Anti-male	0	0	1	1	0	1	0	0
Anti-female	0	0	1	0	0	0	0	1
Gender Identity	3	1	2	0	0	4	0	0
Anti-transgender	3	1	0	0	0	2	0	0
Anti-gender nonconforming	0	0	2	0	0	2	0	0
Multiple-Bias Incidents[5]	1	0	0	0	0	4	0	0
Individual Victim Age Total[6]								
Individual victims 18 and over								
Individual victims under 18								

1 The figures shown in this column for the offense of rape include only those reported by law enforcement agencies that used the revised Uniform Crime Reporting (UCR) definition of rape.   2 The figures shown in this column for the offense of rape include only those reported by law enforcement agencies that used the legacy UCR definition of rape.   3 Includes additional offenses collected in the National Incident-Based Reporting System.   4 The term anti-not Hispanic or Latino does not imply the victim was targeted because he/she was not of Hispanic origin, but it refers to other or unspecified ethnic biases that are not Hispanic or Latino.   5 A multiple-bias incident is an incident in which one or more offense types are motivated by two or more biases.   6 The individual victim age total does not equal the total number of victims because a victim can be an individual, a business, an institution, or society as a whole. In addition, not all law enforcement agencies report the ages of individual victims.

Table 89.   Incidents, Victim Type, by Bias Motivation, 2013

(Number.)

Bias motivation	Total incidents	Victim type					
		Individual	Business/financial institution	Government	Religious organization	Society/public[1]	Other/ unknown/ multiple
Total	5,928	4,696	298	177	171	64	522
Single-Bias Incidents	5,922	4,690	298	177	171	64	522
Race	2,871	2,402	145	107	10	43	164
Religion	1,031	450	87	44	158	5	287
Sexual Orientation	1,233	1,154	25	12	1	4	37
Ethnicity	655	572	35	13	2	5	28
Disability	83	69	4	1	0	6	3
Gender	18	15	1	0	0	1	1
Gender Identity	31	28	1	0	0	0	2
Multiple-Bias Incidents [2]	6	6	0	0	0	0	0

1 The victim type society/public is collected only in the National Incident-Based Reporting System.   2 A multiple-bias incident is an incident in which one or more offense types are motivated by two or more biases.

Table 90.   Known Offenders,[1] by Known Offender's Race, Ethnicity, and Age, 2013

(Number.)

Race/ethnicity/age	Total
Race	5,814
White	3,046
Black or African American	1,410
American Indian or Alaska Native	49
Asian	40
Native Hawaiian or Other Pacific Islander	3
Group of multiple races[2]	407
Unknown race	859
Ethnicity [3]	368
Hispanic or Latino	12
Not Hispanic or Latino	199
Group of multiple ethnicities[4]	23
Unknown ethnicity	134
Age [3]	2,527
Total known offenders 18 and over	1,719
Total known offenders under 18	808

1 The term known offender does not imply that the identity of the suspect is known, but only that an attribute of the suspect has been identified, which distinguishes him/her from an unknown offender.   2 The term group of multiple races is used to describe a group of offenders of varying races.   3 The total number of known offenders by age and the total number of known offenders by ethnicity do not equal the total number of known offenders by race because not all law enforcement agencies report the age and/or ethnicity of the known offenders.   4 The term group of multiple ethnicities is used to describe a group of offenders of varying ethnicities.

Table 91.   Incidents, Bias Motivation, by Location, 2013

(Number.)

Location	Total incidents	Bias motivation							Multiple-bias incidents[1]
		Race	Religion	Sexual orientation	Ethnicity	Disability	Gender	Gender Identity	
Total	5,928	2,871	1,031	1,233	655	83	18	31	6
Abandoned/condemned structure	2	0	0	1	0	1	0	0	0
Air/bus/train terminal	63	31	5	21	4	0	0	2	0
Arena/stadium/ fair-grounds/coliseum	3	1	0	2	0	0	0	0	0
Auto dealership new/used	2	2	0	0	0	0	0	0	0
Bank/savings and loan	11	4	3	1	2	1	0	0	0
Bar/nightclub	121	53	5	44	16	1	1	1	0
Camp/campground	2	1	1	0	0	0	0	0	0
Church/synagogue/temple/mosque	206	13	189	2	2	0	0	0	0
Commercial office building	117	62	17	18	15	3	1	1	0
Community center	1	0	1	0	0	0	0	0	0
Construction site	13	5	3	0	5	0	0	0	0
Convenience store	69	33	10	3	23	0	0	0	0
Daycare facility	3	1	0	1	1	0	0	0	0
Department/discount store	59	29	10	8	10	1	0	1	0
Drug store/Doctor's office/hospital	48	30	11	3	3	0	0	1	0
Farm facility	1	1	0	0	0	0	0	0	0
Field/woods	53	31	5	14	3	0	0	0	0
Gambling facility/casino/race track	3	1	0	0	2	0	0	0	0
Government/public building	107	60	13	15	18	1	0	0	0
Grocery/supermarket	53	32	2	8	10	1	0	0	0
Highway/road/alley/street/sidewalk	1,071	551	92	284	120	15	1	7	1
Hotel/motel/etc.	32	13	6	5	7	1	0	0	0
Industrial site	6	4	0	1	1	0	0	0	0
Jail/prison/penitentiary/corrections facility	71	46	5	14	5	0	1	0	0
Lake/waterway/beach	4	2	2	0	0	0	0	0	0
Liquor store	8	3	0	2	3	0	0	0	0
Park/playground	67	46	7	11	3	0	0	0	0
Parking/drop lot/garage	336	182	28	75	44	0	3	2	2
Rental storage facility	4	1	1	2	0	0	0	0	0
Residence/home	1,865	976	240	397	207	37	2	5	1
Rest area	2	1	0	0	1	0	0	0	0
Restaurant	126	63	9	30	21	1	0	2	0
School/college[2]	234	111	53	45	21	3	1	0	0
School—college/university	100	47	13	23	13	1	1	1	1
School—elementary/secondary	158	92	13	21	27	4	1	0	0
Service/gas station	55	30	6	8	10	0	0	1	0
Shelter—mission/homeless	4	2	0	2	0	0	0	0	0
Shopping mall	9	3	2	2	1	1	0	0	0
Specialty store (TV, fur, etc.)	42	22	6	5	8	1	0	0	0
Tribal lands	4	2	0	0	1	0	0	1	0
Other/unknown	782	276	272	164	48	9	6	6	1
Multiple locations	11	8	1	1	0	1	0	0	0

1 A multiple-bias incident is an incident in which one or more offense types are motivated by two or more biases.   2 The location designation school/college has been retained for agencies that have not updated their records management systems to include the new location designations of "school—college/university" and "school—elementary/secondary," which allow for more specificity in reporting.

Table 92.   Offenses, Offense Type, by Selected State, 2013

(Number.)

State	Total offenses	Crimes against persons						
		Murder and nonnegligent manslaughter	Rape (revised definition)[1]	Rape (legacy definition)[2]	Aggravated assault	Simple assault	Intimidation	Other[3]
Total	6,933	5	15	6	734	1,720	1,925	25
Alabama	6	0	0		2	2	1	0
Alaska	9	0	0		3	1	3	0
Arizona	212	0	0	1	45	46	61	0
Arkansas	34	1	0		6	4	17	0
California	1,012	1		1	149	239	235	0
Colorado	154	0	2		19	37	48	0
Connecticut	172	0	0	0	9	29	71	0
Delaware	13	0	0		3	3	5	0
District of Columbia	80	0	0		16	37	12	0
Florida	82	0	0		13	21	16	0
Georgia	72	0		0	9	22	31	0
Idaho	37	0	0		9	6	10	0
Illinois	123	0	0	0	28	42	18	0
Indiana	78	0	0	0	13	21	30	0
Iowa	15	0	0		6	1	3	0
Kansas	74	0	0	0	3	21	17	0
Kentucky	209	0	0	0	10	42	68	6
Louisiana	23	0	0	0	1	6	2	0
Maine	28	0	0	0	0	8	13	0
Maryland	58	0		0	13	12	6	0
Massachusetts	393	0	2	0	16	72	177	1
Michigan	399	0	3		54	92	152	0
Minnesota	167	0	2		25	38	63	0
Mississippi	4	0	0	0	0	0	0	1
Missouri	116	1	1		21	29	21	1
Montana	37	0	0		3	11	0	1
Nebraska	39	0	0	0	2	13	3	1
Nevada	80	0		1	14	31	9	0
New Hampshire	23	0	0		1	5	7	0
New Jersey	447	0		0	11	26	259	0
New Mexico	12	0		0	2	3	3	0
New York	655	2		1	28	300	3	0
North Carolina	140	0		0	20	34	37	0
North Dakota	63	0	1		4	22	13	1
Ohio	447	0	1	0	11	62	181	2
Oklahoma	45	0	0	0	2	14	13	0
Oregon	75	0	0	0	7	12	15	0
Pennsylvania	110	0	0		11	12	72	0
Rhode Island	8	0	0	0	0	2	1	0
South Carolina	59	0	0		13	16	12	0
South Dakota	18	0	0		2	7	1	1
Tennessee	245	0	2		36	100	47	8
Texas	161	0	0	1	27	65	29	0
Utah	87	0	0	0	7	12	10	2
Vermont	13	0	0		1	4	2	0
Virginia	126	0	0		6	31	20	0
Washington	344	0	1	1	41	76	86	0
West Virginia	63	0	0		4	12	4	0
Wisconsin	65	0	0	0	7	19	18	0
Wyoming	1	0		0	1	0	0	0

Table 92.   Offenses, Offense Type, by Selected State, 2013

(Number.)

State	Crimes against property							Crimes against society[2]
	Robbery	Burglary	Larceny-theft	Motor vehicle theft	Arson	Destruction/ damage/vandalism	Other[3]	
Total	126	174	225	20	36	1,783	60	79
Alabama	0	0	1	0	0	0	0	0
Alaska	0	1	0	0	0	1	0	0
Arizona	8	5	3	0	0	39	1	3
Arkansas	0	0	1	0	1	4	0	0
California	32	19	3	2	7	324	0	0
Colorado	6	1	3	0	0	37	1	0
Connecticut	0	1	12	0	0	41	1	8
Delaware	0	0	0	0	0	2	0	0
District of Columbia	6	1	1	0	0	7	0	0
Florida	2	2	1	1	0	26	0	0
Georgia	3	0	0	0	0	7	0	0
Idaho	0	0	2	0	0	9	1	0
Illinois	3	2	4	0	1	25	0	0
Indiana	1	2	0	0	0	11	0	0
Iowa	0	1	0	0	0	4	0	0
Kansas	0	2	7	0	0	20	3	1
Kentucky	6	13	10	3	2	40	5	4
Louisiana	0	0	4	0	1	8	1	0
Maine	1	0	0	0	1	4	0	1
Maryland	0	1	1	0	2	23	0	0
Massachusetts	3	6	14	0	0	98	3	1
Michigan	2	10	13	0	3	66	4	0
Minnesota	5	1	1	0	0	32	0	0
Mississippi	0	1	2	0	0	0	0	0
Missouri	3	6	4	3	0	19	4	3
Montana	0	1	8	1	0	11	1	0
Nebraska	0	0	1	0	0	15	2	2
Nevada	4	7	0	0	0	14	0	0
New Hampshire	0	2	0	0	0	8	0	0
New Jersey	2	2	1	0	1	145	0	0
New Mexico	0	0	1	0	0	3	0	0
New York	0	26	8	0	5	282	0	0
North Carolina	3	2	3	0	0	41	0	0
North Dakota	0	1	6	1	0	8	1	5
Ohio	10	22	43	6	1	90	10	8
Oklahoma	1	1	1	0	1	11	1	0
Oregon	0	3	1	0	0	37	0	0
Pennsylvania	0	0	0	0	4	11	0	0
Rhode Island	0	1	0	0	0	4	0	0
South Carolina	0	1	5	0	0	10	2	0
South Dakota	1	1	1	0	0	4	0	0
Tennessee	6	2	4	0	1	30	3	6
Texas	6	1	0	0	0	31	0	1
Utah	0	2	10	2	0	16	2	24
Vermont	0	0	2	0	0	4	0	0
Virginia	1	2	1	0	2	60	2	1
Washington	4	11	26	1	2	76	8	11
West Virginia	4	10	14	0	0	12	3	0
Wisconsin	3	1	2	0	1	13	1	0
Wyoming	0	0	0	0	0	0	0	0

1 The figures shown in this column for the offense of rape include only those reported by law enforcement agencies that used the revised Uniform Crime Reporting (UCR) definition of rape.   2 The figures shown in this column for the offense of rape include only those reported by law enforcement agencies that used the legacy UCR definition of rape.   3 Includes additional offenses collected in the National Incident-Based Reporting System.

Table 93.   Agency Hate Crime Reporting, by Selected State and Territory, 2013

(Number.)

State	Number of participating agencies	Population covered	Agencies submitting incident reports	Total number of incidents reported
Total	15,016	295,016,072	1,826	5,928
Alabama	48	1,147,612	4	6
Alaska	33	730,950	1	8
Arizona	81	6,358,545	21	155
Arkansas	265	2,809,536	20	27
California	732	38,324,460	229	843
Colorado	226	5,163,276	48	128
Connecticut	98	3,566,367	48	145
Delaware	58	925,749	11	12
District of Columbia	2	646,449	2	72
Florida	504	19,455,529	41	76
Georgia	499	7,817,674	7	57
Guam[1]	1	0	0	0
Idaho	108	1,611,676	12	32
Illinois	720	12,269,532	38	105
Indiana	134	4,034,953	15	75
Iowa	222	2,958,457	9	10
Kansas	354	2,665,446	30	64
Kentucky	385	4,334,254	77	171
Louisiana	109	3,237,092	6	22
Maine	148	1,328,302	17	25
Maryland	154	5,928,814	20	51
Massachusetts	330	6,496,451	78	350
Michigan	600	9,733,958	141	329
Minnesota	257	4,904,213	39	144
Mississippi	90	1,497,332	2	4
Missouri	621	6,040,074	20	102
Montana	98	1,000,016	12	31
Nebraska	182	1,511,235	10	36
Nevada	5	2,229,342	5	73
New Hampshire	151	1,178,087	16	21
New Jersey	508	8,898,292	140	414
New Mexico	23	888,880	3	12
New York	566	19,515,678	85	615
North Carolina	522	9,845,983	48	118
North Dakota	105	722,021	19	51
Ohio	644	10,376,248	111	370
Oklahoma	328	3,850,568	25	41
Oregon	76	2,301,273	18	66
Pennsylvania	1,375	12,657,821	20	64
Rhode Island	48	1,051,511	7	7
South Carolina	418	4,761,406	39	51
South Dakota	113	767,653	8	13
Tennessee	466	6,495,978	56	196
Texas	1,000	26,304,575	50	132
Utah	131	2,883,607	35	75
Vermont	88	623,447	10	12
Virginia	416	8,258,337	54	119
Virgin Islands[1]	2	0	0	0
Washington	244	6,967,181	80	291
West Virginia	263	1,670,269	17	56
Wisconsin	402	5,691,976	21	50
Wyoming	63	577,987	1	1

1 The 2013 population estimates were not available at the time of publication.

Table 94.   Hate Crime Incidents Per Bias Motivation and Quarter, by Selected State and Agency, 2013

(Number.)

State/agency	Number of incidents per bias motivation							Number of incidents per quarter[1]				Population[2]
	Race	Religion	Sexual orien- tation	Ethnicity	Disability	Gender	Gender Identity	1st quarter	2nd quarter	3rd quarter	4th quarter	
ALABAMA												
Total	5	0	1	0	0	0	0					
Cities	5	0	1	0	0	0	0					
Florence	2	0	0	0	0	0	0	0	1	0	1	39,481
Hoover	0	0	1	0	0	0	0	0	1	0	0	84,139
Prattville	2	0	0	0	0	0	0	1	0	1	0	35,154
Tuscaloosa	1	0	0	0	0	0	0	0	0	1	0	94,126
ALASKA												
Total	8	0	0	0	0	0	0					
Cities	8	0	0	0	0							
Anchorage	8	0	0	0	0	0	0	2	3	3	0	299,455
ARIZONA												
Total	73	30	27	24	1	0	0					
Cities	68	27	25	23	1	0	0					
Apache Junction	1	0	0	0	0	0	0	1	0	0		36,626
Avondale	4	0	0	1	0	0	0	1	1	3	0	78,905
Eagar	0	0	0	1	0	0	0	0	1	0	0	5,034
El Mirage	1	0	0	0	0	0	0	0	0	1	0	32,837
Gilbert	1	0	0	0	0	0	0	1	0	0	0	225,232
Glendale	2	3	1	1	0	0	0	2	0	3	2	234,006
Goodyear	0	0	2	0	0	0	0	1		1	0	71,048
Maricopa	1	0	0	0	0	0	0	0	0	0	1	44,871
Mesa	1	1	0	0	0	0	0	2	0	0	0	456,155
Phoenix	40	12	14	14	1	0	0	25	21	35		1,502,139
Prescott	0	0	0	1	0	0	0	0	0	0	1	40,752
Scottsdale	0	1	0	1	0	0	0	0	0	0	2	225,523
Tempe	1	0	2	0	0	0	0	2	0	1	0	168,501
Tucson	13	6	6	1	0	0	0	8	8	6	4	525,486
Yuma	3	4	0	3	0	0	0	3	5	0	2	96,014
Universities and Colleges	2	0	1	0	0	0	0					
Northern Arizona University	0	0	1	0	0	0	0	0	0	0	1	25,991
University of Arizona	2	0	0	0	0	0	0	2	0	0	0	40,223
Metropolitan Counties	3	3	1	1	0	0	0					
Cochise	0	1	0	0	0	0	0	0	0	0	1	
Maricopa	1	1	0	0	0	0	0	0			2	
Pima	1	1	1	0	0	0	0	0	0	0	3	
Yuma	1	0	0	1	0	0	0	0	1	0	1	
ARKANSAS												
Total	17	0	8	2	0	0	0					
Cities	10	0	3	0	0	0	0					
Bentonville	1	0	0	0	0	0	0	0	0	1	0	39,132
Berryville	1	0	0	0	0	0	0	0	0	1	0	5,417
Cabot	1	0	0	0	0	0	0	0	0	1	0	24,695
England	1	0	0	0	0	0	0	0	1	0	0	2,806
Fairfield Bay	1	0	0	0	0	0	0	0	0	1	0	2,295
Fort Smith	1	0	1	0	0	0	0	0	0	0	2	87,821
Gurdon	1	0	0	0	0	0	0	1	0	0	0	2,184
Marion	0	0	1	0	0	0	0	0	0	1	0	12,258
North Little Rock	1	0	0	0	0	0	0	0	1	0	0	65,398
Pine Bluff	0	0	1	0	0	0	0	1	0	0	0	46,399
Rogers	1	0	0	0	0	0	0	0	1	0	0	59,787
Sherwood	1	0	0	0	0	0	0	1	0	0	0	29,900
Universities and Colleges	0	0	1	0	0	0	0					
University of Arkansas, Pine Bluff	0	0	1	0	0	0	0	0	0	1	0	2,828
Metropolitan Counties	6	0	3	2	0	0	0					
Crawford	2	0	2	0	0	0	0	0	2	1	1	
Faulkner	1	0	0	1	0	0	0	0	1	0	1	
Lonoke	1	0	0	0	0	0	0	1	0	0	0	
Pulaski	1	0	1	1	0	0	0	1	0	1	1	
Sebastian	1	0	0	0	0	0	0	0	1	0	0	
Nonmetropolitan Counties	1	0	1	0	0	0	0					
Greene	1	0	0	0	0	0	0	0	0	1	0	
Pope	0	0	1	0	0	0	0	0	1	0	0	

Table 94.   Hate Crime Incidents Per Bias Motivation and Quarter, by Selected State and Agency, 2013— continued

(Number.)

State/agency	Number of incidents per bias motivation							Number of incidents per quarter[1]				Population[2]
	Race	Religion	Sexual orien-tation	Ethnicity	Disability	Gender	Gender Identity	1st quarter	2nd quarter	3rd quarter	4th quarter	
CALIFORNIA												
Total	374	129	217	115	1	0	7					
Cities	291	117	166	87	1	0	6					
Adelanto	1	0	0	1	0	0	0	1	0	1	0	31,165
Agoura Hills	2	0	0	0	0	0	0	0	2	0	0	20,762
Alameda	0	1	0	0	0	0	0	0	0	0	1	76,206
Alhambra	1	0	0	0	0	0	0	0	0	0	1	84,710
Antioch	2	0	0	0	0	0	0	1	1	0	0	106,447
Arcadia	1	0	0	0	0	0	0	1	0	0	0	57,855
Atascadero	1	0	0	1	0	0	0	0	0	1	1	28,938
Atwater	0	0	0	1	0	0	0	0	1	0	0	28,906
Auburn	1	0	0	0	0	0	0	0	1	0	0	13,779
Azusa	1	0	0	0	0	0	0	0	0	1	0	47,754
Bakersfield	2	1	0	0	0	0	0	0	0	2	1	361,859
Baldwin Park	0	0	1	0	0	0	0	0	0	1	0	76,745
Banning	0	0	0	1	0	0	0	0	0	1	0	30,503
Berkeley	7	1	4	1	0	0	0	6	2	4	1	116,217
Beverly Hills	0	1	0	0	0	0	0	1	0	0	0	34,780
Brentwood[3]	4	0	0	0	0	0	0	0	1	2	1	54,301
Buena Park[3]	0	0	1	1	0	0	0	0	1	0	1	82,632
Burbank	1	1	2	1	0	0	0	1	2	2	0	104,727
Calabasas	0	2	0	0	0	0	0	1	0	0	1	24,114
Camarillo	2	1	0	0	0	0	0	1	1	1	0	66,173
Campbell	1	0	0	0	0	0	0	0	1	0	0	40,549
Carlsbad	1	1	0	1	0	0	0	0	0	3	0	110,505
Carson	1	0	0	0	0	0	0	0	0	0	1	93,415
Cerritos	3	0	0	0	0	0	0	1	0	0	2	49,816
Chico	1	3	0	0	0	0	0	1	2	0	1	88,226
Chino	2	2	2	3	0	0	0	2	2	3	2	80,704
Chula Vista	3	0	1	0	0	0	0	0	3	0	1	255,073
Citrus Heights	1	0	0	0	0	0	0	0	1	0	0	85,337
Claremont	1	1	1	0	0	0	0	2	0	0	1	35,623
Clearlake	1	0	1	0	0	0	0	1	0	0	1	14,951
Clovis	0	1	2	1	0	0	0	0	1	1	2	99,483
Colton	1	0	0	0	0	0	0	0	0	0	1	53,403
Compton	1	0	1	0	0	0	0	0	1	0	1	97,907
Concord	1	0	0	0	0	0	0	0	1	0	0	125,464
Corcoran	1	0	0	0	0	0	0	0	0	1	0	23,290
Corona	0	0	0	1	0	0	0	0	0	0	1	160,159
Coronado	0	1	0	0	0	0	0	1	0	0	0	23,183
Costa Mesa	1	0	0	0	0	0	0	0	0	0	1	112,538
Covina	0	2	1	0	0	0	0	0	3	0	0	48,524
Cupertino	0	0	0	0	0	0	1	0	0	0	1	60,440
Cypress	0	0	0	1	0	0	0	0	0	1	0	49,067
Daly City	0	2	1	0	0	0	0	1	0	1	1	104,536
Dana Point	0	1	0	0	0	0	0	0	1	0	0	34,262
Davis	2	1	4	1	0	0	0	3	4	0	1	66,126
Duarte	1	0	1	0	0	0	0	1	0	1	0	21,759
El Cajon	1	0	0	1	0	0	0	0	1	0	1	102,012
El Cerrito	0	2	1	4	0	0	0	3	1	2	1	24,184
Elk Grove	1	0	0	0	0	0	0	0	0	0	1	160,925
El Monte	5	0	0	0	0	0	0	0	3	0	2	115,591
Emeryville	1	0	0	0	0	0	0	0	1	0	0	10,415
Encinitas	2	1	0	1	0	0	0	2	1	1	0	61,433
Escondido	4	1	1	2	0	0	0	2	2	3	1	148,650
Eureka	1	0	1	0	0	0	0	1	1	0	0	26,881
Fairfield	2	0	0	1	0	0	0	1	0	0	2	108,425
Fontana	1	0	0	0	0	0	0	0	1	0	0	203,427
Foster City	1	0	0	0	0	0	0	1	0	0	0	32,652
Fresno	4	0	3	2	0	0	1	3	3	1	3	508,876
Fullerton	0	1	1	0	0	0	0	1	0	0	1	139,676
Galt	1	0	0	0	0	0	0	0	0	1	0	24,553
Garden Grove	1	0	0	3	0	0	0	0	1	2	1	175,469
Gilroy	0	0	2	0	0	0	0	0	1	1	0	51,240
Glendale	1	0	0	0	0	0	0	0	0	1	0	195,366
Glendora	1	0	0	0	0	0	0	1	0	0	0	50,893
Gridley	0	0	0	1	0	0	0	1	0	0	0	6,563
Hanford	1	0	1	0	0	0	0	1	0	1	0	54,425
Hawaiian Gardens	4	0	0	0	0	0	0	2	1	1	0	14,437
Hayward	0	1	1	0	0	0	0	0	2	0	0	150,955
Healdsburg	1	0	0	0	0	0	0	1	0	0	0	11,483
Hercules	0	0	0	1	0	0	0	0	0	1	0	24,831
Holtville	0	1	0	0	0	0	0	0	0	0	1	6,022
Huntington Beach	0	0	0	0	0	0	1	0	1	0	0	195,842
Imperial Beach	1	0	1	1	0	0	0	1	1	1	0	26,998
Irvine	0	1	0	0	0	0	0	0	1	0	0	235,830

Table 94.   Hate Crime Incidents Per Bias Motivation and Quarter, by Selected State and Agency, 2013— continued

(Number.)

State/agency	Number of incidents per bias motivation							Number of incidents per quarter[1]				Population[2]
	Race	Religion	Sexual orien-tation	Ethnicity	Disability	Gender	Gender Identity	1st quarter	2nd quarter	3rd quarter	4th quarter	
Jurupa Valley	0	1	0	0	0	0	0	0	0	1	0	98,090
Laguna Beach	0	0	1	0	0	0	0	0	1	0	0	23,313
La Habra	0	1	0	0	0	0	0	0	0	1	0	61,740
Lake Elsinore	0	2	0	0	0	0	0	0	0	2	0	56,232
Lake Forest	2	0	0	0	0	0	0	1	0	0	1	79,336
Lakewood	2	0	0	0	0	0	0	0	1	0	1	81,086
La Mirada	1	2	0	0	0	0	0	1	2	0	0	49,150
Lancaster	3	1	0	1	0	0	0	1	2	1	1	159,792
La Quinta	1	1	0	0	0	0	0	1	0	1	0	39,150
Lemon Grove	1	0	1	0	0	0	0	1	1	0	0	26,156
Lemoore	1	0	0	0	0	0	0	1	0	0	0	24,802
Livermore	0	0	0	1	0	0	0	0	0	1	0	84,350
Lodi	0	0	0	2	0	0	0	0	1	1	0	63,639
Lomita	0	0	0	1	0	0	0	0	1	0	0	20,622
Long Beach	3	1	1	0	0	0	0	3	0	1	1	469,665
Los Alamitos	1	0	0	0	0	0	0	1	0	0	0	11,735
Los Angeles	41	29	33	9	0	0	2	21	40	25	28	3,878,725
Los Gatos	2	0	0	0	0	0	0	0	0	1	1	30,351
Lynwood	1	0	0	0	0	0	0	0	0	0	1	71,077
Malibu	1	0	0	0	0	0	0	0	0	1	0	12,891
Manhattan Beach	1	0	0	0	0	0	0	0	0	0	1	35,930
Manteca	1	1	1	0	0	0	0	1	1	0	1	72,261
Milpitas	1	0	0	0	0	0	0	1	0	0	0	69,522
Modesto	0	1	1	1	0	0	0	2	0	1	0	204,252
Montclair	2	0	0	0	0	0	0	1	0	1	0	37,785
Monterey	1	0	1	0	0	0	0	0	0	1	1	29,338
Moreno Valley	1	0	0	0	0	0	0	0	0	0	1	201,284
Morgan Hill	0	1	0	0	0	0	0	0	0	0	1	39,907
Murrieta[3]	3	1	1	0	0	0	0	2	2	1	0	107,768
National City	2	0	1	0	0	0	0	1	0	1	1	59,637
Newark	2	0	0	1	0	0	0	1	1	0	1	43,950
Newport Beach	0	2	1	0	0	0	0	0	0	2	1	87,639
Norwalk	4	1	0	0	0	0	0	0	4	0	1	106,518
Oakland	4	1	4	2	0	0	0	2	4	3	2	403,887
Oceanside	5	1	1	1	0	0	0	2	4	2	0	172,525
Ontario	1	0	0	0	0	0	0	0	1	0	0	168,144
Orange	1	1	1	0	0	0	0	0	1	2	0	140,304
Oroville	1	0	1	0	0	0	0	0	0	1	1	15,581
Oxnard	0	0	1	0	0	0	0	0	0	0	1	202,594
Pacifica	0	1	0	0	0	0	0	0	0	1	0	38,494
Pacific Grove	0	1	0	0	0	0	0	1	0	0	0	15,518
Palmdale	4	1	3	0	0	0	0	3	1	3	1	156,522
Palm Springs	3	1	4	0	0	0	0	4	1	2	1	46,282
Palo Alto	0	0	0	1	0	0	0	1	0	0	0	66,964
Paramount	2	0	0	0	0	0	0	0	1	0	1	54,868
Pasadena	1	1	0	1	0	0	0	0	0	1	2	139,003
Pico Rivera	0	0	1	1	0	0	0	1	1	0	0	63,710
Pinole	0	0	0	1	0	0	0	0	0	1	0	18,848
Placentia	1	0	0	0	0	0	0	0	0	1	0	52,002
Rancho Cordova	1	0	0	0	0	0	0	1	0	0	0	67,634
Rancho Palos Verdes	0	1	0	0	0	0	0	0	0	0	1	42,542
Red Bluff	2	0	1	0	0	0	0	0	1	0	2	14,170
Redding	5	0	1	2	0	0	0	2	2	3	1	91,035
Redlands	0	2	1	0	0	0	0	0	1	0	2	70,282
Redondo Beach	2	0	1	2	0	0	0	1	2	1	1	67,993
Redwood City	0	1	0	0	0	0	0	1	0	0	0	79,707
Richmond	1	0	2	0	0	0	0	0	0	2	1	107,341
Ridgecrest	0	0	1	0	0	0	0	0	1	0	0	28,537
Riverside	11	1	1	2	0	0	1	7	4	0	5	316,423
Rohnert Park	0	0	0	3	0	0	0	2	0	0	1	41,326
Rolling Hills Estates	1	0	0	0	0	0	0	0	0	0	1	8,229
Roseville	0	0	1	0	0	0	0	0	1	0	0	126,236
Sacramento	6	2	6	2	0	0	0	2	5	6	3	478,182
Salinas	0	0	1	1	0	0	0	0	0	0	2	155,742
San Bernardino	2	0	0	1	0	0	0	0	0	2	1	214,322
San Diego	18	12	12	1	0	0	0	7	10	17	9	1,349,306
San Dimas	1	0	0	0	0	0	0	1	0	0	0	33,854
San Francisco	7	3	13	1	0	0	0	4	8	8	4	833,863
San Jose	6	2	6	1	0	0	0	7	1	2	5	992,143
San Leandro	3	0	1	1	0	0	0	2	1	2	0	87,490
San Luis Obispo	1	0	1	0	0	0	0	0	0	2	0	46,095
San Mateo	0	0	1	0	0	0	0	0	0	1	0	100,440
Santa Ana	0	0	1	0	0	0	0	0	0	1	0	332,848
Santa Barbara	1	0	1	0	0	0	0	0	0	1	1	90,006
Santa Clara	0	0	2	0	0	0	0	0	0	2	0	120,150
Santa Clarita	2	0	3	0	0	0	0	2	1	1	1	204,951
Santa Cruz	1	0	1	0	0	0	0	1	0	0	1	62,517

Table 94. Hate Crime Incidents Per Bias Motivation and Quarter, by Selected State and Agency, 2013— continued

(Number.)

State/agency	Number of incidents per bias motivation							Number of incidents per quarter[1]				Population[2]
	Race	Religion	Sexual orien-tation	Ethnicity	Disability	Gender	Gender Identity	1st quarter	2nd quarter	3rd quarter	4th quarter	
Santa Maria	0	0	1	0	0	0	0	0	0	0	1	102,051
Santa Rosa	0	1	2	0	0	0	0	2	1	0	0	171,564
Santee	1	0	1	1	0	0	0	2	0	1	0	55,924
Saratoga	1	0	0	0	0	0	0	0	1	0	0	30,897
Simi Valley	1	1	0	1	0	0	0	1	0	2	0	126,215
Sonora	1	0	0	0	0	0	0	0	0	1	0	4,774
South Gate	0	1	1	0	0	0	0	1	0	1	0	95,591
South Lake Tahoe	0	0	0	1	0	0	0	0	0	1	0	21,243
Stanton	0	0	1	0	0	0	0	0	1	0	0	39,128
Stockton	1	0	1	0	0	0	0	1	0	0	1	299,796
Sunnyvale	1	0	0	0	0	0	0	0	1	0	0	148,160
Taft	0	0	1	0	0	0	0	1	0	0	0	8,839
Tehachapi	1	0	0	1	0	0	0	1	0	1	0	13,607
Temecula	1	0	0	0	0	0	0	0	0	1	0	106,680
Temple City	0	1	0	0	0	0	0	0	0	0	1	36,269
Thousand Oaks	0	1	0	0	0	0	0	0	0	0	1	128,884
Torrance	1	0	0	1	0	0	0	0	0	2	0	147,534
Tracy	4	0	1	1	0	0	0	2	1	3	0	85,174
Turlock	1	0	0	0	0	0	0	0	0	0	1	70,075
Union City	1	0	0	4	0	0	0	1	3	1	0	72,480
Vallejo	1	0	0	1	0	0	0	0	2	0	0	118,336
Ventura	0	1	0	0	0	0	0	1	0	0	0	108,204
Vernon	1	0	0	0	0	0	0	0	1	0	0	115
Victorville	6	0	1	0	0	0	0	2	1	2	2	121,699
Visalia	1	0	1	0	0	0	0	1	1	0	0	127,824
Vista	1	0	1	0	0	0	0	0	1	0	1	96,712
Walnut Creek	1	0	0	0	0	0	0	0	0	0	1	66,149
West Covina	6	0	0	0	0	0	0	3	1	1	1	107,867
West Hollywood	1	0	2	2	0	0	0	1	1	3	0	34,902
Westlake Village	0	2	0	0	0	0	0	2	0	0	0	8,440
Westminster	1	1	1	1	1	0	0	1	1	1	2	91,885
Yorba Linda	1	0	0	0	0	0	0	0	0	0	1	67,492
Yuba City	0	0	0	1	0	0	0	0	0	1	0	65,133
Yucca Valley	1	0	0	0	0	0	0	0	0	1	0	21,214
Universities and Colleges	13	4	10	4	0	0	0					
California State Polytechnic University												
Pomona	0	0	0	1	0	0	0	1	0	0	0	22,156
San Luis Obispo	0	0	1	0	0	0	0	1	0	0	0	18,679
California State University												
Dominguez Hills	1	0	1	0	0	0	0	1	0	1	0	13,933
Long Beach	1	0	0	0	0	0	0	0	1	0	0	36,279
San Bernardino	3	0	0	0	0	0	0	2	0	1	0	18,234
San Jose	2	0	1	1	0	0	0	1	1	1	1	30,448
San Marcos	0	0	1	0	0	0	0	1	0	0	0	10,610
Stanislaus	0	0	1	0	0	0	0	0	0	0	1	8,882
Humboldt State University	0	0	1	0	0	0	0	0	1	0	0	8,116
Marin Community College	0	1	1	0	0	0	0	2	0	0	0	7,058
University of California												
Berkeley	3	2	1	1	0	0	0	1	1	4	1	35,893
Davis	1	0	1	1	0	0	0	0	3	0	0	32,354
Riverside	2	0	0	0	0	0	0	0	1	1	0	20,947
San Diego	0	1	0	0	0	0	0	0	1	0	0	28,294
Santa Cruz	0	0	1	0	0	0	0	1	0	0	0	17,404
Metropolitan Counties	56	7	36	20	0	0	1					
El Dorado	0	0	1	1	0	0	0	1	0	0	1	
Kern	1	0	1	3	0	0	0	1	3	0	1	
Kings	0	0	1	0	0	0	0	1	0	0	0	
Los Angeles	20	3	17	10	0	0	0	14	10	11	15	
Orange	1	0	0	1	0	0	0	1	0	0	1	
Riverside	3	0	0	0	0	0	0	0	1	1	1	
Sacramento	9	1	3	0	0	0	0	2	3	3	5	
San Bernardino	2	0	1	2	0	0	1	1	0	3	2	
San Diego	6	2	3	2	0	0	0	3	2	3	5	
San Luis Obispo	3	0	1	0	0	0	0	0	0	1	3	
San Mateo	0	0	1	0	0	0	0	0	1	0	0	
Santa Barbara	2	0	2	0	0	0	0	1	2	1	0	
Santa Clara	1	0	1	0	0	0	0	0	2	0	0	
Santa Cruz	1	0	1	1	0	0	0	2	0	1	0	
Shasta	4	0	2	0	0	0	0	3	1	2	0	
Sonoma	1	0	1	0	0	0	0	0	0	2	0	
Ventura	1	1	0	0	0	0	0	0	0	2	0	
Yuba	1	0	0	0	0	0	0	0	0	1	0	
Nonmetropolitan Counties	1	0	1	3	0	0	0					
Alpine	1	0	0	0	0	0	0	1	0	0	0	

Table 94.   Hate Crime Incidents Per Bias Motivation and Quarter, by Selected State and Agency, 2013— continued

(Number.)

State/agency	Number of incidents per bias motivation							Number of incidents per quarter[1]				Population[2]
	Race	Religion	Sexual orientation	Ethnicity	Disability	Gender	Gender Identity	1st quarter	2nd quarter	3rd quarter	4th quarter	
Amador	0	0	1	0	0	0	0	0	0	1	0	
Calaveras	0	0	0	1	0	0	0	0	0	1	0	
Lake	0	0	0	2	0	0	0	2	0	0	0	
State Police Agencies	1	0	0	0	0	0	0					
Highway Patrol, Plumas County	1	0	0	0	0	0	0	1	0	0	0	
Other Agencies	12	1	4	1	0	0	0					
Department of Parks and Recreation, Tehachapi District	1	0	0	0	0	0	0	0	0	1	0	
Fontana Unified School District	1	0	0	0	0	0	0	0	0	0	1	
Los Angeles Transportation Services Bureau	2	1	3	0	0	0	0	3	3	0	0	
Port of San Diego Harbor	2	0	0	1	0	0	0	0	1	1	1	
San Francisco Bay Area Rapid Transit												
Alameda County	4	0	0	0	0	0	0	0	2	2	0	
Contra Costa County	1	0	0	0	0	0	0	1	0	0	0	
San Francisco County	1	0	1	0	0	0	0	2	0	0	0	
COLORADO												
Total	54	18	40	15	1	0	0					
Cities	38	14	32	12	1	0	0					
Arvada	2	0	0	0	0	0	0	0	0	1	1	110,792
Aurora	4	0	1	1	0	0	0	1	3	0	2	343,484
Castle Rock	0	0	0	2	0	0	0	0	0	0	2	52,309
Centennial	3	2	1	0	0	0	0	2	2	1	1	104,771
Colorado Springs	3	1	2	1	0	0	0	2	4	1	0	436,108
Commerce City	0	1	0	0	0	0	0	0	0	1	0	49,200
Denver	9	5	15	1	0	0	0	3	13	9	5	648,981
Dillon	0	0	0	1	0	0	0	0	1	0	0	906
Durango	0	0	2	0	0	0	0	1	0	1	0	17,303
Englewood	1	0	0	0	1	0	0	0	0	0	2	31,454
Erie	0	1	0	0	0	0	0	1	0	0	0	19,627
Fountain	2	0	1	0	0	0	0	2	1	0	0	27,163
Glendale	0	1	0	0	0	0	0	1	0	0	0	4,502
Glenwood Springs	0	0	1	0	0	0	0	0	0	1	0	9,715
Golden	0	0	0	1	0	0	0	0	0	0	1	19,334
Grand Junction	4	0	1	0	0	0	0	1	1	2	1	60,167
Greeley	0	0	1	0	0	0	0	0	0	0	1	96,111
Greenwood Village	1	0	0	0	0	0	0	0	1	0	0	14,614
Lafayette	2	0	0	1	0	0	0	0	1	2	0	26,145
Lakewood	1	1	1	1	0	0	0	1	1	0	2	146,298
Littleton	1	0	0	0	0	0	0	1	0	0	0	44,375
Lone Tree	0	0	1	0	0	0	0	0	0	1	0	12,056
Longmont	1	0	1	1	0	0	0	2	1	0	0	89,434
Loveland	1	0	0	0	0	0	0	0	1	0	0	71,325
Monument	0	1	0	0	0	0	0	0	0	1	0	5,800
Pueblo	2	0	0	0	0	0	0	0	0	1	1	108,062
Rifle	0	0	0	1	0	0	0	1	0	0	0	9,306
Snowmass Village	1	0	0	0	0	0	0	1	0	0	0	2,851
Steamboat Springs	0	0	0	1	0	0	0	0	0	1	0	12,008
Telluride	0	0	1	0	0	0	0	0	0	1	0	2,313
Thornton	0	1	2	0	0	0	0	0	0	1	2	125,775
Westminster	0	0	1	0	0	0	0	1	0	0	0	110,093
Universities and Colleges	1	0	2	0	0	0	0					
Colorado State University, Fort Collins	1	0	0	0	0	0	0	0	0	0	1	30,659
University of Colorado, Boulder	0	0	2	0	0	0	0	0	0	0	2	31,945
Metropolitan Counties	10	2	6	2	0	0	0					
Adams	1	0	1	1	0	0	0	1	0	2	0	
Arapahoe	4	2	2	0	0	0	0	6	0	2	0	
El Paso	2	0	0	0	0	0	0	0	0	1	1	
Larimer	0	0	2	0	0	0	0	0	0	0	2	
Mesa	0	0	0	1	0	0	0	1	0	0	0	
Park	1	0	0	0	0	0	0	0	1	0	0	
Pueblo	1	0	0	0	0	0	0	0	0	1	0	
Weld	1	0	1	0	0	0	0	1	0	1	0	
Nonmetropolitan Counties	4	2	0	1	0	0	0					
Cheyenne	0	0	0	1	0	0	0	1	0	0	0	
Garfield	1	1	0	0	0	0	0	0	1	0	1	
Logan	1	1	0	0	0	0	0	0	0	1	1	
Montezuma	1	0	0	0	0	0	0	1	0	0	0	
Pitkin	1	0	0	0	0	0	0	0	0	0	1	
State Police Agencies	1	0	0	0	0	0	0					
Colorado State Patrol	1	0	0	0	0			0	0	0	1	

Table 94.   Hate Crime Incidents Per Bias Motivation and Quarter, by Selected State and Agency, 2013— continued

(Number.)

State/agency	Number of incidents per bias motivation							Number of incidents per quarter[1]				Population[2]
	Race	Religion	Sexual orientation	Ethnicity	Disability	Gender	Gender Identity	1st quarter	2nd quarter	3rd quarter	4th quarter	
CONNECTICUT												
Total	72	20	26	24	3	0	0					
Cities	66	18	21	21	3	0	0					
Bethel	1	0	0	0	0	0	0	1	0	0	0	19,338
Bridgeport	5	1	2	3	0	0	0	2	4	3	2	147,076
Canton	0	0	1	0	0	0	0	0	0	1	0	10,369
Danbury	0	1	1	1	0	0	0		2		1	83,363
Derby	1	0	0	0	0	0	0	0	0	0	1	12,806
East Hampton	0	2	0	0	0	0	0	0	1	0	1	12,934
East Hartford	0	0	1	0	0	0	0	0	1	0	0	51,275
East Windsor	1	0	0	0	0	0	0	0	0	1	0	11,455
Enfield	1	0	0	0	0	0	0		1			44,661
Glastonbury	1	0	0	0	0	0	0	1	0	0	0	34,782
Groton	1	1	0	0	0	0	0	0	1	1	0	9,359
Groton Town	1	0	0	0	1	0	0	0	1	1	0	29,946
Guilford	0	1	0	0	0	0	0			1		22,409
Hamden	0	1	0	0	0	0	0	0	1	0	0	60,829
Hartford	1	1	2	0	0	0	0	2	1	1	0	124,927
Manchester	7	2	0	1	0	0	0	2	2	4	2	58,304
Meriden	2	0	1	0	0	0	0	1	1		1	60,558
Middletown	5	0	1	1	0	0	0	0	3	1	3	47,221
Milford	4	1	0	0	0	0	0		2	4		53,041
New Britain	0	0	1	0	0	0	0	1				73,134
New Haven	5	0	4	1	0	0	0	3	2	4	1	131,071
Newington	1	2	0	0	0	0	0			1	2	30,612
New London	1	0	2	0	0	0	0	3	0	0	0	27,738
New Milford	0	0	0	1	0	0	0	0	1	0	0	27,743
North Branford	1	0	0	1	0	0	0	2	0	0	0	14,369
Norwalk	1	0	1	1	0	0	0	0	0	3	0	87,590
Norwich	1	0	0	0	0	0	0			1		40,485
Old Saybrook	3	0	0	0	0	0	0	0	1	0	2	10,239
Plainville	0	0	1	0	0	0	0				1	17,850
Plymouth	0	1	1	0	0	0	0	0	1	1	0	12,043
Southington	1	0	0	6	0	0	0	3	2	2	0	43,542
South Windsor	0	1	0	0	0	0	0		1			25,871
Stamford	1	2	2	2	1	0	0	2	2	1	3	125,876
Stratford	1	1	0	1	0	0	0	0	1	1	1	52,285
Suffield	1	0	0	0	0	0	0	0	0	1	0	15,908
Torrington	5	0	0	0	0	0	0	1	3	1	0	35,634
Wallingford	2	0	0	2	0	0	0	1	1	2	0	45,185
Waterbury	6	0	0	0	0	0	0	3	1	2	0	109,763
West Haven	1	0	0	0	0	0	0			1		55,349
Willimantic	1	0	0	0	0	0	0	1	0	0	0	17,839
Winchester	2	0	0	0	0	0	0	2	0	0	0	11,019
Windsor Locks	0	0	0	0	1	0	0	0	1	0	0	12,560
Wolcott	1	0	0	0	0	0	0	0	1	0	0	16,735
Universities and Colleges	5	1	2	1	0	0	0					
Central Connecticut State University	0	0	1	0	0	0	0	0	0	0	1	12,091
Southern Connecticut State University	2	0	0	0	0	0	0	1	1	0	0	11,117
University of Connecticut, Storrs, Avery Point, and Hartford[4]	3	1	0	1	0	0	0	2	1	1	1	
Yale University	0	0	1	0	0	0	0				1	11,906
State Police Agencies	1	1	3	2	0	0	0					
Connecticut State Police	1	1	3	2	0	0	0	2	1	4	0	
DELAWARE												
Total	9	0	3	0	0	0	0					
Cities	5	0	2	0	0	0	0					
Dover	0	0	1	0	0	0	0	0	0	1	0	37,402
Milford	1	0	1	0	0	0	0	0	2	0	0	9,872
Milton	1	0	0	0	0	0	0	1	0	0	0	2,687
New Castle	1	0	0	0	0	0	0	0	0	1	0	5,388
Seaford	1	0	0	0	0	0	0	0	0	1	0	7,241
Smyrna	1	0	0	0	0	0	0	1	0	0	0	10,900
Universities and Colleges	1	0	0	0	0	0	0					
Delaware State University	1	0	0	0	0	0	0	0	1	0	0	4,324
Metropolitan Counties	1	0	0	0	0	0	0					
New Castle County Police Department	1	0	0	0	0	0	0	0	1	0	0	
	2	0	1	0	0	0	0					
State Police Agencies												
Kent County	1	0	0	0	0	0	0	1	0	0	0	

Table 94.   Hate Crime Incidents Per Bias Motivation and Quarter, by Selected State and Agency, 2013— continued

(Number.)

State/agency	Number of incidents per bias motivation							Number of incidents per quarter[1]				Population[2]
	Race	Religion	Sexual orien-tation	Ethnicity	Disability	Gender	Gender Identity	1st quarter	2nd quarter	3rd quarter	4th quarter	
New Castle County	1	0	0	0	0	0	0	0	1	0	0	
Sussex County	0	0	1	0	0	0	0	0	0	1	0	
DISTRICT OF COLUMBIA												
Total	18	6	32	4	0	0	12					
Cities	18	6	31	3	0	0	12					
Washington	18	6	31	3	0	0	12	19	21	20	10	646,449
Other Agencies	0	0	1	1	0	0	0					
Metro Transit Police	0	0	1	1	0	0	0	0	0	2	0	
FLORIDA												
Total	40	8	20	8	0	0	0					
Cities	24	7	14	4	0	0	0					
Delray Beach	1	0	0	0	0	0	0	0	1	0	0	62,887
Gainesville	2	0	1	0	0	0	0	0	0	0	3	126,589
Hallandale	2	0	1	0	0	0	0	0	1	0	2	38,710
Homestead	2	0	1	0	0	0	0	2	1	0	0	64,024
Jacksonville	5	0	0	0	0	0	0	3	1	1	0	845,745
Jupiter	1	0	1	0	0	0	0	1	1	0	0	57,826
Lake Alfred	0	0	0	1	0	0	0	0	1	0	0	5,148
Largo	0	0	1	0	0	0	0	0	1	0	0	77,913
Melbourne	1	1	0	0	0	0	0	1	0	0	1	77,277
Miramar	0	0	1	0	0	0	0	0	1	0	0	130,926
North Miami	2	1	3	0	0	0	0	3	1	0	2	61,120
North Miami Beach	0	0	1	0	0	0	0	1	0	0	0	43,417
North Port	0	0	1	0	0	0	0	0	1	0	0	58,699
Orlando	1	0	1	0	0	0	0	2	0	0	0	253,238
Palm Bay	0	1	0	1	0	0	0	0	0	0	2	104,391
Panama City	2	0	0	0	0	0	0	0	2	0	0	36,358
Pembroke Pines	0	0	0	1	0	0	0	0	0	1	0	162,064
Pensacola	0	0	1	0	0	0	0	0	1	0	0	52,454
Pompano Beach	1	1	0	1	0	0	0	0	0	0	3	103,971
Port St. Lucie	1	0	0	0	0	0	0	1	0	0	0	169,877
Sanford	0	0	1	0	0	0	0	0	0	1	0	54,972
St. Petersburg	0	1	0	0	0	0	0	0	1	0	0	247,084
Sunrise	1	0	0	0	0	0	0	1	0	0	0	90,274
Tallahassee	1	0	0	0	0	0	0	0	1	0	0	188,714
Venice	0	2	0	0	0	0	0	2	0	0	0	21,151
Weston	1	0	0	0	0	0	0	0	0	0	1	68,369
Metropolitan Counties	16	1	6	4	0	0	0					
Alachua	0	0	0	1	0	0	0	1	0	0	0	
Brevard	0	0	1	0	0	0	0	0	0	1	0	
Charlotte	1	0	0	0	0	0	0	0	0	0	1	
Clay	1	0	0	0	0	0	0	0	0	0	1	
Collier	1	0	0	0	0	0	0	0	0	0	1	
Flagler	2	0	0	0	0	0	0	2	0	0	0	
Hillsborough	0	0	0	1	0	0	0	0	1	0	0	
Lake	1	0	0	0	0	0	0	0	1	0	0	
Manatee	1	0	0	0	0	0	0	0	0	1	0	
Orange	6	0	4	0	0	0	0	6	2	0	2	
Osceola	0	0	0	2	0	0	0	1	0	1	0	
Palm Beach	0	1	0	0	0	0	0	1	0	0	0	
Pasco	1	0	0	0	0	0	0	1	0	0	0	
Santa Rosa	0	0	1	0	0	0	0	1	0	0	0	
Volusia	2	0	0	0	0	0	0	0	1	0	1	
GEORGIA												
Total	29	5	17	5	1	0	0					
Cities	7	1	12	2	1	0	0					
Atlanta	5	1	12	2	1	0	0	8	11	2	0	451,020
Conyers	1	0	0	0	0	0	0	0	0	0	1	15,465
Villa Rica	1	0	0	0	0	0	0	1	0	0	0	14,307
Universities and Colleges	2	1	3	0	0	0	0					
Kennesaw State University	0	0	2	0	0	0	0	1	0	0	1	24,604
University of Georgia	2	1	1	0	0	0	0	1	0	0	3	34,519
Metropolitan Counties	20	3	2	3	0	0	0					
Cobb County Police Department	19	3	2	3	0	0	0	1	12	8	6	
Henry County Police Department	1	0	0	0	0	0	0	0	1	0	0	
IDAHO												

Table 94.   Hate Crime Incidents Per Bias Motivation and Quarter, by Selected State and Agency, 2013— continued

(Number.)

State/agency	Number of incidents per bias motivation							Number of incidents per quarter[1]				Population[2]
	Race	Religion	Sexual orien- tation	Ethnicity	Disability	Gender	Gender Identity	1st quarter	2nd quarter	3rd quarter	4th quarter	
Total	19	6	4	3	0	0	0					
Cities	18	4	4	2	0	0	0					
Boise	8	1	4	0	0	0	0	2	0	7	4	214,330
Caldwell	1	0	0	0	0	0	0	1	0	0	0	48,069
Chubbuck	0	3	0	0	0	0	0	0	0	0	3	14,224
Coeur d'Alene	2	0	0	0	0	0	0	0	1	0	1	46,023
Hailey	0	0	0	1	0	0	0	0	0	1	0	7,915
Montpelier	1	0	0	0	0	0	0	0	0	1	0	2,520
Nampa	3	0	0	1	0	0	0	2	1	1	0	84,634
Payette	2	0	0	0	0	0	0	1	0	0	1	7,442
Twin Falls	1	0	0	0	0	0	0	0	1	0	0	45,378
Metropolitan Counties	0	1	0	1	0	0	0					
Ada	0	1	0	1	0	0	0	0	1	0	1	
Nonmetropolitan Counties	1	1	0	0	0	0	0					
Cassia	0	1	0	0	0	0	0	1	0	0	0	
Shoshone	1	0	0	0	0	0	0	0	0	1	0	
ILLINOIS												
Total	61	7	29	8	0	0	0					
Cities	48	7	27	6	0	0	0					
Aurora	0	0	1	0	0	0	0	0	0	1	0	200,551
Bartlett	0	1	0	1	0	0	0	0	0	1	1	41,733
Berwyn	1	0	0	0	0	0	0	0	1	0	0	56,838
Carol Stream	0	1	0	0	0	0	0	1	0	0	0	40,376
Champaign	1	0	0	0	0	0	0	0	1	0	0	82,966
Chester	1	0	0	0	0	0	0	0	0	1	0	8,448
Chicago	22	2	18	3	0	0	0	11	10	15	9	2,720,554
Crystal Lake	0	1	0	0	0	0	0	0	0	1	0	40,383
De Kalb	1	0	0	0	0	0	0	0	0	1	0	43,765
Dixon	0	0	1	0	0	0	0	0	0	0	1	15,304
Harvey	1	0	0	0	0	0	0	0	0	0	1	25,408
Irving	1	0	0	0	0	0	0	0	1	0	0	485
La Grange	0	1	0	0	0	0	0	0	1	0	0	15,718
Mokena	1	0	0	0	0	0	0	0	1	0	0	19,130
Moline	1	0	0	0	0	0	0	0	0	1	0	43,172
Morton	0	0	1	0	0	0	0	0	0	1	0	16,462
Normal	0	0	1	0	0	0	0	0	0	0	1	54,241
Pekin	2	0	0	0	0	0	0	1	1	0	0	34,085
Peoria	3	0	2	0	0	0	0	2	1	1	1	115,953
Quincy	1	0	0	0	0	0	0	0	0	0	1	40,841
Rockford	2	1	1	0	0	0	0	0	2	2	0	150,209
Roscoe	1	0	0	0	0	0	0	0	1	0	0	10,700
Skokie	2	0	0	1	0	0	0	0	2	0	1	65,155
Springfield	5	0	0	0	0	0	0	0	2	2	1	117,351
St. Charles	0	0	1	1	0	0	0	1	1	0	0	33,433
Sterling	0	0	1	0	0	0	0	1	0	0	0	15,183
Urbana	2	0	0	0	0	0	0	0	0	1	1	41,598
Universities and Colleges	4	0	0	0	0	0	0					
Northwestern University, Evanston	3	0	0	0	0	0	0	1	0	0	2	21,215
University of Illinois, Springfield	1	0	0	0	0	0	0	0	1	0	0	5,048
Metropolitan Counties	8	0	1	2	0	0	0					
Cook	0	0	0	1	0	0	0	0	1	0	0	
Jackson	1	0	0	0	0	0	0	1	0	0	0	
Lake	1	0	0	1	0	0	0	0	0	2	0	
McLean	1	0	0	0	0	0	0	0	0	0	1	
Peoria	2	0	0	0	0	0	0	0	0	0	2	
Sangamon	1	0	1	0	0	0	0	0	0	1	1	
Will	2	0	0	0	0	0	0	0	0	2	0	
Nonmetropolitan Counties	1	0	1	0	0	0	0					
Cumberland	0	0	1	0	0	0	0	0	1	0	0	
Douglas	1	0	0	0	0	0	0	0	0	1	0	
INDIANA												
Total	49	3	13	9	1	0	0					
Cities	41	0	12	8	0	0	0					
Bloomington	8	0	2	0	0	0	0	1	5	3	1	82,415
Fort Wayne	1	0	0	0	0	0	0	0	1	0	0	254,820
Franklin	1	0	0	0	0	0	0	0	0	0	1	24,034
Goshen	0	0	1	0	0	0	0	1		0	0	32,195

Table 94.   Hate Crime Incidents Per Bias Motivation and Quarter, by Selected State and Agency, 2013— continued

(Number.)

State/agency	Number of incidents per bias motivation							Number of incidents per quarter[1]				Population[2]
	Race	Religion	Sexual orientation	Ethnicity	Disability	Gender	Gender Identity	1st quarter	2nd quarter	3rd quarter	4th quarter	
Indianapolis	29	0	6	8	0	0	0	8	15	16	4	850,220
Mishawaka	0	0	2	0	0	0	0		1	1		47,967
South Bend	2	0	1	0	0	0	0	1		2		100,711
Universities and Colleges	2	1	1	0	0	0	0					
Ball State University	0	1	0	0	0	0	0	0	1	0	0	21,053
Purdue University	2	0	1	0	0	0	0	1	1	1		40,393
Metropolitan Counties	2	1	0	0	1	0	0					
Elkhart	2	1	0	0	1	0	0	0		3	1	
	4	1	0	1	0	0	0					
State Police Agencies												
Henry County	1	1	0	0	0	0	0	2				
Knox County	1	0	0	0	0	0	0				1	
Lake County	1	0	0	0	0	0	0	1				
Monroe County	0	0	0	1	0	0	0			1		
Perry County	1	0	0	0	0	0	0	1				
IOWA												
Total	5	1	3	1	0	0	0					
Cities	2	1	2	1	0	0	0					
Altoona	0	0	1	0	0	0	0	0	0	1	0	15,683
Ames	1	0	0	1	0	0	0	0	0	1	1	61,193
Grinnell	0	0	1	0	0	0	0	0	0	0	1	9,090
Indianola	0	1	0	0	0	0	0	0	1	0	0	14,993
Waterloo	1	0	0	0	0	0	0	0	0	0	1	68,255
Universities and Colleges	0	0	1	0	0	0	0					
Iowa State University	0	0	1	0	0	0	0	0	1	0	0	30,748
Metropolitan Counties	2	0	0	0	0	0	0					
Mills	1	0	0	0	0	0	0	0	1	0	0	
Scott	1	0	0	0	0	0	0	0	0	1	0	
Nonmetropolitan Counties	1	0	0	0	0	0	0					
Ida	1	0	0	0	0	0	0	0	1	0	0	
KANSAS												
Total	38	6	13	5	2	0	0					
Cities	36	5	10	3	1	0	0					
Andover	0	1	1	0	0	0	0	0	1	1	0	12,188
Arkansas City	2	0	0	0	0	0	0	0	1	0	1	12,322
Belleville	1	0	0	0	0	0	0	1	0	0	0	1,928
Cheney	1	0	0	0	0	0	0	0	0	0	1	2,127
Dodge City	1	0	0	0	0	0	0	0	0	1	0	28,265
Gardner	0	1	0	0	0	0	0	0	1	0	0	20,708
Hays	1	0	1	0	0	0	0	0	2	0	0	21,156
Hutchinson	3	1	0	0	0	0	0	1	1	1	1	41,909
Iola	1	0	1	0	0	0	0	0	2	0	0	5,697
Lansing	2	0	0	0	0	0	0	0	0	2	0	11,688
Larned	1	0	0	0	0	0	0	0	0	1	0	4,012
Lawrence	5	2	1	2	0	0	0	1	2	4	3	90,034
Leavenworth	1	0	0	0	0	0	0	1	0	0	0	35,965
Lenexa	1	0	0	0	0	0	0	0	1	0	0	49,777
Louisburg	0	0	1	0	0	0	0	1	0	0	0	4,268
McPherson	1	0	1	0	1	0	0	0	1	2	0	13,245
Mulvane	1	0	0	0	0	0	0	0	0	1	0	6,307
Parsons	2	0	0	0	0	0	0	0	2	0	0	10,278
Pittsburg	1	0	0	0	0	0	0	0	1	0	0	20,395
Pratt	1	0	0	0	0	0	0	0	0	0	1	6,900
Protection	0	0	1	0	0	0	0			1	0	521
Wichita	10	0	3	1	0	0	0	4	4	4	2	386,486
Metropolitan Counties	1	0	2	2	1	0	0					
Douglas	0	0	1	1	0	0	0	0	2	0	0	
Leavenworth	0	0	0	0	1	0	0	0	0	1	0	
Riley County Police Department	0	0	1	0	0	0	0	0	0	1	0	
Shawnee	1	0	0	0	0	0	0	0	0	1	0	
Wyandotte	0	0	0	1	0	0	0	1	0	0	0	
Nonmetropolitan Counties	1	1	1	0	0	0	0					
Ellis	0	0	1	0	0	0	0	0	1	0	0	
Greenwood	1	0	0	0	0	0	0	0	1	0	0	
Marshall	0	1	0	0	0	0	0	1	0	0	0	

Table 94.   Hate Crime Incidents Per Bias Motivation and Quarter, by Selected State and Agency, 2013— continued

(Number.)

State/agency	Number of incidents per bias motivation							Number of incidents per quarter[1]				Population[2]
	Race	Religion	Sexual orien-tation	Ethnicity	Disability	Gender	Gender Identity	1st quarter	2nd quarter	3rd quarter	4th quarter	
KENTUCKY												
Total	113	5	31	15	7	0	0					
Cities	87	4	26	12	4	0	0					
Ashland	3	0	0	0	0	0	0	1	0	2	0	21,432
Bellevue	0	0	1	0	0	0	0	1	0	0	0	5,918
Berea	0	1	1	0	0	0	0	0	1	0	1	14,331
Bowling Green	4	0	2	2	0	0	0	1	2	4	1	61,130
Burkesville	1	0	0	0	0	0	0	0	0	1	0	1,526
Cadiz	0	0	2	0	0	0	0	0	1	1	0	2,624
Carlisle	1	0	0	0	0	0	0	0	1	0	0	1,956
Carrollton	1	0	0	0	0	0	0	0	0	0	1	3,966
Corbin	2	0	0	0	0	0	0	0	0	1	1	7,257
Covington	3	0	3	3	0	0	0	1	4	2	2	40,766
Cynthiana	1	0	0	0	0	0	0	0	1	0	0	6,305
Danville	0	0	1	0	0	0	0	0	1	0	0	16,388
Elizabethtown	2	0	0	0	0	0	0	0	0	0	2	29,470
Elkton	1	0	0	0	0	0	0	0	1	0	0	2,211
Elsmere	1	0	0	0	0	0	0	1	0	0	0	8,478
Flatwoods	1	0	0	0	0	0	0	0	0	1	0	7,412
Florence	1	0	0	0	2	0	0	1	1	1	0	31,434
Frankfort	1	0	1	1	0	0	0	1	1	0	1	27,680
Georgetown	2	0	0	0	0	0	0	0	0	2	0	30,611
Harrodsburg	1	0	0	0	0	0	0	0	0	1	0	8,301
Hazard	1	0	0	0	0	0	0	0	0	1	0	5,455
Henderson	2	0	0	0	0	0	0	0	0	0	2	28,952
Hillview	0	0	1	0	0	0	0	0	0	1	0	9,465
Hopkinsville	1	0	1	0	0	0	0	0	0	1	1	33,253
Leitchfield	1	0	0	0	0	0	0	0	1	0	0	6,814
Lexington	16	1	5	4	1	0	0	5	10	10	2	308,712
Louisville Metro	7	0	4	0	0	0	0	2	4	3	2	671,120
Ludlow	1	0	0	0	1	0	0	0	2	0	0	4,536
Madisonville	1	0	0	0	0	0	0	1	0	0	0	19,761
Morehead	1	0	0	0	0	0	0	0	0	1	0	6,864
Mount Washington	1	0	0	0	0	0	0	0	0	0	1	9,377
Murray	1	0	1	0	0	0	0	0	1	1	0	18,048
Newport	5	0	0	0	0	0	0	0	1	1	3	15,425
Oak Grove	1	0	0	0	0	0	0	0	0	1	0	7,638
Owensboro	2	0	1	1	0	0	0	1	2	1	0	58,304
Paducah	1	0	0	0	0	0	0	0	0	0	1	25,064
Paris	1	0	0	0	0	0	0	0	0	0	1	9,752
Radcliff	2	0	0	0	0	0	0	0	1	0	1	23,177
Ravenna	1	0	0	0	0	0	0	0	1	0	0	595
Richmond	1	1	1	0	0	0	0	1	1	0	1	32,333
Russellville	1	0	1	0	0	0	0	0	1	1	0	6,949
Shelbyville	4	0	0	0	0	0	0	0	1	2	1	14,743
Shepherdsville	0	1	0	0	0	0	0	0	0	1	0	11,534
Shively	0	0	0	1	0	0	0	1	0	0	0	15,511
St. Matthews	2	0	0	0	0	0	0	0	1	0	1	17,768
Vine Grove	1	0	0	0	0	0	0	1	0	0	0	5,298
Williamsburg	1	0	0	0	0	0	0	1	0	0	0	5,258
Winchester	5	0	0	0	0	0	0	1	2	1	1	18,478
Universities and Colleges	1	0	1	0	0	0	0					
Morehead State University	1	0	0	0	0	0	0	0	0	1	0	11,169
University of Louisville	0	0	1	0	0	0	0	0	0	1	0	21,239
Metropolitan Counties	11	0	2	1	2	0	0					
Boone	3	0	0	1	0	0	0	1	2	0	1	
Bullitt	3	0	1	0	0	0	0	0	2	1	1	
Christian	1	0	0	0	1	0	0	0	1	1	0	
Daviess	0	0	1	0	0	0	0	0	0	1	0	
Hardin	1	0	0	0	0	0	0	0	1	0	0	
Meade	1	0	0	0	1	0	0	2	0	0	0	
Shelby	1	0	0	0	0	0	0	0	1	0	0	
Trigg	1	0	0	0	0	0	0	0	0	0	1	
Nonmetropolitan Counties	8	1	0	1	1	0	0					
Calloway	1	0	0	0	0	0	0	0	0	1	0	
Clay	0	1	0	0	0	0	0	0	0	1	0	
Hopkins	1	0	0	0	0	0	0	0	0	1	0	
Knott	0	0	0	1	0	0	0	0	1	0	0	
Knox	1	0	0	0	0	0	0	0	0	0	1	
Lyon	1	0	0	0	0	0	0	0	1	0	0	
Marshall	1	0	0	0	0	0	0	0	1	0	0	
Nelson	1	0	0	0	0	0	0	0	0	1	0	
Ohio	1	0	0	0	1	0	0	1	1	0	0	

Table 94.   Hate Crime Incidents Per Bias Motivation and Quarter, by Selected State and Agency, 2013— continued

(Number.)

State/agency	Number of incidents per bias motivation							Number of incidents per quarter[1]				Population[2]
	Race	Religion	Sexual orientation	Ethnicity	Disability	Gender	Gender Identity	1st quarter	2nd quarter	3rd quarter	4th quarter	
Perry	1	0	0	0	0	0	0	1	0	0	0	
	6	0	2	0	0	0	0					
State Police Agencies												
Campbellsburg	1	0	0	0	0	0	0	0	1	0	0	
Dry Ridge	0	0	1	0	0	0	0	1	0	0	0	
Frankfort	0	0	1	0	0	0	0	0	0	1	0	
Henderson	1	0	0	0	0	0	0	0	0	0	1	
Madisonville	1	0	0	0	0	0	0	0	0	1	0	
Morehead	1	0	0	0	0	0	0	0	0	1	0	
Pikeville	1	0	0	0	0	0	0	1	0	0	0	
Richmond	1	0	0	0	0	0	0	0	0	1	0	
Other Agencies	0	0	0	1	0	0	0					
Montgomery County School District	0	0	0	1	0	0	0	0	0	0	1	
LOUISIANA												
Total	7	6	8	1	0	0	0					
Cities	1	1	5	1	0	0	0					
New Orleans	1	1	5	1	0	0	0	2	3	3	0	377,022
Universities and Colleges	1	0	0	0	0	0	0					
University of New Orleans	1	0	0	0	0	0	0	1	0		0	10,071
Metropolitan Counties	5	5	3	0	0	0	0					
Ascension	3	1	0	0	0	0	0	0	3	1	0	
Calcasieu	0	4	3	0	0	0	0	4	1	1	1	
Iberia	1	0	0	0	0	0	0	0	0	1	0	
Jefferson	1	0	0	0	0	0	0	0	0	1		
MAINE												
Total	12	3	10	0	0	0	0					
Cities	10	3	9	0	0	0	0					
Auburn	2	0	0	0	0	0	0	0	0	2	0	22,948
Belfast	0	0	1	0	0	0	0	1	0	0	0	6,654
Cape Elizabeth	1	0	0	0	0	0	0	0	1	0	0	9,104
Ellsworth	1	0	0	0	0	0	0	0	1	0	0	7,853
Lewiston	0	0	1	0	0	0	0	0	0	0	1	36,422
Machias[3]	0	0	1	0	0	0	0	0	0	0	1	2,173
Mexico	1	0	0	0	0	0	0	1	0	0	0	2,633
Old Orchard Beach	1	0	0	0	0	0	0	0	1	0	0	8,681
Portland	1	1	0	0	0	0	0	0	1	1	0	66,256
Scarborough	0	0	1	0	0	0	0	0	1	0	0	19,252
Searsport	0	0	1	0	0	0	0	1	0	0	0	2,618
Skowhegan	1	0	2	0	0	0	0	1	0	1	1	8,537
South Portland	1	2	2	0	0	0	0	1	2	2	0	25,126
Wiscasset	1	0	0	0	0	0	0	1	0	0	0	3,673
Metropolitan Counties	0	0	1	0	0	0	0					
Sagadahoc	0	0	1	0	0	0	0	0	1	0	0	
Nonmetropolitan Counties	1	0	0	0	0	0	0					
Waldo	1	0	0	0	0	0	0	0	1	0	0	
State Police Agencies	1	0	0	0	0	0	0					
State Police, Somerset County	1	0	0	0	0	0	0	0	0		1	
MARYLAND												
Total	26	15	7	3	0	0	0					
Cities	3	3	1	1	0	0	0					
Aberdeen	0	1	0	0	0	0	0	0	0	1	0	15,039
Annapolis	0	1	0	0	0	0	0	1	0	0	0	38,649
Baltimore	0	1	0	1	0	0	0	1	0	0	1	622,671
Bel Air	1	0	0	0	0	0	0	1	0	0	0	10,314
Frederick	2	0	0	0	0	0	0	0	0	1	1	66,709
Greenbelt	0	0	1	0	0	0	0	0	1	0	0	23,680
Universities and Colleges	2	0	1	0	0	0	0					
St. Mary's College	1	0	1	0	0	0	0	0	2	0	0	1,933
Towson University	1	0	0	0	0	0	0	0	1	0	0	21,960
Metropolitan Counties	19	8	5	2	0	0	0					
Baltimore County Police Department	3	2	0	0	0	0	0	1	0	2	2	
Carroll	2	0	0	0	0	0	0	0	0	2	0	

Table 94.   Hate Crime Incidents Per Bias Motivation and Quarter, by Selected State and Agency, 2013— continued

(Number.)

State/agency	Number of incidents per bias motivation							Number of incidents per quarter[1]				Population[2]
	Race	Religion	Sexual orientation	Ethnicity	Disability	Gender	Gender Identity	1st quarter	2nd quarter	3rd quarter	4th quarter	
Charles	0	0	1	0	0	0	0	0	1	0	0	
Frederick	3	2	0	0	0	0	0	3	0	2	0	
Harford	1	0	0	0	0	0	0	0	0	0	1	
Howard County Police Department	4	0	1	1	0	0	0	0	2	2	2	
Montgomery County Police Department	6	4	2	1	0	0	0	3	5	2	3	
Prince George's County Police Department	0	0	1	0	0	0	0	0	1	0	0	
Nonmetropolitan Counties	1	0	0	0	0	0	0					
Garrett	1	0	0	0	0	0	0	0	0	0	1	
	1	2	0	0	0	0	0					
State Police Agencies												
Frederick County	0	2	0	0	0	0	0	0	1	0	1	
Queen Anne's County	1	0	0	0	0	0	0	1	0	0	0	
Other Agencies	0	2	0	0	0	0	0					
State Fire Marshal	0	2	0	0	0	0	0	0	0	2	0	
MASSACHUSETTS												
Total	146	64	91	42	3	1	3					
Cities	142	57	86	40	3	0	3					
Acton	3	0	0	0	0	0	0	0	2	0	1	22,871
Amesbury	0	1	0	0	0	0	0	0	1	0	0	16,655
Amherst	1	0	0	0	0	0	0	1	0	0	0	39,127
Attleboro	1	0	0	1	0	0	0	0	1	0	1	44,034
Bedford	1	2	0	0	0	0	0	1	0	0	2	13,947
Belmont	0	0	0	1	0	0	0	0	1	0	0	25,421
Beverly	0	1	0	0	0	0	0	0	0	1	0	40,592
Billerica	0	1	0	0	0	0	0	0	0	0	1	41,926
Bolton	0	0	1	0	0	0	0	0	0	1	0	5,060
Boston	73	21	53	15	0	0	3	39	56	40	30	643,799
Braintree	3	0	0	0	0	0	0	0	2	1	0	36,496
Brookline	0	1	0	0	0	0	0	1	0	0	0	59,382
Cambridge	4	3	3	3	0	0	0	6	2	3	2	107,282
Chelsea	1	0	0	0	0	0	0	0	0	0	1	37,454
Danvers	0	1	0	0	0	0	0	1	0	0	0	27,263
Douglas	0	0	1	0	0	0	0	0	1	0	0	8,628
Dover	0	0	1	0	0	0	0	0	0	1	0	5,778
Dracut	4	1	0	0	0	0	0	0	1	2	2	30,533
East Longmeadow	2	0	3	0	0	0	0	0	3	0	2	15,946
Edgartown	1	0	0	0	0	0	0	1	0	0	0	4,252
Fall River	1	0	0	0	0	0	0	1	0	0	0	89,220
Framingham	2	0	0	0	0	0	0	0	0	2	0	70,753
Greenfield	0	0	1	0	0	0	0	0	1	0	0	17,598
Haverhill	2	1	3	2	0	0	0	4	2	1	1	62,249
Kingston	0	1	0	0	0	0	0	0	0	1	0	12,791
Lakeville	0	1	0	0	0	0	0	0	1	0	0	10,939
Lincoln	0	0	1	0	0	0	0	0	0	0	1	6,563
Lowell	0	0	1	1	0	0	0	0	0	1	1	109,449
Lunenburg	1	0	0	0	0	0	0	0	0	0	1	11,149
Lynn	3	2	5	4	2	0	0	1	5	6	4	91,769
Malden	1	2	0	0	0	0	0	0	2	1	0	60,816
Marblehead	1	0	0	0	0	0	0	0	1	0	0	20,209
Marlborough	0	0	0	1	0	0	0	0	0	1	0	39,531
Medford	5	3	0	1	1	0	0	2	4	4	0	57,428
Middleboro	1	0	0	0	0	0	0	0	1	0	0	23,547
Milton	1	2	0	0	0	0	0	0	0	0	3	27,269
Monson	0	0	1	0	0	0	0	0	0	0	1	8,716
Needham	2	0	0	0	0	0	0	0	0	1	1	29,544
New Bedford	0	0	0	1	0	0	0	0	0	1	0	95,156
Newburyport	0	0	1	0	0	0	0	0	0	1	0	17,773
Norton	2	0	0	0	0	0	0	0	0	1	1	19,414
Peabody	0	0	0	2	0	0	0	0	0	2	0	52,178
Pittsfield	0	0	1	0	0	0	0	0	1	0	0	43,992
Plainville	1	0	0	0	0	0	0	1	0	0	0	8,512
Plymouth	9	1	0	0	0	0	0	0	0	6	4	57,893
Provincetown	0	1	0	0	0	0	0	1	0	0	0	2,983
Quincy	6	3	0	4	0	0	0	4	2	4	3	93,490
Randolph	0	0	2	0	0	0	0	0	2	0	0	33,583
Reading	1	0	0	0	0	0	0	0	0	1	0	25,398
Revere	0	2	0	1	0	0	0	0	0	1	2	53,777
Salem	1	0	0	0	0	0	0	0	0	0	1	42,468
Saugus	0	0	1	0	0	0	0	0	0	1	0	27,628
Sharon	0	1	0	0	0	0	0	0	1	0	0	17,935
Shrewsbury	0	0	1	0	0	0	0	0	1	0	0	36,315
Somerville	0	0	1	1	0	0	0	0	0	0	2	77,768

Table 94.   Hate Crime Incidents Per Bias Motivation and Quarter, by Selected State and Agency, 2013— continued

(Number.)

State/agency	Number of incidents per bias motivation							Number of incidents per quarter[1]				Population[2]
	Race	Religion	Sexual orientation	Ethnicity	Disability	Gender	Gender Identity	1st quarter	2nd quarter	3rd quarter	4th quarter	
South Hadley	1	0	1	0	0	0	0	0	0	1	1	17,794
Spencer	0	1	0	0	0	0	0	0	0	1	0	11,801
Springfield	1	0	2	1	0	0	0	3	0	0	1	153,586
Stoughton	0	1	0	0	0	0	0	0	1	0	0	28,186
Swampscott	1	0	0	0	0	0	0	1	0	0	0	13,995
Taunton	2	0	0	0	0	0	0	1	0	1	0	56,264
Waltham	0	1	1	0	0	0	0	0	0	1	1	62,446
Watertown	0	0	0	1	0	0	0	0	1	0	0	33,254
Westborough	1	0	0	0	0	0	0	0	0	1	0	18,563
West Boylston	1	0	0	0	0	0	0	0	0	0	1	7,821
West Springfield	0	1	0	0	0	0	0	0	0	1	0	28,647
Williamstown	0	1	0	0	0	0	0	0	0	0	1	7,682
Worcester	1	0	1	0	0	0	0	0	1	1	0	183,454
Universities and Colleges	4	7	5	2	0	1	0					
Boston College	0	0	1	0	0	0	0	1	0	0	0	14,605
Boston University	0	0	0	1	0	0	0	0	0	1	0	32,603
Bridgewater State University	1	0	0	0	0	0	0	0	0	0	1	11,417
Dean College	0	1	0	0	0	0	0	0	0	0	1	1,322
Emerson College	1	0	0	0	0	0	0	0	0	0	1	4,531
Massachusetts College of Liberal Arts	0	0	1	0	0	0	0	1	0	0	0	1,799
Northeastern University	0	1	1	0	0	1	0	0	0	0	3	27,694
Tufts University, Medford	0	1	1	0	0	0	0	0	0	1	1	10,837
University of Massachusetts												
Amherst	2	3	1	1	0	0	0	3	0	2	2	28,236
Harbor Campus, Boston	0	1	0	0	0	0	0	0	0	0	1	15,874
MICHIGAN												
Total	211	44	49	18	4	3	0					
Cities	161	29	32	12	3	2	0					
Adrian	0	0	1	0	0	0	0	0	1	0		20,759
Albion	1	0	0	0	0	0	0	0	1	0	0	8,524
Alpena	1	1	0	0	0	0	0	2	0	0	0	10,299
Ann Arbor	1	1	1	0	0	0	0	0	3	0	0	116,799
Bangor	0	0	0	0	0	1	0	0	0	0	1	1,857
Bath Township	1	0	0	0	0	0	0	0	0	1	0	11,761
Battle Creek	0	1	0	0	0	0	0	0	0	1	0	61,032
Benton Harbor	3	0	0	0	0	0	0	1	0	2	0	10,039
Benton Township	2	0	0	0	0	0	0	0	0	1	1	14,578
Birmingham	1	1	0	0	0	0	0	1	0	1	0	20,544
Blackman Township	3	0	0	0	0	0	0	0	1	0	2	38,115
Bloomfield Township	1	1	0	0	0	0	0	0	1	1	0	41,791
Brownstown Township	1	0	0	0	0	0	0	0	1	0	0	30,388
Buchanan	1	0	0	0	0	0	0	0	1	0	0	4,419
Buena Vista Township	0	0	1	0	0	0	0	0	0	1	0	8,500
Burton	2	0	0	0	0	0	0	0	1	0	1	29,263
Canton Township	1	1	0	0	0	0	0	0	1	1	0	88,958
Charlotte	1	0	0	0	0	0	0	0	1	0	0	9,046
Chesterfield Township	0	0	0	1	0	0	0	0	0	1	0	43,784
Chocolay Township	0	0	1	0	0	0	0	0	0	1	0	6,029
Clare	1	0	0	0	0	0	0	0	0	1	0	3,095
Clinton Township	4	0	0	0	0	0	0	1	2	0	1	98,071
Coldwater	1	0	2	0	0	0	0	0	2	0	1	10,876
Dearborn	7	2	2	3	0	0	0	7	4	2	1	96,012
Detroit	2	0	1	0	0	0	0	0	0	1	2	699,889
East Grand Rapids	1	0	0	0	0	0	0	0	1	0	0	11,100
Eastpointe	1	0	0	1	0	0	0	0	0	2	0	32,402
Elk Rapids	1	0	0	0	0	0	0	0	1	0	0	1,629
Escanaba	1	0	0	0	0	0	0	0	0	0	1	12,531
Essexville	0	1	0	0	0	0	0	1	0	0	0	3,436
Farmington	1	0	0	0	0	0	0	1	0	0	0	10,514
Ferndale	0	0	1	0	0	0	0	0	0	1	0	20,104
Flint Township	2	0	0	0	0	0	0	0	1	1	0	31,182
Flushing	0	0	1	0	0	0	0	0	0	1	0	8,204
Forsyth Township	1	0	0	0	0	0	0	0	1	0	0	6,278
Franklin	2	0	0	0	0	0	0	0	1	1	0	3,194
Fraser	2	0	0	0	0	0	0	0	1	1	0	14,529
Fruitport	1	0	0	0	0	0	0	0	0	0	1	1,090
Garden City	1	0	0	0	0	0	0	1	0	0	0	27,110
Gerrish Township	1	0	0	0	0	0	0	0	1	0	0	2,942
Grand Blanc Township	2	0	0	0	0	0	0	1	0	0	1	36,793
Grand Rapids	2	0	1	0	0	0	0	1	2	0	0	191,213
Grandville	1	0	1	1	1	0	0	2	0	2	0	15,669
Grayling	1	0	0	0	0	0	0	0	0	0	1	1,872
Grosse Pointe Park	1	0	0	0	0	0	0	0	0	1	0	11,287
Grosse Pointe Woods	0	0	0	1	0	0	0	0	1	0	0	15,760

Table 94.   Hate Crime Incidents Per Bias Motivation and Quarter, by Selected State and Agency, 2013— continued

(Number.)

State/agency	Number of incidents per bias motivation							Number of incidents per quarter[1]				Population[2]
	Race	Religion	Sexual orien-tation	Ethnicity	Disability	Gender	Gender Identity	1st quarter	2nd quarter	3rd quarter	4th quarter	
Hamtramck	1	0	1	0	0	0	0	0	0	1	1	22,017
Harper Woods	1	0	0	0	0	0	0	0	1	0	0	13,922
Hartford	3	0	0	0	0	0	0	1	0	0	2	2,633
Hazel Park	1	0	0	0	0	0	0	0	0	1	0	16,642
Highland Park	0	1	0	0	0	0	0	0	0	0	1	11,591
Holland	1	0	0	1	0	0	0	2	0	0	0	33,354
Huntington Woods	0	2	0	0	0	0	0	2	0	0	0	6,305
Inkster	3	0	0	0	0	0	0	2	0	0	1	24,850
Jackson	1	0	0	0	0	0	0	0	0	1	0	33,378
Jonesville	1	0	0	0	0	0	0	0	0	0	1	2,231
Kalamazoo	4	0	0	0	0	0	0	0	3	1	0	75,352
Kentwood	2	0	0	0	0	0	0	0	0	1	1	50,016
Lake Orion	1	0	0	0	0	0	0	0	0	0	1	3,052
Lansing	2	1	1	1	0	0	0	0	2	2	1	113,907
Lincoln Township	1	0	0	0	0	0	0	0	0	1	0	14,618
Livonia	0	0	1	0	0	0	0	0	0	0	1	95,220
Mackinac Island	0	1	0	0	0	0	0	0	0	1	0	494
Madison Heights	4	1	0	0	0	0	0	1	2	1	1	30,080
Madison Township	0	1	0	0	0	0	0	1	0	0	0	8,567
Marshall	1	0	0	0	0	0	0	0	0	0	1	7,050
Meridian Township	4	0	0	0	0	0	0	0	1	2	1	40,609
Midland	0	0	2	0	0	0	0	1	1	0	0	42,072
Milan	1	0	0	0	0	0	0	0	0	1	0	5,875
Milford	0	1	0	0	0	0	0	1	0	0	0	16,170
Monroe	2	0	0	0	0	0	0	0	1	1	0	20,474
Mount Morris Township	2	0	0	0	0	0	0	1	0	0	1	20,990
Mount Pleasant	3	0	1	0	1	0	0	1	2	2	0	26,238
Muskegon	3	0	0	0	0	0	0	2	0	0	1	36,658
Muskegon Heights	6	0	0	0	0	0	0	0	3	3	0	10,768
Newaygo	1	0	0	0	0	0	0	0	0	1	0	1,961
Northfield Township	1	0	0	0	0	0	0	0	0	0	1	8,387
Northville Township	1	0	0	0	0	0	0	1	0	0	0	28,734
Norton Shores	1	0	1	0	0	0	0	0	0	2	0	23,834
Novi	1	0	0	0	0	0	0	0	0	1	0	57,469
Ontwa Township-Edwardsburg	1	0	0	0	0	0	0		0	1	0	6,585
Owosso	1	0	0	0	0	0	0	1	0	0	0	14,745
Pittsfield Township	1	0	2	0	0	0	0	1	2	0	0	36,091
Portage	1	0	0	0	0	0	0	1	0	0	0	47,387
Port Huron	0	0	2	0	0	0	0	1	0	1	0	29,542
Romeo	2	0	0	0	0	0	0	0	0	2	0	3,597
Roseville	5	0	1	0	0	0	0	1	3	2	0	47,327
Royal Oak	1	0	0	0	0	0	0	0	0	1	0	58,804
Saginaw	4	0	2	0	0	0	0	1	1	2	2	50,580
Saginaw Township	0	1	0	0	0	0	0	0	0	0	1	40,636
Saline	1	0	0	0	0	0	0	0	0	0	1	9,028
Sault Ste. Marie	1	1	0	0	0	0	0	0	0	1	1	14,203
Shelby Township	2	0	0	0	0	0	0	0	0	1	1	75,347
Southfield	2	1	0	0	0	0	0	0	2	0	1	72,755
Sparta	0	2	0	0	0	0	0	0	1	1	0	4,224
St. Joseph	1	0	0	0	0	0	0	1	0	0	0	8,293
Sumpter Township	1	0	1	0	0	0	0	0	0	0	2	9,310
Taylor	1	0	2	0	0	0	0	1	2	0	0	61,836
Three Rivers	1	0	0	0	0	0	0	0	0	0	1	7,712
Traverse City	0	0	1	0	0	0	0	0	1	0	0	14,989
Trenton	1	0	0	0	0	0	0	0	1	0	0	18,483
Troy	2	1	0	0	0	0	0	0	1	0	2	82,608
Utica	2	0	0	0	0	0	0	0	1	0	1	4,765
Van Buren Township	1	1	0	0	0	0	0	0	1	0	1	28,282
Warren	7	1	0	0	0	1	0	0	0	4	5	134,167
Waterford Township	0	1	0	0	0	0	0	0	0	1	0	72,949
Wayland	0	0	0	0	1	0	0	0	1	0	0	4,074
Wayne	4	0	0	0	0	0	0	1	1	1	1	17,232
West Bloomfield Township	5	1	1	2	0	0	0	5	2	2	0	65,840
Westland	1	0	0	1	0	0	0	1	0	0	1	82,554
White Lake Township	0	1	0	0	0	0	0	0	0	0	1	30,585
Woodhaven	1	0	0	0	0	0	0	0	0	0	1	12,652
Wyoming	1	1	0	0	0	0	0	1	0	0	1	73,786
Universities and Colleges	4	4	4	1	1	1	0					
Eastern Michigan University	1	0	0	0	0	0	0	0	0	0	1	23,518
Michigan State University	2	0	2	0	0	0	0	1	0	2	2	48,783
Oakland University[3]	0	3	0	1	1	0	0	1	0	3	1	19,740
Saginaw Valley State University	1	0	0	0	0	0	0	0	0	0	1	10,552
University of Michigan, Ann Arbor	0	1	1	0	0	0	0	1	1	0	0	43,426
Western Michigan University	0	0	1	0	0	0	0	0	0	1	0	24,598
Metropolitan Counties	36	9	9	4	0	0	0					

Table 94.   Hate Crime Incidents Per Bias Motivation and Quarter, by Selected State and Agency, 2013— continued

(Number.)

State/agency	Number of incidents per bias motivation							Number of incidents per quarter[1]				Population[2]
	Race	Religion	Sexual orien- tation	Ethnicity	Disability	Gender	Gender Identity	1st quarter	2nd quarter	3rd quarter	4th quarter	
Eaton	0	1	0	0	0	0	0	0	0	0	1	
Ingham	1	0	0	0	0	0	0	1	0	0	0	
Jackson	1	1	0	0	0	0	0	0	0	1	1	
Kent	2	0	1	0	0	0	0	1	2	0	0	
Livingston	1	0	0	0	0	0	0	0	0	1	0	
Macomb	10	1	1	1	0	0	0	2	5	3	3	
Monroe	4	1	1	0	0	0	0	1	3	2	0	
Oakland	7	2	5	3	0	0	0	5	4	5	3	
Ottawa	4	0	0	0	0	0	0	1	2	0	1	
Van Buren	3	0	1	0	0	0	0	1	1	2	0	
Washtenaw	3	3	0	0	0	0	0	0	2	2	2	
Nonmetropolitan Counties	5	0	1	1	0	0	0					
Missaukee	1	0	0	1	0	0	0	0	1	1	0	
Ogemaw	2	0	0	0	0	0	0	0	0	1	1	
Otsego	0	0	1	0	0	0	0	0	0	0	1	
Tuscola	2	0	0	0	0	0	0	0	1	1	0	
	2	2	3	0	0	0	0					
State Police Agencies												
Cass County	1	0	0	0	0	0	0	0	1	0	0	
Genesee County	1	0	1	0	0	0	0	0	1	0	1	
Jackson County	0	1	0	0	0	0	0	0	0	1	0	
Oakland County	0	1	0	0	0	0	0	1	0	0	0	
Van Buren County	0	0	2	0	0	0	0	0	0	2	0	
Other Agencies	3	0	0	0	0	0	0					
Gerald R. Ford International Airport	1	0	0	0	0	0	0	0	0	0	1	
Huron-Clinton Metropolitan Authority, Lower Huron Metropark	2	0	0	0	0	0	0	0	1	1	0	
MINNESOTA												
Total	83	19	30	11	1	0	0					
Cities	80	19	28	11	1	0	0					
Bemidji	0	0	1	0	0	0	0	0	1	0	0	13,805
Blaine	4	0	0	0	0	0	0	1	2	1	0	60,093
Brooklyn Park	3	0	0	0	0	0	0	1	1	1	0	78,353
Chaska	1	0	0	0	0	0	0		1	0	0	24,158
Columbia Heights	1	0	0	1	0	0	0	1	1	0	0	19,715
Crosby	1	0	0	0	0	0	0	0	1	0	0	2,369
Duluth	1	0	0	0	0	0	0	1	0	0	0	86,211
Eagan	0	2	0	0	0	0	0	0	1	1	0	65,052
Eden Prairie	1	0	0	0	0	0	0	0	0	0	1	62,714
Elk River	1	0	0	0	0	0	0	0	0	0	1	23,351
Faribault	0	0	1	0	0	0	0			1		23,405
Inver Grove Heights	0	1	0	0	0	0	0	1	0	0	0	34,294
Lino Lakes	0	0	1	0	0	0	0		0	0	1	20,910
Mankato	2	2	2	0	0	0	0	0	2	2	2	40,360
Maple Grove	0	0	1	0	0	0	0		1	0	0	65,318
Marshall	1	0	0	1	0	0	0	1	1	0	0	13,370
Mendota Heights	0	0	1	0	0	0	0	0	0	0	1	11,158
Minneapolis	20	4	11	3	1	0	0	6	13	11	9	396,206
Moorhead	1	0	1	0	0	0	0	0	0	1	1	39,322
Plymouth	3	2	2	0	0	0	0	0	3	4	0	73,684
Rochester	2	0	0	2	0	0	0	0	2	2	0	109,675
Roseville	2	0	1	0	0	0	0	0	2	1	0	34,991
Savage	0	0	1	0	0	0	0	0	1	0	0	28,285
Shakopee	0	0	1	0	0	0	0	1	0	0	0	39,214
Shoreview	0	0	1	0	0	0	0	0	0	1	0	25,810
Spring Lake Park	0	0	0	1	0	0	0	0	1	0	0	6,458
St. Anthony	1	0	0	0	0	0	0	0	1	0	0	8,445
St. Cloud	6	0	0	2	0	0	0	0	3	3	2	65,977
St. Louis Park	3	4	0	0	0	0	0	1	4	1	1	46,723
St. Paul	24	4	2	0	0	0	0	0	18	11	1	294,690
Wadena	0	0	1	0	0	0	0	1	0	0	0	4,092
Waite Park	0	0	0	1	0	0	0	0	0	1	0	6,683
West St. Paul	1	0	0	0	0	0	0	0	0	1	0	19,761
Woodbury	1	0	0	0	0	0	0	1				65,259
Universities and Colleges	1	0	0	0	0	0	0					
University of Minnesota, Morris	1	0	0	0	0	0	0	0	0	1	0	1,896
Metropolitan Counties	1	0	1	0	0	0	0					
Hennepin	0	0	1	0	0	0	0	0	1	0	0	
Mille Lacs	1	0	0	0	0	0	0	0	1	0	0	
Nonmetropolitan Counties	1	0	1	0	0	0	0					
Mahnomen	0	0	1	0	0	0	0			1		

Table 94.   Hate Crime Incidents Per Bias Motivation and Quarter, by Selected State and Agency, 2013— continued

(Number.)

State/agency	Number of incidents per bias motivation							Number of incidents per quarter[1]				Population[2]
	Race	Religion	Sexual orientation	Ethnicity	Disability	Gender	Gender Identity	1st quarter	2nd quarter	3rd quarter	4th quarter	
Rice	1	0	0	0	0	0	0	0	1	0	0	
MISSISSIPPI												
Total	2	0	0	2	0	0	0					
Cities	2	0	0	2	0	0	0					
Biloxi	1	0	0	0	0	0	0	1	0	0	0	44,744
Gulfport	1	0	0	2	0	0	0	2	1	0	0	70,863
MISSOURI												
Total	51	11	27	6	1	4	2					
Cities	44	10	23	6	1	4	2					
Branson	0	0	0	1	0	0	0	0	0	0	1	10,918
Clayton	0	1	0	0	0	0	0	0	1	0	0	15,901
Grandview	1	0	0	0	0	0	0	0	0	1		24,630
Independence	1	0	1	0	0	0	0	1	0	1	0	117,381
Joplin	2	0	0	0	0	0	0	2	0	0	0	49,272
Kansas City	30	7	14	5	1	4	2	13	17	21	12	465,514
Raytown	1	0	0	0	0	0	0	0	0	0	1	29,501
Springfield	1	1	1	0	0	0	0	0	3	0	0	163,062
St. Charles	1	0	0	0	0	0	0	0	1	0	0	66,628
St. Joseph	2	0	0	0	0	0	0	1	0	1	0	77,347
St. Louis	4	1	7	0	0	0	0	3	2	2	5	318,563
University City	1	0	0	0	0	0	0	0	0	1	0	35,186
Universities and Colleges	2	0	0	0	0	0	0					
University of Missouri, Columbia	2	0	0	0	0	0	0	0	0	0	2	34,704
Metropolitan Counties	4	0	3	0	0	0	0					
De Kalb	1	0	0	0	0	0	0	0	0	1	0	
Jefferson	0	0	1	0	0	0	0	0	0	0	1	
St. Charles	2	0	2	0	0	0	0	0	2	2	0	
St. Louis County Police Department	1	0	0	0	0	0	0	0	0	1	0	
Nonmetropolitan Counties	1	1	1	0	0	0	0					
Carroll	0	1	0	0	0	0	0	0	0	0	1	
Henry	0	0	1	0	0	0	0	0	0	0	1	
Laclede	1	0	0	0	0	0	0	0	0	0	1	
MONTANA												
Total	25	2	3	1	0	0	0					
Cities	21	2	2	0	0	0	0					
Billings	5	1	1	0	0	0	0	1	2	1	3	107,802
Columbia Falls	1	0	0	0	0	0	0	0	1	0	0	4,721
Great Falls	1	0	0	0	0	0	0	0	0	0	1	58,940
Hamilton	0	1	0	0	0	0	0	0	0	0	1	4,555
Helena	11	0	0	0	0	0	0	11	0	0	0	29,411
Kalispell	2	0	0	0	0	0	0	0	0	2	0	20,665
Missoula	1	0	1	0	0	0	0	1	0	1	0	68,877
Universities and Colleges	1	0	0	0	0	0	0					
Montana State University	1	0	0	0	0	0	0	0	1	0	0	14,269
Metropolitan Counties	2	0	0	1	0	0	0					
Cascade	1	0	0	1	0	0	0	0	0	2	0	
Missoula	1	0	0	0	0	0	0	0	0	1	0	
Nonmetropolitan Counties	1	0	1	0	0	0	0					
Park	0	0	1	0	0	0	0	0	0	0	1	
Silver Bow	1	0	0	0	0	0	0	0	0	1	0	
NEBRASKA												
Total	17	5	8	6	0	0	0					
Cities	14	5	8	5	0	0	0					
Columbus	0	0	1	0	0	0	0	0	0	1	0	22,624
Cozad	0	0	0	1	0	0	0	1		0	0	3,929
Grand Island	0	0	0	2	0	0	0	0	0	2	0	50,441
Kearney	0	1	0	0	0	0	0	0	0	1	0	32,113
Lexington	2	0	0	0	0	0	0	0		0	2	10,204
Lincoln	8	2	4	1	0	0	0	5	3	2	5	267,565
Omaha	4	2	2	1	0	0	0	2	3	3	1	425,076
Sidney	0	0	1	0	0	0	0	1	0			6,831
Metropolitan Counties	0	0	0	1	0	0	0					

Table 94.   Hate Crime Incidents Per Bias Motivation and Quarter, by Selected State and Agency, 2013— continued

(Number.)

State/agency	Number of incidents per bias motivation							Number of incidents per quarter[1]				Population[2]
	Race	Religion	Sexual orientation	Ethnicity	Disability	Gender	Gender Identity	1st quarter	2nd quarter	3rd quarter	4th quarter	
Lancaster	0	0	0	1	0	0	0	0	1	0	0	
Nonmetropolitan Counties	3	0	0	0	0	0	0					
Dawson	3	0	0	0	0	0	0	0	0	1	2	
NEVADA												
Total	31	10	25	7	0	0	0					
Cities	31	10	25	7	0	0	0					
Carlin	1	0	0	0	0	0	0				1	2,457
Henderson	1	0	0	0	0	0	0			1		268,237
Las Vegas Metropolitan Police Department	27	9	23	6	0	0	0	16	13	18	18	1,500,455
North Las Vegas	0	0	1	1	0	0	0		1	1		225,632
Reno	2	1	1	0	0	0	0		1	3		232,561
NEW HAMPSHIRE												
Total	11	5	4	1	0	0	0					
Cities	10	5	3	1	0	0	0					
Ashland	1	0	0	0	0	0	0	0	1	0	0	2,056
Bedford	1	0	0	0	0	0	0	0	1	0	0	21,645
Concord	2	1	0	0	0	0	0	0	2	1	0	42,615
Conway	0	0	1	0	0	0	0	1	0	0	0	10,056
Farmington	1	0	0	0	0	0	0	0	0	1	0	6,799
Hampton	1	0	0	0	0	0	0	0	0	1	0	15,067
Hampton Falls	0	0	0	1	0	0	0	0	1	0	0	2,294
Hanover	0	0	1	0	0	0	0	0	1	0	0	11,195
Keene	0	1	0	0	0	0	0	0	0	1	0	23,236
Londonderry	0	1	0	0	0	0	0	0	1	0	0	24,338
Manchester	1	0	0	0	0	0	0	0	0	0	1	110,411
Newbury	0	0	1	0	0	0	0	1	0	0	0	2,110
Pelham	1	2	0	0	0	0	0	2	1	0	0	13,034
Plaistow	1	0	0	0	0	0	0	0	0	0	1	7,620
Windham	1	0	0	0	0	0	0	1	0	0	0	14,092
Universities and Colleges	1	0	1	0	0	0	0					
University of New Hampshire	1	0	1	0	0			1	0	1	0	15,267
NEW JERSEY												
Total	187	121	64	38	4	0	0					
Cities	180	121	61	38	4	0	0					
Aberdeen Township	8	1	2	0	0	0	0	1	6	1	3	18,150
Allenhurst	0	2	0	0	0	0	0	0	0	1	1	493
Asbury Park	1	0	3	0	0	0	0	1	2	1	0	15,779
Bedminster Township	1	1	0	0	0	0	0	0	2	0	0	8,213
Belleville	0	0	2	0	0	0	0	0	0	1	1	36,229
Brick Township	2	1	0	1	0	0	0	1	2	1	0	75,371
Burlington	0	0	0	0	1	0	0	1	0	0	0	9,865
Burlington Township	0	1	0	0	0	0	0	1	0	0	0	22,750
Caldwell	1	0	0	0	0	0	0	0	0	1	0	7,876
Cinnaminson Township	1	0	0	0	0	0	0	0	0	0	1	16,686
Clark Township	0	1	0	0	0	0	0	0	1	0	0	15,021
Closter	0	0	1	0	0	0	0	1	0	0	0	8,548
Colts Neck Township	3	0	0	0	0	0	0	0	0	2	1	10,075
Cranford Township	0	1	0	0	0	0	0	1	0	0	0	23,165
Delran Township	2	0	0	0	0	0	0	0	1	0	1	16,862
Eastampton Township	0	0	0	1	0	0	0	1	0	0	0	6,103
East Brunswick Township	1	10	2	1	0	0	0	3	4	3	4	48,073
East Hanover Township	0	1	0	0	0	0	0	0	0	0	1	11,350
East Orange	0	1	0	0	0	0	0	0	0	0	1	64,425
East Windsor Township	0	1	0	0	0	0	0	0	0	1	0	27,564
Egg Harbor Township	2	0	0	1	0	0	0	0	2	0	1	43,709
Elmwood Park	1	0	0	0	1	0	0	1	1	0	0	20,077
Evesham Township	7	1	0	0	0	0	0	4	3	1	0	45,798
Ewing Township	1	0	2	0	0	0	0	0	1	0	2	36,449
Fairview	0	0	0	1	0	0	0	0	0	1	0	14,358
Fanwood	0	1	0	0	0	0	0	0	0	1	0	7,447
Fort Lee	2	0	1	0	0	0	0	2	1	0	0	35,900
Franklin Lakes	0	1	0	1	0	0	0	1	1	0	0	10,746
Franklin Township, Gloucester County	0	1	0	0	0	0	0	0	0	1	0	16,740
Freehold Township	0	1	0	0	0	0	0	1	0	0	0	36,048
Galloway Township	0	0	1	0	0	0	0	0	1	0	0	37,304
Glassboro	8	0	2	2	0	0	0	3	2	3	4	19,038
Glen Ridge	0	1	0	0	0	0	0	0	1	0	0	7,626
Gloucester Township	2	0	0	0	0	0	0	0	2	0	0	64,440
Green Brook Township	0	2	0	0	0	0	0	1	1	0	0	7,240

Table 94. Hate Crime Incidents Per Bias Motivation and Quarter, by Selected State and Agency, 2013— continued

(Number.)

State/agency	Number of incidents per bias motivation							Number of incidents per quarter[1]				Population[2]
	Race	Religion	Sexual orien-tation	Ethnicity	Disability	Gender	Gender Identity	1st quarter	2nd quarter	3rd quarter	4th quarter	
Greenwich Township, Warren County	1	0	0	0	0	0	0	0	0	0	1	5,582
Haddonfield	0	1	0	0	0	0	0	0	0	0	1	11,590
Haddon Township	0	0	0	1	0	0	0	0	0	1	0	14,732
Hardyston Township	0	0	1	0	0	0	0	0	0	1	0	8,049
Harrison	0	0	1	0	0	0	0	0	0	0	1	13,975
Harrison Township	1	0	0	0	0	0	0	0	0	1	0	12,616
Highland Park	2	3	3	0	0	0	0	1	4	2	1	14,420
Hightstown	1	1	0	1	0	0	0	0	1	1	1	5,572
Hillsborough Township	1	0	0	0	0	0	0	0	1	0	0	39,037
Hoboken	3	3	1	0	0	0	0	1	2	1	3	52,771
Holmdel Township	2	3	0	0	0	0	0	2	2	0	1	16,657
Howell Township	5	6	4	3	0	0	0	2	7	5	4	51,100
Irvington	0	0	1	0	0	0	0	0	0	1	0	54,246
Jackson Township	2	1	0	0	0	0	0	1	0	0	2	55,817
Jersey City	2	0	2	1	0	0	0	0	3	0	2	256,886
Keansburg	3	0	1	0	0	0	0	1	0	2	1	9,981
Lacey Township	3	0	2	2	1	0	0	1	5	1	1	27,865
Lakewood Township	5	15	0	3	0	0	0	2	6	7	8	92,664
Lawrence Township, Mercer County	0	0	0	1	0	0	0	0	0	1	0	33,172
Little Egg Harbor Township	3	1	0	2	0	0	0	1	2	0	3	20,412
Little Falls Township	0	0	1	0	0	0	0	0	1	0	0	14,504
Livingston Township	2	0	0	0	0	0	0	0	0	2	0	29,621
Logan Township	1	0	0	0	0	0	0	0	0	1	0	6,019
Long Beach Township	0	1	0	0	0	0	0	0	1	0	0	3,068
Lower Township	1	0	0	0	0	0	0	0	0	1	0	22,467
Lumberton Township	2	0	0	0	0	0	0	0	0	2	0	12,516
Mahwah Township	0	1	0	0	0	0	0	0	0	1	0	26,292
Manalapan Township	1	0	0	2	0	0	0	2	0	1	0	39,313
Manasquan	1	2	0	0	0	0	0	1	2	0	0	5,860
Manchester Township	3	0	0	0	0	0	0	0	3	0	0	43,013
Maple Shade Township	1	0	0	0	0	0	0	1	0	0	0	19,291
Margate City	1	0	0	0	0	0	0	0	0	0	1	6,319
Marlboro Township	2	0	0	0	0	0	0	1	1	0	0	40,190
Medford Lakes	0	0	1	0	0	0	0	0	1	0	0	4,196
Medford Township	4	2	1	0	0	0	0	2	1	1	3	23,285
Mendham	0	1	0	0	0	0	0	0	0	0	1	5,029
Middlesex	1	0	0	0	0	0	0	1	0	0	0	13,787
Middletown Township	1	0	0	0	0	0	0	0	1	0	0	66,246
Monroe Township, Middlesex County	8	1	1	1	0	0	0	1	0	2	8	41,356
Montclair	4	2	0	0	0	0	0	2	2	1	1	37,962
Montgomery Township	1	3	0	0	0	0	0	1	1	0	2	22,467
Moorestown Township	1	0	0	0	0	0	0	0	0	1	0	20,706
Morris Township	0	1	0	0	0	0	0	0	0	0	1	22,640
Mount Laurel Township	0	0	0	1	0	0	0	0	0	0	1	41,839
Mount Olive Township	0	0	0	2	0	0	0	0	1	0	1	28,611
Neptune Township	10	0	3	1	0	0	0	0	8	2	4	27,856
Newark	2	0	1	0	0	0	0	0	2	0	1	278,246
New Brunswick	3	1	1	0	0	0	0	3	1	1	0	56,542
New Providence	1	2	0	0	0	0	0	1	2	0	0	12,463
North Brunswick Township	1	0	1	2	0	0	0	1	2	0	1	41,425
Nutley Township	2	1	0	0	0	0	0	0	1	2	0	28,660
Oakland	1	2	2	0	0	0	0	1	2	1	1	12,927
Oceanport	0	1	0	0	0	0	0	0	0	1	0	5,833
Old Bridge Township	1	0	1	0	0	0	0	1	0	1	0	66,528
Palmyra	1	0	0	0	0	0	0	0	0	1	0	7,412
Paramus	0	0	0	1	0	0	0	0	0	0	1	26,628
Parsippany-Troy Hills Township	0	2	0	0	0	0	0	0	0	0	2	53,851
Passaic	2	2	0	1	0	0	0	0	1	2	2	70,445
Paulsboro	1	0	0	0	0	0	0	0	0	0	1	6,034
Pemberton Township	1	0	0	0	0	0	0	0	0	0	1	27,949
Pennsauken Township	0	1	0	0	0	0	0	0	0	0	1	35,788
Pequannock Township	0	1	0	0	0	0	0	0	0	0	1	15,580
Phillipsburg	0	1	0	1	0	0	0	0	0	1	1	14,619
Pine Hill	1	0	0	0	0	0	0	0	0	0	1	10,704
Piscataway Township	0	2	2	0	0	0	0	3	1	0	0	58,259
Pitman	6	1	0	0	0	0	0	1	0	5	1	8,930
Plainsboro Township	0	0	0	0	1	0	0	0	1	0	0	23,256
Point Pleasant	4	1	0	1	0	0	0	1	4	1	0	18,458
Randolph Township	1	0	2	0	0	0	0	0	0	2	1	25,969
Raritan	0	0	2	0	0	0	0	0	0	0	2	7,352
Readington Township	0	1	0	0	0	0	0	0	0	0	1	15,910
Robbinsville Township	2	1	0	0	0	0	0	1	1	1	0	14,046
Runnemede	0	1	0	0	0	0	0	0	0	0	1	8,459
Salem	1	0	0	0	0	0	0	0	0	1	0	5,175
Secaucus	0	2	2	0	0	0	0	0	1	0	3	19,119
Shrewsbury	2	0	0	0	0	0	0	2	0	0	0	3,941
Somerville	0	1	0	0	0	0	0	0	0	1	0	12,174

Table 94.   Hate Crime Incidents Per Bias Motivation and Quarter, by Selected State and Agency, 2013— continued

(Number.)

State/agency	Number of incidents per bias motivation							Number of incidents per quarter[1]				Population[2]
	Race	Religion	Sexual orientation	Ethnicity	Disability	Gender	Gender Identity	1st quarter	2nd quarter	3rd quarter	4th quarter	
South Brunswick Township	0	4	1	0	0	0	0	0	1	2	2	44,575
South Orange	1	0	1	0	0	0	0	1	1	0	0	16,297
South Plainfield	1	0	0	1	0	0	0	1	1	0	0	23,789
Spotswood	0	2	0	0	0	0	0	0	1	1	0	8,459
Toms River Township	0	1	0	0	0	0	0	0	0	1	0	92,332
Totowa	1	1	1	0	0	0	0	0	1	2	0	10,985
Trenton	1	0	1	0	0	0	0	0	1	1	0	84,439
Union Beach	0	0	0	1	0	0	0	0	1	0	0	6,198
Union City	0	1	1	0	0	0	0	1	1	0	0	68,254
Verona	0	1	0	0	0	0	0	0	1	0	0	13,429
Vineland	0	1	1	0	0	0	0	0	1	0	1	60,863
Voorhees Township	2	1	0	0	0	0	0	0	2	1	0	29,284
Washington	3	1	0	0	0	0	0	1	0	2	1	6,408
Washington Township, Gloucester County	2	0	0	0	0	0	0	0	1	1	0	48,110
Washington Township, Warren County	0	0	1	0	0	0	0	0	0		1	6,493
Watchung	0	1	0	0	0	0	0	0	0	1	0	5,844
Weehawken Township	1	0	1	0	0	0	0	0	1	1	0	12,937
West Caldwell Township	0	1	0	0	0	0	0	0	0	1	0	10,878
West Deptford Township	3	1	0	1	0	0	0	3	1	1	0	21,497
West Long Branch	0	1	0	0	0	0	0	0	0	1	0	8,660
West Milford Township	3	0	0	0	0	0	0	2	0	1	0	26,095
Woodbridge Township	1	2	0	0	0	0	0	0	2	0	1	100,568
Woodbury	4	1	0	0	0	0	0	0	0	2	3	10,073
Woodbury Heights	1	0	0	0	0	0	0	1	0	0	0	3,026
Woolwich Township	1	0	0	0	0	0	0	0	1	0	0	11,167
Metropolitan Counties	6	0	2	0	0	0	0					
Camden County Police Department	6	0	2	0	0	0	0	0	4	4	0	
	1	0	1	0	0	0	0					
State Police Agencies												
Ocean County	0	0	1	0	0	0	0	0	1	0	0	
Salem County	1	0	0	0	0	0	0	0	1	0	0	
NEW MEXICO												
Total	6	1	4	1	0	0	0					
Cities	6	1	4	1	0	0	0					
Albuquerque	5	1	4	0	0	0	0	2	1	6	1	558,165
Belen	0	0	0	1	0	0	0				1	7,247
Los Lunas	1	0	0	0	0	0	0	0		1		15,252
NEW YORK												
Total	150	294	122	36	2	6	5					
Cities	95	182	107	26	2	4	3					
Albany	1	2	0	0	0	0	0	0	2	1	0	97,956
Amherst Town	3	0	0	0	0	0	0	0	0	1	2	118,296
Batavia	1	0	0	0	0	0	0	0	0	1	0	15,374
Brighton Town	1	0	0	0	0	0	0	1	0	0	0	36,689
Buffalo	11	1	2	2	0	1	0	6	3	4	4	258,789
Canandaigua	1	0	0	0	0	0	0	0	1	0	0	10,470
Clarkstown Town	1	2	0	0	0	0	0	2	1	0	0	80,705
Cohoes	1	0	0	0	0	0	0	0	1	0	0	16,179
Colonie Town	0	0	1	0	0	0	0	0	1	0	0	78,215
Crawford Town	3	4	0	0	0	0	0	0	1	0	6	9,264
Croton-on-Hudson Village	0	0	0	0	0	1	0	0	1	0	0	8,180
Freeport Village	0	0	0	1	0	0	0	1	0	0	0	43,214
Greece Town	3	0	0	0	0	0	0	0	1	2	0	96,667
Hamburg Town	1	0	0	0	0	0	0	1	0	0	0	45,535
Hyde Park Town	1	0	0	0	0	0	0	0	0	1	0	21,397
Ithaca	0	0	1	0	0	0	0	0	1	0		30,433
Jamestown	2	0	0	0	0	0	0	1	0	0	1	30,658
Liberty Village	0	4	0	0	0	0	0	0	0	0	4	4,285
Middletown	1	0	0	0	0	0	0	0	0	1	0	27,809
Monroe Village	0	2	0	0	0	0	0	0	1	0	1	8,544
Mount Vernon	2	0	0	1	0	0	0	1	1	0	1	68,071
Newburgh	0	0	1	1	0	0	0	0	0	0	1	28,571
New Rochelle	1	2	0	0	0	0	0	1	1	1	0	78,800
New York	44	152	99	17	1	0	1	56	84	81	93	8,396,126
Niagara Falls	2	0	0	1	0	0	0	0	2	0	1	49,574
North Syracuse Village	2	0	0	0	0	0	0	0	1	1	0	6,964
Owego Village	0	0	1	0	0	0	0	0	0	1	0	3,818
Poughkeepsie	0	0	0	2	1	0	1	2	1	0	1	30,778
Poughkeepsie Town	2	1	1	0	0	0	0	0	2	1	2	43,866
Ramapo Town	0	1	0	0	0	0	0	0	0		1	87,204
Rochester	3	1	0	0	0	0	0	0	2	2	0	210,562
Rockville Centre Village	0	1	0	0	0	0	0	0	1	0	0	24,129

Table 94. Hate Crime Incidents Per Bias Motivation and Quarter, by Selected State and Agency, 2013— continued

(Number.)

State/agency	Number of incidents per bias motivation							Number of incidents per quarter[1]				Population[2]
	Race	Religion	Sexual orien-tation	Ethnicity	Disability	Gender	Gender Identity	1st quarter	2nd quarter	3rd quarter	4th quarter	
Salamanca	1	0	0	0	0	0	0	0	0	1	0	5,691
Saratoga Springs	1	2	0	0	0	0	0	0	0	1	2	27,081
Scarsdale Village	0	1	0	0	0	0	0	1	0	0	0	17,564
Schodack Town	0	0	0	0	0	1	0	0	0	1	0	11,573
Sleepy Hollow Village	0	2	0	0	0	0	0	0	1	1	0	9,996
Spring Valley Village	1	1	0	0	0	0	0	0	0	1	1	32,288
Troy	1	0	0	0	0	0	0	0	0	1	0	49,898
Tuckahoe Village	0	0	0	1	0	0	0	1	0	0	0	6,578
Utica	1	0	0	0	0	0	0	0	0	1	0	61,686
West Seneca Town	2	0	0	0	0	0	0	0	1	1	0	44,821
Yonkers	1	3	1	0	0	1	1	2	0	3	2	199,134
Universities and Colleges	8	9	4	1	0	1	1					
Cornell University	1	0	1	0	0	0	0	0	1	1		21,424
Ithaca College	0	0	0	1	0	0	0	0	1	0	0	6,759
State University of New York												
Binghamton	0	2	0	0	0	0	1	0	0	3	1	15,308
Stony Brook	0	2	0	0	0	0	0	0	1	1	0	23,946
State University of New York Agricultural and Technical College												
Alfred	1	0	0	0	0	0	0	0	0	0	1	3,528
Cobleskill	0	0	1	0	0	0	0	0	0	0	1	2,492
Morrisville	0	0	0	0	0	1	0	0	1	0	0	3,095
State University of New York College												
Buffalo	0	0	1	0	0	0	0	0	1	0	0	11,781
Cortland	2	1	0	0	0	0	0	1	1	0	1	7,098
Fredonia	1	0	0	0	0	0	0	0	1	0	0	5,521
New Paltz	2	0	0	0	0	0	0	0	0	0	2	7,655
Oneonta	0	2	0	0	0	0	0	0	0	1	1	6,041
Oswego	0	1	0	0	0	0	0	1	0	0	0	7,921
Potsdam	1	0	1	0	0	0	0	1	0	0	1	4,224
Purchase	0	1	0	0	0	0	0	0	1	0	0	4,240
Metropolitan Counties	41	79	9	8	0	0	1					
Broome	1	0	0	0	0	0	0	0	0	0	1	
Erie	0	0	0	1	0	0	0	0	0	0	1	
Livingston	1	0	0	0	0	0	0	1	0	0	0	
Monroe	1	0	0	0	0	0	0	0	1	0	0	
Nassau	10	28	2	3	0	0	0	9	16	9	9	
Oneida	1	0	0	0	0	0	0	0	1	0	0	
Putnam	0	0	0	0	0	0	1	0	0	1	0	
Suffolk County Police Department	26	50	7	4	0	0	0	11	33	22	21	
Ulster	1	0	0	0	0	0	0	0	0	1	0	
Westchester Public Safety	0	1	0	0	0	0	0	0	0	0	1	
Nonmetropolitan Counties	1	0	0	0	0	0	0					
St. Lawrence	1	0	0	0	0	0	0	0	1	0	0	
	3	8	2	1	0	1	0					
State Police Agencies												
Broome County	0	0	1	0	0	0	0	0	0	0	1	
Dutchess County	0	1	0	0	0	0	0	0	0	1	0	
Franklin County	1	1	0	0	0	0	0	0	1	1	0	
Herkimer County	1	0	0	0	0	0	0	0	1	0	0	
Jefferson County	0	0	1	0	0	0	0	1	0	0	0	
Madison County	0	1	0	0	0	0	0	0	1	0	0	
Nassau County	1	0	0	0	0	0	0	0	1	0	0	
Orange County	0	1	0	0	0	0	0	0	1	0	0	
Otsego County	0	1	0	0	0	0	0	0	0	0	1	
Putnam County	0	0	0	1	0	0	0	0	0	1	0	
Saratoga County	0	1	0	0	0	0	0	0	0	1	0	
Steuben County	0	0	0	0	0	1	0	0	0	0	1	
Ulster County	0	1	0	0	0	0	0	0	1	0	0	
Westchester County	0	1	0	0	0	0	0	0	0	0	1	
Other Agencies	2	16	0	0	0	0	0					
New York City Metropolitan Transportation Authority	2	15	0	0	0	0	0	4	5	4	4	
State Park, Long Island Regional	0	1	0	0	0	0	0	1	0	0		
NORTH CAROLINA												
Total	67	17	23	11	0	0	0					
Cities	51	10	16	8	0	0	0					
Albemarle	1	0	0	0	0	0	0	0	0	0	1	15,946
Asheboro	1	0	0	0	0	0	0	0	0	0	1	25,665
Asheville	5	2	2	1	0	0	0	3	0	3	4	86,445
Burlington	1	0	0	0	0	0	0	0	0	0	1	51,401
Carrboro	1	0	0	0	0	0	0	0	0	0	1	20,709

Table 94.   Hate Crime Incidents Per Bias Motivation and Quarter, by Selected State and Agency, 2013— continued

(Number.)

State/agency	Number of incidents per bias motivation							Number of incidents per quarter[1]				Population[2]
	Race	Religion	Sexual orien- tation	Ethnicity	Disability	Gender	Gender Identity	1st quarter	2nd quarter	3rd quarter	4th quarter	
Chapel Hill	0	0	0	1	0	0	0	0	1	0	0	58,744
Charlotte-Mecklenburg	8	4	6	3	0	0	0	10	4	2	5	837,638
Concord	1	0	0	0	0	0	0	0	1	0	0	82,899
Creedmoor	1	0	0	0	0	0	0	0	0	1	0	4,254
Durham	2	1	3	1	0	0	0	3	0	4	0	242,865
Fayetteville	4	1	0	1	0	0	0	2	1	2	1	202,524
Gastonia	0	1	0	0	0	0	0	0	1	0	0	73,049
Greensboro	3	0	0	0	0	0	0	0	1	0	2	279,343
Greenville	1	0	0	0	0	0	0	0	1	0	0	88,018
Hickory	0	0	1	0	0	0	0	0	1	0	0	40,109
Huntersville	1	0	0	0	0	0	0	0	0	1	0	50,162
King	0	1	0	0	0	0	0	0	1	0	0	6,860
Leland	1	0	1	0	0	0	0	1	0	0	1	15,535
Lilesville	1	0	0	0	0	0	0	0	0	1	0	519
Mint Hill	1	0	0	0	0	0	0	0	1	0	0	24,350
Morganton	1	0	0	0	0	0	0	0	1	0	0	16,852
New Bern	1	0	0	0	0	0	0	0	1	0	0	30,514
Oxford	1	0	0	0	0	0	0	0	0	0	1	8,607
Raleigh	3	0	0	1	0	0	0	0	2	2	0	428,993
Rocky Mount	1	0	1	0	0	0	0	0	1	1	0	57,021
Roxboro	2	0	0	0	0	0	0	0	0	2	0	8,310
Salisbury	1	0	0	0	0	0	0	0	0	0	1	33,626
Siler City	2	0	0	0	0	0	0	1	0	1	0	8,243
Thomasville	1	0	0	0	0	0	0	0	0	1	0	26,866
Wadesboro	1	0	0	0	0	0	0	0	0	1	0	5,673
Wilmington	3	0	1	0	0	0	0	3	0	0	1	110,985
Wilson	0	0	1	0	0	0	0	0	0	0	1	49,737
Wrightsville Beach	1	0	0	0	0	0	0	0	1	0	0	2,551
Universities and Colleges	5	0	4	0	0	0	0					
East Carolina University	1	0	0	0	0	0	0	0	1	0	0	26,947
North Carolina School of the Arts	2	0	0	0	0	0	0	1	0	0	1	880
University of North Carolina												
Greensboro	1	0	2	0	0	0	0	0	0	1	2	18,516
Wilmington	1	0	0	0	0	0	0	0	0	1	0	13,733
Wake Forest University	0	0	2	0	0	0	0	1	0	1	0	7,432
Metropolitan Counties	8	5	2	3	0	0	0					
Buncombe	2	0	0	1	0	0	0	0	0	2	1	
Cabarrus	0	0	0	1	0	0	0	0	0	1	0	
Catawba	1	0	0	0	0	0	0	0	0	1	0	
Guilford	0	0	1	0	0	0	0	0	1	0	0	
Iredell	0	5	0	0	0	0	0	0	2	3	0	
New Hanover	1	0	1	0	0	0	0	0	1	0	1	
Pitt	4	0	0	1	0	0	0	1	1	2	1	
Nonmetropolitan Counties	3	2	1	0	0	0	0					
Rutherford	1	2	1	0	0	0	0	0	2	1	1	
Surry	1	0	0	0	0	0	0	0	0	0	1	
Swain	1	0	0	0	0	0	0	0	0	0	1	
NORTH DAKOTA												
Total	27	5	4	10	5	0	0					
Cities	20	4	4	8	1	0	0					
Beulah	0	0	0	1	0	0	0	1	0	0	0	3,149
Bismarck	0	0	1	5	0	0	0	3	0	2	1	65,850
Carrington	1	0	0	0	0	0	0	0	0	1	0	2,108
Devils Lake	0	0	1	0	0	0	0	0	0	0	1	7,260
Dickinson	0	1	0	0	0	0	0	0	0	1	0	20,347
Fargo	8	2	2	1	1	0	0	2	3	6	3	111,101
Mandan	2	0	0	0	0	0	0	0	0	1	1	19,168
Minot	1	0	0	0	0	0	0	0	0	1	0	44,635
Valley City	1	0	0	0	0	0	0	1	0	0	0	6,580
West Fargo	6	1	0	1	0	0	0	1	2	2	3	28,018
Williston	1	0	0	0	0	0	0	0	0	0	1	19,949
Metropolitan Counties	4	1	0	0	0	0	0					
Cass	0	1	0	0	0	0	0	0	0	0	1	
Grand Forks	2	0	0	0	0	0	0	0	1	0	1	
Morton	2	0	0	0	0	0	0	0	1	1	0	
Nonmetropolitan Counties	3	0	0	2	4	0	0					
Dunn	1	0	0	0	0	0	0	0	0	1	0	
Golden Valley	0	0	0	1	0	0	0	0	0	1	0	
Grant	1	0	0	0	0	0	0	0	0	0	1	
Mountrail	1	0	0	1	3	0	0	0	0	1	4	

Table 94. Hate Crime Incidents Per Bias Motivation and Quarter, by Selected State and Agency, 2013— continued

(Number.)

State/agency	Number of incidents per bias motivation							Number of incidents per quarter[1]				Population[2]
	Race	Religion	Sexual orientation	Ethnicity	Disability	Gender	Gender Identity	1st quarter	2nd quarter	3rd quarter	4th quarter	
Walsh	0	0	0	0	1	0	0	0	0	1	0	
OHIO												
Total	226	17	61	42	24	0	0					
Cities	197	13	51	34	20	0	0					
Akron	5	0	2	1	0	0	0	3	3	2	0	198,405
Alliance	0	0	0	1	0	0	0	0		1		22,144
Ashland	1	0	0	0	0	0	0	1	0	0	0	20,306
Athens	0	0	1	0	0	0	0	1	0	0	0	23,721
Austintown	2	0	0	0	0	0	0	0	1	1	0	36,192
Barberton	3	0	1	0	0	0	0	0	2	1	1	26,245
Bath Township, Summit County	0	0	1	0	0	0	0	0	0	1	0	9,724
Bellefontaine	1	0	0	1	0	0	0	0	1	1	0	13,147
Blue Ash	0	0	1	0	0	0	0	0	0	1	0	12,105
Boardman	1	0	0	0	0	0	0	0	1	0	0	40,277
Bucyrus	0	0	0	1	0	0	0	0	0	0	1	12,007
Butler Township	0	0	0	0	1	0	0	1	0	0	0	7,864
Celina	1	0	1	0	0	0	0	1	1	0	0	10,392
Cincinnati	9	0	1	5	1	0	0	4	0	2	10	296,491
Circleville	1	0	1	0	0	0	0	0	1	0	1	13,491
Clearcreek Township	0	0	0	1	0	0	0	0	0	1	0	14,642
Cleveland	1	0	5	1	0	0	0	1	0	4	2	389,181
Colerain Township	2	0	0	0	0	0	0	0	0	1	1	58,578
Columbus	88	4	17	15	12	0	0	8	22	60	46	816,364
Dayton	5	0	2	1	0	0	0	2	3	1	2	141,167
East Liverpool	1	1	0	0	0	0	0	2	0			11,010
East Palestine	1	0	0	0	0	0	0	0	0	1	0	4,631
Eaton	0	0	1	0	0	0	0	0	0	0	1	8,307
Englewood	0	0	1	0	0	0	0	0	0	1	0	13,455
Fairborn	2	0	0	0	0	0	0	1	0	1	0	32,820
Fairfield	0	1	0	0	0	0	0	0	1	0	0	42,677
Findlay	1	0	1	0	0	0	0	0	1	0	1	41,660
Gahanna	0	0	2	0	0	0	0	0	0	0	2	34,011
Girard	1	0	0	0	0	0	0	0	0	1	0	9,771
Greenhills	1	0	0	0	1	0	0	2	0	0	0	3,591
Grove City	3	0	0	1	0	0	0	1	2	1	0	37,208
Hamilton	0	0	1	0	0	0	0	0	1	0		62,268
Huber Heights	1	1	4	0	2	0	0	1	3	4	0	38,118
Hudson	1	0	0	1	0	0	0	1	0	1	0	22,340
Jackson Township, Stark County	1	0	0	0	0	0	0	0	1	0	0	40,436
Kettering	1	0	0	0	0	0	0	0	1	0	0	55,907
Lancaster	1	0	0	0	0	0	0	0	0	0	1	38,902
Lorain	7	0	0	0	0	0	0	0	5	1	1	63,582
Mansfield	4	0	0	0	0	0	0	0	3	0	1	46,832
Medina	2	0	0	0	0	0	0	2	0	0	0	26,492
Mentor-on-the-Lake	1	0	0	1	0	0	0	0	0	2	0	7,434
Miami Township, Montgomery County	2	0	0	0	0	0	0	0	2	0	0	29,128
Montgomery	2	0	0	0	0	0	0	0	1	1	0	10,305
Montpelier	1	0	0	0	0	0	0	0	0	0	1	4,050
Moraine	0	0	1	1	0	0	0	1	0	0	1	6,317
Mount Vernon	2	0	0	0	0	0	0	1	0	1	0	16,748
Napoleon	1	0	0	0	0	0	0	1	0	0	0	8,663
Nelsonville	1	0	0	0	0	0	0	0	0	1	0	5,334
Niles	1	0	0	0	0	0	0	0	0	1	0	18,950
North Baltimore	1	0	0	0	0	0	0	0	1	0	0	3,492
North Canton	1	0	0	0	0	0	0	0	1	0	0	17,380
North College Hill	2	0	0	0	0	0	0	1	0	1	0	9,340
Norwalk	0	0	1	0	1	0	0	1	1	0	0	16,906
Norwood	1	0	0	2	0	0	0	0	1	1	1	19,052
Ottawa Hills	1	0	0	0	0	0	0	1	0	0	0	4,481
Parma	1	0	0	0	0	0	0	1	0	0	0	80,303
Portsmouth	0	0	2	0	0	0	0	1	1	0	0	20,322
Reynoldsburg	0	1	0	0	0	0	0	0	1	0	0	36,472
Richwood	1	0	0	0	0	0	0	0	1	0	0	2,240
Riverside	2	0	0	0	0	0	0	0	0	1	1	25,115
Solon	1	0	0	0	0	0	0	0	1	0	0	23,105
South Euclid	2	0	0	0	0	0	0	2	0	0	0	21,929
Springfield	3	0	1	0	0	0	0	0	1	3	0	60,012
Springfield Township, Hamilton County	1	0	0	0	0	0	0	1	0	0	0	36,330
Struthers	1	1	0	0	1	0	0	0	2	0	1	10,522
Trotwood	1	0	1	0	0	0	0	0	2	0	0	24,282
Troy	1	0	0	0	0	0	0	0	1	0	0	25,424
Twinsburg	0	1	0	1	0	0	0	0		1	1	18,750
Union Township, Clermont County	1	0	0	0	0	0	0	1	0	0	0	47,066
Upper Arlington	3	0	0	0	0	0	0	0	0	1	2	34,369
Urbana	1	1	0	0	0	0	0	2	0	0	0	11,599

Table 94.　Hate Crime Incidents Per Bias Motivation and Quarter, by Selected State and Agency, 2013— continued

(Number.)

State/agency	Number of incidents per bias motivation							Number of incidents per quarter[1]				Population[2]
	Race	Religion	Sexual orientation	Ethnicity	Disability	Gender	Gender Identity	1st quarter	2nd quarter	3rd quarter	4th quarter	
Vandalia	2	0	0	0	0	0	0	0	1	1	0	15,181
Wapakoneta	1	0	0	0	0	0	0	0	0	1	0	9,812
Warren	3	0	0	0	1	0	0	0	3	1	0	40,474
Warren Township	1	0	0	0	0	0	0	0	0	0	1	5,450
Wooster	1	1	0	0	0	0	0	1	1	0	0	26,468
Xenia	3	0	0	0	0	0	0	1	0	1	1	26,038
Youngstown	1	0	0	0	0	0	0	0	0	1	0	64,938
Zanesville	1	1	2	0	0	0	0	1	2	0	1	25,378
Universities and Colleges	5	0	2	0	0	0	0					
Bowling Green State University	1	0	0	0	0	0	0	1	0	0	0	17,286
Capital University	2	0	1	0	0	0	0	0	0	0	3	3,584
Kent State University	0	0	1	0	0	0	0	0	0	1	0	28,602
Ohio State University, Columbus	2	0	0	0	0	0	0	0	2	0	0	56,387
Metropolitan Counties	13	1	6	6	2	0	0					
Butler	3	0	3	0	2	0	0	3	2	1	2	
Clermont	1	0	0	0	0	0	0	0	1	0	0	
Delaware	1	0	0	1	0	0	0	0	0	2	0	
Franklin	0	0	0	2	0	0	0	1	0	1	0	
Fulton	0	0	0	1	0	0	0	0	1	0	0	
Geauga	1	0	0	0	0	0	0	0	1	0	0	
Greene	2	0	1	0	0	0	0	1	2	0	0	
Lorain	1	0	0	0	0	0	0	1	0	0	0	
Lucas	0	1	1	0	0	0	0	1	0	0	1	
Medina	1	0	0	0	0	0	0	0	0	0	1	
Montgomery	0	0	0	1	0	0	0	1	0	0	0	
Pickaway	1	0	0	0	0	0	0	0	0	1	0	
Richland	1	0	0	0	0	0	0	1	0	0	0	
Stark	1	0	0	1	0	0	0	0	0	1	1	
Trumbull	0	0	1	0	0	0	0	0	1	0	0	
Nonmetropolitan Counties	10	3	2	2	2	0	0					
Ashland	0	0	0	1	0	0	0	0	0	1	0	
Athens	0	0	1	0	0	0	0	0	0	1	0	
Auglaize	1	0	0	0	0	0	0	1	0	0	0	
Hancock	0	0	0	1	0	0	0	0	1	0	0	
Jackson	2	0	0	0	0	0	0	0	0	2	0	
Knox	2	1	0	0	0	0	0	0	2	0	1	
Marion	0	0	1	0	1	0	0	1	0	0	1	
Meigs	0	1	0	0	0	0	0	0	1	0	0	
Ross	2	1	0	0	0	0	0	0	2	0	1	
Shelby	2	0	0	0	0	0	0	0	0	0	2	
Washington	0	0	0	0	1	0	0	1	0	0	0	
Wayne	1	0	0	0	0	0	0	0	0	1	0	
Other Agencies	1	0	0	0	0	0	0					
Cleveland Metropolitan Park District	1	0	0	0	0	0	0	0	0	1	0	
OKLAHOMA												
Total	22	8	7	3	1	0	0					
Cities	20	5	5	3	1	0	0					
Altus	1	0	0	0	0	0	0	0	1	0	0	19,634
Bixby	1	0	0	0	0	0	0	0	1	0	0	23,122
Blanchard	1	0	0	0	0	0	0	1	0	0	0	8,016
Broken Arrow	0	0	0	1	0	0	0	0	0	1	0	102,956
Choctaw	1	0	0	0	0	0	0	1	0	0	0	11,768
Cleveland	0	0	0	1	0	0	0	0	1	0	0	3,224
Elk City	1	0	0	0	0	0	0	1	0	0	0	12,463
Fairfax	1	0	0	0	0	0	0	1	0	0	0	1,373
Heavener	0	1	0	0	0	0	0	0	0	1	0	3,377
Muskogee	1	1	1	0	0	0	0	1	1	1	0	38,884
Norman	3	1	0	0	0	0	0	2	0	1	1	116,970
Oklahoma City	7	2	2	1	0	0	0	3	4	3	2	605,034
Owasso	1	0	0	0	0	0	0	1	0	0	0	31,973
Sapulpa	0	0	1	0	0	0	0	0	1	0	0	20,857
Sayre	1	0	0	0	0	0	0	0	0	0	1	4,556
Skiatook	0	0	0	0	1	0	0	0	0	0	1	7,751
Talihina	0	0	1	0	0	0	0	0	0	1	0	1,112
Tonkawa	1	0	0	0	0	0	0	0	1	0	0	3,150
Universities and Colleges	0	0	2	0	0	0	0					
Southwestern Oklahoma State University	0	0	1	0	0	0	0	0	0	0	1	5,106
University of Central Oklahoma	0	0	1	0	0	0	0	0	0	0	1	17,211
Metropolitan Counties	0	3	0	0	0	0	0					

Table 94.   Hate Crime Incidents Per Bias Motivation and Quarter, by Selected State and Agency, 2013— continued

(Number.)

State/agency	Number of incidents per bias motivation							Number of incidents per quarter[1]				Population[2]
	Race	Religion	Sexual orientation	Ethnicity	Disability	Gender	Gender Identity	1st quarter	2nd quarter	3rd quarter	4th quarter	
Grady	0	1	0	0	0	0	0	0	0	0	1	
Tulsa	0	1	0	0	0	0	0	1	0	0	0	
Wagoner	0	1	0	0	0	0	0	0	1	0	0	
Nonmetropolitan Counties	1	0	0	0	0	0	0					
Roger Mills	1	0	0	0	0	0	0	0	1	0	0	
Tribal Agencies	1	0	0	0	0	0	0					
Tonkawa Tribal	1	0	0	0	0	0	0	0	0	1	0	
OREGON												
Total	32	10	14	9	1	0	0					
Cities	28	8	13	9	1	0	0					
Ashland	1	0	0	0	0	0	0	1	0	0	0	20,455
Beaverton	0	0	1	0	0	0	0			1		93,551
Bend	0	2	0	1	0	0	0	2	0	1	0	79,926
Eugene	6	4	3	2	0	0	0	1	9	1	4	158,499
Newberg-Dundee	0	0	0	1	0	0	0	0	0	1	0	25,647
Newport	0	0	1	0	0	0	0	0	1	0	0	10,029
Portland	1	1	3	1	0	0	0	1	3	2		609,136
Salem	7	1	4	2	0	0	0	9	3	2	0	158,234
Springfield	2	0	0	1	0	0	0	0	1	1	1	60,024
Sutherlin	1	0	0	0	0	0	0	0	1		0	7,747
Tigard	8	0	0	1	0	0	0	2	3	4		50,311
Toledo	2	0	1	0	1	0	0	1	2	1	0	3,461
Metropolitan Counties	2	2	1	0	0	0	0					
Deschutes	1	0	0	0	0	0	0	0	1	0	0	
Jackson	0	1	0	0	0	0	0	0	0	1	0	
Lane	1	0	0	0	0	0	0		1			
Yamhill	0	1	1	0	0	0	0	0	0	1	1	
Nonmetropolitan Counties	2	0	0	0	0	0	0					
Douglas	1	0	0	0	0	0	0	1	0	0	0	
Umatilla	1	0	0	0	0	0	0	0	0	1	0	
PENNSYLVANIA												
Total	44	11	8	1	0	0	0					
Cities	32	5	6	1	0	0	0					
Ferguson Township	0	1	0	0	0	0	0	1	0	0	0	17,807
Johnstown	3	0	0	0	0	0	0	0	1	2		21,954
Lancaster	1	0	0	0	0	0	0	0	1	0	0	59,370
Lewistown	0	1	0	0	0	0	0	0	1	0	0	8,370
Northern York Regional	1	0	0	0	0	0	0	1	0	0	0	67,657
Philadelphia	14	1	0	1	0	0	0	3	11	1	1	1,553,153
Pittsburgh	12	0	3	0	0	0	0	1	3	8	3	307,632
Reading	0	0	3	0	0	0	0	1	1	1	0	88,107
Richland Township, Cambria County	1	0	0	0	0	0	0	0	1	0	0	12,581
State College	0	2	0	0	0	0	0	0	0	0	2	56,612
Universities and Colleges	6	3	1	0	0	0	0					
Lehigh University	1	0	0	0	0	0	0	0	0	0	1	7,080
Pennsylvania State University												
Altoona	1	0	0	0	0	0	0	0	0	1	0	3,863
University Park	4	3	1	0	0	0	0	3	1	2	2	45,783
Metropolitan Counties	1	0	0	0	0	0	0					
Lancaster	1	0	0	0	0	0	0	0	0	1	0	
	5	3	1	0	0	0	0					
State Police Agencies												
Chester County	0	1	0	0	0	0	0	1		0	0	
Franklin County	1	0	0	0	0	0	0	1		0	0	
Indiana County	1	0	0	0	0	0	0	0	1		0	
Lancaster County	1	1	0	0	0	0	0	2	0	0	0	
Skippack County	2	0	1	0	0	0	0	0	3	0	0	
Pike County	0	1	0	0	0	0	0	0	0	1	0	
RHODE ISLAND												
Total	4	2	0	1	0	0	0					
Cities	3	2	0	1	0	0	0					
Central Falls	1	0	0	0	0	0	0	0	1	0	0	19,404
Johnston	1	0	0	0	0	0	0	1	0	0	0	29,068
Newport	1	0	0	0	0	0	0	0	0	1	0	23,874
Providence	0	0	0	1	0	0	0	1	0	0	0	178,887
Warwick	0	1	0	0	0	0	0	0	0	1	0	81,789

Table 94.   Hate Crime Incidents Per Bias Motivation and Quarter, by Selected State and Agency, 2013— continued

(Number.)

State/agency	Number of incidents per bias motivation							Number of incidents per quarter[1]				Population[2]
	Race	Religion	Sexual orientation	Ethnicity	Disability	Gender	Gender Identity	1st quarter	2nd quarter	3rd quarter	4th quarter	
West Warwick	0	1	0	0	0	0	0	0	0	0	1	28,817
Universities and Colleges	1	0	0	0	0	0	0					
University of Rhode Island	1	0	0	0	0	0	0	0	0	1	0	16,451
SOUTH CAROLINA												
Total	33	9	6	3	0	0	0					
Cities	18	7	5	2	0	0	0					
Anderson	1	0	0	0	0	0	0	0	0	0	1	26,812
Belton	0	0	1	0	0	0	0	1	0	0	0	4,222
Chapin	1	0	0	0	0	0	0	0	0	0	1	1,506
Charleston	2	0	0	0	0	0	0	2	0	0	0	127,206
Clover	0	0	1	0	0	0	0	0	0	1	0	5,342
Columbia	1	0	1	0	0	0	0	0	1	1	0	132,240
Dillon	0	1	0	0	0	0	0	0	1	0	0	6,627
Forest Acres	1	0	0	0	0	0	0	0	1	0	0	10,516
Georgetown	1	0	0	0	0	0	0	0	0	1	0	9,072
Goose Creek	1	0	0	0	0	0	0	0	0	1	0	39,425
Greenville	1	0	0	0	0	0	0	0	0	0	1	61,185
Hardeeville	0	0	0	1	0	0	0	0	1	0	0	4,064
Hartsville	1	0	0	0	0	0	0	0	0	1	0	7,877
Holly Hill	1	0	0	0	0	0	0	1	0	0	0	1,259
Honea Path	1	0	0	0	0	0	0	0	0	0	1	3,613
Latta	1	0	0	0	0	0	0	1	0	0	0	1,349
Lexington	1	0	0	0	0	0	0	0	1	0	0	19,547
Manning	0	0	1	0	0	0	0	0	0	0	1	4,034
Mauldin	0	0	0	1	0	0	0	0	0	1	0	24,099
Orangeburg	0	0	1	0	0	0	0	0	1	0	0	13,826
Salley	1	0	0	0	0	0	0	0	0	1	0	412
St. George	1	0	0	0	0	0	0	1	0	0	0	2,139
Summerville	2	0	0	0	0	0	0	1	1	0	0	45,210
Winnsboro	0	6	0	0	0	0	0	2	3	0	1	3,428
Universities and Colleges	2	0	0	0	0	0	0					
The Citadel	1	0	0	0	0	0	0	0	0	1	0	3,499
University of South Carolina, Upstate	1	0	0	0	0	0	0	1	0	0	0	5,561
Metropolitan Counties	8	2	1	1	0	0	0					
Berkeley	2	0	0	0	0	0	0	2	0	0	0	
Fairfield	1	0	0	0	0	0	0	0	1	0	0	
Horry County Police Department	1	0	0	1	0	0	0	1	0	0	1	
Lancaster	0	1	0	0	0	0	0	1	0	0	0	
Lexington	2	0	0	0	0	0	0	1	1	0	0	
Sumter	1	0	1	0	0	0	0	0	0	2	0	
Union	0	1	0	0	0	0	0	0	0	1	0	
York	1	0	0	0	0	0	0	0	1	0	0	
Nonmetropolitan Counties	5	0	0	0	0	0	0					
Chesterfield	1	0	0	0	0	0	0	1	0	0	0	
Colleton	1	0	0	0	0	0	0	0	0	1	0	
Georgetown	1	0	0	0	0	0	0	0	0	0	1	
Hampton	1	0	0	0	0	0	0	0	0	0	1	
Marlboro	1	0	0	0	0	0	0	1	0	0	0	
SOUTH DAKOTA												
Total	10	2	1	0	0	0	0					
Cities	6	1	1	0	0	0	0					
Aberdeen	1	0	0	0	0	0	0	0	0	0	1	26,999
Mitchell	1	0	0	0	0	0	0	0	0	1	0	15,555
Rapid City	0	0	1	0	0	0	0	1	0	0	0	70,406
Sioux Falls	3	1	0	0	0	0	0	1	0	2	1	161,754
Vermillion	1	0	0	0	0	0	0	1	0	0	0	10,892
Nonmetropolitan Counties	4	1	0	0	0	0	0					
Codington	3	0	0	0	0	0	0	1	0	2	0	
Corson	1	0	0	0	0	0	0	0	1	0	0	
Hutchinson	0	1	0	0	0	0	0	1	0	0	0	
TENNESSEE												
Total	59	8	38	81	9	0	1					
Cities	43	4	31	38	8	0	1					
Ashland City	1	0	0	0	0	0	0	0	1	0	0	4,637
Athens	1	0	0	0	0	0	0	0	0	1	0	13,504
Atoka	0	0	0	0	1	0	0	0	0	1	0	8,821

Table 94. Hate Crime Incidents Per Bias Motivation and Quarter, by Selected State and Agency, 2013— continued

(Number.)

State/agency	Number of incidents per bias motivation							Number of incidents per quarter[1]				Population[2]
	Race	Religion	Sexual orien-tation	Ethnicity	Disability	Gender	Gender Identity	1st quarter	2nd quarter	3rd quarter	4th quarter	
Bristol	1	0	2	1	0	0	0	0	0	0	5	26,660
Burns	1	0	0	0	0	0	0	0	0	1	0	1,469
Chattanooga	2	1	0	0	0	0	0	0	0	2	1	172,286
Clarksville	0	0	5	6	0	0	0	1	2	0	8	145,599
Collegedale	1	0	0	0	0	0	0	0	0	1	0	9,468
Covington	1	0	0	12	4	0	0	3	1	5	8	9,076
Dyersburg	1	0	0	0	0	0	0	0	0	1	0	17,013
Elizabethton	0	0	1	0	0	0	0	0	0	1	0	14,220
Fayetteville	1	0	0	0	0	0	0	0	0	1	0	7,155
Franklin	1	0	0	0	0	0	0	0	0	1	0	67,465
Gatlinburg	0	0	0	1	0	0	0	1	0	0	0	4,074
Graysville	2	0	0	0	0	0	0	0	1	1	0	1,512
Greeneville	0	0	1	0	0	0	0	0	1	0	0	15,015
Humboldt	1	0	0	0	0	0	0	0	0	1	0	8,458
Jackson	0	2	2	0	0	0	0	2	0	1	1	67,371
Johnson City	2	0	0	0	0	0	0	1	1	0	0	64,928
Jonesborough	0	0	0	4	1	0	0	0	0	2	3	5,163
Kingsport	2	0	0	0	0	0	0	0	0	1	1	51,496
Knoxville	0	0	0	2	0	0	0	0	1	1	0	183,249
Manchester	0	0	0	2	0	0	0	1	1	0	0	10,258
Mason	1	0	0	0	0	0	0	0	1	0	0	1,611
McMinnville	0	0	0	1	0	0	0	0	0	0	1	13,595
Memphis	9	0	12	1	1	0	1	6	5	9	4	657,691
Milan	1	0	0	0	0	0	0	0	0	0	1	7,789
Millersville	2	0	1	0	0	0	0	0	0	3	0	6,596
Millington	2	0	0	4	0	0	0	0	2	0	4	10,500
Monterey	0	0	0	1	0	0	0	0	1	0	0	2,829
Mount Carmel	0	0	0	0	1	0	0	0	1	0	0	5,422
Munford	0	0	0	1	0	0	0	0	0	0	1	6,036
Murfreesboro	0	0	1	0	0	0	0	0	0	0	1	115,587
Nashville	4	0	1	1	0	0	0	3	1	1	1	635,673
Oliver Springs	1	1	0	0	0	0	0	0	0	2	0	3,250
Paris	0	0	1	0	0	0	0	0	0	0	1	10,168
Pigeon Forge	0	0	0	1	0	0	0	0	1	0	0	6,023
Rossville	0	0	2	0	0	0	0	0	2	0	0	679
Shelbyville	0	0	1	0	0	0	0	0	0	1	0	20,669
Spring Hill	4	0	0	0	0	0	0	2	2	0	0	31,807
Tullahoma	1	0	0	0	0	0	0	0	0	0	1	18,773
Wartburg	0	0	1	0	0	0	0	0	1	0	0	912
Universities and Colleges	4	1	2	0	0	0	0					
Christian Brothers University	1	0	0	0	0	0	0	0	0	0	1	1,603
Southwest Tennessee Community College	0	0	1	0	0	0	0	0	1	0	0	12,220
Vanderbilt University	3	1	1	0	0	0	0	1	1	0	3	12,710
Metropolitan Counties	12	3	4	39	1	0	0					
Hickman	1	0	1	1	0	0	0	0	0	2	1	
Jefferson	1	0	0	0	0	0	0	0	0	1	0	
Marion	1	0	0	0	0	0	0	0	0	0	1	
Robertson	0	1	0	0	0	0	0	0	0	0	1	
Shelby	5	1	3	36	1	0	0	2	7	20	17	
Sullivan	2	1	0	2	0	0	0	1	2	2	0	
Tipton	2	0	0	0	0	0	0	1	0	1	0	
Nonmetropolitan Counties	0	0	1	3	0	0	0					
Bledsoe	0	0	0	1	0	0	0	0	0	1	0	
Henry	0	0	0	2	0	0	0	0	0	1	1	
Lake	0	0	1	0	0	0	0	0	0	1	0	
State Police Agencies	0	0	0	1	0	0	0					
Department of Safety	0	0	0	1	0	0	0	1	0	0	0	
TEXAS												
Total	54	7	44	25	2	0	0					
Cities	46	5	41	21	2	0	0					
Austin	0	0	1	3	0	0	0	2	1	1	0	859,180
Beaumont	3	0	0	0	0	0	0	2	1	0	0	118,177
Bellaire	0	0	1	0	0	0	0	0	0	1	0	17,617
Bellmead	2	0	0	0	0	0	0	0	1	0	1	9,950
Benbrook	1	0	0	0	0	0	0	0	0	0	1	22,157
Brownwood	1	0	0	0	0	0	0	0	1	0	0	18,873
Carthage	0	0	1	0	0	0	0	0	0	1	0	6,918
Commerce	1	0	0	0	1	0	0	1	1	0	0	8,267
Corpus Christi	0	0	1	0	0	0	0	0	0	0	1	314,523
Dallas	3	2	9	4	0	0	0	2	4	9	3	1,255,015
Denison	1	0	0	0	1	0	0	0	1	1	0	22,652

Table 94.   Hate Crime Incidents Per Bias Motivation and Quarter, by Selected State and Agency, 2013— continued

(Number.)

State/agency	Number of incidents per bias motivation							Number of incidents per quarter[1]				Population[2]
	Race	Religion	Sexual orientation	Ethnicity	Disability	Gender	Gender Identity	1st quarter	2nd quarter	3rd quarter	4th quarter	
Denton	1	0	0	0	0	0	0	0	1	0	0	123,260
El Paso	0	0	3	0	0	0	0	2	1	0	0	679,700
Everman	0	0	1	0	0	0	0	1		0	0	6,276
Fort Worth	9	0	2	5	0	0	0	5	1	6	4	789,035
Frisco	1	1	0	0	0	0	0	0	2	0	0	131,769
Gainesville	1	0	0	0	0	0	0	0	0	1	0	16,089
Garland	1	0	1	0	0	0	0	1	0	1	0	235,683
Grapevine	1	0	0	0	0	0	0	0	0	1	0	49,075
Harlingen	1	0	0	0	0	0	0	0	0	1	0	65,885
Houston	4	0	5	4	0	0	0	4	5	1	3	2,180,606
Lancaster	0	0	1	0	0	0	0	0	0	0	1	38,209
Longview	1	0	0	0	0	0	0	0	0	1	0	81,273
Marble Falls	1	0	0	0	0	0	0	0	0	1	0	6,095
McAllen	0	0	1	0	0	0	0	0	1	0	0	136,169
McKinney	1	0	1	2	0	0	0	0	1	1	2	146,869
Mercedes	1	0	0	0	0	0	0	0	0	1	0	16,480
Mineral Wells	0	0	1	0	0	0	0	0	0	0	1	16,717
Pasadena	1	0	0	0	0	0	0	1	0	0	0	153,195
Plano	1	0	0	1	0	0	0	1	0	0	1	275,795
Richmond	0	0	1	0	0	0	0	1	0	0	0	11,841
San Angelo	1	0	0	0	0	0	0	1	0	0	0	96,661
San Antonio	3	0	7	1	0	0	0	3	3	3	2	1,399,725
Springtown	0	0	1	0	0	0	0	0	0	1	0	2,698
Temple	1	0	0	0	0	0	0	0	0	1	0	69,937
Terrell	1	0	0	0	0	0	0	1	0	0	0	16,233
Tyler	1	0	3	1	0	0	0	2	1	0	2	100,033
Victoria	0	2	0	0	0	0	0	0	0	1	1	64,979
Vidor	1	0	0	0	0	0	0	0	0	1	0	10,984
Whitehouse	1	0	0	0	0	0	0	1		0	0	7,919
Universities and Colleges	4	1	0	0	0	0	0					
Amarillo College	1	0	0	0	0	0	0	1	0	0	0	11,530
Southern Methodist University	2	1	0	0	0	0	0	1	1	1	0	10,893
University of Texas, Austin	1	0	0	0	0	0	0	1	0	0	0	52,186
Metropolitan Counties	4	1	2	4	0	0	0					
Collin	0	0	0	1	0	0	0	1	0	0	0	
Goliad	1	0	0	0	0	0	0	0	0	1	0	
Harris	1	1	0	1	0	0	0	1	1	0	1	
Hunt	0	0	0	1	0	0	0	0	0	0	1	
Nueces	1	0	0	0	0	0	0	0	1	0	0	
Travis	1	0	2	1	0	0	0	2	1	0	1	
Other Agencies	0	0	1	0	0	0	0					
Independent School District, Humble	0	0	1	0	0	0	0	1	0		0	
UTAH												
Total	46	10	8	8	2	0	0					
Cities	27	8	4	5	1	0	0					
Bountiful	4	0	0	1	0	0	0	0	1	2	2	42,976
Brigham City	2	0	0	0	0	0	0	1	0	1	0	18,217
Centerville	1	1	0	0	0	0	0	0	2	0	0	16,488
Draper	0	1	0	0	0	0	0	0	0	1	0	44,680
Farmington	2	0	1	0	0	0	0	0	3	0	0	21,582
Grantsville	1	0	0	0	0	0	0	0	0	1	0	9,530
Heber	0	1	0	0	0	0	0	0	1	0	0	12,544
Moab	0	0	0	1	0	0	0	0	1	0	0	5,096
Murray	1	0	0	0	0	0	0	0	0	1	0	48,767
North Salt Lake	0	0	0	0	1	0	0	1	0	0	0	16,815
Pleasant Grove	2	0	0	0	0	0	0	0	0	1	1	34,796
Price	1	0	0	1	0	0	0	2	0	0	0	8,589
Provo	1	0	0	0	0	0	0	0	0	0	1	116,937
Roosevelt	1	0	1	1	0	0	0	0	0	3	0	6,404
Roy	1	1	0	0	0	0	0	0	1	1	0	37,810
Salt Lake City	3	1	1	0	0	0	0	0	3	0	2	190,246
South Jordan	0	1	0	0	0	0	0	0	1	0	0	57,593
South Salt Lake	0	0	1	0	0	0	0	0	0	1	0	24,595
St. George	2	1	0	0	0	0	0	2	1	0	0	76,427
Tooele	0	1	0	0	0	0	0	1	0	0	0	32,241
West Valley	3	0	0	1	0	0	0	1	3	0	0	133,373
Woods Cross	2	0	0	0	0	0	0	0	1	0	1	10,343
Universities and Colleges	3	0	1	0	0	0	0					
University of Utah	3	0	0	0	0	0	0	1	0	0	2	32,388
Utah State University, Logan	0	0	1	0	0	0	0	0	0	0	1	28,786

Table 94.   Hate Crime Incidents Per Bias Motivation and Quarter, by Selected State and Agency, 2013— continued

(Number.)

State/agency	Number of incidents per bias motivation							Number of incidents per quarter[1]				Population[2]
	Race	Religion	Sexual orien-tation	Ethnicity	Disability	Gender	Gender Identity	1st quarter	2nd quarter	3rd quarter	4th quarter	
Metropolitan Counties	6	1	2	0	1	0	0					
Salt Lake County Unified Police Department	0	1	1	0	0	0	0	1	1	0	0	
Tooele	4	0	0	0	1	0	0	1	3	0	1	
Utah	1	0	0	0	0	0	0	1	0	0	0	
Washington	1	0	1	0	0	0	0	0	1	0	1	
Nonmetropolitan Counties	6	1	0	0	0	0	0					
Carbon	3	0	0	0	0	0	0	1	0	2	0	
Emery	0	1	0	0	0	0	0	0	1	0	0	
Summit	1	0	0	0	0	0	0	0	0	1	0	
Uintah	2	0	0	0	0	0	0	0	1	1	0	
State Police Agencies	2	0	1	3	0	0	0					
Utah Highway Patrol	2	0	1	3	0	0	0	2	1	2	1	
Other Agencies	3	0	0	0	0	0	0					
Parks and Recreation	1	0	0	0	0	0	0	0	1	0	0	
Utah Transit Authority	2	0	0	0	0	0	0	0	0	2	0	
VERMONT												
Total	8	1	3	0	0	0	0					
Cities	7	1	2	0	0	0	0					
Bennington	1	0	0	0	0	0	0	0	0	0	1	15,492
Burlington	2	0	1	0	0	0	0	0	1	1	1	42,235
Castleton	0	0	1	0	0	0	0	0	0	0	1	4,649
Colchester	1	0	0	0	0	0	0	0	1	0	0	17,288
Morristown	1	0	0	0	0	0	0	0	0	1	0	5,369
South Burlington	0	1	0	0	0	0	0	0	0	0	1	18,549
Springfield	1	0	0	0	0	0	0	0	0	0	1	9,259
St. Albans	1	0	0	0	0	0	0	0	1	0	0	6,888
Universities and Colleges	1	0	0	0	0	0	0					
University of Vermont	1	0	0	0	0	0	0	0	0	0	1	13,098
State Police Agencies	0	0	1	0	0	0	0					
State Police, St. Albans	0	0	1	0	0	0	0	0	1	0	0	
VIRGINIA												
Total	70	30	12	7	0	0	0					
Cities	30	10	9	2	0	0	0					
Bedford	1	0	1	0	0	0	0	0	0	0	2	5,894
Bristol	0	0	1	0	0	0	0	1	0	0	0	17,641
Charlottesville	1	0	0	0	0	0	0	0	1	0	0	44,187
Chesapeake	4	2	0	0	0	0	0	2	0	2	2	230,577
Christiansburg	1	0	0	0	0	0	0	0	0	0	1	21,581
Danville	0	0	1	0	0	0	0	1	0	0	0	43,133
Farmville	1	0	0	0	0	0	0	0	1	0	0	8,142
Galax	0	0	0	1	0	0	0	0	0	0	1	6,870
Hampton	1	0	1	0	0	0	0	1	0	1	0	136,949
Harrisonburg	3	0	1	0	0	0	0	1	2	0	1	51,767
Hopewell	0	1	0	0	0	0	0	0	0	1	0	22,305
Manassas	1	0	0	0	0	0	0	0	0	1	0	41,512
Manassas Park	0	1	0	0	0	0	0	1	0	0	0	16,332
Newport News	1	1	2	0	0	0	0	0	1	3	0	181,074
Norfolk	3	3	1	0	0	0	0	0	5	1	1	247,303
Poquoson	1	0	0	0	0	0	0	1	0	0	0	12,108
Portsmouth	3	0	0	0	0	0	0	0	0	2	1	97,018
Radford	0	0	1	0	0	0	0	0	1	0	0	16,810
Richmond	0	0	0	1	0	0	0	0	1	0	0	212,830
Roanoke	1	0	0	0	0	0	0	0	1	0	0	97,927
Suffolk	3	0	0	0	0	0	0	0	1	2	0	85,475
Virginia Beach	3	2	0	0	0	0	0	1	1	1	2	450,687
West Point	1	0	0	0	0	0	0	0	1	0	0	3,311
Woodstock	1	0	0	0	0	0	0	0	1	0	0	5,193
Universities and Colleges	3	3	0	2	0	0	0					
Christopher Newport University	1	0	0	0	0	0	0	0	0	1	0	5,186
George Mason University	0	3	0	0	0	0	0	1	0	2	0	32,961
James Madison University	0	0	0	1	0	0	0	1	0	0	0	19,927
University of Richmond	1	0	0	0	0	0	0	0	0	0	1	4,361
Virginia Commonwealth University	0	0	0	1	0	0	0	0	1	0	0	31,445
Virginia Military Institute	1	0	0	0	0	0	0	1	0	0	0	1,664
Metropolitan Counties	31	16	2	3	0	0	0					
Albemarle County Police Department	7	2	0	1	0	0	0	1	5	2	2	

Table 94.   Hate Crime Incidents Per Bias Motivation and Quarter, by Selected State and Agency, 2013— continued

(Number.)

State/agency	Number of incidents per bias motivation							Number of incidents per quarter[1]				Population[2]
	Race	Religion	Sexual orientation	Ethnicity	Disability	Gender	Gender Identity	1st quarter	2nd quarter	3rd quarter	4th quarter	
Amherst	1	0	0	0	0	0	0	0	0	1	0	
Appomattox	0	1	0	0	0	0	0	0	0	0	1	
Arlington County Police Department	1	0	1	0	0	0	0	1	0	1	0	
Chesterfield County Police Department	1	1	0	0	0	0	0	2	0	0	0	
Clarke	1	0	0	0	0	0	0	1	0	0	0	
Fairfax County Police Department	7	5	0	1	0	0	0	3	1	5	4	
Fluvanna	1	0	0	1	0	0	0	0	0	1	1	
Gloucester	1	1	0	0	0	0	0	0	0	0	2	
Henrico County Police Department	2	3	0	0	0	0	0	0	4	0	1	
James City County Police Department	0	1	0	0	0	0	0	0	1	0	0	
Loudoun	2	1	0	0	0	0	0	2	0	1	0	
Powhatan	1	0	0	0	0	0	0	1	0	0	0	
Prince George County Police Department	1	0	0	0	0	0	0	0	1	0	0	
Rockingham	1	0	0	0	0	0	0	0	0	1	0	
Spotsylvania	2	1	1	0	0	0	0	3	0	1	0	
York	2	0	0	0	0	0	0	1	0	1	0	
Nonmetropolitan Counties	6	1	0	0	0	0	0					
Carroll	1	0	0	0	0	0	0	0	0	1	0	
Cumberland	1	0	0	0	0	0	0	0	0	0	1	
King George	0	1	0	0	0	0	0	0	0	1	0	
Louisa	1	0	0	0	0	0	0	1	0	0	0	
Orange	2	0	0	0	0	0	0	1	0	0	1	
Westmoreland	1	0	0	0	0	0	0	0	0	0	1	
State Police Agencies	0	0	1	0	0	0	0					
State Police, Buchanan County	0	0	1	0	0	0	0	1	0	0	0	
WASHINGTON												
Total	158	40	49	32	7	4	1					
Cities	131	32	36	23	5	4	1					
Aberdeen	3	0	0	1	0	0	0	1	1	0	2	16,408
Auburn	5	1	0	3	0	0	1	1	1	4	4	74,565
Bellevue	0	1	0	0	0	0	0	1	0	0	0	127,678
Bellingham	4	0	4	2	0	0	0	2	5	3	0	82,645
Burien	0	1	0	0	0	0	0	1	0	0	0	49,822
Cheney	3	0	0	0	0	0	0	1	1	0	1	11,117
Clarkston	1	0	0	0	0	0	0	0	1	0	0	7,295
Covington	0	1	0	0	0	0	0	0	1	0	0	18,526
Des Moines	4	1	0	0	0	0	0	0	1	2	2	30,684
Everett	1	1	2	2	0	0	0	2	1	1	2	105,129
Federal Way	3	4	4	0	0	0	0	1	3	3	4	92,741
Ferndale	1	1	0	0	0	0	0	1	1	0	0	12,173
Fife	0	0	0	1	0	1	0	0	1	1	0	9,380
Granite Falls	1	0	0	0	0	0	0	1	0	0		3,435
Hoquiam	1	0	0	0	0	0	0	1	0	0	0	8,472
Kalama	1	0	0	0	0	0	0	0	0	1	0	2,316
Kelso	4	0	0	0	0	0	0	1	1	1	1	11,802
Kenmore	0	0	0	1	0	0	0	1	0	0	0	21,531
Kent[3]	8	0	1	0	0	0	0	0	5	2	2	124,359
Lacey	0	1	0	0	0	0	0	0	0	0	1	44,298
Lakewood	3	0	0	0	0	0	0	1	0	0	2	59,057
Maple Valley	0	0	1	0	0	0	0	0	0	1	0	24,644
Mercer Island	0	1	0	0	0	0	0	0	1	0	0	23,969
Mill Creek	0	0	0	0	0	1	0	0	0	1	0	18,806
Milton	0	0	1	0	0	0	0	0	1	0	0	7,076
Mount Vernon	0	1	0	0	0	0	0	0	0	0	1	32,450
Napavine	1	0	0	0	0	0	0	0	0	0	1	1,766
Normandy Park	2	0	0	0	0	0	0	1	0	1	0	6,556
Oak Harbor	1	0	0	0	0	0	0	0	0	1	0	22,288
Olympia	0	0	0	1	0	0	0	0		1	0	48,046
Omak	0	0	1	1	1	0	0	2	1	0	0	4,801
Orting	1	0	0	0	0	0	0	0	0	0	1	6,913
Pacific	1	0	0	0	0	0	0	1	0	0	0	6,911
Pasco	0	0	0	0	1	0	0	0	0	1	0	67,099
Port Townsend	1	1	1	0	0	0	0	1	0	1	1	9,112
Pullman	2	0	0	0	0	0	0	2	0	0	0	31,895
Redmond	1	0	0	0	0	0	0	0	1	0	0	57,263
Renton	10	2	0	1	0	0	0	2	4	2	5	96,657
Seattle	50	14	14	6	3	2	0	19	23	29	18	642,814
Sedro Woolley	1	0	0	0	0	0	0	0	0	1	0	10,652
Shelton	0	0	0	1	0	0	0	0	1	0	0	9,780
Shoreline	2	0	0	0	0	0	0	0	0	0	2	54,762
Spokane	1	0	1	0	0	0	0	1	0	0	1	209,524
Spokane Valley	1	0	0	1	0	0	0	0	1	1	0	90,835
Sunnyside	1	0	0	1	0	0	0	1	0	0	1	16,099

Table 94.   Hate Crime Incidents Per Bias Motivation and Quarter, by Selected State and Agency, 2013— continued

(Number.)

State/agency	Number of incidents per bias motivation							Number of incidents per quarter[1]				Population[2]
	Race	Religion	Sexual orien-tation	Ethnicity	Disability	Gender	Gender Identity	1st quarter	2nd quarter	3rd quarter	4th quarter	
Tacoma	3	0	2	0	0	0	0	2	0	3	0	203,226
Tukwila	1	0	0	0	0	0	0	1	0	0	0	19,765
Tumwater	1	0	0	0	0	0	0	0	0	0	1	18,343
Vancouver	5	0	3	0	0	0	0	2	5	0	1	166,535
Washougal	0	1	0	0	0	0	0	0	0	1	0	14,733
Wenatchee	1	0	0	1	0	0	0	0	0	1	1	32,677
Yakima	1	0	1	0	0	0	0	1	0	0	1	93,589
Universities and Colleges	4	2	2	0	0	0	0					
Eastern Washington University	1	0	0	0	0	0	0	1	0	0	0	12,587
University of Washington	3	2	0	0	0	0	0	0	2	0	3	43,485
Washington State University, Pullman	0	0	1	0	0	0	0	0	0	0	1	27,679
Western Washington University	0	0	1	0	0	0	0	0	1	0	0	14,833
Metropolitan Counties	16	4	9	8	2	0	0					
Benton	0	0	0	0	1	0	0	1	0	0	0	
Chelan	0	2	0	0	0	0	0	0	1	1	0	
Clark	3	0	1	0	0	0	0	1	1	1	1	
Columbia	0	0	0	2	0	0	0	0	2			
Cowlitz	1	0	0	0	0	0	0	0	0	1	0	
King	1	1	1	0	0	0	0	0	1	1	1	
Kitsap	1	0	0	0	0	0	0	0	0	0	1	
Pend Oreille	2	0	1	0	0	0	0	1	0	2	0	
Pierce	2	1	1	2	0	0	0	0	1	4	1	
Skagit	0	0	1	0	0	0	0	0	0	1	0	
Skamania	1	0	0	0	0	0	0	0	0	1	0	
Snohomish	1	0	1	0	0	0	0	0	2	0		
Spokane	1	0	1	3	1	0	0	0	2	1	3	
Stevens	0	0	1	0	0	0	0	0	1	0	0	
Thurston	3	0	1	0	0	0	0	0	1	1	2	
Yakima	0	0	0	1	0	0	0	0	0	0	1	
Nonmetropolitan Counties	6	1	2	1	0	0	0					
Clallam	2	0	0	0	0	0	0	0	0	1	1	
Grant	1	0	0	0	0	0	0	0	0	1	0	
Jefferson	0	1	0	0	0	0	0	1	0	0	0	
Klickitat	0	0	0	1	0	0	0	0	1	0	0	
Lincoln	0	0	1	0	0	0	0	0	1	0	0	
Mason	3	0	0	0	0	0	0	0	0	3	0	
San Juan	0	0	1	0	0	0	0	1	0	0	0	
Other Agencies	1	1	0	0	0	0	0					
Port of Seattle	1	1	0	0	0	0	0	0	0	0	2	
WEST VIRGINIA												
Total	40	6	8	2	0	0	0					
Cities	31	5	5	2	0	0	0					
Barboursville	2	0	0	0	0	0	0	0	1	0	1	4,099
Beckley	3	0	1	0	0	0	0	0	3	1	0	17,593
Buckhannon	1	0	0	0	0	0	0	1	0	0	0	5,649
Charleston	3	3	1	0	0	0	0	1	0	2	4	50,919
Dunbar	0	0	1	0	0	0	0	0	0	0	1	7,834
Fairmont	1	1	0	0	0	0	0	0	2	0	0	18,740
Huntington	4	1	2	1	0	0	0	1	2	5	0	49,172
Martinsburg	1	0	0	0	0	0	0	1	0	0	0	17,589
Morgantown	0	0	0	1	0	0	0	0	0	1	0	31,406
Moundsville	1	0	0	0	0	0	0	0	0	0	1	9,130
Oak Hill	14	0	0	0	0	0	0	0	6	8	0	7,709
Wellsburg	1	0	0	0	0	0	0	0	0	1	0	2,760
Metropolitan Counties	7	0	1	0	0	0	0					
Brooke	4	0	0	0	0	0	0	1	1	2	0	
Fayette	1	0	1	0	0	0	0	0	0	1	1	
Hancock	2	0	0	0	0	0	0	0	0	1	1	
Nonmetropolitan Counties	2	1	2	0	0	0	0					
Harrison	1	1	2	0	0	0	0	0	0	2	2	
McDowell	1	0	0	0	0	0	0	0	1	0	0	
WISCONSIN												
Total	22	5	15	8	0	0	0					
Cities	18	4	11	8	0	0	0					
Algoma	1	1	0	0	0	0	0	0	0	2	0	3,143
Appleton	0	0	2	0	0	0	0	0	2	0	0	73,141
Burlington	1	0	0	0	0	0	0	0	0	0	1	10,502

Table 94.   Hate Crime Incidents Per Bias Motivation and Quarter, by Selected State and Agency, 2013— continued

(Number.)

State/agency	Number of incidents per bias motivation							Number of incidents per quarter[1]				Population[2]
	Race	Religion	Sexual orien-tation	Ethnicity	Disability	Gender	Gender Identity	1st quarter	2nd quarter	3rd quarter	4th quarter	
Fond du Lac	1	0	0	1	0	0	0	0	1	0	1	43,042
Green Bay	1	0	1	0	0	0	0	1	0	1	0	105,107
Janesville	2	0	0	0	0	0	0	0	1	1	0	63,603
La Crosse	0	0	2	0	0	0	0	0	1	1	0	51,741
Madison	3	1	3	5	0	0	0	3	5	2	2	242,523
Merrill	0	0	0	1	0	0	0	0	1	0	0	9,427
Milwaukee	5	1	3	0	0	0	0	1	3	4	1	600,805
Oak Creek	0	1	0	1	0	0	0	2	0	0	0	35,046
River Falls	2	0	0	0	0	0	0	2	0	0	0	15,227
Sparta	1	0	0	0	0	0	0	0	1	0	0	9,623
Wausau	1	0	0	0	0	0	0	1	0	0	0	39,176
Universities and Colleges	0	1	2	0	0	0	0					
University of Wisconsin, Platteville	0	1	2	0	0	0	0	3	0	0	0	8,668
Metropolitan Counties	1	0	0	0	0	0	0					
Dane	1	0	0	0	0	0	0	1	0	0	0	
Nonmetropolitan Counties	3	0	2	0	0	0	0					
Burnett	0	0	1	0	0	0	0	0	0	0	1	
Grant	1	0	0	0	0	0	0	0	1	0	0	
Lincoln	0	0	1	0	0	0	0	1	0	0	0	
Manitowoc	1	0	0	0	0	0	0	0	1	0	0	
Oneida	1	0	0	0	0	0	0	0	1	0	0	
WYOMING												
Total	0	0	0	1	0	0	0					
Cities	0	0	0	1	0	0	0					
Gillette	0	0	0	1	0	0	0	0	0	1	0	31,884

1 Agencies published in this table indicated that at least one hate crime incident occurred in their respective jurisdictions during the quarter(s) for which they submitted a report to the Hate Crime Statistics Program. Blanks indicate quarters for which agencies did not submit reports.   2 Population figures are published only for the cities. The figures listed for the universities and colleges are student enrollment and were provided by the United States Department of Education for the 2012 school year, the most recent available. The enrollment figures include full-time and part-time students.   3 Includes one incident reported with more than one bias motivation.   4 Student enrollment figures were not available.

APPENDIX I: METHODOLOGY

Submitting Uniform Crime Reporting (UCR) program data to the Federal Bureau of Investigation (FBI) is a collective effort on the part of city, county, state, tribal, and federal law enforcement agencies to present a nationwide view of crime. Law enforcement agencies in 46 states and the District of Columbia voluntarily contribute crime data to the UCR program through their respective state UCR programs. For those states that do not have a state program, local agencies submit crime statistics directly to the FBI. The state UCR programs function as liaisons between local agencies and the FBI. Many states have mandatory reporting requirements, and many state programs collect data beyond the scope of the UCR program to address crime problems specific to their particular jurisdictions. In most cases, state programs also provide direct and frequent service to participating law enforcement agencies, make information readily available for statewide use, and help streamline the national program's operations.

Criteria for State UCR programs

The criteria established for state programs ensure consistency and comparability in the data submitted to the national program, as well as regular and timely reporting. These criteria are:

1. A UCR Program must conform to the FBI UCR Program's submission standards, definitions, specifications, and required deadlines.

2. A UCR Program must establish data integrity procedures and have personnel assigned to assist contributing agencies in quality assurance practices and crime reporting procedures. Data integrity procedures should include crime trend assessments, offense classification verification, and technical specification validation.

3. A UCR Program's submissions must cover more than 50 percent of the law enforcement agencies within its established reporting domain and be willing to cover any and all UCR-contributing agencies that wish to use the UCR Program from within its domain. (An agency wishing to become a UCR Program must be willing to report for all of the agencies within the state.)

4. A UCR Program must furnish the FBI UCR Program with all of the UCR data collected by the law enforcement agencies within its domain.

These requirements do not prohibit the state from gathering other statistical data beyond the national collection.

Data Completeness and Quality

National program staff members contact the state UCR program in connection with crime-reporting matters and, when necessary and approved by the state, they contact individual contributors within the state. To fulfill its responsibilities in connection with the UCR program, the FBI reviews and edits individual agency reports for completeness and quality. Upon request, they conduct training programs within the state on law enforcement record-keeping and crime-reporting procedures. The FBI conducts an audit of each state's UCR data collection procedures once every three years, in accordance with audit standards established by the federal government. Should circumstances develop in which the state program does not comply with the aforementioned requirements, the national program may institute a direct collection of data from law enforcement agencies within the state.

Reporting Procedures

Offenses known and value of property—Law enforcement agencies tabulate the number of Part I offenses reported based on records of all reports of crime received from victims, officers who discover infractions, or other sources, and submit these reports each month to the FBI directly or through their state UCR programs. Part I offenses include murder and nonnegligent manslaughter, forcible rape, robbery, aggravated assault, burglary, larceny-theft, motor vehicle theft, and arson. Each month, law enforcement agencies also submit to the FBI the value of property stolen and recovered in connection with the offenses and detailed information pertaining to criminal homicide.

Unfounded offenses and clearances—When, through investigation, an agency determines that complaints of crimes are unfounded or false, the agency eliminates that offense from its crime tally through an entry on the monthly report. The report also provides the total number of actual Part I offenses, the number of offenses cleared, and the number of clearances that involve only offenders under the age of 18. (Law enforcement can clear crimes in one of two ways: by the arrest of at least one person who is charged and turned over to the court for prosecution or by exceptional means—when some element beyond law enforcement's control precludes the arrest of a known offender.)

Persons arrested—In addition to reporting Part I offenses each month, law enforcement agencies also provide data on the age, sex, and race of persons arrested for Part I and Part II offenses. Part II offenses encompass all crimes, except traffic violations, that are not classified as Part I offenses.

Officers killed or assaulted—Each month, law enforcement agencies also report information to the UCR program regarding law enforcement officers killed or assaulted, and each year they report the number of full-time sworn and civilian law enforcement personnel employed as of October 31.

Hate crimes—At the end of each quarter, law enforcement agencies report summarized data on hate crimes; that is specific offenses that were motivated by an offender's bias against the perceived race, religion, ethnic or national origin,

631

sexual orientation, or physical or mental disability of the victim. Those agencies participating in the UCR program's National Incident-Based Reporting System (NIBRS) submit hate crime data monthly.

Editing Procedures

The UCR program thoroughly examines each report it receives for arithmetical accuracy and for deviations in crime data from month to month and from present to past years that may indicate errors. UCR staff members compare an agency's monthly reports with its previous submissions and with reports from similar agencies to identify any unusual fluctuations in the agency's crime count. Considerable variations in crime levels may indicate modified records procedures, incomplete reporting, or changes in the jurisdiction's geopolitical structure.

Evaluation of trends—Data reliability is a high priority of the FBI, which brings any deviations or arithmetical adjustments to the attention of state UCR programs or the submitting agencies. Typically, FBI staff members study the monthly reports to evaluate periodic trends prepared for individual reporting units. Any significant increase or decrease becomes the subject of a special inquiry. Changes in crime reporting procedures or annexations that affect an agency's jurisdiction can influence the level of reported crime. When this occurs, the FBI excludes the figures for specific crime categories or totals, if necessary, from the trend tabulations.

Training for contributors—In addition to the evaluation of trends, the FBI provides training seminars and instructional materials on crime reporting procedures to assist contributors in complying with UCR standards. Throughout the country, representatives from the national program coordinate with representatives of state programs and law enforcement personnel and hold training sessions to explain the purpose of the program, the rules of uniform classification and scoring, and the methods of assembling the information for reporting. When an individual agency has specific problems with compiling its crime statistics and its remedial efforts are unsuccessful, personnel from the FBI's Criminal Justice Information Services Division may visit the contributor to aid in resolving the problems.

UCR Handbook—The national UCR program publishes the *Uniform Crime Reporting (UCR) Handbook* (revised 2004), which details procedures for classifying and scoring offenses and serves as the contributing agencies' basic resource for preparing reports. The national staff also produces letters to UCR contributors, state program bulletins, and UCR newsletters as needed. These publications provide policy updates and new information, as well as clarification of reporting issues.

The final responsibility for data submissions rests with the individual contributing law enforcement agency. Although the FBI makes every effort through its editing procedures, training practices, and correspondence to ensure the validity of the data it receives, the accuracy of the statistics depends primarily on the adherence of each contributor to the established standards of reporting. Deviations from these established standards that cannot be resolved by the national UCR program may be brought to the attention of the Criminal Justice Information Systems Committees of the International Association of Chiefs of Police and the National Sheriffs' Association.

Population Estimation

For the 2013 population estimates used in this publication, the FBI computed individual rates of growth from one year to the next for every city/town and county using 2010 decennial population counts and 2011 through 2012 population estimates from the U.S. Census Bureau. Each agency's rates of growth were averaged; that average was then applied and added to its 2012 Census population estimate to derive the agency's 2013 population estimate.

Population totals for 2000 and 2010 are from the U.S. Census Bureau's decennial population counts.

NIBRS Conversion

Thirty-three state programs are certified to provide their UCR data in the expanded National Incident-Based Reporting System (NIBRS) format. For presentation in this book, the NIBRS data were converted to the historical Summary Reporting System data. The UCR program staff constructed the NIBRS database to allow for such conversion so that UCR's long-running time series could continue.

Crime Trends

By showing fluctuations from year to year, trend statistics offer the data user an added perspective from which to study crime. Percent change tabulations in this publication are computed only for reporting agencies that provided comparable data for the periods under consideration. The FBI excludes from the trend calculations all figures except those received for common months from common agencies. Also excluded are unusual fluctuations of data that the FBI determines are the result of such variables as improved records procedures, annexations, and so on.

Caution to Users

Data users should exercise care in making any direct comparison between data in this publication and those in prior issues of *Crime in the United States*. Because of differing levels of participation from year to year and reporting problems that require the FBI to estimate crime counts for certain contributors, some data may not be comparable. In addition, this publication may contain updates to data provided in prior years' publications.

For information about the FBI's caution against ranking, including warnings about variables affecting crime and characteristics of jusrictions, please see http://www.fbi.gov/about-us/cjis/ucr/ucr-statistics-their-proper-use.

Offense Estimation

Some tables in this publication contain statistics for the entire United States. Because not all law enforcement agencies provide data for complete reporting periods, the FBI includes estimated crime numbers in these presentations. The FBI estimates data for three areas: Metropolitan Statistical Areas (MSAs), cities outside MSAs, and nonmetropolitan counties; and computes estimates for participating agencies that do not provide 12 months of complete data. For agencies supplying 3 to 11 months of data, the national UCR program estimates for the missing data by following a standard estimation procedure using the data provided by the agency. If an agency has supplied less than 3 months of data, the FBI computes estimates by using the known crime figures of similar areas within a state and assigning the same proportion of crime volumes to nonreporting agencies. The estimation process considers the following: population size covered by the agency; type of jurisdiction; for example, police department versus sheriff's office; and geographic location.

Estimation of State-Level Data

In response to various circumstances, the FBI calculates estimated offense totals for certain states. For example, some states do not provide forcible rape figures in accordance with UCR guidelines. In addition, problems at the state level have, at times, resulted in no useable data. Also, the conversion of the National Incident-Based Reporting System (NIBRS) data to Summary data has contributed to the need for unique estimation procedures. A summary of state-specific and offense-specific estimation procedures can be found online at http://www.fbi.gov/about-us/cjis/ucr/crime-in-the-u.s/2013/crime-in-the-u.s.-2013/resource-pages/methodology/methodology.

APPENDIX II: OFFENSE DEFINITIONS

The Uniform Crime Reporting (UCR) program divides offenses into two groups. Contributing agencies submit information on the number of Part I offenses known to law enforcement; those offenses cleared by arrest or exceptional means; and the age, sex, and race of persons arrested for each of these offenses. Contributors provide only arrest data for Part II offenses. These are definitions of offenses set forth by the UCR.

The UCR program collects data on Part I offenses to measure the level and scope of crime occurring throughout the nation. The program's founders chose these offenses because (1) they are serious crimes, (2) they occur with regularity in all areas of the country, and (3) they are likely to be reported to police.

Part I offenses include criminal homicide, forcible rape, robbery, aggravated assault, burglary, larceny-theft, motor vehicle theft, and arson.

Criminal homicide—a.) Murder and nonnegligent manslaughter: the willful (nonnegligent) killing of one human being by another. Deaths caused by negligence, attempts to kill, assaults to kill, suicides, and accidental deaths are excluded. The program classifies justifiable homicides separately and limits the definition to (1) the killing of a felon by a law enforcement officer in the line of duty; or (2) the killing of a felon, during the commission of a felony, by a private citizen. b.) Manslaughter by negligence: the killing of another person through gross negligence. Deaths of persons due to their own negligence, accidental deaths not resulting from gross negligence, and traffic fatalities are excluded.

Rape—In 2013, the FBI UCR Program initiated collection of rape data under a revised definition within the Summary Reporting System. Previously, offense data for forcible rape was collected under the legacy UCR definition: the carnal knowledge of a female forcibly and against her will. Beginning with the 2013 data year, the term "forcible" was removed from the offense title, and the definition was changed. The revised UCR definition of rape is: Penetration, no matter how slight, of the vagina or anus with any body part or object, or oral penetration by a sex organ of another person, without the consent of the victim. Attempts or assaults to commit rape are also included; however, statutory rape and incest are excluded. All rape data submitted in 2013 —whether collected under the revised definition or the legacy definition—are presented in this publication.

Robbery—The taking or attempted taking of anything of value from the care, custody, or control of a person or persons by force or threat of force or violence and/or by putting the victim in fear.

Aggravated assault—An unlawful attack by one person upon another for the purpose of inflicting severe or aggravated bodily injury. This type of assault usually is accompanied by the use of a weapon or by means likely to produce death or great bodily harm. Simple assaults are excluded.

Burglary (breaking or entering)—The unlawful entry of a structure to commit a felony or a theft. Attempted forcible entry is included.

Larceny-theft (except motor vehicle theft)—The unlawful taking, carrying, leading, or riding away of property from the possession or constructive possession of another. Examples are thefts of bicycles or automobile parts and accessories, shoplifting, pocket-picking, or the stealing of any property or article that is not taken by force and violence or by fraud. Attempted larcenies are included. Embezzlement, confidence games, forgery, worthless checks, and the like, are excluded.

Motor vehicle theft—The theft or attempted theft of a motor vehicle. A motor vehicle is self-propelled and runs on land surface and not on rails. Motorboats, construction equipment, airplanes, and farming equipment are specifically excluded from this category.

Arson—Any willful or malicious burning or attempt to burn, with or without intent to defraud, a dwelling house, public building, motor vehicle, aircraft, personal property of another, and the like.

The **Part II** offenses for which only arrest data are collected, are:

Other assaults, also known as other assaults (simple)—Assaults and attempted assaults that are not of an aggravated nature and do not result in serious injury to the victim. Included in this category are stalking, intimidation, coercion, and hazing.

Forgery and counterfeiting—The altering, copying, or imitating of something, without authority or right, with the intent to deceive or defraud by passing the copy or thing altered or imitated as that which is original or genuine; or the selling, buying, or possession of an altered, copied, or imitated thing with the intent to deceive or defraud. Attempts are included.

Fraud—The intentional perversion of the truth for the purpose of inducing another person or other entity in reliance upon it to part with something of value or to surrender a legal right. Fraudulent conversion and obtaining of money or property by false pretenses. Confidence games and bad checks, except forgeries and counterfeiting, are included.

Embezzlement—The unlawful misappropriation or misapplication by an offender of money, property, or some other thing of value entrusted to that offender's care, custody, or control.

Stolen property; buying, receiving, possessing—Buying, receiving, possessing, selling, concealing, or transporting any property with the knowledge that it has been unlawfully taken, as by burglary, embezzlement, fraud, larceny, robbery, and the like. Attempts are included.

Vandalism—To willfully or maliciously destroy, injure, disfigure, or deface any public or private property, real or personal, without the consent of the owner or person having custody or control by cutting, tearing, breaking, marking, painting, drawing, covering with filth, or any other such means as may be specified by local law. Attempts are included.

Weapons; carrying, possessing, and the like—The violation of laws or ordinances prohibiting the manufacture, sale, purchase, transportation, possession, concealment, or use of firearms, cutting instruments, explosives, incendiary devices, or other deadly weapons. Attempts are included.

Prostitution and commercialized vice—The unlawful promotion of or participation in sexual activities for profit, including attempts. To solicit customers or transport persons for prostitution purposes; to own, manage, or operate a dwelling or other establishment for the purposes of providing a place where prostitution is performed; or to otherwise assist or promote prostitution.

Sex offenses (except forcible rape, prostitution, and commercialized vice)—Offenses against chastity, common decency, morals, and the like. Incest, indecent exposure, and statutory rape, as well as attempts are included.

Drug abuse violations—The violation of laws prohibiting the production, distribution, and/or use of certain controlled substances. The unlawful cultivation, manufacture, distribution, sale, purchase, use, possession, transportation, or importation of any controlled drug or narcotic substance. Arrests for violations of state and local laws, specifically those relating to the unlawful possession, sale, use, growing, manufacturing, and making of narcotic drugs. The following drug categories are specified: opium or cocaine and their derivatives (morphine, heroin, codeine); marijuana; synthetic narcotics—manufactured narcotics that can cause true addiction (demerol, methadone); and dangerous nonnarcotic drugs (barbiturates, benzedrine).

Gambling—To unlawfully bet or wager money or something else of value; assist, promote, or operate a game of chance for money or some other stake; possess or transmit wagering information; manufacture, sell, purchase, possess, or transport gambling equipment, devices, or goods; or tamper with the outcome of a sporting event or contest to gain a gambling advantage.

Offenses against the family and children—Unlawful nonviolent acts by a family member (or legal guardian) that threaten the physical, mental, or economic well-being or morals of another family member and that are not classifiable as other offenses, such as assault or sex offenses. Attempts are included.

Driving under the influence—Driving or operating a motor vehicle or common carrier while mentally or physically impaired as the result of consuming an alcoholic beverage or using a drug or narcotic.

Liquor laws—The violation of state or local laws or ordinances prohibiting the manufacture, sale, purchase, transportation, possession, or use of alcoholic beverages, not including driving under the influence and drunkenness. Federal violations are excluded.

Drunkenness—To drink alcoholic beverages to the extent that one's mental faculties and physical coordination are substantially impaired. Excludes driving under the influence.

Disorderly conduct—Any behavior that tends to disturb the public peace or decorum, scandalize the community, or shock the public sense of morality.

Vagrancy—The violation of a court order, regulation, ordinance, or law requiring the withdrawal of persons from the streets or other specified areas; prohibiting persons from remaining in an area or place in an idle or aimless manner; or prohibiting persons from going from place to place without visible means of support.

All other offenses—All violations of state or local laws not specifically identified as Part I or Part II offenses, except traffic violations.

Suspicion—Arrested for no specific offense and released without formal charges being placed.

Curfew and loitering laws (persons under 18 years of age)—Violations by juveniles of local curfew or loitering ordinances.

APPENDIX III: GEOGRAPHIC AREA DEFINITIONS

The program collects crime data and supplemental information that make it possible to generate a variety of statistical compilations, including data presented by reporting areas. These statistics enable data users to analyze local crime data in conjunction with those for areas of similar geographic location or population size. The reporting areas that the program uses in its data breakdowns include community types, population groups, and regions and divisions. For community types, the program considers proximity to metropolitan areas using the designations established by the U.S. Office of Management and Budget (OMB). (Generally, sheriffs, county police, and state police report crimes within counties but outside of cities; local police report crimes within city limits.) The number of inhabitants living in a locale (based on the U.S. Census Bureau's figures) determines the population group into which the program places it. For its geographic breakdowns, the program divides the United States into regions and divisions.

Regions and Divisions

The map below illustrates the nine divisions that make up the four regions of the United States. The program uses this widely recognized geographic organization when compiling the nation's crime data. The regions and divisions are as follows:

Northeast

New England—Connecticut, Maine, Massachusetts, New Hampshire, Rhode Island, and Vermont

Middle Atlantic—New York, New Jersey, and Pennsylvania

Midwest

East North Central—Illinois, Indiana, Michigan, Ohio, and Wisconsin

West North Central—Iowa, Kansas, Minnesota, Missouri, Nebraska, North Dakota, and South Dakota

South

South Atlantic—Delaware, District of Columbia, Florida, Georgia, Maryland, North Carolina, South Carolina, Virginia, and West Virginia

East South Central—Alabama, Kentucky, Mississippi, and Tennessee

West South Central—Arkansas, Louisiana, Oklahoma, and Texas

West

Mountain—Arizona, Colorado, Idaho, Montana, Nevada, New Mexico, Utah, and Wyoming

Pacific—Alaska, California, Hawaii, Oregon, and Washington

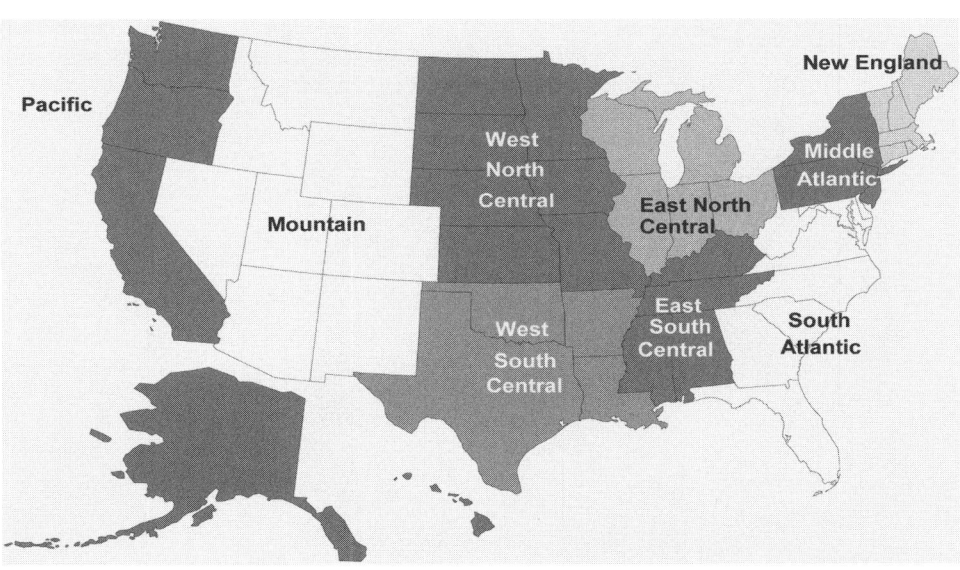

Community Types

To assist data users who wish to analyze and present uniform statistical data about metropolitan areas, the program uses reporting units that represent major population centers. The program compiles data for the following three types of communities:

Metropolitan Statistical Areas (MSAs)—Each MSA contains a principal city or urbanized area with a population of at least 50,000 inhabitants. MSAs include the principal city, the county in which the city is located, and other adjacent counties that have a high degree of economic and social integration with the principal city and county (as defined by the OMB), which is measured through commuting. In the program, counties within an MSA are considered metropolitan counties. In addition, MSAs may cross state boundaries.

Some presentations in this publication refer to Metropolitan Divisions, which are subdivisions of an MSA that consists of a core with "a population of at least 2.5 million persons. A Metropolitan Division consists of one or more main/secondary counties that represent an employment center or centers, plus adjacent counties associated with the main county or counties through commuting ties," (Federal Register 65 [249]). Also, some tables reference suburban areas, which are subdivisions of MSAs that exclude the principal cities but include all the remaining cities (those having fewer than 50,000 inhabitants) and the unincorporated areas of the MSAs.

Because the elements that comprise MSAs, particularly the geographic compositions, are subject to change, the program discourages data users from making year-to-year comparisons of MSA data.

Cities Outside MSAs—Ordinarily, cities outside MSAs are incorporated areas. In 2013, cities outside MSAs made up 6.0 percent of the nation's population.

Nonmetropolitan Counties Outside MSAs—Most nonmetropolitan counties are composed of unincorporated areas.

Metropolitan and nonmetropolitan community types are further illustrated in the following table:

Metropolitan	Nonmetropolitan
Principal cities (50,000+ inhabitants)	Cities outside metropolitan areas
Suburban cities	
Metropolitan counties	Nonmetropolitan counties

Population Groups

The program uses the following population group designations:

Population Group	Political Label	Population Range
I	City	250,000 or more
II	City	100,000 to 249,999
III	City	50,000 to 99,999
IV	City	25,000 to 49,999
V	City	10,000 to 24,999
VI [1,2]	City	Fewer than 10,000
VIII (Nonmetropolitan county) [2]	County	N/A
IX (Metropolitan county) [2]	County	N/A

Individual law enforcement agencies are the source of UCR data. The number of agencies included in each population group may vary from year to year because of population growth, geopolitical consolidation, municipal incorporation, and so on. In noncensus years, the program estimates population figures for individual jurisdictions. (A more comprehensive explanation of population estimations can be found in Appendix I.)

The categories below show the number of agencies contributing to the program within each population group for 2013:

Population Group	Number of Agencies	Population Covered
I	78	58,379,497
II	217	32,344,679
III	484	33,381,466
IV	889	30,734,287
V	1,918	30,507,058
VI [1,2]	9,633	26,639,602
VIII (Nonmetropolitan county) [2]	2,915	27,876,167
IX (Metropolitan county) [2]	2,281	76,266,083
Total	18,415	316,128,839

Currently, 33 states are certified to report data via the NIBRS. Among agencies within those states, more than 38 percent reported all of their statistics via the NIBRS. This represented 30 percent of the U.S. population covered by UCR participants and accounted for 29 percent of all crime reported to the UCR Program.

APPENDIX IV: THE NATION'S TWO CRIME MEASURES

The Department of Justice administers two statistical programs to measure the magnitude, nature, and impact of crime in the nation: the Uniform Crime Reporting (UCR) program and the National Crime Victimization Survey (NCVS). Each of these programs produces valuable information about aspects of the nation's crime problem. Because the UCR and NCVS programs are conducted for different purposes, use different methods, and focus on somewhat different aspects of crime, the information they produce together provides a more comprehensive panorama of the nation's crime problem than either could produce alone.

Uniform Crime Reporting (UCR) program

The UCR program, administered by the Federal Bureau of Investigation (FBI), was created in 1929 and collects information on the following crimes reported to law enforcement authorities: murder and nonnegligent manslaughter, forcible rape, robbery, aggravated assault, burglary, larceny-theft, motor vehicle theft, and arson. Law enforcement agencies also report arrest data for 20 additional crime categories.

The UCR program compiles data from monthly law enforcement reports and from individual crime incident records transmitted directly to the FBI or to centralized state agencies that report to the FBI. The program thoroughly examines each report it receives for reasonableness, accuracy, and deviations that may indicate errors. Large variations in crime levels may indicate modified records procedures, incomplete reporting, or changes in a jurisdiction's boundaries. To identify any unusual fluctuations in an agency's crime counts, the program compares monthly reports to previous submissions of the agency and to those for similar agencies.

The FBI annually publishes its findings in a preliminary release in the spring of the following calendar year, followed by a detailed annual report, Crime in the United States , issued in the fall. (The printed copy of *Crime in the United States* is now published by Bernan.) In addition to crime counts and trends, this report includes data on crimes cleared, persons arrested (age, sex, and race), law enforcement personnel (including the number of sworn officers killed or assaulted), and the characteristics of homicides (including age, sex, and race of victims and offenders; victim-offender relationships; weapons used; and circumstances surrounding the homicides). Other periodic reports are also available from the UCR program.

The state and local law enforcement agencies participating in the UCR program are continually converting to the more comprehensive and detailed National Incident-Based Reporting System (NIBRS).

The UCR program presents crime counts for the nation as a whole, as well as for regions, states, counties, cities, towns, tribal law enforcement areas, and colleges and universities. This allows for studies among neighboring jurisdictions and among those with similar populations and other common characteristics.

National Crime Victimization Survey

The NCVS, conducted by the Bureau of Justice Statistics (BJS), began in 1973. It provides a detailed picture of crime incidents, victims, and trends. After a substantial period of research, the BJS completed an intensive methodological redesign of the survey in 1993. It conducted this redesign to improve the questions used to uncover crime, update the survey methods, and broaden the scope of crimes measured. The redesigned survey collects detailed information on the frequency and nature of the crimes of rape, sexual assault, personal robbery, aggravated and simple assault, household burglary, theft, and motor vehicle theft. It does not measure homicide or commercial crimes (such as burglaries of stores).

Twice a year, Census Bureau personnel interview household members in a nationally representative sample of approximately 90,000 households (about 160,000 people). Households stay in the sample for 3 years, and new households rotate into the sample on an ongoing basis.

The NCVS collects information on crimes suffered by individuals and households, whether or not those crimes were reported to law enforcement. It estimates the proportion of each crime type reported to law enforcement, and it summarizes the reasons that victims give for reporting or not reporting.

The survey provides information about victims (age, sex, race, ethnicity, marital status, income, and educational level); offenders (sex, race, approximate age, and victim-offender relationship); and crimes (time and place of occurrence, use of weapons, nature of injury, and economic consequences). Questions also cover victims' experiences with the criminal justice system, self-protective measures used by victims, and possible substance abuse by offenders. Supplements are added to the survey periodically to obtain detailed information on specific topics, such as school crime.

The BJS published the first data from the redesigned NCVS in a June 1995 bulletin. The publication of NCVS data includes *Criminal Victimization in the United States*, an annual report that covers the broad range of detailed information collected by the NCVS. The bureau also publishes detailed reports on topics such as crime against women, urban crime, and gun use in crime. The National Archive of Criminal Justice Data at the University of Michigan archives the NCVS data files to help researchers perform independent analyses.

Comparing the UCR program and the NCVS

Because the BJS designed the NCVS to complement the UCR program, the two programs share many similarities. As much as their different collection methods permit, the two measure the same subset of serious crimes with the same definitions. Both programs cover rape, robbery, aggravated assault, burglary, theft, and motor vehicle theft; both define rape, robbery, theft, and motor vehicle theft virtually identically. (Although rape is defined analogously, the UCR program measures the crime against women only, and the NCVS measures it against both sexes.)

There are also significant differences between the two programs. First, the two programs were created to serve different purposes. The UCR program's primary objective is to provide a reliable set of criminal justice statistics for law enforcement administration, operation, and management. The BJS established the NCVS to provide previously unavailable information about crime (including crime not reported to police), victims, and offenders.

Second, the two programs measure an overlapping but nonidentical set of crimes. The NCVS includes crimes both reported and not reported to law enforcement. The NCVS excludes—but the UCR program includes—homicide, arson, commercial crimes, and crimes committed against children under 12 years of age. The UCR program captures crimes reported to law enforcement but collects only arrest data for simple assaults and sexual assaults other than forcible rape.

Third, because of methodology, the NCVS and UCR have different definitions of some crimes. For example, the UCR defines burglary as the unlawful entry or attempted entry of a structure to commit a felony or theft. The NCVS, not wanting to ask victims to ascertain offender motives, defines burglary as the entry or attempted entry of a residence by a person who had no right to be there.

Fourth, for property crimes (burglary, theft, and motor vehicle theft), the two programs calculate crime rates using different bases. The UCR program rates for these crimes are per capita (number of crimes per 100,000 persons), whereas the NCVS rates for these crimes are per household (number of crimes per 1,000 households).

Because the number of households may not grow at the same annual rate as the total population, trend data for rates of property crimes measured by the two programs may not be comparable. In addition, some differences in the data from the two programs may result from sampling variation in the NCVS and from estimating for nonresponsiveness in the UCR program.

The BJS derives the NCVS estimates from interviewing a sample and are, therefore, subject to a margin of error. The bureau uses rigorous statistical methods to calculate confidence intervals around all survey estimates, and describes trend data in the NCVS reports as genuine only if

there is at least a 90-percent certainty that the measured changes are not the result of sampling variation. The UCR program bases its data on the actual counts of offenses reported by law enforcement agencies. In some circumstances, the UCR program estimates its data for nonparticipating agencies or those reporting partial data. Apparent discrepancies between statistics from the two programs can usually be accounted for by their definitional and procedural differences, or resolved by comparing NCVS sampling variations (confidence intervals) of crimes said to have been reported to police with UCR program statistics.

For most types of crimes measured by both the UCR program and the NCVS, analysts familiar with the programs can exclude those aspects of crime not common to both from analysis. Resulting long-term trend lines can be brought into close concordance. The impact of such adjustments is most striking for robbery, burglary, and motor vehicle theft, whose definitions most closely coincide.

With robbery, the BJS bases the NCVS victimization rates on only those robberies reported to the police. It is also possible to remove UCR program robberies of commercial establishments, such as gas stations, convenience stores, and banks, from analysis. When users compare the resulting NCVS police-reported robbery rates and the UCR program noncommercial robbery rates, the results reveal closely corresponding long-term trends.

Conclusion

Each program has unique strengths. The UCR program provides a measure of the number of crimes reported to law enforcement agencies throughout the country. The program's Supplementary Homicide Reports provide the most reliable, timely data on the extent and nature of homicides in the nation. The NCVS is the primary source of information on the characteristics of criminal victimization and on the number and types of crimes not reported to law enforcement authorities.

By understanding the strengths and limitations of each program, it is possible to use the UCR program and NCVS to achieve a greater understanding of crime trends and the nature of crime in the United States. For example, changes in police procedures, shifting attitudes towards crime and police, and other societal changes can affect the extent to which people report and law enforcement agencies record crime. NCVS and UCR program data can be used in concert to explore why trends in reported and police-recorded crime may differ.

INDEX

N